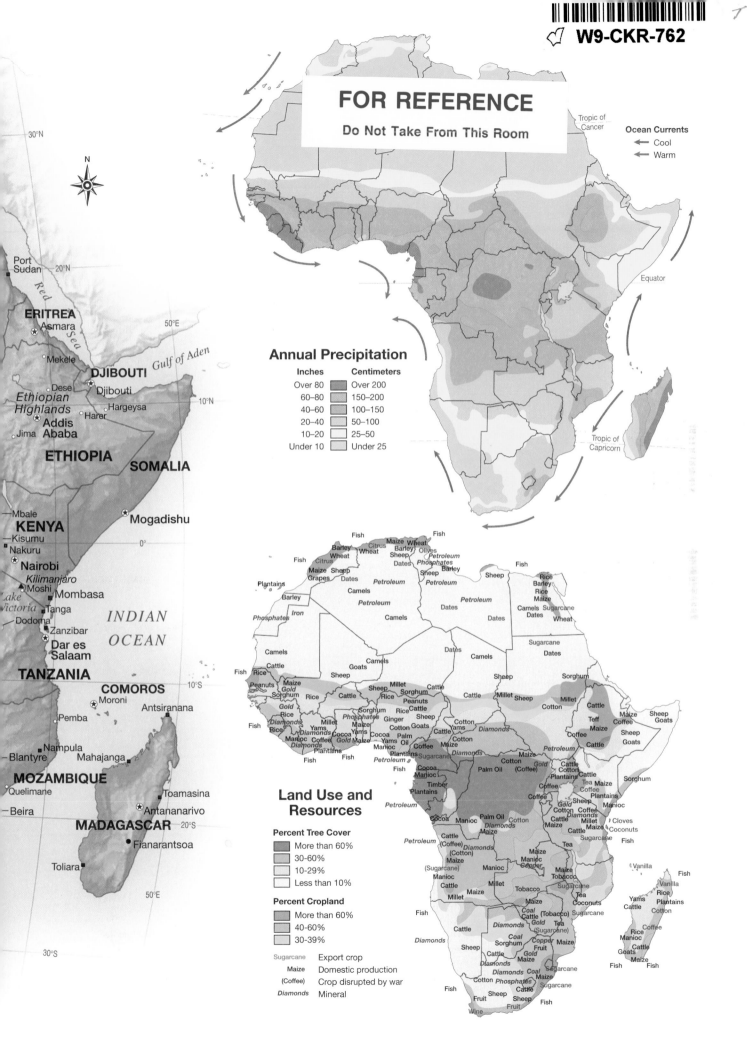

Ocean Currents
← Cool
← Warm

Annual Precipitation

Inches	Centimeters
Over 80	Over 200
60–80	150–200
40–60	100–150
20–40	50–100
10–20	25–50
Under 10	Under 25

Land Use and Resources

Percent Tree Cover
- More than 60%
- 30–60%
- 10–29%
- Less than 10%

Percent Cropland
- More than 60%
- 40–60%
- 30–39%

Sugarcane	Export crop
Maize	Domestic production
(Coffee)	Crop disrupted by war
Diamonds	Mineral

NEW ENCYCLOPEDIA OF

AFRICA

NEW ENCYCLOPEDIA OF

AFRICA

Volume 4

Nairobi–Symbols

John Middleton

EDITOR IN CHIEF

Joseph C. Miller

EDITOR

CHARLES SCRIBNER'S SONS
A part of Gale, Cengage Learning

GALE
CENGAGE Learning

Detroit • New York • San Francisco • New Haven, Conn • Waterville, Maine • London

New Encyclopedia of Africa

John Middleton, Editor in Chief
Joseph C. Miller, Editor

NEW ENCYCLOPEDIA OF AFRICA

John Middleton, editor in chief ; Joseph C. Miller, editor.
    p. cm.
      Includes bibliographical references and index.
      ISBN 978-0-684-31454-9 (set : alk. paper)
      ISBN 978-0-684-31455-6 (vol. 1 : alk. paper)
      ISBN 978-0-684-31456-3 (vol. 2 : alk. paper)
      ISBN 978-0-684-31457-0 (vol. 3 : alk. paper)
      ISBN 978-0-684-31458-7 (vol. 4 : alk. paper)
      ISBN 978-0-684-31459-4 (vol. 5 : alk. paper)
      Africa—Encyclopedias. Middleton, John, 1921-
Miller, Joseph Calder.
      Title.

DT2.N48 2008
960.03—dc22

2007021746

ISBN-10:

0-684-31454-1 (set)
0-684-31455-X (vol. 1)
0-684-31456-8 (vol. 2)
0-684-31457-6 (vol. 3)
0-684-31458-4 (vol. 4)
0-684-31459-2 (vol. 5)

This title is also available as an e-book.
ISBN-13: 978-0-684-31557-7; ISBN-10: 0-684-31557-2
Contact your Gale representative for ordering information.

Printed in the United States of America
2 3 4 5 6 7 14 13 12 11 10 09 08

EDITORIAL BOARD

Joseph Harris
Howard University
Historian

Goran Hyden
University of Florida
Political scientist,
East Africa

Ali Mazrui
State University of New York,
Binghamton
Political scientist,
East Africa

Kelly Askew
University of Michigan
Anthropologist, musicologist,
East Africa

Karin Barber
University of Birmingham
Historian, West Africa

Julia Clancy-Smith
University of Arizona
Historian, North Africa

Mamadou Diouf
Columbia University
Anthropologist, historian, West
Africa

Toyin Falola
University of Texas, Austin
Historian, West Africa

Richard Fardon
School of Oriental and African
Studies, University of London
Anthropologist, Central Africa

Gillian Feeley-Harnik
University of Michigan
Anthropologist, Madagascar

Sally Falk Moore
Harvard University
Anthropologist, lawyer, East
Africa

V. Y. Mudimbe
Duke University
Philosopher, novelist, poet,
Central Africa

Roland Oliver
School of Oriental and African
Studies, University of London
Historian

CONSULTANTS

Peter Geschiere
University of Amsterdam
Anthropologist, Central Africa

Michelle Gilbert
Sarah Lawrence College
Art historian, West Africa

Jane Guyer
Johns Hopkins University
Historian, West Africa

Andrew Hill
Yale University
Paleontologist, East Africa

Michael Lambek
University of Toronto
Anthropologist, East Africa

George Nelson
University of Liverpool
Medicine, East/West Africa

Kimani Njogu
Twaweza Communications,
Nairobi
Director, linguist, East Africa

Abdul Sheriff
Zanzibar Indian Ocean Research
Institute
Historian, East Africa

Wim Van Binsbergen
University of Leiden,
Netherlands
Anthropologist, philosopher,
Southern Africa

Jan Vansina
University of Wisconsin
Historian, Central Africa

John Peel
School of Oriental and African
Studies, University of
London
Anthropologist, West Africa

Paul Richards
Wageningen University and
Research Centre,
Netherlands
Geographer, West Africa

Janet Roitman
University of Paris
Anthropologist,
Central Africa

Parker Shipton
Boston University
Anthropologist, East Africa

Thomas Spear
University of Wisconsin
Historian, East Africa

Dorothy Woodson
Yale University
Librarian, Africa

NAIROBI. Nairobi, the capital of Kenya, is the largest city in Africa between Cairo and Johannesburg. It is also the financial, commercial, communications, and tourist center of eastern Africa, famous as the high-rise backdrop to viewing rhinos and lions at the national game park fifteen minutes from the city center.

Nairobi was founded in 1899 as a convenient stop for the 32,000 Indian laborers and British engineers building the railroad from Mombasa to Lake Victoria. They erected a tent camp 317 miles along the line, and the settlement took its name from a nearby Maasai watering hole. A railway yard and depot were set up, and the camp grew into a small town. In 1905 Nairobi became the capital of the British East Africa Protectorate.

During the first decades of the twentieth century, Nairobi grew as a frontier town and commercial center. Indian merchants, some of whom had been laborers on the rail line, set up bazaars, and Gikuyu people from the surrounding highlands brought agricultural goods to sell. White settlers also came, many of them from the English country set, attracted by the fertile farmlands, temperate weather, and social license epitomized by the scandalous Happy Valley community of British and American settlers. Big-game hunting brought the first tourists to the area, including U.S. President Theodore Roosevelt (1858–1919), who visited in 1909. Roosevelt, white settlers, and adventurers stayed in the Norfolk Hotel, an enduring landmark that still exudes the romanticism attributed to it by writers such as Karen Blixen (1885–1962). A suburb of Nairobi, Karen, takes its name from this illustrious former resident.

As the Gikuyus became a greater urban force, they began to organize politically, especially because their families' lands were being taken by white farmers. Violence ensued after World War II in the form of the Mau Mau revolt. During the state of emergency declared by the British governor in 1952 in response to scattered violence and ubiquitous rumors, thousands of Africans were arrested in a sweep of Nairobi and sent to de facto refugee detention camps in the countryside or detained in the town. The city lived under severe security procedures until the end of the emergency in 1959.

Kenya became independent in 1963, and under the conservative government of Jomo Kenyatta, commerce flourished and the capital grew. In the 1970s, the population of Nairobi increased by 4 percent a year, far outpacing available housing. Shantytowns sprang up around the city. Although Kenyatta and his successor, Daniel arap Moi, made efforts to encourage the building of permanent housing, the official response (especially under Moi's rule) was often to bulldoze the squatters' camps. Moi's successor, Mwai Kibaki, has committed himself to furthering the city's growth.

In the 1990s, the shantytowns were not apparent to the many thousands of tourists who passed through Nairobi each year. Instead, many were struck by the cosmopolitan nature of the modern downtown. Cafés, bars, bookstores, discos, museums, and a university are sprinkled among the glass skyscrapers, and expatriates and well-to-do Kenyans live on lavish estates in the suburbs.

Tourism is by far the largest part of the ever-expanding service sector in Nairobi. The city is the east African safari gateway: Jomo Kenyatta Airport, served by more than thirty international carriers, is one of Africa's largest, and the most popular game parks (Amboseli, Tsavo, and Maasai Mara) are less than a day's drive from the capital. Nairobi's economy also benefits from industries that process food, make cigarettes and beverages, and manufacture plastics and other goods. Though the government is a major employer and the private sector is flourishing, there are not enough jobs in the city and throughout Kenya for the thousands of students who finish secondary school each year.

Unemployment and inadequate housing are the problems that the municipality continues to face in the early twenty-first century. Nairobi's population was about 2.5 million in 2004.

See also **Colonial Policies and Practices; Immigration and Immigrant Groups: European; Kenya: Geography and Economy; Kenyatta, Jomo; Tourism; Urbanism and Urbanization; Wildlife: Hunting, Sport; Wildlife: National Parks.**

BIBLIOGRAPHY

Morgan, William Thomas W., ed. *Nairobi: City and Region.* New York: Oxford University Press, 1967.

Thomas F. McDow

when women were denied the least of rights, let alone publicizing their poetry.

Mririda focuses on the poet's construction of self from her rural life. The originality of the poem's language reflects the strong personality of the poet, and her desire to name herself as a poor, illiterate Berber woman living in a remote mountainous village. "The Affront" is a rebellious poem in which the poet voices her dissent and condemnation of a husband who exploited her and stripped her of dignity. Her divorce from this husband is depicted as a regaining of freedom. That Mririda addresses her mother-in-law, another woman, attests to the notorious power that mothers-in-law used to have. This is strong woman-to-woman language. In the text, the poet speaks of the jewels given by the groom to the bride upon contracting the marriage. These jewels remain the property of the husband, who takes them back in case of divorce. "Did he ever give them to me?" asks the poet; a simple question that raises the whole issue of Moroccan women's legal rights.

See also **Literature: Oral; Literature: Women Writers, Northern Africa.**

BIBLIOGRAPHY

Sadiqi, Fatima. *Women, Gender, and Language in Morocco.* Leiden and Boston: Brill Academic Publishers, 2003.

Fatima Sadiqi

N'AIT ATIQ, MRIRIDA (c. late 19th–early 20th century) Mririda N'Ait Atiq lived in Tassaout, south of Morocco, at the end of the nineteenth and beginning of the twentieth century. She used to sing improvised poems in public markets, where she attracted large audiences. After her death, she was acknowledged as a poet and Moroccans cherish her memory.

Mririda N'Ait Atiq's poems are prototypes of oral literature in which the real subject is the self, a rather unconventional theme within a Moroccan culture emphasizing the group. Two of her poems were translated from French into English. In texture, they bring European ballads to mind, but they also carry a strong Berber flavor in a period

NAMES AND NAMING. To understand personal proper names and naming practices in Africa involves broader issues such as giving, receiving, meaning, reference, use, power, and their "ontological" status. This list may seem needlessly long in light of Western thought, which endorses Alice in Wonderland's introduction and retort: "My name is 'Alice.' What does that mean? Does it have to have a meaning?" Many Anglo-American linguists and philosophers argue that personal proper names do not have lexical meaning but rather function either as conventional "rigid designators" of specific individuals, or as convenient pegs on which to hang contextual information about them.

The situation in much of Africa is semantically and pragmatically different. While the institutions of name-giving, the lexical fields or sets of words from which personal names are taken, and the discursive practices of name use vary significantly throughout Africa, there are transcultural themes in African ideas about names and naming. Those whom one knows or personally knows a lot about—sometimes called "consociates"—are rarely seen as autonomous, independent individuals. In most African thought systems, the "person" is deemed to be created and sustained by numerous constitutive links to other community members, ancestors, vital forces of nature, spirits, or deities. As Laurenti Magesa noted: "Africans do not conceive of personal identity apart from . . . where they come from, what they do, whom they associate with. . . . Human life and activity [are] in constant contact with the lives and activity of other people and with nature" (1997, 82). In brief, names denote and implicate how a person is embedded in a socio-cosmic totality.

Using personal proper names in conversation performs ordinary speech or discourse acts like addressing, identifying, acknowledging, honoring, deferring, distancing, or ingratiating. However, speaking personal names in certain linguistic and cultural contexts can also bring about what seems fantastic in the West; that is, "action at a distance" (somewhat in the way Westerners popularly imagine the forces of gravity or electromagnetic radiation). So, over time certain of one's names become not only metonyms, which index, catalogue, and chronicle one's career, family, or house, they can also become material pathways connecting one with, or severing one from, people, nature, or trans-mundane ("super-human") entities. Contrary to ideas advanced in Western thought, in Africa the relation between the name, the named, and the rest of language and creation is not merely semiotic ("symbolic" and "arbitrary"), but also performative and material.

Given the importance and potency of personal proper names, it is not surprising that naming often takes place in public, festive events, requiring the well-orchestrated participation of numerous, specially designated individuals. Entitlement to confer and receive names and the ceremonial context of naming (often an occasion for exchanging social capital) are crucial aspects of the nominee's adoption and the community's ratification of the nominee's status attainment. Such naming both designates development(s) in one's life course, and publicly valorizes the benefits and obligations inuring in these accomplishments.

Historically in much of Africa, one receives throughout life new names associated with acquiring a destiny, birth, ascribing of caste, attaining puberty, age-set initiation, maternity, paternity, clan filiation, titled or secret-society induction, performing heroic deeds, undertaking a profession, death, or becoming an ancestor. Some notable examples of this kind of naming include taking the name of one's favorite ox (the Nuer), receiving the name of one's pre-birth compact with a specific patron-deity (the Yoruba), receiving a birth name that signifies particular circumstances or happenstances of one's birth (almost pan-African), praising one's heroic deeds (eastern and southern Africa), and receiving posthumously an ancestral or "death name" (Malagasy).

The legacy of colonialism and the ongoing global integration of Western and African ideologies, institutions, and material environments have profoundly affected the prevalence, salience, and cultural context of names and naming in Africa. Many younger people in the early twenty-first century are receiving or taking names from Western media stars or from names of ordinary honorific terms in European languages. It has become commonplace to give and use school, Christian, or Muslim names derived from Euro-American or Arabic repertoires. Often taking a new name from among those common in a religious sect announces and helps effect the abandonment of older "traditional" status obligations and the adoption of new careers: leaving home, becoming an entrepreneur, joining a gang, or living on one's own in town. These newer practices have not obliterated all of the older forms, but have placed those, which do endure, into a new cultural context of gender, class, ethnicity, religious affiliation, markets, and careers, all influenced but not determined by Western ideology and institutions.

See also **Childbearing; Colonial Policies and Practices; Initiation; Symbols and Symbolism.**

BIBLIOGRAPHY

Akinyemi, Akintunde. "Integrating Culture and Second Language Teaching through Yoruba Personal Names." *The Modern Language Journal* 89 (2005): 115–126.

Bloch, Maurice. "Teknonymy and the Evocation of the 'Social' among the Zafimaniry of Madagascar." In *The Anthropology of Names and Naming*, ed. Gabriele vom Bruck and Barbara Bodenhorn. Cambridge, U.K.: Cambridge University Press, 2006.

De Klerk, Vivian, and Irene Lagonikos. "First-Name Changes in South Africa: The Swing of the Pendulum." *International Journal of the Sociology of Language* 170 (2004): 59–80.

Magesa, Laurenti. *African Religion: The Moral Traditions of Abundant Life*. Maryknoll: Orbis Books, 1997.

Orie, Olanike Ola. "Yoruba Names and Gender Marking." *Anthropological Linguistics* 44, no. 2 (2002): 115–142.

Parkin, David. "The Politics of Naming among the Giriama." In *Social Anthropology and the Politics of Language*, ed. Ralph Grillo. London: Routledge, 1988.

Schottman, Wendy. "Baatonu Personal Names from Birth to Death." *Africa: Journal of the International African Institute* 70, no. 1 (2002): 79–106.

HOYT ALVERSON

NAMIBIA

This entry includes the following articles:
GEOGRAPHY AND ECONOMY
SOCIETY AND CULTURES
HISTORY AND POLITICS

GEOGRAPHY AND ECONOMY

Prior to 1800 present-day Namibia was settled by hunter-gatherer and pastoral nomadic groups who lived scattered throughout a region characterized by arid and semiarid conditions in the western, southern, and eastern parts. After 1820 the Oorlam peoples moved into southern Namibia from the northern Cape region in South Africa. They employed a commando style of military organization, and the use of horses and firearms enabled them to rapidly establish domination over the various Nama polities. The latter represented a branch of the much earlier Khoekhoe migrations into southern Africa. In the 1840s the arrival of missionaries and traders stimulated the growth of markets of exchange. Ivory and ostrich feathers were channeled to the Cape market,

as were cattle obtained in raids against Nama and cattle-rich Herero peoples. In return, a range of commodities entered Namibia, including guns and ammunition, ox-wagons, clothes, beads, ironware, and liquor. These developments advanced the frontier of merchant capitalism into southwestern Africa. The rewards of raiding and trading gradually transformed the Nama polities, turning them away from the earlier pastoral nomadic way of life toward a high-risk, high-reward lifestyle, much affected by the exigencies of drought, recurring intergroup tensions, and the insecurity of trade links with the Cape Colony.

In northern Namibia the ability of rulers of the Ovambo kingdoms/polities to sustain a lifestyle dependent on trade, hunting, and raids in present-day southern Angola and northern Namibia was gradually circumscribed by the expansion of the frontiers of Portuguese and German colonialism. An immediate consequence of this development was the emergence of migrant labor, with Oshivambo speakers moving southward in search of wage labor toward the end of the nineteenth and beginning of the twentieth centuries. After 1860, Otjiherero speakers, who had moved into central Namibia possibly in the early 1800s, successfully engaged in a process of repastoralization, managing in the process to free themselves from subjection or tributary relationships with the Oorlam-Nama. A consequence of the emergence of first Oorlam-Nama and then Herero hegemony was the growing marginalization of the San (Bushmen) and Damara peoples and the further transformation of local polities toward market- and consumption-oriented lifestyles.

Although a German protectorate was proclaimed in 1884, effective control over central and southern Namibia was achieved only in the period from the early 1890s to the end of the genocidal war against the Herero and Nama of 1904–1908, which reduced the number of these peoples to an estimated one-third and one-half, respectively, of prewar numbers. During the brief period in which the Germans initiated economic development (1908–1914) in the territory, the outlines began to emerge of what would become a colonial economy premised on resource exploitation and extensive stock farming. The German administration also conducted research into the fields of water conservation, crop cultivation, forestry, and dairy production, aiming to enhance local self-sufficiency. Many

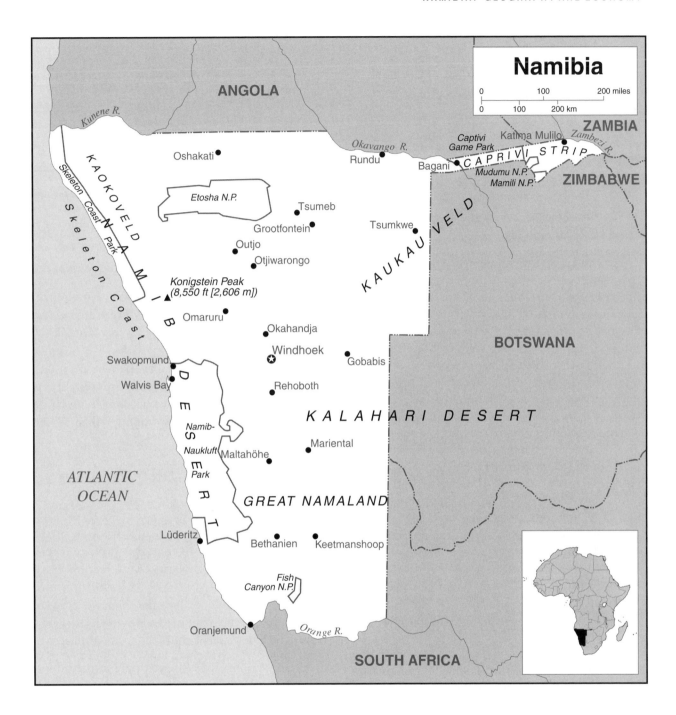

of these initiatives were either neglected or discarded during the South African period, from 1915 to 1990. South African control comprised a period of military administration from 1915 to 1919, followed by the award of a League of Nations mandate over the territory known as South West Africa, which was formally terminated by United Nations–supervised elections in 1990.

Between 1920 and 1960 the major focus of economic activities, apart from mining (copper and diamonds), was stock farming. An extensive program of government-sponsored land settlement for white farmers was launched. Sheep and goats dominated in southern Namibia, and cattle in the central regions. The territory's economic foundations were decidedly shaky until after 1945. The indigenous African inhabitants were restricted to reserves scattered throughout Namibia, or were engaged as migrants in wage labor on mines, farms, and in towns. After 1960 land for settlement was exhausted and the focus shifted toward a massive expansion of the civil service. This process coincided with an ambitious program of development for the African reserves, in particular. The South African government implicitly justified the neglect of the African majority as a consequence of the need to lay the foundations of the modern economy first. From the 1970s onward, funding was directed toward ill-conceived projects and bureaucratic infrastructures in the newly consolidated homelands, constituted on the basis of apartheid, or ethnic separation.

Commercial agriculture for whites continued to receive extensive government support in the form of subsidies, grants, and loans, often explicitly aimed at countering the effects of drought and fluctuating stock prices. Conservation in the colonial period was narrowly conceived of as consisting of a range of parks and game reserves, as well as measures aimed at reclaiming the soil for farming purposes. Extensive exploitation of fishing resources brought the industry to near collapse in the 1970s, whereas the stock farming sector suffered from overgrazing and uneconomic farm units, which contributed toward bush-encroachment and a significant reduction in the carrying capacity of land in the central-northern region. As a whole, the colonial period featured an exploitative economic regime: generous agreements allowed foreign concerns much leeway to extract mineral resources and restricted the other major export product, meat, to the South African market. Namibia represented a captive market for a variety of South African products, particularly in the agriculture and mining sectors.

The postindependence period features de facto political domination by SWAPO (South West Africa People's Organization), who engineered a policy of national reconciliation designed to promote national unity. Whites continue to reside in relatively large numbers in the country and are still the economically dominant element. Apart from a small African elite, the apartheid-era social and economic gaps between the rich and poor persist. Nevertheless, Namibia continues to enjoy relative political and social stability.

See also **Apartheid; Colonial Policies and Practices; Windhoek.**

BIBLIOGRAPHY

Botha, Christo. "The Politics of Land Settlement in Namibia, 1890–1960." *South African Historical Journal* 42 (2000).

Sparks, Donald L., and Roger Murray. *Namibia's Future: The Economy at Independence.* London: Economist Intelligence Unit, 1985.

Werner, Wolfgang. *No One Will Become Rich: Economy and Society in the Herero Reserves in Namibia, 1915–1946.* Basel, Switzerland: P. Schlettwein Publishing, 1998.

CHRISTO BOTHA

SOCIETY AND CULTURES

Namibia, with a population of over 2 million, is one of the world's most sparsely populated countries, and this population is unevenly distributed with some 55 percent living within 93 miles of the northern borders. Most of the rest are found in the central plateau area concentrated in the capital, Windhoek. It is a very young population with more than 40 percent younger than fifteen years old.

Such demographics and Namibia's long history of colonialism, characterized by a substantial and influential settler body, have significantly determined the cultural profile. One of its most noteworthy colonial legacies is that it has one of the most skewed income distribution profiles in the world, with obvious implications for cultural practices. With over 93 percent of its population professing Christianity, it has the highest ratio of Christians on the continent. However, very few belong to independent churches, a situation ascribable, *inter alia*, to demographics, church policy, and indigenous practices, although this is changing as Pentecostal churches—most founded by Africans from other countries—are making inroads. Another striking cultural feature is the exceptionally high illegitimate birth rate and the fact that females are the heads of more than half of all households. These females are supported largely by jobs in the cash sector, remittances from relatives, and earnings from *Shebeens* (typically female-run bars selling traditional and European alcoholic beverages). However, with a nationwide unemployment rate of over 31 percent, more and better-funded male entrepreneurs are getting involved in this informal sector, forcing women to seek other work alternatives, including prostitution. Despite the apartheid colonial policy of trying to promote ethnic homelands, the necessity of migrant work has resulted in most Namibians speaking three or more languages.

Another factor dominating the cultural landscape is the AIDS pandemic. This has resulted in declining life expectancy rates; since 1991 the average has plummeted by more than twenty years. The implications of this are manifested in changing household structures, inheritance practices, and modes of simply getting by. Perhaps the most significant indicator of cultural awareness, however, is the large-scale revival of traditional authorities: chieftainships previously abolished by the colonial authorities as well as former pastoralists and forager groups who have no record of such offices.

Most of the rural population is concentrated in the central northern areas of Ovamboland and in the eastern areas along the Okavango River where intensive agriculture is found. Here the Ovambo speakers, who constitute over 50 percent of the country's total population, occupy the grassy floodplains north of the Etosha Game Park and into Angola. They are part of the matrilineal belt of Central Africa. Divided into eight ethnic groups, their political arrangements have been characterized as feudal. A colonial policy of extensive indirect rule in this region, which served primarily as a labor reserve for the settler economy of the south of the country, further exacerbated these arrangements. Finger millet (*mahangu*) is the principal crop of this region and some Sanga-type cattle are bred, but the major source of cash is migrant remittances that are redistributed through a vast network of *cuca* shops, a variant of *shebeens*. Population pressure has led, in addition to out-migration to central and southern Namibia, to gradual contiguous expansion into the west and the south. Major Wambo groups include the Kwanyama, Ndonga, Kwambi, Mbalantu, Ngandjera, Kwaluudhi, and Eunda/ Nkolonkathi, some of whom still have kings.

Smaller matrilineal groups, engaged in sedentary riverine living, may be found along the Okavango River and in the Caprivi. The Kwangare, Mbunza, Shambyu, Gciriku, and Mbukushu are the most prominent amongst the more than fifty ethnic

groups recorded in the area, whereas the Mafwe and Masubia dominate the Caprivi Strip. Scattered among these peoples are several mobile groups of foragers, or Bushmen.

Beyond the towns, mines, and Ovambo-Okavango area, the dominant mode of subsistence is foraging and pastoralism, as befits the arid nature of the environment. The relationship between pastoralists and foragers is complex, and, given the unpredictability of finding surface water, many people cyclically engage in both herding and foraging, making extensive use of local veld foods. Both processes are extremely variable and have ranged in the past from scavenging and harvesting plants on the coast to the well-documented patterns in several contemporary ethnographies. Several varieties of pastoralism are found, ranging from the agro-pastoralism of the Ovambo speakers, to the capital-intensive ranching of the European settlers, to nomadic pastoralism. Khoekhoegowab speaking nomadic pastoralists dominated the western and southern portions of the country by the fifteenth century. Linguistic evidence suggests that these Khoekhoe pastoralists and foragers are closely related and that their economic differentiation is comparatively recent.

Conventionally, the Khoekhoe are divided into the Damara (/Nu Khoe), the Nama (Hottentot) and the Hai//om. The Damara are Negroid, speak the oldest version of Khoekhoegowab, and used to be forager/pastoralists. An important segment of the Nama are the Orlams, Khoe people who migrated from Cape Colony at the turn of the nineteenth century. These groups are characterized by extremely complex kinship systems, with a strong patrilineal bias. The Hai//om, along with smaller groups of Naron (in the central Kalahari) and Mbarakwengo (on the Okavango), are classified as Bushmen.

The other major category of pastoralists are Herero speakers who, most believe, migrated into the country around the seventeenth century. They occupy a strip of land extending from western Angola through Kaokoland, central Namibia to Botswana. There is linguistic evidence that they are historically related to Ovambo speakers and include groups such as Herero, Mbanderu, Kaokoland Herero, Tjimba-Herero, Himba, Zemba, Hakaona, Tjimba, and Thwa. The

Republic of Namibia

Population:	2,055,080 (2007 est.)
Area:	825,418 sq. km (318,695 sq. mi.)
Official language:	English
Languages:	English, Afrikaans, German, Oshivambo, Herero, Nama/Damara
National currency:	Namibian dollar, South African rand
Principal religions:	Christian 93%, traditional 7%
Capital:	Windhoek (est. pop. 233,529 in 2001)
Other urban centers:	Grootfontein, Katima Mulilo, Keetmanshoop, Luderitz, Ondangwa, Oranjemund, Oshakati, Otjiwarongo, Swakopmund, Tsumeb, Walvis Bay
Annual rainfall:	varies from less than 51 mm (2 in.) in western Namib and lower Orange River valley to less than 102 mm (4 in.) on southern border to over 508 mm (19.8 in.) in the northeast
Principal geographical features:	*Mountains:* Kaokoveld Mountains, Baynes Mountains, Auas Mountains, Huib, Tsaris, Naukluft-Hakos, Joutbertsberge, Khomas Highlands *Rivers:* Orange, Kunene, Okavango, numerous seasonal rivers *Deserts:* Namib, Kalahari
Economy:	*GDP per capita:* US$7,600 (2006)
Principal products and exports:	*Agricultural:* millet, sorghum, peanuts, grapes, livestock; fish *Manufacturing:* meatpacking, fish processing, dairy products *Mining:* diamonds, lead, zinc, tin, silver, tungsten, uranium, copper
Government:	German colony until World War I. Then administered by South Africa under League of Nations mandate until 1966. From 1966 until independence Namibia was under direct authority of the U.N., but South Africa maintained illegal occupation. Independence in 1990. Constitution approved 1990. Multiparty democracy. President elected for a maximum of two 5-year terms by universal suffrage. Bicameral national legislature: 72-member National Assembly elected for 5-year terms by universal suffrage and 26-member National Council nominated for 5-year terms by 13 regional councils. President appoints cabinet from members of National Assembly. For purposes of local government, there are 13 administrative divisions.
Heads of state since independence:	1990–2005: President Sam Shafiishuna Nujoma 1990–2005: Prime Minister Hage Geingob 2005–: President Hifikepunye Pohamba
Armed forces:	President is commander in chief. The National Defense Force, consisting of an army, air wing, and navy, comprises about 7,500 personnel.
Transportation:	*Rail:* 2,383 km (1,477 mi.) *Ports:* Walvis Bay, Lüderitz *Roads:* 55,088 km (34,154 mi.), 7.5% paved *National airline:* Air Namibia *Airports:* Windhoek International Airport; airports at Tsumeb, Grootfontein, Walvis Bay. Numerous airstrips throughout the country.
Media:	4 daily newspapers, 4 weeklies. Radio and television service provided by Namibian Broadcasting Corporation.
Literacy and education:	*Total literacy rate:* 81% (severely disproportional, by race). Since 1990 education has been free, universal, and compulsory to age 16. Higher education is available through University of Namibia, 4 teacher-training colleges, and an agricultural college.

most striking feature among them is their cultural cohesiveness. This has been attributed variously to their traumatic experience as victims of genocide, and to their double-descent kinship system. For example, the largest group, the Herero, has a system featuring seven matrilineal clans (*eanda*) through which individuals inherit cattle and productive property, and twenty exogenous patrilineal clans (*oruzo*) that pass on political office positions and religious items. Historically, the Herero have had a noncentralized political system, but a number

of previously nomadic groups among the Herero and Damara are establishing kingships. Their traditionalism has attracted the interest of anthropologists and tourists.

Most anthropological attention historically has focused on Bushmen or *San*. Major groups, apart from the Khoekhoegowab and Herero speakers, include the !Khu (!Kung; Ju), //Khau//esi (Makaukau; Nogau), /Nu//en, and /Auni. These people have no common name and should be called by their own names. Their status remains subject to considerable debate.

See also **Apartheid; Kings and Kingdoms; Kinship and Descent; Languages: Khoesan and Click; Livestock.**

BIBLIOGRAPHY

Gordon, Robert J. "The Stat(u)s of Namibian Anthropology: A Review." *Cimbebasia* 16 (2002): 1–23.

McKittrick, Meredith. *To Dwell Secure: Generation, Christianity and Colonialism in Ovamboland.* Portsmouth, NH: Heinemann, 2002.

Pendleton, Wade C. *Katutura: A Place Where We Stay: Life in a Post-Apartheid Township in Namibia.* Athens: Ohio University Center for International Studies, 1996.

ROBERT J. GORDON

HISTORY AND POLITICS

In 1750 many parts of present-day Namibia (formerly South West Africa) were linked by trade routes stretching from Angola to Botswana, encompassing the agricultural and cattle-keeping Ovambo kingdoms of northern Namibia, and the very arid lands to the south whose sparse population, largely pastoralist, variously spoke Nama–Damara (Khoekhoegowab), Herero, and San languages. These relations of trade were soon to be reoriented in favor of commerce with the Cape Colony as groups of Oorlams—people of Khoe and San origin, culturally influenced by the Dutch at the Cape—migrated northward across the Orange River. From the 1830s the Oorlam leader Jonker Afrikaner established dominance over most of southern and central Namibia. After his death in 1861, however, the Afrikaners' power crumbled, and groups including Herero speakers under Maharero, based in the central region, established autonomy.

GERMAN RULE

In 1884, after decades of contact with European traders, missionaries, and politicians, Bismarck placed most of Namibia under German "protection" (in 1890 the Caprivi strip was added). The following decade, however, was notable mainly for the rise of the great southern leader Hendrik Witbooi, who gained wide-ranging political power and mounted stiff resistance to German intervention until his defeat in 1894. The new German governor Theodor Leutwein now established control, through a mixture of coercion and agreement, over most African groups except those in the north.

This assault on African political and economic autonomy led to the Namibian War (1904–1908). Much of the African population rose against German rule and overall met with crushing defeat and—according to the general, although still contested, consensus among historians—genocide. In the aftermath most of the Africans of the Police Zone (the center and south) were dispossessed; the exploitation of the colony was hastened by the discovery of diamonds in 1908.

SOUTH AFRICAN RULE

In 1915 South Africa, acting on behalf of Britain in World War I, took possession of Namibia, and shortly thereafter conquered the north by defeating the Kwanyama king, Mandume (1917). Under the Treaty of Versailles (1919) Namibia was declared a mandated territory of the lowest, or "C," status and placed under South Africa—which, although marginally less punitive than the previous regime, nevertheless aimed to retain control over land, mineral resources, and African labor. In the first half of the 1920s segregation on the South African model was introduced, including the creation of reserves. A brief moment of overt resistance was violently repressed (although Africans continued, as before, to employ less confrontational survival and resistance strategies). From the late 1920s, the world depression further facilitated the consolidation of state power. Colonial policy aimed to exclude women from the public sphere, and subjected them to forms of control differing in some respects from those applied to men. Under the exploitative contract labor system, for example, dating from the German period, large numbers of men from the north worked under harsh conditions for short periods in the Police Zone; women from the same region, however, were not allowed to migrate, and were thus largely excluded from the cash economy.

World War II, although preceded by the rise of Nazism among the German population, had little direct effect on Namibia. In 1946, however, the South African government attempted to incorporate South West Africa as a fifth province, using a rigged referendum of the territory to support its case; it was opposed by the Herero chief Hosea Kutako. A decade later, the first truly nationalist organizations emerged, the most widely supported being the South West Africa People's Organization (SWAPO), originating from the Ovamboland People's Organization, founded in 1959. The nationalist struggle gained impetus when, in the same year, at least eleven people were killed by police during a protest in Windhoek. In 1966, with South Africa moving to impose apartheid and Bantustan government in Namibia following the report of the Odendaal Commission (1963), SWAPO embarked on military conflict (through its armed wing, later called the People's Liberation Army of Namibia) in addition to its diplomatic and political campaigning.

In 1971 the International Court of Justice finally ruled South Africa's occupation of Namibia illegal (having failed to do so in 1966). Inside Namibia unrest grew, particularly with the strike of 1971–1972 against contract labor. In 1971 the churches, powerful institutions in a country rendered largely Christian by sustained interaction with missionaries, called for independence. Across the country, especially in the north, repression and militarization increased, and tension grew as South Africa invaded Angola in 1975, following its independence from Portugal.

In the face of international pressure, however, the South African government began to sponsor a form of independence as far as possible under its control. The Turnhalle Constitutional Conference of 1975 was intended to promote a federal structure, based on ethnic categories that had in fact partly been created by colonial rule; it produced the multi-racial, but still white-dominated, Democratic Turnhalle Alliance (DTA).

PEACE PROCESS AND INDEPENDENCE

In 1978 South Africa agreed to a United Nations (UN)–sponsored independence process under UN Resolution 435/1978, a watered-down version of Resolution 385/1976, effectively renegotiated with South Africa by a Western Contact Group consisting of the United States, United Kingdom, Germany, France, and Canada. However, South Africa's immediate attack on the SWAPO base at Cassinga in Angola, killing more than 600, helped to derail the process, and at the end of the year elections were held to install a DTA government,

without international recognition; it repealed some apartheid legislation, but collapsed in 1983. It was replaced in 1985 by a similar multiparty conference leading to what was billed as a transitional government.

The 1980s saw a hardening of positions as right-wing governments took power in the United States and the United Kingdom, and the Soviet Union and Cuba became increasingly involved in Angola; Angolan and Namibian civilians bore the brunt of the renewed fighting. The spy scandal erupted within SWAPO, which detained and tortured hundreds of its members, accused of spying for South Africa. In 1988, however, military stalemate and increased opposition from civil society organizations within Namibia—including trade unions, women's groups, students, and the churches, and reflecting a long-standing politicization of women as well as men—finally led to the implementation of Resolution 435.

Elections at the end of the year gave SWAPO 57 percent of the vote and the DTA 26 percent, and a new constitution was written guaranteeing parliamentary democracy, human rights, and the rule of law. Independence was declared on March 21, 1990, under President Sam Nujoma (succeeded in 2005 by Hifikepunye Pohamba). The country's only deep-water port, Walvis Bay, annexed by Britain in 1878, was transferred from South African to Namibian rule in 1994. Since independence, national elections have been held at five-year intervals, the latest in 2004, when SWAPO, the Congress of Democrats (established in 1999 amid growing disillusionment with the SWAPO government) and the DTA received 76.4, 7.3, and 5.1 percent of the vote respectively.

The independence settlement essentially confirmed the existing distribution of resources and promoted a policy of national reconciliation. Despite some concerns, the political climate remains fairly open, and the state largely peaceful and successful, apart from an armed secession attempt in the Caprivi in 1999, which was followed by a government crackdown involving human rights violations. There has been some postindependence development, although the gap between rich and poor remains wide, and the country has been badly affected by the HIV/AIDS pandemic.

See also **Apartheid; Colonial Policies and Practices: German; Maherero, Samuel; Windhoek; Witbooi, Hendrik.**

BIBLIOGRAPHY

Becker, Heike. *Namibian Women's Movement 1980 to 1992: From Anti-Colonial Resistance to Reconstruction.* Frankfurt: Iko, 1995.

Bley, Helmut. *Namibia under German Rule.* Hamburg: Lit, 1996.

Drechsler, Horst. *Let Us Die Fighting: The Struggle of the Herero and Nama against German Imperialism.* London: Zed Press, 1980.

Hayes, Patricia, et al., eds. *Namibia under South African Rule: Mobility and Containment, 1915–46.* Athens: Ohio University Press, 1998.

Katjavivi, Peter. *A History of Resistance in Namibia.* London: Currey, 1988.

Melber, Henning, ed. *Namibia: A Decade of Independence, 1990–2000.* Windhoek: Namibian Economic Policy Research Unit, 2000.

Vedder, Heinrich. *South West Africa in Early Times.* New York: Oxford University Press, 1938.

Zimmerer, Jürgen. *Deutsche Herrschaft über Afrikaner: Staatlicher Machtanspruch und Wirklichkeit im kolonialen Namibia.* Münster: Lit, 2001.

MARION WALLACE

NANDI

NANDI (?–1827). Nandi, of the Langeni people, was the mother of a Zulu king, Shaka ka Senzangakhona (1787–1828). Just as other chiefly mothers, Nandi had a leadership role and an important personal following in her community. There is much speculation, and disagreement, about key aspects of Nandi's life. This includes her relationships with her husband and her son, and the mourning of Nandi's death. Despite unlikely claims that Shaka was illegitimate, it seems that Nandi was one of Senzangakhona ka Jama's (1757–1816) designated wives. Similarly, many accounts claim that she was banished into exile by her husband, with her son being raised by Shaka's mother's people. Senzangakhona's women resided in least three different royal homesteads, and it was not unusual among other groups in the region for a chief's son to be raised by a maternal uncle. Many of the myths surrounding Nandi have been used as explanations for Shaka's behavior. Mistranslations

of Shaka's name, alleged illegitimacy, and the banishment of Nandi and child by her husband all supposedly resulted in childhood experiences of bullying and ridicule, fuelling vengeance and ambition. Chieftainship allowed Shaka to settle old scores.

Although there are claims that Shaka killed his mother—Fred Fynney, for example, believed that Shaka killed his mother for concealing a child of his—an eyewitness named Madhlebe ka Njinjana, who was one of James Stuarts' informants, asserted that Nandi died a natural death and was not killed by Shaka. Many of the rituals and taboos surrounding Nandi's death and mourning—including bans on cultivation, milking, and pregnancy, *national* mourning, purification ceremonies, watching the grave, sacrifice of oxen, and the inclusion of many ritual burial victims along with Nandi—have been attributed to some aspect of Shaka's personality, but it is more likely that they reflected her importance as mother of the king, especially as procedures were similar to those applied to a king. It was not uncommon for kings or people of rank to be accompanied in death.

See also **Kings and Kingdoms; Queens and Queen Mothers.**

BIBLIOGRAPHY

Bryant, Alfred T. *Olden Times in Zululand and Natal.* London: Longmans, Green and Co., 1929.

Fynney, F. "The Rise and Fall of the Zulu Nation." In *Zululand and the Zulus,* by Fred B. Fynney Pretoria: The State Library, 1967.

Webb, Colin de B., and Wright, John B., eds. *James Stuart Archive* Vol. 2. Pietermaritzburg, South Africa: University of Natal Press, 1979.

Wylie, Dan. *Savage Delight.* Pietermaritzburg, South Africa: University of Natal Press, 2000.

JENNIFER WEIR

NASSER, GAMAL ABDEL

NASSER, GAMAL ABDEL (1918–1970). Gamal Abdel Nasser (Arabic, Jamal 'Abd al-Nasir) was the president of Egypt from 1956 until his death, and was one of the best-known leaders of Egypt and the Arab world. He inspired the short-lived United Arab Republic (1958–1961) of Syria and Egypt, intended as the avatar of a

President of Egypt Gamal Abdel Nasser (1918–1970).
Nasser's Arab-nationalist and anti-colonial foreign policies
were the basis for Nasserism, the political ideology that
became popular among pan-Arab politicians in the 1950s and
1960s. CORBIS

wider Arab political community. On July 23, 1952, he became one of the ninety Free Officers who staged a coup d'état that replaced King Farouk with an eleven-member Revolutionary Command Council. Always in control behind the scenes, Nasser became prime minister in 1954, when he brutally cracked down on the Muslim Brotherhood following an assassination attempt. In 1956, he became president of a socialist one-party state.

Also in 1956, Great Britain and the United States agreed to finance the Aswan High Dam project, but on July 20 the United States abruptly cancelled the offer, followed a day later by Britain. Five days later Nasser nationalized the Suez Canal. In October of that year Israelis occupied Sinai, and French and British troops moved in to the Canal Zone until the Americans forced their withdrawal. Nasser's prestige soared in the developing world, and the dam was completed in 1968 with Soviet assistance. Nasser's survival for eighteen years as Egypt's political leader was a major accomplishment, even if his economic ones—industrialization, land reform, and the rise of a new middle class built on the base of a pervasive police apparatus—were mixed. Even Egypt's defeat in two disastrous wars

with Israel (1967 and 1973) failed to diminish his popularity among the Arab masses.

See also **Egypt, Modern: History and Politics; Farouk, King of Egypt.**

BIBLIOGRAPHY

Nutting, Anthony. *Nasser.* New York: E.P. Dutton, 1972.

St. John, Robert. *The Boss: The Story of Gamal Abdel Nasser.* New York: McGraw-Hill, 1960.

DALE F. EICKELMAN

NATIONALISM. In Africa, nationalism became a dominant ideology during and after World War II. In origins and motivations it may be usefully compared with the anti-imperialist nationalism of subject peoples in other multiethnic empires of the world, notably with those of Austria-Hungary and Ottoman Turkey in somewhat earlier times. Its primary aim was to devise and apply an effective politics of escape from the colonial systems installed by European imperialism, chiefly that of Britain and France. This promise of liberating renewal had obviously to mean different things to different sectors or classes of African society but was to be realized, given the constraints of imperialist policies, by transforming half a hundred subject territories, defined in or shortly before 1901 by frontiers of imperialist partition, into as many sovereign states. In achieving this, it was held, African peoples would be able to reverse the dispossession imposed by European invasion and its consequences.

With many difficulties and much counterviolence against the coercions of the colonial systems, this process of "decolonization," as it later became known, took some forty years to complete. It began in 1951 with the declaration of a "decolonized" kingdom of Libya. It continued across the continent, colony by colony, until 1990, with the formation of a Southwest African republic of Namibia out of its quasicolonial status under white South African rule, and finally in 1993, with the self-liberation of Eritrea from that country's colonial condition within the now-defunct Ethiopian empire. Anticolonial nationalism, in short, was the political force wherewith Africans undertook the task of overcoming the disabilities imposed by imperialist dispossession. Its successes opened an entirely new period in the continent's history. In a real and continuing sense, these gave Africans a means of restoring their own identities. But these achievements inevitably brought a number of wounding disabilities.

As in the internal European empires of the nineteenth century, nationalism had to be the program of newly literate social groupings; this was true even in lands of an ancient Islamic literacy, where the building of a dominant ruling class, or bourgeoisie, was envisaged as the means and guarantee of a liberating modernism. In the minds of the early African advocates of this nationalism—including the Sierra Leonean thinker James Africanus Horton (1835–1883)—Western education, modernizing still more than Christianizing, would enable Africans to stand clear of the "backwardness," as they saw it, to which history had condemned them. Then they could assume their rightful status of self-respect among the peoples of the globe. As another West African visionary, the Gold Coaster S. R. B. Attoh Ahuma (1863–1921), wrote in his then-influential book of 1911, *The Gold Coast Nation and National Consciousness*, "We must emerge from the savage backwoods and come into the open where nations are made."

It was as if the whole long history of African community-formation, before European colonial enclosure, had never existed. This was a nationalism, in short, which thrust precolonial political and constitutional experience into a limbo of the lost. Adjusted to the imperialist and essentially racist ethos of the late nineteenth and early twentieth centuries, nationalism supposed a more or less complete break with the ways in which a majority of Africans were accustomed to think about themselves and their communities. For better or worse, nationalism in practice had to marry liberation with alienation. This produced a coupling that was to prove hard to sustain.

As matters stood, however, this project of a Western-educated few leading the uneducated many became the motor of a political rebirth, of a program of anticolonial change, that seemed the only option to those who advocated it. What other liberating project could induce the imperial powers to give way and eventually withdraw? Edward Wilmot Blyden (1832–1912), the Caribbean nationalist assimilated to West Africa, had answered long before: "An African nationality is the great desire of my soul. I believe nationality to be an ordinance of nature; and no people can rise to an influential position among the nations without a distinct and efficient nationality" (Blyden, v). To that end the enlightened few must lead the ignorant many. It was a powerful line of thought to which surviving kings and chiefs of a historical Africa were able to give only a muffled reply. Some eighty-five years later the rising Nigerian nationalist Obafemi Awolowo (1909–1987) would still find this program a self-evident truth: "Only an insignificant minority have any political awareness" and "this articulate minority are destined to rule the country" (Awolowo, 63). As was said of Indian nationalists, who in some degree set the pace for those of Africa, the spokespersons of this deliberately moderate African nationalism, seeking advance against a still powerful imperialism, "saw in British officials their opponents but in British institutions their hope" (Smith, 782).

Along this route, in substance soon followed by nationalists in all the subject African territories at a time when European imperialism had lost the willingness and now the capacity to prolong its supremacy, even while withdrawal might still be much delayed, nationalism in Africa lost the opportunity to build on the state-forming trends or achievements of the African past. It acquired instead a program of nation-state formation on a pattern set by the English and French revolutions of the eighteenth and nineteenth centuries. The project of nationalism became that of a nation-statism the forms and objectives of which, greatly desirable as they seemed at the time, had to be those of models evolved in western Europe.

That this nation building on an otherwise alien model might repress indigenous political cultures was well enough perceived at the time, and not only by kings or others with a privileged heritage. Yet no other route to effective postcolonial progress appeared to exist or, on the record, seemed likely to emerge. Nation building on the European model became Africa's destiny. For a while, even miniature white-settler minorities like those of Northern Rhodesia (Zambia in 1964) saw themselves as the founders of a nationhood. Even clan-structured peoples whose sense of inherent unity was weak or fractured—the Luo of East Africa would become a significant case, their near-neighbors the Gikuyu another—now began to press forward into the nation-forming arena. Whatever its hybrid origins, the program of nation-statism on the precedents of western Europe carried all before it.

ORIGINS AND EQUIVOCATIONS

But the ambiguities remained. Memorable successes in hastening an end to colonialist overrule were achieved with the promises of a nationalism that had little or no awareness of the needs and constraints of modern nationhood. Such needs and duties might be written into elegant explanations aimed chiefly at non-African audiences, more willing after the lessons of World War II to listen to African voices. But in this immediate postwar era, the ideas of nationalism were powered not by fine rhetoric but by elemental emotions able to inspire the hope of immediate progress.

Very much as among the "submerged nationalities" of nineteenth-century Europe, this power was found in the word "freedom" and its African equivalents, such as *uhuru* in Swahili. Whatever else this freedom might then or later be thought to imply, the slogans of nationalism were accepted as passports to a new and nonracist equality of status and potentials in a world wherein Africans for generations had come to feel themselves woundingly disregarded or despised. So it was that nationalism in its evolved form was above all reactive, drawing its mobilizing strength from currents of self-defense against the racist discrimination that had characterized the rule of all the imperialist powers, if in varying degrees of coerciveness. Yet this mobilizing strength also promised to be creative, not only within the narrow limits of political action but also in cultural struggle, where it might eventually be able to signal the distant onset of a postimperialist culture.

In this creative sense, Africa's nationalism could be understood as a search for identity by peoples long subjected to the suffocating imposition of anonymity. Whatever else nationalism might be thought to imply could have little value; escape from subjection was what mattered. And this was a truth that helps to explain why no one much bothered to investigate the theoretical credentials of the nationalist project. "One thing's certain," exclaimed the Malagasy nationalist Jacques Rabemananjara in 1957 when lecturing a Paris audience: "As we use the word now, nationalism means the unanimous movement of coloured peoples against Western domination. What can it matter if the word should tell or fail to tell the precise nature of the phenomenon we apply it to!" (Rabemananjara, 122). Others down the years would enlarge on the same thought. In 1992 the notable writer Chinua Achebe, recalling that his own people, the Igbo (Ibo) of eastern Nigeria, had generally preferred to organize themselves in small-scale political communities, explained that self-identification by nationhood was only one of the many "suits of clothes" that a people could prefer to wear, and that "Nigerian nationality was for me and my generation an acquired taste"—which, he might perhaps have added, had since gone sour in the mouth (*Guardian*, May 7, 1992).

For many others, also reared in a powerful awareness of their own histories, this taste for new nationality had to prove difficult to enjoy. To the West African Soninke in the modern republic of Senegal, whose remote history had made them the founders of ancient Ghana more than a thousand years earlier, or to Swahili townspeople in east Africa, whose ancestors not much later had founded cities of coral and commercial wealth, the notion that only a wider sense of nationality could provide a passport to self-respect and civilization had to seem strange and even perverse. The Soninke and Swahili were in no sense unique in remembering a prestigious heritage. Yet nationalism, however reductive of historical realities, had come to seem far more useful in its anticolonial and therefore liberating capacities than any celebration of a past that had so thoroughly met with defeat by European invaders. The Soninke in their villages along the lower Senegal River have given little sign of nostalgia for a vanished past; they have accepted their membership in Senegal. The Swahili in their ancient cities recall the tales of their foundation. But their former "civilisation and urbanity are not merely matters of nostalgia for their golden past"; they "give strength in the present and for the future," since "Swahili civilization is not merely backward-looking or a vehicle of silent protest, but a statement of pride in their ability to survive in an oppressive world" (Middleton, 200).

This ambiguity, latent in the claims of modern nationalism, would emerge a little later when these or other peoples pressed gently or less gently into the nation-forming arena in the 1950s. They would then be denounced as the backward-looking agents of what was often, and often ahistorically, perceived as an anachronistic "tribalism." But meanwhile they were awkwardly out of place within an Africa now striving to shake itself free from colonial rule and the prejudices of racist domination. In Nigeria, for example, Igbo "tribalism" would afterward nourish dissent and civil war within the Nigerian nation-state.

But matters seemed different to those Igbo who took a moral and intellectual lead in promoting the concept of a Nigerian nationality during the years when colonial rule seemed so difficult to remove. For them, as for their West African forebears of the 1860s, escape by way of a pan-Nigerian nationalism uniting all "tribes" could be the only useful way ahead. In 1951, with independence from colonial rule looming close ahead, the prominent modern nationalist of Igbo origin Eyo Ita was clear in his belief that any reversion to the multiplicity of Nigeria's many ancient nations would be "out of date," for the future should be one of devotion to a "Nigerian nationality" (*West African Pilot*, January 23, 1951). Six years earlier, when Eyo Ita was the foremost person in the nationalist Nigerian Youth Movement, he told the *West African Pilot* that "the greatest need of Nigerians today is to become a community" and to "evolve a national selfhood," which should be achieved by building "a strong national consciousness" from the "tribal unions" which had begun to be formed during the late 1920s (June 2, 1945).

IDEAS AND PERSONALITIES

These unions or associations, as they were often called, had been seedbeds of nationalism in its emergent anticolonial sense, as had similar entities within the internal European empires of the nineteenth century. They drew their recruits from ethnic- or language-defined groups of country people who had moved to the peripheries of colonial towns, seeking work or relief from hunger. Whether as "urbanized" peasants or migrant laborers, newly mingled peoples came together in these associations, which were initially devoted to the comforts of congeniality and neighborly self-help. Their

directly political purpose took shape later with the emergence of anticolonial activists, both women and men. Their impulse stemmed from the anti-imperialist influences of World War I and, far more confidently, from those of World War II.

Taking encouragement from the growing independence movement in British India, and in a more subtle yet persuasive way from the early World War II European defeats at the hands of a non-European nation, Japan, these anti-imperialist influences counteracted the disunifying impact of a "tribal" past. They spoke for a new nationality principle that would carry all before it. The tribal associations proved to be this principle's handy and effective instruments, as evidenced by their rapid integration into parties of nationalism in British and French territories. Their natural ambiguity, as parties loyal both to a national vocation and to a sense of ethnic separatism, would become apparent somewhat later; for the time being, they did much to enable the nation-building few to achieve a wide audience among the masses. Much the same process occurred under culturally different conditions in northern Africa, including Egypt and Sudan. There, Islam had to face and attempt to resolve an increasingly abrasive contradiction between loyalties to the *umma*, the historical "family of Islam" divisible neither by nation nor ethnicity, and nation-state-forming nationalism, which was inherently separatist.

Along with the steady weakening of European imperialist self-assurance after World War II, the nationalist movements gathered strength. The various miseries that would accompany them in later years would obscure what seemed at the time to be—and what history may eventually confirm as—an irreversible assertion of African self-respect. Behind the rhetoric of national liberation were impressive realities of social, cultural, and even economic advance. In the former British and French colonies, though not elsewhere, substantial gains benefiting most of society were made until economic stringencies worsened after the middle 1970s. As the new nation-states took shape quite rapidly south of the Sahara, beginning with the independence of Ghana in 1957, these gains began to include a widening access to primary schooling and improved quality of education for populations hitherto largely or entirely deprived of any means of understanding the world beyond their frontiers. Fairly large numbers of primary-school age children were in school after the 1970s, when the colonial systems were reduced to Portuguese possessions and South Africa's indirect holdings in the far south.

Effectiveness varied, but here and there educational advances were dramatic. In Somalia, independent since 1960, nationalist initiative produced the invention and dissemination after 1972 of an effective means of writing Somali in a Latin script, Somali as a Cushitic language having proved resistant to an Arabic script. Consequently, a people governed for decades in Italian or English could look forward to governing themselves in their own language, even while the colonial legacy in Somalia degraded into chaos after 1978 in connection with Somali attempts to recover the Ogaden territory from Ethiopia.

Modernizing nationalism likewise strove to expand other public services, notably in health and communications. Many colonies had to begin almost from zero, but rapid if uneven progress was made. Hospitals and medical schools were able to draw upon the graduates of expanding systems of public education. Towns and cities grew vastly, swollen by the arrival of impoverished rural peoples, and there too the nationalist promise of a better life could be initially upheld. If some assets were wasted on ceremonial or merely flamboyant presidential and other displays, efforts were also made to satisfy better the basic social needs of the expanding urban centers. Later on they would become vast cities whose chaotic traffic produced the congestion and pollution problems of Europe and America, but this was scarcely the fault of the nationalists. They had promised modernization, and if modernization created problems, that was only to be expected. Rural peoples might complain of neglect, but they were "backward peoples" low on nationalism's agenda.

The nationalists' programs of modernization in the habits and opportunities of everyday life, at least in the cities, provided new sources of self-respect after the humiliations of the colonial decades. Africans, now traveling the world as citizens rather than servants, found a welcome they had seldom received before. Platforms of worldwide debate, notably the United Nations, heard African men and women who spoke as confident equals. Great academies elected Africans to honored membership. At athletic festivals, Africans won famous prizes. Distant crowds received the same message of equality from touring African soccer teams. As never before, African identities became national identities. Famous runners did not cross the tape as Kalenjin or Gikuyu, Oromo or Amhara; they won their medals as Kenyans or Ethiopians. If Yoruba cities produced soccer players of grand renown, these played as Nigerians. If Fante dance music became popular worldwide, this appeared as Ghanaian music. By the 1970s, if not before, the new nation-states had imprinted their identities deeply into world consciousness.

With this assertion of specific identity, the nationalists secured an African dignity and value very capable of banishing debased racist caricatures and fantasies. With what to the old imperialist world might seem a disconcerting suddenness, there appeared a vivid range of African men and women, politicians or statespersons, scientists or poets, whose innovating self-assertion could not be questioned. In perhaps their greatest achievement, they brought to the world a new sense of African presence, an enlargement that was liberating as much as liberated.

As established leaders of their peoples or insurgent rebels in colonies not yet independent, the best of these men and women achieved fame across the globe. Among the early names on the list were those of Kwame Nkrumah in the Gold Coast colony that became Ghana in 1957, Jomo Kenyatta in Kenya, Benjamin Nnamdi Azikiwe in Nigeria, Félix Houphouët-Boigny in Côte d'Ivoire, Julius Nyerere in Tanganyika (which became Tanzania after formal union with the island of Zanzibar in 1964). They took the world to school in the matter of recognizing Africa, and this education continued as the decolonizing process advanced. After 1970 the hitherto unknown peoples of the Portuguese and Spanish colonies entered the world's consciousness with talented leaders such as Amílcar Cabral (Guinea-Bissau and Cape Verde Islands), Agostinho Neto (Angola), and Eduardo Mondlane (Mozambique). Far in the south, the voice of African self-assertion made itself known and respected through the agency of Nelson Mandela and his colleagues of the African National Congress, bringing with them fresh evidence of renewal in a world increasingly prepared to see colonialism as belonging to the sorrows of a rejected past.

THE LIMITS OF NATIONALISM

The dominant imperial powers, Britain and France, had withdrawn from Africa but with reluctance, demanding in effect that the peoples of the continent transform their colonial states into nation-states, this even as, notably in French West and Equatorial Africa and in British East Africa, strong anticolonial voices began to speak favorably of federal or regional solutions once the British and French had begun seriously to envisage their political withdrawal. Defined by the colonial partition, the new nation-states were obliged to accept from that partition a great deal more than frontiers. Given the social deprivation of most of the former colonies, these emergent states were in practice bound to take over the forms of government designed to meet colonial needs. Although pledged to parliamentary democracy, they found themselves chained to the habits and structures of administrative dictatorship. Neither the imperialist powers nor the nationalists offered long-term programs for development. Therefore, the new governments and their parties were left to accept bureaucratic habits and attitudes already in place even while the clearest minds foresaw that the resultant constrictions on democratic representation must promote the rise of dictatorial ambitions and perversions.

Two arenas of acute difficulty soon became apparent. The first was administrative. Rejecting precolonial precedents, the nationalist bureaucracies proved to be acutely centralizing structures. Colonial government had been resolutely "top-down," all effective power being concentrated at the apex of the administrative pyramid. This necessarily militated against any form of democratic development, whether derived from precolonial African experience or imported from western Europe. In the few countries, most notably Mozambique, where the extremely centralized Soviet model was taken seriously, its impact was disastrous. The new governments found it hard to overcome this centralization of power. Many soon found it impossible. The second difficulty was economic. At least from the mid-1970s all progress in democratic development came into sharp conflict with the economic legacies of the colonial period. Decolonized into a world governed by the needs and interests of the industrialized powers, including the former imperialist powers, African nationalists had to meet the economic terms contingent on their sovereignty, which turned increasingly adverse.

All this combined gradually to ruin the hopes of the nationalists and reduce their nationalism to a caricature of what had been intended. They kept the peace among their nations in all but a few cases, and even in the exceptions the conflicts over frontiers were small. To that end their Organization of African Unity, launched in 1963, had performed as a useful, if limited, forum of intergovernmental diplomacy. Internally, however, many of the new states, for example Zaire and Somalia with many others to follow, found their nationalism swallowed by conflict, or even chaos, as economic stringencies transformed ethnic rivalries, or group rivalries dressed up as "tribalism," to a level of divisive violence against which the state bureaucracies proved increasingly helpless. Just as within the internal empires of nineteenth-century Europe, a liberating nationalism now appeared as a self-defeating scourge. With this decay, nationalists lost the vision and confidence displayed by the pioneers of the 1950s and 1960s. There were exceptions, but generally, it seemed, the nation-statist project had lost its creative power and potential.

A history of these many years of political and ideological decay after the early 1970s would reveal a deepening confusion and defeat. Linked to economic distress, rigidly centralized forms of government had the effect of increasingly confining social power to groups and family structures that could deploy force to use it. While the continent's international terms of trade grew ever more adverse, governments claiming a national vocation collapsed into one or other type of dictatorship by "strong men" or soldiers self-appointed to "save the nation." At best, they struggled against a sea of troubles; at worst, they degraded into banditry. Poverty widened while Africa, as was now realized, could no longer feed itself. Genuine food shortages caused by ecological strain or mistaken policies of development were overtaken or enlarged by internecine piracy and externally promoted subversion, as most tragically during the 1980s in Angola and Mozambique. In the 1990s the disarray of nationalism appeared complete.

At the same time, as the twentieth century came to its end, the possibility of a different if still-distant prospect could be imagined. As a project of anticolonial restitution, nationalist ideology had delivered notable benefits, and the resultant nation-states would survive. But to survive in more than name or habit, they needed to be seriously reformed. There must somehow be an end to the suffocating centralism of these nation-states, derived from their colonial predecessors. Only this, it was now argued in countless debates at many levels, could rescue communities from the costs and losses of sectional strife and open the door to democratic renewal. Only this could enable African peoples to defend themselves in a world whose structures of investment and exchange strongly advantaged those with maturely industrialized economies. New thinking must be required. With all their merits, the nationalists belonged to the period of great-power imperialism. A postimperialist culture must call for other aims and solutions, perhaps regionalist, perhaps federalist, perhaps taking heart from Africa's centuries of precolonial autonomy. Meanwhile, as the millennium dawned, the public scene in most African countries displayed deepening frustration or despair.

Nationalism had encouraged but largely failed to promote political and social unities such as could induce the democratic development of postcolonial nation-states. In case after case observable as the old millennium ended, supposedly national governments were reduced to bureaucratic tyrannies or, in the worst examples, to militarized banditries. Wherever new "national movements" claimed attention, they appeared in practice to represent little more than the clamors of an extremist fanaticism, most obviously among the ancient Islamic communities of the Mediterranean fringe. These "fundamentalists" might promise a new and regenerative social morality, but whatever they achieved in practice was much more often a reversion to aggressive superstition and its destructive consequences. The high ambitions of national liberation, as these had been lived after the 1950s, had now to be set against the often grim realities of everyday life as most Africans found themselves obliged to live it. In the telling case of Angola, for example, the national movement of the 1950s had undoubtedly produced a sense and presence of national purpose, however much ravaged by externally promoted subversions and internal conflicts. But this had now proved too weak to stand against what had become a generalized process of disintegration.

Speaking on a nationwide broadcast of June 1996 to any of his fellow countrymen who would listen to him, the veteran Angolan president, José Eduardo dos Santos, spoke of a record of national failure to overcome a "crisis that everyone recognizes." Apart from offshore oil extraction, there was now "an extreme degradation of social facilities and equipment," superinflation touching an annual rate of 3,000 percent, an uncontrolled eruption of credit in an economy now virtually abandoned to itself. Health and education systems were "in near collapse." Respect for government and its institutions was barely to be found anywhere. He could have added that most people in Angola now lived within a "parallel economy" that was officially illegal, or they scarcely lived at all. "The poverty of the people is extreme," warned dos Santos, "and despair is entering many hearts."

Elsewhere the crisis of structure had sunk to levels sometimes even more chaotic. The relatively old states of Liberia and Sierra Leone were far gone in militarist confusion and self-frustration. In Liberia the republican order established in the nineteenth century by U.S.-backed "Americo-Liberians" had broken down without signs of possible repair: petty warlords relying on easily available automatic weapons repeatedly set their "armies" at each other without the least concern for any national cause. The little central African countries of Rwanda and Burundi were likewise deep in miseries of self-destruction. But elsewhere the picture was happily different: already there were exceptions to the record of failure. The much-abused country of Uganda, whose formal independence from British colonial rule in 1962 had been followed by years of strife, at last entered a period of calm and reconciliation under a regime installed late in the 1980s. As peace gradually returned, this regime brought in constitutional initiatives that were drawn, to an important degree, from precolonial attitudes and arrangements, notably in regard to the devolution of authority whether on the national or local level. Something of the same line of postcolonial innovation, resting on the rural consciousness of past moralities, again proved valuable in an Eritrea released from successive phases of colonial usurpation. At the same time, in the far larger and highly populous republic of South Africa, an end to racist government by the white minorities, achieved early in the 1990s, promised to install a process of democratic social change in the wake of many decades of strife and dictatorship. Once again the necessary solutions were promulgated in terms of administrative decentralization from one or other form of colonial or paracolonial dispossession. Africa, it was argued by the reformists, could save itself if it would now draw upon its own experience and wisdom.

This was a lesson that met with resentment or dismissal by all those for whom Africa's indigenous history remained a closed book. Yet the reformists could and did argue, increasingly during the 1990s, that what they were advocating was no more than a modernized reflection or restatement of the thinking of the anticolonialist pioneers of a century earlier. Africa's own history, they maintained, could produce its own solutions, however perverse this advice might seem to commentators for whom precolonial history retained no more than a decorative or sentimental value. What the pioneering anticolonialist thinker J. E. Casely-Hayford (1866–1930) had proposed, a century earlier, notably in his *Gold Coast Institutions* (1903), could now be seen to possess a startling relevance to Africa's condition.

Hayford had argued in his writings, famous at the time though long forgotten, that colonial or paracolonial forms of rule must in any case fail, in that they would turn their back on the moral and political foundations of indigenous civility. And it was seen in due course that the British and their fellow dispossessors had made no effort, when withdrawing their power, to revitalize and reshape existing native institutions: they had left their colonial institutions in place, being sure that these must remain superior to anything that Africans might be able to devise. Leading African thinkers of the 1990s now argued that solutions of the postcolonial crisis must follow a reversal of this Eurocentric habit of thought: the problems of Africa must demand African solutions. For "the tragedy has been," wrote the leading Nigerian thinker Adebayo Adedeji in an acclaimed judgment of 1992, "that when the opportunity came (in the 1960s) to cast aside the yoke of imperialism, no effort was made to reassert Africa's self-determination by

replacing the inherited foreign institutions and systems of government, and the flawed European models of nation-states, with rejuvenated and modernized African systems that the people would easily relate to and would therefore be credible" (*ACDESS Bulletin* 2, November 1992). How this crucial failure of postcolonial nationalism might now be made good, and by what possible diversities of local initiative and invention, had in fact become the central issues of the whole project of nationalism.

See also **Achebe, Chinua; Azikewe, Benjamin Nnamdi; Blyden, Edward Wilmot; Boundaries, Colonial and Modern; Cabral, Amílcar Lopes; Colonialism and Imperialism; Decolonization; Ethnicity; Houphouët-Boigny, Félix; Kenyatta, Jomo; Mandela, Nelson; Neocolonialism; Nkrumah, Francis Nwia Kofi; Nyerere, Julius Kambarage; Neto, Agostinho; Political Systems; Postcolonialism; United Nations; World War II.**

BIBLIOGRAPHY

Awolowo, Obafemi. *Path to Nigerian Freedom.* London: Faber and Faber, 1947.

Ayandele, Emmanuel A. *The Educated Elite in the Nigerian Society.* Ibadan, Nigeria: Ibadan University Press, 1974.

Blyden, Edward Wilmot. *Liberia's Offering: Being Addresses, Sermons, Etc.* New York: J.A. Gray, 1862.

Cabral, Amílcar. *Unity and Struggle: Speeches and Writings.* New York: Monthly Review Press, 1979.

Coleman, James. "Nationalism in Tropical Africa." *American Political Science Review* 48, no. 2 (June 1954): 404–426.

Coleman, James. *Nigeria: Background to Nationalism.* Berkeley: University of California Press, 1963.

Davidson, Basil. *The Black Man's Burden: Africa and the Curse of the Nation-State.* London: James Currey, 1992.

Hodgkin, Thomas. *Nationalism in Colonial Africa.* London: Muller, 1956.

Hodgkin, Thomas. *African Political Parties.* Harmondsworth, U.K.: Penguin, 1961.

Iliffe, John. *A Modern History of Tanganyika.* Cambridge, U.K.: Cambridge University Press, 1979.

Isaacman, Allen F., and Barbara Isaacman. *Mozambique: From Colonialism to Revolution.* Boulder, CO: Westview Press, 1983.

Joseph, Richard A. *Radical Nationalism in Cameroun: Social Origins of the U.P.C. Rebellion.* New York: Clarendon Press, 1977.

July, Robert W. *The Origins of Modern African Thought.* London: Faber, 1968.

Langley, J. Ayodele. *Pan-Africanism and Nationalism in West Africa, 1900–1945*. Oxford: Clarendon Press, 1973.

Markakis, John. *National and Class Conflict in the Horn of Africa*. Cambridge, U.K.: Cambridge University Press, 1987.

Middleton, John. *The World of the Swahili: An African Mercantile Civilization*. New Haven, CT: Yale University Press, 1992.

Rabemananjara, Jacques. *Nationalisme et problemes malgaches*. Paris: Presence africaine, 1959.

Rotberg, Robert. *The Rise of Nationalism in Central Africa: The Making of Malawi and Zambia, 1873–1964*. Cambridge, MA: Harvard University Press, 1965.

Rothchild, Donald, and Naomi Chazan. *The Precarious Balance: State and Society in Africa*. Boulder, CO: Westview Press, 1988.

Simons, H. J., and R. E. Simons. *Class and Color in South Africa, 1850–1950*. London: International Defense and Aid Fund for Southern Africa, 1983.

Smith, Vincent Arthur. *The Oxford History of India*. Oxford: Clarendon Press, 1961.

BASIL DAVIDSON

NATIONALIST MOVEMENTS. *See* Independence and Freedom, Early African Writers.

NATION-STATES. *See* Political Systems.

N'DJAMENA.

N'Djamena is the capital of the Republic of Chad, situated at the confluence of the Chari and Logone Rivers in the far southwest of the country. The city originated as fishing village that happened to occupy a strategic spot where trans-Saharan caravan routes converged. When the French arrived in the region in 1900, intent on colonization, they built a garrison here and named it Fort-Lamy. From 1903 to 1912, it served as the French base of operations in battles against the peoples of the Sudan. The French forcibly brought in the original civil population—Hausa, Kanuri, and Shuwa Arab—from their homelands elsewhere in the wider region.

The town expanded considerably during the colonial period, attracting immigrants from many ethnic backgrounds who came by choice rather than through coercion. Arabic is now a principal language in urban N'Djamena.

Strategically and geographically located in the center of Africa, N'Djamena was home to the third busiest airport of the French union during World War II, and it is still an important transit center as well as a major stop on the west-east pilgrimage route from western Africa to Mecca.

See also **Chad.**

BIBLIOGRAPHY

Decalo, Samuel. *Historical Dictionary of Chad*, 3rd edition. Metuchen, NJ: Scarecrow Press, 1997.

OLATUNJI OJO

N'DOUR, YOUSSOU

(1959–). Born in Dakar of a *gawlo* (griot of the Tukulor ethnic group) mother and non-griot father, Youssou N'Dour began singing at an early age, earning a reputation as a performer at local traditional outdoor celebrations. Around 1977 he joined the Star Band of Dakar, a resident band at one of Dakar's leading nightclubs. In 1979 he formed his own band, Étoile, which he renamed Super Étoile de Dakar about 1982. He began recording a series of local market cassettes in roughly 1981, and he continued recording over the next several decades, averaging about one album per year.

N'Dour drew on Cuban music (which was prevalent in Francophone Africa), as well as the Wolof drumming that he grew up with. He pioneered a style that he called *mbalax*, after a popular drumming rhythm. His international career took off when he collaborated with British rock vocalist Peter Gabriel in the mid-1980s. In 1988, N'Dour joined Amnesty International's "Human Rights Now!" tour that included Gabriel, Bruce Springsteen, and Sting. Major record labels began releasing and distributing a string of N'Dour CDs. N'Dour became one of the most successful African artists in the world music market and eventually won a Grammy award in 2004 for *Egypt*, a collaboration between Senegalese and Egyptian musicians.

Youssou N'Dour (1959–). N'Dour, a singer and percussionist, won the Best Contemporary World Music Album Grammy Award for *Egypt* in 2005. AP IMAGES

See also **Music, Modern Popular: Western Africa.**

BIBLIOGRAPHY

Cathcart, Jenny. *Hey You! A Portrait of Youssou N'Dour.* Witney, U.K.: Fine Line Books, 1989.

Duran, Lucy. "Key to N'Dour: Roots of the Senegalese Star." *Popular Music* 8, no. 3 (1989): 275–284.

You, Africa! Youssou N'Dour and Super Etoile: The African Tour. Directed by Ndiouga Moctar Ba. California Newsreel, 1994.

ERIC CHARRY

NEOCOLONIALISM. When most of the sub-Saharan African states achieved political independence in the early 1960s, a rift appeared between two groups. One proclaimed a political allegiance to the old colonial powers and the Atlantic powers in general and intended to rely on their support in the states' efforts toward development. The other group emphasized the significance of their liberation from the colonial yoke, choosing nonalignment in international relations, moving closer to the Soviet Union and the radical Arab states—particularly the Egypt of Gamal Abdel Nasser—and declaring themselves socialist. The second group described the first as "neocolonial," coining a word that would become politically popular in the 1960s and 1970s and then fade gradually during the 1980s.

COLONIAL POLICY AFTER WORLD WAR II
This rift was the inevitable result of the varying natures of the national liberation movements that led to the independence of these states. In certain countries, these movements mobilized large masses that often entered into violent conflict with the colonial administration. For these liberation movements, independence had not been granted by the colonial power but had been won in struggle against it. These countries became nonaligned and socialist. A granted independence, on the other hand, had occurred where the leaders of the national liberation movement not only had not antagonized the colonial administration but, won over to its strategies, had not even asked for the independence that was suddenly offered to them. These countries were dubbed "neocolonial."

The neocolonialism debate, therefore, must assess the strategies of the dominant imperialisms. At the end of World War II, the colonial powers—Great Britain, France, the Netherlands, Portugal, and Belgium—intended to maintain and reestablish, by force if necessary, the colonial regimes in Asia and Africa. To this end, they engaged in wars of colonial reconquest in Indochina, Indonesia, Malaysia, and the Philippines, or in the brutal repression of popular protests in the dependent colonies and countries, as with Algeria in 1945; Egypt in 1946; Madagascar in 1947; Kenya in the suppression of the Mau Mau during the 1950s; and the Cameroons in the suppression of the Union des Populations des Camerouns (UPC), also in the 1950s. Yet the colonial powers had to take into account important changes in the development of national liberation movements, whether they dated back to the end of the nineteenth century, as was the case in Asia and Egypt, or had crystallized immediately after World War II, as was the case in most African countries. Confronted with India's size, Great Britain had to rule out military intervention and so was forced to negotiate seriously for the first time, devoting its energies to dividing India up. Elsewhere, though, the strong-arm solution was always considered a possible alternative.

It is often said that the new hegemonic imperialism, that of the United States, advocated decolonization and therefore backed the liberation movements. Yet this claim is certainly wrong. The United States carefully distinguished between two kinds of movements. One kind was the "dangerous" movement, which opted for a policy of radical rupture, linking the recovery of independence to the running of an anti-imperialist, antifeudal social revolution, as in Vietnam and Southeast Asia generally. The other kind consisted of "moderate" movements, which did not challenge the integration of their economy into the worldwide capitalist system. The United States supported its allies against the radical movements, even taking over from the former if necessary, as was the case in Vietnam. Regarding the moderate movements, the United States pressured the two parties to promote negotiation.

The Soviet Union, which on principle supported the demands of every liberation movement, bourgeois or socialist, was isolated by the cold war that the United States decided to impose upon the Soviets after it gained a monopoly on atomic weapons in 1945. Thus, Soviet support remained purely moral until the historic conference held in Bandung in 1955, which offered the USSR the possibility of allying itself with a new bloc of the nonaligned nations in Asia and the Middle East. The formation of this bloc and the financial support that the Soviet Union and China gave it led the colonial powers in Africa to rethink their relation with the continent.

In Africa, the national liberation movements were in no way insignificant, despite the intrinsic weaknesses of the region, with its small and scattered population, low level of urbanization and, especially, of education, almost total lack of local bourgeoisies and so on. Still, the variety of social and historical conditions across the continent gave the movements of each country their own character. On the matter of variation, there has been an emphasis upon the differing attitudes of the colonizers; contrasts have been made, for example, between the assimilationist politics of France (through the French Union) and Portugal and the so-called indirect rule of Britain. These differences, though, are more rhetorical than real in the case of Africa, where in actual practice direct colonial administration was the dominant approach.

INTERNAL AFRICAN CONDITIONS

The distinctive characteristics of internal conditions in Africa are salient. In Africa a number of colonies, protectorates, and a formally independent dominion had significant white populations: Algeria and, to a lesser degree, Morocco, and Tunisia in North Africa; Kenya, Southern Rhodesia (later Zimbabwe), and, especially, the Union of South Africa, in sub-Saharan Africa. Here the national liberation movements were confronted with the issue of the future of the white colonizers. In the extreme cases of South Africa (1948) and independent Rhodesia (1965, formerly British Southern Rhodesia), where the white minority had seized exclusive political power, the movements had to deal with the issue of apartheid (South Africa) and quasi-apartheid (Rhodesia).

Yet, as a whole, the continent had been integrated into the capitalist world as an exporter of tropical agricultural products supplied by a peasantry of small market producers, with mining enclaves here and there, especially in the Belgian Congo and in southern Africa. Through these various forms of capitalist exploitation, the local bourgeoisie was reduced to subordinate mercantile roles, which, moreover, were often carried out by foreign communities of Lebanese or Indians. Furthermore, the statuses of the land, inherited from earlier periods and roughly maintained by colonization, did not permit the formation of latifundiary commercial properties as occurred in Latin America, the Middle East, and northern India. The great landowner class in those areas benefited from integration into the world market and, through the same process, from the support of imperialist domination. This class, which was quickly labeled feudal even though its members were in fact great commercial landowners, failed to take hold in Africa. In its place the colonial administration entered into an alliance with chiefdoms that were supposedly traditional. Some of these really were traditional, and being linked to the political and administrative management of the colony, as in northern Nigeria, for example, they gave the appearance of a feudal system and indirect rule. Yet several others were not traditional, having been created out of whole cloth by the colonizing power, which needed a negotiator who at least seemed to represent the scattered peasantry. The so-called district chiefs in these entities quickly fell into bad repute among the peasants. They were correctly seen as servants without genuine power, in the pay of the administration.

Despite these general shared characteristics, which prevailed throughout sub-Saharan Africa, the degrees to which colonial market capitalism and its forms penetrated local societies were fairly varied and created conditions for national liberation movements that were themselves diverse. One effect of the commercialization of production was the differentiation of the peasantry in the regions where the penetration of capitalism was most advanced. This resulted in the emergence of a relatively well-to-do class of peasants, confronting a semiproletariat of landless workers, many of whom had immigrated from other ethnic regions. This was the case in the colonial Gold Coast (present-day Ghana), western Nigeria, Togo, and Uganda, for instance. The political position of the more well-to-do class was ambiguous: it participated very much in the national liberation movements but adopted moderate, even conservative, positions.

In other regions the creation of a bourgeoisie from elements in the peasantry was hindered for various reasons. In some cases, the social control exercised by the chiefdoms prevented the peasantry from acquiring any historical legitimacy. This was frequently the case in the regions long Islamized, where a class of often religious leaders (the brotherhoods, such as the Mourides in Senegal and the Ansar in the Sudan) monopolized the best lands and assumed the role of partners in the mercantile system. It was equally true in the regions where the precolonial apparatus of state or parastatal control was maintained, as in Uganda, Rwanda, Burundi, and Swaziland.

In other cases the original society, based on equality among lineages, offered strong resistance to the differentiation of access to the soil. This often occurred in central Africa. There, as a result,

the administration was forced to establish venues of pseudo-solidarity among the peasants—that is, village farming communities oriented to commercial production. The results, however, remained poor; commercial production was low and extremely dispersed. Also, the penetration of the market economy remained superficial where distance from the coast considerably reduced an area's profitability, as in the Sahelian region, or where communities were in isolated regions. In some areas a combination of these reasons were at work. In every case the peasantry—inclined to radicalism but without the ability to organize itself—constituted an important reserve labor force that could be mobilized by the national liberation movements.

In these general circumstances, the urban petty bourgeoisie was the catalyst of the national liberation movements. Of course, this class was not isolated from the rest of society. Thus, according to circumstances, it tilted to the left, seeking to establish its principal alliance with the rural masses victimized by the exploitative colonial mercantile system, or to the right, crystallizing the ambitions of the nascent rural bourgeoisie or of the traditional notables and their mercantile partners. In these cases, the weight of ideologically driven decisions was important, sometimes even decisive, in choosing allies. In the French and Portuguese colonies, the metropolitan Communist parties played an important role in this regard, providing training for the African political elite. In the British and Belgian colonies, the influence of the churches—Catholic in the Belgian case, Protestant in the British—was more striking, often moderating or even polarizing the political struggles around the churches' own conflicts, as occurred in Uganda.

If the working-class proletariat was embryonic, it nonetheless existed, playing a role disproportionate to its size. Nearly everywhere, colonization had led to the creation of railway and port infrastructures. Railroad workers were reckoned among the most radical supporters of the postwar trade union movement, especially in the Sudan. In southern Africa the large mining proletariat formed a trade union; in South Africa, the most disciplined members of the African National Congress (ANC) and the Communist Party (PC) come from the mineworkers' union. In this area, therefore, the national bourgeois leadership shared its responsibilities with worker officers. Nonetheless, as a result of various forces, throughout sub-Saharan Africa generally trade unionism was dominated by teachers, nurses, and other government and business employees.

THE NEW NATIONS

These objective facts explain what took place around 1960, when Great Britain and France decided to "decolonize" while trying to transmit power to their political clients. In this period, the anti-imperialist front of Bandung, which supported African struggles for independence, was still in its expansion phase. Followers of Nasser and of Ghana's Kwame Nkrumah chose socialism. The war in Algeria was at its height, forcing the moderates in Morocco and Tunisia to confront France.

In 1951 the Rassemblement Démocratique Africain (RDA) in the French colonies had extricated itself from alliance with the Communists in order to move closer to the power center in Paris. Now, it separated itself from France, adjusting to the anticipated "no" vote of Ahmed Sékou Touré's Guinea in the referendum proposing the establishment of a so-called French community; the vote accelerated the evolution of the RDA elsewhere. The Congolese crisis, sparked by Belgium's refusal to grant its colony independence, crystallized the choices to be made by the various countries in the 1960s between neocolonialism and radical nationalism. Based on whether they supported Congolese radical Patrice Lumumba or moderate Joseph Kasavubu in Léopoldville and the secessionists of Katanga and Kasai, the African states were constituted on two adversarial lines. The radicals, called the Casablanca bloc, formed behind Nasser, Nkrumah, Touré, and Modibo Keita of Mali. The moderate grouping, known as the Monrovia bloc, consisted of the clients of Paris, London, and Brussels. It was during this rift that the neologism "neocolonial" appeared, intended to indicate the choices made by the Monrovia group.

This rift lasted three years, until the Congolese imbroglio was overcome by the call for national unity and the elimination of secessionism in 1963. Haile Selassie then took the initiative of inviting the two African blocs to merge in order to create the Organization of African Unity.

Yet the two groups remained in opposition until the beginning of the 1980s. It is important, however, to relativize the differences in their strategies: although at the time these differences were experienced as opposites, there was common ground. All national liberation movements that became governments shared what might be called an ideology of development, which left a mark on the entire postwar period from 1945 to the 1980s. This ideology, which animated every national liberation movement, held that political independence created the conditions necessary for the modernization of the state, society, and economy in order to reproduce the Western model at an accelerated pace. But while Asia and Latin America involved themselves in the industrialization process during the postwar years, the same cannot be said for Africa, which after three decades of independence still found itself confined to specializations in agriculture and mining. Colonialism and then neocolonialism are largely responsible for this.

The Neocolonial States. The neocolonial option proposed to do more rapidly what colonization was supposed to have initiated already. Political independence was separated from economic and social reform because in these latter two areas, the transformations implemented by colonization were judged to be positive and modernizing, even though insufficient. Therefore, neither social reform—such as agrarian reform—nor a shake-up of economic structures were addressed. Foreign property was allowed to retain its central role in the modern sectors of activity, and the openness of local markets to the world economy was reaffirmed, indeed even reinforced. The integration of sub-Saharan African institutions into the worldwide capitalist system was maintained. Examples include such regional integrations as the western and central African monetary unions, submitting member countries to the management of their money by France, and the community of eastern Africa. For its part the European Economic Community (EEC), the formation of which had begun just prior to the era of African independence with the Treaty of Rome in 1957, supported traditional African agricultural and mining exports (as opposed to African industrialization) by means of the conventions of Yaoundé and then Lomé.

The fact that the neocolonial option was founded upon economic liberalism by no means ruled out strong state intervention on its behalf.

Moreover, such intervention was not devised by the socialists within Africa, but by the colonial powers themselves when they first began instituting a state-run system to supervise the peasantry and to collect and commercialize their market products (through marketing boards, for example). Under the conditions then facing the continent, there was hardly any other way to extract a surplus out of the peasantry. But under neocolonialism such a surplus was intended to finance the administration and the activities of the infrastructure and to feed the profits of foreign capital. The neocolonial state thus maintained, in fact reinforced, the structures of exploitation. Here yet again, there was no means for the new African political bourgeoisie to assert itself and accumulate profits other than through its control of the state. This choice of historical continuity with colonization ruled out democracy for the same reason as in the colonial period: the peasant majority had to be kept under control. Neocolonialism thus favored the single party and the supervision of mass organizations (unions and cooperatives), reproducing the Soviet model in a caricatured way. Few saw the contradiction of neocolonial countries copying the Soviet Union, and the postponement of democracy to a later time was legitimized by the priority given to this type of development.

The neocolonialists assumed axiomatically that development occurred in stages. The "takeoff," to be based on the profits of agriculture and mining, was bound to create by itself, gradually and spontaneously, a market for industry (at first, to take the place of imports, then capable of generating exports), which would attract foreign and local capital, both public and private. The EEC and the World Bank asserted this axiom without hesitation. In fact, however, the automatic transition from one phase to the next has obviously not taken place, the reason being that it presupposed that the state would actively adopt objectives (toward democracy and free enterprise) that were excluded by the neocolonialist option. Certain countries managed to create the illusion of economic success, as with the "miracles" of Côte d'Ivoire, Kenya, and Malawi but they rapidly discovered their limits, which were those of the agro-mining exporter model. The growth and enrichment of the new bourgeoisie offered the prospect of a small industry of import substitution. This new bourgeoisie, which arose from the accentuation of income inequality, and which was grafted on this narrow economic base, could only guarantee the inflated profits of the foreign capital that controlled it, thanks to state protection.

The model did not prepare the way for its own supercession, either economically or politically. On the contrary, it nurtured regressions, including the disenfranchisement of the peoples subjected to the clientelist dictatorships; the intensification of the parasitic character of an urbanization unaccompanied by industrialization; the slower growth, or even decline, of food production; and the increasing corruption of the political bourgeoisie. The clash of these contradictions, slowed by recourse to foreign debt in 1975–1980, was manifested from the beginning of the 1980s. Starting then, the neocolonial states submitted to plans for structural readjustment stemming from exclusive focus on debt service to the detriment of development. Henceforth development was handicapped by, among other things, the collapse of the systems of education, health, and infrastructures; disinvestment; the delegitimization of the state; and the splitting apart of society.

The Radical Nationalist Alternative. Neocolonialism ended in a dramatic (though foreseeable and foreseen) failure, but hopes were also invested in the apparently opposite choice, radical nationalism. The Bandung model, which was popular in Asia and in the Arab world as of the 1950s, inspired a wave of successive movements for Pan-African unity erected on a base of radical liberation movements. Guinea, Ghana, and Mali chose this option in 1960. Later, Tanzania and Congo-Brazzaville (now People's Republic of the Congo) followed suit. Then Somalia, Bénin, Burkina Faso, Zambia, Uganda, Madagascar, and Ethiopia joined, as did the former Portuguese colonies after they gained their independence in 1975; Zimbabwe entered their ranks in 1980 with the establishment of black majority rule.

Theoretical discourse on the significance of radical nationalism takes as its starting point the concept of rupture with colonization as opposed to historical continuity. Rupture sometimes implied moderate social reforms, but above all it involved an attempt at the national level to control the processes for the accumulation of wealth through the mastery of the internal market; the ownership of capital through nationalization; the prioritizing of the public sector and currency management; the reproduction of the work force through the administration of wages and prices; and, at least rhetorically, the acquisition of a technology. The will to speed up industrialization was also declared. The limits of this approach resulted from the fact that it did not envision disconnecting itself from the worldwide capitalist system but instead envisioned forcing that system to adapt to the demands of the internal development of the countries affected. Africa, even more than other regions in the developing world, lacked the means for forcing such coherence. For example, the radical African states also accepted the logic of the Lomé agreements. In these conditions, developmental strategies have not been so different from those enacted in neocolonial countries, despite socialist proclamations and exterior anti-imperialist alliances. The same regressions as in the neocolonial states, again brought about by the refusal to become democratic (based on the same arguments—the need for state intervention and foreign capital and in consequence of social and economic reform—reinforced here by Soviet ideology), have led to similar crises since the start of the 1980s.

CONCLUSION

Neocolonialism has passed through the general crisis of the worldwide capitalist system, neocolonialism's own collapse, and that of its alternative, radical anti-imperialism (in intentions, at least), yet is unable to overcome its own internal limits. The subjugation of Africa to external powers over the entire continent has reduced to nothingness the differences between paths of development asserted during the preceding decades; the Africa of the ruling classes no longer has a plan for development, whether neocolonial or parasocialist. This regression, which has often been described as "fourth-worldization" as opposed to the semi-industrialization of the "third world," creates new openings in the world market and summons a kind of "recolonization" of the continent, cynically carried out by the dominant powers. The neocompradore form that the local state as much as the dominant classes takes in these circumstances—replacing the illusions of radical bourgeois nationalism and neocolonialism—is incapable of convincing society of their legitimacy. Thus, this form entails a political chaos that will be

overcome only when new systems of popular social power succeed in crystallizing around a project that offers an alternative to the utopia of capitalist internationalization.

See also **Colonial Policies and Practices; Colonialism and Imperialism; Decolonization; Haile Selassie I; Lumumba, Patrice; Nasser, Gamal Abdel; Nationalism; Nkrumah, Francis Nwia Kofi; Postcolonialism; Socialism and Postsocialisms; Touré, Sékou; World Bank.**

BIBLIOGRAPHY

Adotevi, Stanislas. *De Gaulle et les Africains*. Paris: Editions Chaka, 1990.

Amin, Samir. "Le développement du capitalisme en Afrique noire." In *En partant du "Capital,"* ed. Victor Fay. Paris: Éditions Anthropos, 1968.

Amin, Samir. *The Class Struggle in Africa*. Cambridge, MA: Africa Research Group, 1969.

Amin, Samir. "Underdevelopment and Dependency in Black Africa: Origins and Contemporary Forms." *Journal of Modern African Studies* 10, no. 4 (1972): 503–524.

Amin, Samir. *Neo-colonialism in West Africa*, trans. Francis McDonagh. Harmondsworth, U.K.: Penguin, 1973.

Arrighi, Giovanni, and John S. Saul. *Essays on the Political Economy of Africa*. New York: Monthly Review Press, 1973.

Benot, Yves. *Les indépendances africaines: Idéologies et réalités*. 2 vols. Paris: F. Maspero, 1975.

Chrétien, Jean-Pierre, and Gérard Prunier. *Les ethnies ont une histoire*. Paris: Karthala, 1989.

Davies, Ioan. *African Trade Unions*. Baltimore, MD: Penguin, 1966.

Gibson, Richard. *African Liberation Movements: Contemporary Struggles against White Minority Rule*. New York: Oxford University Press, 1972.

Gutkind, Peter, and Immanuel Wallerstein, eds. *The Political Economy of Contemporary Africa*. Beverly Hills, CA: Sage Publications, 1976.

Hodgkin, Thomas. *African Political Parties: An Introductory Guide*. Harmondsworth, U.K.: Penguin, 1962.

Lovejoy, Paul E., ed. *The Ideology of Slavery in Africa*. Beverly Hills, CA: Sage Publications, 1981.

Suret-Canale, Jean. *Afrique noire occidentale et centrale*, 3rd. edition. Vol. 2: *L'ère coloniale*; Vol. 3: *De la colonisation aux indépendances*. Paris: Éditions Sociales, 1968.

SAMIR AMIN

NETO, AGOSTINHO (1922–1979).

The anticolonialist revolutionary and first president of independent Angola Agostinho Neto was born at Bengo in the Catete district of western Angola. Neto was the son of a Protestant pastor of Mbundu linguistic origin. In 1947 he left the all-pervasive racism of ruling Portuguese culture in Angola and went to Lisbon to study medicine. With like-minded African students in Portugal at the end of World War II, he began to campaign for Angola's independence. This was necessarily subversive in the eyes of the ruling dictatorship, and Neto was drawn into socialist and communist agitation. In 1958 he returned to Angola and established a medical practice. In 1960 he was arrested by the Portuguese political police, the Polícia International de Defesa de Estado (PIDE) and exiled first to Santo Antão in the Cape Verde archipelago, at that time a Portuguese colonial possession, and then to Portugal.

In 1962 Neto escaped from Portugal and at once assumed leadership of the widespread anticolonial insurrection that had erupted in Angola during 1961. His leadership of the Angolan independence movement, the Movimento Popular de Libertação de Angola (MPLA), was repeatedly confirmed through the years of struggle which brought independence to Angola in 1975, with Neto as president. The nascent Angolan state was at once threatened with disaster by full-scale military invasion from an apartheid-ruled South Africa. Narrowly failing to destroy Angolan independence, the incursion was frustrated and finally defeated by Cuban military intervention.

South African withdrawal still left the Angolans, at the end of 1976, not only riven by their own problems but subject to the destructive miseries of the East-West Cold War and the hostility of the United States. It would not be until the termination of the Cold War in the late 1980s that prospects for eventual reconstruction in Angola could be envisioned. This was too late for the man who had captained Angola's history of self-emancipation. Although disabused of his youthful faith in the Soviet state, Neto remained an unwilling captive of the politics of his time. He died in a Moscow hospital in 1979, leaving the republic he had founded to a difficult survival. A notable poet in Portuguese, Neto produced a volume of verse published initially in Tanzania in 1974 and titled, in its English translation that year, *Sacred Hope*.

See also **Angola.**

BIBLIOGRAPHY

Khazanov, A. M. *Agostinho Neto*, trans. Cynthia Carlile. Moscow: Progress Publishers, 1986.

BASIL DAVIDSON

NEWSPAPERS. *See* **Media: Journalism.**

NGOS. *See* **Nongovernmental Organizations.**

NGŨGĨ WA THIONG'O (1938–).

Ngũgĩ wa Thiong'o, also known as James Ngugi, was born in Kamiriithu in Kenya's Kiambu District. He attended a mission high school and graduated from Makerere University College in Uganda in 1964 with a B.A. in English that was offered by the University of London. A Kenyan scholar, novelist, essayist, and playwright, he is best known for his abandonment of the English language in favor of indigenous African languages as a way of "decolonizing the mind," his attempt to stop the hegemony of colonial culture in postindependence Africa and empower the uneducated peasants and workers who form the bulk of African populations. He launched a successful writing career in English in the 1960s, but after he was detained without trial by the Kenyan government in 1977 for his involvement in indigenous community theater, he started writing in his mother tongue, Gĩkũyũ.

Threatened with assassination in 1982 because of his political engagements in Kenya, he lived in self-imposed exile in Europe and America for over twenty years. His creative works treat the themes of colonialism and neocolonialism, and they sanction armed struggle to resolve crises in colonial and postcolonial Africa. Ngũgĩ renounced

Ngũgĩ wa Thiong'o (1938–). The prolific Kenyan writer is founder and editor of the Gikuyu-language journal, *Mutiiri*. He is a director of the Center for Writing and Translation at the University of California, Irvine. © COLIN McPHERSON/CORBIS

Christianity in the 1970s but continued to use biblical allusions in his novels and plays to support class-based struggles against capitalism. His scholarship and literary essays focus on the intersection of arts, language, and politics. He founded *Mutiiri* a Gĩkũyũ-language journal, and has written children's books in Gĩkũyũ.

See also **Literatures in African Languages.**

BIBLIOGRAPHY

Cook, David, and Michael Okenimkpe. *Ngũg wa Thiong'o: An Exploration of His Writings.* Oxford: James Currey, 1997.

Gikandi, Simon. *Ngũg wa Thiong'o.* London: Cambridge University Press, 2000.

Sicherman, Carol. *Ngũg wa Thiong'o: The Making of a Rebel: A Source Book in Kenyan Literature and Resistance.* New York: Hans Zell Publishers, 1990.

EVAN MWANGI

NIAMEY. The capital of the Republic of Niger, Niamey was originally a small Songhay fishing settlement on the left bank of the Niger River. Because of Niamey's strategic location, the French established a military post there at the beginning of the twentieth century. In 1926 they founded the capital of their colony of Niger there, supplanting the Hausa town of Zinder in that role. Niamey's location on two major regional roadways (the Nigeria-Mali and the Burkina Faso-Chad roads) encouraged its growth and development: by the mid-1970s the population of the city numbered over 220,000, and by 2004, it had grown to an estimated 729,000. Niamey is the commercial center of Niger, producing bricks, cement, ceramics, shoes, and food products. It serves as the processing and export center for the nation's primary agricultural product, peanuts. It is also the center for national culture, hosting a university and the National Museum, which offers natural history displays and ethnological collections.

See also **Niger.**

BIBLIOGRAPHY

Decalo, Samuel. *Historical Dictionary of Niger*, 3rd edition. Metuchen, NJ: Scarecrow Press, 1997.

OLATUNJI OJO

NIANI. Located on the Sankarani River in northeastern Guinea, Niani is claimed by a number of scholars to be the capital, or one of the capitals, of the Mali Empire (thirteenth–sixteenth centuries). Prior to the 1960s, there was considerable debate on the capital's possibly shifting location during the historical development of the polity. D. T. Niane identified Niani as the permanent, imperial capital from the thirteenth to sixteenth centuries, as had several French colonial commentators previously. Other scholars disagreed. Polish excavations at Niani in 1968 and 1973 uncovered the remains of buildings claimed to be the

Audience Hall, Palace, and Mosque of the Royal Quarter occupied during and after the reign of the great Mansa Musa in the fourteenth century. An Arab Quarter less than half a mile away was also excavated. The debate appeared to be settled in favor of Niani as the permanent capital. But in neither area did the radiocarbon dates document an occupation during the thirteenth and fourteenth centuries. No notable exotic or luxury goods were recovered, beyond the glass beads and copper-alloy bangles found at many sites. In the Royal Quarter, several radiocarbon dates ranging from 300–390 BP (uncalibrated), and the presence of tobacco pipes. Despite the lack of confirming evidence, Niani's identification as the imperial capital has become firmly entrenched in the literature.

See also **Guinea; Mansa Musa.**

BIBLIOGRAPHY

Conrad, David. "A Town Called Dakajalan: The Sunjata Tradition and the Question of Ancient Mali's Capital." *Journal of African History* 35, no. 3 (1994): 355–377.

Filopowiak, W. *Etudes Archéologiques sur la Capitale Médiévale du Mali.* Szczecin, Poland: Muzeum Narodowe Szczecin, 1979.

Hunwick, John. "The Mid-Fourteenth Century Capital of Mali." *Journal of African History* no. 14 (1973): 195–206.

McIntosh, S. K., and R. J. McIntosh. "The Early City in West Africa: Towards an Understanding." *African Archaeological Review* no. 2 (1984): 73–98.

Niane, D. T. "Mali and the Second Mandingo Expansion." In *UNESCO General History of Africa*, Vol. 4: *Africa from the Twelfth to the Sixteenth Century*, ed. D.T. Niane. Berkeley: University of California Press, 1984.

SUSAN KEECH MCINTOSH

NIGER

This entry includes the following articles:
GEOGRAPHY AND ECONOMY
SOCIETY AND CULTURES
HISTORY AND POLITICS

GEOGRAPHY AND ECONOMY

GEOGRAPHY

With an area of 489,191 square miles, Niger is the largest country in West Africa. Landlocked Niger has seven neighbors, with Nigeria to the south as the economic and political giant of the region. Two-thirds of the country is desert and form part of the Sahara, whereas the southernmost part of the country, the Sahel, is savanna country where agriculture and livestock raising is possible.

The Niger River, which gave the country its name, runs through the southwest, whereas the other permanent waterway, the Komadougou in the southeast, is a tributary to Lake Chad. In north and central Niger, the Djado Plateau and the Aïr massif make up the only mountainous areas in the country.

The climate is arid and tropical, and from November to January the dry *Harmattan* wind blows from the northeast. It rarely rains in the Sahara, but the Sahelian savanna region receives between 4 and 28 inches of rain annually from May to September. Rains are often erratic, though, and Niger has experienced a series or droughts since the 1960s. Major famines have struck the country at different intervals, 1911–1914; 1930–1931; 1937–1939; 1949; 1973; 1984; and as recently as 2005 a food crisis was badly felt in parts of the country.

Niger has a population of almost thirteen million, unevenly distributed throughout the country. To the north live less than one person per square mile, whereas the density in the areas around Maradi and Zinder to the south is well above 161 per square mile. The population grows at the rate of 3.3 percent annually; 5.6 percent in urban areas. Life expectancy is forty-four years and the GDP per capita is US$230. About a quarter of the population lives in urban settlements. The most important cities are Niamey, the capital on the River Niger, Dosso, Tahoua, Maradi, and Zinder. Agadez to the north was an important city along the trans-Saharan trade routes to Algeria and Morocco. The Hausa are the largest ethnic group and make up about half the population, followed by the Djerma and Songhay (22%), Tuaregs and Fulani (both 10%). Ninety-five percent of the population is Muslim.

ECONOMY

Niger is the poorest country in the world according the *2005 Human Development Report.* Moreover, income disparity remains high. The poorest 20 percent of Nigeriens receive less than 3 percent of the national income.

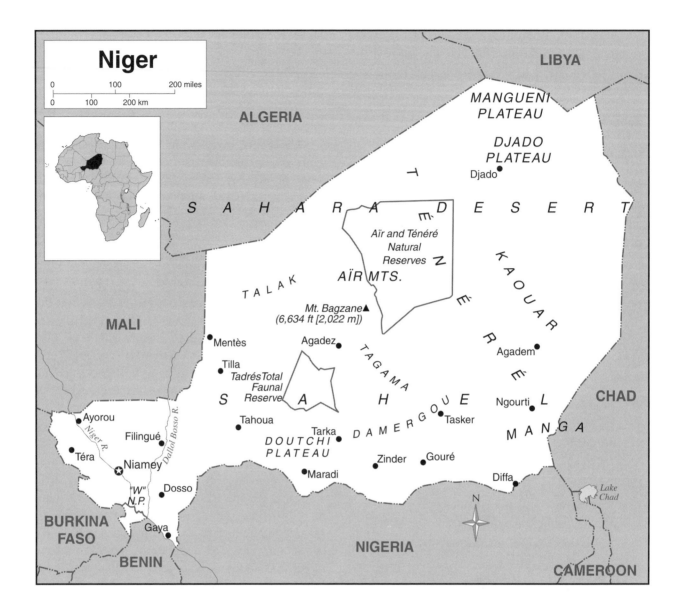

Although world demand for uranium during the 1970s and 1980s gave promise of some prosperity in the country, the decline in demand from the 1990s led Niger's economy to again depend heavily on traditional agriculture and livestock rearing. Agriculture employs about 90 percent of the economically active population and accounts for roughly 40 percent of GDP. Most of the food produced is for domestic consumption, although unregistered trade with Nigeria plays an important role in the economy of the southern region. Most agriculture takes place in the Niger Valley and along the borders with Bénin and Nigeria. The main crops are millet, sorghum, maize, cowpeas, groundnuts, and rice. Cattle are the second-most significant export following uranium, and accounted for 20

percent of export earnings in the late 1990s. Nomadic or seminomadic groups traditionally are the ones to rear extensive livestock.

Livestock production grew considerably in the years following independence, not least because of the growth in demand from Nigeria and the highly populated coastal region. Rain-fed agriculture and livestock rearing are vulnerable to capricious rainfall, however. Droughts in the 1970s and 1980s led to dramatic losses in livestock, and the numbers have not yet reached pre-drought figures. Agriculture also poses a challenge to extensive livestock rearing. Population growth and extension of the cultivated areas have reduced access to pastures and limited mobility. Land degradation seems to result from this.

In general, the competition over land has led to conflicts between farmers and herders, and among farmers themselves. Land reform policies seem not to have alleviated the problems.

The manufacturing sector is negligible. It is mainly processing of agricultural commodities and import substitution, and the modern sector includes a groundnut extraction plant, cotton ginneries, a brewery, a textile factory, and a cement factory. Most activities in manufacturing remain small-scale and artisanal. The sector contributes to less than 10 percent of the GDP.

The 1994 devaluation of the West African Franc (FCFA) favored Niger's exports to Nigeria. Most of Niger's trading is unrecorded, however, and in large parts of Eastern Niger the common currency is the Nigerian Naira and not the FCFA.

Development aid constitutes around 17 percent of GDP. France is the largest contributor. However, political instability and military coups in the 1990s led donors to cut development assistance, and disbursed amounts fluctuated significantly since then. Partly due to the fluctuation in foreign aid, Niger has contracted important debts, and debt service weighed heavily on the state coffers. As a Highly Indebted Poor Country (HIPC), Niger has entered into negotiations over debt relief with International Monetary Fund and the World Bank.

See also **Aid and Development; Debt and Credit; Ecosystems; Famine; International Monetary Fund; Lake Chad Societies; Livestock; Niger River; Production Strategies: Agriculture; Sahara Desert; World Bank.**

BIBLIOGRAPHY

Charlick, Robert B. *Niger: Personal Rule and Survival in the Sahel.* Boulder, CO: Westview Press, 1991.

Gado, Alpha Boureima. *Une histoire des famines au Sahel.* Paris: Harmattan, 1993.

Miles, William F.S. *Hausaland Divided. Colonialism and Independence in Nigeria and Niger.* Ithaca, NY: Cornell University Press, 1994.

Olivier de Sardan, Jean-Pierre. *Les sociétés Songhay-Zarma (Niger-Mali).* Paris: Karthala, 1984.

Raynaut, Claude. *Society and Nature in the Sahel.* London: Routledge, 1997.

Thébaud, Brigitte. *Foncier Pastoral et gestion de l'espace au Sahel.* Paris: Karthala, 2002.

United Nations Development Programme. *2005 Human Development Report.* New York: United Nations Development Programme, 2005.

CHRISTIAN LUND

SOCIETY AND CULTURES

Straddling the Sahara and the Sahel and occupying the intersection of longstanding north-south and east-west trade axes, Niger is characterized by linguistic and ethnic intermingling, mobility, and cross-fertilization. Distinctive ethnically identified practices are counterbalanced by intermarriage, multilingualism, and playful cultural borrowing. The long history of Islam in the region has contributed to a shared culture across people groups and regions—well over 80 percent of the population is Muslim.

Linguistic and cultural differences have historically corresponded with differences in productive practices and economic niches. Sedentary populations have tended to farm the narrow strip of arable land along the southern edge of Niger: Hausa speakers comprise 56 percent of the population, the Zerma-Songhay and Dendi 22 percent. Smaller sedentary groups such as the Kanuri and Manga represent perhaps 5 percent of the population. Nomadic and semi-nomadic populations occupy the more northerly regions include the Tuareg (8%) and Fulani (8.5%). Niger also has small Arab, Toubou, and Gourmantche populations (1.2%).

The occupation of shared territories across ecological zones has contributed to both symbiosis and conflict. Historically, Tuareg nomads could not survive without the agricultural production of their Buzu slaves; Fulani pastoralists relied upon Hausa farmers and merchants for access to pasture and trade goods; and Kanuri traders had close ties with Hausa artisans. Each of these groups has cultural, historical, and political affinities that defy national boundaries. Tuareg populations, for example, are drawn into the political orbit of Libya and Algeria, while Hausa speakers often look to northern Nigeria for patronage and support.

All citizens of Niger share the distinctive legacy of French colonial rule as it was practiced in Niger,

République du Niger (Republic of Niger)

Population:	12,894,865 (2007 est.)
Area:	1,267,000 sq. km (489,191 sq. mi.)
Official language:	French
Languages:	French, Hausa, Djerma, Fulfulde, Kanuri, Tamachek, Toubou, Gourmantche, Arabic
National currency:	CFA franc
Principal religions:	Muslim 95%, remainder Christian and traditional
Capital:	Niamey (est. pop. 700,000 in 2006)
Other urban centers:	Tahoua, Maradi, Zinder, Diffa, Dosso, Arlit, Agadez
Annual rainfall:	varies from 500 mm (20 in.) in the south to 100 mm (4 in.) at Agadez to almost 0 mm in the far north
Principal geographical features:	*Mountains:* Tamgak Mountains, Aïr Massif *Lakes:* Lake Chad *Rivers:* Niger River, other seasonal rivers *Desert:* Ténéré Desert
Economy:	*GDP per capita:* US$1,000 (2006)
Principal products and exports:	*Agricultural:* cowpeas, cotton, peanuts, millet, sorghum, cassava (tapioca), rice, cattle, sheep, goats, camels, donkeys, horses, poultry *Manufacturing:* cement, brick, soap, textiles, food processing, chemicals, slaughterhouses *Mining:* uranium, iron, tin, tungsten, coal, calcium phosphates, gold, some oil
Government:	Independence from France, 1960. Multiple constitutions: 1960, suspended in 1974; revised 1989, suspended in 1991; 1992, suspended in 1996. Most recent constitution, 1999. Multiparty democracy. President elected for 5-year term by universal suffrage. 113-member National Assembly elected for 5-year terms. Local governmental organization based on 8 regions, 36 districts, and 256 communes.
Heads of state since independence:	1960–1974: President Diori Hamani 1974–1987: Lieutenant Colonel Seyni Kountché, chairman of the Supreme Military Council 1987–1989: Colonel (later General) Ali Saïbou, chairman of the Supreme Military Council 1989–1993: President Ali Saïbou 1993–1996: President Mahamane Ousmane 1996–: Colonel (later Brigadier General) Ibrahim Baré Mainassara, chairman of the National Salvation Council 1996–1999: President Ibrahim Baré Mainassara 1996–1999: Colonel Ibrahim Bare 1999–: President Mamadou Tandja
Armed forces:	President is commander in chief. 2-year conscription. *Army:* 6,000 *Air force:* 300 *Paramilitary:* 3,700
Transportation:	Principal transport is by the Niger River to Nigeria, controlled by the Société Nigerienne de Transports Fluviaux et Maritimes. *Roads:* 14,565 km (9,050 mi.), 25% paved *Airline:* Trans Niger *Airports:* 28 airports. International services at Niamey.
Media:	1 daily newspaper: *Le Sahel.* 1 weekly: *Le Sahel Dimanche.* 15 periodicals. 1 book publisher: L'Imprimerie Nationale du Niger. Radio is a state monopoly: Office de Radiodiffusion-Télévision du Niger (also called La Voix du Sahel). Télé-Sahel broadcasts only French-originated television programming. There are 2 other television stations.
Literacy and education:	*Total literacy rate:* 15% (2006). Education is free, universal, and compulsory for 6 years. A great proportion of schoolchildren attend traditional Qur'anic schools. Postsecondary education provided through Université de Niamey, Université Islamique du Niger, École Nationale d'Administration du Niger, Centre Régional de Recherches et de Documentation pour la Tradition Orale.

although they have been differently positioned within the colonial and postcolonial regimes. Despite strong initial resistance to French rule, Zerma speakers benefited more from the employment, education, and infrastructure of the colonial era than other groups and, until recently, dominated political life and the civil service. Hausa speakers bore the economic brunt of peanut cropping under colonialism. This strengthened their affinity with Hausa speakers across the border in British Nigeria and contributed to the emergence of a powerful Hausa merchant class. Tuareg and Fulani pastoralists were at a disadvantage in the colonial and postcolonial periods. Sustained Tuareg resistance to colonial rule contributed to French hostility toward nomadic groups. With the colonial conquest, Tuareg mobility and capacity to dominate agricultural populations were disrupted, whereas the growing commercial economy, based upon sedentary practices, French education, and cash cropping, increasingly passed them by.

Although Niger has a small minority of non-Muslims (including Catholics, Protestants, and those who refuse monotheism of any kind), Islam shapes the spatial and temporal practices of most citizens of Niger. Despite a shared religious culture, including respect for Islamic scholarship in Arabic, strands of cultural and political life antedating Islam continue to have salience. One mark of Islamic religious culture in the region has been a propensity to reconcile local practices, such as spirit possession and bilateral inheritance, with Islam. These deliberate retentions may contribute to ethnic self-assertion, gendered aesthetics, and political inclusiveness. Such adaptiveness is strained as economic discontent, generational tensions, and political critique are increasingly couched in an idiom of religious reform. Reformists may cleanse an existing Islamic Sufi order, promote an alternative Sufi brotherhood, reject Sufism outright, or—most controversially—convert to evangelical Christianity.

Consequently, divisions within each of these ethnolinguistic groups may be more salient than differences between ethnic groups. Almost half of the population of Niger is under the age of fifteen, and growing tension over gerontocratic authority is often more significant than ethnic differences, particularly as education redefines achieved status. Women have become increasingly vocal in promoting their interests, occasionally joining forces with youth and often bridging ethnic divides in the interest of promoting major political change, brokering peace, or arguing for protections for women.

Class and caste are equally important. Precolonial societies across ethnic groups distinguished nobles and Islamic scholars from commoners and slaves. Individuals with similar precolonial socioeconomic roles were often channeled into particular colonial and postcolonial structures, such as the military, the civil service, and the industrial workforce. Members of traditional aristocracies, scholarly clans, merchant classes, and laboring classes may therefore have much in common with one another across ethnic lines because of their positions within the modern political economy, even when their identities are grounded in local ethnic idioms. Distinctions within ethnic groups often have tremendous importance in local politics, whereas, at the national level, unspoken rivalries between ethnic groups may be significant despite crosscutting forms of social differentiation. These competing strands of identity, ethnicity, and interest structure Niger's contemporary politics.

See also **Colonial Policies and Practices; Ethnicity; Islam: Sufi Orders; Law: Islamic; Linguistics, Historical; Sahara Desert; Women: Women and the Law.**

BIBLIOGRAPHY

Alidou, Ousseina. *Engaging Modernity: Muslim Women and the Politics of Agency in Postcolonial Niger.* Madison: University of Wisconsin Press, 2005.

Bovin, Mette. *Nomads Who Cultivate Beauty: Wodaabe Dances and Visual Arts in Niger.* Uppsala, Sweden: Nordiska Afrikainstitutet, 2001.

Cooper, Barbara. *Evangelical Christians in the Muslim Sahel.* Bloomington: Indiana University Press, 2006.

Kimba, Idrissa, ed. *Le Niger: Etat et démocratie.* Paris: L'Harmattan, 2001.

Masquelier, Adeline. *Prayer Has Spoiled Everything: Possession Power, and Identity in an Islamic Town of Niger.* Durham, NC: Duke University Press, 2001.

Meunier, Olivier. *Dynamique de l'enseignement islamique au Niger.* Paris: L'Harmattan, 1997.

Miles, William. *Hausaland Divided: Colonialism and Independence in Nigeria and Niger.* Ithaca, NY: Cornell University Press, 1994.

Olivier de Sardan, Jean-Pierre. *Sociétés Songhay-Zarma, Niger-Mali: Chefs, guerriers, esclaves, paysans.* Paris: Karthala, 1984.

Rain, David. *Eaters of the Dry Season: Circular Labor Migration in the West African Sahel.* Boulder, CO: Westview Press, 1999.

Rasmussen, Susan. *The Poetics and Politics of Tuareg Aging: Life Course and Personal Destiny in Niger.* DeKalb: Northern Illinois University Press, 1997.

Spittler, Gerd. *Les Touaregs face aux sécheresses et aux famines.* Paris: Karthala, 1993.

Stoller, Paul. *Embodying Colonial Memories: Spirit Possession, Power, and the Hauka in West Africa.* New York: Routledge, 1995.

BARBARA M. COOPER

HISTORY AND POLITICS

Several great precolonial empires successively left their imprints on what is present-day Niger. In the fifteenth century, the Songhay Empire to the west and the Bornu Empire to the east wielded much influence. In the nineteenth century, the Fulani Empire of Sokoto was established through a holy war (jihad), stretching from the Niger River to the Hausa states. To the north, the sultanate of the Aïr played an important role since 1400.

French colonial power conquered territory from west to east, gaining the allegiance of many prestigious chiefdoms such as the kingdom of Say, the sultanates of Kebbi and Zinder, and others. In the north, the conquest met fierce resistance from the Tuareg who, led by their chief, Kaocen, organized a general uprising in the Massif Aïr in 1916–1917, which was severely repressed. The pacification of the territory was assured when it became the French Colony of Niger in 1922.

After World War II, French colonial policy softened, allowing Nigeriens to write a new constitution in 1946 that permitted them to elect a representative to the French National Assembly. During this period, the Parti Populaire Nigérien (PPN) of Diori Hamani and the Mouvement Socialist Africain (MSA Sawaba) of Djibo Bakary dominated local political life. A 1956 law then gave Niger's politicians even more voice in the management of their country by establishing a government council presided over by the governor. Its vice president, Bakary, was elected by the Territorial Assembly. Two years later, the new constitution adopted by referendum permitted the creation of a republic with Diori Hamani at its head. Nigerien Independence was proclaimed on August 3, 1960.

The military and an urban elite of Djerma/Songhay ethnic origin, who consigned the Hausa majority and other minority ethnicities (the Fulani, Tuareg, and Kanuri) to minor political roles, dominated the early governments. President Diori (1960–1974) suppressed all political opposition so well that the PPN controlled the entire country. At the end of the 1960s, a rising generation of bureaucrats criticized the inaction of the government, which seemed unable to improve the lot of the rural population. In response, Hamani wanted to call an extraordinary session of the PPN to plan the means of assuring durable development, but

the military coup d'état of April 15, 1974, prevented him from doing so.

The new chief of state, Lieutenant Colonel Seyni Kountché, suspended the constitution and restored order, aiming to alleviate the famine ravaging the country. He built his authority upon an image of integrity that was sorely lacking in the preceding government. Apart from two attempted coups d'état, President Kountché was, from 1974 until his death in November 1987, the master of Niger, which he governed with rigor. In October 1983, he reoriented his regime by designating a civilian prime minister of Tuareg origin, and he frequently changed the responsibilities of his ministers and senior public servants, and carried out new nominations for these positions in order to avoid a feeling of exclusion among members of the political elite. General Ali Saïbou, army chief of staff, succeeded him.

The 1989 to 1999 period was a particularly volatile time politically, involving three coups d'état, voting on four constitutions, elections for four presidents and five national assemblies, and totaling ten different governments in a decade. More liberal, General Saïbou adopted a new constitution in 1989 and created a unique party, the Mouvement National pour la Société de Développement (MNSD). This liberalization of government favored the protest movements of students and unions, leading Saïbou to accept the principle of multiple parties (November 1990) and later to hold a national conference. This conference, which held its first session on July 29, 1991, proclaimed itself sovereign. It suspended the constitution and dissolved the National Assembly and the government but retained the president of the republic. It designated Amadou Cheiffou as prime minister of the transition government and made him responsible for organizing democratic legislative and presidential elections and for managing the country until the installation of the new government.

The Alliance des Forces du Changement (AFC), a coalition of parties opposed to the MNSD, won the legislative elections, and, in 1993, Mahamane Ousmane was elected president of the republic for five years. The supporters of the Kountché regime joined the opposition, and the army withdrew from the political scene. Mahamadou Issoufou was named prime minister but resigned eighteen months later over disagreements with the president. His party, the

PNDS and one of the largest member parties of the AFC coalition, then left the coalition, upsetting the existing alliances. Thus, the AFC no longer held a majority of the seats in the General Assembly and President Ousmane had to dissolve the Assembly.

The new legislative elections, held in January 1994, restored the MNSD to power in a new alliance with the PNDS. The new prime minister was Hama Amadou. In January 1996, the political crisis came to a head when President Ousmane was preparing to again dissolve the Assembly, designate a new prime minister, fire the army chief of staff, and the prime minister was preparing to outlaw the president's party, the Convention Démocratique et Sociale (CDS). In addition, the pressure of a Tuareg rebellion in the north gave the army the political space to stage a coup d'état.

This final coup d'état started a transition to democracy whereby a military junta led by Colonel Ibrahim Baré Mainassara handed over power to an elected civilian government in December 1999 led by Mamadou Tandja, longtime leader of the MNSD. President Tandja's election as a man of mixed Kanuri and Fulani background was politically significant because it freed the government from its perception of preserving Djerma domination of national politics. President Tandja was reelected in December 2004. His rule has emphasized political stability and national reconciliation, though it has been tainted by domestic conflict over food insecurity and the government's close relationship with the International Monetary Fund that has resulted in the government implementing unpopular domestic policies. The 2005 food crisis in Niger in particular made international news and strained Niger's relationship with the United Nations, which the government accused of exaggerating the scale of the food crisis. A new civil society organization formed in 2005, called the Coalition contre la vie chère (Coalition against an expensive life), plans frequents strikes and protests against the government over the rising cost of living in the already poor nation.

See also **Colonial Policies and Practices; Famine; International Monetary Fund; United Nations.**

BIBLIOGRAPHY

Baier, Stephen. *An Economic History of Central Niger.* Oxford: Clarendon Press, 1980.

Di Lorenzo, Amanda, and Enrico Sborgi. "The 1999 Presidential and Legislative Elections in Niger." *Electoral Studies* 20 (2001): 470–476.

Fuglestad, Finn. *A History of Niger, 1850–1960.* Cambridge, U.K.: Cambridge University Press, 1983.

Grégoire, Emmanuel. *The Alhazai of Maradi: Traditional Hausa Merchants in a Changing Sahelian City.* Boulder, CO: Lynne Rienner, 1992.

Niger Country Profile 2007. London: Economist Intelligence Unit, 2006.

Séré de Rivières, Edmond. *Histoire du Niger.* Paris: Berger-Levralt, 1965.

EMMANUEL GRÉGOIRE
REVISED BY NANCY RHEA STEEDLE

NIGER RIVER. At more than 2,500 miles in length, the Niger River is the third-longest river in Africa after the Nile and the Congo Rivers, and the fourteenth-longest in the world. The Niger River Basin is shared by nine countries in West and Central Africa—Bénin, Burkina Faso, Cameroon, Chad, Côte d'Ivoire, Guinea, Mali, Niger, and Nigeria—and is home to approximately 100 million people. It rises in the Fouta Djallon Massif on the Sierra Leone–Guinea border, less than 200 miles from the Atlantic Ocean. From its headwaters, it flows north and east into the southern Sahara and then south and east until it enters the Atlantic Ocean through a broad delta in Nigeria. Among the Mandinka people of Mali it is known as the Joliba, among the Songhay of the great bend in the river it is called the Issa Ber, whereas among the Nupe and Yoruba of Nigeria it is called the Kwara. The name Niger is of uncertain origin but first appears in European literature in the *Description of Africa* (1956) of Leo Africanus in the mid-sixteenth century. It may be related to the Tuareg phrase *egerou n-igereou* used to describe it, meaning river of rivers.

The river has a number of notable natural features. After descending from the highlands of Guinea it becomes a broad, slow-moving mass of water about 3,000 feet wide at Bamako, the capital of Mali, and is joined by other smaller rivers, notably the Sankarani upstream from Bamako and the Bani. This river flows into it in the southern reaches of the next notable feature, the Inland Delta. An immense alluvial plain, the Inland Delta measures up to 30,888 square miles when the heavy annual rains bring floodwaters beginning in late August. Over the ensuing months, this flood creates a massive, shallow lake up to 150 miles wide and 300 miles long and replenishes a number of lakes of more or less permanent character at the northern end of the flood zone, providing abundant freshwater fishing areas. Similar to the Nile in Egypt, this annual flood also lays down a rich layer of silt that provides the region with fertile pasture and agricultural lands.

The flood zone reaches as far north as Kabara, the port of Timbuktu. This northern section of the river, known as the Niger Bend, is the closest major water source to the Sahara desert, which, in former times, rendered it a focal point for commerce and the epicenter of the Sahelian kingdoms of Mali and Gao. It also ensured the importance of Timbuktu as an ideal meeting place for caravan and riverine traffic, and its proximity to the larger flood zone assured its supply of grain. Downstream from Kabara, the Niger becomes narrower again, moving through the gorge of Tossay before turning dramatically south on its journey to the sea. This unusual boomerang course is generally believed to have formed when two ancient rivers joined together as the Sahara began to desiccate after 5000 BCE. Some 250 miles from the Atlantic, the Niger is joined by the Benue River before flowing due south to the sea, through the broad, fan-shaped Niger Delta that is dissected by numerous channels and home to rich mangrove swampland.

The full course of the Niger was not drawn on European maps until after 1830. Until then, European dependence on medieval Arab maps had led mapmakers to posit a connection between the Niger and the Nile—such as al-Idrīsī's theory (1592) of a single river source for both—or to show the Niger originating in a lake (in the general region of Lake Chad) and flowing westward to Senegal. The Scottish traveler Mungo Park (1771–1810) eventually established the west to east flow of the river when he traced its course from Segu as far as Boussa in 1796. In 1830, Captain Hugh Clapperton's (1788–1827) servant Richard Lander (1804–1834) with his brother John (1807–1839) finally established the course of the river below Boussa as it flowed into the Atlantic Ocean.

The lower reaches of the Niger soon became a highway for European—more particularly British—explorers, missionaries, and merchants. Following less successful expeditions by the Lander brothers (1832) and the naval captains William Allen (1792–1864), Bird Allen (1803–1841), and H. D. Trotter (1802–1859) in 1841, the Scottish doctor William Baikie (1825–1864) pushed up the Niger in 1857 into Nupe country, signing a treaty with its emir and creating a more permanent settlement at Lokoja. These expeditions paved the way for the activities of the Royal Niger Company (founded 1886), which, under its chief officer George Taubman Goldie (1846–1925), gained a commercial monopoly as well as political and military influence in the lower Niger region, and thus served as the precursor to more formal British colonial control. By 1903, Brigadier General Frederick Lugard had conquered most of what became Northern Nigeria in an effort to halt French attempts to move into the Niger valley.

Far upstream on the Niger in present-day Mali, the French began to move in from their colony of Senegal in the 1880s, gradually dismantling the Islamic empire established by al-Hajj Umar al-Futī, based at Segu. In 1890, Colonel Louis Archinard (1850–1932) took Segu and seized the royal library that is still kept at the Bibliothèque Nationale in Paris. By the end of the nineteenth century, French forces had completed the conquest of the territories bordering the Niger up to the area the British had conquered in what became Nigeria. By the end of 1960, however, both the British and the French had withdrawn from their colonial territories along the Niger, and four sovereign independent nations had emerged: Guinea, Mali, Niger, and Nigeria.

Many diverse peoples live along the banks of the Niger River and depend on its vital resources for travel and trade. The largest groups are the Bambara (Bamana) in the region between Bamako and Segu in Mali; the Songhay around the northern and eastern reaches of the great bend in the river; the Jerma (Zarma or Zerma) in Niger; the Nupe in central Nigeria, the Igbo (Ibo) along the southern reaches of the river; and the Ijo (Ijaw) in the delta. Also notable are the Sorko—Songhay-speaking fisherfolk, hippopotamus hunters, and boatbuilders—who move up and down the Niger from the Gulbin Khebbi tributary in Nigeria to the Inland Delta in Mali where the Bozo and

Somonou, who engage in similar activities, live. Increasingly, cities dominate the Niger landscape, with more than twelve cities of more than 100,000 inhabitants located within the river's basin. A vast majority of the basin's total population (80%) resides in Nigeria, representing an estimated 60 percent of Nigeria's total population (67.6 million inhabitants) in 2003. The Niger Basin traverses almost all of the possible ecosystem zones in West and Central Africa, sustaining an extensive biological community as well, including 243 species of fish (twenty of which are endemic), a rich array of transmigratory birds, as well as manatees, hippopotamuses, and crocodiles.

The Niger has been a vital artery of communication historically. It is navigable for much of its length by shallow draft boats, the only serious non-seasonal impediments to passage being the rapids at Kolikoro near Bamako, just north of the Mali-Niger border, and at Boussa in Nigeria. During the period of the Songhay Empire (1464–1591) large canoes carried grain to Gao and Timbuktu, and ferried dignitaries and military personnel from one end of the empire to the other. In the early twenty-first century there is still much private river traffic, and a Malian government ferry operates during the high water season between Kolikoro and Gao. Several bridges cross the Niger: two in the Malian capital, Bamako; one at Segu; one at Niamey, the capital of Niger; one at Malanville on the Bénin-Niger border; and many in Nigeria.

Although it represents an extremely important resource for basin inhabitants, the Niger is still only partially exploited. In Mali, a large dam-based irrigation system between Markala and Sokolo built by the French in the 1930s is used to cultivate rice and sugar. Originally coordinated by the Office du Niger, cultivation efforts are increasingly privatized under decentralization initiatives. At Kainji in Nigeria there is a major high dam that was completed in the late 1960s and provides a key source of hydroelectricity for Nigeria and Bénin. Almost all of the oil produced (two million barrels per day) in Nigeria comes from the Niger Delta, accounting for the vast majority of export earnings and contributing to severe contamination of the Delta's water resources. This degradation and inequitable distribution of oil revenues has been the source of notorious recent interethnic conflict and environmental movements. Throughout the Niger River, fishing pressures, sedimentation, and anthropogenic pollutants are threatening this vital natural resource and the services it renders to the basin's peoples. Created in 1980, the Niger Basin Authority (NBA) is one entity that seeks to promote interbasin cooperation and coordination for the river's exploitation and protection.

See also **Gao; Lugard, Frederick John Dealtry; Nile River; Timbuktu; Transportation.**

BIBLIOGRAPHY

Africanus, Leo. *Description de l'Afrique*, trans. A. Epaulard et al. 2 vols. Paris: Maisonneuve, 1956.

Andersen, Inger, et al. *The Niger River Basin: A Vision for Sustainable Management.* Directions in Development Series. Washington, DC: The World Bank, 2005.

Dike, Kenneth O. *Trade and Politics in the Niger Delta, 1830–1885: An Introduction to the Economic and Political History of Nigeria.* Oxford: Clarendon Press, 1956.

Dubois, Felix. *Timbuctoo the Mysterious*, trans. Diana White. New York: Longmans, Green and Co., 1896.

Gramont, Sanche de. *The Strong Brown God: The Story of the Niger River.* London: Houghton Mifflin, 1975.

Hollett, Dave. *The Conquest of the Niger by Land and Sea: From the Early Explorers and Pioneer Steamships to Elder Dempster and Company.* Abergavenny, U.K.: P.M. Heaton, 1995.

Lloyd, Christopher. *The Search for the Niger.* London: Collins, 1973.

Roberts, Richard. *Warriors, Merchants, and Slaves: The State and the Economy in the Middle Niger, 1700–1914.* Stanford, CA: Stanford University Press, 1987.

JOHN HUNWICK
REVISED BY ROSALIND FREDERICKS

NIGER-CONGO LANGUAGES. *See* **Languages: Niger-Congo.**

NIGERIA

This entry includes the following articles:
GEOGRAPHY AND ECONOMY
SOCIETY AND CULTURES, NORTHEAST NIGERIA
SOCIETY AND CULTURES, NORTHWEST NIGERIA
SOCIETY AND CULTURES, SOUTHEAST NIGERIA
SOCIETY AND CULTURES, SOUTHWEST NIGERIA
SOCIETY AND CULTURES, CENTRAL NIGERIA
HISTORY AND POLITICS, NORTHERN NIGERIA
HISTORY AND POLITICS, SOUTHERN NIGERIA

GEOGRAPHY AND ECONOMY

The Federal Republic of Nigeria was formed from the British colony and protectorates of Northern and Southern Nigeria and came into existence on January 1, 1900. It gained its political independence from Britain on October 1, 1960, and became a republic on October 1, 1963. The country lies between 3 degrees and 15 degrees east longitude, and 4 degrees and 14 degrees north latitude. It is bounded on the south by the Gulf of Guinea, on the east by Cameroon, on the north by Chad and Niger, and on the west by Bénin. It has a total land area of approximately 356,669 square miles and a population of roughly 135 million in 2007. The census figures were not without controversy, and a new census was prepared for late 2005. The Federation has grown from three regions (1960) to four states (1963), twelve states (1967), nineteen states (1976), twenty-one states (1987), thirty states (1991), and thirty-six states (1996), and has a federal capital city at Abuja. Until December 1991, Lagos was the capital.

GEOGRAPHY

Old igneous and metamorphic rocks of the basement complex underlie large areas of the country, especially in the northern, central, and western parts. They comprise granitic and basaltic rocks, the latter in areas of volcanic activity such as the Jos, Biu, and Mambilla Plateaus. By contrast, young sedimentary rocks, including sandstone and limestone, underlie the northwestern and northeastern areas, the valleys of the Niger and Benue Rivers, most of the (south)eastern areas, and the coastal belt.

In terms of relief, Nigeria is part of the western lowland zone of tropical Africa. Much of the country lies below 3,300 feet. The main highlands are the Jos Plateau, almost in the center of the country, the Biu and Mambilla Plateaus, and the Adamawa and Mandara Mountains in the eastern borderlands. All are highly dissected. They slope down to upland areas such as the central Hausa High Plains in the north and the Yoruba Uplands in the south. These upland areas are dotted everywhere with striking rocky outcrops and inselbergs. To the northeast and northwest are the lowlands of the Lake Chad depression and the Rima Basin, respectively. In southeastern Nigeria, the sedimentary rocks give rise to a distinctive topography of scarp lands marked by gully erosion and small lakes. The coastal areas are notable for their mix of sand beaches, creeks, and lagoons that merge imperceptibly into the delta of the Niger River.

The Niger River and its principal tributary, the Benue, are the two most important rivers. Both rise outside the country, the former in the Fuuta Jallon highlands of the Republic of Guinea, the latter in the Adamawa highlands of western Cameroon. After their impressive confluence at Lokoja, they continue south to enter the Gulf of Guinea through a large network of creeks and distributaries forming the Niger Delta. Virtually all Nigerian rivers north of the Niger-Benue Valley rise from the Jos Plateau. They include the Sokoto, Kaduna, and Gongola, as well as the Komadugu-Yobe, which drains into Lake Chad. Rivers draining south of the Niger-Benue Valley are usually short and flow either into the Niger-Benue system or directly to the ocean. As in other parts of Africa, rapids and falls are common on Nigerian rivers. These make them unnavigable over any great distance, but indicate some significant potential for hydroelectric development.

Temperatures are high throughout the year. Except on the plateaus, maximum temperatures range from 81 to 104 degrees Fahrenheit, and the minimum from 64 to 77 degrees Fahrenheit. Rainfall is the critical climatic element. It decreases progressively northward from 148 inches per annum in Port Harcourt on the coast to about 25 inches in Maiduguri in the extreme northeast. Seasonal variation in rainfall becomes pronounced as one moves northward, with the dry season varying from less than one month on the coast to as much as seven months in the northeast.

Total rainfall and its seasonality determine soil characteristics and vegetation patterns. Most parts of the country are covered by ferruginous tropical soils derived from both the basement complex and old sedimentary rocks. On the north central Hausa high plains, more fertile soils have developed on the drift deposits covering the basement complex. To the south, clayey and sandy ferralitic soils occur. Low in humus content, they are not the best

soils for agriculture. These become hydromorphic and still less fertile as one moves into the Niger Valley, the Niger Delta, and the coastal creeks and lagoons.

The vegetation pattern changes in consonance with the rainfall and soil conditions. It varies from the mangrove forest of the delta, creeks, and lagoons of the coast, to the rain forest of the southern lowlands, to the succession of the derived Guinea, Sudan, and Sahel grassland belts and the inliers of mountain vegetation on the Jos

and other plateaus. Forests still cover about 10 percent of the land area, and in the south they yield abundant timber that has been exported since colonial times.

ECONOMY

Much of the vegetation has been transformed by human activities, especially through farming and mining, the former now utilizing some 40 percent of the land. In terms of agricultural production, the country can be divided into three broad zones: the southern root crop zone; the northern grain zone; and the middle (mixed crop) belt. The major staples from the southern zone are yams, cassava, and cocoyams. Until the introduction of rice in the twentieth century, corn was the only grain produced in the zone. Agricultural exports are cocoa, palm oil, palm kernels, rubber, and timber. The northern zone produces millet, sorghum, rice, beans, tomatoes, and onions, as well as peanuts and cotton for industrial processing and export. Because of its relative freedom from the scourge of the tsetse fly, this zone, along with the plateau areas, contains most of the major livestock, particularly cattle, goats, and sheep. The middle belt, which can produce both root crops and grains, is emerging as the major food basket of the country. For purposes of enhanced food security, multipurpose irrigation dams have been constructed on many streams and rivers, and aquaculture and fish farm estates have been established in many parts of the country, along with the promotion of lakes and lagoons fisheries. A major cassava export program was launched in 2003 to further stimulate agricultural production in the country.

Mining locations and products are determined largely by geology. Metamorphic rocks of the basement complex offer such metallic minerals as tin and columbite mined on the Jos Plateau; gold, an important export commodity since colonial times; and iron ore, mica, feldspar, marble, and a host of other minerals of as yet unproven economic significance. The sedimentary rocks, especially of the coastal areas and the southeast, yield fossil fuels of various types. Initially, sub-bituminous coal was mined in the Enugu region in the southeast. Since the late 1960s, petroleum has been produced and exported both off- and onshore within the Niger Delta. In 2003, production stood at 849 million barrels per annum, or 2.33 million barrels (mbd) per day. Of this total production, between 79 and 90 percent is exported in any one year. The same area offers large quantities of natural gas, with reserve estimated at over thirteen trillion cubic feet. Major development, production and export of natural gas began in the late 1990s. In 2003, approximately 174 billion cubic meters of natural gas was produced in the course of petroleum mining, 57 percent of which was utilized and 43 percent of

which continued to be flared. Natural gas export promises to bring a renewed upturn to the economy of the country. A West African Gas Pipeline is, as of 2006, nearing completion and links the Republics of Ghana, Togo, and Bénin to Nigeria. It is expected to be a major factor in promoting regional economic integration in the area. There is also abundant lignite. All these are in addition to such industrial minerals as lead, zinc, limestone, kaolin, talc, sand, and clay.

Until the 2,178 mile-long railway network was established by the colonial administration between 1896 and 1927, there was only limited internal exchange or overseas export of any significance. In the early twenty-first century, indifferent management, poor maintenance, road competition, and uneconomic pricing have impaired the operational efficiency of the railways, reducing their relative importance in the nation transportation system. Transportation development, particularly the improvement of the ports of Lagos-Apapa and Port Harcourt in the first two decades of the twentieth century, transformed economic conditions in Nigeria. More ports have since been developed at Tin Can Island in Lagos; at Warri, Koko, Burutu and Sapele in the western delta, at Calabar; and at Bonny and Onne for petroleum shipping. Road development followed after World War I but was closely controlled because of its competition with the railway. Restrictions were relaxed after World War II because the railway proved inadequate for transporting the vastly increased agricultural production from interior locations. Since then the road network has expanded tremendously, amounting in 2003 to some 127,000 miles, nearly half of which are paved comprising largely federal and state roads. Most local government roads are earth roads and suffer greatly from poor maintenance.

Waterways were important for transporting goods during the colonial era. For some months of the year, roughly 5,300 miles of waterways were navigable on the Niger River from the coast up to Jebba, and on the Benue up to Garoua (in Cameroon). The Nigerian government has embarked on dredging the lower reaches of the Niger as a means of further facilitating movement of freight within the Niger-Delta region of the country. Internal air transportation has, since the 1980s, also become important, with the removal of the monopoly previously enjoyed by Nigeria Airways. Many of the state capitals are linked to Lagos and Abuja by a number of private carriers, with many flights each day.

The period after World War II saw the beginning of serious industrialization based on the principle of import substitution. This placed a high premium on port location, and so a high percentage of industrial capacity came to be concentrated in Lagos, to a lesser extent in Port Harcourt, and, since 1992, at the first Export Processing Zone (EPZ) in Calabar. Other important industrial concentrations developed inland in Kaduna, Kano, Jos, Enugu, and Aba. A major strategy to promote and strengthen the growth of small- and medium-scale industries was launched in 2001 by the nation banks that decided to put aside in a special fund 10 percent of their pretax profit for equity participation in such industries. Nonetheless, in spite of consuming a large proportion of the foreign earnings of the country, manufacturing contribution to the gross domestic product (GDP) has declined. It was over 8 percent in 1992 but fell to under 5 percent in 2002.

The weakening in manufacturing growth is closely related to the poor infrastructural situation in the country, especially of electricity and water. This has prompted the government, since the return of democratic governance in 1999, to embark on a major program of privatization and private sector-led economic development based on deregulation of significant areas of the economy. A Bureau of Public Enterprises (BPE) oversees the preparation of many parastatals of the Federal Government for privatization—notably the National Electricity Power Authority (NEPA), the Nigerian Telecommunications Company (NITEL), the Nigerian Ports Authority (NPA), and Nigeria Airways. An area of the economy on which deregulation had the most dramatic impact is telecommunications, where the number of mobile telephones provided by private-sector organizations rose from zero in 2000 to 3.2 million by 2003, and fixed landline telephones rose from 497,000 in 2000 to over 850,000 by 2003.

The gross domestic product in Nigeria in 2003 was 7,180 billion naira at current basic prices. At 121 naira to the U.S. dollar in that year, this came to nearly US$60 billion. After years of virtual economic stagnation for much of the last decade of the last millennium, this represented the beginning of significant growth in the economy. Agriculture provides a significant but declining proportion of the nation gross domestic product, accounting in 2006 for less than 30 percent of the product. By contrast, crude petroleum and natural gas remain the most important sectors of the economy, accounting for over 43 percent of the nation's GDP. There is a determined program to reduce the relative share of this sector in the GDP through more vigorous promotion of non-oil exports. The developmental impact of the national GDP is, however, greatly undermined by the high external debt overhang, in 2006 put at some US$34 billion, for which each year a significant proportion of the nation's budget is dedicated to paying at least the interest on this debt.

The recent surge in the performance of the national economy has been put down to the inauguration in 2003 of the National Economic Empowerment and Development Strategy (NEEDS), a strategy comprising series of socioeconomic reforms that also sets various targets to be met by each sector of the economy—macroeconomic, sectoral, budgetary, external sector, banking, social services, and infrastructure—in each of the first five years of its operation. The strategy established a mechanism for coordinating the performance of all the sectors, as well as an Independent Monitoring Committee that reports on how well the targets and objectives of the various reforms are met. There is growing evidence that the determination of the present administration to vigorously pursue the various reform agenda of NEEDS is already impacting positively on the economy and increasing its attractiveness for foreign direct investment.

See also **Climate; Kano; Lagos; Livestock; Maiduguri; Niger River; Port Harcourt; Production Strategies; Transportation; World Bank.**

BIBLIOGRAPHY

Aina, Tade Akin, and Ademola T. Salau, eds. *The Challenge of Sustainable Development in Nigeria*, Ibadan, Nigeria: Nigerian Environmental Study Team, 1992.

Arya, Pyare L. *Structure, Policies and Growth Prospects of Nigeria*. Lewiston, New York: Edwin Mellen Press, 1993.

Buchanan, Keith M., and John Charles Pugh. *Land and People in Nigeria: The Human Geography of Nigeria and its Environmental Background*. London: University of London Press, 1958.

Federal Office of Statistics. *The Nigerian Statistical Fact Sheets on Economic and Social Development*. Abuja, Nigeria: Federal Office of Statistics, 2004.

Iyoha, Friday E. et al., eds. *Self-Reliance, Politics and Administration in Nigeria*, 2nd edition. Ekpoma, Nigeria: Department of Political Science, Edo State University, 1995.

Iyoha, Milton A., and Chris O. Itsede, eds. *Nigerian Economy: Structure, Growth and Development*. Benin City, Nigeria: Mindex Publications, 2002.

National Planning Commission. *National Economic Empowerment and Development Strategy NEEDS*. Abuja, Nigeria: National Planning Commission, 2004.

Oguntoyinbo, Julius S.; Olusegun O. Areola; and M. O. Filani; eds. *The Geography of Nigerian Development*. Ibadan, Nigeria: Heinemann Educational Books, 1983.

Okonjo-Iweala, Ngozi; Charles Soludo; and Mansur Muhtar; eds. *The Debt Trap in Nigeria: Towards a Sustainable Debt Strategy*. Trenton, New Jersey: Africa World Press, 2003.

Onokerhoraye, Andrew G. *The Impact of the Structural Adjustment Programme on Grassroots Development in Nigeria*. Benin City, Nigeria: Benin Social Science Series for Africa, 1995.

Watts, Michael, ed. *State, Oil, and Agriculture in Nigeria*. Berkeley: Institute of International Studies, University of California, 1987.

AKIN L. MABOGUNJE

SOCIETY AND CULTURES, NORTHEAST NIGERIA

Northeastern Nigeria is characterized by a variety of societies, comprising about ten million people and fifty-five different ethnic groups, most of whom live in the present states of Borno, Yobe, Gombe, Adamawa, and part of Taraba. The languages spoken belong to three out of four African language phyla: the Nilo-Saharan (Kanuri and Kanembu); the Afro-Asiatic (Shuwa Arabs and about sixty Chadic minority languages, e.g., Bole-Tangale, Bade-Ngizim, Bura, Margi, and Mandara); and the Niger-Congo phyla (e.g., Fulfulde, Jukun, and Mumuye). The most widely used languages in trading contexts are Hausa, Fulfulde, and English. Whereas the Muslim town Fulani dominate the region around Jalingo, Yola, and Gombe, the Kanuri people, also Muslim, represent the majority in Borno and Yobe states and have administrative centers in Maiduguri and Damaturu. Bole prevail around Potiskum, and Bura/Babur around Biu.

There are four different cultural areas of northeastern Nigeria. First is the Chad Basin plains which shares a national border with Niger in the north and with Cameroon in the east. For many centuries the Borno Empire, established west of Lake Chad in the fifteenth century, was the leading power of Central Sudan. As part of one of the main trans-Saharan trade routes, the area provided a crossroad for many people and became the center of various networks of trade and social exchange. Assimilation and displacement strategies played a central role in the expansion of the Borno polity; processes which led to the so-called Kanurization of societies living in the area before. As such the Sao, the Badawai, Suwurti, Mower, and Manga are recognized as Kanuri subgroups. Others kept their individual identity (e.g. the Margi) or came into existence as a distinctive ethnic group together with that of the Kanuri (Malgwa/Gamergu, and Mandara). Kanuri society is highly stratified and headed by a royal ruler, the Shehu.

Although dominant in cities and administrative businesses, many Kanuri identify themselves as farmers (millet, guinea-corn, beans). Most rural Kanuri are involved in multiple economic undertakings and perform a handicraft (pottery, raffia plaiting, leatherwork, calabash decoration, or mud-brick-building) along with farming and animal husbandry. They share this multiple economic existence with other people living in the formerly more powerful Emirates (Bade [Bade, Ngizim] and Fika [Bole]). In addition, transhumant Shuwa Arabs live within the area of the Chad Basin plains as sons of the soils (i.e., indigenous). As they were in the westernmost part of the so-called Arabic-speaking Bagara-belt, they reached the area south of Lake Chad in the eighteenth century. After their arrival, they adopted a mixed economy of cattle husbandry and agriculture, and became involved in Borno politics, defending the Muslim state against Fulani jihadists.

The second cultural area is the Gwoza/Mandara mountains, a region southeast of the Chad Basin plains, sharing a border with Cameroon in the east and turning into the Adamawa highlands in the south. Muslims address the societies of that area collectively as Gwoza, Mandara, or kirdi/pagan. These terms refer not only to the peoples' place of origin but also to the religious orientation of most of them, characterized until recently by local religions and cults. The Gwoza Hills are the most northwesterly extension of the Mandara mountains. They are populated by ten major groups (e.g., Guduf, Lamang, Glavda), of which only a few still practice traditional terrace farming. Because the Fulani often exploited them, the Gwoza sought support from the Kanuri and established a kind of patron-client relationship in which the Gwoza are regarded as laborers. Many of the mountain groups are connected through their oral history with the Borno Empire, either because they say they come directly from Borno (Hona, Gude), or more generally from the North (Fali, Bata); some had a tribute-like status with Borno, others have established independent communities and sacred chiefdoms (Fali, Sukur).

Further south lies the Bura-Margi-speaking region, which can be regarded as a transitional zone between the other cultural areas. The Bura, Pabir/ Babur, Margi, Higi, Kilba, and Chibok belong to this language group, many of whom migrated from the northern region. Although they are united by sharing the same language, their culture and religions may differ.

The chiefs of Biu were in close contact with the Jukun from Pindiga (shared cult centers), who are part of societies from the fourth cultural area, the Lower Gongola-Benue Valley. The area is inhabited by a large number of smaller ethnic groups. Some of them, such as the Jukun, the Chamba, and the Bata, tried to establish larger centralized states, but the majority were organized in small-scale chiefdoms or in decentralized political systems based on subsistence farming. Fishermen and artisans from the area are well known, producing famous wooden figurines or working far away from their homes as part-time laborers during farming or fishery seasons, keeping home ties through associations and social clubs. The ethnic groups within the Gombe Emirate, such as the Tangale, Waja and Tula, Kupto, and Kwami— partly Christians and traditionalists—came under Muslim influence in the nineteenth century. The groups have, since the 1950s, been dominantly northernized by Hausa and Fulani settlers.

Besides their heterogeneous cultural background, the people of northeastern Nigeria share a common history connected with the expansion of two Muslim empires, the Borno and Fulani Emirates. Although Borno resisted the jihadist movements of the Fulani at the beginning of the nineteenth century, those wars stopped the expansion of the Borno Empire and gave room for the Fulani to consolidate their political power in the southern and the southeastern regions of northeastern Nigeria. The Fulani are either pastoralists (Wodaabe), settled in towns, or farmers. Both pastoralist and town Fulani own cattle; the pastoralists travel widely with their herds, building temporary houses where grazing conditions are good. The Fulani Emirates are based on hierarchical systems of bureaucracy and taxation derived from the Islamic tradition, and the Emirs are paramount political leaders with great influence on Fulani and non-Fulani communities.

The nineteenth-century jihads between Muslims and non-Muslims have had a great impact on contemporary relations between the different ethnic groups. Considerable tension and competition exist between the Kanuri and Fulani on the one hand, and many non-Muslim groups on the other. Sometimes those potential conflicts are compensated by establishing a joking relationship as in the case of Kanuri and Fulani, which, besides their militant history, allows them to interact in a détente manner.

Because social identity and religious affiliation are closely linked, ethnic and religious tensions are often indistinguishable, and political conflicts are frequently the product of Muslim-Christian antagonism. Direct religious confrontations have been widespread: large-scale violent clashes between different Muslim groups and between Muslims and Christians broke out in Maiduguri in 1982, in Yola in 1984, and in Gombe in 1985. Religious tensions continued throughout the 1990s, strengthened by active Muslim and Christian missionary work. Since the implementation of shari'a Muslim law in most of the northern Nigerian states in 2000, religious motivated clashes increased, culminating in the 2006 riots provoked by the so-called Muhammad cartoons in Maiduguri. In addition, ethnicity and religion are often the decisive criteria for access to government resources, business contracts, and personal careers, emphasizing the great importance of local traditions in the modern state.

See also **Ethnicity; Islam; Lake Chad Societies; Law: Islamic; Maiduguri.**

BIBLIOGRAPHY

Berns, Marla. "Art and History in the Lower Gongola Valley, Northeastern Nigeria." Unpublished Ph.D. diss. Los Angeles: University of California, 1986.

Braukämper, Ulrich. "Towards a Chronology of Arabic Settlement in the Chad Basin." In *Living with the Lake. History, Culture and Economy of Lake Chad*, ed. Matthias Krings and Editha Platte. Cologne, Germany: Köppe, 2004.

Cohen, Ronald. *The Kanuri of Bornu.* New York: Holt, 1967.

Dinslage, Sabine, and Anne Storch. *Magic and Gender. A Thesaurus of the Jibe of Kona.* Cologne, Germany: Ruediger Köppe Verlag, 2000.

Harnischfeger, Johannes. "Islamisation and Ethnic Conversion in Nigeria." *Anthropos* 101 (2006): 37–53.

Hogben, S. J. *An Introduction to the History of the Islamic States of Nigeria.* Ibadan, Nigeria: Oxford University Press, 1967.

Löhr, Doris. "The Malgwa. A Historical Overview and some Ethnographic Notes." *Borno Museum Society Newsletter* 56/57 (2003): 23–44.

Lukas, Renate. "Nicht-islamische Ethnien im Südlichen Tschadraum." Unpublished Ph.D. diss. Frankfurt, Germany: University of Frankfurt am Main, 1973.

Meek, C. K. *Tribal Studies in Northern Nigeria.* London: Kegan Paul, 1931.

Müller-Kosack, Gerhard. Mandara Mountains Home Page. Available at http://www.mandaras.info.

Platte, Editha *Frauen in Amt und Würden. Handlungsspielräume muslimischer Frauen im ländlichen Nordostnigeria.* Frankfurt am Main, Germany: Brandes and Apsel, 2000.

Platte, Editha, and Bosoma Sheriff. Kanuri Studies Association. Available at http://www.kanuri.net.

Neil Kastfelt
Revised by Editha Platte

SOCIETY AND CULTURES, NORTHWEST NIGERIA

Northwest Nigeria occupies a unique place in the history of the country. It was renowned for being the seat of the Sokoto Caliphate and as the center of Islamic learning and activity. The area, which comprises the present-day states of Sokoto, Kebbi, Zamfara, and parts of Niger, had been both the motivator and focus of the Fulani-inspired jihad of Shaikh 'Uthman dan Fodio that began in 1804. Prior to the development of the Sokoto Caliphate and the overthrow of the indigenous *Habe* rulers, the Hausa, who constituted the largest indigenous group, had raided many of their neighbors to the south and west for slaves. Gradually, many of these peoples were absorbed into Hausa culture and became indistinguishable from their overlords. Many of such groups, however, in spite of the jihad in the early nineteenth century and the emirate system, continued to maintain their own identities.

A number of states in this region, including Borgu, Kebbi, Dendi, Zaberma, Arewa, and Gobir, were hostile to the Caliphate. Although the states were initially subjugated, they could not be permanently held. Some modern Hausa-speaking groups do not identify with the Hausa-Fulani. These include the Dendi, Busa, and Tienga. The Dendi are a branch of the Songhay of the middle Niger and speak a language of the independent Songhay family. The Busa and Tienga languages belong to the Mande branch of the Niger-Congo language family.

The Kabbawa, Dakarkari, Kambari, Arawa, Dandawa, Zabarmarwa, Fakkawa, and Dukawa ethnic groups are distinct, although they still retain their linguistic affinity to the Hausa-Fulani. The Kabbawa of Argungu in Kebbi, apart from resisting Fulani conquest, are further distinguished by their maintenance of conspicuous pre-Islamic religious practices, including the Argungu fishing festival and the Uhola festival. The Dakarkari, who are predominant in the present-day Kebbi state, also celebrate the Uhola festival in the towns and villages of the Zuru emirate. It conveys the people's gratitude and commitment to their ancestral god, Asilo, for the rains and good harvests. It is also a puberty rite for young boys and girls.

The first decade of the twentieth century proved unhappy for the Caliphate as it fell in 1903 to British colonial forces. The last decade of the twentieth century, as well as the first decade of the twenty-first, has similarly proved very challenging for the region. The Caliphate continued to suffer severe decline in its eminence. On April 20, 1996, the eighteenth sultan, Alhaji Ibrahim Dasuki (b. 1923) was deposed, arrested, and banished to Jalingo in Taraba State by the military administration. Alhaji Muhammadu Maccido (1928–2006) succeeded him. A similar fate was later to befall the Emir of Gwandu, Alhaji Mustapha Jokolo. He was deposed on June 3, 2005, by the Kebbi State government for negligence of duty, and banished to Nasarawa State. The Gwandu Emirate was the Southwestern half of the Sokoto Caliphate ruled by Mallam Abdullahi Gwandu, the brother of ʿUthman dan Fodio.

A major development in the region was the introduction of the *shariʿa* Islamic law to cover criminal cases. In January 2000, in furtherance of his election campaign promises, Governor Yerima Ahmed Sani (b. 1960) of Zamfara State introduced *shariʿa* law into his state. In swift succession, eleven other northern states followed suit. This created an uneasy constitutional standoff between the Federal Government and the states. The next stage of the crisis began with the formation of the *Hizbah* (*shariʿa* implementation committee) group and the subsequent arrest, prosecution, and conviction of several people for criminal offenses under *shariʿa* law. In March 2000, a *shariʿa* court in Zamfara convicted Buba Bello Jangebe of stealing a cow and had his right hand amputated for the offense. In Sokoto, on October 9, 2001, a *shariʿa* court sentenced Safiya Hussein Tungar-Tudu (b. c. 1967) to death by stoning for committing adultery and for being pregnant out of wedlock. Amina Lawal (b. c. 1973) from Katsina State was to suffer the same fate in March 2002 for the same offense. The men involved in both cases were discharged, for want of evidence. Under *shariʿa* law, pregnancy and childbearing outside of marriage were sufficient evidence for a woman to be convicted for adultery.

Both cases became an international cause, as human rights organizations and foreign governments called on the federal government to intercede on behalf of the convicts. Both cases were won on appeal. The fallout of the introduction of *shariʿa* was the flowering of anti-*shariʿa* uprisings in the region and in several parts of northern Nigeria. These have led to the death of thousands of people as this often took the complexion of ethnoreligious intolerance and antagonisms. Christians and people from other ethnic groups were killed. Homegrown religious fundamentalists and countless numbers of unemployed youths became ready tools in the hands of troublemakers. Unfortunately, the region also has a long, porous border with Niger and Chad; two Islamic nations where poverty and rebellion have created fertile recruiting grounds for Islamic militants that have constituted a menace to Nigeria's security.

Unorthodox Islamic practices have also grown to challenge the dominant Sunni Islamic practices. In December 2000, in Sokoto, the seat of the Caliphate, the *Azalea* sect slaughtered a horse, then shared and consumed the meat, claiming the action to be a revival of a prophetic tradition. It took the intervention of the *Fatwa* Committee of the Nigerian Supreme Council for Islamic Affairs (NSCIA) for the practice to be declared unacceptable. In May 2005, several people were killed when traditionalist Sunnis tried to assert their dominance in the face of growing minority Shiite influence. The furor generated by the polio immunization campaign in 2003 significantly affected social harmony in the area. An Islamic leader alleged that the polio vaccines contained substances capable of rendering Muslim children infertile. The people of the region then developed a serious apathy toward the antipolio exercise. The outcry later proved to be a hoax.

In their day-to-day existence, the people of the region are generally farmers, traders, and pastoralists. They also engage in local crafts, such as weaving and leatherworking. The existence of mineral resources such as limestone, kaolin, salt, gypsum, silica sand, clay, and phosphates makes the area a focus of modern industrialization. The region boasts the Usmanu Danfodiyo University, schools, an airport, hotels, and a network of roads and railway lines. Places of interest include the Sokoto Museum and the *Hubbare*: tombs of Shaikh ʿUthman dan Fodio, his daughter, Nana Asmaʾu (d. 1864), and Sultans Ahmadu Rufai (d. 1873), Hassan Dan-Muazu (d. 1938), and Siddiq Abubakar II (d. 1988). There is also the Waziri Junaidu History Bureau in Sokoto that serves as the repository of the artifacts and intellectual works dating back to period of the Jihad.

See also **Asmaʾu, Nana; Human Rights; Initiation; Languages; Law: Islamic; ʿUthman dan Fodio; Women: Women and the Law.**

BIBLIOGRAPHY

Adeleye, R. A. "The Sokoto Caliphate in the Nineteenth Century." In *History of West Africa*, edited by J. F.

Ade. Ajayi and Michael Crowder. 3d ed. London: Longmann, 1985.

Falola, Toyin. *Violence in Nigeria. The Crisis of Religious Politics and Secular Ideologies.* New York: University of Rochester, 1998.

Kukah, Matthew Hassan. *Religion, Politics and Power in Northern Nigeria.* Ibadan, Nigeria: Spectrum Books, 1993.

Nelson, Harold D., ed. *Area Handbook for Nigeria*, 4th edition. Washington, DC: Government Printing Office, 1982.

Yakubu, Ademola. *The Dialectics of the* Shariʿa *Imbroglio in Nigeria.* Ibadan, Nigeria: Demyaxs Law Books, 2003.

OLUTAYO ADESINA

SOCIETY AND CULTURES, SOUTHEAST NIGERIA

Southeastern Nigeria is about 31,445 square miles, or 8.51 percent of Nigeria's total area. It is bounded by Cameroon on the east, the Bight of Bonny on the south, and the Niger River on the west. Its northernmost towns are Nsukka, Ogoja, and Obudu. It comprises Abia, Anambra, Akwa Ibom, Bayelsa, Cross River, Delta, Ebonyi, Enugu, Imo, and Rivers States.

Southeastern Nigeria includes both coastal and forest regions. The coastal region is intersected by an intricate network of rivers and creeks that are tributaries of the Niger River. These abundant waterways plus frequent rainfall explain why this part is made up of mangrove swamps. Immediately north of the coastal region is dense mangrove forest.

There are more than thirty ethnic and linguistic groupings. They include the Igbo (Ibo), Anang, Efut, Ibibio, Ijo (Ijaw), Ogba, and Ogoni. The Igbo and the Ijaw make up the third and fourth largest ethnic groups in the country at 18 percent and 11 percent, respectively. The Igbo dominate in most of the region while the Ijaw are dominant in the Niger Delta region. A remarkable feature in precolonial times was the absence of centralized political authority. Only the Nri, a subgroup of the Igbo, some western Igbo communities, the Efik, and much later the Ijo were exceptions to this general phenomenon. Secret societies like the Ibibio Ekpo featured prominently in law enforcement among some groups.

Occupations in the zone include farming, fishing, salt making, pottery, weaving, blacksmithing, and wood carving. With the advent of the slave trade in the fifteenth century, the area became a major source of supply and the center of evacuation of slaves to the Americas. With abolition of the slave trade by the mid-nineteenth century, the area became the major palm produce belt of Nigeria. In the twenty-first century, it is the center of crude oil production, which is a major source of conflict and of environmental degradation in the region.

The southeast is also the most Christianized region of Nigeria with the percentage of adherents reaching above 95 percent. The Roman Catholic Church in particular is dominant though many Protestant traditions and Pentecostal groups have made considerable impacts. Traditional religion or animism has significant following in the zone as well.

Following political upheavals soon after independence, southeastern Nigeria made a secession bid under the banner of Biafra from 1967 to 1970. In the first decade of the 2000s, for the most part the peoples are fully reintegrated. Some of Nigeria's largest commercial centers, such as Onitsha, Aba, and Port Harcourt, are located there. The zone has about ten universities, with secondary and primary schools running into thousands. Furthermore, there are four airports, one of which is international. In addition, there are two seaports, Calabar and Port Harcourt. According to the disputed 2006 census, the population of this region is about 37.4 million people, which makes up approximately 26 percent of Nigeria's total population.

See also **Ecosystems; Niger River; Port Harcourt; Slave Trades.**

BIBLIOGRAPHY

Alagoa, Ebiegberi Joe. *A History of the Niger Delta.* Ibadan: Ibadan University Press, 1972.

Forde, C. Daryll, and G. I. Jones. *The Igbo and Ibibio Speaking Peoples of Southeastern Nigeria.* London, 1967.

Talbot, Percy Amaury. *The Peoples of Southern Nigeria.* London: F. Cass, 1969.

Uchendu, Victor. *The Igbo of Southeastern Nigeria.* New York, 1965.

Udo, Reuben Kenrick. "Environments and Peoples of Nigeria." *Groundwork of Nigerian History*, ed. Obaro Ikime. Ibadan: Heinemann Education Books, 1980.

C. OGBOGBO
REVISED BY NANCY RHEA STEEDLE

SOCIETY AND CULTURES, SOUTHWEST NIGERIA

Southwest Nigeria consists of territory lying to the west and south of the Niger River. It occupies seven of Nigeria's thirty-six states (Edo, Ekiti, Lagos, Ogun, Ondo, Osun, and Oyo) and parts of three others (Delta, Kogi, and Kwara). Although as of 2007 results of the proposed 2005 census were not yet known, estimates indicate the population of this region has reached 40 million. The terrain ranges from tropical rain forest to open savanna countryside. There are two seasons, dry and rainy, with roughly 70 inches of rain per annum. The economy is based on agricultural production—including cocoa, kola, rubber, maize, yams, oil palm, and cassava—extensive trade, some industrial production and, historically, considerable activity involving fishing, hunting, and crafts. Two-thirds of the men were farmers in 1950, but the number declined during the oil boom years of the 1970s and 1980s. Women seldom farm, but are involved in wide-ranging trade and marketing networks. Educational attainments of this region's people are the highest in the country.

Yoruba-speaking peoples who spill into the neighboring states of Bénin, Togo, and Ghana dominate the southwest. Other major language groups are Edo (Bini), Egun, Urhobo, Ijo, Ishan, Isoko, and Itsekiri. The term *Yoruba* is applied to a large language-sharing family of peoples who were once known by the names of their political communities or their regional dialects. Some of the more prominent subgroups are Anago, Awori, Egba, Egbado, Ekiti, Ibadan, Ife, Ifonyin, Igbomina, Ijebu, Ijesha, Ketu, Kwara, Ondo, Owo, Oyo, and Shabe. Throughout their history, there has been extensive contact among these groups due to trade, migration, and warfare. Consequently, there has been much cultural blending.

Archaeological evidence indicates stone tool-using inhabitants were in the area between the tenth and second centuries BCE. By the time Ife emerged in the ninth century CE, iron making and agriculture had long been developed. Indigenous urbanism in this region also dates to this time. One small city-state, Ile-Ife, reached an artistic and political zenith between the twelfth and fourteenth centuries, and it is mythologized as the cradle of all Yoruba. Trade was important from earliest times, and external trade expanded rapidly from the seventeenth century with the increase in the New World demand for slaves.

Precolonial Yoruba peoples were organized in hundreds of minor polities ranging from villages and city-states to large centralized kingdoms, of which there were about twenty. From earliest times communities varied in size from tiny hunting and farming camps to great cities inhabited by twenty thousand, and by the 1850s, sixty thousand people. Indigenous capitals were circular, densely settled, and usually protected by earthen walls. At the center were markets and royal compounds that spanned several acres; clustered around them were residences of chiefly and commoner families. Agricultural lands lay outside the walls, and farmers commuted from town to farm.

Political systems consisted of a ruler and council(s) of chiefs who represented important sectors of the society such as descent, military and religious groups, age grades, markets, and secret societies. The presence and relative power of each of these sectors varied from place to place, but they served as a system of checks and balances. The ruler performed rituals, conducted external affairs, kept the peace, and wielded the power of life and death over subjects. Chiefs advised, adjudicated, and administered their families and large compounds of dependents. Palace officials were intermediaries between a ruler and the heads of outlying towns and tributaries. The ancient political systems have survived into the early twenty-first century, although they have few official governmental functions. Indigenous title-holding chiefs now constitute local nobilities and, as such, wield influence in the institutions of the state. Local government is otherwise bureaucratized and modeled mainly on British governmental structures.

Kinship relationships continue to be significant in marking status and regulating the inheritance of land and housing, succeeding to titles, and commemorating important ancestral figures. The extended family is of great importance in the social affairs of individuals, in addition to providing a system of support and security to members. Status is differentiated according to sex, age, and wealth. In the past, elder males held most official positions of familial and civic authority. In the early twenty-first century, class distinctions are calculated according to wealth, education, and occupation.

One of the prominent features of this area is the significance of women in public affairs and their ability to rise to positions of prominence. In some local polities, especially before colonial rule, special titles were reserved for women in markets and chieftaincy hierarchies. They were also active in leading some religious groups. The heavy concentration of women in trade, and now in other professions, gave them and continues to give them an independent source of income that can result in great wealth and thus the ability to influence public affairs.

Introduced religions of Christianity and Islam are embraced in roughly equal proportions. The Portuguese introduced Christianity in the far eastern parts of this region soon after contact in the fifteenth century, but it was not institutionalized until the mid-nineteenth century when Methodist and Church Missionary Society (CMS) missionaries began to proselytize in the far western coastal towns of the region. Indigenous pastors who were freed from slavery, educated in Sierra Leone, and returned to their homelands were the main forces behind the spread of Christianity. Islam slowly entered the southwest from the north centuries earlier through trade, indigenous slavery, and warfare. Today ancient religious practices are performed, or sometimes blended with introduced faiths. The Yoruba system has a pantheon of deities that underpin an extensive system of cults and priests. Their rituals are focused on the life cycle, ecological and civic calendars, and are directed toward appeasing or gaining supernatural favor.

Yoruba are well known for their rich array of art forms. Life-size bronze heads and terra-cottas, sculpted in classical style between 1000 and 1400 CE, have been widely admired for the technical skill and superior artistry that was achieved. Wood and metal sculpture also has gained international prominence. Other art forms are oral literature—especially poetry, proverbs, myth, and oratory—dance, music,

weaving, dyeing, embroidery, pottery, calabash carving, leather- and beadworking, and jewelry- and metalworking. Along with ritual, Yoruba arts are notable contributions to the African diaspora in the Americas and the Caribbean.

See also **Archaeology and Prehistory; Arts: Sculpture; Ceramics; Christianity; Death, Mourning, and Ancestors; Ecosystems; Ife (Ile-Ife); Islam; Kinship and Descent; Niger River; Political Systems: Chieftainships; Production Strategies; Women: Women and Trade.**

BIBLIOGRAPHY

Metz, Helen Chapin, ed. *Nigeria: A Country Study*. Washington, DC: Federal Research Division, Library of Congress, 1992.

Peel, John David Yeldon. *Religious Encounter and the Making of the Yoruba*. Bloomington: Indiana University Press, 2000.

Smith, Robert Sydney. *Kingdoms of the Yoruba*, 3rd edition. Madison: University of Wisconsin Press, 1988.

Trager, Lillian. *Yoruba Hometowns: Community, Identity, and Development in Nigeria*. Boulder, CO: Lynne Rienner, 2001.

SANDRA T. BARNES

SOCIETY AND CULTURES, CENTRAL NIGERIA

Central Nigeria is one of the six geopolitical zones of the modern Nigerian nation. It is situated between Northern Nigeria and Southern Nigeria. In addition to its unique and eclectic cultural features, it possesses cultural influences that are similar to those found in the northern and southern regions. This sociological character makes it a microcosm of the cultural pluralism of modern Nigeria. Central Nigeria is a region in which the cultural patterns of the mainly Muslim North and largely Christian South have mixed with indigenous traditions, rituals, and cultural norms to form a social synthesis that is at once fascinating and combustive.

The region is hardly a cohesive cultural unit; it is a multilingual, multiethnic, multicultural, and religiously pluralistic region. Central Nigeria is composed of at least two hundred different ethnic groups, making it the most ethnically diverse region in Nigeria. The largest of these ethnic groups is the Tiv, with a population of about four million. The Tiv are found in Benue, Nassarawa, and Taraba states. Other major ethnic groups in the region include the Nupe, Igala, Idoma, Gbagyi, Kataf, Berom, Angas, Jukun, Chamba, and Tarok.

A further illustration of Central Nigeria's position as a multicultural and multilingual melting pot is that both Hausa and Yoruba, two of the three major languages of Nigeria, are widely spoken as either the first or second language by several groups in the region. Pockets of Hausa-Fulani migrants, found in several parts of Central Nigeria, speak Hausa. Several other ethnic groups speak Hausa as a second language, owing to their exposure to Hausa traders and Islamic preachers in the period before the Fulani jihad of 1804. The jihad, which resulted in the Sokoto Caliphate, brought the Hausa language—and Hausa-Fulani migrants—to several areas of Central Nigeria that were conquered during the war. These areas include the emirates of Bida, Wase, Ilorin, as well as small states such as Keffi and Nassarawa. Various dialects of the Yoruba language are spoken by the people of Ilorin, Kabba, Bunu, Yagba, and other areas of the Niger confluence zone.

Despite the presence of states and state institutions that are comparable to those of the large kingdoms and empires in the North and the South, most societies in Central Nigeria belong to small states, or are organized into small village units with little central authority or centralized political institutions. While they lack the centrally directed development and efficient administrative fiat of larger polities, these segmentary societies are effective in solving societal problems. What the non- and semi-centralized polities of Central Nigeria lack in centralized authority they make up for by instituting systems of checks and balances in which power is distributed among elders and chiefs whose sway over citizens is negotiated, rather than absolute. These systems ensure that chiefly services and superintending roles are performed in an atmosphere of accountability.

Several religious traditions abound in Central Nigeria, although, due to the region's exposure to Islam in the precolonial period and to Christianity in the colonial period (1900–1960), these two religions claim more adherents than other religions in the area. Despite the presence of a Christian majority and a large Muslim population in the region, various forms of traditional African religions continue to thrive, with many people being devoted to ancestral worship and rituals, and to the cosmic and religious orders preserved from pre-Islamic and precolonial times. One of the fascinating social phenomena of the Central Nigerian area is its abiding religious syncretism. It is common to see people alternate between Christian and traditional Nigerian rituals, and between Islamic and traditional Nigerian practices.

Many rituals, practices, and symbols from traditional religions have been incorporated into the practice of Central Nigerian Islam and Christianity, and vice versa. Many of the region's ethnic groups consist of Christians, Muslims, and adherents of traditional religions, and religious territories hardly correspond neatly to ethnic ones. This trend was furthered in the 1950s and 1960s when many people in traditionally non-Islamic and non-Caliphate areas, such as Igalaland, Ebiraland, and the Tarok Chiefdoms of the Central Plateau, converted to Islam as a result of an Islamization campaign that was funded by Saudi Arabia and run by Northern Nigeria's first premier, the late Sir Ahmadu Bello.

Although adherents of the different religions have largely coexisted in peace, their relationship and interactions with one another are not without occasional tensions. These tensions have sometimes exploded into violent conflict. In the last two decades clashes between Christians and Muslims have become frequent, leading to the destruction of lives and property. The worst of these Christian-Muslim clashes have occurred in Plateau State, the power base of Central Nigeria.

Central Nigeria had no political or legal existence prior to British colonial rule. The British conquered it, along with other regions of what became colonial Northern Nigeria, between 1900 and 1906. Colonial administrative policy implicitly acknowledged that the region was culturally different, and that, unlike the areas of the defunct Sokoto Islamic Caliphate, it was religiously diverse. Nonetheless, throughout their colonial rule the British governed the region as part of the protectorate of Northern Nigeria, with headquarters in Kaduna. The British governed Nigeria through a policy of indirect rule that utilized the indigenous political institutions and, under British supervision, appointed or inherited indigenous officials.

Federal Republic of Nigeria

Population:	135,031,164 (2007 est.)
Area:	923,768 sq. km (356,669 sq. mi.)
Official language:	English
Languages:	English, Hausa, Igbo, Yoruba
National currency:	naira
Principal religions:	Muslim 50%, Christian (Roman Catholic and Protestant) 40%, indigenous beliefs 10%
Capital:	Abuja (Federal Capital Territory; est. pop. 100,000 in 2006)
Other urban centers:	Lagos, Ibadan, Kano, Enugu
Annual rainfall:	Highly variable, 1,700–4,310 mm (70–170 in.) from west to east along the coast; 500 mm (20 in.) in the extreme north
Principal geographical features:	*Mountains:* Mandara, Shebshi, Alantika, Mambilla, Gotel, Jos Plateau, Biu Plateau *Lakes:* Lake Chad, Kainji Reservoir, Tiga Reservoir *Rivers:* Niger, Benue, Katsina-Ala, Gongola, Sokoto, Kaduna, Anambra, Yobe, Benin, Ogun, Escravos, Forcados, Sombreiro, Cross, Kwa, Imo, Calabar
Economy:	*GDP per capita:* US$1,500 (2006)
Principal products and exports:	*Agricultural:* cocoa, peanuts, palm oil, corn, rice, sorghum, millet, cassava (tapioca), yams, rubber, cattle, sheep, goats *Manufacturing:* textiles, cement and other construction materials, food products, footwear, chemicals, fertilizer, printing, ceramics, steel, small commercial ship construction and repair *Mining:* petroleum, natural gas, tin, coal, columbite, iron, gold
Government:	Independence from Great Britain, 1960. Constitution, 1960, sections suspended in 1966. New constitution approved in 1970, suspended in 1983. New constitution approved in 1989, suspended in 1996. Newest constitution 1999; peaceful transition from military rule to a civilian government. Bicameral National Assembly consists of 109-member Senate and 360-member House of Representatives, all elected by popular vote to 4-year terms. President is also elected by popular vote for 4-year term.
Heads of state since independence:	1960–1963: Governor General Benjamin Nnamdi Azikiwe 1960–1966: Prime Minister Abubakar Tafawa Balewa 1963–1966: President Benjamin Nnamdi Azikiwe 1966: Major General Johnson Aguiyi-Ironsi 1966–1975: Lieutenant Colonel (later General) Yakubu Gowon 1975–1976: Brigadier (later General) Murtala Ramat Muhammed 1976–1979: Lieutenant General (later General) Olusegun Obasanjo 1979–1983: President Shehu Shagari 1984–1985: Major General Muhammadu Buhari 1985–1993: Major General Ibrahim Badamasi Babangida 1993: Interim President Ernest Shonekan 1993–1999: General Sani Abacha 1999–2007: President Olusegun Obasanjo 2007–: President Umaru Masa Yar'adua
Armed forces:	Head of state is commander in chief. Voluntary enlistment. *Army:* 60,000 *Navy:* 7,000 *Air force:* 9,000 *Paramilitary:* 2,000
Transportation:	*Rail:* 3,505 km (2,173 mi.), operated by the Nigerian Railway Corporation *Waterways:* 8,575 km (5,316 mi.), principally the Niger and Benue Rivers *Ports:* Lagos-Apapa, Tin Can Island, Delta Port Complex (Warri, Koko, Burutu, Sapele), Port Harcourt, Calabar, Bonny, and Burutu for petroleum shipping *Roads:* 194,394 km (120,791 mi.), 28% paved. Trans-Africa Highway links Lagos with Mombasa. *National airline:* Nigerian Airways (government owned). Air Nigeria (joint government-private venture). Kabo Air and Okada Air (private). *Airports:* Murtala Muhammed International Airport in Lagos. There are 35 other airports with paved runways.
Media:	More than 26 dailies, including *Daily Times, Nigerian Observer, Punch, Nigerian Herald, Nigerian Tribune, New Nigerian.* Almost 100 periodicals. Major Nigerian publishers include Fourth Dimension, Skevium, Nalthouse, and Gaskiya. There are also several multinational publishing companies: Oxford University Press, Longman, Evans, Macmillan, Heinemann, Thomas Nelson. There are several university presses and publishers specializing in local vernacular publications. The government owns Federal Radio Corporation of Nigeria and the Nigerian Television Authority. External radio service provided by Voice of Nigeria. Other outlets include Radio-Television Kaduna and Western Nigeria Radiovision Service. Film production began in 1970.
Literacy and education:	*Total literacy rate:* 51% (2006). Education is free, universal, and compulsory for ages 6–12. 31 universities, including Ahmadu Bello niversity, University of Benin, University of Calabar, University of Ibadan, Obafemi Awolowo University, University of Ilorin, University of Jos, University of Lagos, University of Maiduguri, University of Nigeria, University of Port Harcourt, and Usman Dan Fodio University. Numerous technical schools.

The first major effort to politically detach Central Nigeria from Northern Nigeria and to give it a separate political and social identity came in 1955 with the formation of the United Middle Belt Congress (UMBC). The term Middle Belt was used to denote Central Nigeria because of the region's location in the geographical middle of Nigeria. Although the UMBC was formed primarily to fight for power in the run-up to Nigerian independence in 1960, and although it was dominated by the elite of the Benue-Plateau axis, the organization helped promote a sense of Central Nigerian political and social identity. When Joseph Tarka, a Tiv, became president of the party in 1957, the UMBC became even more assertive in demanding constitutional recognition for Central Nigeria as a separate geopolitical unit under the Nigerian Federation. The UMBC demanded the constitutional creation of a Middle Belt state. It also formed alliances with Southern Nigerian political parties that were sympathetic to the UMBC's call for a separate political identity for Central Nigeria.

For all its agitations, the UMBC's struggle was narrow, and the Hausa-Fulani-dominated Northern Peoples Congress (NPC), the controlling power at the Nigerian political center from 1954, saw Middle Belt agitation as a ploy by Southern political parties to reduce the political clout of Northern Nigeria, and of its dominant political party. The NPC used its power to frustrate the UMBC's demands. With the defeat of the Middle Belt state creation movement, the demand for the constitutional recognition of Central Nigerian political and cultural identity waned and the UMBC as a political party gradually lost its political influence. This state of affairs continued until 1999 when the head of state, General Abdusalam Abubakar (b. 1942), and representatives in a constitutional conference approved a new constitution that created a Central Nigerian geopolitical region along with five others.

See also **Bello, Ahmadu; Ethnicity; Religion and Ritual.**

BIBLIOGRAPHY

Adekunle, Julius O. *Politics and Society in Nigeria's Middle Belt: Borgu and the Emergence of a Political Identity.* Trenton, NJ: Africa World Press, 2005.

Bagudu, Nankin, and C.J. Dakas, eds. *The Right to Be Different: Perspectives on Minority Rights, the Cultural Middle Belt and Constitutionalism in Nigeria.* Jos/Plateau State, Nigeria: League for Human Rights, 2001.

Idrees, Aliyu A., and Yakubu A. Ochefu, eds. *Studies in the History of Central Nigeria Area* vol. 1. Lagos, Nigeria: CSS Limited, 2002.

Kastfelt, Niels. *Religion and Politics in Nigeria: A Study in Middle Belt Christianity.* London: British Academic Press, 1994.

Yoromas, Joses G. "Colonial Legacy, Violence and Democracy in Nigeria: The Case of Middle Belt State." In *Democratisation in Africa: Nigerian Perspectives*, Vol. 2, ed. Omo Omoruyi. Abuja, Nigeria: Center for Democratic Studies, 1994.

MOSES E. OCHONU

HISTORY AND POLITICS, NORTHERN NIGERIA

Northern Nigeria has a long and complex history dominated by Islamic conquest and religious and ethnic conflict. Islam spread into the region about a millennium ago, becoming the main religion and spreading also into what is present-day southwest Nigeria. The centuries after brought the rise of Hausa cities in the region as well as the height of the Songhay Empire, which incorporated parts of Hausaland, and the Borno Dynasty's conquest of Kanem in the sixteenth century. In the seventeenth and eighteenth centuries, Borno controlled the region. Then in 1804 to 1808, an Islamic holy war (jihad) led by ʿUthman dan Fodio created the Sokoto Caliphate, an association of about thirty emirates including Sokoto and Kano, which brought most of the northern region under an unified Islamic government. The consolidation of the caliphate solidified Islam's dominant position in the region in contrast to the southern regions, which are primarily Christian. The slave trade, both trans-Atlantic and trans-Saharan, had major impacts on the region as well, as it depleted the population through forced migration that lasted several centuries and only ended in the late nineteenth century with the advent of British colonialism in the region. The ruling class of this region, dominated by the Hausa-Fulani ethnic groups, for the most part are descendants of the founders of the Sokoto Caliphate and are Sufi Muslims.

Nigeria under British colonial rule was divided into northern and southern protectorates that were ruled differently, one of the many contributing factors to continued conflict and rivalry between the regions in present-day Nigeria. The northern protectorate was governed through a system of Indirect Rule that involved allowing indigenous emirs to continue ruling if they accepted British authority, ended the slave trade, and cooperated with the British colonial authorities. In contrast, the southern protectorate rejected Indirect Rule and embraced Western values, education, and religion. The northern and southern protectorates were joined in a uniform Nigeria in 1914. Then in 1954, Nigeria became a federation of the Northern, Eastern, and Western Regions, reflecting the cultural, religious, and political differences of the dominant groups in these regions. The Northern Region became self-governing in 1959.

Nigeria obtained its independence from Britain in 1960, uniting the regions despite their diverse peoples, histories, and outlooks toward domestic and international politics. Nigeria's political history as an independent state has been dominated by military rule, largely by northerners, with few interruptions by democratic governments. The First Republic, presided over by Prime Minister Abubakar Tafawa Balewa, a northerner, and with a nominal president (Nnamdi Azikiwe), lasted from 1960 to January 1966. Plagued by intense regionalism, declining revenues, and bitter power rivalry, the First Republic moved from one crisis to another until it was overthrown by the military. The first coup, led by Patrick Nzeogwu, was badly planned, and an officer who was not involved in it, Johnson Aguiyi-Ironsi, became the country's head. Nzeogwu and Ironsi were Igbo (Ibo), and both the coups and the policies that followed were interpreted as an attempt to achieve Igbo domination. A countercoup occurred in July 1966, leading to the emergence of northerner Yakubu Gowon as the new head and generating a bitterness that led to the massacre of Igbo in the north, and a secession by the east, led by Odumegwu Ojukwu. The Igbo established the short-lived Republic of Biafra, and a civil war followed to reunite the country.

The 1970s were marked by dramatic changes. The civil war ended in 1970, for a short while abating the danger of ethnicity but introducing the problem of postwar reconstruction and rehabilitation. An oil boom gave the country tremendous opportunities to expand and develop into a regional power. There were coups and countercoups, leading to the

overthrow of Gowon in 1975, and the emergence of the well-liked northerner Murtala Muhammed, who was killed seven months later. Olusegun Obasanjo assumed leadership and became the first Nigerian leader to voluntarily relinquish power to a civilian, northerner Shehu Shagari, who ruled the Second Republic from 1979 to 1983. The later 1980s were dominated by the military, first by northerner Muhammadu Buhari and later by northerner Ibrahim Babangida, who ruled for eight years, during a time of massive corruption and indifference to public opinion. His rule, in fact, destined Nigeria for deep political crisis following his annulment of the 1993 presidential election when Chief Moshood Abiola, a businessman from the southeast, was set to win. Many speculated Babangida's decision to annul the election resulted from pressure by the northern military elite who did not want a southerner in power. At the time, these polls were considered the fairest in Nigeria's history.

Babangida's failure to manage a successful transition led to the inauguration in August 1993 of an interim government, headed by Ernest Shonekan, which was unable to generate trust and offer strong leadership. He was overthrown in November 1993 by General Sani Abacha, whose excessive political style generated domestic protest and international condemnation for human rights abuses and corruption. It was later discovered that Abacha had stolen billions in state revenue, putting the money into Swiss back accounts. In 2005, the Nigerian government started recovering some of these funds.

Abacha's death in 1998, called by some a coup from heaven, led to a landmark transition process to civilian democratic rule, led by Major General Abdulsalami Abubakar. He released political prisoners and oversaw local government elections in December 1998, state legislative elections in January 1999, and federal legislative and presidential election in February 1999. Olusegun Obasanjo was elected president under the banner of his party, the People's Democratic Party (PDP), which also won a majority in the parliament. Obasanjo and the PDP won again in 2003.

Obasanjo's administration faced many major obstacles to restoring democratic governance, reducing corruption, reconciling the country, and promoting development. Early in his administration, he instituted a policy requiring the retirement of over one hundred senior army officials, and worked to create a fair representation of regions and ethnic groups in state appointments, thus reducing the dominance of northerners in national political affairs. In 2000 and 2001, twelve northern, predominantly Muslim states chose to establish Islamic *shari'a* law that fueled religious conflict both among northern groups and along national cleavages as well. Many local conflicts broke out between Christians and Muslims following the introduction of *shar'a* law. It has remained in effect despite outcries, mostly from southerners, that question its constitutional legitimacy.

Controversy over a polio vaccine being administered by the World Health Organization erupted in 2003, pitting northern leaders against the federal government and major international organizations. The northern leaders claimed the vaccine was contaminated and would make girls infertile. Five northern states (Niger, Bauchi, Kano, Zamfara, and Kaduna) banned the vaccine for over a year, allowing a resurgence of the disease in the region and worldwide.

In 2004, an ethnic-religious conflict between predominantly Christian farmers and Muslim settler herdsman in Plateau State led a thousand killings along religious lines, causing the government to declare a state of emergency and to impose martial law. These were not, however, isolated incidents, as official reports estimated that nearly 54,000 people died in sectarian conflict in Plateau State between September 2001 and May 2004. Religious violence also made world headlines in September 2001 when bloody riots in Jos left over a thousand dead, and again in February 2006 after Danish cartoons that depicted the Muslim prophet Mohammad sparked riots in several northern Nigerian cities, leaving many churches burned and several people dead.

Obasanjo's attempts to change the constitution to allow him to run for a third term in the April 2007 presidential election were rejected by the Nigerian Supreme Court in May 2006. Following this judicial defeat, the PDP chose Katsina State governor Umaru Yar'adua as their presidential candidate, a snub to Obasanjo's vice president, northerner Atiku Abubakar, who publicly opposed Obasanjo's attempt to run for a third term. After this falling out, Abubakar was expelled from the PDP and formed a new opposition party, the Action Congress (AC). The other main contender was Muhammadu Buhari of the All Nigeria People's Party (ANPP), who ruled Nigeria in the mid-1980s. All three major candidates were from the north, reflecting behind-the-scenes political negotiations that resulted in an agreement that it was the north's turn to rule after two terms of rule by Obasanjo, a Yoruba from the southwest.

The April 2007 presidential election was marred by corruption, violence, and vote rigging, and was considered illegitimate by both national and international observers. Unsurprisingly, Yar'adua won overwhelmingly. Goodluck Jonathan, the current governor of Bayelsa State in the Niger Delta, is set to be the vice president. Despite widespread fraud and considerable public outcry, the results are likely to stand.

See also **Azikewe, Benjamin Nnamdi; Babangida, Ibrahim Gbadamosi; Bello, Ahmadu; Islam; Lugard, Frederick John Dealtry; Obasanjo, Olusegun; Slave Trades; Tafawa Balewa, Abubakar; 'Uthman dan Fodio; Warfare: Civil Wars.**

BIBLIOGRAPHY

Country Profile: Nigeria. Washington, DC: Library of Congress Federal Research Division, June 2006.

Falola, Toyin, et al. *The Military Factor in Nigeria: 1966–1985.* Lewiston, NY: E. Mellen Press, 1994.

Forrest, Tom G. *Politics and Economic Development in Nigeria.* Boulder, CO: Westview Press, 1993.

Kirk-Greene, Anthony H. M., and Douglas Rimmer. *Nigeria since 1970: A Political and Economic Outline.* New York: Hodder and Stoughton, 1981.

Maier, Karl. *This House had Fallen: Midnight in Nigeria.* New York: Public Affairs, 2000.

Nigeria Country Profile. Washington, DC: The Economist Intelligence Unit, 2007.

Obadare, Ebenezer. "A Crisis of Trust: History, Politics, Religion, and the Polio Controversy in Northern Nigeria." *Patterns of Prejudice* 39, no. 3 (2005): 266–284.

Reynolds, Jonathan. "Good and Bad Muslims: Islam and Indirect Rule in Northern Nigeria." *International Journal of African Historical Studies* 34, no. 3 (2001): 601–618.

Ukiwo, Ukoha. "Politics, Ethno-Religious Conflict and Democratic Consolidation in Nigeria." *Journal of Modern African Studies* 41, no. 1 (2003): 115–138.

TOYIN FALOLA
REVISED BY NANCY RHEA STEEDLE

HISTORY AND POLITICS, SOUTHERN NIGERIA

Nigeria is a vast county of an estimated 120 million people, making it the most populous African nation. Like most African states, it is a country of great cultural and social diversity. As a state, it is a conglomeration of about 250 different ethnolinguistic groups. Of these distinct groups, the three largest and dominant ones are the Hausa/Fulani of the north, the Yoruba of the southwest, and the Igbo of the southeast. Apart from the Yoruba and the Igbo in the south which, have traditionally played an important role in Nigerian politics, some of the medium-size groups in the region include the Ibibio, Ijaw, Efik, and Uhrobo.

DEVELOPMENTS OF 1849–1899

For Africans in the communities that later made up southern Nigeria, the nineteenth century was critical in several ways. All of them came to realize the significance of the familiar saying that weak states invite attack. Group after group, they also came to understand that sovereignty is indivisible. By treaties, agreements, coercion, conquest, or annexation, these communities first lost to foreign authority over their external affairs, then surrendered internal control. Unable or unwilling to confront common foes decisively, they succumbed, under progressive attacks, to forces superior to them in firepower if not in will and guile. As these communities declined and fell, one after another, they paved the way for dramatic changes that affected the course of events well beyond the nineteenth century. For them and for their early-twentieth-century successors, the interplay of the key factors of time, circumstance, and leadership left indelible marks.

Ill-equipped in men and resources to defend themselves against a European incursion, Africans in these groups failed to respond effectively to new changes and challenges in their environment from the beginning of and throughout the nineteenth century. In the end, their largely uncoordinated response failed to deter an enemy seeking to exercise more and more jurisdiction, power, and authority in their lands.

British abolition of the slave trade in 1807 and of slavery in 1833 led to regular patrols in west African waters by a preventive or "humanitarian" squadron. Simultaneously, European traders either persisted in the trans-Atlantic slave trade or sought alternatives in legitimate commerce such as palm produce (palm oil and kernels). About the same time, Christian missionaries began to be active in the region, first along the coast and later in the hinterland. The pursuit of these interests gradually encouraged officials of the British government (in particular of the War, Foreign, and Colonial Offices) to adopt measures in favor of informal empire (through colonies and protectorates) where opportunities encouraged these efforts. As the nineteenth century wore on, British spokesmen such as Joseph Chamberlain (of the Colonial Office) did not hesitate to preach the doctrine of breaking African eggs to make imperial omelets.

How ready, then, were Africans to resist these efforts? In the southwest, the decline and collapse of the Old Oyo Empire and protracted warfare among successor states, in addition to incessant attacks from Dahomey (present-day Bénin), weakened much of Yorubaland. War weariness inclined communities, such as those of New Oyo and Ibadan, and the Ekiti, Egba, Ijebu, Egbado, and Ijesa, among others, to sue for peace through British pressures in the 1880s and 1890s. By 1893, these efforts had brought a measure of peace to parts of Yorubaland.

Events at Lagos and its vicinity resulted in a different solution. In the 1840s, the British feared competition from the French close to Badagri. Moreover, dynastic disputes between claimants to the throne of Lagos created intense rivalries between Kosoko, Akitoye, and Dosunmu and their supporters. Thus, the weak monarchy in Lagos failed to stop creeping British consular jurisdiction from 1851. The annexation (or cession) of Lagos in August 1861 surprised no one.

In the southeast, a similar combination of weakness among the city-states and communities of the Niger Delta and the Cross River plus dynastic rivalries resulted in the establishment of consular jurisdiction in 1849 and its expansion and consolidation thereafter. The declaration, in 1885, of the Oil Rivers Protectorate, renamed Niger Coast Protectorate in 1893, came in the wake of the Berlin Conference, 1884–1885, and Brussels Conference, 1889–1890. Step by step, the era of the "paper protectorate" of the 1880s gave way to one in need of "effective occupation" from the 1890s.

Correspondingly, African rulers, chiefs, and common people, unwilling to cooperate with British consular officials of the 1880s and 1890s, paid dearly for their opposition—mainly through deportation. Notable deportees included Ja Ja of Opobo (1887), Nana of the Itsekiri (1894), Ibanichuka of Okrika (1896), Koko of Nemba-Brass (1896), and Overami, or Ovonramwen, of Bénin (1897). As Ralph Moor, commissioner and consul-general, proclaimed at the end of the 1897 expedition against Bénin, the British crown would brook no rival "king" in any part of the Niger Coast Protectorate.

The new era in the Niger Coast Protectorate tolerated only collaborators, with or without "warrants," who were given minor judicial and administrative roles as members of native courts and councils, the successors, in the 1880s and 1890s, of the informal "courts of equity" begun in the 1850s. About the same time, another fundamental change occurred: from men and measures to principles. In particular, the meaning of a British "protectorate" became more fluid. Its interpretation varied, because the law officers of the British crown said one thing in faraway Whitehall, while the local officials said another.

Along the lower Niger (Idah, Akassa, Onitsha, Asaba, Aboh) a different dispensation occurred during the 1880s and 1890s. The Royal Niger Company, in 1886, received a British charter to combine its trading activities with those of administration (including the dispensation of justice). Its arbitrary exercise of power led to severe confrontations such as the Akassa Raid (1895) and conflict with an Igbo war cult, the Ekumeku (also called the League of the Silent Ones), in Asaba hinterland (1898). The company lost its charter in 1899 as part of new arrangements for the "Niger territories" or "districts," effective from 1900.

DEVELOPMENTS OF 1900–1960

The prevailing environment in southern Nigeria did not favor a meaningful partnership in support of the "indirect rule" of the Lugardian school. In the southern Nigeria of the 1890s and the 1900s, the true "rulers" in central and local institutions were the British officials who dictated polities. The administrators these officials tolerated were collaborators assigned minor executive functions.

In parts of southern Nigeria, advocates of the old order, however, found some refuge in secret societies and cults that met the needs of the informal sector, though prohibited under the Unlawful Societies Proclamation of 1905. Members of secret societies were not immune from detection and punishment by vigilant officials, however. The Ekumeku disturbance in Asaba hinterland in 1898, which recurred in 1903–1904 and 1910, illustrated how entrenched were these conflicts and confrontations between advocates of the old and new orders in southern Nigeria.

Through a variety of means, Britain expanded and consolidated its rule over territories to the west and east of the Niger from 1900. The new era in the government of these territories witnessed various strategies and tactics, which included both diplomatic and coercive measures. The personalities of the British administrators east and west of the Niger were more decisive than those of distant controlling agencies such as the Colonial Office and the British Parliament.

Also, British public opinion failed to change significantly the direction of events in southern Nigeria. Even so, some humanitarian organizations based in the United Kingdom endeavored to make their voices heard. Among these were the Third Party (led by Mary Kingsley, John Holt, and E. D. Morel), the Anti-Slavery and Aborigines Protection Society, and the Native Races and Liquor Traffic United Committee.

In southwest Nigeria, a few unofficial and nominated members of the Lagos legislative council and a vocal press, based in the colony, sought to give vent to criticisms by the chiefs and people of the Colony and Protectorate of Lagos. Less effective outlets for public opinion and criticism were available to those of the Protectorate of southern Nigeria before the 1914 amalgamation.

Thus, agreements, pledges, understandings, and treaties of peace, friendship, and commerce between the Lagos government and the chiefs and people of Yorubaland, between 1886 and 1893, in addition to judicial agreements that supplemented these during 1904–1908, gave more diplomatic cover than was available in the Protectorate of southern Nigeria. Indeed, after the Ijebu's unsuccessful military campaign against the British in 1892, and the bombardment of the alafin's palace at Oyo in 1895, few episodes of that kind occurred in the Protectorate of Lagos.

In the Protectorate of southern Nigeria, British punitive expeditions or patrols were more the rule than the exception. Wherever the British went, Maxim guns, rifles, and seven-pounders went with them. Military campaigns occurred yearly, during the dry season, until 1912. Of these, the most famous was the Aro Field Force, 1901–1902, which covered Arochukwu, Ikot-Ekpene, Itu, Uyo, Abak, Owerri and Bende. One of its major objectives was the destruction of the Aro Long Juju, Chuku Ibinokpabi. The "pacification" of Igboland, however, took much longer, as the Women's Riots of 1929–1930 and Enugu Colliery Incident of 1949 testified.

The various programs of "pacification," expansion, and consolidation of British rule paved the way for a major political event: amalgamation. By 1898, representatives of the British government had agreed on the consolidation of the Niger territories as a conscious policy goal to be implemented gradually, in installments. The deciding factor was economic or financial: to reduce the burden of the public debt on the British Treasury. Northern Nigeria, British officials acknowledged, was then not as economically viable as its southern counterpart, whose resources were needed to support the government of a combined territory. Thus, amalgamation proceeded in stages: The Colony and Protectorate of Southern Nigeria was created in 1906 and that of Nigeria in 1914. Whatever the merits of amalgamation, from the British point of view it was not a creation based on broad Nigerian opinion. The 1914 amalgamation achieved the beginning of "one country," but not of "one people" or "one system" of government. Nigeria's subsequent development, as a multicultural federal state, prevented any precipitate embrace of unitarism among people with different histories and modes of governance.

The southern component of these developments can be briefly examined. At amalgamation, Nigeria comprised two provinces: southern and northern. In 1939, the southern provinces were subdivided into eastern and western. A Nigerian council, 1914–1922, a mere advisory and deliberative body for Northern and Southern Nigeria, performed a cosmetic role along with a legislative council for the colony. Under a new constitution named after Sir Hugh Clifford in 1922, the principle of elective representation was introduced only for electorates in Lagos colony and Calabar municipality. The Richards Constitution (1946), merely expanded the basis of representation in the Central Council to the annoyance of critical Southern politicians. Concessions for responsible government were made under the Macpherson Constitution, (1951) and Lyttelton Constitution (1954), largely because of more agitations by the leaders of southern political parties. Thus, the transition from representative to responsible government through "dyarchy" (of ministerial partnership between British and Nigerian representatives) also witnessed the growth and development of two southern-based parties (known, after 1961, as the National Council of Nigerian Citizens and the Action Group) as well as the Northern People's Congress and the United Middle Belt Congress. From 1954, federalism became a marked feature of Nigeria's constitutional growth and development.

Through several constitutional review exercises, such as the General Conference at Ibadan (1950) and others in Lagos and London between 1953 and 1958, Nigerian politicians and British officials sought to resolve conflicts (including the pace of self-government, the status of Lagos, ethnic minorities, among others) and agreed to independence on October 1, 1960.

POSTINDEPENDENCE PERIOD
Independence, however, failed to resolve the legacy of history of ethnic disparity in Nigeria. The post-independence experiment at national unity failed as the country slipped into political chaos and instability in the early 1960s. Mutual ethnic/regional distrust and political rivalry especially among the three largest ethnic groups, the Hausa/Fulani, the Yoruba, and the Igbo, played an important role in the termination of the First Republic on January 15, 1966, through a bloody military coup that toppled the federal government. Suspicion was rife in northern elite circles that the putsch was an "Igbo coup," designed to eliminate its political power and replace it with Igbo hegemony. Ammunition was given to this perception, first, because the principal architects of the coup were Igbo officers; second, its victims were predominantly northern politicians and military officers; and third, the Igbo officer, Major General Johnson Aguiyi-Ironsi, who replaced as head of state the murdered prime minister, Sir Abubakar Tafawa Balewa, a northerner, pursued policies considered by northerners detrimental to their interest. The

northern desire to redress the political status-quo was directly responsible for the July 29, 1966 counter-coup executed by northern army officers that brought to power a northern officer from the Middle Belt, Lieutenant-Colonel Yakubu Gowon.

The prevailing anti-Igbo sentiment in the north found expression in the pogroms that occurred in parts of northern Nigeria in 1966. The massacre of thousands of Igbo people prompted their mass exodus from the north to their homeland in the Southeast. Considering themselves unsafe in a Nigerian federation, the Igbo declared the secession of the eastern region from the federation on May 30, 1967; and its military governor, Colonel Chukwuemeka Odumegwu Ojukwu, proclaimed the region a sovereign state, the Republic of Biafra. The federal government's attempt to put down the rebellion led to a full-scale, bloody civil war from July 3, 1967, to January 13, 1970. At the end of the war following the capitulation of Biafra, more than 1 million Igbo had been killed.

Aided by a buoyant economy from the oil boom, to a large extent postwar Nigeria achieved national reconciliation and the reintegration of the Igbo. However, disaffection with northern political dominance persisted in southern thoughts and became more expressive from the 1990s as the nation's economy dovetailed. When President Ibrahim Babangida, the military head of state from the north, annulled the result of the acknowledged free and fair presidential election of June 12, 1993, won by a Yoruba leading politician, Chief Moshood Abiola, months of public demonstrations and protests followed in many parts of Yorubaland. The Yoruba saw the unwarranted annulment as northern intention to perpetrate its political dominance.

Since the late 1990s some ethnic-based self-determination organizations in the south have advocated greater sovereignty and even the secession of their respective ethnic groups, though this is not a widely shared value. The militant wing of a Lagos-based Yoruba organization, the Oodua Peoples' Congress, has called for Yoruba nationalism and the willingness to use force to achieve its aim of creating an independent Yoruba state. Separatist agenda has also manifested in the southeast where the cause of Biafra has been revived by an Igbo organization, the Movement for the Actualization of the Sovereign State of Biafra (MASSOB), established in 1999.

Other groups in the south that have felt politically and economically marginalized also began to challenge state authority. The most volatile situation is in the Niger Delta where since the early 1990s a number of ethnic organizations and militias have made demands ranging from greater share oil revenues to ethnic self-determination. The Niger Delta is the region that produces most of Nigeria's oil, yet the vast majority of its people live in abject poverty. In mid-1994, protesting the government's neglect and environmental devastation of their homeland by foreign oil companies, the Ogoni people were met with violent state repression. Government forces killed hundreds of the people and destroyed villages. Leaders of the Movement for the Survival of the Ogoni People (MOSOP), an Ogoni ethnic organization, were arrested, nine of whom were executed on November 10, 1995, after a sham trial. One of those executed was MOSOP's president, Ken Saro-Wiwa, a notable writer and environmentalist.

The Ijaw, also in the Niger Delta, similarly perceive themselves as marginalized and have embarked on a persistence guerrilla-type campaign against government oil interest and foreign oil companies operating in the region. Militant Ijaw organizations such as the Movement for the Emancipation of the Niger Delta (MEND), Niger Delta People's Volunteer Force, and the Egbesu Boys, have been responsible for attacks on oil installations to cripple production. There have also been kidnapping of foreign oil workers by these organizations. Characteristic of the Niger Delta has been numerous violent confrontations between ethnic militias and government forces.

See also **Babanginda, Ibrahim Gbadamosi; Colonial Policies and Practices; Gowon, Yakubu; Ibadan; Ja Ja, King; Lagos; Lugard, Frederick John Dealtry; Postcolonialism; Slave Trades.**

BIBLIOGRAPHY

Ajayi, J. F. Ade. *Christian Missions in Nigeria, 1841–1891: The Making of a New Elite.* Evanston, IL: Northwestern University Press, 1965.

Anene, Joseph C. *Southern Nigeria in Transition, 1885-1906: Theory and Practice in a Colonial Protectorate.* Cambridge: Cambridge University Press, 1966.

Dike, K. Onwuka. *Trade and Politics in the Niger Delta, 1830–1885.* Oxford: Oxford University Press, 1959.

Ekwe-Ekwe, Herbert. *The Biafra War: Nigeria and the Aftermath.* Lewiston, NY: Edwin Mellen Press, 1990.

Falola, Toyin. *The History of Nigeria.* Westport, CT: Greenwood Press, 1999.

Forde, Daryll. *The Yoruba-Speaking Peoples of South-Western Nigeria.* London: International African Institute, 1969.

Nicolson, I. F. *The Administration of Nigeria, 1900–1960: Men, Methods and Myths.* Oxford: Clarendon Press, 1969.

Okechie-Offoha, Marcellina U., and Matthew N. O. Sadiku, eds. *Ethnic and Cultural Diversity in Nigeria.* Trenton, NJ: Africa World Press, 1995.

Oyebade, Adebayo. *The Foundations of Nigeria: Essays in Honor of Toyin Falola.* Trenton, NJ: Africa World Press, 2003.

Tamuno, Tekena N. *The Evolution of the Nigerian State: The Southern Phase, 1898–1914.* London: Longman, 1972.

TEKENA N. TAMUNO
REVISED BY ADEBAYO OYEBADE

NILE RIVER. The Nile is the longest river in the world, flowing south to north, 4,238 miles over 35 degrees of latitude through civilizations of great antiquity. The Nile Basin embraces over 2 million square miles of equatorial and northeast Africa. The river flows through every natural geologic formation, from mountainous highlands to barren deserts, and through eight independent African states—Burundi, Rwanda, Tanzania, Kenya, Uganda, Sudan, Ethiopia, and Egypt. The Nile is unique among the great rivers of the world. The civilizations of dynastic Egypt (3000 BCE–332 BCE), the Kingdom of Kush that flourished in Nubia from 805 BCE to 350 CE, and six hundred years of Greek and Roman rule in Egypt, were as dependent upon the waters of the Nile as the Christian and Muslim states that have succeeded them in the last two thousand years. Humanity cannot survive without water, and so when the inhabitants of the Sahara began to drift out of the desert five thousand years ago to escape its desiccation, their livelihoods and those of their descendants were dependent on the annual Nile flood, producing destruction from too much water, and famine from not enough.

The most southern source of the Nile, the *Caput Nili Meridianissimum,* is a spring in the Kangosi Hills in Burundi. Its eastern and most important hydrological source are the holy springs of Sakala at the foot of Mount Gish in the heartland of the Ethiopian mountainous plateau.

From its southern source in Burundi, not discovered until 1937, the waters of the spring are soon joined by a myriad of streams that coalesce into the Niavarongo and Ruvuvu Rivers to form the Kagera River, which flows into Lake Victoria, the second largest body of fresh water in the world (approximately 35,800 square miles). The lake is situated on a plateau between the two Great Rift Valleys of Africa, from which its waters enter the Victoria Nile at Jinja, 3,400 miles from the Mediterranean Sea and first brought to the attention of Europe by John Hanning Speke (1827–1864) in 1862. The Rwenzori Mountains (the Mountains of the Moon) rise to the west of Lake Victoria, and the Mfumbiro (Virunga) volcanoes form a mountainous dike across the Western Rift Valley. Their northern slopes collect the torrential, tropical rains blown out of the South Atlantic and across the rain forests of the Congo Basin to flow into a series of equatorial lakes—George, Edward, Albert—lying at the bottom of the Western Rift Valley and connected by the Semliki River. At the northern tip of the elongated Lake Albert, the waters of the Nile meet those of the Victoria Nile.

Flowing out of Lake Victoria at Jinja, the Victoria Nile flows north through the marshes of Lake Kyoga before turning west to plunge over the escarpment of the western rift, 142 feet through rock walls only 20 feet wide at Kabarega (formerly Murchison) Falls to flow placidly into Lake Albert. Leaving the lake, the Nile, now known as the Bahr al-Jabal (the Mountain River), proceeds northward out of the Western Rift Valley and into the Sudd (Arabic: *sadd*, barrier), the great swamps of the Nile that fluctuate in size from 5,000 to 12,000 square miles, depending upon the amount of rainfall on the equatorial lakes. In the Sudd, the Bahr al-Jabal meanders hundreds of variable miles while absorbing its western tributaries—the Bahr al-Arab, the Bahr al-Ghazal, and the numerous rivers flowing northeastward from the Congo-Nile watershed, all of which lose most of their water by evaporation and transpiration from the mass of aquatic vegetation. Emerging from the Sudd at Lake No, the White Nile (Bahr al-Abyad) now contains only 14 percent of the total Nile waters (from the agreed standard of measurements formerly taken at Aswan, but now at Dongola) until joined by the significant contribution from the east (14%) of the Sobat River and its tributaries, the Baro and Pibor Rivers. These rivers surge out of the Ethiopian highlands to double the size of the White Nile at Malakal. From there the river flows another 600 miles through flat, arid plains into the reservoir behind the Jebel Aulia dam 30 miles south of Khartoum. Here the basin of the equatorial Nile has brought downriver on average only 28 percent of the total waters available to Egypt at Aswan.

From its eastern source at the springs of Sakala, first seen by a European, Father Pedro Páez (1564–1622) in 1613, the Nile descends down the Little Abbai into Lake Tana and thence 3,260 miles to the Mediterranean. This lake is dotted by islands, upon which are monasteries, churches, and tombs of Ethiopian emperors. Its only outlet is near Bahr Dar on the southern shore. From the lake, the Blue Nile, known in Ethiopia as the Abbai, soon disappears over the lip of Tissisat Falls (an Amharic word meaning "the smoke of fire"), and then careens through a zigzag gorge, gouging out of the Ethiopian plateau a canyon nearly a mile deep, and absorbing thousands of streams and steep-flowing rivers—the Giamma, Muger, Guder, Finchaa, Diddessa, and Balas—to swell the Blue Nile with water and nutrients from the sediments of the highlands. The Blue Nile descends onto the plains of Sudan at the Bumbadi River and into the reservoir of the Roseires Dam at Damazin, 600 miles from Lake Tana. Beyond the dam are flat arid lands between the Blue and White Niles, upon which lie the vast irrigated cotton scheme known as the Gezira (meaning "island"), whereas east of the Blue Nile, the Dinder and the Rahad, two seasonal rivers, break Sudanic plains. Some 1,800 miles from the Mediterranean Sea, the Blue Nile reaches its confluence with the White Nile at the Mugran (Arabic for "meeting"), the spit of sand at Khartoum, carrying 59 percent of the total Nile waters.

From the capital of Sudan, the Nile flows northward through deserts; the inhabitants of Sudan and Egypt congregate along its banks. The river receives no additional water except from the Atbara River, 200 miles north of Khartoum. Rising in Ethiopia, the Atbara is a seasonal, spate river, dry from January to June. During its flood, the Atbara contributes a significant 13 percent to the total annual flow of the Nile. Beyond the Atbara, the Nile makes its great S bend, with its upper point at Abu Hamed and its lower depression at El Debba. It rolls over three cataracts and along the Dongola Reach to flow placidly into the reservoir impounded by the Aswan High Dam (Arabic: Sadd al-'Aali), the waters of which are known in Sudan as Lake Nubia, and in Egypt as Lake Nasser. At Aswan, the Nile is only 287 feet above sea level, yet the water must flow another 730 miles through barrages designed to raise the level of the river for passage into a myriad of irrigation works downstream; beyond Cairo, a labyrinth of canals weaves through the Nile Delta. Forming an inverted pyramid with its pinnacle at Cairo, the river bifurcates into two branches: the Damietta flowing northeast, and the Rosetta passing to the northwest, that form a delta 100 miles deep and 180 miles along the Mediterranean coast. Sixty percent of the population of Egypt live here, and absorb the last of the waters of the Nile.

In 1882, the British occupied Egypt and in 1898 conquered Sudan. Their highest priority was to regulate the historic flows of the Nile waters to prevent flood damage during years of high Niles and famine when its waters did not arrive out of Africa. Nile Control involved creating structures to both conserve water and distribute it to increase irrigated acreage in Egypt to feed its rapidly expanding population. The British built dams in Egypt at Aswan in 1902, in Sudan on the Blue Nile in 1925, and the White Nile in 1937, followed by the Egyptians' completion of the High Dam (Sadd al-'Aali) in 1972 (to provide crucial over-year storage for Egypt that was beyond the capacity of the 1902 Aswan Dam), and more elaborate projects in the Egyptian Master Water Plan of 1981 to capture the reduced Nile flows.

Unlike the British and the Egyptians, the Ethiopians, whose waters contribute to 86 percent of the total Nile flow, did not begin the investigation and development of the Blue Nile and its tributaries until after 1971, when Emperor Haile Selassie established a succession of agencies. Unfortunately, the agencies were primarily make-work projects for civil servants who possessed little interest in and few of the skills required for water development. It was not until 1990 that the Mengistu regime in Ethiopia produced its own Preliminary Water Resources Development Master Plan (PWRD). This plan revived Egyptian fears, believed since the Middle Ages, that Ethiopia could control or divert the Blue Nile waters upon which Egypt was completely dependent. It also raised the controversial question as to who was entitled to the Nile waters—those who use it (historic needs and established rights) or those through whose lands the Nile flows and wish to share it (equitable rights).

In order to reconcile these two incompatible goals, Egypt and six of the riparian states established a council of water ministers, UNDUGU (from the Swahili word *ndugu*, meaning brotherhood), in 1983 to seek a resolution to Nile water usage, without success. In 1992, UNDUGU was restructured and the first International Nile 2002 Conference was launched in 1997. The goal was to meet annually to seek a resolution as to rights to the Nile waters, and to consider the projects of the Egyptian Nile River Action Plan of 1997 that were opposed by some of the states.

Intervention by the World Bank in November 1997 to review the Nile River Action Plan resulted in a new Nile Basin Initiative (NBI) that promoted the concept of shared visions, rather than endless arguments over historic or established rights. Under the patronage of the World Bank, the representatives of the Nile Basin states have since engaged in endless dialogue and discussions that have done much to break down former fears, old animosities, and have produced a more harmonious environment characterized by civil discourse to resolve mutual Nile waters problems. There has been considerable cooperation on small projects, all of which, however, have studiously avoided any division of the Nile waters and has resulted in Egypt, Sudan, Uganda, and Ethiopia embarking quietly on their own ambitious schemes that will require Nile water.

Concerned to feed its burgeoning population and encouraged by the high Nile floods of the 1990s, Egypt launched, without consultation, its Southern Egyptian Development Project to irrigate the vast Toshka depression and the oases of the Western Desert of Egypt. The Egyptians claimed they would provide the additional water for these

schemes by conservation and modernization of their antiquated irrigation system, but the skeptics asserted that additional Nile water would be required from Lake Nasser, the mammoth reservoir behind the Aswan High Dam. Sudan, Uganda, and Ethiopia responded by constructing their own dams to produce hydroelectric power—Sudan at Merowe, Uganda at Bujagali, and the Ethiopian plans for thirteen hydroelectric dams in the Blue Nile Basin. As of 2006 Egypt has raised no objections, for hydroelectric dams do not divert water, just pass it through the turbines and downstream to Egypt where it will be impounded by the Aswan High Dam.

Once the upstream riparian countries embark upon schemes for irrigation that will consume large amounts of water destined for Egypt, which they have consistently threatened to do in order to feed their exploding populations, the unresolved and divisive question of historic or equal rights will be revived. At the beginning of the twenty-first century the utilization of the Nile waters has changed much symbolically, but little in reality. Egypt continues to fund and support projects of the Nile Basin Initiative, which leaves them free to develop their Western Desert with Nile water in what is known as the New Valley. The Ethiopians are left to develop their enormous hydroelectric capacity. That will depend, however, on greater political stability in order to attract the necessary resources from the international community.

See also **Ecosystems; Egypt, Early; Egypt, Modern; Haile Selassie I; Transportation: River; World Bank.**

BIBLIOGRAPHY

Cheesman, Robert E. *Lake Tana and the Blue Nile: An Abyssinian Quest.* London: Macmillan, 1968.

Collins, Robert O. *The Waters of the Nile: An Annotated Bibliography.* London: Hans Zell, 1991.

Collins, Robert O. *The Waters of the Nile: Hydropolitics and the Jonglei Canal, 1900–1988.* Princeton, NJ: Markus Wiener, 1996.

Collins, Robert O. *The Nile.* New Haven, CT: Yale University Press, 2002.

Hurst, Harold Edwin. *The Nile: A General Account of the River and the Utilization of Its Waters.* London: Constable, 1951.

Said, Rushdi. *The River Nile: Geology, Hydrology, and Utilization.* Oxford: Pergamon Press, 1993.

Sutcliffe, J. V., and Y. P. Parks. *The Hydrology of the Nile.* Wallingford, England: International Association of Hydrological Sciences, 1999.

Tevdt, Terje. *The River Nile and Its Economic, Political, Social, and Cultural Role: An Annotated Bibliography.* Bergen, Norway: Centre for Development Studies, 2002.

Waterbury, John. *Hydropolitics of the Nile Valley.* Syracuse, NY: Syracuse University Press, 1979.

ROBERT O. COLLINS

NILO-SAHARAN LANGUAGES. *See* Languages: Nilo-Saharan.

NJINGA MBANDI ANA DE SOUSA

(c. 1582–1663). Little information is available for Njinga Mbandi's early years. It is known that she was baptized into the Catholic faith in 1622 by Portuguese missionaries in what is present-day Angola, taking a Christian name, Ana de Sousa, as was required of converts at the time. In 1624 she turned away from the church and seized power in Ndongo, the principal political and military opponents of the Portuguese in the region, where she claimed a dynastic connection. Opposing interests, shaped mostly by the Atlantic slave trade, led to a break with the Portuguese, who maintained a military presence in the region. The Portuguese set up a puppet rival to the Ndongo throne and expelled her during the period between 1626 and 1629. Njinga ensured her survival through alliances with the feared Imbangala (Jaga) warrior bands, assuming their ideology of war and their laws and rites, which were generally perceived as brutal.

She then withdrew from direct contact with the Portuguese to the eastern area of Matamba around 1630. Njinga created a new basis of power there but never gave giving up her claim to the throne of Ndongo. Matamba became one of the most important states in the region, acting as a broker in the slave trade.

During the Dutch occupation of Angola (1641–1648), Njinga again grew powerful in her remote base in Matamba and maintained her opposition to the Portuguese, who struggled to regain the region. After the Portuguese drove the Dutch out of Angola in 1648, she pragmatically sought reconciliation and sought to establish a balance of power. In 1656 she returned to the Catholic faith. A year later she signed a peace treaty with the Portuguese, ending clashes that had raged for thirty years.

Njinga is remembered in the early twenty-first century as the most important female political figure in Angola's history. She was unscrupulous and unbending in the pursuit of her interests, power-conscious and possessing great diplomatic talent, and at once shrewd and magnanimous. In recent times, she has become a national symbolic figure of African resistance against colonial rule.

See also **Angola: History and Politics; Women: Women in African History.**

BIBLIOGRAPHY

Heintze, Beatrix. "Das Ende des unabhängigen Staates Ndongo (Angola): Neue Chronologic und Reinterpretation (1617–1630)." *Paideuma* 27 (1981): 197–273.

Heintze, Beatrix. *Studien zur Geschichte Angolas im 16. und 17. Zahrhundert.* Cologne, Germany, 1996.

Thornton, John K. "Legitimacy and Political Power: Queen Njinga, 1624–1663." *Journal of African History* 32 (1991): 25–40.

BEATRIX HEINTZE

NJOYA, IBRAHIM MBOMBO

(c. 1873–1933). Ibrahim Mbombo Njoya ascended to the Bamum throne around 1886 in the highlands of what is now western Cameroon after his father, King Nsangu, was killed in a war fought against the Nso kingdom in the same region. Njoya's mother, Queen Njapundunke (d. 1913), acted as regent until he reached adulthood. About 1894, a group of palace servants tried to usurp power. Njoya resisted the uprising with the help of Lamido Umaru, the ruler of the neighboring Islamic Banyo kingdom. In gratitude for Umaru's support, Njoya and his court converted to Islam.

In 1902, Bamum became part of the German colony of Kamerun. Njoya, a pragmatic politician, tolerated the colonial power in order to maintain his kingdom's autonomy. This manipulative strategy allowed him to pursue numerous innovative projects, such as the invention of a Bamum script, the fostering of art production at the palace, and the adoption of new styles of architecture.

The Germans withdrew from Bamum in 1915 as a result of World War I, and the kingdom came under French rule. The French perceived Njoya as a German ally and a threat. In 1924, they stripped him of his powers. Seven years later, they exiled him in Yaoundé, the capital of the colony, where he died. Njoya is remembered as a reformer and innovator, a patron of the arts, and the author and editor of one of the most unusual works of African historiography, a detailed chronicle of the Bamum kingdom.

See also **Cameroon: History and Politics.**

BIBLIOGRAPHY

Geary, Christraud M. *Images from Bamum: German Colonial Photography at the Court of King Njoya, Cameroon, West Africa, 1902–1915.* New York: HarperCollins, 1988.

Njoya, Sultan of Bamum. *Histoire et coutumes des Bamum.* Mémoires de l'Institut Français d'Afrique Noire, Centre du Cameroun. Série: Populations, No. 5, trans. Henri Martin. Dakar, Senegal, 1952.

Tardits, Claude. *Le royaume Bamoum.* Paris: Peeters, 1980.

CHRISTRAUD M. GEARY

NKETIA, J. H. KWABENA (1921–).

A composer, ethnomusicologist, and writer, Joseph Hanson Kwabena Nketia has more than 200 publications and more than eighty musical compositions to his credit. Nketia was educated at the Presbyterian Training College in Akropong, Ghana, and later studied linguistics and social anthropology at the School of Oriental and African Studies in London. He earned music degrees from Trinity College of Music and Birkbeck College in London. He has taught at the Presbyterian Training College, and served as director of the Institute of African Studies and the School of Music, Dance, and Drama at the University of Ghana. He has been professor of music at the University of California, Los Angeles, Andrew Mellon Professor of Music at the University of Pittsburgh, and held visiting professorships at major universities in the United States, Australia, and China. In 1993 he

established and became director of the International Centre for African Music and Dance, based in Ghana.

Nketia has held offices and served on the executive boards of many international organizations. He has also received numerous awards, including the ASCAP Deems Taylor Award for his book *The Music of Africa,* the IMC-UNESCO Music Prize for Distinguished Service to Music, the 2000 Distinguished Africanist Award of the African Studies Association, and the Litt.D. (doctor of letters, *honoris causa*) of the University of Ghana. In addition to studies on the Akan, his own society, Nketia has written many theoretical works in ethnomusicology, with special emphasis on meaning and integrating the scholarly and practical realities of music.

See also **Ghana: History and Politics; Music; Music, Modern Popular.**

BIBLIOGRAPHY

Akrofi, Eric A. *Sharing Knowledge and Experience: A Profile of Kwabena Nketia. Scholar and Music Educator.* Accra, Ghana: AFRAM Publications, 2002.

DjeDje, Jacqueline Cogdell, ed. *African Musicology: Current Trends,* Vol. 2: *A Festschrift Presented to J. H. Kwabena Nketia.* Los Angeles and Atlanta, GA: UCLA International Studies and Overseas Program/ The James S. Coleman African Studies Center and African Studies Association Press, 1992.

DjeDje, Jacqueline Cogdell, and William G. Carter, eds. *African Musicology: Current Trends,* Vol. 1: *A Festschrift Presented to J. H. Kwabena Nketia.* Los Angeles and Atlanta, GA: UCLA African Studies Center/African Arts Magazine and Crossroads Press/ African Studies Association, 1989.

Nketia, J. H. Kwabena. *African Music in Ghana: A Survey of Traditional Forms.* London: Longmans Green, 1962.

Nketia, J. H. Kwabena. *Drumming in Akan Communities of Ghana.* Edinburgh and London: University of Ghana and Thomas Nelson and Sons, 1963.

Nketia, J. H. Kwabena. *The Music of Africa.* New York: W.W. Norton, 1974.

Nketia, J. H. Kwabena. "The Scholarly Study of African Music: A Historical Review." In *The Garland Encyclopedia of World Music: Africa,* Vol. 1, ed. Ruth Stone. New York: Garland Publishing, 1998.

Nketia, J. H. Kwabena. *Ethnomusicology and African Music (Collected Papers)*, Vol. 1: *Modes of Inquiry and Interpretation*. Accra, Ghana: Afram Publications, 2005.

JACQUELINE COGDELL DJEDJE

NKRUMAH, FRANCIS NWIA KOFI

(1909–1972). Francis Nwia Kofi Nkrumah was a Pan-Africanist leader and the first prime minister and president of Ghana. Born in the British colony of the Gold Coast (present-day Ghana), Nkrumah was educated in Roman Catholic missionary schools and attended Achimota College in the colony. He continued his studies abroad, earning degrees from Lincoln University and the University of Pennsylvania, in the United States, and the London School of Economics. While in the United States, Nkrumah read Karl Marx, Vladimir Illich Lenin, and Marcus Garvey. He served as president of the African Students Association and met W. E. B. Du Bois and George Padmore, both ardent Pan-Africanists. In London, Nkrumah wrote and published *Towards Colonial Freedom: Africa in the Struggle against World Imperialism* (1947), a book that set forth his very advanced ideas on fighting colonialism and liberating colonized peoples.

Invited to serve as the secretary-general of the United Gold Coast Convention (UGCC), the initial party formed to participate in negotiations seen as leading the Gold Coast toward eventual independence, Nkrumah returned to the colony in 1947 to put his ideas into practice. In 1949 he split with the UGCC and founded the more radical Convention People's Party (CPP), an organization dedicated to strikes, civil disobedience, and non-cooperation to force independence. The CPP attracted many followers and won local elections. In 1950 Nkrumah was sent to jail for his role in a CPP strike; he was released early in order to take a seat in the Legislative Assembly formed to include Africans. Named prime minister in 1952, he guided the Gold Coast to independence in 1957 as the nation of Ghana.

Nkrumah considered this early and initially distinctive triumph over the colonial system as a blueprint for others and used his position as post-independence prime minister to herald Pan-Africanism as a vehicle to disseminate his theories. Ghana's prosperous economy, based on the high price of cocoa on the world market, was strong enough to support Pan-Africanists abroad and an aggressive development program at home.

Nkrumah saw himself as a leader and spokesman for Africa and Pan-Africanist ideals on the global stage, and he envisaged a united Africa. In 1959 Ghana and the new West African nation of Guinea that had broken from French policies of gradual decolonization agreed to form a union, with Mali (another former portion of French West Africa) to join later. The Ghanaian constitution of 1960 replaced the legacy of British parliamentary rule with a presidential republic and had provisions to surrender the country's sovereignty to a Union of African States. On 1 July 1960, following a plebiscite, Nkrumah became the first president of the Republic of Ghana.

Nkrumah's international reputation grew with the publication of his book *Africa Must Unite* (1963) and the founding of the Organization of African Unity in that same year. Nonetheless, he became less popular and more autocratic in Ghana in the early 1960s, as the country's economy suffered under falling cocoa prices. Nkrumah survived several assassination attempts. After each one he increased his personal control, eliminated rivals through arrest and detention, and in 1964 created a one-party state with himself as president for life.

On February 24, 1966, while Nkrumah was on a trip to Beijing and Hanoi in an ambitious effort to end the growing war in Vietnam, his government was toppled by a military coup. Nkrumah settled in Guinea, where President Sékou Touré appointed him co-president. Though his fall weakened the Pan-African movement, Nkrumah continued to write for the cause. In exile he published *Handbook of Revolutionary Warfare: A Guide to the Armed Phase of the African Revolution* (1968) and *Class Struggle in Africa* (1970), before dying of cancer in 1972.

See also **Du Bois, W. E. B.; Garvey, Marcus Mosiah; Ghana; Touré, Sékou.**

BIBLIOGRAPHY

Budu-Acquah. *K. Kwame Nkrumah*. Accra, Ghana: Service and Method Agency, 1992.

Rooney, David. *Kwame Nkrumah: The Political Kingdom in the Third World*. New York: St. Martin's Press, 1989.

THOMAS F. McDOW

NONGOVERNMENTAL ORGANIZATIONS.

Nongovernmental organizations, or NGOs, have become firmly entrenched in the political, social, and economic fabric of sub-Saharan Africa since the late 1970s. Ranging from Oxfam to the Undugu Society in Kenya, NGOs are, as their name implies, organizations that operate outside the sphere of national government and are vital actors within civil society. Geographically, they are both indigenous to Africa and based in countries elsewhere. Almost all NGOs have some local presence. They range in size from small, grassroots organizations at the community level to large-scale global operations with a network of local field offices throughout Africa. Their membership is equally diverse, ranging from community volunteers (for example, Home Area Associations in Burkino Faso) to professionally staffed organizations such as the World Wildlife Fund. The approach NGOs take in conducting operations is just as varied. Some take a participatory approach, whereas others follow a more top-down strategy. Lastly, NGOs have varying orientations, including humanitarian assistance, research, technical support, managerial support, development, conservation, and famine relief.

PROLIFERATION OF NGOS

The number and role of NGOs in Africa are an outgrowth of the political and economic vacuum that stemmed from the structural adjustment and austerity programs of the 1980s. As African governments faced financial difficulties, they cut social programs and services. Given these conditions, states found it difficult to provide adequate services, including health care, agricultural extension, famine relief, education, and family planning. In many cases the rise of NGOs had its roots in religious organizations, such as missions and churches, which switched their focus from charitable work to community development, health services, and welfare. NGOs also have entered the African civil landscape as a result of the decline in foreign aid transfers. In the wake of the end of the Cold War, Africa has increasingly taken a back seat to efforts to develop other parts of the globe, notably central and eastern Europe. Although funding has dried up for many government programs, European, Asian, and American donors have increased their funding of African NGOs, thus helping to fill this economic vacuum.

Another reason for the proliferation of NGOs is that they perform functions for which national governments are either underfunded or ill-equipped to handle. This is especially true in the case of disaster-relief services, such as famine relief in Somalia, Ethiopia, and the Sahel, and assistance to refugees from civil strife in Rwanda, Burundi, and Democratic Republic of the Congo. The effects of these events are international, and difficult for a single state government to handle. In addition, given the scarcity of funds, aid organizations and donors seek to make the best use of what amounts are available by maximizing the return on their investment. Thus, aid organizations have increased funding to NGOs, which claim to be closer to the people targeted for funds and assistance, and assert that, consequently, they spend less money on overhead. The Canadian International Development Agency and the World Bank have both increased their lending to NGOs. The Kenyan government states that NGOs provide more than one-third of all development funds, as well as almost one-half of family planning services. Therefore, NGOs have become a powerful force in African democratization and development.

NGOs originally stemmed from the two world wars. Oxfam was formed in 1948 and has been involved in Africa since 1954, when it began feeding refugees from the Mau Mau revolt in Kenya. Since the late 1970s, the number of NGOs has increased dramatically. In 1975, there were 124 NGOs in Kenya; twenty years later there were close to 500. It is estimated that, of the 6,000 to 8,000 NGOs working in developing countries, 4,500 work in Africa. They are, however, unevenly distributed in sub-Saharan Africa for various reasons: the local political and economic climate, acceptance of NGOs by local governments, and the willingness of international NGOs to invest in a particular area. Although there are many NGOs in Kenya, Nigeria, Rwanda, Burkina Faso, Senegal, and Zimbabwe, there are few in Ethiopia, Cameroon, Chad, and the Central African Republic.

FOCUS OF NGOS

As NGOs have proliferated, they have changed their focus. The earliest NGOs were largely oriented toward charitable giving, humanitarian services, and agricultural extension, whereas the new crop of NGOs is oriented toward more productive, developmental activities. They include financial management (the Partnership for Productivity in Togo); primary and community-based health care (Tokombere Health Promotion Centre in Cameroon); technical support for agriculture, livestock, crafts, and small-scale businesses (the Centre for Cooperative Research and Training in Rwanda); development-oriented relief services (the Catholic Relief Services of Madagascar); and increased attention to proactive solutions to natural and human-made disasters, such as drought preparedness (the Churches Drought Action in Africa).

The proliferation of NGOs has led to some problems vis-à-vis the state. States fear that NGOs threaten their power by providing services and funding once provided by the state. As NGOs grow in number as well as power, they play a stronger role in policy decisions that may affect how governments interact with communities. For instance, international wildlife NGOs play an increasingly strong role in the conservation of wildlife and natural areas in Africa. Conservation policies, often initiated through NGOs, are carried out by wildlife services of African countries and sometimes lead to conflicts over land and resources that states must confront. The increasing power of NGOs also makes some national governments wary. Thus, NGO autonomy and the political ramifications of the proliferation of NGOs are being challenged by states whose hands are tied by austerity programs, debt, and funding problems. However, the reverse is also true. Many African states welcome NGOs in an effort to secure funding and resources for programs they can no longer support.

Perhaps the best-known NGO in Africa is Oxfam. Founded as the Oxford Committee for Famine Relief to help rebuild Europe after World War II, it has played a pivotal role in Africa. Oxfam had its beginnings in providing food to war-weary people during the Mau Mau revolt. It has subsequently provided funds, assistance, and medical support during the Congo famine of 1961, the Sahelian and Ethiopian famines of 1973, and the 1984–1985 famine in Ethiopia. Oxfam's mission has always been to side with the poor, providing humanitarian assistance regardless of politics. Since its inception, Oxfam has broadened its scope and funds projects, including rural development and family planning, designed to reduce the vulnerability of the poor to natural and human-caused disasters.

Although some of the best-known NGOs are international—such as Oxfam, the World Wildlife Fund, and Médecins sans Frontières (Doctors without Borders)—others are indigenous, locally based organizations that play an important role in African civil society. One such organization is the Undugu Society of Kenya. It works with Kenya's street children and urban poor. Begun in 1973 by a Dutch Catholic priest, Father Arnold Grol (1924–1997), Undugu has more than twenty programs in communities throughout Kenya. It operates youth centers, conducts cleanup campaigns, and provides apprenticeships and employment opportunities to Kenya's urban poor. Undugu has grown over the years and has become a large, registered NGO in Kenya. As such, it must carefully navigate between the goals of the state and its own mission. This relationship highlights the careful balancing act NGOs must perform in order to achieve their goals and objectives.

FUTURE OF NGOS

The future of NGOs in Africa is uncertain. Although the number of NGOs has proliferated since the late 1970s, their quality and effectiveness depend upon a number of political and economic considerations outside their control. International funding is crucial to many NGOs. For example, Kenyan and Zimbabwean NGOs depend on foreign sources for more than 90 percent of their financial support. In addition, the rapid proliferation of NGOs means that they now compete with each other for backing. This may mean that funding will increasingly be based on political, rather than social, considerations. In addition, instability of international funding means that, if political winds change, funding for NGOs also may change, which could endanger long-term relations and programs.

The local political climate is of paramount importance for the growth of NGOs. Given the dependence of NGOs on foreign sources of funding, African governments are often wary about the agendas, directions, and goals of NGOs. NGOs also threaten sources of government financial support. Prior to the 1970s, governments were the main beneficiaries of development funds flowing into Africa. This has changed as donors have shown their preference to finance NGOs rather than national governments. Thus, whereas the enabling environment for NGOs is strong in countries such as Bénin, Ethiopia, and Ghana, in countries such as Zambia and Namibia the political environment is not as friendly. Finally, NGOs face the question of how effective they can be in empowering local communities. In many cases they are successful, as is the Undugu Society, but in other cases, community involvement, though a stated goal of NGOs, is weak. For example, international conservation NGOs call for people's participation in wildlife conservation, yet this is hampered by a lack of understanding of local communities, the need to work with national governments, and the top-down approaches still used by many NGOs. Nevertheless, NGOs are powerful actors in African civil society. They empower local communities and are valuable resources for development, humanitarian assistance, welfare, health services, and family planning.

See also **Aid and Development: Overview; Christianity: Missionary Enterprise; Economic History; Famine; Healing and Health Care: Hospitals and Clinics; Human Rights; Postcolonialism; Refugees; Wildlife.**

BIBLIOGRAPHY

Clark, J.; Michael Brown; Bonnie Ricci; and K. O'Connor. *Non-Governmental Organizations and Natural Resources Management: An Assessment of Eighteen African Countries.* Washington, DC: Private Voluntary Organization-Non-Government Organization/Natural Resources Management System Project, 1993.

Farrington, John, and Anthony Bebbington. *Reluctant Partners?: Non-Governmental Organizations, the State, and Sustainable Agricultural Development.* London: Routledge, 1993.

Igoe, Jim, and Tim Kelsall, eds. *Between a Rock and a Hard Place: African NGOs, Donors and the State.* Durham, NC: Carolina Academic Press, 2005.

Langley, Philip. "Non-Governmental Organisations in Africa and Rural Development." In *Pan African Institute for Development Report* no. 15E. Limbe, Cameroon: Pan African Institute for Development, 1995.

Makombe, Kudzai, ed. *NGO Action on Land: Reflections from East and Southern Africa.* Harare, Zimbabwe: Mwelekeo wa NGO, 2001.

Ndegwa, Stephen N. *The Two Faces of Civil Society: NGOs and Politics in Africa.* West Hartford, CT: The Kumarian Press, 1996.

Ondeine, Barrow, and Michael Jennings. *The Charitable Impulse: NGOs & Development in East & North-East Africa.* Oxford: James Curry, 2001.

Smith, Terence, and Lisa Bornstein. *Northern NGOs in South Africa: Programmes and Partnerships.* Durban, South Africa: University of Natal, School of Development Studies, 2001.

Thomas, Alan; Susan Carr; and David Humphreys; eds. *Environmental Policies and NGO Influence: Land Degradation and Sustainable Resource Management in Sub-Saharan Africa.* London; New York: Routledge, 2001.

Wellard, Kate, and James G. Copestake, eds. *Non-Governmental Organizations and the State in Africa.* London: Routledge, 1993.

DAVID SMETHURST
JEFF PEIRES
REVISED BY DAVID SMETHURST

NONGQAWUSE

NONGQAWUSE (c. 1840–c. 1900). The Xhosa prophet Nongqawuse was an orphan in the Transkei region of southern Africa, raised by her uncle, Mhlakaza, near the Gxarha River. She began to prophesy in April 1856, telling her Xhosa people that they must kill all their cattle, destroy all their corn, and throw away all their magical devices, because the dead were going to rise, bringing with them a new and perfect world. The blind would see, the deaf would hear, and the old would become young. New cattle and corn would appear in abundance, and nobody would ever again lead a troubled life.

After fifteen months of cattle killing (April 1856–June 1857), about 40,000 Xhosa had starved to death, and another 150,000 had abandoned their homes to search for food. The power of the Xhosa kingdom, which had blocked the eastward expansion of the Cape Colony for more than eighty years, was broken, and most of Xhosaland was divided among white English settlers.

The callous manner whereby the Cape Colony governor, Sir George Grey, manipulated the crisis led many Xhosa to conclude that he somehow bribed or deceived Nongqawuse into uttering the fatal prophecies. There is no direct proof of this suspicion, but in any case, other factors tending to produce an atmosphere of crisis need to be taken into account: the military stalemate between the Xhosa and the colonists; the devastating bovine pleuropneumonia (lung sickness) epidemic of 1854–1857, which led the Xhosa to believe that their cattle were bewitched; and the influence of Christianity through Mhlakaza, a lapsed and frustrated Christian convert. Thus, the cattle-killing millennium was not conceived entirely within an indigenous cultural framework, but was a tragic synthesis of Xhosa creation myths and ancestor beliefs with Christian ideas concerning the Resurrection and the Apocalypse.

Historians know almost nothing about Nongqawuse as a person. The only firsthand Xhosa description available states that she was "a girl of about sixteen years of age, has a silly look, and appears to me as if she was not right in her mind" (Peires, 87). She was the only person who saw the spirits of the dead and conversed with them. But her communications were incoherent and were explained to the Xhosa by Mhlakaza, her uncle.

As pressure upon her grew, Nongqawuse became "sick" and stopped talking altogether. Many of her immediate circle, including Mhlakaza, starved to death. Nongqawuse was captured by the colonial police and taken to Cape Town. The authorities tried to get her to implicate the Xhosa chiefs in punishable crimes, but she would not do so. There are no official records concerning her release from custody, but apparently she ended her days quietly, among relatives on a white farm near Alexandria in the Eastern Cape.

See also **Prophetic Movements: Eastern Africa.**

BIBLIOGRAPHY

Gqoba, William W. "The Tale of Nongqawuse." In *Towards an African Literature*, ed. A. C. Jordan. Berkeley: University of California Press, 1973.

Peires, Jeffrey B. *The Dead Will Arise: Nongqawuse and the Great Xhosa Cattle-Killing Movement of 1856–7.* Bloomington: Indiana University Press, 1989.

JEFF PEIRES

NORTHEASTERN AFRICA, CLASSICAL PERIOD, HISTORY OF (1000 BCE TO 600 CE).

The period 1000 BCE–600 CE encompasses a time of profound social and political change in the region of northeastern Africa. These changes, centered on the Nile River in northeastern Africa, involved engagements between the eastern Mediterranean worlds (represented by the twin cultural and military powers of Greece and then Rome) and Africa. Apart from the obvious mercantile, social, and economic implications, this contact would ultimately bring many areas of the region into the eastern Christian world, before the emergence from Arabia of a new socioideological force: Islam.

In Egypt the time period of concern includes the Third Intermediate Period (1070 BCE–525 BCE) and the Late Period, during which time Egypt dominated lower Nubia; political power shifted from the center of religious power at Thebes during the Twenty-First Dynasty to Tanis (in the Delta). From 716–664 BCE Egypt was ruled by the Twenty-Fifth (Kushite) Dynasty, rulers from the Napatan kingdom of the Middle Nile. Assyrian domination followed, and at the beginning of the Twenty-Sixth (Saitic) Dynasty Egypt was a vassal state, but gradually recovered some degree of political and cultural

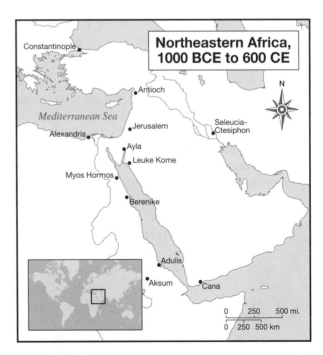

COURTESY OF NIALL FINNERAN

independence. From the sixth century, many Greeks settled in Egypt, as mercenaries in the army and as merchants at the site of Naucratis. With the emergence of Persian power in the east, the Persian king Cambyses invaded Egypt in 525 BCE. During Egypt's Late Period (525–332 BCE) there were vain attempts by Egypt to restore some degree of independence, but in the north of Greece a new power was emerging, a charismatic military genius whose conquests would reshape Egypt and much of the near east: Alexander the Great.

At this juncture one should consider developments southward along the Nile (Kush) in a region historians have often overlooked. During the second millennium BCE two major cultures dominated the region: the C-Group of cattle pastoralists in lower Nubia, and the Kerma polity above the third cataract. Egyptian influence—political, military and cultural—was strong, particularly in lower Nubia. In the eighth century BCE, after the erosion of the Kerma culture, a new center of Kushite political power arose at Jebel Barqal (the "pure mountain"), the site of the Egyptian sacred mountain of Amun, located some 31 miles to the southwest of the fourth cataract. The wider region (known as Napata) contained a number of large temple structures often dedicated to the Egyptian god Amun. The kings of Kush were buried in royal cemeteries at el Kurru and latterly at Nuri, and in time, as historians have seen, came to dominate Egypt (albeit briefly) during the Twenty-Fifth Dynasty.

During the fourth century BCE the Kushite center of Meroë rose to prominence when it replaced the Napatan region as the political center of Kush. Located on the Shendi reach between the fifth and sixth cataracts, its influence is acknowledged by Greek writers such as Herodotus—and latterly by Strabo and Pliny. It is from these sources that the region takes on the identification of Aethiopia, the Greek translation of Kush, meaning *black faces*. Old Testament references to Ethiopia thus refer to the inhabitants of Kush rather than those of the Horn of Africa. Meroitic material culture is vibrant and diverse; steep-sided pyramid structures are a variation on a much older Egyptian theme. Eastern Mediterranean goods (pottery, glassware, and jewelry) abound in funerary contexts, showing strong Hellenistic and then Roman influence, although the fundamental substratum of the material culture remains strongly African.

Eastward, in the Gash Delta in the region of modern Kassala, a long-lived continuum of settlement is seen; from 2000 BCE the site of Mahal Teglinos takes on a degree of socioeconomic complexity that is not mirrored eastward in the Horn of Africa. Here, on the Red Sea coasts and high plateaux of modern Eritrea/northern Ethiopia (the Land of Punt of Egyptian tradition) the emergence of social complexity is a relatively late phenomenon, witnessed by the rise of the Ona culture of central Eritrea, and then slightly later and southward in the mountains of southern Eritrea and eastern Tigray by the emergence of the DMT polity, which is known from unvocalised Epigraphic South Arabian inscriptions, centred on Yeha. The DMT kingdom of the pre-Aksumite period is not a phenomenon to be associated with southern Arabian migration, however, even though inscriptions based upon the Epigraphic South Arabian languages are attested from the fifth and sixth centuries BCE. In these inscriptions South Arabian gods are mentioned, yet arguably only two temple structures, Yeha and Gobochela, really do show strong Sabaean affinities.

The conquest of Persian Egypt by Alexander the Great of Macedon in 332 BCE was followed by the establishment of the Ptolemaic dynasty, effectively Egypt's last independent rulers. The foundation of the city of Alexandria drew Greek conceptions of urban design into an Egyptian environment, yet on the whole a strong ideological syncretic meeting of the Greek and Egyptian worlds emerged. In 30 BCE the Romans arrived, and under Augustus Egypt became one of the most important regions of the Roman Empire. In Alexandria, nascent Christian communities began to flourish in a city with a large Jewish population, and by 312 CE Egypt was one of the most Christianized countries in the world.

Southward, Meroë had been attacked by Petronius' Roman army in 24 BCE, and by circa 350 CE its influence waned in the face of incursions by pastoralist groups as well as an aggressive Aksumite empire to the east. Aksum had come to prominence in the first century CE, and by the mid-fourth century had embraced Christianity. Aksum was engaged, via the Red Sea with trade with the Eastern Mediterranean as well as colonial expansion into Arabia. In the middle Nile the cultural vacuum was filled by the states of Nobadia (in the north), Makhuria and Alwa (to the south). In the north, Byzantine (eastern Roman) hegemony of Egypt continued, but Egyptian Coptic Christianity remained a vehicle for

Theater, or Odeon at the site of Kom el Dikka in Alexandria. This theater was possibly used as a place of instruction during late antiquity. However, the early Christians probably regarded it as a profane place of paganism. COURTESY OF NIALL FINNERAN

popular cultural resistance, an echo of ancient pharaonic glory.

This classical period saw the creation of a rich Graeco-African cultural identity when the whole Nilotic world and African Red Sea system was drawn into the Greek-dominated eastern Mediterranean. The conquest of Egypt in 641 CE by the Islamic armies sweeping in from the Levant—and ultimately conquering the middle Nile region and isolating Christian Ethiopia—fatally fractured the Graeco-African world.

See also **Aksum; Christianity; Desertification, Reactions to, History of (c. 5000 to 1000 BCE); Egypt, Early; Ethiopia and Vicinity, History of (600 to 1600 CE); History of Africa: To Seventh Century; Islam; Kings and Kingdoms; Muslim Northern Africa, History of (641 to 1500 CE); Nile River; Nubia; Tunis.**

BIBLIOGRAPHY

Bowman, Alan K. *Egypt after the Pharaohs, 332 BC–AD 642.* Berkeley: University of California Press, 1986.

Edwards, David N. *The Nubian Past: An Archaeology of the Sudan.* London: Routledge, 2004.

Finneran, Niall. *Alexandria: A City and Myth.* Charleston, SC: Tempus, 2005.

Watterson, Barbara. *The Egyptians.* Oxford: Blackwell Publishers, 1997.

NIALL FINNERAN

NORTHERN AFRICA

This entry includes the following articles:
HISTORICAL LINKS WITH MEDITERRANEAN
HISTORICAL LINKS WITH SUB-SAHARAN AFRICA

HISTORICAL LINKS WITH MEDITERRANEAN

Northwestern Africa, or the Maghreb (the present-day states of Morocco, Algeria, Libya, Mauritania, and Tunisia), was for centuries home to the Carthaginian empire until Carthage was defeated and destroyed by Rome at the end of the Third Punic War in 146 BCE. Thereafter, the Maghreb formed part of the Roman Empire for almost six centuries until the Vandals pushing down from Spain provided new rulers from c. 440 CE until 534. There followed somewhat more than a century of Byzantine rule.

The Muslim Arabs first reached the Maghreb as early as 647 CE, an arrival that inaugurated a period of some twelve centuries during which the Maghreb was destined to be the arena of various Muslim dynasties, the most durable being the Ottoman rule in Algeria and Tunisia from the sixteenth to the nineteenth centuries, and the Moroccan from the seventeenth century to the present. Last in time came the period of French colonial rule followed by independence—Algeria (1830–1964), Tunisia (1881–1956), and Morocco (1912–1956), including a Spanish protectorate in Northern Morocco. This summary chronology suggests that the Maghreb has often throughout history been part of a politico-cultural system centered in some other part of the Mediterranean. Such was demonstrably the case with the Romans, Vandals, Byzantines, and Ottomans, but even the Carthaginian state was created by Phoenicians coming from the Eastern Mediterranean. And many of the early Muslim dynasties in the Maghreb had their roots in the East.

The Maghreb, throughout history, has clearly been involved with other parts of the Mediterranean littoral. The extent and nature of that involvement is partially explained by the Maghreb's distinctive geography. The Atlas mountains crossing Morocco and Algeria before subsiding into foothills in Tunisia configure the Maghreb into a boomerang-shaped island of sorts, surrounded by seas of saltwater and sand (the Sahara). Not surprisingly, the early Muslim Arab conquerors named the region the Western island (*jazirat al-Maghreb*). Within this island where the great majority of the population has always lived there are no navigable rivers and few good natural harbors. Those harbors that do exist usually have only a limited hinterland before being impeded by mountainous or desert barriers. The resulting

juxtaposition of the desert and the sown plus the mountains makes the Maghreb difficult of access from the outside and resistant to unified control from within.

Maghrebi links with its Mediterranean neighbors throughout time may be schematized as follows: The movements into the Maghreb of peoples and ideas, whether conquering armies, migrations, or new religions, have tended to follow the more accessible coastal strip and the more promising sedentary areas unbroken by mountains or desert. Such invasions, if they are to take root, spread from urban and settled areas to other urban and settled areas while usually leaving the nomads and those living in mountain bastions more nearly contained than assimilated.

The prime example of this interrelation between geography and history is the way in which the less mountainous eastern Maghreb, with openings to the sea (such as Carthage in the distant past, and thereafter neighboring Tunis) and an accessible hinterland, has been the most open to movements from other parts of the Mediterranean and the readiest to absorb these intrusions.

Carthage, founded in 814 BCE by Phoenicians coming from the coastal cities of Lebanon, served as the center of a maritime trading empire stringing together other ports along that thin Maghrebi coastal strip and on to Spain. The Roman imperial presence started in the eastern Maghreb and was always most heavily concentrated there. The same held for Christianization. It was the eastern Maghreb that had the greatest concentrations of Christians and produced such Church fathers as Tertullian (c. 155–230), Cyprian (c. 200–258), and Augustine (354–430). Even the Vandals, although invading from Spain into Morocco, thereafter moved eastward and chose Carthage as their capital. So, too, did the Byzantines coming from the east.

The Muslim Arab conquest of the Maghreb came overland via that other sea, the Sahara Desert, and the first important urban settlement, Qairawan (founded in 670), may be seen as a desert port strategically placed where the desert gives way to Tunisia's more accessible hinterland, including the extended eastward-looking coastal plain known as the Sahel. The eastern Maghreb's relative openness to outside influences is further demonstrated by the existence of more Latin speakers in the eastern

Maghreb than farther west during Roman times. Then, during the long centuries of the Arab-Muslim presence, the eastern Maghreb became more quickly and more thoroughly Arabic speaking. Less than 1 percent of the Tunisian population in the early twenty-first century speak Berber, whereas perhaps more than 20 percent in Algeria and more than 30 percent in Morocco remain to this day Berber-speaking.

The Arab conquerors of the Maghreb, although not spared serious resistance from the Berbers, had soon managed to recruit a largely Berber army that not only secured control of the Maghreb but moved on conquer Spain. When in 711 the Berber Muslim general Tariq ibn Ziyad (d. 720) landed his army at the Spanish site to which he gave his name (Gibraltar—Jabel al-Tariq, or mountain of Tariq) he inaugurated a seven-century era during which the Maghreb and the Iberian Peninsula were linked politically and culturally. This was the Maghreb's most sustained link with any part of Europe. The impressive architecture that remains bespeaks the close cultural ties linking Spain and the Maghreb. By the early thirteenth century, however, the Spanish Christian Reconquista (reconquest) had wrested most of Spain from the Muslims. Only Grenada held on until it fell to the Spanish monarchs, Ferdinand (1452–1516) and Isabella (1451–1504), in 1492.

Thereafter, until the era of European colonization, the links between Europe and the Maghreb were limited and usually hostile. Iberian efforts to extend the Reconquista into Morocco were defeated in the following century, leaving only small seaports in Northern Morocco under Christian control—Ceuta and Melilla—both of which remain Spanish territory in the early twenty-first century. That these tiny holdings open to the sea but have little accessible hinterland, yet had been part of the earlier Punic and Roman imperial holdings but never absorbed into Moroccan-based dynasties illustrates the shaping influence of geography. The fate of another seaport, Tangiers, makes this point, as well. The Portuguese held on to Tangiers until 1661 when they ceded it to the British who, persistently pressed by Moulay Isma'il (c. 1645–1727), the early great ruler of the dynasty that still rules in Morocco, abandoned Tangiers in 1684.

By 1574 both Algeria and Tunisia, which had changed hands between Muslim and Christian forces in earlier decades, had become part of the Ottoman Empire, but both were largely autonomous, being just far enough removed from the Ottoman capital in Istanbul to maintain that status.

Thereafter, until the advent of European colonial rule in the nineteenth century, there were no significant invasions of people or ideas from Europe to the Maghreb or vice versa. This age was characterized by a limited amount of trade between Europe and the Maghreb, alongside a distinctive pattern of low-intensity maritime warfare that Europeans have dubbed Barbary piracy. It was, in fact, privateering conducted by both Europe and the Maghreb with elaborate rules including treaties, prize courts, and ransoming of prisoners. Many of these Maghrebi Barbary pirates came from Christian and Muslim areas in the Eastern Mediterranean and beyond. They were based essentially in the major seaports—Rabat and Salé, Algiers, and Tunis and Tripoli (in Libya), and from Algiers eastward their language was usually not Arabic, but Turkish mixed with a Mediterranean lingua franca. Both they and the Europeans with whom they fought and traded had limited impact on the great majority of the Maghreb population.

The age of European colonial rule, by contrast, was long-lasting and penetrated into the Maghrebi countryside. French (and Spanish) rule in the Maghreb brought settlers from the metropole, plus other European countries, in such numbers that they came to constitute between 6 and 10 percent of the total population. They held the political and economic power and imposed their language, their architecture, and their many other institutions on the Maghreb. Interestingly, they failed to impose their religion (Christian proselytism was sporadic and seldom officially encouraged). Islam held firm and served as a major factor in the ultimately successful independence movements.

A significant example of postindependence ties between the Maghreb and Western Europe grows out of a process begun during World War I when Maghrebis were brought to Europe for military service and work in the factories. Such immigration continued thereafter and reached huge numbers following World War II. In the early twenty-first century, an estimated 8–9 percent of the French and 3 percent of the Spanish populations are of Maghrebi origin. This, to evoke yet another historical parallel, may turn out to be most significant invasion of the Maghreb into Europe since Tariq ibn Ziyad took his Berber army into Spain in 711.

The idea of Maghrebi ties with the Mediterranean is not lacking in political controversy. Ideologues during the period of French colonial rule justified France in the Maghreb as a presumably more successful restoration of Rome in Africa. The Maghrebi nationalists who gained independence thought otherwise. A nonpoliticized understanding of Maghreb ties with the Mediterranean would surely find that, although Europe has left its mark on the Maghreb from earliest times to the present, the more long-lived connection has been that coming from the Eastern Mediterranean beginning fourteen centuries ago and never broken since.

See also **Algeria; Carthage; Liberia; Mauritania; Morocco; Rabat and Salé; Sahara Desert; Tripoli; Tunis; Tunisia; World War I; World War II.**

BIBLIOGRAPHY

Abun-Nasr, Jamil M. *A History of the Maghrib*, 2nd edition. Cambridge, U.K.: Cambridge University Press, 1975.

Brown, Leon Carl. "Maghrib Historiography: The Unit of Analysis Problem." In *The Maghrib in Question: Essays in History and Historiography*, ed. Michel Le Gall & Kenneth J. Perkins. Austin: University of Texas Press, 1997.

Gallagher, Charles F. *The United States and North Africa*. Cambridge, MA: Harvard University Press, 1967.

Laroui, Abdallah. *The History of the Maghrib: An Interpretive Essay*. Princeton, NJ: Princeton University Press, 1977.

L. Brown

HISTORICAL LINKS WITH SUB-SAHARAN AFRICA

The historical links between North and sub-Saharan Africa developed mainly through Islam, trade, and war. For the Muslim medieval chroniclers, sub-Saharan Africa came gradually to be conceived as part of the *dar al-Islam* (house of Islam), a concept that included a vast geographical area extending from the Middle East to Southeast Asia, parts of Europe, and Africa. Even though the first attempt to expand the religion of Islam south beyond the Nile Valley met with fierce resistance from the Christian Nubians between 641 and 651 CE, the spread of Islamic influence started to take place slowly in the southern regime of the

Sahara through the trans-Saharan trade in which the *kharijis*, the smallest of the orientations in Islam, became involved in North Africa by the eighth century. Nonetheless, up to the eleventh century CE, Islamic influence was relatively limited and did not go beyond the region of present-day Mauritania under the legalistic Sunni Almoravid state (1073–1147).

By the beginning of the twelfth century, the changing nature of political and religious authority in the Maghreb (North Africa) became more favorable for the spread of Islam into Africa. The Almohad state (1130–1269) that took control from the Almoravids was inclined to a more ascetic form of Islamic practice that was associated with Sufism, especially in rural areas. By the end of the twelfth century, northern and sub-Saharan Africa had already established Sufism and Sunni Islam as one of the most important links that would last to the present. More importantly, Sufism has remained a constant characteristic of rural religious practices due mainly to the sub-Saharan trade and the travels of Sufi scholars who were supported by an elaborate network of *zawiyas* (Sufi brotherhoods). In more urban areas, Sunni Islam was more dominant due to the important role played by the *madrasa* (religious school) system of orthodox Islamic learning.

The gradual spread of Islam into sub-Saharan Africa had a major impact on the already established trans-Saharan trade system that involved the *bilad al-Sudan* (lands of the Blacks, as Muslim historians referred to the West African savanna) regions along the Niger River, the Sahara, and North and sub-Saharan Africa. The advent of Islam had, however, reoriented the economic, cultural, and political direction more toward the north. A certain amount of prejudice and cultural chauvinism was often part of how the *bilad al-Sudan* were perceived among Muslim scholars and rulers in the north, but that did not prevent Muslim traders from venturing into a trans-Saharan trade. The thriving economy of some major urban centers such as in Bornu, Gao, and Glawa was a positive factor for merchants who were attracted by a lucrative trade in gold, copper, and salt.

In assessing the historical North African relationship with the sub-Saharan region, scholars continue to debate whether it was the merchants or the clerics who established links with the Islamic world. This dichotomy is in fact misleading because the distinction between merchants and clerics is blurred. North

African merchants were not immune to religious ideology, and Islam played a very significant role in trans-Saharan trade. The spread of Islamic civilization had not only the effect of bringing sub-Saharan Africa into the orbit of Middle Eastern and Mediterranean civilizations, but also stimulated trade across and beyond the Sahara. It is apparent that the gradual institutionalization of Islam in sub-Saharan Africa also served economic objectives. Islam became part of homogeneous legal discourse and customs that made it more practical for the Muslim traders to enter into transactions in a West African environment, characteristically known for its heterogeneous laws and practices. The introduction of Islam in West Africa created distinct Muslim communities that became part of a complex fabric of society and it was these communities that facilitated and broadened the process of trade.

In addition to Islam and trade, war was also part of how North Africa came into contact with the sub-Saharan regions. The conflict of interpretations about the nature and extent of the Muslim Invasion of Ghana has been part of the debate about the relationship between the northern and the southern regimes of Africa. Due mostly to the scarcity of historical documents, as well as to the politics of Arab chroniclers and colonial historiography, the Almoravid invasion of Ghana in 1076 CE was either glorified by the former or dramatized and blown out of proportion by the latter as part of a destruction of Ghana. A more recent analysis by the Africanist historian Humphrey Fisher in the early 1980s suggests that the whole episode of Almoravid conquest of Ghana may likely be part of a legend fabricated by Arab historians who sympathized with the Almoravid dynasty. Whether part of a historical reality or legend, it did not appear that the Almoravid conquest of Ghana contributed in any serious way to the disruption of the trans-Saharan trade, nor did it damage the relations between the people of sub-Saharan Africa and the Muslim populations in the north. From the eleventh century onward, western and central Africa saw an increasing phenomenon of Islamization of the major monarchies in places such as Takrur (present-day Senegal) and Gao (present-day Mali).

See also **Gao; Ibn Battuta, Muhammad ibn Abdullah; Islam; Maghili, Muhammad ibn ʿAbd al-Karim al-; Muslim Northern Africa, History of (641 to 1500 CE); Niger River; Sahara Desert; Tijani, Ahmad;** Travel and Exploration; ʿUmar ibn Saʿid Tal (al-Hajj).

BIBLIOGRAPHY

Dramani-Issifou, Zakari. *L'afrique noire dans les relations internationales au XVIe siècle: Analyse de la crise entre le maroc et le donrhaï.* Paris: Editions Karthala, 1982.

Fisher, Humphrey J. *Slavery in the History of Muslim Black Africa.* New York: New York University Press, 2001.

Reynolds, Jonathan T., and Erik Gilbert. *Africa in World History: From Prehistory to the Present.* Upper Saddle River, NJ: Pearson Educational, 2004.

Temimi, Abdeljelil. *Etudes d'histoire Arabo-Africaine.* Zaghouan, Tunisia: Ceromdi, 1994.

DRISS MAGHRAOUI

NORTHWESTERN AFRICA, CLASSICAL PERIOD, HISTORY OF (1000 BCE TO 600 CE).

Northwestern Africa, an area that includes the modern countries of Tunisia, Algeria, and Morocco, underwent substantial development from 1000 BCE to 600 CE. The population increased in size, sedentary farmers settled lands formerly occupied by pastoralists, and contact with Mediterranean civilizations brought new ideas, technologies, and economic practices to the region.

FROM SMALL SCALE COMMUNITIES TO UNIFIED STATES

The scant archaeological evidence that exists from the start of this period indicates the presence of small communities practicing both farming and herding. They are often characterized as part of one large Berber population, but it is perhaps better to think of loosely affiliated groups (including the Garamantes) scattered widely throughout North Africa. In Northwestern Africa, members of these communities united into larger kingdoms, called the Massyli, Masaesyli, and Mauri, beginning about 300 BCE. Greek and Latin texts mention prominent rulers about a hundred years later, including Masinissa (of the Massyli; d. c. 148 BCE), Syphax (of the Masaesyli; d. c. 202 BCE), and Baga (of the Mauri; d. c. 200 BCE) who exercised power in a fashion similar to other Mediterranean potentates. They commanded large armies, built capital cities (at Cirta, Siga, and Volubilis), promoted their legitimacy through coinage, and created dynastic alliances through marriage. Most of the population lived in villages, practiced a mixed economy of farming and herding, and spoke the Libyan language, which survives in inscriptions. One intriguing characteristic of Berber culture is the worship of ancestors that may be reflected in the creation of monumental tombs, a number of which were located near prominent settlements in the region. These indigenous kingdoms lasted for about 300 years.

CARTHAGE

800 BCE marks the beginning of external political influences that had a profound role in shaping the cultural and historical trajectory of Northwestern Africa. Phoenicians from Lebanon arrived at Carthage around that time and developed the city into one of the premier harbors of the ancient world. Carthaginians established colonies at ports all along the North African littoral and in Spain, Sardinia, and Sicily to promote trade, especially in metals. Supremacy in shipbuilding and naval warfare were the hallmarks of Punic (the term used to indicate inhabitants of Carthage, rather than ancestral Phoenicians from the Levant) civilization, as the remains of its circular harbor with space for 220 warships still attest. Carthage's territorial advances in Africa brought it into minor conflicts with the indigenous kingdoms, but its ambitions in Sicily generated greater rivalry with Rome. After more than a hundred years of intermittent wars, Rome conquered Carthage in 146 BCE. Contrary to popular belief, Rome did not sow salt into the fields of Carthage (the story is a modern invention)—soldiers destroyed the city center at the time of conquest, then Julius Caesar (100–44 BCE) and his successor Augustus (63 BCE–14 CE) resettled it a century later and made it the capital of the new province of Africa. Rome gradually expanded its hegemony east and west, taking over former Punic areas as well as the lands of the indigenous kingdoms until it controlled all of Northwestern Africa by 50 CE.

NORTHWESTERN AFRICA IN THE ROMAN EMPIRE

Rome ruled Northwestern Africa for 500 years. In the early twenty-first century one can visit hundreds of towns from this period inhabited by the descendants of the Carthaginians and the Berber kingdoms. Many of the towns from this period, such as Iol Caesarea, Sufetula, and Thugga, still contain standing monuments that attest to the wealth created under Roman rule. Certainly, the peace Rome maintained for centuries in the Mediterranean, and the investment of the Roman government in infrastructure such as roads, ports, and aqueducts, provided some of the conditions necessary for growth, but scholars increasingly point to the role of local residents in improving their own communities as the source of much development. The family of Aulus Gabinius Datus, a resident of Thugga, provides one example. An inscription records that this man and his two sons, all of whom had taken Roman names as was common practice, built a monumental temple complex in their town with shrines for three gods—Concordia, Liber Pater, and Frugifer—during the reign of Hadrian (117–138 CE). The size of each structure was impressive, but what is more striking is that the Gabinii chose three divinities whose realms intersected both native African and Roman religions, and therefore were suited to the mixture of the two cultures that had developed in the town.

Most other towns have evidence of private individuals such as the Gabinii who constructed buildings such as baths, temples, shrines, markets, and fountains for their own communities. Private houses of the wealthy demonstrated a similar mixture of local influence and broader Roman domestic arrangements. They generally contained several rooms organized around a courtyard that gave access, as well as provided light and air, to the inner rooms. Decoration, especially in rooms for dining or entertainment, included columns, fountains, statues, and colored mosaic floor pavements. A mosaic showing the arrival of *Dominus Julius*, or Master Julius, by horse to his impressive home while his servants raise animals, hunt, and gather crops represents the polychrome style of North African mosaic floors. This style—with patterns representing gods, hunting scenes, chariot races, and Christian iconography—came to influence mosaic artists elsewhere in the Roman Empire.

The source of this wealth came from the grain fields of the Bagradas River valley in northern Tunisia and the extensive olive orchards to the south and west. The Roman Empire created an enormous demand for grain and olive oil, and also for fish sauce, wine, and fine pottery. African landowners invested heavily in surplus production and

Overview of the town of Thugga. The town of Thugga overlooks the fertile Bagradas valley in northern Tunisia. The reconstructed temple and theater stand out in the center left and center right, while the walls of ancient houses are visible lower down the hillside. PHOTOGRAPH BY DAVID STONE

reaped the benefits of a large export market. Archaeological evidence documents extensive olive plantations in the steppe regions of Tunisia and Algeria, production areas for ceramic jars used in shipping, and massive harbor facilities. In the port areas of Rome, archaeologists have located the remains of African merchants' stalls and broken jars used to transport oil and fish sauces to Roman consumers.

The role of North Africa in creating this market should not be underestimated: certainly, Roman conquerors provided peaceful conditions and North Africa's proximity to Italy made shipping relatively inexpensive, but the region was not naturally fertile. Ecologically, the region straddles arid, semiarid, and Mediterranean zones, and annual precipitation levels can vary significantly. African farmers had to work hard to produce a substantial surplus. The agricultural system was neither wholly African nor Roman, but the product of a fusion of the two cultures, just as, for instance, irrigation techniques in the region of Cillium, which relied on aqueducts along with cross-wadi walls to nourish the crops, depended on both Roman and

African technologies. Political and economic rewards were available to Africans who participated in the Roman economy—a good example is Aulus Gabinius Datus again, who made money by leasing agricultural land to local farmers. Those like him used their wealth to gain prestige by running for office, erecting buildings in their towns, and sponsoring gladiatorial games for their fellow citizens. It was rare but not impossible for an African to become a Roman senator, and one African, Septimius Severus (145–211) from Lepcis Magna in Libya, became emperor in 193 CE.

EARLY CHRISTIANITY

North Africa had a significant impact on early Christianity, both before and after it replaced paganism as the official religion of the Roman Empire in the early 300s CE. Roman authorities persecuted the earliest members of the African church, just as they persecuted Saint Perpetua, who wrote a vivid account of the events that led to her death and martyrdom in 203 CE. Saint Augustine (354–430) is the best-known African cleric, whose writings contributed to the establishment of the Christian doctrines, but others such as

Tertullian (c. 155–230), Lactantius (c. 240–c. 320), and Cyprian (d. 258), were also important. The appointment of Caecilian (d. c. 330) as bishop of Carthage in 311 CE instead of Donatus (d. c. 355), who was favored by most of the dioceses of Africa, provoked a major schism within the church that lasted 100 years.

END OF CLASSICAL PERIOD

The history of Northwestern Africa at the end of this period, as Rome's authority weakened, is one of political upheaval. Vandals (from Germany) invaded the region in the 430s CE. Byzantine forces from Constantinople arrived to take Africa back a hundred years later, and Arabs conquered the entire coast of North Africa in the late 600s. In the aftermath, the orientation of North Africa toward the Mediterranean that persisted throughout the Classical period shifted to the Middle East and the centers of Arab rule. The diminished trading network in the Mediterranean reduced the need for significant surplus production and exports, and over time the size of the population decreased.

See also **Desertification, Reactions to, History of (c. 5000 to 1000 BCE); Morocco, History of (1000 to 1900) Muslim Northern Africa, History of (641 to 1500 CE); Northeastern Africa, Classical Period, History of (1000 BCE to 600 CE).**

BIBLIOGRAPHY

Brett, Michael, and Elizabeth Fentress. *The Berbers.* Malden, MA: Blackwell, 1996.

Camps, Gabriel. "Aux origines de la BerbÈrie: Massinissa ou les dèbuts de l'histoire." *Archèologie-Epigraphie* 8 (1961): 3–320.

Dunbabin, Katherine. *The Mosaics of Roman North Africa.* Oxford: Clarendon Press, 1978.

Lancel, Serge. *Carthage: A History.* Malden, MA: Blackwell, 1995.

Mattingly, David J. "Oil for Export? A Comparative Study of Olive-Oil Production in Libya, Spain, and Tunisia." *Journal of Roman Archaeology* 1 (1988): 33–56.

Ridley, R. T. "To Be Taken with a Pinch of Salt: The Destruction of Carthage." *Classical Philology* 81 (1986): 140–146.

Stone, David, and Lea Stirling, eds. *Mortuary Landscapes of North Africa.* Toronto: University of Toronto Press, 2006.

DAVID STONE

NOUAKCHOTT. Nouakchott, the capital and largest city of Mauritania, is located six miles inland from the Atlantic Ocean. It is situated on a salt flat, and parts of the city lie under sea level. The city's population (a mix of Arab and sub-Saharan ethnic groups) was in 2006 variously estimated at between 700,000 and 800,000 inhabitants. Many of these people are rural migrants who fled from poverty and deteriorating environmental conditions elsewhere in the country. Until 1957 Nouakchott had been a tiny settlement, consisting of a fort and an airstrip. In that year, the French selected it as the capital of the colony of Mauritania, which until then had been administered from Saint-Louis across the border in Senegal. Following independence in 1960, essential national infrastructure and institutions were created in the city: two great mosques (one built in the Moroccan and the other in the Saudi style), a national stadium, a wharf on the Atlantic (1966), and a deep-sea harbor (1986), the last financed by the People's Republic of China. Much of the city consists of low-density shantytowns that sprawl across the desert. In 2006, oil from offshore fields forty miles from the city began flowing to world markets, and to China in particular, and hopes have been raised that the resulting revenue will solve the city's social and economic problems.

See also **Colonial Policies and Practices; Mauritania.**

BIBLIOGRAPHY

Kjeilen, Tore. "Nouakchott. Place of Winds." Available from http://i-cias.com/mauritania/nouakch.htm.

Pitte, Jean-Robert. *Nouakchott, capitale de la Mauritanie.* Paris: Université de Paris-Sorbonne, 1977.

ERIC S. ROSS

NUBIA. Since the early Middle Ages, the toponym Nubia has been applied to that portion of the Nile Valley that lies immediately upriver from Egypt. It is not a political term, for there never was any single nation specifically called Nubia, and in the early twenty-first century, the region is divided between the republics of Egypt and Sudan. Nubia takes its name rather from a distinctive ethnic group who call themselves Nubians and who speak languages of the Nubian family.

The Nubian-speaking peoples seem to have migrated from the Kordofan and Darfur regions of western Sudan to the Nile Valley in a series of waves, beginning perhaps two thousand years ago. Initially they settled within the territories of the Sudanese empire of Kush, became its subjects, and absorbed much of the culture of the riverine farmers along the Nile. Gradually, as their numbers became predominant, their languages supplanted the older, Meroitic language of Kush. By the time the empire of Kush broke up in the fourth century CE, all of the peoples of southern Egypt and northern Sudan spoke Nubian languages and were called Nubians. The northern boundary of Nubia was, and still is, just to the south of Aswan in Egypt; the southern boundary was somewhere well to the south of present-day Khartoum, perhaps around Sennar.

For about two centuries after the fall of Kush, there is almost no historical record relating to the Nubians and their country. Extensive archaeological excavations have shown that in the northernmost part of Nubia (commonly called lower Nubia), a fairly powerful kingdom persisted and still carried on some of the traditions of Kush. It derived its prosperity from trading with Byzantine Egypt. In the sixth century CE when Christian missionaries from Byzantium entered the country, they found three well-established Nubian kingdoms. In the north, on the borders of Egypt was Nobadia; farther upstream and centered in the Dongola region was Makuria; and in the region around the confluence of the Blue and White Niles was Alodia, known in later medieval texts as Alwa.

All three of the Nubian kingdoms accepted the Christian faith with extraordinary rapidity, and conversion was complete by the end of the sixth century. The Nubian church became, and for nearly a thousand years remained, an integral part of the Coptic Orthodox Church of Egypt, and all its bishops were appointed by the Coptic Patriarch of Alexandria. The conversion set the stage for a flourishing of religious architecture, art, and literature, which were the hallmarks of medieval Nubian civilization.

Less than a century after the Christianization of Nubia came the Arab conquest of Egypt. The conquerors also twice invaded Nubia, in 642 and 652, but on each occasion the invasion was repulsed. The Arab commander, Abdallah ibn Sa'd (d. 656), then concluded a treaty with the kingdoms of Nobadia and Makuria that guaranteed the Nubians against any further Arab incursions or any forcible imposition of Islam for the next six hundred years. In exchange for the guarantee of peace, the Arabs received an annual tribute of slaves. This document, called the *baqt*, laid the foundations for medieval Nubian peace and prosperity.

Sometime in the eighth century, the two kingdoms of Nobadia and Makuria were merged under a single king whose capital was at Dongola. There was not a complete merger of administrations, however; the two regions were always separately named in documents, and each had its own administrative hierarchy. Nobadia, the northern region, was a free trade zone in which Arab traders were allowed to travel and even to settle, and where Egyptian coinage was in circulation. Administration was in the hands of a representative, or viceroy, called the eparch of Nobadia. Makuria was much more directly ruled by its king: here all foreign commerce was a royal monopoly and no money was in circulation. The peoples of Nobadia and Makuria spoke different, though closely related, Nubian languages, as do the present-day inhabitants of those regions.

The united kingdom of Nobadia and Makuria prospered for several centuries through trade with Islamic Egypt, sending gold, ivory, slaves, ebony, and ostrich feathers, and receiving in exchange fine textiles, glassware, glazed pottery, and wine. At the same time, the Nubians made elaborate, decorated pottery of their own, adorned with designs derived from medieval manuscript illumination. These vessels, together with the brightly colored paintings on church and cathedral walls, were the outstanding artistic achievements of medieval Nubian civilization.

The weakening and eventual destruction of the Christian kingdoms began when the Mamluk sultans seized power in Egypt in 1250 CE. They repudiated the *baqt* treaty and launched a series of incursions into Nubia, none of which, however, resulted in any lasting conquest. Much more destructive in the long run were the mass migrations of nomad Arab tribes, some from Egypt and some directly from the Arabian peninsula. In the fourteenth and fifteenth centuries, these tribes overran the territories of Alwa and most of Makuria, and the formerly unified kingdoms were divided into a series of petty, warring principalities under Arab warlords. Throughout these regions, the Nubian languages were gradually replaced by Arabic.

The far north, including Nobadia and the northern part of Makuria, was spared the Arab invasions because of the extreme desert conditions of the Nile hinterland. Here, a splinter Christian kingdom called Dotawo persisted until the end of the fifteenth century, after which the historical record was silent for several centuries. Archaeological evidence has shown, however, that when lower Nubia was annexed to the Ottoman Empire in the latter half of the sixteenth century, there was no surviving trace of either the medieval Christian kingdoms or of the Nubian church. Gradually, in the seventeenth and eighteenth centuries, the Nubians converted to Islam as Islamic teachers from northern and western Africa came to settle among them. The people continued to speak Nubian rather than Arabic, as they continue to do to the present day.

The twenty-first century Nubians are thus a linguistic enclave, surrounded on all sides by Arabic speakers, some of whom were also speakers of Nubian languages until a few centuries ago. The name Nubia, which once applied to the whole of southern Egypt and northern Sudan, has come to be applied only to the area actually occupied by Nubian speakers. However, a large part of Nubia was flooded in the 1960s with the building of the Aswan High Dam, and the inhabitants have been resettled in distant regions in Egypt and Sudan. There are about 1.2 million Nubian speakers remaining, equally divided between Egypt and Sudan.

See also **Nile River; Slave Trades: Northeastern Africa and Red Sea; Sudan: Society and Cultures; Travel and Exploration: Arab; Uganda: Society and Cultures.**

BIBLIOGRAPHY

Adams, William Y. *Nubia, Corridor to Africa*. Revised edition. Princeton, NJ: Princeton University Press, 1984.

Dafalla, Hassan. *The Nubian Exodus*. London: C. Hurst, 1975.

Edwards, David. *The Nubian Past*. London: Routledge, 2004.

Fernea, Robert A., and George Gerster. *Nubians in Egypt*. Austin: University of Texas Press, 1973.

Welsby, Derek. *The Medieval Kingdoms of Nubia*. London: British Museum Press, 2002.

WILLIAM Y. ADAMS

Sam Nujoma (1929–) at UNESCO headquarters in Paris, September 2004. Nujoma was the first president of Namibia, serving from 1990 to 2005. He continues to serve as president of the South West African People's Organization. DANIEL JANIN/AFP/GETTY IMAGES

NUER. *See* **Ethnicity.**

NUJOMA, SAMUEL SHAFIISHUNA

(1929–). Samuel Shafiishuna Nujoma was born in Ongandjera in the far north of Namibia. He attended a Finnish mission school before relocating to Walvis Bay, the principal port of the then United Nations trust territory of South West Africa (1946), and later to Windhoek (1948), the territory's capital, under South African rule. He was fired from the South African Railways (1957) for union organizing and then worked as a city clerk while attending night school.

In 1958 Nujoma helped to found, and was elected president of, the Ovamboland Peoples Organization, a party from his home region. In 1959 he helped mobilize resistance to the forced removal of blacks from Windhoek as part of South Africa's local implementation of apartheid. In March 1960 he fled into exile; the newly founded South West African Peoples Organization (SWAPO) elected him president. In June 1960, he appeared before the U.N. Committee on South West Africa. He was arrested on his return to Windhoek and was deported. He subsequently established SWAPO provisional headquarters in Dar es Salaam, Tanzania, and embarked on armed struggle. The following three decades Nujoma spent galvanizing international support for Namibian independence and directing SWAPO's military activities.

As South Africa moved toward democratic rule and heeded World Court injunctions to relinquish its control of the territory, Nujoma returned from exile in September 1989 and was chosen president-elect in balloting by the Constituent Assembly on February 16, 1990. However, he did not assume office until the date of Namibia's official independence, March 21, 1990. As president of Namibia, Nujoma has received widespread praise for his steady-handed stewardship of democracy. He chairs weekly cabinet meetings and is personally involved in agricultural and drought relief projects. He delegates the tasks of daily governance to his prime minister.

See also **Apartheid; Namibia; Postcolonialism; Windhoek.**

BIBLIOGRAPHY

Good, Kenneth. *Realizing Democracy in Botswana, Namibia, and South Africa.* Pretoria, South Africa: Africa Institute of South Africa, 1997.

Katjavivi, Peter H. *A History of Resistance in Namibia.* London: Currey, 1988.

JOSHUA BERNARD FORREST

NUMBER SYSTEMS. Through the ages the people of Africa have invented hundreds of numeration systems, both spoken and symbolic, that use body parts or objects to count or to represent numbers.

VERBAL NUMERATION

The most common way to count bigger quantities—without inventing completely new number words—is to combine existing number words and rely on the arithmetic relationships between the involved numbers.

In the Makhuwa language of Mozambique, *thanu* (five) and *nloko* (ten) are the basic number words of the system of numeration. One says *thanu na moza*, or five plus one, to express six. Seven becomes *thanu na pili*, or five plus two. To express twenty, one says *miloko mili*, that is, tens two or 10×2. Thirty is *miloko miraru*, or tens three.

The most common basic number words in Africa are the words for ten, five, and twenty. Some languages, such as Nyungwe (of Mozambique), use only the basic number word ten. Others such as Balanta of Guinea-Bissau use five and twenty as basic number words. The Bété language of Côte d'Ivoire uses three basic number words: five, ten, and twenty. For instance, fifty-six is expressed as *golosso-ya-kogbo-gbeplo*, that is, twenty *golo*] times two [*so*] plus [*ya*] ten [*kogbo*] (and) five [*gbe-*] (and) one [*blo*]. The Bambara of Mali and Guinea have a ten-twenty system. The word for twenty (*mugan*) means one person, the word for forty (*debe*) means mat, referring to a mat on which husband and wife sleep together: jointly they have forty digits.

As languages are never static, variants for number expressions may be found over time, or different combinations may be used in different regions. For instance, among the Huku of Uganda, the number words for thirteen, fourteen, and fifteen may be formed by addition of one, two, or three to twelve. Thirteen is expressed as *bakumba igimo*, meaning twelve plus one. The decimal alternatives $10 + 3$, $10 + 4$, and $10 + 5$ were also known.

A particular case of the use of addition to compose number words is the duplicative principle whereby both parts are nearly equal. For instance, among the Sango of Congo, seven is expressed as *na na-thatu* $(4 + 3)$, eight as *mnana* $(4 + 4)$, and nine as *sano na-na* $(5 + 4)$.

In several African languages, along with additive and multiplicative principles, subtraction has also been used in forming number words. For example, in the Yoruba language of Nigeria, sixteen may be expressed as *eerin din logun*, meaning four until one arrives at twenty.

In those contexts where it was necessary to have number words for relatively large numbers, there often appear completely new number words or ones that express a relationship with the basic number word of the numeration system. For instance, among the Bangongo of Congo, one says *kama* (100), *lobombo* (1,000), *njuku* (10,000), *lukuli* (100,000), and *losenene* (1,000,000).

GESTURE NUMERATION

Gesture counting was common among many African peoples. Many variants have been invented. For instance, the Yao of Malawi and Mozambique represent one, two, three, and four by pointing with the thumb of their right hand at one, two, three, or four extended fingers of their left hand. Five is indicated by making a fist with the left hand. Six, seven, eight, and nine are indicated by joining one, two, three, or four extended fingers of the right hand to the left fist. Ten is represented by raising the fingers of both hands and joining the hands. The Shambaa of Tanzania and Kenya use the duplicative principle. They indicate six by extending the three outer fingers of each hand, spread out; seven by showing four on the right hand and three on the left; and eight by showing four on each hand.

To express numbers greater than ten, the Sotho of Lesotho employed different men to indicate the hundreds, tens, and units. For example, to represent 368, the first person raises three fingers of the left hand to represent three hundreds, the second one raises the thumb of the right hand to express six tens, and the third one raises three fingers of the right hand to express eight units. In fact, here we deal with a positional system, as the position of each man determines whether he indicates units, tens, hundreds, thousands, and so on.

TALLY DEVICES

Many types of tally devices were used in Africa. An example of using knotted strings can be found among the Makonde of Mozambique and Tanzania; pregnant women tied a knot in a string at each full moon

to keep track of when they were about to give birth. In order to register the age of a person, two strings were used. A knot was tied in the first string at each full moon; once twelve knots had been tied, one knot was tied in a second string to mark the first year and so on.

OTHER VISUAL NUMERATION SYSTEMS

A variety of numeration systems in Africa are written in one way or another. The Fulani of Niger and Nigeria place sticks in front of their houses to indicate the number of cows or goats they possess. One hundred animals are represented by two short sticks placed on the ground in the form of a V. Two crossing sticks, X, symbolize fifty animals. Four sticks in a vertical position, | | | |, represent four; two sticks in a horizontal and three in a vertical position, — — | | |, indicate twenty-three animals. For example, the following was found in front of the house of a rich cattle owner:

VVVVVVXII,

showing that he had 652 cows.

The Akan peoples of Côte d'Ivoire, Ghana, and Togo used money weights, that is to say, they used stone or metal figurines or vegetable seeds as coins. Many figurines display graphic signs representing numbers. Although in the languages spoken by the Akan peoples, such as Anyi, Baule, Aboure, Attie, and Ebrie, only the basic number word ten is used, base five is also found as a basic number expression on their money weights:

$$5 = \bigcirc$$
$$6 = 5 + 1 = \bigcirc$$
$$7 = 5 + 2 = \bigcirc_c \cdot$$
$$8 = 5 + 3 = \bigcirc_\epsilon$$
$$9 = 5 + 4 = \bigcirc_-$$

Duplication may be observed in the transition from one of the expressions for six: $6 = \wedge\wedge\wedge\wedge$ to an expression of twelve: $12 = 6 + 6 = \wedge\wedge\wedge\wedge$.

See also **Geometries; Knowledge: Overview; Mathematics; Research: Overview; Symbols and Symbolism: Overview.**

BIBLIOGRAPHY

Gerdes, Paulus. "On Mathematics in the History of Sub-Saharan Africa." *Historia Mathematica* 21 (1994): 345–376.

Gerdes, Paulus, and Ahmed Djebbar. *Mathematics in African History and Cultures: An Annotated Bibliography*. Cape Town, South Africa: African Mathematical Union, 2004.

Gerdes, Paulus, and Ahmed Djebbar. *Les Mathématiques dans l'Histoire et les Cultures Africaines: Une Bibliographie Annotée*. Lille, France: Union Mathématique Africaine and Université de Lille I, 2004.

PAULUS GERDES

NURSING. *See* Healing and Health Care: Medical Practitioners.

NWAPA, FLORA (1931–1993).

The Nigerian writer Flora Nwapa was born in eastern Nigeria at Oguta. She received her primary and secondary education at Archdeacon Crowther's Memorial Girls School and CMS Girls School in Lagos, took an arts degree at University College, Lagos, in 1957, and in 1958 was awarded a diploma in education at Edinburgh University. Upon returning to Nigeria she took a post as a women's education officer and subsequently accepted positions as a teacher of English and geography at Queen's School, Enugu, and as assistant registrar at the University of Lagos. Following the Biafran War (1968–1970), Nwapa served for five years on the East Central State Executive Council.

Nwapa published her first novel, *Efuru*, in 1966. Published in London by Heinemann, *Efuru* is a portrait of a fiercely independent Igbo (Ibo) woman who secures a respected place in her rural society, not as a wife and mother but as an autonomous trader and a devotee, eventually a priestess, of Uhamiri, the divine lady of the lake. It was the first English novel to be published by a black African woman and thus marks Nwapa's dual significance as one of Nigeria's most important novelists and as a foundational figure in African women's writing. In addition to *Efuru*, Nwapa has published four novels: *Idu* (London, 1970), *One Is Enough* (Enugu, 1981), *Women Are Different* (Enugu, 1986), and *The Lake Goddess* (Trenton, NJ, 1995). She has also authored *Never*

Again, a memoir of the Biafran War (Enugu, 1975); two collections of short stories, *This Is Lagos, and Other Stories* (Enugu, 1971) and *Wives at War, and Other Stories* (Enugu, 1980); and numerous books for children.

Nwapa was also a publisher. In 1977, discontented with the Euro-American monopoly on the publication of African literature, Nwapa established her own publishing house, Tana Press, which was dedicated to publishing works by African women and books for children. The entrepreneurial spirit that animated Nwapa's decision to establish the Tana Press, a spirit that emerged from her conviction that African women could liberate themselves only by securing their economic independence, weds one of the central achievements of Nwapa's life to the social ethic and aspiration of many of her characters. The recipient of numerous awards during her lifetime (including the Officer of the Order of the Niger in 1982 and the Ife Merit Award for Authorship and Publishing in 1985), Nwapa died of pneumonia on October 16, 1993.

See also **Literature: Popular Literature.**

BIBLIOGRAPHY

Adeola, James, ed. *In Their Own Voices: African Women Writers Talk*. Portsmouth, NH: Heinemann, 1990.

180°: New Fiction by South African Women Writers. Cape Town: Oshun Books, 2005.

IAN BAUCOM

NYERERE, JULIUS KAMBARAGE (1922–1999).

In Tanzania Julius Kambarage Nyerere is popularly known as *Mwalimu* (teacher), because that was his original profession and lifelong passion. Nonetheless, he went on to lead the nationalist struggle for Tanganyikan independence from British rule. Independent in thought and innovative in his actions, he has based his political career on the pursuit of liberation and social advancement in Africa.

In the early days of independence, Nyerere, like many of his contemporaries, believed in the variously defined African socialism. In the late 1960s and early 1970s, he relentlessly and singlemindedly pursued a policy of *ujamaa* (socialism and self-reliance) in

Julius Nyerere (1922–1999). Nyerere held the position of president of Tanzania and earlier Tangasnyika from the country's founding in 1964 until his 1985 retirement. He is known by the Swahili name *Mwalimu*, which means "teacher," because of his first occupation. Pierre Verdy/AFP/Getty Images

Tanzania. Despite its proclaimed enabling intentions, this policy resulted in the disruption and dislocation of agricultural production, neglect of industry, and intensification of external dependence. Nyerere refused to acknowledge these failures.

Nyerere also had some notable successes. Propelled by his unwavering commitment to social justice, he supported liberation struggles in southern Africa and beyond, and turned the Tanzanian capital of Dar es Salaam into a haven for liberation movements throughout Africa. In the 1970s Nyerere was one of the most articulate and committed believers in global interdependence and a defender of the developing world's failed quest for a New International Economic Order. He later became the first chairman of the South Commission, established in 1987. The commission's primary task was to study the many problems and common experiences of the southern countries—a phrase used at the time to distinguish the poorer nations of the tropical regions from the northerly industrial nations—and draw lessons for regional cooperation with the hope of attaining a collective self-reliance.

Although Nyerere established authoritarian rule in Tanzania, many who perceived him as a benevolent dictator believed that he was driven by good but misguided intentions. Others believe that he was essentially Machiavellian. In any case, his personal integrity is generally acknowledged. After he relinquished the presidency he became converted to democracy and multiparty rule. He was skeptical about party proliferation, however, and was equally suspicious of Western motives in making democracy a condition for economic aid. In retirement, as "Father of the Nation," Nyerere agitated for prudent and honest government as well as fair play in politics.

Nyerere wrote extensively on political and social issues, and even after retirement from the presidency in 1985, he remained an ardent defender of the interests of the developing world. He consistently opposed the structural adjustment policies of the International Monetary Fund and World Bank, believing that such policies—focused on debt repayment—were devastating to the fragile economies of the developing world. Nyerere devoted his life to the fight for African freedom, human dignity, and global social justice, although critics have claimed that his passion for these goals, and his inability to tolerate dissent, frequently clouded his judgment on how to attain them. In his later years he developed leukemia, and died while undergoing care for that disease in a London hospital on October 14, 1999.

See also **Dar es Salaam; International Monetary Fund; Nationalism; Postcolonialism; Socialism and Postsocialisms; Tanzania: History and Politics; World Bank.**

BIBLIOGRAPHY

Duggan, William Redman, and John R. Civille. *Tanzania and Nyerere.* Maryknoll, NY: Orbis Books, 1976.

Hatch, John Charles. *Two African Statesmen: Kaunda of Zambia and Nyerere of Tanzania.* Chicago: Regnery, 1976.

Mungazi, Dickson A. *We Shall Not Fail: Values in the National Leadership of Seretse Khama, Nelson Mandela, and Julius Nyerere.* Trenton, NJ: Africa World Press, 2005.

Nyerere, Julius. *Freedom and Unity*. Dar es Salaam, Tanzania: Oxford University Press, 1967.

Nyerere, Julius. *Freedom and Socialism*. Dar es Salaam, Tanzania: Oxford University Press, 1968.

Nyerere, Julius.*Freedom and Development*. Dar es Salaam, Tanzania: Oxford University Press, 1974.

Nyerere, Julius. *Crusade for Liberation*. Dar es Salaam, Tanzania: Oxford University Press, 1979.

Smith, William Edgett. *We Must Run While They Walk: A Portrait of Africa's Julius Nyerere*. New York: Random House, 1971.

MWESIGA BAREGU

OBASANJO, OLUSEGUN (1937–).

Born in Abeokuta, Ogun State in southwestern Nigeria, Olusegun Obasanjo was educated at Baptist Boys' High School, Abeokuta. He enlisted in the Nigerian army in 1958 and received his military training at the Mons Officers' Cadet School, Aldershot, England, and at other military institutions in Britain and India. He was commissioned second lieutenant in the Nigerian Army in 1959 and achieved the rank of general by 1979. Obasanjo served in the Congo in 1960 and in the Nigerian civil war (1967–1970). As commander of the Third Marine Commando Division, he took the surrender of the Biafran forces in January 1970. In 1973 Obasanjo was appointed federal minister of works and housing, and in 1975 as chief of staff (Supreme Headquarters). He was head of state of the Federal Republic of Nigeria (1976–1979) and has the distinction of being the only Nigerian leader, to date, who has willingly relinquished power at the end of his designated tenure in office. Obasanjo is a member of the Inter Action Council of Former Heads of States and Governments, member and cochairman of the Commonwealth Eminent Persons Group on South Africa, and founder and chairman of the Africa Leadership Forum and Foundation. Obasanjo's numerous published books include *My Command* (1980), an account of his experiences in the Nigerian civil war.

Obasanjo was a vocal opponent of Nigeria's dictatorial head of state during the 1990s, Sani Abacha. He was arrested in Lagos in March 1995 on the charge of concealment of treason and, after a

Olusegun Obasanjo (c. 1937–). Olusegun Obasanjo served as Nigeria's president twice. The first time, he was a military ruler. The second time, he was elected by the people. AP IMAGES

secret trial, was sentenced to life imprisonment (later commuted to fifteen years). Released with Abacha's death in June 1998, he ran for the presidency in

1999 as candidate of the People's Democratic Party and was elected with in excess of 60 percent of the popular vote, but failed to garner the support of his own home district. In 2003 he again ran for office, in a campaign that pitted his southern, Christian supporters against a Muslim candidate from the north of the country. He won with a substantial majority, but the religious polarization engendered by the campaign caused some disquiet in the international community.

See also **Government: Military; Postcolonialism.**

BIBLIOGRAPHY

Eke, Kenoye Kelvin. *Nigeria's Foreign Policy under Two Military Governments, 1966–1979: An Analysis of the Gowan and Muhammed/Obasanjo Regimes.* Lewiston, NY: E. Mellon Press, 1990.

Fawole, W. Alade. *Nigeria's External Relations and Foreign Policy under Military Rule, 1966–1999.* Ile-Ife, Nigeria: Obafemi Awolowo University Press, 2003.

Kolawole, Dipo, ed. *Nigeria's Foreign Policy since Independence: Trends, Phases, and Changes.* Lagos: Julius and Julius, 2004.

A. L. MABOGUNJE

Milton Obote (1924–2005) in Nairobi, July 28, 1985. Obote is considered the founding father of independent Uganda. His leadership was toppled by Idi Amin and, after a return to rule, he was overthrown a second time. Obote was granted political asylum in Zambia after his second overthrow. AFP/GETTY IMAGES

OBOTE, MILTON (1924–2005). Apollo Milton Obote, born in northern Uganda near Akoroko, studied at Makere University in Kampala for one year before he was expelled by colonial officials for political activity. He then worked in Kenya as a laborer and salesman, joining Kenya's nationalist political organizations in the early 1950s, at the time of the Mau Mau uprising. Upon his return to Uganda as the colony began to move toward independence in the mid-1950s, Obote became active in the Uganda National Congress Party (UNCP) and set up local branches in his home area.

Elected to the newly formed Legislative Council in 1958, Obote was critical of British colonial policy. When the UNCP split the next year, Obote established the Uganda People's Congress (UPC) to oppose the traditionalist-royalist Kabaka Yekka (KY) party, which sought to reestablish the Buganda Kingdom, the largest and most influential of the historic kingdoms in Uganda. After the UPC's defeat in 1961, however, the party formed a loose alliance with KY, and Obote was elected prime minister under the colonial government in early 1962. Britain granted independence later that year, and a quasi-federal system was established with the Bugandan king, Mutesa II, as president and Obote as prime minister. In this post Obote was important in organizing the East African Community.

Accused of gold smuggling with army officer Idi Amin in 1966, Obote moved to consolidate power, suspending the constitution and declaring himself executive president. He managed to rule Uganda without Bugandan support by using the army to dismantle the kingdom and force Mutesa into exile. Though the army was his means of centralizing power, it twice proved his undoing. He alienated the military with his political shift to the left, announcing the Common Man's Charter in 1969 and the nationalization of 60 percent of the foreign interests in 1970.

While Obote was out of the country in 1972, Idi Amin escaped the house arrest Obote had imposed on him, led an army coup, and took over the government. Obote spent the Amin years in exile in Tanzania and returned to Uganda after the Tanzania People's Defense Force pushed Amin's army out of the Kagera Salient and Amin's regime fell in 1979.

Obote was elected president of Uganda in 1980. He faced the difficult task of reviving a ruined economy and restoring order to a lawless country in the wake of Amin's mass killings and deportations. Unable to control an increasingly ruthless army and faced with a rebellion led by 1980 electoral contender Yoweri Museveni, Obote lost favor with Ugandans. He was deposed in 1985 by the army (which was in turn overthrown in 1986 by Museveni's National Resistance Army). Obote escaped to exile in Zambia. Although his return to Uganda was occasionally rumored in succeeding years, Obote died of kidney failure in 2005, in South Africa.

See also **Amin Dada, Idi; Museveni, Yoweri; Uganda.**

BIBLIOGRAPHY

Ingham, Kenneth. *Obote: A Political Biography.* New York: Rutledge, 1994.

Thomas F. McDow

ODUNDO, MAGDALENE (1950–).
Magdalene Anyango N. Odundo was born in Kenya and has lived in England since 1971. Although her work owes a debt to African sources, inspirations, and methodologies, its refinement and sophistication is made possible by the incorporation of modern European and North American technologies as well as its circulation within an international art market.

Odundo moved to England to continue her education; she received her bachelor of arts degree in 1976 from the West Surrey College of Art and Design and her master of arts degree in 1982 from the Royal College of Art in London. Pivotal to her development as a ceramic artist was a trip to northern Nigeria in 1974, where she spent three months learning the hand-building method of coiling from village women potters, a process that is millennia old in Africa. Odundo meticulously uses coiling to build the upper sections of her pieces in a laborious process that sometimes takes weeks to complete.

Her working method also synthesizes other ceramic traditions she admires, from the highly polished blackware distinctive of Pueblo artists of San Ildefonso to slip methods of antique Greek and Roman pottery. She has drawn on them to finish her own works with a labor-intensive sequence of burnishing, applying slip, and lightly burnishing again to achieve a high surface luster. The vessels are fired in a gas kiln in an oxidizing atmosphere to turn them a lustrous red-orange, or in an oxidizing followed by a reducing atmosphere to turn them a rich charcoal-black. The unexpected variations in color and explosions of iridescence on their surfaces distinguish Odundo's work and reveal her mastery of the firing process.

Odundo's ceramic forms draw on a range of art historical precedents such as the complex shapes of ancient Cyprus; the severe geometry of Cycladic figurines; the elegant contours and precise details of Attic vases; the heavy, energetic forms from Jomon Japan; and the finely decorated waisted vessels of the Nupe of northern Nigeria. Odundo also is attracted to the metaphoric capacity of vessels, especially the ways they reference the bodies of women. Some evoke the swelling belly of pregnancy or, through small decorative nodes, vertebrae as well as nipples and an umbilicus. Although Odundo's pots may stand in for people, they often look like women by borrowing essential aspects of their adorned appearance, as well as the ways their bodies have been reshaped to conform with various cultural standards of beauty, African or European.

See also **Art; Arts.**

BIBLIOGRAPHY

Berns, Marla C. *Ceramic Gestures: New Vessels by Magdalene Odundo*. Exhibition catalogue. Santa Barbara: University Art Museum, University of California, 1995.

Cooksey, Susan; Linda Arbuckle; and Augustus Casely-Hayford. *Resonance and Inspiration: New Works by Magdalene Odundo*. Exhibition catalogue. Gainesville: Samuel P. Harn Museum of Art, University of Florida, 2006.

Hill, Rosemary. *New Works: Magdalene Odundo*. Swansea, Wales: Swansea Museums Service, Swansea City Council, 1987.

Joris, Yvonne G. J. M., ed. 1994. *Magdalene Odundo: African Beauty—A Retrospective*. Exhibition catalogue. 's-Hertogenbosch, Netherlands: Stedelijk Museum voor Hedendaagse Kunst.

Slayter-Ralph, Anthony, ed. *Magdalene Odundo*. Hampshire, U.K.: Lund Humphries, 2004.

Vaizey, Marina. *Magdalene Odundo: Clay Forms*. Bowness-on-Windermere, U.K.: Blackwell House/Lakeland Arts Trust, 2001.

MARLA C. BERNS

OGOT, GRACE

OGOT, GRACE (1930–). Known to her neighbors as Nyasembo ("the lady from Asembo"), Grace Emily Akinyi Ogot was born in Asembo location in Nyanza Province, western Kenya. She was the first Kenyan woman and the first writer to win international attention as a novelist. Ogot went to local schools before attending Ng'iya Girls' School for her intermediate schooling. She then went to Butere in western Province for high school. Thereafter she trained as a nurse at Maseno CMS Hospital, then proceeded to Mengo in Uganda before obtaining a scholarship which took her to Middlesex Hospital in Britain, although initially her parents doubted the wisdom of a single woman going overseas. Determined, she nevertheless overcame these obstacles, becoming subsequently a tutor at Maseno, a midwife in Kisumu, and a journalist. In the latter capacity she worked for the BBC as an Overseas broadcaster in the early 1960s. Ogot married the historian Bethwell Allan Ogot in 1959.

Ogot's first book was *Land without Thunder*, a collection of short stories. Her first novel was *The Promised Land*. This is a story, set in the 1930s, of a couple who move from Kenya into Tanzania only to become embroiled in issues of personal jealousy and materialism. Her other works include *The Strange Bride*, *The Graduate*, *The Other Woman*, and *Land without Tears*. Her writing style is evocative of vivid imagery and aims to capture the formalities of traditional Africa. She has also experimented with the creation myths from her village in *Miaha*. Many of Ogot's stories are based on the theme of migration: from home to elsewhere in the world, including the United States.

See also **Kenya; Literature: Women Writers, Northern Africa; Media: Journalism.**

BIBLIOGRAPHY

Kanogo, Tabitha. *African Womanhood in Colonial Kenya 1900–1950*. Athens: Ohio University Press, 2005.

E. S. ATIENO ODHIAMBO

OGUNDE, HUBERT ADEDEJI

OGUNDE, HUBERT ADEDEJI (1916–1990). The Nigerian actor and playwright Hubert Adedeji Ogunde was born in Ososa in Ogun State of Nigeria, where he was educated. He was a pupil teacher in Ijebu-Ode from 1932 to 1940. He served in the Nigerian police force from 1941 to 1945, after which he established the Ogunde Theater and the Ogunde Record Companies in 1946. He later expanded his scope with the establishment in 1966 of the Ogunde Dance Company and the Ogunde Film Company. He wrote and presented over fifty plays in addition to making several films. His folk opera and musical morality plays performed in Yoruba are frequently seen on stage, television, and cinema houses in all parts of Nigeria.

Ogunde founded and became president of the Nigerian Dramatists and Playwrights Association. He was also a founding member of the Association of Nigerian Theater Artists. Until his death, he led the Nigerian National Troupe. He was honored in 1982 with membership in the Order of the Niger (MON), and the Universities of Ife and Lagos awarded him honorary degrees in 1985 and 1986 respectively.

See also **Popular Culture: Western Africa; Theater.**

BIBLIOGRAPHY

Anyanwu, Mike, and Adavi Abraham, eds. *A Journey Fulfilled: Impressions and Expressions on Hubert Ogunde*. Ibadan, Nigeria: Caltop Publications, 1994.

Hubert Adedeji Ogunde (1916–1990). Nigerian actor, playwright, theatre manager, and musician Hubert Adedeji Ogunde on tour in London with eight of his dancers, all of whom were his wives. Ogunde worked first as a teacher and police officer before getting his start in the theatre. WESLEY/KEYSTONE FEATURES/GETTY IMAGES

Clark, Ebun. *Hubert Ogunde: The Making of Nigerian Theater.* New York: Oxford University Press, 1979.

C. OGBOGBO

OLYMPIO, SYLVANUS EPIPHANIO

(1902–1963). Sylvanus Epiphanio Olympio was the first president of an independent country to be overthrown by the wave of military coups of the late 1960s. His political career flourished at the height of African optimism, and his violent end marked the beginning of African disillusionment with the nationalist politics of the independence era.

Born to a wealthy family, he was educated in the German system prevalent in Togo and studied at the University of Vienna and the London School of Economics and Political Science. He had a successful career with the United Africa Company, rising to district manager for Togo, a post he held from 1928 to 1938. At that time, it was the highest post held by an African working for a colonial multinational company.

He entered politics, was banished from Togo, but returned after World War II when President Charles de Gaulle of France allowed elections in French African colonies, including Togo, controlled as a United Nations trust territory. Olympio was president of the Territorial Assembly from 1946 to

Sylvanus Olympio (1902–1963) at New York International Airport (now LaGuardia Airport), March 1962. As the prime minister and first president of Togo, Olympio had a pro-Western foreign policy. He visited the United States to meet with President John F. Kennedy and was friendly with most of Togo's neighbors, except for Ghana. EXPRESS NEWSPAPERS/GETTY IMAGES

personnel, and it was the army's enmity that destroyed him. He was killed on January 13, 1963, as he was fleeing to the American Embassy in Lomé.

See also **Decolonization; Togo.**

BIBLIOGRAPHY

Kokouvi Agbobli, Atsutse. *Sylvanus Olympio: Un destin tragique.* Abidjan, Côte 'Ivoire: Livre Sud, Senegal NEA, 1992.

Tété-Adjalogo, *Têtêvi G. Histoire du Togo: Le régime et l'assassinat de Sylvanus Olympio, 1960–1963.* Paris: NM7, 2002.

                                             ALEXANDER GOLDMAN

ORACLES.   *See* **Divination and Oracles.**

ORAL LITERATURE AND TRADITIONS.   *See* **Literature: Oral.**

ORANGE FREE STATE.   *See* **Cape Colony and Hinterland, History of (1600 to 1910); South Africa, Republic of.**

1952, when his party lost power to the Parti Togolais du Progrès (PTP), which was supported by the colonial authorities.

Olympio came to power as prime minister under French decolonization policies again in 1958 and campaigned for Togolese independence, which was achieved in 1960. In 1961 he was elected first president of the new republic. His authoritarian rule, coupled with austerity measures taken to balance the budget, made him unpopular in some quarters. Because his government was largely composed of Ewe people from southwestern Togo, northerners felt they were excluded. Juvento, a radical branch of his party, wanted Togo to cut itself off from France completely, while Olympio was attempting to bring in foreign investment (there was significant investment in the phosphate industry in 1962), and he suppressed Juvento's leaders ruthlessly. Finally, he refused the army's demands for more pay and more

ORGANIZATION OF AFRICAN UNITY.   The organization of African Unity (OAU) is the symbol and embodiment of the various Pan-African movements that originated in the African diaspora between 1900 and 1945. The leading figures of the movements were African Americans, West Indians, and Africans: the American educator and writer W. E. B. Du Bois, the father of Pan-Africanism and the driving spirit of the Pan-African Congress (1900, 1919, 1921, 1927, 1945); Henry Sylvester Williams; Marcus Garvey, founder of the Universal Negro Improvement Association; George Padmore; and Kwame Nkrumah, the first president of Ghana. It was after the 1945 Pan-African Congress in Manchester, England, that Pan-Africanism took on an African dimension aimed at self-government and independence. However, between the 1900 Pan-African Congress and the historic Conference of Independent African States in Addis Ababa,

Ethiopia, in 1963, which led to the founding of the OAU, many attempts were made to achieve freedom, independence, and unity in Africa.

The major landmarks in the struggle for African solidarity and unity are:

- The National Congress of British West Africa (1920–1930)
- The Ghana-Guinea Union of November 1958, which Mali joined in April 1961
- The Pan-African Movement for East and Central Africa (PAFMECA)
- The Casablanca Group (January 1961), composed of Ghana, Guinea, Mali, Morocco, Egypt, and Algeria
- The Monrovia Group (May 1961), composed of Liberia, Nigeria, Cameroon, Chad, Côte d'Ivoire, Congo (Brazzaville), Dahomey (present-day Bénin), Upper Volta (present-day Burkina Faso), Gabon, Central African Republic, Ethiopia, Liberia, Malagasy Republic (Madagascar), Mauritania, Sierra Leone, Somalia, Tunisia, and Senegal. The Brazzaville Group (October 1960) joined the majority of English-speaking African countries outside the Casablanca group in May 1961 to form the Monrovia Group.

These attempts at regional cooperation culminated in the creation of the OAU on May 25, 1963, at Addis Ababa. The charter of the OAU was designed on that date by the thirty-two leaders of the independent African states.

PRINCIPLES AND OBJECTIVES

The principles and objectives of the OAU are stated in articles II and III of the charter: (1) to promote the unity and solidarity of the African states; (2) to coordinate and intensify their cooperation and efforts to achieve a better life for the peoples of Africa; (3) to defend their sovereignty, territorial integrity, and independence; (4) to eradicate all forms of colonialism from Africa; and (5) to promote international cooperation, with due regard for the Charter of the United Nations and the Universal Declaration of Human Rights.

To achieve these aims member states agreed to harmonize their policies through cooperation in politics, diplomacy, defense and security. Member states also agreed to the following principles: the sovereign equality of all member states; noninterference in the internal affairs of states; peaceful settlement of disputes; condemnation of subversion; emancipation of the African territories still under colonial rule; and affirmation of a policy of nonalignment. The founding members states envisaged a unity "transcending ethnic and national differences." Membership was open to all of "the continental African States, Madagascar and other islands surrounding Africa."

INSTITUTIONS

Article XX of the charter created six specialized commissions, subsequently reduced to three by a 1965 amendment: the Economic, Social, Transport, and Communications Commission; the Educational, Cultural, Health, and Scientific Commission; and the Defense Commission.

When necessary, ad hoc commissions were established by the OAU to aid in its peacemaking efforts. They included the Ad Hoc Committee on the Algero-Moroccan Dispute, created in 1963; the Ad Hoc Committee on Inter-African Disputes (the 1979 Uganda-Tanzania conflict); and the commission established by the OAU resolution on the Tanganyka military mutiny of 1964, which made possible the replacement of British troops (which had been invited by the government) with Nigerian troops.

The headquarters of the OAU General Secretariat was located at Africa Unity House in Addis Ababa, Ethiopia. The General Secretariat was the permanent organ responsible for servicing OAU meetings and implementing decisions and resolutions adopted by the OAU heads of state and government. It housed the OAU archives and coordinated the activities of member states in the fields stated in the charter. Since the signature in 1992 of the Abuja Treaty establishing the African Economic Community (AEC), the General Secretariat also served as the secretariat for that body. The General Secretariat was headed by the secretary-general, assisted by five assistant secretaries-general appointed under articles XVI and XVII of the charter. The main policy organs were the Assembly of the Heads of State and Government and the Council of Ministers.

CONFLICT PREVENTION, RESOLUTION AND MANAGEMENT

Since its establishment, the OAU seldom condemned unconstitutional rule, military takeovers, abuse of human rights or interfered in serious ethnic conflicts, on the grounds that these were matters internal to the governments concerned in accordance with Article III.2 of the charter. This situation changed after the 1990 Addis Ababa Summit, which reviewed key post–Cold War developments, noted Africa's poor economic performance in the 1980s and articulated Africa's understanding of the economic and political dimensions of the post–Cold War era and its implications for democracy, economic policy, and regionalism in Africa.

The main internal conflicts in the 1980s and 1990s were in Angola, Burundi, Mozambique, Rwanda, Sudan, and South Africa. In this connection, the African subregional organizations that were considered irrelevant to peacemaking became increasingly involved, notably in the ECOWAS intervention in the Liberian conflict (August 1990); IGADD in Sudan; SADC in Lesotho, ad the OAU/UN mediation in Lusaka, Zambia, on Angola. Despite the lack of financial and logistical resources and the inability of the existing mechanisms within the OAU to manage conflict, following the renewal of interethnic conflict and the overthrow of the democratically elected government, the OAU took the unprecedented step of calling for economic sanctions to restore constitutional rule and other conditions conducive to social and political stability.

After the Dakar (1992) and Cairo (1993) Summits, the OAU began to address the difficult problems of interstate and intrastate conflicts and created the mechanism for conflict management and resolution in 1993 to replace the Commission of Mediation, Conciliation, and Arbitration and the Defense Commission which had been ineffective in managing conflicts. The OAU Peace Fund was created to support the conflict management activities of the new mechanism.

Recognizing the gravity of the conflicts within the continent, the 1993 Cairo Summit declared "No single internal factor has contributed more to the socio-economic problems on the continent than the scourge of conflicts within and between countries." A Charter Review Committee was established to make recommendations on reform and restructuring of the OAU in light of the organization's conflict management mandate, the organization requirements of the African Economic Community and its new development orientation. In this connection the United Nations Development Program provided funds for management consultancies for the restructuring of the secretariat and for the organizational and human resource improvements of the weaknesses in the OAU management and "to harmonize policies and strategies in economics, politics, security, education and culture, science and technology for Africa's development and peace" (RAF/87/101 *Improvement of the OAU Administrative and Management Capability* and RAF/82/003 *The Strengthening of the OAU General Secretariat*).

DEVELOPMENT STRATEGIES: REGIONAL ECONOMIC INTEGRATION

In economic policy and development, the OAU actively participated in developing the following:

- The Lagos Plan of Action and Final Act of Lagos (1980)
- Africa's Priority Program for Economic Recovery (APPER) (1986–1990)
- The African Alternative Framework for Structural Adjustment for Social and Economic Recovery and Transformation (AAF-SAP) (1989)
- Establishment of the African Economic Community in Abuja (1990)

These major initiatives were the OAU's responses to the broad provisions of the charter, to Africa's development crisis of the 1980s, and the general underdevelopment of the continent. The African Economic Community was viewed as part of the strategy to address these problems in cooperation with the Regional Economic Communities.

The philosophy underpinning the African Economic Community (AEC) was free trade, export-led growth, privatization, and competitive industrialization based on comparative advantage. The strategy of regionalism was confirmed in the Declaration of the OAU Algiers Summit of July 1999, which while noting that globalization was an irreversible process stressed that regionalism was essential for Africa's development in the new millennium.

HUMAN AND PEOPLES' RIGHTS

The adoption of the Charter of the Human and Peoples' Rights and the establishment of the African Commission on Human and Peoples' Rights were achievements of the OAU. The charter incorporates the principles of the Universal Declaration of Human Rights as well as African values such as cultural rights and peoples' rights. The Preamble reads: "We convinced that it is henceforth essential to pay particular attention to the right to development and that civil and political rights cannot be dissociated from economic, social and cultural rights in their conception as well as universality." After a difficult start, reporting by member States improved, as well as cooperation with nongovernmental organizations. By late 1990 more than one hundred petitions were received but were not publicized. The draft protocol proposed on the African Court on Human and Peoples' Rights was considered by the Council of Ministers in May 1997, February 1998 and in June 1998 when the council reviewed a report on the financial implications of the draft protocol on the proposed court.

ACHIEVEMENTS AND FAILURES

The OAU has been criticized on many counts: failure to promote pan-African unity, pan-African socialism, and regional economic integration. It has also been criticized for preferring continental unity and ignoring the African diaspora; for failing to end apartheid and neocolonialism and for failure to take a firm position against military coups d'etat that have plagued Africa from 1960s to the 1990s. Most of these criticisms ignore the resource constraints and limited capabilities of the OAU, and the conservative nature of the charter, six of the seven principles in Article III were aimed at preserving the sovereignty of member states and the sanctity of the inherited boundaries. Only fundamental changes in Africa's domestic and external environment would have made the radical changes implied by the critics possible. On the credit side, Africa's skillful use of the UN platform to promote decolonization and to press for sanctions against South Africa's apartheid regime and various economic initiatives articulated periodically stand out. The OAU Liberation Committee whose headquarters were relocated from Addis Ababa to Dar-es-Salaam, gave strong and consistent support to the Liberation Movement in collaboration with the Frontline States.

On governance, the OAU finally took action in the late 1990s by requiring African governments that came to power by unconstitutional means to restore constitutional rule and the doctrine of non-recognition of such regimes was enunciated 9AHG/Dec. 141 ad 142 (XXXV) (1999).

The Constitutive Act of the African Union, which replaced the OAU, was approved at the Summit in Togo (1999). The union itself was created at the 2002 Summit in Maputo, Mozambique, opening a new chapter in Africa's continuing struggle for peace, development, and democracy.

See also **Addis Ababa; Aid and Development; Cairo; Cold War; Dakar; Diasporas; Du Bois, W. E. B.; Economic Community of West African States (ECOWAS); Garvey, Marcus; Human Rights; Nationalism; Postcolonialism; Refugees; United Nations; Warfare.**

BIBLIOGRAPHY

Amate, C.O.C. *Inside the OAU: Pan Africanism in Practice.* New York: St. Martin's Press, 1986.

Cervenka, Zdeneke. *The Unfinished Quest for Unity: Africa and the OAU.* New York: Africana, 1977.

Gassama, M. I. S. "The OAU Does Care." *New African* 317 (April 1994): 20.

Geiss, Immanuel. *The Pan-African Movement.* New York: Africana Publishing Company, 1974.

Langley, J. Ayo. *Pan-Africanism and Nationalism in West Africa, 1900–1945.* Oxford: Clarendon Press, 1973.

Mbuyinga, Elenga. *Pan-Africanism or Neocolonialism: The Bankruptcy of the OAU.* London: Zed Press, 1982.

Organization of African Unity. AHG/Dec.1 (XXVIII). *Decision on a Mechanism for Conflict Prevention, Management and Resolution.*

Organization of African Unity. CM/Dec. 384 (LXVII). *Progress Report of the Secretary General on the Establishment of the African Economic Community.* Doc. CM/2043.

Organization of African Unity. CM/Dec. 392 (LXVII). *Interim Report on the Activities of the African Commission on Human and Peoples' Rights.* Doc. CM/2056.

Organization of African Unity. CM/Dec. 461(LXX). *Decision on the Progress Report of the Secretary General on the Implementation of the Restructuring of the OAU General Secretariat.* Doc. CM/2107, Rev. 1.

United Nations Development Program New York: RAF/ 87/101. *Improvement of the OAU Administrative and Management Capability* (1987–1993).

United Nations Development Program New York: RAF/ 87/104. *Establishment of the African Economic Community.*

Wolfers, Michael. *Politics in the Organization of African Unity.* London: Methuen, 1976.

J. AYODELE LANGLEY

ORTHOGRAPHIES. *See* Writing Systems.

OSEI BONSU (c. 1779–1823).

Osei Bonsu became king of the Asante following a period of conflict in the region, which is part of present-day Ghana. The prior *asantehene* Osei Kwame (1777–1803) had been forced to abdicate, and his successor, Opoku Fofie, died a few weeks after coming to the throne. Osei Bonsu restored domestic stability. Concerning himself with regulating trade with the European establishments on the coast, Osei Bonsu engaged in successful campaigns against the Fante in 1806–1807, 1811, and 1816. Once the Asante gained effective control of trade routes from the northern hinterlands to the coast, several European emissaries came to negotiate trade and friendship. Numerous Muslim traders and clerics also came to the capital at Kumasi.

Osei Bonsu continued and improved centralizing bureaucratic reforms begun in the mid-eighteenth century. Though the king remained primus inter pares in relation to state rulers of the Asante confederation, Osei Bonsu appointed civil officers in Kumasi and provincial administrators who were directly responsible to him. Their close regulation of external trade ensured economic prosperity for the nation. Notwithstanding such achievements, Osei Bonsu was disappointed by the British failure to sign a treaty of trade and friendship negotiated in 1820. In fact, at the time of his death and before his successor, Osei Yaw Akoto, came to the throne, Asante was at war with the British.

See also **Colonial Policies and Practices.**

BIBLIOGRAPHY

Bowdich, Thomas. *Mission from Cape Coast Castle to Ashantee.* London: Cass, 1966.

Dupuis, Joseph. *Journal of a Residence in Ashantee,* 2nd edition. London: Cass, 1966.

Owusu-Ansah, David. *Islamic Talismanic Tradition in Nineteenth-Century Asante.* Lewiston, NY: Edwin Mellen Press, 1991.

Wilks, Ivor G. "Aspects of Bureaucratization in Ashanti in the Nineteenth Century." *Journal of African History* 7, no. 2 (1966): 215–232.

Wilks, Ivor G. *Asante in the Nineteenth Century: The Structure and Evolution of a Political Order.* Cambridge, U.K.: Cambridge University Press, 1975.

DAVID OWUSU-ANSAH

OSEI TUTU (c. 1636–1717).

Osei Tutu was the first Asante king, ruling from about 1685 to his death in 1717. Succeeding his uncle, Obiri Yeboah of the Oyoko clan, as *kumasihene* (ruler of Kumasi, one of the Akan towns of the time) about 1685, Osei Tutu continued his predecessor's wars of expansion, and succeeded in consolidating the territorial base of the Oyoko dynasty. He united the military forces of the nuclear Asante states for the conquest of Denkyera (1699–1701). The military union provided the framework of subsequent Asante federation and the machinery for Asante political expansion. In the course of the eighteenth century, it resulted in the creation of greater Asante, embracing most of present-day Ghana and eastern Côte d'Ivoire.

Osei Tutu built up Kumasi as the capital of the Asante kingdom and introduced enduring incorporative institutions for its further growth. First was the Golden Stool, the seat or throne used in the ritual installation of the *asantehene.* Mystically incorporating all existing stools, it became the supreme shrine of the Asante people, embodying their collective soul. Identified with the nation, it defined an Asante as its subject. Second, *odwira* (first fruits), an annual national festival, was given precedence over other festivals; it brought together all Asante for both secular and ritual purposes. Third was a set of laws that the Asante regard as the framework of their nationhood.

The Asante union established by Osei Tutu remains intact, recognized in the constitutions of

Ghana since 1959 as the Ashanti Regional House of Chiefs. Relations between the *asantehene* and the heads of the constituent state remain modeled on rules promulgated by Osei Tutu. The rites of communion with the ancestral spirits culminating in the annual *odwira* festival are still observed, and the Golden Stool is known as the stool of Osei and Poku, his immediate successor.

See also **Kings and Kingdoms.**

BIBLIOGRAPHY

Adjaye, Joseph K. *Diplomacy and Diplomats in Nineteenth Century Asante.* Lanham, MD: University Press of America, 1984.

Freestone, Basil. *Osei Tutu: The Leopard Owns the Land.* London: Dobson, 1968.

Reindorf, Carl Christian. *A History of the Gold Coast and Asante* [1895]. Basel, Switzerland: Basel Mission Book Depot, 1951.

Wilks, Ivor G. *Asante in the Nineteenth Century: The Structure and Evolution of a Political Order.* New York: Cambridge University Press, 1975.

NANA ARHIN BREMPONG

OSHITELU, JOSIAH OLUNOWO

(1902–1966). Born in the small Yoruba town of Ogere in Ijebu Province, southwestern Nigeria, Oshitelu was a teacher and catechist at an Anglican school when in 1925 he had a series of visionary experiences involving the revelation of seals of power and the holy names of God. This led to his suspension by his church, and in 1929 he set up his own congregation. When the great *Aladura* (praying) revival broke out in Ilesha and Ibadan in 1930–1931, Oshitelu became associated with it but eventually went his own way. A book of prophecies of imminent divine judgment brought him briefly into conflict with the colonial authorities. During the 1930s, as Oshitelu's Church of the Lord began to spread in Nigeria and farther afield, Oshitelu established an annual festival of Mount Taborar at the Ogere headquarters. At these festivals he dispensed healing and other blessings, and delivered revelations. These made him a considerable public figure, though he was careful to avoid controversy. The Church of the Lord appointed Oshitelu its Primate, and became a coherent body under him. On his

death in 1966 the church, with some 15,000 members in Nigeria, passed without dispute to the leadership of his designated successor, Emmanuel Adejobi (1919–1991).

See also **Festivals and Carnivals; Nigeria; Prophetic Movements.**

BIBLIOGRAPHY

Turner, Harold W. *African Independent Church*, 2 vols. Oxford: Clarendon Press, 1967.

J. D. Y. PEEL

OTTOMAN EMPIRE. *See* Colonial Policies and Practices.

OTTOMAN NORTHERN AFRICA, HISTORY OF (1500 TO 1850).

The sixteenth century started in North Africa with political fragmentation and Portuguese and Spanish outposts along the Atlantic and Mediterranean coasts. With the conquest of Granada in 1492 the Islamic presence on the Iberian Peninsula ended. North Africa became the frontier between Christians and Muslims. The *Marinids*, who controlled Morocco until 1465 were overthrown by their *Wattasid* branch (which reigned until 1549). But the *Abdalwadids* (or *Zayyanids*) still reigned in the region of Tlemcen in western Algeria (1236–1554), and the *Hafsids* governed *Ifriqiya* (present-day Tunisia) and eastern Algeria (1229–1574). There is in the whole of the Maghrib a lack of balance between the unruly tribes in the countryside *siba* and the towns and their pacified surroundings under the courts' authority, which lasted until the twentieth century.

However, the Christian threat produced an Islamic revival during the fifteenth and sixteenth centuries and provoked strong Muslim resistance. The tribes in southern Morocco were organized against the Portuguese and the Wattasids by the *Sa'dis*, who claimed descent from the Prophet Muhammad as *shurafa'*. The Wattasids followed a policy of coexistence with Portugal and Spain. In other regions resistance was organized by religious leaders, chiefs of mystical orders, and holy men. The Europeans, however, used far more advanced military technologies, namely firearms, while the North Africans lagged behind for some time in this regard. Nevertheless, the *Sa'dis* forced the Portuguese out of southern Morocco (1537–1557) and turned against the Wattasids, overthrowing them in 1549. They were successful in defending Morocco against Ottoman attacks in the following years until 1554.

HABSBURG VERSUS OTTOMANS

The sixteenth century around the Mediterranean was characterized by a sharp conflict between Habsburg and the Ottomans, with the western Mediterranean and the Balkan as the central areas of fighting. The Emperor Charles V tried several times to conquer Algiers and Tunis (between 1534 and 1541); the last attempt was in 1574. By that time, the Ottomans had occupied Egypt (1517) and extended their rule toward North Africa. Two brothers, 'Aruj and Khairaddin Barbarossa—corsairs who in 1516 made Algiers their base for fighting against the Spaniards—helped the Ottomans in 1520 by offering allegiance to the sultan in exchange for military support.

Khairaddin Barbarossa built the Ottoman naval force for sultan Süleyman the Magnificent and started conquering the eastern Maghrib; his successor Dragut (Turghud) finished the Ottoman occupation of the North African coast (1554–1556). Between 1536 and 1587, the regions along the coast were governed by Ottoman *beglerbegs*, or military governors. But Morocco resisted Ottoman pressure. A French-Ottoman commercial agreement, directed against Charles V, laid the ground for French interests in the southern shore of the Mediterranean (1536). Later, in 1694, the French founded the Compagnie d'Afrique to develop their commercial activities in the region and to negotiate agreements. The Knights of St. John of Jerusalem handed over Tripoli to the Ottomans in 1551, this being in line with Venetian losses in the eastern Mediterranean.

In Morocco, the Sa'di *sharif* Ahmad al-Mansur (1578–1603) imposed his rule on the whole country by building up a professional army with Spanish and Turkish mercenaries and the use of firearms. He overturned the empire of Songhay (present-day Mali) along with Timbuktu and Gao in an attempt to provide the state with foreign resources: gold and slaves. As an opponent of the Ottomans and due to his control of the trans-Saharan commercial routes, including the gold trade, he was a privileged diplomatic partner for England and Spain. After his death, however, Morocco was again divided between several *maraboutic* Berber principalities. Rabat and Salé, the twin towns at the Bou Regreg, enriched by piracy, became an independent corsairs' republic.

Between 1609 and 1614, up to 275,000 *moriscos* (former Muslims who had been forced to convert to Christianity) were expelled from the Iberian Peninsula after several rebellions. Most of them settled in North Africa, bringing with them the urban Hispano-Moorish culture and thus enriching North African urban culture.

OTTOMAN RULE AND MILITARY REPUBLICS

In 1587, three Ottoman *beyliks* were established in Algiers, Tunis, and Tripoli, administered by governors sent by the Sublime Porte. Piracy generated the main revenue, coming from ransoming Christian captives and from money for peace collected from Christian ports and countries. The special role played by Christian renegades on the Muslim side is worth noting. Quite often they were experienced army officers, sailors, or engineers. Algiers, especially notorious for its corsairs, was bombarded in retaliation several times by both the British (in 1622, 1655, and 1672) and the French (1665), as was Tripoli.

After an intermediate regime of commanders of the Ottoman corps (1659–1671), the troops in Algiers rebelled in 1689 against the Ottoman governor and installed a kind of military republic. The *dey* (maternal uncle) was chosen among the officers as ruler. Algiers acted independently from the Ottoman sultan, but recognized him as caliph, so that the Ottomans did not interfere. The local populations were to a large degree autonomous in their local affairs and governed by their own leaders. Therefore, they accepted the *deys* as the rulers of the country, helped by the fact of low taxes and by the *deys*' securing the support of influential *sufis*. The Algerian *deys* stayed in power until the French occupation in 1830. By the end of their rule, they nevertheless suffered from the decline in revenue coming from piracy. For compensation they had to heavily increase taxes causing conflicts with the tribal communities.

In Tunis, the situation was quite similar. By the end of the sixteenth century, the Turkish militaries seized power and installed a *dey*, becoming de facto

Stairs to the mosque Sidi ʿAbdarrahman in Algiers. The mosque, which was built in the beginning of the 12th century AH/18th century CE, is one of the few remaining buildings from Ottoman times. PHOTOGRAPH BY GERHARD ENDRESS, BOCHUM

autonomous. Privateering activities financed the state. Enslaving Christians was common, like elsewhere in North Africa. Tunis especially profited from the influx of the expelled Andalusian *moriscos* in artisan and agricultural activities at the beginning of the seventeenth century. The old Jewish

Shrine of an unknown saint in the medina, Arabic for "town," of the Moroccan port of Asilah. After a long Portuguese and Spanish occupation, the port was reconquered by the ʿAlawite Sultan Moulay Ismail in 1691. Courtesy of Sandra Petermann, Mainz

community and European merchants, recently installed under various treaties, acted as intermediaries between the two shores of the Mediterranean.

Out of the Ottoman military, the Muradi *beys* emerged as the new rulers, establishing a hereditary dynasty, by subduing several warrior tribes and extending the control of Tunis over the interior. With indigenous support, they counterbalanced the Turkish institutions and resisted several attempts by the *deys* to restore their old power with the help of the *dey* of Algiers. However, the Muradi *beys* did not renounce their Ottoman allegiance. Also recognizing the Ottoman caliphate, the Husaynids *beys* came to power in 1706, shortly after a successful Ottoman coup against the Muradi *beys*. The dynasty overcame a civil war caused by internal conflicts and organized its support from local notables and the body of ʿulama, Muslim scholars, breaking at the same time the power of the great tribes. Trade with Europe increased and manufacturing

developed on a larger scale. The end of corsair activities and the imposition of free commerce by European forces led to intense reform activities, especially after the French invasion of Algeria in 1830 and the Ottoman installation at Tripoli in 1835. By this time, a Tunisian national identity emerged. The Husaynid *beys* stayed in power until 1957.

Tripoli and its hinterland had been in Ottoman possession since 1551. Here also, an army officer, the head of the cavalry Ahmad Qaramanli, seized power in 1711 and established a dynasty that reigned until 1835. Privateering and the trans-Saharan trade provided the state's revenue. Napoleon's conquest of Malta and Egypt in 1798 led to an opening of the country for European trade, but also for rivalry between England and France for supremacy in the region. A tribal rebellion with the support of the British ended the Qaramanli era and reinstalled the Ottomans in Tripoli.

THE ʿALAWITES OF MOROCCO

From 1631 on, the *shurafaʾ* of the Hasani-Filali branch from Tafilalt conquered eastern Morocco and then rebuilt the sharifian empire by expanding to the north, subduing the Berber *maraboutic* principality of Dilaʾiyya, taking Fez and re-conquering Marrakesh. They established the dynasty of the ʿAlawites still in power in Morocco in the twenty-first century. Throughout the seventeenth and eighteenth centuries, firm and successful ruling by the Alawite sultans alternated with anarchy. The ʿAlawites did not resort to *marabouts* for support. Instead, they put their own sharifian descent to the fore to gain politico-religious legitimacy and relied on armed forces, who helped them by ending the foreign occupation of ports. Regularly, the sultan had to fight rebellions and to play off one group against the other. Expeditions toward western Algeria failed. The economy was in decline due to internal warfare and political instability. A decentralization strategy and a technique of power, which negotiated but did not command, stabilized the dynasty both internally and externally, and was based on the sultan's dual power as military and religious leader, as sultan and *amir al-muʾminin* (commander of the faithful). Foreign contacts and trade were deliberately restricted to a few ports (Essaouira and Tangier).

THE FRENCH INVASION IN ALGERIA

Following a diplomatic incident and due to internal political problems, France invaded Algeria in 1830, conquering the whole country in a long-lasting and brutal war. This occupation, which led to the integration of the country into metropolitan France, shocked the political and cultural order of North Africa and provoked profound changes, not only in Algeria, but also in its neighboring countries. Morocco supported the Algerian resistance, but suffered a heavy defeat by the French in the battle of Isly (1844). Algeria's indigenous structures in education and administration were completely destroyed, its economy transformed into a colonial one, large parts of the population proletarianized and uprooted. The emir ʿAbd al-Qādir fought for nearly twenty years against the French, before being arrested in Morocco and exiled in 1847. From all countries in the region, only Morocco remained fully sovereign.

See also **ʿAbd al-Qādir; Algeria; Christianity; Fez; Gao; Islam; Marrakesh; Morocco; Rabat and Salé; Timbuktu; Tripoli; Tunis; Warfare: Internal Revolts.**

BIBLIOGRAPHY

Abun-Nasr, Jamil M. *A History of the Maghrib in the Islamic Period.* Cambridge, U.K.: Cambridge University Press, 1987.

Julien, Charles André. *History of North Africa: Tunisia, Algeria, Morocco, from the Arab Conquest to 1830.* New York: Praeger, 1970.

Laroui, Abdallah. *The History of the Maghrib: An Interpretive Essay.* Princeton, NJ: Princeton University Press, 1977.

JÖRN THIELMANN

OUIDAH. A slave trading center of the Hueda people, Ouidah (Whydah) was conquered by Dahomey in 1727 and became infamous as a "port" of the slave trade from the late seventeenth to the nineteenth centuries. Ouidah is estimated to have been the embarkation point for well over 1 million persons sold into the Middle Passage and is second only to Luanda as a departure site for the Atlantic trade. The city stands some three miles from the beach, from which goods and human cargoes were ferried to ships anchored offshore. Ouidah attracted a diverse population drawn from ethnic groups in the hinterland of what are present-day Bénin, Nigeria, and Togo, and from European nations that included Holland, France, Britain, and Portugal. In the early nineteenth century numbers of persons from Brazil, including many manumitted slaves, settled in Ouidah and founded a commercial community that maintained cultural practices from Portugal and Brazil. In the colonial period these Afro-Brazilian "Aguda" used their literacy and commercial skills to become administrators and leading merchants, even as the focus of commerce moved eastward to the cities of Cotonou and Porto-Novo. Bypassed by development, Ouidah nevertheless had a population of about 25,000 in 2006. An important destination for heritage tourism, Ouidah is also the seat of the ancestral family homes of many prominent families.

See also **Slave Trades.**

BIBLIOGRAPHY

Law, Robin. *Ouidah: The Social History of a West African Slaving "Port," 1727–1892.* Athens: Ohio University Press, 2004.

EDNA G. BAY

OUSMANE SEMBÈNE. *See* Sembène, Ousmane.

OVERPOPULATION. *See* Demography: Population Data and Surveys.

P

PAINTING. *See* Arts.

PALEONTOLOGY. *See* Prehistory.

PAN-AFRICAN AND REGIONAL ORGANIZATIONS. *See* Organization of African Unity.

PASHA, EMIN. *See* Schnitzer, Eduard.

PATON, ALAN (1903–1988). The South African writer Alan Stewart Paton was born in Petermaritzburg. Paton worked as a teacher in rural Natal before being appointed principal of the Diepkloof reform school near Johannesburg. While touring similar reformatories in Europe and America in 1946 he wrote *Cry, the Beloved Country*, a passionate denunciation of South Africa's racial policies that has remained in print ever since its publication in 1948, has twice been filmed, and turned into a musical (*Lost in the Stars*) with a score by Kurt Weill.

Although Prime Minister D. F. Malan attended the premier of the 1950 film in Johannesburg,

Paton's anti-apartheid liberalism cost him his position at Diepkloof, and he turned full time to writing, eventually producing two more novels (*Too*

South African author Alan Paton (1903–1988). In 1953, Paton founded the South African Liberal Party, which spoke out against apartheid legislation introduced by the National Party.
Pictorial Parade/Getty Images

Late the Phalarope [1953] and *Ah, but Your Land Is Beautiful* [1981]), short stories, biographies, literary and political essays, and two volumes of autobiography. Paton was a leading figure in the Liberal Party from 1953 until its disbandment in 1968 as a result of legislation banning mixed-race political parties. Sidelined politically by the intensified polarization of South African politics in the last two decades of apartheid, in his moral integrity and commitment to his beloved country and to interracial harmony, Paton played a significant role not only in South African culture but in the history of race relations worldwide.

See also **Apartheid; Literature: Popular Literature; South Africa, Republic of: Society and Cultures.**

BIBLIOGRAPHY

Alexander, Peter F. *Alan Paton: A Biography.* Cape Town, South Africa: Oxford University Press, 1994.

Callan, Edward. *Alan Paton.* Boston: Twayne, 1982.

SIMON LEWIS

PATRIARCHY AND PATRILINY. *See* **Kinship and Affinity; Kinship and Descent; Marriage Systems.**

PAWNING. *See* **Children and Childhood; Debt and Credit: Entrustment.**

PEASANTS

This entry includes the following articles:
OVERVIEW
CENTRAL AFRICA
EASTERN AFRICA
SOUTHERN AFRICA
WESTERN AFRICA

OVERVIEW

The reference to African farming populations as "peasantries" seems more apposite to some times and places than to others. The term only reached a tentatively general acceptance among scholars in

the 1970s. And it is a matter of controversy how useful it is to draw more attention to the similarities between African farmers and, for example, Chinese or medieval European peasantries, than to the differences. The similarities are clear: these are usually family-based enterprises, using non-mechanized technologies for cultivation and processing, producing for both home consumption and regional markets. The differences hinge on two characteristics generally taken as definitional of peasantries: they are generally assumed to comprise "part" economies and societies that "orient their production toward their own consumption and [also] toward the fulfillment of obligations to the holders of political and economic power over them" (Saul and Woods, 240). Political subordination has usually entailed sedentarization and the imposition of measures of control and appropriation: legal naming, census enumeration, taxation and military service. Due to controls on movement, peasant production tends toward the intensive end of the extensive-intensive continuum of land use. Only in a few African societies did farmers of the past submit to state control of resources, and in even fewer places did they practice intensive agriculture. Ethiopia is the single fairly unambiguous case. Hence the sense of unease among scholars about grouping the past and present rural economies of Africa, for comparative purposes, with the classic peasantries of the world.

To add to the confusion that the inexact application of the term "peasant" might bring, the French term *paysan* has a different enough connotation from the English term "peasant" to have been generally accepted in the literature on French West and Equatorial Africa long before controversy arose in Anglophone circles. A *paysan* was someone who made a living from the *pays*, the countryside. One of the early classic studies of African farmers, by Paul Pélissier, was entitled *Les paysans du Sénégal: Les civilizations agraires du Cayor à la Casamance* (1966). The famous Belgian schemes for modernizing agricultural techniques in the Congo during the colonial period were called *paysannats*. Ironically, the cultivators of the Zaire River basin are perhaps among the least likely, in all of Africa, to fit neatly into a "peasant" mold. Where they developed intensive techniques (as they did in fishing) it was in non-state political structures, and the centralized polities were more based on the profits of trade than of production. But in relationship to a French-speaking colonial government, all rural producers could conveniently be assimilated to the concept of *paysans*.

Indeed, it was really the changes at the end of the colonial era that made English-speaking scholarship warm to the analytical prospect of "peasants." Whatever the situation in the past, African cultivators were by then definitively integrated into state structures and world markets, and as a result many were practicing more intensive and specialized agriculture than their forebears. In 1955 M. G. Smith wrote of the Hausa economy of Northern Nigeria that it was based on "two differing interest groups, the peasants and their rulers" (4). In 1961 Lloyd Fallers—working from his study of one of Africa's stronger state structures and more intensive agriculture systems, the Baganda—posed the question bluntly: "Are African cultivators to be called 'peasants'?" Rural-based political movements in the 1960s made it clear that, whatever they were called, African farmers were ready to make some claims against the state and to react to markets, taxes, duties, and other institutions of the world economic system in a fashion that seemed closer to peasant politics than to anything else.

By that time, however, a great deal of new research had been published on the history of employment of rural-based populations outside of agriculture altogether, or on European-owned farms. Oscillating migration in South Africa was simply the most formalized version of a general pattern of male and youth employment for long periods of time outside of their home areas. And in the 1970s it became clear that in several places small rural producers were being forcibly removed, with radically changed rights to land. In South Africa the resulting settlements began to be referred to as "rural slums," because occupants had neither jobs nor the bases for a life of self-provisioning This finding about the proletarian element in rural life put a dent into another of the diacritics of a peasantry: family-based cultivation. In fact, it was suggested by Ester Boserup in 1970 that African farming was better depicted as feminized farming than as household production. In brief, scholarship had no sooner become more or less comfortable with the idea of a peasantry "than they were confronted with the fact that in vast parts of Africa peasants had already been made into proletarians" (Cooper, 284). Both workers and farmers migrated to jobs and to land.

The debates about terminology may seem sterile, but in fact they have been productive, because each effort at definition has drawn African cases into a different comparative context with respect to the rest of the world. Robert Netting, for example, abandoned the criterion of state subjection altogether, to pursue the criterion of intensive household production. As a result, some African local economies figure alongside Chinese and Swiss farming while others do not. Sara Berry, by contrast, emphasized the particular nature of African state intervention, regardless of the intensity of agricultural technique. She argued that the relationship between African farmers and postcolonial states is a partial one, where the state intervenes in production but only enough to produce uncertainty rather than decisive change. Other work, particularly in west Africa, with its tradition of production for commercial markets, suggests that cultivators of food for rapidly growing urban populations are indeed intensifying and also accommodating to government, but in ways that come forward from their own history rather than primarily through either political subjection or adoption of well-known world techniques of intensification such as irrigation or manuring.

Specialists were still debating these issues in the 1980s to expand the terms for analyzing the social, political, and technical dynamics of rural livelihoods in Africa. But during the 1980s and 1990s African farmers departed further and further from a classic peasant model. They lost markets for their major products, such as cocoa, coffee, cotton, and palm products, for complex reasons: steep competition from Asia and from subsidized western farmers; civil disorder; natural catastrophes due to climate or disease; and negative policies. At the same time, the expanding sectors of African national economies have been largely in extractive industries: timber, oil, diamonds and coltan (amongst many other minerals). So state structures are increasingly independent of people's work in the rural sector, in favor of royalties from industries that employ very few people. The two conditions taken together—adverse circumstances and the rise of natural resource economies—has resulted in one of the highest urbanization rates in world history as former peasants turn to the urban informal sector to make a living and protect their lives.

The idea of a peasantry fits less well when rural producers are no longer the backbone of social economies. And yet it may still be useful, combined with other concepts that set the comparative frame in other ways. West Africa, with its long tradition of commerce and urban life, is particularly challenging for posing questions that tease out the separate influences of factors that the term "peasant" groups together and that remain compelling: the techniques and social organization of rural production; the relationship the state to its resource base and its producers; and the engagement of African farmers and artisans with various markets in a rapidly changing global political economy.

See also **Agriculture; Production Strategies.**

BIBLIOGRAPHY

Berry, Sara. *No Condition Is Permanent: The Social Dynamics of Agrarian Change in Sub-Saharan Africa.* Madison: University of Wisconsin Press, 1993.

Boone, Catherine. *Political Topographies of the African State: Territorial Authority and Institutional Choice.* Cambridge, U.K.: Cambridge University Press, 2003.

Boserup, Ester. *Woman's Role in Economic Development.* New York: St. Martin's Press, 1970.

Cooper, Frederick. "Peasants, Capitalists, and Historians: A Review Article." *Journal of Southern African Studies* 7, no. 2 (1981): 284–314.

Fallers, Lloyd. "Are African Cultivators to Be Called 'Peasants'?" *Current Anthropology* 2 (1961): 108–110.

Guyer, Jane I. *An African Niche Economy: Farming to Feed Ibadan, 1968–1988.* Edinburgh: Edinburgh University Press, 1997.

McCann, James C. *People of the Plow: An Agricultural History of Ethiopia, 1800–1990.* Madison: University of Wisconsin Press, 1995.

Mkandawire, Thandika, and Charles Soludo. *Our Continent, Our Future.* Trenton NJ: Africa World Press, for Council for the Development of Social and Economic Research in Africa, 1999.

Netting, Robert McC. *Smallholders, Householders: Farm Families and the Ecology of Intensive, Sustainable Agriculture.* Stanford, CA: Stanford University Press, 1993.

Pélissier, Paul. *Les paysans du Sénégal: Les civilisations agraires du Cayor à la Casamance.* Saint-Yrieix, France: Fabrègue, 1966.

Saul, John S., and Roger Woods. "African Peasantries." In *Peasants and Peasant Societies,* ed. Teodor Shanin. Harmondsworth, U.K.: Penguin Books, 1971.

Smith, M. G. *The Economy of Hausa Communities of Zaria.* London: H. M. Stationery Office for the Colonial Office, 1955.

JANE I. GUYER

CENTRAL AFRICA

Peasants are small-scale tillers of land and keepers of livestock whose ultimate economic and social security lies in their land rights and family labor teams. They may hire extra labor or work for wages, but the focus of their lives is the family farm and the satisfaction of family needs. Self-sufficiency and autonomy are highly valued ideals that are never attained, and peasants are always part of a larger social system in which they occupy a subordinate political position. Peasants must regularly provide food or labor for public works projects, and they must perform military service. They are obliged to pay tribute, rent, or tax in one form or another to their ruling classes.

Radical scholars postulated that the proletarianization of the peasantry was a logical outcome of the process of peasant differentiation under capitalism, and thus saw peasants as a transitory category of rural Africans. Poor peasants were expected to abandon their increasingly small and infertile plots of land and become dependent on wages, whereas rich peasants would expand production and become capitalist farmers. However, there has been no uniform process of peasant differentiation, and the uneven pace of development has produced different outcomes in different countries. Peasant societies in Central Africa resemble those in southern Africa in many ways, but capitalist economic development in southern Africa has a longer history and has had a greater social impact.

There are more European settler farmers in South Africa and Zimbabwe than in Botswana, Zambia, or Malawi, and wherever European farmers have settled in large numbers, large-scale farming enterprises have developed, rendering many peasants landless in the process. In such countries, wars of liberation have been fought over land and over democratic rights. Central African peasant societies farm on a small scale, using hand tools and, occasionally, ox-drawn implements. Malawi, Zambia, and Mozambique have a combination of large estate, plantation, and peasant agriculture. In these countries, peasants are not separate from the capitalist economy. In fact, the viability and growth of peasant farming depends on peasants' participation in the capitalist economy. Remittances and savings of migrant workers, as well as the sale of produce in the towns and cities, play a crucial role in peasant societies. Equally important in the past was the role played by the colonial and national governments in promoting sections of the population and helping them make the transition to market-oriented farming.

FROM WAGE LABOR TO PEASANT FARMING IN ZAMBIA

In Zambia, the involvement of state agencies in farmers' training and credit programs, and even the marketing of produce, was crucial in pushing peasants further into the capitalist economy. The Zambian economy long relied upon the copper mines as the major employer and earner of foreign exchange. The contribution of peasant farmers to the national economy was so low that the farmers were generally dismissed as subsistence producers. The steady decline in the mining industry and in the national economy generally since the 1970s has made peasant farming more important for the survival of the low-income sections of the population. It has also made the movement from wage employment to peasant farming feasible. Zambian government statisticians estimate the urban population to be about half of the national total.

Although the country may appear to be urbanized, it is common for people to straddle the urban and peasant economies as a matter of necessity. Recent population trends have indicated a slowing rate of urbanization, a shrinking of the population of the once rapidly growing Copperbelt towns, and an increase in population of small towns as they assume some of the people leaving the large cities. Although small towns are able to support all sorts of nonagricultural commercial and informal sector activities, they also enable residents to do some farming, especially of seasonal food crops.

Zambian government policies were based on the neoliberal preference for efficient, highly capital-intensive plantations and greenhouses for much of the 1990s. State subsidies for peasant farmers were discontinued under pressure from the World Bank and IMF, and many of the small-scale maize producers reverted to subsistence farming. A combination of maize shortages, the high cost of aviation fuel, and even a political backlash from citizens fed up with foreign agribusiness dominating their agricultural economies has forced the Zambian government to reconsider providing supportive services to peasant farmers in the early twenty-first century.

PEASANTS UNDER SOCIALISM IN MOZAMBIQUE

Peasants in Mozambique have experienced the problems of both capitalist- and socialist-oriented development, as well as the stress caused by prolonged war, drought, and famine. Beginning in the colonial period, peasant society was influenced by the migration of male laborers to the gold mines and farms in South Africa, to farms in southern Rhodesia (now Zimbabwe), and to Portuguese-owned plantations in Mozambique. In some areas the forced production of cotton also disrupted village life. As a result, self-provisioning was greatly undermined, thereby making wage labor and the purchase of food common in many Mozambican peasant societies.

After Mozambique's independence in 1975, the Marxist Mozambique Liberation Front (FRELIMO) government tried to stop its citizens from working in the South African mines in a campaign against exploitative capitalist relations. Agricultural production soon fell due to the lack of resources for farm implements, fertilizers, and other inputs. The campaign put peasant societies under economic stress. For Mozambicans, as for Malawians and Zambians, security lay in creative straddling of the urban and rural economies by both peasants and the urban poor, thereby blurring the distinction between peasant and proletarian. Peasants attempting to protect their autonomy against the socialist state continued to use the tactics developed during the colonial period. Thus, if government-controlled corn prices were lower than those for beans, peasants planted beans. When the cassava price was deregulated, they switched to cassava. When money became worthless as a result of prolonged economic crisis, barter became the norm. Corn was exchanged for fruits and vegetables, even by government agencies. Under such circumstances, peasants could prosper, until the civil war reached their village.

During the civil war of the 1980s, many of Mozambique's peasant societies were destroyed. People fled to neighboring countries or were displaced internally, separated from their families. In the chaos of the civil war, especially attacks by the Mozambique Resistance Movement (RENAMO) on rural communities, the parallel economy became more important, as did the Mozambican peasants' dependence on international relief and labor migration to South Africa. Thousands of Mozambicans risked the electrified fence and the wild animals in Kruger National Park to find security, though not a normal life, in South African refugee camps.

THE LAND QUESTIONS IN SOUTHERN AFRICA'S PROLETARIANIZED PEASANT SOCIETIES

In the 1980s, researchers in rural southern Africa found that wages, remittances from migrant workers, and pensions, rather than self-provisioning agriculture, provided most rural people with their livelihood. This would seem to suggest that the process of proletarianization had been completed and that there were few peasant societies left in southern Africa of the labor reserves. Although Swaziland and Botswana, more than Lesotho and South Africa, could claim to be predominantly peasant societies, the practice of rural-urban straddling remained evident across the whole region. By the end of the 1990s, the shortage of land in all these countries made peasant farming unviable, and made the unfinished business of land reform a priority for certain governments.

In Zimbabwe, Namibia, and South Africa, where the white settlers occupied the best agricultural lands and where the economic role for black people was defined as labor migration, rather than farming, by the colonial states, the pressure for land reforms has mounted. An unprecedented violent land restitution campaign in Zimbabwe in 2000 saw black elites taking over white farmers' lands, or turning them into smaller peasant farms. Although it may appear that Zimbabwe is a special case because of its authoritarian regime, it is likely that even those countries that do not have a white settler population to accuse for their land hunger, massive unemployment, landlessness, and urban slums cannot happily co-exist with the policies of wealth creation that favor capitalist farming over peasant production, and flowers for export over maize for local consumption. It is not feasible for people to be landless and jobless at the same time. Peasants may be more viable than proletarians in the long run because the farmers can ride out the worst periods of recession and unemployment by reverting to small-scale commercial or subsistence farming.

In Zimbabwe, as elsewhere, rural farm workers and tenants still hope for their land rights. If the democratically elected South African government were to transfer large tracts of land to the rural population, viable peasant agriculture could be reestablished even in this industrialized African economy.

In general, the experience of Lesotho, which turned from a grain-exporting peasant economy into a food-importing labor reserve for South Africa, exemplifies the sort of underdevelopment that other parts of rural southern Africa have experienced under colonialism. The Eastern Cape and the Orange Free State also recorded periods of growth in colonial-era peasant farming that contributed to capital accumulation in South Africa. The boom ended when both the human and the livestock populations exceeded the carrying capacity of the available land. The land laws of 1913 and 1936 decreased the ability of African peasants to sustain their growth even more because the peasants were not allowed to obtain land outside their reserves. Although the Nationalist party government's Tomlinson Commission of 1955 noted that Africans in the rural reserves needed more land, there was never a major redistribution of property. Some of the problems experienced by the rural population were a consequence of government policies.

In the early twenty-first century, black former landowners in ex-peasant communities are strongly demanding that the new government correct the wrong policies of the past. Peasant societies in both Central and southern Africa need more than land reforms for their well-being and development. As a part of the early twenty-first-century global economy, they participate in a market where anything from secondhand American clothes to electronic goods from Taiwan may be exchanged for their crops, and where fluctuations in international currency exchange rates may render them poorer overnight. In the final analysis, the fate of peasant societies depends on the success of their national and regional economies.

See also **Agriculture; Economic History; Gender; Production Strategies.**

BIBLIOGRAPHY

Bundy, Colin. *The Rise and Fall of the South African Peasantry.* Berkeley: University of California Press, 1979.

Chipungu, Sam N. *The State, Technology, and Peasant Differentiation in Zambia: A Case Study of the Southern Province, 1930–1986.* Lusaka: Historical Association of Zambia, 1988.

Macintosh, Maureen. "Mozambique Case Study." In *Agricultural Pricing Policy in Africa*, ed. Charles Harvey. London: Macmillan Education, 1988.

Moyo, Sam. "The Politics of Land Distribution and Race Relations in Southern Africa, Identities Conflict and Cohesion Programme Paper Number 10." Geneva: United Nations Research Institute for Social Development, 2004.

Murray, Colin. "Lesotho: From Granary to Labour Reserve." In *Transformations on the Highveld: The Tswana and the Southern Sotho*, ed. William F. Lyle and Colin Murray. London: David Phillip, 1980.

Sandbrook, Richard. *The Politics of Africa's Economic Recovery.* Cambridge, U.K.: Cambridge University Press, 1993.

Saul, John, and Roger Woods. "African Peasantries." In *Peasants and Peasant Societies: Selected Readings*, 2nd edition. ed. Theodor Shanin. Oxford: Blackwell Publishers, 1987.

OWEN SICHONE

EASTERN AFRICA

The term "peasantry" gained currency in eastern Africa during the 1960s, coincident with the rejection of the colonial denotation of African agricultural producers as "natives." In the policy arena of the 1980s and 1990s, the term "peasantry" was increasingly supplanted by "smallholders."

Peasants in eastern Africa, as elsewhere, are identifiable by three main characteristics: sedentary agricultural practices, an internal social organization based on family labor, and external subordination to state authorities as well as the regional or international markets through which the value of their surpluses are channeled. The geographical incidence of peasant societies has been variegated due to the availability of a suitable combination of factors associated with ecology, population density, the nature of state power, and external influences including market demand and the spread of world religions.

Many parts of eastern Africa, specifically areas of low rainfall, poor drainage, or tsetse infestation, have been sparsely populated and poor in natural resources, making the historical development of surplus production and the emergence of surplus-extracting elites and peasantries unlikely. Even where the natural resource base and population densities have been favorable, peasantries have not arisen without sufficient infrastructure and agricultural innovations making surplus extraction physically feasible. The stimulus of the market and the organizational role of the state in developing roads and communications has been critical.

PRECOLONIAL PEASANTRIES
Despite the drought-prone nature of northern Sudan, the use of waterwheels and plows created localities of relatively high agricultural productivity and the possibility of tribute-paying peasants in successive agrarian kingdoms of the Nile Valley dating back more than three thousand years. Peasants performed labor services and paid taxes in kind. The system of taxation was structured to gather goods of potential export value, such as cotton. In the fourteenth century CE, the elites of most of these agrarian kingdoms adopted Islam. Market influences emanating from the Mediterranean began to undermine the foundations of the kingdoms in the eighteenth century. Merchants grew in power, amassing land by foreclosing on indebted peasants and switching to reliance on the labor of imported slaves from the south for large-scale plantation production.

Ethiopia, strongly identified with peasant agriculture throughout its long-recorded history, combined the power of a highland state and church to form an enduring apparatus of surplus extraction. The adoption of ox plows sometime before 1000 BCE and cultivation of many crops unique to Ethiopia, for example enset, or "false banana" (*Ensete ventricosum*), and teff (*Eragrostis tef*) resulted in higher-yielding agriculture and more densely populated settlements than in the surrounding, drier lowlands. The Aksum kingdom flourished from 100 to 700 CE marked by the

Aksumite king Ezana conversion to Christianity around 330 CE It is apparent that although slave labor was used in Ethiopia during the last millennium, the constraints placed on active engagement in slave trading by the Christian scriptures restricted the spread of slavery. Thus, the family labor system of the Ethiopian peasantry predominated.

Environmental and climatic extremes of the regions to the south—namely, the arid lowlands of Ethiopia, Somalia, northern Kenya, and northern Uganda, as well as the dry-wetland complex of southern Sudan—proved to be a barrier to the establishment of high-yielding sedentary agricultural systems. At relatively low levels of population density, pastoralist forms of livelihood and tribal social organizations were most common. The pastoralist belt, spanning the width of eastern Africa and running through southern Sudan and Ethiopia, Somalia, and the drier parts of Kenya, Uganda, and Tanzania, demarcated a clear boundary line between the different agrarian traditions of the northern and southern zones of eastern Africa.

Hoe agriculture was associated with the kingdoms and tribute-paying peasants of various high rainfall areas in Kenya, Uganda, and Tanzania that European explorers encountered in the mid- and late nineteenth century. In the intralacustrine region where Uganda, Tanzania, and Rwanda meet, Tutsi pastoralists ruled over peasant cultivators. In other areas—for example, Uhaya, Uchagga, and Usambara, in Tanzania; and Buganda, in Uganda— the ruling class was not occupationally distinct from those it ruled. The wealth of these agrarian kingdoms rested on extremely high-yielding banana plantain production. In the dryer savanna areas, there was a complex mosaic of tribal communities practicing a mixture of shifting cultivation, pastoralism, and hunting and gathering. During the nineteenth century, these communities were increasingly subject to slave raiding and to the economic stimuli of traders associated with the Omani commercial empire that had become eventually headquartered itself on Zanzibar Island.

PEASANTRIES DURING THE COLONIAL PERIOD

Colonial annexation encompassed all eastern African territories with the exception of Ethiopia. The imposition of European rule incorporated the existing peasantries and created peasant societies in ecological zones which had hitherto posed obstacles to generating and collecting surpluses. The result was the peasantization of vast expanses of eastern Africa. Peasantization was accomplished through colonial taxation, increasingly collected in cash rather than in kind, and through the attendant introduction of new crops and promotion of peasant commodity production. A similar process of monetization and widening surplus appropriation took place in Ethiopia under Menelik and later Haile Selassie as the country developed into an imperial state in which tax collection became more standardized.

Hut and poll taxes and tariffs on external trade were the main forms of colonial taxation. Peasants were obliged to be in possession of cash earned by selling either their labor or commodities to pay taxes. In many areas, colonial government officials or missionaries introduced cash crops such as coffee, cocoa, cotton, tea, and tobacco. Irrigation schemes were devised to facilitate the spread of cotton cultivation in the Sudan and sugar and banana production in southern Somalia along the Juba and Shabelle Rivers. Furthermore, investment in transport infrastructure was vital. Railroads from coastal entrepots were built at the turn of the century to tap the main commodity-producing regions of the hinterland. Road building was a continual colonial preoccupation in up-country districts. Given the vulnerability of peasants to harvest fluctuation, particularly in agricultural systems where food surpluses were neither large nor reliable, colonial famine prevention was a necessary counterbalance to government taxation policy.

Whereas slavery was outlawed and peasant societies expanded dramatically during the colonial period, it should be stressed that peasant production was not ubiquitous throughout eastern Africa. Various agricultural patterns evolved. For the first half of the twentieth century, Uganda and Ethiopia represent the clearest examples of states whose policies fostered the conditions for maintaining and taxing peasant production. In Sudan, it was originally the intention of the British to create an extensive peasantry associated with the new irrigation works, but the emergence of an indigenous rural landowning class was not checked, and labor tenancy followed. In Kenya, European settlers succeeded in getting colonial government support for the appropriation of land and the creation of an African tenant class in the service of European planters. In Tanganyika (part of present-day Tanzania), peasant production was encouraged in various areas, while other areas of European land appropriation gave rise to a plantation sector which siphoned African labor from the more remote parts of the country where peasant commodity production was not considered viable because of the lack of transport infrastructure.

INDEPENDENCE AND AFTER

Most eastern African countries gained their political independence during the 1960s. In many countries, the new ruling elites successfully mobilized peasant support for their struggle against the colonial powers. Independence resolved political tensions while creating new economic contradictions. Colonial governments had tended to operate with tightly restricted budgets and skeletal staffing, and they had few welfare goals. Postcolonial governments, however, won support on the basis of promises of far-ranging improvements to the living standards of the national population. They sought to modernize through industrialization and they did so amidst rapid urbanization. Their taxation strategies had to accommodate heavy state expenditure. Yet peasants associated taxation, particularly poll taxes, with colonialism, and the new national governments risked deep unpopularity by imposing such taxes. Governments increasingly relied on indirect taxation exacted through control of the terms on which peasants marketed commodities. Peasant producer prices were depressed relative to world market prices, boosting government revenues.

In the 1960s and 1970s, many countries had considerable success in achieving their welfare goals. Investment in health care and education led to measurable improvements in infant mortality rates and peasant life expectancies in rural areas. One outcome was a steady increase in population and, consequently, demographic pressure on land. In some countries, the problem of decreasing rural land availability was alleviated when peasants migrated to urban jobs. But in other countries, the strain was very severe and expressed itself in an increasing incidence of food shortages culminating in devastating famines, such as the ones experienced in Ethiopia and Sudan in the mid-1970s and then repeated less than a decade later in the 1980s.

The mid- to late 1970s was a period of economic crisis arising from the oil price boom. Given the vast distances over which African agricultural goods are transported to shipment points, the oil price rise dealt a severe blow to the international competitiveness of commodities produced by peasants on the continent. Peasants in many eastern African countries lost significant amounts of their share in international markets for their major export crops which translated into diminished tax revenues, cutbacks in social services and a rapid decline in the social and economic welfare of many segments of the rural population. East African governments' heavy reliance on external donor funding and increasing foreign indebtedness ensued.

Against a background of economic uncertainty, the political legitimacy of many eastern African states was questioned in the 1980s and early 1990s both internally and externally. Sudan, Uganda, Ethiopia and Somalia experienced civil disorder and military upheaval. More generally, an increasing reliance on foreign aid made the eastern African states subject to the World Bank and IMF's insistence on domestic policy reform.

Structural adjustment programs were implemented throughout the region beginning in the 1980s. Market liberalization was a central component of the programs, justified in terms of the need for the comparative advantage of smallholders' commodity production in the world market to emerge. However, these policies were implemented at a time when the terms of trade for eastern Africa's most important peasant commodity exports were extremely low. Peasant farmers, squeezed by rising costs of agricultural inputs while cash crop incomes fluctuated along a downward tendency, started shifting away from the commercial production of their traditional cashcrops. Men's income from cashcropping diminished, undermining their role as the family cash earner. A surge in income diversification, particularly on the part of women and youth, was weighted towards non-agricultural goods and services. Retaining an agricultural subsistence base, rural producers generated income from trading, beer-making, prepared snacks, hair styling and handicrafts, to name but a few activities, many of which had not previously been commoditized.

Non-agricultural income-earning combined with individualization of economic activity is currently dissolving long-standing agrarian divisions of labor as well as economic rights and responsibilities within peasant families. The force of international markets and the weakness of East African governments are sidelining peasant producers' prominence in the economies of the eastern African nation-states. One could argue that the peasantization of eastern Africa initiated at the outset of European colonialism in the late nineteenth and early twentieth centuries is, roughly a century later, being reversed. The social, economic, cultural and welfare implications of "depeasantization" on rural dwellers, who still constitute a major portion of the population in eastern Africa, has yet to be fully fathomed.

See also **Agriculture; Aksum; Archaeology and Prehistory; Climate; Colonial Policies and Practices; Economic History; Ecosystems; Haile Selassie I; Labor; Law; Menelik II; Nyerere, Julius Kambarage; Postcolonialism; Production Strategies; Refugees.**

BIBLIOGRAPHY

Bahru, Zewde. *A History of Modern Ethiopia, 1855–1974.* London: James Currey, 1991.

Brett, Edwin Allen. *Colonialism and Underdevelopment in East Africa: The Politics of Change, 1919–1939.* London: Heinemann, 1973.

Bryceson, Deborah Fahy. *Food Insecurity and the Social Division of Labor in Tanzania, 1919–1985.* New York: St. Martin's Press, 1990.

Bryceson, Deborah Fahy. *Women Wielding the Hoe: Lessons from Rural Africa for Feminist Theory and Development Practice.* Oxford: Berg, 1995.

Bryceson, Deborah Fahy. "African Peasants' Centrality and Marginality: Rural Labour Transformations." In *Disappearing Peasantries: Rural Labor in Africa, Asia and Latin America,* ed. Bryceson, Deborah Fahy, Christobal Kay, and Jos Mooij. London: Intermediate Technology, 2000.

Iliffe, John. *A Modern History of Tanganyika.* Cambridge, U.K.: Cambridge University Press, 1979.

Kapteijns, Lidwien, and Jay Spaulding. "History, Ethnicity, and Agriculture in the Sudan." In *The Agriculture of the Sudan,* ed. G. M. Craig. New York: Oxford University Press, 1991.

Kitching, Gavin. *Class and Economic Change in Kenya: The Making of an African Petite Bourgeoisie, 1905–1970.* New Haven, CT: Yale University Press, 1980.

Little, Peter D. *Somalia: Economy without State.* Oxford: James Currey, 2003.

McCann, James. *From Poverty to Famine in Northeast Ethiopia: A Rural History, 1900–1935.* Philadelphia: University of Pennsylvania Press, 1987.

Pankhurst, Richard. *Economic History of Ethiopia, 1800–1935.* Addis Ababa, Ethiopia: Haile Sellassie I University Press, 1968.

DEBORAH FAHY BRYCESON

SOUTHERN AFRICA

In both the colonial and postindependence periods, many African countries have experienced substantial population resettlement. Resettlement is distinguished from other kinds of population movement in that relocation is compulsory. People are either forced by the authorities to move from their homes or, as in the case of refugees, they feel constrained to flee in order to escape violence or famine. In Africa, the major causes of resettlement have related to dam construction and agricultural schemes, the establishment of socialist villages, and the refugee crisis, with some 50 million people uprooted since World War II.

South African society has historically been organized along the lines of the administrative and territorial separation of race groups. South Africans have been legally divided into four separate race groups: black, colored, Indian, and white, with the whites having been accorded ownership of or control over approximately 87 percent of the land surface. Resettlement has occurred principally in terms of this policy of racial separation, reaching its height during the apartheid years.

CAUSES OF RESETTLEMENT UNDER APARTHEID

The Surplus People Project, a nongovernmental organization, argues that, up to 1982, the apartheid policy was responsible for the resettlement of more than 3.5 million people. Several important causes led to this resettlement:

- Black farm laborers were turned off or left white-owned farms (1,129,000 people)

- Removals occurred under the Group Areas Act, which set aside separate residential areas for the different official race groups (834,000 people)

- Urban relocation was government policy. Black people staying in towns or cities in South Africa were required to live in officially proclaimed black townships, usually on the outskirts of the city. A number of these townships were deproclaimed, with people being resettled in newly established centers within the homelands (also known as reserves or bantustans), which had been set aside for black occupation (730,000 people)

- Homeland consolidation and "black spot" (black settlements) removals were undertaken. The government sought to make the homelands as geographically consolidated as possible. Black spots anomalously situated in nonhomeland South Africa were redefined, and people had to move to enable the political jigsaw to fit together (614,000 people).

Betterment planning sought to combat erosion and improve agriculture in the homelands through what planners saw as a more rational land-use plan. Settlements were divided internally into separate arable, grazing, and residential areas, with people having to move into newly established residential areas, particularly from the 1950s through the 1970s. Betterment planning has been by far the largest single cause of resettlement in South Africa, accounting for the displacement of at least 3 million people. Agricultural settlement schemes were established with the intention of creating jobs and promoting commercial agriculture for both white (e.g., the Vaalharts Irrigation Scheme) and black farmers (e.g., the Mooifontein maize project in the homeland of Bophuthatswana). These schemes, however, did not involve the compulsion to move integral to the definition of resettlement.

Finally, not to be discounted as a cause of resettlement is the flight from violence. The civil war in Mozambique led to a considerable number of people seeking safety in neighboring countries, including South Africa, where a number of Mozambican refugees have settled permanently. Violence in some black townships and rural areas in South Africa similarly led to sporadic flight from these areas, whether on a temporary or more permanent basis.

At least 7 million people thus felt the impact of resettlement during the apartheid era—largely for political reasons. They were overwhelmingly people other than those legally defined as white.

SPATIAL CHANGE AND SOCIOECONOMIC DISRUPTION ARISING OUT OF RESETTLEMENT

Involuntary resettlement is an almost universally disruptive and stress-inducing process that involves both geographical and social displacement. Relationships predicated on kinship or territorial ties are disrupted as associates are separated from one another in new residential patterns; people's access to and distance from basic resources such as arable and grazing land, water, and wood, are changed, often for the worse. People may either lose their jobs as a result of the move, or have to travel much further to work, and find themselves further from basic social services. Involuntary resettlement thus places people at risk of impoverishment.

The greater the degree of spatial change, the greater the disruption and the necessary adjustment. While people undergoing resettlement in South Africa almost always found themselves in denser and more socially diverse settlements than before, the scale of socio-spatial change varied according to the type of settlement situation. Betterment-planning areas usually experienced the least such change, for in such cases people were moved within their own settlement areas (usually a move of not more than a mile or two). In many cases people found themselves with less arable land—in some cases, even no land—as planners sought to implement what they saw as a more rational land-use plan, re-zoning land they regarded as unsuitable for cultivation.

A related kind of resettlement involved the removal of black communities from their home areas to *trust* land, acquired by the state from white farmers for black occupation under the 1936 Native Trust and Land Act. These trust areas (over which the state retained ownership) were often considerable distances from the home areas and involved a much greater degree of change and disruption. A number of these areas subsequently became unofficial receiving areas for people moved out of non-homeland areas for various reasons, and therefore became overcrowded.

Group Areas removals and urban relocation involved greater distances than betterment resettlement, while yet allowing some—but by no means all—people to be close enough to their former homes to keep contact with their former associates and to keep their jobs. While state housing was provided for many of these relocatees, people found themselves having to spend more on accommodation, on travel to work, and on goods at local shops, because they lived farther from urban shopping areas. Urban relocation to homeland towns usually involved greater distances and socioeconomic disruption than Group Areas removals, as well as placing people under often unpopular homeland administrative systems.

The greatest spatial change and suffering was experienced by those people moved to closer settlements in the homelands. They either were moved to these areas or had to move there to find a place to stay as they were turned off of or left white-owned farms, black spots, or urban areas. Closer settlements usually arose in a fairly ad hoc fashion with minimal planning and service provision, and incomers generally had to construct their own accommodation. The homeland of Qwaqwa provides the most extreme case of a closer settlement. Between 1969 and the mid-1980s, the population of this homeland of 298 square miles increased from roughly twenty-four thousand inhabitants to nearly half a million, as people streamed in from the rest of South Africa, whether officially designated as citizens of this southern Sotho apartheid homeland or not. In the vast majority of cases, obtaining any arable land was simply out of the question under such severe population density. Many people moved as separate families or even individuals, as circumstances permitted or dictated. Kin and colleagues accordingly were scattered widely. With minimal if any socioeconomic continuity, people had to start forging new relationships in conditions of severe overcrowding and impoverishment—often leading to conflict within, and restructuring of, primary social units.

RESETTLEMENT AS NECESSARY TO SET RIGHT THE INJUSTICES OF APARTHEID

Setting right the injustices of the past in a post-apartheid society, by putting dispossessed people of color back on the land, will, paradoxically, require further resettlement. To argue that such resettlement will necessarily result in people being economically and socially better off, simply because

they will be receiving land, and because the cause is now just, and resettlement in principle voluntary, may, however, be dangerously naïve.

The complexities involved when trying to counteract the fundamental upheaval caused by involuntary resettlement in combination with seeking to improve people's conditions, are frequently too much for both officials and local communities to handle. As a result, many resettlement projects are poorly planned, coordinated, implemented, and monitored, resulting in inadequate consultation, financing, and provision of land, resources, and services—often leaving people impoverished, disrupted, and conflicted. Many of these problems would not vanish merely because of the demise of apartheid.

TYPES OF RURAL RESETTLEMENT IN POST-APARTHEID SOUTH AFRICA

Most post-apartheid resettlement (as opposed to individual families moving into newly built housing developments) has taken place in the rural areas, in the following ways:

- Land restitution. Where people were turned off their land by racially discriminatory legislation, the state seeks to restore them to their land, or where this is not feasible, to compensate them financially.

- Land redistribution. Land grants have been provided to enable families, initially below a certain income level, to acquire land. People were encouraged to pool their grants and move onto farms in groups. Recent policy initiatives have emphasized distributing land to fewer people, targeting emerging commercial farmers.

- Reversing betterment planning. In some places, people have begun moving out of centralized residential areas, back to their original, pre-betterment sites.

- Land invasion. In some situations, people have moved onto unoccupied, state-owned land. The state has not expelled them, providing emergency services, with their de facto presence eventually becoming acknowledged.

- In addition to the above situations, where land is being restored or reclaimed, forced (and now illegal) evictions from commercial farms and conservation areas continue to occur, much as in apartheid times.

Some 88 percent of the 48,825 restitution claims settled by March 2004 relate to urban claims. They were settled by financial compensation, and will thus not involve any resettlement. In one of the highest profile cases of the reversal of apartheid urban resettlement, families expelled from District Six in Cape Town were in 2005 granted title deeds to newly constructed properties in their former area, and have started the process of going home.

PROBLEMS CONFRONTING RESETTLED COMMUNITIES IN POST-APARTHEID SOUTH AFRICA

But "going home" is not without its problems. Group resettlement, even when voluntary, constitutes an upheaval, calling for the social and economic (re)constitution of what may turn out to be new communities, more or less from scratch. In South Africa, both officials and resettling people are in a state of initial adaptation. Many officials who have to implement resettlement are negotiating a young bureaucracy, with its new set of power relations, conventions, and procedures—amid significant shortages of resources and experience. The resettled community has to negotiate new local level institutions and procedures, both among its own members, and in relation to officialdom. This is particularly difficult, as with the restitution case of Riemvasmaak in the Northern Cape Province, where the inhabitants of the original settlement, who had been ethnically diverse, had been resettled to three different destinations. Coming home saw these divisions being self-maintained, which seriously weakened effective community leadership, and consequently, the ability to negotiate development initiatives with outsiders.

Resettled communities need to get back on their economic feet. For this, an integrated livelihood strategy, incorporating agriculture as well as other rural and non-rural livelihoods, is necessary. In a number of cases, the land has lain idle because of its new occupants being unable to obtain the necessary equipment, services, advice, or credit. There have been, however, promising cases of creative sharecropping, whereby neighboring white farmers provide expertise and equipment to help new land reform groups start up, in exchange for a portion of

their crop. While initial assistance and training is necessary to get people skilled, productive, and integrated into their regional economic setting, it is crucial that such support is managed and weaned so as not to generate dependency.

Land reform has moved at a relatively slow pace during the first decade of South Africa's democracy—in response to a largely urban driven political agenda, a switch from a poverty-oriented to a more commercial agriculture focus in the land reform program, and an adherence to a willing buyer-willing seller approach to land exchange. With signs at the 2005 Land Summit, and in 2006, that government may be moving away from a purely voluntary, market-driven approach to land exchange, land expropriation may become a reality. The pace of the movement of land from white to other hands—and with it, the frequency of restorative resettlement—may thus increase. But, as the scale of resettlement increases, so will the social and economic challenges that go with it.

See also **Agriculture; Apartheid; Economic History; Gender; Production Strategies; Refugees.**

BIBLIOGRAPHY

Cernea, Michael. "Risks, Safeguards and Reconstruction: A Model for Population Displacement and Resettlement." In *Risks and Reconstruction: Experiences of Resettlers and Refugees*, ed. Michael M. Cernea and Christopher McDowell. Washington, DC: The World Bank, 2000.

De Wet, Chris. "Moving Away from Apartheid: Recent Rural Resettlement in South Africa." In *Development: Theory, Policy and Practice*, ed. Jan Coetzee, Johann Graaff, Fred Hendricks, and Geoffrey Wood. Cape Town: Oxford University Press, 2001.

Hall, Ruth; Peter Jacobs; and Edward Lahiff. *Final Report. Evaluating Land and Agrarian Reform in South Africa*. Cape Town: Program for Land and Agrarian Studies, University of the Western Cape, 2003.

James, Deborah. *The Road from Doornkop*. Johannesburg: South African Institute of Race Relations, 1984.

Lund, Francie. *Lessons from Riemvasmaak for Land Reform Policies and Programs in South Africa*, Vol. 2: *Background Study*. Cape Town: Program for Land and Agrarian Studies, University of the Western Cape, 1998.

Niehaus, Izak. "Relocation into Phuthadijhaba and Tseki: A Comparative Study of Planned and Unplanned Removals." *African Studies* 48, no 2 (1989): 157–181.

Platzky, Laurine, and Cherryl Walker. *The Surplus People: Forced Removals in South Africa*. Johannesburg: Ravan Press, 1985.

Sharp, John. "Relocation and the Problem of Survival in Qwaqwa." *Social Dynamics* 8, no 2 (1982): 11–29.

Western, John. *Outcast Cape Town*. Minneapolis: University of Minnesota Press, 1981.

CHRIS DE WET

WESTERN AFRICA

As an important category for social science and historical research, peasants has lost significance especially among those supporting political and economic transformation in Africa in general and West Africa in particular. With the decline in Marxist analyses of rural questions, debates about the proper definitions and conceptualizations of peasants and peasantries have faded. There seems to be a general use of the term "peasant," meaning rural populations engaged in some forms of food production. However, there continues to be a series of debates as to their place and contributions to economic development. The end of the twentieth century has seen earlier generalizations about land abundance in West Africa give way to an increasing focus upon land scarcity, land competition, rural productive intensification, and labor migration.

WEST AFRICAN PEASANTS AND CONTEMPORARY HISTORY

There has been scholarly discussion as to the origin, form, and trajectories of peasantries, especially in western Africa where the characteristic patterns of centralized land holding did not exist on a broad scale. In general, West Africa's rural populations have been seen to suffer from the new neoliberal world order. This is very different from the hopes and aspirations of what had been West African socialism first under the leadership of Kwame Nkrumah, Ahmed Sékou Touré, and Modibo Keita, and then under the leadership of Amílcar Cabral. There had been a broad hope with the analysis of Amílcar Cabral, the leader of the African Independence Party of Guine and the Cape Verde Islands (PAIGC) in Guinea-Bissau, who articulated how African peasantries could play a progressive, nontribal and nonethnic political role following independence. Followers of the revolutionary Franz Fanon similarly hoped that the burgeoning neocolonial tendencies of the 1960s could be arrested using alternative political models. Guinea (Conakry) during the mid-1960s attempted to emulate the Chinese communist model while carrying out an imitation cultural revolution.

The emphasis upon peasantries and their potential for revolution never captured its former place with the end of the Indochina War, the death of Chinese Communist leader Mao Zedong, and China's shift to capitalism. Instead of soldiers leading new forms of liberation, being a soldier has led to an alternative to rural employment with greatly enhanced possibilities of enrichment. Robert Buijtenhuijs has termed these predatory wars. "Although involving peasants, and in cases such as Liberia or Somalia (where child soldiers are numerous) the sons and daughters of peasants, their motivations are not those of peasants fighting for their livelihoods or for control of land. In fact, as the rebellion unfolds, peasants' interests are progressively undermined" (2000, 115). Notions of progressive politics in the third world based upon local people and authentic leadership have given way to rethinking globalization or efforts to reexamine the state and possibilities for diminishing or ending poverty. Whether or not ideas about peasants will continue to be central in this context is highly problematic.

PEASANTS AND LAND

In the contemporary period, land has increased economic, social, and political value due to its growing scarcity and due to economic instability. There is a growing conflict, often violent, in which farmers are opposed to other farmers, national governments are claiming land for the state in opposition to local people, herders and farmers argue over rights for cattle to pass through cultivated areas, whereas migrants see their rights whittled away by local people who wish to reassert control over this resource. All too often the conflicts are framed in extreme ethnic terms. Land has become a key contested resource despite increased economic diversification. Claims to land usually take the following forms:

1. Customary claims have usually been based on first settlement and clearance of bush land, converting it into farmland and establishing some kind of covenant with the spirits of the area through regular offerings and sacrifices.

2. Claims asserted through conquest, either native kingdoms or through colonial conquest.

3. Claims based upon long-term use. These claims can be highly contested depending in part the type of land tenure system at work. In general, women do not establish ownership on the basis of their use.

4. Government programs, development projects, titling projects have allocated land generally favoring those who are powerful or are well-networked to those in power.

Given the importance of herders and herding in West Africa it has been difficult for them to establish long-term rights to the land that they have used for decades if not centuries. And of course in drought periods they can move extraordinarily long distances with their herds disrupting more settled peoples.

ENVIRONMENT AND DEVELOPMENT

Understanding West African peasants, farmers, and herders has led to a series of interrelated debates on strategies for development, understanding new forms of conflict and warfare, and environmental conservation and degradation. These are quite different from earlier debates about the possibilities of profound social transformations. The signal postindependence event responsible for shifting debates and discussions about West Africa was the Sahelian drought and famine from 1968 through 1974. In attempting to formulate first emergency and then longer term responses to this famine, Western nation policy makers attributed the famine to an inexorable desertification hastened by the farming and herding practices of West Africa's dryland populations.

It didn't take long for a new literature to emerge situating the drought and famine in colonial strategies, in pushing cash crop cultivation northward, in restricting pastoral movements leading to overgrazing and in general to the neglect of West Africa's arid and semiarid lands. These lands were framed as backward, stagnant, and inflexible in comparison to the more southerly populations upon whom development aspirations were placed. This continued the long historical patterns of shifting power, wealth, and influence toward the coasts and away from the interior.

Development discourses have proliferated and range from privileging local knowledge and responses to environment or more conventionally the requirement for external assistance with clear targets. Lost sight of in such broad considerations is precisely how under varying conditions different groups of people at different scales respond, adapt, change to the conditions of which they are partly responsible and those outside their control. Thus in the complex interplay between multilateral and bilateral donor institutions, the United Nations and its multiple parts, national political elites, opposition parties, and a whole host of secular and religious nongovernmental organizations ignore how and why rural populations change.

The signature programs resulting from this period were the Senegal River Development projects, a parallel project for the Gambia River, increased use of the Niger River for irrigation and greater interstate cooperation for economic and social development. The general vision of state-driven development has given way to decentralization, privatization of state agencies, greater participation by beneficiaries, or the cancellation of large state projects (for example the two dams on the Gambia River). The creation of high value newly irrigated lands on the Senegal River led to intense conflict over rights of access between minority and majority populations in Mauritania. Poorer peasants suffered disproportionately in the conflicts. In the upper Senegal River Basin peasant associations fought a long and ultimately successful series of battles to have their associations benefit from development planning and not be incorporated into large-scale, state-dominated plans All too often those who can benefit from increased agricultural intensification are not the poorest or most vulnerable.

PEASANT LABOR

The almost universal application of a series of structural adjustment programs sponsored by the World Bank and International Monetary Fund (IMF) and supported by a range of bilateral donors has led to increased blurring of the more stable categories of rural western Africa: rural/urban, elder/youth, male/female, cash crops/food crops, agriculture/trade, and wage labor/family labor. Rural and/or peasant West Africans have had to diversify into nonagricultural activities due to changing national and local economies. As monetary income remains essential for access to education, health care, travel, religious ceremonies and even agriculture most rural producers seek wage labor or trade opportunities locally, regionally, nationally and internationally.

Thus the migration flows long documented in the West African literature continue. However, West African peasant families continue to be disadvantaged in the global context of labor flows due to relatively weak education and training. Agriculture often requires nonagricultural income to support the purchase of seeds, fertilizer, pesticides, ox and plow, and even tractors and requires successful off-farm employment. The global context for peasant labor has changed. Nonetheless West African peasant farmers continue to engage in commercial crop production including cocoa, groundnuts, coffee for international markets and vegetables, kola nuts, bananas, pineapples and other fruits and grains including rice, maize and millet for regional and national markets. The maintenance of peasant labor no longer is of particular strategic utility. African peasant labor, skilled in production of limited crops, has become noncompetitive in the production of food or suffers from first world subsidies for export crops (cotton, rice) or from international competition (coffee, cocoa, groundnuts). Indeed, illegal activity is often seen as necessary to complement other livelihood strategies.

In the context of changing environmental conditions, shifting demands of a world market, and pressures to force African farmers to produce for export, peasants have resisted, acquiesced, and adopted to these circumstances. However, it is difficult to think of peasants as a single group or category, the authentic local struggling against brutal external forces. Peasants are differentiated by wealth, by gender, by generation, by positionality with respect to the market and by religion. They are also characterized by ingenuity, experimentation, and adaptability and change in their agricultural systems. The wealthier tend to diversify in the form of nonfarm business activities including trade, transport, shop keeping, brick making, etc. while the poor seek wage work. In turn, women's land rights and access opportunities become more vulnerable.

Therefore, the incorporation and significance of peasant agency in research and development strategies have been difficult. From the standpoint of, for example, the World Bank or from national governments, peasants are to follow the best economic policies promoted by both or either for production and marketing. In place of single or simple solutions, complexity has become commonplace. The notion of the unitary peasant household has taken a severe beating in the hands of contemporary feminist thinkers. Development projects and strategies have had negative or hidden consequences for women. Men own or control most land and other resources while women do much of the work, especially in the production and processing of food crops. And even the latter generalization does not hold for large numbers of Hausa-speakers in Niger and Nigeria who practice wife-seclusion, which prevents women from direct participation in agriculture. In Côte d'Ivoire with cotton prices falling in 1985–1986, male cotton farmers pressured their wives to shift labor from food crops to cotton. Generational conflicts are, like gender, at the heart of households and render difficult any single reading of household interests.

THE FUTURE OF WEST AFRICAN PEASANTS?

Aside from ongoing poverty, one of the critical issues for peasants will be land tenure. Land will continue to constitute a key political, social, and cultural asset, conferring great power and authority upon those who control access to this resource. Businesspeople, customary chiefs, and politicians are keen to accumulate and invest in land, as a source of profit for current and future generations, as well as an asset of value in cementing political alliances. The land issue is open to considerable political manipulation. In Côte d'Ivoire, for example, the large number of migrants from neighboring countries seeking land to farm has generated heated debate regarding the issue of who can claim Ivorian nationality and associated land ownership rights. The expulsion of Burkinaabe from Côte d'Ivoire combined with increased cotton cultivation and use of animal traction in the South West has led to large amounts of monetarised land transactions. In general, competition over land has intensified regional, national, and international conflicts.

Overall in West Africa, less than 5 percent of land is formally titled, being concentrated in cities and project areas. The vast majority of land is subject to a variety of local administrative systems, often an amalgam of local, customary and state regulation, but with considerable room for confusion and contradiction between competing claims, leading to negotiation, dispute, land grabbing, and conflict. Typically, peasants in western Africa assert their right to use land, not to own it. Nonetheless, land is lent, rented, occasionally pawned, and, increasingly, sold. Land sales are relatively infrequent in rural areas where land quality is poor, where the population density is low, or where there is no ready access to markets. By contrast, a series of factors have contributed to an increased but an uneven pace of land sales in the savanna areas. Where there are competing demands for land, particularly in growing peri-urban areas and other areas having better soil for agriculture, proximity to water for irrigation, and greater access to markets, land sale become more likely. Processes of commoditization and intensification are mixed. They increase productivity but they hasten processes of enclosures restricting resources to the better off. Given the high percentage of rural populations that remain vulnerable to hunger and famine continued attention ought to be given to those populations.

Large numbers of West African peasants, like most rural dwellers, engage in efforts to maintain diverse and changing livelihood portfolios including highly risky efforts to traverse the Atlantic to Europe. West African rural populations are more closely integrated into the global economy but not on conditions of their choosing.

See also **Cabral, Amílar Lopes; Ecosystems; Gender; International Monetary Fund; Labor; Nkrumah, Francis Nwia Kofi; Production Strategies; Touré, Sékou; United Nations; World Bank.**

BIBLIOGRAPHY

Adams, Adrian, and J. Sow. *A Claim to Land by the River: A Household in Senegal, 1720–1994.* New York: Oxford University Press, 1996.

Barker, Jonathan. *Rural Communities Under Stress: Peasant Farmers and the State in Africa.* Cambridge, U.K.: Cambridge University Press, 1989.

Bassett, Thomas J. *The Peasant Cotton Revolution in West Africa: Cote d'Ivoire, 1880–1995.* Cambridge, U.K.: Cambridge University Press, 2001.

Bernstein, Henry. "African Peasantries: A Theoretical Framework." *Journal of Peasant Studies* 6, no. 4 (1979): 421–443.

Bryceson, Deborah Fahy. "Peasant Theories and Smallholder Policies: Past and Present." In *Disappearing Peasantries? Rural Labour in Africa, Asia and Latin America,* ed.

Deborah Bryceson, Cristobal Kay, and Jos Mooij. London: Intermediate Technology Publications, 2000.

Buijtenhuijs, Robert. "Peasant Wars in Africa: Gone with the Wind?" In *Disappearing Peasantries? Rural Labour in Africa, Asia and Latin America,* ed. Deborah Bryceson, Cristobal Kay, and Jos Mooij. London: Intermediate Technology Publications, 2000.

Derman, William. *Peasants, Serfs and Socialists: A Former Serf Village in the Republic of Guinea.* Berkeley: University of California Press, 1973.

Hyden, Goren. *Beyond Ujamaa in Tanzania: Underdevelopment and an Uncaptured Peasantry.* London: Heinemann, 1980.

Klein, Martin, ed. *Peasants in Africa: Historical and Contemporary Perspectives.* Beverly Hills, CA: Sage, 1980.

Isaacman, Allan. "Peasants and Rural Social Protest in Africa." In *Confronting Historical Paradigms: Peasant Labor and the Capitalist World System in Africa and Latin America,* ed. Fred Cooper et al. Madison: University of Wisconsin Press, 1993.

Mortimore, Michael. *Roots in the African Dust: Sustaining the Drylands.* Cambridge, U.K.: Cambridge University Press, 1998.

Schoeder, Richard. *Shady Practices: Agroforestry and Gender Politics in the Gambia.* Berkeley: University of California Press, 2000.

Toulmin, Camilla. *Negotiating Access to Land in West Africa: Who Is Losing Out?* In *Citizenship, Identity and Conflicts over Land and Water in Contemporary Africa,* ed. Bill Derman, Rie Odgaard, and Espen Sjaastad. London: James Currey, 2007.

Watts, Michael. *Silent Violence: Food, Famine and the Peasantry in Northern Nigeria.* Berkeley: University of California Press, 1983.

BILL DERMAN

PENTECOSTAL CHURCHES. *See* Christianity: African Instituted Churches.

PEREIRA, ARISTIDES MARIA

(1924–). Aristides Maria Pereira was president of Cape Verde. Born in Boa Vista, in the Cape Verde archipelago, of Roman Catholic parents, Pereira completed his secondary education in Santiago, Cape Verde, before joining a Portuguese trading company. In 1956 he became one of the six founding members of the Partido Africano de Independência

Aristides Maria Pereira (1924–). Although he promised to lead Cape Verde with democratic and socialist values, after his election as president, Pereira (right) allied with China and Libya. He put in place economic plans to help peasants, but the country remained hard hit by poverty. AP IMAGES

da Guiné e Cabo Verde (PAIGC), the anticolonial movement launched clandestinely by Amílcar Cabral.

When armed resistance finally proved necessary to the movement's survival as well as to its eventual success, Pereira played a leading role in the guerrilla war that led to independence for Guinea-Bissau in 1974, and for Cape Verde a year later. He then returned to Cape Verde and was elected president of the new republic. An architect of his country's modernization and democratization, he also acted as a skilled diplomat on the continental scene. In 1990 Pereira presided over the introduction of a multiparty system in Cape Verde. When he and his party were voted out of office in legislative elections in 1991, Pereira and his colleagues accepted this verdict without complaint, seeing their defeat as a logical development of the democratic principles for which they had fought, and for which many of them had risked or lost their lives.

See also **Cabral, Amílcar Lopes; Cape Verde: History and Politics.**

BIBLIOGRAPHY

Davidson, Basil. *The Fortunate Isles: A Study in African Transformation.* London: Hutchinson, 1989.

BASIL DAVIDSON

PERRY, RUTH SANDO (1939–). Ruth Sando Perry was born in Grand Cape Mount County in 1939 on Liberia's northwest coast. Although from a Muslim family (her father held the title of AlHaji), she was educated at St. Theresa Convent High School and received a degree in education from the University of Liberia. She married McDonald Perry, a judge and legislator, and had seven children, but was left a widow at a comparatively young age. She worked as a teacher and in banking, and was elected senator from Grand Cape Mount County during the administration of President Samuel K. Doe (1986–1990). When the Liberian civil conflict began to engulf the country in the early 1990s, Perry was one of the organizers of the women's peace movement, active in organizations such as the Liberian Women's Initiative (LWI) and the Mano River Union Women for Peace Network (MARWOPNET), both of which were instrumental in bringing the warring factions to the peace table. At the Abuja II conference in 1996, she was elected chairperson of the six-member Council of State. Her formidable charge was to oversee the Economic Community of West African States (ECOWAS) plan for disarmament, demobilization of armed combatants, and elections, in one year. She was the first woman to deliver a keynote address to the Summit of African Heads of State in Harare in July of 1997. Perry continues to work as an advocate for Liberian women and girls and has founded several nongovernmental organizations (NGOs).

See also **Economic Community of West African States (ECOWAS); Nongovernmental Organizations; Women: Widows.**

BIBLIOGRAPHY

African Women and Peace Support Group. *Liberian Women Peacemakers: Fighting for the Right to be Seen, Heard and Counted.* Trenton, NJ: Africa World Press, 2004.

MARY H. MORAN

PERSON, CONCEPTS OF. This entry considers the African cultural construction of personhood, comparing it with European versions of the concept. There are vast differences between African cultures across space and time, but here "African" refers to features that many, if not most, African cultures have in common, whether on the African continent or throughout the African diaspora. Similarly, "European" refers to societies sharing a European language and culture, whether in Europe or not, including many people on the North American continent. Comparisons such as those attempted in this essay are about cultural forms and social actions. People can live in more than one culture at one and the same time and may experience no difficulty "being African" and "European," just as many people can speak two or more different languages.

While the "category of the person" is probably a universal feature of human culture, its form and conception are constructed in a variety of culturally specific ways. These differences that can be attributed to the ways in which ideology, history, and social organization affect the interpretations people make of their experience of self and other. In the disciplines of philosophy and anthropology the term "personhood" is used as a shorthand for describing and interpreting different solutions to a universal existential dilemma: the problem of reconciling the lived experience of changing physical bodies and sets of discordant experiences with the sense that there are unifying themes mediated through a single entity, which one calls a person. Philosophers tend to seek justifications for choosing among different concepts of personhood, while anthropologists have pioneered the investigation of different vernacular concepts of the person, located across time and space. Both disciplines attempt to understand the underlying assumption or grounds that enable people to say the movement of a body through time and space and the accumulation of a set of experiences denote a single person, or exhibit a definable personhood, the characteristic or quality of being a person.

All peoples have evolved theories as well as commonsense understandings of the person that provide guides to classifying different people and categorizing the experience of self and other. These theories explain why people act the way they do, interpret their experiences, and predict their actions and fates. The terms these theories use are derived from religious and moral concepts or from cosmology. They encode ideas about physical and social growth and development, motivation and personality, and the consequences of action.

CONTRASTS BETWEEN AFRICAN AND EUROPEAN CONCEPTS OF PERSONHOOD

In most, if not all cultures, vernacular concepts of the person use the body as a model for constructing the person. Ideas about the person entail descriptions of the capacities and powers that persons have to carry out their actions and locate these powers and capacities in the image of the body. Hence it is not surprising to find similarities between the African and European concepts of personhood. For comparative purposes, however, the differences count far more than the shared ideas and attitudes. There are at least four significant differences between the African models of the person, such as the Iteso have, and European models of personhood.

First, in the traditions of European societies dualistic models using categories such as body and soul (in religion) or the body and mind (in psychology and philosophy) define the basic terms of a theory about the person that makes a radical distinction between physical capacities and powers on the one hand and mental and moral capacities and powers on the other hand. In many African cultures mental and moral capacities and powers are located in the body rather than opposed to the body. Among the Iteso people of Kenya and Uganda, for example, the heart, *etau*, is the seat of emotions, while the head, *akou*, is the seat of experience. The head guides the heart, which provides vitality and energy to the body. At first sight the Iteso model appears very similar to European commonsense discourse about the person, in which the heart is often made equivalent to the soul or is the seat of emotions, and the mind is located in the activities of the brain, operating through the senses found primarily in the head.

Many African cosmologies of the person also include the concept of the double, an entity that defies categorization as either spiritual or corporeal. In West African Akan cosmology the double seems to have all the attributes of the body but moves within the world of the dead. Witches attack and eat the double of others, resulting in the illness and death of the corporeal body. The double seems to be the source of life force and power in the real world, and those who are successful are said to have a heavy double (even as their physical body tends to expand to reflect their success).

The European model tends to be more metaphorical; it uses bodily experience as a metaphor for certain experiences, such as emotions, which are not thought of as being actually embodied, rather than define specific powers as an activity of the embodied person, as the Iteso model does. This is an instance that shows how the dualistic emphasis of European culture and cosmology shapes the use of the body as a model for experiencing the world, in contrast to more monistic African models.

Second, in the European view each person is customarily defined as separate from other persons. Hence, the powers and functions of the person are restricted to the single bounded individual. People are defined by their ability to influence and affect others, rather than by the set of social relationships in which they take part. In contrast, among the Iteso people and many other peoples throughout Africa and the world, the body is not simply a container of powers and attributes set in a world with other bodies containing their own attributes and powers. For the Iteso the body is at most separated from other persons as the end points of relationships. The Iteso model of personhood recognizes both the effects of one person on another and the relationships that bind one to, or divide one from, another. This model operates in a large portion of Iteso ritual and ceremony, which is devoted to defining, creating, or maintaining relationships, "making paths," among persons.

The model of the person among the Iteso and in other African societies is not dualistic, nor are people seen as isolated from other persons. No people, African or otherwise, has been known to think about the person only in terms of effects or relationships. The contrast drawn here is one of emphasis and degree rather than an absolute one. Yet one may say that the Iteso and most other African concepts of personhood are relational rather than material, and that the boundaries of the body are defined as more permeable and less discrete in Africa than in many European settings. Marilyn Strathern called this relational form of personhood the "dividual," emphasizing the way that personhood can be conceived of as "partible" as opposed to the indivisible European concept of the person. Though she was writing about Melanesia, the concept is widely applicable in many African cultures.

A third difference between European and African concepts of the person such as those held by the Iteso has less to do with body image and personal experience than with ideas about action and agency, the ways in which actions are conceived and the judgments made about the person who undertakes or is affected by an action. One feature that people in both settings share is that they show a lively awareness of differences in character and disposition. The Iteso have a well-developed vocabulary that distinguishes various emotional states and dispositions, although shame plays a greater role than guilt in their attribution of emotions to themselves and others. Yet the reactions to and judgments people make about seemingly similar emotional states and motives can be very different. Early on, American children may learn the moralizing rhyme, "Sticks and stones can break my bones but names will never hurt me." Later they learn that words can indeed hurt, but also that hurtful words can be rescinded and relationships often repaired. For the Iteso the disposition is permanent and not a transient state of affairs. An apparent statement of homicidal intent such as "I could kill you for that" is taken as an unambiguous expressed desire that will be acted upon as soon as circumstances permit. Hence, even though Iteso recognize differences in character and disposition, they do not define emotional states and their relationship to actions as Europeans do. A similar contrast could be drawn between Iteso and European ideas about love and passion. The romantic concept that "being in love" overwhelms other cognitive and emotional capacities is not so prevalent in Iteso thinking about and judgments made of persons.

The fourth and final contrast to be drawn between the African example of the Iteso and European concepts of the person has to do with ideas about fate and destiny. In capitalist society the historical tendency has been increasingly for the fate of the person to be seen as a growth from within rather than an imposition from without. Fate is increasingly seen as a matter of personal responsibility and not the product of external, often extrahuman, even supernatural, forces. This development, termed "disenchantment" by the German sociologist Max Weber, is manifested in the individualism characteristic of social relations under capitalism and is connected to a worldview that is often mechanistic and materialist in a reductionist sense.

By contrast, African concepts of the person are far more often articulated in a worldview that defines individual fate as not only imposed from without, but the responsibility and concern of coalitions activated during circumstances of crisis and focused on resolving the breaches in social relations that are perceived as an underlying cause of the misfortune that it has been the fate of the afflicted person to suffer. In many African cultures, because the spirit world and the physical world are permeable and coexistent, the body is in contact with a host of external spirits and paranormal agents such as witches, healers, ancestors, and genies. In some cases foreign spirits can take control of the body, either after being summoned by a ritual setting or without warning. Individual fate, health, and wealth are often determined by the actions of these external and unpredictable agents, and much effort is placed in appeasing or attempting to direct their actions.

THE STUDY OF PERSONHOOD IN AFRICA

The literature on personhood in Africa owes its inception to Marcel Mauss's seminal essay on the concept of the person, "Une catégorie de l'esprit humaine: La notion de la personne, celle de moi" (1939). In this essay Mauss reminded his audience that etymologically "person" derives from the ancient Latin *persona*, which referred to the mask and role performed by an actor in a play. Mauss argued that the Roman concept of the person evolved into what he termed "la personne morale," which refers to the social definition of the person in terms of its status and roles and rules governing actions and social relationships. Relying on evolutionary assumptions, Mauss postulated distinct stages in the development of concepts of the person, culminating in the evolution of the "moi," the individual self, which he believed to be characteristic of capitalist societies. There is some justification for applying to whole societies the traits that Mauss attributed to each of his theoretical stages. The contrast between the extreme individualism attributed to capitalist society and the more socialized concept of personhood and social relations in Africa and elsewhere seems valid and is reflected in the contrasts between African and European concepts of personhood drawn above. What is

untenable in Mauss, however, is the assumption that non-European or noncapitalist societies had no concept of individual selfhood.

For any society, the distinction between what the anthropologist Meyer Fortes termed "person" and "individual" is critical for understanding the significance of concepts of personhood in everyday life. Looking at it from the objective side, it is the distinctive qualities, capacities, and roles with which society enable the person to be known to be, and also to show oneself to be the person one is supposed to be. Looked at from the subjective side, it is a question of how the individual, as actor, knows oneself to be—or not to be—the person he is expected to be in a given situation and status. The individual is not a passive bearer of personhood; he or she must appropriate to him- or herself the qualities and capacities of personhood, and the norms governing its expression.

The distinction between person and individual transforms Mauss's evolutionary framework into a form of analysis that seeks to understand behavior not as it has evolved from one society to another but in terms of context and social situation, in relationship to everyday life. One of the most significant aspects of the concept of the person addressed by Meyer Fortes's distinction between person and individual is the complex and changing relationship between the socially prescribed and the individually experienced, in which locally based, vernacular interpretations about personhood are developed.

There are no better examples of how Africans distinguish between person and individual than those described in Fortes's essays on personhood among the Tallensi people of Ghana. In "On the Concept of the Person among the Tallensi" (1973), Fortes showed that African solutions to the dilemma of identity as manifested in concepts of the person have epistemological and social dimensions; norms defining the person are generally experienced only by deviations from them or failures to conform to them—just as individuality is experienced only through conformity to or deviation from norms. This is not just a matter of conformity but rather is part of an elaborate cosmology and set of social ideas that Tallensi use to make sense of social and individual experiences. Fortes illustrated this concept in *Oedipus and Job in West*

African Religions (1959), his study of Tallensi interpretations of fate and destiny.

The inability or failure to live up to the most fundamental aspects of Tallensi concepts of the person, such as exhibiting the capacity to bear children, are interpreted as the product of an impersonal agency called *nuor-yin*, which Fortes translated as "evil prenatal destiny." Illnesses are more usually attributed to conflict between living persons or the result of failure to propitiate the ancestors. Other Tallensi spirits are related to healthy growth and development and to the quality of life in community and kinship group. With these elements taken together, Fortes described a very elaborate cultural complex through which people interpret their life in society and their experience of one another, and through which they debate about the ultimate ends of existence and the means through which to achieve them.

The Tallensi view represents the best-described example of a widespread and complex concept of the person that has not only been evoked by anthropologists and historians of religion but is the cultural framework for some of the most important African novels and stories, such as Wole Soyinka's *The Interpreters*, Ben Okri's *The Famished Road*, and Buchi Emecheta's *Joys of Motherhood*. In the first of these examples, a novel of social change, all the main characters represent a different Yoruba power or *orisha*, and through this device Yoruba concepts of the person are connected to contemporary events. The protagonist of Okri's book is a child born of an evil prenatal destiny, and the novel tells the story of his adventures in a world in which he did not choose to live. Emecheta's novel ends with the core of an Igbo (Ibo) person, her *chi*, afflicting her ungrateful children. Each of these novels is a major work of African fiction. They show in different West African social and cultural settings how West African ideas about personhood, agency, and fate are used to organize everyday experiences and provide an armature for products of the imagination ranging from popular culture and forms of religiosity to imaginative literature itself.

Alma Gottlieb's 2004 work has contributed to the literature on personhood by examining the culture of babies among the Beng of Côte d'Ivoire. The Beng believe that babies have returned from the world of the dead, and that many babies' peculiar characteristics are a holdover from that world. Their cries for example, are interpreted by diviners who translate their desires for money and jewelry and other luxuries they were familiar with in the afterlife.

In addition the vast literature on topics such as witchcraft and sorcery and spirit possession are relevant to discussions of African concepts of personhood. Witchcraft and sorcery beliefs are forms of moral discourse, exhibiting African ideas about the nature and use of power and about good and evil. It has often been noted that inversion characterizes the image of the witch, that witches seem to have attributes and practices that invert the most fundamental moral norms of society. This is the domain of culture that Thomas O. Beidelman called the "moral imagination," in which people think through their most profound aspirations and fears. Contemporary literature increasingly focuses on the relationship between witchcraft and modernity. African concepts of personhood are challenged by money economies in which the individual agency and capitalist profit conflicts with the ideology of social distribution of wealth.

Iteso culture can provide an example of spirit possession, where multiple "persons" inhabit the same body. Women assume male attributes and powers in the Iteso cult of possession, and they set up spheres of social life that are exempt from male domination, at least when cult groups meet. Many of the problems that women say are caused by possession, such as the death and illness of children, are precisely those fundamental aspects of Tallensi personhood that Fortes described as the product of an evil prenatal destiny. In cults of possession, male interpretations of these problems are marginalized, as women assume male prerogatives and acquire the symbols of male power. One may say that the shifting definitions of gender and the person displayed in cults of possession are used to constitute epicenters of power, in terms of which women define the causes of their affliction and acquire means to deal with their difficulties in asserting all the attributes of the adult person. Cults of possession are a privileged arena in which the discrepancies between person and individual are articulated.

In contrast, Adeline Masquelier argued that spirit possession is not simply a form of communicative freedom and empowerment. *Bori* practitioners in Niger not only must negotiate their relationship with Muslim and masculine dominated community, but they often struggle with their multiple forms of personhood as the relationship with the spirit itself is often fraught with tension. In some cases the spirit directly criticizes its host during possession, and the possessed must attempt to fulfill the spirit's economic and spiritual demands for sacrifices when the host regains control of his or her body.

The literature on the concept of the person in Africa shows the importance of relating work done within different disciplines and on seemingly different aspects of African life. Academic disciplines tend to fragment deleteriously the ways in which Africans conduct their lives, unless they use integrative points of view embodied in concepts like that of personhood.

See also **Economic Systems; Gender; Literature; Philosophy and the Study of Africa; Religion and Ritual; Soyinka, Wole; Spirit Possession; Witchcraft.**

BIBLIOGRAPHY

Beidelman, Thomas O. *The Moral Imagination in Kaguru Modes of Thought*. Bloomington: Indiana University Press, 1986.

Dieterlen, Germaine, ed. *La notion de personne en Afrique noire, Paris 11–17 octobre 1971*. Paris: Éditions du Centre national de la recherche scientifique, 1973.

Fortes, Meyer. "On the Concept of the Person among the Tallensi." In *La notion de personne en Afrique noire, Paris 11–17 octobre 1971*, ed. Germaine Dieterlen. Paris: Éditions du Centre national de la recherche scientifique, 1973.

Fortes, Meyer. *Religion, Morality, and the Person: Essays on Tallensi Religion*. Cambridge, U.K.: Cambridge University Press, 1987.

Gottlieb, Alma. *The Afterlife Is Where We Come From: The Culture of Infancy in West Africa*. Chicago: University of Chicago Press, 2004.

Jackson, Michael, and Ivan Karp, eds. *Personhood and Agency: The Experience of Self and Other in African Cultures*. Washington, DC: Smithsonian Institution Press, 1990.

Karp, Ivan. "Power and Capacity in Rituals of Possession." In *Personhood and Agency*, ed. Michael Jackson and Ivan Karp. Washington, DC: Smithsonian Institution Press, 1990.

Lambek, Michael, and Andrew Strathern, eds. *Bodies and Persons: Comparative Perspectives from Africa and Melanesia*. Cambridge, U.K.: Cambridge University Press, 1998.

Lienhardt, G. "Self: Public and Private, Some African Representations." In *The Category of the Person: Anthropology, Philosophy, History*, ed. Michael Carrithers, Steven Collins, and Steven Lukes. Cambridge, U.K.: Cambridge University Press, 1985.

Masquelier, Adeline. "From Hostage into Host: Confessions of a Spirit Medium in Niger." *Ethos* 30, no. 1–2 (2002), 49–76.

Mauss, Marcel. "Une catégorie de l'esprit humaine: La notion de la personne, celle de moi." *Journal of the Royal Anthropological Institute* 68 (1939): 263–282.

Moore, Henrietta, and Todd Sanders. *Magical Interpretations, Material Realities: Modernity, Witchcraft, and the Occult in Africa*. London and New York: Routledge, 2001.

Riesman, P. "The Person and the Life Cycle in African Social Life and Thought." *African Studies Review* 29, no. 2 (1986): 71–198.

Strathern, Marilyn. *The Gender of the Gift*. Berkeley: University of California Press, 1988.

Turner, Victor Witter. *The Drums of Affliction: A Study of Religious Processes among the Ndembu of Zambia*. Oxford and London: International African Institute, 1968.

IVAN KARP
REVISED BY SASHA NEWELL

PHILIP, JOHN (1775–1851). John Philip, a Scottish missionary who campaigned for the rights of the indigenous people of southern Africa, was born in Kirkcaldy, Fife. He studied at Hoxton Theological College and ministered in Aberdeen from 1804 to 1818. After being appointed a director of the London Missionary Society (LMS) he arrived in Cape Town to investigate LMS affairs in 1819 and became superintendent of missions in 1820.

Convinced that the indigenous population was oppressed by settlers, Philip collected evidence that supported his views while travelling extensively between 1820 and 1826. After unsuccessfully lobbying the colonial government, he left for England in 1826 to muster support for the civil rights of the Khoikhoi. He solicited the help of the antislavery movement, and his *Researches in South Africa* was published in 1828. This prompted the passage in 1829 of a parliamentary measure to "effectively secure to all the natives of South Africa, the same freedom and protection as are enjoyed by other free people of that Colony whether English or Dutch." Philip returned to Cape Town to increased enmity from settlers and the colonial government in 1829.

Philip believed that the Griqua polity beyond the Cape Colony frontier could, with LMS help, become a model for other indigenous groups. He visited mission stations within and beyond the colony between 1832 and 1833 and vigorously promoted his plan for the establishment of independent states east and north of the colony from 1838. After a war in 1846 that saw Griqua lands annexed, Philip withdrew from public affairs and retired.

In a racially contested order Philip was demonized after his death and came to be portrayed as a meddling and ignorant outsider to further the aims of colonial nationalists, and segregationist and apartheid ideologues. Historians have molded and remolded Philip's image for more than a century, and, although still contested, it can be said that his *Researches* was a pioneering liberal interpretation of colonial race relations.

See also **Apartheid; Cape Town; Colonialism and Imperialism.**

BIBLIOGRAPHY

Bank, Andrew. "The Great Debate and the Origins of South African Historiography." *Journal of African History* 38, no. 2 (1997): 261–281.

Bank, Andrew. "The Politics of Mythology: The Genealogy of the Philip Myth." *Journal of Southern African Studies* 25, no. 3 (September 1999): 461–477.

Gailey, Harry A. "John Philip's Role in Hottentot Emancipation." *Journal of African History* 3, no. 3 (1962): 419–433.

MacMillan, William Miller. *Bantu, Boer and Briton: The Making of the South African Native Problem.* London: Faber and Faber, 1929.

Philip, John. *Researches in South Africa: Illustrating the Civil, Moral and Religious Condition of the Native Tribes.* London: James Duncan, 1828.

Ross, Robert. *Adam Kok's Griquas: A Study in the Development of Stratification in South Africa.* Cambridge, U.K.: Cambridge University Press, 1976.

JIMMY PIETERSE

PHILOSOPHY. The African mind has been deeply engaged over the ages with fundamental questions about the world and human experience. This is evident from the rich resources of speculative thought in African oral traditions and, in places, from long-standing written records of philosophical reflection. This entry is mostly concerned with traditional modes of thought.

These modes of thought are philosophical in the sense that they attempt answers to questions displaying the high abstractness and generality characteristic of philosophy. For example, many of the oral traditions offer ideas on questions of the following kinds: What is the explanation of the order in the cosmos? What is the nature of human personality? What, from an ontological perspective, is the significance of death for the human species? Are human beings subject to an overarching destiny and how does such an idea stand with moral responsibility? What is the criterion of goodness for an individual as well as a community? And what is the role of extra-human beings, such as the Supreme Being and the ancestors, in foundation of morality and its enforcement? Detailed generalizations about the doctrines entertained by Africans about these issues must await particularistic philosophical studies of the multifarious peoples of Africa.

COSMOLOGY AND ONTOLOGY

Certain articles of belief, however, would appear to be almost universal on the continent. Thus, there is nearly everywhere belief in a hierarchy of existents, at the top of which is a Supreme Being or power postulated to account for the orderliness of phenomena. Next, below the Supreme Being, are a variety of extra-human beings of diverse powers and tendencies that can be tapped by humans, the next in the hierarchy, if they know how. Below the human species come, in a descending order, the world of the lower animals and plants and the realm of inanimate reality. The universality of this picture of the world is limited only by rare cases, such as the system of the Central Luo, who, according to Ugandan poet, scholar, and philosopher Okot p'Bitek, do not postulate a Supreme Being at all. The rest of the scheme, however, remains in place even in that case.

What modes of conceptualization does this worldview evince? The question calls for some prior conceptual unraveling. In what sense, for example, is the generally postulated Supreme Being supposed to account for the cosmos or, more strictly, for the order therein? It should be noted that what strikes the African mind is the order of the cosmos, not its sheer existence. This hypothesis is in close harmony with the radically empirical bent of African cosmological thinking.

In terms of detail, African cosmologies are heterogeneous, though in terms of diction they are almost always mythopoeic. The Akans of Ghana are somewhat of an exception to this remark, for their cosmology is given expression in, to adapt an apt phrase of the Ghanaian philosopher and public man, J. B. Danquah, "*drum stanzas*" astringent in their verbal economy. Drum stanzas are versified aphorisms rendered on "talking drums." Some of the most profound metaphysical ideas of the Akan are contained in drum "texts" of this kind, famous for their compressed expression.

To take an example: The Creator created things. What did he create? He created Order, Knowledge, and Death (Danquah 1968, 70). More characteristic is the Yoruba account of what happened "in the beginning." In one famous version the present-day town of Ile-Ife was the scene of creation. The Supreme Being sent an agent with a packet of loose earth to go and spread upon the land, which was just a watery marsh, and solidify it for human habitation. Being thirsty on the way, the agent drank liberally of an available palm wine and was overtaken by slumber *re infecta*, whereupon the Supreme Being sent another agent, who promptly accomplished the task.

The intriguing drama of the Yoruba myth is matched by the elaborate symbolism of that of the Dogon: The process of creation takes place in a cosmic egg of two partitions, each containing a pair of twin beings that are "direct emanations of God" (Griaule and Dietelen 1954). Each twin being contains both male and female principles, symbolizing the fundamental role of opposites in all phenomena. As in the Yoruba story, something goes wrong, and the male element in one of the twin beings bursts out prematurely, an aberration that results in the creation of the earth, with manifold imperfections. God then intervenes with some rescue work, which defines various details of the cosmology.

These summaries do not capture the mythopoeic richness of the Yoruba or Dogon accounts of first things, but they do provide a basis for raising a question of philosophical interpretation: Do these accounts espouse a notion of creation out of nothing or one of the introduction of order into a preexistent manifold of indeterminacy? A myth is a metaphor, and its explication ought to reflect its format. By this criterion, the sense in which the appeal to the Supreme Being in the Yoruba myth seems to be intended to account for the world is that in which an architect accounts for the form of a building. Whether empirically warranted or not, such an idea of a cosmic architect is, conceptually, more empirically oriented than that of a creator ex nihilo. The same would seem to be even more evidently true of the Akan and Dogon doctrines.

How universal is this empirical orientation in cosmology in Africa? Unanimity is not at hand. Some authors see a doctrine of ex nihilo creation in some African traditional talk of God. Thus E. E. Evans-Pritchard maintains that the Nuer of southern Sudan characterize creation by the use of language that can only mean that God created the world out of nothing. J. J. Maquet is positive that the Banyarwanda of Rwanda believe that the world was created by God out of nothing. According to him, they are clear on this because they say that before creation there was nothing. And indeed, even of the Akan, Kwame Gyekye has asserted that their doctrine of origins is one of divine creation out of nothing. The possibility that the various peoples of the vast continent of Africa do not share one mode of cosmological reflection cannot, of course, be discounted. But a thorough appraisal of the issue is unlikely without a conceptual analysis of existence in the languages concerned.

In this last connection the observations of Alexis Kagame, the late Rwandan philosopher and linguist, about how the concept of existence is rendered in the languages spoken "throughout the Bantu zone" are of the greatest philosophical interest. According to Kagame, the analogue of the verb "to be" in these languages is expressed by either of two roots: *li* and *ba*. But these words by themselves, unlike the English verb "to be," are incomplete and incapable of expressing the notion of existence in any context. One has to add the adverb of place *ho* for this purpose. So that, ignoring idiomatic niceties, the notion of "exists" is expressed by means of either *liho* or *baho*, meaning "is there," "is at that place." Remarkably, the word *ho* has exactly the same function in the rendition of the concept of existence in Akan. Gyekye (1995, 179) provides lucid testimony to what he calls the "locative implication" of the Akan expression for "exists." To express the notion the Akan say *wo ho*, where *wo* has the same semantic incapacities as the Bantu *li* or *ba*. Existence, therefore, is essentially spatial in both the Bantu and Akan conceptual frameworks. The ontological implications of this concept of existence are many.

For example, if existence is spatial, an existent creator must be in space, and cannot therefore be said to have created space; nor, consequently can he (she, it?) be said to have created the universe out of nothing. Further, the notion of a spiritual substance in the sense of Descartes as a nonextended, nonspatial entity is self-contradictory, on the same hypothesis. Spirits are spoken of in the African worldview only in the sense of entities conceived of in physical imagery but not subject to all the constraints of space and time. They might be called quasi-material or quasi-physical. Ghosts and the ancestors belong to this class. They are all regular parts of the African hierarchy of beings outlined earlier. It does not make sense, therefore, to set up here a distinction between the natural and the supernatural, and call them or any "spirits" supernatural.

HUMAN PERSONALITY

The notion of quasi-materiality just introduced is also important for understanding the ontology of personhood in African philosophy. Given the present state of philosophical data about the various peoples of Africa, it is not judicious to generalize continentally with too much confidence. But from various accounts, the following provisional generalization appears supportable: A person is generally held to consist of two distinct, though not ontologically discontinuous, types of elements. One is material, the other quasi-material. The first is uniformly characterized as the body, but the second is multiple and subtly variegated in description.

The Yoruba, for example, distinguish between the life force, which they call the *èmí*, and the individuality principle, which they call *orí-inú*. The *èmí* is thought of as a life-giving entity that flows directly from God to animate the otherwise inert assemblage of bodily essentials. But life is not just life. For good or ill, there is always a unique direction imparted to life by the combination of character, potentiality, and circumstance. The *orí-inú* is the postulated entity in the makeup of a person that is held to be responsible for this dimension of human life. One may call it, for short, its destiny. With dramatic vividness, the Yoruba traditional myth of human incarnation tells of the *orí* kneeling down before God to receive the apportionment of its destiny before departure to its earthly abode. (In an alternative scenario, the *orí* proposes and God disposes.)

Once brought upon the earth through the intimacy of man and woman, psycho-physiological functions assume a cardinal importance in the life of an individual. And to account for these the Yoruba point to the *opolo*, the brain, as the physiological basis of the power of reasoning and to the *okàn*, the heart, as the basis of will and emotion. As far as the basic ontological differentiation of constituents is concerned, though certainly not in terms of detail, this Yoruba analysis of personhood is typical of the notions entertained on the same subject in West Africa by the Mende of Sierra Leone, the Dogon of Mali, and the Akan of Ghana.

A basically similar conception of human personality is encountered elsewhere in Africa. In his survey of concepts of personhood among the peoples of the Bantu area, which, by his reckoning, "covers roughly one-third of the African continent," Kagame finds a common inventory of the constituents of personhood. First, there is an animating principle that makes a human being a sentient being. This he calls, in translation, the "shadow." (One of the components in the constitution of a person in the Akan conception, by the way, is *sunsum*, which literally means "shadow.") Second, there is what he calls the principle of intelligence, and, third, the heart, which, almost exactly as in the Yoruba case, is the seat of will and emotion and constitutes the mechanism for the integration of the total personality. By E. E. Evans-Pritchard's account in his *Nuer Religion*, the Nuer too resolve the human person into "three component parts, *ring*, flesh, *yiegh*, breath or life, and *tie*, intellect or soul" (144).

Of all the groups noted, the Lugbara have the longest inventory of personhood, but each constituent is intriguingly analogous to some item in the previous inventories. John Middleton noted in his *Lugbara Religion* (1960) that the Lugbara conceive a person to consist of *rua* (body), *ava* (breath), *oriandi* (soul), *endrilendri* (shadow), *adro* (guardian spirit), and *tali* (personality).

The ontological status of the postulated components of personhood noted in the above accounts raises subtle issues. For example, all the authors cited, with the arguable exception of Evans-Pritchard and Middleton, speak directly or indirectly of the non-bodily constituents of human beings as spiritual or immaterial. The standpoint of this discussion, on the other hand, is that African modes of thought dispense with sharp ontological dualisms, such as that between the physical and the spiritual or the natural and the supernatural. The issue, of course, is an open one, and is likely to be debated for a considerable time to come.

IMMORTALITY AND MORALITY

The foregoing considerations about personhood have implications for African conceptions of immortality. It is safe to say that practically all African societies—though not all traditional Africans, for indigenous skeptics exist—communally entertain beliefs in immortality and cherish expectations of it. Equally universally, the African world of the dead is conceived to be continuous with and analogous to the world of the living, sometimes even reproducing its basic political order. This empirical connotation of the afterlife is generally noted by scholars, but its consequences for the ontological status of the inhabitants of the postmortem realm are rarely realized. At all events, one thing should be clear. If the inconsistencies of Cartesian dualism, in which an immaterial, non-spatial soul is supposed to be housed in the space of a material body, are not to be gratuitously attributed to African traditional metaphysics on an even grosser scale, it must be recognized that African conceptions of the beings in question do not fit any Western scheme of the material and the spiritual. Of these departed immortals, the best description, to adapt a phrase of Evans-Pritchard's, might be that they are "shadowy replicas of the living" (1956, 160).

The immortals just spoken of are, of course, the ancestors. Not only are they in some respects essentially similar to the living, but also they are regarded as being in constant interaction with the living sectors of their lineages, of which, usually, they remain highly venerated members. For most traditional Africans, the ancestors are tireless guardians of the morality and well-being of the living, rewarding virtue and punishing error in their own para-physical way. It should not, however, be inferred from their impact on the enforcement of morals that they are viewed as the basis of morality in African society.

One of the safest generalizations about African ways of thought is that morality is founded therein purely upon the necessity for the reciprocal adjustment of the interests of the individual to the interests of the community. This perspective on ethics is connected with the well-known communalist ethos of African traditional societies. So deep does this emphasis on community run that the very concept of a person includes a requirement of basic communal respectability. Moral thinking in such societies habitually focuses on the imperatives of the harmonization of interests, to which the individual is oriented from early childhood through widely irradiating circles of kinship.

Moral rightness or wrongness, on this showing, is understood in terms of human interests. But no ethical understanding, of itself, ensures the infallible practice of its precepts. Hence there is the need for sanctions against deviations from rectitude. It follows that the moral importance of the departed ancestors or the various extra-human powers, or even the Supreme Being, can only consist in their being regarded as sources of sanctions designed to reinforce a wavering will to virtue. The same applies to the moral role of living elders, parents, and civil authorities. None of these can be called the foundation of morals. It is, therefore, misleading to suggest, as is so often done, that morality rests on religion in African thought.

In this discussion no mode of thinking has been attributed to Africans in any unique sense. The claim has been that African traditional philosophy has an empirical (which, to be sure, does not mean an empiricist) orientation, and that, combined with the communalism of African society, this gives rise to an ethics based exclusively on considerations regarding the harmonization of human interests. Such philosophies of morals are not peculiar to Africa, being encountered in various ethical systems in the East and the West. Again, the empirical orientation is known, for example, in British empiricism, though there it comes along with a theory of "ideas" which, if it were imported into, say, an Akan conceptual framework, would produce quite a meaningless result.

Léopold Senghor, however, in his philosophy of Négritude, maintained that Africans have a special way of knowing. Among Africans there is a feeling of unison not only between person and person but also between person and object. Arising from this is a mode of knowing the external world that he called "participatory." "Classical European reason is analytical and makes use of the object. African reason is intuitive and participates in the object" (Reed and Wake 1965, 34). It seemed that, for Senghor, this difference had its basis not just in culture but in physiology: "...the modes of knowledge...are different and linked to the psycho-physiology of each race" (33).

Anxiety at this apparent attribution to the African psyche of a constitutional indisposition to analysis was reduced when, in reaction to criticism, Senghor explained, "In truth every ethnic group possesses, along with different aspects of Reason, all the virtues of man, but each has stressed only one aspect of reason, only certain virtues ... we must maintain the Negro-African method of knowledge but integrate into it the methods that Europe has used throughout her history" (Senghor 1964, 75). Any remaining objection to Senghor's thesis in this moderated form must be to detail rather than principle.

Another point that Senghor made about African ways of thinking has a logical interest. As is well known, he approved of the dialectical, but not the materialistic, part of the dialectical materialism of the Marxists. In the matter of dialectics he remarked, "Negro-African reason is traditionally dialectical, transcending the principles of identity, non-contradiction and the excluded middle" (Senghor 1964, 75).

Two questions arise. Can any communication take place among humans in the absence of these principles? And does African thinking dispense with or "transcend" them? Regarding the first some (including the present writer) say no; others yes. Regarding the second, it can be said that at least Akan thinking does not try to trifle with those "laws of thought." On the contrary, the Akans are very insistent on them. Any Akan with a moderate reputation for wisdom will tell you that *Nokware mu nni abra*, that is, truths don't conflict (Non-contradiction). If one tries to evade both the affirmative and the negative of a proposition, one will invite upon oneself the commentary: *Kosi a enkosi, koda a enkoda!* "He won't stand and he won't lie down either" (Excluded Middle). As for Identity, even babies when they are being given their names are customarily enjoined to say of that which is white that it is white and black that it is black. Truth-telling is what is being symbolically advised here in the first place. But if what is white might conceivably have been also not white, the advice is pointless. The law of identity, then, is a presupposition of, at least, the imperative of truth-telling.

It is, of course, not impossible that, as in Western society, some in African society have tried to play fast and loose with these "laws of thought." But that would be thanks to individual idiosyncrasy rather than cultural identity. In these logical matters African and Western modes of thought display similarity, not difference.

On the whole, however, the radically empirical character of African thought stands out and is responsible for some significant conceptual disparities with Western thought. These await comprehensive investigation.

See also **Ife (Ile-Ife); Myth and Cosmology; Philosophy and the Study of Africa; Religion and the Study of Africa; Senghor, Léopold Sédar.**

BIBLIOGRAPHY

Abraham, Willie E. *The Mind of Africa.* Chicago: University of Chicago Press, 1962.

Appiah, Kwame Anthony. *In My Father's House: Africa in the Philosophy of Culture.* New York: Oxford University Press, 1992.

Danquah, J. B. *The Akan Doctrine of God,* 2nd edition. London: Frank Cass, 1968.

Evans-Pritchard, E. E. *Nuer Religion.* New York: Oxford University Press, 1956.

Eze, Emmanuel Chukwudi. *Achieving Our Humanity: The Idea of the Postracial Future.* New York: Routledge, 2001.

Gbadegesin, Segun. *African Philosophy: Traditional Yoruba Philosophy and Contemporary African Realities.* New York: Peter Lang, 1991.

Griaule, Marcel, and Germaine Dieterlen. "The Dogon of the French Sudan." In *African Worlds: Studies in the Cosmological Ideas and Social Values of African Peoples*, ed. Cyril Daryll Forde. New York: Oxford University Press, 1954.

Gyekye, Kwame. *An Essay on African Philosophical Thought: The Akan Conceptual Scheme*, 2nd edition. Philadelphia: Temple University Press, 1995.

Gyekye, Kwame. *Tradition and Modernity: Philosophical Reflections on the African Experience.* New York: Oxford University Press, 1997.

Harris, William T., and Harry Sawyer. *The Springs of Mende Belief and Conduct: A Discussion of the Influence of the Belief in the Supernatural among the Mende.* Freetown, Sierra Leone: Sierra Leone University Press, 1968.

Horton, Robin. *Patterns of Thought in Africa and the West: Essays on Magic, Religion, and Science.* Cambridge, U.K.: Cambridge University Press, 1993.

Idowu, E. Bolaji. *Olodumare: God in Yoruba Belief.* London: Longman, 1962.

Kagame, Alexis. "The Empirical Acceptation of Time and the Conception of History in Bantu Thought." In *Cultures and Time*, ed. Louis Gardet et al. Paris: The UNESCO Press, 1976.

Kagame, Alexis. "The Problem of 'Man' in Bantu Philosophy." *The African Mind: A Journal of Religion and Philosophy in Africa* 1, no. 1 (1989).

Kaphagawani, Didier N. "African Conceptions of a Person: A Critical Survey." In *A Companion to African Philosophy*, ed. Kwasi Wiredu. Malden, MA: Blackwell, 2004.

Little, Kenneth. "The Mende in Sierra Leone." In *African Worlds: Studies in the Cosmological Ideas and Social Values of African Peoples*, ed. Cyril Daryll Forde. New York: Oxford University Press, 1954.

Maquet, Jacques Jerome Pierre. "The Kingdom of Ruanda." In *African Worlds: Studies in the Cosmological Ideas and Social Values of African Peoples*, ed. Cyril Daryll Forde. New York: Oxford University Press, 1954.

Menkiti, Ifeanyi. "Person and Community in African Traditional Thought." In *African Philosophy: An Introduction*, ed. Richard A. Wright. Lanham, MD: University Press of America, 1984.

Middleton, John. *Lugbara Religion: Ritual and Authority among an East African People.* Oxford: Oxford University Press, 1960.

O'Donohue, John. "A Bantu Philosophy: An Analysis of Philosophical Thought among the People of Ruanda, Based on *La philosophie bantu-rwandaise de l'être* (Brussels, 1956) by M. l'Abbe Alexis Kagame." *Journal of African Religion and Philosophy* 2, no. 1 (1991).

p'Bitek, Okot. *African Religions in Western Scholarship.* Nairobi, Kenya: East African Literature Bureau, 1970.

p'Bitek, Okot. *Religion of the Central Luo.* Nairobi, Kenya: East Africa Literature Bureau, 1971.

Reed, John, and Clive Wake, eds. *Leopold Sedar Senghor: Prose and Poetry.* London: Oxford University Press, 1965.

Senghor, Leopold Sedar. *On African Socialism.* New York: Frederick A. Praeger, 1964.

Tempels, Placide. *Bantu Philosophy.* Paris: Presence Africaine, 1959.

Wiredu, Kwasi. "The Concept of Mind with Particular Reference to the Language and Thought of the Akans." In *Contemporary Philosophy: A New Survey*, Vol. 5: *African Philosophy*, ed. Guttorm Fløistad. Dordrecht, Netherlands: Martinus Nijhoff, 1987.

Wiredu, Kwasi. "Morality and Religion in Akan Thought." In *African American Humanism: An Anthology*, ed. Norm R. Allen, Jr. Buffalo, NY: Prometheus Books, 1991.

Wiredu, Kwasi. "The African Concept of Personhood." In *African-American Perspectives on Biomedical Ethics*, ed. Harley E. Flack and Edmund D. Pellegrino. Washington, DC: Georgetown University Press, 1992.

Wiredu, Kwasi. "Death and the Afterlife in African Culture." In *Person and Community: Ghanaian Philosophical Studies*, ed. Kwasi Wiredu and Kwame Gyekye. Washington, DC: The Council for Research in Values and Philosophy, 1992.

KWASI WIREDU

PHILOSOPHY AND THE STUDY OF AFRICA

EUROPEAN PHILOSOPHY AND THE STUDY OF AFRICA

Plato and Aristotle say relatively little about Africa. Aristotle refers in his works on natural history to biological and meteorological curiosities from Egypt and Ethiopia, as when, for example, in book 4, chapter 4 of *De Generatione Animalium*, he remarks that "monstrosities occur more often in regions where the women give birth to more than one child at a time, as in Egypt"; or, in book 2, chapter 14 of *De Caelo*, he reports that different stars are visible in Egypt than can be seen farther north; or in book 1, chapter 5 of the *Historia Animalium*, where he reports that there are flying snakes, without feet, in Ethiopia. He also observes, in book 1, chapter 1 of *Metaphysics*, that the mathematical arts originated in Egypt, because the priests had the time to develop them (this is part of a general argument for the view that theoretical knowledge is the fruit of leisure). In the *Politics*, he discusses various features of the Egyptian constitution and social structure as well as observing that in Ethiopia social position is said to be determined by height. Egypt is important to Aristotle because, as he says in book 7, chapter 10 of the *Politics*, the Egyptians appear to be the most ancient of all peoples and to have laws and a constitution that have existed from time immemorial.

Plato says rather less, but in the *Phaedo* he does refer to the Egyptian practice of embalming, and in the *Laws* the Athenian Stranger remarks on the superiority of Egyptian laws limiting innovation in music and painting. In the *Statesman*, the Eleatic Stranger refers to the priestly powers of the Egyptian monarchs; in the *Timaeus*, there are a few remarks about the warrior caste in Egypt. Egypt is most frequently invoked in Plato, however, when characters in his dialogues swear "by the dog of Egypt."

There is, in fact, fairly little discussion of Africa or African ideas, beliefs, and practices in the works of the major writers of the European philosophical canon, even in Saint Augustine, who was, of course, born in Roman North Africa in Tagaste (though, it should be said, some of the heresies he combated originated, as he did, on the African continent).

This fact should be relatively unsurprising. While the European philosophical canon reflects in many obvious ways the particular traditions of the cultures of those who wrote it, much of that work proceeded on the assumption that it was addressing the most general questions about the nature of reality, questions whose answers did not depend on where you asked them or on accumulating particular facts knowable only in particular places. When Aristotle in the *Metaphysics* asks the most general question about Being, he is not asking a question whose answer requires evidence from Africa: scholars project he would have been interested in any answers to his questions that came to him from Africa (as he was in the natural historical works), but on the central questions of metaphysics he relied largely on his own arguments and Greek texts.

The first philosophers in the European tradition to take cultures and nations as topics of serious philosophical reflection were in the European Enlightenment, and probably the most important of these were Johann Gottfried von Herder (1744–1803) and George Wilhelm Friedrich Hegel (1770–1831). Both of these philosophers made contributions to the philosophy of history that reflected a sense of the profound *philosophical* significance of national or cultural traditions. Nevertheless, for two major reasons, much of the very little the Enlightenment philosophers had to say about Africa and Africans was negative.

First, by the mid-eighteenth century it had become conventional to distinguish between the "Negro" population, which is mostly found in present-day sub-Saharan Africa, and the mostly lighter-skinned Arabic-speaking North African populations of the Maghreb, and the well-known negative observations of many philosophers of the European Enlightenment about Africa were associated with a negative view of the Negro race. Few contemporary readers are likely to be undisturbed when they discover the moments when Africa is banished from Hegel's supposedly universal history and when David Hume declares, in the essay on "National Characters," that blacks are incapable of eminence in action or speculation (likening in the same place Francis Williams, the Jamaican poet, to a "parrot who speaks few words plainly").

Second, very little was known in Europe about the intellectual life of non-Muslim Africa until late in the nineteenth century; and it is, of course, the intellectual life of this part of the continent that European philosophy would need to address, if it were to take up the possibility that African peoples had something to contribute to the evolution of human understanding.

As a result, the philosophical engagement of the European tradition with Africa had essentially to wait until the period after World War II: then two forces combined to give salience to the question of how philosophy should take its place in Africa. First, the critique of scientific racism that had begun in the first part of the century was continued and extended in the face of the Nazi Holocaust and the recognition that racism had led to moral catastrophe on an unprecedented scale in the heart of the "civilized world." Second, an increasing number of African scholars trained in European philosophy began to teach in the new African universities in the 1950s and 1960s.

NON-EUROPEAN LITERATE TRADITIONS

In North Africa, where Muslim philosophers are able to draw on a long literate philosophical tradition that itself goes back to Plato and Aristotle, one is dealing with work that belongs within the world of philosophy in Arabic; while these works are plainly African in location, this article will not address them further, since to do so would require substantial contextualization within the world of Arab cultures and of Islam.

For similar reasons, the literate philosophical traditions of Ethiopia, which go back to the translation into an Ethiopian language (probably in the fifth century CE of a Greek text, *The Physiologue*), constitute a substantially distinct tradition—one that has been excavated by Claude Sumner working in Addis Ababa. *The Physiologue* is largely a work of Christian natural theology. The later *Book of the Philosophers* is a sixteenth-century translation of a (probably ninth-century) Arabic collection of philosophical sayings, heavily influenced by Greek (and, more particularly, Platonic and neo-Platonic) sources. *The Life and Maxims of Skendes* has a similar history—a Greek original, translated into Ethiopic from an Arabic version. It is only when one examines the seventeenth-century treatises of Zara Yiqob and his student Walda Heywat that one begins to get a distinctive and original Ethiopian tradition, which Sumner has characterized as rationalist.

COLONIAL LEGACIES

The role of academic philosophy in sub-Saharan Africa cannot be understood without acknowledging the radical differences between the colonial and postcolonial educational histories of Anglophone and Francophone states—differences that themselves reflect differing national approaches to philosophy and to colonial education in Britain and France.

When, in the early part of this century, Gottlob Frege replaced Hegel as the tutelary spirit of English philosophy, Continental historicist modes of thought were largely expelled from the philosophy faculties of English (though, curiously, not from Scottish) universities. In England, the most influential body of philosophical practice through the mid-century derived from the transfer, through such figures as Ludwig Wittgenstein and Alfred Ayer, of the logical positivism of the Vienna Circle to Oxford and Cambridge into the context provided by the critique of idealism which had been begun by Bertrand Russell. The tradition that resulted came to be known as "analytical philosophy." Analytical philosophy was centered in the philosophy of language and in epistemology, and its method was conceptual analysis.

In France, on the other hand, historicism survived and was supplemented by the introduction of Husserlian phenomenology, under the influence of Jean-Paul Sartre. Metaphysics and ontology remained central topics, and a good deal of intellectual effort was also devoted to normative questions and, in particular, to political philosophy in a broadly Marxist tradition.

This difference in approach to philosophy was exacerbated by the differing approaches to education in general and colonial education in particular. In France and in the Francophone states, philosophy was a central part of secondary education for those with a serious vocation to intellectual life. Philosophy was also central to university education. Because French colonial policy aimed to create a class of "evolved" Africans, fully educated to the highest standards of French civilization, it was natural that philosophy should gain the attention of some of the most successful African students in the Francophone educational systems, and given the centripetal pull of Paris, it is unsurprising that significant numbers of them were educated in philosophy there.

The difference with the Anglophone world could not be more striking. Philosophy was almost exclusively a university subject, and it was the province, almost everywhere except Oxford, of a relatively small number of students. (At Oxford, many students studied some philosophy, but there, too, relatively few specialized in that subject exclusively.) And the aim of colonial education was not, on the whole, to create "black Englishmen." Even if it had been, philosophy would not have played a central role in the process, since philosophy was not regarded as central to an English education at home.

As a result it is important to distinguish the trajectories of philosophy in Anglophone and Francophone spheres. (The Portuguese devoted no resources to tertiary education in their colonies and few to the tertiary education of their colonial subjects; contemporary philosophical traditions in Angola, Guinea-Bissau, and Mozambique owe much to the influence of Marxism in the anticolonial movements in Lisbon, where figures such as Agostinho Neto and Amílcar Cabral were educated.)

FRANCOPHONE PHILOSOPHY

Négritude. The essential background to modern African philosophy in French is in the theories of Négritude. While the Négritude movement is rightly seen as the product of the extraordinary convergence of Léopold Sédar Senghor, of Senegal, and Aimé Césaire, from the Antilles, who coined the term that gave the movement its name, the first philosophical statement of Négritude was made by Jean-Paul Sartre, in the essay "Black Orpheus." Sartre framed Négritude in the existentialist terms he had developed in *Being and Nothingness.* Négritude was the "being-in-the-world-of-the-Negro." And, Sartre argued within the historicizing narrative of Marx, the movement was the anti-thesis to European racism and a stage in a dialectical process that would produce in the end a synthesis in which both race and class would be transcended.

Senghor went on to articulate the movement as the basis for an understanding of African cultural and intellectual life that was to endure through decolonization, and for him, at least, the key to Négritude was a fundamental difference between European and African modes of experiencing the world. For Senghor (following the French anthropologist Lucien Lévy-Bruhl) Africans engage the world cognitively not, like Europeans, with reason but with their emotions, knowing objects in the world by "participating" in them.

Bantu Philosophy. The second major source of modern Francophone philosophy is in the work of Placied Tempels, a missionary priest in what was the Belgian Congo, now Zaire. The first French edition of *La philosophie bantoue*, which was written originally in Dutch, was published in the Belgian Congo in 1945. (An English-language version was published by Présence Africaine in 1959.) Tempels argued that the thought of the Bantu-speaking Luba had at its center a notion of Force, a notion that occupied the position of privilege of the notion of Being in Western (by which, as a Catholic, he meant Thomist) thought; and his articulation of that notion owed a good deal to the French philosopher Henri-Louis Bergson.

There has been much controversy both about Tempels's methods and his claims about the thought of Bantu-speakers. But his work provided an influential model of how philosophy in Africa might be conceived. He constructed what was later to be called an "ethnophilosophy": exploring and systematizing the conceptual world of a culture, as expressed in the central concepts embedded in its language. As a result, a significant amount of academic philosophical work in Africa in the postwar period has been in the form of ethnophilosophy, which amounts, in effect, to adopting the approach of a folklorist: studying the "natural history" of traditional folk-thought about the central issues of human life. Among the most influential of Tempels's followers was the Rwandan intellectual Alexis Kagame, whose *La philosophie bànturwandaise de l'être* (1957) sought to extend Tempels's work in his own Kinyarwanda language. But there has also been a significant body of work in what V. Y. Mudimbe has called the "school of Tempels," much of it by Catholic clerics concerned with missiology.

Where Senghor's Négritude had insisted on a distinctive African epistemology, ethnophilosophy has tended to insist that what is distinctive is African ontology and ethics, focusing, in particular, on the role of belief in spirits and ancestors in understanding reality and in shaping normative life.

Critique. Criticism of Négritude and of ethnophilosophy developed in parallel with each of them. Frantz Fanon argued implicitly against Négritude in *Les damnés de la terre* (1961) when he insisted that African culture should be seen as shaped by political struggle, not by an essence reflected in folklore. (Though Fanon was born in the French Antilles, he died an Algerian citizen, and his political writings were grounded in his experience of colonialism and decolonization in his adopted country.) But perhaps the most philosophically substantial critique begins in the *Essai sur la problématique philosophique dans l'Afrique actuelle* (1971) of the philosopher Marcien Towa and reaches its apotheosis in the work of the Béninois philosopher Paulin J. Hountondji.

Sur la philosophie africaine: Critique de l'ethnophilosophie (1977)—which has also been influential in its English translation, *African Philosophy: Myth and Reality* (1983)—collects some earlier essays in which Hountondji had mounted an assault on ethnophilosophy, an attack that is fundamental within the Francophone tradition in that it opposes assumptions common to Négritude and to ethnophilosophy. Hountondji makes his major objections to ethnophilosophy in the first three essays, which appear in their original order of publication.

Beginning with a recapitulation of Césaire's political critique of Tempels as a "diversion," he moves on to discuss the work of Kagame, whose *La philosophie bàntu-rwandaise de l'être* "expressly and from the outset, establishes its point of view in relation to Tempels's work as an attempt by an autochthonous Bantu African to 'verify the validity of the theory advanced by this excellent missionary'" (39). While endorsing some of Kagame's specific criticism of Tempels, Hountondji objects to what he calls their shared "unanimism," their conviction that there is a collective system of thought at the heart either of black African cultures generally (Négritude) or of particular cultures in Africa (Tempels, Kagame), and to their conviction that the articulation of this body of thought would constitute an African (or Bantu, or Rwandan) philosophy. (He refers at one point to "the description of an implicit, unexpressed world-view, which never existed anywhere but in the anthropologist's imagination" [p. 63].)

Along with his attack on ethnophilosophy's unanimism, Hountondji has an unflattering analysis of its motivations. Ethnophilosophy, he alleges, exists "*for a European public*" (45). It is an attempt to cope with feelings of cultural inferiority by redefining folklore as "philosophy," so as to be able to lay claim to an autochthonous philosophical tradition.

The most original of Hountondji's objections to the ethnophilosophers derives from an essentially Althusserian view of the place of philosophy. Hountondji cites a passage from *Lénine et la philosophie* where Louis Althusser says that philosophy "has been observed only in places where there is also what is called a science or sdences—in the strict sense of theoretical discipline, i.e., ideating and demonstrative, not an aggregate of empirical results" (97), and then Hountondji himself goes on to argue that if "the development of philosophy is in some way a function of the development of the sciences, then . . ., we shall never have, in Africa, a philosophy in the strict sense, until we have produced a history of science" (98; meaning by "science" here, of course, systematic knowledge in the French sense). Hountondji then develops in Althusserian language an insistence on the development of a critical tradition. The project of philosophy is not one of describing concepts but one of engaging with them in order to seek out the truth. Hountondji essentially argues that African philosophers cannot commit themselves to a singular heritage, because there isn't one—this is part of the critique of unanimism—and then argues that there is, in any case, no reason to hold to ideas because they come from "our" (African) traditions, unless they can stand up to critical ("scientific") scrutiny.

In later work, Hountondji has moved away from some of the universalism of the essays in *Sur la philosophie africaine*, examining in a more pragmatic spirit the possible roles of philosophy in Africa and exploring the ways that philosophy in Africa can address the project of intellectual modernization, a task that requires the development of a critical sociology of knowledge in countries that are, like all African countries, in "the periphery" of the world-system. For these purposes, Hountondji has now come to concede that the materials of ethnophilosophy can provide a useful starting point.

A final crucial figure in the development of the Francophone tradition is the Zairian philosopher, philologist, and novelist V. Y. Mudimbe, whose work has had a significant impact in the English-speaking world, both through Anglophone translations and commentary and through those of his own works that have been published in English since he has come to be based in the American academy. Mudimbe's work can be seen as a vast and systematic interrogation of the various Western discourses about Africa. In *L'autre face du royaume* (1973), for example, he conducted a scathing attack on ethnology, which he called a "langage en folie"; and in *The Invention of Africa* (1988), probably his best known theoretical work, he pursued a rigorous examination of anthropology and of African studies, arguing that Africa, as a subject of inquiry, is an invention of a Western episteme. Mudimbe's explicit methodological debt to Michel Foucault is substantial; he is pursuing an archeology, in the Foucauldean sense, of Africanist knowledge.

ANGLOPHONE PHILOSOPHY

Because of the very different roles that philosophy occupies in British and French cultures, the history of philosophy, in the strict sense, in Anglophone Africa cannot be said to have been as central to late colonial and postcolonial intellectual life as it has been in the Francophone areas of the continent. Nevertheless, two important streams of Anglophone thought can be identified that are distinctive.

Conceptual Analysis. First, there is a tradition of conceptual analysis of African concepts and conceptual systems that is somewhat different from the tradition of Francophone ethnophilosophy because its engagement with those concepts and systems is critically argumentative, in rather the sort of way that Hountondji can be taken to have been proposing. This tradition's earliest text is probably *The Akan Doctrine of God: A Fragment of Gold Coast Ethics and Religion* (1944), by the Ghanaian political leader Joseph Boakye Danquah, who took a doctoral degree in philosophy at London University. This text explores Akan conceptions against an Aristotelian background, and while it celebrates Akan traditions, it does so, in contrast to Tempels, by finding them close to European (Aristotelian) notions rather than remote from European (Thomist) conceptions.

Since Danquah's work was by a distinguished Anglophone African public figure—it was he who invited Kwame Nkrumah to take up the leadership of the independence movement—it is somewhat puzzling that his work has had so much less influence than the English translation of Tempels's *La philosophie bantoue*, which appeared in 1959. It is tempting to speculate that in the period of African independence it suited American, European, and African intellectuals to focus on a text that made an exciting claim for the distinctiveness of African thought rather than a more careful exploration of connections between ideas in one African cultural

zone and early European philosophy. This may also account for the rather substantial success of *The Mind of Africa* (1962) by the Oxford-trained Ghanaian philosopher Willie E. Abraham. This book sought to characterize African modes of thought in the manner that Hountondji was later to criticize as unanimist, focusing, as it did, on features of the intellectual life of African cultures such as ethical communitarianism and the belief in ancestral spirits. (Abraham's work has the advantage over Tempels's, however, that many of the generalizations he makes are both quite intelligible and roughly ethnographically correct.)

Since these works a number of Ghanaian philosophers, among them Kwame Gyekye in his *An Essay on African Philosophical Thought: The Akan Conceptual Scheme* (1987) and Kwasi Wiredu in his *Philosophy and an African Culture* (1980) and *Cultural Universals and Particulars: The African Perspective* (1996) have explored questions in epistemology, ontology, metaphysics, ethics, and the philosophy of religion with careful attention to a particular (Akan) conceptual world; and Barry Hallen and J. O. Sodipo in their *Knowledge, Belief, and Witchcraft: Analytic Experiments in African Philosophy* (1986) have carried out an extended exploration of Yoruba epistemology. Other work of this sort has been carried out in other traditions.

If this work is not the sort of descriptive (and often exoticizing) ethnophilosophy that Hountondji was criticizing, it is also not what the Kenyan philosopher Odera Oruka identified as "sage philosophy," something that he and his students pioneered, which entails the detailed exposition of the views of "wise elders" untrained in the methods and the themes of European philosophy. This work is unlike ethnophilosophy in identifying the philosophical systems it explores as the product of (culturally situated) individual thinkers, but it is also unlike the works of Gyekye, Wiredu, and Hallen and Sodipo (all of whom draw to varying degrees on respectful conversation with philosophically untrained interlocutors in the languages they discuss) in that it does not seek to engage in conceptual analysis of its own. (Oruka went on, later, to characterize the work of Gyekye, Wiredu, and Hallen and Sodipo as "hermeneutical," engaged with the philosophical exploration of an African language "to help clarify meaning and logical implications.")

Nationalist-Ideological Philosophy. Oruka also identified a significant body of philosophical writing as "nationalist-ideological": and it is here that one finds the second body of distinctive Anglophone writing. For many of the African political leaders of the independence generation wrote works of political theory. Nkrumah published one work that was somewhat technical in its philosophical style while he was president of Ghana, a book entitled *Consciencism: Philosophy and Ideology for DeColonization* (1964). While the most interesting of the philosophical claims in this work are hard to defend—they include an attempt to defend the compatibility of materialism and belief in spirits by way of a doctrine of categorical conversion that is far from clear—Nkrumah insisted, like Senghor, on the African roots of his ideas, and especially of his socialism. After his fall from power, Nkrumah published a substantial body of further work on decolonization and on non-colonialism, including *Neo-colonialism: The Last Stage of Imperialism* (1965) and *Class Struggle in Africa* (1970).

Less philosophically opaque work in political theory can be found in the writings of Kenneth Kaunda of Zambia (for example, *A Humanist in Africa*, 1966, and *Kaunda on Violence*, 1980) and Julius Nyerere of Tanzania (*Nyerere on Socialism*, 1969). These compare favorably in originality and clarity with analogous Francophone work, such as the extensive Marxist works of President Sékou Touré of Guinea, though none of them has had the influence of the work of Frantz Fanon.

It is, finally, worth insisting that in the discussion of philosophy in Africa, this article has focused on arguments and trends *distinctive* of philosophy in Africa; there have, of course, been philosophers in Africa trained in Europe and North America who have pursued the standard fare of the traditions in which they were trained. African philosophy journals, such as the Anglophone *Second Order*, have published articles on Aristotle and Locke on substance, for example; and Francophone philosophers, like V. Y. Mudimbe, have taught and written about Michel Foucault. This work constitutes the bulk of what Odera Oruka dubbed "professional philosophy."

Given the peculiar circumstances of the intellectual trained in a Western philosophy with very little historical engagement with Africa (almost none of it positive), it is not surprising that since decolonization began there has been a very substantial discussion alongside all the work this article has described on the question "What is African philosophy?" This can often usefully be glossed as asking what African philosophers with Western trainings should be doing. Tsenay Serequeberhan excerpts most of the crucial essays in this debate in his *African Philosophy: The Essential Readings* (1991). This article provides a sketch of the wide variety of answers that Africa's philosophers have implicitly endorsed in their practice over the last few decades.

See also **Cabral, Amílcar Lopes; Césaire, Aimé; Fanon, Frantz; Kagame, Alexis; Kaunda, Kenneth; Neto, Agostinho; Nkrumah, Francis Nwia Kofi; Nyerere, Julius Kambarage; Philosophy; Religion and Ritual; Senghor, Léopold Sédar; Touré, Sékou.**

BIBLIOGRAPHY

Abraham, Willie E. *The Mind of Africa*. Chicago: University of Chicago Press, 1962.

Danquah, Joseph Boakye. *The Akan Doctrine of God: A Fragment of Gold Coast Ethics and Religion*. London: Cass, 1968.

Gyekye, Kwame. *An Essay on African Philosophical Thought: The Akan Conceptual Scheme*, rev. edition. Philadelphia: Temple University Press, 1995.

Hallen, Barry, and J. O. Sodipo. *Knowledge, Belief, and Witchcraft: Analytic Experiments in African Philosophy*. Stanford, CA: Stanford University Press, 1997.

Hountondji, Paulin J. *African Philosophy: Myth and Reality*, trans. Henri Evans. London: Hutchinson University Library for Africa, 1983.

Hountondji, Paulin J. "Démarginaliser." Introduction to *Les savoirs endogènes*. Dakar, Senegal: Codesria, 1994.

Kagame, Alexis. *La philosophie bàntu-rwandaise de l'être*. New York: Johnson Reprint Corp., 1966.

Kaunda, Kenneth D. *Kaunda on Violence*, ed. Colin M. Morris. London: Collins, 1980.

Mudimbe, V. Y. *The Invention of Africa: Gnosis, Philosophy, and the Order of Knowledge*. Bloomington: Indiana University Press, 1988.

Nkrumah, Kwame. *Consciencism: Philosophy and Ideology for De-Colonization*. London: Heinemann, 1970.

Nyerere, Julius K. *Nyerere on Socialism*. Dar es Salaam, Tanzania: Oxford University Press, 1969.

Oruka, Odera H. *Trends in Contemporary African Philosophy.* Nairobi, Kenya: Shirikon, 1990.

Oruka, Odera H. *Sage Philosophy: Indigenous Thinkers and the Modern Debate on African Philosophy.* New York: E. J. Brill, 1990.

Serequeberhan, Tsenay, ed. *African Philosophy: The Essential Readings.* New York: Paragon House, 1991.

Sumner, Claude. *Classical Ethiopian Philosophy.* Addis Ababa, Ethiopia: Commercial Print. Press, 1985.

Wiredu, Kwasi. *Philosophy and an African Culture.* Cambridge, U.K.: Cambridge University Press, 1980.

KWAME ANTHONY APPIAH

PHOTOGRAPHY

This entry includes the following articles:
AESTHETICS AND SOCIAL SIGNIFICANCE
HISTORY
PHOTOJOURNALISM

AESTHETICS AND SOCIAL SIGNIFICANCE

Research in visual cultures and media anthropology has taken considerable interest in the photographic practices and discourses of non-Western cultures. Contemporary research has shown that technical media like photography do not constitute fixed, stable units; technological hardware provides only a necessary, but in no way a sufficient condition for how photography will be used and what cultural concretion it will receive. So while, on the one hand, photography lastingly shapes patterns of sociocultural interaction and human sensory perception, it is itself culturally shaped. It is integrated in local practices and concretized in specific ways, in accordance with cultural milieus.

HISTORY AND TECHNOLOGY

Although photography was invented in 1839, at the dawn of European imperialism when scientific exploration and colonization of Africa were already well under way, it was not until the 1920s that the first locally manufactured cameras appeared in the Gold Coast and Nigeria. The main modification to the European models was the integration of a darkroom into the camera body. This permitted production of a negative on printing paper and immediate processing; this negative was then snapped again in front of the lens—producing, after processing, the positive. This extremely practical and ingenious technique, popularly known as "wait and get" photography, led to a new type of ambulant actor who offered comparatively cheap portraits and passport pictures to the growing number of urban poor and peasants from remote areas visiting the towns. The result was a democratization of access to individual photographic representations which had been an exclusive privilege of the urban elites. However, the majority of Africans first encountered photography while taking identity photos, thus being subjected to the public eye of the colonial state that sought to impose individual identities and responsibilities where corporate ones had prevailed. The colonial state used the new technology of reproduction to identify, oversee, and control its subjects more effectively. In doing so, it opened a new discursive field and created a practice of identifying the photographic portrait and its subject "in truth."

Thus early urban African photography led during the 1940s to a period that many photographers refer to today as the Golden Age of the black-and-white studio photography. Electrification reached more and more towns, permitting installation of artificial studio lights. European, American, and Asian companies introduced medium-size cameras (for roll film) and low-cost enlargers. The customers diversified, as did their reasons for requesting pictures for "future remembrances." Photographers were increasingly invited to cover their clients' rites of passage (baptisms, initiations, "outdoorings," weddings, and funerals) as well as local political events such as the enstoolement of a new king or the dedication of a new building. Some work of this generation—mainly from Francophone West African countries—was exhibited and published in catalogs and books in the 1990s (Alex Acolatse, Seydou Keita, Malick Sidibe, Samuel Fosso, Salla Casset, August Azaglo). In South Africa, and to a lesser extent in Nigeria, magazines such as *Drum* stimulated the development of African photojournalism.

Another structural change in the history of photography occured in the 1980s when manual black-and-white photography was gradually replaced by quasi-industrial color photography. The new laboratories, mostly run by foreigners of Asian or

Head of a pharaoh. This photograph was taken at the Egyptian temples of Abu Simbel in 1852 by French poet and novelist Maxime du Camp. Between 1844 and 1864, du Camp and others inspired by orientalism published albums illustrating Egyptian antiquities. MAXIME DU CAMP/HULTON ARCHIVE/GETTY IMAGES

European background and supported by significant capital, took over the market in developing and printing. Studio photographers lost their former monopoly, and more and more studios were forced to close down. A similar situation existed in postwar Europe; instead of leading to large-scale amateur photography, as happened in Europe, in Africa, however, a new actor was brought onto the scene: the young "roving" photographer who often served as an agent for one of the color labs. Compared with the highly stylized and often enlarged black-and-white photographic images of earlier decades, the production of color photographs was more heterogeneous, without retouching, smaller and impressive in volume.

In the early years of the twenty-first century, digital photography reached Africa, yet it is too early to say much about the new practices that evolve with this technological change. In Uganda,

for example, photographers made use of the Adobe Photoshop computer program to rework digital portraits thereby reintroducing (digital) practices of retouching that allow them to beautify and idealize the depicted person in a new way. In addition, the fast spread of cheap mobile phones combined with a digital camera may finally lead to large-scale amateur photography as it evolved in Europe in the 1870s and 1880s.

SOCIAL AND CULTURAL EMBEDDEDNESS

In the early days, local beliefs about stealing souls and shadows made for considerable resistance to photographers. Picture taking was feared because it was thought to make people weak or their blood thin or even to kill them. In many African languages, the word for "negative" is the same as for ghost or spirit, and cameras were often literally referred to as "shadow-catching machines."

Yet, in the nineteenth century, Western explorers and missionaries calculatingly employed technical media—the book, the printing press, film, the gramophone, and photography—to demonstrate their own and their God's extraordinary power. They made use of the camera as a magical instrument to heal as well as to harm, as medicine, as a photographic gun to kill, or as an apparatus "to steal souls." The travelers' and missionaries' reports of the nineteenth century exhibit a conspicuously large number of variations of these scenes of media-technological superiority; they suggest that Europeans possessed a (technical) knowledge enabling them to magically dazzle the others. Thus, in Africa, it was Europeans who initially placed photography in a context of power, healing, killing, sorcery, and witchcraft. They converted technology into magic. However, the initial fear seems to have abated quickly. Photography has become widely accepted and integrated into the local canon of pictural traditions.

Early photographers in Africa found themselves in direct competition with other image makers. In order to compete, they blended their European and Indian aesthetic legacies with existing local conventions. But they also offered services to people who until then had been deprived of having their likenesses preserved. Since in Ghana, for example, potters had imagined and rendered the dead long before the coming of photography, it was not surprising that photographers would attempt to emulate that custom, too. In the long run, they drove the potters out of business. Photographers started to depict their customers in the locally idealized manners and produced images that were considered appropriate to be displayed on walls. Photography became a practice of splitting off the ideal from the idiosyncratic self, thus transforming images of individuals into virtually eternal image allegories and potential objects of religious veneration. All over the continent, photography increasingly became integrated into ancestor worship.

This tendency to assimilate photography into the realm of "tradition" was paralleled by the new practice of keeping photo albums, and not only by young people. Photo albums allowed people to construct biographies in a new way. The presentation of photo albums became part of the protocol of visiting and hospitality. The visitor is symbolically introduced to the life and family of the host or hostess by flipping through his or her collection of photographic stand-ins. Finally, photography became important in what one might be tempted to call a custom of "generalized image circulation and exchange." People appreciate giving and receiving pictures as reminders of events, as signs of friendship or love, as indicators of modernity and social achievement. This exchange is, however, subtly regulated by social distance and proximity. People are eager to give out their pictures to a person who lives far away, and ever less willing as the proximity increases. In hierarchical as well as conflictual relations, pictures are not exchanged at all. The growing significance of photographs within this system of image circulation and exchange is connected to people's increased migration and mobility. Here, pictures clearly serve as substitutes for absent persons as well as for events in which one was not able to participate, thus symbolically counteracting the loss of social cohesion. Sometimes photographs are used for healing and harming. Along the Kenyan coast, for example, socalled *waganga* use photographs to diagnose as well as to identify persons who are attacking and harming their clients. In love magic, photographs are widely "worked on" to bring back a beloved who has run away or fallen in love with another person. In the 1950s, when photography spread through the villages of western Kenya, many people feared that

their likenesses would be used by witches or sorcerers to kill them. As a means to counter this threat, the practice of holding a Bible while being photographed evolved as a protective device.

As elsewhere in the world, African photography serves the purpose of preserving memories of happy times—even creating them. Photography (and videography) are deeply embedded into a culture of performance and conspicious consumption where social positions are negotiated. During feasts like weddings marking the life cycle, as well as Christmas and Islamic celebrations, photographs are used not only to document a particular ritual passage, but the act of photography itself becomes part of a more comprehensive ritual of self-representation. Photography "crowns the situation," as a photographer in Mombasa put it. During weddings, for example, the quantity and quality of photographs produced and distributed among the guests and relatives serves as an index of a host's social standing. As in a *potlatch*, his status can be raised or be destroyed. And, in addition, photographs will be used to remember this event.

However, as Islamic fundamentalism spreads, men are making greater attempts to control and limit the circulation of women's photographs. The Islamic interdiction of representing a person is heavily debated among scholars and believers. In Lamu, a center of Islamic scholarship, for example, photographs of women are no longer to be seen in studio display cases. However, paradoxically, the increasing segregation of men and women has allowed a few female photographers to become professionals and to specialize in taking pictures and video recordings of women during feasts.

One of photography's main functions is to provide a means to remember. Picture taking, and to a lesser extent writing, has in many significant ways replaced other bodily forms of memory and has become one of the primary means by which Africans remember. A contemporary practice consists of remembering events by clothes and clothes by photographs. That photography in Africa is linked to clothing can also be seen in the fact that, at least in some West African countries, many photographers started out as tailors. The boundaries of these two professions often overlap; both are highly experienced in creating appearances. In some areas, a kind of repertory of photographic gestures are meant to visualize proverbs or adages; others are expressions of suffering as well as of wishes and desires. Here, however, the viewer must be familiar with the local canon of body gestures in order to understand the motive or to guess the event that is to be remembered by a particular photograph.

AESTHETICS

A comparison between late-nineteenth-century black-and-white pictures and later color ones reveals a continued focus on the human figure. Landscapes and other motifs are almost completely lacking. The composition is mostly formal, characterized by the desire for centrality, frontality, balance, and completeness. The main subject is nearly always in the center of the picture and in full figure, whether sitting or standing, singly posed or in a group. Writing about Nigeria, Stephen Sprague (1978) emphasized that the model for such body posing and image framing might have derived from conventions of sculpture. Nigerian photographers are less interested in depicting individual idiosyncrasies than social types. The Yoruba ideal of *jijora* postulates a mimetic balance between abstraction and individual likeness. Ghanaian photo criticism stresses the preservation of body integrity: no body parts are to be cut off in the framing or cropping of a photograph, or else the photographer will have "killed his image." Other aesthetic criteria used by Ghanaians as well as by Kenyans to evaluate photographic appearances of persons include the ideals of coolness, roundness, and smoothness.

Since the mid-twentieth century, retouching has been standard practice in beautifying black-and-white photographs. An investgation of retouched negatives is particularly illuminating as it reveals African ideals of beauty. Retouching with graphite pencils as it was done in Ghana lightened the complexion and was mostly done to facial wrinkles. An old Ghanaian photographer put it: "Retouching can make you young and moreover change your face entirely." With regard to scarifications, opinion differs. Some photographers retouch them, too, because they consider them to be "savage tribal marks" of olden days; others, however, refuse to do so, since they feel that the photographed persons might no longer be recognizable. Retouching is also done to protruding veins and bones, especially collarbones, since their visibility is thought to signify malnutrition and poverty. Faces are usually made fuller and rounder. The eyes, especially the corneas, are lightened, as "white eyes" suggest coolness, calm, and kindness, whereas "red eyes" are associated with heat, disorder, and witchcraft. Retouching is supposed to "cool" one's face by transforming it into a mask of the cool. As on statues, neck rings, denoting prosperity, sometimes are drawn on the negatives. They serve as indices of body prosperity.

With the introduction of color film, which does not lend itself to retouching, the practice was gradually disappearing. However, practices of photo montage which were extraordinarily popular in the Golden Age of black-and-white photography continued to be practiced also in the era of color photography. Human figures are excised from an already existing picture, placed on a new image and photographed again. Through this technique of montage photographers became image magicians, and studio names such as Magic Photo Studio or Mr. Magic referred to this uncanny aspect of photomontage that allowed to turn photography into a wish-fulfilling machine while likewise profiting from its indexicality. The most common practice was probably the rematching of body and head which was usually done when a person had died without leaving behind a full-figure picture. The image of the head was then taken from an identity shot and mounted on the body of somebody else. In addition, villagers and migrant workers who had no good clothes for a photo session were able to order their likenesses on the bodies of elegantly dressed men.

Such montage techniques were sometimes integrated into ritual contexts, such as the Yoruba twin cult. When one of the twins had died, before they had been photographed together, the surviving one was photographed alone and the photographer printed the negative twice, so that the two twins appeared to be sitting together. This was supposed to maintain their spiritual integrity. If they were of opposite sexes, the surviving twin was photographed in male and once in female clothing. Sprague noted that such photographs were increasingly replacing earlier wooden *ibedji* sculptures and kept on altars. Some of these photomontages are quite obvious, some are more subtle, and others are so sophisticated that it is nearly impossible to determine how the pictures came into being. One encounters montages such as a newlywed couple on a television screen or a woman inside a beer bottle. Sometimes double exposures consist of one subject in two poses: a man reading a book and lighting a cigarette. This multiplying device could be seen as an image allegory or as a local response to the puzzling experience of an age termed by Walter Benjamin as the "age of technical reproducibility."

African photo studios provide their customers with many hand props and clothes. In Ghana, coats and ties are supplied; they are often completed by prestigious *kente* cloths, royal sandals, hats, umbrellas, watches, imitations of gold ornaments and ceremonial swords. One Asante photographer declared himself to be a "kingmaker." He had on hand all the items necessary to dress men as chiefs and women as queen mothers. In the monarchistic Asanteman, following the death of a queen mother, women of all social classes hurry to photographers' studios to dress and be shot as queen mothers themselves. Elsewhere backdrops are used with painted Durbar scenes including a royal umbrella, in front of which a customer may be photographed seated on a chief's stool.

The environment of African photo studios and their hand props and backdrops reflect, above all, a male gaze. Nearly all studio owners and roaming photographers are men, and only a few have allowed female apprentices to acquire photographic skills and to work for them. These woman are in subordinate positions that do not permit them to influence the setting. Yet, as already mentioned, at the Kenyan coast within the Islamic context, female photographers emerged that specialized in taking pictures of women.

Painted backdrops with landscapes, clouds, and bourgois living room interior were originally introduced by Europeans. They were first copied by local artists and then continuousely adapted to the tastes of African studio visitors. Each decade developed its own favorite motifs, such as urban scenes with multistory buildings, city streets lined with street lights, skyscrapers, airports and airplanes, parks and benches, waterfalls and national tourist sites, and "room dividers" laden with the icons of modernity and social promotion (refrigerator, TV, sound system, mobile phones and VCR). Whereas in some parts of Africa perspectives prevail that make no attempts at realism, a strong tendency to trompe d'oeil compositions in which people interact with their painted environment has emerged in Ghana and Nigeria. Here, the photographic practice has shifted from providing simple symbolic presences to that of true illusions.

African photography forms part of what Susan Vogel has called "new functional art"; it has had a significant impact on other pictorial arts (such as painting and sculpture). Studio photography in Africa does not attempt to document social reality. Instead, it is considered to be a way of seeing the world and improving one's standing in the world.

In its more than 150 years of existence, African photography has left an immense legacy of visual documents and chronicles revealing shifts in identity formations (individual as well as collective ones), social memories, human desires, ambivalences, memento mori, and much more. In the twenty-first century photographic archives are not yet part of African cultural scenarios. African photography has only since the 1990s been officially recognized as an art through the increasing number of exhibits in Europe and the United States. Individual artists such as Malick Sidibe, Seydou Keita, Samuel Fosso, N.V. Parekh, and Philip Kwame Apaya have entered the international art market. Various photographic archives of African photo studios have been bought by Western art dealers whereas in Africa very few people realize that they are losing a treasure that allows to trace a visual history "from below."

See also **Art: Regional Styles; Communications; Festivals and Carnivals; Film and Cinema; Islam; Witchcraft; Women: Women and Islam in Northern Africa; Women: Women and Islam in Sub-Saharan Africa.**

BIBLIOGRAPHY

Behrend, Heike. "'Feeling Global': The Likoni Ferry Photographers in Mombasa, Kenya." *African Arts* 33, no. 3 (2000): 70–77.

Behrend, Heike. "Fragmented Visions: Photo Collages by Ronnie Okocha Kauma and Afanaduula Sadala in Kampala, Uganda." In *Photography and Modernity in Africa*, ed. Heike Behrend and Jean-Francois Werner. *Visual Anthropology* 14, no. 3 (2001): 301–320.

Behrend, Heike. "'I Am Like a Movie Star in My Street': Photographic Self-Creation in Postcolonial Kenya." In *Postcolonial Subjectivities in Africa*, ed. Richard Werbner. London: Zed Books, 2002.

Behrend, Heike. "Photo-Magic: Photographies in Practices of Healing and Harming in Kenya and Uganda." Spec.

issue, ed. Birgit Meyer, *Journal of Religion in Africa* 33, no. 2 (2003): 129–145.

Buckley, Liam. "Self and Accessory in Gambian Studio Photography." *Visual Anthropology Review* 16, no. 2 (2001): 71–91.

Buckley, Liam. "Objects of Love and Decay: Colonial Photographs in a postcolonial Archive." *Cultural Anthropology* 20, no. 2 (2005): 249–270.

Pinney, Christopher, and Nicolas Peterson, eds. *Photography's Other Histories.* Durham, NC: Duke University Press, 2003.

Sprague, Stephen. "Yoruba Photography. How I See the Yoruba See Themselves." *African Arts* 12, 1978: 1, 52–59.

Wendl, Tobias, and Heike Behrend. *Snap Me One! Studiofotografen in Afrika.* Munich: Prestel, 1998.

Wendl, Tobias. "Entangled Traditions: Photography and the History of Media in Southern Ghana." *RES: Anthropology and Aesthetics* 39 (2001): 78–100.

HEIKE BEHREND
TOBIAS WENDL

HISTORY

Although the in-depth history of photography in Africa has yet to be written, recent studies reveal the complex nature of the dissemination and use of this technology on the African continent, and the interactions of photographers of different backgrounds. Perhaps most importantly, scholars have begun to examine the circulation of images in different material forms, such as photographic prints, book illustrations, and postcards. The impact that the dissemination of image objects may have had on photographic practice still needs to be explored. At this point, one can only delineate major developments, discuss the work of important photographers, and examine the European and American views of Africa that affected the images of that continent. Both foreign and indigenous practitioners were linked through their interest in the actual technology, through situations in which photographers learned from each other, and through the flow of image objects.

THE EARLY YEARS

In the mid-nineteenth century, several historical and technical developments coincided. The first photographic process, the daguerreotype, was introduced in 1839. Over the next decades, photographic technology developed from the cumbersome early processes, such as the calotype and the wet-collodion process, to the dry-plate process of 1871 that facilitated the taking of pictures. Another breakthrough occurred with the invention of handheld cameras in the late 1870s and finally with the arrival of celluloid film in 1885 and box cameras in the 1890s.

The second half of the nineteenth century was a period of systematic exploration and subjugation of the African continent, and the growth of physical anthropology and ethnography as disciplines that began to use photography. By the turn of the twentieth century, both professionals and amateurs were practicing photography around the globe. Images had a wide distribution, first through photographic albums and in the forms of lithographs and engravings, and then through halftone reproductions in contemporary books and on collotype postcards.

European travelers, artists, scientists, and professional photographers began taking images in Africa after the introduction of the first photographic processes in 1839. The nineteenth-century fascination with Egypt drew artists and photographers to the Nile River. Adventurous travelers along the African coast also used photography, among them a helmsman by the name of Vernet traveling with Charles Guillain (1808–1875) to Madagascar and the east African coast in the years 1845 to 1848. His daguerreotypes are now in the archives of the Musée du quai Branly, Paris.

STUDIOS AND EXPLORERS

This phase of photography gave way to the establishment of photographic studios. Europeans opened commercial photographic studios in Egypt and in South Africa in the Cape as early as the 1840s. Studios opened in other cities, from Freetown in Sierra Leone to Luanda in Angola in the 1860s, a development closely tied with the growth of towns along the African coast and the regular service of shipping lines that connected them. Studio photographers catered mainly to expatriate patrons who wanted their portraits taken; some of them also traveled extensively and sold collectible photographs such as city views, images of African villages, and sets of native types to residents and travelers passing through well into the first two decades of the twentieth century. One of the best-known among many is François-Edmond Fortier (1862–1928; French) who was based first in Saint-Louis and then in Dakar (in Senegal). His large series of postcards circulated widely at the time and continue to be appreciated. In East Africa, many photographers were originally from India, where indigenous photography had begun early on. Goans settled on the Kenyan and Tanzanian coasts and in Zanzibar, and established large commercial studios and also published postcards.

As studio photography flourished along the coasts, several famous explorers and travelers began to employ photography during their expeditions to the interior of Africa. John Kirk (1832–1922), a botanist on David Livingstone's Zambezi expedition of 1858 to 1862, took some of the earliest images of buildings, boats, and vegetation in the interior of Africa. Later on, the Nile brought photographers into eastern and Central Africa, among them the Austrian artist Richard Buchta (1845–1894), whose pictures of the upper Nile and northern Uganda, taken during 1878–1879, became famous and were distributed in both albums and print.

ANTHROPOLOGISTS, MISSIONARIES, AND PROFESSIONAL PHOTOGRAPHERS

From the 1880s, photography proliferated and the pace of African exploration increased in conjunction with imperial claims, scientific projects, and the effort to place peoples under colonial rule. By then photography was no longer the domain of a few specialists. Military personnel, colonials, scientists, and missionaries produced images that served multiple functions, from personal mementos to research and propaganda to entertainment for audiences at home. According to their backgrounds and interests, photographers often emphasized particular aspects of their experience and followed certain preoccupations and photographic conventions.

Anthropologists early on developed a standardized code of representation of Africans as racial specimens, producing some of the most dehumanizing images of them. Their collections, among them the images of the German anthropologist Gustav Theodor Fritsch (1838–1927), who conducted research in southern Africa from 1863 to 1866 and in Egypt from 1898 to 1899, remain in many archives and ethnographic museums. The tradition of the traveler and anthropologist as photographer has continued into the present. Among the most famous are Leo Frobenius (1873–1938; German), Robert Sutherland Rattray (1881–1938; British) in Ghana,

Charles Gabriel Seligman (1873–1940; British) in Sudan, and Pierre Verger (1902–1996; French) in Bénin.

Photographers of different backgrounds were also eager to contribute to science and followed anthropological conventions in their photography, relying on photographic instructions written for amateurs. Melville William Hilton-Simpson (1881–1936; British) accompanied the Hungarian explorer Emil Torday (1875–1931) to Central Africa in 1907–1908 and, after 1912, also photographed in Algeria. The Austrian merchant Rudolf Oldenburg (1879–1932) purposefully produced photographic records in Guinea and Cameroon to serve anthropology. He sold series of prints to many ethnographic museums in the German-speaking part of Europe. From 1909 to 1915 the German American taxidermist, collector, and mammalogist Herbert Lang (1879–1957) created a fabulous set of images of the Mangbetu that is now in the American Museum of Natural History in New York.

The work of missionary photographers reflected the missions' emphasis on civilizing their charges. Because missionaries were often the first Europeans to reach an area, their images are of great importance to historical and cultural studies. The African American missionary William Henry Sheppard (1865–1927) was the first visitor to the Kuba kingdom. His photographs are now at Hampton University in Virginia. A few of the missionary photographers were women. Anna Rein-Wuhrmann (1881–1971; Swiss), for example, created evocative portraits of nobility in the Bamum kingdom of Cameroon, where she worked for the Basel Mission from 1911 to 1915. Her images, now in the Basel Mission Archive in Switzerland, are beautifully composed, rising beyond mere documentation.

After World War I, anthropological interest in the study of race declined. Nevertheless, the conventions and requirements of anthropological and ethnographic photography still influenced the type of imagery produced. Austrian travel writer and photographer Hugo Bernatzik (1897–1953) created magnificent images of people in Guinea and Sudan. He was one of several traveling photographers who sought recognition as both an artist and an anthropologist. Whereas some professional photographers claimed ethnographic expertise, others made more or less exoticizing images that circulated in books,

Photographer Peter Magubane (left) with Nelson Mandela. One of the most unusual African journals, *Drum*, employed the famed photojournalist Magubane in the latter half of the twentieth century. Professional photographers from all over Europe had already begun taking images in Africa. WILLIAM F. CAMPBELL/TIME LIFE PICTURES/GETTY IMAGES

exhibitions, and other forms. Two photographers whose works have had a major impact to this day are Casimir Zagourski (1881–1944; Polish) and Michel Huet (1917–1997; French). Zagourski was based in Léopoldville (present-day Kinshasa) in the Belgian Congo (present-day Democratic Republic of the Congo); he created evocative series of the peoples in Central Africa that he marketed in the form of postcards and lager exhibition prints. Huet's imagery had a wide impact, as his numerous black-and-white and color postcards were sold in West Africa for decades and were seen by many both in and outside of the continent.

NEWS AND PROPAGANDA PHOTOGRAPHY

One of the major uses of photography for the colonial governments in Africa was as a tool for propaganda. Even before 1914 the German Reichskolonialamt mandated that all photographs by colonials in government service be presented to the office, which retained the right to keep images that might serve its purposes. In the 1920s new genres of photography, such as photo reportage and news photography, came into their own, increasing the already major pictorial output on Africa to a flood of images

from the continent. In the 1930s and 1940s colonial picture services, such as the Belgian Centre d'Information and Documentation (later Congopresse), and research institutions, such as the Institut Français de l'Afrique Noire, headquartered in Dakar, hired documentary photographers. Photographers worked for magazines, for example George Rodger (1908–1995; British) and Eliot Elisofon (1911–1973; American) for *Life*, and Volkmar Kurt Wentzel (b. 1915; American) for *National Geographic*. One of the most unusual journals was *Drum*, first published as *African Drum* in 1951 in Cape Town, South Africa. Among *Drum*'s main photographers was Jürgen Schadeberg (b. 1931; South African). *Drum* also employed African photojournalists, among them Ernest Cole (1940–1990; South African) and Peter Magubane (b. 1932; South African), whose fame drew attention to the contributions of African photographers.

Photographers from countries of the North Atlantic rim have been taken to task for creating denigrating and stereotypical images of Africans, among them those engaged in the documentation of racial difference. Indeed, there are many instances when photographic subjects, especially women, were coerced to pose for the photographer.

However, recent studies present a more complex reading, moving beyond simplistic assumptions and focusing on the many different ways in which photographic encounters unfolded in the past on the African continent.

See also **Dakar; Film and Cinema; Freetown; Livingstone, David; Luanda; Media; Nile River; Saint-Louis; Travel and Exploration: European.**

BIBLIOGRAPHY

Ackermann, Andreas, Ute Röschenthaler, and Pater Steigerwald, eds. *Im Schatten des Kongo: Leo Frobenius: Stereofotografien 1904–1906.* Frankfurt: Frobenius-Institut, 2005.

Albrecht, Michael, et al., eds. *Getting Pictures Right: Context and Interpretation.* Cologne, Germany: Köppe, 2004.

Edwards, Elizabeth, ed. *Anthropology and Photography, 1860–1920.* New Haven, CT: Yale University Press, 1992.

Geary, Christraud M., ed. "Historical Photographs of Africa." *African Arts* 24, no. 4, special issue (1991).

Geary, Christraud M. *In and Out of Focus. Images from Central Africa, 1885–1960.* Washington, DC: Smithsonian National Museum of African Art, 2003.

Hartmann, Wolfram; Jeremy Silvester; and Patricia Hayes; eds. *The Colonising Camera: Photographs in the Making of Namibian History.* Athens: Ohio University Press, 1999.

Landau, Paul, and Deborah Kaspin, eds. *Images and Empires: Visuality in Colonial and Postcolonial Africa.* Berkeley: University of California Press, 2002.

Pierre Fátúmbí Verger: Dieux d'Afrique. 1995. Paris: Editions Révue Noire.

Theye, Thomas, ed. *Der geraubte Schatten: Die Photographie als ethnographisches Dokument.* Munich: C. J. Bucher, 1989.

CHRISTRAUD M. GEARY

PHOTOJOURNALISM

Apart from the traditions of studio photography, it is the documentary style that has been the hallmark not only of South African photography but also of Angolan, Mozambican, and others. Besides the works of Western photographers such as Carter Sudan, James Nachtwey, and Don McCullin reporting as cultural outsiders from a continent of crisis and war, there has been a strong tradition of professional African photographers documenting everyday life for more than half a century. Even though there is still hardly any research on the history of early African documentary photography, its linkage to the development of journalism in general indicates an interesting history still to be written.

African photojournalism emerges in the Anglo- and Lusophone countries, mainly in Southern Africa. Before 1940, references to this kind of photography are scarce. Documentary photography still seems to be a sideline of studio photographers. A 1920 book contains photographs taken by the following photographers: George Da Costa of Nigeria; Wlawin Holm, who had a studio in Lagos and was the first Nigerian member of the Royal Photographic Society of Great Britain; and Alphonso and Arthur Lisk-Carew of Sierra Leone. Not later than the 1940s and 1950s, politically charged photojournalism began to flourish.

Photographers such as David Goldblatt, Peter Magubane, Santu Mofokeng, and Jürgen Schadeberg were active in South Africa. The photo-essays of the magazine *Drum*, which was the most important organ publishing their photos, gained the status of icons in the recent South African history (an equal status may be attributed to *The Namibian* in Namibia or *Notícias* in Mozambique). Goldblatt's series on everyday life in the 1950s and 1960s, and of Afrikaners in the 1970s, questioned the conditions of society. The work of South African photographer John Liebenberg had a strong impact on the political struggle for independence in Namibia in the 1980s. Liebenberg was one of the few photographers reporting from the wars on Namibia's border and in Angola. Under conditions of a sometimes fragile freedom of the press, the works of many photographers were first distributed by international press agencies such as Reuters. Some of today's icons of African press photography first made the covers of North American magazines such as *Time* or *Spiegel*. Especially during the 1980s, these works gave a face to conflicts that were difficult for journalists from abroad to reach.

Since the end of apartheid in the early 1990s, as well as the end of some regional wars, the role of documentary photography in Southern Africa has changed. Free press and easy access to global markets created a copious setting from which some photographers of international reputation originated (such as Luís Basto [b. 1969] or Guy Tillim [b. 1963], who won the DaimlerChrysler Award for Photography in 2004).

Typically, the ties between the different national scenes of photography are close. Photographers from South Africa work in Angola and Namibia, and vice versa. Luis Basto, who has his roots in one of the most vital scenes of African photography in Maputo, Mozambique, lives and works as well in Zimbabwe and South Africa. In the Lusophone countries of Angola and Mozambique, documentary photography was flourishing long before independence. The most prominent figure in Maputo is Ricardo Rangel (b. 1924). In 1952, he became the first nonwhite journalist to join the staff of a newspaper in Mozambique, at *Notícias da Tarde*. In 1970, Rangel was one of the founders of *Tempo*, the country's first color newsmagazine. At *Notícias*, where he worked from 1977, he minted more than one generation of photojournalists: Kok Nam (b. 1939), the prominent figure of the second generation, is followed by photographers such as Sérgio Santimano (b. 1956), and a third generation such as Rui Assubuji (b. 1964) and Luís Basto.

As in Mozambique and South Africa, documentary photography generally not only serves to accomplish political means but also contributes to an archive of everyday life. In Angola, a country with an equally distinct tradition of documentary photography, the Angola Information and Tourism Centre (CITA) was founded in 1949 and launched a huge campaign to document all aspects of Angola daily life. The still-famous slogan—Vamos descobrir Angola (Let's discover Angola)—led to an archive of more than 150,000 prints. After independence in 1975 the archive, now named En Foto, was taken over by the Ministry of Information and was finally privatized in 1991 under the name A Photo. Many other archives, especially those of individual photographers or groups, have been lost in war. The Pinto Afonso family is one example. The three Afonso brothers, José (called Zé) (1940), Ruy (1946), and Joaquim (1950), founded the famous studio Foto Ngufo in 1968 in Luau on the border with former Zaire that still exists in Luanda. As many of their colleagues in Angola and other war-torn countries, they lost nearly all their negatives, which did not stop their passion for photography. Today it is the third generation of Afonsos with Karina (1977), Marly (1979), Iris (1986), Sérgio (1975), and Rogério Pinto Afonso (1978) making themselves a name not only in photography but also in new media such as video.

FROM STUDIO PHOTOGRAPHY TO PHOTOGRAPHY IN CONTEMPORARY ART

Photography plays a major role within contemporary African art. Early studio photography and more recently documentary photography have become integral parts of the major international exhibitions of African art. At the same time, these two early genres of African photography also influence the work of contemporary visual artists. Besides the plurality of styles of expression, the tradition of studio photography and the documentary style are the two major lines of tradition that may be identified in many contemporary works of art.

Even though commercial studio photography for a local audience has more or less come to a halt, studio photography as means of artistic expression is picking up. The most prominent example is Samuel Fosso (b. 1962) whose self-fashioning studio portraits indicate the blurred line between commercial photography and modernist museum art. In his self-portraits, he experiments with expanding his identity by disguising it. He masquerades as different fictional or historical archetypes. Another artist in this conceptual, performative, and self-reflexive style of photography is the London-based Nigerian artist Rotimi Fani-Kayode (1955–1989).

African studio photography does not simply become art. It also has become a strong element in the widely shared visual archive, as well as its iconographic tradition being adopted within other genres. In her 2003 work "Better Lives," the South African artist Sue Williamson showed refugees from Angola, Sudan, and the Democratic Republic of the Congo formally posed as if in the studio of a photographer. Williamson takes the general setting of studio photography and restores the dimension of time: The portrayed are filmed while listening to recordings of their own voices telling their own paths of life. The exhibited work displays the photo prints combined with text as well as the video.

In "From the Inside" (2001), Williamson spoke to HIV/AIDS patients and painted some of their experiences on walls in prominent locations. The exhibited work consisted of black and white portraits in documentary style confronted with color prints of the photos she took of the walls. Photography, at first a mere means of documentation of conceptual art projects, has turned into an integral part of these art projects and products themselves.

The Nigerian photographers' collective, Depth of Field (DOF), is a notable example of contemporary African photography on the edge between documentation and postmodern art. Uche James-Iroha, Kelechi Amadi-Obi, Toyin Sokefun, and Amaize Ojeikere joined forces in 2001 at the IVième rencontres de la photographie africaine in Bamako, Mali. Toyosi Odunsi and Emeka Okereke joined the collective in 2003. They document the pulsating daily life in the streets of Lagos and the urban domestic settings, and some of them stage their photographs in order to create images that seek to approach reality with the help of staging. DOF proves the discursive potential of post-twentieth-century photography in Africa. A new generation self-consciously draws upon the lines of tradition of African studio, as well as the documentary style.

In the context of new media art becoming more important in Africa since the end of the 1990s, photography has not replaced by video as one might expect, but, on the contrary, gained more ground. As the members of DOF expand photography into modern art, many African artists who first started with sculpture, plastics, and the like subsequently turned to photography. Photography became an integral part of the conceptual projects of visual artists including those of South African Jane Alexander (b. 1959), Cameroonian Pascal Marthine Tayou (b. 1966), or Beninese Romuald Hazoumé (b. 1962).

Alexander's different series of digital photos are a montage of the disturbing characters one knows from her three dimensional installations into photos she takes of streets and other places in her vicinity. Tayou documents everyday life in his Cameroonian home village using a perspective literally from the ground and dust, where he also picks up the materials for his installations made out of litter. Hazoumé equally follows the material of his scrap masks made of plastic containers when he records the huge piles of plastic vessels tied to motorbikes or bicycles of itinerant traders or smugglers on the Bénin-Nigerian border. Photography has become a means for contemporary artists not only of documentation but also to adjust their work by linking it to everyday life in Africa.

Photography thus still keeps the promise of capturing the ephemeral realities we are confronted with.

EXHIBITING AFRICAN PHOTOGRAPHY

African photography has found an audience in Africa and globally not only by distributing the products of nineteenth and twentieth century commercial studio photography or the publication of African press photography in African and worldwide papers and journals, but also as a genre of modern art. African photography has been exhibited as part of contemporary African art as early as 1960 when the Nigerian photographer Dotun Okunbanjo (b. 1928) exhibited his work in London. He subsequently organized the First International Photographic Exhibition in 1961 in Lagos. But it was only in the 1990s that a number of exhibitions, first in Europe and most notably the 1994 Bamako Biennale, followed. The Bamako Photography Festival Rencontres africaines de la photographie was Africa's first and only festival for contemporary photography, now taking place every two years.

The first major exhibition in the United States devoted exclusively to African photography was In/sight: African Photography 1940 to the Present in the Guggenheim Museum New York in 1996. In this show, curated by the New York-based Nigerian Okwui Enwezor, studio and documentary photography were still dominant, whereas his 2006 show Snap Judgments at the International Center of Photography in New York marks the shift toward photography as an integral part of contemporary visual arts. Another milestone along this path is the 1998 exhibition L'Afrique par elle-même (Africa: A Self-Portrait) at the Maison-Européenne, the impetus for which came from the Paris-based magazine Revue Noire. Founded in 1991, it was the pioneering press for contemporary art in the 1990s and devoted a wide space in its publications to African photography (among it in 1998 was the 432-page article, "Anthologie de la Photographie Africaine.").

Many other international exhibitions such as The Short Century: Independence and Liberation Movements in Africa, 1945-1994 (1996 at the Villa Stuck in Munich, Germany) curated by Enwezor, or Africa Remix (2004 Kunstpalast Düsseldorf) curated by Simon Njamy, have had substantive sections of African photography but were not exclusively devoted to this medium. The Austrian Kunsthalle Wien organized two major shows with regional focus: The 2001 exhibition Flash Afrique: Photography from West Africa and 2006 Black Brown White: Photography from South Africa, both curated by Thomas Miesgang and Gerald Matt. Another major exhibition with a strong emphasis on African photography was Fault Lines: Contemporary African Art and Shifting Landscapes, organized by the Institute of International Visual Arts (inIVA) in London for the 2003 Venice Biennale.

Besides the international exhibitions, there have also been some major exhibitions within Africa itself, mainly in South Africa and Mali. Since 1994, the Bamako Biennales have become the major event for Pan-African photography. Founded by the French photographers Françoise Huguier (1942) and Bernard Descamps (1947), the first festival 1994 has been mainly devoted to the works of Keïta and Sidibé. The second festival in 1996 broadened the range for photo-reportage. The third biennale in 1998 continued on this path addressing questions on representation, self-representation, and artistic freedom. The fourth biennale, Memories of a Millennium and the fifth in 2003, Rencontres, Sacred and Profane Rites, explored both the history and the context of photography in Africa.

In South Africa, there have been a number of smaller and bigger exhibitions on photography since the end of apartheid in 1994. The South African National Gallery (SANG) has undertaken two key exhibitions of South African photography: the 1997 show PhotoSynthesis: Contemporary South African Photography, and in 1999, Lines of Sight: Perspectives on South African Photography that also traveled to the Bamako Biennale in 2001, as well as Decade of Democracy in 2004. Curated by Emma Bedford, the latter also devoted a large part of its exhibits to photography.

See also **Apartheid; Art; Lagos; Media: Journalism.**

BIBLIOGRAPHY

Enwezor, Okwui, ed. *The Short Century: Independence and Liberation Movements in Africa, 1945–1994.* Munich, Germany: Prestel, 2001.

Enwezor, Okwui, ed. *Snap Judgments: New Positions in Contemporary African Photography.* Göttingen, Germany: Steidl Publishing, 2006.

Matt, Gerald, ed. *Flash Afrique: Photography from West Africa.* Göttingen, Germany: Steidl Publishing, 2002.

Matt, Gerald, and Thomas Miesgang, eds. *Black, Brown, White: Photography from South Africa.* Nürnberg: Verlag für moderne Kunst, 2006.

Njami, Simon, ed. *Africa Remix. Contemporary Art of a Continent.* Ostfildern-Ruit, Germany: Hatje Cantz Publishers, 2005.

Saint Léon, Pascal Martin, ed. *Anthologie de la Photographie Africaine.* Paris: Revue Noire, 1998.

Z'Graggen, Bruno, and Grant Lee Neuenburg, eds. *Iluminando vidas Ricardo Rangel und die mosambikanische Fotografie.* Basel, Switzerland: Christoph-Merian-Verlag, 2002.

ULF VIERKE

PHYSICIANS. *See* **Healing and Health Care: Medical Practitioners.**

PIDGINS. *See* **Languages: Creoles and Pidgins.**

PILGRIMAGES, ISLAMIC. The *hajj* or pilgrimage to Mecca in the Arabian Peninsula is obligatory for every Muslim who has reached puberty and has sufficient means to perform it at least once in life. It occurs between the seventh and tenth day of the Dhu-al-Hajja when as many as 2.5 million pilgrims from all over the globe congregate in what is arguably one of the most spectacular annual human gatherings in the world.

To most Muslims, the hajj is a religious, social, and sometimes political rite of passage. It signifies the climax of the believer's long devotional journey toward the Creator that for many also sanctifies an upward social mobility. African Muslims, especially those from West Africa, began very early after the spread of Islam and in increasing numbers to perform the pilgrimage, undertaking a long and arduous journey. Some of the many skeletal remains scattered at different places along the trans-Saharan trade route that some African historians highlight as proof of the high volume of African slaves sold in North African markets and beyond may well belong instead to West African pilgrims. Unlike slaves where health, body build, and age were always taken into account in determining who would make it safely to the other end of the Saharan desert, pilgrims were their own masters. Any person with sufficient means was able to embark on this hazardous journey regardless of age or the state of health. Indeed, elderly pilgrims and those with chronic diseases undertook the journey precisely because of the likelihood that they might die en route to Mecca, or while performing the rites there, convinced that thus they would have satisfied this religious requirement and attain salvation.

By the turn of the second millennium CE, Islam, which had already been firmly established in North Africa, began to take root in Africa south of the Sahara. Not long after, the kings and later, local clerics and ordinary people of Takrur, Mali, Songhay, Kanem-Bornu, Bagirmi and Dar Fur regularly performed the hajj. They traveled along the North African littoral or trekked across the Saharan desert to meet in Cairo. From there they continued their journey toward Mecca in ever growing numbers, accompanied by Egypt's own official pilgrimage caravan. The kings accomplished this feat for spiritual reasons as well as political expediency, often in spectacular ways that captured the imagination of their Middle Eastern contemporaries.

In 1324, the Malian monarch Mansa Musa went on pilgrimage with a huge entourage and so much gold that the value of this precious metal depreciated considerably in Egypt where he stopped en route. The Egyptian historian al-Maghrizi wrote six years later of another West African caravan of over 5,000 pilgrims that passed through Cairo. There was an equally important road to Mecca crossing the Sudanic belt from the Atlantic shores in the west to the port of Swakin on the Red Sea in the east. Following the example of his father and grandfather in performing the hajj more than once, *Mai* or King ʿAli ibn Umer ibn Idris Aloma of Kanem-Bornu near Lake Chad took this route in his fourth pilgrimage in 1667. He led a caravan of enormous size, including 15,000 slaves, often taken for security or as exchange for provisions.

Personal spiritual adulation and enhanced prestige were not the only benefits accruing to pilgrims. Many West African and Saharan Muslim kings or revivalists commenced their journey toward religious fame and political leadership by first performing the pilgrimage. The leader of the first jihadist rising among the Sanhaja Berbers early in the eleventh century was a pilgrim, a certain Shaykh Tarsina. Returning from pilgrimage in 1035, his son-in-law and successor Yahya ibn Ibrahim took as companion and adviser ʿAbdallah ibn Yasin, who became the future leader of one of the most successful revivalist movements in north West Africa; the Almoravids. Late in the fifteenth century the famed king of Songhay on the Niger Bend, Askiya Mohammed, declared jihad against his non-Muslim neighbors to the south but only after performing the pilgrimage to Mecca and acquiring on the way the title of Caliph of the Lands of the Blacks.

Again, the founding fathers of the nineteenth century Muslim states on the Niger Bend and the Upper Volta river had made the pilgrimage; Seku Ahmadu of Hamdullahi, Shaykh ʿUmar Tal of Dingiray, and Shaykh Mahmud of Wahabu. Shaykh ʿUthman dan Fodio, the leader of the well-known Fulani jihad in what is now Northern Nigeria did not himself perform the pilgrimage. However, he read widely on the subject in classical literature, had many visionary encounters with the Prophet Mohammed, listened to returning pilgrims telling their rich and gratifying stories, and wrote so extensively and emotionally on the subject that the effect on him was to launch a vigorous and successful jihad in 1804. One of his opponents, Shaykh Muhammad al-Amin al-Kanemi successfully defended his kingdom, Bornu, against the Fulani aggression, mainly because, unlike the Fulani leaders, he had actually performed the hajj. As a pilgrim, al-Kanemi stood on firmer spiritual and moral ground than his adversaries.

Just as it empowered kings and jihadists, pilgrimage was often used by the embattled as an excuse for flight from disagreeable situations. In medieval times, many learned men in Morocco, Algeria and Tunisia, including the renowned historian Ibn Khaldun, found it expedient to leave the domain of an oppressive Muslim ruler on the pretext of performing the pilgrimage to Mecca. In 1903 the last ruler of the Sokoto caliphate, Sultan al-Tahiru called on his Muslim followers to escape with him to Mecca, now that the infidel British had control over Northern Nigeria. Fearful of mass depopulation of the region, the British authorities blocked the religious exodus and fought and killed the sultan.

Long after colonialism had been established in Africa, colonial authorities remained nervous over the exposure of their Muslim subjects to revolutionary ideas while on pilgrimage. Accordingly, they used excuses such as control of epidemics, pilgrims' lack of sufficient funds, smuggling, or border disputes to forbid or severely curtail pilgrimage to Mecca. Before World War I, French authorities in West Africa not only made pilgrimage illegal but also arrested those who clandestinely attempted to make the journey. However, during the war, especially after the Ottoman Sultan called on all Muslims to fight the infidels, the French, the Italians, and the British colonial authorities found themselves in the awkward position of having to facilitate pilgrimage to Mecca, if only to offset the pro-Ottoman sentiment of their Muslim subjects. In Ethiopia, the Italians promoted Islam and encouraged pilgrimage because of the war, but also to weaken the Ethiopian church. Recently, hajj management has become an important government undertaking in independent African states with sizeable Muslim populations, just as it had been in the past. Presidents and prime ministers have replaced medieval kings, and airplanes rather than camels are the preferred means of transport.

In the past, West African pilgrims took several years before they finally arrived at Mecca. While in route they settled temporarily and engaged in petty trading, farming, menial jobs, or amulet-making and selling. Many established themselves permanently in villages and small towns along the way, though their commitment to finish the journey to the holy land remained strong. They became thus "permanent pilgrims," as one perceptive writer has described these diasporic West Africans currently living in the Sudan.

Once the hajj rituals are completed, many African pilgrims, especially those from poor countries like the Sudan, Nigeria, Niger, and Mali, stay behind in Mecca for study or for the purpose of earning enough money for the trip home, something the Saudi authorities find increasingly disconcerting. To add to the Saudis' troubles, many West African pilgrims are believed to smuggle in huge quantities of narcotics and contraband currencies, or engage in

charlatan practices of healing, or claiming to transform paper into bank notes or base metals into gold.

Besides helping create a sense among Muslims of worldwide solidarity and unity, the hajj has also facilitated the spread of the *turuq*, or religious fraternities, in Africa. The leaders and founders of the different *turuq* in many African countries with Muslim populations became affiliated with religious brotherhoods while on pilgrimage. The Shadhiliyya and the Ahmadiyya in the Sudan, the Salihiyya in Somalia, and the Tijjaniyya in Nigeria and the Sene-Gambia were all propagated by returning pilgrims who had obtained their necessary credentials in Mecca from known shaykhs of the respective fraternity. Indeed, the political, intellectual and sectarian history of Islam in Africa as elsewhere cannot be adequately understood without reference to this free-flow of Muslim mystics, clerics, thinkers, political hopefuls and, of course, pilgrims between Mecca and other parts of the Muslim world. The significance of the hajj will only grow stronger as more and more of the estimated 300 million African Muslims become financially able to participate in this important annual sacred journey.

See also **Ibn Khaldun, Abd al-Rahman; Islam; Kanemi, Muhammad al-Amin al-; Mansa Musa; Slave Trades; Transportation: Caravan; 'Uthman dan Fodio.**

BIBLIOGRAPHY

Birks, J. S. *Across the Savannas to Mecca.* London: C. Hurst & Co. 1978.

Fisher, H. J. "The Early Life and Pilgrimage of al-Hajj Muhammed al-Amin the Soninke." *Journal of African History* 11, no. 1 (1970): 51–69.

Kickey, J. V.; G. R. Staat; and D. B. McGraw. "Factors Associated with the Mecca Pilgrimage among the Bokkos Fulani." *Journal of African and Asian Studies* 14, no. 3–4 (1979): 217–230.

al-Naqar, Umar. *The Pilgrimage Tradition in West Africa.* Khartoum: University of Khartoum Press, 1972.

Works, Arthur John, Jr. *Pilgrims in a Strange Land: Hausa Communities in Chad.* New York: Columbia University Press, 1976.

Yaba, Christian Bawa. *Permanent Pilgrims: The Role of Pilgrimage in the Lives of West African Muslims in Sudan.* Washington, DC: Smithsonian Institution Press, 1995.

ISMAIL H. ABDALLA

PLAATJE, SOL

PLAATJE, SOL (1876–1932). The South African writer Sol Plaatje was born in Boshof in the Orange Free State of South Africa and received his elementary education at the Lutheran Church Missionary School in Barkly West. He worked as a pupil-teacher and as a mailman before he was sent to Mafeking in 1898 to serve as an interpreter for Lord Edward Cecil at the Court of Summary Jurisdiction and then in the Native Affairs Department.

Plaatje was in Mafeking when the Anglo-Boer war broke out in 1899. During that year, he kept a journal of the Boers' siege as they attempted to gain independence from the British. Having discovered himself as a writer, Plaatje left government service in 1901 to begin a newspaper, *Koranta ea Becoana* (The Tswana Gazette). The paper was printed in both Tswana and English and was the first Setswana newspaper. In 1908, Plaatje returned to Kimberly to found a second newspaper, *Tsala ea Batho* (The Friend of the Bechuana).

Plaatje's interest in politics grew through his journalism, and in 1912 he helped to organize the South African Native National Congress (SANNC), which later became the African National Congress (ANC). Elected the group's first general secretary, he was key in their first action in opposition to the Native Land Act of 1913. The colonial government had passed an act to prevent Africans from owning land or living in territories that the British had declared their own. As a member of the SANNC, Plaatje went to London as part of a protest delegation. Though unsuccessful with the British government, Plaatje stayed in England to lecture on racial problems in South Africa while he worked at the University of London as a language assistant. Fiercely believing in the preservation of his culture, Plaatje also wrote three books during his three years in London: *Native Life in South Africa Before and Since the European War and the Boer Rebellion; The Sechuana Phonetic Reader*; and *Sechuana Proverbs, with Literal Translations and Their European Equivalents*, all of which he published in 1916.

A scathing observer of the happenings in his country, Plaatje wrote in *Native Life*:

> What have our people done to these colonists, we asked, that is so utterly unforgivable, that this law should be passed as an unavoidable reprisal? Have we not delved in their mines, are not a quarter of a million of us still laboring from them in the depths of the earth in such circumstances for the most niggardly pittance? . . . Have we not obsequiously and regularly paid taxation every year, and have we not provided the Treasury with money to provide free education for Dutch children in the "Free" State and Transvaal, while we had to find additional money to pay the school fees for our own children?

Plaatje continued to travel in order to make known the worsening racial tensions in South Africa. In 1919 he joined another SANNC delegation to the Versailles Peace Conference, despite the conference's refusal to acknowledge their presence. That year in Paris, he also attended the Pan-African Congress before he returned to London, where he met British Prime Minister David Lloyd-George and made an appeal on behalf of Blacks in South Africa. In 1921, Plaatje traveled to the United States to meet with publishers of the American edition of *Native Life in South Africa*. That year he also published his *The Mote and the Beam: An Epic on Sex-Relationship 'Twixt White and Black in British South Africa*.

In 1923, Plaatje returned to South Africa and earned a living as a journalist while he continued to

Solomon Plaatje (1876–1932). Plaatje was fluent in at least seven languages, and he was the first writer of the Chuana language.

work for the preservation of his native Setswana language. He translated Shakespeare's *Comedy of Errors* into Setswana *Diphoshophosho*, and *Julius Caesar* into *Dintshontsho tsa Bo-Julius Kesara*. His final novel, *Mhudi: An Epic of South African Native Life a Hundred Years Ago*, was published in 1930. Plaatje died of pneumonia during a trip from Kimberly to Johannesburg.

See also **Literature; Media: Book Publishing; Media: Journalism.**

BIBLIOGRAPHY

Plaatje, Sol. *Native Life in South Africa: Before and since the European War and the Boer Rebellion*. Johannesburg: Ravan Press, 1982.

Rall, Maureen. *Peaceable Warrior: The Life and Times of Sol T. Plaatje*. Kimberley, South Africa: Sol Plaatje Educational Trust, 2003.

Willan, Brian. *Sol Plaatje, South African Nationalist, 1876–1932*. Berkeley: University of California Press, 1984.

SARAH VALDEZ

PLANTATION ECONOMIES AND SOCIETIES.

Many of sub-Saharan Africa's most important agricultural export crops—coffee, cocoa, sugar, tea, palm oil, tobacco, sisal, and bananas—are typically associated with plantation agriculture. However, in most African countries, plantations have not become a dominant feature of the agricultural economy and rural society as is the case in tropical South America and Southeast Asia. Where they have become the dominant institution in the agricultural economies, the centralized, hierarchical, and regimented production systems that typify plantations have resulted in social, economic, and ecological problems that are difficult to resolve. Sub-Saharan Africa's ecology, high land-to-labor ratio, social institutions, and technologies combine to make the production of export commodities under plantations uneconomic. As a result, most of Africa's agricultural commodities are produced by small farmers with holdings considerably smaller than 125 acres. Nonetheless, plantations have been important in the development of agricultural exports and the introduction of new crops and technologies into Africa. Their role remains significant for some key exports for several African states.

Plantations are a special type of large farm, normally more than 240 acres, which is distinguished by the way that production is organized and channeled. Modern plantations are social and economic institutions run by merchant or industrial capital for the production of tropical export crops. Among their key features are specialization in one or two tropical crops for export, with some processing of the export crop done on the plantation; there is some preference for perennials or tree crops. Typically, plantations maintain a large, disciplined, unskilled labor force with sharp differences between managerial-technical staff and field labor. Plantations often depend upon imported labor, which must be housed and fed. Thus, labor costs are the highest factor in total cost of production. The failure of plantations to dominate the continent's production of agricultural exports highlights the indigenous social institutions, ecology, and history of infrastructure development in Africa, which made plantations profitable only in cases where they received considerable direct and indirect concessions and subsidies from the colonial or postcolonial state. These were in the form of cheap or free land, coerced labor, export monopoly, and price guarantees or subsidies.

ORIGINS AND EVOLUTION OF PLANTATIONS IN SUB-SAHARAN AFRICA

The African islands of Cape Verde, São Tomé e Príncipe, Bioko (Fernando Póo, Equatorial Guinea), Zanzibar, Mauritius, and Réunion have the longest history of plantations. Early sugar plantations on Cape Verde and São Tomé e Príncipe were crucibles for the development of the classic plantation systems of the tropical Americas. Early attempts by the Portuguese in the late fifteenth and the sixteenth centuries to establish sugar plantations based on slave labor did not last due to slave insurrections, poor processing technologies, and the more favorable land conditions and greater control over labor that was possible in the Americas. The sugar plantations established by French and Dutch planters in southern Africa and the Indian Ocean proved more successful. This was due in part to better technology, improved cane varieties, and the ability to import indentured labor from South Asia and Indonesia following the collapse and abolition of slavery in the early and mid-eighteenth century. Sugar plantations are still important in South Africa, Swaziland, Madagascar, and Mauritius.

Europeans and creole African traders established plantations in the eighteenth and nineteenth centuries along the upper Guinea coast from the Casamance River in Senegal in Guinea and Sierra Leone. Sugar, groundnuts, and palm oil were the main exports upon which these were based. As economic institutions they were short-lived since production reverted back to indigenous small farmers with Europeans and creoles acting as buyers and middleman. The growing demand by Europe for plant oils used in soap manufacture and as lubricants in the early pre-petroleum industrial age led to the establishment of large oil palm plantations in West Africa in the early nineteenth century. These plantations were established and managed by African and creolized African elites. In Dahomey the kings and court officials established palm plantations worked by slaves. The same was true in the neighboring Yoruba chiefdoms of Egba and Ijehu. Slave revolts in the latter half of the nineteenth century and eventual conquest by France and Britain in the last decade of the nineteenth century put an end to this West African plantation system. Around the same time, another indigenous plantation system arose on the Swahili coast on the island of Zanzibar. Here the sultan of Zanzibar and the Omani-Swahili elite established clove and coconut plantations also worked by slaves. While the labor regime had changed, these plantations remained at the end of the twentieth century.

The heyday of plantations in Africa was the early part of the twentieth century, particularly before World War I. Portuguese planters and bankers established large cocoa and coffee plantations in São Tomé and Príncipe; coffee plantations in Angola; and cotton, sugar, and coconut plantations in Mozambique. German companies established cocoa, banana, and coffee plantations in their West African colonies of Kamerun (present-day Cameroon) and Togo. In German-ruled Tanganyika (present-day Tanzania) sisal and coffee plantations were established. In southern Africa and the Indian Ocean, sugar has been the main plantation crop, dominating the agricultural-export economies of Swaziland, Réunion, and Mauritius. The Belgian colony of the Congo produced many of the same plantation crops—rubber, coffee, oil palm—but state-supported companies preferred to coerce African farmers to produce them rather than invest in the capital and management structure of large settler-run plantations. The large Kenyan coffee and tea estates were under settler control. Low-cost land grants, protected markets, and laws forbidding Africans from growing coffee made white-owned plantations viable ventures despite the inherent diseconomies of this system in a free market.

Plantations continued in some cases even under socialist state ownership, as was the case in Angola, São Tomé and Príncipe, Mozambique, and Tanzania. The collective and industrial character of plantation production of cocoa, coffee, coconut, tea, and sisal appealed to the Marxist notion of a rural proletariat which could participate in the management of the plantation under state ownership. These nationalized plantations failed to match the earlier and already low production levels of the colonial planters. The added costs of state patronage and bureaucratic management did little to improve incomes for the workers or profits for the state. The experience of state-owned plantations illustrates how the plantations' social and political characteristics, useful in the control of a populace and natural resources, may override any economic rationale for profitable production of export crops. The contemporary agro-industrial plantation in Africa exemplifies this.

In contemporary sub-Saharan Africa, plantations are an important exception to the smallholder production which predominates. For example, coffee and cocoa, the most valuable agricultural exports in sub-Saharan Africa, are in the early twenty-first century predominantly produced by African smallholders. The modern agro-industrial plantation is best represented by the efficiently managed and technologically advanced sugar estates of Mauritius, Swaziland, and South Africa. Other agro-industrial plantations were established by multinational corporations such as Unilever for oil-palm production in West Africa, and Firestone Rubber for plantations in Liberia. A Japanese company in Liberia operates the largest single rubber (*Hevea brasiliensis*) plantation in the world. Civil strife in that small country over ten years has reduced rubber production to the occasional and uncontrolled tapping of existing trees with little maintenance and no investment. Tobacco plantations in Malawi, Zimbabwe, and South Africa still employ large labor forces and are linked to multinational tobacco corporations. While southern African and Indian Ocean sugar and tobacco estates are still competitive and benefit from significant research and development, labor remains a problem. Plantation work is a low-status and onerous job that is avoided when other options are available. As economies develop and the rights of laborers are affirmed, obtaining and managing a highly regimented labor force on the estates becomes a problem. Migrant laborers are one option, but increasingly the agro-industrial plantation is being supplanted by the system of contract growers dependent upon a centralized processing unit or sugar mill.

In Equatorial Guinea and São Tomé e Príncipe, the plantation has survived even under state ownership. The expatriate planters are now being invited back, and new investors, including international development banks, are being wooed. In Somalia, banana plantations were a major element in the national export economy until the total breakdown of security in the early 1990s. Even in times of terrible drought, Somalia's banana plantations were always assured a supply of water.

African agricultural entrepreneurs supported by multinational fruit export companies have revived plantation systems in Côte d'Ivoire for the production of pineapple and bananas. A state-owned company for the promotion of rubber production in Côte d'Ivoire also established large industrial rubber plantations, but even here the emphasis is increasingly being placed on organizing and providing technical support to smallholders while providing central processing and purchasing services. Foreign companies in Côte d'Ivoire continue to play an important role in the export of plantation crops, but they are increasingly moving out of plantation production and concentrating on the processing and evacuation of the product for export. There is also a trend toward greater control over plantations by national investors or parastatal companies. Plantations owned by large multinationals are more likely to have labor unions which can press for higher wages and improved housing and health conditions. The multinational companies in turn are working hard to reduce labor costs and overcome labor scarcity by investing in labor-saving technologies, as has already happened in tropical America.

FUTURE TRENDS FOR PLANTATION SYSTEMS IN SUB-SAHARAN AFRICA

Studies of plantation economies in Africa, Asia, and tropical America conclude that plantations will continue their downward trend. Prices for the traditional tropical export crops grown on plantations have been declining or stagnant since the mid-1980s. Africa's productivity in these crops is declining relative to competitors in Asia and America. Africa's products even face competition from temperate crops grown in industrialized countries. For example, production of sugar beet and maize sweetener all contribute to the depressed prices for sugar. Guaranteed export quotas and prices such as those the European Union extends to the former colonies is one reason that Mauritius, Swaziland, and Réunion can continue to depend on export income from sugar plantations. Palm oil and coconut oil face similar competition from soybean, corn, and rapeseed oils. Tobacco prices for African planters have remained stable, thanks to the growing markets of China, eastern Europe, and the former Soviet Union, but they, too, face stiff competition from new producers. Plantation production of fresh fruits such as pineapples and bananas requires efficient post-harvest handling, packaging, and transport infrastructures, conditions that are still lacking in many African states. With more efficient marketing and handling facilities, smallholders could meet the demand for tropical exports without the heavy investment and management infrastructure of a plantation. This trend is already apparent as established plantations are evolving into centralized processing units for small farmers referred to as "outgrowers."

For nearly all tropical export crops grown in Africa, there seem to be few, if any, economies of scale derived from large-scale plantation production. Economies of scale are, however, clearly present in the processing and evacuation of the product for export. Nonetheless, a well-organized system for grading, transporting, and pricing the output of small producers has shown itself to be more efficient than plantation systems, as the comparison of West African cocoa production from plantations and small producers has shown.

As a source of employment it is unlikely that large plantations can extend their contribution. A curious feature of plantation economies is that plantations often experience labor shortages in areas of high rural unemployment. This has much to do with the nature of the labor regime that essentially defines plantations. Africa's peoples have traditionally lived in societies where land is abundant and where, with the exception of cases such as feudal Ethiopia and the Zanzibari sultanates, central authorities were seldom able to regiment or deny farmers access to the land and control of their own labor. As a result, only rarely and through some form of coercion were African farmers obliged to become plantation laborers. Where plantations did predominate, such as in the case of insular Africa, plantation labor was composed primarily of migrants brought to work as slaves or indentured laborers. Countries such as São Tomé e Príncipe and Equatorial Guinea, where the plantation system came to dominate society, are still coping with the polarized institutions and inherent social and economic problems produced by the plantation.

Mauritius was a classic sugar plantation society facing social instability and high unemployment at the time of independence. The planters were mainly based in the country and were able to use the export and industrial infrastructure as well as the capital and management experience generated by its sugar industry to diversify into industry. Herein lies perhaps the most important contribution that plantations can make to sub-Saharan Africa's economic development. In the early stages of development, plantations can provide a basis upon which to build an export infrastructure and managerial experience that can eventually be used to diversify the economy around the major plantation crops. However, there are serious social and political inequities entailed in the labor regimes of many plantation systems. Plantations tend to monopolize an inordinate share of natural resources, land, water, and vegetation in those sectors where they predominate. Growing concern for environmentally sound production is also promoting to greater importance African smallholder production with its traditional use of crop diversity and low levels of external inputs. While a combination of social, economic, and ecological factors argue against any expansion of plantation production in Africa, a

particular appeal of the plantation sector has been its centralized production, which can provide a more reliable source of tax revenue in countries where plantations are not themselves recipients of government subsidies. It is the strong linkage between centralized political power and plantation systems that continues to promote this system in many African countries. As a counterbalance, technological advances in crop production and new modes of management and communication are increasingly able to provide the means to coordinate production of tropical export crops without the economic and social cost of hierarchical and centralized systems of production that are embodied in the plantation.

See also **Agriculture; Economic History; Labor: Plantation; Labor: Trades Unions and Associations; Land: Tenure; Production Strategies: Agriculture; Réunion; Slavery and Servile Institutions; Zanzibar Sultanate.**

BIBLIOGRAPHY

Beckford, George L. *Persistent Poverty: Underdevelopment in Plantation Economies of the Third World.* New York: Oxford University Press, 1972.

Chembezi, D. "Modelling Acreage Response with Risk Consideration: The Case of Malawi." *Agricultural Systems* 36, no. 4 (1991): 427–438.

Davies, S. "Plantations and Rural Economy: Poverty, Employment, and Food Security in Kenya." *IDS Bulletin* 18, no. 2 (1987): 15–20.

Epale, Simon J. *Plantations and Development in Western Cameroon, 1885–1975: A Study in Agrarian Capitalism.* New York: Vantage Press, 1985.

Evans, Julian. *Plantation Forestry in the Tropics: The Role, Silviculture, and Use of Planted Forests for Industrial, Social, Environmental, and Agroforestry Purposes.* New York: Oxford University Press, 2004.

Fall, B. "Économie de plantations et main-d'oeuvre forcée en Guinée-Française: 1920–1946." *Travail, capital, et société* 20, no. 1 (1987): 8–33.

Giusti, Jorge. *The Kenya Plantation and Agricultural Workers' Union.* Geneva: International Labour Office, 1987.

Kimaro, D. N.; B. M. Msanya; and Y. Takamura. "Review of Sisal Production and Research in Tanzania." *African Study Monographs* 15, no. 4 (1994): 227–242.

Kirk, Colin. *People in Plantations: A Review of the Literature and Annotated Bibliography.* Brighton, U.K.: Institute of Development Studies at the University of Sussex, 1987.

Lele, Uma J. *Smallholder and Large-Scale Agriculture in Africa: Are There Tradeoffs Between Growth and Equity?* Washington, DC: World Bank, 1989.

Loewenson, Rene. *Modern Plantation Agriculture: Corporate Wealth and Labor Squalor.* Atlantic Highlands, NJ: Zed Books, 1992.

Maddox, G. H. "Famine, Impoverishment, and the Creation of a Labour Reserve in Central Tanzania." *Disasters* 15, no. 1 (1991): 35–42.

Mendis, P. "A Survey of Estate Size and Tea Productivity Debate in India, Sri Lanka, and Kenya." *Marga* 11, no. 4 (1991): 72–79.

Ndegwe, N. A. "An Appraisal of 'Turnkey' Oil Palm Production in Rivers State, Nigeria." *Agricultural Administration and Extension* 29, no. 3 (1988): 185–196.

Ogbu, O. M., and M. Gbetiouo. "Agricultural Supply Response in Sub-Saharan Africa: A Critical Review of the Literature." *African Development Review* 2 (1990): 83–99.

Pryor, E. L., and C. Chipeta. "Economic Development Through Estate Agriculture: The Case of Malawi." *Canadian Journal of African Studies* (1990): 2450–2474.

Sajhau, Jean-Paul. "Employment, Wages, and Living Conditions in a Changing Industry: Plantations." *International Labour Review* 125, no. 1 (1986): 71–85.

Sajhau, Jean-Paul, and Jürgen von Muralt, eds. *Plantations and Plantation Workers.* Geneva: International Labour Office, 1987.

Tiffen, Mary, and Michael Mortimore. *Theory and Practice in Plantation Agriculture: An Economic Review.* London: Overseas Development Institute, 1990.

Vaughan, Megan, and Graham H. R. Chipande. *Women in the Estate Sector of Malawi: The Tea and Tobacco Industries.* Geneva: International Labour Office, 1986.

PABLO B. EYZAGUIRRE

PLANTS

This entry includes the following articles:
DOMESTICATION
IMPORTED SPECIES
VARIETIES AND USES

DOMESTICATION

With its diverse array of climates and environments, sub-Saharan Africa is home to a wide range of indigenous domesticated plants and methods of crop production. The domesticated plants of sub-Saharan Africa can be divided into three major agro-environmental complexes: the savanna, Ethiopian, and forest margin (see Table 1).

The savanna complex is the most widespread and characteristic of the three groups and is composed of a wide range of oils, fruits, pulses, and cereals adapted to the grasslands and woodlands encompassing much of sub-Saharan Africa. The most economically significant crops are the cereals including sorghum, pearl millet, fonio, and rice. Sorghum is undoubtedly the most important crop, grown over more acres than any other African food plant. Botanists have identified four wild and five domesticated races of sorghum, each of which has a specific geographical area of distribution. However, all belong to the same biological species, *Sorghum bicolor.*

The Ethiopian complex is composed of a small group of crops native to Ethiopia. These include teff, the principal cereal of Ethiopia; coffee (*Coffea arabica*); noog, an edible oil plant; enset, a banana-like plant rich in carbohydrates; a number of root and legume crops; and possibly finger millet.

Crops of the forest margin complex include oil palm, yam, guinea millet, kola nut, coffee, cowpea, and other plant foods first domesticated in the savanna/tropical forest ecotone or within the tropical forests of western Africa.

The origins of these domesticates remain poorly studied. This is due in part to a past focus by archaeologists on early hominid and Iron Age studies rather than the Neolithic (stone-tool-based food production), as well as problems in the archaeological recovery of African domesticates, many of which preserve poorly. Nevertheless, this has not prevented scholars from formulating numerous theories to explain the origins of sub-Saharan African plant domestication.

In general these theories can be placed within two major groups. The first group argues for the independent domestication of plants in distinct biogeographical regions. During the first half of the twentieth century, the Russian agronomist Nicolai I. Vavilov proposed Ethiopia to be one of eight world centers of origin for cultivated plants. He was soon followed by other agronomists, geographers, botanists, cultural anthropologists, and archaeologists who also considered Ethiopia as well as the western and eastern Sahel to be independent centers of plant domestication where local hunter-gatherer

Major cultivated plants of sub-Saharan Africa

Latin name	Common name
Plants of the Savanna Complex	
Colocynthis citrullus	Watermelon
Digitaria exilis	Fonio
D. iburua	Black fonio
Oryza glaberrima	African rice
Pennisetum glaucum	Pearl millet
Polygala butyracea beniseed	Black
Solanum aethiopicum	African tomato
Sorghum bicolor	Sorghum
Voandzeia subterranea	Earthpea
Plants of the Ethiopian Complex	
Avena abyssinica	Tetraploid oats
Catha edulis	Chat
Coffea arabica	Arabica coffee
Eleusine coracana	Finger millet
Ensete ventricosum	Enset
Eragrostis tef	Teff
Guizotia abyssinica	Noog
Plants of the Forest Margin Complex	
Brachiaria deflexa	Guinea millet
Coffea canephora coffee	Robusta
Cola acuminata	Kola nut
Dioscorea bulbifera	Air potato
D. rotundata yam	White guinea
Elaeis guineensis	Oil palm
Lablab niger	Hyacinth bean
Plectranthus exculentus	Hausa potato
Solenostemon rotundfolius	Piasa
Sphenostylis stenocarpa	Yampea
Vigna unguiculata	Cowpea

SOURCE: Adapted from Harlan, Jack R. "Indigenous African Agriculture." In *The Origins of Agriculture: An International Perspective*, edited by C. Wesley Cowan and Patty Jo Watson. Washington, DC: Smithsonian Institution Press, 1992.

Table 1.

populations devised methods of domesticating, producing, and processing wild plant foods.

The second and more prevalent group of theories views the physical migrations of agriculturalists and the spread of crops through cultural diffusion as the main stimuli for the establishment of agriculture. One of the most common themes has been to argue for the migration of farming peoples from the Near East who introduced domesticated plants and agricultural methods (not to mention their genes) to the indigenous foragers of northern and eastern Africa. Alternatively, scholars have suggested that the "idea" of Near Eastern farming was introduced through stimulus diffusion to those northern African populations who were "preadapted" to cereal agriculture in that they were already intensive grain collectors. Once African groups established farming, they subsequently introduced agriculture to neighboring populations.

Perhaps the most common and influential example of the use of migration theory to account for the spread of agriculture in African populations relates to the purported movements of Bantu-speaking populations out of western Africa. These iron-using farming communities are often argued to have been responsible exclusively for introducing agriculture to much of Central, East, and southern Africa over a two-thousand-year period.

Why foraging populations would shift to food production was a question initially rarely asked by researchers, probably because it was commonly assumed that once foragers were introduced to farming they would readily accept it as an inherently better way of life. However, environmental change at the end of the Pleistocene or mid-Holocene epochs was to become one of the most common explanations, as it was argued that regional shifts from humid to more arid environments forced hunter-gatherer populations to turn to alternative modes of food procurement, including plant domestication. Some archaeologists have considered demographic and social stress as causal explanations for independent plant domestication, while others have concentrated upon uncovering the processes involved in the change from foraging to farming rather than on any specific cause.

Historical linguistic evidence suggests that as early as eight thousand years ago, proto-Nilo-Saharan-speaking peoples in southern Egypt and Sudan were engaged in the cultivation of cereals of unspecified type, with sorghum or pearl millet being grown by 5000 BP (before the present). Direct archaeological evidence for the origins of savanna complex crops is meager. At the site of Nabta in southern Egypt, excavations have uncovered numerous charred remains of wild plants, including seeds of sorghum. Securely dated at around 8000 BP, the seeds are, however, morphologically wild, although biochemical data suggest they may be cultivated. At the Neolithic site of Kadero in central Sudan, grain impressions of sorghum and finger millet were found on pottery shards dating to the seventh millennium BP.

Since it is impossible at these early Neolithic sites to be certain if the cereals represent wild or cultivated species, the earliest secure evidence for any African food crop comes from India—not Africa—where dates of around 4000 BP for sorghum are interpreted by some scholars to represent a minimum age for African cultivation. However, the earliest unequivocal evidence for domesticated sorghum (*S. bicolor*) in Africa dates to around 2200 BP from such Sudanese sites as Jebel Moya and Meroë. Similarly, in the savanna regions of western Africa, the earliest dates for sorghum, pearl millet, and rice come from the site of Jenné-jenno, situated along the Niger River in Mali and dating to around 2000 BP.

On historical linguistic grounds, the spread of savanna complex domesticates south into eastern Africa is argued to have taken place soon after 5000 BP. However, direct archaeological evidence for any cultigens is conspicuously absent until the arrival of Bantu-speaking, iron-using farming communities around two thousand years ago. The same can be said for Central and southern Africa, where the earliest direct evidence of sorghum and millet dates to no earlier than the first millennium CE.

Except for finger millet, which may have been initially domesticated outside Ethiopia, the unique crops of the Ethiopian complex evidently were not introduced during prehistoric times to other regions of Africa, as were cultigens of the savanna complex. Historical linguistic data propose that by 7000 BP "proto-Cushites" in the northern and central Ethiopian highlands were cultivating such cereals as teff and finger millet, while in the southern highlands early Omotic-speaking peoples were engaged in the domestication of enset.

Because of the lack of archaeological research on the Ethiopian Neolithic, there is remarkably little direct archaeological evidence for early cultivation. In the 1970s, excavations at Gobedra rock shelter in northern Ethiopia produced surprisingly fresh-looking uncharred seeds of cultivated finger millet from strata bracketed by radiocarbon dates of 9000 and 5000 BP. However, later radiocarbon accelerator dating of the actual seeds indicated they are intrusive and are only about one thousand years old.

Excavations at the site of Ona Nagast on Bieta Giyorgis hill overlooking the ancient capital of Aksum have produced the first direct evidence for domesticated teff. Here teff as well as lentil and grape seeds were recovered from strata dating to around 400–700 CE. Another team of researchers excavating in the domestic area of ancient Aksum have discovered the first remains of noog, as well as a range of unspecified pulses and crops of Near Eastern origin, dating to around the sixth century CE. These finds, however, only provide minimal age estimates for the cultivation of Ethiopian complex crops, which surely are of much greater antiquity.

Turning to crops of the forest margin complex, historical linguistic evidence suggests a great antiquity for many of these plants, especially the yam and oil palm. However, as with the other two complexes, direct archaeological evidence for these crops is very limited. Charred oil palm nuts and cowpeas dating to about 2,500 years ago have been recovered from Kintampo period and other sites in Ghana, Liberia, and Nigeria and are assumed to be cultivated varieties (although this still remains uncertain). Virtually nothing is known about the origins of yams and other tubers, as preservation problems have so far prevented archaeologists from recovering the remains of these important domesticates.

Research into the origins of sub-Saharan Africa's domesticated plants was still in its infancy at the close of the twentieth century, as only a handful of archaeological sites had provided direct evidence for the age and distribution of early domesticates. Many more problem-oriented, long-term archaeological projects will be needed before there is a significant improvement in the database necessary to test the various hypotheses generated to explain the evolution of African plant domestication.

See also **Agriculture; Archaeology and Prehistory; Demography; Ecosystems; Linguistics, Historical; Production Strategies.**

BIBLIOGRAPHY

Bard, Kathryn A., and Rodolfo Fattovich. "The I.U.O./ B.U. Excavation at Bieta Giyorgis (Aksum): An Interim Report." *Nyame Akuma* 44 (1995): 25–27.

Bower, J. "Early Food Production in Africa." *Evolutionary Anthropology* 4 (1995): 130–139.

Clark, J. Desmond, and Steven A. Brandt, eds. *From Hunters to Farmers: The Causes and Consequences of*

Food Production in Africa. Berkeley: University of California Press, 1984.

Harlan, Jack R. "Indigenous African Agriculture." In *The Origins of Agriculture: An International Perspective,* ed. C. Wesley Cowan and Patty Jo Watson. Washington, DC: Smithsonian Institution Press, 1992.

Harlan, Jack R; Jan M. J. de Wet; and Ann B. L. Stemler; eds. *Origins of African Plant Domestication.* The Hague: Mouton, 1976.

Phillipson, David W. *African Archaeology,* 2nd edition. Cambridge, U.K.: Cambridge University Press, 1993.

Phillipson, David W. "The B.I.E.A. Aksum Excavations, 1995." *Nyame Akuma* 46 (1996): 24–33.

Shaw, Thurstan, et al., eds. *The Archaeology of Africa: Food, Metals, and Towns.* London: Routledge, 1993.

Sutton, John E. G., ed. "The Growth of Farming Communities in Africa from the Equator Southwards." *Azania* 29–30 (1994–1995). Special double volume.

STEVEN BRANDT

IMPORTED SPECIES

Since the earliest times, Africa's farmers have exploited their geographical proximity to other continents and their ever-increasing engagement with global neighbors to experiment with exotic species of plants. African farmers drew on traditions of creativity and innovation they first applied to indigenous crops to experiment with new plants, to domesticate some to their own preferences before adopting them as staples, and to reject entirely others they deemed unattractive.

Nile Valley farmers integrated wheat, barley, lentils, and peas from southwest Asia into their repertoire of domestic grains and vegetables by the fifth millennium BCE, and cannabis at an undetermined but similarly early date. Neighbors in the Red Sea hills, Ethiopian highlands, and a moist strip of the Mediterranean coast soon replicated their success. These early seed trials preceded more difficult transfers of perishable cuttings of food crops from tropical South Asia, including sugarcane, starchy plantains, and sweet bananas before 400 BCE. Farmers in East and Central Africa found plantains to be a crop ideally suited to moist forests, where the exotic plant produced more food with less labor than that required for indigenous starches such as African yams and ensete. By 1000 CE, these farmers had acquired through intensifying Indian Ocean trade a new,

highly productive variety of plantains which they used to pioneer highland environments unsuitable for the older types, an Asian species of yam they planted on ground too wet for the African species, and the beach-tolerant coconut. Islamic horticulturalists added citrus plants to courtly herbaria in North Africa, but for limited medical use. In general, early African farmers used foreign species to supplement, rather than completely supplant, indigenous crop plants.

Fifteenth-century maritime explorers from western Europe and the traders who followed them introduced an incredible variety of new plant species collected throughout the world in order to provision themselves, but African farmers stole some for themselves. Africans adapted and then adopted many new fruits and vegetables from the Americas including maize, cassava (also known as manioc), peanuts, common (or kidney) beans, chile peppers, pumpkins, squashes, pineapples, papayas, guavas, and tomatoes. From Asian origins, they took mangos, ginger, and a species of rice distinct from their indigenous type. Women tested new plants in their kitchen gardens, where they could evaluate their qualities and requirements and adapt them to their preferences. Africans generally had little regard for Northern European garden plants, which fared particularly poorly in Africa's tropical environments, and they adopted few of the non-food plants introduced from abroad—except tobacco, which rapidly captured African addicts. But maize's popularity was even greater, racing across the continent as farmers eagerly converted plots of sorghum and millet to the quickly maturing exotic. Some found they could take two harvests per year, and all recognized that maize's covered ears protected grain from loss to birds or spillage. But by the eighteenth century, increasingly sporadic rainfall deprived it of the regular watering it needed to thrive, and maize farmers everywhere found themselves vulnerable to hunger, debt, violence, and enslavement.

Heightened inequality in nineteenth-century Africa coerced people to farm crops with little or no nutritional significance but which had parts that middlemen could convert into cash on world markets. Slaves, forced laborers, and peasant farmers enjoyed little if any choice to work with new foreign crops from the Americas, including a new species of cotton, a new latex-producing tree, a new species of groundnut, the fibrous sisal, and cocoa for chocolate. Plantation owners took coffee out of its native Ethiopia to colonize new highlands in East and Central Africa, where tea from Asia also thrived. On East African islands, slaves also produced cloves and vanilla beans originally from Southeast Asia, and they carried the burden of a new expansion of sugarcane culture. Everywhere the European concessionaires and their African partners maximized their profit margins by pushing the costs to build transportation infrastructures needed to move raw goods into taxes levied on the farmers themselves, and they routed the course of roads and railways to connect ports with the ecological regimes the cash crops demanded.

Cash cropping of imported species came at the expense of food security because these crops were so labor-intensive they left little time for food gardens, and they exhausted African soils rapidly enough to require constant clearing of new plots. Many farmers turned to the cassava that they had previously shunned as only a famine food, but now the hardy crop filled their bellies with little work, which was particularly dear in the aftermath of the 1918 flu pandemic. Farmers also turned to petrochemical fertilizers and pesticides to artificially sustain fragile cash-crop economies and ecologies, which only deepened their dependence on expensive imported technology amid long-term decline in prices for their own agricultural products. By the end of the twentieth century, Africans had lost their food self-sufficiency and were importing more food than they exported.

Other colonial-era plant introductions produced equally disastrous, if unintended, long-term consequences for Africans. Most notorious is the water hyacinth, whose aggressive growth chokes once navigable inland waterways and starves fish of oxygen. No less pernicious is azolla, with fernlike leaves that matt together to provide an ideal breeding ground for the mosquitoes that transmit the malarial parasite and improve the habitat for the snail that harbors the agent of bilharzia. On the vast savannas of southern and eastern Africa, the seeds of foreign grasses first introduced by outsiders to improve pastures with more biomass now travel as hitchhikers as herders move their livestock away from dry-season bushfires made more violent by the new grasses' sensitivity to drought and away from the expanding frontier of barren land exhausted by the nutrient-demanding invasive species.

Plant scientists have most recently developed new varieties of established African crops. Multinational corporations' laboratory scientists engineered maize genes to program their patented plants to produce their own pesticide and to tolerate their companies' particular brand of weed-killers. Collaboration between African agronomists, foreign researchers, and expert farmers was the hallmark of the project to combine the best characteristics of Asian and African species of rice, which could not intermingle genes on their own. Their open-source "new rice for Africa" (NERICA) offers an optimistic model for developing Africans' agricultural aspirations in the future.

See also **Agriculture; Livestock; Slavery and Servile Institutions; Soils; Travel and Exploration.**

BIBLIOGRAPHY

Alpern, Stanley. "The European Introduction of Crops to West Africa." *History in Africa* 19 (1992): 13–41.

Isaacman, Allen. *Cotton Is the Mother of Poverty: Peasants, Work, and Rural Struggle in Colonial Mozambique, 1938–1961.* Portsmouth, NH: Heinemann, 1995.

McCann, James C. *Maize and Grace: Africa's Encounter with a New World Crop, 1500–2000.* Cambridge, MA: Harvard University Press, 2005.

Rossel, Gerda. *Taxonomic-Linguistic Study of Plantain in Africa.* Leiden, The Netherlands: Research School CNWS Publications, 1998.

Vansina, Jan. "Histoire du manioc en Afrique Centrale avant 1850." *Padieuma* 43 (1997): 255–279.

Bernd, Heine, and Karsten Legère. *Swahili Plants: An Ethnobotanical Survey.* Cologne, Germany: R. Knöppe Verlag, 1995.

J. D. LA FLEUR

VARIETIES AND USES

Throughout sub-Saharan Africa, the savannas, woodlands, and forests supply many products essential to the well-being of rural communities. Over two-thirds of Africa's 600 million people rely directly or indirectly on forests for their livelihoods, including food security. A survey conducted among the various ethnic groups in Burkina Faso and Bénin has shown that more than two-thirds of all plant species are put to use. Even urban dwellers receive a host of inputs from plant-based resources. In addition, a range of plants is important in export markets. Plant products are largely from natural systems, or their modified derivatives, not from planted exotic species, except in the obvious case of crops such as maize and cassava. Natural or seminatural systems are the primary source of energy, as firewood and charcoal, and a crucial source of cash income and subsistence. Important products include poles and construction materials, timber, tool handles, household utensils, wild foods, medicines, leaf litter, and grazing. In addition, natural systems have a service role in controlling soil erosion, providing shade, modifying hydrological cycles, and maintaining soil fertility. Religious and cultural customs that relate to designated areas and certain tree species are vital to the spiritual well-being of rural communities.

Species use is highly selective, providing the preferred species are available. In a village in Malawi, nearly ninety tree and shrub species were identified as being used for various purposes.

WOOD PRODUCTS

Firewood. Approximately 600 million people in Africa depend on biomass for their cooking needs. Women are the principal collectors and consumers of firewood for domestic uses and are highly species selective, where choice has not been eroded by deforestation. The characteristics of favored firewood plants include: burning with a hot flame, producing little smoke, and having long-lasting embers. Dry wood of small dimensions is preferred, because it is easier to collect and transport than wood of living trees. Men are generally responsible for the collection of larger quantities and diameters of firewood, such as for brick burning or fish smoking. They often use a sledge or cart to transport the wood and are not so particular about the species collected.

Traditional beliefs forbid the use of certain species. For example, in Malawi it is taboo to use the wood of *Psorospermum febrifugum* for fires, because it is believed that its smoke causes family conflicts (its local name means trouble stirrer).

The forests and woodlands are a vital source of firewood and charcoal for urban populations. Whereas fuelwood markets are relatively uncommon in rural areas, urban households are generally dependent on the market to meet their energy needs. In Mozambique, annual household fuelwood consumption is estimated at 52.5 million cubic feet. In Tanzania, around 91 percent of all domestic energy consumed in the country is from fuelwood. Some industries also rely on wood for fuel. The cheapest source of fuel for the Malawian tobacco industry is wood. Wood for tobacco curing, accounting for an estimated 17 percent of the country's total energy consumption in the late 1970s, comes from the unlicensed clearance of woodlands.

Timber. There are many fine timber species in sub-Saharan Africa. One of the most important in eastern and southern Africa is *Pterocarpus angolensis*. It is durable, works well, and shrinks little in drying. Another notable species is *Dalbergia melanoxylon*, considered one of the best turnery woods in the world, and used for making musical instruments. It is the world's most valuable timber, fetching close to US$6.098 per cubic foot in the international market for sawn timber. Many species face overexploitation. For example, the accessible stock of *P. angolensis* has been felled in southern Malawi, and the furniture industry relies on supplies from across the border in Mozambique. Because of armed conflict that kept loggers out in Mozambique, it still has large stocks of valuable indigenous hardwoods, and commercial logging operations have increased since the cessation of the war. The timber is being exported as logs to South Africa, Portugal, and Germany.

The humid tropics contain the greatest extent of timber for the international market, and logging is important in the economies of countries in the area. For example, in Cameroon, the industry generates 28 percent of all nonpetroleum export revenues. The forests of the tropics region were opened to logging, and agriculture began to expand into forested areas in the 1970s. Although some countries have been extensively logged, the forests in others have been protected because of infrastructure limitations or armed conflict.

The supply of construction materials for local use is still a vital role of woodlands and forests, though in places where the resource has become

Truck carrying wood for fuel. Wood serves as the basis for domestic energy in sub-Saharan Africa. Additionally, plants and woodlands are used for food, medicine, timber, firewood, household utensils, and other implements that sustain the livelihoods of the 600 million people in the region. PHOTOGRAPH BY B. M. CAMPBELL

degraded, the large diameter posts of durable timber traditionally used have become scarce. House and barn construction requires many poles of different dimensions, weights, and durability, as well as rope fiber for tying them together and grass for thatching, which has to be replaced at frequent intervals. Rope fiber, made by peeling strips from beneath the bark, needs to be strong, long, and easily separated from the tree stem and the bark.

Household Implements and Curios. Wood is the principal material for making domestic implements: hoe and axe handles, pestles and mortars, cooking sticks, plates, bowls, bows and arrows, drums, knobkerries, walking sticks, harnesses, and oxcarts. It is also important for carved curios, an important income earner and sometime source of foreign exchange. The woodcarving industry in Kenya, characterized primarily by carved bowls, rhinoceroses, and giraffes, is the largest of its kind in Africa, generating an estimated US$20 million/

year in export revenue. As with firewood, specific attributes are required of the wood for each express purpose. Drawing on Malawian examples, hunting tools, such as knobkerries and arrows, are made from dense heartwoods such as that of *Swartzia madagascariensis*, and bows are made from light, durable, and flexible woods such as *Diplorhynchus condylocarpon* and *Cordia abyssinica*. For axe and hoe handles, species with woods having interlocked grain at the root collar, and that are strong, resist splitting, and sand to a smooth finish, such as *Julbernardia paniculata*, are preferred. *Terminalia sericea* is the preferred species for yokes, because of its flexibility.

WILD FOODS
The woodland of the Lubumbashi region in Democratic Republic of the Congo reportedly produces more than fifty edible plants, including fruits of *Strychnos* and *Chrysophyllum bangweolense*; drupes of *Vitex*, *Parinari*, and *Uapaca*; flowers and seeds

of *Stenostylis*; tubers of *Dioscorea*; bulbs of *Cyanastrum johnstonii*; and young shoots of *Adenia gummifera*. Whereas the consumption of fresh fruit is still important, in some areas the use of other edible woodland products has declined. In southern Zimbabwe, there has been a shift from foodstuffs gathered in woodlands toward weeds and pests collected from arable and disturbed land. Indigenous foods are of great importance in the diet of rural people; their role in the cash economy appears to be much more variable.

Fruit. Wild fruits are abundant in tropical forests and woodlands. In Tanzania, eighty-three species of indigenous fruit trees have been recorded. Although children primarily consume them, adults will also eat wild fruits while they are walking through the bush, herding animals, or collecting other products. Wild fruit is not normally a major constituent in the diet, but is an important vitamin and nutrient supplementary source of food. Many fruits are a major source of iron, and some have a high crude protein and calcium content. Wild fruits are more important in remote areas and are especially important during times of famine. *Grewia flavescens* fruits, ground and made into a porridge, comprised nearly 25 percent of the food items during the dry season in a remote communal area in northern Zimbabwe after a major drought.

Mushrooms. Many woodland types have abundant and diverse mushroom populations. In Malawi, sixty species of edible fungi have been documented. In a village in the Kasungu district of Malawi, 16 percent of journeys to the woodlands in a six-month period were for mushroom collection—second only to firewood collection trips. During the rains, mushrooms are widely sold along roadsides, particularly by women and children.

Insects. Insects, such as caterpillars and termites, are widely consumed in Africa and constitute a valuable source of protein, vitamins, and energy. They are often eaten as a relish to supplement a generally starchy staple diet. Although woodlands are well-known as a source of honey, their value as the major source of edible caterpillars in Africa is less widely recognized. To rural people, however, this is a resource of great importance that influences public attitudes toward conservation. A survey of public attitudes toward Kasungu National Park in Malawi found that the resources the majority of

people wanted to harvest from the park were honey and caterpillars.

Fourteen species of edible caterpillars are recorded in Kasungu district, Malawi, of which four species are preferred, partly because of taste, partly because of availability. Caterpillars are consumed fresh but also are dried and stored for up to six months; they are an important source of protein. In Zimbabwe the availability of caterpillars is reported to have diminished markedly; of an estimated fourteen species that were commonly consumed in the past, most of the species have decreased in abundance and some are rare. Caterpillars are harvested by shaking a tree or a branch, though there are cases reported of people cutting trees to obtain them.

Traditional management practices by local chiefs to control the collection season for caterpillars are recorded from Zambia and from Democratic Republic of the Congo, where a magical fetish is used to prevent collection until the caterpillars have nearly reached their maximum size. Customary regulations among the Yansi people in Democratic Republic of the Congo prohibit the cutting of live branches from certain tree species during caterpillar collection. Yansi women burn savanna woodland to promote leaf regrowth and thereby increase caterpillar abundance.

As commercial harvesting for local markets or export has escalated, these controls have weakened under massive demand for the seasonally available resource. The quantities harvested are immense. In southwestern Democratic Republic of the Congo, commercial harvest of dried caterpillars averaged 185 tons per year. Mopane worm sales of 1,600 tons per year are recorded in South Africa, whereas in Botswana, a single businessman was recorded buying 5,000 bags of mopane worms. Harvesters are mainly women, who collect an average of 40 pounds (wet weight) of caterpillars per hour; the caterpillars are then eviscerated, dried, and sometimes smoked for a longer shelf life. Surveys from mopane woodlands in South Africa show that harvesters can earn US$715 in seven weeks, almost 95 percent of the average farm worker's income in this area. Because each bag contains about 80,000 caterpillars, and up to six hundred women are recorded harvesting from one area of *Colophospermum mopane* woodland, there is concern that edible caterpillars are too profitable for their own good.

Baobab tree. Baobab (*Adasonia digitata*) trees are found in the dry savannas of Africa and India. Local peoples use the bark for cloth and rope fibers and its leaves for condiments and medicines, in addition to eating its high-vitamin fruit. PHOTOGRAPH BY B. M. CAMPBELL

Leaves and Roots. Wild plant leaves and roots are another important source of food derived from woodlands and forests. Rural households in Lushoto, Tanzania, consume at least fifteen species of wild leaves. In central Zambia, ten species of edible wild leaves and four species of edible roots were recorded.

Honey and Beeswax. Apiculture is a traditional occupation throughout the woodlands and savannas, but rapidly disappearing forests have led to a decline in honey and beeswax production in some areas. Productivity estimates from Tanzania indicate that 1 square mile can support 44 bee colonies producing 0.1 ton of beeswax and 1.3 tons of honey per year. Honey and beeswax are important foreign currency earners; in Tanzania they generate about US$ 1.7 million each year. Tanzania's exports are destined for the Middle East, Japan, Germany, and the United Kingdom.

MEDICINES

Woodlands and forests, to diviners and herbalists, are much more than the sum of species with various uses. They are also a link with the supernatural world. Use of traditional medicines for strengthening, protection, or purification rituals is particularly important during periods of conflict, social upheaval, or uncertainty, when it is important to draw on supernatural power. In rural areas, plants are used to protect homes and crops; in hunting or warfare, to promote success (or failure of opponents). An example from Zimbabwe is the key role played by *mhondoro* spirit mediums during the liberation war in that country. Traditional medicines are also used and traded in urban areas for medical, symbolic, and traditional religious purposes, and it is important to understand the background of the magical use of traditional medicines. High unemployment, a psychologically stressful environment, and crowded living conditions are features of many urban areas in Africa. Additionally, labor migration creates the need for men to maintain relationships with wives, or to find girlfriends in the urban environment. The protective and cleansing functions of medicinal plants offer one way of dealing with this conflict-ridden and competitive environment, where individuals become polluted through proximity to undesirable people, discarded medicinal charms, or the activity of sorcerers. It is not surprising, therefore, that employment opportunities for traditional healers are increasing. With the rise of HIV/AIDS there has been a further expansion of traditional medicine, as those infected seek cures for their ailments. In Zimbabwe, the urban demand for traditional remedies is reflected in a higher ratio of traditional healers to total population (1:234) than in rural areas (1:956). In Ethiopia, forests, woodlands and cultivated lands are supplying 75 to 90 percent of Ethiopia's rural population's requirements for traditional medicine.

The roots, leaves, and bark of many different species are used in health care, both as medicine and for magic. Plant material combinations are used in self-treatment of common ailments, such as coughs, headaches, sores, and diarrhea. In a number of African languages the words for tree and medicine are the same or similar.

In Malawi, traditional birth attendants offer plant medicines to women for contraceptives, for barrenness, and for childbirth. Traditional healers are consulted for more serious complaints, and they travel long distances to find materials they need. The general lack of formal health-care facilities in the rural areas means that people are more dependent on plant medicines that are normally regarded by the locals as more effective than European methods. The disappearance of woodlands makes it harder to find the traditional materials and is

Ouagadougou market. A man kneels at a market in Ouagadougou (Burkina Faso), where traditional medicines are made available. The success of these markets is a reflection of the popularity of traditional medicine used in many African countries. PHOTOGRAPH BY B. M. CAMPBELL

Ethiopian coffee ceremony. An Ethiopian woman pours coffee during a coffee ceremony in a room filled with frankincense. Frankincense is an aromatic resin extracted from the Boswellia plant and used internationally in perfumery and aromatherapy. PHOTOGRAPH BY B. M. CAMPBELL

identified by rural people as a factor in reducing their well-being.

In addition to the importance of medicinal plant compounds for local use, some are internationally marketed, such as quinine, which earns foreign currency for Tanzania. *Prunus africana* in Cameroon has a retail value in the order of US$220 million per year. Medicinal plants appear to be widely traded, although in-depth information is lacking, mostly because herbalists do not wish to divulge information on their trade. Urban traditional herbalists frequently purchase their supplies from wholesale collectors who move far afield in search of prized species. There is an informal export trade in medicinal plants, such as from Mozambique to neighboring countries, mostly South Africa and Zimbabwe.

OTHER USES
Small-scale farmers often use leaf litter from forests and woodlands to increase soil fertility in arable lands. Leaf litter is of particular value to farmers who lack access to other soil fertilizing inputs, and is critical to those who have no land other than their home yards.

The flush of leaves that occurs in many woodlands during the dry season is a vital forage resource at a time when grasses are desiccated, a month or two before the rains. During this time cattle may spend up to 60 percent of their feeding time on trees. The new leaves are high in crude protein and mineral content. Cattle, goats, and wild animals browse leaves from regeneration, short trees, and shrubs.

A wide range of other useful products comes from trees, including tannins, dyes, oils, resins, and gums.

Many of these products are unknown outside the area in which they are used, and there exists a high potential for added value and commercialization. But there are also well-known products in the international market; from Ethiopia, 2,000 tons of plant extracts (such as gum arabic, frankincense, myrrh) worth about US$200,000 are exported each year.

SERVICE FUNCTIONS OF WOODLANDS AND FORESTS

Other benefits of woodlands and forests include soil retention, stream-flow regulation, shade, and shelter from strong winds. Woodlands often provide watershed protection to soils prone to erosion by heavy seasonal rains, and rapid regrowth from well-developed rootstocks provides bush fallow for shifting cultivation. Water conservation is a frequent justification for protection, and trees play a role in protecting the source of streams.

SPIRITUAL AND CULTURAL VALUES

Throughout sub-Saharan Africa, trees and woodlands are important in the spiritual and cultural life of local residents. Territorial cult religions, in which the spirits of ancestors are believed to guard natural resources are common to most of the indigenous people of the region. There are various rules and taboos that govern the use of resources; these must be obeyed, or misfortune and disaster are predicted to result. Sacred groves, often burial sites for ancestors, are used for a variety of important cultural and religious ceremonies.

EMPLOYMENT

Jobs in enterprises based on inputs from forests and woodlands are an important part of total employment in some countries. In Malawi, these enterprises are estimated to employ over 150,000 people, perhaps 15 percent of the total number employed in the small- and medium-scale enterprise sector. In Cameroon, the logging industry employs over 34,000 people. In Kenya, woodcarving involves more than 60,000 woodcarvers, providing significant household income for about 300,000 dependants. Sales of honey and beeswax in Tanzania involve about 2 million rural people.

See also **Agriculture; Ecosystems; Disease: HIV/AIDS; Food: Supplies and Distribution; Forestry; Healing and Health Care: African Theories and Therapies; Lubumbashi; Production Strategies: Agriculture; Religion and Ritual; Taboo and Sin; Trade, National and International System.**

BIBLIOGRAPHY

Banda, ASM, and Hilary de Boerr. "Honey for Sale." In *Indigenous Peoples and Protected Areas: The Law of Mother Earth*, ed. Elizabeth Kempf. London: Kogan Page, 1993.

Campbell, Bruce M. "The Use of Wild Fruits in Zimbabwe." *Economic Botany* 41, no. 3 (1987): 375–385.

Campbell, Bruce. M., ed. *The Miombo in Transition: Woodlands and Welfare in Africa*. Bogor, Indonesia: Center for International Forestry Research, 1996.

Cunningham, Anthony B. *African Medicinal Plants: Setting Priorities at the Interface between Conservation and Primary Health Care*. Paris: U NESCO, 1993.

Cunningham, Anthony B.; Brian Belcher; and Bruce M. Campbell, eds. *Carving out a Future: Forests, Livelihoods and the International Woodcarving Trade*. London: Earthscan, 2005.

DeFoliart, Gene Ray. "Edible Insects and Minilivestock." *Biodiversity and Conservation* 4 (1995): 306–321.

Fleuret, Anne. "The Role of Wild Foliage Plants in the Diet: A Case Study from Lushoto, Tanzania." *Ecology of Food and Nutrition* 8, no. 2 (1979): 87–93.

Gauslaa, Y. "Management and Regeneration of Tropical Woodlands with Special References to Tanzanian Conditions: A Literature Review." *Lidia* 2 (1989): 37–112.

Gelfand, Michael, et al. *The Traditional Medical Practitioner in Zimbabwe*. Gweru, Zimbabwe: Mambo Press, 1985.

Holden, S. "Edible Caterpillars: A Potential Agroforestry Resource?" *Food Insects Newsletter* 4 (1991): 3–4.

Lan, David. *Guns and Rain: Guerrillas and Spirit Mediums in Zimbabwe*. Berkeley: University of California Press, 1985.

Lowore, Janet, et al. *Community Use and Management of Indigenous Trees and Forest Products in Malawi*. Zomba: Forestry Research Institute of Malawi, 1995.

Malaisse, Francoise. "The Miombo Ecosystem." *Natural Resources Research* 14 (1978): 589–606.

McGregor, Joann. "Gathered Produce in Zimbabwe's Communal Areas: Changing Resource Availability and Use." *Ecology of Food and Nutrition* 33, no. 3 (1995): 163–193.

Mkanda, Francis X., and S. M. Munthali. "Public Attitudes and Needs around Kasungu National Park, Malawi." *Biodiversity and Conservation* 3 (1994): 29–44.

Morris, Brian. "Woodland and Village: Reflections on the 'Animal Estate' in Rural Malawi." *Journal of the Royal Anthropological Institute* 1, no. 2 (1995): 301–315.

Muyay, Tango. "Insects as Human Food." trans. D. Turk. *Food Insects Newsletter* 4 (1991): 5–6.

Pegler, David Norman, and G. D. Piearce. "The Edible Mushrooms of Zambia." *Kew Bulletin* 35, no. 3 (1980): 475–491.

Quin, P. J. *Foods and Feeding Habits of the Pedi; with Special Reference to Identification, Classification, Preparation, and Nutritive Value of the Respective Foods.* Johannesburg, South Africa: Witwatersrand University Press, 1959.

Schoffeleers, J. M. *Guardians of the Land: Essays on Central African Territorial Cults.* Gweru, Zimbabwe: Mambo Press, 1978.

Williamson, Jessie. *Useful Plants of Malawi.* Revised edition. Zomba: University of Malawi Press, 1975.

Wilson, Ken. "Trees in Fields in Southern Zimbabwe." *Journal of Southern African Studies* 15, no. 2 (1989): 369–383.

BRUCE M. CAMPBELL

POETRY. *See* Literature: Epics and Epic Poetry; Literature: Modern Poetry.

POHAMBA, HIFIKEPUNYE (1935–). Hifikepunye Pohamba was born in Okanghudi in the northern region of Namibia, and was educated by Anglican missionaries. In the early 1960s he helped to found the South West Africa People's Organization (SWAPO), which led the struggle against South Africa for independence. Pohamba was SWAPO's representative on the African continent, taking time off to study politics in the Soviet Union. He served time in exile, in prison, and under house arrest because of his SWAPO involvement.

Hifikepunye Pohamba (1935–). The president of Namibia puts flowers on the tombs of Cuban soldiers who have died in Africa's wars, Colon cemetery, Havana, September 2006. Once whipped in public and imprisoned for his political activism, Pohamba took office in 2005, echoing the views of Namibia's founding president, Sam Nujoma. ADALBERTO ROQUE/AFP/GETTY IMAGES

After Namibia achieved independence in 1990, Pohamba held several cabinet posts under President Samuel Nujoma, including minister of public lands. He is a member of the radical grouping within SWAPO, Namibia's dominant political party. In that position, he advocated the expropriation of lands from white farmers. In 2004, Pohamba, with the support of President Nujoma, became SWAPO's presidential nominee. In the November election in that year, Pohamba won 76 percent of the vote.

Pohamba was inaugurated as president in March 2005. In his inaugural address, he stated that his priorities include fighting corruption, spurring economic growth through education and skills development, combating HIV/AIDS, and advancing workers' and women's rights. In the early months of his presidency, he visited the United States to seek assistance from Washington and investment from American businesses. In February 2006 he inaugurated the new Anti-Corruption Commission.

See also **Apartheid; Namibia: History and Politics.**

BIBLIOGRAPHY

Economic Intelligence Unit. *Country Report: Namibia.* London: Economic Intelligence Unit, 2005.

Good, Kenneth. *Realising Democracy and Legitimacy in Southern Africa.* Pretoria, South Africa: Africa Institute of South Africa, 2004.

MICHAEL LEVINE

POINTE-NOIRE. Pointe-Noire is the second largest city and principal seaport of Congo (Brazzaville). It is located at 95 miles north of the mouth of the Congo River, and 245 miles west of Brazzaville. Its site was chosen in 1921 as the terminus of the Congo-Ocean railway, which links Brazzaville, on the Congo River, to the ocean. Work on the artificial harbor began in 1934 and was completed in 1939.

From 1950 to 1958, Pointe-Noire was the capital of Moyen Congo, a territory of French Equatorial Africa, but it lost that status to Brazzaville, which became the political capital of the independent Republic of Congo. Pointe-Noire, however, remained the largest economic and industrial hub of the Republic of Congo, endowed with the largest deep sea port of the region.

The importance of Pointe-Noire lies in its position as the natural ocean outlet of a vital communication axis of equatorial Africa stretching all the way to Chad and centered around the 321-mile Congo-Ocean railway. Since the 1970s, oil refining and offshore drilling have become its most important economic activities, culminating with the construction within the Nkossa offshore oil field of the largest drilling platform ever built.

Besides oil, Pointe-Noire has the potential for considerable diversification of the Congo economy if the government is able to attract sound partners to operate and develop tourism and major industrial projects in the Republic of Congo (e.g., development of a magnesium smelter to produce magnesium alloys for the global automotive industry, rehabilitation of the old potash mine of Holle, energy and gas production from and further development of the 168,000-acre eucalyptus forest plantation).

With the influx of people displaced from neighboring regions by the country's successive civil wars and with an important West African immigration, the population of Pointe-Noire was estimated to be 800,000 in 2002.

Pointe-Noire is the home of the great Congolese poet, Tchicaya Utam'si and includes the Loango Kingdom in its vicinity, which was one of the components of the Kingdom of Kongo and as such supplied a fair amount of slaves to the Americas through the loading port of Luanda.

See also **Brazzaville; Congo, Democratic Republic of the; Energy.**

BIBLIOGRAPHY

Chippanio, Nino, ed. *Tchicaya, notre ami.* Association des Anciens Fonctionnaires de l'UNESCO (AAFU), 1998. Distributed by Presence Africaine Editions, Paris.

"Congo (People's Republic)." In *The Atlas of Africa,* ed. Regine Van Chi-Bonnardel. New York: The Free Press, 1973.

Institut de Recherche et Developpement (IRD) au Congo. "Pointe-Noire." 2005. Available from http://www.congo.ird.fr/.

EMMANUEL DONGALA

POLITICAL MOVEMENTS. *See*
Government; Independence and Freedom, Early African Writers; Nationalism; Political Science and the Study of Africa; Political Systems.

POLITICAL PARTIES. *See* Government;
Independence and Freedom, Early African Writers; Political Systems.

POLITICAL SCIENCE AND THE STUDY OF AFRICA. Political science is
relatively new to the African scene. Whereas anthropologists and historians were actively involved in the study of Africa during the colonial period (although historians tended to study only European history in Africa), political scientists began their first explorations on the eve of independence, in the 1950s.

A major reason for this difference is that the colonial powers did not encourage the study of politics. The subject was taboo to colonial administrators, who wanted to keep their colonies free from politics because it was associated with African nationalism and opposition to colonial rule. Having it recognized and confirmed by academics was not only against policy but also an admission that things were not the way they were supposed to be in the colonies. Academics from the colonizing countries, notably Britain and France, therefore, did not take an active interest in political phenomena in Africa. To the extent that politics was studied at all in the colonial period, it features subtly in the publications of anthropologists and historians.

This situation changed in the 1950s when American scholars were prompted by the emerging Cold War to study other continents including Africa, a continent that fascinated many political scientists because they could detect the strength of nationalism there. Working primarily under the auspices of the Committee on Comparative Politics of the Social Science Research Council and the newly established Fulbright Program, American political scientists set off to study African nationalism and the transition from colonialism to independence. They included David Apter (b. 1924),

Margaret (Peggy) Bates (b. c. 1941), Gwendolen Carter (b. 1906), James S. Coleman (b. 1926), Gus Liebenow, and Carl Rosberg (b. 1923), all of whom made their mark on the study of African politics in subsequent years.

The early focus on decolonization and nationalism gave way in the 1960s to other themes in the study of African politics. During the 1960s and 1970s, political scientists were particularly interested in three areas that reflected the political events and trends in Africa south of the Sahara. The first was ethnicity. African states had been created by the colonial powers with little regard for precolonial boundaries. Most colonial states consisted of many ethnic groups. It was natural, therefore, that political scientists concerned themselves with the role of the ethnic factor in politics in the newly independent states. For instance, in his study of politics in the Congo (later Zaire, present-day Democratic Republic of the Congo), Crawford Young, one of the pioneers of this genre, concluded that ethnicity is not a primordial factor in African politics but is malleable and adjustable to social circumstances. Nelson Kasfir confirmed this several years later in a study of ethnicity in Ugandan politics.

The second theme was the role of the military in African politics. Many African governments had been overthrown by the military in the late 1960s and early 1970s, and these events attracted scholarly interest. Much of the literature in this area centered on the question of whether the military was a stabilizing or destabilizing force, and whether its officers were better placed than civilians to provide the necessary competence for governing Africa's modernizing societies. Scholars who have contributed to an understanding of the military in African politics include Samuel Decalo and Robin Luckham.

The third theme that emerged in the 1960s as significant among political scientists related to Africa's role in the global economy. African states had gained political independence during this time, but their economies remained bound to the former colonial powers. Studies of international political economy tended to emphasize the neocolonial character of African states, that is, their extensive dependence on external economic forces that limited their sovereignty. Students who drew their theoretical and ideological inspiration from Marxism dominated this area. Although not political scientists per se, Samir Amin (b. 1931), an Egyptian, and Walter Rodney (b. 1942), a citizen of Guyana, were particularly influential. Also notable were Colin Leys, a Briton, and such African scholars as Issa Shivji, Mahmood Mamdani, and Okwudiba Nnoli.

In the 1980s, scholarly interest among political scientists crystallized in a focus on the African state. Much of this interest stemmed from what was perceived as the inability of states in Africa to perform the roles conventionally associated with such institutions. States were not successful in maintaining law and order. Nor did they do a good job of collecting public revenue. In promoting development, they tended to do particularly poorly. What were the reasons for such poor performance, and what were the consequences for society? In answering this and related questions, scholars began to see that there was an informal side to African politics that could not be ignored. What mattered were not the formal rules but informal relations among key political actors. The concept of neopatrimonialism was generally adopted to refer to this most prominent aspect of African politics: the personalized nature of rule and the inclination to use patronage to secure support. Scholars whose names are associated with this orientation include Jean-Francois Medard, a French scholar, Thomas Callaghy, Naomi Chazan, René Lemarchand, and Donald Rothchild.

Some of this emphasis continued into the 1990s, but it has taken second place to the study of efforts by African countries to democratize their political systems. Africa south of the Sahara, just as other regions of the world that were not democratic prior to 1990, has been under pressure to create more open polities, in which party competition is permitted and the rule of law is adhered to. This transition has not been easy, and political scientists not only have taken an academic interest in this set of issues but have also served as consultants and advisers to international organizations concerned with funding and supporting these efforts in African countries. Political scientists who have written on this subject include Joel Barkan, Michael Bratton, Larry Diamond, John Harbeson, Richard Joseph, and Nicolas van de Walle.

Most of political science scholarship on and in Africa has been in response to challenges facing national development on the continent. This remains the case in the beginning of the twenty-first century. Recent research has been inspired by the neo-institutionalist paradigm that has become influential in both economics and political science. Thus, empirical studies have focused on the political economy of both political and economic reform in Africa. This, however, has not precluded a continued interest in the role of informal institutions, such as patron-client relations, and their role in shaping politics on the continent.

Although most young African academics were ideologically opposed to the role that the United States played in Africa during the Cold War days, many received their academic training in U.S. universities, often under the guidance of the first generation of American Africanists. A professional association—the African Association of Political Science—was started in 1973 with headquarters in Dar es Salaam, Tanzania. Now headquartered in Harare, Zimbabwe, it is affiliated with the International Political Science Association and has two representatives on the latter's governing council. Its membership is drawn from all over the continent, including northern Africa. It works through local chapters, which exist in some, but not all, countries. African scholars who have made a contribution to the discipline at large include Claude Ake (b. 1939) and Peter Ekeh from Nigeria, Michael Chege and Ali Mazrui (b. 1933) from Kenya, George Nzongola-Ntalaja from Democratic Republic of the Congo, Issa Shivji from Tanzania, Mahmood Mamdani (b. 1947) from Uganda, and Sam Nolutshungu from South Africa.

See also **Cold War; Colonial Policies and Practices; Decolonization; Naturalism; Neocolonialism.**

BIBLIOGRAPHY

Bates, Robert H.; Valentin Y. Mudimbe; and Jean O'Barr, eds. *Africa and the Disciplines.* Chicago: University of Chicago Press, 1993.

Coleman, James S., and C. D. R. Halisi. "American Political Science and Tropical Africa: Universalism vs. Relativism." *African Studies Review* 26, no. 3/4 (1983): 25–62.

Hyden, Goran. "Africanist Contributions to Political Science." *PS-Political Science and Politics* 34, no. 4 (2002): 797–800.

Sklar, Richard L., and C. Sylvester Whitaker. *African Politics and Problems of Development.* Boulder, CO: Lynne Rienner, 1991.

GORAN HYDEN

POLITICAL SYSTEMS

This entry includes the following articles:
STATES
CHIEFTAINSHIPS
ISLAMIC

STATES

STATE FORMATION IN SUB-SAHARAN AFRICA

The most distinctive contribution of Africa south of the Sahara to the study of political systems is the huge variety of its decentralized and autonomous systems of governance. These include bands of foragers; autonomous village governments by the leaders of their households; Houses (aggregates based on fictive common kingship and residence); federations of Houses (including confederations legitimized by a fictive common genealogy or, in Eastern Angola, dynastic webs); collective governance in vicinages, that is, polities encompassing adjacent settlements that cooperate for a limited set of common purposes, as in Eastern Angola; large-scale segmentary lineage systems; federations of such lineages (northern and northeastern Africa); clans as associations of lineages legitimized by putative descent; collective government by those initiated into the upper subset of a hierarchical set of sodalities; republics ruled by big men (men influential because of their wealth) appointed for a limited term by their peers within a dominant oligarchy; extensive territorialized societies such as Poro in West Africa; a hierarchy of such societies (Maniema); hierarchical or crosscutting title-holding sodalities (Igbo, Ekoi); territorial shrine associations (Zambia); and age-sets (East Africa, Côte d'Ivoire). A variety of more or less stable forms of urban governments may be added to this list, such as governance by negotiation between the leaders of the various occupational groups with crosscutting membership present in the city (Middle Niger Bend), between the big men of the town's major houses (Calabar, Congo River towns), or even

governance by formal moieties as in Lamu. Besides these, there also existed genuine territorial chiefdoms and segmentary kingdoms (clusters of chiefdoms founded by a single dynasty, as with the Alur and Zande) that are reminiscent of the federations of Houses already mentioned. Frequently, individual polities combined several different governing institutions into a system of their own.

Whatever the actual system in use though, ideology was the glue that held a polity together. Power was believed to derive from supernatural entities that protected the members of a polity against disasters and provided the fertility necessary for their current well-being and future reproduction. Those entities were thought to empower the collective or individual leadership of the polity to which legitimacy was given for as long as the leadership remained successful in warding off calamities. Such empowerment was made visible, and hence concrete, through a variety of rituals, shrines, charms, and/or initiations.

Ideology also allows one to distinguish between collective (acephalic, heterarchic) and individual (cephalic, monarchic) leadership. In many cases, the government was a collective, even though a hereditary or elected spokesperson represented the whole polity in its dealings with outsiders. Such spokespersons were not decision makers, however, because they were not believed to be endowed with any supernatural power of their own. That stands in sharp contrast to genuine chiefs who were decision makers, as their power derived from a particular supernatural endowment bestowed on that individual. Chiefs inherited the gift of fertility from their forebears or/and were specially chosen by the spirits. In most cases, their installation in office was sanctioned by the invisible world through a ritual initiation that, it was believed, only the chosen one could survive. Thus, despite the presence of a ruling council of some sort, many territorial chiefdoms were actually governed by such a chief who made the final decisions. Moreover, in many chiefdoms or kingdoms, several institutions could be combined into a single system. For instance, chiefdoms and Poro could coexist (Mende), and in the Luba state, governance consisted of a combination of a king and his court and the Bumbudye secret society. Such mixes were the most distinctive feature of all centralized states in Africa because they grew out of such decentralized and/or collective systems.

CENTRALIZATION

The expression territorial state in sub-Saharan Africa refers only to a centralized political system that encompasses a large common territory and/or a sizeable population. Outside of the Mediterranean world, the first large territorial states emerged in Ethiopia by the first century CE, in West Africa from the sixth or seventh century onwards, in Southeast Africa by the twelfth century, and in Central Africa by the fourteenth century. These states were all monarchies in which the king was perceived as the concrete embodiment of the abstract notion of state. African territorial states had deep local roots. They were the product of a gestation lasting for several centuries, during which time they gradually took shape as a result of the interaction of several major factors. But apart from being a stable, sedentary community, or its nomadic equivalent (stable transhumance), and apart from an ideology that involved an unspoken social contract between the rulers and the ruled, no other single specific input was required. Hence, each state resulted from a different mix of inputs. Many of them arose in areas that encompassed several ecotones (the frontiers where different environments meet) and were endowed with a favorable climate for agriculture or/and for stock raising, were free from at least some of the major scourges such as malaria or sleeping sickness, and contained rich soils as well as essential resources such as salt or metal ores. Denser populations sometimes benefited the rise to larger-scale and more centralized polities, as did a higher degree of specialized know-how, including local economic specializations that resulted in brisk trade, and large occupational and symbiotic groupings (often erroneously called castes) that either interacted as equals or were tied to each other in a social hierarchy. More often than not, significant social stratification, a hallmark of all centralized states, rested on unequal ownership of precious goods. Thus pastoral or agropastoral societies tended to develop patronage systems based on the lending of cattle, whereas elsewhere the big men (rarely women) of subordinate groups accumulated wealth from tributes and/or trade, and banded together to form local aristocracies. Long distance trade hastened such developments when prominent local leaders amassed or monopolized exotic objects endowed with great symbolic value.

Centralization in such states resulted from their ideology. Just as each state developed from preexisting institutions, it also crafted a new ideology that built on preexisting convictions. The result everywhere was that paramount leaders were deemed to be endowed with a specific supernatural power essential for the survival and the reproduction of the whole society. This power cast them as protectors of their subjects, and legitimized the ruling houses and each individual ruler. Indeed, the very existence of the state rested on an unspoken social contract whereby subjects submitted to obedience and gave gifts to the rulers (in many cases symbolized by the so-called noble tribute of special animals) in return for protection against calamities such as droughts or epidemics. This contract was acted out during annual ritual festivals in which representatives of all the population groups of the realm participated, and, even more importantly, during the installation ceremonies for new rulers. Moreover, royal power—objects, emblems, and the body of the rulers themselves—constantly reminded everyone that supernatural power resided with the ruler, even in many officially Muslim states such as the Hausa states with their New Year festivals, or Bornu with its *mune* power object.

Although ideology was essential to centralization, it was usually accompanied by the threat of physical coercion. But not always: thus the huge Lunda polity was a commonwealth, not a single state, because the only link common to the participating polities was their shared acceptance of the Rund ruler as their paramount. In general, the threat of force was represented by a body of armed men residing at the center of the realm. Small permanent units of professional warriors or pages stationed at the royal court often sufficed. Other troops were raised from the general population only in case of foreign wars or of a major secession. But because there were so few professional soldiers, and because their armament was not better than that of potential rebels, such arrangements were inefficient. Cavalry existed only in the Sahel, and allowed both rulers and aristocrats to easily dominate the bulk off the population, at least before the introduction of effective firearms. Some states, however, did create more efficient military institutions, usually by creating a royal standing army. Perhaps Rwanda saw the most developed form of these in the shape of self-sustained, multiple, standing armies that managed their own lands and herds and were based on a hereditary draft. Although this prevented secession, Rwanda occasionally succumbed to severe civil wars in which its armies fought each other.

Even though ideology and the threat of coercion held the state together, they were in most cases not powerful enough to withstand the centrifugal trends towards autonomy for more than a few centuries. After that, the state broke up and disappeared or spawned smaller successor states. Hence, the career of a state consisted of two or more centuries of gestation, followed by an efflorescence for another two or three centuries, followed by its dissolution into smaller scale states. In consequence and contrary to the expectations of neo-evolutionary theorists, the portions of the continent occupied by large-scale territorial states grew slowly over a long span of time.

As every large territorial state in sub-Saharan Africa grew out of a wide variety of preexisting institutions, its growth was fostered by the mix of different catalysts. For instance, the gestation of Mapungubwe and its successor began two to three centuries before the territorial state gelled (when the ruler's residence, including a sacred space probably devoted to rainmaking, was set apart from all others). And precisely when Mapungubwe emerged, the local climate deteriorated. Scholars have long debated whether the dominant force in its emergence was the growth of cattle herds and the rising powers the patronage leaders enjoyed as a consequence, or the contemporary growth of intercontinental imports in preciosities in return for exports of gold and ivory. They have also wondered how much the concomitant change in climate (less rain, hence greater importance of rainmaking?) contributed to the results. In the early twenty-first century it is understood that climate, cattle, and trade all played an essential part in the emergence of this state. This can be compared to the rise of Rwanda where the ideology and the emphasis on cattle patronage were similar, and the role of the climate remains unclear, but where long-distance trade was absent and a high population density all played a major role in the kingdom that emerged there in the seventeenth century.

This slow gestation of states over centuries ensured that no large-scale territorial state was a carbon copy of another. For example, the neighboring kingdoms of Burundi and Rwanda were quite dissimilar, despite their vicinity and their similar initial conditions. Initially Burundi's social stratification was different from Rwanda's, and the differences increased over time. Burundi did not develop the same institutions of patronage, nor the same instruments of coercion, as Rwanda, and it never became as centralized as its neighbor. Yet because they both started from similar initial situations and since the same factors were dominant in their development, one would expect similar outcomes. Such cases point to deficiencies in existing explanations for the rise of territorial states and, more generally, in neo-evolutionary theory.

See also **Aksum; Ethiopia and the Horn, History of (1600 to 1910); Ethiopia and Vicinity, History of (600 to 1600 CE); Initiation; Postcolonialism; Production Strategies; Religion and Ritual; Urbanism and Urbanization.**

BIBLIOGRAPHY

Keech McIntosh, Susan. *Beyond Chiefdoms. Pathways to Complexity in Africa.* Cambridge: Cambridge University Press, 1999.

Levtzion, Nehemiah. *Ancient Ghana and Mali.* London: Methuen, 1973.

Pwiti, Gilbert. "Southern Africa and the East African Coast." In *African Archaeology*, ed. Ann Brower Stahl. Oxford: Blackwell, 2005.

Vansina, Jan. *Paths in the Rainforests: Towards a History of Political Tradition in Equatorial Africa.* Madison: University of Wisconsin Press, 1990.

Vansina, Jan. *How Societies are Born: Governance in West Central Africa before 1600.* Charlottesville: University of Virginia Press, 2004.

JAN VANSINA

CHIEFTAINSHIPS

African chieftainships include a wide range of political and ritual offices that draw legitimacy from local histories and culturally specific logics. In the twenty-first century African chiefs constitute an extremely heterogeneous group that includes the rulers of centralized precolonial kingdoms such as the *Kabaka* of Buganda in Uganda as well as the neotraditional rulers of Igbo autonomous village communities in Nigeria, whose offices are circum-scribed by a community-endorsed local constitu-tion. Legitimated by the real or imagined tradition of individual groups, contemporary chiefs represent African communities and localities in a variety of ways. While the members of the institutionally complex BaFokeng Tribal Administration retain control over land and labor in South Africa, the *Sultan* of Sokoto also speaks as a religious leader on behalf of northern Nigerian Muslims and the *Litunga* of Lozi has established himself as a voice of political opposition within the Zambian state.

Despite its association with traditional legiti-macy, chieftaincy is an extremely dynamic modern phenomenon. While the constitutions of several countries, including Ghana, Zambia, Uganda, Namibia, and South Africa, have been amended since the 1990s to include government-recognized Councils or Houses of Chiefs, political entrepre-neurs from societies with weaker traditions of cen-tralization also claim chiefly status in many African states. The number of modern chieftainships in Africa further increases as many African communi-ties bestow chiefly titles on both insiders and out-siders to honor and reward them. The increasing number of African chiefs and their growing politi-cal voice have inspired a debate about chiefs that focuses on their historical role vis-à-vis their com-munities and the African colonial and postcolonial state.

CHIEFTAINSHIP AND EUROPEAN RULE

In many precolonial African polities, groups distin-guished by different histories, cultures, languages, occupations, and gender had their own representa-tives, who negotiated the status of their localities within wider networks of cooperation and compe-tition, in centralized states and societies, vis-à-vis the center. Often different forms of representation overlapped, and parliamentary institutions as well as diverse positions of authority and leadership, in modern times referred to as chieftainship, played important roles in complex systems of governance (Izard 1985).

During the expansion of European interests to Africa, many African rulers were co-opted into the colonial states. This practice reflected the African experience with multiple forms of authority as well as past European successes. In India and Malaya,

the British had recognized local rulers as princes and thus forged politically successful alliances that they hoped to replicate in Africa. However, because they perceived African societies as less affluent and centralized than those they had encountered in Asia, the British usually referred to African rulers as chiefs. As the term was popularized, a wide range of often very dissimilar offices was subsumed under the category of chieftainship.

Where local chieftainships were not destroyed, they were utterly transformed by colonial rule. The British colonial officer Frederick Lugard developed the principle of indirect rule, which suggested that the active participation of chiefs in the colonial administration ensured the legitimacy of the colo-nial state. In return, their participation in the state empowered chiefs vis-à-vis their communities. The British integration of chiefs into the colonial state was followed to a lesser degree by other European administrators who shared the belief that the strat-ification of societies under chiefly rule contributed to the social and political development of Africa.

CHIEFTAINSHIP AND SOCIAL CHANGE

While indirect rule proved successful in many parts of Africa that had previously been highly central-ized, it met with resistance in many African com-munities where the powers of precolonial rulers had been tempered by other institutions or balan-ces which were removed by the colonial state. Where chieftainship was introduced to societies with flat or intricately balanced hierarchies in the attempt to centralize them, it contributed to the hierarchization of African societies. Also, where women had access to chieftainships, colonial administrators tended to ignore them or to reduce their importance, effecting a masculinization of local and traditional politics. In some societies, especially those with strong egalitarian traditions, such policies led to revolt (Afigbo 1972).

In colonies where Africans holding chiefly office were able to participate in local, regional, and even central government, chieftainship became a charter for the competition for power. For this reason, it became increasingly important both for state officials and local communities to control the access to chiefly office. In parts of Africa, the desire of local groups and political entrepreneurs to obtain recognition for a chieftainship led to the "invention of tradition" (Hobsbawm and Ranger 1992). Elsewhere, both colonial officials and African intellectuals asserted their understandings of what constituted legitimate chiefly authority by producing local histories and carrying out research into political traditions (Watson 2001).

CHIEFTAINSHIP AND NATIONALIST POLITICS

In many colonial societies chieftainship became an important political asset at a time when Africans with Western educational qualifications were increasingly excluded from decision-making on the basis of racist ideologies. As the colonial state propped up the often despotic policies of chiefs, and as chiefs passed on authoritarian state policies, many African intellectuals perceived chieftainship and European over-rule as deeply entwined. Even where chiefs had not compromised themselves by close co-operation with the colonial state, educated Africans often perceived chieftainship as quaint and inefficient. When the various movements for African independence gained momentum in the 1940s and 1950s, African educated elites as well as political observers expected the political independence of Africa to lead to a modernization of African societies along Western lines and believed that educated Africans rather than chiefs were the future rulers of Africa (Crowder and Ikime 1970).

During the decade of decolonization in the 1960s African chiefs lost many of their privileges to elected councils and to members of the educated and political class. Even where the new constitutions foresaw the representation of chiefs, individual chiefs often opposed the dominant nationalist party and the speed of decolonization. This was particularly the case in countries such as Ghana, which moved toward independence under a clear agenda of social reform. However, although radical African leaders deposed or exiled disobliging chiefs, chiefs who supported the government of the day could often mobilize state support in disputes with local malcontents or with rival communities. Although the state remained the more powerful partner in the relationship with the chiefs, chiefs remained important political actors in many post-colonial states (Rathbone 2000).

CHIEFTAINSHIP AND THE POSTCOLONIAL STATE

Since the 1980s, chieftainships have gained power and influence particularly in Anglophone African states. Several authors have associated this phenomenon with Africa's administrative and political problems, arguing that chiefly authority expands or maintains its power to the detriment of the modern state apparatus. Jeffery Herbst suggests that the continuing control of many chiefs over the allocation of land prevents African states from asserting their control in the rural areas. Similarly, Mahmood Mamdani argues that rural power continues to be represented by the decentralized despotism of the local chiefs whose legitimacy is entrenched by references to community and culture. Other authors have suggested that while traditional authority inevitably poses a challenge to the political and administrative process in Africa, chiefs also act as mediators between their communities and the state.

State bureaucracies, especially in Anglophone African states, have a tradition of controlling and managing chiefs. They also serve as spaces for the collaboration and assimilation of elites. According to Jean-François Bayart, chiefs have established or widened their access to the state through their access to the administration in many African states. Meanwhile, state representatives have increasingly sought communally based traditional or neotraditional legitimacy for their own ends. In contemporary Nigeria, the private ties between politicians, administrators, and chieftainship make a demarcation between chiefly and state politics increasingly difficult. Chiefly status no longer just informs the hierarchies of the local administration but is closely associated with political power on the state and federal level. Thus the expansion of chieftainship, even into previously chiefless societies, is not only an indication of state shortcomings but also reveals the state's ability to affect local political structures indirectly (Nolte 2002).

THE FUTURE OF CHIEFTAINSHIP

The increased presence of chiefly authority, especially in relatively successful and strong African states such as South Africa, Ghana, and Uganda, suggests that chieftainship may not always undermine the state or its institutions. The resurgence of chieftainship in South Africa is particularly interesting in this context, as chieftainship in the colonial and apartheid state was an instrumental part of maintaining racially and culturally separate communities. The fact that chieftainship continues to hold a prominent place within the South African majority government was partly due to the state's need to incorporate the sectional and socially conservative interests linked to chieftainship. However, at the same time the constitutional endorsement of chieftainship reflects wider cultural and political trends toward multiculturalism and the desire for community and authenticity (Oomen 2005).

The ability of contemporary chieftainship to transcend parochialism is illustrated by the fact that many African communities bestow honorary chieftainships on both insiders and outsiders to honor and reward them, and government agents, development workers, school proprietors, and even academics throughout Africa hold honorary or "development" chieftainships. Such titles reflect both the contributions of the now chiefs to "their" communities and the wider political, economic, and educational structures in which they are embedded, and which enabled them to make the contributions for which they were rewarded with chieftainships. As honorary chieftainship embeds national and international actors in diverse local contexts, it becomes a resource with which African communities attempt to access and manage national and international developments. At the same time, the very rootedness of chieftainship retains and reformulates local differences.

See also **Colonial Policies and Practices; Ghana; Kings and Kingdoms; Lugard, Frederick John Dealtry; Postcolonialism.**

BIBLIOGRAPHY

Afigbo, A. Eberechukwu. *The Warrant Chiefs: Indirect Rule in South-Eastern Nigeria, 1891–1929.* London: Longman, 1972.

Bayart, Jean-François. *The State in Africa: The Politics of the Belly.* London: Longman, 1993.

Crowder, Michael, and Obaro Ikime, eds. *West African Chiefs: Their Changing Status under Colonial Rule and Independence.* New York: Africana, 1970.

Hafkin, Nancy J., and Edna G. Bay, eds. *Women in Africa.* Stanford, CA: Stanford University Press, 1976.

Harneit-Sievers, Axel. *Constructions of Belonging: Igbo Communities and the Nigerian State in the Twentieth Century.* Rochester, NY: University of Rochester Press, 2006.

Herbst, Jeffery. *States and Power in Africa: Comparative Lessons in Authority and Control.* Princeton, NJ: Princeton University Press, 2000.

Hobsbawm, Eric, and Terence Ranger. *The Invention of Tradition.* Cambridge, U.K.: Cambridge University Press, 1992.

Izard, Michel. *Gens du Pouvoir, Gens de la Terre: Les Institutions Politiques de'l Ancien Royaume du Yatenga.* Cambridge, U.K.: Cambridge University Press, 1985.

Lugard, Frederick. *The Dual Mandate in Tropical Africa.* Edinburgh and London: Blackwood, 1922.

Mamdani, Mahmood. *Citizen and Subject: Contemporary Africa and the Legacy of Late Colonialism.* Princeton, NJ: Princeton University Press, 1996.

Nolte, Insa. "Chieftaincy and the State in Abacha's Nigeria: Kingship, Political Rivalry and Competing Histories in Abeokuta during the 1990s." *Africa* 72, no. 3 (2002): 46–89.

Oomen, Barbara. *Chiefs in South Africa: Law, Power and Culture in the Post-Apartheid Era.* Oxford: James Currey, 2005.

Rathbone, Richard. *Nkrumah and the Chiefs: The Politics of Chieftaincy in Ghana 1951–1960.* Oxford: James Currey, 2000.

van Rouveroy van Nieuwaal, E. Adriaan B., and Rijk van Dijk, eds. *African Chieftaincy in a New Socio-Political Landscape.* Münster: Lit Verlag, 1999.

Vaughan, Olufemi. *Nigerian Chiefs: Traditional Power in Modern Politics.* Rochester, NY: University of Rochester, 2000.

Watson, Ruth. *"Civil Disorder Is the Disease of Ibadan": Chieftaincy and Civic Culture in a Colonial City.* Oxford: James Currey, 2001.

INSA NOLTE

ISLAMIC

There is no distinctive Islamic political system, but there is a Muslim political tradition that involves the competition and context over both the interpretation of symbols and control of the institutions, formal and informal, that produce and sustain them. The forms of political contest and discourse as well as the meanings of traditions vary widely throughout Muslim Africa and the Muslim world, but a constant is the invocation of ideas and symbols that Muslims in different contexts identify as Islamic in support of their organized claims and counterclaims.

Muslims throughout northern and sub-Saharan Africa, both in Muslim majority countries such as Egypt, Morocco, Mauritania, and Somalia, and countries in which Muslims coexist with Christians and others, such as Nigeria and Sierra Leone, or where they form a distinct but significant minority, such as Kenya, have a heightened consciousness of forming part of a world community and use this awareness to amplify their voice and political strength. At times, some Muslims resort to violence to advance their goals, as the 1981 assassination of Egypt's President Anwar al-Sadat indicates. Extremist groups in Algeria, Egypt, and elsewhere continue to threaten state officials, intellectuals, journalists, and foreigners with kidnapping or assassination in the hope of forcing governments to make strategic concessions. Yet other Muslims groups in many of the same countries call for democratization, thus indicating that Muslims can use existing political systems to reflect their political views and pressure governments to reform.

Rulers, for their part, routinely invoke Islamic imagery and ideas to legitimize their rule and to defend themselves against Muslim critics. Acceding to pressure to ban the consumption of alcohol, for example, is an easy accommodation, as is the implementation of dress codes.

LINKING RELIGION AND POLITICS

Most discussions of Islam and politics assume that Islam makes no distinction between the religious and political realms. Western scholars—and, to a significant extent, Muslims—emphasize the inseparability of the two by comparing Muslim with Christian political thought. Although the metaphor changed in early and medieval Christian writings, the idea of a separation of powers remained constant: God's and Caesar's due, the Pope's and Emperor's swords, the ecclesiastical sun and imperial moon. In Islamic thought, in contrast, the frame of reference has been the indivisibility of the whole: *din wa-dawla*, religion and state.

This view of indivisibility finds support in more than forty references in the Qur'an to the need to obey "God, his Prophet, and those of authority among you" (for instance, 4:59). It also builds on the example of the Prophet, at once a spiritual leader and the head of a political community. Yet politics and religion became separable not long after the death of the Prophet and the establishment of dynastic rule. Some argue that this functional separation had taken place by the ninth century, with the establishment of schools of law and the emergence of an interpreting class of religious scholars—the *'ulama*—who possessed semiautonomous sources of financial and political support. It can also be argued that the division of spiritual and temporal powers occurred even earlier—on the death of the Prophet in 632 CE.

Most Muslim debates about religion and politics concern the role of Islamic law, the *shari'a*, in society. Some countries regard it as the sole source for all legislation; others regard it as only a source, and such distinctions are written into constitutions. Yet in practice this distinction is more complex. Politicians and jurists sometimes claim that the *shari'a* is fixed and immutable, but in practice its interpretation makes it flexible and adaptive. Thus Moroccan personal status law is based on the *shari'a* as interpreted by a set of codified rules, the *Mudawwana*, which actually makes major innovations in the personal status of women, for example. These reforms are possible because the monarchy can claim to base its interpretation of what is considered there the *shari'a*'s real intent. In such debates, such issues as the role of women in society, so-called proper Islamic dress, alcohol, and Islamic banking sometimes assume prominence because they are hot button issues easy for a wide public to understand.

SACRED AUTHORITY

The key to understanding the intricate and intersecting relationships between Islam and politics in Africa, as elsewhere, lies in understanding the nature of sacred authority. Use of this term may appear to reaffirm the conventional assumption of the indivisibility of religion and politics. A more satisfactory view is to regard sacred authority as one kind of authority among others, because not all authority is based on religion. Control of the military, intelligence (Arabic, *mukhabarat*), and security apparatuses has little to do with religion. Moreover, sacred authority does not assume that religion and politics are completely independent spheres of activity. They are separable spheres that intersect and overlap according to context. The intersection occurs when groups or states vie to manipulate religious language and symbolism to induce or compel obedience to their wishes.

The bearers of sacred authority, including but not limited to the *ulama*, serve as go-betweens but also represent specific social and economic interests. Sufi shaikhs in the African countryside often represent the interests of the peasantry, for instance, and the *ulama* in countries such as Morocco and Egypt often defend the interests of the bazaar or *suq* merchants, whereas Islamist groups may represent the interests of disenchanted and relatively nonmobile middle-class professionals. But values and interests are not radically divorced from each other, and, of course, values can be interests and interests can be valued. Disagreement over where morality ends and politics begins—or, to put the point somewhat differently, over what constitutes the nature of morality in a Muslim society and who creates and controls it—is intensely political.

NETWORKS OF AUTHORITY

No one group in Muslim societies monopolizes sacred authority. Kings, presidents, military officers, bureaucrats (dealing specifically with religious issues and otherwise), *ulama*, shaikhs, and non-traditionally educated intellectuals all compete for sacred authority. To complicate matters further, several or all may exercise authority simultaneously—one individual's sacred authority is not exclusive of another's, yet all competitors share certain underlying characteristics.

First, all Muslim leaders are conditioned by the modern world, and distinctions between fundamentalists, traditionalists, and modernists are misleading if they ignore the common ground on which they all stand. Real differences in type of education, social position, and ideology exist among them, but none has remained unaffected by normative and technological changes.

Second, the development of a standardized language inculcated by mass higher education, the mass media, travel, and labor migration has objectified and irrevocably transformed Muslim relations to sacred authority, making it easier to contest established political authority. Thus in southwest Nigeria, Muhammad Jumat Imam (1896–1960) proclaimed himself the Mahdi-Messiah in December 1941 and

proceeded to construct a new movement that assumed the style of a Sufi *tariqa* (religious order), including a shrine for its founder that has become the focal point for regional pilgrimage. Imam nominated himself as the preeminent religious authority, and regarded others as lacking knowledge of English and Arabic, which he possessed. The spread of British colonial education, with its access to employment in the colonial government, had already begun profoundly to influence Islamic education and the nature of religious authority by the 1930s.

Third, the combined effect of criticizing the religious status quo and the belief that sacred texts are directly apprehensible has been a potent challenge to exclusivist ideas of authority, resulting in a fragmentation of sacred and political authority. This has led to an opening up of the political process and heightened competition for the mantle of authority.

The beneficiaries of modern mass education are often less willing to collaborate with the state system that made their education possible in the first place. Many are attracted to Islamist groups such as the Muslim Brotherhood (in Egypt and the Sudan), Tunisia's Hizb al-Nahda (the Renaissance Party, formerly the Mouvement de Tendance Islamique (MTI) in Tunisia), and the Front Islamique du Salut (FIS) in Algeria. These groups are led by so-called new intellectuals, who have usually not received a traditional religious education. The groups and their leaders have become self-conscious Islamic actors who inevitably compete for authority with other self-proclaimed Islamic actors—especially the *ulama* and, increasingly, the state.

Sufi groups as well are never apolitical. They challenge the *ulama*'s exclusive control over religious knowledge and sometimes challenge the state's self-ascribed right to speak for Islam. In some contemporary societies, such as parts of West Africa, Sufi orders have taken a pronounced political role. French colonial authorities were concerned that the Ottomans and rival colonial powers could use religious orders to weaken French rule in the Maghreb and sub-Saharan Africa. As a whole, however, the hierarchies of dominance established by Sufi *tariqa*s formed a pervasive and popularly understood organizational framework in some countries, including Morocco and Senegal.

Fourth, the contenders for Islamic authority have been predominantly male, but women are not entirely excluded. 'Ulama and preachers of sermons (khatibs) are exclusively men, but women in some regions play influential roles in Sufi movements. In the case of Africa, women often play significant roles in religious education. Moreover, as with the Muridiyya in Senegal, even if women have no formal position in a religious order, their prestige and status are guaranteed by their inheritance, equal to that of their brothers, of their father's baraka, and some have acquired their own disciples. In Senegal, Sokhna Magat Diop, eldest daughter of a Muridiyya leader, succeeded her father and led a branch of the brotherhood for decades. In the western Sudan and West Africa since at least the sixteenth century, women have become religious scholars, established their own religious schools (khalwas), and initiated new members into the orders.

RADICALISM AND MODERNITY

The ideas of many contemporary radical Islamists mirror the secular ideologies with which they compete. Morocco's 'Abd al-Salam Yasin (b. 1928), whose own movement combines many structural elements of a Sufi brotherhood with high-technology means of Internet dissemination, argues that there have been no Islamic governments since the time of the Prophet Muhammad and his first successors. Similar to other radicals—although in Yasin's case his movement is nonviolent—contemporary Muslim societies have been de-Islamized by imported ideologies and values. These cause social and moral disorder, and Muslim peoples are further subjected to injustice and repression by elites whose ideas and conduct derive more from the West than from Islam. Yet the content of Yasin's talks and writings suggests that his principal audience is young, educated, and already familiar with the secular, imported ideologies against which he argues. His key terms, derived from Qur'anic and Arabic phrases, are more evocative for his intended audience than the language and arguments of both the secular political parties and the traditionally educated religious scholars. His daughter Nadia, a leading spokesperson for the movement, drives home this notion even more by

writing and speaking primarily in French—and by breaking the gender stereotypes associated with many Islamic movements.

In spite of claims to authenticity and uniqueness, contemporary Islamic politics, both conventional and radical, have much in common with their secular and non-Islamic counterparts and, similar to them, must be seen in the rapidly shifting economic and social contexts in which their advocates and carriers operate. Whether in northern Nigeria, Somalia, North Africa, Sierra Leone, or Egypt, these debates over principles and practice are now global, and as likely to occur in Europe or North America as northern or sub-Saharan Africa.

See also **Islam; Law: Islamic; Sadat, Anwar al–; Symbols and Symbolism.**

BIBLIOGRAPHY

Eickelman, Dale F., and James Piscatori. *Muslim Politics.* Princeton, New Jersey: Princeton University Press, 2004.

Launay, Robert. *Beyond the Stream: Islam and Society in a West African Town.* Berkeley: University of California Press, 1992.

Lauzière, Henri. "Post-Islamism and the Religious Discourse of 'Abd al-Salam Yasin." *International Journal of Middle East Studies* 37 (2005): 241–261.

Paden, John. *Religion and Political Culture in Kano.* Berkeley: University of California Press, 1973.

Piscatori, James. *Islam in a World of Nation-States.* New York: Cambridge University Press, 1986.

Soares, Benjamin. *Islam and the Prayer Economy: History and Authority in a Malian Town.* Ann Arbor: University of Michigan Press, 2005.

Villalón, Leonardo A. *Islamic Society and State Power in Senegal: Disciples and Citizens in Fatick.* New York: Cambridge University Press, 1995.

DALE F. EICKELMAN

POLLUTION. *See* **Ecosystems; Taboo and Sin.**

POLYGAMY. *See* **Family; Kinship and Affinity; Marriage Systems.**

POPULAR CULTURE

This entry includes the following articles:
POLITICAL IDEOLOGY
CENTRAL AFRICA
EASTERN AFRICA
NORTHERN AFRICA
SOUTHERN AFRICA
WESTERN AFRICA

POLITICAL IDEOLOGY

Relationships between popular culture and political ideology are complex and multifaceted. Symbolic productions—speeches as well as objects—are connected to the exercise of political power: craftwork and works of art, including such mass products as postage stamps, banknotes, printed portraits of politicians, televised images, and such group or individual behavior as the distribution of a press photo or a televised image, the sidewalk radio (street gossip, the rumor mill), and so on, are linked to the practice of political power. Today, especially in Nigeria and Ghana where local video production is expanding very rapidly, new technologies transform the relationship between local and global political culture. Even if access to the Internet is still limited to urban Africa, the electronic circulation deeply changes ways people locally produce and access culture as well as popular culture relationships with local politics. National media were also transformed not only by democratization, which offered much more space for expression, even if often making media and urban rumor mill almost undistinguishable, but also by new access that the Internet offers to the global culture. All over Africa cartoons, both published in local newspapers or printed as booklets and circulating over the Internet, gained new meaning and new power as image makes them understandable without reading skills. Cartoons are a new field of inquiery on which research is not yet well advanced, the best way to keep informed is either by checking specialized bibliographies, such as one compiled by John Lent (2004), or via Internet research. Nevertheless, even if technological change transforms accessibility to the production and to the comsumption of popular culture, one of its central caracteristics remains. It is the ability to reverse meanings, to capture official symbols, and give them new subversive meaning in the process of sharing and talking about the reception. Performance and oral circulation (even if today orality is postscriptural) are essential for relating popular culture and politics, and for making new meaning happen.

For example, in Democratic Republic of the Congo (DRC) in 1990, at the beginning of the process of democratization, the fifty-zaire bill was put into circulation. New notes are routinely introduced in order to adjust the nominal value of the currency for inflation. The image on this note—the mountain gorilla, a protected species—entered into the realm of international ideology. The sidewalk radio, soon followed by a press recently freed from censorship, seized upon an alleged admission by the state that this new currency would only be monkey money (worthless money). The popular indignation over the image of the gorilla on a banknote bears witness to a long cultural memory in Zaire, since most Zaireans were born after 1960. The word *macaque* (a genus of monkeys) was the common racist insult in the colonial era. It stuck so strongly in people's minds that a banknote with a monkey image on it was taken as synonymous with calling ordinary people *macaque*, just as whites had done before independence. People felt they were being called uncivilized, savages, persons without political existence, mere fodder for the state. There followed a long and spirited public discussion, with the participation of various experts and witnesses, including several former government ministers, regarding the alleged presence of Satanic symbols on the banknotes. Their presence was thought to prove the existence of a pact binding the forces of evil to the president and to two or three other personalities whose positions illuminate the partnership between culture and politics. The spiritual head of the Kimbanguist church, the most famous musician in the country, and eventually the president's personal Senegalese marabout, all came to be involved. Except for President Mobutu Sese Seko, all died within a few years, which lent support to the rumor.

Some people refused not only to accept the fifty-zaire note, but even to touch it, for fear of being thereby delivered to Satan through the agency of the market. The unrest lasted for several months because, sharing a fundamentally Christian imagination, the people acknowledged Satan as the generic figure of all evil including sorcery. Some particularly wide-ranging views included Islam because of the role of the Senegalese marabout.

The arts were involved because of Franco, a famous singer whose work supported the government as often as criticizing it. Mobutu, the marabout, and Franco, were believed to have become rich because they sacrificed not only their family members but also the entire population of the DRC.

It is imperative to situate popular culture in Africa within the historical context of industrialized and urbanized societies, and to link it directly to the economy, market societies, and commodification. Yet this last characteristic, which appears in the better works on popular culture in sub-Saharan Africa, seems to be put forward more timidly and with some hesitation with regard to the popular arts.

In the context of Africa's contemporary societies, delimiting the field of popular culture is particularly difficult. Where Islam and Christianity have advanced noticeably, secularization is weak. These religions favor the broad participation of diverse social strata, without alleviating or suppressing social inequality. Within the African Christian churches, some prayer meetings are held at the Intercontinental Hotel, while others take place on a dusty piece of land. In Nigeria, everyone dances to the music of a modern orchestra (Ebenzer Obey) at a great traditional feast (the enthronement of the oba of Ondo). Nevertheless, some dance in the festival hall while others dance the same steps in the streets.

Contemporary African societies are consumer societies. Even if the majority of the population does not have the means to live the internalized values, many cultural goods originate in local or global mass culture. Literate culture, whether Western or Muslim, is accepted as the model of high culture, which seems to separate it from the nationalist objectives of the state. In that culture originated the intentional confusion of democracy and acculturation, of social distinction and cultural and political betrayal. One forgets that even the most traditional rituals today incorporate manufactured objects acquired in the market, and the most modern politics never fails to resort to the most traditional symbols. Examples are the plastic dolls in the Yoruba Ibeji ritual and the battle between the African National Congress and the Inkatha Freedom Party in South Africa over the question of the modern legitimacy of traditional Zulu men's appearance including arms-carrying in the industrial centers of South Africa.

Social actors do not consciously consult a set of norms of behavior that regulates what they do or defines who they are. Nevertheless, they are as a rule aware that such norms exist. Because of this awareness, Jomo Kenyatta, for example, could use published ethnographies to construct a cultural bible of traditional practices and values. In everyday life, social actors do not behave as Yoruba, Swahili speakers, or Kinois (inhabitants of Kinshasa) even if, in certain circumstances, particularly in the context of mass tourism or in the face of political enemies, they behave especially like Yoruba, Zulu, or Kinois. Festive behaviors are ways to parade distinctions of cultural, social, or political status. Examples include the highlife in Lagos and Ghana, dance clubs in the cities of the Belgian Congo in the 1920s and 1930s, and the Zulu immigrant workers' Inkatha gatherings.

RELIGIOUS THOUGHT

In twenty-first-century Africa, the religious is the central site of the development of social thought. It is a place of identification, where one interprets a particular statement according to a norm, a totality. Fabian has drawn attention to the relation between popular culture and the place of the secular in the religious thought of the African Christian churches. Identity, legitimacy, and authority are actively debated within various churches and religious groups, as well as by African philosophers. In the DRC the testimony, a life narrative presented publicly in order to attest to divine intervention, is laden with these matters. Numerous testimonies circulate in photocopies and on cassettes along with model examples taken from the Western charismatic movements. They offer a new ethic and a new aesthetic of daily life. The proselytism of Muslim and Christian fundamentalists emphasizes the presence of a global framework. They circulate audiocassettes and videocassettes, books, and other materials to even the most remote corners of Africa.

The paradigm constructed around the relations between sin and healing, grace and forgiveness, emerges as the dominant structure for bringing meaning to popular culture, especially in relation to politics. The new dynamic of transformation operates largely on society's base, but there is also increasing participation of both traditional and modern intellectuals as well as politicians. It has been correctly claimed that industrialization and new technologies do not lead to the obliteration, but rather to the expansion, of popular cultures in contact with mass culture, they integrate the culture of the elites and the elites themselves. The measure of contemporary popular culture is the international market, the global culture.

COMMUNICATION

Popular forms of communication are communication inherently post-scriptural because they refer to writing even though they are distinct from it. The visual has grown rapidly in popular culture because television and videocassettes have been added to the printed, photographic, and painted images that have been part of daily life for two or more generations. The distinction between communication and the arts is arbitrary but nonetheless useful, because the media are increasingly mass produced and are increasingly dominated by capital and by international cultural products. South Africa has long led in this regard, whether one considers the press, television, or music. Elsewhere, this is above all the case with music. Up to the 1970s this industry was essentially local, even if the capital and production was foreign. Music, video to a lesser degree, the press, and publishing are torn between integration into a global market, which was interrupted by an economic crisis, and the informal distribution of foreign mass cultural products acquired with no regard to copyright ownership.

One cannot speak of communication without also speaking about African languages, many of which escape the standardization imposed by writing and, especially, printing. Creolization and code switching allow language to be closer to the real world and to better express representations while participating in globalization. Creole and pidgin are as much the materials as the grammars of popular culture. It is impossible to understand the cultural dynamic without understanding their function. In a recent paper Denis Constant Martin, while presenting a very telling comparison between South African and Brazilian experience, draws our attention to the danger of a romanitic view of creolization, which can also be a negation of racial inequality.

The sidewalk radio (gossip) is a literary genre and a medium of communication particularly important for the functioning of every political regime. The popular comic strip and, since the liberalization in 1990, the popular press, and especially the satirical cartoon that depends heavily on it, are genres virtually ignored by researchers. Possibly they should be considered a single medium. In the DRC, where there has almost never been a free press, the free Kinois press of 1990 was assimilated into the sidewalk radio. The overwhelming majority of readers learn what is in the newspaper by perusing copies spread out on the ground by the seller, who is constantly surrounded by a tight circle of readers. As a result, the circulation of information is the responsibility of the sidewalk radio, the orality of which is postscriptural.

Radio and television, as well as videocassettes, where foreign television programs are found, require special attention because of their growing presence in popular culture. In the absence of any local alternative, the power of state controlled radio can be almost unlimited as demonstrated by the "Radio mille collines" in Rwanda at the time of the genocide.

As far as TV and video are concrned, foreign programs such as *Dallas*, Bollywood, and Brazilian soap operas circulating on cassettes and VCD, the action films of Bruce Lee, and videocassettes of sports competitions, such as soccer and wrestling, are the material of popular culture in the same way that secondhand clothing is the material of appearance. The soundtrack is usually unintelligible; the spectators who watch the image have to reconstruct the meaning, taking into account their own aesthetic of reception. Paul Richards and Stephen Ellis suggest that the violent action films watched by young people at the mobile video shows in Liberia and Sierra Leone constitute a point of initiation into violence. In Lubumbashi, the DRC, the young people who prefer these films appreciate them only for their violent scenes. Videos offer a virtual reality where, by proxy, one has useful experiences. The men who attend the showings of erotic films, or more often now, view pornography on the Internet, offer a similar reason for it: they get technical training there.

From about 2000, the digital revolution allowed the explosion of the local radio and TV

"Parlementaires débout," acryllic on canvas. During the 1990s in Kinshasa, young people evolved into a powerful pressure group in support of the political opposition. Educated but too poor to buy newspapers, they gathered around street vendors, reading papers free of charge and discussing them. Their opinions spread quickly by word of mouth because vendors set up stands near bus stops. They were called Standing MPs. FROM THE COLLECTION OF B. JEWSIEWICKI

stations as well as local "professional" and amateur video recording. In most African cities theaters collapsed and video is today the most popular private as well as public leisure, which is available all over African cities in small informal halls. In the 1980s and 1990s, the demand for North American, followed by Indian and Brazilian, soap operas educated local public's taste, making it ready for local production. Today in English speaking West African, mainly in Nigeria and Ghana, thousands of video films are made every year. In Lagos alone, no less than seven new DVDs are launched every Monday and between 20,000 and 50,000 copies sold for about $1.00 each, but the average budget of such a production is betwen $10.00 and $30.00. A video film's commercial life is very short (less than a month), which means that if the previous one was successful a very similar video will be made few months later. Video production and distribution are under tremendous pressure from illegal

duplication, as is music industry. It makes the production and consumption life span of any new product even shorter than a month. It means that most of mass consumption products live in social memory rather than in works available to be viewed again and again.

In the 1990s, African photography underwent a profound transformation of production and reception. The studio photographers almost disappeared when the availability of cheap automatic photo cameras met locally the industrial development and printing of photographs. Today, thousands of young men offer unprofessional but cheap services, widely available and fully dependent on the client's aesthetic taste. In place of familly albums, photograpy is today ephemeral and dispensable.

As in the case of the free, private press almost undistinguishable from sidewalk radio, locally produced photograpy, music, and video are rather ephemeral material supports of social and cultural memory rather than art products to be preserved and carried from one generation to the other. That new locally made mass culture is fully available to political and religious propaganda, but given its low price an ideological monopoly seems unlikely.

POPULAR ARTS AND LETTERS
Popular arts and letters constitute another specific sphere. The internal logic of the field of popular culture does not justify this division, but the international market, where a work of popular art can be appropriated as a curio, something to be collected or displayed, makes the arts a separate field because they have a distinct market. The biggest problem has little to do with the pertinence of the Western bourgeois distinction between art and craft. Rather, it has to do with the impossibility of separating, using internal criteria, the aesthetic of the beautiful and the epistemology of the true; of what is socially pertinent and what is merely pleasant to look at. To forbid ourselves an aesthetic appreciation of the popular arts of Africa would be discrimination. Nonetheless, one must be explicit regarding the appropriation of objects detached from their context.

At the heart of what is considered Western art is its separation from what is commercial and thus might be considered less profound, less intimate. This separation, which resembles the deeply held conviction of many Catholic missionaries for whom every belief system, even the "heathen" can be religious, contains a grain of monotheism. Popular arts in contemporary Africa operate in a context of commodification. Neither the material used nor the amount of time an artist works escapes it; objects circulate through market exchange, and the subsistence of the artists is worked out through the market. The artists forced to leave the market because of a lack of buyers, as has happened to many popular painters in the DRC, suddenly find themselves unable to work in their chosen field. Without a canvas, without paints, they become farmers, unskilled laborers, or traveling vendors; a fact that does not authorize us to question their inner need to paint. Should favorable circumstances arise, with some start-up capital or an advance on a commissioned work, they will become painters again.

In the long run, new technologies, new materials, and new possibilities of commercialization favor the expansion of popular arts in spite of economic poverty. Popular arts do not deteriorate when artists incorporate new contributions and challenges. Studio photography has stimulated rather than supplanted the practice of portrait painting. There is no indication that radio and video have marginalized popular theater. The phonograph, the radio, and the cassette recorder have made the expansion of popular music possible. New instruments, new techniques for recording and pressing disks and then cassettes, and local and international capital have transformed the artisanal activities of musicians into an industry. Music and popular painting have changed, thanks to commodification and new markets offering possibilities for expansion. The number of artists has exploded, thus making possible the affirmation of new talents. Popular paintings and the words of contemporary songs offer a reflection of society: they discuss social values and propose social norms.

Often of populist inspiration, research on popular culture emphasizes the political critique, the subversive character of the text. Yet it must be admitted that at least as often, songs praise the incumbent regime, conveying its values and transmitting its structure. Franco, one of the most popular contemporary Zairean musicians, sang as much to glorify the Mobutu regime as to criticize it. Decorated with the country's highest distinction for his praise, he was stripped of that honor and imprisoned for his criticism.

Song, as genre, takes a more systematic interest in social questions and great existential problems than in political struggles. Its political impact is most acute when a metaphor focusing on social justice or social harmony meets with a political situation. The proverbial use of a song title, passage, or tune shows that it enjoys lasting success. Sometimes the subversive reading of a song or of a series of songs, where the words and music often fit together, is due to the zeal of the censor, who, catching a whiff of subversion, thereby creates a political reading of the message. The ban was specifically against songs in "local languages," but actually against songs in Gikuyu, specifically new cassette versions of Mau Mau songs. In response, Bob Marley cassettes were played, especially "Fight the Power," until music was banned in matatus at which point both types were played, but only when the vehicles were moving. "Etike Revo Wetin," a song with Wole Soyinka's lyrics that was issued in reaction to the Nigerian elections of 1983, is an example of a song popular long after the political event to which it referred.

APPEARANCE

Appearance is fully registered in popular culture, often serving as an instrument of political confrontation and propaganda. Produced in great quantities, the printed fabric that drapes the female body is an important vehicle of the political image in many parts of Africa. In many places political parties and political organizations will have cloth produced with their political slogans. Supporters then wear the cloth and become walking promotors of the political party's message. Monarchs, heads of state, and Pope John Paul II have had their likenesses exhibited on such textiles.

In authoritarian political regimes, citizens deprived of any real exercise of voting power often have to express their support for the rulers through dress made of fabric distributed free of charge by businesses anxious to show their support of the regime in a public place. By the late twentieth century, such a display of support had become limited to specific political manifestations; to wear such clothing every day had become an admission of poverty.

The name of a fabric, of a specific pattern, or of an article of clothing can carry a political message. In Zambia in the 1990s, chiluba was a jacket typically made from secondhand clothing. Frederick Chiluba, the first democratically elected president, symbolized Zambia's transition to a market economy. The object and its name together take on political significance. To be sure, chiluba commemorates the new liberty by reference to the dress and the new managerial style of the president. People remember well the austerity of life under the previous regime and the austere dress of Kenneth Kaunda. Nevertheless, the fact that chiluba comes from salaula (to select from a pile, in the Bemba language) that is to say used clothing imported from the West, recalls the profound economic crisis that the country experienced. It is possible that the collective memory still recalled the mercantilist liberation preceding the colonial period, during which time only the leaders were affluent enough to wear used clothing from Europe. If such was the case, the derision directed toward these same leaders in the colonial literature would still be alive in the people's memory, and chiluba would signify a reproach for what people experienced as recolonization.

Whether in Nigeria, South Africa, or the DRC, the grammar of various modes of appearance lies at the heart of political representations. An example is the South African debate of the early 1990s over what constituted legitimate attire for a Zulu worker at political gathering. In Mobutu's Zaire, the 1972 ban on suits and ties for men and on slacks and short skirts for women was part of politics of authenticity, which included the banning of Christian first names. At the same time, by virtue of bourgeois and Christian missionary norms, decency as decreed by civil servants dictated that women had to wear bras, even during the most traditional village ceremonies.

The importance of one's physical bearing and manner of dress is an urban fact. In the cultural milieu of the DRC, elegant appearance indicates one's lifestyle, as does the origin of the upscale ready-to-wear clothes one wears. The phenomenon is comparable with highlife appearance in Nigeria and Ghana. There are several specific manifestations of it in South Africa. It combines appearance with a lifestyle, music, the places of leisure one frequents, and so on. The musicians in vogue are often its leaders; for example, Papa Wemba in then Zaire, as seen in the film based on his life story, *La vie est belle*. They launch a fashion, a musical style, a dance step. The popular culture of appearance follows the same tendency as elsewhere in the industrial world: at the level of everyday social life, aesthetics takes over from ethics.

Along with appearance, it should be mentioned that whether and how people drink and smoke can be a sign of identity, the political calling card of a Muslim or a member of an African Christian church. Alcohol, tobacco, and hemp, as well as the places where they are consumed, whether they are established bars or clandestine spots, are political places par excellence. For several governments, keeping people supplied with beer and cigarettes and keeping these commodities affordable in relation to the buying power of low salaries have been properly political issues. Controlling and infiltrating the places where they are consumed has had a definite influence on political stability. Group and individual identities are asserted, confronted, and negotiated there.

SPORTS SPECTACLES

Sports competitions, as well as the gatherings, the demonstrations, and the public appearances of political personalities, are another domain of popular culture. There is a fundamental difference between the urban spectacle considered here and performance in the preindustrial rural context. The invention of leisure activities and their specific organization in a time and place set aside for this purpose have in two ways altered the meaning and the form of the spectacle, the product instead of the performance. On the one hand, there is a sharp separation between the audience and the performers; on the other hand, the management of leisure activities is directly associated with the management of a society that is expected to be rational. The spectacle of sports draws close to the political spectacle because the two are essentially occasions to publicly construct and confront collective identities, in principle nonviolently.

The fact that the sports arena constitutes a preferred location for political gatherings is not just a matter of its being able to accommodate large crowds. Since the colonial period, the use of sports, especially soccer matches, as spectacle has been considered a way to channel social energies toward political objectives. This practice of depoliticization inevitably reveals its political character. Numerous major political events have begun at a sports competition. At first, it had to take the place of the urban performance of "tribal" dances. However, it was quickly seized upon by the logic of the construction of identity that prevailed in both black and white colonial popular culture. In the Belgian Congo, a model colony at that time, the first anticolonial urban riot took place in 1957, at the close of a soccer match between a Congolese and a Belgian team. It had already been indicated that, on certain occasions, in the words of the Belgian newspaper *La Libre Belgique*, "in the mind of the crowd, the game quite rapidly took on the look of an interracial clash." In its June 25, 1957, edition, *La Libre Belgique* indicated that the white colonials, not having appreciated the victory won by the Congolese team a little earlier, had "publicly

uttered some unsportsmanlike remarks regarding the Congolese players." Thus, as happened all over the world, soccer stadiums became specific locations for confrontations over identity and points of political uprisings. *La Libre Belgique* therefore reconsidered its correspondent's assertion. In its June 21 edition, the newspaper had painted a picture of the culture, or rather the absence of culture, of the black spectators responsible for the incidents. It stated that only a few hundred highly advanced people were able to truly appreciate the match; 80 percent of the other Congolese did not know anything about the sportsmanlike ideal of fair play. Four days later, the newspaper acknowledged the responsibility of the European spectators but made no reference to European culture.

New technologies today make it possible to replace the actual spectacle with the quasi-virtual and portable one of the video recording. Itinerant small businessmen equipped with a television monitor, video recorder, and electric generator have put video recordings within the reach of millions of viewers, who are increasingly isolated by civil wars, the destruction of communications networks, and poverty. Consider the Congolese example of the wrestling matches in Lubumbashi. The local popular culture, in particular that of the young, has invested these competitions with the ideal of individual self-affirmation, achieved through one's own strength. Yet this strength must be protected and increased by recourse to magical powers that come from the villages or from foreign places. In contrast with what happens in a video spectacle of a wrestling match, in this case the opponents show off and praise not only their physical power but also, in fact especially, their so-called magical power. The spectators are under the illusion of having privileged access to the grammar of individual success. Thus, in the popular culture structured by the market and by commodification, sports competitions, in whatever form the spectacles are produced, retain their role as the places where identity is constructed and confronted.

See also **Art; Creoles; Film and Cinema; Globalization; Kaunda, Kenneth; Kenyatta, Jomo; Kinshasa; Lagos; Languages; Literacy; Literature: Popular Literature; Lubumbashi; Media; Mobuto Sese Seko; Music, Modern Popular; Photography; Soyinka, Wole; Sports; Theater.**

BIBLIOGRAPHY

Appiah, Anthony. *In My Father's House: Africa in the Philosophy of Culture.* New York: Oxford University Press, 1992.

Barber, Karin. *West African Popular Theater.* Bloomington: Indiana University Press, 1997.

Barber, Karin, ed. *Readings in African Popular Culture.* Bloomington: Indiana University Press, 1997.

Coplan, David. *In Township Tonight: South Africa's Black City Music and Theater.* London: Longman, 1985.

Hartmann, Wolfram; Jeremy Silvester; and Patricia Hayes; eds. *The Colonizing Camera: Photographies in the Making of Namibian History.* Cape Town, South Africa: University of Cape Town Press, 1999.

Hyden, Goran, and Michael Leslie, eds. *Media and Democracy in Africa.* Oslo, Norway: Nordic Africa Institute, 2002.

Jewsiewicki, Bogumil, et al. *A Congo Chronicle. Patrice Lumumba in Urban Art.* New York: Museum for African Art, 1999.

Jewsiewicki, Bogumil, and V. Y. Mudimbe. *History Making in Africa.* Middletown, CT: Wesleyan University Press, 1993.

Landau, Paul, and Deborah Kaspin, eds. *Images and Empires: Visuality in Colonial and Postcolonial Africa.* Berkeley: University of California Press, 2002.

Lent, John A. *Comic Art in Africa, Asia, Australia, and Latin America 2000: An International Bibliography.* New York: Praeger, 2004.

MacGaffey, Wyatt. *Art and Healing of the Bakongo, Commented by Themselves.* Bloomington: Indiana University Press, 1991.

Martin, Denis Constant, "A Creolizing South Africa? Memory, Hybridity, and Creolization. (Re)imagining the South African Experience." *International Social Science Journal* 187 (2006): 165–176.

Vail, Leroy, and White Landeg. *Power and the Praise Poem: Southern African Voices in History.* Charlottesville: University of Virginia Press, 1991.

Werbner, Richard, ed. *Postcolonial Subjectivities in Africa.* London: Zed Books, 2002.

White, Bob. *Ndule: Political Culture and the Politics of Dance Music in Mobutu's Zaire.* Durham, NC: Duke University Press, 2007.

White, Louise; Stephan Miescher; and David W. Cohen; eds. *African Words, African Voices: Critical Perspectives in Oral History.* Bloomington: Indiana University Press, 2001.

BOGUMIL JEWSIEWICKI

CENTRAL AFRICA

Before describing the popular culture of Central Africa, it is necessary to discuss the contentious concept of popular culture itself. The definition of popular combines such diverse meanings as produced for the masses, vulgar or common, favored by the people, and pertaining to people as a whole. Popular culture cannot be limited to the idea of prepackaged mass consumer culture, for it often includes social movements produced precisely in resistance to such hegemonic top-down forces. But neither is it simply subculture, for the heart of the concept is its encompassment of the group as a whole. Nor, despite its apparent connection to contemporaneity, may it be opposed to traditional culture, because any kind of folk culture would, by definition, fall within the category of popular. Indeed, insofar as popularity invokes collectivity, it is difficult to strictly differentiate popular culture from the culture concept itself.

Although a taxonomic classification of this fluid term proves rather fruitless, the heuristic value of the concept becomes apparent when examined in relation to temporality. Johannes Fabian (b. 1937) suggests in his 1998 work that popular culture can only be observed in moments, in specific temporal contexts, interstices of creative freedom in the face of dominating influence of cultural status quo. It is useful to think of popular culture in terms of the process of adoption (much like fashion) of a behavior or belief that spreads through a social group along the paths of preexisting relationships. This is why popular culture is often linked to power, for it is always involved in the process of cultural change, and so always a threat to the powers that be. It is at once, dialectically, the force through which hierarchical power is maintained and challenged.

Because the concept can encompass practically any aspect of culture, it would be impossible to treat the diversity of important genres of popular culture in Central Africa with any depth: sports (especially football and basketball), theater (often televised or sold on videotape), music, dance, bar culture, independent churches, women's savings groups, witchcraft, dance, urban slang, and fashion. Instead, a single example, the *sapeurs*, may illustrate how popular culture works in Central Africa.

The sapeurs are a movement of primarily unemployed, criminally engaged youth devoted to

Congolese sapeurs attend a funeral in Paris. Congolese men use every public occasion to compete in elegance. Gesture, mannerism, brand names, the quality of fabric, and harmony of colors all are carefully performed and evaluated. Their reputation within transnational networks stretching from Paris to Brazzaville is at stake. COURTESY OF ALEXANDER NEWELL

dressing well. The movement began in the 1980s in Brazzaville, but was quickly adopted across the river in Kinshasa, where it became associated with Papa Wemba (b. 1953), a Congolese music star whose international popularity carried la Sape all over sub-Saharan Africa as well as through immigrant populations in Europe. To dress well within this movement means to dress in European and American clothing, especially *haute couture* designer labels. The link between the sartorial and the legitimation of authority has a long history in Central Africa, and European dress has been of significant symbolic importance since earliest contact, valued as much for its rarity as its connection with exotic and powerful foreigners.

Clubs organized around the art of dress began as early as the 1950s, but it was not until the 1980s that they reached their ultimate form as the SAPE: the Société des Ambianceurs et Personnes Élégantes. This was a hierarchically organized system of rival clubs that challenged each other in duels of appearance. Competition took place through the *Danse des Griffes* (the dance of labels),

in which the clothing and brand are performed and embodied. Sapeurs display themselves in all forms of public space, including weddings, funerals, sporting events, and cafes, but they are most intimately associated with the *nganda*, unlicensed bars run primarily by women. These are crucial social sites for exchanging information and goods, but above all places where *on fait le show* (one makes a show), spending ostentatiously to impress peers. Such clandestine drinking establishments have been the primary urban public space and site for cultural resistance since at least the 1920s, though women sold homebrewed alcohol illegally from their homes to migrant laborers long before this. The women who work in the nganda are at once scandalous for breaching gender norms and revered for their sexual power and financial success. Although sapeurs are mostly male, some women compete *à la garçonette*, dressing in men's clothes and facing off directly with the men. Photographs that are purchased, collected, and displayed by sapeurs carefully document appearance and attendance at important public events.

Justin-Daniel Gandoulou, the primary ethnographer of the movement, describes the SAPE as the result of the cultural surgery that colonialism performed upon Central Africa, slicing away at indigenous values and replacing them with European ones. However, through the lens of popular culture it is also possible to interpret the SAPE as a vibrant local movement built upon preexisting cultural tradition. Although the SAPE is devoted to the imitation of European style, it incorporates the Congolese religious concept of *ngolo* (life force), believed to be passed through the clothes and embodied by the actors. As a sapeur in Paris said, "*La Sape* is a religion. We do not believe in one overarching God, but in a sense we are all gods, gods of la Sape." The SAPE is also a form of cultural resistance, aimed against both the local elite and French hegemony. In Brazzaville, Congo youth challenged the legitimacy of the Mbochi political establishment that took over power through military force, emphasizing their own cultural superiority. When the elite's efforts to quell the movement failed, some politicians even hired sapeurs as sartorial advisers. In more recent years, the SAPE has become a means of forging and expressing national identity, as sapeurs from different African countries claim superior understanding of the art of dress, resulting in stylistic differentiation and competition along nationalist lines.

This example highlights the complexity and polyvalency of popular culture, as well as its utility as a theoretical concept. The SAPE is at once the prototypical trickle-down consumption of mass culture and a form of resistance against class hierarchy and cultural hegemony. In effect, they appropriate and claim ownership over the very symbols of hierarchy that were used to assert dominance over them in the past. It combines elements of so-called traditional culture, as well as historical ethnic rivalries with foreign symbols of modernity, urban identity, and nationalism. The concept of popular culture allows these contradictory valences to be understood as elements of one and the same historical process of local cultural interaction with global forces and hierarchy within Central Africa.

See also **Art; Dance; Film and Cinema; Kinshasa; Literature: Popular Literature; Media: Cinema; Media: Radio and TV; Music, Modern Popular; Theater; Youth.**

BIBLIOGRAPHY

Fabian, Johannes. *Moments of Freedom: Anthropology and Popular Culture.* Charlottesville: University Press of Virginia, 1998.

Friedman, Jonathan. "The Political Economy of Elegance." *Culture and History* 7 (1992): 101–125.

Gandoulou, Justin-Daniel. *Dandies à Bacongo: Le Culte de l'Élégance dans la Société Congolaise Contemporaine.* Paris: Editions L'Harmattan, 1989.

MacGaffey, Janet, and Rémy Bazenguissa-Ganga. *Congo-Paris: Transnational Traders on the Margins of the Law.* Bloomington: Indiana University Press, 2000.

Martin, Phyllis M. *Leisure and Society in Colonial Brazzaville.* Cambridge, U.K.: Cambridge University Press, 1995.

SASHA NEWELL

EASTERN AFRICA

Popular culture generally refers to communicative expressions that grow from, are possessed by, and are significantly associated with the people. Neither elitist nor traditional, it is unofficial in the Bakhtinian sense: novel, syncretic, and urban-oriented (though drawing from rural-based arts). It transcends ethnic, geographic, and national boundaries because it can be disseminated by electronic and print media, or by roving performers beyond the boundaries of its place of creation. Popular culture raises the consciousness of the people insofar as it opens avenues for self-reflection and comprehension. Indeed, it is recognition of this consciousness-raising role that has set in motion major popular cultural movements linking culture with social change in eastern Africa.

MUSIC AND POETRY

In eastern Africa, popular culture did not come with Western colonialism. On the eastern African coast there is evidence of the tremendous influence of the Arab and Indian culture in decorations and *taarab* music going back to 900 CE. Whereas colonial and postcolonial popular culture is clearly distinctive in its innovativeness, within the traditional setup limited innovation was allowed. *Gicandi* dialogue poetry among the Gikuyu, *gungu* on the islands of Lamu and Pate, and *kibati* oral poetry on Pemba operated within a poetically consistent canonicity convention. They were public performances of spontaneous poetic dueling.

Popular culture grows out of a convergence of thought and practice between the alien and the local, or between cultural intellectuals and the ordinary people. During the move for independence, the precolonial culture was collaboratively reactivated and redefined to reflect the ongoing struggle. The Mau Mau songs of Kenya, the Pungwe and Chimurenga songs of Zimbabwe, music and dance about dictatorship in Uganda, and the liberation poetry of Mozambique, though created for political mobilization through the efforts of an elite, were appropriated by the people and made an integral part of their culture.

Most East African secular musicians focus on relationships as the principal domain of concern, be it in the popular *taarab* music of the coast, the rumba derived from West African rhythms, the reggae rhythms taken from the Caribbean, or the *benga* beat from upcountry Kenya. Political and social commentaries are also made to a significant degree through popular songs, which are available in all languages, but more so in the region's major languages—notably Swahili, English, Dholuo, Gikuyu, Ganda, and Luhya. Religious music has taken root over the years and has adopted fast-paced styles to address issues of faith. Meanwhile, secular songwriters focus in their compositions on love, marriage, betrayal, money, power, life, and death.

POPULAR ARTS

Popular culture stems from the need for self-expression and may serve a variety of intrinsic and extrinsic functions. For example, popular arts in the form of concerts, theater, stickers, music, fiction, art in bars, and *matatu* and *daladala* taxis (in Kenya and Tanzania, respectively) are being used for financial advantage. Moreover, every major town has an array of commercial popular entertainment in the form of American, Indian, British, and Chinese movies, records, cassettes, novels, and television dramas. The region is replete with evidence of Western mass culture, especially in the world of film, and there is an overwhelming urge to develop an indigenous film and video/DVD industry. Images from Western popular culture are manifest almost everywhere in eastern Africa. In addition, tourist art—such as carvings, baskets, paintings, and performances of music, dance, masquerade, and acrobatics, provided either through the ministries of tourism and culture or the informal sector— is financially motivated. Political leaders and government bureaucrats ensure that troupes perform

forms of traditional dances modified to fit the occasion. The cast may be rewarded individually or collectively after the performance.

There are also non-financially motivated popular art forms, such as those found in home decorations, paintings, and recreational music and dance. Moreover, the elite, in pursuance of developmental policies and consciousness-raising, promote the growth of developmentalist theater as a way of reaching the people. Indigenous theater styles and *ngonjera* (poetic drama) were used to propagate the Ujamaa philosophy in Tanzania, and nongovernmental organizations are using popular culture to an impressive degree in the transmission of political and health-related messages in Uganda.

Popular theater that is people-based may also be seen as subversive, as happened in the 1977 Kamiriithu Theatre Project in Kenya, which led to the detention of Ngũgĩ wa Thiong'o and the exile of most of his associates. Ngũgĩ and his team had set out to revive the Kamiriithu Community Educational and Cultural Centre by working with laborers and peasants to make adult education a liberating process. The collaboration was seen as a threat to the political establishment.

Popular culture is essentially dynamic, free, ever changing, and playful (by bridging the performer-audience gap), and it resists containment. It challenges and collapses the dichotomies between traditional and modern, foreign and indigenous, official and unofficial. In all cases, alien popular culture is localized, appropriated, and redefined through being assigned new meanings and modes of representation. That is precisely what the popular Beni dance did after growing out of the European brass tradition. The Beni, a militaristic mime, combined indigenous dance forms and the colonial military parade.

THE NOVEL

In a 1982 article on the Tanzanian popular novel, Rajmund Ohly (d. 2003) asserted that the popular novel is generally simple; targets the emotions rather than the intellect; is easy to read; and sets out to entertain rather than to educate. A more sympathetic view of the popular novel in East and Central Africa would view it as emanating from the

Western elite novel on the one hand, and from the oral narrative on the other, but rebelling against them by not conforming strictly to their conventions. The urban novel in Tanzania is almost exclusively rendered in Swahili, the national language, and there is a visible influence of the Western detective novel in, for instance, those of Mohammed Said Abdulla (b. 1918) and Faraji Katalambula. Some popular fiction in Tanzania and Kenya also appears in newspaper serials.

The Ugandan urban novel is mainly available in English and Ganda. Okello Oculi (b. 1942), Eneriko Seruma (b. 1944), Michel Kayoya (b. 1943), and Davis Sebukima have written on love, wealth, alienation, prostitution, and unemployment in postcolonial Ugandan cities. Okot p'Bitek (1931–1982) uses gentle, genial satire in his popular narrative poetry, which carries the rhythm of indigenous oral poetry, to reflect the cultural and political alienation of the African people in the region, especially in the urban areas. His popular poetry includes "Song of Lawino" (1966), "Song of Ocol" (1970), "Song of Prisoner" (1971), and "Song of Malaya" (1971). P'Bitek was the founder of the Gulu Festival and director of Uganda's National Theatre and Cultural Centre. He went into exile when Idi Amin took over leadership in Uganda. Alumidi Asinya has written *Abdulla Salim Fisi* (1977), a beast fable on the career of Idi Amin.

In Kenya the urban novel is predominantly in English and Swahili. Struggles in the economy are central to these novels. In *Voices in the Dark* (1970), for example, Leonard Kibera (1942–1983) depicts the struggles of the present-day urbanite through the eyes of Gerald Timundu, a radical playwright in love with the daughter of a wealthy businessman. As the novel develops, readers witness the contrasts between the emerging political and economic elite on the one hand, and the beggars who are the main characters in Timundu's plays on the other. The negative attitudes, values, and practices of the people on Etisarap (Parasite) Road are subjected to satirical treatment.

The foremost Kenyan urban novelist is Meja Mwangi (b. 1948). His novels *Kill Me Quick* (1973), *Going Down River Road* (1976), *The Cockroach Dance* (1979), *The Bread of Sorrow* (1987), *The Bushtrackers* (1979), and *Weapon of Hunger* (1989)

explore urbanicity, especially as it relates to unemployment, economic and social stagnation and regression, and crime and punishment in the lives of the majority of the people. There are ethnic and racial tensions, dislocations and uncertainties, illicit drink, drugs, prostitution, and intra- and interclass criminality in settings replete with individualism. These issues also are treated in the works of Charles Mangua (b. 1942), especially in *Son of Woman* (1971), *A Tail in the Mouth* (1972), and *Kanina and I* (1994); and those of Mwangi Ruheni (b. 1934), in *What a Life!* (1972), *What a Husband* (1979), *The Future Leaders* (1973), and *The Minister's Daughter* (1975). A wide range of Kiswahili novels exist, as well, and the foremost novelist in this language is Said Ahmed Mohamed (b. 1947).

In recognition of the place of the crime novel in the region, Heinemann Publishers launched the Spear series in 1975 and published such titles as *The Ivory Merchant* (1976), *Lover in the Sky* (1975), and *Mystery Smugglers* (1975) by Mwangi Gicheru (b. 1948); and *A Prisoner's Letter* (1979) by Aubrey Kalitera. These titles now appear under the East African Educational Publishers Spear series. There are other popular novels in the Spear series, including *Life and Times of a Bank Robber* (1988) by John Kiggia Kimani; *Agony in Her Voice* (1982) by Peter Katuliiba; *Unmarried Wife* (1994) by Sitwala Imenda; *The Girl Was Mine* (1996) by David Karanja (b. 1971); and *My Life in Crime* (1984) and *Son of Fate* (1994) by John Kiriamiti. East African Educational Publishers also started the Peak series in 1995 and published *From Home Guard to Mau Mau* by Elisha Babu; *Hearthstones* (1995) by Kekelwa Nyaiywa; and *Links of Chain* (1996) by Monica Genya. These works are fast-paced and critical of the region's social and political direction.

Macmillan publishers started the Pacesetters series in 1977 and Trendsetters in 1995. Personal, social, and political betrayal, urban crime, corruption, poverty, wealth, misuse of power, and human relationships are some of the themes covered in this series. Some of the popular novels in the Pacesetters series include *Child of War* (1985) by Ben Chirasha of Zimbabwe (b. 1957); *Thorns of Life* (1988) by David Maillu (b. 1939); *Poisoned Bait* (1992) by James Ngumy; *The Shadow of a Dream* (1991) and *Desert Storm* (1992) by Hope

Dube; *Double Dating* by Walije Gondwe (Malawi's first female novelist); and *Love on the Rocks* (1981) and *Rassie* (1989) by Andrew Sisenyi of Botswana.

Longman (Kenya) launched the Crime series in which it published *The Men from Pretoria* (1976) by Hilary Ng'weno; and *Master and Servant* (1979) by David Mulwa. These titles now appear in the Longhorn Masterpiece series. Other Masterpiece popular novels include *Shrine of Tears* (1993) by Francis Imbuga (b. 1947), and *The Mixers* (1991) and *Two in One* (1984) by Mwangi Gicheru.

The slowly changing patterns of life among the Maasai people are depicted in popular form in the writings of Henry Ole Kulet. In *To Become a Man* (1990), for example, he depicts the cultural and social expectations of Maasai youth. In *Moran No More* (1990), through the experiences of Roiman, he portrays the challenges posed to Maasai youth, caught up in the cultural, social, political, and economic dynamics of postcolonial Kenya. Kulet also depicts the tensions between cultural expectations and postcolonial reality in his other novels, such as *Is it Possible?* (1971), *Daughter of Maa* (1987), and *The Hunter* (1985).

Longhorn has published the fiction of Yusuf Dawood, the writer of the *Sunday Nation* column "Surgeon's Diary," which first appeared on May 25, 1980. Some of the stories in the "Surgeon's Diary" have been published in *Yesterday, Today, and Tomorrow* (1985), *Behind the Mask* (1995), and *Off My Chest* (1988). Dawood has also written *The Price of Living* (1983) and *Water Under the Bridge* (1991). In his novels and short stories, he examines the relationship between surgeons and their patients, their different problems and how they cope with them, ethical behavior, wealth, and power. In *The Price of Living*, for instance, he explores the relationship between morality, money, and power. The character Maina Karanja judges success through the eyes of money and power in a world that is shaped through competition and immorality. As he comes to find out, there are things that money cannot buy.

Money and power is also the subject of Sam Kahiga's (b. 1943) *Paradise Farm* (1993). This popular fiction is a portrayal of the intense, though at times turbulent, love between Joe and Janet in the Kenya highlands, Nairobi, Mombasa, and the dark alleys of New York's Harlem where the novel reaches its climax. *Paradise Farm* is also about the

difficult search for the meaning of life, race relations, and supernatural forces that influence the activities and experiences of human beings.

Another interesting novel in the Longhorn Masterpiece series is *Sunrise at Midnight* (1996) by Ongoro wa'Munga. In this novel, a business magnate, Carlysto Baronner Sakwa, conspires with the prime minister of an island kingdom to persuade the old and sick founder of the nation to declare himself king so that they can start a dynasty between them. In the process, Carlysto grabs 14,000 acres of land from his clansmen, plans the death of many citizens who are opposed to his activities, and attempts to force his daughter to marry the prime minister's son. The daughter, however, commits suicide rather than succumb to a forced marriage. Moreover, before the king becomes fully manipulated, the nation is saved by one of his close confidants, Mrs. Patricia Odiero. On learning the truth about his prime minister, the king restores power to the people.

The Oxford University Press New Fiction from Africa series included *Murder in Majengo* (1976), a crime thriller by Marjorie Oludhe Macgoye (b. 1928). Also in the 1970s, Foundation Books started its African Leisure Library series, and John Nottingham launched the Afroromance series.

It has been claimed that, whereas Onitsha market literature (printed initially in the market town of Onitsha, Nigeria) is fresh, vigorous, and imaginative, Kenyan popular fiction is pornographic and cynical. Kenyan popular fiction has been called escapist, compensatory, and titillating fantasizing, and accused of evading social issues, uncritically approving of capitalist values of competition, individualism, and money worship, or indulging sex and sadism. The Tanzanian authorities have accused author David Maillu of being pornographic, and his novels have been withdrawn from circulation. His Comb books, such as *Unfit for Human Consumption* (1971), *Troubles* (1974), *After 4:30* (1974), *My Dear Bottle* (1973), and the 850-page narrative poem *The Kommon Man* (1975), are so sexually explicit as to be devoid of artistic appeal. He is, however, more aesthetically conscious and optimistic in perception when writing for children. Under the Pyramid series, he has written, among other titles, *The Last Hunter*

(1992), *Journey into Fairyland* (1992), and *The Government's Daughter* (1996).

The claim that popular fiction in the region is cynical is only partly true and cannot, in any case, be made with regard to the popular novel in Swahili or other African languages, an area that is here best represented by Gakaara Wanjau (1921–2001), who wrote in Gikuyu for over fifty years. He provided the framework for the Gikuyu writings by Ngũgĩ wa Thiong'o. *Kwani?* A literary journal founded by Binyavanga Wainaina (b. 1971) publishes upcoming writers in a language that is youthful, playful, and syncretic, whereas *Jahazi*, a journal published by Twaweza Communications in Nairobi, publishes critical essays in arts, cultures, and performance. The humorist Wahome Mutahi (1955–2004) consolidated satirical writings in the *Sunday Nation*, as well as in his novels and plays.

See also **Amin Dada, Idi; Art, Regional Styles: Eastern Africa; Arts; Dance: Social Meaning; Film and Cinema; Languages; Literature: Popular Literature; Literatures in African Languages; Media: Radio and TV; Music, Modern Popular: Eastern Africa; Ngũgĩ wa Thiong'o; Theater: Anglophone Central and Eastern Africa.**

BIBLIOGRAPHY

Arnold, Stephen H. "Popular Literature in Tanzania: Its Background and Relation to 'East African' Literature." *Kiswahili: Journal of the Institute of Kiswahili Research.* 51, nos. 1–2 (1984): 60–86.

Barber, Karin. "Popular Arts in Africa." *African Studies Review* 30, no. 3 (1987): 1–78.

Lindfors, Bernth. "A Basic Anatomy of East African Literature." In *Design and Intent in African Literature*, ed. David F. Dorsey, et al. Washington, DC: Three Continents Press, 1982.

Liyong, Taban Lo, ed. *Popular Culture of East Africa: Oral Literature.* Nairobi, Kenya: Longman, 1972.

Mlama, Penina Muhando. *Culture and Development: The Popular Theatre Approach in Africa.* Uppsala, Sweden: Scandinavian Institute of African Studies, 1991.

Ngugi wa Thiong'o. *Decolonising the Mind: The Politics of Language in African Literature.* London: J. Currey, 1986.

Njogu, Kimani. *Reading Poetry as Dialogue: An East African Literary Tradition.* Nairobi, Kenya: Jomo Kenyatta Foundation, 2004.

Ohly, Rajmund. *Aggressive Prose: A Case Study in Kiswahili Prose of the Seventies.* Dar es Salaam, Tanzania: Institute of Kiswahili Research, 1981.

Ohly, Rajmund. "Swahili Pop Literature: The Case of Munda Msokile." *African Marbugensia* 15, no. 1 (1982): 43–55.

Searle, Chris. "The Mobilisation of Words: Poetry and Resistance in Mozambique." *Race and Class* 23, no. 4 (1982): 305–320.

KIMANI NJOGU

NORTHERN AFRICA

Taking popular culture in northwestern Africa as Amazigh (or, for Europeans, Berber), as distinct from urban and other Arabic-speaking elites, most of the culture produced in Amazigh societies is oral in character, apart from a specific form of writing the Amazigh language in the religious school system. The people, who lead either nomadic or sedentary lifestyles, used to live in rural or outlying areas before the establishment of the French protectorate in Morocco in 1912. Arabic, as the language of the Qur'an, enjoyed great symbolic prestige and was thus the medium of established culture. Culture was therefore a hybrid model, with the coexistence of a written—essentially religious—culture, and a popular—predominantly oral—culture. Expressed in rituals and festivals, the popular culture contributed to the transmission of value systems and thence to the construction of social relations and the building of society. Among these, various poetic genres, whether chanted or ritualized, and centered around music and dancing, were the most important and highly developed. They were themselves classified according to the social status of those performing them and the themes expounded.

Although the popular culture has been completely altered following the onset of Moroccan nationalism and the complex and distinct processes of colonization and decolonization, Amazigh cultural traditions have taken advantage of the particularly favorable situation in Morocco and adapted to the changes. In addition to maintaining the traditional practice in villages, various new forms have emerged in an urban context. The exclusion of Amazigh culture from any official recognition and the disdain for those promoting it in the eyes of Arab and Westernized circles played a decisive part in this cultural dynamic. Individuals or groups, whether settled in towns or remaining in rural environments, continued to perform, invent or develop, or transform the traditions of their local cultures without any involvement by the state authorities. This freedom to express themselves led to the emergence of a new popular Amazigh culture in Morocco when it became independent.

The tradition of itinerant professional singers, or *Rwais*, provides a fascinating illustration of this inventiveness. Although their appearance could be located in the second half of the nineteenth century, they have evolved within an independent tradition, which, with the growth of emigration from the countryside, has developed into an authentic urban tradition, as well. They perform in both country and city, and at a variety of venues (weddings, public places, markets, and theaters). When one considers the context in which they emerged, this tradition has undergone a vast number of changes in every aspect: the composition of the troupe, the inclusion of women, costumes, tempo, and the introduction of new instruments. Rwais' transformation can thus be regarded as a developing tradition, related to the settlement of Ishelhiyn (Chleuh) in the towns.

The group consists of a leading musician, who both sings and plays the *rribab* (a single chord, stringed instrument), with male accompanists playing other instruments such as the *lutar* (lute), the *allun* (tambourine), and the *naqqus* (bell), and repeating the chorus, along with women who act as both chorus and dancers. Before the inclusion of women at the end of the 1930s, effeminate boys took those parts.

In this way, within the context of this cultural movement, various musical bands made up of those who had come from the country or their children who had been born in the city, were formed from the beginning of the 1970s. They brought together traditional music and modern instruments, and joined a new urban musical scene. The Izenzaren in Agadir, Usman in Rabat, and Archach in Casablanca are well-known examples.

Other traditions of rural origin, such as *ahwash*, also took hold in the towns. *Ahwash* is the name for a genre typically found in the High Atlas, Anti-Atlas, and Souss regions along the desert's edge, combining poetry, music, and dance. It was performed at particular festivals and rituals by the villagers themselves and gave rise to impromptu poetic contests known as *tanddamt*. Despite being primarily a village tradition, and allowing for the

fact that the conditions in which it was created and performed were not available in towns, a number of individuals from these regions attempted to continue with it wherever they settled. Ahwash bands were thus formed, such as *lferqt n Meàmura* (the band from Mamora). Mamora is the name of a forest near Rabat, and the name represents a pivotal moment in the relationship between emigrants and their cultural heritage. A group of individuals from the southern Anti-Atlas met every Sunday in that forest and performed a particular dance. The founders of the movement named it after the place where they met.

Commercial production (via publishing houses and the spread of audiocassettes), plus a major consumer market for cultural materials, contributed to the appearance of other new media, such as videos. Thus publishing companies, based in both Morocco and France (such as Boussivision, Wardavision, and Ayyuz), have produced videos in Amazigh. The main actors and directors involved are from the Rwais tradition. Since 1994, around one hundred films have been made in Amazigh. They deal with social problems in films such as *Tamghart n wurgh* (*The Woman in Gold*), *Argaz bu krât temgharin* (*The Man with Three Wives*), or present oral storytelling (*Butfunast, The Cow Man*; *Hemmu uNamir*, a character in Berber mythology) or the biographies of particular artists (the film *Tihhya* is a biography of the singer Fatima Tabaâmrant). They also represent the debate between religions (*Ran kullu ddunit, They All Love Life*) or they tell didactic tales such as *Lkenz ur itkmmaln*, (*Inexhaustible Treasure*). Despite the unexceptional technical quality of several films, public enthusiasm for them has been enormous. National television began to broadcast a number of these films such as *Tuf tanirt* (*More Beautiful Than an Angel*) in July 2004.

With form and content of this kind, the cultural revival of the Amazigh can be seen in the future within the context of the production and reproduction of a new popular culture. It also demonstrates the process of cultural expression and assertion necessary in any struggle to be accepted by a dominant culture as different, something typical of minority group resistance within a nation-building endeavor.

See also **Art; Dance; Festivals and Carnivals; Film and Cinema; Literature: Oral; Literature: Popular**

Literature; Media: Radio and TV; Music, Modern Popular; Theater.

BIBLIOGRAPHY

Amarir, Omar. *Amalou, quelques arts poétiques marocaines* (en arabe). Casablanca, Morocco: Imprimerie Dar al-Kitab, 1978.

Carter, Sandra G. "Moroccan Berberity, Representational Power and Identity in Video Films." *Gazette* 63, no. 2–3 (2001): 41–262.

Chottin, Alexis. *Corpus de musique marocaine II. Musique et danses berbères du pays chleuh.* Paris: Heugel, 1933.

Galand-Pernet, Paulette. *Recueil de poèmes chleuhs I. Chants de trouveurs.* Paris: Editions Klincksieck, 1972.

Jouad, Hassan, and Bernard Lortat-Jacob. *La Saison des fêtes dans une vallée du Haut-Atlas.* Paris: Le Seuil, 1978.

Lakhsassi, Abderrahmane. "Amazighité et production culturelle." In *Usages de l'identité amazighe au Maroc,* ed. H. Rachik. Casablanca, Morocco: Najah El-Jadida, 2006.

Lefébure, Claude. "Ousman: la chanson berbère reverdie." In *Nouveaux enjeux culturels au Maghreb.* Paris: CRESM and CNRS, 1986.

Lortat-Jacob, Bernard. *Musiques et fêtes au Haut-Atlas.* Paris: Mouton-EHESS, 1980.

Rovsing Olsen, Miriam. "Chants du mariage de l'Atlas marocain." Ph.D. diss. Université Paris-x, Nanterre, 1984.

Schuyler, Philip D., "Rwais and Ahwash: Opposing Tendencies in Moroccan Berber Music and Society." *The World of Music* 21, no. 1 (1979): 65–80.

ABOULKACEM AFULAY EL KHATIR

SOUTHERN AFRICA

Popular culture in Africa, as elsewhere, is associated sociologically with "modernization," "industrialization," "urbanization," "social (class) differentiation," and even "capitalist penetration." in brief the urban, class-structured society that results from migration and wage labor as opposed to the "rural/traditional" forms tied to organic, autonomous, self-sufficient communities possessing access to the means of production. Social anthropology has, however, demonstrated that this dichotomy does not accord with the situation on the African ground. Rural people are thoroughly integrated into the wage economy even if they are not migrant laborers, and in South Africa forced population movements created as well the phenomenon of "rural urbanization." In the towns, conversely, rural styles of performance are maintained and elaborated by people for whom home (as opposed to residence) will always be somewhere in the countryside.

Cape Town, settled by the Dutch in 1652, was by the eighteenth century both a great port of call and a seat of empires with many layers, both polished and rough-hewn, of cosmopolitan, hybridized culture. In seaside taverns, at creole "rainbow balls," and even on rural Dutch plantations, slave musicians from the East Indies, India, Madagascar, and the interior of southern Africa (Khoesan and Bantu) learned to perform on violins, woodwinds, horns, snare and bass drums, and guitar. The music and the dancing rapidly localized as distinctive syncretic Cape (*kaapse*) styles, expressing the experience of race and place, emerged in South Africa's "mother city." Even distinctive institutions such as the illegal house-tavern, where black and brown people were sold and even served their grog in the back kitchens of private houses, originated in Cape Town under Dutch East India Company rule in the seventeenth century. In the late nineteenth century, immigrant Irish vice police in Cape Town gave these taverns the Gaelic sobriquet that has stuck ever since: *shebeens* (little shops).

The forms of indigenous popular culture associated with nineteenth- and twentieth-century South Africa virtually all have their origins in the cultural fusion of European and African forms that accompanied the colonial penetration of the interior and the resulting growth of farms, towns, mining camps, and their associated black ghettos. Often first on the scene from the outside were Christian missionaries, who brought European hymnody and forms of display (school concerts and plays) into an African environment in which a capella choral music and group dance were the dominant form in both religious and recreational contexts. Starting more than a century ago and continuing to the present, formidable African choirs have made world tours and enlivened political, religious, ceremonial, and competitive local events.

The emergence of a distinctively South African Afro-European performance culture was further enhanced by the influences of the English music hall and the American minstrel and light operatic traditions that touring companies brought from abroad starting in the latter half of the nineteenth century. The urban workplace as well as the small-town churches spread this choral music-and-movement form to non-Christian rural labor migrants, who soon developed it into a range of thoroughly local styles. Among these, the *isicatamiya* of Zulu-speaking Natal, researched by Veit Erlmann and David B. Coplan, has been brought to the world by the Durban-based, Grammy Award–winning Ladysmith Black Mambazo.

South African popular culture in general entered its second phase of development with the rise of the "Diamond City" of Kimberley in the 1870s and Johannesburg, "City of Gold," in the late 1880s. The pattern of segregated urban life and culture established in these centers remained the template for popular cultural development even at the end of the twentieth century. Among the white population, those of English and the "better" class of Dutch descent continued to import their cultural forms and interests from Europe. The rural and urban working-class Afrikaners (including the "Coloured people" of mixed racial descent), however, developed games, cuisine, and styles of foil speech, performance, and sociability that were strongly influenced by the indigenous people among whom they lived and upon whose labor they depended. But it is only after the formal dismantling of apartheid in the 1990s that Afrikaans culture is being liberated from its fitfully hegemonic, racially exclusive governmentality and is jostling with renewed creative energy for a place among the other indigenous language cultures of the land.

Black popular culture was likewise produced and organized around markers of transforming social identity, and the display of cultural capital necessary for the establishment of claims to urbanized status and class mobility. In the domain of performance culture this led to the emergence, by the 1920s, of a range of petit bourgeois and working-class styles, venues, and occasions of concertizing, popular dance, and local jazz music. For the small professional and salaried class, it was ballroom dance, choir music, mission church sodalities, football clubs, and boxing. For laborers, it was raucous, "honky-tonk" *marabi* African jazz, urbanized rural-style dance competitions, and independent African folk gospel churches. Of course there was social movement. Domestic servants, eager to acquire Western cultural

capital, were the most ardent enthusiasts of ballroom dance. Middle-class Africans, attuned to Count Basie and Duke Ellington, began to enjoy the localized compositions of an emerging, distinctively African dance band and entertainment world. From this world developed the "classic" South African jazz called *mbaqanga*, or simply "African jive," of the postwar period, made famous abroad by performers such as Miriam Makeba and Hugh Masekela.

This world was nearly destroyed by the enforced removal of black people from the inner-city and near-suburban residential "locations" to distant, anomic government "townships" such as Soweto in Johannesburg and Mamelodi in Pretoria during the 1960s. But with characteristic reconstitutive social creativity, black people made homes and communities bloom amid the barren, squalid rows of four-room brick "matchbox" houses. American, specifically African American, popular culture was once again mobilized to produce resilient, rough, and energetic new cultural styles and forms that not merely reflected but challenged repressive social experience. The way was opened for the emergence of a popular dance-balladry and theater that examined dislocations within black community life and stubbornly protested the political dispensation that so severely exacerbated them. So in the 1970s and 1980s, the meaning of "popular" in South African black culture shifts political gear from the expression of social reality to its active rejection. The youth culture of the time, fueled by the "black consciousness" of its African-American materials and models, made modernist rebellion into a nationalist cultural style. The expressions of this style not only in performance, but also in dress, funerals, leisure, education, and political activity, played a large role in creating the modes of solidarity that kept the anti-apartheid mass democratic movement moving through the dark and tortuous tunnel to the light of the 1990s.

As liberation approached, television, previously neither much directed at nor much watched by township residents, began to play a leading role in the conscious development of new popular cultural models for a self-creating society. The transformation of SATV into a genuinely public broadcaster has not only democratized language programming to better serve all of the country's eleven official languages; it has also sponsored the scripting and production of local dramatic and comedy series that focus unblinkingly, if somewhat naively, on salient issues of a tumultuous, dynamic, democratizing society. On SABC radio, democratization has enabled a host of new regional, metropolitan, and community stations serving previously neglected audiences to find airspace. Further, a new quota that requires 25 percent of all music played over the radio to feature South African performers has begun to reinvigorate South African music and spur the reworking and development of stylistic blends and influences from elsewhere in Africa, Latin America, and the United States into the familiar framework of popular local genres.

As the struggle for liberation began to achieve its political (if not yet social) aims, the energies of militant township youth that had been absorbed in this struggle found in part a new focus in the creation of a performance- and media-oriented youth popular culture. "Culture clubs" and youth clubs sprang up in black communities throughout the country's urban areas, and by the early 1990s almost half of township youth were involved in associations of this kind. Their hope is that the educational, vocational, and cultural programs of these clubs can make up in some measure for the failings of their schools, and offer at least the possibility of a way out of the cycle of violence, poverty, and stagnation that rules life in the townships and shantytowns in the midst of South Africa's remarkable political renaissance.

Starting in the early 1990s, township youth answered the call for a new popular culture that would celebrate the end of apartheid and the materialistic symbolism of black achievement. This culture, at first thoroughly hedonistic and celebratory, was best represented by its musical expression in *kwaito*, a blend of African-American "house," rap, and 1980s township dance beats, and introduced (through Yfm radio in Johannesburg) new sexual, media, consumer, and class politics to the country. With the aging of the "Y generation," this popular culture has also matured, and focuses on burning social issues as well as pleasure, fantasy, and the self-image and aspirations of the new, mushrooming black middle class.

See also **Apartheid; Cape Town; Dance; Diasporas: Music; Johannesburg; Ladysmith Black Mambazo; Makeba, Miriam; Masekela, Hugh; Media: Radio and TV;** Music, Modern Popular; Theater; Urbanism and Urbanization; Youth.

BIBLIOGRAPHY

Allen, L. "*Kwaito* versus Cross(ed)over: Music and Identity during South Africa's Rainbow Years, 1994–1996." *Social Dynamics* 30, no. 2 (2004): 82–111.

Ansell, G. *Soweto Blues: Jazz, Popular Music & Politics in South Africa.* New York and London: Continuum, 2004.

Coplan, David B. *In Township Tonight! South Africa's Black City Music and Theater.* London: Longman, 1985.

Coplan, David B. "Sounds of the 'Third Way': Ethnic Identity and the African Renaissance in Contemporary South African Music." *Journal of Black Music Research* 1 (Spring 2002): 107–124.

Coplan, David B. "God Rock Africa: Thoughts on Politics in Popular Black Performance in South Africa." *African Studies* 64, no. 1 (July 2005): 9–28.

Erlmann, Veit. *African Stars: Studies in Black South African Performance.* Chicago: Chicago University Press, 1991.

Erlmann, Veit. *Nightsong: Performance, Power, and Practice in South Africa.* Chicago: Chicago University Press, 1996.

DAVID B. COPLAN

WESTERN AFRICA

Popular culture describes a complex and variable range of phenomena. Throughout West Africa, examples of popular culture are found both in forms generally recognized as part of the arts—such as music, song, theater, video film, sculpture, painting, portrait photography, and writing—and also in a wide range of different mediums that includes coffin making, joking and storytelling, hairstyles, hand-dyed and factory-printed cloths, house decoration, commercial billboards, and television soap operas. This diversity is often fluid, seemingly ephemeral, as it responds to changing social conditions and possibilities.

But such an obvious yet ambiguous term as popular culture proves resistant to easy definitions. *Popular culture* is a description open to social contestation. Furthermore there has been much debate on the overloaded assumptions entailed by the use of the term culture, especially in its intersections with the processes of globalization. This is a debate that is particularly applicable to localized forms of popular culture that often appropriate and reconstitute products, ideas, and social practices from across local, regional, and international boundaries.

Popular culture as a term has gained currency in emphasizing the contrast between the actions of the mass of people compared to the elites in West Africa who control the infrastructures and institutions. The term identifies social practices situated or generated at the level of ordinary, often economically impoverished, people. However, these masses are not homogeneous, but differentiated into social layers. Indeed, the producers of this popular culture often lie within the skilled classes, usually literate or semi-literate, sometimes migrants, and, at the outset of the twenty-first century, often adherents of Christianity or Islam. Moreover, the contrast between the masses and the elites is highly ambiguous and ambivalent. For example, football in West Africa, which is sponsored and encouraged by the state, generates a mass appeal—especially with the recent international successes of the Cameroon, Ghanaian, and Nigerian national teams—that situates it within the umbrella of popular culture. Other examples are the state-sponsored cultural exhibitions of The First World Festival of Negro Arts held in Dakar in 1966 or the Second World Black and African Arts and Culture (FESTAC) festival held in Nigeria in 1977, both of which presented a range of popular and elite cultural forms. At times, popular culture seems critical of elite social ideologies, as demonstrated by Fela Anikulapo-Kuti's criticism of the Nigerian government in his Afro-beat music, resulting in his twenty-month incarceration in 1984. At other times, it seems indifferent to the existing political order, or aspiring toward elite status, as the popularity of wearing factory-printed cloths embellished with Rolls-Royce logos, Mercedes Benz cars, or photographic portraits of political rulers attests. The elites and the masses often share many aspects of the same popular culture as the pidgin poems of Major-general Mamman Vatsa (1940–1986), a former member of the supreme military council of Nigeria, demonstrate. But popular culture provides a means for people to participate in and relate to events within society. Such is the scope of popular culture in West Africa, regionally and historically, that the emphasis will be on a few salient examples and inevitably much more will be omitted.

Popular culture has always been a dynamic feature of West African societies, and precedes the colonial period. Masquerade is one such expression and is found all over West Africa. It takes many forms and is situated in many different and often overlapping contexts. Some contexts can be understood in terms of the construction of social categories and the legitimation of political authority. It can provide entertainment, as well as present the views of the ordinary people. In this context it is sometimes used to castigate and satirize the activities of the elite groups, whether it is elders, eminent chiefs or, nowadays as likely, local politicians.

However, the advent of the colonial enterprise at the end of the nineteenth century in West Africa engendered new social formations. This was particularly evident in the urban areas where the various bureaucracies required for administering the colonial enterprise produced new social groupings, acquiring new skills and often with an added emphasis on literacy. The urban conurbations themselves developed or expanded to accommodate the exigencies of colonial rule and provided a fertile ground for the development of popular culture across West Africa. West African urban populations were diverse and heterogeneous in comparison to the rural areas, although the rural populations also were affected by the new transport infrastructures, commodity crop production, and the expansion in various mediums of mass communication. Change and innovation in religious expression also played its part in shaping new forms of popular culture. Mass conversion to Islam and to Christianity at the beginning of the twentieth century led to new and dynamic forms of religious organizations, such as new associations of Islamic brotherhoods, and the Independent African churches. The development of new roles and contexts of identity cut across prior social boundaries to create innovative forms and traditions. These combined with different forms of mass communication to create novel and potent forms of local popular culture.

In Francophone West Africa, the colonial state intervened far more directly with the development of a state-sponsored, cosmopolitan-based culture that maintained close links to the European metropolises. With the onset of independence, many of the Francophone countries, such as Mali, Senegal, and Guinea-Bissau, persisted with a strategy of state intervention in music, performance, and dance, but with a new emphasis on developing popular regional idioms as part of the project of nation-building.

Hereditary griot traditions derived from the Manding and Wolof kingdoms persisted as forms of popular culture in a range of arts that encompassed music, dance, masquerade, storytelling, woodcarving, and leatherworking, although now with the added patronage of business entrepreneurs and, in Senegal, of the Islamic brotherhoods as well as the nation state. In Senegal, however, the colonial separation of popular and elite culture was maintained after independence, although for very different purposes. President Léopold Senghor (1906–2001), in his development of the concept of Négritude, directed state resources into supporting an elite culture and establishing government-funded art, dance, and music schools.

The dynamic development of the Islamic brotherhoods has been paramount in Senegal and the role of the *marabout* (holy men) founders of these brotherhoods, such as Cheik Ahmadou Bamba of the prominent Mouride brotherhood, are celebrated in many mediums. The popular art of painting on glass, derived from Islamic North Africa at the beginning of the twentieth century, produced many devotional pictures of these Islamic brotherhood leaders. Glass painting was an art form inspired by the then-costly photographic reproductions that it copied, as well as by chromoliths and postcards. Its similarity to photography in recording the world, its devotional intent, and its provenance from northern Africa may have made it acceptable to the brotherhoods, despite Islamic prohibitions on figurative representations. However, its subject matter soon encompassed all aspects of social life, often from a humorous and lively viewpoint. Its sources of imagery also drew upon popular Islamic prints from Cairo, and even from French comic books such as Tintin.

The composition of glass painting retains the formal portrait representations of photography with its frontal axis, symmetry, and shallow ground. The forms are outlined in black ink and then filled with evenly rendered and bright enamel colors. Spaces and shapes are intentionally flattened and perspectives tilted to accommodate the fields of uniform color. The picture is painted on the underside of a thin sheet of glass, where it is protected. However, the color gives the appearance of the image floating on the surface, and achieves a luminous and saturated quality. It was learnt by apprentices from masters of the craft and provided a cheap means of reproduction. By the 1950s, its original consumers had replaced it through easy access to studio photography and small printing works that could offer cheap mechanical reproduction. Now demand is maintained by tourists and its gradual incorporation as a commodity into international art markets. However much of this style of religious imagery is now disseminated in the mural paintings that adorn surfaces in the urban areas, although the repertoire has been extended to include other iconic figures, such as Malcolm X and Bob Marley, as well as other prominent individuals, both local and international, who are deemed relevant to the artists who produce them.

When state support in Senegal was withdrawn toward the end of the 1970s, some artists, such as the co-operative group Laboratoire AGIT-Art, sought to bridge the gap with popular culture by producing avant-garde art that incorporates masks and similar artifacts in their work. They situate these works in unexpected public contexts, such as in busy markets, and, at one level, compete with the signboards and barbers' signs that are vigorous manifestations of popular art.

The separate state-managed and entrepreneurial popular culture trajectories of Francophone Africa contrast with the development of such traditions in Anglophone West Africa, where there tended to be less state intervention. However, elite elements contributed to innovative forms of popular culture. Ghanaian concert parties are an example of this interplay between the elites and the masses. These concert parties derived initially from comic plays that were performed at the end of the school year for the Ghanaian colonially-educated elite during the 1920s. The plays gained in popularity, and the format shifted to incorporate an eclectic range of elements from church nativity plays, Akan tales about the trickster spider Ananse, and Hollywood movies and vaudeville, all spoken in the local language. In the 1960s and 1970s, fifty or sixty groups operated in the country, although with the onset of television, cinema, and the disapproval of emerging Pentecostal churches, the groups' numbers have declined.

The Independent African churches with their reshaping of Christianity to West African contexts have also precipitated new forms of popular culture. In Lagos in Nigeria, the Yoruba Church of the Lord (one of a cluster of Independent African churches known as the Cherubim and Seraphim) commissioned Hubert Ogunde (d. 1990) in 1944 to compose native air operas. The enormous success of these religious productions encouraged him to form his own traveling company two years later. He wrote, produced, and presented productions (including musical arrangements), and took on the role of actor-manager for his ensemble. He promoted his first play by advertising for paid actresses who made up the bulk of his ensemble. It was the first time that actresses were billed to appear as professional actresses in their own right in Yoruba theater.

His plays proved to be a great success with enormous popular appeal. This he achieved by drawing on concert party traditions, using indigenous musical instruments, and also referring to the *egungun* masquerade tradition of *apidan* or *alarinjo* theater, especially in the opening glees with which his performances started. His productions centered around topical themes of the day, whether a craze for an exorbitantly expensive and fashionable cloth, or about a strike in Jos for which he was briefly arrested by the colonial authorities. His arrest made him a national hero in the struggle for an independent Nigeria.

By the 1950s, his outstanding success in both the urban and rural areas led to the formation of many rival traveling theaters, such as those of E. K. Ogunmola (1925–1973) and Duro Lapido (1931–1978). The competing groups introduced new elements, such as spoken (instead of sung) Yoruba and English dialogue to broaden their appeal, the use of popular folklore as a new theme, and the introduction of Western instruments to draw on highlife and juju influences. In the 1970s and 1980s many of the troupes appeared regularly on local radio and television. A number of films were also made, such as Ajani Ogun (1976), produced by Ola Balogun and featuring Duro Lapido, and Aiye (1980) with Hubert Ogunde. The filmic explorations of contemporary concerns and their relations to the past garnered even greater audiences.

New forms of popular theater were not confined to the urban areas. In Benue State, Nigeria, among the Tiv people, *Kwag Hir* (which translates as marvelous thing) puppet theater developed in the late fifties from a long tradition of resistance to colonial authority. Kwag Hir combines a long-established form of storytelling about the magical world of *adzov* (which also legitimized the popular resistance) with innovative, jointed puppet figures in theatrical performances. It articulates a Tiv sense of identity in placing the contemporary world in this mythical world of adzov—whether the story enacted is about the construction of a new road, or a lake from a popular folktale. It is a popular theater that provides through performance a counterpoint in the construction of ethnicity within Nigeria, such that is described as Tiv traditional theater in state-sponsored tours.

Apart from Christianity and Islam, other local religions and cults provide dynamic and popular forms of culture in both the urban and rural areas. New deities have developed this century, such as Mami Wata, a river goddess with long flowing hair who is found throughout West Africa, although in different forms. She is associated with a contemporary lifestyle enjoying fast living, popular music, sweet drinks, and smoking. Some devotees perform their rituals with a harmonica or guitar. Mami Wata's appearance and her associations with a modern lifestyle have provided a basis for describing the dangers and seductions of urban living. Mami Wata imagery appears in music, in paintings in bars, and elsewhere.

Other innovative forms have emerged such as the Odelay societies in Freetown, Sierra Leone, that are also concerned with the contemporary lifestyle of the young. In this multi-ethnic urban setting, gangs of young men have formed Odelay secret societies settled in marginal areas of the city. These groups espouse a freethinking lifestyle, much influenced by the precepts of the Jamaican religion of Rastafari, which includes the smoking of marijuana. Group identity and prestige centers on the masquerade processions through the city that form the core of their activities. These processions are ritual events in which Odelay societies engage in physical and aesthetic contests with other Odelay societies. The masquerades have two forms that either emphasize their powerful fighting capabilities as creatures of the bush, loaded with potent and dangerous medicines, or elaborate a fanciful and ornate appearance using rich materials and decorations.

Other masquerades and processions found in Freetown include the lantern festivals. These developed during the nineteenth century in the Senegal and Gambian regions, and had spread to Freetown by the 1930s. The lanterns, lit by candles within wire structures, range from simple hand-held figures to elaborate mobile floats representing ships, human figures, animals, cars, mosques, and other objects. In Freetown, lantern festivals usually take place at the end of Ramadan and are sponsored by the Young Muslim Men's Association whereas in Gambia, the festivals are a Christian affair.

In the central region of Segou, Mali, Muslim youth associations participate in complex puppet theaters. These theatrical arenas are a communal space in which to represent masquerade and even to elaborate on its forms while adhering to the precepts of Islam, drawing on performance traditions from a range of different ethnic groupings. Such performances invoke and shape collective memory and contribute to the reproduction of group identities along different dimensions that include ethnicity, occupation, gender, youth, and elder. The performances also provide a discourse on these relationships both in past and in present day circumstances. With the seeming dominance of the world religions and various forms of revivalism (such as Pentecostalism and Wahhabiyya in Christianity and Islam, respectively) in many parts of West Africa, popular art forms that are tied to localized religious or ritual ideas and practices would seem to be in decline. However, there has been a shift in the production and consumption of these art forms from mainstream society to youths who utilize it as part of the cultural repertoires in asserting collective and individual youth identities. The forms are now autonomous and not directed at the behest of older generations. Throughout southeastern Nigeria at Christmas and the New Yam festival, masquerades make their appearance and assert youth identities. At Arondizuogu in Imo State the Ikeji festival is spectacularly celebrated by youth and ritual specialists performing masquerades—in ways that are not condoned by an older generation that adheres to stricter forms of Christianity, whether orthodox and Pentecostal. Moreover, these events are videoed and distributed over a wide area on mass media compact discs as part of this shared youth culture.

Clothing and fashion have played an important part in popular culture. One such example is adire cloth (an indigo resist dye cloth produced in the Yoruba-speaking area of southern Nigeria). The starch resist is applied freehand or through cut metal stencils. The process was further developed with the access to factory-woven cotton shirting, which provided a more even ground. In the 1930s and 1940s, adire flourished in a dazzling array of images, often set in squares side by side, on the same cloth. These images depicted geometric images, frogs, watches, umbrellas, Qur'an boards, sugar lumps, and even the pillars of the Ibadan Municipal Town Hall in a cloth named *Ibadandun* (Ibadan is sweet—meaning that life is good there). A popular design was Olokun, named after the Yoruba river goddess. One of the most striking was *Oloba* (It has King, meaning that the cloth portrays a king) that contained a central oval over which was written King George and Queen Mary. It was a form of popular visual culture that took account of and participated in the diversity of the colonial world.

By the 1960s its appeal had diminished and was replaced by Kampala, a form of wax resist dyed cloth that has molten wax poured on it before the dyeing process takes place. This process probably stems from dyeing techniques used in Senegal and Sierra Leone by the Manding diaspora. It was introduced into Nigeria during the civil war at the time of the Kampala peace conference—an example of the way popular culture links and encapsulates historical events.

The gaining of independence among West African countries renewed the emphasis on local dress and fabrics. In Nigeria, the male *agbada*, a long sleeved gown, became necessary for important occasions, irrespective of status. Hausa and Nupe embroidery of the top pocket and neck opening crossed ethnic boundaries and religious divides to become essential to the finish of any agbada. Hausa embroidery consists of a range of patterns based on Islamic calligraphy, such as the simpler long triangular shapes of "Three Knives," or the squares known as "Houses," to more elaborate combinations. In Mali in the 1980s there was a revival of the Bogolan, a mud-dyed cloth, which derived from

Bamana traditions of fabric dyeing. It was used in state-sponsored cultural drama and dance productions in the 1960s, and gradually gained in popularity and transcended its original ethnic boundaries to become an emblem of Mali nationality.

Printed images and words have played their part in shaping popular culture. For example, there are the Indian prints that inspired Mami Wata imagery; prints of Al-Buraq, the Islamic horse that took Mohammad to Jerusalem and up to heaven; and the posters and picture calendars that present collective images of associative life. The printed word has effloresced throughout the urban conurbations of West Africa. Onitsha market literature (printed initially in the market town of Onitsha, southern Nigeria) of the 1950s and 1960s is one example where a vigorous and direct reworking of English produced stories and pamphlets that described the protagonists overcoming the difficulties of adversity, or the trials of love to gain success in the urban environment.

Its audience was a new literate class composed of semi-skilled clerks, primary school teachers, small scale entrepreneurs and traders, mechanics, and taxi drivers. Its stories drew on plots and dramas of popular foreign films (Indian, American Hollywood, Hong Kong) that catered to the cosmopolitan aspirations of this social layer. Although Onitsha market literature died out during the Nigerian civil war at the end of the 1960s, resulting in a flourishing literary tradition that exploited the qualities of Nigerian English for a local audience

In contrast to printed matter that can be produced comparatively easily by small entrepreneurs, film requires a large capital outlay. This has shaped film's trajectories in West Africa. Before the 1960s, filmmaking remained in the hands of Europeans, although some West Africans gained technical experience working for the British Colonial Film Unit, or in Francophone West Africa, working for the French filmmaker Jean Rouch (d. 2004). It was only with independence that filmmaking in West Africa has flourished.

With independence, France initiated a new policy of economic and cultural cooperation with its former colonies, which encouraged West African filmmakers in their productions. These filmmakers adapted the medium to represent African realities and concerns, and attracted mass audiences.

Anglophone West Africa developed an independent cinema industry that has mainly produced feature films that blend comedy and melodrama. By the 1990s, filmmaking in West Africa was characterized by a diversity of themes and styles.

Mass access to video recorders has resulted in a shift to low-cost video productions that have inspired a burgeoning video market, superseding film. Both Ghana and Nigeria are major production centers, and Nigeria alone produces over a thousand videos a year. The Nigerian market is an intensely competitive one and, due to the ease with which videos can be pirated, profits have to be made within the first few weeks of distribution. There are no governmental or international subsidies and, at the outset in the late 1980s and early 1990s, local cultural commentators viewed video producers with hostility. However, entrepreneurial producers cater directly to local audiences, producing videos in English as well as in the main language groups. Due to the speed of production and consumption, and the range of choices engendering an ethos of innovation and change (as well as imitation of successful formats), topical issues are incorporated into the narratives and themes of many of the videos.

The Issakaba series of five films directed by Lancelot Oduwa Imasuen (b. 1971) and made between 2000 and 2002 is based on the emergence of the Bakassi Boys (of which Issakaba is an anagram with one vowel added), who formed in 1999 as a local vigilante group to counter the prevalence of armed robbery at Ariaria Market in Aba, one of the major trading cities of southern Nigeria. The Bakassi Boys expanded rapidly to become a popular vigilante movement in eastern Nigeria, often collaborating with police or security forces as part of a widespread response to rising levels of personal insecurity and increased violent crime. The Issakaba films traced the rise of such vigilante groups, outlining the ways in which they drew on precolonial ideas of administering justice, of age-grade forms of social organization in which the youth were responsible for policing within local communities, as well as forms of protection in the use of medicines and the seeking out of wrongdoers in the community. The dramatic and immediate narratives set out in vivid terms the battle between good and evil. Although the Bakassi Boys' popularity was initially widespread, and such vigilante groups were accepted, the predatory actions of some of these groups led to a debate about their legitimacy in Nigeria. As the films developed they also reflected on the ambiguity of power and its capacity for corruption. Venal and evil vigilante groups are represented from the second Issakaba film onwards. The topicality of Nigerian videos and their direct dramatic narratives of local issues and dilemmas are a key aspect of their mass appeal. Their popularity has led to their export throughout the continent, even to countries such as Ghana (which has its own thriving video industry), as well as internationally to the Nigerian diaspora and beyond, leading it to be described as Nollywood.

Photography is perhaps the most widely dispersed popular art form in West Africa. The first cameras were on sale in 1839, and by the end of 1840s West African photographers were utilizing the medium. As a popular art, portraiture photography dominated and offered new forms of commemoration, remembrance, and self-presentation. In the Yoruba-speaking area of Nigeria, photographic portraits of individuals has replaced twin carvings (known as *Ibeji*) as a visual representation more amenable to the strictures of Islam and Christianity, both of which reject Ibeji wood carvings as pagan practice. Many West African photographers, such as Seydou Keita (b. 1920) or Malick Sidibe (b. 1935) (who practiced in Mali in the 1940s and 1950s), have studios, but are also mobile in seeking out new clients. Photographic compositions both inscribe local social practices, and, in the negotiation of representation with the sitter, delineate local aesthetic preferences, such as the use of textile patterning in Seydou Keita's work, or in the playful qualities of contemporary fashion trends captured by Malick Sidibe.

See also **Achebe, Chinua; Art; Body Adornment and Clothing; Dance; Film and Cinema; Freetown; Kampala; Kuti, Fela; Literature: Popular Literature; Mami Wata; Masks and Masquerades; Music, Modern Popular; Ogunde, Hubert Adedeji; Photography; Rouch, Jean; Senghor, Léopold Sédar; Soyinka, Wole; Theater.**

BIBLIOGRAPHY

Barber, Karen, ed. *Readings in African Popular Culture.* Bloomington: Indiana University Press, 1997.

Behrend, Heike, and Jean-François Werner. "Photographies and Modernities in Africa." *Visual Anthropology* 14, no. 3 (2001): 241-342.

Bettelheim, Judith. "The Lantern Festival in Senegambia." *African Arts* 18, no. 2 (1985): 50-53.

Diawara, Manthia. *African Cinema: Politics and Culture (Blacks in the Diaspora).* Bloomington: Indiana University Press, 1992.

Drewal, Henry, and Margaret Drewal. *Gelede: Art and Female Power Among the Yoruba.* Reprint edition. Bloomington: Indiana University Press, 1990.

Haynes, Jonathan. *Nigerian Video Films.* Revised and expanded edition. Athens: Ohio University Press, 2000.

Jeyifo, Biodun. *The Yoruba Popular Traveling Theatre of Nigeria.* Nigeria Magazine, Lagos: Federal Department of Culture, 1984.

Nunley, John. *Moving with the Face of the Devil: Art and Politics in Urban West Africa.* Chicago: University of Illinois Press, 1987.

Picton, John. *The Art of African Textiles: Technology, Tradition and Lurex.* London: Lund Humphries Publishers, 1995.

Roberts, Allen; Mary Roberts; Gassia Armenia; and Ousmane Gueye. *A Saint in the City: Sufi Arts of Senegal.* Los Angeles: University of California Los Angeles, Fowler, 2003.

Secretan, Thierry. *Going into the Darkness: Fantastic Coffins from Africa.* London: Thames and Hudson, 1995.

Sprague, Stephen. "Yoruba Photography: How the Yoruba See Themselves." *African Arts* 12, no. 1 (1978): 16-29.

Vogel, Susan. *Africa Explores: 20th Century African Art.* Munich: Prestel Pub, 1991.

CHARLES GORE

POPULATION. *See* **Demography; Disease; Family: Economics.**

PORT HARCOURT. Like other "new towns" in eastern Nigeria such as Enugu, Aba, or Umuhaia, Port Harcourt was founded in direct response to British colonial imperatives (whether administrative or commercial) and quickly came to exemplify a distinctive culturally heterogeneous form of cosmopolitan African urbanism. In the early twenty-first century it is the capital of Rivers State and the largest and most important political and commercial center in the entire oil-producing Niger Delta. Its official population is 1.5 million but this figure is meaningless because there is no census from the late twentieth or early twenty-first century. The greater metropolitan area—consisting of four local government areas—is at least twice that figure.

Port Harcourt was established in 1913 as a sea outlet for the coal deposits discovered to the north in 1909 in Udi Division, near Enugu. It was attractive to the colonial state because of its natural harbor in the creeks of the Niger Delta and as a site for a railhead. The city was named after Lewis Harcourt who served as secretary of state for the colonies before World War I. Located in the heart of a maze of creeks and swamps, much of the land is low lying and was thought to be uninhabitable. But beginning in the 1960s the city expanded enormously into areas of dubious quality for housing and social occupation. The main township near the port (usually called "town") comprised the original native location and was characterized by some imposing stone "Big Men" residences. The caliber of this section of the city has deteriorated and become marked by endemic poverty and gang activity. Between 1913 and 1919 the colonial state acquired land upon which the new city was to be developed, laid out government residential areas (GRAs) for both the colonial officials and local Nigerian elites, and established a European-dominated framework for urban administration and governance.

The period from 1920 to World War II was one of rapid growth—the city grew from 7000 in 1921 to 73,000 in 1953—in which differing ethnic communities established social networks and forms of nascent political organization. In the key period after the war up through the constitutional debates of the mid-1950s local government was handed over to Nigerians in the city and the franchise extended. Port Harcourt played a key role in the emergence of a pan-Ibo political movement even though it was the only important Ibo-speaking center located on land not identifies with either of the major Onitsha or Owerri Ibo subgroups. The city was a sort of neutral ground and became in 1948 the headquarters of the pan-Ibo movement and necessarily a centre of Ibo wealth and entrepreneurial skills. By 1953, 77 percent of the population was Ibo.

In the period before the civil war (1966) Port Harcourt was a multiethnic city driven by intense competition and conflict between the Ibo majority and the non-Ibo minority (Ijaw, Ikwere, Ogoni)

and by persistent hostilities between Catholics and Protestants. By 1965 the municipality was Nigeria's second largest harbor and the nation's second largest industrial center; the population at least doubled between 1953 and 1963. The industrial, social, and ethnic composition of the city was radically transformed, however, by three sets of processes after 1960. The first was the Biafran War. While Ibo and certain non-Ibo minorities were involved in the separatist struggle, the effect of the conflagration was to vastly reduce the dominance of the Ibo community in the city. Correspondingly the vast growth of Port Harcourt slums represents a massive in migration by ethnic minorities. Second, the discovery of oil and gas—by 1963 nine fields had been discovered and the first refinery was opened in 1965—made Port Harcourt Nigeria's premier oil city. Enormous oil wealth was brought to the city and population exploded during the oil boom of the 1970s but urban infrastructure failed to keep pace. The third force has been the proliferation of evangelical Protestantism since the 1970s and the transformation of the urban morphology by the rise of mega churches.

Contemporary Port Harcourt, with a population probably close to 4 million, is a rough and tumble oil town marked by enormous wealth and poverty existing cheek by jowl. Traffic jams and massive pollution compounded by poor drainage and sanitation are endemic and the slum world of the city has become home to criminal and gang activity and increasingly interethnic violence associated with struggles over access to oil (the debate over resource control), local elections, and political thuggery. Port Harcourt was once dubbed the Garden City but it has become a massive oil town with minimal city infrastructure, almost no urban governance, and a deep culture of political corruption and violence.

See also **Colonial Policies and Practices; Nigeria; World War II.**

BIBLIOGRAPHY

Wolpe, Howard. *Urban Politics in Nigeria: A Study of Port Harcourt.* Berkeley: University of California Press, 1974.

MICHAEL WATTS

PORT-LOUIS. The capital and principal port of Mauritius since 1730, Port-Louis is situated on the northwestern part of the island. It is the seat of government, the most populous town (160,000 in 2004), a proportion (some 30,000) of which is ethnic Chinese, mostly descended from immigrants from China's Guangdong Province brought as indentured workers in the nineteenth century, and the main trading center of the island. Its primary industry is the processing of textiles and sugar for export.

Protected from storms by a range of mountains, and therefore a safe harbor, the site that became Port-Louis was visited first by Europeans (Portuguese) in 1498. They did not leave much of a mark, however, except that their visits to the island are believed to have caused the extinction of a large bird, called the dodo. One hundred years later, the Dutch had no difficulty laying claim to the island and the port. Their colony never thrived, however, and they abandoned it in 1710.

The French arrived in 1721 and established Port-Louis as the capital of this island addition to their colonial holdings in India. The port was probably named after King Louis XV (r. 1715–1774), although it may have taken its name from a Breton port near Lorient. Under French rule, Port-Louis rapidly developed into a major Indian Ocean port. It also became an important naval base and a center for regional trade.

The city was designed by Bertrand François La Bourdonnais, who was named administrator of the port in 1736. La Bourdonnais called for the construction of government buildings, aqueducts, hospitals, and schools, along with commercial structures such as granaries and the infrastructure of the early port. In the early twenty-first century it remains the island's largest port, and home to the Mauritius Institute, a public library, and the national Museum of Natural History.

See also **Mauritius: Geography and Economy.**

BIBLIOGRAPHY

Sacerdoti, Emilio. *Mauritius: Challenges of Sustained Growth.* Washington, DC: International Monetary Fund, 2005.

Simmons, Adele S. *Modern Mauritius: The Politics of Decolonization.* Bloomington: Indiana University Press, 1982.

Wright, Carol. *Mauritius.* Newton Abbot, U.K.: David & Charles, 1974.

JESSE A. DIZARD

PORTO NOVO. The official capital of the People's Republic of Bénin (formerly Dahomey), Porto Novo was formerly Ajase, capital of the Yoruba state of Popo. It was called Hogbonou by its Gun (Goun or Egun) inhabitants, and Aklon by the Ahori (Awori).

In the eighteenth century, Ajase (as it was then known) became an important seaport for the Oyo slave trade with the Europeans. In about 1752, the name was changed to Porto Novo by Portuguese merchants. Following the decline of the Oyo empire (1820s), Porto Novo faced attacks from nearby Dahomey, and Egba Badagry and Lagos to the east. In the nineteenth century, dynastic rivalries in Porto Novo and competition among European powers led to its being ceded by Portugal to France. In 1863, the king of Porto Novo sought French protection against Abomey (the capital of Dahomey).

Porto Novo became a French protectorate in 1882. The late nineteenth and early twentieth centuries witnessed the immigration of a sizable number of returnees from enslavement in Brazil. The French abolished the institution of kingship following the death of King Toffa in 1908. In 1970, the Beninese political figure Sourou-Migan Apithy called for the cession of Porto Novo to Nigeria.

Since the 1970s, Porto Novo has been surpassed in economic importance by the deep water seaport of Cotonou. Nevertheless, it remains the national capital, with its administrative buildings such as the library, the National Archives, and the sciences division of the Institut d'Enseignement Supérieure du Bénin. Its population in 2004 was estimated at 234,300.

See also **Bénin.**

BIBLIOGRAPHY

Akinjogbin, I. A. *Dahomey and Its Neighbours, 1708–1818.* Cambridge, U.K.: Cambridge University Press, 1967.

Decalo Samuel. *Historical Dictionary of Dahomey (People's Republic of Bénin)*. Metuchen, NJ: Scarecrow Press, 1970.

OLATUNJI OJO

PORTUGUESE COLONIES. *See* Colonial Policies and Practices: Portuguese.

POSTCOLONIALISM.

The Ghanaian philosopher Kwame Anthony Appiah was the first to ask if the prefix *post* in postcolonial was the prefix *post* in postmodern. In so doing he pointed to the issues of history, economics, culture, and politics that sit squarely at the center of postcolonialism as a concept, experience, and political program.

Both parts of the term—*post* and *colonial*—have been hotly debated. Traditionally, *post* has had a strictly temporal definition; indicating a decisive break between *then* and *now* or *before* and *after*. The idea of what the prefix *post* could mean underwent a conceptual sea change with the advent of postmodernism. The epistemological break with modernism was accompanied by a shift in the meaning of the prefix *post*. In the postmodern episteme, *post* referred to a ruptural point between two moments in intellectual history. Thus the *post* came to represent the overcoming of a paradigm, rather than a chronological moment; indicating that a previous intellectual authority has been negated.

The term *colonial* has been subject to similar kinds of intellectual challenges. At one time colonialism simply referred to formal political rule of one state (usually European) over another (usually African, Asian, or Latin American). Colonized persons were subjects, rather than citizens, and did not enjoy any rights of political self-determination. Colonialism thus referred to the takeover of territory in order to appropriate the material resources and exploit the labor of another country. This process required that the colonized country surrender its political and cultural independence.

Colonialism was also marked by racial and national divisions. Colonial subjects were largely nonwhite and non-European whereas the agents of colonialism were largely white and citizens of Germany, France, Belgium, England, or Portugal. Settler colonies like South Africa, Zimbabwe, and Kenya were the paradigmatic examples of the ways in which racial discrimination was critical to the exercise of colonial rule.

Postcolonialism was, thus, first understood in its temporal dimension. The concept first gained currency in the period after the formal departure of the European colonial powers from Africa. It referred to the granting of political freedoms in the form of representative government and the transformation of colonial subjects into free and independent political citizens. The postcolonial state was marked by its racial composition (African rather than European) and its economic composition (usually socialist—e.g., Julius Nyerere's African socialism). Postcolonial African nations also sought to demonstrate their cultural independence from the West. Senegal's first postindependence president, Léopold Senghor, in concert with Caribbean intellectuals, developed the concept of Négritude, which celebrated the unique contribution of Africa and African peoples to the development of civilization.

The concept of postcolonialism, in its strictly temporal dimension, did not adequately address the continuities of power that attended formal decolonization, however. Although France allowed formal decolonization, it nevertheless exercised continued economic and political control over its former dependencies like Senegal and Côte d'Ivoire. Former British colonies like Ghana and Nigeria suffered under a crippling debt burden. They could not operate independently of Western-dominated institutions like the International Monetary Fund, the World Bank, and the World Trade Organization.

Thus the notion of postcolonial was supplanted by the idea of neo-colonial. Neo-colonialism was an idea that developed to explain how countries could be postcolonial (formally politically independent) and still economically and culturally dependent.

Neocolonialism did not, however, provide adequate conceptual tools to understand the cultural legacies of colonialism—in particular how the racial and national divisions that were the basis of colonial rule worked to construct north and south, civilized and savage, traditional and modern as binary oppositions that worked to define "the West" and "the rest of the world." The concepts of othering, orientalist discourse, and the binary construction of Orient and Occident first developed by Edward Said in *Orientalism* (1978) to explain British cultural domination in Asia were equally relevant to understanding how the idea of Africa developed as what V. Y. Mudimbe in 1988 called the "constitutive outside" of the West.

Postcolonial studies offer a different reading of the *post* that underplays its strictly temporal meanings while highlighting its epistemological dimensions. In this way postcolonial theory establishes a degree of continuity with postmodernism. Postcolonial studies proceeds from the notion that colonialism is the "always present underside within colonialism itself" (Mishra and Hodge 1991, 284). In other words, rather than seeing colonialism as something that was either external to the West or that had an impact only on the politics, culture, and society of the colonized countries, postcolonial studies sees colonialism as having played a deep and enduring role in the development of the politics, society, economics, and culture of the metropole.

This concept of the postcolonial has many intellectual antecedents. The Caribbean experience and Caribbean intellectuals provided many of the concepts and ideas that were later reworked by postcolonial scholarship about Africa. Walter Rodney (1974) and Eric Williams (1944) were among the first to suggest the importance of colonialism and slavery to the development of Western capitalism. C. L. R. James, likewise, drew important connections between the Haitian revolution and the French Revolution, arguing that "the slaves in St. Domingue by their insurrection had shown revolutionary France that they could fight and die for freedom" (1989 [1938], 120). Scholars like Frantz Fanon (1967) and Aimé Césaire (2000) likewise wrote of the importance of colonized subjects for the construction of the Western self; paying particular attention to the ways in which Whiteness, as a racial identity, is dependent upon Blackness as its binary opposite.

African nationalism also played a critical role in the conceptual evolution of postcolonialism. African nationalism was central to the political transition from colony to independent state. Moving beyond the temporal, however, African nationalism first

brought forward the idea that societies are not always coterminous with nations and, thus, that the nation-state need not always be the privileged unit of analysis. Postcolonial scholarship has borrowed heavily from this tradition. Paul Gilroy's 1993 concept of the black Atlantic focuses on diaspora populations and transnational communities. Gilroy drew upon a long tradition of African scholars and activists who defined themselves as part of a larger international black community and developed theoretical frameworks and political programs that encompassed the whole of the African diaspora.

See also **Césaire, Aimé; Colonial Policies and Practices; Colonialism and Imperialism; Fanon, Frantz; Government; International Monetary Fund; Law; Modernity and Modernization: Antimodern and Postmodern Movements; Neocolonialism; Nyerere, Julius Kambarage; Political Systems; Senghor, Léopold Sédar; Socialism and Postsocialisms; World Bank.**

BIBLIOGRAPHY

Césaire, Aimé. *Discourse on Colonialism*, trans. Joan Pinkham. New York: Monthly Review Press, 2000.

Fanon, Frantz. *Black Skins/White Masks*. New York: Grove, 1967.

Gilroy, Paul. *The Black Atlantic: Modernity and Double Consciousness*. Cambridge, MA: Harvard University Press, 1993.

James, C. L. R. [1938]. *The Black Jacobins*. New York: Vintage, 1989.

Mishra, Vijay, and Bob Hodge. "What is Post(-)colonialism? In *Colonial Discourse and Postcolonial Theory*, ed. Patrick Williams and Laura Chrisman. New York: Columbia University Press, 1991.

Mudimbe, V. Y. *The Invention of Africa*. Bloomington: Indiana University Press, 1988.

Rodney, Walter. *How Europe Underdeveloped Africa*. Washington, DC: Howard University Press, 1974.

Said, Edward W. *Orientalism*. New York: Pantheon Books, 1978.

Williams, Eric. *Capitalism and Slavery*. Chapel Hill: University of North Carolina Press, 1944.

ZINE MAGUBANE

POSTMODERNISM. *See* **Modernity and Modernization: Antimodern and Postmodern Movements.**

POTTERY. *See* **Arts; Ceramics.**

PREHISTORY

This entry includes the following articles:
CENTRAL AFRICA
EASTERN AFRICA
ETHIOPIA AND THE HORN
SAHARA AND NORTHERN AFRICA
SOUTHERN AFRICA
WESTERN AFRICA

CENTRAL AFRICA

At the crossroads of the continent, Central Africa is one of the least known regions from an archaeological perspective. In the absence so far of early hominids fossils, pebble tools and flakes similar to Early Stone Age artifacts in other regions have been reported in various locations but their dating remains unsure.

At Senga, on the Semliki River, near the border between the Democratic Republic of the Congo (DRC) and Uganda, a date of 2.3 million years has been tentatively suggested for a Plio-Pleistocene stone-artifact assemblage of the Oldowan type; however, it was disturbed and redeposited.

The subsequent Acheulean industrial tradition, with its very characteristic pear-shaped handaxes, seems restricted to the periphery of the rainforest in Central Africa. The best-known site is Kamoa, in southern Katanga. Comparison with other regions suggests that the age of this material may be between 400,000 and 300,000 years. The Acheulean is followed by an industry designated generally as the Sangoan. Characterized by robust tools referred to as picks and core-axes, it includes many utilized flakes and scrapers. It occurs through Central Africa, but unmixed, stratified assemblages are lacking.

Dramatic climate oscillations between warm-wet and cold-dry conditions during the Pleistocene have induced vegetation changes, altering the way of life of the local population. During the driest episodes, the equatorial rainforest shrunk, to form some small isolated pockets, as desert and grassland extended.

During one of those climatic changes, sometime between 300,000 and 250,000 years, Sangoan industries were gradually replaced by those known as Lupemban, in Equatorial Africa.

To stress the continuity between the two, one speaks generally of the Sangoan-Lupemban Industrial Complex. Typical Lupemban artifacts are finely worked bifacial tools, long lanceolate points and core-axes. They are abundant around Kinshasa and in northern Angola. Unfortunately no site has provided so far the Lupemban in an undisturbed, well stratified layer. At the opposite end of DRC, at Katanda, on the Semliki River, several Middle Stone Age industries have been recovered and tentatively dated around 80,000 years. One-sided barbed bone harpoon-heads are reported to be associated with these industries but their age and their association remain controversial.

Middle Stone Age industries were gradually replaced by microlithic industries considered typical of the Late Stone Age. Early evidence for microlithic techniques comes from the Matupi Cave in northeast RDC, dating back to 35,000 years ago. Further south, the microlithic industries of Katanga and Angola are typologically related to the one further east in Zambia.

In the western part of Central Africa, the gradual reduction of the Lupemban artifacts leads to an industry called Tshitolian. It extends from the savanna on the southern fringe of the rainforest, in Angola and Congo, to Gabon and Cameroon. Various triangular, crescent, trapezoidal, and leaf-shaped microliths are common and may have been used as arrow-points.

In the northeastern corner of Central Africa, at the rock shelter of Shum Laka in the Grassfields of Cameroon, a microlithic industry in quartz has been dated around 30,000 years and continued until 7,000 years ago with little change. Then, ceramics and later, around 4,000 years, a macrolithic industry on basalt with chipped hoe-like artifacts with ground blades appeared at Shum Laka. During that period, evidence of the use of oil-producing plants, the palm oil and the *Canarium*, are present in increasing numbers in the archaeological record, not only in Shum Laka but throughout Central Africa, suggesting the practice of arboriculture.

Around the mid-fifth millennium BCE, if not earlier, peoples in the western part of Central Africa, from Cameroon to Angola, began to make pottery and axe/hoes ground-stone artifacts. Village sites have been discovered from around Yaoundé in Cameroon, from western Central African Republic, from Gabon and Lower Congo. In the deep pits of unknown function usually associated with those settlements, one finds also, in a few instances, bones of sheep or goats as evidence of domestic livestock, and more surprisingly, at Nkang, in Cameroon, indications that the banana was already grown there by that time. The sites are generally regarded as evidence for expansion southward of the ancestors of the present-day Bantu-speaking people. Near Bouar, in Central Africa Republic, hundreds of megalithic monuments were also erected with stone slabs during this period.

By the end of the last millennium BCE, iron working began to appear, spreading probably from the North. Furnaces, slag and tuyeres from those early metallurgists have been recovered from Rwanda, Central Africa Republic, Cameroon, Gabon, and both Congos. Archaeological surveys of the Congo River and its tributaries in the interior of the equatorial forest have also yielded various pottery traditions and deep pits during the same general period. In contrast, in the savannas southwest of the rainforest, iron, and copper working are dated back only to the first centuries CE in the Copperbelt.

In most of Central Africa, there is little archaeological evidence for the following centuries, up to the arrival of the first Europeans. In northern Cameroon, around Libreville in Gabon and around Kinshasa and the lower portion of the Congo valley, limited archaeological research has led to the identification of several pottery groups whose distribution seems to correspond to various polities and trade routes. It is only much further upstream, along the Congo River, in the center of Katanga, that an archaeological sequence spanning over 1,300 years from the Early Iron Age to the present-day Luba population is available. It testified to the emergence in the Upemba depression, a vast floodplain dotted with scores of archaeological sites, of a complex hierarchical polities with a hereditary rich minority manipulating elaborate symbols of power, like ceremonial axes, iron anvils and sea shells. The masterful execution of many grave goods in clay, iron, copper, ivory, bone and shell indicate the presence of specialized artisans.

Changes in rituals and in the material culture occurred over time but there is clear continuity in some other aspects of the archaeological record. It shows that the present Luba ethnic group is the result of a long and complex cultural process. Further archaeological research in other parts of Central Africa could provide more precise information on the past of its many present-day inhabitants.

See also **Agriculture; Archaeology and Prehistory; Ceramics; Congo, Republic of; Congo River; Climate; Libreville; Metals and Minerals; Production Strategies; Uganda.**

BIBLIOGRAPHY

Brooks, Alison S., and Catherine C. Smith. "Ishango Revisited: New Age Determination and Cultural Interpretations." *African Archaeological Review* 5 (1987): 65–78.

Casey Johanna. "Holocene Occupations of the Forest and Savanna." In *African Archaeology*, ed. Ann Brower Stalh. Malden, MA: Blackwell Publishing, 2005.

Clist, Bernard. "Archaeology in Gabon." *African Archaeological Review* 7 (1989): 59–95.

Cornelissen, Els. "On Microlithic Quartz Industries at the End of the Pleistocene in Central Africa: The Evidence form Shum Laka, NW Cameroon." *African Archaeological Review* 20 (2003): 1–24.

de Maret, Pierre. "From Pottery Groups to Ethnic Groups in Central Africa." In *African Archaeology*, ed. Ann Brower Stahl. Malden, MA: Blackwell Publishing, 2005.

Eggert, Manfred K. "The Central Africa Rain Forest: Historical Speculation and Archaeological Facts." *World Archaeology* 24 (1992): 1–24.

Lavachery, Philippe. "The Holocene Archaeological sequence of Shum Laka Rock Shelter (Grassfields, Cameroon)." *African Archaeological Review* 18 (2001): 213–247.

Van Noten, Francis, ed. *The Archaeology of Central Africa.* Graz, Austria: Akademische Druck-u. Verlagsanstalt, 1982.

PIERRE DE MARET

EASTERN AFRICA

The archaeological record of sub-Saharan eastern Africa includes the cultural and technological evolution of humanity from its genesis. Although it is known that the earliest hominids had a geographical range beyond East Africa, the region possesses some of the earliest known and best preserved Australopithecine fossils in the world. Discoveries made throughout the Central Rift Valley demonstrate the presence of the semiarboreal *Australopithecus afarensis* hominids more than four million years ago in the then-mosaic woodland and savanna regions of the subcontinent. The most complete and best-preserved specimen is Lucy, a young adult female *A. afarensis* discovered in the Hadar region of central Ethiopia. Lucy's skull shares many common features with apes, such as a protruding brow-ridge, cranial capacity of only 450 cubic centimeters, and broad cheekbones. However, her appendages indicate that the hominid line diverged from apes significantly, especially in the aspects of her limited ability to walk upright (referred to as bipedalism) and reduced reliance on brachiating her arms for movement. Footprints preserved in volcanic ash found at Laetoli in northern Tanzania dated to 3.6 million years ago confirms the presence of an upright-walking hominid in East Africa at this time.

Hominids that postdate *A. afarensis* in eastern Africa include *A. aethiopicus*, *A. garhi*, *A. robustus*, and *A. bosei*, the latter two of which are robust species with large browridges and molars thought to be adapted for masticating starchy and woody vegetation. Anthropologists believe that these species of hominids represent genetic dead ends, and the ancestors of the modern *Homo* lineage more likely hail from the more gracile southern African hominid living at the same time named *A. africanus*, or the northeast African variant, *A. garhi*. The later East African Australopithecine fossils have been dated to between 2.7 and 1.0 million years ago.

Archaeological evidence for tool production and usage in the form of Olduwan unifacial choppers has been linked to upright-walking and larger-crania *Homo habilis*. These hominids begin the period that is typically referred to as the Early Stone Age (ESA). Paleoanthropological and archaeological evidence from the Lower Omo Valley in Ethiopia, Koobi Fora in northern Kenya, Olduvai Gorge in Tanzania, and Uraha in Malawi show that the cranial capacity of *H. habilis* is 50 percent larger than that of the Australopithecines, whereas postcranial skeletal morphology indicates this hominid is a fully bipedal organism. *H. habilis* lived contemporaneously with some *Australopithecines* from 2.4 to 1.5 million years ago.

Homo erectus fossils have been found throughout Eurasia and Africa, but Turkana Boy, found at

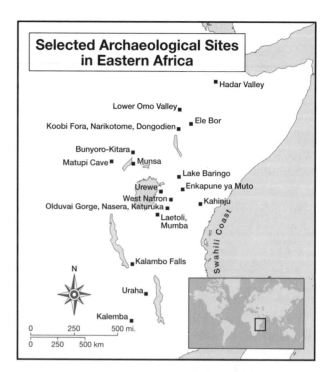

MAP COURTESY OF DAVID K. WRIGHT. DATA AVAILABLE FROM USGS/ EROS, SIOUX FALLS, SD

Narikotome, northern Kenya in 1984, represents perhaps the most complete fossil of the species. The earliest members of this lineage are sometimes called *H. ergaster*, but not all scientists subscribe to this nomenclature. The brain sizes of these hominids typically achieved 1,000 cubic centimeters at adulthood, and there are relatively few postcranial differences between *H. erectus* and *H. sapiens*. Enlarged brains are thought to have allowed for more sophisticated tool production techniques to evolve. Acheulian hand axes can be traced to 1.4 million years ago in parts of East Africa, most notably West Natron, Tanzania. Eventually, hand axes were distributed throughout the Old World and were still being made by *H. erectus* in the last 100,000 years.

The beginning of the Middle Stone Age (MSA) is typically recognized as occurring around 300,000 years ago, at sites across East Africa and beyond. The MSA was characterized by flake technology, as opposed to the ESA where the tools produced were fashioned from the cores of stones. The ability to begin making a tool with a clear template as to its eventual outcome, and replicate the production of that tool systematically, demonstrates the achieving of another evolutionary milestone in hominid thought processes. Archaeological sites around Lake Baringo, Kenya, and in Mumba, Tanzania, are the earliest dated MSA sites in the world.

After 50,000 years ago, the appearance of Later Stone Age (LSA) blade-based technologies are traced across the whole of eastern Africa. Matupi Cave, in Democratic Republic of the Congo, has a charcoal radiocarbon age of greater than 40,000 years associated with LSA tools. The site of Kalambo Falls in Zambia has an archaeological sequence spanning from the ESA through the LSA, separated by alluvial lenses demonstrating successive reoccupation of the area and evolving hunting and food-gathering strategies of the region's inhabitants. Other sites, such as Nasera and Naisiusiu at Olduvai Gorge in Tanzania, Enkapune ya Muto and Norikiushin in Kenya, and Kalemba in eastern Zambia, are transitional LSA sites. LSA industries are associated exclusively with anatomically modern *Homo sapiens*, and employed a wide range of raw materials including bone, antler, wood, shell, and ivory.

The production of projectile pointed weaponry across East Africa after 50,000 years ago marks a dramatic change in the subsistence and settlement strategies of the inhabitants of the region. The ability to hunt large, migratory mammals without having to stab them with a spear opened up new ecological niches and allowed modern humans to spread from sub-Saharan Africa to every corner of the globe. LSA archaeological sites from across East Africa indicate that the trade of obsidian used for the production of sharp-edged tools occurred across hundreds of kilometers. For example, the site of Mumba Höle in Tanzania has obsidian that traveled 320 kilometers from the Kenyan Rift Valley. This evidence shows that LSA humans traveled great distances across a wide range of ecological habitats as part of their survival strategies.

Hunting and gathering remained the primary mode of subsistence in East Africa until after 4,000 years ago, when archaeological and linguistic evidence show that cattle and goats entered with Cushitic- and Nilotic-speaking people from north of the region. The sites of Dongodien near Lake Turkana, Ele Bor in southern Ethiopia, Enkapune ya Muto near Nairobi, and Kahinju in Tsavo, Kenya each have evidence demonstrating that limited numbers of domesticated animals were kept by the inhabitants of these sites, even as they continued to hunt wild animals. By 2,000 years ago, pastoralism had reached south of the Zambezi River Valley and became the predominant mode of subsistence across East Africa.

Farming was introduced to portions of East Africa around 2,500 years ago. The earliest crops found in the region were probably yams, and various species of millet (*Eleusine* sp.) and bananas (*Musa* sp.). Evidence from Munsa in central Uganda suggests that bananas were cultivated as early as 6,000 years ago. With the exception of certain crops, such as finger millet and possibly bananas, all domesticates present in East Africa are believed to have been introduced from elsewhere. The origins of plant cultivation techniques in East Africa are poorly understood, but most early crops are associated with Bantu-speaking horticulturalists who arrived in the region in intermittent migrations from the West African forests after 2,500 years ago.

Around 2,500 years ago, evidence for early iron production is also found at various archaeological sites across the region. The sites of Urewe in southwestern Kenya, as well as several sites in Rwanda, eastern Democratic Republic of the Congo, southern Uganda, and Katuruka in northwestern Tanzania, show that western Lake Victoria was a center of early iron innovation in East Africa. North of the Zambezi River, the arrival of iron technology, agriculture, and Bantu speakers did not occur as a package. Instead, diffusion of technologies and agricultural practices spread across the region unevenly as groups intermarried and migrated, bringing their ideas and innovations with them. In the course of these movements, vast social networks developed between the ecotones across East Africa.

The rise of hundreds of independent city-states along the Swahili Coast of the Indian Ocean was brought about by regional and international trade of consumable goods and luxury items. The interlacustrine kingdoms, such as Bunyoro-Kitara in Central Uganda, also participated in the intercontinental exchange networks in which goods traveled thousands of miles, across continents and oceans. Archaeological evidence from these sites indicates that local elites in urban areas were able to command resources in the form of ivory, animal skins, and eventually slaves, for export to locations across the Indian Ocean from 1,500 years ago until

500 years ago. In return, the merchants would facilitate the movement of imported cloth, glass beads, and coastal shells to the interior portions of the subcontinent.

The arrival of Portuguese warships after 500 years ago marked a dramatic change in the political governance and relations between East Africa and the rest of the world. The subjugation of the region due to persistent naval attacks and tribute extraction by successive European and Arab colonizers eroded the foundations of indigenous power dynamics. The once-thriving coastal ports along the Indian Ocean littoral and fiefdoms of the Great Lakes region were abandoned as the maritime slave trade accelerated and strained intercommunity relations across the region. Over the last four million years, East Africa has been the incubator of the biological and technological evolution of humanity. The archaeological heritage of East Africa is unsurpassed in terms of its antiquity, and the importance of the region toward shedding light on the shared human experience cannot be understated.

See also **Agriculture; Archaeology and Prehistory; Ivory; Leakey, Louis and Mary; Metals and Minerals; Production Strategies; Slave Trades; Zambezi River.**

BIBLIOGRAPHY

Ambrose, Stanley H. "Small Things Remembered: Origins of Early Microlithic Industries in Sub-Saharan Africa." *Archaeological Papers of the American Anthropological Association* 12, no. 1 (2002): 9–29.

Clark, J. Desmond. "The Middle Stone Age of East Africa and the Beginnings of Regional Identity." *Journal of World Prehistory* 2 (1988): 235–305.

Connah, Graham. *African Civilizations: Precolonial Cities and States in Tropical Africa, An Archaeological Perspective.* Cambridge, U.K.: Cambridge University Press, 1987.

Ehret, Christopher. *An African Classical Age: Eastern and Southern Africa in World Prehistory History, 1000 BC to AD 400.* Charlottesville: University Press of Virginia, 1998.

Kusimba, Chapurukha M. *The Rise and Fall of Swahili States.* Walnut Creek, CA: Alta Mira Press, 1999.

McIntosh, Susan Keech, ed. *Beyond Chiefdoms: Pathways to Complexity in Africa.* Cambridge, U.K.: Cambridge University Press, 1999.

Mitchell, Peter. *African Connections: Archaeological Perspectives on Africa and the Wider World.* Walnut Creek, CA: Alta Mira Press, 2005.

Phillipson, David W. *African Archaeology.* Cambridge, U.K.: Cambridge University Press, 2005.

Rightmire, G. Philip. "Patterns of Hominid Evolution and Dispersal in the Middle Pleistocene." *Quaternary International* 75 (2001): 77–84.

Willoughby, Pamela R. *The Evolution of Modern Humans in Africa: A Comprehensive Guide.* Walnut Creek, CA: Alta Mira Press, 2006.

DAVID K. WRIGHT

ETHIOPIA AND THE HORN

The Horn of Africa has the longest archaeological record in the world. The earliest fossils of hominids and tools were found in Ethiopia. The earliest complex societies and states in sub-Saharan Africa appeared in the Eritrean-Sudanese borderland, Eritrea, and northern Ethiopia. However, the region is still largely unexplored from the archaeological viewpoint, and there are great geographical and chronological gaps in the record. In particular, the social, economic, and cognitive development in late prehistoric time (c. 10,000–1000 BCE) is almost completely unknown in most of the Horn.

Remains of early hominids were mainly found along the Awash and Omo Valley (Ethiopia), and include different species of Australpithecines, such as *Ardipithecus Ramidus* (c. 4.4 Myr [million years]), *Australopithecus afarensis* (c. 3.5–3.0 Myr, *Australopithecus anamensis* and *Australopithecus garhi*, as well as the earliest representatives of genus Homo (*Homo habilis*, c. 2.5–1.4 Myr; *Homo Ergaster*, c. 2.0–1.6 Myr; *Homo erectus*, c. 800,000–600,000 years ago) and the oldest *Homo sapiens sapiens* (Omo I, Omo II, c. 200,000/100,000 years ago).

The oldest stone artifacts, dated to c. 2.6–2.3 Myr were found in Hadar region and Omo Valley (Ethiopia). Evidence of the Oldowan industry, dated to 1.5–1.2 Myr, were also found at Melka Konture and Gadeb in central Ethiopia. The earliest evidence of the Acheulean industry, dated to c. 1.4 Myr, was also found at Konso Gardula (southern Ethiopia).

About 200,000 years ago, Middle Stone Age industries replaced the earlier ones and survived up to about 20,000 years ago. Main sites of this age are Gademotta, Melka Konture, Porc Epic, K'one, and Bodo in Ethiopia, and Midhishi and Gud Gud in Somalia.

Late Stone Age industries, such as the Magosian, with reduced artifacts in size appeared in the late Pleistocene. Later Stone Age industries with microlithic tools, dating to roughly 10,000–4000 BCE, were recorded in Ethiopia, Eritrea, and Somalia. They included industries related to the Wilton complex of eastern and southern Africa in the highlands and along the coast in Ethiopia, Eritrea, and northern Somalia, and the Eibian and Doian industries in Somalia. A local industry with backed blades, dated to approximately 9000–2000 BCE, was identified in the Afar region and spread southwards along the Great Rift Valley. Another industry from Logghia (Afar), dated to around 7000–5000 BCE, may be intrusive because of some similarities to Epipaleolithic industries of the twelfth millennium BCE in the Nile Valley and northern Africa.

Most likely, human groups in eastern Ethiopia were already exploiting local wild cereals in the late Pleistocene and were thus preadapted to cultivation, but no sure evidence of an independent domestication of plants was found so far. Marine shells from the Red Sea, Indian Ocean, and Arabian Gulf from burials dating to the fifth to fourth millennia BCE at Lake Besaka in Middle Awash Valley, about 311 miles from the coast, suggest that a network of exchanges between the highlands and the coast existed at this time.

The archaeological record suggests that food production spread into the Horn of Africa from the Eritrean-Sudanese lowlands and, perhaps, the Arabian Peninsula in the fourth to the second millennia BCE. Some local plants, such as tef (*Eragrostis tef*) and ensete, or false banana (*Musa ensete*), may have been cultivated in late prehistoric time, although paleobotanic evidence of these plants dates to historical time (first millennium BCE–first millennium CE).

Millet, sorghum, cattle, and sheep-goats represent the earliest evidence in the Eritrean-Sudanese lowlands from sites of the Butana Group (c. 3800–2700 BCE) near Kashm el Girba. In the third to first millennia BCE, pastoral people with domestic barley, ziziphus, and legumes (Gash Group, c. 2700–1500/1400 BCE), agro-pastoral people with domestic sorghum (Jebel Mokram Group, c. 1500/1400–800 BCE), and again pastoral people (Hagiz Group, c. 800 BCE–300/400 CE) occupied the lowlands. Rock pictures of longhorn and shorthorn cattle suggest that pastoral people occupied the highlands in

Eritrea in late second to early first millennia BCE (Naturalistic Style; Iberic Style). Sedentary and/or semisedentary people finally occupied the highlands in Eritrea (Ona Culture, late second to early first millennia BCE) and northern Ethiopia, respectively, since the second millennium BCE.

The earliest evidence of domestic cattle from Lake Besaka in eastern Ethiopia dates back to the mid-second millennium BCE. Rock pictures of cattle and fat-tail sheep suggest that pastoral people with Afro-Arabian cultural traditions occupied the eastern and central Horn of Africa, as far as Eritrea, northern Somalia, and southern Ethiopia, since the late third millennium BCE (Ethiopian-Arabian style). Sedentary or semisedentary people were also settled near Harar on the highlands (Ethiopia) and at Assa Koma in the Afar region (Djibuti) in the second millennium BCE.

Complex societies arose in the Eritrean-Sudanese lowlands and Eritrean highlands in the third to the early first millennia BCE, most likely as a consequence of the progressive inclusion of northern Horn of Africa into a network of interregional exchanges between the Nile Valley, Arabian Peninsula, and African hinterland.

Evidence of these early complex societies is the Gash Group (c. 2700–1500/1400 BCE) and the Jebel Mokram Group (c. 1500/1400–800 BCE) in the Gash Delta (Kassala), and the Ona Culture (c. late second to early first millennium BCE) in the region of Asmara. A clear-cut size hierarchy of the settlements and administrative devices, such as clay stamp seals, tokens and clay sealings, characterized the Gash Group. A size hierarchy of settlements, too, characterized the Jebel Mokram Group, but no administrative device was recorded in the sites of this cultural unit. The scale of social complexity of the Ona Culture is still uncertain, but the discovery of a rich tomb points to the existence of powerful elite.

In the mid-first millennium BCE, Eritrea and northern Ethiopia were included in the South Arabian area of economic and cultural influence and an early state, modeled on the Sabean one, emerged in the region. In the late first millennium BCE, this state was replaced by the Kingdom of Aksum (c. 400 BCE–800 CE) that dominated the southern Red Sea in Roman and Byzantine times.

Complex societies finally arose in central and southern Ethiopia beginning in the late first millennium CE. They were characterized by megalithic stelae with carved decorations that may be ascribed to different populations living in these regions in the tenth to fifteenth centuries CE.

See also **Agriculture; Archaeology and Prehistory; Art, Genres and Periods: Rock Art, Eastern Africa; Harar; Human Evolution; Metals and Minerals; Production Strategies.**

BIBLIOGRAPHY

Barnett, Tertia. *The Emergence of Food Production in Ethiopia.* Oxford: Archaeopress, 1999.

Brandt, Steven A. "The Upper Pleistocene and Early Holocene Prehistory of the Horn of Africa." *The African Archaeological Review* 4 (1986): 41–82.

Chavaillon, Jean, and Marcello Piperno, eds. *Studies on the Early Paleolithic Site of Melka Kunture, Ethiopia.* Florence: Istituto Italiano di Preistoria e Protostoria, 2004.

Clark, John Desmond. *The Prehistoric Cultures of the Horn of Africa.* New York: Octagon Books, 1972.

Fattovich, Rodolfo. "Remarks on the Late Prehistory and Early History of Northern Ethiopia." In *Proceedings of the Eight International Conference of Ethiopian Studies* I, ed. Taddese Beyene. Addis Ababa, Ethiopia: Institute of Ethiopian Studies, 1988.

Fattovich, Rodolfo. "The Peopling of the Northern Ethiopian-Sudanese Borderland between 7000 and 1000 BP: A Preliminary Model." *Nubica* 1/2 (1990): 3–45.

Finneran, Neal. "A New Perspective on the Late Stone Age of the Northern Ethiopian Highlands: Excavation at Anqqer Baahti, Aksum, Ethiopia 1996." *Azania* 35 (2000): 21–51.

Finneran, Neal. "Excavations at the Late Stone Age Site of Baahti Nebait, Aksum, Northern Ethiopia." *Azania* 35 (2000): 53–73.

Graziosi, Paolo. "New Discoveries of Rock Paintings in Ethiopia." *Antiquity* 138 (1964): 91–99, 187–190.

Joussaume, Roger. "L'art rupestre de l'Ethiopie." In *Préhistoire Africaine*, ed. Colette Roubet, Henri-Jean Hugot, and Georges Souville. Paris: Editions Association pour la diffusion de la pensée française, 1981.

Joussaume, Roger. *Tiya–L'Éthiopie des mégalithes.* Chauvigny: Association des Publications Chauvinoises, 1995.

Schmidt, Peter R., and Matthew Curtis. "Urban precursors in the Horn: Early 1st-Millennium BCE Communities in Eritrea." *Antiquity* 75 (2001): 349–359.

Semaw, Sileshi. "The World's Oldest Stone Artefacts from Gona, Ethiopia: Their Implications for Understanding Stone Technology and Patterns of Human Evolution between 2.6–1.5 Million Years Ago." *Journal of Archaeological Science* 27 (2000): 1197–1214.

RODOLFO FATTOVICH

SAHARA AND NORTHERN AFRICA

Humans may have inhabited northern Africa for more than 1 million years. There are sites of about that age in Southwest Asia, and it is likely that people reached the Levant from East Africa through the area that is present-day Egypt. There is, however, no convincing evidence for human presence in northern Africa at such an early date.

LOWER PALEOLITHIC (EARLY STONE AGE, 2,500,000–270,000 BP)

Both hand axes and human fossils have been found at the site of Ternifine, Algeria, associated with the remains of animals that lived during the early Middle Pleistocene (500,000 BP [before present]). Paleomagnetic readings indicate an age for Ternifine of between 730,000 and 600,000 BP. Somewhat later, but still during the Middle Pleistocene, human bones and artifacts were found in Morocco at Sidi Abderrahman and at the Thomas Quarries. The human remains in all three of these sites have been identified as *Homo erectus* (the genus of the species *Homo* that immediately preceded early *Homo sapiens*), and the associated archaeology includes bifacially flaked, leaf-shaped Acheulean hand axes. Slightly later, the earliest archaic Homo sapiens (or evolved *H. erectus*) occur in the later part of the Middle Pleistocene at the sites of Rabat and Salé in Morocco, both estimated to be around 400,000 years old.

Hand axes occur widely throughout North Africa, from the Red Sea to the Atlantic and from the high beaches of the Mediterranean southward. In the Sahara they are frequently associated with spring and lacustrine sediments that record several wet episodes, tentatively dated between 450,000 and 300,000 BP. A few localities have yielded crude hand axes that may be older but have not been dated. It is unlikely that Oldowan or other very early artifacts will be found in the Sahara; people needed time to develop the technical skills required to live there, even during periods of increased moisture. For even during the wet periods, the Sahara was at best a wooded savanna, very different from the tropical and subtropical world occupied by earlier groups in eastern and southern Africa. There were frequent droughts, which would have required a major adjustment in the way people used the area and, if they were to survive, required that they be able to move elsewhere to available water.

MIDDLE PALEOLITHIC (250,000–40,000 BP)

Around 250,000 years ago the remarkable behavioral conservatism that characterized the Acheulean for over a million years was broken by the appearance of a new lithic (stone tool) technology that marks the beginning of the Middle Paleolithic. Human remains have been found in several Middle Paleolithic sites in north Africa. Physically, all of them are heavily muscled and almost fully modern *H. sapiens*, though different from their Neanderthal contemporaries in Europe and Southwest Asia in shape and size of teeth and in details of cranial and postcranial skeleton.

Two varieties of Middle Paleolithic culture have been described in North Africa: the Mousterian and the Aterian. The Mousterian is similar to the Mousterian in Western Europe and is characterized by tools made on blanks removed from a prepared stone core using a special technique known as Levallois, and retouched into side-scrapers, points, and pieces with an irregular or denticulated edge. The Aterian culture differs from the Mousterian primarily in the presence of tanged points or knives and bifacially flaked leaf-shaped or foliated pieces. It is believed that these foliated pieces and tanged points were hafted, perhaps in a special way and for a function that is as yet unknown.

The Aterian and Mousterian may be contemporary. Both occur in deposits dated to the last interglacial period (c. 125,000 BP), and at the Haua Fteah in Libya the Aterian occurs interbedded between two Mousterian horizons. It has been suggested that the specialized Aterian tools are for specific tasks and that they have behavioral rather than chronological significance.

The Middle Paleolithic settlement system has been studied in some detail in the Egyptian Sahara. Although a limited number of sites are preserved, it is clear that Middle Paleolithic groups occupied the desert only during periods of greatly increased moisture, when they repeatedly utilized a variety of settings for different purposes. Some sites functioned as quarries from which raw materials for stone tools were obtained; many sites, particularly those on the shores of the lakes, were secondary workshops where these groups shaped many of their tools; some were kill-butchery sites; and others, back from the lakes, may have been where they spent the night (to avoid the large nocturnal predators that hunted near the lakes). This pattern persisted throughout the Middle Paleolithic in this area, a period of more than 100,000 years, lasting from perhaps 250,000 to 70,000 BP.

In both the Maghreb (western North Africa) and the Sahara, Middle Paleolithic sites contain numerous bones of medium- to large-sized animals: rhinoceros, giraffe, horse, and various antelopes and gazelles. A few of the sites also contain grinding stones, which may have been used to process plant foods. In the Nile Valley wild cattle, gazelle, and hartebeest occur commonly, but there is one site with numerous fish bones, some of which come from very large deepwater species. It is among the earliest good evidence for fishing known anywhere.

The end of the Middle Paleolithic is not well dated in North Africa. In the Maghreb the Aterian may have survived until 30,000 BP, but in the eastern Sahara there are no known sites that date between 65,000 and 10,000 BP, and it seems that the Sahara was hyperarid and unoccupied throughout the last two European glacial periods (65,000 to 13,000 BP). The latest dates for the Aterian in the central Sahara (western Libya) come from Uan Afuda Cave where there are four TL and OSL dates ranging from 90,000 to 69,000 BP, and an OSL measurement of 61,000 BP from Uan Tabu Cave. All of the dates have large standard deviations between 7000 and 10,000 years, and thus do not necessarily conflict with the dates from eastern Sahara. The Nile Valley, however, seems to have been used during the early part of this period (from c. 60,000 to 50,000 BP) by a late Middle Paleolithic complex characterized by numerous Upper Paleolithic-style tools, particularly end scrapers, together with typical Middle Paleolithic sidescrapers and denticulates made with Middle Paleolithic technology.

UPPER PALEOLITHIC (40,000–20,000 BP)

Typical Upper Paleolithic technology, distinguished by the production of numerous long blades from prismatic cores and by a tool kit which emphasized retouched blades, end scrapers, burins (a kind of gouge), and borers, appears at a few sites in the Nile Valley around 40,000 BP and at two sites in Libya dated 35,000 BP. One of the Nile Valley sites, near Nazlet Khater in Middle Egypt, yielded a fully modern but robust *Homo sapiens* skeleton that in several features resembles a much later population found in many Late Paleolithic sites in the Nile Valley and the Maghreb, where they are known as the Mechtoid type. The Upper Paleolithic people were very efficient hunters, much more effective than those of the preceding Middle Paleolithic. Their prey often consisted of large gregarious animals, such as hartebeest, wild cattle, and gazelle. The Maghreb apparently was not occupied during the Upper Paleolithic, but why it was not used during these ten thousand and more years is not known. Presumably its climate was as favorable as that of coastal Libya and the Nile Valley.

LATE PALEOLITHIC (20,000–12,000 BP)

Around twenty thousand years ago, in the Nile Valley, coastal Libya, and the Maghreb, a new lithic technology appeared that emphasized the production of small bladelets. These bladelets were often steeply retouched along one edge, sometimes to form a point at the distal end. This change in technology and typology marks the onset of the Late Paleolithic in North Africa. By 16,000 BP some groups were retouching their bladelets to make geometric microliths (an artifact the largest dimension of which is less than 30 mm.) that were probably used to make composite tools in which several microliths were mounted and used together on a haft or shaft. These composite tools are a further indication that these groups were developing an increasingly competent technology.

There are numerous Late Paleolithic sites everywhere in North Africa (except the Sahara). Some of these sites have yielded interesting data on the food economy of the time. Along the Nile River, groups favored wide, sand-filled embayments that were inundated by water during the seasonal floods. The yearly round began with the onset of the summer flood when the catfish moved to the edge of the floodplain, where they spawned. During this period they were easily taken in large numbers, and the sites used at this time contain numerous fish bones and occasional burned pits for smoking and preserving the fish. A few weeks later, when the flood receded, aquatic plants grew in the marshy areas of the floodplain, and vast stands of nutsedge occurred on the moist, sandy slopes of the embayments.

In the winter months, the carbohydrate- and fiber-rich marsh and sedge tubers could be eaten, but they first had to be parched and ground to remove the toxins and break up the fibers. The sites used in the winter contain charred tubers and grinding stones used to process the tubers. Numerous bones of ducks and geese of species that are winter visitors to the Nile also occur in these sites, in far greater quantities than the occasional bones of wild cattle, hartebeest, and gazelle, indicating that large-mammal hunting was not an important economic activity while those sites were in use. Sites occupied during the late spring were located at rock outcrops along major stream channels, where freshwater mussels were found.

In Libya and the Maghreb the known Late Paleolithic sites often contain numerous animal bones, particularly those of the Barbary sheep, which seem to have been intensively hunted. Sea level during the maximum of the last glacial (c. 20,000 to 13,000 BP) was around 100 meters lower than today, and it is highly likely that the now drowned coastal area of that period was the main center of occupation for many Late Paleolithic groups. If so, the food economy in those sites was probably very different from that indicated by the upland sites we now know, which were probably only seasonal hunting camps.

The Late Paleolithic in the Maghreb is known as the Iberomaurusian, while in the Nile Valley it is known by a variety of other names: Gemian, Halfan, Kubaniyan, and Sebilian, for example. There are many similarities and some important differences between the archaeological complexes found in the two areas. In both, the sites share a similar lithic technology and typology, but the Iberomaurusian, except for minor changes through time, is characterized by continuity that can be traced for a period of almost ten thousand years. In the Nile Valley, on the other hand, not only are there regional differences that account for some of the variety of names given to these lithic complexes, but through time there also seem to have been a number of changes in style that may indicate the periodic intrusion of new groups into the valley.

During the Late Paleolithic the Nile was a narrow ribbon of life bounded on both sides by extreme deserts. It was not rich in resources, the river being perhaps only 15 percent as large as today, and it supported a very restricted fauna. There appears to have been considerable competition for these resources: many of the Late Paleolithic skeletons found in the Nile Valley show evidence of violence, some of it approaching true warfare in its intensity and character.

Around 12,500 years ago, rainfall at the headwaters of the Nile increased, and the river became a huge stream with enormous floods; it began to down cut and flowed in a wide, deep channel. The ecology of the valley changed: the vast stands of nutsedge were much reduced, the wide embayments were no longer flooded, and different strategies for fishing had to be developed. Small camps of simple Terminal Paleolithic fishers, hunters, and gatherers are the only known sites in the Nile Valley between 11,500 and 7000 BP.

The end of the Iberomaurusian in the Maghreb is not well understood. The early Holocene, from around 12,000 to 10,000 BP, saw some groups expanding into the desert beyond the mountains, which probably indicates an increase in local precipitation. Regional diversity in the lithic tool complexes is also evident, but it is not clear if this is due to increased isolation or if it resulted from the appearance of new groups.

In some parts of the Maghreb, particularly in Tunisia and eastern Algeria, a new lithic complex known as the Capsian appeared. Bone tools were much more common, and in some of the Capsian sites there was a shift from backed bladelets to geometric microliths, while in other areas there was a change from bladelet production to large blades, often retouched into end scrapers, burins, and backed pieces; the changes in technology indicating a change in culture. The food economy also altered: animals were hunted, but great quantities of edible snails also were collected and eaten. The appearance of the Capsian may coincide with a change in population; the rugged Mechtoids disappear and are replaced by a more gracile Mediterranean type. It

is not clear if this was an evolutionary shift or a population replacement.

NEOLITHIC (10,000–4800 BP)
Around 12,000 BP the summer monsoons, which some five hundred years earlier in the uplands of East Africa had produced the increased flow in the Nile, expanded northward and brought rainfall to the hyperarid southern Sahara. Precipitation was much lower than during the last interglacial, when permanent lakes were widespread in the Sahara, but it was sufficient to form ephemeral lakes or playas. Human populations soon expanded into this area, some probably following the rains northward while others may have moved westward from the Nile Valley. In the eastern Sahara most of these earliest sites are small and date to around 9500 BP Most contain rare sherds of pottery with complex, comb-impressed, rocker stamped designs, perhaps among the earliest known. They also yield numerous bones of gazelle and hare and, in almost every site, a few bones of cattle. These cattle are of particular interest because they have been identified as domestic, used primarily for milk and blood, and thus served as a reliable and renewable food resource that may have permitted life in the desert. At first, the cattle herders seem to have used the desert only seasonally, after the summer rains, returning either to the south or to the Nile when it became too dry to live in the desert.

Around 8000 BP large villages appear, and they began to dig large, deep wells that, together with the collected plant remains, made it possible to live in the desert year-round. Their houses were oval brush- or mat-covered huts with shallow saucer-shaped floors. Near these houses, even those dating around 8000 BP and later, there are deep bell-shaped storage pits. Comb impressed pottery is also present, but rare. They also intensively collected a wide variety of wild plants, including sorghum and millet. One site, dating 8000 years ago, yielded over 20,000 identified plant remains, including 118 species of grasses, legumes, tubers and fruits, and 10 species of trees. The plant foods were an important component in their diet, and probably played a key role in their ability to live in the desert during the winter and late spring when other foods were scarce. It is likely that the large storage pits were where the plant foods were kept for later use. Today these plants live far to the south in the Sahelian zone, and their presence in southern Egypt indicates that the northern limit of the Sahel was at least 310 miles farther north than in the twenty-first century.

There are suggestions of increased social complexity in the eastern Sahara beginning around 6500 BP. Megalithic alignments were erected to mark the then positions of stars and star clusters of importance to later Predynastic and Old Kingdom cosmology, as were circles of upright stones that may have served as simple astronomical devices, and cattle were buried in pits under stone-covered tumuli. The Neolithic in the eastern Sahara endured for almost four thousand years and represents a remarkably successful adaptation to a very harsh environment. It finally ended around 4800 BP when the summer rains began to shift to the south and the area was again hyperarid and uninhabitable.

In western Libya, the first pottery and domestic cattle occur around 7500–7000 BP, while farther west in the south-central Sahara there are radiocarbon dates of over 9000 BP at two sites with pottery and bifacial arrowheads. Elsewhere in the central and western Sahara, a Terminal Paleolithic persists until around 8500 BP when pottery, ground stone, and bifacial arrowheads appear, often associated with human remains that have been identified as Mechtoid. Apparently there was an east-to-west spread of domestic animals, and a south-to-north movement of pottery making. If the dates for the early pottery in the south-central Sahara are correct, an early independent development of ceramics must have occurred in sahelian Africa.

The Neolithic in the Maghreb, indicated by domestic animals (sheep, goat, and cattle), plants (wheat and barley), and pottery, began around 6000 BP, or slightly before. A part of the Neolithic may have reached this area by sea; some of the pottery resembles the Cardial Neolithic pottery found along the northern Mediterranean coast, from Greece westward. Other Neolithic influences may have come along the southern Mediterranean coast, from Southwest Asia by way of the Nile and Libya. A Neolithic Capsian tradition emerged in the Maghreb and the northern Sahara in which many of the lithic tools of the Terminal Paleolithic Capsian culture were still used and snail collecting remained an important economic activity.

As recently as 7000 BP the Nile was occupied by small groups of people living by fishing, collecting, and hunting, in ways not very different from the Late Paleolithic. Between 6400 and 5400 BP, however, a developed Neolithic appeared suddenly in Lower Egypt, and around 5800 BP in Upper Egypt. The early Neolithic in Lower Egypt (as seen at Merimde and Fayum) seems to involve simple egalitarian societies: burials are within the villages and lack grave goods, all the houses are similar in size and contents, and there is no evidence of social differentiation.

Some 310 miles south, in Upper Egypt, the Badarian sites are smaller than Merimde and the houses are simple huts, all about the same size, but there are differences in size between the villages; most are small hamlets that cluster around larger communities. The most important difference from Lower Egypt, however, is the treatment of the dead: Badarian burials are in special cemeteries and some graves are far richer than others; all features indicative of emerging social stratification that may have been a critical step in the development of pharaohnic Egypt.

It has been generally assumed that the development of complexity in the Nile Valley during the early and later Neolithic was the result of stimulus from Southwest Asia. Most of the domestic plants and animals which formed the economic base of the Egyptian Nilotic Neolithic are Southwest Asian, the pottery is well made, polished, and resembles pottery from southwest Asia, and the transformation to complexity began in that area before the process becomes evident along the Nile. There is, however, a strong possibility that the rise of complexity seen first in the Badarian of Upper Egypt may have been related to the increasing aridity in the eastern Sahara, and the consequent movement of people from that area to the Nile Valley. As noted above, there are indications of emerging social complexity in the eastern Sahara well before it is evident along the Nile. From whatever source or sources, it was the rise of social complexity along the Nile which eventually led to the first Pharaonic civilization.

See also **Agriculture; Archaeology and Prehistory; Art, Genres and Periods: Rock Art, Saharan and Northern Africa; Egypt, Early; Human Evolution; Metals and Minerals; Nile River; Rabat and Salé.**

BIBLIOGRAPHY

Balout, Lionel. *Préhistoire de l'Afrique du Nord: Essai de chronologie*. Paris: Arts et métiers graphiques, 1955.

Biberson, Pierre. "e Paléolithique inférieur du Maroc atlantique." In *Publications du service des antiquités du Maroc*. 1961.

Camps, Gabriel. *Les civilisations préhistoriques de l'Afrique du Nord et du Sahara*. Paris: Doin, 1974.

Clark, John Desmond. *The Prehistory of Africa*. London: Thames & Hudson, 1970.

Close, Angela E., ed. *Prehistory of Arid North Africa: Essays in Honor of Fred Wendorf*. Dallas, TX: Southern Methodist University Press, 1987.

Cremaschi, Masuro, and Savino Di Lernia, eds. *Wadi Teshuinat Paleoenvironment and Prehistory in South-Western Fezzan (Libyan Sahara)*. Edizioni All'Insegna del Giglio. Milano: C.N.R. Quaderni di Geodinamica Alpina e Quaternária, 1998.

Di Lernia, Savino, ed. *The Uan Afuda Cave: Hunter-Gatherer Societies of Central Sahara*. Universita Degli Studi di Roma "La Sapienza," Arid Zone Archaeology, Monographs 1. Edizioni All'Insegna del Giglio, 1999.

Hassan, Fekri A., ed. *Droughts, Food and Culture: Ecological Change and Food Security in Africa's Later Prehistory*. New York: Kluwer Academic/Plenum Publishers, 2002.

Klees, Frank, and Rudolph Kuper, eds. *New Light on the Northeast African Past: Current Prehistoric Research: Contributions to a Symposium, Cologne 1990*. Cologne: Heinrich-Barth-Institut, 1992.

McBurney, Charles B. M. *The Stone Age of Northern Africa*. Hamondsworth, U.K.: Penguin, 1960.

Vaufrey, Raymond. *Préhistoire de l'Afrique*, Vol. 1: *Le Maghreb*. Paris: Masson, 1955.

Wendorf, Fred, et al., eds. *The Prehistory of Wadi Kubbaniya*, Vol. 2: *Stratigraphy, Paleoeconomy, and Environment*; Vol. 3: *Late Paleolithic Archaeology*. Dallas, TX: Southern Methodist University Press, 1989.

Wendorf, Fred, et al. *Egypt during the Last Interglacial: The Middle Paleolithic of Bir Tarfawi and Bir Sahara East*. New York: Plenum Press, 1993.

Wendorf, Fred, et al. *Holocene Settlement of the Egyptian Sahara*, Vol. 1: *The Archaeology of Nabta Playa*. New York: Kluwer Academic/Plenum Publishers, 2001.

FRED WENDORF

SOUTHERN AFRICA

Africa, south of the Zambezi River, was part of the Africa-wide dispersal of the earliest species of humankind and, subsequently, of early representatives of true humans and of modern people. The evidence is in relevant fossils at paleontological and archeological sites. Stone artifacts occur widely in the landscape and are an important record of some 2 million years of human occupation by Stone Age peoples. The subcontinent was distant from centers of agriculture and metallurgy and it is only in the last two thousand years that farming of domestic animals and crops was introduced leading to the progressive disappearance of hunter-gatherer lifeways, a process still not complete. It was the end fifteenth century opening of the maritime trade route around the southern tip of the continent that saw the beginnings of historical documentation of the land and its peoples.

EARLY HOMINIDS (HOMININS)

In the 1920s and 1930s the pioneering research of Raymond Dart and Robert Broom provided the initial fossil evidence for the presence of a chimpanzee-sized creature with an upright posture that on many anatomical characters could be claimed to be representative of the lineage of humankind and not the apes. Known informally as the australopithecines from the name of the genus *Australopithecus*, given to the original specimen found at Taung in the Northern Cape Province, it was only in the 1940s that their antiquity and significance became generally accepted. Since then related finds have been made in East and North Africa showing a continentwide distribution.

The southern African fossils with the exception of that from Taung come from the infillings of solution caverns in dolomite rock. The caverns have variously served as fall-traps, shelters, and dens for carnivores such as large cats and hyenas that preyed on the australopithecines and other animals. The Taung child may have been taken by a bird of prey. A number of particularly productive sites such as Sterkfontein and Swartkrans, both near Johannesburg in Gauteng Province have been investigated for decades and newer fossil localities have been discovered in ongoing research. The result is that there are more than 500 specimens representing various elements of the skeleton available for study. Based primarily on dental characters the South African australopithecines divide into gracile (from graceful) and robust forms. The gracile form is the older dating in the range 3 million to 2.5 million years and the robust form with its large cheek teeth is known from deposits in the 2 million to 1 million years. The brain size of both forms is marginally above the upper limit for the Great Apes or one third that of modern humans. The robust australopithecines fossils are found in deposits that include the remains of true humans who are presumed to be the makers of the stone tools found in those deposits.

EARLIER, MIDDLE, AND LATER STONE AGES

The oldest stone tools from any datable context in southern Africa come from the site of Sterkfontein and are the simple cores and flakes classified in the Oldowan industry. More widespread in the landscape and also included in the earlier Stone Age are artifacts of the continentwide Acheulian industry dating from 1.5 million years. Most Acheulian sites are in river valleys and around springs and pans rather than in the uplands, and caves were rarely occupied. The classic occurrences are associated with the gravels of the Vaal River where tens of thousands of typical large bifacial Acheulian hand axes and cleavers have been exposed through mining for alluvial diamonds. The human remains associated with the Acheulian sites are those of *Homo egaster* (*H. erectus* in some classifications) and, at the more recent sites, *H. heidelbergensis* (archaic *H. sapiens* in some classifications).

The transition from the Early to the Middle Stone Age may have begun by some 400,000 years ago but was certainly complete before 200,000 years. The Middle Stone Age is a technological stage that lacks the large handheld bifacial artifacts of the Acheulian and the reliance is on flakes and blades struck from prepared or Levallois cores that could be hafted. Many if not most Middle Stone Age sites in southern Africa, including both open-air and cave sites, date to the period 130,000 to 60,000 years ago, a period of population expansion. Associated human remains have been assessed as anatomically modern supporting other fossil and genetic evidence that sub-Saharan Africa was the center for the emergence of modern humans. Among the southern African populations that show deep genetic roots are the San and their ancestry may reach back to the Middle Stone Age.

The Late Stone Age began some 22,000 years ago and is characterized by small (often less than

0.98 inch) stone flakes and bladelets. These served as parts of light composite tools such as arrows. Tools were made in bone and wood and plant resins were used to mount the stone bits. Much of the material culture recovered from Late Stone Age archaeological sites can be associated with that of the contemporary San hunter-gatherers linking prehistory to the ethnographic present.

There are an estimated 30,000 rock art sites that date to the Late Stone Age and this art tradition survived into the nineteenth century. It includes both paintings and engravings and most depictions are of animals, humans, and signs. There is a unity in the art throughout the whole region that sets it apart from the art of Central Africa. This unity is a reflection of a shared shamanistic belief system and San ethnography has been invaluable in understanding the metaphors in the depictions and the meaning of the art.

HERDERS, EARLY FARMERS, AND STATE FORMATION

In the last two thousand years, fat-tailed sheep and later other domestic animals were introduced from eastern Africa and herding became the established way of life among the Khoekhoen (Hottentots) in the drier western half of the subcontinent. Their descendants such as the Nama of Namibia continue in this tradition. Only the wetter eastern half of the subcontinent is suitable for cultivation of African domesticates and this is where early farmers with iron technology, a mixed economy and particular styles of pottery settled in the same period. These Iron Age farmers represent the expansion of speakers of the Bantu language subfamily into the subcontinent.

From 900 CE in the Limpopo valley elite centers exploiting resources such as ivory and gold and controlling trade with the east coast emerged among the farming communities. The sites of Schroda, K2, and, by 1200 CE, Mapungubwe, represent stages in the emergence of kingdoms that were precursors to the rise of Great Zimbabwe to the north. Great Zimbabwe, the Monomotapa of history, was a powerful African state that declined with the Portuguese disruption of Arab monopoly of east coast trade.

Prehistoric times ended with the expansion of and the influence of the colonial farming frontier. Resistance to this expansion led to the rise of the Zulu military state and to disruptions and

Rock painting from Game Pass Shelter at Kamberg in KwaZulu-Natal Province, South Africa. This painting is a good example of the shamanistic beliefs illustrated in San rock art. It depicts a dying eland (the largest of the African antelope) with back legs crossed, head down, and hair erect on its back. The man holding the eland's tail has an animal head, crossed ankles, and hair erect. He is a shaman who, in a trance, visits the spirit world where he obtains power to make rain, heal the sick, and other tasks. COURTESY OF DEACON ARCHIVES

internecine wars. The reverberations are felt into the twenty-first century.

See also **Agriculture; Archaeology and Prehistory; Art, Genres and Periods: Rock Art, Southern Africa; Johannesburg; Metals and Minerals; Zambezi River; Zimbabwe, Great.**

BIBLIOGRAPHY

Blundell, Geoff, ed. *Origins: The Story of the Emergence of Humans and Humanity in Africa.* Lannsdowne: Double Storey, 2006.

Dart, Raymond A. "'*Australopithecus africanus*': The Man-Ape of South Africa." *Nature* 115: 195–199.

Deacon, H. J., and Janette Deacon. *Human Beginnings in South Africa: Uncovering the Secrets of the Stone Age.* Walnut Creek, CA: Altamira Press, 1999.

Lewis-Williams, J. David. *Discovering Southern African Rock Art.* Cape Town: David Philip, 1990.

H. J. DEACON

WESTERN AFRICA

Many aspects of the archaeological record of western Africa remain poorly known. Despite well-developed traditions of archaeological research in some countries, even basic chronological and cultural historical information is lacking for many areas. The material considered here ranges from the earliest indications of human occupation of the region, through the advent of food producing societies, to the growth of urbanism and the study of sites associated with the arrival of the Europeans on the West African coast in the fifteenth century.

Western Africa, as it is considered here, includes the area south of the Tropic of Cancer and west of the countries of Cameroon and Chad, bordered to the west and the south by the Atlantic Ocean. The region encompasses the continent's climatic and vegetational extremes, ranging in parallel bands from tropical rain forest along the coast to the

Sahara desert in the north. In the past, the rainfall and relative humidity have varied from drier to substantially wetter. These climatic changes influenced human settlement and adaptations, at times enabling the habitation of regions that are today unsettled, or allowing the cultivation of certain crops beyond their current habitats. Not surprisingly, ecological change has frequently been examined as a source of transformation in past human societies.

The earliest human settlement of western Africa remains poorly known. The region lacks the extensive exposures of Pliocene and Pleistocene deposits that have provided clues to human origins in other parts of Africa. Only a handful of fossil finds provide evidence of pre-*Homo sapiens* hominid occupation. The first was excavated in the 1960s from a poorly dated context in eastern Chad, 124 miles west-southwest of Largeau. The other discovery consists of a fossilized jaw and seven teeth, recovered in 1995 from a site near Koro Toro, also in Chad. These remains, over three million years old, have been classed as *Australopithecus afarensis*, a species known from a number of finds in Ethiopia and the East African Rift Valley and are the first example of an Australopithecine recovered west of the Rift Valley and thus substantially expands the range of these early hominids.

THE STONE AGE

Additional information on the early human settlement of western Africa has been gleaned through the study of stone tools. The Early Stone Age is characterized by simple flaked tools, including industries known as Oldowan and Acheulian. Middle Stone Age industries incorporate more refined flaking technology, are more variable, and are considered to reflect increasingly specialized adaptations to local conditions. The Late Stone Age continues the trend toward increasing diversity including small, flaked stone implements called microliths that may have been hafted, or mounted on wood, to make composite tools such as arrowheads. Some locales include pottery and ground stone tools in the later portion of the Late Stone Age. In many instances earlier or simpler technologies persisted along side more recent and complex industries. For this reason, patterns of technologies during the Stone Age, as well as later periods, are best characterized as mosaics of varying local patterns.

Early Stone Age tools have been widely unearthed in western Africa, particularly from sites in the Sahara and the Jos Plateau in northern Nigeria. Isolated finds have been noted from other areas, but are absent in Sierra Leone, Liberia, and coastal Côte d'Ivoire. This apparent void in human habitation could, however, be the result of the poor state of archaeological research in the region rather than an actual absence of remains. It should be noted, though, that the majority of the artifacts reported are surface finds, or from secondary deposits and erosional surfaces, rather than systematic excavation. Given the evidence for early human ancestors stretching back several million years in eastern and southern Africa, it is reasonable to assume that portions of West Africa were also occupied by stone tool makers more than two million years ago.

The Middle Stone Age of West Africa is only slightly better documented than the Early Stone Age. In the Sahara, two flaked tool industries include scrapers, points, and blades struck from prepared stone cores. Similar finds in sub-Saharan West Africa feature heavy quartz flakes, picks, choppers, and scrapers. These implements, interpreted by some as part of a specialized woodworking toolkit, are represented by the stratified sequence at Asokrochona in southern Ghana. Although dates are limited, West African Middle Stone Age sites may probably be widely bracketed between 200,000 and 30,000 years ago. In other parts of Africa, the Middle Stone Age appears to have begun 200,000 to 250,000 years ago. Some researchers have suggested that these Middle Stone Age sites are associated with the emergence of anatomically modern *Homo sapiens*, but the lack of both fossil evidence of human remains and well-dated assemblages leaves West Africa's role in emergence of early Homo sapiens murky.

The Late Stone Age is better known from a variety of more securely dated assemblages. Stylistically, the stone tools that characterize the period are more diverse, a feature that has been interpreted as an indicator of adaptations to varying environments. During the phase of hyperaridity in the region between 20,000 and 12,000 BP, the desert extended well south of its current boundaries and evidence of human habitation is absent north of the latitude of the Senegal River or Lake Chad. With the onset of increasingly wet conditions after 12,000 BP, the Sahara was reoccupied.

Limited material is similar to earlier assemblages from northern Africa, suggesting that resettlement of portions of the Sahara was from the north. Rock paintings of elephants and wild buffalo in areas that are now extremely arid may date to this period. Pottery occurs on sites throughout the Sahara 10,000 to 4000 BP. Harpoons, remains of fish, hippopotamus, and crocodile, are common on many Saharan sites between 7500 and 4500 BP. These finds have led some researchers to infer a shared cultural adaptation to aquatic or riverine environments.

By 4000 BCE, Saharan sites include evidence for the herding of domesticated cattle, goats, and sheep. It is unclear how these herding adaptations relate to the aquatic and the hunting and gathering economies. They may represent varied components of a mixed economy by culturally and environmentally adapted populations. The origin of the domesticated stock has been viewed alternatively as an introduction from southwest Asia, or the result of indigenous domestication and breeding of wild cattle from North Africa. Sheep and goats were introduced, as they have no wild African progenitors.

The Late Stone Age occupation of southern savanna and forest was not interrupted by arid conditions. The Iwu Eleru rock shelter, currently just within the forest zone in southwest Nigeria, is one of the best-described sites there. The earliest levels are dated to over 10,000 year ago. Excavation produced numerous microliths that may have been inserted into arrow shafts, or hafted for use as cutting tools. Comparable finds are characterized by sizable accumulations of marine shells. As is the case of the Saharan sites, the more recent Late Stone Age occupations in the south include ceramics and in some instances appear to continue up until the first millennium CE.

AGRICULTURE

Western Africa was the site of independent domestication of a wide variety of plants, including sorghum, African rice, millets, oil palm, and over sixty species of yam. Millet, for example, was likely first manipulated in the arid northern regions, whereas yams were more likely cultivated along the forest-savanna margin of the time. Detailed reconstruction of the origins of food production is bedeviled by diverse terminology and an array of varying interpretations. The word Neolithic has been used to denote food production, particularly agriculture, and a suite of associated social and technological innovations including polished ground stone tools, pottery, sedentary village life, and stock herding. In West Africa, such an appellation is problematic, as some features clearly occur independently of others. Ceramics, for example, have been dated as early as 8000 BCE in some locales, whereas the earliest incontrovertible evidence for domesticated plants does not occur for another six thousand years.

Early evidence for the use of domesticated cereals comes from the cultivable margins of the desert, or Sahel. Impressions of domesticated pearl millet (*Pennisetum americanum*) and Guinea millet (*Brachiaria deflexa*) are reported from the site of Karkarichinkat South in eastern Mali, dated between 2000 and 1500 BCE. Evidence for the harvesting of pearl millet is also evidenced at the site of Dhar Tichett in central Mauritania between 1000 to 900 BCE. At this site, dramatic reliance on domesticated grains coincides with increasingly arid climatic conditions. Signs of pearl millet, sorghum (*Sorghum bicolor*), and African rice (*Oryza glaberrima*) from third century BCE contexts at the site of Jenné-jeno, Mali in the inland Niger Delta indicate that domesticated plants were an important aspect of subsistence in portions of the Sahel and northern savanna by the first millennium BCE.

In the forest and savanna regions to the south, the gradual intensification of sedentary life and food production after 2000 BCE is illustrated by more than two dozen sites in Ghana and Côte d'Ivoire, collectively referred to as the Kintampo complex. A more sedentary lifestyle with intensified agriculture is illustrated by sizable settlements and house remains. Evidence for animal husbandry consists of remains of sheep or goats from Kintampo and Ntereso. Modeled figures on ceramics and clay figurines include representations of animals that some believe represent cattle and sheep.

METAL TECHNOLOGY

Similar to the origins of food production, the advent of metal technology in western Africa presents a varied and increasingly complex picture. With notable exceptions, Iron Age assemblages superseded the Late Stone Age without any intervening era characterized by the smelting of copper or bronze. Whereas early research tended to attribute the diffusion of iron technology from Classical North Africa or Meroe in the Republic of the Sudan, more recent interpretations have underscored indigenous innovation and variation.

Finds in the areas around Akjoujt in Mauritania and in the Agades region of Niger indicate copper-producing technology between the eighth and third centuries BCE, whereas a similar technology spans the last two millennia BCE in Niger. These industries are based on the exploitation of native copper that was extracted from local rocks and melted. Neither of the industries involved the smelting of metal ore, and their relationship to later iron working traditions is uncertain.

The earliest conclusive evidence for iron production dates to the first millennium BCE. Sites in Niger produced evidence of small-scale iron smelting, along with flaked and polished stone tools, and one, at Ekne Wan Ataran, includes several dozen habitation sites representing a shift to larger more permanent settlements than found during preceding periods. To the south, iron artifacts and evidence for smelting dating to the first millennium BCE have also been recovered in Nigeria and Cameroon. Associated with some of the Nigerian material are the distinctive Nok terra-cotta figures that have been found in an elongated swath some 300 miles long, south and west of the Jos Plateau in Nigeria. Sites have shown evidence of iron production during the last centuries BCE in Mali, Chad, Ghana, and Senegal.

URBANISM AND SOCIOPOLITICAL COMPLEXITY

Initial theories explaining the origins of urban growth, social stratification, and trade in western Africa often focused on trans-Saharan Arab contacts and the role of Islam subsequent to the eighth or ninth centuries CE. Increasing evidence has shown, however, that large, complex Iron Age sites, predate extensive contact with North Africa. Jenné-jeno has produced evidence of a large settlement by the third century BCE. The town expanded rapidly during the middle of the first millennium CE when a wall one mile long enclosed it. In other parts of the inland Niger Delta, tumuli, or large earthen mounds containing burial chambers, human sacrifices, and rich grave goods, have been identified and dated between 600 and 1000 CE. These features, along with evidence of interregional trade and growing homogeneity of material culture over a wide area, may provide indications of increasing centralized political authority later manifest in the ancient empires known as Ghana (eighth to tenth centuries) and Mali (thirteenth to fifteenth centuries).

Thousands of similar tumuli and megaliths dot the landscape at about the same time further to the west in the Senegambia. These tumuli vary substantially in size and construction, ranging from small sandy rises a few feet across to sizable mounds 262 feet in diameter with exterior layers of fire baked earth. Many tumuli concentrate in the northeast, south of the Senegal River. It is within this region that the Takrur trading empire arose by the tenth century CE.

Other Senegambian megaliths occur farther south as shaped laterite columns three to ten feet in height, often arranged in circular patterns. Many of the complexes are substantial. The site of Sine in central Senegal, for example, has some nine hundred stones placed in fifty-four overlapping circles. The archaeological research undertaken thus far affords little insight into the settlement and social context in which the sites were constructed. Available dates place the megaliths and the more southern tumuli between the sixth and eleventh centuries CE, whereas the northern tumuli appear to be more recent.

Further indications of increasing sociopolitical complexity come from the southern savanna and northern forest of Nigeria, in areas that are today occupied by Yoruba-speaking peoples. Archaeological sites dot the region, many including complex networks of walls, earthen banks, and distinctive potsherd pavements made from pebbles and broken ceramics placed on edge. One of the most important sites is Ile-Ife, known in Yoruba traditions as the place where the world was created. Archaeological evidence indicates that initial settlement of the site may date to before 1000 CE. Other discoveries, dating to the fourteenth and fifteenth centuries, include copper alloy casts and terra-cotta sculptures. Some of these are reminiscent of the earlier Nok sculptures found to the north.

One of the most interesting, though enigmatic, sites of the West African forest is Igbo Ukwu, located east of the Niger River in southern Nigeria, a region inhabited by the Ibo-speaking people in the early twenty-first century. The site consists of a ritual disposal pit, a reliquary, and a burial, all dated to the ninth or tenth century CE. The spectacular assemblage of cast bronze objects and over 150,000 imported glass beads would seem to attest to social stratification, yet indications of urbanization and centralized political authority are absent in the region until the recent past.

See also **Agriculture; Archaeology and Prehistory; Ceramics; Ife (Ile-Ife); Jenné and Jenné-jeno; Metals and Minerals; Niger River.**

BIBLIOGRAPHY

Connah, Graham. *African Civilizations*, 2nd edition. Cambridge, U.K.: Cambridge University Press, 2001.

Davies, Oliver. *West Africa Before the Europeans.* New York: Methuen, 1967.

DeCorse, Christopher R. *An Archaeology of Elmina: Africans and Europeans on the Gold Coast, 1400–1900.* Washington, DC: Smithsonian Institution Press, 2001.

DeCorse, Christopher R., ed. *West Africa during the Atlantic Slave Trade: Archaeological Perspectives.* New York: Leicester University Press, 2001.

McIntosh, Susan K., and Roderick J. McIntosh. *Annual Review of Anthropology* 12 (1983): 215–258.

McIntosh, S. K., and R. J. McIntosh. *African Archaeological Review* 11 (1993):73–107.

Shaw, Thurstan; Paul Sinclair; Bassey Andah; and Alex Okpoko; eds., *The Archaeology of Africa: Food, Metals and Towns.* London: Routledge, 1993.

CHRISTOPHER DECORSE

PREMPEH, AGYEMAN (c. 1871–
1931). Agyeman Prempeh, after winning a war of succession (1884–1888) to the Asante Golden Stool, from 1888 to 1896 engaged in restoring peace among the central Asante and asserting his authority over the rebellious northern provinces, with some success. Concurrently, the British were consolidating their rule on the Gold Coast colony just to the south, and their hesitation about further imperial expansion kept the Asante disunited. Prempeh's refusal of their offer of protection led the British to invade Kumasi in 1896 and exile Prempeh to Sierra Leone and, in 1900, to the Seychelles Islands.

Agyeman Prempeh (1871–1931). Prempeh I was regarded as king by the Asante, but the British did not recognize him as ruler of all Asante.

In exile (1896–1924), Prempeh learned English and was baptized in the Anglican Church, taking the name Edward. Owing to his exemplary life, the pressure of Asante nationalism, and the requirements of indirect rule that the British acknowledge historic rulers in their colonies, the British allowed Prempeh to return to Kumasi in 1924 as a private citizen. Since the Asante still regarded him as their king, and the British needed his help to advance indirect rule, he was installed as *kumasihene* (ruler of Kumasi) in 1926. Although not recognized by the British as ruler of all Asante (*asantehene*) he accomplished the political and legal reorganization of the Kumasi state between 1926 and his death in 1931, and created the conditions for the restoration of the Asante confederacy on January 31, 1935.

See also **Colonial Policies and Practices; Kumasi.**

BIBLIOGRAPHY

Braffi, Emmanuel K. *The Esoteric Significance of the Asante Nation.* Kumasi, Ghana: E. K. Braffi, 1984.

Ghana National Archives. *The Life of Nana Prempeh I, 1872–1931, Incorporating History of Nana Prempeh's Adventure during His Thirty Years of Captivity, Namely Elmina, Sierra Leone, and Seychelles.* Accra, Ghana: n.d.

Lewin, Thomas J. *Asante before the British: The Prempean Years, 1875–1900.* Lawrence: Regents Press of Kansas, 1978.

Tordoff, William. *Ashanti under the Prempehs.* London: Oxford University Press, 1965.

NANA ARHIN BREMPONG

PRETORIA.   Modern Pretoria has been the administrative capital of South Africa since 1910, when the country was established as the Union of South Africa, in a compromise that distributed judicial authority to Bloemfontein in the Orange Free State and seated the Union legislative body in Cape Town. The origins of Pretoria go back to the 1840s, when *voortrekker* migrants from the British Cape Colony settled in the Transvaal on the banks of the Apies River. Pretorius named the city for his famous father, Andries, who is remembered primarily for two reasons. In December 1838 he led some 500 *voortrekkers* (an Afrikaner term for "pioneers") into the Zulu kingdom in Natal. There, beside the Ngome River, he led his party to victory against an attacking Zulu force that has been estimated to be 10,000 strong. This battle is commemorated in Pretoria on the engraved stone walls that circle the Voortrekker Monument, a massive, elaborate structure erected in the 1940s to honor all who participated in the Great Trek. In January 1852 he negotiated with the British the Sand River Convention, which established the SAR as an independent Afrikaner territory.

The city—known originally as Pretoria Philadelphia—was founded in 1855 by Marthinus W. Pretorius, the first president of the South African Republic (SAR) (1857–1877), as a meeting place for the Afrikaner parliament, the Volksraad. As the Afrikaner capital the city was at the center of political and military battles between the Afrikaners and the British at the end of the nineteenth century. The British occupied Pretoria during the South African War (1898–1902); the peace treaty, the Peace of Vereeniging, was signed there on May 31, 1902.

Pretoria abounds in monuments to Afrikaner history, including statues of the two Pretoriuses, father and son; a statue of Paul Kruger (president of the SAR, 1883–1900); and a statue of Louis Botha (commander of the Boer forces during the South African War; later first prime minister of the Union of South Africa, 1910–1919).

Pretoria is the largest city in geographical extent in South Africa, though only the fourth most populous: two million people live in the greater metropolitan area, but only about half that number reside in the city proper. Cape Town, by contrast, had 3,092,000 inhabitants in 2000, according to United Nations estimates, while Durban is home to an estimated 3.7 million and Johannesburg has an estimated 3.2 million. The sharply segregated residential patterns of Pretoria continue to reflect a history of apartheid that dates back to the beginning of the century: whites, blacks, Cape Coloured people, and Indians each congregate in largely separate neighborhoods that surround the center of the city, which is occupied primarily by the offices of the national government and those of the Guateng (successor to the Transvaal state) Provincial Administration, as well as commercial and industrial enterprises.

The latter include food processing, engineering, and—most important—diamond, iron, and steel mining companies: the general area where Pretoria is located is one of the most abundant in minerals in South Africa. Industry in the city is facilitated by the national rail system, as well as by the nearby international airport. So, too, is tourism: tourists come to see not only the monuments but also the famous jacaranda trees—there are 70,000—which produce their purple blooms in October and November. Other attractions include the National Zoological Gardens of South Africa, known especially for its work in wildlife conservation, and the important collections of South African art and old Dutch masters on exhibit at the Pretoria Art Museum. The University of South Africa, the University of Pretoria, and the world-renowned Onderstepoort Veterinary Research Institute are in Pretoria. Not surprisingly, this city—where Nelson Mandela was inaugurated in 1994—also serves as the headquarters for a number of

Afrikaner political organizations, including the Conservative Party of South Africa, which has sought to establish an independent Afrikaner state.

See also **Apartheid; Cape Town; Kruger, Paul; Mandela, Nelson; South Africa, Republic of.**

BIBLIOGRAPHY

Hattingh, P. S., and A. C. Horn. "Pretoria." In *Homes Apart: South Africa's Segregated Cities,* ed. Anthony Lemon. Bloomington: Indiana University Press, 1991.

McCarthy, Jeff J. *Pretoria: From Apartheid's Model City to a Rising African Star?* Johannesburg, South Africa: Center for Development and Enterprise, 1998.

MARGARET ALISON SABIN

PRODUCTION STRATEGIES

This entry includes the following articles:
OVERVIEW
AGRICULTURE
PLOW FARMING
HUNTING AND GATHERING
PASTORALISM
MINING, MODERN
ARTISAN PRODUCTION
PERIPATETIC PRODUCTION

OVERVIEW

For the most part, traditional African societies—whether hunters and gatherers, pastoralists, or farmers—have been rural peoples whose livelihood depended on the land.

NATURAL CONSTRAINTS

The deserts were areas of limited resources, which placed constraints on the peoples who lived there. Their dependence upon elementary technology made these groups especially vulnerable to natural conditions. The regional variability of rainfall was one particularly decisive factor in their survival. Desert peoples like the Khoesan of the Kalahari were forced to forage for food and search daily for scarce water supplies. Sometimes Africans were enslaved by nomadic pastoralist groups, as in the Sahara.

In the Sahel, rainfall is limited to two or three summer months. This region, which lies directly to the south of the Sahara and extends from the Atlantic coast to the semi-desert of the Horn of Africa, was best suited to transhumant cattle pastoralists (Tuaregs in the west, Maasai and Somali in the east) who moved their livestock seasonally up and down according to the rains. A similar ecosystem exists along the northern border of the Kalahari, which is inhabited by Tswana cattle pastoralists. In the intertropical zone, a longer rainy season is followed by a brief humid season in the winter months. This climate permitted the development of grasslands. The economic complementarity between agriculture and the raising of large and small livestock here ensured a relative degree of prosperity. The staple crops were cereals much less nutritive than wheat: sorghum and millet, then corn (maize) introduced by the Portuguese. In the equatorial zone proper, abundant rains give rise to the great forests, long inhospitable to agriculture except in the form of root crops (originally yams, then manioc introduced by the Portuguese). This was the territory of hunting, fishing, and foraging peoples such as the Pygmy groups, for whom the dense forests provide a refuge even today. It was not until the twentieth century that colonizers established plantations in this region for the cultivation of export crops (cocoa and coffee).

In east-central Africa the stark division of the continent into climatic zones is moderated by the effect of higher altitudes, which result in a better balance of temperatures and rainfall and which gradually gave rise to agropastoralist societies such as the Gikuyu in Kenya and the Tonga of Zambia. Their economies, too, were based on the complementarity between cattle-keeping and farming. From the sixteenth to the twentieth centuries, maize, imported from the Americas, progressively transformed these agrarian societies by shifting productive energies to a crop that could be grown not only for subsistence but also for export. Beginning in the early twentieth century, an analogous role was played by rice, which originally grew in Africa, then was imported in great quantities by the colonial powers.

The ecological vulnerability of much of Africa's regions is accentuated by other unfavorable conditions. The climate characteristically provides too much or too little rain. The soils are generally poor: in the arid regions, rapid evaporation causes mineral salts to rise to the surface and form hard lateritic crusts that have to be broken up with a pick before the land can be farmed. In the wet zones, on the other hand, the rains leach the nutrients from the soils, so that they form heavy humid lateritic clays. In addition, in many areas sleeping sickness, which affects both humans and livestock and has been known from earliest times, militates against keeping large livestock, whose dung could be used as fertilizer. The only fertilizer traditionally used here resulted from the practice of burning the ground cover off fields prior to planting—the ashes provide some soil nutrients. To avoid sterilizing the soils, cultivated land here therefore needs to be left fallow for long periods, on the order of fifteen to twenty-five years. This implies a semi-itinerant farming system. The traditional unit of production was made up of all the local members of two or more successive generations—the household or village collective. They would periodically move off as a group to clear new lands when the current farm became less productive. This practice explains how a relatively small number of people could clear vast expanses of land. For example, the Gabonese forest today is entirely second-growth, not primary; this is believed to be the result of human activity, although people have never been many.

Except in the Nile Valley, Africa has no vast alluvial plains comparable to the river deltas of Asia. There are no fertile volcanic soils except in very limited areas, such as in northern Rwanda or the slopes of Mount Cameroon. Irrigation was known, but appears rarely to have been developed, despite archaeological evidence discovered in the Sahel. This is probably because settlement along the river banks was interdicted by ancient, recurrent endemic diseases: malaria (known since prehistoric times), bilharzia (caused by parasitic worms and resulting in blood loss and tissue damage), and oncocerchiasis, also called "river blindness."

DEMOGRAPHIC FACTORS

The birthplace of humanity, Africa, was no doubt populated for millions of years by groups of hunters and gatherers. *Homo sapiens sapiens* is far more modern, about 300,000 years ago, whose modern descendants could be the Khoesan-speaking peoples now limited to the desert regions. Our knowledge of these peoples begins around 8000 BCE with the beginning of the desertification of the Sahara. The peoples of the Sahara migrated southward, giving rise among others to the linguistic groups of the Nilo-Saharan family (for example, the Songhay). From this first migration, sometime around 1000 BCE, there arose a linguistic group on the interior Nigerian plateau, between the Niger and Benue Rivers, and in the Congo Basin. This great language family, called Niger-Congo, gave rise to the Bantu-speaking peoples who progressively spread out over central, western, and southern Africa. There is ample evidence of iron working having developed here rather earlier than among contemporaneous peoples while, apparently, still stone tools were in use at the same time. The iron-working people were farmers who spread the use of iron across the continent. They created the first great intercontinental trade routes, exchanging two commodities that were universally necessary but not universally available. Salt, produced only in the desert, around the great lakes of the eastern Rift, and on the coasts, was exchanged for the iron that was needed to manufacture that widely used farming tool, the hoe.

The Bantu expansion was stimulated by the arrival of the banana, brought by the Indian Ocean trade toward the end of the first millennium CE, and then by the introduction of the new plants from the Americas (cassava, maize, beans). These new crops completely transformed rural agriculture in the Congo Basin, stimulated a marked population increase, and made possible the formation of the great empires of the African interior. Unfortunately, the slave trade—particularly the Atlantic slave trade—dealt a harsh blow to this demographic growth throughout the eighteenth century. The massive European penetration of the continent in the nineteenth century and the first phase of the colonial era, in turn, caused a further demographic recession, largely because of the uncontrollable spread of major endemic diseases (rinderpest, a cattle disease introduced on the eastern coast in the 1880s; sleeping sickness; and venereal disease). The result was that, by the end of the nineteenth century, the total population of sub-Saharan Africa had achieved the same level as five centuries earlier (about 100 million).

SOCIAL FACTORS

Naturally, given the diversity of the African environment, there has never been a single, uniquely African form of social organization. However, at a certain level of generalization, the modes of organization that exist show some undeniable similarities. The reason for this is twofold. First is the long history of cross-cultural contacts within sub-Saharan Africa, arising from more or less long-distance regional trade (for example, salt for iron, salt for gold, farm products for the products of pastoralists, or yam for meat in the rainy forest). Second, the continent as a whole has undergone successive shared experiences: the Bantu expansion during the first millennium BCE; the spread of Islam beginning in the eighth to tenth centuries; contact with the West since the mid-1500s; direct European colonization during the nineteenth and twentieth centuries; and independence, gained largely through the efforts of a single generation (1956–1980).

Within this difficult context, African agrarian societies built up social institutions designed to protect their environment, conserving much in order to maintain a balance among the needs of production, demographic uncertainties, and political imperatives. Marxist scholars of the 1960s and 1970s viewed these institutions as "modes of production," but it is less reductionist today to speak of them as total social systems: although production is a major concern for these societies, it is not their only preoccupation. In these preindustrial societies, everything was expressed in social and ideological terms: beliefs, institutions, and rules of life made up a complex whole in which it is impossible to isolate what is deterministic of economic imperatives and what is determined by them. Furthermore, today it is known that these social and ideological structures do not survive only as a part of a particular mode of production, but have remained in place long after that mode of production has disappeared.

It is clear, however, that rural preindustrial societies were initially organized for survival: to provide food, shelter, and clothing, and to guarantee the continuity of the household were the overriding imperatives. Subsistence concerns had an impact upon production for profit. Use values were the main values appreciated by African societies, versus market values known only by the world market located outside the African subcontinent. An entire series of effects arise from this fact, which the analysis of modes of production helped us to understand.

The mode of production defined by Marx makes a distinction between two levels: the productive forces (the means of production) and the social relations of production. In rural Africa, productive forces were limited to the generalized use of the hoe. Although the rock art of the Sahara demonstrates that the wheel was known, it was not adopted outside of Ethiopia. This had important technological consequences because the wheel was useful not only for transport but above all as an energy source, enabling the use of the plow or intensified irrigation techniques. The reasons why Africans did not adopt the wheel are many and controversial. They include a recognition of the fragility of the environment (as the unhappy experiments with industrial agriculture during the 1950s and 1960s confirm); weak demographic pressure, which failed to generate a need to intensify production; the frequent weakness of hierarchical societies that could support specialization of production beyond the subsistence level; the lack of a perception of the individual that would encourage the development of an entrepreneurial spirit—in brief, a whole constellation of ideological and social structures.

These structures were a part of the social relations of production in a system wherein, whether one was a farmer, a pastoralist, or a hunter-gatherer, the single most important means of production was the land. The land was therefore protected. Truly inalienable and sacred, the land was a gift from the gods and the ancestors and could be neither bought nor sold. Placed in the care of a ritual specialist, the "chief of the land," access to land was the condition upon which the survival of the community was based. Such access was often strongly inegalitarian: the most powerful lineages controlled it. But in principle, no one could be deprived of access to it: one needed only to put oneself under the protection of one of the dominant lineages, either as a dependent or as a slave, in order to participate in the subsistence of the group.

The mistaken Western view that this kinship-based organization of production was egalitarian arose largely from an outmoded belief that household- or village-based communities lived in an amiable "primitive communism." In agricultural societies, and even more so among pastoralist groups, there was a clear inequality between elders and youngers, dominant and dependent lineages, masters and slaves, men and women, aristocrats and commoners. This inequality was great even in groups that lacked a state hierarchy. In equatorial Africa, the Pygmy hunting groups served the Bantu farming communities. In exchange for their meat they received a very small portion of the Bantu agricultural harvest. Even within the dominant lineages, a sometimes fierce hierarchy existed between the elders—the keepers of knowledge and power—and the juniors, from whom respect and labor were expected. In order to maintain social and political equilibrium, it was the elders who negotiated marriage exchanges between lineages. They alone possessed the cattle needed for the bridewealth required for a junior to acquire a wife. Therefore women were only used as political and economic tools of production and reproduction.

Lacking technology, the productive force was limited to what an individual could produce with his hands and a hoe. But the hoe was, without exception, a tool used exclusively by women. This was because a man's wealth was measured not in goods but in the people, particularly the women, that he possessed, or in the livestock that served as the means of exchange for women. In this system, women were simultaneously prized and despised. They were prized because, without exception, they did the bulk of the farm work (and, in pastoralist societies, were responsible for milking the cattle), and also because their fertility was the best indicator of the reproductive success of the group. But they were also despised because, even in matrilineal systems where they had a relative right to inherit power, they almost never exercised that power directly. Slaves or free, young women generally constituted the lowest social level of any group, subordinate to the mother-in-law and to the men, young and old, of the family unit.

THE ROLE OF TRADE

Exchange has always played an important role in old former societies: exchanges of women, of goods, and of slaves, whether on the local, regional, or international level. Local exchanges were most often handled by women, who had direct responsibility for the household's subsistence. Indeed, in certain regions such as the Gikuyu states, it was only colonialism that displaced the women from their earlier role as merchants. But in broader markets, where

goods from distant venues acquired a higher value due to their rarity, commerce was controlled by the chiefs. The chiefs conducted transactions among themselves, through intermediaries who were their direct dependents, or entrusted the trade to carefully controlled outsiders. The ancient empires of the savanna (Ghana, Mali, Songhay) built their wealth on the gold and salt trades. They did not directly control production: salt was brought in by the Arabs, while gold was locally mined by small producers. Similarly, between the twelfth and fifteenth centuries, the ruler of Great Zimbabwe controlled the trade of gold, from regions that were not necessarily under his rule, for the rare goods (including Chinese pottery) that came to him by caravan from Sofala on the Indian Ocean.

For some time scholars contended that the power of these states was derived from exclusively external elements, and two nearly impermeable systems were distinguished: "rural communists" on the one hand, and state aristocracies on the other. Today this analysis appears too simplistic. Certainly, in Africa there is less evidence of the state's direct exploitation of the peasantry than was the case in medieval Europe where the wealth of the sovereigns, based primarily on the trade in wheat, required the direct exploitation of the peasantry. But the power of the state was directly felt by the peasantries of the great medieval African empires, which participated in the slave trade as much as in the trade of gold. All the products to be traded had to be handled, transported, and transformed. At the time of the Atlantic slave trade, the ruler of the ancient kingdom of Dahomey (present-day Bénin) built up his authority by alternating his military and mercantile power, as many other slave trading small kingdoms. Every dry season, he led his army in raids on the neighboring people, from whom he took prisoners of war who then were sold as slaves. During the rainy season, he negotiated with Europeans for the arms and prestige goods that he needed to maintain his power. Nearby, during the same period, one of the fundamental bases of the Asante king's wealth was his control of the neighboring Jula merchant communities and the kola nut trade that they monopolized. These nuts had to be gathered, processed, and transported by local peasants. The formation of the early African states cannot be conceived of as independent of the local societies upon which they were built, because what we call a "state" was essentially a capital city and an army. Most of the time, the soldiers were simply the subjects of the ruler and could be drafted at his command. The capital city was inhabited by people whose activities were only marginally agricultural: their existence, and the existence of a court, presupposes the existence of a rurally based provisioning complex where the peasantry—dependents or slaves—was directly involved, and craftsmen highly developed, often among professional casted people. This was similarly the case in eastern Africa, where under the influence of Swahili culture and the domination of the Omani sultanate, a complex economic and political organization developed as early as the eighteenth century, with many interconnections between the coastal urban trade and the non-Muslim hinterland providing ivory and slaves.

FUTURE PROSPECTS

Nonetheless, it remains surprising that these often highly elaborate and powerful societies did not in the precolonial past make the transition from subsistence-based to production-based economies. Surely this was in part because their ensemble of social values was based on a different conceptual universe in which their ideas of poverty, time, wealth, and value were not the same as those of Western societies. Doubtless, too, the linkage between internal production processes and the external resources available to the states did not develop in Africa in the same way that it did in the West. The great merchant systems of Africa foundered with the disappearance of the foreign markets upon which they depended (the Muslims of the Mediterranean, the Atlantic slave trade). This underscores the importance of a third factor: these societies found themselves dependent on foreign markets, long before colonial conquest, a situation that time and again served to thwart the internal dynamism of African states.

One final point must be made. Certainly, institutions and ideologies inherited from the past often appear maladaptive to the new economic and political conditions that arose from the events of the past two centuries. Nonetheless we must reject the outmoded paradigm of tradition versus modernity. The description above was not standstill for centuries and generations. Traditional societies were never static. Concepts and circumstances were constantly evolving over time. Rural societies, formerly described as "stateless," were based on subsistence agriculture governed by power relationships linking village to village, indeed family to family via marriage exchange, with the flow of women ensuring good neighborly relations as well as the readjustment of kinship ties. This (exclusive) type of rural patriarchal organization saw its sphere of influence decline drastically over the course of time, with the continent gradually being subject to a variety of economic situations, involving inter-regional relations, war, slavery, and trade of all kinds. States emerged, theocratic states, trade and slaving empires, warlord territories.

Furthermore, in contrast to Native Americans, Africans have been open to foreign contacts since the beginning of history. Internal economic and political structures were in contact with the rest of the world from an early stage and for a long time these relations involved continuously looking outwards in order to effect economic renewal: exporting gold, then slaves, raw materials, and today oil. Without always being aware of it, African societies for centuries played a major role in the world economy. Thus Africa provided the whole world with slaves, via the Indian Ocean, the Mediterranean, and across the Atlantic. This exploitation also transformed the inner structures, so that slavery and the slave trade gradually became important aspects of African societies themselves.

It would require another article to detail the strategies by which customary political authorities have adapted in order to retain a portion of their economic power, and above all how these strategies involved not only adaptation but also the innovation of rural peoples seeking a place in this new context: A new acceleration occurred with the introduction of Western mercantile capitalism, then the intrusion of Western modern capitalism long before the so called "colonial imperialism" of the end of the nineteenth century, It interfered at least one century beforehand, as early as the Industrial Revolution emerged in western Europe. The immediate precolonial and colonial era, characterized by the introduction and development of cash crops and plantations grown for export, gave rise to the internal social reorganization of powerful groups. A new class of entrepreneurs has arisen, for example, on the cocoa plantations of the Gold Coast (present-day Ghana), or among the Hausa pastoralists who sold livestock to the colonial settlements on the western coast of Africa. A plantation economy based on slavery developed in eastern Africa. Modern land laws and private property were introduced long before colonialism. Moreover, local notables admirably knew how to use "modernization" to strengthen their own power. This process did not only act practically, but also ideologically. African thoughts and representations evolved along with the changing world they were aware of.

Since independence, these trends have continued wherever they have not been thwarted or interrupted by war. Finally, since the 1970s, corresponding to the great global recession, the impoverishment of the lands has inspired the invention of new modes of production. Thus the need to supply the towns tends more and more to reorganize production and exchange of subsistence goods: market gardens and farms within or surrounding urban areas are springing up. Meat markets are being developed for the pastoralists. All these modes of production, called "informal" by the Western economists who understand them poorly, still await serious study and analysis.

See also **Agriculture; Economic History; Economic Systems; Ecosystems; Kalahari Desert; Kinship and Affinity; Kinship and Descent; Land; Languages; Linguistics; Historical; Livestock; Sahara Desert; Salt; Slave Trades; Soils; Zimbabwe; Zimbabwe, Great.**

BIBLIOGRAPHY

Alpers, Edward. *Ivory and Slaves: Changing Patterns of International Trade in East Central Africa in the Later Nineteenth Century.* Berkeley: University of California Press, 1975.

Anderson, Benedict. *Imagined Communities.* New York: Verso, 1983.

Berry, Sara. "The Food Crisis and Agrarian Change in Africa." *African Studies Review* 27 (1984): 59–112.

Bohannan, Laura, and George Dalton, eds. *Markets in Africa.* Evanston, IL: Northwestern University Press, 1972.

Boserup, Esther. *Women's Role in Economic Development.* London: Earthscan, 1969.

Comaroff, Jean, and John L. Comaroff, eds. *Millennial Capitalism and the Culture of Neoliberalism.* Durham, NC: Duke University Press, 2001.

Coquery-Vidrovitch, Catherine. "The Political Economy of the Peasantry and Modes of Production." In *The Political Economy of Contemporary Africa,* ed. Immanuel Wallerstein and T. Hopkins. Beverly Hills, CA: Sage, 1977.

Coquery-Vidrovitch, Catherine, and Paul Lovejoy, eds. *The Workers of African Trade.* Beverly Hills, CA: Sage, 1985.

Glassman, Jonathon. *Feasts and Riot: Revelry, Rebellion, and Popular Consciousness on the Swahili Coast, 1856–1888.* Portsmouth, NH: Heinemann, 1995.

Goody, Jack. *Technology, Tradition, and the State in Africa.* New York: Cambridge University Press, 1971.

Hanson, Holly Elisabeth. *Landed Obligation: The Practice of Power in Buganda.* Portsmouth, NH: Heinemann, 2004.

Iliffe, John. *The African Poor: A History.* Cambridge, U.K.: Cambridge University Press, 1987.

Klein, Martin, ed. *Peasants in Africa: Historical and Contemporary Perspectives.* Beverly Hills, CA: Sage, 1980.

Meillassoux, Claude, ed. *The Development of Indigenous Trade and Markets in Africa.* New York: Oxford University Press, 1981.

Méillassoux, Claude, ed. True*The Anthropology of Slavery: The Womb of Iron and Gold.* Chicago: University of Chicago Press, 1991.

Méillassoux, Claude, ed. *Maidens, Meals, and Money: Capitalism and the Domestic Community.* New York: Cambridge University Press, 1991.

Moore, H. L., and Megan Vaughan. *Cutting Down Trees: Gender, Nutrition and Agricultural Change in the Northern Province of Zambia, 1890–1990.* London: J. Currey, 1994.

Palmer, L., and N. Parsons, eds. *The Roots of Rural Poverty in Central and South Africa.* London: Heinemann, 1977.

CATHERINE COQUERY-VIDROVITCH

AGRICULTURE

The various ways that sub-Saharan agrarian systems are socially organized and technically executed have a direct bearing upon their productivity. It is imperative to understand the production constraints inherent in all agroecological systems—extensive as well as intensive—before rational attempts are made to solve the early twenty-first century African food crisis. Agricultural growth depends on the efforts made by local governments to understand farmers' extensive knowledge and time-proven practices, and the needs and priorities that these generate. "The effectiveness of new technologies will greatly depend upon their being locally managed, reasonably priced, fairly low-risk, appropriate in terms of seasonally available labor, and, above all, promising and profitable" (Linares 1997, 21).

Different crop combinations, agricultural practices, and new cultivars have already increased, or will hopefully do so in the future, food production by African smallholders. The tragic effects of poverty, food insecurity, landlessness, and diminishing resources on rural and urban dwellers must be reversed through applications that encourage sustainability. Only then will sub-Saharan peoples achieve the peace and prosperity they so badly need and deserve.

PROMISING PRACTICES
A number of production techniques hold great promise for increasing yields, ensuring soil fertility, and making best use of dwindling land and forest resources. The following are only some of the numerous practices that Africans, as well as other world farmers, have instituted in the effort to assure sustainability. They demonstrates the ability of small-farm holders to experiment, improvise, and innovate with crop combinations that are best adapted to multiple and often immediate needs.

Intercropping. Also known as mixed cropping, the term refers to the procedure, widespread in the tropics, whereby farmers plant different crops in the same field at the same time. An estimated 80 percent of the total cultivated area in West Africa is under this regime. Paul Richards (1985, 64–72) points out that in the forest zone, twenty to thirty crop species are planted in the same parcel during one season, and in the savanna, ten to fifteen species. Often, men work on the principal crop and women perform the intercrops, either in a regular pattern, or at random. Particular attention is given to combinations of plants that ripen either sequentially or simultaneously. In the western corner of West Africa, rice is commonly intercropped with millet, maize, and cassava, whereas in the rest of West Africa, yam and cassava are often interplanted with maize. In some Sierra Leone communities, the rice upland farm is planted with additional crops such as cucumber, cassava, and maize, grown

for subsistence, and *egusi* (melon) and *beniseed* (sesame) are grown for sale. Groundnut farms are also intercropped with cassava and maize here.

Among the many advantages of intercropping are: better yields, a larger diversity of available foodstuffs, less risk of total loss, more effective seasonal distribution of labor, increased uptake of plant nutrients, and greater control of soil erosion, weeds, and pests. Most importantly, mixed cropping is well adapted to poor soils, allowing higher plant densities than monocropping. Moreover, it is subject to constant improvement through the introduction of new varieties, better use of fertilizers, and more targeted planting patterns and schedules. Thus, intercropping has considerable economic and social potential, not only for improved household nutrition, but also for the cultivation of commercial crops that contribute much-needed cash to the family.

Market-gardening. Growing vegetables for household consumption and sale in neighboring town markets in small, intensely irrigated parcels of land, often close to home, enhances food security and adds to family income. Because it can be combined with daily chores, gardening is often a female pursuit, carried out communally or individually, depending on access to inputs such as water and fertilizer. In the Casamance region of southern Senegal, the women living in a community near the town of Bignona have for several years cultivated vegetables during the dry season in a large, fenced, communal garden, divided into individual parcels measuring 33 feet by 3 feet that each woman works. They plant mostly imported vegetables (onions, tomatoes, and lettuce), plus a few indigenous African leafy vegetables such as *yahatou* (the African eggplant) and *bissap* (red calyx). Some species are grown in nurseries from packaged seeds, then transplanted. Each parcel is irrigated twice daily with water from a well dug up by agricultural extension services. What the women progressively harvest they take to sell in the market in Bignona, making a significant profit.

Thirty-five kilometers away, in the outskirts of Ziguinchor, the capital of Casamance, a woman will borrow a rice field that has been harvested, and hence holds residual water, in order to grow vegetables during the dry season. In payment, she will help the owner's wife transplant rice during the rainy season. Using supplementary irrigation from

Growing vegetables in the off season. A young Jola woman waters her home garden where she grows vegetables in the off season for sale in the market. Maize is one of the most important crops of the region. PHOTOGRAPH BY OLGA F. LINARES

wells that men dig for a fee, and generous amounts of fertilizer purchased from an extension agency, a woman grows sweet potatoes, the usual imported vegetables, some of the aforementioned native species, plus perhaps *gombo* (okra). She uses the crops she harvests to feed the family, and sells the surplus in one of the city markets, earning the equivalent of one or two hundred U.S. dollars a year, a fortune by local standards.

In the nearby country of the Gambia, a veritable garden boom has taken place, financed initially by international donor agencies. Hundreds of women's communal vegetable gardens line the shores along the Gambia River Basin, replacing the men's groundnut fields as the main source of cash. Up to 80 percent of the women earn more from their gardens than their husbands do from their groundnuts. This brings them power and prestige, but gardening has also increased female workloads and

aggravated marital conflicts, as husbands often ask their wives for loans, whereas the latter try hard to protect their earnings. Even then, market gardening by women has, here as elsewhere, been a highly successful option for increased household security. Such gardening has flourished in the face of variable rainfall, government austerity measures, a devaluation of the local currencies, and increased land and labor shortages.

Development programs have consistently ignored women's productive potential as subsistence and commercial farmers. Extension services have failed to provide them with technical training, affordable inputs, transportation facilities, or credit to pay for wells, tools, new cultivars, and improved seed. There is much that can be done to encourage innovation and improve the conditions under which women toil in their gardens or out in the fields. In fact, it may be impossible to achieve a turnaround in African agriculture without increasing support for women farmers.

Urban and Periurban Agriculture. Urban farming—the growing of food crops in community lands and parks, unused city spaces, roadsides, terrain not suitable for house construction, and periurban zones—plays a central subsistence role in the informal economies of many African cities. Half of the urban migrants to Ouagadogou actively farm; almost two-thirds of urban households in six towns surveyed in Kenya grow at least part of their food within or in adjacent city spaces; in low-income areas of Lusaka, 45 percent of families grew crops on in their back and/or front yards or in the periphery of the city, with an additional 15 percent cultivating at both sites; a survey of 51 cultivators, spread in four different areas of the city of Lomé, revealed that in two zones, 85 percent of urban dwellers farmed on a permanent basis, whereas in the other two zones 38 percent did so part-time only. Put differently, in the city of Beria, in Mozambique, 88 percent of the green spaces in the city are farmed by families, and in Zaria, Nigeria, 66 percent of the area of the city is used for cultivation.

In the developing economies of the Third World, urban agriculture provides jobs—especially for recent immigrants—is a source of healthy food, and brings much-needed income. It is a time-consuming, intensive endeavor that makes rational use of empty space, and promotes efficient utilization of water, fertilizer and other resources. Urban agriculture brings a myriad of ecological benefits to city residents by helping to recycle waste, prevent erosion, create green spaces where useful animal species can thrive, and facilitate experimentation with new seed varieties and other planting materials. In addition, it fosters interethnic cooperation in gaining access to land, and in the formation of complex networks of economic interdependence between producers, middlemen, and consumers. In short, urban farming creates added value in both social and biological terms.

Two different examples illustrate how urban farming is conducted. In Lomé, the Togolese capital, food crops for household use are usually grown during the rainy season, whereas vegetables and ornamental plants for sale are cultivated throughout the year. Farmers cultivate either administrative lands, reserved for the construction of public buildings such as schools and hospitals, or private properties that they own, rent, or borrow. Growing food crops is mainly a family endeavor. Commercial crops, however, may be grown by nuclear family members, with or without the additional help of friends and hired workers. Most farmers buy seed, mostly grains, whereas planting materials for root crops (cassava, sweet potato, taro) are saved after the harvest, or acquired from relatives. Food crops grown include maize, string beans, groundnuts, tomatoes, gumbo, and peppers. Vegetables grown for the market include foreign imports—such as lettuce, carrots, cucumber, tomatoes, green peppers, celery, spinach, onions, eggplant, and cabbage—and native species—*gboma* (a *Solanaceae*), *adémè* (a *Tiliaceae*), *fontètè* (an *Amaranthecea*). The latter are conserved in the ground, or as dried seed kept in closed jars. Women specialize in the sale of certain products—such as two or three kinds of green vegetables—acting more often as intermediaries rather than producers. Profit margins are small, but the sale of vegetables provides jobs and some income to family members, contract workers, and female traders. Growing household crops obviously improves family nutrition, and reinforces social relations through gifts and exchanges. Hence, in Lomé, urban agriculture allows numerous farming families to survive, provides food for those otherwise employed, among other benefits. Government or private initiatives that facilitate cooperation among

producers, extend them credit facilities, make inputs affordable, and protect their products through tariffs, will enhance the contribution that this form of livelihood can make to the welfare of city residents.

Another example of the way in which city farming may be conducted involves periurban cultivation of rice parcels and upland fields in a nine-mile radius from Ziguinchor, the capital of Casamance, in southern Senegal. The city is encircled by lowlands that are inundated with water during the rainy season where rice is cultivated, and slightly raised uplands that are planted with millet and sorghum, and more recently with groundnuts and maize. The seventy-five households surveyed cultivated a total of 158 clusters of fields measuring from a few hundred to several thousand square feet. Half of these are planted with rice (the bottomlands), another 24 percent with upland crops, and 26 percent with fruit trees or household crops. Over half of the Ziguinchor farmers are women: they cultivate mostly rice and upland fields that are often borrowed, and do so usually with the help of hired hands. Male-headed households, on average larger than those headed by women, cultivate either all three, or only two types of fields that they either own or rent. Many men are self-employed, or they work in the public sector, using the labor of their wives, unmarried children, sundry relatives, and wards to prepare their fields. Despite considerable investment in time and money, only one of the households in the sample was self-sufficient in rice; the rest had to purchase imported Southeast Asian rice to feed their families for several months each year. Nevertheless, given the large size of families and the small salaries householders make, there would not be enough to eat without home-grown rice, complemented by millet and sorghum.

Home Gardens. These are small (0.25–1.2 acres), permanently cultivated parcels, located in the backyards of, or close to dwellings, planted with multipurpose agricultural crops, trees, shrubs, herbs, spices, medicinal plants, fish ponds, and animals, and managed by household members. They contain a high number of species, arranged in layers. Root crops and herbs occupy the ground, annuals or small perennials the next level up, bushes and trees an intermediate layer, and large trees the upper canopy. Home gardens maintain and enhance agricultural biodiversity by serving as a refuge for endangered crop varieties, as places to experiment with new cultivars, and as ongoing systems for crop evolution. Most importantly, they ensure a continuous supply of edible foods, firewood, medicinal plants and spices, and household construction materials. Often, they also produce marketable surpluses. Although frequently managed by women, in some societies men may also be involved in their upkeep.

In Ghana, home gardens occur in all agroecological zones and are planted with fruit trees, vegetables, and other products. In moist and semideciduous forests, home gardens contain many species (93 to 104), and are multistoried: the uppermost canopy consists of trees (mango, oil palm, avocado); the next level of annual and perennial species (plantain, citrus, soursop, papaya, and guava); the third story of vegetables (eggplant, cocoyam, yam, and cassava) plus medicinal plants; and the ground layer of creeping plants such as sweet potato. Three crops—plantain, yams, and millet—are represented by several species: thirteen, eight, and two, respectively. Thus, they are important sites for the conservation of underutilized fruits, indigenous tree varieties, and wild species.

The ethnicity and gender role of Ghana's home gardeners vary among regions, as does their educational level, their household size, their engagement as part- or full-time cultivators, their methods of land preparation, and the percent of crops they grow for subsistence versus for sale. In all areas, however, home gardens perform the double function of improving family nutrition and increasing the household budget.

In northwest Tanzania, small (averaging 1.48 acres) multistoried home gardens, found around homesteads, include crops and livestock. The major crops planted are banana and coffee, but over fifty other crops are grown as well, including several species of beans, sweet potatoes, cassava, taro, and yams. Livestock is kept in homestead sheds, mostly for their manure, and is grazed in adjacent communal land. The home garden is managed by family labor: women sow and weed beans and maize, and men prune the coffee trees, remove old leaves from banana trees, and lop or cut down trees. An average garden produces 179 pounds of coffee, 105 bunches of banana, and 265 pounds of beans a year; if manured, the same parcel may produce twice as much. At present, the system is under threat due to land fragmentation under rapid

Maize harvesting. A Jola woman from Ziguinchor, the capital of the Casamance in southern Senegal, harvests maize from her home garden for household consumption. PHOTOGRAPH BY OLGA F. LINARES

population growth, pest outbreaks, decreasing soil fertility, and low coffee producer price. In view of their potential to recycle nutrients and prevent erosion, and to ensure household food security, home gardens deserve to be improved through techniques such as integrated pest management and the inclusion of fast-growing plants that fix nitrogen and improve the soils.

PEASANT CROP REVOLUTIONS: MAIZE, CASSAVA, AND COTTON

Development experts often assume that West African rural farmers are conservative and unwilling to change. The recent and dramatic expansion of maize, manioc, and cotton cultivation—three introduced New World crops—into this region contradicts this view. As individuals, or as members of households and communities, peasant farmers have increased domestic and commercial production of these crops in a truly revolutionary manner, with important results for feeding the African poor and generating much needed cash.

Maize (Zea mays). Maize production has greatly expanded in postindependence Africa, becoming the most important food crop consumed by rural and urban dwellers alike. It is the staple of eastern and southern African populations—where seven countries account for 70 percent of its production, and up to 40 percent of the calories consumed—but maize cultivation has also increased significantly in the western countries. In the Nigerian savanna belt, for example, production increased from about one million tons in 1964 to nearly two and a half million tons in 1994. Reasons for this are the use of high-yielding crop varieties, and cheap fertilizer encouraged by extension services, plus government investment in technology and infrastructure. In Kenya and Zambia, maize production grew fivefold from the 1980s or so, and in Malawi the surface area that was planted in hybrids expanded in eight years from 3 to 30 percent of the maize areas. Even then, however, maize production has failed to keep up with population growth, or to increase rural incomes significantly. For these reasons, governments must do more to develop and disseminate new varieties and technologies, to strengthen delivery systems for seed and fertilizer, and to liberalize the marketing of maize.

Cassava or Manioc (Manihot esculenta crantz). At present, cassava is the second most important source of calories for African populations. It is cultivated in about forty countries, producing more carbohydrates per hectare than any other staple. Because it grows in poor soils, is resistant to drought and locust invasions, is easily propagated by stem cuttings, can be planted at any time of the year, and may be stored underground for months, to be progressively harvested as needed, the cultivation of cassava has rapidly spread throughout the continent. Although the roots contain low levels of protein, cassava may be eaten with other supplementary foods; the leaves, often prepared as a vegetable, are rich in proteins and contain important vitamins and minerals. For all these reasons, cassava has become primarily a rural food

Maize cobs. A Jola woman from the village of Falmere in the Casamance region of southern Senegal carries maize cobs home to cook. PHOTOGRAPH BY OLGA F. LINARES

staple, particularly useful as a famine reserve crop, as well as a cash crop produced for urban consumption; its industrial use as starch, and as feed for livestock, are of minor importance. In some countries such as Nigeria, improved high-yielding Tropical Manioc Selection varieties (or TMS) have increased production by 40 percent without fertilizer. They have transformed cassava from a low-yielding famine food to a high-yielding food staple that also holds great promise as livestock feed and industrial raw material.

Cotton (Gossipium sp). In Côte d'Ivoire, the cotton revolution was the outcome of negotiations by farmers with agricultural experts, administrators,

Collecting cassava leaves. A young Jola man from the village of Katinong in the Casamance region of southern Senegal collects cassava leaves to be cooked as a vegetable. Cassava is a woody shrub native to South Africa that is typically cultivated annually for its edible, starchy root. PHOTOGRAPH BY OLGA F. LINARES

merchants, and representatives of the cotton industry in an effort to adopt new farming technologies and high-yielding varieties. As more and more farmers engaged in the intensive monocropping of this cash crop, yields per acre increased by 1.6 percent per year in the years 1965–1984, and the area planted in it by 6.9 percent. Although cotton production fell in the mid-1980s as a result of World Bank structural adjustment policies removing farm subsidies, it resurged again in the 1990s when a vigorous peasant cooperative movement transformed the terms of trade between producers and the powerful French-controlled Ivorian company for the development of textile fibers (Compagnie Ivoirienne pour le Developpement des Textiles or CIDT). The result was better prices and more organizational autonomy. Despite this agricultural success story, however, growing cotton has not improved dramatically peasant livelihoods.

CHALLENGES FACING THE AGRICULTURAL SECTOR

If the rural smallholder farmers of sub-Saharan Africa, who represent about 64 percent of the population, are to develop sustainable and intensive agricultural systems capable of feeding themselves and urban dwellers, pressing economic, social, and biotechnology problems need to be addressed. Local governments must increase significantly their investment in agriculture in myriad and well-known ways: by insuring farmers' property rights to land and other resources, by extending them credit to buy equipment and fertilizer, by improving their access to markets, by offering price incentives and better terms of trade and, most importantly, by training farmers in the appropriate use of new science and biotechnologies that improve soil fertility, provide better access to water, conserve natural resources, and encourage the development and adoption of resistant, high-yielding crop varieties. To succeed, all new approaches must be built upon the strengths exhibited by efficient and innovative traditional agricultural practices, such as those outlined above, that are based on sound indigenous knowledge and time-proven procedures. Only then may Africa's food crisis be reversed, restoring agricultural self-sufficiency and security to the population at large. A productive and sustainable agriculture that is securely anchored in local expertise, and on existing social relationships and institutions, empowers farmers to make decisions that will allow them to escape the vicious cycle of poverty, and set them on the path to healthy economic growth.

See also **Agriculture; Ecosystems; Family; Gender; Labor; Livestock; Plants; Soils; Urbanism and Urbanization; Women.**

BIBLIOGRAPHY

Bassett, Thomas J. *The Peasant Cotton Revolution in West Africa: Côte d'Ivoire. 1880–1995.* Cambridge, U.K.: Cambridge University Press, 2001.

Bennett-Lartey, S. O., et al. "Aspects of Home Garden Cultivation in Ghana." In *Home Gardens and Agrobiodiversity*, ed. Pablo B. Eyzaguirre and Olga F. Linares. Washington, DC: Smithsonian Books, 2004

Bricker, Gary, and Soumana Traoré. "Traditional Urbanization in Upper Volta: The Case of Ouagadougou, a Savannah Capital." In *Development of Urban Systems in Africa*, eds. Robert A. Obudho, and Salah El-Shakhs. New York: Praeger, 1979.

Byerlee, Derek, and Carl K. Eicher. *Africa's Emerging Maize Revolution.* Boulder, Colorado: Lynne Rienner Publishers, 1997.

Eyzaguirre, Pablo B., and Olga F. Linares. "Introduction." In *Home Gardens and Agrobiodiversity*, eds. Pablo B. Eyzaguirre and Olga F. Linares. Washington, DC: Smithsonian Books, 2004.

Kouvonou, F. M.; B. G. Honfoga; and S. K. Debrah. 1999. "Sécurité alimentaire et gestion intégrée de la fertilité des sols: contribution de maraîchage périurbain a Lomé." In *Urban Agriculture in West Africa: Contributing to Food Security and Urban Sanitation*, ed. Olanrewaju Smith. Ottawa, Canada: International Development Research Centre, 1999.

Linares, Olga F. "Cultivating Biological and Cultural Diversity: Urban Farming in Casamance, Senegal." *Africa* 66, no. 1(1996): 105–121.

Linares, Olga F. "Agrarian Systems." In *Encyclopedia of Africa South of the Sahara*, Vol 1. Ed. John Middleton. New York: Holiday House, 1997.

Memon, Pyar Ali, and Diana Lee-Smith. "Urban Agriculture in Kenya." *Canadian Journal of African Studies* 27, no. 1 (1993): 25–42.

Nindi, Benson. "Agricultural Transformation in Sub-Saharan Africa: The Search for Viable Options." *Nordic Journal of African Studies* 2, no. 2 (1993): 142–158.

Nweke, Felix I.; Dunstan S.C. Spencer; and John K. Lynam. *The Cassava Transformation: Africa's Best-Kept Secret.* East Lansing: Michigan State University Press, 2002.

Richards, Paul. *Coping with Hunger: Hazard and Experiment in an African Rice-farming System.* London: Allen and Unwin, 1987.

Richards, Paul. *Indigenous Agricultural Revolution: Ecology and Food Production in West Africa.* Boulder, Colorado: Westview Press, 1985.

Rugelama, G. H.; A. Okting'Ati; and F.H. Johnsen. "The Homegarden Agroforestry System of Bukoba District, North-Western Tanzania. 1. Farming Systems Analysis." *Agroforestry Systems* 26 (1994): 53–64.

Sanyal, Bishwapriya. "Urban Cultivation amidst Modernization: How Should We Interpret It?" *Journal of Planning Education and Research* 6, no. 3 (1987): 197–207.

Schilter, Christine. *L'agriculture Urbaine à Lomé: Approches Agronomiques et Socio-économiques.* Paris: Éditions Karthala, 1991.

Schroeder, Richard A. " 'Gone to their Second Husbands': Marital Metaphors and Conjugal Contracts in the Gambia's Female Garden Sector." *Canadian Journal of African Studies* 30, no. 1 (1996): 69–87.

United Nations Development Programme. *Urban Agriculture: Food, Jobs and Sustainable Cities.* New York: United Nations Development Programme, 1996.

OLGA F. LINARES

PLOW FARMING

The plow has a long history in Africa as an instrument of agricultural production, primarily to prepare the soil for planting. Through much of that history, its use was limited to North Africa and parts of the Nile Valley. In the nineteenth century it was widely adopted across Southern Africa. In the twentieth century European colonial administrations promoted its use in East, Central, and West Africa. Adoption was slow, but farmers throughout the cereal, groundnut, and cotton growing regions of Africa have increasingly taken it up. Its use remains confined to a minority of farmers in sub-Saharan Africa.

The plow originated in Southwest Asia following the domestication of cattle and of wheat and barley. By 3000 BCE it was deployed throughout the valleys of the Tigris-Euphrates and the lower Nile, where it ensured the productivity, which underpinned the civilizations of Sumer and Pharaonic Egypt. Animal-drawn plows increase the output of human labor and may double the surface area worked by an individual farmer. Thus, it is an instrument of extensification rather than intensification. While oxen were favored as draft animals, African peoples have also used horses, donkeys, buffalos, and camels. The first plows were made entirely of wood. Iron tips then followed. These plows, sometimes called "scratch" plows, break the surface of the earth, but do not penetrate deeply nor turn the soil.

From the upper Nile Valley the plow spread westward to the Maghreb and southward to present-day northern Sudan Republic and to the Ethiopian Highlands, where its initial adoption, probably by Kushitic-speaking peoples, has been dated to no later than the second millennium BCE. Originally, the plow was associated with wheat and barley, with comparatively dense populations, and with the ready availability of draught animals. However, both Sudanese and Ethiopian farmers have also used plows to cultivate cereals of African origin—sorghum, bullrush millet, finger

Folk painting representation of traditional Ethiopian plowing. The Amharic caption to this painting reads, roughly, "by plowing they are preparing [the soil]." Contemporary Ethiopian and Eritrean farmers continue to use "scratch" plows, which were first used in early agricultural systems in Southwest Asia. FOLK PAINTING, PERSONAL POSSESSION, DONALD CRUMMEY

millet, and téf. The surpluses, which they produced, supported a succession of states.

Where wheat and barley did not thrive, where populations were less dense, where draught animals were not available, and where other production systems satisfied local need, the plow made little headway. Many Ethiopians and Sudanese opted for alternative strategies. Some Ethiopians based their livelihood on the cultivation of a semi-permanent root crop called *enset*, for which the plow offers no advantages.

European imperialism provided the impetus for the modern adoption of the steel moldboard plow, which turns over the soil at the same time as it breaks it. Plows were adopted rapidly by African farmers across southern Africa, in the Ciskei and among the Sotho from the 1850s onwards, and among the Tswana in the 1880s and 1890s. The impulse was modernization represented by European missionaries and the opening of markets for agricultural produce. Elsewhere, adoption was later. In the 1920s, in Nigeria, Guinea, and Mali administrations promoted the plow to increase groundnut and cotton production. By 1928 about 4,000 farmers in Guinea were using plows, in neighboring Mali about

2,500 were doing so by 1932, and by 1936 the Nigerian number was about 1,000 farmers. Numbers grew slowly and spasmodically. As of the late twentieth century perhaps 10 to 20 percent of West African farmers used ox-drawn plows, their adoption boosted by readier availability of credit to purchase oxen, primarily in the cotton and groundnut regions of the Sahel—Senegal, Mali, Burkina Faso, Niger, Chad—and the northern provinces of Côte d'Ivoire, Ghana, Bénin, Nigeria, and Cameroun (Starkey). In East Africa, the numbers were probably similar.

Adoption was never a linear process and involved changes in the gender division of labor and the holding of landed property. However, in contrast to the failed tractor mechanization schemes of the 1960s and 1970s, animal-drawn plows have proved a viable option for an increasing number of African farmers.

See also **Agriculture; Gender; Soils.**

BIBLIOGRAPHY

Pryor, Frederic I. "The Invention of the Plow." *Comparative Studies in Society and History* 27, no. 4 (1985): 727–743.

Starkey, P. H. "The Introduction, Intensification and Diversification of the Use of Animal Power in West African Farming Systems: Implications At Farm Level." In *Animal Power in Farming Systems. Proceedings of Networkshop Held 17–26 September 1986 in Freetown, Sierra Leone*, ed. P. H. Starkey and F. Ndiamé. Eschborn: Vieweg, n.d.

DONALD CRUMMEY

HUNTING AND GATHERING

Articulated relations of property, production, labor, and exchange have, generally in scholarly history, been erroneously treated as being absent from hunter-gatherer social formations. Equally inhibiting to an understanding of these relations has been a tendency, when such relations are addressed, to equate production in such societies with energetics rather than social processes. An adequate discussion of this subject thus requires that attention be given to two interrelated subtopics: first, the received model of hunting society and its critique; second, the new model with emphasis on institutions of land tenure upon which production is based and the social relations that govern exchange systems.

The means of production in hunting-gathering systems are varied and complex. Methods of hunting include the use of snares, spears, bow and arrows, net traps, pitfalls—sometimes in conjunction with animal drives and running an animal to ground. Snares and simple pitfalls are placed in paths habitually used by particular species (ranging in size from small mammals to hippopotamuses); unobtrusive barriers of brush are often erected to ensure that the prey does not sidestep the trap. These methods plus bow-and-arrow hunting are usually carried out by one man acting alone, although small hunting parties are not infrequent. By contrast, net traps and pitfall drives require the cooperation of a large number of people. In both methods, the trap—net or pit—is established at a suitable location and is attended by several persons (usually men); animals are driven to this location by many other persons (among them women and children) who, having fanned out at some distance away, force the prey to run into the traps where they are killed with clubs and spears. Spear hunting is most successfully carried on with dogs trained to bring prey to bay; during the twentieth century, horses have been used to chase animals and spear

them from the mount. The gathering of plant foods, on the other hand, requires little other than carrying devices—bags, slings, pouches—and a sharpened stick to dig tubers.

Archaeological and historical evidence increasingly demonstrates that few peoples have relied solely on these methods for at least several centuries. Almost all societies in which hunting-gathering has been important during this time, certainly all in Africa, have engaged to some degree in animal husbandry based on some combination of cattle, sheep, and goats, either as owners of livestock or as herders for others. Sorghum, millet, sweet-reed (a kind of sugarcane), cowpeas, and melons have been widely grown for an equally long time; cassava and maize were added by Europeans from the sixteenth century. The degree to which these domesticated products play a role in hunter-gatherer economies and the length of time they have done so is hotly contested by adherents of the received and new models, and indeed in many cases the question cannot yet be satisfactorily answered.

THE RECEIVED MODEL

Hunter-gatherer societies were initially characterized by nineteenth-century scholars who based their theories on the work of French sociologists and British and American evolutionary anthropologists. In both of these theoretical frameworks, a distinction was made between simple, "mechanical" societies and complex, "organic" ones—the former functioning entirely according to the static (mechanical) rules of nature, the latter evolving through the interposition of social (organic) rules between persons and nature. The economic form of mechanical society was said to be hunting and gathering: its attributes were listed as small, self-sufficient groups of individuals, all possessing identical abilities and skills; mobility of individuals among groups restricted only by ecological factors; reciprocal access to resources and land, all held collectively; undeveloped material culture limited in variety and amount by nomadic life; and division of labor based only upon age and sex. In this economic form, production—as the creation of artifactual products through acts of labor—could not exist; humans were themselves the instruments of production, in Marx's sense of being the direct means of harvest with few tools (other than rudimentary ones of stone, bone, and wood) intervening in the process. This model was posited to be the original form of human society and, thus, was seen as the initial, "Stone Age" stage of human social evolution.

This theoretical approach held that, while the intervention of social rules produced the whole range of organic agricultural and industrial societies known in the nineteenth century, the imperative, mechanical rules of nature did not allow hunting-gathering societies to evolve. Thus, peoples in Africa, Asia, the Americas, and Australia encountered by Europeans from the sixteenth century onward who appeared to subsist entirely or substantially by hunting and gathering were thought to be relics of the Stone Age. As such they were studied for the light they might throw on the origin of human society.

Although, in the early twentieth century, this model was temporarily abandoned, it was revived in the 1960s by, principally, American anthropologists working in the new paradigm of evolutionary ecology. In its new form it was called variously the hunting model, the band level of sociocultural organization, or the foraging mode of production. But the attributes of the original model were largely unchanged. Two significant contrasts, however, distinguish the revived model from the original. First, and most important, it acknowledged the existence of production among hunter-gatherers—although it was a restricted kind of production with division of labor still based solely on "natural ascriptions" of age and sex, and individuals were still viewed as instruments of production subservient to nature. Second, while in the nineteenth century the lives of hunter-gatherers were usually thought to be "nasty, brutish, and short," now anthropologists set out to demonstrate that theirs was "the original affluent society." These anthropologists, like their predecessors, turned to living peoples as a window through which to witness Paleolithic affluence. While at first apparently successful, their results were soon shown to be flawed by the constrictions of the model.

These efforts stimulated a reexamination of supposedly simple hunter-gatherer relations of production. This led to the formulation of a new model which articulates these relations with the other domains of social life. This model proposes that production in hunter-gatherer societies (as in all other societies) is the emergent result of the interplay of social status, land entitlement, propinquity of other peoples, investment opportunity, and the historicity of the region in which it takes place. In the first instance, hunter-gatherer access to the forces and means of production resides in kinship practices which are, in turn, ineluctably enmeshed in relations to land.

THE NEW MODEL
Land Tenure.
In contrast to the ecological concept of territory, which focuses on productivity and the means of production, the constitution of land tenure locates people within the social matrix of relations to the land upon which productive activity must take place. A number of hunter-gatherer societies in Africa share structural elements of property relations and tenure in common. Property law in these societies defines not so much rights of persons over things, as obligations owed between persons with respect to things. Being in a property relationship involves being bound within a set of reciprocal obligations among persons and things; entitlement to land and rights to its use must be subject to a complex of claims arising from this social matrix. It is not, however, land itself that is inherited. What actually is inherited is a set of status positions binding individuals to a network of obligations owed among persons through which they are entitled to land.

Among southern African Khoesan, a person's primary entitlement is that person's birthplace; there is a very high probability that this birthplace will be in at least one parent's entitlement. An individual's tenure in land is acquired bilaterally through a regional kinship net defined initially by birth into a local descent group and later reinforced by marriage. East African Okiek divide land into lineage-owned, patrilineally transmitted tenures; the local group is a significant association of identity which incorporates affines (relatives by marriage) into its residential units. The Lese-Dese and the Efe pygmies of central Africa respectively organize themselves as segmented patrilineages and exogamous patrilians each with its own traditionally transmitted tenure. It is thus apparent that hunter-gatherer kinship is a form of conjectural history the elements of which—both the positions potentially open to persons and the connections among these positions—are subject to manipulation in conjunction with wider social and economic concerns.

Social Relations of Exchange. Exchange networks play important integrative roles in this social-spatial structure. While land is owned communally, the means of production—weapons, tools, containers, transporting devices, as well as the products of individual labor—are private property. This private nature of production makes possible the specialization of productive activity and the consequent necessary interdependence of producers via exchange. Among the Khoesan-speaking Zhu, 62 percent of reciprocal exchange occurs between grand relatives and 82 percent between great-grand relatives; a high proportion of this exchange is associated with marriage negotiations. Comparable statistical data are not available for eastern and central Africa, but the outlines of reciprocal exchange appear similar. Historically, this dialectic between independent private production and dependent community sociality formed extensive exchange networks that tied together diverse, disparate goals and strategies—the political conditions of their labor—of families, homesteads, kin, and neighbors.

If political practice is that activity which produces and transforms social relations, it becomes evident that, among the people discussed, kinship is the arena in which political practice takes place. Exchange, then, is the product of strategies oriented toward the satisfaction of material and symbolic interests and organized by reference to a determinate set of economic and social conditions. It emerges as relationships that can be read in different ways by participants in them. In keeping with the necessary interdependence of private producers via exchange, no local descent group can independently reproduce itself within the parochial limits of a single land tenure. For this reason, a significant number of marriage ties are negotiated with strategically placed collateral affines in adjacent and nearby tenures. Adults with mature children choose to gain strength through intensified exchange and other forms of cooperation with people in specific tenures because they are concerned with finding spouses in those tenures for their children.

There is also "foreign" exchange. Exotic products are transferred over distances far greater than those to nearby tenures; a web of extensions of individual relationships stretches for hundreds of kilometers through many hands. Persons closer to each other in any direction along the network are closer relatives or affines; those farther away, both in geographical distance and along the links of transfer chains, are progressively more tenuously related. Marriage negotiations form part of the strategies employed to tie desirable trade partners more closely together and to give generational continuity to these arrangements. Partnerships are passed in inheritance from parent to child, and inheritors strive to solidify anew those partnerships that offer continuing advantageous access to material and social resources. That is, the role of exchange in the reproduction of the conditions of production is an incorporative one; it is through delicate, complex balancing of individual interests in a fluid field of options that the parochial bounds of local groups are opened to a necessary wider social sphere.

See also **Anthropology, Social, and the Study of Africa; Kinship and Descent; Land: Tenure; Marriage Systems; Plants: Domestication.**

BIBLIOGRAPHY

Bailey, Robert. *The Behavioral Ecology of Efe Pygmy Men in the Ituri Forest, Zaire.* Ann Arbor: Museum of Anthropology, University of Michigan, 1991.

Barnard, Alan. *Hunters and Herders of Southern Africa: A Comparative Ethnography of the Khoisan Peoples.* Cambridge, U.K.: Cambridge University Press, 1992.

Berry, J. W., et al., eds. *On the Edge of the Forest: Cultural Adaptation and Cognitive Development in Central Africa.* Berwyn, PA: Swets of North America, 1986.

Kratz, Corinne A. *Affecting Performance: Meaning, Movement, and Experience in Okiek Women's Initiation.* Washington, DC: Smithsonian Institution Press, 1994.

Wilmsen, Edwin N. *Land Filled with Flies: A Political Economy of the Kalahari.* Chicago: University of Chicago Press, 1989.

EDWIN N. WILMSEN

PASTORALISM

Pastoralism has a long history in Africa, stretching back over thousands of years, and a very wide distribution. Yet it has varied so much that it is difficult either to define or to categorize. Rather than establishing "types" of production, it is better to see communities as occupying different points along a continuum stretching from "pure" subsistence pastoralism, where households are entirely dependent on livestock both for subsistence and for the creation and maintenance of social bonds, to its opposite, the complete absence of livestock in the local economy. While both extremes exist, the majority of African communities occupy points in between, with pastoralists clustering between "pure" pastoralism and forms of mixed economy where livestock may not be vital to subsistence but are nonetheless of great cultural and social importance. Because pastoralists are highly adaptable and responsive to changes in their environment, both communities and individual households may shift their position along the continuum: even within fully pastoral societies households vary in the size of their herds and the extent to which they are dependent on them.

In the past, the social mobility of pastoralists and the adaptive potential of pastoralism as a strategy were supported by the fact that pastoralism rarely existed in isolation. Pastoralists usually maintained close exchange relations with communities of cultivators and hunter-gatherers. Such networks offered pastoralists access to alternative food supplies to supplement the product of the family herds in times of dearth and to places of refuge if herds were destroyed by drought or disease. They also enabled households to expand their labor force by absorbing outsiders in good times and to slough off members in bad times, thus maintaining a balance between human and animal populations. The expansion and contraction of the boundaries of pastoralism, as individuals and households joined or left, was a common feature of regional interaction, and makes it essential to view pastoralism as but one of a number of interdependent production strategies linked to different but mutable ethnic identities. More recently, however, these patterns of regional interaction have been affected by land pressures and political instability and, to some extent, superseded by the development of direct links between pastoralists, the state and national economies. Pastoralists under pressure are now more likely to relocate to settlement schemes or refugee camps or simply to move to town in search of work than to be absorbed into neighboring

communities; and supplementary food can be obtained from local shopkeepers for cash rather than from trading partners by exchange.

PASTORAL RESOURCES

As a production strategy, pastoralism involves the combined management of four main resources: livestock, land (grazing), water, and labor. Differences in the nature of and interrelation between these resources, and in the ways that each is utilized and controlled, shape individual pastoral systems and create the very wide variations between them.

Cattle, sheep and goats, and camels are the animal staples, though the last are not found below Somalia and the arid areas of northern Kenya. Often different types are kept together, though herded separately; cattle and small stock (sheep and goats) being the most common combination. All four types have different breeding characteristics, tolerances to disease and drought challenges and grazing requirements: mixing herds maximizes resource use and extends the range of subsistence. Sheep and goats, the "small change" of the pastoral economy, are especially useful as they are hardy, multiply fast, and can be slaughtered for meat without compromising the core of the herd. The age/sex composition of cattle and camel herds is designed to maximize milk production and breeding potential.

Grazing and water are closely related, the latter a scarcer and more important resource. Cattle and small stock require water at least every other day and this places constraints on the mobility of the herds. Strategies of pastoral expansion have usually concentrated on securing control of the permanent water points without which large areas of grazing are inaccessible. Access to water is also more strictly controlled by particular communities or neighborhoods, while grass is "free." With some exceptions, African pastoralists are not strictly nomadic. Rather, they are seasonally transhumant, moving their herds from dry season grazing reserves with permanent water to the more extensive pastures that become available once the rains have come. Modern developments have changed patterns of movement. Bore-holes and pipelines have created new permanent water points and may even allow pastoralists to settle; but the dry season reserves that are crucial to survival may be diverted to non-pastoral use, especially if they have high agricultural potential. Movement may further be limited by the spread of private fenced pastures to which general access is forbidden. The development of modern pastoral infrastructures—water delivery systems and pasture improvement, for example—increases the likelihood that common resources will be privatized, and this is perhaps exerting the greatest pressure for change on pastoralism.

The distribution of labor in pastoral societies depends crucially on the interdependence between people and their herds. There must be sufficient labor to manage and protect the herds, but the size of the labor force depends on the amount of food available. Imbalances occur when there are either too many animals or too many people, but these can be evened out to some extent by transfers between households. Richer households may either loan out animals to poorer families with a surplus of labor or they may adopt or co-opt others to help with the herding. Transfers of this kind also help to spread risk and to maximize the number of people with access to pastoral resources. However, the extent and frequency of loaning varies. "Pure" subsistence pastoral communities often prefer to concentrate livestock in fewer hands and, in effect, either absorb or force out households that cannot maintain themselves independently.

Pastoralism is a skilled, arduous, and uncertain business, reflecting an often harsh and unpredictable environment. The division of labor is usually by age and gender. Children herd small stock close to home while cattle and camels are herded by young men and elders, sometimes in camps far removed from the homestead. Although herd management is typically the province of men, women play a crucial part in milking and ensuring that their families are fed, and they have definite, if varying, rights both in particular animals and over their product. Women must be given animals to milk and they may hold these in trust for their sons. In some cases, however, women control animals and even herds outright.

OTHER FACTORS

Apart from maintaining access to the four resources discussed above, pastoralists also have to take other considerations into account when shaping their strategies. The first of these is the risk of losses from drought, disease and predation.

The incidence of drought varies widely. In some arid areas, partial or total rain failure is a regularly recurring event, punctuated by catastrophic droughts extending over several years. Elsewhere, drought is less common but the more disastrous when it occurs, since local pastoralists may be ill-prepared. The impact of drought should be seen as a process rather than an event, however. Animals will die of starvation, but the long-term risk is that, with herd productivity drastically lowered, household heads will have to liquidate assets in order to feed their families. During droughts, the terms of trade turn dramatically against pastoralists as livestock prices or values drop. Once lost, assets are difficult to regain and herd-owners thus become caught in a downward spiral towards destitution. This has been the pattern in many areas since the major droughts of the 1970s.

Disease presents another challenge. Although there has been no epidemic comparable to the great rinderpest pandemic that destroyed ninety percent of infected herds from Eritrea to South Africa in the 1890s, four major diseases, rinderpest, bovine pleuropneumonia, tick-borne East Coast Fever and trypanosomiasis, carried by tsetse fly, still take their toll. While disease can be controlled by vaccination, by avoiding known foci, and by the elimination of vectors by dipping and bush clearance, the ideal of a managed, disease-free pastoral environment has faded since the days of massive government intervention in mid-century. African pastoralists have come to accept western veterinary care, but maintaining artificial immunity requires infrastructure that many states cannot reliably maintain and pharmaceuticals that may be beyond the financial reach of many households. Without the natural immunity conferred by a continuous low level of infection, herds become extremely vulnerable to epidemic outbreak. Especially in areas beyond the reach of regular veterinary care, pastoralists thus continue to accept losses, especially among young stock, as the inevitable price of herd security.

Livestock raiding has always been part of pastoralism. Being relatively valuable and mobile, animals are attractive targets and difficult to safeguard. The pattern and intensity of raiding varies, however, and has recently been complicated by growing poverty, the expansion of markets for stolen stock and increased access to modern weapons. In some regions, local warfare remains virtually endemic, but there are also areas where stock theft is now highly professional and sometimes state-sponsored. Even in more stable countries, individual thefts remain common. There is little that pastoralists can do beyond arming themselves and forming local militias or using their contacts with central government to demand a higher level of general policing and security.

Having herds guarantees not only physical survival but also social reproduction. Livestock underpin social and cultural identities, provide the means to marry and to create the support networks that are vital both to survival and to the accumulation of wealth and influence, and are a visible sign of success and status. As bride wealth given to the wife's family by her husband's, animals create links between households and support marriages that guarantee the future. Animal sacrifices mark the major events in the lives of individuals and communities and mediate between people and God. Livestock exchanges that enable households to grow and link them cooperatively with others are a very important part of the total production system, and herd owners will want to maintain a reserve of animals to meet these obligations.

The need to balance subsistence requirements, social obligations, and risks, together with the equation of livestock with wealth and status, explains pastoralists' determination to build up large herds. However, they have been under pressure from developmentalists to modernize production and to reduce herd size, on the grounds that "overstocking" degrades the environment and that it is more advantageous to concentrate on quality than on quantity. Given the continuing uncertainty of life and the lack of guaranteed outlets and alternatives in many areas, pastoralists have been unconvinced by these arguments; and their skepticism is often justified. Moreover, a better understanding of the dynamics of grassland ecology has led to a re-evaluation of the claim that pastoralists misuse pasture and destroy their own environment by refusing to accept herd limitation.

COMMERCIAL PASTORALISM

Although pastoralism in Africa is still predominantly linked to subsistence, herd owners have increasingly entered the market to acquire cash for tax and to fund education, veterinary care, and food and consumer purchases. Generally, this requires the sale of several beasts a year, but not necessarily the planned off-take characteristic of fully commercial production. Livestock raising for the market was first established by white settlers, but has been taken up by Africans who have sufficient capital. Enterprises concentrate on beef production, and to a lesser extent on dairy and wool. The transition to large-scale commercial ranching is not easy. The herd profile for beef production, for example, with its focus on regular off-take, is almost the opposite of that of a subsistence herd that maximizes growth and security. Finding a viable market can also be difficult. While there is a large and growing demand for meat (and to some extent dairy products) among urban populations, the local market is served by pastoralists who sell to meet their cash needs rather than by commercial enterprises. Export is regional rather than international, since African enterprise can rarely compete with the major overseas producers. Moreover, state involvement in livestock production and marketing has not always been a success.

THE FUTURE OF PASTORALISM

Pastoralism is a resilient form of production, and still offers the best means of survival in the arid regions of Africa. It is, however, under stress, though popular images of impoverished pastoralists are only part of the picture. Extreme subsistence specialization with its large herds does seem to be diminishing as more households move towards a sedentary mixed economy or "small-holder" pastoralism with fewer but higher yielding animals and a wider subsistence and commercial base. Yet production systems need to be viewed in the long term, and there have been trends both toward and away from pastoral subsistence. In Eastern Africa, for example, livestock keeping seems to have become more widespread and more specialized in the century before the 1970s; but this may now be reversing itself as drought, population pressures, and political instability reduce access to resources. Pastoralists will have to adopt new strategies and identities, but pastoralism itself will survive.

See also **Disease: Viral and Infectious; Famine; Labor: Child; Livestock: Domestication; Marriage Systems; Trade, National and International Systems; Water and Irrigation.**

BIBLIOGRAPHY

Anderson, David, and Vigdis Broche-Due, eds. *The Poor Are Not Us.* Oxford: James Currey, 1999.

Fratkin, Elliot. *Ariaal Pastoralists of Kenya.* Boston: Allyn & Bacon, 1998.

Fratkin, Elliot; Kathleen Galvin; and Eric Roth; eds. *African Pastoralist Systems.* Boulder, CO: Lynne Reiner, 1994.

Hodgson, Dorothy, ed. *Rethinking Pastoralism in Africa.* Oxford: James Currey, 2000.

Hutchinson, Sharon. *Nuer Dilemmas.* Berkeley: University of California Press, 1996.

Peters, Pauline. *Dividing the Commons.* Charlottesville: University Press of Virginia, 1994.

Stenning, Derrick, *Savannah Nomads.* Oxford: Oxford University Press, 1959.

RICHARD WALLER

MINING, MODERN

The mineral industry, which dates at least to ancient Egypt, has been an important activity on the African continent. It played a significant role in the trade between Africa and the rest of the world in medieval times and was a source of growth for empires in the West Africa region from the tenth through the fourteenth centuries. In the twenty-first century, the mining industry continues to be an important source of revenue for national and local governments, provides employment and business opportunities to citizens, and provides foreign exchange and foreign direct investments in the continent. The mineral industry remains key to future economic growth of several African countries.

The continent is endowed with mineral resources; the U,S, Geological Services ranks Africa as first or second in quantity of world reserves for bauxite, cobalt, diamond, phosphate rock, platinum-group metals (PGM), vermiculite, and zirconium. In 2001 the continent was estimated to host 30 percent of total worldwide reserves of PGM, chromium, manganese, cobalt, zirconium, bauxite, vanadium, titanium, tantalum, and copper.

In 2004 Africa's share of total world production was about 63 percent for PGM, 48 percent for diamonds, 30 percent for phosphate rock, 23 percent for gold, 20 percent for uranium, 5 percent for coal, and less than 5 percent for copper.

The PGM are concentrated in southern Africa (South Africa and Zimbabwe), copper in Central/southern Africa (Zambia, Democratic Republic of the Congo [DRC], and South Africa), bauxite in West Africa (Guinea), and diamonds in Central and southern Africa (Botswana, South Africa, Angola, DRC, Central African Republic). The main producers of gold in Africa are South Africa, Ghana, Mali, and Tanzania.

The mineral industry is subdivided into industrial exploitations and artisanal and small-scale mining, which is largely informal. Significant number of people in rural areas, particularly in West and Central Africa, are involved in the mining of gemstones, gold, and other precious and semi-precious stones and metals. Artisanal mining is used as a temporary or permanent source of rural income for the poorest. It has been also used in the past years to fuel conflicts in Central and West Africa. The situation has fortunately evolved, and local and international initiatives including the Kimberley process and Diamond for Development Initiative are being implemented not only to prevent negative aspects linked to artisanal mining but to increase its benefits to rural citizen while mitigating its negative aspects.

HISTORICAL EVOLUTION OF THE MINERAL INDUSTRY

The prospect of economic benefit is the impetus for mineral resources exploration and development. However the conditions under which investors access the resources and develop them, the risk involved, and market access for products are key issues in the modern mining industry. These conditions influence the type of mineral activities developed, and their nature and structure.

From the 1960s to 1980s, several African countries went through a period of nationalization. In doing so, governments were motivated by the objectives of deriving a fair share of the benefits from the exploitation of their resources, which are viewed in many ways as national heritage. In addition, in a number of countries the dominant political ideology was one of state control of production

Front loader dumping ore into a truck in a chamber of an underground gold mine, East Africa. Underground chambers in pre-colonial Africa allowed only shallow access to deposits and could not be emptied in the case of a flood. Therefore, mines had to be abandoned when the limited technical means for retrieving ore were reached. Not until 1888, when the process of amalgamation was developed, could the remaining ore be recovered and the industry prove truly profitable. BOWATER/MIRA.COM/DRR.NET

assets—a philosophy thought to lead to more rapid industrialization and faster growth than reliance on free markets. This ideology was applied to mining assets and state-owned corporations took over ownership and management control in the majority of countries. However by the 1990s evidence showed that the nationalization did not result in increased value added or higher contribution of the mining industry to national income. Rather, it resulted in lost making operations being subsidized by public finance. These operations were not contributing to the reduction of poverty, and were draining resources that otherwise could be used for other national priorities such as the improvement of human development indicators and infrastructure.

Zambia and DCR constitute example of countries that took the path of nationalization. Zambia produced 750,000 tons of copper in 1973 (10% of world production) when the assets where still primarily held by private companies from South Africa and the United Kingdom. The nationalization occurred in the early 1980s with the creation the Zambia Consolidated Copper Mines (ZCCM), and by the year 2000 the country's production fell to about 257,000 tons of copper or about one-third of the production in 1973. Since then Zambia has privatized its mining assets and the output in 2006 was over 500,000 tons.

DCR was at its independence in 1960 the world's fourth largest producer of copper and was supplying 55 percent of the world's cobalt. In 1967 the country nationalized the assets of the Belgian mining company Union Minière and created the Générale des Carrières et des Mines (Gecamines). At the time of independence the reported copper production of Union Minière there was 301,000 tons versus 73,300 tons or less than one-third in 2004. In the mid-2000s, the Gecamines in DRC was undergoing restructuring.

THE TWENTY-FIRST CENTURY

Poor results from state ownership resulting from low investment, inadequate management of operations, and revenues to deal with vagaries of commodities cycles, and the need to attract new investment that could not be financed by the state-led governments in Africa to swing back toward private mining. This accelerated after the fall of the Berlin wall in the beginning of the 1990s, and a number of African countries have since reformed their mineral legislation to introduce competitive provisions. With the acceleration of globalization further reforms were introduced to both respond to increased competitionand to align mineral legislation and practices to the evolving paradigm of environmental stewardship, good governance, and transparency. As a result a number of African countries are in their third generation of mineral legislation.

The combination of a better investment climate in Africa, the favorable geology in a continent largely underexplored, and the availability of venture capital for exploration have led to a dramatic increase in exploration spending on the African continent from both major and junior mining companies. African share of world mineral exploration spending has been increasing since the beginning of the 1990s; in 2003 for the first time the total exploration budget for Africa as reported by mining companies according to the Metals Economics Group was more than that of Australia. Since then Africa—with a share of global exploration budget of 16 to 17 percent—is the third destination for exploration expenditures after Latin America and Canada. According to the Metals Economics group, the mineral exploration budget in Africa was $374 million in 2003 (17.1% of world total), $572 million in 2004 (16.1%), $833 million (17%) in 2005, and $1.1 billion (16%) in 2006.

The improved investment climate and general trend of divesture by governments in mining operations have led to increased acquisition of previously state-owned mineral assets, and increased investments and production by private companies. Increased exploration led to successful discovery of world-class mineral deposits and increased production of mineral resources, including mining in countries where industrial mining was marginal or absent. Mali and Tanzania, both of which had limited industrial mineral production in the 1980s, have become important producers of gold. Significant mineral development occurred in Ghana and Namibia. The privatization of ZCCM also resulted in increased production of copper from Zambia.

The private actors in the mineral industry in Africa are also evolving thanks to globalization and the rise of companies from developing countries. Private investment in the mineral sector in Africa was the business of Western companies up until the 1980s; this is changing with increasing number of companies from China, India, Brasil, and Russia. The end of apartheid has led to a dramatic increase in activities from South African companies or with former South African companies listed in stock exchanges outside of Africa. In the early 2000s South African companies are enjoying a leading role in gold and diamond mining in Africa.

In spite of these changes and increased exploration and production, African countries face significant challenges to transform the mineral industry into an engine of growth and development. Africa is an important producer of raw or semi-processed mineral products, however it is not benefiting from the higher value of downstream processed, semi-finished, and finished products from minerals. According to UNCTAD, ores and metal originating from Africa ranged from 3 to 5 percent of world total in value between 1998 and 2003. The gap in the vast resources and reserves of the continent, and its share of the global trade, reflects the constraints to the development of the sector, including policies restraining value-added activities, limited infrastructure, and relatively limited oversight capacities. At the same time, it represents a vast opportunity of mineral industry–stimulated development if the appropriate frameworks and conducive investment climate are put in place.

One of the challenges in the development of the mineral industry is the necessity of moving from mining as an enclave in the national economy to mining as an integrated part of national/regional economies taking into consideration sustainability perspectives on socio-economic and environmental matters. This challenge encompasses sustainable benefits for communities living around mineral projects through the use of mineral revenue to drive positive economic and social changes in areas that may otherwise lack opportunities, environmental management at all stage of the mineral development cycle from exploration to exploitation and closure, the management of revenues when commodities prices are high or low, redistribution of the revenues between central, regional, and local governments, and measures on good governance and transparency, which are also aimed at reducing the resource curse and at using mining revenues for poverty reduction.

Another constraint relates to the need for infrastructure. Mineral projects often require large infrastructure to transport supplies and equipment to the production site, and in return to ship the ore or concentrate to clients. The scale of production needed to amortize the large sums of capital needed for the mineral sector requires reliable transport systems including roads, railroads, and port infrastructure. Moreover mineral production requires substantial power and water, more so when processing is involved. The quasi-general insufficiency of such infrastructure hampers the development of the sector, dictates the type of commodities mined, and limits developmental impact of the sector, including reducing downstream activities and the multiplier effects. One of the issues in infrastructure is the limited availability or lack of integrated multidimensional strategies, coupled with short, medium, and long-term plans devised in a participatory way to create a backbone of infrastructure servicing not only the mineral industry but also other economic opportunities in areas of mineral endowment. As a result mining companies often negotiated individual agreements with host countries to find tailored solutions to bottlenecks to their individual projects. The situation is evolving both inside some countries but also at the subregional/regional levels where subregional/regional infrastructure development programs are being discussed and developed.

A significant challenge is the ability of public institutions to play the role of effective regulator capable of setting the right policies, monitoring and controlling their application, ensuring that the public institutions are getting the fair share from the revenues derived from mineral production, and efficiently managing the revenues to stimulate growth and alleviate poverty.

Some countries such as South Africa and Botswana have successfully managed these challenges, and other countries are addressing them with various levels of success. It is encouraging to notice that numerous African countries (14 out 22) have committed to the principles and criteria of the Extractive Industries Transparency Initiative (EITI), which intends to collect, reconcile, and audit revenues from minerals as declared received by government and paid by companies. Nigeria and Guinea have published mineral revenue data under EITI, and several other African countries are expected to publish similar data in the coming years.

See also **Apartheid; Capitalism and Commercialization; Globalization; Economic Systems; Labor: Industrial and Mining; Metals and Minerals.**

BIBLIOGRAPHY

Extractive Industries Transparency Initiative. Available from http://www.eitransparancy.org.

Metals Economics Group. Available from http://www.metals economics.com.

United Nations Conference on Trade and Development. Available from http://www.unctad.org.

BOUBACAR BOCOUM

ARTISAN PRODUCTION

Artisan production refers to the work of skilled craftspeople engaged individually or in small workgroups using relatively simple tools to produce useful and/or decorative objects and is distinguished from industrial production by the small scale and dispersed locations of production, and the absence or simplicity of the division of labor. The term is sometimes extended in Africa to include other small-scale forms of production using simple technologies, for example, artisan fishing and artisan diamond mining.

Although artisans are part of all African societies, the items produced and the cultural significance of artisan production varies. Artisans produce agricultural tools such as hoes and cutlasses; household utensils such as cooking pots and storage baskets; decorative objects such as wall plaques and paintings; ceremonial objects such as masks and walking sticks; textiles with culturally significant designs; pottery; children's toys; musical instruments; and jewelry. Artisans utilize many kinds of materials, organic and inorganic. Plant-derived materials are widely used; examples include palm fronds to make baskets and mats; wood to carve ceremonial objects; seeds to make jewelry; and gourds to make household containers. Blacksmiths utilize iron as their primary raw material, and in some societies metalsmiths make beautiful ceremonial objects and jewelry from gold, silver, and bronze.

In rural Africa, most artisans practice their craft part-time. Where climates are seasonal, people who are full-time farmers during the rainy season turn to their other occupations as artisans after the harvest. Artisan production provides an important source of income in these communities. In urban centers, artisans are more likely to practice their craft year-round, and as a sole or primary occupation.

Tools recovered from archeological sites across the continent, rock paintings in the Sahara, and artifacts from Egyptian tombs all speak to the antiquity of artisan production. Precolonial artisan production varied widely, both between and within particular societies. Whereas most artisans operated in relatively unstructured situations, blacksmiths, metalworkers, and weavers were more likely to be organized in guild-like groups to manage critical natural resources, regulate production and trade, recruit and train new workers, and secure their position in society. The majority of artisans were men, but women also played an important role, often in particular crafts such as spinning and embroidery. Most artisan production was for local exchange and use, but in some cases, such as textiles from precolonial Hausaland, goods were distributed over long distances, including across the Sahara into North Africa.

In some societies, the leading artisans were closely linked to royalty, producing objects that celebrated the accomplishments of rulers and recorded events of historical significance. The magnificent bronze statues, busts, and plaques from precolonial Bénin, produced using the lost-wax technique, are a notable example of court art.

After the colonial conquest, artisan production was adversely affected by the implementation of forced labor and taxation. Young men who left their home communities as wage laborers were less likely to learn and practice traditional trades. Imported goods marginalized some artisans, such as indigenous textile producers who were forced to compete with relatively cheap, colorful, manufactured textiles. Western education and missionary activity cultivated a taste for imported goods. Wearing European-style clothing became a symbol of civilization and assimilation. As part of their civilizing mission, missionaries often banned or destroyed objects of spiritual or cultural significance.

Certain groups of artisans benefited from new markets created through increased economic activity or the growth of interregional trade. Blacksmiths, for example, benefited from the growth of the colonial agricultural and mining economy, and from their new access to scrap iron and steel as a cheap and adaptable raw material. Woodworkers also found new opportunities, such as producing furnishings for schools and churches.

The marginalization of certain artisan groups increased after independence as a result of the growth of local import-substitution industries and the increased availability of imported goods in both rural and urban areas. Manufactured textiles mostly replaced artisan textile products; imported costume jewelry supplanted locally produced jewelry; and cheap plastic goods increasingly replaced artisan pottery, baskets, and calabashes.

Some artisan producers successfully adapted to the new forms of competition by creating new designs or making use of manufactured production inputs. Instead of using leather to make their shoes, several shoemakers turned to plastics or to rubber from old tires. Tin cans and other scrap metals were used to make everything from cooking pots to small oil lamps.

The development of Africa's tourist industry and growing international interest in African artifacts has opened new market opportunities. Craft producers such as wood carvers, metalworkers, basketmakers, and textile artists have responded to this demand with increased production, new designs and raw materials, and new marketing arrangements to reach a mostly non-local clientele. Adaptations to the growth of the international and tourist markets have ranged from the mass production of cheap, standard-design carvings and crafts, to the creation of distinctive, high-value pieces by skilled artisans.

Internal African markets largely drive the demand for some products. The revival of interest in African cultural heritage has fostered increased interest in and demand for culturally significant products, such as Ghana's kente cloth.

Before the 1970s, policymakers paid little attention to artisans, who were considered a marginal and declining factor in an envisaged new industrial economy. Groundbreaking studies of the informal economy challenged these assumptions and showed that the vitality of urban economies depended as much on informal as on formal economic activities. These studies showed that artisan production provided employment for many workers, was a source of cheap, sustainably produced goods, helped workers to learn new skills, and contributed significantly to economic growth. The two sectors were found to be closely linked; artisans produced goods such as concrete blocks, and services such as motor-vehicle repairs for formal sector enterprises. With growing recognition of the informal economy, some artisans were able to gain increased access to loans and support to build their businesses. During the 1980s, economic recession and structural adjustment affected most African countries. Numerous factories closed and millions of workers lost their formal-sector jobs and were forced to rely on informal sources of income. Recent studies of livelihoods have confirmed that many African households rely on multiple sources of income, including work as artisans, for survival.

African artisan production continues to evolve early in the new millennium. Some artisans will have a secure future because of African cultural revival, tourism, and international marketing opportunities. So too producers who modify their products in response to changes in consumer demand, or who readily adopt new raw materials and tools. Prospects for other artisans, such as village potters producing traditional water and cooking pots, are less promising.

See also **Arts; Body Adornment and Clothing; Ceramics; Textiles; Tourism.**

BIBLIOGRAPHY

Birks, Stace, et al. *Skills Acquisition in Micro-Enterprises: Evidence from West Africa.* Paris: Organisation for Economic Co-operation and Development, 1994.

Clarke, Duncan. *The Art of African Textiles.* San Diego, California: Thunder Bay Press, 1997.

Cunningham, Anthony; Brian Belcher; and Bruce Campbell, eds. *Carving out a Future: Forests, Livelihoods and the International Woodcarving Trade.* London: Earthscan, 2005.

Mack, John. *Africa: Arts and Cultures.* London: British Museum Press, 2000.

ROBERT STOCK

PERIPATETIC PRODUCTION

Textbooks in anthropology often reproduce a simplistic typology of productive strategies. Rural people are often described as being hunter-gatherers, agriculturists, or pastoralists. However, there seem to be (1) a fair number of hybrid production strategies combining various types of production; and (2) communities that are not engaging in hunting, herding, or agriculture. Instead, these communities earn their incomes from supplying services to other, food-producing communities. Minority groups, which scholars have referred to as peripatetics in comparative analyses, and service nomads fit into this type of production strategies. Communities like the Waata and the Thwa of eastern and southern Africa, both of which display a hunter-gatherer background; the "gypsy-like" Yibir, Dupi, and Fuga from the Horn of Africa; and casted craftsmen like the West African LawBe, the Saharan Inaden, and the Sudanese Halab make their living entirely or periodically by supplying services to a dominant population. Groups formed around the turn of this century, such as the Nigerian Yan Goge, wandering urban musicians, and the Karretjies, itinerant sheepshearers in the semiarid South African Karroo, show that minority groups are increasingly entering this niche.

These groups share common features. Aparna Rao described them as "primarily nonfood producing, preferentially endogamous, itinerant communities, subsisting mainly on the sale of goods and/or more or less specialized services to sedentary and/or nomadic customers." Peripatetics usually are generalists offering services to host populations that range from fortune-telling to ritual activities to handicrafts. This does not prevent some peripatetics from occasionally hunting or herding small stock, and others from migrating only occasionally. Typically, their activities are held in contempt by the dominant societies. Furthermore, all these groups are despised minorities within a larger setting and experience marked forms of symbolic and sometimes even violent rejection. However, their position is ambiguous; although deemed to be outcasts and thought to be antisocial, they frequently are courted as diviners and ritual specialists who are indispensable for the spiritual well-being of their clients. A common denominator of peripatetic producers is their extreme flexibility: new markets are eagerly explored and exploited, new clients are courted and others discarded, and food-producing strategies are integrated into the portfolio of household economies or abandoned without much hesitation.

HALAB

Traditionally the Halab, or Nile Valley gypsies, were associated with manufacture of metal goods. In addition they acted as veterinarians and livestock traders. As entertainers they generated income as musicians, snake charmers, monkey trainers, and tightrope walkers. Halab women earned money as diviners and healers. In the first decade of the 2000s Halab in Omdurman, Sudan, specialize in forging, thus extending their traditional skill in ironwork. Their small-scale enterprises are located within the informal sector and typically are small, family-based businesses that hire day laborers. They produce metal drums, pans, troughs, and water tanks, mainly from recycled metals, as well as simple machines (e.g., coffee grinders and sausage machines).

The endogamous Halab are despised in Sudan. Their access to rural resources has been legally restricted, and they are forced to be mobile. Urban Halab are more sedentary, although the dominant population sees them as rather unstable and mobile.

LAWBE

The LawBe are one group of casted craftspeople in West Africa's Sahel. In the past they were nomadic, traveling from village to village, whereas in the early 2000s there is a marked tendency for the group to settle in towns. LawBe mobility is not confined to the territory of one host society, and they cross ethnic boundaries rather frequently. They offer their services to a number of patrons, who are obliged to show generosity to craftsmen who continuously supply them. Casted people are even entitled to small donations from their customers beyond payment for their goods. Occasionally they are given small plots of land to supply their households, but typically they do not have property rights in the land they till. LawBe men produce wooden utensils, mortars, pestles, milking equipment, and occasionally canoes. Frequently they travel to villages where they know they can buy trees to be used for carving. They obtain permission to cut trees at the fringe of the village and later work them into goods for sale. LawBe women are hairdressers and have a reputation of being prostitutes. Like other groups of casted craftspeople of the Sahel, the LawBe are endogamous. In the twenty-first century their woodcarving economy has been boosted by tourists' demand for exotic, hand-carved items.

YAN GOGE

The Yan Goge, the "children of the bowed lute," are itinerant entertainers in the Hausa towns of northern Nigeria and are culturally linked to the Sahelian griot tradition. With the griots they share the marginalized position of entertainers in a Muslim context. The Yan Goge are people who have been estranged from their traditional social context due to personal fate or to societal pressures against professional musicians and dancers. They are organized in several smaller groups: male dancers, female dancers, musicians, praise singers, and a manager. Their clients are wealthy urban dwellers and, since the late twentieth century, political parties that rely on the praise singers to popularize their programs and hope for the advertising effect of the dance companies. Additional income is earned from prostitution, shoe shining, and in-between jobs, such as taking odd bits of information as oral or written accounts from a customer to a specified person or group.

YIBIR

The Yibir are part of the *sab*, a despised group of hunters, beggars, and craftsmen among the Somali. I. M. Lewis estimated that about 1,300 individuals existed in the early 1960s. Some of them are attached to noble Somali pastoralists, and others offer services to various households. In the late nineteenth century a traveler described them as beggars, buffoons, fortune-tellers, tanners, saddlers, and producers of charms. Soothsaying, magic, surgery, hairdressing, and circumcision are other income-generating activities. They were entitled to customary gifts that allegedly had to be paid as a form of symbolic blood money because a major Yibir ancestor was killed by an early Somali hero. In return for these obligatory alms, they blessed their clients. The Somali attribute great supernatural powers to the Yibir and fear their curse. The Yibir are strictly endogamous. They trace their ancestry to pre-Islamic times and mention a pagan sorcerer as their ancestor, a fact that is not highly esteemed in an Islamic context. Apparently they use an argot to protect themselves or to cause curiosity among their clients. Many Yibir have settled in towns of northern Somalia, where they earn their livings as craftsmen and merchants.

FUGA

The Gurage of Ethiopia call all despised craftsmen Fuga and then differentiate them into blacksmiths, tanners, and the Fuga proper, the woodworkers. In other southwestern Ethiopian groups, such as the Kambata and Janjero, tanners and potters are subsumed under the term *Fuga*. The Fuga are not confined to tribal territories and move about to offer their services in various southern Ethiopian societies. From the perspective of the sedentary farmers, they are nomads who have no settled abode, yet in actuality they may oscillate between sedentary and mobile periods. Several authors have reported that they use an argot for communication among themselves. In most Ethiopian host societies they were prohibited from owning land and thereby were barred from investing labor and capital in agriculture; in a few societies they were permitted to hold small sections of rented land. Due to this legal discrimination they were forced to generalize their service activities: among the Gurage they specialized in woodworking, felling trees, cutting wood, and constructing parts of homesteads. Among the Kambata they served as potters and leatherworkers and earned additional income as musicians at weddings and funerals and as ritual experts. As was typical for southern Ethiopian minorities, they were despised and feared at the same time. They were circumcisers and performers of funeral rites and were considered indispensable when a curse on a field had to be removed. At the same time they were described as irreligious by members of the dominant societies and were suspected of turning into hyenas at night.

WAATA

In the nineteenth century Philipp Viktor Paulitschke described the Waata of Ethiopia and Kenya as "nomadic gypsies," who occasionally hunted and at other times acted as musicians. Enrico Cerulli translated the word *Waata* as "wandering magician" in

Tigrinya. Waata groups who in the early 2000s live among the Boran, Sidamo, Gabbra, Orma, and coastal Bantu of Ethiopia and Kenya are generally described as foragers. Although all ethnographies report that they do some hunting and gathering, they engage in numerous other activities: they tan skins make pottery, act as grave diggers, and offer ritual services. The endogamous Waata are held in contempt for breaking food taboos, being irreligious, and pursuing a life "outside culture," yet they are indispensable in many rituals of their host societies. The pastoral nomadic Gabbra of northern Kenya do hardly any ritual without significant contribution by the Waata. The latter follow a complex pattern of spatial mobility; as long as the economy of their hosts flourishes, they will attach themselves to patrons; when it declines, they will survive as foragers for some time.

THWA

The Thwa of southwestern Angola are small-scale pastoralists who earn a major part of their living by offering services to diverse host populations. The men are ironsmiths who produce bracelets and various types of knives and spears; the women are expert potters. The Thwa conduct rituals for spirit-possessed clients and cure various diseases. In order to conduct these rituals, they move to the client's household for some weeks. According to their traditions, they have experienced a complex history of shifts between various modes of production. During the ivory boom of the nineteenth century, they became expert elephant hunters and either acted as hands for commercial hunters or hunted on their own account and exchanged the ivory later on, according to their oral traditions. These traditions still convey an expert knowledge of elephant hunting. After the ivory boom was over, they found new income-generating activities in a growing demand for iron products, pottery, and ritual services among rich pastoral and agropastoral neighbors. The Thwa are despised and are frequently accused of thievery and sorcery by members of other communities. They are strictly endogamous; should a man from another group have a liaison with a Thwa woman, he has to undergo a costly purification. Most of the services delivered by Thwa are paid for in livestock, and since healing spirit-possessed customers has become a good business, their livestock holdings have expanded considerably.

MAJOR STRATEGIES WITHIN THE PERIPATETIC MODE OF PRODUCTION

The peripatetic niche is determined by various factors: the dominant mode of production, the dynamics of the natural environment and the social environment, and the technological capacity and options. Some occupational activities occur often and are frequently combined. In the field of handicrafts, smithing, leatherwork and tanning, pottery, and weaving are typical for peripatetics. They frequently offer ritual services like circumcision, grave digging, magical curing, fortune-telling, and divination. Begging and various kinds of entertainment also provide income. Many of these activities are not highly regarded by the dominant population but are urgently needed to fulfill certain material or spiritual needs. Peripatetics in Africa frequently use subsidiary food-producing strategies. They occasionally hunt and gather, pursue small-scale horticulture on rented fields, or raise small stock. Frequently the dominant population restricts their access to resources, and they are not entitled to own resources in their own right. Because they are always dependent on a large number of clients, they are mobile. The degree of mobility is determined by the density of potential customers in an area. Some peripatetics live directly attached to their clients and migrate with them, whereas others follow independent migratory cycles. The Yibir of the Somali and the Tuudi smiths of the Tubu have been reported to negotiate between warring tribes or factions. Typically, peripatetics are deemed to be neutral and nonaligned, indispensable qualities for brokers within a multiethnic setting. The Fuga, the Waata, and the Manna of Ethiopia did not take part in wars of the dominant societies, and the nyeenyBe craftsmen of the Wolof had a special status during times of violent conflict. In many contexts these lowly regarded communities are attributed an ideal go-between status.

Peripatetic groups are generally assigned ritual powers by the host society, and this belief in their supernatural capacity defines other income-generating strategies for them. In many West African societies peripatetics are deemed to be experienced sorcerers and magical healers. The Aouloube, casted craftsmen among the Malian Tukulor, are reported to be specialists in curing venereal diseases, and the Enkyagu, smiths of the Marghi in northern Nigeria, act in addition as cicatrizers of females, diviners, doctors, and grave diggers. The Awka, traveling smiths among the Nigerian Igbo (Ibo), act as agents of a famous oracle and earn income as diviners, circumcisers, and healers. The Fuga of the Ethiopian Gurage, the Janjero, and the Kambata are indispensable specialists in rites of passage, organize burials, and conduct circumcisions. Their skills as healers and producers of magical potions are frequently used by members of the host society. The Thwa of southern Angola specialize in healing spirit possessions. They produce the most effective charms and amulets to repulse sorcery and evil spirits. Joseph Berland emphasized that "[...] their flexibility and resourcefulness, and facility at utilizing a repertoire of strategic patterns of spatial mobility" is typical (2000, xx).

Many peripatetic minorities have clung to an original language in spite of their minority status or have developed an argot to shield internal communication against a hostile social environment. Yet many of them act within a multiethnic setting and consequently are bi- or even trilingual. This "language policy" ensures that they are conversant in the cultural codes of several host societies and at the same time maintain "secret knowledge" against outsiders. This ambiguity is reflected in the myths of origin of many African peripatetic societies. These myths integrate them into dominant tales of genesis and cultural development, and at the same time explain their marginal economic and social situation. An early ancestor of the Fuga was said to have offered a mythical king rotten meat, and therefore was cursed. The ancestor of the Yibir, a pagan witch doctor, fought with a Muslim Somali ancestor and tried to kill him with magic. An ancestor of the West African LawBe craftsmen had the impudence to wound Muhammad in a fight. Pollution and sin are dominant themes in these tales of origin and explain the low status of these groups but also underline their ambiguous role between purity and impurity and between life and death.

AN EVOLUTIONARY PERSPECTIVE ON PERIPATETIC SOCIETIES

The cases in which foragers move into a peripatetic niche, combining generalized productive strategies with spatial mobility, are rather frequent in Africa and Asia. The hallmark of their economy and social organization is flexibility, which allows them to adapt optimally to their clients' changing demands. Many hunter-gatherers, like the Waata, Dorobo, and San, pursue foraging strategies in times of stress and adopt nonfood-producing strategies when the economy of the dominant society flourishes.

However, African peripatetic groups did not develop solely out of forager societies, which have been losing ground to food-producing societies. Other peripatetics originated in a peasant setting, driven from their land by war, famine, or expropriation. The itinerant sheepshearers of the South African Karroo, the Karretjies, are just one example. Urban unemployment and poverty, a flourishing informal sector, and a growing refugee population seem to open new fields for the emergence of peripatetic groups. The Halab of Khartoum, as specialized ironworkers, and the Yan Goge of northern Nigeria, as professional itinerant entertainers, show that peripatetic strategies are an option for the urban as well as the rural future.

Peripatetic economic strategies and social organization in Africa have not been important topics of anthropological research. Ethnographers frequently deal with them only in passing and mainly reproduce the opinions of host societies about them. There is very little knowledge from within. Due to their mobility patterns, which are not confined to tribal territories, and their despised status, research on peripatetics is difficult. However, more scientific interest in this specific mode of production may elucidate new perspectives on economic change and the transmission of knowledge, and could have an impact on the development of crafts in many African societies.

See also **Capitalism and Commercialization; Economic Systems; Initiation; Ivory; Livestock; Metals and Minerals; Prostitution; Spirit Possession; Women.**

BIBLIOGRAPHY

Berland, Joseph C. "Nature, Nurture, and Kinship: Body Fluids and Experience in the Social Organization and Identity of Peripatetic People." In *Culture, Creation, and Procreation: Concepts of Kinship in South Asian Practice*, ed. Monika Böck and Aparna Rao. New York: Berghahn Books, 2000.

Bollig, Michael. "Ethnic Relations and Spatial Mobility in Africa: A Review of the Peripatetic Niche." In *The Other Nomads: Peripatetic Minorities in Cross-Cultural Perspective*, ed. Aparna Rao. Cologne: Böhlau Verlag, 1987.

Bollig, Michael. "Hunters, Foragers, and Singing Smiths: The Metamorphoses of Peripatetic People in Africa." In *Customary Strangers: New Perspectives on Peripatetic Peoples in the Middle East, Africa and Asia*, ed. Joseph Berland and Aparna Rao. Westport: Praeger Publishers, 2004.

Casimir, Michael J. "In Search of Guilt: Legends on the Origin of the Peripatetic Niche." In *The Other Nomads: Peripatetic Minorities in Cross-Cultural Perspective*, ed. Aparna Rao. Cologne: Böhlau Verlag, 1987.

Casimir, Michael. J. "'Once Upon a Time': Reconciling the Stranger." In *Customary Strangers: New Perspectives on Peripatetic Peoples in the Middle East, Africa and Asia*, ed. Joseph Berland and Aparna Rao. Westport: Praeger Publishers, 2004.

Casimir, Michael. J., and Aparna Rao. *Mobility and Territoriality*. New York: Berg Publishers, 1992.

Cerulli, Enrico. "Folk-Literature of the Galla of Southern Abyssinia." *Harvard African Studies* 3 (1922): 200–214.

Dahl, Gudrun. *Suffering Grass: Subsistence and Society of Waso Borana*. Stockholm: Department of Social Anthropology, 1979.

De Jongh, Michael. "No Fixed Abode: The Poorest of the Poor and Elusive Identities in Rural South Africa." *Journal of Southern African Studies* 28, no. 2 (June 2002): 441–460.

Dupire, Marguerite. "A Nomadic Caste: The Fulani Woodcarvers. Historical Background and Evolution." *Anthropos* 80, no. 1–3 (1985): 85–100.

Hallpike, C. R. "The Status of Craftsmen Among the Konso of South West Ethiopia." *Africa* 38 (July 1968): 258–269.

Hallpike, C. R. *The Konso of Ethiopia: A Study of the Values of a Cushitic People*. Oxford: Clarendon Press, 1972.

Hayden, R. M. "The Cultural Ecology of Service Nomads." *The Eastern Anthropologist* 32, no. 4 (1979): 297–309.

Lewis, I. M. *A Pastoral Democracy: A Study of Pastoralism and Politics Among the Northern Somali of the Horn of Africa*. London: Oxford University Press, 1961.

Olofson, Harold. "Children of the Bowed Lute: Organization and Expressive Culture of the Hausa Urban Itinerant Entertainers." *Anthropos* 75, no. 5–6 (1980): 920–929.

Paulitschke, Philipp Viktor. *Ethnographie Nordost-Afrikas*. Berlin: Dietrich Reimer, 1893.

Rao, Aparna. "The Concept of Peripatetics: An Introduction." In *The Other Nomads: Peripatetic Minorities in Cross-Cultural Perspective*, ed. Aparna Rao. Cologne: Böhlau Verlag, 1987.

Rao, Aparna. "Vanishing Culture and Struggles on Survival: The Crises in Peripatetic Lifestyles." *Bulletin for*

Urgent Anthropological Research 41 (2001–2002): 63–80.

Shack, William A. "Notes on Occupational Castes Among the Gurage of South West Ethiopia. " *Man* 64 (March/April 1964): 50–52.

Streck, Bernhard. "Local Strangers: The Nile Valley Gypsies in the Ethnic Mosaic of Sudan." In *Customary Strangers: New Perspectives on Peripatetic Peoples in the Middle East, Africa and Asia*, ed. Joseph Berland and Aparna Rao. Westport: Praeger Publishers, 2004.

MICHAEL BOLLIG

PROPHETIC MOVEMENTS

This entry includes the following articles:

CENTRAL AFRICA

The terms "independent" and "prophet" designate contrasting modes in Africa's Christian evangelization by Africans. With the caveat that those modes are not always separable, a convenient shorthand is to think of the independent mode as proclaiming new goals, and the prophet mode as proclaiming new gifts or new revelations. "Ethiopian," "Pan-Africanist," and "separatist," on the one hand, and "Zionist," "healing," and "spiritual," on the other, mark an approximately similar distinction. Hence, the constitution of Jordan Msumba's Last Church of God and His Christ proclaimed new goals when it declared, around 1925 in colonial Nyasaland (Malawi), that "Africa [was] in need of a church that would correspond with her God-given customs and manners" (Rotberg, 341). And when beautiful hymns and the gift of healing erupted from the visions of Alice Lenshina, in colonial Northern Rhodesia (Zambia) of the 1950s, a huge prophet movement was born—but, to recall the caveat, Lenshina's movement evolved into the independent Lumpa Church. That the Lumpa Church ended in 1964 amid millennarian prophesying, and through bloody confrontation with the newly independent government, shows that both modes have political resonance.

Even so, the essence of any religion is the content of its promise, and the promise of Christianity in all its forms is salvation. Therefore, the fundamental question about Africa's Christian evangelization of itself is "Salvation from what, and for what?" Every central African evangelizer's biography has intersected with the economic, political, and religious realities of a vast region subject to British rule from the 1890s until the 1960s. Therefore, picture first the peoples of Nyasaland, Northern Rhodesia, and Southern Rhodesia (now Malawi, Zambia and Zimbabwe, respectively) as suddenly dispossessed of land and sovereignty, and as thenceforth linked with one another, with South Africa, and with the world economy. Now add colonial taxation as an early tool of labor recruitment to mines, farms, and other enterprises, thus moving men out of their villages, often on foot, back and forth across the length and breadth of the region. Think of the Zambian Copperbelt, the Zimbabwean coal mines, and the South African gold mines not only as places of work and of new urban experiences, but also as places that both inspired and met new needs, individual and collective, secular and spiritual.

Insert South Africa again, therefore, this time as a luxuriant garden of churches, some representing "mainline" Christianity and others, a great variety of energetic nonconformisms. The term "Zionist," for one mode of African Christianity, is taken from an American Pentecostal mission to South Africa, with headquarters in Zion City, Illinois. The Watch Tower Bible and Tract Society (whose adherents at first called themselves Bible Students and after 1931, Jehovah's Witnesses) made many converts there, black and white. Now add periodic crises as well: harsh mobilizations during two world wars; widespread joblessness in the 1920s and again in the 1930s; the (successfully contested) establishment in the 1950s of the Central African Federation and, with it, settler domination of all three territories. Finally, add not simply Christianity but diverse and sometimes competitive Christianities—against the background of the first to take root, the Church of Scotland and Free Church of Scotland missions to Nyasaland (separate Presbyterian entities after the "Disruption" of 1843), established at Blantyre and Livingstonia in 1875–1876.

Catholics, Anglicans, Baptists, Methodists, and various nondenominational Protestant evangelicals followed soon thereafter, along with scores of others, including imports from America such as Seventh Day Adventists and the African Methodist Episcopal Church, in addition to Pentecostal groups and the Watch Tower Bible and Tract Society. All missions built networks of churches and schools; all manned them largely by training African evangelists and catechists. Now, bisect the whole with a thoroughgoing color bar. Its significance in matters religious is well conveyed by the lifelong Zambian Free Churchman Paul Mushindo, who for fifteen years collaborated with Rev. R. D. McMinn on the creation of a Bemba Bible: "McMinn...loved me as a man loves his best tool.... He often said, 'Mushindo is my right hand'" (Fields, 13). Some chose not to rise above such contradictory bonds but to annul them. The earliest missionaries had little success in the environment of religious choice that prevailed until full "pacification" in the 1890s (which, in Southern Rhodesia, included the defeat of the Chimurenga Rising, inspired by the Shona prophetess Nehanda and her colleagues). In the midst of the rapid growth that then ensued, the exit routes from mission Christianity became visible right away. By 1900, Nyasaland had its first independent church. John Chilembwe established the churches and schools of the Providence Industrial Mission, with the encouragement of the missionary radical Joseph Booth and with the support of African-American Baptists. Chilembwe's preaching against colonial exactions of all kinds and against the constant indignities of the color bar laid out the political and economic routes away from missions. He embraced the religious and cultural forms that the missionaries at Blantyre purveyed while disputing their sole authority to purvey them. In addition, he advanced a Protestant ethic for Africa that owed much to the teachings of Booker T. Washington, his American contemporary.

Between the mid-1900s and mid-1910s, other mission-educated Africans increasingly joined more specifically religious disputes. Missionary magazines such as *Livingstonia News* depict an emerging map of long-term dissensus: the meaning of baptism; long probation before baptism; slow ordination of Africans; increasing church dues and school fees; proper interpretation of the Bible; material inequality between black and white Christians; the missions' community of interest with colonial regimes; the missionaries' support of wartime mobilization; and finally—not least—the cultural content of European Christianity. Were indigenous customs and tastes in religious expression condemned as "pagan" by the Bible or merely by authoritarian missionaries? What of participation in traditional ceremonies, the use of African beer, and polygamy (men and women differing)? Was witchcraft not an evil from which to seek deliverance? And did full-scale African Christians not have a legitimate say?

To varying degrees like Livingstonia in this regard, Protestant missions generally deemed such issues fundamental enough to help define entrance into, discipline within, and dismissal from the Christian community. They preached salvation as the highest good and held that there was "no salvation outside the church." But, at the same time, their principles held that, of the many called, few would be chosen—slowly—even as missionaries continued a steady sifting-out. In sum, not surprisingly for groups that had begun institutional life as breakaway sects, the doors of the churches were narrow for coming in and wide for going out. Protestant missions grappled with salvation at those doors.

Catholic missions displayed a different institutional structure and heritage. Salvation was to be grappled with inside the church, sinners and saints together. Hence, they baptized far more freely and more easily took a pragmatic posture on cultural issues other than divorce. That many Catholic missionaries were of peasant origin, unlike their mainly city-reared Protestant brethren, surely affected the tone of Christian life. It mattered, too, that their money demands were small. Congregational self-reliance was not their missionary ideal; and in any case, costs could be kept relatively low. An unmarried priesthood could do without the expensive domestic establishments that elsewhere evoked the color bar—and it did not at first attract African would-be emulators. Perhaps most consequentially of all, the early emphasis of Catholic missions was on the rapid development of churches rather than of schools—and, correspondingly, of catechetical teaching by rote rather than preparation for firsthand encounters with the Bible. Bible literacy invites diverse interpretation that in turn invites schism.

Such differences do not mean, however, that Catholic missions escaped all religious dissent and invention. For example, in the 1920s, when interest in schooling was becoming widespread and resolute, they became vulnerable to complaints. That catechists began losing respect, compared with their better-educated Protestant counterparts, made the weaknesses of the initial strategy obvious. Likewise, they were not always fully protected against new revelation. In the 1930s, Catholics were among those who welcomed the *bamucapi* medicine men to deal with economic and interpersonal stress, phrased in the idiom of witchcraft. And in the 1950s, Lenshina's movement drew large numbers of people earlier claimed as Catholic. Meanwhile, the Catholic magazine *Le Petit Écho* reported on a short-lived Catholic movement that arose in the same era and area. Emilio Mulolani, a third-generation Catholic, apparently rediscovered through ultra-asceticism the antinomian heresy that faith alone, not obedience to the moral law, was necessary for salvation. The private communal life and public parades of his mixed coterie of young men and women led to public turmoil and a quick response by the Catholic Church. Mulolani was sent to Rome for a psychiatrist and a new confessor. But such dramas were uncommon. The Protestants' early-developed, long-lived map of religious invention had no full-scale Catholic counterpart.

As suggested earlier, the idiom of witchcraft as a manifestation of evil is one strand in the story of indigenous thought patterns that produced various inspirations, variously related to all of the mission Christianities. Since none of the Christianities approached spirits, possession, exorcism, divination, and witchcraft with pragmatic ease, solutions fell to others. In a spectacular sweep during the intense public crisis of the Great Depression, *bamucapi* from Nyasaland and Northern Rhodesia (many of them returned labor migrants and some, former mission pupils) pressed whole villages at a time to confess witchcraft, renounce it by surrendering their amulets for public destruction, and partake of a communal meal treated with a special medicine. Then and later, missionaries and officials sometimes held on only by using similar tactics preemptively.

In Southern Rhodesia, the public crisis of those same years converged with the private crisis of a Shona artisan, Johane Masowe (born Shoniwa Mutedza Tandi Moyo). Masowe's crisis led to visions and millennarian expectation, and then, like John the Baptist's, to continuous preaching and baptizing despite many arrests. He baptized by total immersion in rites called "Jordans" that drew large followings in many localities and, inevitably, drew the attention of the police, who considered him subversive. Anglican by birth, Masowe addressed his new revelation not only to ceaseless demands by Europeans for church dues and taxes throughout the Great Depression but also to other practical problems. To cure spirit illnesses and witchcraft, he conducted services of healing, confession, and the surrender of amulets. To cure material unease, he proclaimed an ethic of self-sufficiency through skillful labor within a close community of the saved. With their schools and workshops, the Masowe Apostles (also called the Korsten Basketmakers) have prospered as well as suffered persecution. They are a large group in the early 2000s (estimated at some 500,000), with a history that spans nine countries.

Think of Masowe's revelation and career as spanning the continuum between the visible spirit of capitalism and the invisible spirits of Europe and Africa. At one extreme of that continuum are neo-traditional inspirations that are bound to Christianity by their explicit rejection of it. In Malawi, the Church of the Black Ancestors provides an example. Founded in the late 1960s, it preaches the restoration of lapsed ancestor observances and the prestige of elders, once powers within communities of kin. But, whatever success it may achieve, the very notion of mobilizing a church, through the voluntary recruitment of individuals, presupposes the organizational mode of the imported religion it rejects.

No African Christian initiative so fully illustrates the whole continuum as does the African "Watchtower" or "Kitawala." Because it has a phenomenally broad geographic scope and was for decades controlled by Africans, it embodies the ungeneralizable diversity of independent and prophet churches as a phenomenon. Besides, Watchtower ideas and methods have influenced and inspired other religious initiatives. Its origin in the region goes back to *1907*, when Elliott Kenan Kamwana, a former prize pupil at Livingstonia, returned to Malawi from South Africa. There, with the religiously peripatetic Joseph Booth, he had studied the teachings of an American, Charles Taze Russell, founder of the Watch Tower Bible and Tract Society. In Kamwana's version of Russell's ideas, the end of the world would mean British defeat and the end of Africans' living as powerless strangers in their own lands. Preaching, furthermore, that missions had withheld Bible truth and baptism while demanding money from the people, he baptized many thousands by total immersion—"without preparation," said the missionaries, who besides detected new and unsettling connotations of the rite.

Thus did Kamwana plant the first charge of a millennarian explosive—both religious and political—that repeatedly shook all three territories. In 1917, police in Southern Rhodesia planted the next two, when they expelled seven mine laborers who continued their "subversive" activities as they returned on foot to their villages in Northern Rhodesia and Nyasaland. With stunning effectiveness in the war-ravaged north of Northern Rhodesia, Watchtower preaching and baptizing announced the coming Kingdom—and denounced the one ruled by collaborating chiefs and the British. Thereafter, the result of the colonial governments' continued exclusion of the society's missionaries was to lend Watchtower ideas a protean adaptability according to place, time, and the interests of preachers and their hearers. Only two features of those ideas can be generalized. First, all Watchtower congregations adhered, in one way or another, to the society's principle against political engagement and allegiance to governments of this world. Therefore, all were persecuted for noncompliance with the mobilizations of World War II. Second, virtually all adopted the society's practice of baptism by total immersion, a practice that converged with the practical need for deliverance from witchcraft. In that way, the rite was free to take its proper place alongside other interests that baptism into a Christian community connoted for many villagers. It typically did so. (On occasion, however, witchcraft eradication predominated—spectacularly, in the murders connived at during 1925 by Shaiwila, a chief in Northern Rhodesia, and Tomo Nyirenda, a migrant laborer from Nyasaland).

Like indigenous African Christianity as a whole, the Watchtower exhibits a body of imported ideas undergoing continual modification as they percolate through an immense region. Some had political themes on the surface, as in the role many Watchtower preachers played in the Copperbelt strike of 1935, whereas healing and interpersonal concerns predominated in others. The militant revival of 1917 had both. Hanoc Sindano, among the boldest veterans of 1917, formed a law-abiding community of the saved, called Jerusalem, that lasted into the 1950s. We find the Bible rejected or else made central (with the Old and New Testaments taken together, valued unequally, or read with different emphases). Organization followed overseas models, indigenous ones, or a synthesis of both. Thus, for example, while Livingstonia hesitantly adapted to the absence of men by instituting the office of deaconess, Watchtower deaconesses evangelized so prominently that colonial officials and chiefs collaborated in the enactment of rules designed to end their missionary travels. (By contrast, despite Lenshina's role as its prophetess, men were the powers in the Lumpa Church, as in the nearby missions and in most independent and prophetic churches.)

Some groups expressed open contempt for constituted authority, African or European; others took care to obey every law that conscience permitted; still others were jostled into antigovernment conflicts by passing circumstances or heavy-handed officials. Some aspired to, while others rejected, European cultural habits in matters as diverse as marriage, dress, housing, and education. Some groups ran quiet, and others ecstatic, worship services. The codes of conduct taught ranged from antinomian violation of established rules to teachings indistinguishable from those of the missions. Hence, the reports in areas remote from one another were that nighttime funeral drumming, fought for decades by European missionaries, ceased instantly as a result of Watchtower conversions in a locality. Elsewhere, however, some groups practiced ritual incest, a rite called the "baptism of fire." When, in the 1930s, the society's missionaries were at last allowed conditional freedom to evangelize, they struggled for many years to stamp out that notorious rite. Despite this and other deviations, they nevertheless found as well a broad base of experienced leaders and committed members on which, and with whom, to rebuild. Today, there are many Jehovah's Witnesses in all three countries, and the Luapula area of Zambia was said in the 1970s to have the highest concentration of Jehovah's Witnesses in the world. During the region's struggles for independence as well as in the postindependence era, they have attracted suspicion and suffered persecution. Quite different political regimes have opposed the political disengagement they affirm as their Anabaptist heritage.

In summary, it can be said that independent and prophet churches are endlessly diverse in doctrine, practice, leadership, and organizational forms. That diversity has prevailed not only between different churches in different places but also within individual churches over time. What all share with one another is their common heritage in post-Reformation Christianity, whose keynote is boundless variety as a result of internal change, schism, and fresh evangelization. Today that heritage finds expression in such marked activity in both overseas and indigenous churches that one can speak of a "second Christianization" in the region.

This continuing process of Christianization reflects a history of peoples and ideas in motion. Central Africans carried with them different understandings of the urban and rural worlds in which they lived. Through the force of beliefs and actions they attempted to perpetuate existing spiritual domains as well as to construct new ones. Based upon their experiences and circumstances, they aligned themselves with different religious orders. They sought salvation and explanation. In the twenty-first century Central Africans are confronting a series of new devastating crises exemplified in the manifestations of HIV/AIDS, a progressive incurable disease. The disease has become the basis for structuring indigenous beliefs including witchcraft, notions of spirit, and the powers of Christian beliefs. Arsenals of prophetic and Christian practices are being mounted against it and since there are no cures, it allows for more elaborate religious configurations. The number of Christians and their beliefs has been steadily changing.

In the 1890s, only a relative handful of people professed Christianity. Proportions in 1993 were estimated at 75 percent in Malawi (out of a population of 9.3 million persons), at 50 to 70 percent in Zambia (out of a population of 8.53 million persons), and at 55 percent in Zimbabwe (out of a population of 10.64 million persons). Since published estimates of the larger denominations in Malawi account for only about 200,000 church members, the large remainder undoubtedly reflects the work not only of missions but also that of at least ninety churches created between 1900 and 1979 outside mission auspices. Likewise, Zambia and Zimbabwe are home to many overseas missionary groups too small to be reported, as well as to a comparably effervescent indigenous creativity. Therefore, if a century ago Europeans could speak of "planting" Christianity in the region, it must be said that in the twenty-first century African indigenous churches, as a group, represent the transplanting that has enabled Christianity to flourish.

See also **Blantyre; Chilembwe, John; Christianity; Disease: HIV/AIDS, Social and Political Aspects.**

BIBLIOGRAPHY

Dillon-Mallone, Clive Mary. *The Korsten Basketmakers: A Study of the Masowe Apostles, an Indigenous African Religious Movement.* Manchester: Manchester University Press, 1978.

Fields, Karen E. *Revival and Rebellion in Colonial Central Africa.* Princeton, NJ: Princeton University Press, 1985.

Linden, Ian, and Jane Linden. *Catholics, Peasants and Chewa Resistance in Nyasaland, 1889–1939.* Berkeley: University of California Press, 1974.

Marwick, Max G. "Another Modern Anti-Witchcraft Movement in East Central Africa." *Africa* 20, no. 2 (1950): 100–112.

Ranger, Terence O. *Revolt in Southern Rhodesia, 1896–97: A Study in African Resistance.* Evanston, IL: Northwestern University Press, 1967.

Richards, Audrey I. "A Modern Movement of Witch-Finders." *Africa* 8, no. 4 (1935): 448–461.

KAREN E. FIELDS
REVISED BY GEORGE CLEMENT BOND

EASTERN AFRICA

Eastern Africa has a long history of prophetic movements and cults, some linked to indigenous or traditional deities and spirits, some to Christianity, and others to Islam. These movements were reported from the earliest periods of colonial administration and missionary endeavor. Some were recognized as efforts to overcome drought, famine, and other natural disasters; others were considered to be anti-European, often as atavistic manifestations of heathen superstition, and as destructive of the order brought about by colonial administrations and therefore to be put down by force. It has often been held that these movements were early examples of resistance to colonial overrule, but many were in existence

Legio Maria prophet-healers at Efeso (Ephesus). Efeso is one of three Legio holy sites and the place where Bikra Maria (the Virgin Mary) is believed to be buried. The fly-whisk, a device traditionally used by African leaders and healers to bless and to cleanse, is used to sprinkle congregants with holy water. Kenya, 2005. PHOTOGRAPH BY MATTHEW KUSTENBAUDER

long before the Europeans arrived. Although some have indeed been part of resistance movements, all have been more than mere responses to colonial rule and have been concerned also with divisions and conflicts within and between local societies and their various elite and commoner groups.

A distinction should also be made between healers and diviners, who are consulted by individual clients, and prophets and reformers, who attract and lead wide groups of followers and whose activities have political aims and consequences. Most of the recent prophetic movements have had as their immediate aim the purification of Christian and Muslim religious institutions, with the ultimate intended consequence of reforming and cleansing the whole of society. In some movements a

religious ideology of restoration has been paramount; in others the emphasis has been on political and military resistance.

THE EARLIER PROPHETS
The earliest movements were those led by the prophets of the Nuer and Dinka peoples of southern Sudan. Of these, the most famous was the Nuer prophet Ngundeng Bong (d. 1906), who in the 1870s built an immense earthen pyramidal mound where divine power became manifest to and in him. He claimed the ability to predict the future and to purify his people, who saw in his person the presence of divinity. He and the many other prophets were the central ritual experts and peacemakers of the Nuer and Dinka people, concerned mostly with

finding adequate land and pasturage in the ever-changing riverine environment of the southern Nile region and protecting their peoples from drought, plague, and famine. Nonetheless, the British colonial administration saw them as hostile, and tried for many decades to weaken the prophets and to destroy their pyramids.

A second prophetic movement was that which guided the Maji-Maji rebellion against the Germans in southern Tanganyika in 1905–1907. In response to a repressive policy of forced labor and cotton planting, armed protest galvanized around a powerful prophet, Kinjikitile, who united the disparate peoples. Kinjikitile was possessed by the spirit Hongo and delivered prophetic utterances from the high deity Bokero at a pool of mystically powerful water, the drinking of which was believed to make fighters immune to German bullets and inspired the consumers to join together to expel the German administration. Determined to retain their colonial holdings, the Germans used their superior weaponry to crush the movement, killing more than 75,000 people.

A third early prophetic movement was the Yakan cult among the Lugbara of northwestern Uganda, in which the prophet, Rembe (d. 1919), was not Lugbara but Kakwa. Here much the same pattern emerged: a cult, centered on a prophet who was believed to possess divinely given knowledge and mystical power, was transformed into a movement with an anticolonial ideology that inspired an armed uprising. The Lugbara first sought Rembe in the 1880s, as they wanted his help fighting epidemics of human and cattle sicknesses. They also wanted his assistance resisting the influx of Europeans and Arabs that was destroying the traditional ways of local life and livelihood. When these epidemics reappeared, Rembe was again called to Lugbaraland in 1915. There he established himself at a pool in which there lived a rainbow-colored serpent. While possessed, Rembe received messages from the serpent. Women and men from a wide area drank the pool's water, which was held to make them unaffected by bullets, to bring back the ancestors and dead cattle, and to cause Europeans and Arabs to vanish. The movement culminated in a small revolt in 1919 that was soon put down by the colonial powers. Rembe was taken to the Sudan and hanged at Yei. The overt similarities with the Maji-Maji cult are striking, but there appears to have been no historical connection between them.

A longer-lasting movement was that known as Nyabingi among the Kiga people of southwestern Uganda. This dates back to the mid-nineteenth century with the appearance of mostly female prophets who were possessed by the goddess Nyabingi. In its early phase, the cult opposed the growing strength of the rulers of Rwanda and Ankole, and its leaders united local territorial and descent groups into wider defensive groupings. With the arrival of Europeans, a Nyabingi prophetess named Muhumusa arose around 1910 to lead the general resentment against the use of Ganda agents by the new British administration. She was deported and imprisoned until her death in 1945. The cult continued, however, and launched attacks upon Ganda agents and Christians. In the late 1920s these foreign agents were finally withdrawn and strategically replaced by local Kiga, who were predominantly Christians and unsupportive of the Nyabingi movement, which then died out.

There were also early Islamic movements: that led by Mahdi Ahmed (1844–1885) in the Sudan; that of Sayyid Muhammad Abdallah Hasan (known by the British as the Mad Mullah) of Somaliland; and the movement led by Muslim reformers among the Swahili of the east African coast in the later years of the nineteenth century. The first two were overtly political, the aim being mainly to oust the colonial (and Christian) conquerors from Muslim lands. The third was concerned more with purifying the Islam practiced by patrician merchants of the coastal towns and with bringing former slaves into the mainstream of coastal society. The most famous reformer was Sayyid Saleh ibn Alwy ibn Abdullah Jamal al-Layl (known more familiarly as Shaykh Habib Swaleh, 1844–1935), who came to the town of Lamu from the Comoro Islands about 1880 and built the great Riyadh Mosque that has attracted pilgrims and scholars from throughout eastern Africa and beyond ever since.

LATER CHRISTIAN MOVEMENTS

Other prophets have been reported from all parts of eastern Africa throughout the twentieth century. They have been linked to the advent of Christianity in Africa in the sense that the leaders have either been considered emissaries of indigenous divinities sent to

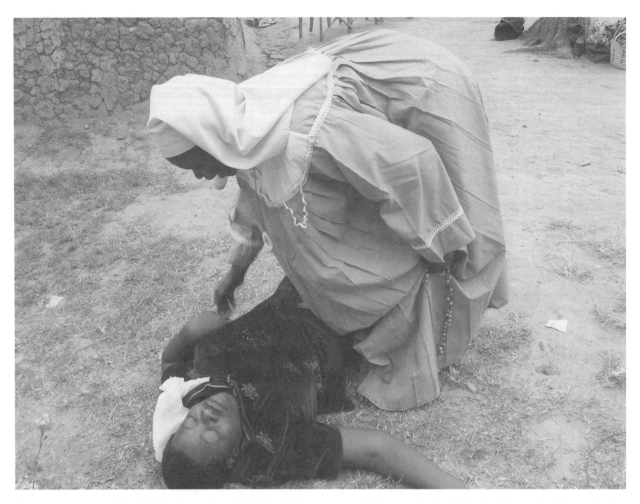

Woman possessed by spirits during Legio services. A senior Legio Maria member holds her losali (rosary) while praying for another woman, who has been carried outside a prayer meeting to be released from the spiritual forces. Those most frequently possessed by spirits during Legio services are women. Kenya, 2005. PHOTOGRAPH BY MATTHEW KUSTENBAUDER

oppose Christianity, or have been African Christians attempting to purify and Africanize Christianity that was brought and controlled by European missionaries. Virtually all, at one time or another, became overtly political and held the aim of freeing their members and local societies from colonial rule (and later from postcolonial governments), and so became part of resistance movements.

Certain common or widespread processes in the histories of these movements exist. One was that prophets have usually been concerned with fighting witchcraft and sorcery, which are the signs of societal and cultural confusion and disintegration. As reformers, prophets have tried to purify society from evil by appealing to traditional moral concepts. However, the basic criterion for defining

these leaders as prophets has been their ability to transcend local social and religious groups and moralities and to construct new moral systems that are acceptable to culturally diverse groups over wide areas. In many cases traditional divinities have come to be seen as outmoded and ineffective on their own. As a result, the old notions of spirit possession, ancestral spirits, and mystical power have often been incorporated into Christianity, a universal religious framework that provides prophets with greater legitimacy and wider social networks upon which to draw.

Many of these movements have been local and temporary, but others have been long lasting and have entered history and tradition as events of central importance in African history. The successive prophetic cults and movements among the Gikuyu of central Kenya are an example of this. Here the first reported movements were overtly political associations, such as Harry Thuku's Young Kikuyu Association in the early 1920s, which was concerned with offsetting the effects of land alienation and improving the treatment of laborers. Soon there appeared in this and other associations a breach between older and younger people, the former adhering to traditional religious beliefs and the latter to Western education and Christianity. In 1929 the so-called circumcision controversy defined these conflicts more clearly. This was a conflict between Gikuyu and the European missions (especially the Church of Scotland and the Africa Inland Mission) that wanted to stop the practice of the clitoridectomy of girls. This led not only to conflict between Gikuyu and the Europeans, but also between the more traditional landowning elders (supported by the administration) and younger, educated, and generally landless men and women (considered untrustworthy citizens by the administration). Most Gikuyu Christians left the missions and established their own churches and schools. The two most important factions were the African Independent Pentecostal Church, linked to the Kikuyu Independent Schools Association, and the more radical and antimission African Orthodox Church, which established the Kikuyu Karinga Educational Association and was linked to the leading political group of the time, the Kikuyu Central Association.

While this overtly Christian controversy was raging, another strand appeared in the form of the 1920s movement *Watu wa Mungu* (People of God). Gikuyu seers who refused European clothing and objects and who worshiped facing Mount Kenya, where dwelt the traditional Gikuyu High God, led the movement. Watu wa Mungu became linked to the highly political Kikuyu Central Association, whose secretary-general was Jomo Kenyatta (his book, *Facing Mount Kenya*, had its dustcover showing Kenyatta wearing the attire of the Watu wa Mungu). Although details are unreliable, there seems to have been an historical link between the seers of Watu wa Mungu and the leaders of the later Mau Mau revolt. The conflict is perhaps one of the most frequently cited examples of anticolonialist resistance, but it is important to note that the internal struggle between landed and landless Gikuyu was at the time equally as important.

There have been many other and similar prophetic movements in Kenya. One such movement for which there is reliable information was that known as Mumbo among the Gusii of western Kenya. They believed in Mumbo, a god who had homes in the sky and in Lake Victoria and who appeared in a vision to a prophet called Onyango among the Luo to the immediate northwest. Onyango began preaching in 1913 and claimed that the great serpent had swallowed him and then spat him out, telling him to preach to the people against adopting European religion and ways. Mumbo took the form of an immense snake linking sky and lake and promising a future of ease and prosperity to those who accepted its message. Adherents were to sacrifice to it and follow certain rules: to wear skins instead of European-style clothes; not to wash or cut their hair; and to perform traditional dances. Also, they were allowed or perhaps encouraged to smoke *bhang* (hashish). In the early 1920s the cult's message spread among the Gusii, who had suffered military defeat by the Kenyan administration in 1905–1908 and heavy losses of men recruited into the Carrier Corps—a military unit of Africans created for the sole purpose of carrying supplies to the Indian Army forces fighting against German East Africa during World War I. Also, their indigenous political leaders had been ignored by the administration and young educated men had been appointed in their place. The cult spread quickly in the 1930s after a period of drought and famine. There were several Gusii prophets of Mumbo, the two most powerful being a former prophet called Zakawa and a woman called Borairiri. The cult made sporadic appearances and attacks in 1933, in 1938, and again in 1947 until it was banned in 1945, after which time it mostly died out. Its message was bitterly opposed to the European administration and mission Christianity; hostility was largely directed against local administrative chiefs and officials.

A later movement was the *Dini ya Msambwa* (Religion of the Ancestor) among the Luhya of western Kenya, an area that had suffered from external interference since the time of the Arab-Swahili slave raiders of the mid-nineteenth century. Mumia (1871–1971), chief of the Luhya subgroup called

Wanga, had been a central figure in the trade with the coast in slaves and ivory, and welcomed the British colonial administration, carefully placing many of his close kin as subchiefs throughout Luhya. During the interwar years European settlement had increased throughout Kenya, with European farmers taking more land for themselves and continually demanding more labor. The first third of the twentieth century brought little prosperity to the Luhya and little hope for their future as independent peasant farmers.

In the late 1930s a prophetic leader, Elijah Masinde (d. 1987), appeared. A former Quaker mission convert from the Bukusu subgroup of the Luhya, his aims were to expel the European administrative, settler, and mission presence, and to return to the traditional religion of the Luhya while retaining European material wealth. The movement spread rapidly within and beyond the Bukusu, with sporadic outbursts of destruction of European property and threats to mission supporters. The word *basambwa* means those ancestors to whom offerings are made, and *Msambwa* was the related term used to describe the creator divinity, Wele. Wele was associated with Mount Elgon and a lake near its peak, which the movement referred to as Zion. The water of the lake purified sinners and gave strength to the movement's members by making them immune to bullets, among other things. Other minor prophets and mediums, mostly men, assisted Masinde. Throughout their teaching, continual reference was made to the Bible and its accounts of a millenarian society in which foreign oppressors had no place. In 1945, Masinde was committed to Mathari Mental Hospital, and although he was soon released he quickly lost his former influence. By the 1950s or so the movement had spread widely, but was no longer a Bukusu-only movement. It was proscribed after Kenyan independence, in 1968.

The Dini ya Msambwa also led in the 1950s to religious activity and prophecy among the Pokot, north of the Luhya; they followed a prophet of their own, Lukas Pkech. The aims were similar to the Dini ya Msambwa, and ended in 1950 with a military confrontation at Kolloa in which Pkech, many of his followers, and several European administrative and police officers were killed. The Kenyan administration exacted heavy penalties and the movement came to an end.

Both Mumbo and Dini ya Msambwa were clearly political resistance movements with religious ideologies, the latter incorporating Christian themes but at heart advocating a return to tradition. Any purification of Christianity was a tangential aspect of its aims and activities; reversion to or revival of the traditional faith remained central. Christians were counted as enemies, although their Bible could be used as text to support prophecies made by Masinde and the other leaders.

A tendency toward violent resistance among other prophetic movements of the time and in the region accentuates the uniqueness of *Legio Maria*, a nonviolent prophetic movement that began among the Luo of southwestern Kenya. Founded by Catholic lay member Simeo Ondeto (1920–1991) in 1963, the year of Kenya's independence, Legio Maria has creatively combined conservative Catholicism, traditional religion, and charismatic manifestations of the Holy Spirit. It is the largest secession from the Roman Catholic Church anywhere in Africa, with membership estimates as high as two million. At first, followers regarded Ondeto as a prophet, sent by God to heal their sicknesses and to show them the secret to wonderful things. He was called *hono* (the man who can do miracles), and his followers believed that he could prophesy, cure the sick, raise the dead, make the blind see and the crippled walk, and cast out evil spirits. He was said to know what was happening in other places and to know what was in a person's heart. Eventually, Legios came to believe that their prophetic leader was, in fact, Jesus Christ reincarnated in African skin and come to save them from their suffering. In the early 2000s, images of Baba Messias Ondeto (Simeo Ondeto) and his mother, Bikra Maria (the Virgin Mary), adorn the altars of Legio Maria churches as well as the necks of Legio followers. Their elaborate services, based on the pre-Vatican II Latin mass, prominently feature healing rituals, exorcism, deliverance from witchcraft, prophecies, glossolalia (speaking in tongues), dream interpretation, visions, and spirit possession.

Kenya's history as a settler colony was a central factor in the formation and orientation of radical movements such as Mau Mau, Mumbo, and Dini ya Msambwa, whose prophets confronted the

Casting out evil spirits after the mass. Members of the Legio Maria congregation at Efeso circle round a large wooden cross in the center of the compound following celebration of the mass, sung mostly in Latin. The worshippers kneel while those with special gifts of healing and exorcism cast out evil spirits and cleanse the members with holy water. Kenya, 2005. PHOTOGRAPH BY MATTHEW KUSTENBAUDER

social dislocation caused by colonial rule by brazenly ordering the British out. Uganda, on the other hand, had few white settlers and a different colonial history. There the best-known movement was that known as *Abalokole* (the saved ones), first among the Kiga and Hororo of southwestern Uganda and later among the Ganda and other groups. The movement began in the Ruanda Mission, an offshoot of the (Protestant) Church Missionary Society that had long worked among the Ganda. It established a mission at Kabale in 1921, and many of its members were Canadian Pentecostals. After the Nyabingi revolts of the late 1920s, in which men supplanted the traditional female diviners, the women moved to the Kabale mission. During the 1930s the movement developed into a full-scale revival, largely under the guidance of a medical

doctor, Joe Church (1899–1989). Membership required public confession of sins, repentance, and the renunciation of alcohol, personal adornment, and dancing; charismatic behavior in the form of trance and glossolalia was common. Salvation was sent by Christ and was not considered as resulting from an individual's act of will. The movement established itinerant teaching teams, some three-quarters of the members being women. It spread rapidly to Buganda and then to the rest of the country, and reached the Lugbara of far northwestern Uganda in the late 1940s as a women's movement. In Buganda during World War II, some of its leaders were imprisoned for advocating civil disobedience and nonpayment of taxes. However, the (British) bishops refused to expel Balokole members and retained them in the Church of

Uganda on the premise that they were sincere, if misguided, Christian reformers. Balokole members and supporters have since played an important role in church affairs throughout Protestant Uganda. Abalokole has had few directly political aims but was intended to purify the church by the moral sanctification of church members and by Africanizing the church hierarchy. Nonetheless, it has exerted considerable influence in the choice of political leaders throughout southern Uganda.

A final movement that may be mentioned is the Holy Spirit Movement among the Acholi of northern Uganda. This prophet-led millenarian movement began in 1985, when it was believed that the Christian God sent a spirit called Lakwena (Messenger) to Uganda, where he spoke through an Acholi woman named Alice Auma (1956–2007). Functioning in the style of the traditional spirit medium, Alice set up a shrine at Opit, where she offered cleansing rituals to Acholi soldiers rejected by their communities for committing indiscriminate acts of violence in Uganda's bloody civil war. After a short-lived Acholi-led military coup, it became apparent that the Acholi people themselves were the targets of a punitive campaign launched by the rebel-leader-become-president, Yoweri Museveni, and his National Resistance Army. Lakwena responded, shifting tactics from a nonviolent healing mission to a violent one by deploying a military arm of the movement, the Holy Spirit Mobile Force, to fight the Uganda government. Its aim was to cleanse first the nation and then the world of evil, and to establish a new social order in which humans, the spirits, and the forces of the environment would live together in peace. Alice guided a number of highly successful military engagements on Lakwena's instructions until late 1987, when, on their march to take the capital, the force was defeated by the national army just 31 miles from Kampala. Alice fled across the border to Kenya, where she lived in refugee camps until her death in 2007.

Alice Lakwena's Holy Spirit Movement may best be understood as a religiously based restorationist movement that responded to and was shaped by the particularities of Ugandan social history. Christian apocalyptic imagination, combined with traditional religious practices, played a critical role in reestablishing a sense of human agency by providing a redemptive framework for interpreting past events and directing future action. In the case of Alice, religion was not simply a tool used for political gain. Instead, the imaginative religious discourse espoused by the Holy Spirit Movement held an explanatory power and promised solutions for the problems of Acholi society that no political discourse could match. Operating within the synthesized framework of traditional Acholi religion and newer Christian apocalyptic, Alice and her followers engaged in religiously sanctioned violence that was seen as a just punishment on those who defied the moral order through indiscriminate acts of killing and as a necessary remedy for the purification of the people and the transformation of society. Alice's holy war, highly proscribed by a set of religious interdictions, was carried out by her Holy Spirit Mobile Forces as the primary means of creating order out of disorder. The destruction of their land, the loss of their livelihoods, and the deaths of their sons supplied the ominous apocalyptic signs of impending doom, and many Acholi looked for a prophet who would rescue them from extermination, give them justice against their enemies, and heal their broken society. Alice Lakwena appeared on the scene for such a time as this, announcing a truly prophetic and millenarian vision by which God's kingdom and judgment would come on earth to set all things right.

CONCLUSION

Despite their differences in beliefs, symbols, and social consequences, these and other eastern African movements shared certain basic features.

Prophets were believed to be emissaries sent by a divinity (God), often coming from outside the particular society. A problem was that of the identity of the divinity concerned, whether traditional, Christian, or Islamic. The first was tied to a particular society, the others were universal. Yet most of these movements conceived of divinity as forming a single source of power: the differences were in their respective congregations.

Prophets were always sacred persons, given knowledge and power by the divinity and not by their followers (here prophets differ from priests). A prophet had the ability to contact the divinity whether by possession and glossolalia, or by the rainbow snakes that linked earth and sky. For this reason, they were formidable and strange figures. The often-reported prophetic behavior was the reversal of everyday comportment in matters of attire, food, sexuality, and frequently of gender. Prophets were not limited by ordinary constraints of time and space, and their superhuman deeds were proof of a divine connection—they traveled through the air; they assumed the forms of humans and animals; they prophesied at night or in the wilderness; they were able to turn bullets into water.

Prophets came in response to crises, to signs of breakdown or threat to a society's sense of order, certainty, and accepted traditions. Their message was one of purification and reform in order to restore those traditions and forms of society as the people imagined them once to have been. The prophetic messages were typically restatements of these traditions, by reconstruction and recombination of traditional elements deemed the opposite of those of the present day. Throughout the history of eastern Africa, it may be assumed that there were countless would-be prophets, each with their own ambitions and messages. Most of them either failed or remained local figures, vanishing from historical memory. A few, however, were accepted and gained a significant following.

In the cases presented earlier, there already existed certain basic conditions: the wretchedness and uncertainty in the lives of peasant farmers or urban laborers under the colonial or postcolonial regimes; long and dangerous epidemics striking humans and livestock; an increasing uncertainty about women's roles; worsening change and conflict in the relations between old and young, men and women, rich and poor, landed and landless, educated and noneducated, indigenous and stranger, and free and slave or ex-slave.

These conditions, however, had persisted for long periods without the appearance of popular prophets or reformers. For this there was need of a flash point, a sudden impulse for people to act together to set perceived wrongs right, as with the Kenya missions' deciding to stop Gikuyu clitoridectomy or the German administration's imposition of compulsory cotton planting. These are examples of what historian Marcia Wright referred to as a "prophetic moment" (124) when a prophet was sought or appeared with a message

that purported to reveal the divine truth and the meaning behind the current conditions and events. The prophet's presence and message transformed a human historical event into a moral and spiritual one; it removed the actors from everyday time and space, and convinced them that they were endowed with the creative power of the divinity as manifest in the prophet's person. The sacred was typically defined in terms of the opposite of the everyday, and the prophet's adherents were told to reverse or invert their normal behavior so as to remove themselves symbolically from everyday earthly authority and to share in the divinity. To reform society, the movement's members had themselves to be reformed through the process of a *rite de passage*, or rite of transformation, only after which could the transformed persons begin to reform society and to make it as it had been and should again become.

See also **Death, Mourning, and Ancestors; Dreams and Dream Interpretation; Ethnicity: Eastern Africa; Famine; Kenyatta, Jomo; Lakwena, Alice; Musevini, Yoweri; Myth and Cosmology; Religion and Ritual; Thuku, Harry; Witchcraft; World War I; World War II.**

BIBLIOGRAPHY

Allen, Tim. "Understanding Alice: Uganda's Holy Spirit Movement in Context." *Africa* 61, no. 3 (1991): 370–399.

Allen, Tim. *Trial Justice: The International Criminal Court and the Lord's Resistance Army.* New York: Palgrave Macmillan, 2006.

Anderson, Allen. *African Reformation: African Initiated Christianity in the 20th Century.* Trenton, NJ: Africa World Press, Inc., 2001.

Anderson, David M., and Douglas H. Johnson, eds. *Revealing Prophets: Prophecy in Eastern African History.* Athens: Ohio University Press, 1995.

Behrend, Heike. *Alice Lakwena and the Holy Spirits: War in Northern Uganda, 1985–97.* Athens: Ohio University Press, 1999.

Berntsen, John L. "Maasai Age-Sets and Prophetic Leadership, 1850–1910." *Africa* 49, no. 2 (1979): 134–146.

Brown, L. Carl. "The Sudanese Mahdiya." In *Protest and Power in Black Africa*, eds. Robert Rotberg and Ali Mazrui. New York: Oxford University Press, 1970.

de Wolf, Jan J. "Dini ya Msambwa: Militant Protest or Millenarian Promise?" *Canadian Journal of African*

Studies/Revue Canadienne des Études Africaines 17, no. 2 (1983): 265–276.

Hansen, Holger Bernt, and Michael Twaddle, eds. *Religion and Politics in East Africa: The Period Since Independence.* Athens: Ohio University Press, 1995.

Hopkins, Elizabeth. "The Nyabingi Cult of Southwest Uganda." In *Protest and Power in Black Africa*, eds. Robert Rotberg and Ali Mazrui. New York: Oxford University Press, 1970.

Johnson, Douglas H. *Nuer Prophets: A History of Prophesy from the Upper Nile in the Nineteenth and Twentieth Centuries.* New York: Oxford University Press, 1994.

Middleton, John. "The Yakan or Allah Water Cult Among the Lugbara." *Journal of the Royal Anthropological Institute of Great Britain and Ireland* 93, no. 1 (1963): 80–108.

Muga, Erasto. *African Response to Western Christian Religion: A Sociological Analysis of African Separatist Religious and Political Movements in East Africa.* Nairobi, Kenya: East African Literature Bureau, 1975.

Murray, Jocelyn. "The Kikuyu Spirit Churches." *Journal of Religion in Africa* 5, fasc. 3 (1973): 198–234.

Packard, Randall M. "Chiefship and the History of Nyavingi Possession among the Bashu of Eastern Zaire." *Africa* 52, no. 4 (1982): 67–86, 90.

Robins, Caroline. "Conversion, Life Crises, and Stability Among Women in the East African Revival." In *The New Religions of Africa*, ed. Bennetta Jules-Rosette. Norwood, NJ: Ablex, 1979.

Shadle, Brett L. "Patronage, Millennialism and the Serpent God Mumbo in South-West Kenya, 1912–34." *Journal of the International African Institute* 72, no. 1 (2002): 29–54.

Spear, Thomas, and Isaria Kimambo, eds. *East African Expressions of Christianity.* Athens: Ohio University Press, 1999.

Wipper, Audrey. *Rural Rebels: A Study of Two Protest Movements in Kenya.* New York: Oxford University Press, 1977.

Wright, Marcia. "Maji Maji: Prophecy and Historiography." In *Revealing Prophets: Prophecy in Eastern African History*, eds. David Anderson and Douglas H. Johnson. Athens: Ohio University Press, 1995.

MATTHEW KUSTENBAUDER

SOUTHERN AFRICA

In southern Africa, a distinction is to be drawn between two kinds of prophetic activity, namely the messianic and the healing. Messianic prophets proclaim a message of great social upheaval; they predict widespread suffering and/or deliverance that will introduce a social utopia, such as the restoration of an ideal past, by means of some superhuman cosmic intervention. Although we can trace such visionary prophets among the Xhosa of the eastern Cape back to the first decades of the nineteenth century, it was in the 1850s that they achieved historical prominence at a time when, having endured a number of damaging epidemics, British colonists were squeezing the Xhosa economically and politically. The prophet Mlanjeni encouraged Xhosa resistance with the assurance that British bullets would harmlessly dissolve into water. In 1856, the visions of a young woman, Nongqawuse (d. 1928), actively promoted by William Goliath, her uncle, urged the Xhosa to destroy existing stocks of grain and cattle in anticipation of a more plentiful renewal of resources and a complete social reformation. This great transformation was to be ushered in by the return of the ancestors from the dead as new people, the idea of bodily resurrection being derived from an acquaintance with Christian teaching. All of the Xhosa messianic prophets drew inspiration from an association with missionary Christianity and headed antiwitchcraft movements. As the prophets were unifiers, at least in intent if not always in result, their message was concerned with societal healing.

The messianic prophet seems to have been notably absent among the Zulu people, despite the claims sometimes made on behalf of Laduma Madela (b. c. 1908). Recent evidence reveals that Laduma, among several others, has set himself up as a specialist heaven-herd: someone who herds and drives away lightning and hail from people, dwellings, livestock, and crops. This function rested on the Zulu belief that the Lord of the Heavens, when annoyed, hurled down bolts and pellets from above. The damage could be avoided by ritually diverting the storm to a different location. Those who provide protection by controlling celestial violence in this way may not qualify for recognition as prophets, yet they claim to ensure deliverance from impending disaster, admittedly on a more reduced scale than the Xhosa prophets.

Healing prophets in southern Africa work on an even narrower stage. Their primary concern is with the welfare of the individual. Here the gift of prophecy is mainly that of discernment: the ability to see beneath the surface of things, and to reveal the source of affliction or misfortune. To this extent, they are not unlike African diviners. However, they are empowered not by the ancestors but rather by the Holy Spirit. Almost without exception, they can be described as Christian prophets, though some are more Christian than others, and they operate within the ranks of the African Independent Church (AIC) movement, more particularly within the larger Zionist component of that movement.

The AICs in southern Africa took two divergent forms, as they arose from different sets of circumstances in the experience of the colonized: missionary discrimination and repression of workers. The discriminatory practices of the missionaries produced churches called Ethiopian, the first of their kind appearing in 1892. Although the missionaries preached a Christian creed of egalitarianism, they were reluctant to promote black pastors to positions of responsibility and refused to interact with them as equals. The educated lower clergy eventually rebelled by establishing separate African churches in Johannesburg that were free from white control but in all other respects were replicas of their parent bodies. Ethiopia was chosen as a rallying point because it was the biblical prototype of Africa and because contemporary Ethiopia embodied the ideal of political independence. In 1904, the first charismatic Zionist church appeared among exploited farm workers in a remote rural area. As a response to conditions of near enslavement, the workers adopted a Pentecostal strain of religion, imported from working-class America by a white missionary, which empowered them with the Holy Spirit to provide a novel form of spiritual healing that was neither scientific nor African. Although prophecy was not an original element of the received package, it was soon introduced once the influence of the white missionary had been removed.

Since the beginning of the twentieth century, the AICs have grown and spread geographically throughout southern Africa, following the migrant routes from the South African mines to present-day Zimbabwe, Zambia, Malawi, and Democratic Republic of the Congo. According to the official enumeration in 1990, AIC members constituted 30 percent of the total African population in South Africa alone. Because they are most numerous in northeastern South Africa and are heavily concentrated in the densely populated urban areas around Johannesburg and Durban, their proportional representation in these cities was 40 percent or greater. There is an unmistakable correlation between AIC expansion and the transformation of rural migrants into settled urban populations. Although no exact figures are available, there is every indication that this development has favored the growth of Zionist, rather than Ethiopian, churches.

There are several thousand Zionist churches in existence at any time, some expanding and others declining, and new ones arising at a rate faster than those dying out. Nobody can claim to speak for Zionists in general because, lacking a semblance of central organization or an agreed canon of orthodoxy, they are characterized by wide variation of belief and observance, and by obsessive disunity. Many retain a sense of authenticity and orthodoxy by tracing historical links to the first Zionist foundation and by preserving the tenets of the early founders. These groups take pride in calling themselves Christian Zionists and distance themselves from new Zionists, whose pretensions they disparage. New Zionists are undoubtedly in the majority, if only because anyone inspired by a spiritual vision and prophetic message can set up a church and woo followers by borrowing selected elements of Zionism, mixing them with features of African religion, and reconstructing these to fit the founder's esoteric design. Still other charismatic churches are not Zionist in any sense. Also of spontaneous prophetic origin, these other churches are attempts to adapt traditional religion to modern needs, and are often led by several generations of a particular family. Some—for example, the Zion Christian Church near Pietersburg, under the leadership of Engenas Lekganyane (d. 1948); and the Nazareth Baptist Church outside of Durban, identified with Isaiah Shembe—are spectacularly large, although both churches exaggerate the sizes of their followings. Most Zionist churches are of modest size because of an inherent tendency to segment and subdivide, to which even the large traditional churches are not entirely immune.

While the range of differences expressed in Zionism defies generalization, some salient features may be singled out for comment, predominantly in connection with Christian Zionists. Most Zionist churches seek to alleviate the condition of the poor, with varying success. The two main strategies are economic uplift and healing. The first is an economic package blending a disciplined way of life, sobriety, abstemiousness, hard work, financial saving, and mutual support. The maintenance of discipline is entrusted to a preaching hierarchy: the preacher, who addresses a local congregation, may recruit converts; an evangelist, who, in addition to a preaching function, has the right to baptize and process entry into full church membership; and a bishop, who oversees several congregations that are typically headed by a minister. These positions can be embellished at will with the addition of contingent offices. The preaching function draws on the Bible as a source of moral precepts and exemplary precedents. At the Christian end of the Zionist spectrum, married men monopolize the preaching ranks; newer Zionists admit women to the ministry, and even allow female bishops. The ministry, however, is unspecialized; without wages or formal training, incumbents must work for a living, and because leaders are seldom more than barely literate, education is not a qualification for office. Apart from founding a church of one's own, entitlement to office rests upon experience, endurance, and an ability to recruit followers.

Healing draws on a different kind of expertise, that of the prophet. Here the difference between Christian and new becomes more manifest. Later strains of Zionism restored ancestors to their healing role, commonly in some form of partnership with the Holy Spirit, and prophets in their healing work derived their insights into the nature of illness and remedy from these twin sources. With this goes a marked tendency for prophetic healing to become the dominant or sole concern of these newer churches, to the virtual exclusion of Bible-centered preaching; prophet leadership then becomes the norm, with corresponding female ascendancy. Mainstream Christian Zionists recognize both male and female prophets, but male prophets are given a better hearing, and all prophets are subordinate to the male preaching hierarchy. Healing power and prophetic inspiration are derived from the Holy Spirit alone, and healing is not divorced from preaching. Preachers are charged with drawing on the Bible to stir up the enthusiasm of the

congregation and to arouse the Holy Spirit among them, in such a way as to build up a wave of spiritual power than can be used by the prophet to heal the sick. A major concern is alleviating the damage done to individuals by sorcery, and equipping them with symbolic protective devices suffused with the power of communal prayer.

Such prophets cannot operate independently of the congregation to which they belong and from which they derive the inspiration of the Holy Spirit. They would be disowned by the congregation and labeled diviner should they engage in private or commercial healing. Nor do they have complete freedom within the congregation to expose individual moral lapses too zealously, to the point of alienating a member or potential member. The ministry, concerned primarily with group conservation and growth, would intervene to tone down such excesses. Conversely, prophets are capable of stage-managing the denunciation of corruption or an abuse of authority on the part of an officeholder, and can raise the specter of some future accident, vaguely foreseen, as a spur to the restoration of good behavior. Preachers and prophets complement one another, not least in the exercise of mutual control.

Prophets among the new Zionists, similar to the prophet founders of large churches, are much less subject to such communal restraints. Their prophetic gift has not emerged from a congregation or church structure, but was a personal possession that later wove itself into a church. While Zionist prophets are arguably not diviners *manqué*, they openly don the mantle of the Zulu heaven-herd and can be seen encircling residences with prayer, blessed water, and lit candles in the gloom of a gathering storm. A more permanent feature of this prophetic protection against all kinds of mystical attack is the attachment of specially treated flags to poles outside, or tucked beneath the rafters within, the house. Zionists thus believe that they live within a protective canopy provided by charismatic prophet-leaders, or by the efficacious interaction of their congregation's prophets and preachers.

See also **Johannesburg; Nongqawuse; Religion and Ritual.**

BIBLIOGRAPHY

Comaroff, Jean. *Body of Power, Spirit of Resistance: The Culture and History of a South African People.* Chicago: University of Chicago Press, 1985.

Daneel, Martinus L. *Old and New in Shona Independent Churches*. Vol. 2. The Hague: Mouton, 1974.

Fogelqvist, Anders. *The Red-Dressed Zionists: Symbols of Power in a Swazi Independent Church*. Uppsala, Sweden: Uppsala Research Reports in Cultural Anthropology, 5, 1986.

Kiernan, James P. *The Production and Management of Therapeutic Power in Zionist Churches within a Zulu City*. Lewiston, New York: Edwin Mellen Press, 1990.

Peires, Jeffrey Brian. *The Dead Will Arise. Nongqawuse and the Great Xhosa Cattle-Killing Movement of 1856–7*. Bloomington: Indiana University Press, 1989.

Sundkler, Bengt Gustaf Malcolm. *Bantu Prophets in South Africa*. London: Oxford University Press, 1976.

West, Martin Elgar. *Bishops and Prophets in a Black City: African Independent Churches in Soweto, Johannesburg*. Cape Town, South Africa: David Philip, 1975.

JAMES P. KIERNAN

WESTERN AFRICA

Prophetic movements have not dominated the landscape in western Africa to the same extent as they have in eastern and Southern Africa. Nevertheless, a number of prophetic movements did emerge from around 1920 onward, marking the most dramatic growth of Christianity in twentieth-century West Africa. It has been noted that the growth was uneven—prophetic churches are abundant in Nigeria and Ghana. Côte d'Ivoire recognizes the prophetic Harrist church, together with Islam, Protestantism, and Roman Catholicism, as one of four official religions. But in other West African countries, such as Sierra Leone, Senegal, and Mali, prophetic churches have made little impact. This no doubt has to do with the dominance of Islam in these countries, but it is also likely that colonial policies and the presence of Roman Catholicism produced a buffering effect. All across Africa, and indeed within Christianity as a whole, prophetic movements have been more likely to spring from the Protestant churches.

CHRISTIAN PROPHETIC MOVEMENTS

The prophet-healing churches in Ghana are popularly referred to in Akan as Sunsum Sore or Spirit churches. Perhaps no other of Ghana's Spirit churches has as long and colorful a pedigree as the Musama Disco Christo Church (Army of the Cross of Christ), founded by a former Methodist catechist and schoolteacher, Joseph William Egyanka Appiah (1893–1948), who later became known to his followers as Prophet Jemisimiham Jehu-Appiah. Similar to many breakaway groups, the Musama Disco Christo Church (MDCC) began in 1919 as a prayer fellowship within one of the mission churches, the Methodist Church of the Central Region of the Gold Coast (present-day Ghana). When Appiah and his followers were asked to leave the Methodist Church in 1922 for their so-called occult practices of prophesying, healing, and speaking in tongues, the group established the MDCC, claiming to have received this name by divine revelation. Three angels visited Appiah, and they told him that he would be a king. Indeed, the movement constructed for themselves a holy city, which they named Mozano (my [God's] city). In it, Appiah reigned as the spiritual head of a dynasty, taking the title *Akaboha* (King) I. His bride and the cofounder of the movement, Abena Bawa, became the Prophetess Natholomoa Jehu-Appiah and also the *Akatitibii* (Queen mother) of the church. The MDCC borrows its elaborate church structure from traditional Fanti royal courts, yet it notably bans the use of ancestor rituals. It emphasizes divine healing and has an elaborate hierarchy of angels, who are to be petitioned in prayer. It has its own special language for greetings between church members, each of who receives a unique heavenly name (no two are alike) from the head of the church upon his or her conversion. Borrowing heavily from practices contained in the Old Testament, members gather once a year at a holy shrine, where the *Akaboha* enters once a year to offer prayers before an Ark of the Covenant and make sacrifices on behalf of the people. The office of *Akaboha*, comprising both spiritual and political duties, is inherited through the Jehu-Appiah family line. Appiah's grandson currently holds the title of *Akaboha* III.

Whereas Appiah's prophetic visions led him to found a city and become a king, William Wadé Harris (1865–1929) was called to the life of a wandering evangelist. Perhaps one of the first and greatest of the prophets to emerge in all West Africa, Harris had a lasting impact in Ghana and is regarded as the father of Christianity in Côte d'Ivoire. He embarked upon his most successful preaching journey across southern Côte d'Ivoire and Ghana between the years 1913 and 1914. In Ghana he challenged traditional priests, many of whom were converted after apparently recognizing the superiority of the power of the Christian God over traditional deities, ancestors, and nature spirits. It is said that over one thousand new people came to hear Harris preach each day, until opposition from Catholic missionaries caused him to flee. In Côte d'Ivoire, he is thought to have converted and baptized well over 120,000 people in one year. Such was the enthusiasm surrounding Harris's ministry that the French colonial administration imprisoned him for a short time and thereafter kept him under close watch. Eventually, under pressure from Catholic missionaries, the French authorities deported him from Côte d'Ivoire in 1914. Harris returned to his native Liberia and to neighboring Sierra Leone, where he preached with little success until his death in 1929.

Harris's career is characteristic of other prophetic movements in western Africa in that his prophetic calling began in Anglophone West Africa and later spread to neighboring Francophone countries. Harris, an indigenous Grebo, was a well-educated, middle-class Liberian disillusioned with the country's black American rulers and the missionaries who had employed him as a teacher in the Episcopal church. While in prison in 1910 on charges of treason (he symbolically raised the Union Jack in place of the Liberian flag, signaling that native Liberians would fare better under British colonial rule), Harris experienced a vision that changed his life. The angel Gabriel appeared to him with the message that he was to be a prophet, commissioned by God to preach the gospel in a more African way. Upon his release, Harris became a peripatetic proclaimer in the biblical style of John the Baptist—he went about barefoot, adorning himself in a simple long white calico robe and turban. Armed only with cross, calabash, and Bible—the essential tools of his prophetic calling—Harris preached the absolute sovereignty of God, healing from disease, and the rejection of traditional religions. He encouraged people to burn their fetishes and idols, and strongly condemned the consumption of alcohol. Contrary to the practice of the mission churches that required a long probationary period before initiation, Harris baptized converts

on the spot, often baptizing entire villages at once, thereby minimizing potential social tensions. These villages ever after retained a Christian character.

With the exception of supporting polygamy, which he practiced himself, Harris's teaching was similar to that of the European missionaries. He urged his converts to await Christian missionaries with Bibles and had no intention of establishing his own church. When he arrived in Côte d'Ivoire in 1914, there were probably only a few hundred Catholics throughout the entire country. Many converts joined the Catholic Church as a result of his preaching. When the first Methodist missionaries arrived in 1924 they were pleasantly surprised to find thriving village churches started by Harris that came to form the backbone of the Methodist mission, thus the Methodist Church dates its founding in Côte d'Ivoire to Harris's 1914 preaching tour. Nevertheless, disputes over polygamy and compulsory church dues discouraged some Harris Christians from joining the mission churches. Women, who occupied a prominent role since the movement's inception, founded a number of prominent Harrist churches. Marie Lalou (d. 1951) started the Deima Church, the second largest Harrist church in Côte d'Ivoire. Grace Tani (d. 1958), a former diviner who had been converted by Harris, established the Church of the Twelve Apostles in western Ghana.

At about the same time but farther east in the Niger Delta, an adult Anglican convert by the name of Garrick Sokari Braide (c. 1882–1918) began his prophetic career. A poor fisherman and trader with little formal education, he received a vision in 1912 as he knelt at the communion rail. After that, Braide embarked upon an extraordinarily successful public ministry of preaching and healing. The similarities between Braide's career and that of Harris are noteworthy. Both men were charismatic figures credited with the power to heal and make rain. Given the name Prophet Elijah II by his followers, Braide was also a fiery preacher who called people to renounce their traditional practices and to believe in God. Enthusiastic public response to his preaching aroused resentment within the Anglican church mission (CMS) and anxieties within the colonial government. Crowds flocked to listen to Braide, and his disciples carried the message all over the Niger Delta and deep into the Igbo interior. Braide railed against the evils of alcohol consumption with the result that trade in spirits declined dramatically, drawing the attention of colonial authorities who felt the pinch from decreased tax revenues. Furthermore, zealous converts frequently smashed traditional shrines, which angered the shrines' devotees who complained bitterly to the authorities. In 1916, however, Braide's prophetic career came to an abrupt end. Colonial officials with written support from the Anglican Bishop, James Johnson, arrested Braide. Although Braide himself never assumed leadership of his own church (Anglicans were the primary beneficiaries of Braide's converts), his preaching and healing ministry did result in the creation of new churches. While Braide was still in prison, some 40,000 of his followers formed the Christ Army Church. Shortly after his release in 1918, Braide died, perhaps a victim of the worldwide influenza epidemic.

In western Nigeria, 1918 also marks the emergence of the Aladura movement, the name given to an aggregation of churches that took root among the Yoruba peoples of western Nigeria. In that year, Joseph Shadare (d. 1962) organized an Anglican prayer group (aladura is a Yoruba word meaning praying people) at Ijebu-Ode, Nigeria to provide support and healing for victims of the influenza epidemic. The group largely comprised members of the younger Christian elite, who called themselves the Precious Stone Society. Dissatisfied with Western religious forms and lack of spiritual power, they were strongly influenced by the divine-healing literature of the fundamentalist Faith Tabernacle Church based in Philadelphia in the United States. Although some of its first members had prophetic visions, the group's main activities centered on faith healing, prayer protection, and observing a strict moral code. In 1922 they broke with the CMS due to their disapproval of infant baptism and the use of medicines.

The Aladura movement experienced its greatest period of expansion, however, under a Yoruba prophet-healer named Joseph Ayodele Babalola (1906–1959). Another prophet with a short but influential preaching career, Babalola left his job as a road construction driver to preside over a massive revival and healing movement in 1930. Similar to the other prophets before him, Babalola heard a voice ordering him to preach and to heal. The ensuing

revival resulted in thousands of conversions and great bonfires in which people burned their charms and traditional religious objects. Rumors of witch-hunting and opposition to Western medicine circulated, drawing opposition from all sides—traditional leaders, colonial administrators, and missionaries. The government responded by rounding up Babalola and the leaders of the movement and placing them in jail. Shortly after their release, Babalola sought help from the Pentecostal Apostolic Church of Great Britain. When the missionaries arrived in 1932, however, problems arose over the missionaries' use of Western medicines—clearly contrary to doctrines of divine healing—their exclusion of polygamists, and their assertion of full control over the movement. In 1941 the ablest leaders, including Babalola and Isaac B. Akinyele (1882–1964), formed their own Christ Apostolic Church, which by the 1970s had several hundred thousand adherents, its own schools, and had spread as far west as Ghana.

Another well-known Aladura church is the Eternal Sacred Order of Cherubim and Seraphim Society, or simply the Cherubim and Seraphim. It was founded in 1925 by Moses Orimolade Tunolashe (d. 1933), a Yoruba prophet, and Christiana Abiodun Akinsowon, an Anglican girl from the Lagos elite who had experienced visions and trances. The Cherubim and Seraphim, similar to the Precious Stone Society, started out as an Anglican prayer group. It emphasized revelation through dreams and visions, divine healing instead of traditional charms and medicine, and protection from witchcraft. Members believed that the Archangel Michael was their captain, and they were known for their distinctive white robes. They permitted Western medicine, and they also permitted polygamy. Intense criticism by Anglican priests forced a separation in 1928, the same year in which the founders parted. Further dissension produced some fifty-two splinter groups, which spread widely in Nigeria and west to Dahomey (present-day Bénin), Togo, and Ghana. The Cherubim and Seraphim continues to exert its influence in Nigeria in the early twenty-first century, where nearly all of the fifty-two groups have reunited under the Baba Aladura, Dr. G. I. M. Otubu.

The Church of the Lord (Aladura), established by Josiah Olunowo Oshitelu (d. 1966), an Anglican catechist and schoolteacher, is another important

Aladura church. In 1925, through fasting and devotions, Oshitelu experienced many unusual visions in which he was called to be a prophet. Within a few years, he was preaching judgment on idolatry and traditional charms and medicines, uttering prophecies, and healing through prayer, fasting, and holy water. An associate of Babalola during the 1930 revival, he also claimed to have been given the power to detect witches. On the question of polygamy, however, Oshitelu broke with the Christ Apostolic Church, eventually taking seven wives. After Oshitelu's death in 1966, Apostle Adeleke Adejobi (1921–1991) assumed leadership of the Church of the Lord (Aladura; CLA). An indefatigable leader and bridge-builder, Adejobi oversaw the establishment of CLA churches in Freetown, Sierra Leone, and Accra, Ghana. He was instrumental in the creation of the Organization of African Instituted Churches (OAIC), based in Nairobi, and served as its first chairman. He improved cooperation among the Aladura churches, forming the Nigeria Association of Aladura Churches, which had over 1,200 member churches by 1996. In 1975, the CLA became one of the few AICs to join the World Council of Churches. Founded at Ogere, Nigeria in 1930, the CLA has since spread to north and east Nigeria, Ghana, Liberia, Sierra Leone, Togo, the United States, the U.K., and Germany, claiming nearly 2.5 million members.

The Aladura movement continues to grow and it encompasses many small secessions, ephemeral groups, and prophet-healers. Following the end of colonialism in West Africa in the late 1950s, new movements began to appear with names such as Spiritual Healing Church of the Lord, and True Church of God. One such later movement that has now surpassed the earlier Aladura churches is the Celestial Church of Christ (CCC), first started by a former Methodist named Samuel Oscoffa (1909–1985) in Bénin. In 1947 he had a divine revelation while paddling his fishing canoe in the coastal lagoons. Having received angel instructions, Oscoffa began preaching and soon gained notoriety as a great healer and wonder worker—he was even said to have raised the dead. In 1952, poor Gun fishermen carried the message of the CCC to Lagos, where it gained adherents among the Yoruba middle class. As with members of most of the previous Aladura churches, CCC members wear distinctive white gowns, remove their shoes in worship, and permit polygyny. However, miraculous healings, ecstatic speech, and traditional prayer rituals that combine Catholic, Anglican, and Muslim practices may account for the increased popularity of the CCC over the older Aladura churches. As of 2004 it claimed to have had five to six million members with some 2,000 congregations in Nigeria and still others in western Africa, Europe, and North America.

MILLENARIAN MOVEMENTS

Though Christianity proved the more fertile soil for prophetic ideas to take root, both it and Islam were incubators of millenarian expectation. In Christianity, such expectation was identified with the idea that upon Christ's return evil would be destroyed, the earth made new, and all would enjoy a thousand-year reign of peace, justice, and prosperity. Likewise, Islam pictured the return of the Mahdi, a savior figure who would vanquish the Antichrist and establish the rule of Islam over all the earth. The millenarian ideas and expectations of these world religions articulated well with Africans' hopes for a community cleared of witches and the need to cope with the rapid social, economic, and spiritual changes triggered by colonization.

One example of a Christian millenarian movement in western Africa is the Brotherhood of the Cross and Star (BCS) in eastern Nigeria, which was founded in Calabar in 1956 by Olumba Olumba Obu (b. 1918). Starting out as a prayer and Bible study group, the movement has been one of the fastest growing in Nigeria, with well over two million adherents in West Africa, the United States, Great Britain, Germany, Australia, India, and the Caribbean. Although the BCS began to take shape along similar lines with the Aladura churches, the group diverged when it developed messianic and syncretistic tendencies. Consequently, both the older mission churches and the Aladura churches look upon BCS with disdain. To members of the movement, Obu is not only a healer and miracle worker but also God in human form, the Messiah. He is referred to by his followers variously as the Universal Teacher, His Holiness, King of Kings and Lord of Lords, or simply OOO, the letters that adherents paint on their cars and houses for protection. Obu's coming marks the eighth and final incarnation of God in world history—the previous seven manifestations of God being in the form of

Adam, Enoch, Noah, Melchizedek, Moses, Elijah, and Jesus. Although the group does not consider itself to be a church, it uses the Christian scriptures and supplements them with Obu's own revelations and pronouncements. Members say that their central doctrine is to love all people without discrimination, which they attempt to achieve through its centers (known as bethels) for worship, teaching and healing, and a wide range of social programs. In recent years, tensions have mounted over who will succeed OOO, who is said to have gone blind and is now rarely seen outside his compound. Obu's eldest son, also named Olumba Olumba Obu, was appointed in 2001 by his father as his successor, however that move has been challenged by Obu's daughter, Ibum, who is supported by some BCS bishops.

Long before any significant Christian presence made itself felt there, a storm surge of millenarian expectation that had been churned up within Islam's heartland crashed upon the mixed communities of West Africa. The result was the nineteenth century jihad movements led by zealous reformers such as 'Uthman dan Fodio, Abi Bakr ibn Sa'id, and al-Hajj 'Umar. It is important to recognize that in orthodox Islamic belief, self-proclaimed prophets are subject to the charge of heresy. This is because of Islam's teaching about the Prophet Muhammad—he is said to be the seal of the prophets. For this reason, these movements are referred to as reform movements or millennial movements, even though they functioned much the same way in Islam as the prophetic movements functioned within Christianity.

Initiated in 1804, dan Fodio's reform movement swept through Hausaland, located in what is now northern Nigeria. A pious cleric, Shehu 'Uthman dan Fodio (1754–1817) fought to eradicate pre-Islamic, pagan elements from the practices of Islam in Hausaland. His education included many works by well-known Sufi luminaries, whose charismatic example left their mark on the shehu's own religious exercises and mystical visions. A revival at al-Azhar, that great center of learning in Egypt, suffused the shehu's message with a sense of urgency and helped him to see his mission within the context of worldwide Islam. As the great teacher al-Maghílí did three centuries earlier, dan Fodio came to believe that he was the *mujaddid* of

the thirteenth Islamic century (which began in 1784 CE), the precursor to the *Mahdi*, chosen by God to purify Islam. His belief was supported by his mystical visions, in which he was given guidance by the Prophet Muhammad and 'Abd al-Qādir al-Jiláni, the twelfth-century founder of the Qádiriyya Sufi order. On one occasion, after dan Fodio observed silence in prayer for an entire year, he received a vision of the Prophet Muhammad. In another vision, the Prophet brought the shehu before God's throne, where he was presented to 'Abd al-Qādir who appointed him as his earthly representative, saying, "This man belongs to me." Not only did these encounters provide instruction, they also confirmed the divine origin of his calling. His community, meanwhile, conducted themselves with the knowledge that their victory was assured by the Prophet Muhammad and the Sufi saint, mediated through the shehu's leadership. The most decisive vision came when dan Fodio was given the so-called Sword of Truth by al-Qādir and told to draw it against the enemies of God. After such a vision, the jihad seemed inevitable. By means of a wide network of alliances and through a series of well-calculated military campaigns, dan Fodio succeeded in replacing most of the Hausa kings—branded as pagans by the reformers—with emirs loyal to the architects of the revolution. Having firmly secured the centers of power, the shehu and his followers set out to revive Islamic orthodoxy through the establishment of the *Shari'a* and the introduction of Islamic political structures and social institutions under the administration of a new caliphate based at Sokoto. Dan Fodio's jihad had far-reaching consequences as its example inspired similar revolutions aimed at purifying the religion throughout the mixed-Islamic kingdoms of West Africa for at least the next century.

Another important reformer who patterned his own career of jihad on that of dan Fodio's was al-Hájj 'Umar Tal al-Fútí (c. 1794–1864), who established the Tukolor empire in Futa Toro in Senegal in the mid-nineteenth century. Deeply steeped in the devotions of the Tíjáníyáh Súfi brotherhood, he was also exposed to radical Wahhabi teachings when he undertook the pilgrimage to Mecca in 1826. Wahhabism sought to eliminate what it considered to be syncretic practices in Islam—images, prayers to saints, the veneration of local holy sites, and the use of fetishes, amulets, or charms. The fires of reform were further stoked within al-Hájj 'Umar following his return from Mecca in 1832, when he stopped in Sokoto for a period of six years as the guest of Muhammad Bello, the son and heir of 'Uthman dan Fodio. After Bello's death in 1837, al-Hájj 'Umar returned to his home in Futa Toro, where in 1852 he declared a formal jihad that was waged for the next ten years against his non-Muslim neighbors. Al-Hájj 'Umar's jihad was successful; however his empire never achieved the glory of dan Fodio's Sokoto. Pressured by encroaching French colonial forces and dogged by anti-Tukolor rulers agitating from within, al-Hájj 'Umar eventually died in battle in 1864.

More recently, a genuinely prophetic movement emerged in West African Islam. It culminated in the Maitatsine Riots, which rocked northern Nigeria between 1980 and 1985, leaving more than 8,500 people dead. The sect's founder, Alhaji Muhammadu Marwa (c. 1922–1980), who hailed from Cameroon, proclaimed himself a prophet (contrary to the teachings of orthodox Islam). In 1962, Marwa was arrested and banished to Cameroon but he seems to have returned to Nigeria shortly thereafter. In 1975 he was again arrested on charges of political agitation after attracting a large following. By 1980 Marwa was besieged by controversy because he claimed to be a prophet, discarded Qur'an exegesis based in classical Arabic for his own bizarre brand of interpretation, and rejected the *sunna* of the Prophet. Central to his preaching was a rigorous rejection of affluence and Western material culture. Marwa's religion, appealed to a nonliterate crowd and had a decidedly anti-Hausa bias. Non-sect members, especially affluent ones, were regarded as infidels. In fact, his title, maitatsine, derives from the Hausa word *tsini* and means The Anathematizer. It is reported that the Maitatsine vigorously attacked his detractors declaring, "Allah ta tsini," "May God damn you." More than twenty years after the riots were put down and Alhaji Marwa was martyred in Kano by the military police, scholars still puzzle over the peculiarity of the movement. Reports of ritualized human butchery on the part of Maitatsine in order to make magic charms reveals as much about the resilience of animist culture and ideas as it does about the synthetic quality of Islamic (or Christian for that matter)

beliefs and practice in western Sudan. Whatever the case, the Maitatsine Riots that bubbled and seethed in Kano in the 1980s will be remembered as a highly exceptional and heterodox instance of prophetism in West African Islam.

PENTECOSTALISM

More recently, since the 1970s there has been a great proliferation of new churches, many of which are situated in the Evangelical or Protestant tradition. In particular, the rise of global Pentecostalism has made its strongest impact on the continent in western Africa, especially in the cities of Nigeria and Ghana, where everything from informal and makeshift prayer houses to multi-million-dollar mega-churches thrive. These new Pentecostal and charismatic churches are strongly influenced by movements based in the United States and Great Britain, and many of them are led by women and youth. The founders and pastors of the mega-churches are typically educated, whereas the entrepreneurs of smaller storefront churches with names such as "Glad Tidings Tabernacle," "Signs and Wonders Church," and "Hebron Divine Power Center" are usually not. In either case, personal charisma is the most necessary qualification for leadership. Although many preach a gospel of spiritual and material prosperity, not all do. An important continuity with the earlier prophetic movements is that the new Pentecostal churches attempt to speak to people on the most basic, existential level. They offer an encounter with God, in which healing from sickness and deliverance from evil is achieved by means of God's powerful spirit. Unlike many of the prophetic movements, however, nearly all would consider the need for a conversion experience in which one makes a personal decision to accept Jesus Christ and affirmation of the Bible as the literal and inerrant Word of God as essential tenets of the Christian faith. The Pentecostal churches also compete with some of the older so-called Spirit churches and other independent churches for members, many of whom are drawn to promises of prosperity and a way to exercise control over the myriad challenges that confront people living in contemporary Africa.

See also **'Abd al-Qādir; Accra; Bello, Muhammad; Braide, Garrick Sokari; Christianity; Dance: Social**

Meaning; Freetown; Harris, William Wadé; Kano; Literature: Oral; Music; Musical Instruments; Oshitelu, Josiah; Religion and Ritual; Spirit Possession; 'Uthman dan Fodio.

BIBLIOGRAPHY

Agbeti, J. Kofi. *West African Church History*. 2 vols. Leiden, The Netherlands: Brill, 1986, 1991.

Anderson, Allan H. *African Reformation: African Initiated Christianity in the 20th Century*. Trenton, NJ: Africa World Press, 2001.

Babalola, E. O. *Christianity in West Africa*. Ibadan, Nigeria: Scholar Publications International, 1976.

Baeta, C. G. *Prophetism in Ghana: A Study of Some "Spiritual" Churches*. London: SCM Press, 1962.

Crumbley, Deidre Helen. "Impurity and Power: Women in Aladura Churches." *Africa* 62, no. 4, (1992): 505–522.

Crumbley, Deidre Helen. "Patriarchies, Prophets, and Procreation: Sources of Gender Practices in Three African Churches." *Africa* 73, no. 4 (2003): 584–605.

Fernandez, James W. *Bwiti: An Ethnography of the Religious Imagination in Africa*. Princeton, NJ: Princeton University Press, 1982.

Gaiya, Musa. *Pentecostal Revolution in Nigeria*. Copenhagen, Denmark: Centre of African Studies, University of Copenhagen, 2002.

Gifford, Paul. "Liberia's Never-Die Christians." *The Journal of Modern African Studies* 30, no. 2 (1992): 349–358.

Gifford, Paul. "Deliverance and the Prophetic." In *Ghana's New Christianity: Pentecostalism in a Globalising African Economy*. Bloomington: Indiana University Press, 2004.

Haliburton, Gordon MacKay. *The Prophet Harris. A Study of an African Prophet and His Mass-Movement in the Ivory Coast and the Gold Coast 1913–1915*. New York: Oxford University Press, 1973.

Hastings, Adrian. *African Christianity*. New York: Seabury, 1976.

Hastings, Adrian. *A History of African Christianity: 1950–1979*. New York: Cambridge University Press, 1979.

Hastings, Adrian. "From Agbebi to Diangienda: Independency and Prophetism." In *The Church in Africa: 1450–1950*. New York: Oxford University Press, 1994.

Ibrahim, Jibrin. "Religion and Political Turbulence in Nigeria." *The Journal of Modern African Studies* 29, no. 1 (1991): 115–136.

Isichei, Elizabeth. "West Africa c. 1900 to c. 1960." In *A History of Christianity in Africa: From Antiquity to the Present*. Trenton, NJ: Africa World Press, 1995.

Isichei, Elizabeth. "African Initiated Churches: The Prophetic Model." In *The Religious Traditions of Africa: A History*. Westport, CT: Praeger, 2004.

Kalu, O. U. "Waves from the Rivers: The Spread of the Garrick Braide Movement in Igboland, 1914–1934." *Journal of Niger Delta Studies* 1, no. 2 (1977): 296–317.

Ludwig, Frieder "Elijah II: Radicalisation and Consolidation of the Garrick Braide Movement 1915–1918." *Journal of Religion in Africa* 23, Fasc. 4 (1993): 296–317.

Mary, André. "Pilgrimage to Imeko (Nigeria): An African Church in the Time of the 'Global Village.'" *International Journal of Urban and Regional Research* 26, Iss. 1 (2002): 106–120.

Ndiokwere, Nathaniel I. *Prophecy and Revolution: The Role of Prophets in the Independent Churches and in Biblical Tradition*. London: SPCK, 1981.

Offiong, Essein A. "Schism and Religious Independency in Nigeria: The Case of the Brotherhood of the Cross and Star." In *New Religious Movements in Nigeria*, ed Rosalind I. J. Hackett. Lewiston, NY: E. Mellen Press, 1987.

Omoyajowo, Akin. "The Aladura Churches in Nigeria Since Independence." In *Christianity in Independent Africa*, eds. Edward Fasholé-Luke, et al. London: Rex Collings, 1978.

Omoyajowo, J. Akinyele. *Cherubim and Seraphim: The History of an African Independent Church*. New York: NOK, 1982.

Opuku, Kofi A. "Changes within Christianity: The Case of the Musama Disco Christo Church." In *Christianity in Independent Africa*, eds. Edward Fasholé-Luke, et al. London: Rex Collings, 1978.

Peel, John D. Y. *Aladura: A Religious Movement among the Yoruba*. London: Oxford University Press, 1968.

Ray, Benjamin C. "Aladura Christianity: A Yoruba Religion." *Journal of Religion in Africa* 23, Fasc. 3 (1993): 266–291.

Sanneh, Lamin. *West African Christianity: The Religious Impact*. Maryknoll, NY: Orbis Books, 1983.

Shank, David. *Prophet Harris, the "Black Elijah" of West Africa*. New York: Brill, 1994.

Turner, Harold W. *History of an Independent African Church: Church of the Lord (Aladura)*. 2 vols. London: Clarendon, 1967.

Walker, Sheila S. *The Religious Revolution in the Ivory Coast: The Prophet Harris and the Harrist Church*. Chapel Hill: University of North Carolina Press, 1983.

MATTHEW KUSTENBAUDER

PROSTITUTION. Few aspects of women's work are as mystified as prostitution in modern Africa. Even after an eighteenth- and nineteenth-century vision of African sexual license had vanished from polite society, social scientists and reformers looked at prostitution in Africa and saw it as "natural" and "cultural"—confusing Africans' public tolerance for what women had to do to survive with a cultural condoning of the sale of sex for money. Following from this, a range of observers from the 1950s onward have looked at the sale of sexual relations in Africa and labeled and hierarchized them without regard for the strategies that informed the ways women practiced prostitution. An emphasis on which women were in bars, who formed short-term liaisons, who did not demand cash and who did was replaced, by the 1980s, by studies of HIV/AIDS and risk behaviors that created new hierarchies based on researchers' imaginings of how much choice women had of their customers.

In all of these cases, prostitutes were located in generalized notions of culture, but never in their families, households (those headed by themselves and those headed by husbands and lovers), and homesteads. Indeed, a close reading of the literature on prostitution in twentieth-century Africa reveals the flaws in such hierarchies: women went from bars to short-term liaisons in an evening; they demanded cash when their need for it was urgent and did not demand cash when they were negotiating another kind of relationship with a man. What women sought from their customers had less to do with the woman's personality and culture than it did with the labor market of the place where she worked: demanding cash from a man with low wages may have been far more advantageous than trying to establish a long-term relationship with him; forming a short-term liaison with a man whose job included housing might have been extremely advantageous to women who worked in cities where rents were high.

For most prostitutes in Africa, past and present, sex work was a way to earn money; a successful Nairobi prostitute who worked in the 1940s explained that most prostitutes did not seek jobs "because it was unlikely a woman would find a job that paid as much as 30 boyfriends" (White, 202). The absence of pimps throughout the continent enabled women to keep most of their earnings; even where there were taxi or rickshaw drivers, touts or go-betweens to arrange sexual encounters, these were usually paid by the man, not the woman. The kind of prostitution a woman chose to practice, however—whether she was on the street, in a house, or sitting outside her house—had to do with whom she was earning money for.

Streetwalking is generally considered the most contemptible form of prostitution, the work chosen by down-and-out desperate women whose moral character is even lower than those who work as prostitutes indoors. Such a crass generalization has little to support it, however. Streetwalkers maintained to this researcher that while working on the streets was difficult, the rewards were worth the difficulties—the streets were a place to earn a lot of money in a reasonably short period of time. If a woman was sending money home to support family and kin in depressed rural Africa, streetwalking was often the best strategy. The greatest risk, streetwalkers maintained, was repeated police harassment; they claimed they had more control over the customers they chose—and refused—than did women who "stayed inside their rooms."

For these reasons, streetwalking was a form of prostitution that homeless women could practice until they earned a month's rent, and hence it was the way many immigrants to urban Africa entered city life, but it was not a form women abandoned once they could rent accommodations. Indeed, many women rented rooms in areas where it was nominally illegal for Africans to live in order to be close to the most lucrative markets: men returning from work or men in cars ("a man with a car cannot tell you he has no money") were well worth a monthly investment of rent several times greater than it would have been in African areas.

But the risks and high financial costs of streetwalking meant that most women did not stay in it very long. As a form of prostitution into which women were often driven by crises at home, many women returned home and abandoned prostitution when the crisis had passed. Maasai women in early colonial Kenya, for example, whose cattle-keeping families had been devastated by the rinderpest epidemics of the late 1890s, were numerous among Nairobi's prostitutes in the first decade of this century; when Maasai herds were restocked by about 1911, Maasai women left prostitution and returned to the homes they had subsidized for years. At other times—in port cities when fleets arrived or during wartime—many prostitutes engaged in streetwalking briefly because the financial rewards were so high.

Women who stayed inside their rooms—a form of prostitution that had various names throughout the continent—have been mystified again and again. These women helped construct the mystification, maintaining that "no one could tell I was a prostitute." But there was much to support this fiction: unlike streetwalkers, these women were invisible to authorities and thus free from police harassment and public condemnation. As important was that these women provided a range of services to their customers, of which sexual relations was only one. A man who spent the night with a prostitute in her room in Nairobi from the 1920s on could expect breakfast and bathwater heated for him; men on the Zambian Copperbelt from the 1920s to the 1950s referred to the women they visited in their rooms as "good friends" who could cook for them and do their laundry. Such services were strategic; if women asked for payment when the encounter ended, she could charge for every cup of tea provided. Such a strategy produced a slower rate of accumulation than streetwalking did, but almost all women agreed that in the long run earnings in the aggregate were worth the wait, even including the times men refused to pay or delayed payment as long as they could.

More to the point, they were not selling sexual relations but domestic relations, those that men could only obtain through marriage. What men purchased when they visited and were served by a woman in her room was not only a fiction of marriage rights, but a vision of the proper relations of women to men. In northern Nigeria, *karuwai*—who were generally divorced women who lived together and catered to men's needs—sang, cooked, and had sexual relations with men in exchange for money. In much of the region, where divorce was frequent, men frequently stated a wish to marry *karuwai*, not to save them from a life of degradation, but because only women who had been *karuwai* knew how to look after a man. Where these prostitutes did not live together, they

tended to be well-regarded, if not respected, members of their communities. In 1930s and 1940s Johannesburg, before the intense segregation of apartheid was in place, prostitutes in urban yards blended into neighborhoods of shopkeepers, families, and migrant laborers. Many colonial and postcolonial officials observed the social service these women provided by allowing the migrant labor system to function smoothly, which did not require the higher wages a family presence would.

But the women who chose such a deferential form of prostitution seem to have done so because they were earning money for the most radical of lives: these women were not supporting families in rural Africa, and only occasionally were they supporting any kin but their children in town. Rather, they had established themselves as independent heads of households. The slow and steady saving by the women who stayed inside their rooms, measured in cups of tea and nights of conversation, was for women who had for the most part cut their ties with rural households and kin.

In very many cases, these women took their slowly acquired earnings from prostitution and invested in urban property, sometimes in legal townships and more often in squatters' settlements, where the risks of losing one's investment could be offset by the high rents charged there. It was this particular relationship of prostitutes to laboring men, and the states for whom they labored, that was most troubled: the same women officials saw as protecting the migrant labor system also provided the accommodation that gave a sense of place and belonging to the very laborers the states wanted to maintain as migrant. Thus when there have been attacks on prostitutes who practiced this form of prostitution, it has invariably been on the status and legality of these women's property ownership rather than anything to do with their prostitution.

Prostitution in Africa does not simply break down into neat dichotomies of women in their homes and on the streets. African prostitutes go to bars and nightclubs, of course. One well-known and frequently cited vision of that life comes from Cyprian Ekwensi's 1960s Nigerian novel *Jagua Nana*, in which the heroine is herself both a loyal lover to one man and a prostitute and which points to some of the ambiguities of successful nightclubbing and successful prostitution.

Indeed, most working streetwalkers maintain that going to bars or nightclubs is only a good strategy when used occasionally. Being well known in one bar could lower a woman's nightly earnings considerably, as men could argue that they should be charged what their friend paid last month. Besides, the overhead costs of a night on the town are not always easily recouped.

In many parts of Africa (as in many parts of the world, in fact) a form of prostitution developed that responded to several economic factors, including the density and high rents of the urban areas poverty of the rural areas. The form of prostitution in which women sat outside their rooms has often scandalized observers, who were at worst horrified to hear women calling low prices out to men passing by, and at best called it "commercialized prostitution," a telling comment on what some social scientists thought about women who stayed in their rooms. But in fact most women sat outside their rooms because their rooms were too small for anything but a bed; often the rooms were illegal structures added to urban housing and measuring under forty square feet.

The women who sat outside, known as *wazi-wazi* in Nairobi (from the Swahili word for open, as in exposed) or *tu tu* in west African towns (for the number two, as in two shillings), did so to make themselves and their prices well known. Other established local prostitutes were horrified by women shouting out low prices: these prices fixed pay rates for women. There was no negotiating and no need to prepare tea or food. "If a man knew in advance that he could go with me for 1 shilling, he would.... I wouldn't have to spend money on tea in the hopes that he would give me a few pennies in the morning" (White, 197). This was a form of prostitution favored by women who were supporting families at home—often they were the daughters of cash-crop producers impoverished by the decline in commodity prices during the depression. Often they came to Africa's cities in groups, living close together. They did not care for the niceties of looking after men, or of blending into the neighborhood: in Nairobi, *wazi-wazi* women were remembered for being the first prostitutes to fight fiercely with men if they refused to pay; they would call in their neighbors for physical support. The small rooms were tolerable for these women because they did not intend to stay for long. *Tu tu* prostitutes in Abidjan, Accra, and other west African towns had a fixed price and no protracted urban relations and could take their earnings back to northern Ghana and Burkina Faso whenever they liked. As an old woman said of the women from northwest Tanzania who dominated the *wazi-wazi* form in Nairobi in the late 1930s, "They didn't want to be rich here, they wanted to be rich in Tanganyika" (White, 114).

This form of prostitution combined its most aggressive aspects and was practiced by women who were earning as the most dutiful of daughters; it was generally engaged in by individual women for only a short time. It provided high earnings at tremendous social costs to the women, and for it to be financially successful required high male employment. But as rural households faced decline after decline, this form of prostitution became the choice of many rural women seeking to better the conditions of their families.

Prostitution in Africa—like prostitution anywhere else—is not a form of social pathology or cultural predisposition. It is one of the ways that women's work supports their families, and the specifics of the ways women in Africa have prostituted themselves have to do with the specific kinds of families they are supporting and creating, and the specific kinds of support their families require at the time.

See also **Disease: Sexually Transmitted; Gender; Labor: Migration; Sexual Behavior; Urbanism and Urbanization: Overview; Women.**

BIBLIOGRAPHY

Bujra, Janet M. "Women 'Entrepreneurs' of Early Nairobi." *Canadian Journal of African Studies* 9, no. 2 (1975): 213–234.

Chauncey, George W., Jr. "The Locus of Reproduction: Women's Labour in the Zambian Copperbelt, 1927–1953." *Journal of Southern African Studies* 7, no. 2 (1981): 135–164.

Cohen, Abner. *Custom and Politics in Urban Africa: A Study of Hausa Migrants in Yoruba Towns.* Berkeley: University of California Press, 1969.

Hollmann, Ellen. *Rooiyard: Sociological Survey of an Urban Native Slum Yard.* Rhodes-Livingston Papers. Cape Town: Oxford University Press, for Rhodes-Livingstone Institute, Livingstone, Northern Rhodesia, 1948.

COLONIALISM AND THE
STRUGGLE FOR DEMOCRACY

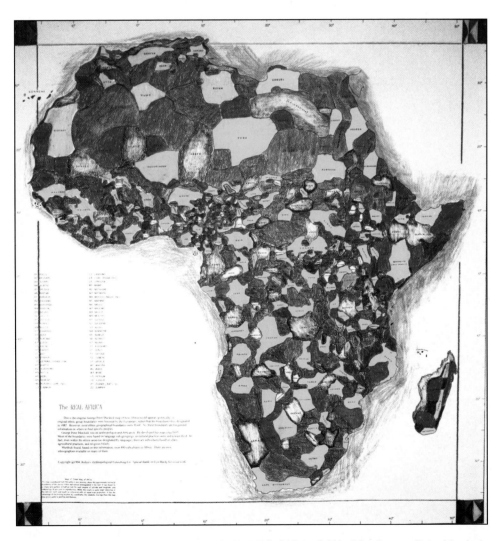

"The Real Africa." Based on the original "1855 Tribal Map of Africa" by George Peter Murdock, this map, hand-colored by Lyn Hardy, represents how Africa would appear politically if original ethnic group boundaries had been implemented rather than colonially designated borders. Published by Robyn's Anthropological Consulting Co., 1994, from the original *, Map 1-Tribal Map of Africa, in Africa: Its Peoples and Their Culture History* by George Peter Murdock. New York: McGraw-Hill, 1959. Size: 49 x 51 cm. Courtesy Robyn Michaels

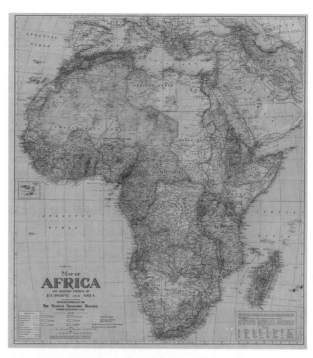

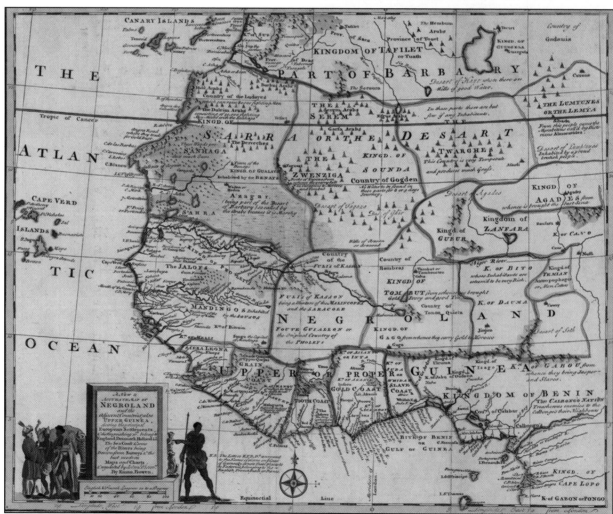

CHOCOLAT LOMBART

1883-1885. — Expédition au Congo de l'explorateur français de Brazza. Une attaque de nuit du campement.

TOP LEFT: Trading card showing French explorers attacked in the Congo. The melodramatic juxtaposition of the dark, savage "other" and the "enlightened" European is typical of colonial views. The legacy of the Franco-Italian Pierre de Brazza, the subject of this card and creator of the colony whose capital bears his name, remains contested, with some Congolese honoring him as a founding father and others charging him with rapine and pillage. © STEFANO BIANCHETTI/CORBIS

BELOW: Waterhole in the slave building, Janjanbureh (Georgetown), McCarthy Island, Gambia. Slaves awaiting transport had only this river water to drink. Slavery existed in Africa for centuries, but European exploitation for the New World institutionalized it on a gigantic scale. © MICHAEL MARTIN

TOP LEFT: Remnants of French nuclear test, Algeria. The 1960–1966 tests in the Sahara Desert were among the last manifestations of French rule in this North African colony, which ended in 1962. Elsewhere in Africa, France has continued to intervene in the affairs of its former colonies. © MICHAEL MARTIN

BOTTOM LEFT: Anti-corruption billboard in Kisoro, Uganda. Personal appropriations of funds, particularly from foreign donors and investors, have funded politics of patronage in many African countries. "Structural adjustment" programs required by the World Bank and International Monetary Fund since the 1980s have encouraged some governments to address such "corruption." © IVAN VDOVIN/JAI/CORBIS

TOP RIGHT: Jomo Kenyatta. Kenya's revolutionary leader, imprisoned by the British for his alleged Mau Mau affiliation, became the republic's first president in 1964. JASON LAURÉ/ LAURÉ COMMUNICATIONS

BELOW: Egyptian presidents. Iconic images of Presidents Mubarak, Nasser, and Sadat on display in Cairo. Egypt has had but three leaders since 1954. Authoritarian rulers have manipulated foreign governments and domestic electoral processes to remain in power for long periods in many African nations. © MICHAEL MARTIN

TOP LEFT: Protest in Bénin. Beninese students display scatological disrespect toward the visiting French interior minister (later president) Nicolas Sarkozy in 2006. Restrictions on immigration were the immediate flashpoint, but French military interventions and economic policies have been harshly contested in the postcolonial era. AP IMAGES

BOTTOM LEFT: Protest at the World Bank, 2007. World Bank and International Monetary Fund policies requiring reductions in spending by indebted African governments have motivated protests around the world. In one such protest, in Washington, DC, the group known as Debt, AIDS, Trade, Africa (DATA) dramatizes the claim that such policies impede access to education for Africans. AP IMAGES

TOP RIGHT: Angolan teen soldier, 1993. Portuguese disengagement amid the absence of a functional government led to prolonged civil war in Angola, fueled by competing foreign economic interests. Here, as in Liberia and Côte d'Ivoire, hard-pressed governments and factions have made use of ever-younger youths and children. AP IMAGES

BOTTOM RIGHT: Samburu ranger. The Samburu cattle herders of northern Kenya fend for themselves in a remote area. In this region, desertification, Somali civil wars, and weak government institutions leave them largely reliant for security on tactics derived from many years of protecting livestock from earlier marauders. © MICHAEL MARTIN

Southall, Aiden W., and Peter C. W. Gutkind. *Townsmen in the Making: Kampala and Its Suburbs.* Kampala: East African Institute of Social Research, 1957.

White, Luise. *The Comforts of Home: Prostitution in Colonial Nairobi.* Chicago: University of Chicago Press, 1990.

LUISE WHITE

PROVERBS. *See* Literature: Proverbs and Riddles.

PSYCHOLOGY AND THE STUDY OF AFRICA.

Following Helen Dunmore, writing in London's *Times* (who holds that truths are unraveled in fictions), psychologists would do well to include literature in a broad spectrum of ways of knowing about (individual) human nature. This broad spectrum would include the disciplined means of the systematically representative survey and carefully controlled experiment, along with emerging strands of enquiry within social psychology such as discourse analysis. Each of these ways may contribute to deeper knowledge, though each way is also sometimes considered to be insufficiently narrow in itself. In European and North American nations, such different pathways tend to be compartmentalized, and this separation may be reflected also in Africa. However, it may be useful to draw into the project of continuing to develop a psychology in Africa a consideration of the large and growing corpus of African literary work in the two largely separate worlds of English and French.

In 2006 J. C. Munene of Uganda's Makerere University called upon applied psychologists "to resume interest in African Affairs the way Professor Berry, Jahoda, etcetera, did in the sixties and early seventies." Munene noted that "well-funded departments in European and American Universities" could "focus on current African problems that the World Bank, IMF, and Northern governments are funding rather profusely. The current areas include poverty, HIV/AIDS, macro-and microeconomics, governance, corruption, capacity building, etcetera. Such a psychology could be free from attractive but long-term goals of searching for an African Psychology...." In this call, Munene

implies that there has been some relaxation of the pace of work set in the early postcolonial phase that was summed up by Wober (1976). That phase seemed unsatisfactory to some, who felt it imported concepts and methods mostly alien to the people to whose lives they were applied.

There has since been a huge increase in the number of universities in Africa, and also in the psychology departments they house. Much of the work that has come from these places has found a forum in the *Journal of Psychology in Africa* (published in South Africa by the National Inquiry Services Centre); as well as this outlet for Africa-based research in the field, the Organization for Social Science Research in Eastern and Southern Africa (OSSREA) has compiled a CD (2006) offering "a database of documents (most of them with full text) and their bibliographic references. The publications include books, research publications, official documents, abstracts, workshops and newsletters." OSSREA appears to have no counterpart in West and in Saharan Africa, partly because neither English nor French has prevailed as a language of academic expression in those regions, nor has any single African language emerged as the vehicle for such a forum.

Psychological teaching and research has thus spread throughout Africa, building on the narrower start established up until the 1960s mostly by expatriate workers. One way of taking stock of progress and of looking for where and how to go forward may be to list some of the major topics that were reviewed by Wober and to consider what these may mean for the world at large and, conversely, what developments in the wider world of psychology may have to offer for understanding and for policy advice in Africa.

Five areas of psychological functioning may be examined. These include: early child physical and cognitive development; the notions that there are different types of human ability and that the profiles and levels of abilities developed in a population differ across cultures; an emerging view that the human condition may better be evaluated in terms of psychological measures—of well-being—than by the more usual economic indicators such as GNP; in societies where powerful and different traditions (of modernity and of traditional culture) overlap, what this double consciousness may entail for individuals in terms of developing attitudes that may either recognize logical contradictions and drive toward some kind of cognitive resolution, or who may, on the other hand, develop an approach that may compartmentalize and live in two or more seemingly contradictory worlds; and whether the incidence and forms of mental ill health and individual adjustment to society show vital differences between cultures, or whether universals of dysfunction may be identified.

EARLY CHILDHOOD PHYSICAL AND COGNITIVE DEVELOPMENT

The picture portrayed in the 1976 analysis was that, in many African societies, babies showed high degrees of vitality and promise for mental development. However, after a late weaning and a displacement from much significant one-to-one relationship with one or both parents, tested cognitive abilities fell behind levels observed in other populations worldwide—both those that were literate and some non-literate, such as among Inuit and South Sea Island peoples. Some analysts took what others considered a racist view: that a genetic blight had descended upon Africa's populations. Others considered that poor nutrition and health, as well as a relative lack of individual cognitive support (encouragement to read and write, as well as to sing, dance, and participate in stories—which experiences are highly fostered in many African societies) are first and preferred lines of explanation for any seeming cognitive deficits. A new summary of current research on these matters would be useful; it would point to whether and how cognitive development may have improved or not; it would help direct investments in teaching, nutrition and health care, as practical matters.

In the last decade, expensive machines for examining brain function have been used in wealthy countries, more so in America and Europe than in Africa, and it would be useful to see what these techniques might reveal amongst young African children—comparing the middle classes with the poor. There are signs that poor nutrition at an early age hampers development of pathways that connect the left and right sides of the brain, thus retarding the emergence of coordinated intellectual functioning. Any positive results of such study would be of universal significance, underlining the unity and robustness of humankind; on the other hand, any deficits discovered

would point to remedial measures that would deserve urgent attention.

DIFFERENCES IN MODELS OF INTELLIGENCE

Robert Sternberg (1999) has drawn from research in Africa and in other continents to support the notion that intelligence is not a universal construct but takes different shapes and natures in different cultures. He has gone on to develop ideas on how intelligence may be successfully maximized—and it follows that these strategies will also take different forms in different cultures. Lessons may emerge here on the matter of conflict resolution and reconciliation.

MEASURES OF WELL-BEING

The economist Lord Layard (2003) has shown that multinational surveys reveal that happiness increases markedly with national prosperity at the lowest and ascending levels of prosperity until a turning point is reached, at which further gains in prosperity—measured by GDP—correlate only weakly with further increases in happiness. Of the 55 countries surveyed, only three are in Africa—Nigeria, Ghana and South Africa—and all three stand at the turning point at which it becomes harder to increase happiness merely by increasing the national GDP. Layard seems to imply that happiness is a uniform construct; however, much of what is shown in literature suggests that happiness is made up differently in different cultures. What this variation may entail for economic planning and policy remains to be debated—and much deeper and widespread study of the architecture of happiness could well be carried out in Africa.

IS COGNITIVE DISSONANCE NECESSARILY DISSOLVED?

The American psychologist Leon Festinger (1957) theorized that "when there is an inconsistency between attitudes or behaviors (dissonance), something must change to eliminate the dissonance. In the case of a discrepancy between attitudes and behavior, it is most likely that the attitude will change to accommodate the behavior." Dissonance may be likely to occur among people in African societies that have been greatly changing in the twentieth century, and where individuals have different models from traditional and evolving cultures of career development and ideal personality acquired. If there is an element in traditional culture that discounts the need to resolve dissonance, this background may have important consequences for behavior and design in modern roles and workplaces. Some older studies have held that dissonance resolution was strongly at work. Other studies—as by Wober in Nigeria—implied that resolution was by no means such an imperative. Ayanna Gillian (2003), a Tobagan scholar, has argued this as it applies not only to Caribbean but also to advanced industrial populations such as in the United States. Whatever strategies to resolve or accommodate cognitive dissonance, are adopted nowadays by individuals when confronted by logically conflicting cultural norms in different African cultures and at different levels within them will bear strongly on how societies adapt to their current problems, and the matter calls for substantial study.

PATTERNS OF ADJUSTMENT OF THE SELF TO SOCIETY

Different cultures define and deal with personally and socially dysfunctional feeling and behavior in different ways. Ben Okri (1991) vividly described a culture in which a spiritual world is not only recognized but that also infuses normal life. Conditions that secularized European and North American societies would label delusional or paranoid are normal, if problematic in Okri's world; they have implications for the adaptation of European forms of democracy in Africa, and for the practice of psychiatry. The arrival of the twenty-first century is most unlikely to have seen traditional faiths disappear. On the contrary, Africa as a fountain of faith has given strength to a Christendom flagging in Europe—an African is now Archbishop of York—and the world of Islam has also been reinforced in Africa south of the Sahara.

Institutions in the European mould may lack courage or facilities to conduct surveys or deploy expensive brain scanning equipment amongst peoples who have suffered natural disasters and civil wars; yet knowledge that could lead to a better life could be increased by research at such locations. Not least, the rest of the world and Africa itself may learn more about how its societies practice reconciliation after wars and revolutions.

See also **Children and Childhood: Infancy and Early Development; Literacy; Person, Concepts of; Research: Social Sciences.**

BIBLIOGRAPHY

Dunmore, Helen. "Truths Are Unravelled in Fictions." September 23, 2006. Available from http://www.timesonline.co.uk/article

Festinger, Leon. *A Theory of Cognitive Dissonance.* Evanston, IL: Row, Peterson, 1957.

Gillian, Ayanna. "Thoughts on Cognitive Dissonance." September 3, 2003. Available from http://www.rootswomen.com/ayanna

Layard, Richard. "Happiness: Has Social Science a Clue?" Lionel Robbins Memorial Lectures 2002/3, London School of Economics, delivered on March 3–5, 2003. Available at http://cep.lse.ac.uk/events/lectures/layard/RL030303.pdf

Lynn, Richard. *Race Differences in Intelligence: An Evolutionary Analysis.* Augusta, Georgia: Washington Summit, 2006.

Munene, John C. "Applied Psychology in Africa." Available from http://www.iaapsy.org/drafts

Okri, Ben. *The Famished Road* London: Jonathan Cape, 1991.

Sternberg, Robert J. "The Theory of Successful Intelligence." *Review of General Psychology* 3 (1999): 292–316.

Wober, Joseph Mallory. *Psychology in Africa.* London: International African Institute, 1976.

JOSEPH MALLORY WOBER

PUBLIC HEALTH. *See* **Healing and Health Care.**

PUBLISHING. *See* **Media: Book Publishing; Media: Comic Art; Media: Journalism.**

PUNT. *See* **Nubia.**

QADHDHAFI, MUAMMAR (c. 1940–).

Born into the Qathadfa tribe and educated in Libya, Muammar Buminyar Qadhdhafi has seven children from two marriages. Qadhdhafi engineered a military coup on September 1, 1969, that toppled the conservative Sanusi monarchy. Qadhdhafi was highly influenced by his political mentor, the late President Nasser of Egypt. The untimely death of Nasser in 1970, coupled with the hostility he experienced from Nasser's successor, prompted Qadhdhafi to develop and promote his own Third International Theory that he based on *People Power*. His system embodies two parallel structures: People's Committees, which are chosen from the populous and tasked with administering the country; and Revolutionary Committees that oversee them and promote Qadhdhafi's ideology. The Revolutionary Committees are not bound by any legal structure and are accountable only to the Libyan leader.

Colonel Qadhdhafi's years as dictator have been turbulent and destabilizing for Libya and the world. He has been accused of fomenting global terror, assassinating opponents, and launching wars on his neighbors. His belligerent foreign policy prompted attacks on Libya by Egypt and the United States and, from 1992 until 2003, a United Nations' embargo for having downed civilian airliners in Scotland and Niger. The embargo was lifted and relations with the U.S. and the West were reestablished after the colonel assumed responsibility and paid billions of dollars in compensation to the victims. With his position secure,

Libyan leader Muammar Qadhdhafi (c. 1940–).
Qadhdhafi holds no public office or official title, but in official press releases he has been given lengthy titles including "Brotherly Leader and Guide of the Revolution." © KHALED EL-FIQI/EPA/CORBIS

he has turned to promoting his ideology in Africa and grooming his children to succeed him. Libya continues to be one of the least free countries in the world.

See also **Libya; Nasser, Gamal Abdel; Warfare.**

BIBLIOGRAPHY

African Studies Center, University of Pennsylvania. "Libya Page." Available from http://www.africa.upenn.edu/Country_Specific/Libya.html.

El-Kikhia, Mansour O. *Libya's Qaddafi: The Politics of Contradiction*. Gainesville: University Press of Florida, 1997.

MANSOUR EL-KIKHIA

QUAQUE, PHILIP

QUAQUE, PHILIP (1741–1816). The cleric and educator Philip Quaque, also called Philip Lweku, was the first African to be ordained a priest in the Church of England. Born at Cape Coast (modern Ghana) during the slaving era, he was a protégé (some sources implausibly say the son) of the local chief, Caboceer Cudjoe, who maintained good relations with the British and helped preserve Cape Coast within the British sphere of influence. At the age of thirteen Philip was sent to England for education, sponsored by the Society for the Propagation of the Gospel in Foreign Parts, known after its initials as SPG. During his study in England he was ordained first as deacon of the Anglican church by the bishop of Exeter at the Chapel Royal in St. James on March 25, 1765, then as priest on May 1, 1765, by the bishop of London. He married an English woman, Catherine Blunt, in London in 1765, and returned to Cape Coast in 1766 as the Reverend Philip Quaque, with the official title of "Missionary, School Master, and Catechist to the Negroes on the Gold Coast." He went there in the joint service of the SPG and the Company of Merchants Trading to Africa, an association of British merchants engaged in the slave trade. Quaque was also designated chaplain at Cape Coast Castle. He died at Cape Coast on October 17, 1816, aged seventy-five.

Quaque's career can be divided into two aspects. The first part centered on his religious duties as missionary and chaplain, and it was the less distinguished of the two. As chaplain at Cape Coast Castle, with responsibility sometimes extending to other British coastal trading castles at Dixcove, Sekondi, and Komenda, Quaque propagated "fortress Christianity," with the inevitable consequence of sealing the religion from any genuine indigenous response. Second, fortress Christianity, tied to the vestiges of medieval Christendom, targeted chiefs and rulers, the fittest of the fit, as alone worthy of Christian baptism. Since these chiefs and rulers acted from political expedience, they resisted baptism for fear of compromising their authority by unwittingly conceding sovereignty to some foreign Christian monarch. After some forty-five years of dogged attempts, Quaque finally wrote to London in October 1811 admitting failure as a missionary. He was beaten by what he called African indifference.

The second aspect of his career concerned his educational work, and there also he had mixed success. As an organized institution, Quaque's school was for the most part an ad hoc affair. He tried but failed to construct a new building for the school, and enrollment fluctuated wildly, between sixteen at its highest to one or none at all. The elitist shadow of fortress Christianity had fallen over it, too. In 1789 Quaque was reporting that the school was being reestablished in the fort as a charity boarding school for needy mulatto children. However, the reports of progress the school was making by 1791 proved premature, for decline soon set in. Support for the work from the European Castle community and its African clients was lost, and Quaque felt the local population was too hostile to the school to fill the gap. However, one tangible result of the school was the few individuals who were trained there and who in turn became teachers, thus perpetuating the tradition of primary school education at Cape Coast and in other Fante areas.

Quaque himself paid a personal price for having become the advocate of fortress Christianity. He lived under the constraints of castle politics, cultivated English manners and customs, and abandoned the Fante tongue for English. He relied on translators in his dealings with Africans. In less challenging times, all of that might have turned him into nothing more curious than an eccentric, but in those early years eccentricity was tantamount to cultural rejection. Garrisoned in his trading enclave, Quaque failed to become an effective mediator between Africa and Europe. On the African side, he complained often of unreasonable demands and expectations. His second and third wives after the death of Catherine Blunt in November 1766 were African, and that entailed extended family duties and obligations. Yet Quaque resented those duties and obligations as unwarranted, so Westernized had he become.

It is the unalterable nature of the duties and obligations of African family life that offers a rare glimpse into how Africa's encounter with Europe would falter in cultural misunderstanding. Quaque could have served as a transitional figure to great consequence, but he did not.

However, Quaque's proximity to chiefs and rulers allowed him to observe at close hand the nature and functioning of indigenous institutions, and their responses to Western influences. His position at the strategic intersection of Cape Coast, the center of Fante politics, and Kumasi, the hub of Asante power makes him extremely valuable as a source in understanding late-eighteenth- and early-nineteenth-century political relations in that part of western Africa. Similarly, his comments on the ambivalent attitude of chiefs and other members of the political aristocracy to the European presence at Cape Coast reveals the limited value of chiefs, whom Quaque said created obstacles rather than providing bridges, in efforts to establish Christianity in Africa. In Quaque's judgment, chiefly authority thus filled an ambivalent role in facilitating Western contact with Africa, while, on the other hand, it deflected it, too. Such a mixed verdict is appropriate to Quaque himself.

See also **Christianity; Colonial Policies and Practices; Education, School.**

BIBLIOGRAPHY

Bartels, F. L. "Philip Quaque, 1741–1816." *Transactions of the Gold Coast and Togoland Historical Society* 1 (1995): 153–177.

Priestley, Margaret. "Philip Quaque of Cape Coast." In *Africa Remembered: Narratives by West Africans from the Era of the Slave Trade,* ed. Philip D. Curtin. Madison: University of Wisconsin, 1967.

LAMIN SANNEH

QUEENS AND QUEEN MOTHERS.

Men dominate in African monarchies: The model of a king's authority is based on patriarchal authority exercised by heads of descent groups and households. However, in most monarchies, one or two high-ranking women participate in the exercise of royal power and occupy a position complementary to that of the king. It should be noted that, in the published literature, the translations into English of indigenous terms for these positions are often both confused and confusing.

There are a few known instances in Africa of women ruling in their own right as queens. The Lovedu of the Transvaal are the best-known example; others include the Merina and Sakalava of Madagascar. In each of these cases their gender is ambiguous: the Merina use a non-gender-specific term: the person who rules; the Sakalava queen was spoken of familiarly as if a sexually promiscuous woman, yet addressed in male terms and given the prerogatives of a man, and she was prohibited from bearing children. It is perhaps significant that in these three cases, women took over from previous reigns of men in the nineteenth century, when the kingdoms were coming under colonial rule. These changes may have been related to efforts to evade direct colonial administration by removing the seat of indigenous kingship to a less obviously political (non-male) context.

In Sierra Leone, British colonial authorities installed female paramount chiefs, but women among the Mende and Sherbro seem always to have exercised leadership in the public domain—as founders of towns, lineage heads, officials in the Sande secret society, and later as land chiefs. Indeed in Sierra Leone, the position of paramount chief was a colonial invention.

THE RAIN-QUEEN

The classic case of a woman ruling in her own right in Africa is that of Mujaji, the Rain-Queen of the Lovedu, a small kingdom in the Transvaal, South Africa. Mujaji I came to the throne about 1800, following previous reigns of male kings; her successors have all been women who have exercised little political authority. With only the powers of persuasion, not of coercion, these queens rely on strategy, diplomacy, and power derived from their control of rain medicine throughout the region, so they have a reputation for being able to turn the clouds into rain. Their mystical powers are said to have originated as a consequence of royal incest: Mujaji is rumored to have been conceived through incest between her mother and her mother's own father, the previous king.

The Rain-Queen occupies the center of a complex network of political links and obligations expressed in the idiom of kinship. Symbolically she is both masculine and feminine. She has no husband and should bear no children, but she has many wives, given to her by chiefs and nobles in return for rain. She allocates these wives to nobles, and the children of this union recognize her as their father. She dies by her own hand, taking poison, and is buried secretly at the royal mausoleum far from ordinary eyes. (The Rain-Queen was the subject of H. Rider Haggard's novel *She: A History of Adventure* [1887] that concerns a mythical queen of fair complexion, rumored to have powers over the intrepid explorers who penetrated her secret realm.)

EGYPT'S QUEEN

In ancient Egypt, there was usually only one male, native-born king at any given time, though occasionally there was a co-regent. A number of queens acted as regent and ruled on behalf of their young sons. Though there are a number of unresolved ambiguities concerning her reign in the Eighteenth Dynasty of the New Kingdom, Queen Hatshepsut (d. 1482 BCE; ruled 1479–1485 BCE) was undoubtedly the most influential woman Egypt ever knew. New Kingdom queens had a more public position than during the Old and Middle Kingdoms—they had a range of secular and religious titles, owned their own estates, and were associated with various goddesses and cults. Hatshepsut was the eldest daughter of Pharaoh Tuthmosis I. She married her half-brother Tuthmosis II (d. c. 1479 BCE) and when he died was regent for her stepson/nephew Tuthmosis III (d. c. 1450 BCE). After a short time as regent, she was officially transformed into a female king: She took a royal name limited to kings and made offerings directly to the gods—a prerogative of the divine pharaohs. She rewrote her history to include her own divine conception and birth, carried male regalia including the false beard traditionally worn only by a king, and dressed in male clothing. She never attempted to establish a solo reign. Tuthmosis III was the junior partner in the co-regency, and when Hatshepsut died, Tuthmosis III reigned alone.

Hatshepsut's rule was prosperous and included many building projects—including the Deir el-Bahri temple at Luxor. Following her death, at the end of the reign of Thuthmosis III, there was a determined effort to delete Hatshepsut's name from history. Her rule was omitted from the official king list and her name and most of the monuments showing her as king were destroyed and recarved with the name of her father or husband, Thutmose I and II—though images of Hatshepsut as queen consort (the correct place for a female royal) were not defaced. Fourteen hundred years later, Cleopatra VII (69–30 BCE) inspired myths and legends as the ambitious and bewitching Egyptian queen of Hellenistic and Roman Egypt. The daughter of King Ptolemy XII (117–51 BCE) of Macedonian descent, Cleopatra ruled as co-regent with her brother-husband; and when he died she proclaimed her infant son allegedly the child of Julius Caesar; 100–44 BCE as co-regent and essentially ruled Egypt alone.

OTHER AFRICAN REGNANT WOMEN

Although most African monarchies do not have regnant queens, in most of them certain senior women serve important roles as royal wives, queen mothers, queen sisters, or as regents for immature kings-to-be who are too young to be given the powers of rulership. Such women are deemed to be essential ingredients of royal power and authority. Symbolically and politically these female office-holders' behavior largely resembles gender relations in the wider society in which men dominate in the political sphere, yet are dependent on women for nurturing and regeneration. Regnant women, further, are often given symbolic attributes of sacredness and of maleness. These women's positions complement that of a male king and their role may also allow them to supplement, modify, soften, or even publicly correct a king's behavior or political decision.

There are many variations on how their basic principle is realized in actual organization and behavior. The male and female elements of a single kingship may be separated in space, time, political and ritual status, legal roles, and a great number of symbolic attributes and forms of behavior. The Lozi of Zambia divide their kingdom into north and south and have two identical capitals twenty-five miles apart: The southern one is ruled by a sister of the king (who has her own chiefs, councilors, and army) and is a sanctuary from the king's anger. Among the Akan of Ghana and the Nyoro of Uganda, queen mothers or official sisters exercise secular authority similar to that of senior chiefs. Among the Luba of Zaire, such women more resemble spirit mediums or tomb guardians. The queen mother of the Shi of eastern Democratic Republic of the Congo (who holds as her private domain approximately half the land in the kingdom) may rule as regent for years until her son comes of age and is powerful enough to end her rule. She is a symbolically complementary aspect of the kingship, and both she and her son share a single essence that embodies both masculine and feminine traits.

In a parallel fashion, the Aluund (Lunda) king of southwestern Zaire is both a father and the nurturing female who possesses regenerative power for his people. He is secluded and symbolically sexless, and without bodily orifices. Outside everyday ordinary human and social exchange a senior wife guards his body, and it is believed that the well being of this body symbolically reflects the unity and well-being of the people, animals, and crops.

Kings in Africa almost always have (or had) many wives following the model of the polygynous family. To have many wives was a symbol of high status, and children could enhance the influence of their father, or (in a patrilineal kingship) build up his lineage. The wives, as representatives of their various clans, could exercise influence on behalf of their own clan heads, but at the same time they jointly bound the kingdom together. Royal spouses were given different titles and were attached to the king in various ways. Among the Swazi, representative headmen from throughout the country provided the bridewealth for the kings' main wife (who was rarely, if ever, his first wife). A king's wives seldom reigned alongside the king as did his sister or mother, and it should be noted that the indigenous term designating a king's wife is frequently used metaphorically for the numerous attendants who serve the king, regardless of their sex.

Among the Luba of Democratic Republic of the Congo, important female office holders include certain of the king's wives and the Mwadi, a female spirit medium who incarnates the spirit of a deceased king and inherits his emblems, titles, and residence. Forbidden to have sexual relations and provided with wives of her own, the Mwadi was treated as though she were a king herself. At the beginning of the colonial period, there were said to be at least four reigning Mwadi wielding greater authority than the then-ruling king.

The role of the queen mother among the Asante and other matrilineal Akan peoples of Ghana have attracted both scholarly attention and flights of imagination. To begin with, she is not a queen mother in the English sense of the term—that is, she is not the actual mother of the ruling king (she may, indeed, be his sister) and she is neither a woman who rules nor is she the king's wife. Further, she is not a high priestess of a cult associated with women and the moon (as has been fancifully asserted by some writers). Her authority is respected, but she has little formal power. And although the term queen mother is a gender-specific one for chief (*ohene* plus the female suffix), the *ohemmea* is not simply a female chief. Her royal status is that of a man: She adjudicates issues as the only woman among men; she dresses as a man; and (in Asante) when she is married, unlike other women, she is not bound exclusively to her husband.

The Akan kingship structure is replicated at different levels of Akan society: the word ohemmea was adopted originally for an elder woman in the king's lineage, but the title in the last three or four decades of the twentieth century has been used far more loosely to refer to honorary queen mothers, market queen mothers, queen mothers of seamstresses, prostitutes, and the like. The Akan queen mother is symbolically and politically important, but she is not the symbol of the kingship as is the king. Rather, whether or not she actually has children, she personifies nurturing motherhood; and is the affective link to the matrilineal ancestors. She is also the first publicly to weep for the previous year's dead in the annual royal purification rite, and is invoked in arbitrations as the symbolic creator and destroyer and the ultimate arbiter in decision-making.

The queen mother is also appealed to as an advocate and protector to fugitives from the king's court, and performs these functions without undermining the kingdom's stability. In Asante her judicial court is less costly than that of the king, and the members of her court are men. In the past in some Akan kingdoms, the queen mother took part in rites pertaining to women: puberty, naming rites for infants, and ridding the town of pollution. Politically most important is that she symbolizes the lineage that produced the king, and her wisdom (that is, her knowledge of genealogy that is held to derive from her biological role in reproduction) enables her to legitimize the selection of the king and to advise and rebuke him should he misuse his power as king. She continues to reign whether or not the ruling king's position falls vacant, and she must take part in the selection of his successor.

The Ganda of Uganda, who are patrilineal, exemplify the complex field of roles played by royal women. The kingship is divided between one being the living ruler and the wife or wives, one of whom will bear the future heir to the kingship in a palace at Mengo, the kingdom's capital in Kampala, and the other being the deceased king with a palace in the form of a complex of royal shrines several miles away. The gender-neutral title of Kabaka is used for the regnant king and the effigy of the deceased king, as well as for several women, including the queen mother (his actual mother), the queen sister (the senior of his sisters or half-sisters), and, it seems, the chief wife who is in charge of the king's charms. Also important is the royal midwife, who is the queen mother's sister. There is no royal clan. The king belongs to his mother's clan. After the king's accession his mother is traditionally forbidden to see him, and she may bear no further children. She becomes queen mother with her own lands, subjects, palace, and court officials. Ganda princesses, including the queen sister, who undergoes her brother's accession rite jointly with him, must have no children and are called by male names. At her brother's death, the queen sister retires to guard his relic (his jawbone) in his shrine

and acts as a medium when he is consulted by his successors. These women, although highly powerful in a temporal sense, owe the king neither tribute nor political obedience, yet together they form an integral part of the total kingship.

A widespread but not universal concept associated with kings and these female royal kin is that of an original act of royal incest from which the line of kings has descended. The brother-sister or father-daughter incest that figures in the royal myths of origin removes the actors from an ordered moral world, and their offspring are thereby set apart, given the dangerous status of the sacred, and placed above the everyday conflicts of interest within the kingdom itself. Luc de Heusch (1972) suggests that this incest sacralizes sexual relations and fertility throughout the kingdom, and has to do with the perceived opposition and complementarity of the sexes. Monarchy, he says, is founded on the sacred triad of king, sister, and mother.

Other well-known examples of queen mothers are found in the kingdoms of Mundang in Chad, those of the Cameroon Grasslands, the Bénin of Nigeria, and Zululand. They differ primarily only in detail from those described above. The kings were (and are) surrounded by a proliferation of courtiers and titled officials, as well as by their queen mothers, sisters, and consorts. These women held (and hold) uniquely prestigious and powerful positions in the political hierarchy of the kingdom. Their status was equivalent to that of high-ranking male chiefs, they generally possessed their own court with chiefs and retainers, and their power was often expressed visually in art and ritual regalia.

See also **Gender; Kings and Kingdoms; Kinship and Affinity; Kinship and Descent.**

BIBLIOGRAPHY

Boeck, Filip de. "Of Trees and Kings: Politics and Metaphor among the Aluund of Southwestern Zaire." *American Ethnologist* 21, no. 3 (1994): 451–473.

Cohen, Ronald. "Oedipus Rex and Regina: The Queen Mother in Africa." *Africa* 47, no. 1 (1977): 13–30.

Feeley-Harnik, Gillian. "Issues in Divine Kingship." *Annual Review of Anthropology* 13 (1985): 273–313

Gilbert, Michelle. "The Cimmerian Darkness of Intrigue: Queen Mothers, Christianity, and Truth in Akuapem History." *Journal of Religion in Africa* 23, no. 1 (1993): 2–43.

Haggard, Henry Rider. *She: A History of Adventure.* London: Longmans, 1887.

Heusch, Luc de. *The Drunken King or The Origin of the State,* trans. Roy Willis. Bloomington: University of Indiana Press, 1972.

Kaplan, F., ed. *Queens, Queen Mothers, Priestesses and Power: Case Studies in African Gender.* New York: The New York Academy of Sciences, 1977.

Krige, E. Jensen, and J. D. Krige. *The Realm of a Rain-Queen: A Study of the Pattern of Lovedu Society.* London: Oxford University Press, 1943.

MacCormack, Carol. "Mende and Sherbro Women in High Office." *Canadian Journal of African Studies* 6, no. 2 (1972): 151–164.

Ray, Benjamin C. *Myth, Ritual, and Kingship in Buganda.* New York: Oxford University Press, 1991.

Roberts, Mary Nooter, and Allen F. Roberts, eds. *Memory: Luba Art and the Making of History.* New York: Rosen Publications, 1996.

Roehig, Catharine, ed., with Renee Dreyfus and Cathleen Keller. *Hatshepsut: From Queen to Pharaoh.* New York: The Metropolitan Museum of Art and Yale University Press, 2005.

Tyldesley, Joyce. *Hatshepsut: The Female Pharaoh.* London: Penguin Books, 1996.

MICHELLE GILBERT

RABAT AND SALÉ.

Rabat, the Pearl of Morocco, overlooks the Atlantic Ocean and the mouth of the Oued Bou Regreg river where it faces the city of Salé. During the French protectorate (1912–1956), Rabat became the country's royal and administrative capital. The colonial authorities, urban planners, and architects intended it to be a showcase and a masterpiece of planning. They were partly successful. A half a century after independence, the two towns form Morocco's second-largest urban agglomeration. They lie midway in an urban belt stretching from Kenitra to the industrial capital of Casablanca. The cities manifest most problems of uncontrollable massive urbanization. Salé, once a center of refined urban culture, has become largely an impoverished dormitory town for its sister city.

The area of the Bou Regreg includes Neolithic remains, neo-Punic relics of a fourth century BCE Carthaginian trading post, and some ruins and inscriptions of a Roman settlement, Sala Colonia; these are on the left bank of the river on a site called Chellah where a fourteenth century cemetery of the Muslim Merinid dynasty remains intact. The Roman frontier town was along the fortified borders, the last outpost of Rome's North African empire.

In 1799, Rabat and Salé had a combined population of 25,000–30,000. Rbatis and Slawis, inhabitants of Rabat and Salé, were considered part of the country's urban elite. Their Jewish communities, integrated and economically important, had been moved out of the madina proper (the traditional Muslim town) into *mallahs*, separate Jewish quarters. By the end of the nineteenth century, Rabat and Salé had become the country's third largest urban agglomeration.

See also **Morocco.**

BIBLIOGRAPHY

Abu Lughod, Janet. *Rabat, Urban Apartheid in Morocco.* Princeton, NJ: Princeton University Press, 1980.

Brown, Kenneth L. *People of Salé: Tradition and Change in a Moroccan City (1830–1930).* Manchester, U.K.: Manchester University Press, 1976.

KENNETH L. BROWN

RABEMANANJARA, JACQUES (1913–2005).

Born in Maroantsetra on the island's east coast, Rabemananjara attended the seminary in Antananarivo, and later the Sorbonne. In Paris, he met the principal actors of the *Négritude* movement, the major black Pan-African cultural movement of the era, and the founders of its signature journal, *Présence Africaine*. He was a major figure at the two Congresses of black writers and artists organized by the group in 1956 (Paris) and 1959 (Rome). Elected to represent Madagascar in the French National Assembly in 1946 under the banner of the Democratic Movement for Malagasy Renewal (MDRM), which he cofounded, he was barred from serving and accused of instigating the 1947 revolt against the

French in his homeland. Sentenced to life in prison, he wrote his best poetry there, including *Antsa* (1956), *Lamba* (1956), and *Antidote* (1961), although he had begun publishing a decade earlier (*Sur les marches du soir*, 1940).

Rabemananjara's considerable *œuvre* cuts across genres. In addition to eight books of poetry, he also wrote plays (*Les dieux malgaches*, 1947; *Les boutriers de l'aurore*, 1957; *Agape des dieux Tritiva: Une tragédie*, 1962), political essays (*Témoignage malgache et colonialisme*, 1956; *Nationalisme et problèmes malgaches*, 1958), and historical tales (*Le prince Razaka*, 1995). Dubbed the Cantor of Négritude, Rabemananjara nonetheless cuts a distinctive profile across the landscape of that movement, with his revolutionary poetry counterbalanced by evocative theater that is rooted in the legends of his Madagascar's precolonial past. In 1988, the French Academy awarded him the Grand Prize of Francophonie for his lifetime work.

See also **Césaire, Aimé; Literature: Modern Poetry; Senghor, Léopold Sédar.**

BIBLIOGRAPHY

Boucquey de Schutter, Eliane. *Jacques Rabemananjara.* Paris: Seghers, 1964.

Bourjea, Serge. "Jacques Rabemananjara: à la croisée du cri et du silence." *Six conférences sur la littérature africaine de langue française*, ed. Wolfgang Leiner. Tübingen, Germany: Attampto, 1981.

Kadima-Nzuji, Mukala. *Jacques Rabemananjara, l'homme et l'œuvre.* Paris: Présence africaine, 1981.

Koenig, Jean-Paul. *Le Théâtre de Jacques Rabemananjara.* Paris: Présence africaine, 1989.

ALIKO SONGOLO

RABIH BIN FADLALLAH (??–1900).

The slave trader and marauder Rabih bin Fadlallah is also called Rabih Zubayr, and in French accounts he is referred to as Rabah, Rabbi, or Rabat. He was born in Salamat al-Basha, on the southeast side of Khartoum on the upper Nile River. He belonged to the Hamaj group of the southern Blue Nile. As a young man, Rabih joined a Sudanese battalion of the Turco-Egyptian army then claiming control in the region. He went to the province of Bahr al-Ghazal in the late 1850s as assistant head of a private slave-trading company, one among many then ravaging the region. When his company was taken over by the government, Rabih was employed by Zubayr Rahma Mansur, the biggest of the slave traders. After Zubayr's departure to Egypt in 1875, Rabih was employed by Sulayman ibn Zubayr. Following Sulayman's defeat by government forces in 1879, Rabih reassembled the remainder of his slave army and fled southwest to Azande territory along the Oubangui-Chari rivers, on the margins of the equatorial forest. Moving west toward Lake Chad in the early 1880s, he raided non-Muslim groups such as the Banda, Kreish, and Sara in that region. After defeating a French expedition in 1891, Rabih occupied Bagirmi. In 1894 he invaded Bornu, where he was joined by Haiyatu, ruler of Adamawa, who married his daughter, thus carving out the rudiments of a warlord empire around and to the south of Lake Chad. In 1899 Haiyatu was killed by Rabih's son Fadlallah. During the same year Rabih defeated a French force at Togbao. In response, the French sent an expedition under the leadership of Émile Gentil, the governor of Chari, near Lake Chad. After a series of skirmishes, Rabih was killed at Lakhta on April 22, 1900.

See also **Nile River; Slave Trades; Zubayr, Rahma Mansur al-.**

BIBLIOGRAPHY

Adeleye, R. A. "Rabih b. Fadlallah, 1879–1893: Exploits and Impact on the Political Relations in Central Sudan." *Journal of the Historical Society of Nigeria* 5, no. 2 (1970): 223–242.

Cordell, Dennis. *Dar al-Kuti and the Last Years of the Trans-Saharan Slave Trade.* Madison: University of Wisconsin Press, 1985.

Hallam, W. K. R. *The Life and Times of Rabih Fadl Allah.* Ilfracombe, U.K.: Stockwell, 1977.

Hill, Richard. *A Biographical Dictionary of the Sudan*, 2nd edition. London: Cass, 1967.

AHMAD ALAWAD SIKAINGA

RACE. *See* **Human Evolution.**

RADAMA I

RADAMA I (1793–1828). Radama I was the second king of the Merina kingdom of central Madagascar. The son of Adrianampoinimerina, founding ruler of the Imerina kingdom in central Madagascar, Radama reigned between 1810 and 1828, and was responsible for two developments critical to the kingdom's history: its expansion from Antananarivo, the capital, into an island-spanning empire, and an uneasy alliance with the British government. The two developments were intimately connected. Actively negotiated by Radama I in 1816, the British alliance provided the king's peasant army with military training and equipment and his administration with a literate elite trained in schools run by the London Missionary Society. In exchange Radama agreed to ban the large export trade in slaves from his kingdom, cleverly conciliating the British while at the same time undercutting political opponents who benefited from the trade. The social price of Radama's military campaigns was paid by the peasantry through prodigious death rates in his army and the loss of male labor to increasingly feminized Merina households. He was opposed most vocally by women, who staged a revolt in 1822 when Radama cropped his plaited hair in the European fashion. Sometimes called Madagascar's Napoleon, Radama was in his mid-thirties when he died of an unknown disease.

See also **Andrianampoinimerina; Antananarivo; Ethnicity; Ranavalona, Mada; Slave Trades: Indian Ocean.**

BIBLIOGRAPHY

Jolly, Alison. *Lords and Lemurs: Mad Scientists, Kings with Spears, and the Survival of Diversity in Madagascar.* Boston: Houghton Mifflin, 2004.

Valette, Jean. *Études sur le regne de Radama Ier.* Antananarivo, Madagascar: Impr. Nationale, 1962.

PIER M. LARSON

RADIO. *See* **Media: Radio and TV.**

RAIN FORESTS. *See* **Ecosystems: Tropical and Humid Forests; Forestry.**

RAMPHELE, MAMPHELA (1947–). Mamphela Ramphele is a South African political activist, and educator. When she was a medical student at the University of Natal Medical School in the late 1960s she was involved in the South African Students' Organisation (SASO), where she met the anti-apartheid activist Steve Biko. She earned her medical degree in 1972. She emerged as a leader in the Black Consciousness movement of the 1970s, and was banned to a remote location. Biko was killed by South African government security forces in 1977, and their child was born after his death. While she was banned, Ramphele organized a medical center, childcare program, and other community projects. After the banning order was lifted in 1984 she earned a doctorate in social anthropology, writing a dissertation that examined the lives of South Africa's migrant workers. She wrote about legal issues and poverty in South Africa in a series of books that exposed the reality of apartheid, including the Noma Award–winning *Uprooting Poverty: The South African Challenge* (1989, coauthored with Francis Wilson). In 1996 she was named vice-chancellor of the University of Cape Town, where she became the first woman and the first black to hold that position. In 2000 she joined the World Bank as a managing director. She has received numerous honorary degrees and other awards.

See also **Anthropology, Social, and the Study of Africa; Apartheid; Biko, Steve; South Africa, Republic of; World Bank.**

BIBLIOGRAPHY

Ramphele, Mamphela. *Across Boundaries: The Journey of a South African Woman Leader.* New York: Feminist Press, 1996.

Ramphele, Mamphela. "Political Widowhood in South Africa: The Embodiment of Ambiguity." *Daedelus* 125, no. 1 (1996): 99–117.

KATHLEEN SHELDON

RANAVALONA, MADA (c. 1788–1861). Mada Ranavalona was queen of Madagascar, who ruled from 1828 until her death in 1861. She was the daughter-in-law of Andrianampoinimerina, who reunited the Merina kingdom on the plateau of Madagascar around 1797. Ranavalona called herself Rabodonandrianampoinimerina, "the beloved daughter of Adrianampoinimerina." She was a blood relative and the wife of Radama I (r. 1810–1828), who extended the Merina kingdom through much of the island. Radama had not chosen a successor when he died, and Ranavalona became queen, consolidating her power with the Merina military leaders and nobles. Putting to death any rivals, she became an absolute monarch determined to uphold Malagasy tradition and avoid interference by the European powers that Radama I had favored (while nonetheless adopting European dress and manufactured goods such as firearms, sugar, and alcohol).

She terminated British protection. When negotiations about trade with the British resumed in 1836, the queen's position was to allow trade only at ports controlled by Malagasy governors. There the traders were subjected to interference and put under the jurisdiction of Malagasy law, including forced labor and *ganguin*, ordeal by poison; the British withdrew. Britain and France bombarded the port city Tamatave (present-day Toamasina); when the queen impaled the heads of the corpses on the beach, the European powers turned back. Ports were opened again only in 1853.

While Radama I had welcomed Christianization by the London Missionary Society, Ranavalona persecuted Christians at various times by suppressing their religion, murdering them, and exiling missionaries. She persecuted them because Christian teachings undermined devotion to ancestral idols and to an oligarchy ruling a highly stratified society based on slavery. In 1835 all Malagasy were forbidden from converting to Christianity, and in 1836 and 1840 the queen brutally martyred Protestant Christians.

The borders of the Merina kingdom established by Radama I remained essentially in place during Queen Ranavalona's reign, but control was consolidated. Some ethnic groups (Sakalava and Ambongo in the west, Tanala in the south, and Antanosy to the southwest) retained their independence. In the south the Antesaka rebelled in 1852 and were massacred by Merina troops. By this time the Merina army had degenerated from the organization established by Radama I into a group of unscrupulous plunderers.

For the imported manufactures she lost by closing the ports the queen relied on a shipwrecked Frenchman, Jean Laborde, who set up a small industrial city, employing over a thousand laborers. The items they manufactured included guns, tiles, cement, and ribbons; he also built a zoo and a wooden palace for the queen. His future, however, was tied to the ill-fated "Lambert Charter." Jean Lambert, a French businessman-adventurer, made a secret agreement in 1857 with the queen's son, Prince Rakoto, to allow for development of the island under a French protectorate. Upon discovery of the plot, the suspicious and superstitious queen banished all Europeans, tortured Christians, and asked for confessions by criminals and sorcerers, murdering and imprisoning over a thousand people. Upon her death, Prince Rakoto became Radama II, having been designated by the aged and ailing queen as her heir.

See also **Andrianampoinimerina; Antananarivo; Christianity; Ethnicity; History of Africa: To Seventh Century; Queens and Queen Mothers; Radama I; Slave Trades: Indian Ocean.**

BIBLIOGRAPHY

Edouwaye, Flora, ed. *Queens, Queen Mothers, Priestesses, and Power: Case Studies in African Gender.* New York: New York Academy of Sciences, 1997.

Gow, Bonar A. *Madagascar and the Protestant Impact.* New York: Africana Publishing Co., 1980.

Kottak, Conrad Phillip. *The Past in the Present: History, Ecology, and Cultural Variation in Highland Madagascar.* Ann Arbor: University of Michigan Press, 1980.

Raison-Jourde, François. *Les souverains de Madagascar: L'histoire royale et ses résurgences contemporaines.* Paris: Karthala, 1983.

NANCY G. WRIGHT

RANSOME-KUTI, OLUFUNMILAYO

(1900–1978). Also known as Olufunmilayo Anikulapo-Kuti, she was born into a Christian Yoruba family with Sierra Leonean connections and trained as a teacher in England. In 1925, she married the prominent cleric and educator Reverend Israel Oludotun Ransome-Kuti (1891–1955). In the period from 1946 to 1948, her career as pastor's wife and teacher took a dramatic turn when she emerged as the militant leader of Abeokuta Women's Union, which launched mass demonstrations of market women against the taxation policies of Alake Ademola II (1872–1962), the traditional ruler of Abeokuta who was forced into temporary exile.

This campaign was the highpoint of Ransome-Kuti's activist career, but she could not translate local success into a larger national political role. The National Council of Nigeria and the Cameroons (NCNC) executive refused to sponsor her candidacy in the regional elections of 1956 and 1957. Two attempts to run as an independent resulted in defeat, ultimately leading to her expulsion from the NCNC. She then launched the Commoners' People's Party, another short-lived venture. Meanwhile, her efforts in the 1950s to establish an autonomous umbrella women's movement, the Federation of Nigerian Women's Organization, also failed.

After Nigeria's independence (1960), Ransome-Kuti withdrew from national politics but remained active in Abeokuta public life. An outspoken critic of corrupt and autocratic leaders, she set a family tradition of radicalism followed by her three sons: Olikoye, a lawyer (1927–2003); Fela, an Afropop musician (1938–1997); and Beko, a physician (1940–2006).

See also **Kuti, Fela; Nigeria.**

BIBLIOGRAPHY

Johnson-Odim, Cheryl, and Nina Emma Mba. *For Women and the Nation: Funmilayo Ransome-Kuti of Nigeria.* Urbana: University of Illinois Press, 1997.

Mba, Nina. "Olufunmilayo Ransome-Kuti." In *Nigerian Women: A Historical Perspective,* ed. Bolanle Awe. Ibadan, Nigeria: Bookcraft, 2001.

LARAY DENZER

RAS TAFARI. *See* Haile Selassie I.

RAVALOMANANA, MARC (1949–).
Marc Ravalomanana was born into a family of humble means in Imerikasina, less than twenty miles from Madagascar's capitol of Antananarivo. He was educated in Imerikasina by missionaries. He then attended a Protestant secondary school

Marc Ravalomanana (1949–). Ravalomanana was a wealthy businessman who founded Madagascar's largest dairy company, TIKO. He was mayor of the island's capital before becoming president. AP IMAGES

in Sweden, where students were under stringent discipline. Throughout his life, he has been an ardent Christian.

In the early 1970s, Ravalomanana became a businessman. At first he sold yogurt on the streets of the capital. Then, with the assistance of the Protestant Church, Madagascar, he obtained a loan to buy a factory. Eventually, Ravalomanana became a multimillionaire whose company, TIKO, has a monopoly on dairy product sales in Madagascar. Additionally, he gained ownership of the Malagasy Broadcasting System, which controls MBS TV and Radio MBS.

Ravalomanana entered politics in 1999 when he was elected mayor of Antananarivo and received credit for his cleanup of the city. But the president demonstrated an authoritarian streak when he had more than one hundred homes bulldozed in September 2000 on the grounds that they were unsightly, an action that raised a national controversy.

In December 2001 Ravalomanana ran for president of Madagascar against the incumbent, Didier Ratsiraka (b. 1936). Both claimed victory. Ratsiraka declared martial law as Ravalomanana's supporters, concentrated in the cities, disrupted vital transportation links. In July 2002, after the United States and France had recognized Ravalomanana's parallel government, Ratsiraka fled to France. Ravalomanana liberalized Madagascar's economy, attracted foreign investment, secured donor aid, and obtained debt relief. But although the economy revived, the poor, hurt by rising prices, did not share in the benefits. The president attempted to limit France's great influence in Madagascar by improving relations with English-speaking nations.

Concurrent with serving as president, Ravalomanana is also vice president of the Protestant Church. He was reelected president of Madagascar in December 2006.

See also **Antananarivo; Madagascar; Media: Radio and TV.**

BIBLIOGRAPHY

Luxner, Larry. "Madagascar's Pro-business President Cited Country's Achievements." *Washington Diplomat.* March 2005. Available from www.luxner.com.

"Uneasy Run-up to Madagascar Election." *Afrol News.* September 8, 2006. Available from www.afrol.com/articles.

MICHAEL LEVINE

RAWLINGS, JERRY

(1947–). Born the illegitimate son of a Ghanaian (Ewe) mother and a Scottish pharmacist father in Accra, Jerry Rawlings (John, as he was named at birth) attended the prestigious Achimota Secondary School as the Gold Coast colony gained independence under Kwame Nkrumah before joining Ghana's air force as a flight cadet in 1967.

Angry at the corruption and economic incompetence of the I. K. Acheampong-F. W. K. Akuffo military regime (1972–1979) that succeeded the initial wave of civilian nationalist politics, Rawlings led an unsuccessful mutiny on the night of May 14, 1979, for which he was imprisoned. He was freed from jail on June 4 to head the Armed Forces Revolutionary Council (AFRC). The AFRC carried out a radical and sometimes violent populist program of "house-cleaning," which included the execution of eight senior officers and former officers, before handing over power to a freely elected civilian government, headed by President Hilla Limann, on September 24, 1979.

Disillusioned with the Limann administration, Rawlings seized power by coup d'état on December 31, 1981. His initially radical neo-Marxist Provisional

Jerry John Rawlings (1947–) addresses the United Nations, September 2000. Rawlings became Ghana's president twice in one year. On May 15, 1979, he was involved in a coup that led to his arrest and imprisonment. Then, on June 4, 1979, he came into power again after the military government was overthrown. TOM MIHALEK/AFP/GETTY IMAGES

National Defence Council evolved into a pragmatic, authoritarian administrative regime and implemented an International Monetary Fund/World Bank structural adjustment program commonly regarded as the most successful in Africa. Accused by his political opponents of extensive human rights abuses, Rawlings nonetheless retained sufficient popularity to win a reasonably free and fair presidential election in November 1992. He was reelected to office in 1996, and during his two terms in office managed reasonably well in the difficult balancing act that is politics in this region of Africa. Constitutionally barred from seeking a third term in office, Rawlings retired from the presidency following the elections of 2001, and was succeeded in office by John Kufuor. Since leaving office, Rawlings has become involved in the fight against disease in Africa, notably in campaigns to eradicate malaria and HIV/AIDS.

See also **Disease: HIV/AIDS, Social and Political Aspects; International Monetary Fund; Kufuor, John; Postcolonialism; World Bank.**

BIBLIOGRAPHY

Gyimah-Boadi, E., ed. *Ghana under PNDC Rule.* Senegal: Codesria, 1993.

Jeffries, Richard. "Ghana: The Political Economy of Personal Rule." In *Contemporary West African States,* ed. Donal B. Cruise O'Brien, John Dunn, and Richard Rathbone. New York: Cambridge University Press, 1989.

Jeffries, Richard, and Clare Thomas. "The Ghanaian Elections of 1992." *African Affairs* 92 (July 1993): 331–366.

Okele, Barbara E. *Four June: A Revolution Betrayed.* Enugu, Nigeria: Ikenga Publishers, 1982.

Rothchild, Donald, ed. *Ghana: The Political Economy of Recovery.* Boulder, CO: Lynne Rienner Publishers, 1991.

Shillington, Kevin. *Ghana and the Rawlings Factor.* New York: St. Martin's Press, 1992.

RICHARD JEFFRIES

REFUGEES. The forced displacement of populations and the social processes of incorporation, integration, and exclusion in sub-Saharan Africa have been continuous phenomena since ancient times. Had there been state boundaries in Africa then, such forced migrants would have been regarded as refugees according to definitions in use now, especially those set out in the 1969 Organization of African Unity (OAU) Convention Governing Specific Aspects of Refugee Problems in Africa. This Convention incorporates and expands on the definition of the term refugee as laid down in the 1951 United Nations Convention and Protocol Relating to the Status of Refugees. The African Charter on Human and Peoples' Rights (that came into force in 1986) reaffirms the right of asylum and the Convention on the Rights of the Child (1990) makes specific provision for the protection and education of child refugees. The integration of the African continent into the global state system, and of its refugees into the international legal and humanitarian regime, has adversely affected the traditional processes of incorporation and integration of the stranger.

MIGRATION AND REFUGEES IN THE PRECOLONIAL PERIOD

Throughout the known history of the African continent, factors including environmental changes, famine, disease, and competition for resources have led to wars, flight, and resettlement.

In western Africa, the Islamic religious duty to make the *hajj* became a force for the movement and permanent displacement of people across the continent along routes leading to the Red Sea ports as many people were unable to complete the journey to Mecca, or to return home.

From at least the ninth century CE, trade in human beings became another major cause of involuntary population movements. The Arab slave trade affected large sections of the continent and was a cause of displacement within and beyond it. Although different from plantation slavery, domestic and military slavery, as practiced by many African societies, continued into the twentieth century; Mauritania legally abolished this institution only in 1972. Slaves became members of families through marriage, but they continued to occupy lower socioeconomic positions within the societies in which they lived. For example, the classical Arab word *ab'ed*, meaning slave, is still used by Arabic speakers to designate all peoples of sub-Saharan African descent.

From the fourteenth century, the introduction of arms and the capture and sale of slaves by Europeans, and by Africans to Europeans, caused further large-scale movements of people, including the loss of millions of the most able-bodied from throughout western Africa. The British abolished the slave trade in their colonies in 1807. In its attempts to enforce the abolition, the British navy patrolled the seas of western Africa, capturing slave ships en route to the Americas. Rather than being returned to their homelands, the human cargoes were deposited in Freetown, a colony established for liberated slaves in 1787.

COLONIALISM AND FORCED MIGRATION

Throughout the eighteenth and nineteenth centuries, competition among the European powers for trade and influence on the African continent, culminating in the Treaty of Berlin (1885) that defined the boundaries of colonial governments, further disrupted African communities. World

War I (1914–1918), which included local battles for control, drew Africans into European conflicts. This process was continued during World War II (1939–1945).

Although slavery had been officially abolished, the need for labor in the colonies continued. This problem was addressed in Sierra Leone, for example, by paying local leaders to recruit workers to what, in practice, constituted forced labor migration. Throughout the colonial period, Africans were forcibly dispossessed of their land, such as with the Land Apportionment Acts (1930, 1931) in Rhodesia.

The extraction of resources, both mineral and agricultural, required substantial labor forces, and throughout sub-Saharan Africa, people needed to earn cash because of the imposition of various systems of taxation. In many cases, the search for paid employment forced workers to travel great distances. Mozambicans and Malawians went to work in the mines of South Africa, and thousands of Nigerians went to work on the Gezira Scheme in Sudan.

FORCED MIGRATION, DECOLONIZATION, AND THE COLD WAR

Decolonization following World War II was rarely a peaceful process. Major independence wars—beginning with Algeria and including all the major Portuguese colonies, Kenya, and the still unresolved colonial situation of the Western (Spanish) Sahara (that has been claimed and occupied by Morocco with the support of France, the United States, Britain, and other nations that support the war for this territory)—all produced refugees.

At the conclusion of the World War II, the world was partitioned into new zones of influence. Supporting the movement toward the independence of African colonies for both strategic and material advantages, the superpowers competed for ideological control. Both the Soviet Union and the United States were eager to have access to the uranium and cobalt resources in the Belgian Congo (later known as Zaire, now the Democratic Republic of the Congo). This newly independent country became the first subject of superpower competition in Africa; in one way or another, almost all European nations were involved in the war, which broke out soon after the Congo declared independence on

June 30, 1960, and led to the death and displacement of unknown numbers of people.

Much of the fighting in the Horn of Africa from the mid-1960s to the mid-1990s was exacerbated by the Cold War, during which the superpowers financed and armed various governments, as they have done throughout Africa. Haile Selassie, emperor of Ethiopia, for example, received more than half of the U.S. military aid allocation to sub-Saharan Africa, a good deal of which he spent in the war against Eritrean independence. U.S. support of the emperor was small, however, compared with the funds the Soviet Union bestowed on the military regime that overthrew him in 1974. The region has been awash with weaponry and displaced persons ever since.

In 1976, when the Soviet Union and the United States switched sides in the Somali/Ethiopian conflict, a catastrophe was precipitated in Somalia that continues to the present day. The original problem, however, stemmed from the postindependence division of Somalis among four countries: Kenya, Ethiopia, Djibouti, and Somalia itself. In 1978, Siad Barre (1919–1995) invaded the Ogaden, launching the first of many waves of refugees in and out of Ethiopia.

In the first decades following independence, the issue of self-determination was probably the principal source of conflict on the continent, creating refugees and enormous numbers of internally displaced persons. Examples included the wars in Sudan, Ethiopia, and Nigeria. Other disputes over the arbitrary boundaries created by the colonialists and defended by the OAU include the wars fought in pursuit of greater Somali and the war between Upper Volta (present-day Burkina Faso) and Mali in 1974.

The second largest number of refugees in the latter half of the twentieth century came from southern Africa. The protracted wars for independence in Mozambique and Zimbabwe produced thousands of refugees. The apartheid system in South Africa forcibly uprooted millions within the state itself and forced thousands of others to seek safety in neighboring countries and abroad, as well as destabilized its neighbors and caused large-scale forced migration in the region, especially from Mozambique, Angola, and Namibia.

EXPULSIONS

Mass expulsions of minority groups, orchestrated by many newly independent states, were another major cause of forced migration in the late twentieth century. The expulsion by Idi Amin Dada of 40,000 Asians from Uganda in 1972 was perhaps the most widely publicized, but in post-Amin Uganda in the 1980s, Milton Obote's government adopted a scorched earth policy in the north, sending more than 350,000 of its citizens into exile in Kenya, Sudan, Zaire, and elsewhere. Nigeria, in 1983 and 1985, expelled some three million migrant workers.

Guineans were expelled from the border area of Senegal in 1965; Ghanaian fisherman who had lived in Sierra Leone for generations were ousted in 1967; in 1969, Ghana expelled 200,000 migrant workers from Nigeria, Niger, and Upper Volta, following the introduction of the Aliens Compliance Order; and in 1971, Zambia expelled 150,000 migrants, mostly Rhodesians (Zimbabweans), Botswanans, Zairians, Tanzanians, and Somalis. Perhaps the most violent ouster, which led to a cascade of displacements, began in 1989 with Mauritania's expulsion of its black populations, including large numbers of migrants from sub-Saharan Africa. This triggered revenge killings of Mauritanian traders scattered throughout Senegal.

INDEPENDENT AFRICA'S RESPONSE TO FORCED MIGRATION

In 1969, the OAU promulgated the Convention Governing Specific Aspects of Refugee Problems in Africa. Incorporating all the provisions of the 1951 United Nations Convention (as amended by the 1967 protocol), the OAU definition of refugee was broadened from applying only to individual persecution to include "every person who owing to external aggression, foreign domination or events seriously disturbing public order in either part or whole of his country of origin or nationality is compelled to leave his place of habitual residence in order to seek refuge in another place outside his country of origin or nationality" (Article I [2]).

By 1993, forty-three states had ratified the 1969 OAU Convention. South Africa was in the process of doing so, and Zimbabwe, Swaziland,

and Sudan had introduced domestic legislation incorporating, to varying degrees, the provisions of the Convention. However, at least three major factors have rendered the protection and incorporation of refugees problematic.

Refugees and the Interests of States. The OAU Convention was written in the context of the formation of states that sought to establish their legitimacy and to consolidate internal control of their populations. The cornerstone upon which the OAU was built was the sanctity of existing borders and the principles of territorial integrity and noninterference in the internal affairs of member states. The Convention puts the interests of states above the protection of refugees. States have the right to determine when the circumstances that gave rise to flight have ceased to exist, and the Convention denies refugee status to any persons "guilty of acts contrary to the purposes and principles of the OAU or the UN." It forbids any "subversive action" against any member of the OAU (Article III [1] and [2]). Seeking to ensure the depoliticization of refugees, it advises that they be settled away from borders, denies them freedom of speech and association, and declares the granting of asylum to be a humanitarian, and not "an unfriendly" act, in relation to the state of origin (Article II [2]).

Refugee Status as Temporary. The founders of the OAU apparently believed that, once the colonial wars had ended, there would be no more situations on the continent that could give rise to forced migration. Whereas the 1951 UN Convention did not mention repatriation except in negative terms forbidding the *refoulement* (forced return) of a refugee, Article V of the OAU Convention specifically includes provision for voluntary repatriation and rehabilitation once conditions in the country of origin permit.

Whereas the 1951 UN Convention provides for favored treatment of refugees, including the right to education, employment, and ownership of property, and Article 34 recommends that states facilitate their assimilation and naturalization, the emphasis upon repatriation in the OAU Convention has allowed its signatories to ignore these provisions (even though it includes all of the rights of the UN Convention), and has led African states to regard refugee status as temporary. This assumption has had enormously negative consequences on traditional practices concerning the incorporation of the stranger and has, with few exceptions, both directed the development of state policy toward refugees and legitimized the approach to refugee assistance orchestrated by the international humanitarian establishment.

Assisting African Refugees. Whenever there is movement across borders, the first to assist the refugees are the local people. Islamic law makes the granting of asylum a religious duty on the part of both the individual and the polity. Most refugees in Africa have never received international assistance but have settled among their hosts, on whose goodwill their security and economic survival depend. All African societies have some method of incorporating the stranger into their membership, but the subject has been inadequately researched. In southern Africa, for example, the chiefdoms made provision for strangers, whose status depended on their class and on whether they were coming in as individuals or as members of a large group with a leader of their own. During the wars of 1820–1837, which spread from Zululand to the High Veld, and north and south along the coast from the Save River to Mthatha, thousands of Africans were displaced and scattered. Some were absorbed as individual refugees into other communities; others were accepted as groups under their own leaders to whom land was allocated. Still others established conquest states, such as those of the Nguni under Soshangane (c. 1750–1859), the Ndebele under Mzilikazi, and the Kololo on the Zambezi River. The aftereffects of slavery and colonialism undermined the capacity of African societies to incorporate and integrate involuntary migrants into their communities.

At least one society, the Luo of Kenya, made special provisions for refugees. They recognized three categories of strangers: prisoners of war (*wasumbini*); migrants (*jodak*), who were provided land and could marry within the community; and refugees (*jomotur*). Refugees were either attached to individual families, especially when the numbers were small, or, after consultation with the elders, settled separately in parts of clan land that were not under cultivation.

INTERNATIONAL POLICIES AND AFRICAN RESPONSE

Given the poverty of most host states in Africa, it is generally assumed that international aid is required, and the OAU Convention calls for burden sharing. However, rather than channeling this assistance through governments, the Office of the UN High Commissioner for Refugees (UNHCR) and its implementing partners, foreign nongovernmental organizations, have become the main conduits for international funds.

Although the major solution to the refugee problem in Africa promoted by UNHCR up to the 1980s was local integration, its policy of settling refugees in camps had the opposite effect: creating islands of destitution. This approach, rather than allowing refugees to be incorporated into and to contribute to their host's economy, froze the refugees in a state of permanent marginality in their host societies and perpetuated their image and label as outsiders. Thus, in order to receive international assistance, states were increasingly forced to stop the spontaneous settlement of refugees among their own populations and to comply with the international policy of encampment in order to make the refugees countable and visible. This created great insecurity among self-settled refugees and led to serious violations of the fundamental rights of refugees, including the regular use of the military to force them into camps.

This approach, which continues to the present day, has been justified on the grounds of security. However, the refugees who represent the greatest security risks for host states are seldom forcibly encamped. For example, refugees from South Africa enjoyed freedom of movement in the countries that hosted them, even though South Africa mounted military operations on the host countries' soil. At least two nations—Sierra Leone and Guinea—declined offers of international assistance. Guinea received large numbers of refugees from the liberation war in Guinea-Bissau, but withstood pressure to establish a UNHCR office there. Tens of thousands of Fula-speaking people fled Sékou Touré's Guinea and were peacefully received by Sierra Leone. They were not labeled as refugees, no international assistance programs were mounted, and no camps were set up for them. The government permitted their integration into the national economy, and their leadership was absorbed into the

Sudanese refugees in UN camp. Chadian boys play football as the sun comes down over Habile IDP (Internally Displaced People) Camp, Chad, near the border with Sudan, April 2007. Tensions between Chad and Sudan had risen over the last few weeks following border clashes that left 17 Sudanese dead after a Chadian army attack. URIEL SINAI/GETTY IMAGES

local Islamic religious community. In the early twenty-first century, although unknown numbers of unassisted refugees are living among their hosts in rural and urban areas. integration as a solution has been largely abandoned, and, increasingly, the people are effectively warehoused in camps.

GROWING RESTRICTIONISM IN AFRICA

Since the end of the Cold War, there has been a growing tendency for African states to adopt the industrialized countries' anti-integration and restrictionist policies toward refugees. The OAU Convention provides for the recognition of refugee status en masse by nationality. From the late twentieth century on, refugee status on an individual basis is increasingly being adjudicated by UNHCR, rather than states, despite the states' having ratified the Convention. Over the same period, as a consequence of donors' frustration with the failure of the camp policy to make refugees self-sufficient, UNHCR has been involuntarily repatriating refugees, notably the Rwandans.

CONCLUSION

Since the thirty-fifth anniversary in 2004 of the promulgation of the OAU Convention on refugees,

sub-Saharan Africa has continued to be a major theater of involuntary population movements, most recently from Democratic Republic of the Congo, the continuing crises in Sudan, and displacements from Liberia, Sierra Leone, Côte d'Ivoire, and Togo. According to UNHCR, at the end of 2004, approximately 2.75 million of the world's 9.2 million refugees were being hosted in Africa. The violation of human rights, conflicts between states, ethnic strife, struggle for religious hegemony, natural disasters, lack of democratic practice, failure of development, global economic inequalities, and ideological rivalries have all contributed to the degeneration of Africa into an arena of conflict and turmoil. It is evident that conventional attempts to resolve the refugee phenomenon through encampment have only served to create problems.

The challenge for the future is to address the fundamental political issues that have beset the continent and have led to forced displacement on an unparalleled scale. From the international perspective, donors must review the impact of current aid policies on the region. Since the early twenty-first century, the overall position of refugees in Africa has not improved, and in many cases has worsened, with refugees being redefined as threats to security. Without major changes in the bureaucratic and political interests that have stymied the reform of the refugee regime, there seems little prospect of a better life for refugees in Africa.

See also **Amin Dada, Idi; Colonial Policies and Practices; Decolonization; Human Rights; Labor: Migration; Nongovernmental Organizations; Obote, Milton; Organization of African Unity; Slave Trades; United Nations: United Nations in Africa; Warfare; World War II.**

BIBLIOGRAPHY

Allen, Tim, and Hubert Morsink, eds. *When Refugees Go Home: African Experiences.* London: James Currey, 1993.

Anand, Renu M. *African Refugees: An Overview.* New Delhi, India: Khama Publishers, 1993.

Brooks, Hugh C., and Yassin El-Ayouty, eds. *Refugees South of the Sahara: An African Dilemma.* Westport, CT: Negro University Press, 1994.

Deng, Frederick M. *Protecting the Dispossessed: A Challenge for the International Community.* Washington, DC: The Brookings Institute, 1993.

Goodwin-Gill, Guy S. *The Refugee in International Law.* Oxford: Oxford University Press, 1983.

Greenfield, Richard. "The OAU and Africa's Refugees." In *The OAU after Twenty Years*, ed. Yassin El-Ayouty and Ira William Zartman. Oxford: Praeger, 1983.

Hamrell, Sven. *Refugee Problems in Africa.* Uppsala, Sweden: The Scandinavian Institute of Africa Studies, 1967.

Hansen, Art, and Anthony Oliver-Smith, eds. *Involuntary Migration and Resettlement: The Problems and Responses of Dislocated People.* Boulder, Colorado: Westview Press, 1982.

Harrell-Bond, Barbara. *Imposing Aid: Emergency Assistance to Refugees.* Oxford: Oxford University Press, 1986.

Kuhlman, Tom. *Burden or Boon? A Study of Eritrean Refugee in the Sudan.* Amsterdam: VU University Press, 1990.

Leopold, Mark. *Inside West Nile: History and Representation on an African Frontier.* Oxford: James Currey, 2005.

Lischer, Sarah Kenyon. *Dangerous Sanctuaries: Refugee Camps, Civil War, and the Dilemmas of Humanitarian Aid.* Ithaca, New York: Cornell University Press, 2005.

Loescher, G. *UNHCR and World Politics: A Perilous Path.* Oxford: Oxford University Press, 2001.

Malkki, Liisa. *Purity and Exile: Violence, Memory, and National Cosmology among Hutu Refugees in Tanzania.* Chicago: University of Chicago Press, 1995.

Rogge, John, ed. *Refugees, A Third World Dilemma.* Totowa, New Jersey: Rowman and Littlefield, 1987.

Platsky, Laurine, and Cherryl Walker. *The Surplus People: Forced Removals in South Africa.* Johannesburg, South Africa: Ravan Press, 1985.

Shack, William A., and Elliott P. Skinner, eds. *Strangers in African Societies.* Berkeley: University of California Press, 1979.

Verdirame, Guglielmo, and Barbara Harrell-Bond. *Rights in Exile; Janus-Faced Humanitarianism.* New York: Berghahn Books, 2005.

BARBARA HARRELL-BOND
MARK CHINGONO
ENOCH OPONDO
REVISED BY BARBARA HARRELL-BOND AND MARK LEOPOLD

RELIGION AND RITUAL. The religions of Africa, both indigenous and introduced, have been the subjects of much argument and misunderstanding, due mostly to misleading accounts written on the basis of European classifications and definitions and failure to analyze them as systems of thought and action of particular societies in particular social and historical contexts. There has also often been misunderstanding because there is no word in most African languages that may directly be translated by the English word "religion," most words so translated being better understood as "custom," "proper moral behavior," or some such reference to ethical or collective values; most African societies do not construct rigid boundaries between the "religious" and other forms of shared and valued thought and behavior.

A linked question commonly asked about African religions is that of their "truth" or theological validity, a question that reflects early Eurocentric views, held especially by Christian missionaries, that African religions were composed of "fetishes," "black magic," "juju," "words of the devil," and so on. These views had no foundation in reality or history and typically reflected the view that "world" religions, being literate and possessing sacred books, are "higher" and thus both truer and with greater cultural and historical value than those of Africa, which are "lower" and so less true and of less value. Perhaps a theologically valid question, it easily leads to failure to understand the nature and importance of religion in Africa.

Another frequent question is whether there is one or are many indigenous religions in the continent.

NEW ENCYCLOPEDIA OF AFRICA

Many non-African observers and some modern Afrocentric African scholars claim that there is only one; others, including most Africans themselves, maintain that there are as many as there are particular societies, each with its own culture and system of morality. There is also the question of whether African religions are unique or are essentially similar to those of the remainder of the world. It is clear from at least most anthropological research that the religions of African peoples are comparable with those found elsewhere in their social uses and functions, even though they vary in cultural detail both from others and also among themselves. The indigenous religions of Africa should be evaluated as similar in function, although not necessarily in theology, origins, or history, to those from anywhere else, whether literate or not. However, most accounts have rigidly separated indigenous or local religions from the so-called world religions of Christianity and Islam, even though all have existed side by side in some parts of the continent for many centuries and have influenced one another in many ways.

Historians have little knowledge of indigenous African religions before the earliest colonial contacts, apart from the scattered records of travelers and from archaeological excavations, both sources that present grave difficulties of interpretation. It should not be assumed that the religions in Africa have ever been, or are, unchanging. As African societies undergo changes, as they have done throughout history, so do their religions, as social constructs, also change.

MYTH

Every known African religion has its corpus of myths, of which there have been many analyses and interpretations. "Myth" is a Eurocentric notion, but so long as the popular fallacy that a myth is merely an untrue story is discarded, it is a crucial part of religion—or of politics—for analysis and understanding, even if, again, there may be no precise term for it in any particular African language. Myths are typically held by those who tell and listen to them to be "true" accounts of the past or the present, of ancestral origins and of historical events, and are used to resolve what people consider to be the moral and social paradoxes and contradictions of past or present. The past is thereby used to explain and give

meaning to the present, and as paradoxes and contradictions change over time, so are the relevant myths and their interpretations likely to change to accommodate them. Myths are thus "true" in a moral sense, as providing a cosmology, a representation of a society and its place in the world, both in the past and in the twenty-first century. No myths of any particular people have fixed versions or interpretations: tellers shape them to vagaries of the present and the memories of their listeners, who, as participants in the telling, give them meanings that they find relevant to their own problems: men, women, and children, rich and poor, old and young, may—and usually do—find different meanings in a single mythical recitation.

A problem throughout Africa resolved by myth is the cosmogony or creation of the world by Divinity (a less ethnocentric term than the more usual "God") and the subsequent formation of the particular society, which is usually held to have been done by some kind of heroic ancestors. Creation and societal formation may be related in a single myth or separately, but all African peoples have such myths, some simple and others elaborate, and all with similar elements: divine creation *ex nihilo*, the appearance of sacred or semi-sacred heroic figures often using magic to form society, and the later historical growth of that society, now peopled by "ordinary" living people. These myths place Divinity and the living in their present relationship, which many, perhaps most, myths state arose from separation of sky (the usual place of Divinity) and earth; the moral fault for the separation was human disobedience of Divinity, so that humans were separated (as in the Tower of Babel myth), given their own non-divine languages and cultures, and made subject to the vagaries of sickness, death, and divisiveness. In essence these myths define space and time, which entered human awareness after the separation, when "history" began. Other universal problems of African cosmology include those of the similarities and relations between women and men, and between human and nonhuman animals. These myths have many forms, those of tales of moral and immoral behavior and the rewards of each perhaps being the most widespread.

In brief, myths are statements about the validation of the distribution and exercise of power and authority among the living. They explain the world and human society within it, and time and space in human experience, so that the world becomes controllable and the future perhaps at least possibly predictable. This world is generally accepted as divinely made and inspired, its meanings perhaps unknowable by ordinary people but knowable at least in patches by those whose skills, learning, sanctity, and devotion make that possible. One of the most common errors made in accounts of African religions is to assume that Africans lacks sophisticated and devout thinkers. To the contrary, theological or cosmological argument (however different from Western forms) is one of the central areas in all African thinking and argument.

THE STRUCTURES OF RELIGION
In all indigenous African religions the believed or accepted identities of mystical agents that can affect living people are essentially similar. They are headed by a Creator Divinity, in most cases considered male and dwelling in the sky, often ruling in conjunction with some form of Mother or Earth Goddess. Divinity is typically defined as otiose or remote, having created the world and then retired from the living, although most African religions hold that Divinity continues to determine both an individual's fate or destiny and the time and manner of death. Divinity is usually given attributes by the theological argument known as the *via negativa*, being defined by criteria that are the opposite of those defining the living: being everlasting, beyond life and death, omnipotent, beyond human comprehension or control, responsible for all life, death, disease, or whatever fates may befall the living.

Whether in a particular myth the identity of Divinity is that of an indigenous African religion or that of Islam or Christianity, the attributes used by the living to describe Divinity are everywhere similar in this regard. But there is one crucial difference. In the former religions Divinity is that of the particular society and essentially cares only for His own creatures, helps and punishes them, and is unconcerned with others. On the other hand in both Islam and Christianity Divinity is usually considered by devotees to be universal, caring for all humankind. It is clear that this development in belief is, at least usually, linked to the widening of

a given society's sense of identity and boundaries in the context of modernization and change.

Below Divinity there is typically thought to be an array of lesser mystical or spiritual beings of various kinds and with various powers. They act as intermediaries between Divinity and the living, and it is among them in the many ways that these figures are thought of that are found the principal differences between African religious systems. These intermediaries may be divided into those that are living and those that are not. The former category comprises priests, diviners, and other religious functionaries, many given sacred qualities by formal initiation and appointment. The nonliving essentially comprise spirits and ancestors of many kinds.

Spirits are refractions or aspects of Divinity, under divine authority, holding many powers over the living, not immediately known to or understood by them, and only occasionally partially accessible to them. They are usually considered to be without number, without known shape, to be invisible, inaudible, and unsmellable, although at times they may choose to become visible, or audible, and smellable, and to take on shapes perceptible to the living. They may be associated with particular places where either they dwell or may be contacted by the living at shrines placed for them. They may be great or small in power, be male or female, be associated with particular alien groups, or have their own languages and other distinguishing features.

Then there are ancestors, recognized as mystical intermediaries in most indigenous religions, although their influence fades with Islamic or Christian conversion. A dead person does not automatically become an ancestor but is made so by the performance of mortuary rites. Only a few of the dead may be selected: those remembered in genealogies; men who have begotten children or only sons; or women who have been first-borns and so held to resemble men. Which ones are selected and made individual ancestors, to whom sacrifice or prayer may be made, varies among societies. In the literature various terms are used to distinguish what one might call the effective dead (usually known as shades, ghosts, or ancestral spirits) from those who are forgotten as individual beings. The effective dead are typically considered as members of the clans, lineages, and families of their living descendants; they may be able to been seen and heard; and both protect and punish the living for disloyalty or harm to the group, which persists over the generations. In most African societies the descent group remains the basic and long-lasting social unit, and relations within it, and thus between living and ancestors must be those of mutual trust and support against other clans and lineages.

Contact and communication between living and nonliving are at the heart of almost all indigenous African religions. Contacts are of two main kinds. One is initiated by the living, or more precisely by their ritual intermediaries such as priests; the other is initiated by spirits, ancestors, or Divinity. There are many kinds of living mediators: priests, diviners, prophets, rainmakers, seers, and elders are given sacrificial sacred authority. Few are full-time specialists or professionals. Some act by virtue of genealogical position and age, for instance the heads of lineages who may sacrifice to the ancestors; others are given power and skill by rites of initiation. All, at least while acting as mediators, possess some degree of sacredness, not an innate quality but given by training and initiation.

These various roles involve the possession and exercise of power and authority, which may be important politically as well as ritually. There are typically found two main categories of living mediators, to be distinguished as priests and prophets of various kinds. Both are important holders of religious and political authority: following the German sociologist Max Weber's classic typology, priests are given forms of bureaucratic authority, prophets forms of charismatic authority. But the distinction is not always very clearly marked, and to be effective each may acquire elements of both forms. Both involve forms of knowledge that may be learned from teachers, invented, acquired from spirits, inherited from ancestors, bought from other practitioners, shared, sold, lost, or forgotten. Religious knowledge, in Africa as elsewhere, is one element in many forms of social and mystical relationships between living people or between the living and the dead, spirits, or Divinity. In particular, ritual, possession, divination, and witchcraft are associated with knowledge that may be sacred, secret, mystical, or evil, or may be more technical (such as

knowledge of healing herbs). Undergoing a religious rite brings change in social status and in knowledge of oneself: new spiritual experiences can bring new knowledge. One may see these religious figures in this light: they possess a secret knowledge, they are attributed sacredness in varying degrees, and they exercise various forms of power and authority beyond those of ordinary people. As everywhere, the boundary between religious and political position and authority is often slight.

SACRIFICE AND POSSESSION

Sacrifice takes many forms, may be largely secret or confined to a narrow congregation, and is intimately linked to the exercise of lineage, familial and political authority.

Ritual communication initiated by the living is of many kinds: prayer, sacrifice, vision, prophecy, silent devotion; that initiated by the mystical agents of Divinity almost always takes the form of possession or sickness of the living. Both forms of communication involve a change, temporary or permanent, in the social and psychological personality of the living vis-a-vis both mystical agents and other living people. There are in general two main kinds of sacrifice: that performed regularly at stated intervals or on regular occasions, and that performed as needed to restore physical, psychological, or moral harm health. Both involve purification, the one from the pollution of an existing condition and the other from that of taboo, sin, misdemeanor, or the malevolence of others, and all involve some form of transformation or re-formation of a person or group (as a congregation).

Sacrifices made as part of rites of transition or transformation are generally known by Arnold van Gennep's term as *rites de passage*. The most widespread rites are at initiation and at death; others occur at birth, marriage, the reaching of various age and generation classes and grades, the gaining of political or religious positions such as king or priest, and the purification or de-pollution of person or congregation. The central part of these rites is the period of seclusion, when the initiands are symbolically, and often physically, separated from the everyday world and then undergo transformation. This period typically begins and ends with rites of sacrifice, which "make sacred" and so purify those passing into a new grade or status. The phase of seclusion may be long or short but seems invariably marked by forms of symbolic reversal, such as eating normally tabooed foods, wearing normally forbidden or different clothing, or other symbolically reversed observances such as going into an ecstatic state or psychological dissociation.

At death there occur rites of disposing of the corpse (usually by burying, burning, or exposure), of transforming the deceased into an ancestor, and of purifying the mourners so as to re-form the local group that has been disrupted by the death. Rites may be elaborate and drawn out, or simple and short. Which they are is determined mainly by the status of the deceased, a king or chief having the former and infants the latter.

Sacrifices for physical, psychological, and moral healing appear to be universal in African societies. Their central feature is usually oblation, or an offering, typically that of a living animal, although some involve only the offering of non-animal foods. The oblation is typically offered to the dead and to spirits, less commonly to Divinity. Animal sacrifice follows a common pattern: consecration of the animal for sacrifice; identification with the person for whom the rite is being performed, so that it will carry with it his or her pollution from sin or misdemeanor; killing and immolation; and consumption by the congregation, whose members thereby share food with the dead or other agents and with one another, so redefining and strengthening the bonds that unite them. The sin that has led to sickness is carried away by the immolation and the breach of kinship and solidarity that has occurred is mended.

The other principal form of ritual communication is possession, the "seizing" of a living person by Divinity, a spirit, or an ancestor. The victim typically enters a state of trance or of violent physical seizure while the body and mind are taken over by the possessing agent. There are two main forms of possession: in one it is a sign of a mystical link between agent and victim that singles the latter out as being joined to the world of spiritual powers and so to possess mystical power; in the other possession gives the victim the power of divination and mediumship, of being the mouthpiece of a powerful being. As part of professional skill, possession may be self-induced by dancing, hyperventilation, drugs or other means of dissociation.

Although both men and women may be possessed, the majority in Africa are reported to be women. Well-known examples are the *bori* cult of Northern Nigeria and the *zar* cult of northeastern Africa, in which women possessed by the *bori* or *zar* spirits form cult groups. As with sacrifice, possession brings about the purification and change of moral and social status of the victim, such as being removed from everyday uncertainties and obligations of familial or other authority and coming under the greater authority of the possessing spirit. Possession is still little understood as a physiological and psychological phenomenon. It takes place, voluntarily and involuntarily, induced by the self or by others; often the possessed person, especially if also a medium, has little or no recollection of being possessed.

A necessary part of sacrifice is divination to determine the mystical agents to whom the oblation must be made. Divination takes many forms, which may be divided into mediumship and oracular divination, although the distinction is often hazy. Mediumship typically involves possession or trance, and with practice a diviner can easily enter trance. Diviners often wear clothing or eat foods that represent the "wilderness," linked to Divinity and its powers, whence comes their knowledge. They are often featured by non-African travelers, writers, and filmmakers as "witchdoctors" in order to show them as "primitive." Oracular divination involves the use of devices such as the throwing of pebbles or shells or the examining of animal entrails, which the diviner interprets as having hidden information about the causes of sickness or harm.

To understand sacrifice in African religions (as in any other), the complex notions of sin, taboo, atonement, and restitution must be considered. They concern purity, pollution, and danger, and essentially involve the breaking or abandonment of culturally determined symbolic boundaries that are established and validated by myth and tradition. Breaching a taboo, associated especially with the differences between divine and human, between human and animal, and between women and men, rarely appears to be taken as a purposeful and heinous act. However, deliberately harming others, breaching ordered boundaries through misdemeanor or disobedience that destroys amity, trust, and identity of lineage and neighborhood groups, may be considered sin. It may lead to sickness or other response from Divinity, ancestors or spirits that must be cured by atonement or sacrifice.

THE PROBLEM OF EVIL

Notions that might properly be translated as "evil" are part of all African religions. Evil comes in many forms: as sudden or cruel death, as undeserved sickness, as unfortunate event or coincidence, as unexpected poverty or failure, as bad dreams or visions. The occurrence of evil may be unexpected, may spring from sense of guilt, or may be retribution for an antisocial act. To explain and counter forms of evil, people usually use divination to identify its senders, who in small-scale interpersonal communities are thought likely to be other people rather than spirits or Divinity. Harm sent as justifiable retribution, punishment, or "teaching" by the dead is typically diagnosed by diviners and removed by expiatory sacrifice. Harm that is malevolent and unmerited is typically attributed to other persons, those known in the literature as witches and sorcerers.

It used to be held by non-African Christian and Muslim travelers and missionaries that African peoples are characterized by witchcraft and its terrors. This is an exaggeration, although there have been instances in history of mass witch epidemics, at times of serious and sudden disasters, that have been countered by prophetic reformers. There is no reliable evidence of any actual existence of witches; what do exist are belief, fear, suspicion, and accusation of actual people thought to practice witchcraft, who may be sought out and punished by so-called witch doctors or witch-hunters. The distinction between witches and sorcerers—and so between the processes of bewitchment and ensorcellment—is not found in all African societies. It is more rarely made in European societies, and so Christian observers have tended to confuse and conflate the terms. General anthropological usage is that a witch has an innate mystical power to harm others merely by volition (there may also be physical manifestations of the power, such as red eyes, a gray complexion, or bodily deformities), whereas a sorcerer harms others by the deliberate use of material substances, usually known in the literature as "medicines" or "fetishes." Both may be men or women.

It appears universal in African societies that bewitching and ensorcellment are held to be expressions of envy, jealousy, or hatred between rivals, whether kin or unrelated neighbors. Evildoer and victim must generally, therefore, know each other, and divinatory procedures are based on this fact. Suspected or accused witches and sorcerers are typically made to withdraw the sickness or misfortune; they may at times also be punished, ostracized, or even killed, especially in cases where the same person is accused on many occasions. It follows that witchcraft and sorcery accusations will be found as much in modern urban settings as in the more "traditional" rural ones: it is not merely a consequence of lack of education or refusal to be converted to Islam or Christianity.

European travelers and missionaries have tended to characterize African religions as being largely devoted to "magic," especially to "black" magic and sorcery. This term, with its implications of superstition and "primitive" thought, is used essentially to refer to beliefs and practices that the observer cannot accept as being "natural" or "religious," an ethnocentric view that is best discarded.

PROPHETS AND REFORMERS

No African society or social group is unchanging, and African history is filled by the comings of prophets who have tried to reform or reshape a society and its religion in the face of wide disaster, whether natural or man-made. It is typical for the sources of disaster to be thought to lie outside the particular community and so to need exterior help beyond the capabilities of the group's own ritual experts. Therefore prophets also typically come from outside the community, claiming their charismatic authority is given by Divinity; they stand above any particular group, so that they can rebuild the identity and well-being of the "besieged" community. Historians know little of past prophets but may assume that most failed and left no record of their activities. During the twentieth century most prophets were Christian with new messages from the Christian Divinity; indeed, many earlier missionaries were themselves at first taken to be prophets.

Christianity and Islam—both prophetic religions—are of great antiquity in Africa, both northern and sub-Saharan, but their spread throughout the entire continent, especially that of Christianity, is a relatively new phenomenon. In the twenty-first century Africa is the scene of the most rapid and widespread rate of Christian conversion to Christianity in the world. If one looks at the religious thought and behavior of any particular people in sub-Saharan Africa, and whether the group claims adherence to an indigenous faith, to Islam, or to Christianity, it is clear that except for a few geographically remote peoples almost every religion has come to include elements of all these faiths, amalgamated, perhaps uneasily, into single living religious systems. It also becomes clear that virtually every such religious system exhibits the structure of mystical agents that has previously been described, despite cultural variation between the societies concerned.

Christianity came first to sub-Saharan Africa at Aksum in the fourth century and has persisted in Ethiopia ever since. Islam spread along the northern and eastern coasts of the continent beginning in the seventh century and on its eastern coasts from the ninth century. Christian priests came to Africa with the Portuguese in the fifteenth century during the colonial period, at first as chaplains to coastal European trading posts and then as priests to the kings of Kongo and Bénin. Later, during the eighteenth and nineteenth centuries, Christian missionaries entered the interior and spread across the continent.

The Christian missions of the colonial period in the first half of the twentieth century were almost all in the hands of non-Africans of diverse churches and sects, with differing aims and methods and with varying conversionary impact. African adherents generally held lower positions in these mission hierarchies despite pious protestations of "brotherhood" and equality. Non-African missionaries held greater overall authority yet paradoxically were locally dependant upon their inferiors, and both sides knew it. The consequence was that during the mid- and late twentieth century missions tended to divide, and in the early 2000s most European missionaries have given way to African priests working in association with European-based mission sponsors and to leaders of the ever-growing African independent, separatist, and Pentecostal churches, in which the leaders exercise essentially charismatic authority outside or in contradiction to more bureaucratic or formal political authority.

Much has been written on "religious syncretism" but its precise meaning remains unclear. Other than any presumed primordial "ur-religion," all religions of which anything is known are syncretic blends from many sources, although devout believers of any religion rarely care to admit such debts to others. In Africa the term has come to have the rather explicit meaning of a mingling of local religions with either Christianity or Islam; the more devout converts to a world religion may be adamant in shunning "heathen" belief and ritual, but most ordinary people appear to accommodate one or the other according to the situation of the moment.

There is more to conversion to one of the universalist religions of the Book than a "change of heart." It is also a matter of the widening scale of local and culturally discrete societies that in the twenty-first century become parts of larger economic and political systems. One consequence is the realization that local divinities lose their power, and so others with wider power over many societies may be accepted. The obvious such divinity is the Christian or Islamic God, and many people come to adhere to Him. Yet they may at times still appeal to their traditional community or family divinities to help them in traditional situations and with traditional problems in these spheres of their lives. If it appears more likely that, for example, a sickness may best be removed by traditional reconciliatory ritual among intimates, then that is followed; the opposite holds true for help with conflicts or tensions with strangers or with invisible "markets" or "nations." In these situations the comprehensiveness of Islam or Christianity may appeal to a community.

Linked to the growth of Pentecostalism and other Christian faiths have gone changes in the importance of beliefs and practices to do with witchcraft and sorcery and their removal. It is widely held that new changes in social position, wealth, and power on these transcending scales, seen by the poor and weak as morally undeserved, are due to witchcraft and sorcery by the newly rich and powerful. As with "traditional" witch beliefs, accusations follow envy and resentment. They may also be resolved by new forms of exorcism of accused witches and sorcerers by Christian, especially Catholic, priests.

CONCLUSION: THE NATURE OF RELIGIONS IN AFRICA

There are three main conclusions to be drawn about religion in Africa. First, there are as many indigenous religions as there are distinct societies; second, the former distinction made between "indigenous" and "introduced" religious beliefs and rites has grown increasingly difficult to maintain, as people have moved between them and also formed new faiths based on elements of both; and third, African religions are essentially similar to all others throughout the world, even though they reflect or express local peculiarities. It is from the detail of these local variations that the nature, functions, and histories of African religions may best be understood, both by Africans who wish to learn of the cultural and religious variety and richness of their continent and by non-Africans who wish to learn from Africa to widen their knowledge of the world as a single whole.

See also **Anthropology, Social, and the Study of Africa; Christianity; Death, Mourning, and Ancestors; Fetish and Fetishism; Healing and Health Care; Initiation; Islam; Judaism in Africa; Myth and Cosmology; Prophetic Movements; Religion and the Study of Africa; Spirit Possession; Taboo and Sin; Vodún; Witchcraft.**

BIBLIOGRAPHY

Blakeley, Thomas D.; Walter E.A. van Beek; and Dennis Thomson; eds. *Religion in Africa: Experience and Expression.* Portsmouth, NH: Heinemann, 1994.

Evans-Pritchard, E. E. *Nuer Religion.* Oxford: Clarendon Press, 1956.

Gifford, Paul. *African Christianity.* Bloomington: Indiana University Press, 1998.

Griaule, Marcel. *Conversations with Ogotemmêli: An Introduction to Dogon Religious Ideas.* London: Oxford University Press, 1965.

Heusch, Luc de. *Sacrifice in Africa: A Structuralist Approach*, trans. Linda O'Brien and Alice Morton. Bloomington: Indiana University Press, 1985.

Horton, Robin. *Patterns of Thought in Africa and the West.* Cambridge, U.K.: Cambridge University Press, 1993.

King, Noel Q. *African Cosmos: An Introduction to Religion in Africa.* Belmont, CA: Wadsworth, 1986.

MacGaffey, Wyatt. *Modern Kongo Prophets.* Bloomington: Indiana University Press, 1983.

Mbiti, John S. *African Religions and Philosophy.* Garden City, NY: Doubleday, 1970.

Meyer, Birgit. *Translating the Devil: Religion and Modernity among the Ewe in Ghana.* Trenton, NJ: Africa World Press, 1999.

Mudimbe, V. Y. *Tales of Faith: Religion as Political Performance in Central Africa.* London: Athlone Press, 1997.

Parrinder, Edward Geoffrey. *Religion in Africa.* New York: Praeger, 1969.

Ray, Benjamin. *African Religions: Symbol, Ritual and Community.* Englewood Cliffs, NJ: Prentice-Hall, 1976.

Taylor, John. *The Primal Vision: Christian Presence Amid African Religion.* London: SCM Press, 1963.

JOHN MIDDLETON

RELIGION AND THE STUDY OF AFRICA.

During the 1990s, a review of academic disciplines devoted to the study of Africa omitted the academic study of religion, although religion featured prominently in discussions of anthropology, philosophy, and art. As an interdisciplinary academic discipline, religious studies has been established in African university departments, beginning with the University of Ibadan, Nigeria, in 1949. Since 1992, religious studies has been supported by a professional society, the African Association for the Study of Religion.

African religion has emerged as an important field of inquiry for academic study, following a long history of denigration and neglect. European, North American, and African researchers have recovered indigenous beliefs and practices, frequently denied the status of religion by European colonizers, as significant religious resources and illuminating reference points for understanding the religious dimensions of the human experience. Increasingly, Africa has been recognized as an interreligious environment, with distinctive indigenous, Christian, and Muslim formations, whereas the religious creativity of the African diaspora has extended the understanding of global transformations of religion.

Indigenous African religions, in all of their variety, are a powerful religious force in the world.

According to statistics compiled by Adherents. com, African traditional and diasporic religions account for the religious affiliations of 100 million people, ranking eighth in this website's accounting of the major religions of the world (Adherents. com, 2005). Of course, African adherents of Christianity and Islam are substantially represented in these "world religions," with more members of the Church of England in Nigeria than in England and more Muslims living in Nigeria than in Saudi Arabia. While African indigenous religions have established a global presence in diaspora, the global religions of Christianity and Islam have assumed a variety of local forms in Africa as African religions.

However, during European expansion into Africa, European Christians—travelers, missionaries, and colonial agents—had considered that Africans had no religion. In southern Africa, for example, beginning around 1600, European observers reported that indigenous Africans, whether Khoesan in the Western Cape, or, later, Xhosa, Zulu, or Sotho-Tswana along an advancing colonial frontier, lacked any trace of religion. Because the observers recognized a variety of religions, based on the eighteenth century convention of classifying religions into Christianity, Judaism, Islam, and Heathenism, they were not saying only that Africans lacked Christianity: They were asserting that Africans represented an absence of religion, a deficit of a human faculty that might distinguish them from the beasts that perish, and therefore that Africans were not fully human. Muslim observers, as well, tended to represent sub-Saharan Africans as lacking religion, describing Africans as *kuffar* ("unbelievers") or seeing them as perpetuating the pagan era of *jahiliyah* associated with pre-Islamic Arabia. But the European denial of African indigenous religion, which functioned as a corollary of conquest and colonization, had a more sustained impact on Africa.

With a history in European Christian controversies over the religious significance of material objects, a contest between good relics and evil *feitiços*, the Portuguese term for made objects used in witchcraft, the terms fetish and fetishism were injected into these early representations of African religion as an allegation of the absence of religion. Denial of religion, as a strategic intervention in Africa, occurred elsewhere on the continent. As

religion was taken as a basis of responsibility and trust, in the mercantile trading zone of West Africa, European traders reported that they could do business with African Christians and African Muslims because they possessed a religion, but they could not do business with adherents of indigenous African religion, whom they called fetishists, because they allegedly had no religion. In this context of intercultural trade, lacking religion meant that fetishists were unable to value material objects in exchange relations, as they undervalued trade goods while overvaluing the objects they used in rituals.

Ironically, during the late nineteenth century, European theorists transformed this alleged absence of religion, evoked by the term fetishism, into the notional origin of religion. Through an evolutionary schema adapted as much from the philosophical speculations of Auguste Comte as from the scientific investigations of Charles Darwin, scholars of religion argued that reports about the fetishism, animism, or totemism of African natives provided evidence for the primitive origin of religion of all humanity. African religion, according to the formulation of Edward B. Tylor in *Primitive Culture* (1871), was symptomatic of animism, a mistaken belief in supernatural beings, which marked the original primitive religion.

Whereas this search for the origin of religion presumed that Africans did not live in the same historical time as modern Europeans, the eight textual traditions identified by F. Max Müller (1823–1900) in 1870 as major world religions implied that Africans did not live in the same geographical space with other religions in the world. Although Müller himself was sensitive to this exclusion, observing that his list of world religions defined by sacred texts left out much of the religious creativity of humanity, the logic of identifying world religions only as literate meant that African religion could register only as a residual category, as primitive or primal, with a place in human prehistory, perhaps, but no recognized claim on space in the contemporary religious world.

Recent understandings of religion in Africa—seeing them as both indigenous and mobile, as both anchored in place and crossing boundaries—have challenged earlier assumptions about religious origins and the classification of religions. During the twentieth century, as European and North American anthropologists were devoting ethnographic attention to African religion, not as an imaginary origin of humanity but as a way of life in its own right, African scholars provoked important debates about the notion of religion. The influential theologian John Samuel Mbiti (b. 1931) who rendered all of African life as notoriously religious, was challenged by the Ugandan poet and scholar Okot p'bitek (1931–1982) for illicitly smuggling ancient Greek philosophical and implicitly Christian categories into Africa.

However, the presence of God in African religion was of not only theological interest. As anthropologist Robin Horton (1971) argued, political, social, and economic changes that expanded the scope of human interaction and moved people from small, local religious engagements to larger religious transactions had to be overseen by a transcendent deity. Missionary religions, whether Christianity or Islam, could provide such a macrocosmic solution, but indigenous religious resources could also be expanded. Although the absence of sacred texts justified an earlier dismissal of African religion, the study of religion in Africa has revitalized our understanding of religious texts to include oral tradition, ritualized memory, and performative practices of social reproduction.

African indigenous religion has been engaged in three spheres: the home, the polity, and the knowledge and power of ritual specialists. Religious practices have been devoted to building up a home as a sacred domestic space, protected by ancestors from antisocial agents—referred to in English as witches—who might draw upon supernatural forces or techniques to disrupt the stability of the domestic space. Indigenous rituals have been drawn into strengthening, and mediating, the authority of leadership in African social relations. With the massive disruptions of African domestic life and political organization under forces of colonization, modernization, and now globalization, the most mobile, transportable mode of indigenous religion has been the ritual specialist. In popular perception, and sometimes in academic analysis, the ritual specialist is regarded as the essential carrier of indigenous African religion. The most visible expressions of African indigenous religion are found in the specialized practices of herbalists, healers, and diviners, who provide spiritual goods

and services, but also in the publicity of African "shamans," such as the West African Malidoma Patrice Somé and the South African Vusamazulu Credo Mutwa, who emerged during the 1990s within the global network of New Age spirituality as representatives of African religious authenticity.

In contemporary Africa, with a long multireligious history that has seen the development of substantial Christian and Muslim traditions, modern states have, in many cases, replicated the colonial legacy of denying indigenous religion. Generally, indigenous ritual specialists have had to be organized, and certified, to gain formal recognition as legitimate religions within African states. For the study of religion, these struggles over religious legitimacy shift the politics of category formation, the basic questions of defining religion or denying religions, from the colonial era to the present.

African religion, in all of its diversity, has provided a rich field of inquiry for understanding religion under globalizing conditions. On the one hand, local African traditions, whether indigenous, Christian, or Muslim, have been profoundly transformed by the incursions of new transnational forces. Whereas Arabizing Islamists and Americanizing evangelicals have had an enormous impact on the religious life of Muslims and Christians in various parts of Africa, new media have become essential parts of African religious life. For the study of religion, these developments have encouraged attention to the importance of media, with special attention to local African religious mediations of global popular culture.

Conversely, in the African diaspora, indigenous African religion has led a kind of alternative life, a transnational life in the Atlantic world, which has invigorated scholarship in religion. Recent research on Vodún, Santeria, Candomblé, and other diasporic forms of African religion have been at the forefront of developments in theory and method in the study of religion. The study of African diasporic religion has been situated in contact zones, those spaces of intercultural relations and asymmetrical power relations, in which creolization and hybridity have emerged as new modes of African religious creativity under difficult conditions.

Africa, which Hegel placed outside of history and generations of European religious scholars subjected to denial or neglect, has become increasingly important to the history of religions. Likewise, attention to religion has been recognized as important for understanding the dynamics of African life, from art to politics. The historical study of African religion, with special attention to a history of the present, is crucial for both the study of Africa and the study of religion.

See also **Christianity; Fetish and Fetishism; Islam; Judaism in Africa; Religion and Ritual; Vodún; Witchcraft.**

BIBLIOGRAPHY

Adherents.com. "Major Religions of the World." Available from http://www.adherents.com/Religions_By_Adherents. html.

Adogame, Afe, and Frieder Ludwig, eds. *European Traditions of the Study of Religion in Africa.* Wiesbaden, Germany: Harrassowitz Verlag, 2004.

Bates, Robert H.; Vumbi Yoka Mudimbe; and Jean O'Barr; eds. *Africa and the Disciplines: The Contributions of Research in Africa to the Social Sciences and Humanities.* Chicago: University of Chicago Press, 1993.

Chidester, David. *Savage Systems: Colonialism and Comparative Religion in Southern Africa.* Charlottesville: University Press of Virginia, 1996.

Chidester, David. "'Classify and Conquer': Friedrich Max Müller, Indigenous Religious Traditions, and Imperial Comparative Religion." In *Beyond Primitivism: Indigenous Religious, Traditions and Modernity,* ed. Jacob K. Olupona. London and New York: Routledge, 2004.

Ellis, Stephen, and Gerrie ter Haar. *Worlds of Power: Religious Thought and Political Practice in Africa.* Oxford: Oxford University Press, 2004.

Hackett, Rosalind. *Art and Religion in Africa.* London: Cassell, 1996.

Horton, Robin. "African Conversion." *Africa* 41 (1971): 85–108.

Mbiti, John S. *African Religions and Philosophy.* London: Heinemann, 1969.

P'Bitek, Okot. *African Religions in Western Scholarship.* Nairobi: Kenyan Literature Bureau, 1971.

Pietz, William. "The Problem of the Fetish, I." *Res: Anthropology and Aesthetics* 9 (1985): 5-17.

Ranger, Terence. "The Local and the Global in Southern African Religious History." In *Conversion to Christianity: Historical and Anthropological Perspectives on a Great Transformation,* ed. Robert Hefner. Berkeley: University of California Press, 1993.

Setiloane, Gabriel M. *The Image of God among the Sotho-Tswana.* Rotterdam, The Netherlands: A.A. Balkema, 1976.

Setiloane, Gabriel M. *African Theology: An Introduction.* Cape Town, South Africa: Lux Verbi, 2000.

Tylor, Edward Burnett, Sir. *Primitive Culture.* 2 vols. New York: Harper, 1958.

Westerlund, David. *African Religion in African Scholarship.* Stockholm, Sweden: Almqvist & Wiksell, 1988.

DAVID CHIDESTER

RÉPUBLIQUE CENTRAFRICAINE.
See **Central African Republic.**

RESEARCH

This entry includes the following articles:
OVERVIEW
BIOLOGICAL SCIENCES
SOCIAL SCIENCES
HISTORICAL RESOURCES
RESEARCH FUNDING
SCHOLARLY ETHICS

OVERVIEW

The aims, methods, and achievements of humanistic and social scientific Africanist research may be divided into three overlapping periods: until just before World War II; from the mid- until the late-twentieth century; and from then into the early twenty-first century. These periods correspond to broad changes in the history of colonialism and postcolonialism, the kinds of information and knowledge sought, and the identities of the researchers. Most research on the societies and cultures of Africa, their ecologies and economies, and their position in world history has taken place during the colonial interlude and its immediate aftermath. It has reflected both the nature of whatever information and knowledge has been needed or fashionable at a given time and also the theories and methods of the observers and analysts who collected that information and constructed that knowledge from it. And for almost all the past century and a half most researchers have been non-African; African scholars have only recently attained or been accorded equal rank and reputation.

RESEARCH UNTIL WORLD WAR II

Until the early twentieth century, most work on Africa was by individual scholars in Europe who relied on reports from the field by travelers, missionaries, and colonial officials; few actually visited the continent. Historians reconstructed colonial contact as part of European history; anthropologists were essentially ethnologists interested in the origins and movements of African peoples and the past links between ecology, economy, language, and forms of social organization; missionaries, who wrote many of the early ethnographies of these peoples, emphasized the Africans' languages and religions. Few other academic disciplines were concerned with Africa, except for archaeologists, classicists, and philologists interested in early Egypt and Greek and Roman Africa.

During the early twentieth century the disciplines interested in Africa were being given their modern forms. Anthropology led the way, with the beginnings of professional field research within tropical Africa by pioneer field workers such as Bronislaw Malinowski (1884–1942), Alfred Radcliffe-Brown (1881–1955), Gerard Lindblom (1887–1969), Richard Thurnwald (1869–1954), Leo Frobenius (1873–1938), Charles Seligman (1873–1940), such scholarly missionaries as Roscoe and Junod, and a few colonial administration anthropologists such as R. S. Rattray and C. K. Meek; all either worked in Africa in the first quarter of the century or taught students who did. In 1909 Arnold van Gennep (1873–1957) published his seminal work on rites of passage, demonstrating that individuals made social transitions according to a single pattern of removal, passage through a liminal state of vulnerability, and reintegration in a new status. Marcel Mauss (1872–1950) showed in 1925 that the gift is everywhere a central form of exchange and social relationship; and E.E. Evans-Pritchard (1902–1973) in 1935 showed the error of former definitions of African modes of thought as prerational and prelogical. Africans could no longer be held to be intellectually different from those researching them and so became collaborators in the field rather than mere objects of observation by outsiders.

The wider importance of these developments was Western academics' realization of the comparability of African, European, and other societies, thereby ending the former European view of Africans as primitive and exotic. In addition, this period saw the emergence of three theoretical innovations that were to structure research in virtually all disciplines. One was the method known as functionalism, which analyzed the coherence of interrelationships among forms of political, domestic, and religious behavior both with one another as well as with intellectual frameworks of customs, beliefs, moralities, artistic, and dramatic activities. The second was the publication in 1928 by the International African Institute (London) of the International African Alphabet, which created a single orthography for unwritten languages in Africa that facilitated intersocietal comparison and the recording of texts in African languages. The third was the accompanying realization that all research on present-day populations demanded the researcher's use of local languages and dialects: reliance on interpreters was inadequate.

THE SECOND HALF OF THE TWENTIETH CENTURY

After World War II it became obvious that the colonial interlude was ending, and the colonial powers realized that they needed more information if they were either to plan for its peaceful ending or to prolong it as long as possible, even by military means. Funded programs of Western research on Africa were increased, often through rapid growth of European and colonial universities and of other institutions focused on the continent. Most indigenous African institutions of learning were mainly concerned with the study of Islam and its history and not seen as contributing to the overriding goal of modernizing the continent. Among the principal innovators were geographers, who came to emphasize the field of tropical human geography and ecology; archaeologists, who moved from previous interests in stone and iron technologies to studying early forms of social organization; and anthropologists, who made detailed analyses of systems of social organization and religion so as to fill gaps in their knowledge of African societies, and shifted from small hunting-and-gathering groups, once thought primal, to the elaborate kingdoms of West and Southern Africa. Little was known about most of the two thousand or so societies of the continent beyond their approximate territorial positions and linguistic affiliations, and it was important to classify, analyze, and compare their social, political, and religious systems at all periods, although with sadly little concern for modern processes of change.

Historians had this general anthropological framework on which to build and began to turn from the Eurocentric history of colonialism to include the responses to external contact by the African societies themselves, thereby moving from the study of what had happened to Africa to the ethnographic study of what had happened in Africa, or what history Africans had made for themselves. This was no easy task due mainly to the lack of written documentation of events, but by the 1960s historians, led by Roland Oliver (b. 1923), Jan Vansina (b. 1929), John Fage, and others were carrying out studies of the reactions of African societies to European trading and colonial and missionary activities. Other disciplines followed the same path, from a quest for the different and the exotic to understanding the everyday: religions, economies, philosophy, art languages, literature, psychology, and other aspects of life familiar to modern Westerners.

At first most of the peoples selected for research, especially by anthropologists, were rural, those at the time usually referred to as tribes that could easily be defined as coherent, hence intelligible, cultural entities. Attention to the complexities of their structures focused largely on forms of descent and kinship, their patterns of cultural behavior, ideologies, and religious beliefs and rituals. However, after World War II interest grew in changing forms of wealth and stratification, population movements, colonial-era labor migration, and the growing cities and towns as centers of modern industrial and political organization. Many cities were capitals of eighteenth- and nineteenth-century African kingdoms, but most were modern settlements of the colonial era, inhabited not only by Africans (usually temporary immigrants from surrounding rural areas) but also by Europeans and others who considered themselves culturally distinct from Africans. These centers of industrial, mining, administrative and commercial developments were thought hardly to be African at all, so dominant among European scholars was the image of changeless rural villages. The towns presented new problems of study very different from those of tribal areas (a widespread question was whether their inhabitants were tribesmen or townsmen), and in many cases the colonial powers did not always want outsiders to look at the increasingly squalid conditions prevailing in them or new forms of social and political unrest.

Almost all social-scientific academic research until the independence of most colonies in the later part of the twentieth century was, of course, necessarily carried out under the constraints of colonial authorities. Local administrations formally controlled the research permitted, although their actual oversight was in fact usually slight: they had other matters to attend to. They seem usually to have considered academic research to be impractical and too slow in producing results; many maintained staffs of their own to undertake research on local problems. Behind this skeptical view was often the fear that these outsiders might produce criticism of administrative policies and practices: several anthropologists were expelled from urban areas, notably from the Northern Rhodesian Copperbelt, for studying poverty, trades unions, and other urban organizations in critical ways.

Geographers and anthropologists were considered safe by colonial authorities so long as they kept to the rural areas, where it was accepted that they could not do much harm by studying indigenous forms of social and political organization. Historians were safe as well, so long as they devoted themselves, as indeed they usually did in any case, to the precolonial and early colonial periods; economists could be useful but most were unable to see beyond contemporary European and American theories or to analyze local African systems of production and exchange; sociologists found it difficult to use their European experience to understand African cities; psychologists were baffled by problems of rationality, morality, and the family; and political scientists were too attracted by the problems of newly independent national governments to observe what was happening at the local levels of politics. Humanists such as art historians, musicologists, and literary critics were more easily tolerated, although many African writers who began to write and publish before independence in the 1960s incurred administrative disapproval as being anti-European.

Most researchers in the later twentieth century were British and French scholars of many disciplines who became specialized Africanists, training and sending out their own students to make local studies. An immediate intention was to fill the gaps in knowledge of individual African societies so as to complete the ethnographic and historical map of the continent, but the work varied among the metropolitan countries. British scholars concentrated on the history of colonial rule (from the viewpoint of the colonizers) and on the ethnography of still little-known African peoples, most researchers coming from only a few universities (especially London and Oxford) or sponsored by learned societies with specialized African interests (the Royal Geographical Society, founded in 1831; the Royal African Society, 1901; the International African Institute, founded in 1926 by Lord Lugard, an important colonial administrator; and the African Studies Association of the United Kingdom, 1960); several specialized research institutes were based in Africa itself (especially those in Livingstone and then Lusaka, Kampala, Lagos, and Freetown), and the many missionary and medical societies.

In France most research comprised colonial history and cultural ethnography; and one or two universities and scholarly institutes, among others the Societe des Africanistes, 1930, and the Institut Francais de l'Afrique Noire, founded in Dakar in 1939 and later extended to other French colonies, also provided researchers who worked in most French colonies. After World War II, French researchers of many disciplines were largely divided between those interested in African thought and ideology (Marcel Griaule, 1898–1956; Germain Dieterlen, 1903–1999; and others) and those concerned with urbanization and modernization (Georges Balandier, b. 1920; Claude Meillassoux, b. 1925; Catherine Coquery-Vidrovitch). The Ecole Pratique des Hautes Etudes, The Centre National des Recherches Scientifiques, and the Musee de l'Homme, all in Paris, had world reputations.

In Belgium, after the founding of the Tervuren Museum in 1910, most research in the Belgian colonies was linked to art and museum collections, although later there were established ethnographic and historical research institutes in the Congo and Rwanda-Burundi. German research centered on linguistic work, under the famed scholars Carl Meinhof (1857–1944) and Diedrich Westermann

(1875–1956), as well as material culture, but the loss of Germany's colonies in 1918 and the later Nazi period led to a general lack of interest in the continent. Italian research was limited almost entirely to the Horn of Africa. The Salazar dictatorship in Portugal had little interest in the African populations of its colonies and research on them was limited to a few descriptive ethnographies.

The United States took little interest in Africa until the second half of the century, when it became evident that ex-colonial nations could be used as partners in the Cold War. Previously the leader was Melville Herskovits (1895–1963), whose interest in American populations of African descent led him back to Africa in search of the roots of cultures that survived in the New World, and who established a research center at Northwestern University in 1948. At Stanford University the linguistic taxonomist Joseph Greenberg (1915–2001) grouped Africa's some two thousand languages into five super-families that still structure linguistic research on the continent. The Rockefeller, Carnegie, and Ford Foundations, which had funded earlier British research from the 1930s, helped to open Africanist centers in Boston, Los Angeles, Wisconsin, and elsewhere.

The political situation in South Africa had always seriously affected research in both rural and urban communities and groups. Government researchers concentrated on work that would assist various developments to maintain apartheid, or on ethnological studies without immediate political significance; others, in particular anthropologists such as Isaac Schapera (1905–2003), Hilda Kuper (1911–1992), and Monica Wilson (1908–1982), produced ethnographies that have become classics, many of them based on research in the then British High Commission territories of Bechuanaland, Swaziland, and Basutoland. Many moved to Britain and the United States where they became leaders in many universities (such as the distinguished anthropologists Meyer Fortes, 1906–1983; and Max Gluckman, 1911–1975) and inspired a growing group of resident researchers as the rigidity of the regime lessened near the end of the century.

The then-USSR was less concerned with Africa than were Western Europe and North America, although it had long-standing interests in Ethiopia and South Africa. Toward the end of the century other countries became increasingly involved, in particular the Netherlands with an emphasis on anthropology at the University of Leiden, the Scandinavian countries, and Japan.

In brief, by the formal end of colonial overrule in Africa—gradually from the 1960s through the 1980s—the knowledge of Africa was patchy, with relatively little information on most of its societies, their cultures, or their histories. It was held mainly by competitive European scholars and formed neither a coherent corpus of knowledge nor any deep understanding of the subjected continent equal to that held, whether in Europe or elsewhere, about the Near East, Asia, or Southeast Asia. Africa remained little known and little understood by the outside world and indeed by its own scholars of the time.

THE TURN OF THE CENTURY AND AFTER

In the wake of colonial overrule, the later twentieth and early twenty-first centuries have turned to researching information about African countries and their inhabitants needed by postcolonial nations and global commercial and other interests. The issues of research center on who can best supply that information, and who owns and controls what is discovered, thus following organizational and cultural developments in contemporary African societies, cities, and nations. The former longstanding pattern of many separately distinguishable ethnic groups mostly based on forms of descent has almost everywhere given way—though in differing degrees—to one of groups' being newly organized as a consequence of their territorial dispersal and intermingling to form new populations. Rules of land tenure and property ownership, forms of exchange, patterns of kinship and marriage, notions of time and space, and religious belief and practice have all been deeply affected by adaptations to modern cash economies and political citizenship. Anthropologists have largely given up ethnographic studies of individual societies (the former tribes) as these have almost all lost their colonial boundaries due largely to population movements to the growing cities and the consequent shifts in personal and social orientations once known as detribalization.

Most recent anthropological research has focused on such social problems as the growth of poverty, unemployment, and slums or informal settlements, the breakdown of traditional forms of organization and religious behavior, changes in patterns of gender, marriage, rank and authority, wars, famines, and disease. Many historians, however, have continued essentially to study European history as it has been played out in Africa, but availability of recently collected archives has led to greater emphasis on local responses to outside contact. Economists have joined anthropologists in studying nonmarket forms of trade and exchange, and political scientists have continued their earlier studies of national governments and international relations. All these fields of research differ from those of earlier periods in one basic way: they are of concern to African communities and groups rather than to extracontinental colonial rulers. Much of the funding and personnel involved in contemporary research still come from outside Africa, but African governments and institutions are interested as never before and exercise greater control and guidance than in previous periods.

However, in recent years both popular and academic interests in African studies have lessened and governmental and foundation support in Europe and America has declined. There appear to be several reasons: first, foreign government support has dropped with the end of the Cold War, in which the global antagonists wanted information about the continent and had to provide means of obtaining it; second, the increase in conflicts among political rivals in Africa have made carefully thought-out research projects difficult to pursue; third, individual researchers find projects dangerous and often impossible in environments of deteriorating public health and security; and last, beyond Africa's new reputation for violence, poverty, and political instability, commercial and financial interest have shifted to parts of the world other than Africa.

Whereas Europeans conducted almost all scientific research, in the widest sense, in colonial Africa, and controlled both higher education and funding in Africa and Europe, in the postcolonial era African scholars have themselves increasingly been able to hold higher educational and research positions and to publish their research findings. With the approach of independence in the 1950s, African scholars were students in Europe and in North America, where they found welcome in the then-Negro (now historically black) colleges and universities. The first generation returned to African universities and research institutes to replace European expatriate staff and faculty. The second generation could also obtain full positions in their own right in non-African institutions throughout the world, and many did so as the research institutions of the continent were allowed to drift by governments with other priorities, including primary education. The third generation of African scholars has begun to ask significantly different questions from those of their teachers, setting themselves in a wider postcolonial context and defining problems more from local African viewpoints than from the European and American ones that have continued to dominate international scholarship on the continent.

Much has been written about the "brain drain" of the first and second generations of African scholars. It may often have had—and still does have—deleterious consequences for research in Africa itself, but acceptance of these researchers throughout the world is also an important marker of the end of Africa's intellectual, scholarly, and scientific isolation. This process should not be seen merely in crude terms of African scholars' taking over from non-African ones: rather it has been a process of amalgamation, of fellowship, of collaboration, of equality, and of the abandonment of previous long-standing racialism. It has also marked global acceptance of the worth and value of Africans' thinking, an acceptance paralleled by recognition of and reliance on African statesmen, politicians, scientists, and religious leaders.

THE CONTEXTS AND METHODS OF RESEARCH

Research in Africa, of whatever disciplines, has always faced certain problems either not found everywhere else or at least not to so marked an extent. Among them have been the general background of neglected education and scholarship, difficulties for foreign researchers of cultural interpretation and translation, fewer and less adequate research facilities, and limited means of dissemination of knowledge produced among the people it concerns. The intellectual and moral positions of African researchers remains one of disparity between the African cultures that they study and the Western intellectual tools that they bring to the task. This paradox goes back to the colonial situation in which most research was by non-African scholars attached to the formal Eurocentric academic disciplines of European (and American) scholarship. African scholars of equal ability and distinction first saw their role as presenting an Afrocentic inversion of Western research paradigms imposed on them, much of it consciously anticolonial and often anti-European. Scholars of the 1940s and 1950s such as Fanon, Senghor, Diop and then literary writers such as Achebe, wa Thiongo, Soyinke, and their modern followers have always provided important counterweights to the dominance of research in Eurocentric terms.

Many internationally renowned scholars such as Léopold Senghor, Jacob Ajayi, V. Y. Mudimbe, Joseph Ki-Zerbo (b. 1922), Paulin Hountondji (b. 1942), Ali Mazrui (b. 1933), and others have attempted to build a single integrated field of African studies that includes African, European, and North American ideas and institutions and recognizes common training and standards of achievement. Important factors in the advancement of research by African institutions have been the spread of modern education and literacy at both school and university levels and the recent explosion of new media in most African countries. Until the later twentieth century, Western-style education and literate communication were associated only with the new elites of most countries, often antagonistic to traditional holders of authority. In recent years, however, the power of new elites, growing literacy of mass populations, and electronic (nonliterate) media have provided support for local research institutions and scholars. Research had previously been of little concern to anyone except scholars themselves, but in recent years they have become of importance to a more general public, and this popular interest has influenced the research projects funded by governments and scholarly and commercial institutions.

Methods of research within Africa itself have changed with Africanization of the enterprise. At the basis of all research in Africa, whether by African or non-African scholars (although this similarity is not always acknowledged), have been and remain the problems of comprehension and translation across linguistic and cultural divides. Although these gaps are found everywhere in humanities and social science research, they appear to be most marked in Africa, due largely to the lack of long experience of research and to the Eurocentric colonial-era view of African people as culturally, morally, and even intellectually inferior. The European tradition of limiting research data to information in documents written either by non-Africans or African writers highly educated in Christian or Islamic scholarship is perhaps acceptable in writing the history of European intentions in Africa (the subject of most historical writing on Africa, such as that on the slave trades or early missionary activity), but is clearly inadequate for understanding the impact of outsiders' actions and incapable of revealing Africans' histories per se, without extremely cautious and respectful methodologies.

Anthropologists have worked for almost a century on methods of understanding how Africans themselves envisage their societies and histories and on problems of understanding the prominence in Africa of collective memory, but few others have troubled to learn from them, even though they are required for understanding of documents and even archaeological materials. The consequence has been—and remains—a distinction between disciplines concerned with European colonial history and those concerned with comparative knowledge of African societies and cultures, whether of today or of the past.

In recent years a marked increase in African universities and in educational and commercial institutions largely independent of non-African connections and personnel has greatly broadened the range of research fields in Africa beyond the social sciences and humanities. Studies in scientific fields that need costly laboratory facilities have been marginal, as facilities of this sort have been scarce and underfunded across the continent, outside South Africa and some northern African countries. Researchers have tended to use those in Europe and North America and thus contributed to priorities there. This relative neglect of the experimental sciences has presumably reflected African university policies favoring teaching needs that have not demanded highly expensive facilities; however, in recent years this situation has radically altered.

The social efficacy and intellectual productivity of research depend on disseminating results. There are many means of doing so: books, journals, photographs and films, speech recordings and music, radio and television, novels and personal memoirs, and museums and exhibitions, all aimed at different recipients and markets. Scholarly books have almost always been published by non-African university and government presses, as well as by a handful of specialist commercial presses. European and American institutions have therefore largely controlled the reports of research, whoever may be the actual researchers, and have tended to favor issues familiar to their primarily external markets.

The same bias toward non-African concerns has existed with regard to scholarly journals and newspapers; the latter, although published locally, have only recently been controlled by African proprietors and editors. Ethnographic photography and cinema have been sporadic within Africa, usually as adjunct to conventional research conducted in literate formats, though in recent years an African commercial cinema has come to flourish. Recordings of speech and music have a long history in linguistics and ethnomusicology, and for many years non-African commercial recording companies have published popular music in African cities. Radio transmitters are long established throughout the continent and reach the majority of the population; television is also widely established but generally reaches only urban communities. Novels and memoirs have a very long history, originally by European writers; but recently more African writers, aware of scholarly research findings, have entered the commercial novel field with immense success, although they have often found it difficult to publish within Africa itself. Finally, dissemination of research findings has been by museums and various national and international exhibitions. Europeans' collection and often virtual looting of African art and artifacts have histories of central importance to knowledge of African cultures abroad, both in the museum world and the worldwide system of art markets, but these processes of collection have been on the commercial fringes of research itself.

See also **Achebe, Chinua; Anthropology, Social, and the Study of Africa; Cold War; Colonial Policies and Practices; Dakar; Demography; Diop, Alioune; Fanon, Frantz; Freetown; Kampala; Kinship and Affinity; Lagos; Land: Tenure; Lusaka; Ngũgĩ wa Thiong'o; Senghor, Léopold Sédar; Soyinke, Wole; Time Reckoning and Calendars; World War II.**

BIBLIOGRAPHY

Bates, Robert H.; V. Y. Mudimbe; and Jean O'Barr, eds. *Africa and the Disciplines: The Contribution of Research in Africa to the Social Sciences and Humanities.* Chicago: University of Chicago Press, 1993.

Epstein, Arnold Leonard, ed. *The Craft of Social Anthropology.* London: Tavistock, 1967.

Evans-Pritchard, Edward E. *Anthropology and History.* Manchester, England: Manchester University Press, 1961.

Fyfe, Christopher, ed. *African Studies since 1945.* London: Longman, 1976.

Gaillard, Gérald. *The Routledge Dictionary of Anthropologists.* London: Routledge, 2004.

Goody, Jack. *The Expansive Moment: The Rise of Social Anthropology in Britain and Africa, 1918–1970.* New York: Cambridge University Press, 1995.

Guyer, Jane. *African Studies in the United States: A Perspective.* Atlanta: African Studies Association Press, 1996.

Kloos, Peter, and Henri J. M. Claessen, eds. *Current Anthropology in the Netherlands.* Rotterdam: Anthropological Branch of the Netherlands Sociological and Anthropological Society, 1975.

Moore, Sally Falk. *Anthropology and Africa: Changing Perspectives on a Changing Scene.* Charlottesville: University Press of Virginia, 1994.

Mudimbe, Valentin Y. *The Invention of Africa: Gnosis, Philosophy, and the Order of Knowledge.* Bloomington: Indiana University Press, 1988.

Mudimbe, Valentin Y. *The Idea of Africa.* Bloomington: Indiana University Press, 1994.

Vansina, Jan. *Oral Tradition as History.* Madison: University of Wisconsin Press, 1985.

Vansina, Jan. *Living with Africa.* Madison: University of Wisconsin Press, 1994.

JOHN MIDDLETON

BIOLOGICAL SCIENCES

African biological research is one of the positive legacies of European colonial rule over Africa. After a long and tortuous period beyond the Renaissance, scientific research became part of European culture as a means of both survival through understanding and taking protection from the elements, as well as for prosperity in what was becoming an increasingly intra-European competition for economic success. This is the tradition that was passed on to the European colonies with various levels of commitment and investment. And these were the origins of formal African biological research.

THE PRE–WORLD WAR II COLONIAL PERIOD

A major change occurred in the cultural ecology of Africa through the continent's colonization by European powers. The changes wrought by the European colonization of Africa were of greater magnitude than anything that affected Africa before or since. Its most positive legacy was probably to bring Africa into contemporary world civilization, not least in the field of biological research.

The first European biologists came to Africa in expeditions. They concentrated on compiling a taxonomic database, which included much information that was new to formal European science. With respect to the international nomenclature of plants and animals, the introduction of African flora and fauna constituted new scientific information.

The early colonial collections of biological specimens were destined for exhibition in European museums. Later, live specimens were sent to European zoos. The British Museum (Natural History) in South Kensington, London, like its French, Belgian, Spanish and Portuguese counterparts, continues to house rich collections of African animals and plants.

By the end of World War I, there was a shift from a pure collecting zeal to seeking some understanding of the ecological relationships of the diverse components of the African biota. The historical scientific expeditions that came to Africa to collect specimens of animals and plant life were increasingly replaced by groups who tried to study relationships of African plants and animals to each other, and the balance between them in their various environmental contexts. In the late 1920s the British Graham Expedition to Lake Victoria resulted not only in the naming of a new tilapia species, *Tilapia esculenta* (now *Oreochromis esculentus*), but also in determining the effect of newly introduced gill nets, the mesh sizes of which were deemed by the Graham expedition to be too small for the continued survival of the endemic Lake Victoria species. Edgar B. Worthington undertook perhaps the most important of the investigations of the inland waters of Africa in 1929 and 1932; reports of the latter included the results of a 1930–1931 expedition sponsored by Cambridge

University. One member of that Cambridge expedition was a young graduate, Leonard C. Beadle, who in 1950 became the first professor of biology at Makerere, the pioneer institution of higher learning for the whole of East and Central Africa situated in Kampala (Uganda) since its founding in 1922. The results of some of these expeditions continued to be published into the 1990s.

THE POST–WORLD WAR II PERIOD
World War II brought about a major change in the political ecology of Africa. With the returning African war veterans who had fought and died alongside their white compatriots, particularly in Burma and Malaysia, the distinction between the rulers and ruled became somewhat blurred. Agitation for independence was in the air. As the victors of World War II, the major European colonial powers were Britain, France, and Belgium, with Portugal and Spain being reduced to a relatively minor role. The Axis Powers of Germany and Italy were required, as a consequence of their defeat, to cede their colonial territories to the Allies as mandated territories. The truth, however, was that both victor and vanquished were economically severely damaged.

With the sweep of socialism in Europe, there was an anticipatory mood of political independence in the colonies. India and Pakistan became independent in 1947. These were followed ten years later with the first African colony to attain independence: Gold Coast (now Ghana).

These events were not without due effect on the development of African biology. Colonial scholars and administrators felt an urgent need to redefine the structures of research along more pragmatic lines. In the British Colonial Office, the buzzword of the time was federation. French colonial philosophy was revolving along the same line, except that the French preferred to regard Francophone colonies as part of Metropolitan France. Thus, before the granting of independence to Ghana and later Nigeria, the idea of a West African Federation was put forward. In Central Africa, Roy Welensky (1907–1991) and his white-dominated Central African Federation was undermined by African political leadership, in particular by Dr. Hastings Kamuzu Banda of Malawi.

These various political moves did not occur without impact on the organization and running of research in Africa. Thus in the immediate postwar East

Africa, the East African High Commission was formed in 1948, a kind of joint high command of the three British East African Governors of Kenya, Uganda, and Tanganyika and their Zanzibar counterpart, the British Resident. Under this body, instruments of economic advancement and integration were formed, such as the East African Currency Board, the East African Posts and Telecommunications Corporation, the East African Railways and Harbours Corporation, and the East African Airways Corporation.

At the same time, a number of research institutes were set up. These were the East African Medical Research Organization at Mwanza in Tanzania and the East African Agricultural and Forestry Research Organization and the East African Veterinary Research Organization, both at Muguga, a few miles northwest of Nairobi, Kenya. Both the East African Leprosy Research Organization and the East African Trypanosomiasis Research Organization were situated in Tororo, Uganda. The East African Freshwater Fisheries Research Organization was established at Jinja, Uganda, on the shores of Lake Victoria, and the East African Marine Fisheries Research Organization was founded in Zanzibar. All these organizations were engaged in the fields of applied biological research.

One seed for the future expansion of biological research and knowledge was in the founding and expansion of higher learning institutions: Ibadan in West Africa and Makerere in East Africa became the nuclei of a wide catchments base of higher education that, in the case of Makerere, transcended national boundaries. Thus, in the early 1950s students attending Makerere came not only from the four East African states of Kenya, Uganda, Tanganyika, and Zanzibar, but also from Malawi and Zambia. In Southern Rhodesia (present-day Zimbabwe), a Federal University College at Salisbury was founded during this phase of the colonial era, although in reality this was a white-dominated institution.

THE EARLY POSTINDEPENDENCE PERIOD
By the 1960s, many African countries were either politically independent or on their way to becoming so. Most African countries that gained independence had a national university, or the nucleus of one. In rare cases, a few countries banded together to support a federal university. The University of

Botswana, Lesotho and Swaziland (UBLS) is a case in point. Subsequently, both UBLS and the University of East Africa yielded to national political pressures to become national universities. The University of East Africa also started as a federal university, shared between Kenya, Uganda, and Tanzania, with constituent university colleges of Dar es Salaam, Makerere, and Nairobi. It split in 1970, with each to become a separate university.

In the early postindependence period, an interest in more fundamental, theoretical aspects of biology was taking shape in the universities. Although applied aspects of these fundamental studies were not necessarily relegated to other institutions, the freedom—indeed, desire—to take a longer view of biological research was both healthy and necessary. New linkages with universities in Europe, and to a lesser extent in America, led to international partnerships between universities and research institutions. Granting bodies such as Ford, Rockefeller, Nuffield, Wellcome, and Munitalp Foundations began to significantly support university research in Africa. The Rockefeller Foundation, in particular, developed a program to support the indigenization of East African universities with training scholarships and fellowships for African academic staff. In the wake of this, strong growth in contemporary biological research took place in a number of African countries.

Both the number and the quality of publications in biological research began to rise significantly, and there was worldwide recognition of African biological research. More and more conferences were held in Africa as a mark of respect for the research quality emanating from the continent. The International Symposium on Comparative Endocrinology was held in Kenya in 1974. This was both an acknowledgement of the quality of the research carried out on this fundamental aspect of biology in Africa, and was also recognition of the potential for new biological insights that could be forthcoming through understanding of tropical endocrine mechanisms. By the mid-1970s African biological research reached its peak and institutions such as the International Centre for Insect Physiology and Ecology (ICIPE) and the International Laboratory for Research in Animal Diseases (ILRAD), which later became the International Livestock Research Institute (ILRI), attained enthusiastic international support.

THE LATE POSTINDEPENDENCE PERIOD

The 1980s and 1990s saw a general decline in African university research. Many factors contributed to this situation. The improved health of African nations resulted in reduced infant and child mortality rates and a consequent dramatic increase in the number of young people in the general population. This produced political pressure on African governments to increase the level of enrolment in public universities. At the same time, financial and equipment resources for scientific research diminished. Competition for international funds became greater worldwide, demanding ever-higher quality of research proposal and supporting references. University staff remuneration decreased. Thus, whereas in 1963 academic staff in the East Africa enjoyed salaries that were slightly higher than their British equivalents (largely to attract British expatriates to work in the newly independent ex-colonies), these salaries became less than a fifth of those enjoyed by their British contemporaries in British universities by the 1980s. By the 1990s, this had dropped to less than a tenth of their British colleagues.

The post-Gorbachev era brought a sharp rejoinder to African countries that North American and European countries were demanding a much more rigorous level of financial and political accountability and transparency as a precondition of the release of budgetary support. More market-oriented approaches became necessary in the management of both governmental and university institutions. In the mid-1990s, however, African biological research had yet to recover to its earlier postindependence boom. As of 2007 the situation has yet to change significantly. There is far too little national government support for research in the universities. It is hoped that once the reorientation in the general economy has taken place, modern tools of communication will see a resurgence of African biological research and the growth of biological knowledge to a hitherto unprecedented level.

See also **Banda, Ngwazi Hastings Kamuzu; Colonial Policies and Practices; Knowledge; Postcolonialism; Socialism and Postsocialisms; World War II.**

BIBLIOGRAPHY

Beadle, Leonard C. *The Inland Waters of Tropical Africa: An Introduction to Tropical Limnology.* London; New York: Longman, 1981.

Graham, Michael. *The Victoria Nyanza and Its Fisheries.* London: The Crown Agents for the Colonies, 1929.

Partnerships for Strengthening Conservation Biology in Africa. Report of a Workshop held in Nairobi, Kenya, 10–13 September 2001. Available from www.aaas.org/international/africa/conservationbiology/report.shtml.

Worthington, Edgar Barton. *A Report on the Fisheries of Uganda Investigated by the Cambridge Expedition to the East Africa Lakes 1932–33.* London: The Crown Agents for the Colonies, 1932.

Worthington, Edgar Barton, and Stella Worthington. *Inland Waters of Africa.* London: Macmillan, 1933.

MOHAMED HYDER

SOCIAL SCIENCES

THE ANTHROPOLOGICAL APPROACH

Africa was long conceived by most Europeans to be an unknown continent inhabited by strange creatures. As there had been contacts with the outside world, travelers knew better. Later, during the colonial period, some administrators and missionaries wrote detailed working accounts of the peoples with whom they were in contact. There were hundreds of languages unknown to Europeans. The ways of life of the people with whom they had contact were completely unfamiliar. Then, anthropologists took up the task of writing scholarly descriptions with the goal of identifying the location, customs, and ideas of the many peoples who lived on the continent. The aim of ethnography was to describe these ways of life intelligibly to European rationalists. Some monographs attempted to describe the whole culture of a people in one book. Other writings were structured around particular themes such as marriage and family, religion, migration, or economy.

Having built up a collection of descriptions of many particular peoples, anthropologists began to compare aspects of the social arrangements they saw, matrilineal and patrilineal kinship groups, peoples with chiefs, and some without. These anthropologists generated theoretical frameworks to analyze the differences discovered. Social anthropology itself developed out of this literature. Leading thinkers in the field examined such matters as African political systems, African systems of kinship, and African systems of thought. Much of this work was done during the colonial period, 1890–1960 for most of Africa, except South Africa. The work reflected a strong interest in reconstructing the organization of these societies as they were thought to have existed in precolonial times. Inevitably, the colonial period had brought about the disruption of many traditional ways without endowing Africa with the values, practices, and economic assets of an industrial society. Some anthropologists idealized the folk cultures of the African past and deplored the tragedy of their disintegration. Anthropologists in the early twenty-first century are concerned to describe the Africa they see before them, the mixture of old ways and modern introductions, and how it got to be the way it is.

Since independence, largely after the 1960s, there has been a considerable change both in the ways anthropologists have approached African affairs, and in the situations of African societies.

Anthropologists tend to describe particular aspects of lives, rather than trying to capture the whole of a culture or of a people. They are much less occupied than their predecessors with distinguishing what is indigenous from what is modern. A classic topic of interest in earlier African studies is the nature of kinship and family. A 1997 collection of essays inspects contemporary issues in the context of life among a number of peoples in Western Kenya and Eastern Uganda (Weisner, Bradley, and Kilbridde 1997). The families and households about which they write belong to different ethnic groups and speak many different languages. Occupationally they are diverse. They comprise herders, traders, laborers, and urban dwellers. They come from an area of high population density. The common focus of these scholars is on the African family in crisis, and on change and adaptation. They emphasize that the crisis with which they are concerned is not simply a product of European or North American imagining, but is a concern of Africans themselves. The essays are organized around Africans' themes of economy, human development, gender and fertility, the elderly, and health.

Both before and after independence, many anthropologists conducted studies of the economic activities of households and communities. These were local projects, aspects of the societies whose affairs they were observing in other dimensions as well. Thus, anthropologists, not professional economists, produced much of the earliest economic data. Examples include books on economic changes in South African native life, labor migration, farming, exchange, investments and the impact of money, markets in Africa, the economies of the Hausa in Northern Nigeria, and innovators and entrepreneurs among cacao farmers in Nigeria.

Economy and gender studies have received a good deal of recent attention. Among other books, Jane Guyer has written about the division of labor, resources and income in farm families in Southern Cameroon (1984), and in 2004 she published a wide-ranging book on economy, currencies, exchange and transactions in Africa. Sara Berry wrote on economy and social relations in an extended Yoruba community, *Fathers Work for their Sons* (1985).

A reader on *African Market Women* and their roles in economic development appeared in 1995, edited by Bessie House-Midamba and Felix K. Ekechi. In 1997, Ann M. O. Griffiths published a book on gender and justice in an African community (*In the Shadow of Marriage*). A 2005 reader, edited by Oyeronke Oyewumi with many African contributors, is *African Gender Studies.*

On the political front several books written since the 1990s have stood out because they convey the circumstances dramatically. One is an account of Hutu refugees in Tanzania written by Liisa Malkki (1995).

Another was written about the war in Sierra Leone, *Fighting for the Rain Forest* by Paul Richards (1996). Another is by Andrew Apter, who addresses *The Pan-African Nation: Oil and the Spectacle of Culture in Nigeria* (2005). And the third and fourth are two books by James Ferguson, one an ethnographic study of a development project in Lesotho (*The Anti-politics Machine* 1994) and, in an unusual project for an anthropologist, the attempt to understand Africa's place in the world order today, a book titled *Global Shadows* (2006). The global context is now pertinent to the anthropology of Africa even in the most local studies.

THE POLITICAL DIMENSION

Political scientists became actively interested in African studies after independence principally because of the opportunity to observe and understand the

processes of forming new states. David Apter wrote pathbreaking books on Ghana and Uganda in 1963 and 1967, and another on the politics of modernization in 1965. Aristide Zolberg wrote on the Côte d'Ivoire in 1964 and on the party-states of West Africa in 1966. There was a conference on African socialism in 1962 (Friedland and Rosberg, 1964). Lionel Cliffe wrote on one-party Tanzania and its elections (1967). Donal Cruise O'Brien wrote on an Islamic brotherhood, the Mourides of Senegal and their political and economic organization (1971). In 1971, Robert Bates wrote about Zambian mineworkers, about their unions, parties, and their connection with political development. Five years later he published a book on the rural responses to industrialization in Zambia (1976). These were all directly and indirectly concerned with the formation of the postcolonial state and its *dirigiste* character.

At around the same time another theme began to emerge as a dominant analytic concern of political scientists: the multiethnic character of African countries. The recognition of political fault lines in the new states became the focus of analysis. In this vein, Crawford Young published *The Politics of Cultural Pluralism* (1976). Richard L. Sklar in an article on "The African Frontier for Political Science" made the point that in most African states there was a "state behind the state," namely that the traditional political organization of its ethnic groups had persisted not only through the colonial period but continued to be politically important after independence. C. S. Whitaker had confirmed continuities such as these in his book on the politics of tradition in Northern Nigeria (1970).

Economic development did not occur in Africa by donors and by Africans, as had been expected. A number of works address this apparent anomaly. But development was not the only locus of disappointment in this discipline. Personal rule has been characteristic of many African regimes. What Robert H. Jackson and Carl G. Rosberg had to say in 1984 about this the failure of expected liberal democracy is devastating. They argue that, "Among the most important practices in personal regimes are conspiracy, factional politics and clientelism, corruption, purges and rehabilitations, and succession maneuvers...taken together they appear to accurately characterize the kind of politics to which politicians in the great majority of sub-Saharan countries have resorted over the past two decades" (28).

The earlier optimistic emphasis on the organization of the postcolonial state, and on the political potential of ethnic pluralism, has given way to a focus on crime, violence, conflict, corruption, and inequality. There have been works on violence in Nigeria, the spread of political violence in Congo-Brazzaville, the so-called politics of the belly in the state in Africa, the criminalization of the state, and disorder as a political instrument. Other analyses abound.

A more hopeful outlook has reappeared in the early twenty-first century. After publishing *States and Power in Africa* (2000), Jeffrey Herbst joined with Greg Mills, a South African scholar, to write *The Future of Africa: A New Order in Sight?* (2003). The question mark is significant, but they base their conception of the new order on the emergence of two continent-wide organizations, the African Union, and a program for development called the New Partnership for Africa's Development (NEPAD). They pin great hopes on both. NEPAD is a genuinely new departure. It has a permanent secretariat and a mechanism for peer review. It plans to institute a new aid and government regime to strengthen government budgeting, central bank operations, and corporate governance, and to encourage foreign investment throughout the continent. The South African government is taking the lead in pushing this program forward. Foreign countries, such as Canada, have launched a NEPAD fund. Herbst and Mills, although applauding the objectives of NEPAD, worry about implementation of even the most well-considered plans, given the unsettled conditions in many African countries, and knowing that the goals of NEPAD have not yet been widely accepted in Africa.

THE ECONOMIC DIMENSION

The initial problem that confronted professional economists when they wanted to address the economic situation of African countries was that reliable, quantitative information and the data necessary to construct annual statistical series were not available for the colonial era.

That lack has been somewhat ameliorated in the era of independence; from the 1960s on, data collection improved. From that time forward a new topic preoccupied the few economists interested in Africa: development studies. Aware of the close relationship between the political stability and capital formation, there was a postcolonial effort to measure indicators of economic improvement.

A special feature, namely heavy regulation, was incorporated in the macroeconomic models of African economies. Standard small, open economies have been enlarged to incorporate various aspects of the control regimes common to Africa. One of these features has been the temporary effects of shocks created by commodity booms and busts. This recognition of the fragility of dependent economies in turn produced policy changes on which new theoretical analyses were founded. Thus, the African experience changed aspects of the general economic model of small open economies. In the 1980s, a new set of events invited analysis and provided other insights that could be applied comparatively elsewhere, namely the nature of the socialist decline and its economic effects.

The diversity of situations, country to country, in the markets for labor, credit, and land provided economists with many opportunities for comparisons within the continent. Such policy diversity in otherwise similar economies created the opportunities for research, as were the economy of households. Because rural households in Africa are sites of both production and consumption, gender-specific aspects of decision-making processes there brought a further new dimension into economic analysis generally.

Professional economic research on Africa became more feasible in the 1990s with the development of an African Economic Research Consortium. This included scholars from many European and American institutions. The Oxford Centre for the Study of African Economies, led by Paul Collier, has involved a number of African scholars, Oyejide and Ajayi at Ibadan, Ndulu and Wangwe at Dar es Salaam, and Kanbur and Elbadawi at the Research Department of the World Bank.

There continue to be limitations on the statistical data, vital to contemporary economics, available. There are official and unofficial markets, and the unofficial sector is difficult to track. To the extent that gross national product (GNP) can be calculated, the per capita GNP on the continent has not been growing but rather declining. Africa attracts little new foreign direct investment, and the investment it draws has, in recent years, been focused on mineral extraction and to new oil finds. Isolated, highly technical, high-investment industry does not, however, translate into prosperity for the population as a whole.

The United Nations Human Development Index gives a sense of the continuing high levels of poverty in Africa. Applied research by economists will continue to follow Africa's problems and progress. The World Bank and the International Monetary Fund monitor economic developments in Africa, and the Bank has sponsored some major research. Under the leadership of Paul Collier and Nicholas Sambanis, a large volume was assembled on the causes of civil war (2005). It included a substantial number of African scholars as contributors. The group used an economic model of civil war, applying it in a series of country case studies. The general argument of the designers of the model was that "it is not political and social grievance that leads to civil war, but rather, for given levels of grievance, it is the opportunity to organize and finance a rebellion that determines if a civil war will occur" (Collier and Sambanis 2005). This study contains a vast amount of data about the countries and wars they address. It is also self critical, calling for a need to refine the model and to improve the basic measures used to test it. Keeping up with events, Augustin Kwasi Fosu and Paul Collier have more recently edited a book on postconflict economies in Africa (2005).

See also **Anthropology, Social, and the Study of Africa; International Monetary Fund; Political Science and the Study of Africa; Postcolonialism; Psychology and the Study of Africa; World Bank.**

BIBLIOGRAPHY

Achebe, Chinua. *Things Fall Apart.* New York: Knopf, 1992.

Apter, Andrew. *The Pan-African Nation: Oil and the Spectacle of Culture in Nigeria.* Chicago: University of Chicago Press, 2005.

Apter, David. *Ghana in Transition.* New York: Atheneum, 1963.

Apter, David. *The Political Kingdom in Uganda*, 2nd edition. Princeton, NJ: Princeton University Press, 1997.

Bates, Robert H. *Unions, Parties and Political Development: A Study of Mineworkers in Zambia.* New Haven, CT: Yale University Press, 1971.

Bates, Robert H. *Rural Responses to Industrialization: A Study of Village Zambia.* New Haven, CT: Yale University Press, 1976.

Bates, Robert H. *Markets and States in Tropical Africa: The Political Basis of Agricultural Policies.* Berkeley: University of California Press, 1981.

Bates, Robert H. *Beyond the Miracle of the Market: The Political Economy of Agrarian Development in Kenya.* Cambridge, U.K.: Cambridge University Press, 2005.

Bates, Robert H.; Vumbi Yoka Mudimbe; and Jean O'Barr; eds. *Africa and the Disciplines.* Chicago: University of Chicago Press, 1993.

Bayart, Jean-Francois. *The State in Africa: The Politics of the Belly.* New York: Addison Wesley, 1993.

Bayart, Jean-Francois; Stephen Ellis; and Beatrice Hibou. *The Criminalization of the State in Africa.* Bloomington: Indiana University Press, 1999.

Bazenguissa-Ganga, Remy. "The Spread of Political Violence in Congo-Brazzaville." *African Affairs* 98, no. 390 (1999): 389–411.

Berry, Sara. *Fathers Work for Their Sons.* Berkeley: University of California Press, 1985.

Bohannan, Paul. *Migrant Labor and Tribal Life.* London: Oxford University Press, 1947.

Bohannan, Paul. *The Tiv of Central Nigeria.* London: International African Institute, 1953.

Bohannan, Paul. *Tiv Farm and Settlement.* London: H. M. Stationery Office, 1954.

Bohannan, Paul. "Some Principles of Exchange and Investment among the Tiv." *American Anthropologist* 57 (1955): 60–70.

Bohannan, Paul, and George Dalton. *Markets in Africa.* Evanston, Illinois: Northwestern University Press, 1962.

Bohannan, Paul, and George Dalton, eds. *Markets in Africa.* Garden City, NY: Doubleday and Company, 1965.

Bohannan, Paul, and Laura Bohannan. *Tiv Economy.* Evanston, Illinois: Northwestern University Press, 1968.

Chabal, Patrick, and Jean-Pascal Daloz. *Africa Works: Disorder as a Political Instrument.* Bloomington: Indiana University Press, 1999.

Collier, Paul, and Nicholas Sambanis, eds. *Understanding Civil War*, Vol. 1: *Africa.* Washington, DC: The World Bank, 2005.

Colson, Elizabeth. *Marriage and Family among the Plateau Tonga of Northern Rhodesia.* Manchester, U.K.: Manchester University Press, 1958.

Comaroff, Jean. *Body of Power, Spirit of Resistance: The Culture and History of a South African People.* Chicago: University of Chicago Press, 1985.

Comaroff, Jean, and John Comaroff. *Of Revelation and Revolution*. Chicago: University of Chicago Press, 1991.

Comaroff, John, and Jean Comaroff. *Ethnography and the Historical Imagination*. Boulder, Colorado: Westview Press, 1992.

Comaroff, John, and Jean Comaroff, eds. *Modernity and its Malcontents: Ritual and Power in Postcolonial Africa* Chicago: University of Chicago Press, 1993.

Comaroff, John, and Jean Comaroff, eds. *Civil Society and the Political Imagination in Africa: Critical Perspectives*. Chicago: University of Chicago Press, 1999.

Cruise O'Brien, Donal B. *The Mourides of Senegal: The Political and Economic Organization of an Islamic Brotherhood*. Oxford: Clarendon Press, 1971.

Evans-Pritchard, Edward Evans. *The Nuer*. Oxford: Clarendon Press, 1940.

Evans-Pritchard, Edward Evans, and Fortes, Meyer, eds. *African Political Systems*. London: Oxford University Press, 1940.

Falola, Toyin. *Violence in Nigeria: The Crisis of Religious Politics and Secular Ideologies*. Rochester, NY: University of Rochester Press, 1998.

Ferguson, James. *The Anti-Politics Machine*. Minneapolis: University of Minnesota Press, 1994.

Ferguson, James. *Global Shadows*. Durham, NC: Duke University Press, 2006.

Fortes, Meyer. *The Dynamics of Clanship among the Tallensi*. London: Oxford University Press, 1945.

Fortes, Meyer, and Germaine Dieterlen, eds. *African Systems of Thought*. London: Oxford University Press, 1965.

Fosu, Augustin Kwasi, and Paul Collier, eds. *Post-Conflict Economies in Africa*. New York: Palgrave Macmillan, 2005.

Griffiths, Anne M.O. *In the Shadow of Marriage*. Chicago: University of Chicago Press, 1997.

Guyer, Jane. *Family and Farm in Southern Cameroon*. Boston: Boston University, African Studies Center, 1984.

Guyer, Jane. *Marginal Gains: Monetary Transactions in Atlantic Africa*. Chicago: University of Chicago Press, 2004.

Herbst, Jeffrey, and Greg Mills. *The Future of Africa: A New Order in Sight?* Oxford: Oxford University Press, 2003.

Herskovits, Melville. *Dahomey, an Ancient African Kingdom*, 2 vols. New York: J. J. Augustin, 1938.

Hill, Polly. *The Migrant Cocoa Farmers of Southern Ghana*. Cambridge, U.K.: Cambridge University Press, 1963.

House-Midamba, Bessie, and Flix K. Ekechi. *African Market Women*. Westport, Connecticut: Greenwood Press, 1995.

Jackson, Robert H., and Carl G. Rosberg. "Personal Rule." In *Readings in African Politics*. ed. Tom Young. Bloomington: Indiana University Press, 2003.

Kuper, Leo, and Michael Garfield Smith, eds. *Pluralism in Africa*. Berkeley: University of California Press, 1969.

Magubane, Bernard. "Pluralism and Conflict Situations in Africa: A New Look." *African Social Research* 7 (1969): 559–654.

Malkki, Liisa H. *Purity and Exile*. Chicago: University of Chicago Press, 1995.

Middleton, John. *Lugbara Religion*. London: Oxford University Press, 1960.

Moore, Sally Falk. *Anthropology and Africa*. Charlottesville: University of Virginia Press, 1994.

Mudimbe, Vumbi Yocha. *The Invention of Africa*. Bloomington: Indiana University Press, 1988.

Ocholla-Ayayo, Andrew B. C.; Joshua Akong'a; and Simiyu Wandibba. *African Families and the Crisis of Social Change*. Westport, CT: Bergin and Garvey, 1997.

Oyewumi, Oyeronke, ed. *African Gender Studies*. New York: Palgrave Macmillan 2005.

Radcliffe-Brown, Alfred R., and Daryll Forde, eds. *African Systems of Kinship and Marriage*. London: Oxford University Press, 1950.

Richards, Audrey I. *Land, Labour and Diet in Northern Rhodesia*. London: Oxford University Press, 1939.

Richards, Paul. *Fighting for the Rain Forest War, Youth and Resources in Sierra Leone*. Portsmouth, NH: Heinemann, 1996.

Rothchild, Donald, and Naomi Chazan, eds.*The Precarious Balance: State and Society in Africa*. Boulder, CO: Westview Press, 1988.

Schapera, Isaac. "Economic Changes in South African Native Life." *Africa* 1 (1928): 170–188.

Schapera, Isaac. *A Handbook of Tswana Law and Custom*. London: Oxford University Press, 1938.

Smith, Michael Garfield. *The Economy of the Hausa Communities of Zaria* London: H. M. Stationery Office, 1955.

Van de Walle, Nicholas. *African Economies and the Politics of Permanent Crisis 1979–1999*. Cambridge and New York: Cambridge University Press, 2001.

Weisner, Thomas S.; Candace Bradley; and Philip Kilbride; eds. *The Politics of Tradition: Continuity and Change in Northern Nigeria, 1946–1966*. Princeton, NJ: Princeton University Press, 1970.

Wilson, Godfrey, and Monica Wilson. *The Analysis of Social Change*. Cambridge, U.K.: Cambridge University Press, 1948.

Young, Tom, ed. *Readings in African Politics.* Bloomington: Indiana University Press, 2003.

Zolberg, Aristide. *One-Party Government in the Ivory Coast.* Princeton, NJ: Princeton University Press, 1964.

Zolberg, Aristide. *Creating Political Order: The Party-States of West Africa.* Chicago: Rand McNally, 1966.

SALLY FALK MOORE

HISTORICAL RESOURCES

Virtually all scholarly inquiry by historians into the past of sub-Saharan Africa has taken place since the 1950s. Before this, anthropologists and linguists, and to a lesser degree archaeologists, had touched on the continent only as it happened to affect their own work, but there were few trained historians made sustained efforts to bring the study of Africa into the larger historiographical enterprise. Beginning in the 1950s, however, Africa's approach to national independence brought with it the desire to provide the numerous incipient states with pasts of their own that would justify their new autonomy. As a result, historians trained in other fields began to retrain themselves and turn their attention to Africa. Soon they became the first crop of historians specifically imbued with an interest in Africa.

Thus, from the beginning, in terms of the initial rationale with which historians approached the study of the past in Africa, the subject has emulated the course of historical study in other times and places. That is, the interest in the past was not entirely disinterestedly intellectual but was also part of a larger and more practical nationalist enterprise. Also from the beginning, Africanist historians were in a hurry to make up for lost time, and the resulting compression of the course of African historical studies into a short period rendered it peculiarly amenable to it being treated as a true microcosm of the ways in which the study of the past are otherwise organized and pursued.

Not surprisingly, although the body of evidence that has been used to study Africa's history resembles its counterparts in other regional fields of the discipline, the ways in which its parts have been used have varied according to circumstances. In particular, the relatively late beginning of the study, and the fact that both more and less evidence is available than for other areas of the world, has created a set of historiographical norms that differ in important ways from those developed elsewhere and earlier.

WRITTEN SOURCES

Written sources have typically been the predominant form of evidence that has been unearthed and studied. Such evidence for Africa south of the Sahara can be traced as far back as the *Periplus* of the Red Sea, which provided information about large parts of the east coast of Africa in the first century CE. This early look at the area proved to be an aberration, however, and it was not until several centuries later that the Islamic conquest of northern Africa led to a more sustained interest in, and records of, areas immediately to the south of the Sahara.

Several centuries later again, the Europeans—first the Portuguese and then other nations—began to creep down the west coast of Africa and then up the east coast. Almost always their settlements hugged the beaches and islands, but occasionally they spread inland along some rivers. The result was that snatches of information about the surrounding areas were recorded both in chronicles and in local records. Eyewitness accounts of events at these settlements were of course recorded, but regrettably, the former have proved more interesting to historians despite their necessarily hearsay character. Equally unfortunately, little original material has survived from the Portuguese outposts, where the tenure of Europeans began earliest.

Concurrent with these records were the reports of missionaries, who followed the secular authorities and often expanded their interests well beyond those areas accessible to civil and military administrations or merchants. As a consequence, missionary records are of especial importance, but they have yet to be extensively quarried, at least for the period before formal colonial rule, sometimes because they were written in Latin and because access to religious archives tends to be more difficult, but also because of a mistaken impression that the missionaries confined themselves largely to doctrinal matters of only limited appeal.

With the imposition of formal colonial rule, usually late in the nineteenth century—and the exploration that preceded and succeeded it—the amount of written documentation increased a great deal, although it often requires deft interpretation because of the persistent but unrecognized ignorance of the colonial authorities about much in the societies they were attempting to understand and govern. Withal, the body of written evidence for and from this period far surpasses the sum total of all other forms of written materials for previous periods. Naturally, that has been what historians have most extensively and intensively used, whether they are concerned with the colonial period proper or with its antecedents.

In dealing with this evidence, certain things need to be considered. Up to the late nineteenth century, almost all the available data could be classed as travel accounts, and to a lesser, but still underappreciated, degree that remained true even through the colonial period. As a genre, travel accounts require special handling. They were written to appeal to a particular audience; were often seen through a triumphant Christian and Eurocentric (and, earlier, Islamic) optic, which tended to peculiarize and demean that with which it was not familiar; and—at least early on—competed with the genre of imaginary voyages. Inevitably, and even in the twentieth century, such accounts tended to produce information that was at once stereotyped, implausible, and woefully culture-bound.

Using earlier sources critically requires more than separating the unlikely from the likely, or the obviously false from the possibly true. It requires a thorough understanding of what concepts of true and false meant at the times such accounts were produced, and how these premises affected their tenor and content. Often, it also requires consulting many versions of the same text as it worked its way from travel notes to edited compilation, or later to typescript, to an eventual published version. These principles apply to both secular and religious writings, which distortions were much more similar than different. It also requires other kinds of similarly elusive knowledge—for instance, about the expected audience for these works and the implications of this consideration for their content. Many of them were written to raise funds for exploration, conquest, or missionizing, not to mention justifying the considerable expenditures of colonial rule, or simply to cover for official

performance below the standards that superiors demanded but seldom funded—all clear cases where it would have been tempting for authors to gild whatever lilies they were trying to germinate in the minds and purses of their readers. Many also were written in atmospheres of controversy, as authors and nations competed for priority of discovery or reputation as civilizers or modernizers of their native wards.

Another problem, more structural than cultural, that confronts historians is that, until at least the eighteenth century, unacknowledged and wholesale borrowing by one writer from earlier ones was regarded not only as acceptable but as an esteemed hallmark of erudition. It often took modern historians of Africa several decades of using these materials before this antiquated notion became unavoidably apparent to modern historians. Recognizing later writers' ample appropriations from earlier sources means that what was once considered corroborative written testimony is very often no more than the illusion created by this European cultural trait manifesting itself again and again.

Awareness of such characteristics has led to a more sustained interest in critically analyzing these sources, rather than simply treating the evidence as unproblematic. At the same time, this has meant that historians have recognized the need to be less sure about the reliability of their sources.

ARCHIVES

African historians have availed themselves of the numerous archives concerned with Africa in one degree or another. The variety of these is surprisingly great. Most important are formal governmental archives, whether housed in the former colonizing nations in Europe or in their former colonies. In addition to these, local and specialized archives—such as ecclesiastical, business, and educational depositories—exist in very large numbers and are beginning to be exploited to a greater degree. To facilitate this interest, an impressive number of archival guides has been published since the 1950s. An added advantage in using archival materials is that, with the passing of time, documents for the entire colonial period, entirely closed in the sensitive years of late colonialism when the field took shape, have become open in most archives.

Typically, a wide variety of information is to be found in such archival materials, so they have been heavily used by economic, social, and political historians of the colonial period. One of its advantages lies in its presentation of data in very raw form, allowing historians to reconfigure it to their own intellectual specifications. This primary character is seldom the case for the large body of testimony in the archives on the precolonial past that consists largely of the testimony of Africans. Colonial authorities, who were interested in arranging local administrative structure, elicited the testimony and fit the material to their own needs. Many local informants soon grasped the implications of the colonizers' interest and often were able to turn the naiveté of their powerful inquisitors to their own advantage by offering precisely what they perceived that their new colonial rulers desired. Those who became most adept at this manipulation gained distinct advantages in the new colonial system, which only encouraged greater use of the practice.

A long-time source of particular importance for African historians is the extensive body of anthropological or ethnographic literature that began to be formally compiled early in the twentieth century. Here, too, the purpose was largely to understand better what were thought to be the rigid, traditional norms of the newly colonized societies, in order to create a reliable framework of predictable behavior under the new administrative structures. Like archaeology, anthropology during the colonial period operated with certain, now largely outdated, premises in hand, particularly as they related to the origins of African states and other political entities.

These illusions established another case where the Africans who were being subjected to such scrutiny were not loath to turn it to their advantage by providing the same kinds of answers to anthropologists as to the civil authorities, regardless of whether they were true in any objective sense. These complex negotiations have imposed on historians who use these materials the onus of understanding their contexts as thoroughly as their apparent content. Often this critique involves consulting missionary and local administrative materials for balance, as well as making recourse to surviving papers of the anthropologists who published such ethnographies in order to understand how they often went about their business as government agents, rather than exclusively as disinterested scholars.

ORAL SOURCES

Historians, not only of Africa but also elsewhere, frequently have made use of written accounts without realizing that very often these were merely the last renditions of information that had been transmitted orally for unknown periods of time from one mouth—and one generation—to the next before being committed to writing. Nearly all the sources from early Christianity, early Islam, and the High Middle Ages, as well as from such places as India, Southeast Asia, and pre-Columbian America, fall squarely into this category of written mythologized knowledge. In few such cases have historians had the advantage of being able to discern this chain in being, and certainly not in process. One of the critical differentiating characteristics of African historiography has been that the creation and use of oral data of various kinds in Africa are far more susceptible than elsewhere to observation; therefore, its dynamics are more easily understood there.

Intensive collection of oral data by historians began in the late 1950s and peaked in the following two decades. During that time, enormous amounts of material were collected in the field by interrogating authorities treated as informants and piecing together whatever information they provided with other oral data, written records, and whatever further relevant evidence seemed to exist. This massive collation was seen as—and indeed was—necessary if any substantial local knowledge of most parts of Africa before, at the earliest, the mid-nineteenth century was to be preserved. Many of the available written sources—colonial, missionary, anthropological—had relied on such testimony, which practitioners of oral historiography during these two decades often noted approvingly.

Along the way, a strong sense of camaraderie and of privileged distinctiveness developed among these practitioners that encouraged many oral historians to confer on the data they collected certain privileges and immunities from routine standards of criticism that they would not have considered suitable for forms of historical evidence that they had not personally created. Therefore, and unfortunately, the personal notes containing these data have often failed to reach the public domain. The failure to deposit these research materials at an early stage can be compared to the actions of archivists who refuse access to the materials under their control or of users of archives who are reluctant to identify their sources adequately. In this case, though, there is the crucial additional disadvantage that these materials were often in formats (such as audiotapes) that were too vulnerable to the passage of time to survive and to be made accessible for later use.

The effect is that a significant proportion of the writing on precolonial Africa that has appeared since the 1950s has been based on evidence that is now, and unnecessarily, unavailable. The recent crises in many African archives mean that large bodies of written documentation have been destroyed or scattered. Thus, in a period of less than forty years, an extraordinary amount of evidence has disappeared, which renders some Africanist historical scholarship dangerously exempt from disciplined attempts at refutation.

Oral data, more than any other genre of evidence, require special care in their production and interpretation. This need arises largely from the fact that historians are necessarily active participants in their creation rather than simply acting as interpreters and transmitters of a written record that they cannot change. The temptations and opportunities to influence unduly, mostly inadvertently, the orally derived record as it is being made, combined with the general inaccessibility of the results noted above, have combined to cast into doubt much of this work on grounds that it cannot be tested. On the other hand, the production of a large body of methodological literature in response to the opportunities and challenges provided by research on oral and other forms of evidence has been one of the principal contributions of Africanist historical scholarship to the larger discipline.

ARCHAEOLOGY

Archaeology was probably the first historical academic field in modern times to turn its attention seriously to Africa, since archaeological investigation began well before the end of the nineteenth century. The unfavorable combination of a climate destructive of all but the most stable materials and use of mostly temporary building techniques has meant that fewer human structures are available in Africa than in many areas of the world favored with stone techniques of construction. Even so, there are many spectacular remains scattered throughout the continent, and some of these, such as Great Zimbabwe in southern Africa and numerous sites in western Sudan and in the interlacustrine area (Uganda and vicinity), attracted archaeologists' attention early on.

Initially, the interpretation of these sites and others tended to position itself firmly within the intellectual trends of the early twentieth century, with their strong racial biases. As a consequence of this very limiting focus and the unavailability of epigraphic evidence, the temptation was to impute these sites manifesting buildings in stone, or, later, metallurgy, to various groups of immigrant outsiders. Since then, new techniques, such as radiocarbon dating, and an increasing realization that most of the putative exogenous builders never existed in the first place have transformed these views, so that it is now conventional wisdom that builders developed these sites in response to specific conditions and entirely on the basis of their own technologies.

Likewise, the discovery toward the end of the colonial years of new sites, less spectacular in their lithic monumentality but more suggestive in the new ranges of African creativity, such as Igbo-Ukwu and Nok in Nigeria, has forced fuller appreciation of the character, antiquity, and spread of indigenous societies and skills within Africa, particularly south of the Sahara. Inevitably, the trend has been to show that more, and more varied and sophisticated, cultures developed earlier, and did so independently rather than as a result of radiating from one of two centers outside the continent—or even within it.

One of the most important of these developments has been the archaeological discovery that Africans developed iron metallurgy many centuries earlier than once supposed, and in a number of local variations, suggesting that, whether or not the notion was invented only once, it was quickly and routinely adapted to local requirements. These discoveries, in turn, combined with other evidence, have forced changes in earlier hypotheses as to the timing and directions of the spread of the Bantu languages, and the people speaking them, throughout central, southern, and eastern Africa.

LINGUISTICS

This naturally brings us to consider another category of evidence important for the earlier centuries, even millennia, of the African past that has developed from the study of the continent's numerous languages and language families. Translation work began very early, with the devising of dictionaries as far back as the sixteenth century by missionaries seeking to facilitate the spread of Christian doctrines. By the middle of the nineteenth century, philologists had discerned the great Bantu language family, if not yet quite delineating its complexities, and linguistic study has proceeded apace ever since.

The methodologies of modern historical linguistics are specialized, and the principles and arguments of this highly technical discipline are not easily absorbed by those not specially trained. As a result, historians of Africa have found themselves perpetually in thrall to the hypotheses about languages, not particularly needing to concern themselves with contexts and processes of speaking. Sometimes these have been based on too superficial a study of an inadequate samples of speech patterns—at least as determined by later work. As a result, the conclusions of historians about the passages of language, and therefore—or so it is often held—of correlated peoples and cultures throughout Africa have undergone a surprising number of sea changes in a very short time. Taking into account recent experiences and proceeding more provisionally will mean that the work and conclusions of linguistics will continue to be of special importance as evidence for historians in any attempts to discern the broader patterns that characterized Africa before either written or oral—or even archaeological—evidence begins.

Historians, as well as linguists, benefit from the production of African-language dictionaries and grammars. Comparing word forms and meanings from one ethnic group to another, for instance, is a useful way to supplement and test other forms of evidence about origins and subsequent mutual relationships over time. The Africans' propensity to borrow words from other languages, including the languages of the colonizers, created patterns in the resulting modern forms of languages that also raises interesting questions and provides insights into issues of social and economic relationships both before and during the colonial period.

PHOTOGRAPHS AND FILMS

Large collections of photographs relating to Africa taken during the colonial period have long existed, in public and private archives, as well as in museums. However, only since the 1980s have scholars taken a serious interest in colonial photography. Most of these collections have yet to be organized and studied, but such an effort is at present one of the primary objectives of Africanists in both anthropology and history. Such photographs not only depict the Africans as subjects, but also offer important insights on the cultural outlooks of the colonial photographers, many of whom were Africans.

In like fashion, films from and about Africa have come to be treated as historical sources as well as entertainment. In particular, those films produced for ethnographic and propaganda purposes reaching back to the beginning of the twentieth century, are used in the early twenty-first century to understand the cultural norms and activities that they preserved, as well as the preferences of the audiences for whom they were intended. Most films created by Africans are of more recent vintage, but even these will eventually be used to trace historical aspects of the periods and places involved.

ANCILLARY EVIDENCE

In other ways, Africanist historians have innovatively sought ancillary evidence from disciplines that historians in other fields seldom consult. For instance, both musicological and ethnobotanical evidence has been considered in attempts to understand better the ebb and flow of early African history. This imaginative inclusiveness has been required by the scantiness of standard lines of evidence; nonetheless, experience has shown clearly that, when practiced cautiously, such appropriation of the fruits of research conducted through the frameworks of other interdisciplines can have the particular value that comes when independent lines of investigation converge.

ELECTRONIC RESOURCES

As might be expected, Africa has not been excluded from the remarkable recent proliferation of electronic resources relating to past and present. For Africa, the forms that digitization has taken are similar to those for other areas of the globe. Archives and other materials are being digitized apace, as have been rare printed materials and official publications. Large databases of materials relating to slavery and the slave trade have been assembled, and Web-based access to a large number of historical and current African newspapers is now routine. Most of the major U.S. African studies centers have websites with far-reaching linkages to electronic and print resources in African studies.

CONCLUSION

In less than a lifetime, the scholarly study of African history has progressed from virtual nonexistence to a discipline comparable to any other field of history, including support by a vast and complex panoply of diverse resources and reasonably rigorous methods for using them. Although most of the source materials existed by the 1950s, many of them, in particular the collections of oral testimony, are largely products of the subsequent flowering of interest in Africa's past. This range of sources is not peculiarly different from those used in other fields of history, although the balance among them naturally differs because the historical particularities of the evidence for African history makes it unlike that of any other cultural area, just as all of these areas have created sources of comparable uniqueness among themselves. Evidence in every regional or cultural—or national—field of history is the distinctive product of the historical communities that created it. Definitions of historical evidence developed, however appropriately, by nineteenth-century Europeans to understand themselves as creators of modern nations, have been gradually adapted to the quite different narratives developed to understand Africans as themselves. As Africans continue to develop ways to present their own understandings in modern academic terms, they will surely identify still other kinds of evidence of their pasts.

Thus, in the early years of the twentieth-first century there seems to be some inclination to regroup and to consider many of these sources, and their uses, anew. Such reassessment is a common practice in the larger field of history; the difference is that there it has taken as long as several centuries, whereas in African history historians find themselves looking at their own work from the vantage point of their own later experiences and those of the still emerging range of other Africanist disciplines, whether historians or not.

See also **Anthropology, Social, and the Study of Africa; Archaeology and Prehistory; Colonialism and Imperialism; Communications: Electronic; Education, School; Historiography; History and the Study of Africa; Linguistics, Historical; Linguistics and the Study of Africa; Literature: Oral; Media: Book Publishing; Photography; Prehistory; Travel and Exploration: European (Since 1800).**

BIBLIOGRAPHY

American Historical Association. *Guide to Historical Literature*, 3rd edition, Vol. 1. ed Mary Beth Norton. New York: Oxford University Press, 1995.

Fage, John Donnelly. *A Guide to Original Sources for Precolonial Western Africa Published in European Languages*, revised edition. Madison: University of Wisconsin African Studies Program, 1994.

Heintze, Beatrix, and Adam Jones, eds. *European Sources for Sub-Saharan Africa Before 1900: Use and Abuse.* Stuttgart, Germany: Franz Steiner, 1987.

Henige, David. *Oral Historiography.* London: Longman, 1982.

International Council on Archives. *Guide to the Sources of the History of the Nations. B: Africa.* 8 vols. Zug, Switzerland: Inter Documentation Company, 1970–1983.

Jewsiewicki, Bogumil, and David S. Newbury, eds. *African Historiographies.* Thousand Oaks, California: Sage, 1986.

Miller, Joseph C., ed. *The African Past Speaks.* Folkestone, England: Dawson, 1980.

Neale, Caroline. *Writing "Independent" History: African Historiography, 1960–1980.* Westport, Connecticut: Greenwood Press, 1985.

Robertshaw, Peter, ed. *A History of African Archaeology.* London: James Currey, 1990.

Shaw, Thurstan, et al., eds. *The Archaeology of Africa: Foods, Metals, and Towns.* London: Routledge, 1993.

Vansina, Jan. *Oral Tradition as History.* Madison: University of Wisconsin Press, 1984.

DAVID HENIGE

RESEARCH FUNDING

With the exception of a few of Africa's more developed countries like Egypt and South Africa, domestic funding for research has been very limited, if not totally nonexistent. There are several reasons for these limits.

During colonial days, research funding was available to European scholars and scientists in their respective home countries. There was no need to set up separate funding facilities in the colonies.

Efforts at establishing national research funding facilities focused on agriculture and medicine after African countries became politically independent. Social sciences and humanities were not priorities. The focus was on action and application, not discovery and reflection. In countries like Mozambique and Tanzania that turned to socialism in the 1970s, political mobilization, rather than greater expertise, mattered most.

Since the 1980s, the problem for African nations has been shortage of public funds. Structural adjustment policies forced African governments to cut down on public spending in all categories, leaving money for only a reduced set of priorities. Funding research was pushed even further down the list. Additionally, continued inefficiency in public management caused an even greater decline in funding, even of critical sectors like agriculture and health.

Other priorities and a lack of appreciation of the importance of research in policy-making circles in African countries, therefore, are major reasons why domestic funding facilities have either not been established or have dried up. The dire circumstances under which scholars and scientists in African countries typically work has also been a contributing factor. Their salaries have been inadequate. Those who can pursue concentrations other than research, therefore, do. Many moonlight in business ventures. Accepting consultancies for foreign embassies and firms has been particularly popular. Although these activities may have amounted to commissioned research, they have distracted scholars in Africa from publishing in academic journals and thus establishing a national or international recognition in scientific circles. The number of Africans who have bucked this trend is few. In recent years, with greater pressure on public universities to increase admission of students, heavier teaching loads have often exacerbated the

situation. Neither time for, nor interest in, research has been available there.

It is no surprise that, in the straitened political and economic circumstances of most African countries, foreign funding of research has been dominant. The primary backers in the social sciences have been two main U.S. philanthropies (the Ford and Rockefeller Foundations), Canadian International Development Research Center (IDRC), and the Swedish Agency for Research Cooperation with Developing Countries (SAREC). Their approach has entailed independent or joint funding of specific projects or programs, such as the African Economic Research Cooperation (AERC) project that supports economic research and graduate education, based in Nairobi, Kenya. They also run their own research competitions focused on practical issues, such as population, or a broader set of social science issues. The urgency of Africa's needs in these areas of applied research has effectively limited knowledge to flows from modern European and North American science into Africa, rather than expanding global understanding to include inputs from Africa.

These international foundations have also been instrumental in establishing two regional Africa-based research councils: the Council for the Development of Social Science Research in Africa (CODESRIA), based in Dakar, Senegal, and catering for the region as a whole, and the Organization for Social Science Research in Eastern Africa (OSSREA), headquartered in Addis Ababa, Ethiopia, and responsible for funding and promoting research in eastern and southern Africa. Over a thirty-year period beginning in 1975, these agencies spent approximately US$100 million on funding social science research in Africa. Although there have been times that one or more of these agencies indicated that it will cease funding these councils —and the availability of funding has varied over the years—none of them has abandoned this mission altogether. Their funding has become institutionalized.

While funding for research on agriculture in Africa has stagnated in recent years, financing has grown in support of medical research. Much of the funding for agricultural research has been channeled through the various agencies that make up the Consultative Group for International Agricultural Research (CGIAR), financed by the World Bank and many bilateral donor agencies. The CGIAR centers, such as the International Institute for Tropical Agriculture (IITA) in Ibadan, Nigeria, fund national research centers or individual researchers in these countries. Funding for agricultural research has declined globally since the beginning of the twenty-first century, although some centers like the World Agroforestry Center in Nairobi have fared relatively well.

Medical research has benefited primarily from the global interest in the AIDS epidemic in Africa. National research institutions in Africa have provided funding for work on a broad variety of issues. These include better understanding the HIV viruses and the value of local herbs for drug development. The United Nations AIDS Programme (UNAIDS) and various public and private institutions such as the Bill and Belinda Gates Foundation have been particularly active in this field. Sociologists and anthropologists interested in prevention or counseling issues have also gained from these funding agencies.

Compared to other regions of the world, funding for research in Africa is limited, both internally and externally. Little appreciation in policy-making circles and a scarcity of financial resources, as well as competing priorities among researchers, help explain this state of affairs.

See also **Addis Ababa; Aid and Development; Dakar; United Nations; World Bank.**

BIBLIOGRAPHY

James S. Coleman, and David Court. *External Assistance and Universities in the Third World: The Rockefeller Foundation Experience.* Oxford: Pergamon 1991.

William S. Saint. "Universities in Africa: Strategies for Stabilization and Revitalization." *World Bank Technical Paper* Number 194. Washington DC: The World Bank, 1992.

GORAN HYDEN

SCHOLARLY ETHICS

Africanists and development practitioners alike tend to perceive sub-Saharan Africa as a conundrum where, for some development workers, every good idea seems to have gone wrong. Representations of African predicaments on the global scene conjure up images of a continent torn apart by civil wars, epidemics, famines, uncontrolled urbanization, and a whole host of other socioeconomic and political pathologies. Intellectual and media

constructions of the area suggest scenarios in which the continent might be drifting back to some "dark ages." The question is why several decades of development intervention in sub-Saharan Africa have failed to improve and enhance the quality of life and the life chances of most of the people on the continent. Why has the dominant neoclassical paradigm, based on the modernization theory, failed to produce the much talked about "development" for the continent?

This entry sketches out the different trajectories of development theories and praxis in sub-Saharan Africa. It questions the underlying linear approach inherent in modernization theory and its aspiration for some teleological outcome that is a finished product. It argues that the failure to situate culture and history in the processes of negotiating, accepting, and internalizing foreign notions of development could be responsible for the weakness in establishing development effectiveness. Due to the existence of institutional pluralism, the recurrent dichotomy between "traditional" and "modern" has emerged as a constraint and has been driving the development agenda. Development interventions aim at transforming traditional societies into modern nation-states. The entry notes the weakness of social science analysis and research to serve as a predictive science that informs policy making. The explanatory power of social sciences has served as an analytical tool for working with such categories as ethnicity, tribalism, corruption, and pluralism. The complexity provided by these categories is sometimes held accountable for the failure of development intervention. The entry situates the responsibility of the African elite in the production of society. It also examines the extent to which civil society has been able to produce a counterdiscourse or a critique of the postcolonial state as the latter articulates its vision of society.

The dominant development paradigm assumes that economic growth is the basis of all development. This paradigm gave new impetus to modernization theories that were premised on the concept of social engineering. The core tenet of the social engineering approach was to formulate development planning in terms of transplants of Western institutions and products to the developing countries. This approach sought to fill the "objects gap" (the lack of modern technological inputs). Under conditions of induced development, the assumption was that the benefits of development would eventually trickle down from the progressive elite to the common people. As a result of oversimplification, it became more a question of identifying the progressive elites to serve as vectors of change. Social research has abundantly demonstrated the inadequacies of the trickle-down approach but has failed to change the trajectory of development intervention in sub-Saharan Africa.

From a historical perspective, the early days of colonial rule in sub-Saharan Africa sought to maintain law and order, finance the colonial enterprise, and pursue the civilizing of the "natives." According to Frederick Lugard, the chief architect of British indirect rule, social research was desirable when it served to resolve pressing concerns of administrators, educators, health and welfare workers, or traders working for the good of Africans. It is not surprising that a key function of research under colonial rule was to provide guidance to administrators for troubleshooting. The development of British structural-functionalism, with its emphasis on situational variations in behavior and processes of social conflict, is a case in point.

The critical factor in this approach was to use the social sciences to facilitate the diffusion of Western technology by overcoming resistance to change arising from traditional values and institutions. In the process, social analysis either became very normative (restatement of customary laws) or pursued village and area studies that had a limited policy formulation role. The anticipated output of these studies was to access and assess the validity of local norms, social structures, and practices.

In summary, early social science research fostered the goals of the colonial enterprise. Local knowledge systems and practices were carefully filtered, using "repugnancy clauses" as gatekeepers. The construction of development discourse has survived essentially as a missionary discourse.

The shift of focus to emphasize poverty reduction in the late 1960s coincided with the rise of neo-Marxist analyses in political economy. In a September 1973 speech, Robert McNamara drew attention to the existence of over 100 million families having tiny landholdings with conditions of cultivation too poor to contribute significantly to production. This "wake-up call" led to some adjustments in the approach to development intervention but no significant change in the underlying assumptions. The

basic assumptions still called for the modernization of traditional societies and their incorporation into national and world economies.

The critical shift during this period was the movement away from filling the "objects gap" to one that sought to fill the "policy gap." Failures in development theory and praxis were attributed to weak institutional policies and capacity. Development economics identified market failures and attributed market distortions to state policies. Different scholarly analyses characterized the state as "predatory," "strong," "weak," "soft," or "overdeveloped" and tried to explain the stifling of civil society and markets. The bottom line of this neoliberal approach was to get the state off the back of civil society and to allow the "invisible hand" of the market to allocate scarce resources.

The inadequacies of growth and market models produced inequalities in the distribution of wealth. Social scientists contested the organizing powers of the market and demonstrated the role of culture in the "commodification" of things. When growth models were subjected to critical social analysis, it could easily be demonstrated why the anticipated outcomes could not be achieved due to cultural constructions of these concepts. Arjun Appadurai, editor of *The Social Life of Things: Commodities in Cultural Perspective* (1986), characterized these cultural processes as the "social life of things." In the same vein, Igor Kopytoff's essay "The Cultural Biography of Things: Commoditization as Process," in Appadurai's *The Social Life of Things*, examines the cultural biography of things. The contributions of social research exposed the limits of the totalizing discourse of the market.

Even before these analyses demonstrated the limits of the market, international funding agencies, such as the World Bank, commissioned participatory poverty analyses (qualitative analyses that integrate the perceptions of the poor by different groups in society and what represents poverty in a given cultural context). These analyses mapped out the structural and endemic patterns of resource exclusion that create constraints leading to poverty. Other agencies, such as USAID, devised the New Directions mandate (1973–1975) integrating social analysis in project planning. The new direction sought a "social soundness analysis" of projects, a forerunner of the social assessment advocated by the World Bank. Its goals were

- To assess the relevance of local values, beliefs, and social structures to the technological package under consideration
- To promote cultural integration by fitting innovations into existing social patterns
- To get the impressions villagers and others have of their own circumstances
- To evaluate the impact of programs upon people and their way of life

This interest in social research was driven by the realization that development impact can be internalized if it is grounded in the culture and history of the people. With all these analyses, social research was still relegated to mitigating impacts in project implementation.

To what extent has the African elite contributed to the articulation of a development paradigm that responds to African predicaments? Antonio Gramsci, in *Selections from the Prison Notebooks* (1971), suggested that a viable civil society could emerge only when there are "organic intellectuals" with the capacity to articulate a counterdiscourse to that of the state. Rather than accept the state's vision of society uncritically, the organic intellectuals had the historic role to provide a counterdiscourse to that of the state, serving as a countervailing force to the state's excesses. Consequently, if numerous organizations and groups exist in civil society but lack the capacity to articulate a counterdiscourse to that of the state, that civil society would be considered underdeveloped.

If the organic intellectuals play a critical role in the conception of society, to what extent has the African elite provided an alternative vision to that of the state? A rapid overview of the contribution of Africanist scholars to development theories points to the following trends:

- Most of the critical literature is written by African scholars living in the diaspora or not living in their country of birth.
- Those home-based African scholars who contribute to the ongoing debates on development tend to focus on other countries.
- The few who engage in producing a counterdiscourse to that of the state are either co-opted

to become state elite or are silenced. A classic African aphorism says it all: *la bouche qui mange ne parle pas* (the mouth that eats does not speak).

Although African responses to these development paradigms were forcefully stated by scholars such as Samir Amin in his essay "Underdevelopment and Dependence in Black Africa: Origins and Contemporary Forms," (1972) and Adebayo Adedeji's work, their impact on policy formulation in sub-Saharan Africa has been marginal. At the Economic Commission for Africa (ECA), Adedeji was the driving force behind the Lagos Plan of Action, which was endorsed by the Organization of African Unity (OAU), yet it was never fully implemented by the member governments. The ECA further proposed an African alternative to the structural adjustment programs that has not been adopted by African policymakers. The agenda is still driven by foreign development assistance. The fact that International Monetary Fund–sponsored structural adjustment programs have not been debated in any of the parliaments in sub-Saharan Africa shows to what extent they have very little social legitimacy or a local constituency for their implementation.

Part of the problem arises from the weakness of civil society in most countries to hold political regimes accountable for the implementation of their development agendas. In some instances, a strong voice has emerged from ecclesiastical society, criticizing the regime in power for having institutionalized the "structures of sin." These counterdiscourses fade away when they are subsumed into ethnic or regional politics. This accounts for the fact that, unlike Latin America, a consistent exposition of the critical tenets of Liberation theology has failed to emerge in sub-Saharan Africa.

It is not unusual that the concept of the common good seems to mean different things to public servants. The overriding goal of those seeking public office is to get access to and control over the common good. In his *L'état en Afrique: La politique du ventre* (1989), Jean-François Bayart convincingly demonstrated that public office is perceived through metaphors of "belly politics" or "eating the state." Because the state is seen as a resource base, it is therefore not surprising that the participants in "belly politics" devise strategies that allow them to privatize the common good. In sub-Saharan Africa, the common good is a vanishing resource. The dominant institutional frameworks serve to legitimize the privatization of the common good. Under these predatory structures, the capture of power represents access to the common good. The consolidation of power defines membership in a strategic manner that highlights exclusionary principles weighted in terms of ethnicity and regionalism. Donor-driven reforms of policy frameworks, without the political will to implement a change agenda, do not produce results on the ground. The driving force is to use public office to accumulate resources.

This entry's analysis demonstrates how several decades of development intervention have failed to reduce poverty in any substantive manner in sub-Saharan Africa. First, the social engineering paradigm of neoclassical theories has not brought about the trickle-down effect of economic growth. Second, a weak civil society in most of sub-Saharan Africa has failed to challenge the policies of the state elite. Third, a weak institutional framework has failed to mold the leaders who are committed to an accountable management of the common good. Under these circumstances, is there a need for new development paradigm?

In the late 1980s, a group of Africans and Africanist scholars set out to search for a new development paradigm. They concluded that a new concept of modernization should be formulated from the vantage point of African predicaments. This yearning to capture the precariousness and instability of the human condition in sub-Saharan Africa is driven by a sense of hopelessness among Africanists and development practitioners. There is a pervasive sense of Africa's irrelevance in the emerging trends and processes of globalization. How can the Africans chart a new pathway that responds to the continent's predicaments? Is there a need for a new paradigm?

A change of paradigm, without an enabling environment for development effectiveness, will not automatically put the continent on a trajectory of growth and improved quality of life. The constraints on a conducive environment are overwhelming but surmountable. First, there is need for visionary leadership to refocus institutions to be at the service of the people. Where such strong and committed leadership cannot be developed, development intervention should focus on strengthening existing institutions and developing new ones that are accountable to their

users. This second step of setting an appropriate institutional framework should aim at producing a vibrant civil society that ensures the respect of constitutional rights and duties. The guiding principle should be to bring government to the doorsteps of the people. Third, the development community and bilateral donors must allow home-grown institutions and organizations to develop their own culture and legitimacy. Development impact can be sustainable only if it is internalized by the beneficiaries.

In summary, there must be a relocalization of the sources of political power and the mechanisms to ensure accountability. This will create an environment conducive to investment in institutions that will mold future leaders. With a vibrant civil society and strong institutions, a new development paradigm could then be articulated along the following conceptual lines: good governance, inclusive growth, and the sustainable management of the common good. This could be the framework for solving the African development conundrum.

See also **Anthropology, Social, and the Study of Africa; History and the Study of Africa; International Monetary Fund; Lugard, Frederick John Dealtry; Organization of African Unity; Political Science and the Study of Africa; World Bank.**

BIBLIOGRAPHY

Adedeji, Adebayo, ed. *Africa within the World: Beyond Dispossession and Dependence.* London: Zed Books, 1993.

Bates, Robert; V. Y. Mudimbe; and Jean O'Barr; eds. *Africa and the Disciplines: The Contributions of Research in Africa to the Social Sciences and Humanities.* Chicago: University of Chicago Press, 1993.

Bayart, Jean-François. *L'état au Cameroun.* Paris: Presses de la Fondation nationale des sciences politiques, 1979.

Davidson, Basil. *The Black Man's Burden: Africa and the Curse of the Nation-State.* London: James Currey, 1992.

Dilley, Roy, ed. *Contesting Markets: Analyses of Ideology, Discourse, and Practice.* Edinburgh: Edinburgh University Press, 1992.

Escobar, Arturo. "Anthropology and the Development Encounter: The Making and Marketing of Development Anthropology." *American Ethnologist* 18, no. 4 (1991): 16–40.

Geschiere, Peter. "Chiefs and Colonial Rule in Cameroon: Inventing Chieftaincy, French and British Style." *Africa* 63, no. 2 (1993): 151–175.

Himmelstrand, Ulf; Kabiru Kinyanjui; and Edward Mburugu; eds. *African Perspectives on Development: Controversies,*

Dilemmas, and Openings. New York: St. Martin's Press, 1994.

"Intellectuels africains." *Politique africaine*, no. 51 (1993).

Moore, Sally Falk. *Anthropology and Africa: Changing Perspectives on a Changing Scene.* Charlottesville: University Press of Virginia, 1994.

Robins, E. "The Strategy of Development and the Role of Anthropologist." In *Practicing Development Anthropology*, ed. Edward C. Green. Boulder, CO: Westview Press, 1986.

Werbner, Richard. "South Central Africa: The Manchester School and After." In *Localizing Strategies: Regional Traditions of Ethnographic Writing.* Edinburgh: Scottish Academic Press, 1990.

C. F. FISIY

RESETTLEMENT. *See* Refugees.

RÉUNION

GEOGRAPHY

Réunion is the westernmost of the Mascarene Islands situated in the southwestern Indian Ocean. The island has a surface area of 1,557 square miles and lies almost 500 miles east of Madagascar at 21 degrees south latitude and 55 degrees east longitude. The landscape is generally mountainous and dominated by three principal peaks, which are surrounded by three wide valleys, or *cirques*, that are drained by several rivers. The island, which was created by volcanic activity, still has an active volcano which has erupted several times since 1925.

Réunion's climate is tropical at lower elevations but moderated by the southeast trade winds; the climate is cool above 1,500 meters altitude. A rainy season lasts from November to April while the months from May to October are dry. The local topography influences rainfall patterns; the windward side of the island receives from 157 to 307 inches of rain each year, while northern and western areas receive only 24 inches per year. Forest originally covered much of the island, but only 35 percent of its surface area remains forested.

PEOPLE

Réunion was uninhabited before the seventeenth century. Permanent settlement of the island (originally known as the Ile de Bourbon) by French colonists began in 1663 and continued under the auspices of the French East India Company. The legal status of the island's earliest non-European residents is uncertain, but slavery was institutionalized by the early 1690s. An estimated 200,000 slaves reached the island from East and West Africa, India, Madagascar, and Southeast Asia between the late seventeenth century and the 1830s. Following the abolition of slavery in 1848, indentured laborers were brought to the island from India, China, Africa, and Indo-China. Considerable intermarriage over the years has blurred the ethnic distinctions that once characterized the island's population. In 2006 Réunion had an estimated 787,584 inhabitants. French is the island's official language, but most Réunionnais speak Creole. The population is predominantly Roman Catholic, with smaller numbers of Hindus, Muslims, and Buddhists.

HISTORY

Réunion's political and economic history since its colonization has been dominated by France. During much of the eighteenth century, the Ile de Bourbon and the neighboring Ile de France (Mauritius) served as a base from which French interests in India were supported. In 1767 control of the Iles de France et de Bourbon passed to the French Crown. Following the French Revolution in 1789, the Ile de Bourbon's name was changed to Réunion and a colonial assembly was created. Local opposition to the French National Assembly's abolition of slavery in 1794 led to a period of *de facto* independence that lasted until 1803 when metropolitan control was re-established. In 1810 a British expeditionary force captured Mauritius and Réunion. The Treaty of Paris in 1814 ceded Mauritius and its dependencies to Britain while restoring Réunion to France. In 1848 the French government's decision to abolish slavery in France's colonial empire led to the emancipation of some 62,000 Réunionnais slaves; the same year the colony was permitted to elect deputies to the National Assembly. In 1946 Réunion, together with other former colonies such as Guadeloupe and Martinique, became an integral part of France when it was designated as a *département d'outre-mer.*

ECONOMY

During the eighteenth century, Réunion's economy was focused on the production of the foodstuffs needed to feed the population of the Iles de France et de Bourbon and coffee for export to France. Sugar replaced coffee as the island's chief export early in the nineteenth century, and dominated the local economy well into the twentieth century, accounting for 85 percent of export earnings in some years. Réunion also exports rum, molasses, vanilla, and flower oil extracts used to manufacture perfumes.

In the late twentieth century, service industries and manufacturing supplanted agricultural as the most important sectors of the island's economy. In 2000 an estimated 73 percent of the island's gross domestic product (GDP) came from services compared to 19 percent from industry and 8 percent from agriculture. The island's natural beauty has led the government to encourage the development of tourism as a means of relieving high unemployment and poverty rates. One-third of the local labor force is unemployed, while the French government provides welfare payments to 75 percent of the population. A five-year regional development plan for the island was implemented in 1994, with almost one-half of the cost to be met by the European Union.

GOVERNMENT

The people of Réunion have a heritage of opposition to metropolitan rule. Negotiations during the latter part of the twentieth century over the nature of the relationship between France and Réunion have been framed by the emergence of an independence movement on the island. The momentum for self-determination is fueled by the feeling among many Réunionnais that they do not receive the same social and welfare benefits that French citizens in metropolitan France enjoy and that the mother country is interested in the island primarily for its own benefit.

See also **Colonial Policies and Practices: French; Creoles; Economic History; Mauritius; Plantation Economies and Societies.**

BIBLIOGRAPHY

Aldrich, Robert, and John Connell. *France's Overseas Frontier: Les départements et territoires d'outre-mer.* Cambridge, U.K.: Cambridge University Press, 1992.

Allen, Richard B. "The Mascarene Slave Trade and Labour Migration in the Indian Ocean during the Eighteenth and Nineteenth Centuries." In *The Structure of Slavery in Indian Ocean, Africa and Asia*, ed. Gwyn Campbell. London: Frank Cass, 2004.

Chane-Kune, Sonia. *Aux origines de l'identité réunionnaise.* Paris: L'Harmattan, 1993.

Desport, Jean-Marie. *De la servitude à la liberté: Bourbon des origines à 1848.* La Réunion: Océan Editions, 1989.

Ho, Hai Quang. *Contribution à l'histoire économique de l'île de la Réunion.* Paris: L'Harmattan, 1998.

NANCY G. WRIGHT
REVISED BY RICHARD B. ALLEN

RHODES, CECIL JOHN (1853–1902).

Cecil John Rhodes was born the third of six sons of an impecunious Anglican vicar in Bishop's Stortford, England. At seventeen, after a cursory education, he immigrated alone to Natal in southeastern Africa, where he farmed cotton before moving to the diamond fields at Kimberley in the Cape Colony. There, Rhodes rose rapidly in power and wealth. By age thirty-six he controlled most of the diamond riches of South Africa and many of the gold mines of the Witwatersrand. Rhodes went back and forth to Oxford from 1873, finally receiving a pass degree there in 1881.

Elected to the parliament of the Cape Colony in 1881, Rhodes served as prime minister from 1890 to 1896. With his wealth and his overweening imperial ambitions, he also sponsored the conquest of Southern Rhodesia (present-day Zimbabwe) from 1890 through 1897 through a private corporation, the British South African Company. That conquest spilled over into Northern Rhodesia (present-day Zambia), Nyasaland (present-day Malawi), and even Mozambique. Rhodes was also responsible for the ill-starred Jameson Raid of late 1895, a filibustering attempt to subvert Afrikaner rule in the Transvaal, an area that contained most of the fabulous gold wealth of the region. This raid helped turn Afrikaners against English speakers in South Africa.

Rhodes, however, is unjustly blamed for fomenting the Anglo-Boer War of 1899–1902; by 1899 Rhodes was no longer the key English-speaking

Cecil John Rhodes (1853–1902). Rhodes, a businessman and founder of the diamond company DeBeers, colonized the state of Rhodesia, which was named after him. Rhodesia later became Zambia and Zimbabwe. HULTON ARCHIVE/GETTY IMAGES

RHODESIA. *See* Zambia; Zimbabwe.

RIDDLES. *See* Literature: Proverbs and Riddles.

RÍO MUNI. *See* Equatorial Guinea.

RITUALS OF REBELLION. *See* Festivals and Carnivals.

ROCK ART. *See* Art, Genres and Periods: Rock Art, Eastern Africa; Art, Genres and Periods: Rock Art, Saharan and Northern Africa; Art, Genres and Periods: Rock Art, Southern Africa.

imperialist leader in South Africa. In the Cape Colony, Rhodes sponsored racist legislation that deprived Africans of the right to vote. He also helped to inaugurate the infamous mining-compound system. He introduced scientific citrus growing to South Africa and was an early environmentalist. Rhodes also established the scholarship system that bears his name, and which has numbered among its recipients a U.S. president and the prime ministers of several English-speaking nations of the British Commonwealth.

See also **Cape Colony and Hinterland, History of (1600 to 1910); Metals and Minerals: Gold and Silver.**

BIBLIOGRAPHY

Rotberg, Robert I. *The Founder: Cecil Rhodes and the Pursuit of Power.* New York: Oxford University Press, 1988.

ROBERT I. ROTBERG

ROUCH, JEAN (1917–2004). Trained as a civil engineer, Jean Rouch came to the colony of Niger to help build roads during World War II. There, he became interested in the spirit possession practices of the Songhay people and embarked on doctoral research on Songhay religion under the supervision of anthropologist Marcel Griaule (1898–1956). In 1960, Rouch became a researcher at the Centre National de la Recherche Scientifique and his doctoral thesis, a detailed compendium of Songhay religious beliefs and practices, was published as *La religion et la magie Songhay.*

Rouch also wanted to document the lives of African people through film. When filming a hippopotamus hunt, he lost his tripod in the Niger River. He continued to film with a handheld camera, thus ushering a style of filmmaking that would become known as *cinéma-vérité* and in which nonactors, real settings, and handheld cameras are used. Rouch went on to chronicle a half century of profound social transformations in West Africa and produced over 120 films, including the famously controversial *Les maîtres fous,* a documentary about spirit possession. He elaborated a filming style through which the

French filmmaker Jean Rouch (1917–2004) directing the 1961 film *Chronique d'un été (Chronicle of a Summer).* Rouch's interest in Africa began when he worked as a civil engineer in Niger in 1941. THE KOBAL COLLECTION; THE PICTURE DESK, INC.

passion as well as controversy for its depictions of Africans and African religion.

Much has been written about Jean Rouch's accomplishment as an ethnographer, a filmmaker, an innovator, and a follower of the spirits. There is nonetheless general agreement that Jean Rouch was a great experimenter, willing to take risks, to innovate, and to follow the drama of life to its most revealing or troublesome climaxes, testing the limits of our imagination in the process.

On February 18, 2004, anthropologist and filmmaker Jean Rouch died in a car crash in Niger, where he was attending a film festival, some sixty years after first coming to Niger to work as a civil engineer.

See also **Media: Cinema; Spirit Possession.**

BIBLIOGRAPHY

Eaton, Mick, ed. *Anthropology, Reality, Cinema: The Films of Jean Rouch.* London: British Film Institute, 1979.

Stellar, Paul. *Cinematic Griot: The Ethnography of Jean Rouch.* Chicago: University of Chicago Press, 1992.

ADELINE MASQUELIER

camera was used as a catalytic force to stimulate reactions from cinematic subjects and combine fiction with reality. Filming became a form of *anthropologie partagée* or ethnofiction. Two of the finest examples of what Rouch called ethnofiction are *Jaguar* and *Moi, un noir.* He developed an influential theory of ethnographic filmmaking through which the cinematic experience was conceived as a collaboration between filmmaker and subject.

Rouch was hailed by some for his critical depictions of colonialism and condemned by others for his portrayal of Africa in its violent rawness, but his influence on anthropology and filmmaking is widely acknowledged. He taught as a visiting professor at Harvard University for four years, and from 1986 to 1991 was director of the Cinémathèque Française. In Niger, where he returned every year, Rouch became a legend whose work provoked

RWABUGIRI (1840–1895). Kigeri Rwabugiri is renowned as the great warrior-king of late-nineteenth-century Rwanda. But his reign from about 1865 to 1895 was as important for structural transformations within Rwanda as for his external wars.

Rwabugiri came to power as the result of a complicated set of events that amounted to an internal coup. Having acceded by power, Rwabugiri ruled by force. Within the state he appointed administrative authorities (including Hutu and Twa) dependent on his favor as a counterweight to powerful Tutsi political lineages; he thus consolidated power at the central court and increased the arbitrary power of the monarch.

Nonetheless in song and memory, Rwabugiri is best remembered for his external military campaigns, especially to areas west and north of Rwanda. In fact, the booty and rewards resulting from those campaigns (cattle, women, and political position) made possible the expansion of power at the central court. Yet despite the vast area attacked, relatively few regions were permanently annexed; one must distinguish the full incorporation of conquered regions (the geographical expansion of Rwanda) from military occupation (often of brief duration) and simple raids.

Rwabugiri's death marked not only the end of an era of energetic expansion and the consolidation of royal power but also an end to Rwanda's status as an independent monarchy. Shortly after his death many of Rwanda's greatest military heroes perished in two battles fought against troops associated with the Congo Free State. The court thereafter followed a policy of collaboration with the European intruders, a policy that, though not without tension and political manipulation on both sides, served the objectives of both the Rwandan elites and the colonial powers.

Although the luster of Rwabugiri's reign was built on incessant battles externally and a constant campaign against entrenched power within, his enduring reputation is also based on the decline that came after. His reign served as both the culmination and the terminal point of the long process of building royal absolutist hegemony in the state structures of Rwanda.

See also **Kings and Kingdoms; Kingship.**

BIBLIOGRAPHY

Kagame, Alexis. *Les milices du Rwanda précolonial.* Brussels: Academie Royale des Sciences, 1963.

Kagame, Alexis. *Un abreégé de l'histoire du Rwanda*, Vol. 2. Butare, Rwanda: Éditions universitaires du Rwanda, 1975.

Newbury, Catharine. *The Cohesion of Oppression: Clientship and Ethnicity in Rwanda, 1860–1960.* New York: Columbia University Press, 1988.

Newbury, David. "Les campagnes de Rwabugiri." *Cahiers d'études africaines* 14 (1974): 181–191.

Newbury, David. "Rwabugiri and Ijwi." *Études d'histoire africaine* 7 (1975): 155–175.

DAVID NEWBURY

RWANDA

This entry includes the following articles:

GEOGRAPHY AND ECONOMY

Rwanda is a small country (10,169 square miles) in the Great Lakes region of Africa with a population estimated to be 9,907,509 (2007). It borders Democratic Republic of the Congo (DRC) on the West, sharing Lake Kivu with this neighbor, Tanzania on the east, Uganda on the North and Burundi on the South. As of January 2006, the country reduced the number of provinces from twelve to five, the new provinces being Eastern, Northern, Western, Southern, and the City of Kigali. The elevation ranges between 3,117 feet and 14,825 feet above sea level. The country has a two large forest reserves, and number of distinct geological and environmental regions. A large, central plateau area dominated by hills gives the country its nickname, *la pays de milles collines* (the land of a thousand hills). The northwest is mountainous with a volcanic chain, the Virunga Range, straddling its borders with DRC and Uganda; savannas make up the northeast and east; a large hilly plateau comprises the east; the Nile-Zaire crest watershed is in the west; and a large marsh is to the south. Rwanda has a temperate climate with two rainy seasons (February–April, November–January) and two dry seasons. It is a republic with a president and a newly established multiparty system.

THE PEOPLE

Kinyarwanda (the only indigenous language), French, and English are Rwanda's national languages. Ninety-four percent of the people are Christian, 4.6 percent are Muslim, and 0.01 percent follow indigenous beliefs. The population is made up of three ethnic groups—Hutu, Tutsi, and Twa— who live, intermingled, throughout the country. Precolonial Rwanda was created by the conquest and assimilation of neighboring kingdoms, and the populations of these kingdoms were assimilated as either Hutu if agriculturalist, or Tutsi if pastoralist, and the predominantly forest-dwelling pygmies were incorporated as Twa. Typically, the breakdown is 15 percent Tutsi, 84 percent Hutu, and 1 percent Twa, and they are all assumed to be physically distinct. These numbers are misleading because ethnicity is identified through the father, the rate of intermarriage is high, and, because Rwanda was created by the conquest and assimilation of neighboring kingdoms, the physical differences within the ethnic groups differ dramatically by class and region.

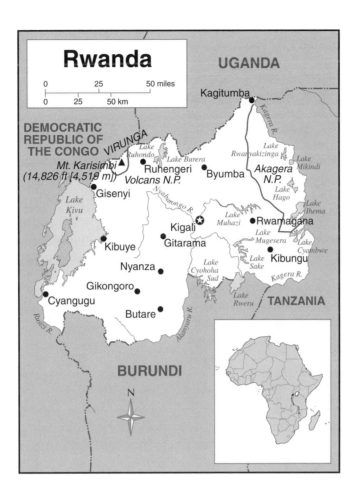

Rwanda has the highest population density in Africa and has a 2.5 percent birthrate. Forty-one point nine (41.9) percent of the population is under fifteen years of age and the average life expectancy is 43.9 years of age—42.1 for males, 45.6 for females. Sixty-four percent of the population is literate, with more literate males (70.5%) than females (58.8%).

THE ECONOMY

Roughly 45 percent of Rwanda's landmass is arable, and 81.5 percent of its population is defined as rural. Agriculture accounts for 40.1 percent of the GDP, industry for 22.9 percent, and services for 37 percent. Overseas development aid provides 20.3 percent of GDP. The main crops are beans, bananas, sorghum, and sweet potatoes (mostly for home consumption), as well as some livestock production, also predominantly for home consumption. Coffee, tea, and pyrethrum are the main export crops, and Rwanda also exports a small amount of hides and tin ore. Most Rwandans, more than 90 percent, are still predominantly subsistence agriculturalists. As in many sub-Saharan African societies, the majority of the day-to-day agricultural tasks are done by women, while heavy agricultural work is shared by men and women. Cash crops, coffee, tea, and pyrethrum are controlled by men, but farmed by women. Coffee is a smallholder crop, with 80 percent of households growing coffee, while tea and pyrethrum are grown on government-owned plantations. In the gender division of labor, women do the majority of agricultural work and have control over crops kept for household consumption, and men control the cash generated through cash crops and any subsistence crops that are sold.

See also **Ecosystems: Savannas.**

BIBLIOGRAPHY

Centre national de la recherche scientifique. *Les milieux tropicaux d'altitude: Recherches sur les hautes terres d'Afrique Centrale.* Talence, France: Centre d'Etudes de Geographie Tropicale, 1981.

Université Nationale du Rwanda. *Atlas du Rwanda.* Nantes, France: Association pour l'Atlas des Pays de Loire, 1981.

United Nations Development Program. *Human Development Report 2005. International Cooperation at a Cross-roads: Aid, Trade and Security in an Unequal World.* New York: United Nations Development Program. 2005.

VILLIA JEFREMOVAS

SOCIETY AND CULTURES

In 1994 Rwanda shook the world's conscience when close to 1 million people, mostly ethnic Tutsi, were killed through state-sponsored violence. Land-grabbing by powerful elites loyal to President Habyarimana, high population densities, abject poverty and unemployment, the invasion from Uganda by the Rwandan Patriotic Front (RPF), and the manipulations of ruthless Hutu demagogues, were prominent causal factors. In the first decade of the 2000s, despite the introduction of far-reaching economic, social, and political changes, Rwanda has many features that point to continuity with the past, most notably the centralization of political power and an elite scramble for limited resources. As ever, Rwanda is also known for its dense, interdependent networks of kinship, administration, and commerce.

Rwanda's precolonial history too was dominated by struggles over resources, mainly land and cattle. History before 1900 revolved around the interaction of three populations: farmers (called Hutu) cleared and managed land on a clan basis; herders (called Tutsi) took advantage of the region's lush pasturelands; while a population known as Twa lived primarily in forested regions. Although these social categories had permeable boundaries, competition for resources did occur, especially between herders and farmers. Resolving their conflicts required the presence of a central authority, which, when it emerged, took the shape of an aristocratic herder dynasty. After creating a (Tutsi) kingdom, this Nyiginya dynasty organized its court around an ideology and rituals of kingship, the deployment of permanent armies, and the cementing of allegiances through the cattle contract (*ubuhake*). The first systematic differentiation between Tutsi and Hutu may have developed in the context of militarization.

A major administrative reorganization and expansion of the court's influence occurred in the second half of the nineteenth century, when King Rwabugiri and his courtiers accumulated vast herds of cattle, mostly through incessant conquest and terror. This resulted in the emergence of farmers with insufficient or no land, whose only survival strategy was to hire themselves out as day laborers (*abacancuro*). Pauperized herders also emerged. But it was farmers, not herders, upon whom the court imposed the notorious *uburetwa* labor tax without which farmers could not access land. The imposition rigidified the Hutu-Tutsi differentiation; *Ubuhake* and *uburetwa*—the tools that forged the classification—remained central organizing principles until the end of Belgian colonial rule. Belgium not only built upon the classification, but also racialized it.

At the onset of the twentieth century, Rwanda was divided into two polities with distinctive land-cum-political regimes. Roughly, there were regions controlled by the Tutsi Nyiginya court and regions that remained outside its influence. The latter included the northwest of contemporary Rwanda and a few Hutu kingdoms. These regions became part of present-day Rwanda when Belgian colonists assisted the court with its quest to annex them and bring about administrative unification. Before unification, regions ruled by the central court were governed by a land tenure system known as *isambu*, which specified that land invariably belonged to the Tutsi king (*mwami*). In contrast, in regions outside the court's influence, land was held by corporate lineages in a system of clientship known as *ubukonde*. Under *ubukonde*, lineage and nonlineage members could request land from the lineage head. Following administrative unification, only the king retained the right and power to allocate land.

The Hutu social revolution of 1959 brought down the Tutsi kingdom and Belgian colonialism, and removed the pillars of serfdom. The cattle contract (*ubuhake*) and associated *uburetwa* labor tax were abolished, as was the right to grazing lands (*ibikingi*) previously reserved for royal herds. More land thus became available for cultivation. But the country's new Hutu leaders pursued clientelistic agendas and showed little interest in alleviating poverty. The one official strategy to combat poverty was the prohibition of distress land sales by the poor, which was a restriction easily circumvented. Unlawful sales escalated in the late 1980s, by which time serious inequalities in land ownership and access had become entrenched. By the mid-1980s, half the country's productive land was controlled by about 15 percent of the population, mostly Rwandans in commerce, government, and the aid industry. In 1989, the collapse of the coffee price on the world market brought economic disaster for Rwanda's smallholder farmers—and drove many to the brink of despair, especially in densely populated regions.

As Hutu extremists manipulated the despairing population, it emerged that the conquests and administrative unification of the 1920s had left a permanent legacy: northern Hutu viewed southern Hutu as "Other," as Tutsi. Relatively dormant in the early days of independence, north-south antagonism resurfaced in the mid-1960s after a United Nations (UN) report reprimanded President Kayibanda, a southerner, for running a corrupt regime and favoring Rwanda's southern Hutu. Habyarimana's coup of 1973 ended the corrupt Kayibanda regime, but the process of favoritism simply changed course; international aid now flowed toward the northwestern prefectures of Gisenyi (Habyarimana's home region) and Ruhengeri. On seizing power, Habyarimana's northern Hutu elite vowed to restore the pre-Tutsi culture the north had lost. While this restoration scheme found little support in South Rwanda, where cross-ethnic relations and marriages had become common, the legacy of the north-south divide became apparent during the genocide, when South Rwanda initially resisted the calls for genocide.

In October 1990, the Rwandan Patriotic Front (RPF), its fighting force composed mainly of exiled Tutsi, invaded Rwanda from Uganda. The four-year war that ensued galvanized Hutu extremists to launch their anti-Tutsi propaganda and murderous militia forces. Following the assassination of President Habyarimana in April 1994, by which time a fragile peace agreement had been signed in Arusha, Hutu Power extremists mobilized a nationwide militia, the *Interahamwe*, to exterminate Tutsi and Hutu sympathetic to conciliation. Their propaganda claimed to expose the country's "real" problem: ethnicity, or the danger of a return to the old order under a Tutsi

aristocracy. The essentialist, racist category of "the evil Tutsi" was operationalized for the sake of safeguarding political privilege. Hutu Power extremists used an effective public information system, mainly via Radio Mille Collines, to incite the Hutu population to genocide.

During the horror of 1994, the Catholic church also emerged as actively siding with Hutu Power. Historically, the state and the church had developed in symbiosis, both acting as channels to power, influence, and wealth. In colonial times, the state-church alliance favored the Tutsi, regarded as the country's noble rulers, but church leaders dropped this favoritism in the late 1950s by championing "social Catholicism" and the Hutu cause. However, Tutsi priests continued to be prominent in the clergy until the early 1990s. When, following the RPF invasion, several Tutsi priests were arrested and some killed, along with other Tutsi and Hutu moderates, the church by and large remained mute. The scene was thus set for acts of complicity and participation in the genocide by some clergy. The Catholic church has yet to recover its authority, as the postgenocide explosion of Christian sects testifies.

Some 800,000 people were killed in one hundred days. Besides the fear of being killed should they refuse to join the killers, ordinary people also killed for economic gain, often for possession of a victim's land. The killing frenzy ended when the RPF forces defeated Rwanda's regular army, and some 2 million Hutu fled to eastern Zaire (present-day Democratic Republic of the Congo [DRC]) and western Tanzania. With the UN-run camps provoking regional instability, the bulk of the refugees would later be expelled and repatriated. They were expelled from the DRC in 1997, after Rwanda invaded its "big neighbor," and later from Tanzania following action taken by the local authorities. It is increasingly acknowledged, however, that the Arusha Accords, which had proposed a structure for power sharing in Rwanda, had been imposed on a country not ready for multipartyism.

Since the RPF's military victory in July 1994 Rwanda has seen power become increasingly centralized in the hands of a ruling minority intolerant of political opposition. This tightening of control

Republic of Rwanda

Population:	9,907,509 (2007 est.)
Area:	26,338 sq. km (10,169 sq. mi.)
Official languages:	French, Kinyarwanda, English
Languages:	French, Kinyarwanda, English
National currency:	Rwanda franc
Principal religions:	Christian 94%, Muslim 5%, other 1%
Capital:	Kigali (est. pop. 800,000 in 2006)
Other major urban centers:	Gitarama, Butare, Ruhengeri, Gisenyi
Annual rainfall:	1,770 mm (70 in.) in the west, 760 mm (30 in.) in the northeast and east
Principal geographical features:	*Mountains:* Virunga Mountains (highest peak, Mount Karisimbi) *Lakes:* Ruhondo, Muhazi, Mugsera, Ihema, Rwanye, Burera, Rugwero, Cyohoha, Kivu *Rivers:* Kagera, Ruzizi, Nyabarongo, Rukarara, Mwogo, Biruruma, Mokungwa, Base, Nyabugtogo, Akanyaru
Economy:	*GDP per capita:* US$1,600 (2006)
Principal products and exports:	*Agricultural:* coffee, tea, pyrethrum (insecticide made from chrysanthemums), bananas, beans, sorghum, potatoes, livestock *Manufacturing:* cement, agricultural products, small-scale beverages, soap, furniture, shoes, plastic goods, textiles, cigarettes *Mining:* tin, tungsten, beryl, amblygonite, columbite, tantalite
Government:	Former German, then Belgian colony. Independence from Belgian-administered U.N. trusteeship, 1962. Constitutions adopted in 1962, 1978, and 1991. Civil war begun in 1990, genocide of roughly 800,000 Tutsis and moderate Hutus in 1994. The Tutsi rebels defeated the Hutu regime and ended the killing in 1994, but 2 million Hutu refugees fled the country.
Form of government:	Republic. Council of ministers appointed by president, who is elected by popular vote for 7-year term. Bicameral parliament consists of 26-member Senate and 80-member Chamber of Deputies.
Heads of state since independence:	1962–1973: President Grégoire Kayibanda 1973–1994: President Major General Juvénal Habyarimana 1994: President Théodore Sindikugbabo 1994–2000: President Pasteur Bizimungu (Major General Paul Kagame held actual power) 2000–: President Paul Kagame
Armed forces:	Armed forces consist of an army and a small air force and comprise about 25,000 soliders.
Transportation:	*Waterways:* some commercial navigation on Lake Kivu *Roads:* 14,008 km (8,704 mi.), 9% paved. External shipping through Burundi to Dar es Salaam and through Uganda to Mombasa. *National airline:* Air Rwanda *Airports:* International facilities at Kigali. Smaller airports at Gisenyi, Gabiro, Butare.
Media:	1 daily newspaper, 10 nondailies, 9 periodicals, including *Hobe* (monthly), *Imvaho* (weekly), *Kinyamateka* (biweekly business magazine), and *La Relève* (monthly). 5 book publishers, principally in French. 8 radio stations, 2 television stations.
Literacy and education:	*Total literacy rate:* 70.4% (2006). School system was destroyed in the fighting of 1994. Educational services resumed in September 1994. 6 years compulsory. Postsecondary education provided by Université Nationale du Rwanda, Institut Africain et Mauricien de Statistique et d'Economie Appliquée, École Technique Officielle Don Bosco.

from the center was first expressed in 1995 when (Hutu) Prime Minister Twagiramungu and other Hutu ministers left the post-genocide government. A further wave of high-profile departures occurred in early 2000. These turbulent episodes stifled civil society, while human rights groups became subject to pressure and cooptation by government.

During its first decade in power, the RPF-led government introduced numerous reforms, some spectacularly innovative. In 2002 government revived a traditional participatory justice system, known as *gacaca*, to speed up the trials of those accused of participation in the genocide. This ambitious experiment, however, has turned out to be slow, unpopular, and hampered by the absence of trained judges and survivor fears of repercussion. Another experiment was the villagization (*imidugudu*) initiative launched in 1996. Although villagization had failed elsewhere in Africa, *imidugudu* initially received significant foreign support. The official justification for *imidugudu* was that putting an end to the legacy of dispersed settlements and ever-fragmenting plots would enhance agricultural productivity. The scheme, however, has been implemented only in part, and without proof of productivity enhancement.

Demographic change has also led to new legislation. The 1999 Inheritance Law has abolished gender discrimination for women who are legally married, and for their offspring. While the law marks a positive step toward institutionalizing gender parity, two major caveats must be noted. First, since most unions in Rwanda are common-law unions not legally registered, young women and girls are easily labelled illegitimate, which disqualifies them from inheriting property. Second, the inheritance law cannot be applied retrospectively. It does not apply to the daughters and women whose fathers and husbands died in the genocide.

Most ambitiously, government has embarked on a major land reform program, which hinges on the consolidation of fragmented family plots and the granting of land titles. Although aiming to bring about better soil management and productivity, and to reduce the prevalence of land disputes (escalated since the genocide), the new legislation may result in up to half a million households losing what little land they have while nothing is done to curb the power of the country's *nouveaux riches*, who engage in land speculation. The promotion of professional pastoralism, and local authorities' right to expropriate arable land not properly managed, a central feature of the 2005 Land Law, are factors likely to fuel tension. To offset the fears of land dispossession, government has pledged—but without guarantees—that the poor who exit from agriculture will benefit from a robust boost in off-farm employment and income-generating activities.

Despite the horror of 1994, Rwanda maintained strong continuities with the past during the first decade of the 2000s. Two are particularly noteworthy: the centralized control by elites over the main means of production, land in particular, and the power of local authorities. The postgenocide state imposes firm parameters, but gives local administrators discretion in how to interpret and apply them.

See also **Ethnicity; Human Rights; Refugees.**

BIBLIOGRAPHY

Eltringham, Nigel. *Accounting for Horror: Post-Genocide Debates in Rwanda*. London: Pluto Press, 2004.

Newbury, Catharine. *The Cohesion of Oppression: Clientship and Ethnicity in Rwanda, 1860–1960.* New York: Columbia University Press, 1988.

Pottier, Johan. *Re-Imagining Rwanda: Conflict, Survival and Disinformation in the Late 20th Century.* Cambridge, U.K.: Cambridge University Press, 2002.

Van Hoyweghen, Saskia. "The Disintegration of the Catholic Church of Rwanda: A Study of the Fragmentation of Political and Religious Authority." *African Affairs* 95 (1996): 379–401.

Vansina, Jan. *Antecedents to Modern Rwanda: The Nyiginya Kingdom.* Oxford: James Currey, 2004.

JOHAN POTTIER

HISTORY AND POLITICS

In 1897, when the Germans entered Rwanda, Rwanda was a kingdom created by the conquest and assimilation of neighboring kingdoms and its borders were similar to those of Rwanda in the early twenty-first century. The population spoke Kinyarwanda and was divided into three ethnic groups: Hutu, Tutsi, and Twa. The process of precolonial conquest and assimilation had incorporated agriculturalists as Hutu, pastoralists as Tutsi, and the pygmy forest dwellers as Twa. While the majority of Twa were forest dwellers, they also specialized as potters and a small number were members of the royal court. Both Tutsi and Hutu farmed land and kept cattle; the difference was in the social importance that was placed in the activities. The elites and the peasantry comprised both Tutsi and Hutu. The kingdom had administered recently conquered regions through Indirect Rule, assimilating these regions into the central power structure over time, leaving both Hutu and Tutsi lords in power.

The precolonial kingdom saw a turbulent transformation of land, labor, and power relations. Over an estimated 600 years, the system changed from one in which the king was a first amongst equals with power vested in clans to one in which land, labor, and power were vested in a hierarchy of individual patron-client relationship with the king at the apex. This centralization culminated with Kigeri Rwabugiri's (1860–1895) brutal suppression of a civil war between two major clans, the Ega and the Nyginya, leaving power in the hands of a tiny aristocratic elite. Queen Mother Kangogera's killing of Rwabugiri's heir, Mibambwe Rutarindwa (1895–

1896), and the enthronement of Kangogera's son, the child king Yuhi Musinga (1896–1931), created a legitimacy crisis. Kangorera and her brothers saw the Germans as a means to consolidate and expand their power; therefore, the court accepted the German flag. The German presence was small, only ten European administrators and foreign soldiers, so the Rwandan central court had considerable power during this period and the power structure within the country was not substantially changed.

GERMAN COLONIAL RULE: 1898–1919

Although nominal German rule lasted from 1898 until 1919, effective German rule lasted from 1907 to 1916 (Germany lost the country to Belgium during World War I). Until 1907, the German presence was concerned with punitive expeditions to consolidate borders and to buttress the power of the African elites. After 1907, the German residency attempted to make this colony economically viable by building infrastructure using *corvée* labor, decreeing the planting of cash crops, tutoring the kings in modern political rule, and allowing missionaries to convert the population to Christianity.

The Rwandan king, the royal court and its internal factions, the Notables, rebel lords, and the peasantry in both kingdoms all used colonial rule and the presence of missionaries to their own advantage: The colonial administration required large amounts of labor for its projects, making its demands through the local hierarchy, giving Notables and chiefs an excuse to increase their demands on their subjects. Musinga and Kangogera needed the Germans to rule. They used the Germans to execute enemies, to enforce taxes and labor service, to expand their own powers, and to keep the missionaries in check. Nevertheless, they were also often at odds with the German administrators. The Belgian missionaries, Le Societé des Missionaires d'Afrique, had an uneasy relationship with the German colonial state and the Central Court for two reasons: Belgium was a competitor in the region; and the missionaries acted as champions of the Hutu peasantry against aristocratic Tutsi exploitation. Despite Musinga's resistance to the German rule, the German support of aristocratic abuse of power made a link between the colonial regime and the crown in the eyes of the population.

BELGIAN COLONIAL RULE: 1919–1962

Belgium took Rwanda by force in mid-1916, was given governance by the Treaty of Versailles in 1919, and was formally confirmed as the colonial authority by the League of Nations in 1924. From 1924 until 1962, Rwanda was governed as a League, and then as a UN protectorate. The Belgians found the indigenous political organization hard to understand and administer, so they set about reforming the system, reducing the numbers of chiefs, simplifying the system, and purging the Hutu lords from power. Convinced that they were ruling over racially separate castes stratified by aptitude, the Belgians promulgated the ideology that the Tutsi were racially superior invaders and were the natural rulers of Rwanda. Consequently, the Belgians set about educating a cadre of local administrators of Tutsi aristocratic lineage, using racial and class criteria to choose this cadre, and purging the Hutu lords from political power. The Belgian administration deposed Musinga in 1931 because he frustrated the Belgian reforms and refused to be baptized, or to appoint or promote Christian lords, and put his son, Mutara Rudahigwa (1931–1959), on the throne. Rudahigwa and his court used the new ideology of Tutsi racial superiority to consolidate even more power into the hands of the new chiefs and the aristocratic class. New taxes, new forms of labor service, new obligatory crops, and new exactions were implemented, and the court used these new forms to accumulate wealth and extract labor. The Belgians deplored the abuses of the chiefs but both the Belgian government and the Rwandan chiefs used the pretext of custom to extract more from the peasantry.

The post–World War II period saw a change in the colonial and church bureaucracy that affected internal Rwandan ethnic relations and the attitude of the colonial administrators. The prewar bureaucracy and church were more often drawn from the European aristocracy who saw Tutsi privilege as a bulwark against communism. The postwar functionaries—who were drawn from a middle class—saw Tutsi privilege as abusive and retrograde. The postwar church created a new Hutu educated class and gave them positions in church organizations, but the court excluded them from political power.

As the country approached independence, the church and the Belgian colonial regime in Rwanda veered from its pro-Tutsi policy to a strong pro-Hutu stance. In 1959 ethnic violence was unleashed by a series of political events starting with the death of Rudahigwa, the enthronement of his brother, Kigeri Ndahindurwa (1959–1962), by a Tutsi extremist group, and the supposed killing of a Hutu party functionary during the lead-up to the elections. Hutu elements attacked and persecuted or killed the Tutsi aristocracy and its adherents. Tutsi commoners, who represented the majority of Tutsi, were not targeted at this time. With considerable support from the Belgians, the Parmahutu (Parti du Mouvement de l'Emancipation Hutu), a Hutu extremist party, won the UN-supervised 1962 elections in the midst of this violence, and deposed Ndahindurwa.

THE FIRST REPUBLIC (1962–1973)
AND THE SECOND REPUBLIC (1973–1994)

The election of a Hutu extremist party that promulgated a racist philosophy that the Hutu were the natural inhabitants of Rwanda and that the Tutsi were interlopers, headed by Gregoire Kayibanda (1962–1973), and the attempted invasions by Rwandan Tutsi exiles between 1961–1965, transformed the ethnic politics. Kayibanda responded to these attacks with violence against the general Tutsi population, peasant and elite, and thousands fled over the border to Uganda, the Congo, Burundi and Tanzania. During this regime, the Hutu of central Rwanda consolidated land and power into the hands of a tiny minority, whereas the Hutu of the north controlled the army but were excluded from political power. As the regime lost credibility, it tried to use ethnic violence to maintain its hold on power and to diffuse the growing class consciousness. The beleaguered Kayibanda regime tried unsuccessfully to use the 1972 massacre of the Hutu elites in Burundi as an excuse to incite ethnic violence against the Tutsi in an attempt to bolster its position. In a bloodless coup, the northern Hutu General Juvenal Habyarimana (1937–1994) established the second republic when he overthrew Kayibanda and took power in a popular palace putsch in 1973. This coup stopped the anti-Tutsi violence until 1990.

From 1973–1986, Habyarimana's regime was able to extend benefits to a portion of the population, most commonly, but exclusively, Hut; however, much of this was done on the basis of foreign aid and the strength of the coffee economy. Land, labor, power, and wealth were concentrated in the hands of a small number of Hutu families from the north. By 1989, the regime was no longer able to deliver the economic, social and political benefits that characterized the early years of the second republic and was under criticism for corruption, nepotism, and a lack of human rights. In 1989, a fall in coffee prices prompted a recession. Most small farmers lost 50 percent of their income in that year. The loss of coffee income affected the Rwandan treasury to the extent that the International Monetary Fund imposed a draconian Structural Adjustment program (SAP). This led to the sale of food reserves, the lifting of price controls, privatization, currency devaluation, a wage freeze, and job losses.

Exacerbated by a severe drought in 1989, food prices skyrocketed and starvation ensued. Other factors, such as the bourgeoning population coupled with a lack of new lands, and the centralization of lands through distress sales, served to discredit the government. The Rwandan Patriotic Front (RPF) a Ugandan-based group formed mostly by Tutsi refugees or their descendents who had fled to Uganda between 1959 and 1965, invaded in 1990 and came close to collapsing the regime. This invasion also provided an excuse for the Habyarimana regime to deflect criticism by resorting to anti-Tutsi extremism. Between 1990 and 1993, it had limited success despite a vicious propaganda campaign. When it was clear that they were losing the war, the Habyarimana regime was forced to the bargaining table and, in 1992, signed the Arusha Accords. The RPF, which negotiated from a position of strength against a divided and fractious coalition of different political parties, was able to gain an agreement that would have given the RPF effective control over the army. The regime responded by intensifying anti-Tutsi propaganda and violence. An extremist group, the Reseau Zero, began to plan the eradication of the Tutsi, just as plans for the turnover of power were launched. The assassination of Burundian President Melchior Ndadaye (1953–1993) a Hutu who had been elected with 80 percent of the popular vote by a Tutsi-dominated army, added fuel to the propaganda campaign.

FROM 1994 TO THE PRESENT

On April 6, 1994, Habyarima was killed when his airplane was shot down. Although there is a considerable amount of speculation on who attacked the airplane, with all sides from the French, the RPF, and the Hutu extremists being blamed, the perpetrators have never been identified. The extremists from the "Reseau Zero" group used this as an excuse to perpetrate genocide against the Tutsi population and to kill moderate Hutu in the political opposition. For the first three days, this killing was confined to areas controlled by the extremists. However, over the next three weeks it spread throughout the country. Ironically, the center of the old Tutsi-dominated kingdom was the last area to be affected by the killing. Over 100 days, 500,000–800,000 people were killed, most by the militias and the army, but also by common people. In order to explain the genocide, the role of such complex and important factors as economic recession, structural adjustment programs, population explosion, civil war, the loss of legitimacy by the political elites, the international political struggle for influence waged by the French, the impact of the Arusha Accords, and the assassination of Ndadaye must be taken into account.

While the world community hesitated, the Rwandan Patriotic Front resumed the civil war and by July 1994 had pacified the country, by conquering and driving out the pre-existing Rwandan army and militias thereby stopping the killing of the Tutsis, and established a military regime with Paul Kagame (b. 1957), at that time the vice president and minister of defense effectively in charge of the country. In 2000 Kagame declared himself president and in 2003 was elected president in the first national elections since 1961. The current parliament has the distinction of achieving near gender parity, with 49 percent of the deputies being women. Twenty-three out of eighty seats in the main house of the parliament have been earmarked for women, the other female deputies were elected amongst the fifty-three candidates who are elected through universal suffrage by secret ballot. There are also two seats earmarked for youth and one for a disabled deputy.

See also **Colonial Policies and Practices; International Monetary Fund; Postcolonialism; Queens and Queen Mothers; Rwabugiri.**

BIBLIOGRAPHY

Chrétien, Jean-Pierre, trans. *The Great Lakes of Africa: Two Thousand Years of History.* New York: Zone Books, 2003.

Des Forges, Alison L. "Defeat Is the Only Bad News: Rwanda under Musiinga, 1896–1931." PhD diss, Yale University, 1972.

Des Forges, Alison L. *Leave None to Tell the Story: Genocide in Rwanda.* New York; Washington, DC; London; Brussels; Paris: Human Rights Watch and International Federation of Human Rights, 1999.

Dorsey, Learthen. *Historical Dictionary of Rwanda.* Metuchen, New Jersey: Scarecrow Press, 1994.

Jefremovas, Villia. *Brickyards to Graveyards: From Production to Genocide in Rwanda.* Anthropology of Work Series. New York: SUNY Press, 2002.

Lemarchand, Rene, *Rwanda and Burundi.* London: Pall Mall Press, 1970.

Newbury, Catherine. *The Cohesion of Oppression: Clientship and Ethnicity in Rwanda 1860–1960.* New York: Columbia University Press, 1988.

Reyntjens, Filip. *L'Afrique des Grands Lacs en Crise: Rwanda, Burundi: 1988–1994.* Paris: Karthala, 1994.

VILLIA JEFREMOVAS

S

SAAD, SITI BINTI (1880–1950). Among the most famous performers in East African history, the Zanzibari taarab musician Siti binti Saad and her band were the first Swahili speakers to have their voices and music recorded and produced on gramophone disc in 1928. Saad was the lead vocalist in the band, but Mwalim Shaaban Umbaye composed the majority of the songs. Mbaruku Effandi Talsam played violin, oud (a lute-like stringed instrument), and flute, accompanied by Subeti bin Ambari and Budda bin Swedi on violin and drums. While taarab is a distinct musical genre blending sounds from throughout the Indian Ocean, it is perhaps most similar in sound to small orchestras from Egypt. Saad's music is sometimes compared to that of the famous Egyptian songstress Umm Kulthum.

Saad's band is widely credited with transforming taarab from a form of courtly praise music, associated largely with the Omani ruling elite on the island of Zanzibar and adjoining coastal towns, into a genre for popular entertainment. One important element of this involved transforming the language of taarab from Arabic to Kiswahili. Through the distribution of Saad's recordings, taarab became popular not only in Zanzibar but also throughout colonial Tanganyika, Kenya, the Belgian Congo, and Nyasaland (present-day Malawi). The gramophone discs pressed from their recordings sold more than 72,000 copies between 1928 and 1931, allowing the recording company EMI to nearly double its East African sales figures.

The popularity of the music created by the band was rooted in the fact that members sang not only about love but also about struggles for justice and economic and social empowerment widespread in colonial East Africa. At a time when Africans were typically prohibited from using newspapers or political platforms to voice their concerns, Saad's band used its music to raise social and political issues and stimulate public debate. Saad was also the first woman to perform publicly a musical genre that had been exclusively male.

See also **Music, Modern Popular; Popular Culture: Eastern Africa; Zanzibar.**

BIBLIOGRAPHY

Fair, Laura. *Pastimes and Politics: Culture, Community and Identity in Post-abolition Urban Zanzibar, 1890–1945.* Athens: Ohio University Press, 2001.

Shaaban, Robert. *Waasifu wa Siti binti Saad* [1958]. Dares Salaam: Mkuki na Nyota, 1991.

LAURA FAIR

SAADAWI, NAWAL EL- (1931–). Nawal el-Saadawi, a doctor of medicine, a writer, and a feminist, was born in Kafr Tahla, a small Egyptian village on the bank of the Nile. A woman of strong political convictions, she fought to free Egypt from the British. In 1963 she became Minister of Health, and in 1968 founded and edited the controversial *Health Magazine.* In 1971 she established the Arab Women's Solidarity Association

Nawal el-Saadawi (1931–). Egyptian feminist, writer, activist, and physician Nawal el-Saadawi guides a demonstration against the Euro-Mediterranean Summit in Barcelona, November 2005. Her political activism has often conflicted with her career aspirations, causing her to be terminated from several prominent positions. © GUIDO MANUILO/EPA/CORBIS

(AWSA). As its president, she organized many international conferences, the last of which in Cairo in 2005. A constant critic of the Egyptian regime, she was arrested in 1981 and jailed by order of President Anwar al-Sadat. She was compelled to leave Egypt in 1993, and went to the United States where she accepted a position at Duke University. While at Duke she started the first part of her autobiography, *A Daughter of Isis* (1999). (The second part, *Walking through Fire*, appeared in 2002.) In 1999 she was allowed to return to Egypt. She has received numerous honorary degrees and awards, and her books have been translated into thirty languages.

For Nawal el-Saadawi writing gradually became more important than medicine because "writing became a weapon with which to fight the system" (*Daughter of Isis*, Zed Books, 1999, 292). She writes primarily in Arabic; her husband Atef Hetata has been her English translator. Among her many books are *The Hidden Face of Eve* (1980), *Memoirs from the Women's Prison* (1995), *Woman at Point Zero* (1982), *The Fall of the Imam* (1988), and *The Nawal el Saadawi Reader* (1997).

See also **Cairo; Egypt, Modern: History and Politics; Literature: Popular Literature; Literature: Women Writers, Northern Africa; Sadat, Anwar al-.**

BIBLIOGRAPHY

Malti-Douglas, Fadwa. *Men, Women, and God(s): Nawal El Saadawi and Arab Feminist Poetics.* Berkeley: University of California Press, 1995.

SONIA LEE

SADAT, ANWAR AL- (1918–1981). Anwar al- Sadat was the third president of Egypt. Born in Mit Abu al-Kum, in Minufiya governorate, north of Cairo, Sadat graduated from the Egyptian Military Academy in 1938. During World War II, he engaged in anti-British activities for which he was imprisoned twice in 1942 and from 1946 to 1949, respectively.

Egyptian president Anwar al-Sadat (1918–1981). Sadat was awarded the Nobel Peace Prize with Israeli Prime Minister Menachem Begin in 1978 after signing the Camp David Accords. The agreements made Sadat unpopular with many Muslims and Arabs, but they improved Egypt's relations with the United States. GEORGES BENDRIHEM/AFP/GETTY IMAGES

Sadat joined the free-officers movement and participated in the July 1952 coup that deposed King Farouk and established a republican system. He assumed several governmental positions until Gamal Abdel Nasser appointed him vice-president in 1969. Following Nasser's death in September 1970, Sadat became president in October. He soon consolidated his power and in 1973 led a successful war against Israel.

With his legitimacy enhanced, Sadat steered Egypt away from Nasser socialist policies, liberalized the economy, established a relatively pluralistic system, and maintained a pro-U.S. foreign policy. Faced with domestic economic difficulties and a growing popular discontent, Sadat sought peace with Israel. He visited Jerusalem in 1977 and then engaged in peace negotiations, with U.S. mediation. In 1987 Sadat, along with Israel prime minister Menachim Begin, shared the Nobel Prize for Peace. In 1979 he signed with Israel a peace treaty that, although welcomed in the West, met with internal opposition in Egypt. Deteriorating economic conditions and the suppression of increasing dissent created a highly volatile political situation. Sadat was assassinated by Islamic militants on October 6, 1981, while reviewing a military parade commemorating the 1973 October War.

See also **Egypt, Modern: History and Politics; Nasser, Gamal Abdel.**

BIBLIOGRAPHY

Hirst, David, and Irene Beeson. *Sadat*. London: Faber and Faber, 1981.

Sadat, Anwar. *In Search of Identity: An Autobiography*. New York: Harper and Row, 1978.

EMAD SHAHIN

SAHARA DESERT

This entry includes the following articles:
GEOGRAPHY AND HISTORY
CARAVAN ROUTES

GEOGRAPHY AND HISTORY

The largest desert in the world, the Sahara stretches across the African continent from the Atlantic to the Red Sea, covering about 3.3 million square miles. It has been the major barrier to, as well as the major avenue for, contacts between the Mediterranean and sub-Saharan cultures of Africa.

In prehistoric times, the region had wetter, savanna-like climatic periods. Vestiges of human culture from the Upper Paleolithic and Neolithic periods (more than ten thousand years ago), in the form of rock pictures, tools, and artifacts, have been found in parts of the Sahara. The current extension of the desert stems from about 3,000 BCE. There have been some variations in the climate during this period, but descriptions from the earliest periods of recorded history closely match current conditions.

About one-fifth of the desert is covered by sand (the *erg*). The rest is mostly rock and gravel plains, with two major mountain masses: Ahaggar in the north, and Tibesti in the center (in Algeria and Chad, respectively). The Nile cuts through the eastern edge of the desert. The exact boundaries of the Sahara have been unstable as the desert has expanded in drier periods and receded in wetter periods, as it did in the late Middle Ages. As of the twenty-first century, the desert is expanding southward, not least because of human-initiated changes in the ecology of the desert's edge.

THE PEOPLE OF THE SAHARA

The population of the Sahara is about 2.5 million, living in oases or in the moister highlands. The main population groups are Arab, Berber, and Teda (or Toubou). A continual merger of and change in ethnic identities, however, makes it useful to consider these distinctions primarily as linguistic ones.

The Arab-speaking peoples live mainly on the northern edge of the desert, the major groups being the Bedouins of the Libyan Desert and the Chaamba of Algeria. In the west—southern Morocco, Mauritania, and parts of Mali—the majority language is Hassaniyya, an Arabic dialect with a strong Berber influence. The Hassaniyya speakers (called Moors) are internally divided between the *bidan* (whites), who traditionally had a higher social status, and vassals, with the *haratin* (freemen) in the lowest positions.

Only a minority of the Berber people live in the Sahara proper, but many Berber groups (Shluh, or Tashelhayt, Tamazight, and Znaga) live on the desert edge in the north and west. The largest group of Berber speakers in the Sahara, however, is the Tuareg (between one-half and one million).

The Tuareg cover the region from the Niger River bend in the west to the Azben (Aïr) highlands (now part of Niger) in the east, with some small Tuareg groups living in neighboring countries. They can be divided into the northern groups, namely the Kel Ahaggar and Kel Ajjer (primarily in Algeria), and the southern groups, consisting of the Kel Adrar near the Niger River bend, the Iwellemmedan to their east, and the Kel Azben. Of these, the Iwellemmedan is numerically the largest group.

The Teda inhabit the eastern part of the desert, in Kawar (Niger) and in northern Chad. Historically, they also lived on the northern edge; thus, they inhabited the Kufra Oasis until the nineteenth century and had a strong presence in Fezzan (both in Libya). The Teda are closely related to the people to the south of the Sahara, in particular the Daza, in language and culture. The main Teda areas in the desert proper are the Tibesti and Ennedi mountain regions. Smaller groups of sub-Saharan peoples, such as the Kanuri in Kawar, also inhabit the desert.

The Tuareg categorize their peoples into three classes: nobles (*imajeghan*), freemen (*imghad*), and vassals. The vassals may often be people from the southern desert edge (*bella* in Niger). These might be former slaves or subjugated neighbors who have adopted the Tuareg language. Some clans (such as the *ineslemen* among the Tuareg) are devoted to religious practice, and many desert centers are repositories of great Islamic learning. In particular, Shinqit in the Western Sahara has produced many Islamic scholars of world renown.

ECONOMY AND TRADE

The economic basis for life in the desert is twofold: pastoralism—in camels, goats, and sheep—and trade. Some of the oases support a permanent settlement through date production and a limited garden agriculture. Most oasis towns, however, are closely linked with the surrounding pastoral population, or serve as centers in local or long-distance trade.

The most important commodity in local or regional trade is salt, which is exchanged for millet or other foodstuffs in the south. Salt is extracted by mining, desalination of seawater, or evaporation of groundwater. The Tuareg salt trade continues to the twenty-first century, unlike most of the long-distance trade.

Contacts and trade across the Sahara go back to prehistoric times. It was, however, the introduction of the camel to the Sahara in the first centuries CE that made regular and extensive trade possible. The main commodities were gold and slaves, but spices, leather, and later ostrich feathers also went north, whereas weapons, horses, textiles, and paper went south. The Saharan populations benefited from this trade by providing marketplaces in the oases, or by collecting toll and protection money from foreign traders. These revenues could be transformed into political capital, because the group that controlled the trade route could also control its neighbors. The revenues could also be invested in agricultural production in the desert-side regions.

The development of roads across the desert over the last half century has changed the nature of contacts, allowing lorries to transport goods, although at a cost often superior to that of the camels. Improved contacts has also made the desert an avenue for illegal migration northwards, often destined for Europe.

POLITICAL HISTORY

The political history of the Sahara is the history of its insertion into the affairs of its desert-side neighbors. Early sub-Saharan kingdoms, such as Ghana in the west and the Zaghawa in the east (Chad), probably had a strong presence in the Sahara. The desert also served as a refuge for political and religious groups. Thus, the Berber-based Ibadi Muslims of the Maghreb retreated into the Sahara when Sunni and Shia groups defeated them in the tenth and eleventh centuries. There they formed an independent state in the Fezzan and have survived as independent communities to the early twenty-first century in Wadi Mzab, Algeria, and Jabal Nafusa, Libya.

Another religious movement of the Sahara was the Almoravids (al-Murabitun), formed by Berbers of the western Sahara from southern Morocco and perhaps as far south as the Senegal River. Originally a movement of religious reform, it conquered the western Maghreb and Spain in the mid-eleventh century, ruling there for a century.

Further east, the new sub-Saharan kingdoms stretched across the desert. During the last half of the thirteenth century, the central Sahara, as well as Fezzan to the north, was ruled by the *mai* (king) of Kanem. This was, however, the only period when the southern states controlled the north. In the west, the period of the great medieval empires came to an end when the sultan of Morocco moved an army across the desert in 1591 and conquered Timbuktu. However, real power soon reverted to the local population, in particular to the Tuareg.

In the central regions, the kingdom of Bornu, heir to Kanem, maintained its control over the desert regions and its trade until the seventeenth century. Then, the Tuareg of Azben under the Kel Owey defeated the Bornu army and maintained overall political control over the region until the onset of colonialism.

In the eastern Sahara west of the Nile Valley, outside control was limited, and the Teda clans ruled unchallenged. Only in the nineteenth century was the region brought into a more united framework. This was achieved through a religious movement, the Sanusiyya Sufi brotherhood, who worked among the Bedouin from the 1840s, and linked the northern and southern edges of the eastern Sahara into a trading network.

European colonization of the Sahara started about 1850, in Algeria. Several religious-based groups and leaders were active in resisting conquest, including Ma' al-'Aynayn (c. 1830–1910) in western Sahara, the Rahmaniyya in southeastern Algeria, and the Sanusiyya in the east. The western desert (Tuwat, Algeria) was occupied only in 1900, the central Sahara (Azben and Kawar) in 1905–1906, whereas the French took Tibesti and Ennedi in 1911–1913. Most of the desert came under French control except Saqiyat al-Hamra' and Río de Oro (Spanish-controlled from 1884), Libya (conquered by Italy in 1911–1931), and the deserts of Egypt and the Sudan (controlled by Britain from 1882 and 1898, respectively).

The French administrative divisions were preserved as national boundaries after independence in 1960–1962. In the Western Sahara, Spanish withdrawal in 1976 led to conflict between Morocco, which claimed the region, and the Polisario guerrilla movement, which demanded an independent nation. As U.N. mediation was unsuccessful, the region remained under Moroccan control.

On the economic level, the major event of the twentieth century, apart from the destruction of the trans-Saharan trade, was the discovery of rich mineral resources under the desert, in particular oil, phosphate and uranium, iron, and bauxite. At the same time, the integration of these regions into modern states was accompanied by an increased sedentarization, and often the impoverishment, of the desert populations. Disastrous droughts in the 1970s and 1980s only exacerbated these social and economic problems, leading in the 1990s to a number of revolts by Tuareg and other desert groups in Mali, Niger, Chad, and elsewhere.

See also **Agriculture: World Markets; Boundaries, Colonial and Modern; Climate; Desertification, Modern; Ecology; Ecosystems: Deserts and Semi-Deserts; Energy: Domestic; Livestock: Domestication; Production Strategies: Agriculture; Production Strategies: Overview; Slave Trades: Northern Africa and Sahara; United Nations: United Nations in Africa.**

BIBLIOGRAPHY

Bernus, Edmond. *Touaregs nigeriens: Unité culturelle et diversité régionale d'un peuple pasteur.* Paris: Editions de l'Office de la recherche scientifique et technique outre-mer, 1981.

Briggs, Lloyd Cabot. *Tribes of the Sahara.* Cambridge, MA: Harvard University Press, 1960.

Chapelle, Jean. *Nomades noirs du Sahara: Les Toubous.* Paris: Plon, 1957.

Cleaveland, Timothy. *Becoming Walata: A History of Social Formation and Transformation.* Portsmouth, NH: Heinemann, 2002.

Hamani, Djibo. *Au carrefour du Soudan et de la Berberie: Le sultanat Touareg de l'Ayar.* Niamey, Niger: Institut de recherches en sciences humaines, 1989.

Lhote, Henri. *Les Touaregs du Hoggar.* Paris: A. Colin, 1984.

Norris, Harry T. *The Arab Conquest of the Western Sahara: Studies of the Historical Events, Religious Beliefs, and Social Customs Which Made the Remotest Sahara a Part of the Arab World.* London: Longman, 1986.

KNUT S. VIKØR

CARAVAN ROUTES

Whether composed of human porters or animals, caravans have crisscrossed the continent for millennia. Starting in 3000 BCE, however, irreversible desertification made trans-continental travel increasingly challenging. The earliest documented routes were frequented by so-called *Garamantes* who presumably organized expeditions on horse-drawn chariots between the Punic North and Central Africa in search of information, fabled carbuncle gemstones, and occasionally enslaved Africans. Archaeologists identified two "chariot routes": an eastern branch connecting northern Libya to the markets of the Central Sudan, and a western route from northwestern Algeria through Mauritania and ending in the Niger River bend. Trans-Saharan trade would evolve along these two axes and a third one linking the Western Sudan to Egypt.

Two events in the Common Era revolutionized overland communication while transforming the Sahara Desert's social landscape. The first was the introduction of the camel, or single-hump dromedary, after the second century. This resourceful domestic animal became the engine of caravan transportation, enabling inhabitants to adopt nomadic pastoralism and trade across the northern half of the African continent. By the sixth century, camel caravans were supplying gold to Byzantine Carthage, capital of Ifriqiya. The second event was the spread of Islam beginning in earnest in the eighth century. Aside from creating a Muslim world, Islam provided a code of law, a common language and a script that promoted civil society while favoring far-flung exchanges. In Western Africa a group known as the Wangara specialized in the gold trade and organized trans-Saharan trade in a vast area from the Middle Niger to the Central Sudan. In the major towns of tenth-century Fatimid Ifriqiya, Ibadi Muslims played a significant role in proliferating Islamic knowledge as well as in trans-Saharan commerce. At the same time, pockets of Jewish communities, residing in North African oases since the second century, would endure as key players in caravan trade.

The expansion of trans-Saharan trade in the latter part of the first millennium was linked to an increased demand for metal. West and Central Africans needed copper and brass to manufacture tools and equipment. They also depended on Saharan rock salt as a mineral supplement, while dates, cowry shells, beads, foreign pottery and glassware, textiles and other manufactured goods were in frequent demand. For northerners, access to West African gold was of primary interest before ivory, and enslaved Africans. Saharan residents also relied on trade for foodstuffs, namely cereal, as well as other essentials such as cotton cloth and wood. The Middle Niger River region, stronghold of the great medieval empires wherein lie the gold, became an epicenter of trans-Saharan traffic and cross-cultural exchange. Starting with Ghana, African rulers thrived on commerce by protecting routes, taxing caravans and negotiating terms of trade with camel-owning Sanhaja (so-called Berber) nomads.

By the ninth century, the two central routes were from Zawila in northern Libya southward to Kanem, near Lake Chad, and from the northern Maghribi terminus of Sijilmasa to Awdaghust in medieval Ghana. A central axis linked towns such as Gao and Tadmekka to North Africa via Ghat in the central Sahara. In the Western Sudan, these routes reached outlying markets such as Jenné, the main *entrepôt* for transshipment to the Niger River. While, in the Maghrib, towns such as Tuwat and Wargla became key trade centers. The eleventh-century Almoravid crusaders, interested in proselytizing as much as in gold, channeled a portion of trans-Saharan traffic westward causing the demise of Sijilmasa. In the eastern Sahara, caravans circulated along the so-called Forty Day Road between Dar Fur and Egypt, a route still used in the twentieth century.

Travel from one Saharan coast to the other, routine during the fall and winter months, took on average forty to ninety days depending on caravan itineraries, sizes, and loads. Caravaners navigated with the North Star as their main referent, while environmental and political variables determined precise itineraries. Salt, the caravan currency par excellence, was mined mainly in Awlil, then Idjil in the west, Teghazza, and later Taodenni in the center, and Bilma in the east. These were all necessary stopovers at different points in time, while the last two salt-pans are still active. By the first centuries of the second millennium, a number of Saharan oases emerged to replace some of the older markets along caravan routes. Some of these include Tafilelt in the northwest, Wadan, Shingiti, Tishit and Walāta in the western Sahara, Timbuktu in the south-central Sahara, Agadez and Takedda to the east, and Murzuk and GhadamËs in the north-central Sahara. Through this last town traveled caravans between Timbuktu, the Fezzan and occasionally Egypt. Commerce radiated to desert-edge markets including Kano, Katsina, Zinder, and Bornu in the center-east. Some towns, such as Shingiti and Takedda, doubled as rallying points for pilgrimage caravans that combined commerce with religious duty. Until the end of the eighteenth century when this tradition became infrequent, multiple trans-Saharan caravan routes led to Mecca via Cairo, either through Morocco and Libya or northern Nigeria and the Sudan.

From the fourteenth to the eighteenth century, trans-Saharan commerce flourished. The Ottoman occupation of North Africa stimulated caravan trade, while the stifling Moroccan conquest of Songhay in 1590s would cause a shift eastward toward the powerful city of Bornu. It was especially in this period that caravans sometimes numbered in the tens of thousands of camels. Aside from the goods and enslaved Africans already mentioned, paper and book manuscripts were pricey objects traded across the Sahara, as were horses, while enslaved Africans would eventually replace gold as the most valuable export. From the seventeenth century onward, the increased presence of Europeans on the North and West coasts of Africa began to impinge on the direction and nature of commerce.

By the nineteenth century trans-Saharan trade involved European commerce located in major port cities such as Tripoli (Libya), Mogador (Morocco) and Saint-Louis (Senegal). In exchange for imported cotton-cloth, writing paper, metalware (from coins to firearms) and miscellaneous goods, Africans chiefly sold ostrich feathers, ivory, gum Arabic and other plant products, as well as leather to European merchants. Maritime traffic, however, did not replace the ships of the desert even after the European conquest of the Sahara. In the late nineteenth century, the French toyed with the idea of constructing a trans-Saharan railway line from Algiers to Saint-Louis, via Timbuktu, but this pipedream never saw the light of day. Colonization engendered a gradual decrease in the trans-Saharan slave trade, although it lasted until into the early twentieth century. Whereas neither the French in the west, the Italians in Libya, nor the British in the east ever mastered the art of caravanning, they relied on local experts to conduct their expeditions. In the late nineteenth century, the French imposed a pass system to tax and monitor the circulation of caravans, including those peddling slaves.

In the next decade trucks competed with camels on major routes, but caravans continued profiting from trans-Saharan commerce. However, by the 1970s the truck had largely replaced the caravan, and in the early 2000s places such as Sebha in Libya are central fueling stations for transcontinental motor caravans. Contraband oil from Algeria is smuggled into Mali and Niger, whereas passenger trucks in the other direction transport West and Central African economic refugees seeking passageway to prosperous Europe. Yet small camel caravans still circulate in the Saharan interior, supplying dwindling numbers of nomads and oases inhabitants, while some continue as old, transporting precious Saharan salt.

See also **Cairo; Kano; Saint-Louis; Slave Trades; Timbuktu; Transportation: Caravan; Tripoli.**

BIBLIOGRAPHY

Abitbol, Michel. "Juifs maghrèbins et commerce trans-Saharien du VIIIe au XVe siècle." In *Le sol, la parole et l'écrit. Mélanges en hommage à Raymond Mauny*, ed. Jean Devisse. Paris: Société française d'histoire d'outre-mer: diffusion, L'Harmattan, 1981.

Austen, Ralph. "The Trans-Saharan Trade: A Tentative Census." In *The Uncommon Market: Essays in the Economic History of the Atlantic Slave Trade*, ed. J. Hogendorn and H. Gemery. New York: Academic Press, 1979.

Austen, Ralph. "Marginalization, Stagnation and Growth: Trans-Saharan Caravan trade, 1500-1900." In *The Rise of Merchant Empires: Long-distance Trade in the Early Modern World, 1350–1750*, ed. James Tracy. Cambridge, U.K.: Cambridge University Press, 1990.

Devisse, Jean. "Routes de commerce et échanges en Afrique occidentale en relation avec la Méditerranée: Un essai sur le commerce africain médiéval du XIe au XVIe siècle." *Revue d'Histoire Economique et Sociale* 50, no.1 (1972): 42–73; no. 2 (1972): 357–397.

Lewicki, T. "Pages d'histoire du commerce trans-Saharien: les commerçants et les missionnaires Ibâdites au Soudan occidental la fin du 6e et au 9e siècle." *Cahiers d'études africaines* 2 (1962): 513–535.

Lhote, Henri. "Route antique du Sahara central." *L'encyclopédie mensuelle d'Outre- mer* 11 (1951): 300–305.

Lovejoy, Paul, and Steve Baier. "The Desert-Side Economy of the Central Sudan." *International Journal of African Historical Studies* 8, no.4 (1975): 551–581.

Mauny, Raymond. "Une route préhistorique travers le Sahara occidental." *Bulletin de l'institut français d'afrique noire* 17 (1947): 341–357.

McDougall, Ann E. "Salt, Saharans and the Trans-Saharan Slave Trade: Nineteenth Century Developments." In *The Human Commodity: Perspectives on the Trans-Saharan Slave Trade*, ed. E. Savage. London: F. Cass, 1992.

GHISLAINE LYDON

SAHEL. *See* Desertification, Modern.

SAʿID BIN SULTAN (1791–1856). The first sultan of Zanzibar of the Bu Said dynasty, Saʿid bin Sultan was born in Oman in the ruling Bu Said family. He succeeded his father in 1804 as a joint ruler with his elder brother Salim (d. 1824). However, power lay with their cousin Badr, who acted as regent until his assassination in 1806. Saʿid then assumed total control and adopted the secular title of "Sultan" (instead of the religious "Imam").

Saʿid visited Zanzibar in 1828 after consolidating his position in Oman. Here, too, he had to overcome resistance to Omani rule, especially from Mombasa. He moved his administrative capital to Zanzibar in 1840 where he resided (with periodic visits to Muscat) until his death in 1856.

Saʿid developed Zanzibar into a major commercial port whose trading network extended even to America, Europe and China. He introduced clove trees on the islands, thus laying the foundation for Zanzibar's main export to the world. Saʿid's third contribution was co-operation with the British in their attempts to end slavery; the treaties of 1822 and 1845 paved the way towards that goal at least by limiting slavery. Finally, Saʿid's initiative of sending trading caravans into the interior of the East African mainland, a practice carried on by his successors, has been a major factor in the development and spread of Swahili, the region's *lingua franca*.

See also **Islam; Ivory; Mombasa; Slave Trades; Zanzibar; Zanzibar Sultanate.**

BIBLIOGRAPHY

Farsi, Abdalla Saleh. *Seyyid Said bin Sultan*. New Delhi: Lancers Books, 1986.

Said-Ruete, Emily. *Memoirs of an Arabian Princess* [1888]. London and The Hague: East-West Publications, 1994.

FAROUK TOPAN

SAINT HELENA. Saint Helena and its dependencies, a British-held island territory in the South Atlantic, consists of Saint Helena itself, Tristan da Cunha, Ascension, and several other smaller and uninhabited islands.

The island of Saint Helena lies 1,150 miles west of the coast of Angola and has an area of 47 square miles with its highest point 2,700 feet above sea level. It is a crater surrounded by high cliffs with only a few landing areas, at the largest of which is the capital, Jamestown. The island, then uninhabited, was discovered and named by the Portuguese navigator João da Nova Castella (d. 1509) on May 21, 1502, the anniversary of the death of Saint Helena. After a Dutch occupation, the British East India Company took possession in 1659, importing laborers and slaves from Cape Town and using it as a provisioning station for ships sailing to and from India. The British Crown took control during the exile of Napoleon Bonaparte there from 1815 until 1821, and, except for a few later years under the British East India Company, the island continues to be governed by a British-appointed governor to the present day. The opening of the Suez Canal in 1869 and the coming of steamships weakened its economy. Its population in 2007 is some 7,500, of whom about 1,000 live in Jamestown, and is composed mainly of people of African (50%), British (25%), and Asian (25%) descent; all use the English language.

The internal, low-lying crater area is fertile and inhabited, settlement being in the form of many small farms; the only town is the capital. The staple foods include fish, potatoes, and vegetables, and the inhabitants keep livestock. For many years the island depended economically on the export of flax, hemp, and wool, and on the sale of lace and craft-goods to passing ships. In recent years the population has become increasingly impoverished and there has been steady emigration to Great Britain, South Africa, and the Falkland Islands. Saint Helena is largely dependent upon British develop-ment aid and remittances from emigrants. It main link to the outside world is by a quarterly ship from Britain and occasional passing vessels from South Africa.

Saint Helena's dependencies are Tristan da Cunha and Ascension islands. The former, an archi-pelago of several small islands, lies some 2,500 miles southwest of Saint Helena and the same distance from Cape Town, and has an area of 38 square miles. It was discovered by the Portuguese sailor Tristão da Cunha (1460–c. 1540) in 1506, was annexed by Britain in 1816 and made a dependency of Saint Helena in 1938. In 1961, volcanic action led the total population to move to Britain, but two years later some two hundred of them returned to the island; there were about 300 in 2007, all in the single settlement of Edinburgh. The island depends on development aid from Britain, on fishing, and on the sale of postage stamps through agents in Saint Helena and Britain.

The lone island of Ascension lies 700 miles northwest of Saint Helena and has an area of 34 square miles. It was discovered and named on Ascension Day 1501 by João da Nova Castella and has been a dependency of Saint Helena since 1922. The island is barren except for the small settlement of Green Mountain, in which lives the entire population (the administrator and staff from Saint Helena and the personnel of British and American weather and satellite tracking stations).

Saint Helena and its dependencies form one of the few remaining colonies of Great Britain. Despite attempts through the United Nations to give the colony independence, its remoteness from the African mainland, its lack of economic self-sufficiency, and the refusal of its people to consider themselves African, make political independence unlikely and virtually impossible.

See also **Cape Town; Production Systems; Slave Trades; Travel and Exploration: European.**

BIBLIOGRAPHY

Gosse, Philip. *St. Helena, 1502–1938.* London: Cassell, 1938.

Teale, Percival. *St. Helena: A History of the Development of the Island with Special Reference to Building Civil and Military Engineering Works.* New Haven, CT: Yale University Press, 1974.

JOHN MIDDLETON

SAINT-LOUIS. Located where the Senegal River meets the Atlantic Ocean, Saint-Louis emerged as a strategic West African Atlantic port town in the seventeenth century. Inhabitants of the mainland Wolof states named the island N'dar. In 1659 French slave traders erected a fort on the island making it one of the earliest fortified European trade posts in Africa. Governed by royal mercantile com-panies in the eighteenth century, a permanent settle-ment of European merchants, black African fisher-man, traders, and boatmen, as well as elite women known as *signares,* the *métis* children of Afro-European unions and their slaves grew up around the fort. In the nineteenth century the population grew to include a majority of Muslim Senegalese.

Despite two brief periods of British occupa-tion, Saint-Louis became the seat of French impe-rialist interests in West Africa. With the end of the Napoleonic Wars in 1817, French merchant firms returned to the island to capitalize on the export of "legitimate" goods such as gum Arabic and peanuts. In the 1860s French soldiers launched wars of conquest into the interior from Saint-Louis and proponents of colonialism viewed Saint-Louis as the place from which the French civilizing mission would spread. In addition to serving as the administrative capital of Sénégal until 1960, France established electoral institutions in the colonial towns and extended voting rights to the urban adult male population regardless of race. Saint-Louis residents developed a flourishing urban political culture in colonial Sénégal. The end of French rule and the transfer of the capitol of the Republic to Dakar in 1960 marked a decline in the social, political and economic prominence of Saint-Louis, Sénégal.

See also **Senegal; Slave Trades.**

BIBLIOGRAPHY

Bonnardel, Regine. *Saint-Louis du Sénégal: Mort ou Naissance.* Paris: Harmattan, 1992.

Clark, Andrew F., and Lucie Colvin. "Saint-Louis." *Historical Dictionary of Senegal.* Metuchen, NJ: Scarecrow Press, 1994.

Johnson, G. Wesley. *The Emergence of Black Politics in Senegal: The Struggle for Power in the Four Communes.* Stanford, CA: Stanford University Press, 1971.

Searing, James F. *West African Slavery and Atlantic Commerce: The Senegal River Valley, 1700–1850.* Cambridge, U.K.: Cambridge University Press, 1993.

HILARY JONES

SAKALAVA. *See* Madagascar.

SALIH, TAYEB (1929–).

Born in the north of Sudan, the Sudanese writer Tayeb Salih began to study science in Khartoum and continued in London where he specialized in international business before becoming director of the British Broadcasting Company Arabic Service. Married with three children, Salih subsequently moved to Doha, Qatar, where he ran the Ministry of Information, and then to Paris, where he worked in various roles for the United Nations Education, Scientific, and Cultural Organization (UNESCO). Despite writing only a modest output (only five books in a very short period of time), Salih has had an immense influence on modern Arab fiction. Even more than the formal renaissance in which he took part at the end of the 1950s with other writers of his generation, his central place in contemporary Arab literature is based on the themes included in his writings.

Beginning with his first book, *The Wedding of Zein* (1967), Salih, from an African Islamic background yet completely at ease with European culture, asks questions of those born in so-called traditional societies regarding the past and obscurantism. In *Season of Migration to the North* (1969), universally acclaimed as a masterpiece, this ultimately pessimistic strain of thought is broadened to the subject of confrontation with the West. Reviving this very topical theme in Arab literature via a subtle exchange with William Shakespeare's *Othello*, Saleh has had an influence on generations of Arab and Western readers with this prophetic work on the difficulties of the dialogue between civilizations.

See also **Literature: Popular Literature; Sudan: Society and Cultures.**

BIBLIOGRAPHY

Hasan, Wail S. *Tayeb Salih: Ideology and the Craft of Fiction.* Syracuse, NY: Syracuse University Press, 2003.

Salih, Tayeb. *Season of Migration to the North,* trans. Denys Johnson-Davies. New York: Penguin Classics, 2003.

YVES GONZALEZ-QUIJANO

SALT.

Salt is found or can be made almost everywhere in Africa. Historically, sea salts produced by evaporation in coastal pools or by boiling brine (West, Central, and East African coasts) were most common; a few lagoons produced layers thick enough to be cut in bars (Mauritania, Senegal, and Somalia), resembling Saharan rock salt. Desert salt slabs, mined from subsoil strata formed from ancient lake beds, varied in quality and formation—Mauritania's shallow Ijil mine produced thick salt with more magnesium than Mali's Teghaza/Taodeni fragile bars dug from underground galleries. Nor were desert salts necessarily rock salt: salt-crusted *sebkhas* produced bitter natron, a valued salt cure for animals; other sources had industrial uses (dying, tanning). Niger's salt oasis, Kawar (bordering Libya and Chad), used a brine-boiling process to manufacture pure salt-cones. Inland lake, brine-based industries also flourished in the more humid east and south (Kenya, Tanzania, Uganda, and Zimbabwe), and rock salt was mined in Angola. Where alternatives were lacking, vegetable salts made from drying and burning plants, filtering the ash, and boiling the resulting brine, satisfied basic needs. An important Nigerian variation on this manufacturing process used mangrove tree trunks.

It is said that humans can live without gold but not without salt: herein lies the key to understanding the unrivaled role salt has played in African economies. Animals naturally process salt from licks and grasses, making salt accessible to humans in urine, blood, and milk products; initially, societies with animal-based diets needed little additional salt to satisfy biological needs. But those needs grew as grains, legumes, fruits, and vegetables became more central to food consumption. Archaeologists suggest that the development of agriculture some 8,000 years ago led to increased production of and trade in salts, though there is tangible evidence of this only for the past two-to-three millennia. Although the majority of exchange was probably locally and regionally based involving foodstuffs and craft-products, research focused more on long-distance luxury trades such as those of the Sahara and highlighted slaves, copper, and gold among goods purchased with desert salts from ancient through modern times. Salt featured prominently in medieval stories of silent trading for African gold, giving rise to the notion of salt-starved Africans willing to part with gold for an equal measure of salt. Salt was similarly central to more recent accounts of Saharan slave trading, slaves being rumored as worth the value of their foot measured in salt. Underlying the myths was an element of truth: the most sought-after salts in Africa were Saharan and, for centuries, these salts were used to purchase the most sought-after goods in Europe and Asia—gold and slaves.

Need was also socially conditioned: salts were unequal in quality, taste, and consistency. Preferences developed, often a factor of social class. Rock salt (the salt of choice for the rich) was usually higher priced than sea salt; both invariably replaced vegetable salts when available and affordable. Markets and prices reflected local demand. Salts more easily stored and transported were preferred, but use also played into demand: animals' needs were best met with varieties of earth salts; the different chemical compositions of various rock, sea, and even vegetable salts gave them specific medicinal uses. Particular rock salt layers were associated with good or bad luck. In the West African Sahel, it was both money and a measure of value, especially in the grain trade.

At various times and places, salt paid soldiers, purchased food, honored guests, and bought brides.

Control of salt was competitive and political: rulers taxed merchants and transporters if they could not otherwise monopolize the industry. State revenues came to depend on salt. Transporting and marketing salt was profitable for all. Salt—from mine to market—was labor intensive; industries everywhere were subsidized by the hierarchical and caste-like social structures of many African societies, and slave and servile labor was widely used. Europeans tried—and failed—to compete. Only when colonial investment in transport (steamships, railways, and roads) reduced the cost of delivering European-produced salts enough to render indigenous varieties prohibitively expensive were they at all successful. Even then, customary usage and local market networks secured a place for some African salts well into the twentieth century. In the early twenty-first century, Saharan salts retain cultural and spiritual significance: in Niger, traveling with the annual salt caravans marks a boy's passage to manhood; in Mali, salt is a divine gift and the trek to Taodeni's *sebkha* leads a man to Allah. In much of Africa, salt is both a symbol of past wealth and a promise for the future: sea salts of West, eastern, and especially Southern Africa are infinite resources for modern technology to develop.

See also **Archaeology and Prehistory; Money: Commodity Currencies.**

BIBLIOGRAPHY

Connah, Graham. *Kibiro. The Salt of Bunyoro, Past and Present*. London: British Institute of East Africa, 1996.

Lovejoy, Paul E. *Salt of the Desert Sun*. Cambridge, U.K.: Cambridge University Press, 1986.

McDougall, E Ann. "Salts of the Western Sahara: Myths, Mysteries and Historical Significance." *International Journal of African Historical Studies* 23, no. 2 (1990): 221–251.

Sutton, Inez. "Salt in Kenya: A Survey of the Literature." *Journal of Eastern African Research and Development* (1994): 163–182.

Vikor, Knut S. *The Oasis of Salt. The History of Kawar*. London: C. Hurst, 1997.

E. ANN MCDOUGALL

SAMBA, CHÉRI

SAMBA, CHÉRI (1956–). The Zairian painter David Samba wa Mbimba-N'zinga-Nuni Masi was born on December 30, 1956, at Kinto-M'vuila, a village in southern Zaire (then the Belgian Congo). His family included both Protestants and Catholics. Although raised in a matrilineal Kongo culture, Samba acknowledged the authority of his father, a blacksmith, over the children of the family. At age sixteen he moved to Kinshasa, where he became an apprentice to a painter. In 1975 he opened his own studio, where he produced multiple versions of paintings that appealed to the people; their subjects included the *mbanda* affair (the "battle of women," or the "battle of rivals," in which wives of the same man quarrel in public), and the siren known as Mami Wata. Samba's work first received broad recognition after he was featured at an exhibition in Kinshasa at the 1978 International Congress of African Studies. In 1979 he took the professional name Cheéi Samba. Three years later he participated in the Paris exhibition "Faces and Roots of Zaire." In 1989 he achieved international fame through his participation in the exhibition "Magicians of the Earth," also in Paris. Between 1990 and 1997 his paintings appeared in more than thirty exhibitions of contemporary art in North America, Europe, and Japan.

Samba is a grassroots intellectual who refused to be labeled by his ethnic heritage or by the term "African," because he opposes any irreducible specificity and wants his paintings to appeal universally. Samba is a self-proclaimed postcolonial explorer of the contemporary West. He has the typical ethnologist's gaze, concealing his surprise while facing the exotic West under the claim of knowing the natives of modernity better than they know themselves.

Samba's paintings explore the exoticism of modernity in a way that invites comparison with Paul Gauguin's gaze at the "primitive" other. Their paths cross as they travel in opposite directions. Gauguin was caught up in the desire to discover the primitive within himself, becoming so involved in fantasy that he lost himself. Samba hunts the modern, hoping to become more modern than the natives of modernity, the Westerners. The two men paint and repaint—that is how they communicate with the world—presenting themselves as primitive and modern, respectively.

Samba works within a modernity that calls itself universal without losing its specific origins. As soon as he could afford to do so, he traveled back and forth between the modernity of Kinshasa and the place of its origins in the West. The child of

colonial rationality, Samba cannot refrain from comparing the two modernities. He retains the naï veté of the good student who is surprised that the world is not exactly as he was taught it would be. He finds that sin has not only corrupted the modernity of Kinshasa but also that the white man was a sinner a long time before. It is not Samba himself, nor the African invented by the colonial gaze, who has made modernity depraved. The perversion and immorality he discovered at the heart of modernity fascinate him, and he seems to enjoy putting his brush to it. By painting both white man and black bourgeois as sinners, he hopes to remove the stain of the original sin of the colonial encounter's having corrupted modernity.

Samba the artist—for a long time he saw himself as a brush worker, moralist, and witness hurling images in the face of the world—could only revolt against the aesthetic of modernity. The world is his audience. He does not hide, and he is not intimidated. He seized the contemporary aesthetic of visual culture and its techniques so that modernity would be his. He owned it, he used it, he called himself supermodern.

According to V. Y. Mudimbe in *Les corps glorieux des roots et des êtres* (1994), Samba's aesthetic is not "the art of remaking and interpreting." Rather, it is a "strategy and technique of destroying the forms of discourse and of power" in the arts and in the image of the African.

In the late nineteenth century, the stories told by travelers and explorers invented an Africa, an African, whom the Westerner pretended to initiate into modernity in order to repay the debts incurred by colonizing. To remove the mark of this invention, to cease to be modern because someone else had devised it, Samba invented the former colonial master, invented the West. Samba has mastered his destiny by seeing clearly through modernity as colonial logic, the logic of invention of the other. In his paintings he is the inventor of modernity, inventor of himself. What is more authentic, and also more subversive of the colonial logic, than a subject who claims that he is the inventor of his master?

This is why the West has been seduced by Samba's work and has admitted him to the ranks of contemporary painters. Samba is a typical explorer, sometimes naive, sometimes insolent, who certainly depends on the natives for his very existence even as he proclaims himself a Prometheus of the new humanity. One century after Gauguin was forced to go to the land of the primitive in order to be credible in the nascent world of industrial modernity, Samba made Gauguin's voyage in the opposite direction, and won fame first in France and later in the United States.

From the moment Chéri adopted the nickname that transformed him into Samba—the public persona—he did not stop writing stories of Africa's reception in the West and of the West's in Africa. Thanks to his impertinence, Samba's work escapes from the rigidity of the Western classification system and from a purely emotional level of reception accorded to precolonial African arts.

Samba is the first popular African painter whose success in the West is assured by the professional market. His work has followed the path of other "modern" artists who have been legitimated by the value placed on their work by galleries and museums, a seal of approval that transforms something pleasing to the eye into a serious investment. For those reasons he escaped the destiny of contemporary African artists working for local clients, who are categorized in the West as makers of curios, not artists.

See also **Art; Mami Wata; Popular Culture.**

BIBLIOGRAPHY

Jewsiewicki, Bogumil. *Chéri Samba: The Hybridity of Art/ L'hybridité d'un art.* Westmount, Québec: Galerie Amrad African Art Publications, 1995.

Mudimbe, V. Y. *Les corps glorieux des mots et des êtres: Esquisse d'un jardin africain à la bénédictine.* Montreal: Humanitas and Présence Africaine, 1994.

Samba, Chéri. *J'aime Chéri Samba/sous la direction,* ed. André Magnin. Paris: Fondation Cartier pour l'art Contemporain, 2004.

BOGUMIL JEWSIEWICKI

SAMORI. *See* **Touré, Samori.**

SAN. *See* **Languages: Khoesan and Click.**

SAND PAINTING. *See* Arts.

SANUSI, MUHAMMAD IBN ʿALI AL- (1787–1859).

Muhammad ibn ʿAli al-Sanusi was a North African religious leader and founder of the Sanusiyya Sufi brotherhood.

The Sanusiyya brotherhood became the dominant Islamic order in the eastern Sahara (Libyan Cyrenaica, northern Chad, and surrounding regions) soon after its founding in 1841. While it later became known for its resistance to colonialism, its primary goal was to promote Islamic piety and social advance among the Bedouin.

Its founder, Muhammad ibn ʿAli al-Sanusi was born near Mustaghanim, present-day western Algeria, and pursued his studies in Fez and Cairo. In Mecca, he met the Sufi reformer Ahmad ibn Idris, and became his most prominent follower. At Ibn Idris's death in 1837, he set out for North Africa, and in 1841 founded the first lodge of the brotherhood that came to take his name, in al-Bayda in Cyrenaica.

From then until his death in 1859, al-Sanusi divided his activity between building the order in the Sahara, and writing some fifty books, mostly from Mecca and Medina. He wrote several works on Sufism, but was also a strong advocate of *ijtihad,* "new interpretation," in Islamic law. His brotherhood continued under the leadership of his son and his grandson, the later King Idris of Libya.

See also **Cairo; Fez; Idris, Ahmad ibn; Islam: Sufi Orders.**

BIBLIOGRAPHY

Evans-Pritchard, E. E. *The Sanusi of Cyrenaica.* Oxford: Oxford University Press, 1949.

Triaud, Jean-Louis. *La Légende noire de la Sanûsiyya: Une confrérie musulmane saharienne sous le regard français (1840–1930).* Paris: Éditions MSH, 1995.

Vikør, Knut S. *Sufi and Scholar on the Desert Edge: Muhammad b. ʿAli al-Sanusi and His Brotherhood.* London: Hurst, 1995.

KNUT S. VIKØR

SÃO TOMÉ E PRÍNCIPE

This entry includes the following articles:
GEOGRAPHY AND ECONOMY
SOCIETY AND CULTURES
HISTORY AND POLITICS

GEOGRAPHY AND ECONOMY

The twin island republic of São Tomé e Príncipe, located in the Gulf of Guinea, comprises a total area of 386 square miles. Former cocoa plantations and forests that are intersected by many small streams cover these mountainous, volcanic islands. The highest mountain is the Pico de São Tomé at 6,640 feet. The climate is tropical and humid, with an average annual temperature of 81 degrees Fahrenheit in the coastal lowlands. Annual precipitation varies from 39 inches in the northern lowlands to 201 inches on the southern slopes of the mountain in São Tomé. The dry season runs from June to September. The total population was estimated at 199,500 in 2007, of which about 6,000 live on Príncipe, approximately one-fifth the size of São Tomé with an area of 55 square miles.

The Portuguese successfully colonized uninhabited São Tomé from 1493, establishing the first plantation economy in the tropics, based on sugarcane and slaves brought from the African mainland to the islands. Initially, the transit slave trade from western central Africa to the Gold Coast had also been important for the economy of the new colony, but from 1520 sugar became the major contributor to the flourishing economy. By the end of the sixteenth century, Luanda had replaced São Tomé as an entrepôt for the slave market. At that time, annual sugar production reached a peak of 12,000 tons. However, by 1610 sugar production had dropped to 900 tons due to emerging competition from Brazil, the poor quality of the local sugar, and assaults on the plantations by runaway slaves.

In the seventeenth century, the plantation economy virtually disappeared, and Creole smallholders—descendants of white settlers and African slave women—cultivated the former plantation lands for subsistence and the provisioning of ships. By then, the local Creole society and culture had been firmly established. The introduction of coffee (1787) and cocoa (1822) paved the way for the reemergence of the plantation economy in the archipelago. From the mid-nineteenth century, a new wave of

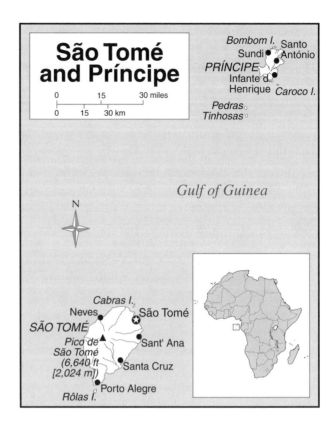

Portuguese colonists established large coffee and cocoa plantations, and dispossessed the landholding Creoles. When slavery was abolished in 1875, the Portuguese replaced the slaves with contract workers from Angola, Cape Verde, and Mozambique. By the end of the nineteenth century, Portuguese planters owned 90 percent of the land, and cocoa had surpassed coffee as most important export crop.

In 1909 cocoa reached the highest annual production ever, at 30,300 tons. The same year, a British campaign against the harsh living conditions of the contract workers on the islands culminated in a boycott of São Tomé's "slave cocoa" by William Cadbury and other British chocolate manufacturers. Thereafter, cocoa output gradually decreased due to plant disease, soil exhaustion, and competition from West African smallholders. Notwithstanding, cocoa has remained the country's dominant export crop. Until the 1940s, the indentured laborers outnumbered the local Creoles, who refused to work on the estates.

By independence in 1975, following the anticolonial military coup d'état against the post-Salazar *Estado Novo* in Lisbon, São Tomé e Príncipe became a socialist one-party state based on the Soviet model. In September 1975, the regime nationalized the Portuguese-owned estates and subsequently regrouped them into fifteen state-owned agricultural enterprises. Due to mismanagement and ill-allocated investments, cocoa output dropped from 10,000 tons in 1974 to 3,400 tons in 1984. State investments in the diversification of the economy also failed due to similar shortcomings. Consequently, the country became completely dependent on foreign aid. The economic failure forced the regime to liberalize the economy and finally introduce multiparty democracy in 1990. In the 1990s, a cocoa rehabilitation project financed by the World Bank with US$40 million failed completely. As a result, the plantations were dismantled and the lands distributed to former plantation workers. In 2003 cocoa export was still at a meager 3,500 tons. Since 2000 the development of tourism has produced some encouraging revenues, whereas fishery and agriculture have lagged behind their targets. Offshore oil deposits that have been developed since 1997 are now the greatest hope for economic profits. Oil production is expected to start in 2010. Until then, the country's economy remains the smallest in Africa, with GDP estimated at US$71 million and GDP per capita at US$1200 (2003).

See also **Agriculture; Creoles; Economic History; Geography and the Study of Africa; Plantation Economies and Societies.**

BIBLIOGRAPHY

Hodges, Tony, and Malyn Newitt. *São Tomé and Príncipe. From Plantation Colony to Microstate.* Boulder, CO: Westview Press, 1988.

Seibert, Gerhard. *Comrades, Clients and Cousins. Colonialism, Socialism and Democratization in São Tomé and Príncipe*, 2nd updated edition. Leiden, The Netherlands, and Boston: Brill Academic Publishers, 2006.

GERHARD SEIBERT

SOCIETY AND CULTURES

The total population of these equatorial islands is estimated at 199,579, according to 2007 estimates. About half the population is younger than fourteen years. Annual population growth is 3.13 percent. Life expectancy at birth is sixty-seven years. About 6,000 people live on the island of Príncipe. Due to ongoing rural migration the urban population grew from 45 percent in 1991 to 55 percent in 2001. São Tomé and Príncipe is a Creole society whose origins stem from the late fifteenth century when Portuguese colonists and African slaves settled on the hitherto uninhabited archipelago. The largest sociocultural group is the Forros, descendents of mixed unions between white settlers and African slave women in the sixteenth century and of slaves freed in subsequent centuries. The Angolares, who are mainly fishermen, are descended from runaway slaves from the sugar plantations in the sixteenth and seventeenth centuries, who constituted a maroon community in the south of São Tomé. The descendants of contract workers from Angola, Mozambique, and Cape Verde, who arrived in the islands between 1876 and the 1960s, locally known as Tongas, have gradually assimilated into forro society. Since independence the colonial boundaries between these groups have been blurred. Notwithstanding, many contract workers from Cape Verde have largely maintained a distinct identity of their own. On Príncipe the Cape Verdian community constitutes the majority of the population.

Apart from the official language, Portuguese, four Portuguese-based Creole languages are spoken in the country. Portuguese is understood by almost everyone. However, in daily life it is the dominant language only of the urban middle class. The principal Creole is the *lunga santomé*, or forro, spoken by 73.5 percent of the population. *Ngola* is the Creole of the Angolares, spoken by an estimated 5 percent of the population, while *Lung'iye* is the Creole language of the natives of Príncipe, spoken by 1.6 percent of the population. The three local Creole languages stem from a common origin, which was the contact language between Portuguese settlers and African slaves that emerged in the early sixteenth century. Although structurally similar, the three Creoles are not mutually intelligible. The fourth Creole spoken in the islands is *crioulo*, the language of the local Cape Verdian community.

Seventy percent of the population are baptized in the Roman Catholic faith, introduced by the Portuguese in the late fifteenth century. Despite its long presence, in practice local Catholicism has been largely limited to baptism and some rites, like funerals and processions. The annual feasts of the local Catholic saints are also important sociocultural events in the islands. The Seventh-Day

Adventist Church was introduced in 1937 and is the oldest Protestant church, with 2,418 members in 2001 (1.8%). About 6 percent of the population belongs to Pentecostal churches, whereas 2 percent are members of the New Apostolic Church. More than 3 percent of the population belongs to other churches, and almost 20 percent claim to be without religion. African cults like the spirit possession cult *djambí* and beliefs in witchcraft and divination coexist with Christianity.

The local kinship system is bilateral; that is, individuals reckon descent through both sexes on both sides of their families. Three distinct types of conjugal union exist, namely the Christian-style marriage, the co-residential customary union, and the visiting relationship. Only 3 percent of the population is formally married since marriage is largely restricted to the educated elite. Most men, whether married or not, are polygynous in practice, having more than one woman. The dominant type of conjugality is the co-residential customary union known as *união de facto*. A customary union might last for life, but mostly customary unions tend to be rather unstable. Separation in the case of the visiting relationship is also frequent. Therefore serial unions are very common, particularly among the poor majority. Due to the virtual absence of the monogamous marriage, the high incidence of multiple and serial customary unions and visiting relationships, about one-third of the households are female headed. Whereas the mother is expected to assume the principal responsibility for bringing up the children, due to poverty or emigration child-shifting or fostering by other female relatives is quite common.

República Democrática de São Tomé e Príncipe (Democratic Republic of São Tomé and Príncipe)

Population:	199,579 (2007 est.)
Area:	1,001 sq. km (386 sq. mi.)
Official language:	Portuguese
National currency:	dobra
Principal religion:	Catholic 70%, Evangelical 3%, other
Capital:	São Tomé (est. pop. 56,166 in 2005)
Other urban centers:	on São Tomé Ribeira Alfonso, Neves, Porto Alegre; on Príncipe: Santo Antonio, Infante Don Henrique
Main islands:	São Tomé, Príncipe
Annual rainfall:	varies from 1,000 mm (40 in.) in northern lowlands to 3,800–5,000 mm (150–200 in.) in highlands
Principal geographical features:	*Mountains:* Pico de São Tomé
Economy:	*GDP per capita:* US$1200 (2003 est.)
Principal products and exports:	*Agricultural:* cocoa, coconuts, palm kernels, copra, cinnamon, pepper, coffee, bananas, papayas, beans, poultry; fish. *Manufacturing:* textiles, soap, beer, fish processing
Government:	Former Portuguese colony. Independence from Portugal, 1975. Constitution adopted in 1975. New constitution approved in 1990 and again in 2003. Multiparty parliamentary democracy since 1990, single party previously. President and 55-seat unicameral Assembleia Nacional are directly elected by universal popular vote to serve 5-year terms (president limited to 2 successive terms). Prime minister (post introduced in 1990) is appointed by the president. President appoints Council of Ministers on the proposal of the prime minister. For purposes of local government the 2 islands constitute 2 districts, divided into 12 counties (11 on São Tomé).
Heads of state since independence:	1975–1991: President Manuel Pinto da Costa. 1991–2001: President Miguel Trovoada. 2001–: President Fradique Bandeira Melo de Menezes
Armed forces:	President is commander in chief. Armed forces consist of army, coast guard, and presidential guard.
Transportation:	*Ports:* São Tomé. *Roads:* 320 km (199 mi.), 68% paved. *National airline:* Linhas Aéres de São Tomé. *Airports:* International facilities at São Tomé
Media:	Main periodicals: *Diaírio de República*, Povo (intermittent publication), *Revoluçao* (government weekly), *O Independente*, *Nova República*, *O Pais Hoje*, *O Parvo*. No book publishing. 6 radio stations, 2 television stations. Radio Nacional de São Tomé e Príncipe is government-owned.
Literacy and education:	*Total literacy rate:* 68.1% (2006). Free, universal, and compulsory education up to secondary level. No facilities for higher education.

The dominant typical dwelling in the country is a wooden house on stilts, with two or more rooms and a roof of corrugated sheet. Such single-family wooden houses represent two-thirds of the 34,000 dwellings and dominate in the dispersed settlements, locally called *lúchans*, the few small towns, and the populous neighborhoods on the outskirts of the capital. The kitchen is outside the house in a separate shack. The centers of the small towns and of the capital are predominantly constituted by two-story brick buildings, mostly constructed in the modern colonial period. Since the late 1990s modern two- and three-story apartment buildings have been erected on new construction sites outside the capital. On the former cocoa estates people still live in the overcrowded quarters for contract workers that were constructed about a hundred years ago. Wooden houses have no tap water or toilet. Only a very few have a latrine on the compound. More than half of all dwellings have no electricity.

See also **Christianity; Colonial Policies and Practices: Portuguese; Creoles; Kinship and Descent; Slave Trades; Slavery and Servile Institutions; Witchcraft.**

BIBLIOGRAPHY

Hodges, Tony, and Malyn Newitt. *São Tomé and Príncipe: From Plantation Colony to Microstate.* Boulder, CO: Westview Press, 1988.

Seibert, Gerhard. *Comrades, Clients and Cousins: Colonialism, Socialism and Democratization in São Tomé and Príncipe*, 2nd edition. Leiden and Boston: Brill Academic Publishers 2006.

GERHARD SEIBERT

HISTORY AND POLITICS

In 1470, Portuguese navigators discovered the uninhabited islands of São Tomé and Príncipe in the Gulf of Guinea. In the late fifteenth century, the Portuguese succeeded in establishing a colony in São Tomé. Among the first white settlers were deported Jewish children, who had been forcibly separated from their parents, and convicts. The colonists engaged in regional slave trade with Elmina and established sugarcane plantations, with the labor of slaves brought from the African mainland. Due to the small number of white colonists, the Portuguese Crown safeguarded the settlement by encouraging unions between slave women and white male settlers. As early as 1515, a royal decree freed these African wives and their children. Consequently, a group of free native Creoles gradually emerged, the *forros*. The encounter between the Catholic Portuguese culture and Africans of various cultures resulted in the development of a distinct Creole society with its own language and character.

From the beginning of the colonization, slaves revolted and escaped into the inaccessible mountainous interior. The greatest slave revolt occurred in 1595. The runaway slaves established a Maroon community in the mountains and frequently assaulted the plantations. After their final defeat in the late seventeenth century, the Maroons, who later became known as Angolares, enjoyed some autonomy until 1878.

The collapse of the sugar industry in the mid-seventeenth century drastically reduced the number of whites and, consequently, the remaining Creoles became steadily more African by blood. Until the mid-nineteenth century, the leading Creole families dominated the local Catholic clergy and the São Tomé town council. In addition, the *forros* were in control of the former plantation lands that the Portuguese had abandoned. The competition of the family factions among the Creole elite for power provoked constant political instability in São Tomé. Due to the frequent turmoil, from 1753 to 1852 the residence of the Portuguese governor was transferred to the small island of Príncipe.

The introduction of coffee (1787) and cacao (1822) to the islands paved the way for a second colonization that began around 1850 when Portuguese planters started large-scale coffee and cocoa cultivation. When slavery was abolished in 1875, the Portuguese planters replaced the slaves with contract workers from Angola, Cape Verde, and Mozambique. These indentured laborers outnumbered the native Creoles until World War II. The latter refused to conduct manual work, which they considered beneath their status as free Africans, on the plantations. By 1898, the Portuguese owned 90 percent of the land and had established the infrastructure for an effective recolonization. As a result, the former landowning *forro* elite became marginalized both economically and politically. They worked almost exclusively in the lower ranks of the colonial administration.

Following rumors that the colonial government wanted to oblige the Creoles to work on the plantations, depriving them of their intermediate position within the highly stratified colonial society, the Creoles waged a spontaneous uprising in February 1953. On the orders of the governor, white settlers put down the revolt using excessive violence, killing numerous innocent and unarmed people. In 1960, Creole students abroad founded the Comité de Libertação de São Tomé e Príncipe (CLSTP, based in Accra, Ghana), the first nationalist group demanding independence. Following the coup that toppled Nkrumah in 1966, the CLSTP was expelled from Ghana and virtually ceased to exist. Not until 1972 did a few *forro* nationalists form the Movimento de Libertação de São Tomé e Príncipe (MLSTP) in Malabo (Equatorial Guinea).

After the Portuguese Revolution of April 25, 1974, the succeeding leftist regime in Lisbon promised independence to all of Portugal's colonies. When São Tomé e Príncipe became independent on July 12, 1975, the country became a constitutionally one-party state governed by the MLSTP. Due to the turmoil preceding independence, at the time most of the 2,000 Portuguese residents had departed. With the assistance of Cuba and former socialist countries, the MLSTP tried to organize both state and society according to the socialist blueprint. The regime became increasingly authoritarian and oppressive, and nationalized the entire economy, including the plantations. However, due to mismanagement and a lack of trained cadres, the plantations rapidly deteriorated, and investments in the diversification of the economy failed.

Forced by sheer economic necessity, from 1984 the regime gradually shifted away from its socialist dogmas and approached western countries for assistance. Following the signing of a Structural Adjustment Program with the IMF in 1987, the economy was liberalized and in late 1989 the MLSTP decided to introduce multiparty democracy. In its first democratic elections, the major opposition party Partido de Convergência Democratíca (Democratic Convergence Party, PCD) swept the ruling party, meanwhile reconstituted as MLSTP/PSD with a liberal orientation, out of office. In the early elections of 1994, the MLSTP/PSD returned to power and has ruled through changing coalitions until April 2006. Legislative and presidential elections have been held regularly and peacefully. Therefore, despite election campaigns affected by vote-buying and widespread corruption by office holders, the performance of multiparty democracy has been considered a success. In the economic field, despite a considerable inflow of development aid, the performance of the democratically elected governments has lagged far behind the programs, and consequently mass poverty has increased in recent years.

See also **Colonial Policies and Practices; Creoles; Postcolonialism; Slavery and Servile Institutions.**

BIBLIOGRAPHY

Garfield, Robert. *A History of São Tomé Island 1470–1655: The Key to Guinea.* San Francisco: Mellen Research University Press, 1992.

Hodges, Tony, and Malyn Newitt. *São Tomé and Príncipe. From Plantation Colony to Microstate.* Boulder, CO: Westview Press, 1988.

Seibert, Gerhard. *Comrades, Clients and Cousins. Colonialism, Socialism and Democratization in São Tomé and Príncipe.* 2nd updated edition. Leiden, The Netherlands and Boston: Brill Academic Publishers, 2006.

GERHARD SEIBERT

SARBAH, JOHN MENSAH (1864–1910).

The foremost politician in the Gold Coast (present-day Ghana) at the turn of the twentieth century, John Mensah Sarbah was born on June 3, 1864. His father was John Sarbah, a wealthy merchant of Cape Coast and member of the Legislative Council recently created to broker growing British colonial ambitions with African professional and entrepreneurial interests. The younger Sarbah attended Wesleyan High School, Cape Coast, and later studied law at Lincoln Inn, London, where he became a barrister in 1887 at the age of twenty-three. He returned to the Gold Coast to establish a legal practice. Sarbah led the fight against the Municipal Ordinance of 1888 as part of the efforts by educated Africans to claim political rights in the British protectorate of the time and soon became known as a formidable defender of African interests against colonialism. He was one of the organizers of the Fante National Political Society in 1889, a nationalist organization advocating the preservation and modernization of traditional customs.

In 1891 Sarbah established a newspaper, *The Gold Coast People*, and soon distinguished himself as an authority on the traditions of the Fante communities of the coastal region, the subject of his two major books, *Fanti Customary Laws* (1897), and *Fanti National Constitution* (1906). He led the opposition to the 1892 Land Bill that proposed transferring the administration of public lands from the chiefs to the British Crown, and joined in the formation of the Aborigines Rights Protection Society (ARPS) in 1897 to sustain this opposition. When a modified version of the proposed law called the Concessions Bill was to be debated in 1900, he was appointed an extraordinary member of the Legislative Council and acted as broker for the ensuing negotiations. He became a regular member in 1901, the same year in which he established the *Gold Coast Weekly* newspaper. Sarbah opposed the 1906 Native Jurisdiction Bill that was drafted to institutionalize Indirect Rule. It aimed to vest powers of local administration in the chiefs, to the exclusion of the educated men such as Sarbah, an idea he considered alien to the democratic traditional constitutions of the Fante. He was prominent in the Fante Public School Company, which in 1903 established the Mfantsi National Education Fund. In 1905 this founded what became the famous Mfantsipim Secondary School, a training ground for future generations of political opponents of British colonial rule.

Sarbah lost favor with the public when an amendment to the Native Jurisdiction Bill enhancing the power of chiefly courts recognized by the British was passed in August 1910, and he died in November before it was known how much he had achieved in getting the bill modified to preserve the jurisdiction of the British courts in the multiple legal environment of the protectorate.

See also **Ghana; Media: Journalism.**

BIBLIOGRAPHY

Edsman, Björn M. *Lawyers in Gold Coast Politics c. 1900–1945: From Mensah Sarbah to J. B. Danquah.* Uppsala: University of Stockholm, 1979.

Kimble, David. *A Political History of Ghana: The Rise of Gold Coast Nationalism, 1850–1928.* Oxford: Clarendon Press, 1963.

Sarbah, John Mensah. *Writings of John Mensah Sarbah.* Bristol: Thoemmes, 2004.

C. OGBOGBO

SARO-WIWA, KEN (1941–1995). Ken Saro-Wiwa was born in Bori, in the oil-rich Niger Delta region of Nigeria's southern coast. His father was Chief Jim Wiwa (1904–2005) of the Ogoni people, a minority group whose homeland was in the Delta. He attended the University of Ibadan and Government College at Umuahia, both in Nigeria. During the mid-1960s he taught at Nigeria's University of Lagos.

In the late 1960s and early 1970s, Saro-Wiwa held a series of government posts, including

Ken Saro-Wiwa (1941–1995). Saro-Wiwa was a member of the Ogoni people, an ethnic minority whose homeland in the Niger Delta has long been used for oil extraction. As a minority rights activist, he led a nonviolent campaign against the environmental damage created by foreign oil companies, most notably Shell. © REUTERS/CORBIS administrator of the port of Bonny in the Delta, and commissioner of works, land, and transport. After losing the latter post in 1973, Saro-Wiwa turned his attention to writing poetry, novels, short stories, and plays. His *Sozaboy: A Novel in Rotten English* (1985), a novel based on the Biafra War (also known as the Nigerian Civil War), was his most highly regarded work. His most popular works were his scripts for the television soap opera, *Basi and Company*, about fifty million Nigerians watched this program in the 1980s.

In 1990 Saro-Wiwa turned his attention to the vast environmental damage inflicted by foreign oil companies, particularly Shell Oil, which for over three decades had been profitably drilling for oil in the Niger Delta on Ogoni lands. In 1991 he formed the Movement for the Survival of the Ogoni People (MOSOP), which demanded that the companies relieve the environmental degradation they had caused, sought more autonomy for the Ogoni, and asked for a larger share of the oil profits for the Ogoni. In 1993, MOSOP organized a demonstration of 300,000 Ogoni, more than half of the Ogoni population. MOSOP's activities were always peaceful, in line with Saro-Wiwa's strong commitment to nonviolence.

Saro-Wiwa, also a critic of Nigeria's dictatorship, was barred from going abroad on speaking engagements in 1992 and was arrested for treason in 1993. In 1994 he and eight others were charged in the deaths of four Ogoni leaders believed to be government collaborators. Convicted in a trial widely seen as rigged, the defendants were—over international protests—hung in November 1995. Subsequently, a number of the prosecution's witnesses stated that the government had bribed them for their testimony.

See also **Literature: Popular Literature; Nigeria: History and Politics.**

BIBLIOGRAPHY

McLuckie, Craig W., and Aubrey McPhail, eds. *Ken Saro-Wiwa: Writer and Political Activist.* Boulder, CO: Lynne Rienner, 2000.

Na'Allah, Abdul Rasheed, ed. *Ogoni's Agonies: Ken Saro-Wiwa and the Crisis in Nigeria.* Trenton, NJ: Africa World, 1998.

Saro-Wiwa, Ken. *Sozaboy: A Novel in Rotten English.* London: Longman, 1985.

Saro-Wiwa, Ken. *A Month and Day: A Detention Diary.* New York: Penguin, 1995.

MICHAEL LEVINE

SASSOU-NGUESSO, DENIS (1943–).
Born in Edou in the northern area of the Republic of the Congo (also known as Congo Brazzaville), Denis Sassou-Nguesso became a soldier at the age of seventeen and received military training in Algeria and France. He joined the ruling party, the Parti Congolais du Travail (PCT; Congolese Party of Labor), soon after its formation in 1969.

In 1970, Sassou became a member of the Military Committee of the Party, of which he later became vice president. In 1979, the committee

Denis Sassou-Nguesso (1943–). In January 2007, a panel of French judges reopened an investigation into whether Republic of the Congo president Sassou's government played a role in the disappearance of 353 Congolese refugees. © PATRICK ROBERT/ CORBIS

selected him to succeed Joachim Yhombi-Opango (b. 1939) as president of the nation. In the early 1980s he introduced a Marxist-Leninist-style constitution and strengthened ties with the Soviet Union, while retaining good relations with France. In 1989, as the communist governments of Eastern Europe collapsed, he instituted economic liberalization and a democratization process that included the legalization of opposition parties in 1990. In the country's 1992 presidential election, he finished third with 17 percent of the vote.

Sassou left for France in 1994, remaining abroad until 1997, when he came back to run in the presidential election again. In June 1997, a month before the scheduled election, fighting broke out between government forces and Sassou's private militia. After four months of violence, the insurgents, aided by Angolan troops, were victorious, and Sassou became president again. However, fighting broke out once more in the latter half of 1998. A national conciliation dialogue was held in 2000–2001, and a new constitution that increased the presidential term from five to seven years was approved by popular referendum in January 2002. Two months later, Sassou won the presidential election with 90 percent of the vote, but his major opponents were excluded from running.

See also **Congo, Republic of: History and Politics; Military Organizations: Militias; Youth: Soldiers.**

BIBLIOGRAPHY

Amnesty International. "Republic of Congo: A Past that Haunts the Future." April 9, 2003. Available from http://web.amnesty.org.

Economic Intelligence Unit. *Country Report: Congo Brazzaville.* London: Economic Intelligence Unit, 2005.

MICHAEL LEVINE

SAVANNAS. *See* **Ecosystems: Savannas.**

SAVIMBI, JONAS (1934–2002). The Angolan opposition leader Jonas Savimbi was born to a Protestant church worker in Portuguese Angola who was also a railroad station master, and educated in the Catholic schools of the colony. He received a scholarship from the United Church of Christ to study medicine in Lisbon and, by the end of his education, was able to speak six languages. Though there is no record of his having pursued a doctoral degree, Savimbi has referred to himself as "doctor." During his student years, as colony after African colony received political independence, Savimbi attended a 1961 conference in Uganda, where he met Tom Mboya, a Kenyan resistance leader, who recommended he collaborate with Holden Roberto to form a group to resist continued Portuguese rule, the Union of Angolan Peoples. In 1962, Roberto and Savimbi headed the National Front for the Liberation of Angola (FNLA) by bringing together a number of other fragmented resistance groups. Savimbi attended the United Nations that year as a

Rebel leader Jonas Savimbi (1934–2002). During a 1986 visit to the White House, Savimbi was told by U.S. president Ronald Reagan, who supported Savimbi in the fight against Angola's Marxist-inspired government, that victory by UNITA, the group Savimbi led, "electrifies the world." AP IMAGES

representative of FNLA but left the group to establish his own National Union for the Total Independence of Angola (UNITA).

During Savimbi's year of transition between the two liberation groups, he went to China to train as a guerrilla. He envisioned a resistance movement that would have both social and military programs and would not be formed around the issue of ethnicity, as FNLA reflected primarily the interests of the northern Angolan Kongo peoples. Nonetheless, UNITA was dominated by the Ovimbundu people of southern Angola, the country's largest ethnic group, and fundamentally opposed itself not only to the Portuguese, but also to FNLA, as well as to the third resistance movement in the colony, Agostinho Neto's Luanda-based Popular Movement for the Liberation of Angola (MPLA). Of the three liberation movements, UNITA was the weakest at the time that Portugal's colonial presence in Africa collapsed in 1974. At that point, Savimbi promised a place for the Portuguese settlers in the former colony, no socialization of private property, and disengagement from the Cold War.

In practice, Savimbi's plans were not so simple to implement. He made three attempts to bring the three opposition groups together but did not succeed. Despite Savimbi's neutralist intentions, the struggle of UNITA was, from the onset, enmeshed in Cold War politics. With the United States shipping arms to UNITA and the USSR supplying aid to the MPLA, the groups fought one another in a struggle that escalated out of control as both groups increased their numbers of weapons and soldiers in order to remain competitive. Cuban soldiers were brought into Luanda, and the West retaliated by mobilizing troops in South Africa. Foreign involvement increased, bringing in France, China, and several Arab states, while the country's boundaries were in constant flux.

It became apparent by the late 1980s that only negotiations would settle the dispute in Angola, and José dos Santos, the MPLA recognized president of the nation, proved receptive to discussion. With the prevailing influence being wielded by the United States, the mutual withdrawal of Cuban and South African troops was agreed to. Namibia was declared independent in 1990, and open elections were held in 1992, with supervision by the United Nations. UNITA and the MPLA signed a peace treaty, but when Savimbi lost in the elections of 1993, he rejected the results and returned to guerrilla warfare. UNITA claimed more than two-thirds of the country, including valuable diamond mines, which as of the late 1990s supplied Savimbi and his forces with some US$1 million weekly.

Throughout the late 1990s Savimbi was the target of dozens of failed assassination attempts, but when death came for him, on February 22, 2002, it was not at the hands of an assassin. He died in battle against government troops in the province of his birth, Moxico, in the remote southeastern corner of the country. Many doubted the report of his death, so his body was placed on display in the town of Lucusse, not far from where he had died.

See also **Angola: History and Politics; Neto, Agostinho.**

BIBLIOGRAPHY

Windrich, Elaine. *The Cold War Guerrilla: Jonas Savimbi, the U.S. Media, and the Angolan War.* New York: Greenwood Press, 1992.

SARAH VALDEZ

SCARIFICATION. *See* **Arts; Body Adornment and Clothing.**

SCHNITZER, EDUARD (1840–1892). Eduard Schnitzer, born in Oppeln, Prussian Silesia, was awarded a medical degree from Berlin University in 1864. From 1864 to 1875, he traveled under Turkish Governor Ismaïl Hakki Pasha in Asia Minor, Arabia, and North Africa extensively, worked in Anatolia and Albania, developed highly skilled knowledge of local languages and cultures, changed his name to that of Emin Pasha, and probably became a Muslim. In 1875, he returned home with the widow of a former employer (whom he claimed to have married) and her four children. Soon thereafter, he abandoned them and fled to Egypt. There, he met General Charles George Gordon, then governor of the Equatorial Province of the Sudan, and was appointed his personal physician. When Gordon

German explorer Emin Pasha (left), formerly Eduard Schnitzer, with British American journalist turned explorer, Henry M. Stanley. The illustration was drawn in 1891. Schnitzer was a doctor of medicine, a naturalist, and an African traveler and administrator. He changed his name while traveling under Turkish Governor Ismaïl Hakki Pasha in Asia Minor, Arabia, and North Africa. PHOTOGRAPH BY MANSELL/TIME & LIFE PICTURES/GETTY IMAGES

became governor of the whole Sudan, Emin succeeded him in 1879 in the Southern Region thereof, called Equatoria (present-day Uganda).

The remoteness of the province, 1,500 miles south of Khartoum, seemed to have suited Emin. Besides remarkable administrative achievements there

(amongst others successfully hindering the slave trade), his work mainly focused on ethnography and natural sciences. His travels led him to the Nile and the Great Lakes in Northern East Africa. In 1883 the Mahdist revolt in Sudan blocked any passage from Equatoria to Egypt and obliged Emin to retreat southward with his troops, which included Italian traveler G. Casati (1838–1902), establish new headquarters near Lake Albert, and appeal to the Western world for help. After previous aborted trials, the famed explorer Henry Morton Stanley led the Emin Pasha Relief Expedition during 1887–1889, a mission financed by a committee led by William MacKinnon (1823–1893). The journey took the expedition across Africa from the mouth of the Congo River to Bagamoyo on the east coast (present-day Tanzania), by way of Lake Albert. It was one of the most costly expeditions ever undertaken in Africa, both in men and materials. Moreover, since it had never been clear whether Emin needed replenishment of his supplies or rescue from his province, the situation was bedeviled by misunderstandings, vacillations, and a mutiny by Emin's troops.

Eventually, some conservatively estimated 1,500 men, women, and children set off for the coast in April 1889. They reached Bagamoyo in December, leaving most of the troops behind. Emin did not wish to accompany Stanley back to Europe, and his fall from a balcony induced the British explorer to leave the German doctor behind. In 1890, Emin joined a German expedition to the territories claimed as German East Africa (present-day Tanzania). In October 1892, while he was exploring the Congo Basin Region, Arab slave traders murdered him.

See also **Congo River; Gordon, Charles George; Nile River; Stanley, Henry Morton; Travel and Exploration: European.**

BIBLIOGRAPHY

Casati, Gaetano. *Ten Years in Equatoria and the Return with Emin Pasha*, trans. J. Randolph Clay. London, Warne, 2 vol., 1898; reprint: New York: Negro Universities Press, 1969.

"Emin Pacha (Eduard Schnitzer." In *Enzyklopädie der Endecker und Erforscher der Erde*, vol. II, ed. by Dietmar Henze. Vol. II, Graz: 1983, pp. 166–170; vol. IV, Graz: 2000, p. 744.

Holt, P. M. "Emīn Pasha." In *Encyclopédie de l'Islam, nouvelle édition*, vol. II, Leyde-Paris, 1977, pp. 713–714, and vol. V, Leyde-Paris, 1986, p. 1241.

Jephson, Arthur J. Mounteney. *Emin Pasha and the Rebellion at the Equator*. London, Sampson Low, Marston, Searle and Rivington, 1890; reprint, New York: Negro Universities Press, 1969.

Jones, Roger. *The Rescue of Emin Pasha*. London: Allison and Busby, 1972.

Middleton, Dorothy, ed. *The Diary of A. J. Mounteney Jephson: Emin Pasha Relief Expedition, 1887–1889*. London: Cambridge University Press, 1969.

Newman, James L. *Imperial Footprints: Henry Morton Stanley's African Journeys*. Washington DC: Brassey's, 2004.

Peters, Carl. *New Light on Dark Africa: Being the Narrative of the German Emin Pasha Expedition, its Journeyings and Adventures among the Native Tribes of Eastern Equatorial Africa, the Gallas, Massais, Wasukuma, etc., etc., on the Lake Baringo and the Victoria Nyanza*. London: Ward, Lock and Co., 1891.

Schweitzer, Georg. *Die Tagebücher von Dr. Emin Pascha*, ed. F. Stuhlmann. Hamburg/Braunschweig/Berlin, 3 vol., 1917–1922.

DOROTHY MIDDLETON
REVISED BY MATHILDE LEDUC-GRIMALDI

SCHREINER, OLIVE (1855–1920).

The South African writer Olive Schreiner was born in South Africa on March 24, 1855. After spending her childhood at a Lutheran mission station in the eastern Cape Colony, she moved in 1872 to the diamond-mining town of Kimberley, where she began to write her first novel, *Undine* (eventually published in London in 1929). The tragic narrative of a European woman's revolt against the patriarchal strictures of colonial society, *Undine* prefigures Schreiner's lifelong interest in the confined condition of women in the highly disciplined male world of the Victorian empire. In 1881 after working for several years as a governess, and with the manuscript of *Undine* complete but unpublished, Schreiner moved to London, where, in 1883, she published a second manuscript, *The Story of an African Farm*, under the pseudonym Ralph Iron. The novel, which remains Schreiner's best-known work, was an immediate success and brought her no little celebrity. While in London, Schreiner also published a collection of allegories and dream narratives entitled *Stories, Dreams, and Allegories* (1890) and wrote *From Man to Man*, a novel detailing the lives of two sisters trapped in the institutions of marriage and prostitution.

In 1889 Schreiner returned to South Africa, where in 1894 she married Samuel C. Cronwright. Together they wrote *The Political Situation* (London, 1896), a jeremiad against the commercial

Author Olive Schreiner (1855–1920) in 1901. Schreiner wrote *The South African Question by an English South African* to explain to the public why there should not be a war between the Boer and the British. MANSELL/MANSELL/TIME & LIFE PICTURES/ GETTY IMAGES

franchise. That same year she left South Africa once again, though she returned in 1920, the year of her death.

At once an accomplished prose stylist and one of the nineteenth century's most important critics of patriarchy and imperialism, Schreiner left a legacy that rests both on her lyric evocations of the sparse geographics of the eastern Cape and on her examination of the pinched lives that a politicized landscape afforded its frequently rebellious female inhabitants.

See also **Literature; Women: Women and the Law.**

BIBLIOGRAPHY

Clayton, Cherry. *Olive Schreiner.* New York: Twayne, 1997.

Clayton, Cherry, ed. *Women and Writing in South Africa: A Critical Anthology.* Marshalltown, South Africa: Heinemann, 1989.

First, Ruth. *Olive Schreiner: A Biography.* Foreword by Nadine Gordimer. New Brunswick, NJ: Rutgers University Press, 1990.

Horton, Susan R. *Difficult Women, Artful Lives: Olive Schreiner and Isak Dineson in and out of Africa.* Baltimore, MD: Johns Hopkins University Press, 1995.

IAN BAUCOM

interests monopolizing the mineral wealth of the country. Increasingly devoted to political causes, Schreiner began to lecture extensively at women's congresses and to defend the cause of the Boers in the Anglo-Boer war. Her anti-imperial defenses of the Boers form the centerpiece of a collection of prose entitled *Thoughts on South Africa* (London, 1923). During the war she also composed *Woman and Labour*, an extensive study of the disenfranchisement of women from capitalized labor. The sole original manuscript of the twelve-chapter book was, however, burned by British soldiers during the Anglo-Boer War (1898–1092), so in 1899 Schreiner recomposed one chapter from memory. That chapter, under the original title, was published in 1911.

During the final years of her life, Schreiner became increasingly involved in the women's suffrage movement and also began to devote herself to racial enfranchisement. In 1913 she resigned from the Women's Enfranchisement League when it refused to endorse a demand for a nonracial

SECRECY. *See* **Knowledge.**

SECRET SOCIETIES. In Africa secret societies are typically associated with West Africa. In the literature they are sometimes referred to as cult associations or secret cults. Such secret organizations are thought to have control over certain medicines or magical materials, but those terms do not carry all the meanings found in local vernaculars. The pidgin English term *juju* is often preferred in African conversation and popular literature. Throughout West Africa these societies or cults are linked to masks and to certain recurring images of raw power, such as the leopard. As the vernacular terms indicate, the core of these institutions is esoteric knowledge about curing, or more generally of protecting and promoting life. When the members of the secret society, those who have been initiated and paid their fees, observe the rules of the society then they are protected from certain malign forces. The elements of this basic form have been taken up, developed, and elaborated in different ways.

In the Upper Guinea Coast, the Poro society of the men and the Sande, or Bundu, society of the women are notable for their complex and lengthy initiation ceremonies coordinated over quite large areas and embracing several ethnic groups. Where these institutions prevail all adult men are initiates of the Poro society and all adult women initiates of the Sande society. The initiation itself takes place over a period of several months in a concealed part of the forest from which uninitiated people, apart from the novices themselves, are excluded. There a house or houses are built to accommodate the novices and those looking after them as well as those initiates who merely wish to exercise their prerogatives and enjoy a few days away from the routines of everyday life and work.

The procedure is punctuated by the appearance in the town or village of the masked figure, colloquially the Poro devil or Sande, devil of the society and which signifies that the novices are undergoing one of several transformations in their progress towards their eventual return to the village and normal life as an initiated adult. The Poro masked figure drawn out of the forest by its attendants projects an awesome sense of untamed force. The Sande mask that of femininity and fertility. Political functions have been attributed to secret societies such as Poro in terms of the control of trade or of the exploitation of the natural resources in the forest, including fisheries, which are a common good. Poro can institute a rule, for example with respect to harvesting palm fruits, breach of which will automatically remove the protection of Poro "medicine" from the offender.

Poro and Sande are universal in so far as they embrace the entire adult population but there are other secret societies alongside Poro and Sande, membership of which is limited though open to both men and women and whose distribution is not nearly as extensive as Poro and Sande. Thus the Humoi society cures and protects its members from the consequences of breaches of rules of sexual conduct and gender relationships, the consequences of which may affect people other than the

offenders. The Humoi society also concerns itself with matters of health and illness and its services may be called upon to restore the fertility of the land of a village. On a smaller scale, the owner of a "medicine" may initiate an apprentice into the secrets of his medicine and so authorize the novice when he has paid over the fees to practice that particular cure, and that person, in turn, may initiate a novice in the secrets of the cure so producing a network of initiates. An initiate on returning to his community will require a licence to practice in the chiefdom from its paramount chief but can expect to be guaranteed exclusive rights in the chiefdom.

Hierarchy and ranking is endemic in secret societies and initiates progress in seniority as further secrets are revealed to them on the payment of the appropriate fees. Because of the idiom of secrecy much of what happens does not make any symbolic sense to those involved but there is the assurance that someone further up the hierarchy must know. Though even here there may be limits as in the case of a secret cult among the Chamba of eastern Nigeria where the final mystery of the cult was hidden under an inverted pot. However, the last person who knew the secret precautions that had to be put in place before the pot could be safely lifted died before he had passed them on to an initiate. Other secret societies constitute a powerful political elite with responsibilities in relation to the paramount ruler, for example, for his installation rites on succession to the office and title as in the case of the Ragbenle society of the Temne of Sierra Leone or the Ogboni society of the Yoruba whose members comprised the traditional councils of the Yoruba kings of Nigeria.

Secret societies of some antiquity nevertheless undergo changes in response to the impact of world religions. So a version of the Ogboni society appeared among middle class Christian Yoruba as the Reformed Ogboni society, and in the Upper Guinea Coast the Poro society has waned before the spread of Islam. At the same time the Sande or Bundu society has continued to evolve and flourish in the same way that the women's *bori* and *zar* possession cults of northern Nigeria and the Sudan have done. The old Creole population of Freetown in Sierra Leone which looked to England for inspiration rather than the dark interior of Africa established among themselves Masonic lodges. At the same time elements of West African secret societies such as Ekpe from the southeast of Nigeria, as a consequence of the Atlantic slave trade, have been identified in a secret society known as Abakua, in Cuba, while Ogboni symbolism has been detected in *condomble* ceremonies in Brazil.

In the 1980s among the communities of the Niger Delta area of Nigeria there emerged a new secret society known as Egbesu, drawing its membership from the socially and politically excluded, which is actively resisting the central government and the international oil companies. Membership cuts across the numerous ethnic groups of the delta and the Egbesu spirit secured protection for its cult members from the physical attacks of the police and army. This secret cult is a movement that appeals to and seeks to awaken a moral community with its roots in a precolonial era whose rights to their land and its resources have been usurped by what are defined as alien powers.

Nigerian university student associations became heavily politicised in the 1980s as a direct response to radical changes in public finances but were then destroyed by the government. In their place appeared violent secret associations offering magical protection to their members who were targeting corrupt senior university office holders. These secret societies of students are outlawed and publicly demonized by associating them with armed gangs and ritual killings.

In West Africa there is a curious link between some of these late modern vigilantes and the much older traditions of hunting and of associations of hunters. This is especially true of the groups variously known as the *Yendaba* among Hausa speakers, the *Benkadi* of Burkina Faso, the *Donzo* of Côte d'Ivoire, and the *Kamajo* in Sierra Leone. Such associations appear in situations where there is a significant rural-urban dimension to resistance and conflict. However, it is important to note that the leaders of the insurgents in the forest are often drawn from the educated but politically excluded urban youth for whom the forest has no appeal except as a base from which to conceal and then project themselves. They invoke the secret and mysterious powers of the hunter because they know that it plays effectively on precisely those fears of the dark savagery of the forest, the source of the power of the old secret societies, which haunt the urban elites. Hence national political leaders seek to reassure their urban supporters by urging a distinction between the traditional "real hunters" and these modern politicized "fake hunters."

At the end of the twentieth century vigilantes came to prominence in many parts of Africa. While on the one hand they take on the responsibility of cleaning up the neighborhood, literally and metaphorically, and of promoting the claims of local people against those of outsiders by, for example, controlling access to markets including the labor market, their position is very ambiguous. In West Africa the positive reputation of "area boys" in the local community they seek to protect is undermined by their secret links with powerful individuals in the political and commercial classes for whom they act as enforcers. In east Africa, though the *sungusungu* groups of vigilantes are more transparent they only enjoy a quasi-legal status that leaves them vulnerable to prosecution. To the extent that vigilantes have to conceal their identities they may be considered to be secret societies, but clearly they are not an outgrowth of that idiom of mysterious secrecy that is such a powerful theme in West African culture.

See also **Age and Age Organization; Body Adornment and Clothing; Diasporas; Initiation; Masks and Masquerades; Religion and Ritual; Witchcraft.**

BIBLIOGRAPHY

Fardon, Richard. *Between God, the Dead and the Wild. Chamba Interpretations of Religion and Ritual.* Edinburgh: Edinburgh University Press for the International African Institute, 1990.

Ferme, Mariane C. *The Underneath of Things. Violence, History, and the Everyday in Sierra Leone.* Berkeley: University of California Press, 2001.

MacCormack, Carol P. "Sande: The Public Face of a Secret Society." In *The New Religions of Africa*, ed. Bennetta Jules-Rosette. Norwood, NJ: Ablex, 1979.

CHARLES JEDREJ

SEKHUKHUNE I (c. 1810–1882).

Sekhukhune I was the paramount chief of the Pedi and a military leader in northeastern Transvaal. He was born about 1810 to Sekwati (r. 1775–1861), ruler of the Marota (also called the Pedi) of the Transvaal region of South Africa. During Sekwati's reign, Boer incursions into the territory sparked wars of resistance by the indigenous peoples of the region. In 1852, after the Boers had denied Sekwati's people access to the Tubatse River, Sekhukhune succeeded in sneaking under Boer fire to fetch water for his people. This established Sekhukhune as a leader and earned him his name (from *khukhuna*: to creep). On Sekwati's death, Sekhukhune claimed the right to rule, but was challenged by his half-brother, Mampuru.

To secure his claim, Sekhukhune led a bloody fight against Mampuru and his supporters, ultimately prevailing. He then expanded his empire by arranging a number of strategic marriages, by conquest, and by offering protection to refugees of the violence of war. He attempted to end European influence by expelling Christian missionaries from his territories and burning the mission at Maandagshoek to the ground. These and other incidents incited renewed Boer attacks, this time with the help of Swazi fighters. When another of Sekhukhune's half-brothers (Dinkwanyane) was killed, Sekhukhune retaliated by attacking the Boer-held Burger's Fort.

In February 1877 Sekhukhune secured peace by agreeing to pay a war indemnity of 2,000 cattle and by agreeing to subject his people to the authority of the South African government. He reneged on the deal, but in April of 1877 the Transvaal was annexed by the British. Sekhukhune again led his people in revolt, but was defeated by a force of two British regiments and some 8,000 Swazi allies. Sekhukhune was captured and sent to Pretoria; his son and heir was killed during the fighting.

In 1881 Transvaal gained its independence. Sekhukhune was released and went to live in the Lulu Mountains. There, in August 1882, he was killed by his former rival for power, Mampuru. Mampuru was arrested by the British and hanged in Pretoria. To reduce the threat of resistance, the British broke up the Marota people into two groups. Half were resettled at Molaletsi, in the Lydenburg district, the other half were moved to Mooggelegen, in the Middleburg district.

See also **Christianity; Missionary Enterprise; Refugees.**

BIBLIOGRAPHY

Hunt, D. R. "An Account of the Bapedi." *Bantu Studies* 5 (1931): 275–326.

SARAH VALDEZ

SEMBÈNE, OUSMANE (1923–2007).

In 2004 Ousmane Sembène's film *Moolaadé* (winner of the Cannes 2004 Un Certain Regard category) was named Best Foreign Film by the American National Society of Film Critics. On June 19, 2006, Sembène was elevated by the Senegalese government to the rank of *Trésor humain vivant* (a living human treasure) and on November 9, 2006, the French government bestowed on him the *Legion d'honneur*. Sembène died in June 2007 after a long illness.

Of modest birth in Casamance, southern Senegal, Sembène inscribed his name in world history. Expelled in 1936 for disciplinary reasons, his formal education ended in middle school. From 1938 to 1944 he worked as an apprentice mechanic and a bricklayer. As a French citizen, Sembène, like many young Africans of his generation, was called to active duty into the army to liberate France from German occupation in 1944. Upon his discharge in 1946, he returned to Dakar, joined the construction worker's trade union, and witnessed the first general strike that paralyzed the colonial economy for a month and ushered in the nationalist struggle in French Africa. The strike is the subject of Sembène's most well-known novel *Le bois des bouts Dieu* (*God's Bits of Wood*, 1960).

In 1947 Sembène left Dakar and migrated to the Mediterranean city of Marseilles until 1960, the year Senegal was granted independence. As a black African docker who knew how to read and write, he was soon identified by labor union leaders who enrolled him in the Confédération Générale du Travail (CGT), the largest and most powerful left-wing workers' union in postwar France. After backbreaking work unloading ships during the day, at night and on weekends Sembène enthusiastically attended seminars and workshops on Marxism and joined the French Communist Party in 1950. These experiences informed the author's first novel *Le docker noir* (*The Black Docker*, 1956. It was also in the midst of such intense political activism that Sembène discovered communist artists and writers: Richard Wright, John Roderigo Dos Passos, Pablo Neruda, Ernest Hemingway, Nazim Hikmet, Claude McKay, and Jacques Roumain, from Haiti. Sembène became also involved with the international Communist youth organization Les Auberges de jeunesses and discovered the Communist theater Le Theatre Rouge.

Senegalese film director, producer, and writer Ousmane Sembène (1923-2007). Sembène is considered the father of African cinema. His works dealt with subjects that promoted justice and dignity for Africans, including his best-known novel, *God's Bits of Wood*, which was based on his participation in a 1947 Senegalese railroad strike. CORBIS

By the early twenty-first century he was best known as a filmmaker; Sembène used only cinema to bring home what the widespread illiteracy in the continent did not allow him to accomplish through his writing. Sembène was nearly forty years old when, in 1962, he became interested in filmmaking. In 1963 his short *Borom Saret* ushered Senegal and Africa into the landscape of world cinema, sixty-eight years after the invention of cinematography, and sixty-three years after the Lumiere brothers' *L'arroseur arrosé* was screened in Senegal. Sembène's films thus transformed Africa from a consumer of its own images made elsewhere into a "producer" of its own images. However, it was with *Mandabi* (*The Money Order*), based on his short story with the same name, in 1968, that Sembène's dream to reconnect with Africa's

masses came true. For the first time, an African film-maker used an African language (Wolof, the dominant language in Senegal), hence setting a trend to be followed by all filmmakers on the continent).

At the international level, Sembène, unequivocally recognized as the father of African cinema, received countless awards and distinctions. His images are intended not only for entertainment and profit, but also to promote freedom and social justice and restore pride and dignity to African people. Rejecting a mere imitation of Hollywood's narrative techniques, Sembène also borrowed from the rich heritage of African oral narratives, handed down by the griots, to usher in a genuinely African film aesthetics.

See also **Dakar; Film and Cinema; Labor: Trades Unions and Associations.**

BIBLIOGRAPHY

Gadjigo, Samba. *Ousmane Sembène: The Life of a Revolutionary Artist.* California Newsreel. Available from http://www.newsreel.org/articles/OusmaneSembène.htm.

Murphy, David. *Sembène: Imagining Alternatives in Film and Fiction.* Trenton, NJ: Africa World Press, 2000.

SAMBA GADJIGO

SENEGAL

This entry includes the following articles:
GEOGRAPHY AND ECONOMY
SOCIETY AND CULTURES
HISTORY AND POLITICS

GEOGRAPHY AND ECONOMY

The Senegalese economy is influenced, though not determined, by a marked north-south geographical zonation. Semiarid lands to the north are dominated by agropastoral lifeways, whereas sub-tropical forested areas to the south are characterized by rain-fed agriculture, wood extraction, and fishing. Port cities located along the narrow coastline provide opportunities for trade. Together with mining activities, they offer some degree of diversity to an otherwise predominantly agricultural economy. Out of the potential 60,000–70,000 hectares of cultivable land, only about half are in use in the early twenty-first century. Since the 1980s, commercial

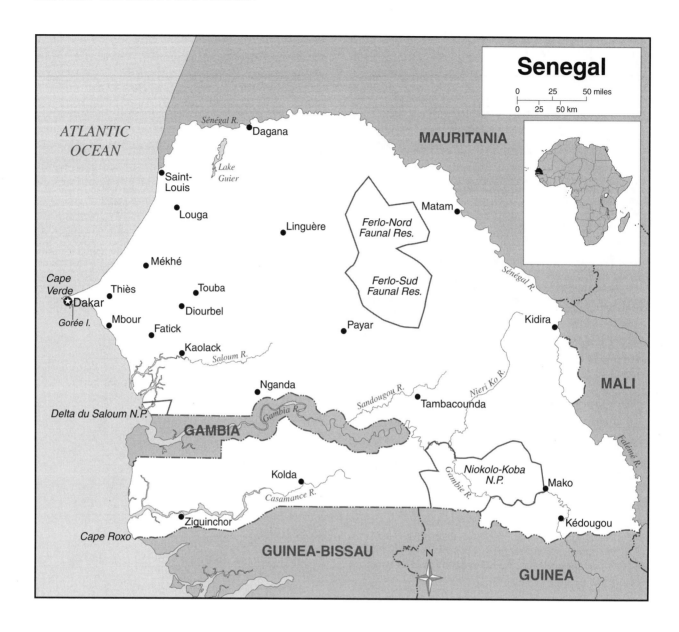

fishing and the mining of phosphates have grown significantly, comprising respectively 30 and 16 percent of export earnings. Light industries contribute about 15 percent of gross domestic product (GDP), less than the service sector, however, which has grown to provide more than 50 percent of GDP. Tourism is also an important source of foreign exchange. Despite these recent developments, the Senegalese economy still suffers from serious structural problems, including a stagnant agricultural sector (Berthelemy et al 1997) and a lack of peasant participation in rural development (Niang 2005).

The geography and economy of the country can be best understood using a regional perspective. With a total area of 75,749 square miles, Senegal forms the westernmost corner of Africa within the so-called tropical belt. Marked contrasts in rainfall nevertheless exist, with a low precipitation of less than 11.8 inches to the north, in the semidesertic Sahel region, to a high of more than 39 inches to the south, in the low-lying and swampy Casamance Region. Built on a Tertiary sedimentary subsidence basin, the country is relatively flat (averaging 197 feet), except for the Fouta Djallon region to the southeast, with elevations of up to 1,411 feet. A

249 mile-long submerged coast has low sandy plains interrupted by wide valleys formed by the Senegal and Casamance rivers, with drier upper valleys to the east, in the Ferlo and Sine-Saloum. Several major geographic/economic regions, not necessarily corresponding to administrative units, can be defined.

THE SAHELIAN-SUDANIC REGION
The Sahelian-Sudanic Region to the north, including the Fouta Toro along the middle valley of the Senegal River, has a long dry season lasting up to ten months. The herbaceous vegetation is composed of extensive savannas interspersed with low shrubs and bushes. This is the domain of agropastoral peoples such as the Fulani (or Peul), who constitute 20 to 45 percent of the inhabitants. Following the seasons, the Fulani move with their troops of zebu cattle, sheep, and goats from the flooded valley of the Senegal River to the drier margins covered with pasture and bushes. Besides the important role played by herding, the Fulani also cultivate millet, green beans, and melons near their encampments during the rainy season, and in the floodplains and marigots of the river during the dry season. They regularly exchange milk and other bovine products for cereals with neighboring Wolof and Toucouleur cultivators. During the long drought of the 1970s, many Fulani lost a large number of their animals, a fact that drove them to settle in the valley and floodplain.

THE OUALO (WALO)
Stretching from the city of Saint-Louis on the Senegal River Delta east to Dagana is a land of numerous *marigots*, or tributaries, dunes, and swamps. Here, a number of important irrigation projects, including Richard Toll, begun as early as the 1940s, were created in an effort to boost rice production. In the early twenty-first century, these projects are coordinated by a government/private agency, Société d' Aménegement et d'Exploitation de Terres du Delta du Fleuve Sénégal (SAED), and are still focused on the planting of rice and tomatoes. SAED regrouped mostly Fulani, but also Wolof and Toucouleur cultivators, into cooperatives and furnished them with seed, fertilizer, and other inputs. SAED also served as an intermediary between peasant farmers and buyers of their agricultural products. The SAED-sponsored projects have met with limited success due to salinization problems and poorly maintained irrigation works that have lowered production, and inadequate opportunities for commercialization.

CENTRAL SENEGAL AND THE FERLO
Inhabited by Fulani, Moor, and Wolof herders, this sparsely inhabited, dry region has suitable pasture and limited farming opportunities only in the rainy season. It is located along the northern half in the interior of the country to the south of the riverbanks and to the east of the groundnut basin. In the past, cities such as Thies were relatively important cultural and centers thanks to the region's rich phosphate resources and developed railway system.

THE SINE SALOUM
This region, also known as the Groundnut Basin, extends from Louga in the savanna about 124 miles from Dakar to the Sine-Saloum river, a semiarid zone roughly the same distance to the south. The predominant soils is light and sandy and therefore ideally to the cultivation of groundnuts (such as peanuts), which accounts for 40 percent of all farmed land. The Kaolack district produces about half of the country's groundnuts, followed in importance by the Thies and Diourbel districts. Groundnuts are cultivated by independent Sereer cultivators, often using animal traction, and dependent upon a fodder tree that loses its leaves during the rainy season, the Apple-ring Acacia or Winter thorn *Acacia Albida*, to restore soil fertility, and by Wolof farmers belonging to the Mouride brotherhoods. This crop provides more than 50 percent of the country's agricultural production, and though continues to be an important commercial crop, its export value has decreased considerably, becoming secondary to fishing and phosphate exports. Nevertheless, groundnuts still play an important role in providing in rural incomes and is central to the operation of mills producing oil for domestic use and export.

EASTERN SENEGAL
The largest of the Senegalese administrative regions is a low-lying land of extensive savannas, hills, and plateaus 984–1,312 feet high inhabited largely by Fulani, but also Malinkes and much smaller groups such as the Bassaris, Coniaguis, and Bedik. They practice a short-term fallow agriculture, centered on groundnuts, millet, and sorghum on the light soils of the flatlands and plateaus, and grow rice in

the depressions temporarily flooded during the rainy season. Here, and in Upper Casamance, cotton is an important commercial crop, providing 3 percent of the country's export earnings and managed by a private company (Société de Développement des Fibres Textiles; SODEFITEX). Only two large towns exist: Tambacounda (called Tamba) and Kedougou. With about 100,000 inhabitants, the economy of Tamba is mostly agricultural, but mining plays an important role in the region near Kedougou. About half of the eastern region is delimited by the Niokola-Koba National Park. Covered by savannas, bamboo forests, Guinea woodland trees, and seasonal swamps, the park is the best-protected conservation area in the country, providing the economy with earnings from tourism.

THE CASAMANCE

Located in southwest Senegal, and cut off from the rest of Senegal by the ex-British colony of The Gambia, the Casamance region forms a long corridor extending 224 miles from west to east. It is subdivided into two principal administrative zones: Ziguinchor in Lower Casamance and Kolda in Upper Casamance. The domain of a rich sub-Guinean forest, it is the rainiest region of the country, even after several decades of diminishing precipitation. The low-lying river basins of Lower Casamance, traversed by numerous tidal channels known as marigots, are lined by mangrove vegetation and allow for an ancient and productive wet and upland rice agriculture, practiced mostly by the Jola (Diola) peoples who live in large villages amongst oil palm groves, silk-cotton trees, Borassus palm, acajou (*Khaya Senegalensis*), and numerous planted mangos. Toward the Middle and Upper Casamance regions, the mangrove forest disappears and is replaced by a degraded sudanic vegetation. Here, the Manding populations, sedentary Fulani, and more recent immigrants from Guinea-Bissau cultivate dryland cereals such as millets, sorghum, and groundnuts as a commercial crop.

PORT CITIES

Saint-Louis. The fourth largest city of Senegal (population approximately 180,000) is located on an islet in the Senegal Estuary. An administrative and commercial center with a small trade in groundnuts, skins, and gum, Saint-Louis is an industrial locus for sugar production. It is also

one of the largest fishing centers in West Africa. The principal Wolof and Lebou inhabitants are fishermen, the Fulani are pastoral farmers, and the Maures, who emigrated from Mauritania, are merchants and shopkeepers. The city suffered an economic decline when the capital was transferred to Dakar in 1957, but it is still an important commercial and tourist center.

Dakar. Situated on the Cape Verde Peninsula (*la Petite Côte*), Dakar (population 2.4 million in 2005), is the densely settled (7,076 persons per square mile) administrative and economic capital of Senegal. Its westernmost position in the African continent has helped it to become one of the busiest Atlantic commercial ports, serving Mauritania and Mali, as well. With more than 1,236 miles of protected waters, a fifth of which have been dredged to depths of more than 36 feet, the port handles in excess of 10 million tons of cargo each year. In the city, refined sugar, groundnut oil, fertilizers, cement, and textiles are important manufactured products, whereas oil refining, flour milling, and fish canning are other major industries. Dakar is a major administrative zone, the seat of the National Assembly and the presidential office, and a renowned academic center with a splendid university and a research institution (Institut fondamental d'Afrique noire; IFAN) of world status.

Ziguinchor. Placed at the entrance to the Casamance River in southern Senegal, Ziguinchor, the fifth largest city in the country, is a port town. Located in a rice-growing area, the city produces groundnut oil, frozen fish, and orange juice, and serves as an outlet for the groundnuts that are shipped from the hinterlands to other cities to be processed. The city is also an important groundnut milling factory. Although the Jola constitute more than 60 percent of the larger Ziguinchor region, they are only 35 percent of the city's population, which has numerous immigrants from Guinea-Bissau and Mauritania, who buy and sell agro-alimentary and manufactured goods.

See also **Dakar; Ecosystems; Port-Louis; Production Systems; Saint-Louis; Tourism.**

BIBLIOGRAPHY

Berthelemy, Jean-Claude; Abdoulaye Seck; and Ann Vourc'h. 1997. *Growth in Senegal: A Lost Opportunity.*

Paris: Development Centre of the Co-Operation Organization for Economic Development.

Church, Ronald J. Harrison "Senegal: The Ancient Base." In *West Africa: A Study of the Environment and Man's Use of It*, 6th edition. New York: John Wiley and Sons, 1968.

Freud, C.; Ellen Hanak-Freud; Jacques Richard; and Pierre Thenevin. *L'arachide au Sénégal: un moteur en panne.* Paris: Editions Karthala, 1997.

"Les régions du Sénégal." Available from senegalaisement. com/senegal/regions.html.

Niang, Mamadou. *Participation Paysanne et Developpement Rural au Sénégal.* Dakar: Council for the Dedelopment of Social Science Research in Africa (CODESRIA). 2005.

Santoir, Christian. "Peul et aménagement hydro-agricoles dans la vallée du fleuve Sénégal." In *Pastoralists of the West African Savanna*, ed. Adamu Mahdi and Anthony H.M. Kirk-Greene. Manchester, U.K.: Manchester University Press, 1986.

OLGA F. LINARES

SOCIETY AND CULTURES

In contrast with many of its neighbors, Senegal has experienced the gradual emergence of a sense of a distinctly *Senegalese* society and culture among important segments of the population, reflected in a vibrant national culture of popular music and other forms of artistic expression. Nevertheless, as elsewhere on the continent, sociocultural pluralism remains a central defining feature of the country. Three major overlapping cleavages comprise the key features of Senegalese society: social stratification, ethnolinguistic identities, and religion.

The vast majority of Senegalese belong to a set of core Sahelian social groups; the major exceptions being the Diola and other groups of lower Casamance and some much smaller groups in the extreme southeast. Sahelian social structures share a number of key features, including an elaborate system of social stratification that distinguishes individuals of noncasted or noble birth from a variety of casted groups. Though the term caste is debated by scholars, these groups share important definitional elements: they are endogamous; their interactions are regulated by relations of hierarchy; and they are occupationally defined, with an individual's occupation transmitted by birth and not by actual economic activity. To varying degrees, the Sahelian societies also maintain a system of stratification between freeborn and slave

individuals, and in some cases this distinction continues to have a significant impact in regulating social interactions.

The caste system is occasionally called into question in public discourse and plays an increasingly marginal role in public life, but it remains central to personal relations and, notably, to marriage patterns. Marriage across ethnicity that respects caste lines is thus more easily accepted than cross-caste marriage within a given ethnic group. There are also many shared cultural values across Sahelian societies, reflected in an elaborate moral terminology with equivalents across languages, and that are frequently correlated with the system of social stratification.

The largest ethnic group in Senegal is the Wolof, comprising some 40 percent of the population. The historical emergence of the Wolof language as the Senegalese lingua franca, and its overwhelming dominance in urban areas, has resulted in highly fluid and permeable boundaries to Wolof ethnicity and contributed significantly to an ongoing process of ethnic Wolofization in much of the country. The second-largest ethnolinguistic group in Senegal is composed of the HaalPulaar, or speakers of Pulaar (also known as Peul, Fulani, and Fulfulde). Historically, Pulaar speakers comprised distinct communities, including the pastoral Peul or Fulani, the settled Tukulor people of the Senegal River valley, and various smaller groups. Although these distinctions sometimes remain salient at the local level, at the national level the shared HaalPulaar linguistic identity has become the dominant sociopolitical force, a phenomenon driven largely in reaction to the encroaching role of the Wolof language. The third major ethnic grouping in Senegal is the Seereer (also spelled Sereer or Sérère). This group is likewise an amalgam of a variety of historically distinct groups, and the sociopolitical salience of the identity seems also to emerge in reaction to the spread of Wolof. Strikingly, however, the people grouped as the Seereer speak a variety of mutually unintelligible languages.

In addition to these three main ethnic groups, a number of groups who speak Mande languages also belong to the Senegalese Sahelian core. These include the Mandinka, Soninké, Bambara, and Sarakholé. The most important of the non-Sahelian ethnic groups is the Diola (Joola) of the

---

République du Sénégal (Senegal)

Population:	12,521,851 (2007 est.)
Area:	196,190 sq. km (75,749 sq. mi.)
Official language:	French
Languages:	French, Wolof, Pulaar, Serer, Diola, Mandingo, Soninke
National currency:	CFA franc
Principal religions:	Muslim 94%, Christian 5%, traditional 1%
Capital:	Dakar (est. pop. 2,400,000 in 2005)
Other urban centers:	Diourbel, Kaolack, Kolda, Louga, Rufisque, Saint-Louis, Thies, Tambacounda, Ziguinchor
Annual rainfall:	varies from 300–500 mm (12–20 in.) in north to 1,000–1,500 mm (40–60 in.) in south
Principal geographical features:	*Rivers:* Senegal, Casamance, Gambia, Saloum, Soungrougrou, Falémé, Koulountou, Niéri Ko, Sandougou, Kayanga, Mayel-Samou, Siné *Lakes:* Lac de Guier
Economy:	*GDP per capita:* US$1,800 (2006)
Principal products and exports:	*Agricultural:* peanuts, millet, corn, sorghum, rice, cotton, tomatoes, green vegetables, cattle, poultry, pigs, fish *Manufacturing:* agricultural and fish processing, fertilizer production, petroleum refining, construction materials, ship construction and repair *Mining:* phosphates, iron ore, gold, some oil
Government:	Independence from France, 1960. Constitution approved in 1963, revised in 1991 and 2001. Multiparty republic. President elected by universal suffrage for 5-year term. Unicameral 120-member Assemblée Nationale elected for 5-year terms by popular vote. President appoints prime minister, who appoints Council of Ministers in consultation with the president. For purposes of local government there are 11 regions, 34 departments, and 320 rural councils.
Heads of state since independence:	1960–1980: President Léopold Sédar Senghor 1981–2000: President Abdou Diouf 2000–: President Abdoulaye Wade
Armed forces:	President is commander in chief. 2 years obligatory enlistment. *Army:* 12,000 *Navy:* 700 *Air force:* 650 *Paramilitary:* 4,000
Transportation:	*Rail:* 904 km (560 mi.), state owned *Waterways:* 1,000 km (621 mi.), Senegal River (all year); Saloum and Casamance Rivers (part of the year) *Ports:* seaports: Dakar, Saint-Louis; riverports: Kaolack, Matam, Podor, Richard-Toll, Ziguinchor *Roads:* 13,850 km (8,587 mi.), 29% paved *National airlines:* Air Sénégal provides internal service. Senegal holds a share of Air Afrique. *Airports:* Yoff International Airport at Dakar, smaller international airports at Cap Skirring, Zinguinchor, Saint-Louis. 16 other small airports and airstrips throughout the country.
Media:	Principal daily newspaper: *Le Soleil.* Principal monthly: *Le Démocrate.* Book publishers include Les Nouvelles Éditions Africaines and the Institut Fondamental d'Afrique Noir, affiliated with the Université de Dakar. Radio and television broadcast through the Office de Radiodiffusion-Télévision du Sénégal. 28 radio stations, 1 television station. Senegal is a major producer of feature films in Africa. Film production supervised by the government.
Literacy and education:	*Total literacy rate:* 39% (2006). Education is free, universal, and compulsory for ages 6–12. Secondary education offered through teacher-training and technical schools. Postsecondary education provided by Université de Dakar, Université de Saint-Louis, Université Cheikh Anta Diop de Dakar, Université des Mutants, École Nationale d'Administration du Sénégal, Institut African de Développement Economique et de Planification, École Inter-États des Sciences et Médecine Vétérinaires.

---

lower Casamance, south of the Gambia. Since the 1980s, a sense of marginalization from the dominant national Sahelian culture has fed resentments and sparked an ongoing low intensity separatist movement among the Diola and related groups in Casamance. The small community of Moors established in many areas the country, and whose identity is linked to neighboring Mauritania regardless of their actual birth or citizenship, were the targets in 1989 of the most significant ethnic conflict in postindependence Senegal. In addition, small communities of Lebanese, and to a lesser degree of Cape Verdians, constitute significant presences in urban areas.

Religion may present the most significant distinguishing feature of Senegalese society and culture. Some 94 percent of the Senegalese population is Muslim today. Although Islam has been present in the region from the tenth century and by the colonial conquest constituted a majority in many areas, the demographic preponderance in the early twenty-first century is the result of a significant expansion under colonial rule. The remaining 6 percent of the Senegalese population are almost all Catholics, with most being concentrated among the Diola and neighboring communities in the Casamance and among portions of the Seereer. Historically there have been close and peaceful ties between Muslims and Christians, with ethnicity—and even more importantly, caste—usually serving as a more significant influence than religion on marriage choice.

Senegalese Muslims are in the large majority (some 90% or more) followers of the Sufi traditions often referred to as Islamic mysticism. Each Sufi community or order, sometimes referred to as brotherhoods, teaches a particular set of ritual litanies and other practices. In the Senegalese context, adherence to one of these orders is a core element of most individual's identity. The major orders in Senegal were established by charismatic religious figures active at the time of the colonial implantation. The most important of these are led by three major families: the Mbacké family, founders of the Mouride order, and the Sy and Niasse families, affiliated with the Tijaniyya order. Other orders of some significance include the Qadiriyya (widespread and with a long history in West Africa but a minority in Senegal), and the indigenous Layène order, most of whose followers come from the Wolof-speaking Lebou people of the Cape Vert Peninsula. There are numerous other religious families, including other branches of the Tijaniyya, and in general the force of generational change means that today all religious families in the country are marked by a degree of fragmentation of authority, and hence of the allegiance of disciples.

Although Sufism is a widespread and ancient tradition in the Muslim world, a distinctive national form of religious social organization based on Sufism has become well established in Senegal. This is centered around membership in local level social groups known as daairas, based on a shared relationship with a specific religious guide or marabout. This identity is reinforced in an elaborate and widespread system of ceremonies and rituals that make up a colorful and defining feature of the Senegalese cultural landscape.

As with all societies on the continent, Senegal is subject to a number of influences shaping the evolution of its historical and traditional sociocultural norms. In religious terms, the global context of a seemingly growing conflict between Muslim societies and Europe and North America has so far not significantly affected interreligious relations in the country, but there are indications that it is producing shifts in the Sufi system as proponents of a more Islamist or reformist form of religious practice increase their credibility and impact. In addition, Senegal is increasingly a diasporic society at many levels. In addition to established communities of Senegalese laborers and merchants in Europe, the United States, and African countries such as Gabon, Côte d'Ivoire, and more recently South Africa, there are a high number of Senegalese intellectuals and professionals occupying positions in European and North American universities and in international organizations. These expatriates play a significant role in the Senegalese economy for large numbers of families, and hence serve as vehicles for social and cultural change. The centrality of emigration in the social imagination undoubtedly helps to fuel the waves of youthful Senegalese embarking on increasingly risky endeavors to seek their fortunes abroad, with as yet unexplored consequences for Senegalese society and culture.

See also **Ethnicity; Kinship and Descent; Marriage Systems; Slavery and Servile Institutions.**

LEONARDO A. VILLALÓN

HISTORY AND POLITICS

The singularity of the Senegalese political experience has been noted since its independence. At independence it inaugurated a quasi-democratic system in a continent where, prior to the political crises of the late 1980s, democratic movements were rare. Senegal's precocity has been attributed to the historical trajectory of political, cultural, and religious factors, and to social and political actors who, over a very lengthy period, had constructed a Senegalese territory and culture that was distinct from the authoritarianism that fractured the rest of the African continent.

This culture was the product of a cumulative history that spanned the precolonial, colonial, and postcolonial eras. It arose from multiple discourses, the best known being Léopold Sédar Senghor's négritude movement and Cheikh Anta Diop's

Afrocentrist thesis of a black ancient Egypt. Accounts of the identity, or identities, of Senegal, while celebrating the exemplary nature of Senegalese democracy, disclose as well a troubled history and major contemporary crises that signal the end of an historic sequence: the nationalist compromise.

PRECOLONIAL ANTECEDENTS

Senegal's physical dimensions were the product of colonial conquest and the formation of the French colonial empire. The original colony, which achieved independence in 1960, was governed by an administrative practice whose influence is apparent in the twenty-first century. The colonial territory brought together the previously separate territories of the precolonial societies, but this unification failed to eliminate the distinctive genealogy and geography of indigenous Senegalese societies. The region's high degree of integration into the Atlantic colonial economy was achieved through a process of adjustment on the part of the colonized and the strategies of accommodation adopted by the colonizers.

The Senegambian territory of the precolonial period was an open space. Its development had been influenced by numerous factors: continuous migrations; the mingling of populations; and social, cultural, political, and economic institutions that were differentially affected by the imperial designs of the Wolof empire of ancient Ghana and the states of the western Sudan. These Sahelian empires were reinforced by the first incursions of Islam in the region, which occurred around the ninth century.

Islam and its various leaders had a profound impact on the two types of communities that existed in precolonial Senegambia: hierarchical societies and the so-called egalitarian societies. The first were structured by institutions based on an unequal access to resources and power and included the Wolof, Tukulor, Mandinka, Soninke, and some, but not all, of the Serer groups. This type of organization exemplifies one of the political modalities of Senegal: the disassociation between the cities that formed political centers and the territories of their subordinate village communities. This disassociation gave rise to the terms of political legitimization as well as to the pluralism that sustains a more or less effective local autonomy in the presence of a broader regional power. From this has arisen a perpetual tension within the Senegalese political system: a tension between the centrally based political actors and the local arbiters of legitimacy; between those who employed violence and those who attempted to escape from it. These precolonial tensions are reflected in the political systems that came after.

Precolonial modes of incorporation, imposed by conquerors that came from outside the region, established the terms by which power could be exercised. They gave rise to a political trajectory that never succeeded in overriding the variability of social and cultural expression that characterized the Senegambian region. From the outset, the political systems arising from precolonial imperial conquest displayed a marked distinction between the dominators and the dominated in terms of differential access to wealth, social prestige, and political power. An ongoing process of social fragmentation contributed to the development of a system of political participation and administration based on the patronage and clientelism that was characteristic of the Muslim communities.

As for the egalitarian societies (which included the Serer peoples of the northwest, some Malinke groups, the Diola, Manjak, Balanta, Bainuk, Basari, and Konagi), authority appears to have been relatively diffuse. In general the regulation of these groups was accomplished through a variety of political and juridical institutions. The central ideology underlying these institutions—of production, reproduction, and redistribution—was ultimately based on the control of the land. Resistant to Islam because of its assimilationist policies, these so-called egalitarian societies entrenched themselves in their "traditional" religions; many later converted to Christianity, which was more open to local influences.

The Senegambian region's progressive involvement in the Atlantic slave trade gave rise to the political reorganization of the territory and the reconfiguration of local socioeconomic structures. The importance of the slave trade for the newly developing economic regions marked a significant break from what had gone on in the trans-Saharan trade. The coastal communities benefited from this new Atlantic trade, obtaining their independence from those indigenous empires that had previously exercised political dominance over them.

The hierarchically organized societies were, in geographic terms, better defined than the egalitarian communities. They were better integrated even though their political equilibrium was precarious. As the violence precipitated by the slave trade became more widespread, the hegemony of royal authoritarianism became more secure as these hierarchies extended their political control to encompass local peasant communities. The leaders of such smaller communities faced a single choice: to lose their power or to be incorporated into the patronage network as clients. The heavy militarization of states and very coercive centers precipitated a militant response within the Islamic communities. The Muslim response was to reinvent a history for the region and to reconfigure the idea of community. To accomplish this, Muslim leaders dedicated themselves to the difficult enterprise of breaking down the boundaries of indigenously defined ethnic territories—to produce, through force, a transethnic community.

In the majority of the hierarchically ordered societies, by the era of colonial conquest, two coalitions confronted one another in the struggle for power and the control of communities and resources. These were the aristocratic elites and their allies and clients on one side, and on the other, the leaders of the Muslim communities, the marabouts (Muslim religious teachers who often established brotherhoods of followers). The peoples of the egalitarian societies that lived in proximity to the slave-raiding states (the Serer of the northwest) and the slave brokers who lived along the rivers of the south (Balanta, Bainuk, Diola) retreated to increasingly inaccessible locations and adapted their social, economic, and cultural structures to a spirit of resistance, irredentism, and exaggerated ethnocentrism.

Political regions were redefined and social ideologies were reorganized, particularly at the time of the abolition of the Atlantic slave trade. These transformations, like the earlier reformulation of hegemonic codes under the pressure of power struggles during the expansion of Islam, resulted in a certain fluidity in the exercise of political power. They help to explain the methods employed during the period of colonial conquest and pacification: the co-optation of the hierarchical societies in conjunction with the repression of the more rebellious egalitarian societies.

The organization of the colonial administration was influenced by the conditions of conquest and by the political and social structures that were in place in the conquered societies. Although the colonizers proclaimed a generous policy of assimilation, colonial practice in fact successfully subordinated the preexisting political structures to the needs and goals of France.

THE INVENTION OF AN INDIGENOUS SOCIETY

The indigenous societies known today are the product of French colonial domination and of cumulative adjustments by the individual Senegalese societies that were faced with administrative policies of enclosure and forced labor. To accomplish its goals, the colonial administration had to accommodate Senegambian conditions. The colonial state was very selective in the way in which it went about integrating Senegambian societies into its new order. This selectivity was economically motivated around the groundnut, which in the second half of the nineteenth century became the principal cash crop of the colony of Senegal.

The groundnut economy was restricted to two zones: the central region between the Senegal and Gambia Rivers (and its peripheries), and the urban markets. This geography provided the basis for the dualistic political and administrative organization of the Senegalese colonial society that distinguished between French subjects, who were regulated by the Code de l'Indigénat, and French citizens, who were natives of the Four Communes of Saint-Louis, Gorée, Rufisque, and Dakar.

From the French colonial perspective, it was imperative that the first group (subjects) be restricted to indigenous territorial enclosures, under the supervision of a colonial administrator. Initially, the colonial administration had left these enclosures in the hands of the traditional chiefs; later they were entrusted to the marabouts, who had very quickly asserted themselves as the major groundnut producers. Chief of the community and of the territory, the marabout was the centerpiece in the new hierarchy, the guarantor of a regime that was based on absolute obedience. Early on, the colonial administration had contrasted the disorder of the so-called fetishist societies, whose rituals, customs, and chiefs they did not understand, to the organization of these Islamic brotherhoods. The latter seemed to possess values similar to those of the colonizers, particularly a strong sense of subordination to the state and to its leaders.

In the rural areas beyond the groundnut-growing region, the difficulty of identifying leaders in the egalitarian societies and of recruiting them into the colonial system had resulted in an absence of integration and a situation of chronic tension. The situation in the 1980s and 1990s in the Casamance tragically illustrates how this situation has continued to exist. There, a separatist movement has turned to armed rebellion, acknowledging no allegiance to the central Senegalese state.

The variety of mechanisms of colonial engagement with local forms of power, and the centrality of the groundnut in the developing colonial geography and ethnology, encouraged the emergence of a political and economic model based on Wolof and Muslim organizational forms. This was especially true in the groundnut-growing regions, in which the Mouride and Tijani Muslim brotherhoods had their greatest success, and where the political directives and voting recommendations of the Caliph (Muslim leader) were incontestable. The integration of these maraboutic hierarchies into the colonial administration was accomplished in two ways. The first method was associative: Muslim leaders were included in the parades and celebrations held by the colonizers. Second, these same leaders officiated in locally held Muslim religious ceremonies. The marabouts thus became identified as the indispensable mediators between the powerful and the rural populations.

The interface between the political, the religious, and the commercial that forged the distinctive shape of Senegalese politics thus appears as the fruit of a long historical accumulation. When the French government abolished the status of "subject" at the end of World War II and granted citizenship to all Senegalese, the marabouts assumed an even more important political role than they had previously held. Their undeniable status as political entrepreneurs in the final decade of colonization had a great influence on the construction of the postcolonial state and the configuration of the relations between the state and the society.

THE CONSTRUCTION OF AFRICAN SOCIALISM, 1960–1980

At the time of independence, when metropolitan politics were extended to the whole of the colonial territory, the country's elites were divided into two political parties: the Section Française de l'Internationale Ouvrière (SFIO) of Lamine Guèye and the Bloc Démocratique Sénégalais (BDS) of Léopold Sédar Senghor and Mamadou Dia. This reflected the two modalities (hierarchical societies integrated with the central power, egalitarian polities in the rural regions) that characterized the Senegalese colonial state. The peoples who had originally had exclusive rights of citizenship voted for the SFIO (the "Red" party), and the former subjects voted for the BDS (the "Greens": the color associated with Islam and with the land). The battle between the Reds and the Greens dominated Senegalese political life for ten years, from 1948 to 1958, when the two principal parties fused to form the Union Progressiste Sénégalaise (UPS).

In the fusion of the Red and Green parties, which produced postcolonial Senegal, a continuity of the colonial project can be seen, as well as a continuation of the ways in which social, political economic, religious, and ethnic networks were articulated. The nationalist project of the postcolonial era found it difficult to eliminate the differences that existed between rural and urban zones in terms of political activism, alliance formation, mobilization of the electorate, and definitions of identity. Despite repeated political crises arising from disputes over political and economic options and international politics, Senegalese political life was relatively unchanging over the first two decades of independence. Although earlier social structures had been thrown into disarray, the colonially imposed territorial borders and the economic emphasis on groundnut cultivation remained unchanged.

Senegalese leaders joined with other African nationalists in their vision of nation building. They insisted on the viability of the nation as a unit of political organization, on the incontestability of a workable African socialism. Above all, they shared the prevailing attitudes toward modes of mobilization and of militarization. African socialism, first associated with the négritude movement, provided the terms on which economic, political, and social activity were based. It legitimated bringing economic decisions under the control of political elites.

The close identification of power holders with the state itself, as opposed to the powerless masses, fostered the very pedagogic style that was adopted by the national leadership. The ideology underlying this pedagogical style of rule was one that envisioned a unified state structure, administered from above through local intermediaries who possessed ethnic, religious, or ancestral legitimacy. The national political discourse strongly invoked traditional values of respect and submission (of sons to fathers, juniors to elders, women to men) and excluded social juniors from the political and economic sphere. The state reinforced the old colonial imposition of geographical unity, assumed control over the administration of the economy, and consequently assumed a paternalistic role that excluded all expressions of dissonance and dissidence.

On the whole, reacting to internal and external economic constraints and employing a system heavily reliant on patronage, the Senegalese postcolonial state was constituted as the sole source of political discourse as well as the sole locus of control and access to economic and financial resources. The ruling class thus monopolized the dispensation of social prestige. It eroded all other sources of discourse and autonomous practices of economic accumulation. The political administration of the economy and society accelerated the growth of patronage through the practice of nepotism and the widespread practice of buying and selling allegiances. The role of Wolof groups in the government declined. Postcolonial conditions accentuated the role of the Islamic brotherhoods in the political and economic goals of mobilizing the rural populations and the urban peripheries.

Paradoxically, because their rationalization was based on invocations of indigenous values, the dynamics of political unification opened the door to the first stirrings of dissent against the nationalist project. Certain segments of society had always managed to escape assimilation into the state, and by the late 1970s efforts to eliminate the rights of these groups were already in the works.

The drought that began in the early 1970s, the global recession caused by the oil crisis of the time, and the crisis affecting groundnut and phosphate (Senegal's principal exports) brought economic recession to Senegal. The central cause of this was the structural-adjustment policies of the International Monetary Fund (IMF) and the World Bank. Neither the relaxation of the state's central control (through the nomination of a prime minister and co-optation of a new political generation in 1971), nor the Senghorian experiment with multiparty democracy (which began in 1974), nor the liberalization of the economy was able to curb the economic downturn and the fiscal crisis. Structural-adjustment policies encouraged a twofold contradictory tendency: the accession of technocrats to positions of power and the reaffirmation of ideological, ethnic, and religious claims to the land. Seemingly bored with the challenge of solving Senegal's problems, Senghor resigned from office in 1980. He returned to his farm in Normandy and waged a successful campaign for election to the Académie Française.

THE ACCESSION OF THE TECHNOCRACY AND OF THE IDEOLOGY OF AUTONOMY

Three factors were involved in the establishment of the new political configuration. First was the rising tendency for aspirants to power to base their claims on expertise, rather than on the politics of patronage. Second was the devolution of state power in the face of pressures imposed by the moneylenders (the IMF and the World Bank). Third was the development of new terms of association. Evidence of these factors and the decline of the central state can be seen in the sudden rise of technocrats to positions of power and the decline in the importance of nationalism as the prevailing ideology in the land. Further evidence is found in the ongoing Casamance secessionist crisis; the easing of control which allowed limited multiparty politics (and resulted in the pre-electoral, electoral, and postelectoral riots of 1988); the bloody episodes of the Senegalese-Mauritanian border conflicts; the ideological activities of the Set-Setal (a youth movement that arose in the cities during the early 1990s and expressed its views through wall murals and statues); and the assassination of one of the members of the Senegalese Constitutional Council.

Structural-adjustment programs opened up spaces in the economy for illegal, parallel, and informal markets and activities. In dismantling the old organizations of the central state and its administration these programs have, in the same stroke, destroyed all the existing mechanisms for social regulation. Arbitration and social and ideological compromise occur only spasmodically. The slow agony of dealing with the bureaucratic class, the unkept promises of opportunities for the bearers of modernity (students and apprentices) to enter the ruling class, and the endemic corruption of the older elites have all contributed to discrediting the concept of nationalism.

Abdou Diouf, who succeeded Senghor as president in 1981, tried in vain to undo the political and patronage-based constraints that have resulted in the failure of Senegal's economy, in part by basing government appointments on technical competence rather than on political considerations. By this means, as well as through his pioneering vision and his efforts to satisfy his international creditors, his administration achieved a certain state of grace. Notably, Diouf removed virtually all restrictions on the press and on the formation of opposition political parties. But the unkept democratic and economic promises, and the severity of the economic and social crisis, nonetheless precipitated an infernal cycle of student strikes and repressions, which culminated in violence during the 1988 elections.

The difficulty of staging political action and the government's failure to achieve full democracy provoked a resurgence in the invocation of ethnic identities. Calls for solidarity are deliberately invoked in public politics, which solicit allegiance in terms of ethnicity, or religious or regionally defined identities. At the same time, new political actors have arrived on Senegal's political and social scene, drawn from groups that had been previously disdained in the old nationalist discourse: young people, women, and marginal social groups.

In dismantling the administration, structural-adjustment policies succeeded in drying up the old systems of redistribution and patronage, but no economic upturn followed. As a result, the technocracy was unable to establish its own credibility, nor could it revive the old patronage networks or produce its own political economy. The result has been chronic instability and agreements and compromises that accomplish nothing.

Diouf was confirmed as president in the 1983 elections and again in 1988 and 1993. The latter two elections were seriously marred by allegations of voter fraud; widespread urban rioting broke out, and the leading opposition candidate, Abdoulaye Wade, was briefly imprisoned. Pushed by donor nations, Diouf formed a coalition government that included Wade. In the run-up to the 2000 elections factional quarrels broke out in Diouf's Partie Socialiste, thereby splitting the vote and forcing a runoff between Diouf and Wade, which Wade won with 58 percent of the vote. Diouf relinquished office with dignity and alacrity.

After forty years of rule by the same political party, Wade's appeal was straightforward: *Sopi*, or "change" in Wolof. Six years into his first term in office, Wade has few positive changes to boast about, and no dearth of changes for the worst—from increases in rural poverty to power outages in the capitol. He seems particularly to have lost favor in the urban areas that had strongly backed him in the 2000 elections.

The extraordinary explosion of pluralism in Senegalese public life has accompanied an economic and ecological crisis that has accelerated the migration of people to the interior and beyond national borders, to traditional territories based on ethnic or religious associations. Disputed territories are not only being redefined on the international frontiers (as in the Senegal-Mauritania conflict) but also internal divisions are being redrawn according to repeated affirmations of ethnic identifications within a particular region, to the exclusion of and discrimination against outsiders. The separatist claims of the Mouvement des Forces Démocratiques de la Casamance (MFDC) illustrate this situation.

Such movements are justified in the idioms of the land in precisely the same terms as were used by both the colonial-era ethnography and the nationalist modernization movements in their efforts to accomplish their goals of repression, enclosure, or mobilization. These new movements have ushered in an era that has seen the rejection of the old nationalist institutions and defiance of its power. Nonetheless, they follow the long-standing historical tradition of recruiting membership into autonomous organizations on the basis of shared ethnic background, place of residence, or religious affiliation.

The secessionist movements began with the formation of alliances among rural youths and women, groups that had been excluded from participation in the cooperative system that had formed the vector for the nationalist goal of integrating the peasantry into the postcolonial state. Trapped in the clientalist system that had long enervated Senegalese politics, these rural cooperatives were controlled by the most undemocratic segment of the population. Working at the grass-roots level, activist groups built upon local dissent and developed strategies for the redefinition of the state. Taking over the role of the collective, these new organizations bore within themselves the seeds of a new social conscience that was highly critical of the state projects. They eroded the efficacy of the clientalist system and participated in the dissolution of the policies of centralization, enclosure, and submission to administrative rule.

The state's treatment of Casamance separatism gave focus to the ongoing problem. The impression—perhaps false—is that in order for the state to free itself of the political demands of the region, Casamance separatism must be accepted. Some Casamance partisans reject the concept that this is, indeed, a part of Senegalese territory. The region, taken as a whole, is perceived by many to be a region apart. This view is so widely held that both sides of the dispute—the administration and the MFDC—invoke a history of conflict over the legitimacy of claims that the territory is rightfully part of the state. By 2007 the Casamance confrontation was the longest lived secessionist movement in Africa. Despite repeated peace agreements signed by both the government and spokesman for the rebellion, sporadic violence continued. The human cost includes some 64,000 people driven from their homes since the 1980s. Senegal's troubles in the Casamance consist of the recourse to violence because the people are excluded from participating in the primary political sphere and are only seen by the center as the stakes of secondary politics. Paradoxically, this situation maintains the centrality of the old hierarchical Islamo-Wolof model in the organization of Senegalese politics and claims to social legitimacy. This separatist attitude may be contagious for other areas that are predominantly occupied by traditionally egalitarian groups, most notably in the northern region of Senegal.

See also **Colonial Policies and Practices; Dakar; Diop, Cheikh Anta; Diouf, Abdou; Famine; Gorée; International Monetary Fund; Islam; Nationalism; Postcolonialism; Saint-Louis; Senghor, Léopold Sédar; Slave Trades; Socialism and Postcolonialisms; World Bank.**

BIBLIOGRAPHY

Cruise O'Brien, Donal; Momar-Coumba Diop; and Mahmadou Diouf. *Construction de l'État au Sénégal.* Paris: Karthala, 2002.

Diop, Momar-Coumba, ed. *Gouverner le Sénégal: Entre lájustement structurel et développement durable.* Paris: Karthala, 2004.

Diouf, Mamadou. *Histoire du Sénégal: Le modèle Islamo-Wolof et ses peripheries.* Paris: Maisonneuve & Larose, 2001.

Foltz, William J. "Sénégal." In *Political Parties and National Integration in Tropical Africa,* ed. James S. Coleman and Carl Rosberg. Berkeley: University of California Press, 1964.

Gellar, Sheldon. *Democracy in Senegal: Tocquevillian Analytics in Africa.* New York: Palgrave Macmillan, 2005.

Schaffer, Frederic C. *Democracy in Translation: Understanding Politics in an Unfamiliar Culture.* Ithaca, NY: Cornell University Press, 1998.

MAMADOU DIOUF
REVISED BY WILLIAM J. FOLTZ

SENGHOR, LÉOPOLD SÉDAR (1906–2001).

The poet, philosopher, and first president of Senegal (1960–1981) Léopold Sédar Senghor was the first person of African descent elected to the 300-year-old Académie Française, the highest honor France bestows. Among African leaders Senghor stands alone. He was the embodiment of what appear to be irreconcilable qualities: he was as African as he was European, as much a poet as a politician, as much a traditionalist as a revolutionary.

Born in Ndijtor, near Joal, in Senegal, Senghor was sent by his father to the white man's school so that he might become "civilized." Senghor (as he later wrote) was thus torn away from the mother tongue, from the ancestor's skull, from the "tom-tom" of his soul. He studied for the Catholic priesthood, but because he protested against racism he was obliged to leave the Dakar seminary. After finishing his studies in a public high school in 1928, Senghor won a scholarship to study in France, where his closest school friend was Georges Pompidou, who later became the nation's president.

Senghor's greatest ambition was to become a "black-skinned Frenchman," but it was not long before he realized that was impossible. He then began his quest for his "Africanness"—his *négritude,* as he put it. He rediscovered his "childhood kingdom" and wrote prizewinning poetry exploring his African soul. After being imprisoned by

Senegal president Léopold Sédar Senghor (1906–2001). Senghor was the first African to become a member of Académie Française, France's official organization to rule on matters of French language. MYCHELE DANIAU/AFP/GETTY IMAGES

the Nazis during World War II, Senghor was elected deputy from Senegal to the French National Assembly, serving in Paris from 1946 until Senegal's advance toward independence in 1958.

Senghor was first elected president of post-independence Senegal in 1960, and retired from his office in 1980. He first advocated the establishment of a European-African Federation: Eurafrica. When the independence movement seemed unstoppable, he called for a union of French-speaking African states, but the rising tide of micro-nationalism in the late 1950s defeated these ideas. Senghor devoted the rest of his career to developing a theory of civilizations converging into a universal, global culture. In the midst of an increasingly fragmented world, Senghor stands as the prophet of multicultural federalism. He died on December 20, 2001, in France.

See also **Literature; Senegal: History and Politics.**

BIBLIOGRAPHY

Bourges, Herve. *Léopold Sédar Senghor: lumière noire.* Paris: Mengès, 2006.

Brunel, Pierre. *Léopold Sédar Senghor.* Paris: Adpf, 2006.

Hymans, Jacques Louis. *Léopold Sédar Senghor: An Intellectual Biography.* Edinburgh: Edinburgh University Press, 1971.

Senghor, Léopold Sédar. *Nocturnes*, trans. John Reed and Clive Wake. London: Heinemann, 1969.

Spleth, Janice. *Léopold Sédar Senghor.* Boston: Twayne, 1985.

Vaillant, Janet. *Black, French, and African: A Life of Léopold Sédar Senghor.* Cambridge, MA: Harvard University Press, 1990.

JACQUES LOUIS HYMANS

SEROTE, MONGANE (1944–). The South African writer-politician Mongane Walter (Wally) Serote was born in Johannesburg and brought up in the townships around the city. Serote became a journalist and soon fell foul of the apartheid authorities. In the late 1960s and early 1970s his powerful poetry established him as one of the leading literary proponents of black consciousness; his first book *Yakhal'inkomo: Poems* (1972) won him the Ingrid Jonker Prize in 1973. Following a master's degree in creative writing at Columbia University in New York, he lived in exile, first in Botswana, then in London where among other achievements for the African National Congress (ANC)'s cultural office he convened the important Conference for Another South Africa in Amsterdam in 1987. In addition to maintaining a steady output of poetry, Serote also wrote one of the most complex and interesting "struggle novels" *To Every Birth Its Blood* (1981). He returned to South Africa in 1990, and since 1994 has been an ANC member of parliament and chair of the parliamentary Committee on Arts, Science and Technology. In the latter capacity he has been closely associated with the South African chapter of the African Renaissance. Serote's long poem *History Is the Home Address* (2005) indicates his continued belief in culture as a weapon in the struggle to free black South Africans from the debilitating effects of apartheid and its legacy.

See also **Apartheid; Johannesburg; Literature; Media: Journalism.**

BIBLIOGRAPHY

Ernst, Ulrike. *From Anti-Apartheid to African Resistance: Interviews with South African Writers and Critics on Cultural Politics Beyond the Cultural Struggle.* Hamburg, Germany: Lit Verlag, 2002.

Moslund, Sten Pultz. *Making Use of History in New South African Fiction: Historical Perspectives on Three Post-Apartheid Novels.* Copenhagen: Museum Tusculanum Press, 2003.

SIMON LEWIS

SEXUAL BEHAVIOR. Until the late twentieth century, sexuality was a research area cloaked in mystery, fraught with anxiety, mired in taboos and sanctions. Some works of African fiction have provided insight into sexual manners and mores, as have "Dear Doctor" columns in African magazines and newspapers, and some scholars have buried issues of sexuality within other material. But Western social scientists have with good reason been uncomfortable asking questions about intimate behavior, not to mention writing about it. Writing about African sexuality is problematic: there is a minefield of Western myths and stereotypes about the curious customs, the easy-going sex-as-transaction, the promiscuity. Does the intent of scholarship justify showcasing these, of engaging in prurience to understand and explode such stereotypes? Or, as John Caldwell and his colleagues have asked, is the problem a Western view that stifles discussion of different patterns of sexual behavior? Certainly it is crucial to frame such practices sociologically, understanding the social, political and economic stressors implicated in different or exaggerated behavior. There is also the problem of labeling; given, for example, the size of Africa and its diversity of cultures, is there a distinct African sexuality?

While the study of African sexuality is far from complete, the state of silence has begun to change, for several reasons: the feminist perspective, which has expanded to include women's sexual desires as well as their use of sexuality to their best advantage; highly publicized concerns about female sexual surgery; the blossoming of queer theory; and research into HIV/AIDS, as it has decimated entire African villages. All of these areas involve issues of control, and all demand attention to what goes on in the sphere of erotic activity.

To understand sexuality, one must begin with the premise that sexual behavior is not just "natural"; it is socially and culturally constructed. Cultural rules and regulations intersect with sexual practices as people negotiate the social arena. From one African society to another, even within the same African field situation, there are variations in attitudes and conduct based on gender, ethnicity, class, religion, and so on. What is "normal" varies, but there is always a norm, which is tied into moral attitudes, highlights morally disapproved behavior, marshals moral disapproval, and provides social deterrents. Sexual relations are always ordered.

HETEROSEXUAL ACTS AND BEHAVIORS

There is an interesting controversy in the literature. Caldwell holds that one can posit a general system of African sexuality, which contrasts with the Eurasian system: that people in many African societies are not guilt ridden about sex, that they enter sexual relationships casually and treat sex much like a transaction. Foreign religions and administrative and educational systems introduced Eurasian notions of morality, but there is no indigenous religious or moral focus on the sex act. While the broader area of sexual relations is affected by moral forces, what is central here, in contrast to the Eurasian system, is reproduction. On the contrary, according to Suzette Heald, one needs to focus on coitus itself in order to understand the power attributed to it, because the act is fraught with danger. To many cultures sexual control epitomizes social and moral behavior. In all societies there are prescriptive and proscriptive rules to ensure that continuity in the social order is maintained. Coitus can be disruptive especially when its occurrence breaks rules, for example because the partners are forbidden, or the correct ritual has not been followed. Generally it is the elders who have a vested interest in preserving continuity in the social order. In many East African societies, it is taboo to discuss sex publicly, and husband and wife may never refer to the act directly. The Ganda in Uganda only have sex in the dark, as it is indecent to see one's partner naked.

Whichever side one takes, given the cultural construction of sexuality one must acknowledge that individual African cultures do have their respective cookbooks of appropriate acts and behaviors and of who constitute appropriate partners. Among the Asaba in southeastern Nigeria, where children live in exogamous lineages and after age eight are sexually segregated, children know little about sex. A woman's premarital chastity both brings her family honor and ensures her future daughters' proper upbringing. Yet among the neighboring Ijaw (Ijo), as in much of the continent, premarital pregnancy is not an issue. And among the !Kung of the Kalahari Desert, where there is little privacy, children learn about sex from watching their parents' lovemaking and practice it themselves well before marrying. In eastern Africa, premarital sexuality is typically permitted, so long as pregnancy does not occur.

The significance men and women place upon sex reflects cultural values. Among the Kgatla of Botswana, it is regarded as a duty binding together husband and wife. Both Kgatla men and women speak openly about sex and acknowledge it as a pleasurable activity; it is important in its own right. Among the !Kung, the articulate Nisa related in Marjorie Shostak's *Nisa: The Life and Words of a !Kung Woman* (1981), girls and women need and want sex—that without it their minds don't develop normally. But in many areas, women are not expected to enjoy sex. For example, in Kenya, where coitus is understood as the cornerstone of marriage, necessary for health and sanity, and instrumental for women who may exchange sex for money with male partners, men do not work hard to increase their female partner's pleasure. Among the Gusii in Kenya, coitus is an act which the woman resists, while the man is expected to cause her pain. In the Sudan, where there are severe penalties for a woman initiating or showing interest in sexual intercourse, she engages in a series of maneuvers and sex signals. Through the smoke ceremony, for example, she permeates her skin with spices; while this is clearly understood by her husband as an invitation, she must be passive in sex and hide her orgasms. In the Copperbelt of Zambia, there is a flank celebration of marital sex in popular songs, endorsing the pursuit of sex for its own sake, which includes the woman's pleasure.

The significance placed on sex also reflects economic realities and power. For example, there is the expectation that men will provide for wives and children. In urban Namibia, many men live in bad economic straits with poor prospects. Frustrated and angry, some young men express their maleness by coercing women in their sexual interaction through dominance and violence. Women may use sexuality as an economic resource, in the normal course of their relationship with men, and it can cost men plenty in the city. Low-income women in urban areas in Kenya, Nigeria, Ghana, and Senegal sell sex to survive. In the traditional interpretation, female sexuality provides a service and is based on reciprocity; in the urban milieu women may manipulate sex to cultivate patrons who will further their interests. Both represent an economic exchange and the woman's use of her sexuality to her own benefit. The "outside women" serve as alternatives to polygynously married wives.

While scholars have some information on frequency of coitus and specific practices, it is hard to know how accurate it is. Scholars know that a polygynous man observes a strict rotation among his wives to ensure fairness and thus harmony: the wife who cooks for him sleeps with him. Does this mean he engages in sex every night? Members of some cultures report that they have sexual relations several nights per week, and on those nights they do so two to three times, the last at dawn before getting up. The Gusii told Robert LeVine that the first night of marriage, a man is expected to have six to twelve orgasms. This may be an example of an idealized norm; it may be simple exaggeration.

While the Kgatla report a preference for a woman with a fairly wide vagina, which has been "worked loose," in much of Africa people report the desirability of friction in sex. This has been institutionalized in Central and southern Africa (including Zaire, Zambia, Malawi, Zimbabwe, and South Africa), where women use intravaginal herbal and other agents to create a condition referred to as "dry and tight"—to contract the vagina, make it warm, and prevent vaginal secretion during intercourse. In Zambia these are among several types of "love medicine" that women use to enhance the stability of their relationships with men and to reduce feelings of vulnerability. The medicines are rubbed on the body, eaten by the woman or the man, inhaled, or thrown into bathing water. The most important are luck medicines, used to ensure a man's love and economic support.

Men also report using love medicines to make conquests and increase their feelings of potency.

In sub-Saharan Africa, sex takes place most frequently in one of two ways: with the woman on her back, the man on top and his legs between hers, or both on their side, facing one another. A third position is vaginal penetration from behind. There are some reports of masturbation, and of anal penetration, for example in the Sudan in cases where the woman has been infibulated and her husband cannot penetrate her vaginally. Lovemaking generally does not include kissing, except among those with European experience. And while penile penetration seems to be the primary focus, some, like the Kgatla and the Azande, report foreplay or genital fondling.

Sexual activity is defined by social and economic context, and cultural sanctions and taboos exact behaviors to maintain the structures of power. There are taboos against discussing sex with men of different generations, or in public, or with the opposite sex; against sexual intercourse at certain times, for example, when a woman is menstruating, or with certain classes of people, such as members of the same or adjacent generations, a husband's brother, or a father's young widow. The postpartum taboo on sexual relations is common in traditional contexts. Among the Yoruba in southwestern Nigeria, until the mid-1970s prolonged abstinence was the norm, and child spacing was accomplished through female sexual abstinence, while the husband sought out other women—prostitutes, girlfriends, or wives. Yet the period of abstinence has been dramatically shortened because men are conceding women's sexual needs.

African notions of sex include mystical ideas, as sex carries magical potency. In perusing central African court records, anthropologist A. L. Epstein found that women filed complaints against husbands engaging in unseemly practices (cunnilingus, intercourse with her when asleep, appropriating her menstrual cloth for success in gambling). To avoid supernatural dangers, one must observe taboos and respect social boundaries. By violating the boundaries, people confuse categories and provoke explosive responses. Extramarital liaisons, pursued by both men and women, represent such a violation, although for men they are widely accepted as more permissible. According to male-defined sexual ideology, most Africans consider that sexual access

to a plurality of women is a male right, while married women are expected to maintain fidelity. In fact, both men and women have rather flexible definitions of marital status. West African men of the elite class have commonly engaged in outside marriages, which are informal though often stable marriage-like unions with women, coincident with the men's formal marriages. Their wives, however, do not have this option and often dare not divorce lest they lose status, so they engage in adultery. Among the Maasai of Kenya, extramarital relations are adulterous when they occur between a woman and any man from an age-set junior to her husband's. They violate group boundaries, disrupting relations among men's age-sets and between men and their wives by upsetting the inequality in social relations. A woman caught in the act is severely punished by her husband. Earlier in the twentieth century, on the Copperbelt, mining compound life was insecure for the wives of miners, so these women sought to stabilize their financial situations, which in many cases included selling their sexual services, while their husbands looked the other way.

In Kenya, Luo men are puritanical about their wives' adultery, unlike the men of the Copperbelt or the Nupe of Nigeria. Nyakyusa women in Malawi and Tanzania must maintain exclusive relations with their husbands except during initiation ceremonies and when they accompany a bride to her husband's house; as long as penetration does not take place, on those occasions husbands can make no complaint. Among the !Kung, where married women regularly take lovers ("Having affairs is one of the things God gave us"), and some affairs are long-term, discretion is advised to avoid fights or marital dissolution. Elsewhere in southern Africa, when men are adulterous and neglect their wives, the women take lovers—but their infidelity is regarded as more serious than the men's.

Sexual surgery is practiced in a variety of African countries, the highest recorded frequencies in Burkina Faso, Djibouti, Eritrea, Ethiopia, Gambia, Mali, Somalia, and Sudan. Variously termed female circumcision, female genital mutilation, sexual surgery, it has gained a prominent place in Western public discourse regarding "the other." The surgery may range from the least extensive, cliteridectomy, simply cutting the hood of the clitoris, to the most radical, infibulation, which aims to leave the woman with as small an opening as possible for the passage of urine and menstrual blood. Many say that the primary rationale for sexual surgery is cultural, religious, for the sake of cleanliness, purity, to control women's sexual passions—to keep the young girl pure, the married woman faithful. But the current debate juxtaposes the defender/opposer view, with some defenders arguing that wider violations of women's rights are not addressed and others that the surgery does not degrade women but in fact "creates" them.

A simple way of dealing with the evidence of extramarital sex is to use some kind of birth control, but the cultural centrality of having babies has obviated its use. In Ghana, for example, and throughout much of Africa, as men and women do not share equally in decisions of a sexual nature, men dominate decisions about contraception. Men do not use condoms because, they believe, condoms inhibit pleasure. And because they believe condoms are meant for illicit sex, men resist using them with regular partners. Yet the majority of men who patronize prostitutes also refuse to use condoms.

SAME-SEX PARTNERS

Using sex as a resource, as a way of negotiating society, of surviving better socially and economically, may not be common in Africa among individuals of the same sex, given the centrality of procreation to economic and social adulthood, but it does exist and there is evidence that it predates European colonization. The age-grade system among the Nyakyusa of Tanzania and Malawi was institutionalized spatially as the basis for village organization; homosexual relations were said to be common within boys' villages, beginning among those of ten to fourteen and continuing until marriage. In pre-European times, Azande boys and youths engaged in gay sex. They also took boy-wives, a legal union based on marriage and following the same taboos, in which they had sex between the thighs. Boy-marriage was given up, it was said, in part due to a breakdown in the sanctions against extramarital sex. According to some accounts, homosexual sex was expected among pubescent Bantu youths in southern Africa, although it was probably rare among adults.

Across the continent among the Hausa in Nigeria, there are men who have constructed a different kind of sexual identity. Known as 'yan daudu, men who act like women, they constitute a gay subculture. Among the Hausa, where there is extreme sexual segregation and men have their work roles and women theirs, 'yan daudu do both: they assume women's roles, although still marry and have children. They present themselves as womanlike without sacrificing a male sexual identity: they cook and sell food, normally the occupational role of women, and they participate in parties, which Hausa men would disdain as not proper. At the same time, they wear men's clothing, they are addressed as men, they marry and have children and they are discrete about their sexual engagement with men. Some 'yan daudu live with karuwai (prostitutes) as a cover.

In the all-male company towns of the Copperbelt and South Africa, homosexual relationships were used as resources. Miners had sexual relationships with boys known as "the wives of the mine." These mine marriages followed a set of rules: they occurred only between senior men and young boys and they were not casual. The "wives" took on women's behavior, carrying out domestic duties for their partners for which they were generously remunerated. The predominant act of coitus was based upon adolescent Nguni, Xhosa, and Zulu premarital sex play; this took place only between the thighs, the senior "breathing out" into the young boy's legs, the latter behaving with womanly decorum by only receiving. (One cannot say, however, that anal sex was not practiced by African men. It is the case that in the Sudan, men penetrate their infibulated wives anally; moreover, beginning in the late nineteenth century nearly one-third of all court cases in Zimbabwe involved sodomy.)

Many of the "wives" agreed to mine marriages because their income enabled them to pay bridewealth at home and become "full men." The boy continuing on in the mine would at some point let his husband know he wanted his own "wife," perhaps tired of his nonejaculatory role. Thus for many, homosexuality was one phase in the life cycle. In the late nineteenth century, these mine marriages almost came to be regarded as the norm in South Africa, and they also emerged among Mozambican workers in the early twentieth century. The mine administration condoned the marriages to steady productivity. In South African mine culture at the beginning of the twenty-first century, men speak of their need for sex as an important aspect of their masculinity within the context of dangerous living and working conditions. Men consider sex important to their physical well-being, and as they are away from wives and girlfriends, they negotiate sexual identities as needed—including homosexual relationships.

There is less in the literature about lesbian sex, but it too is recorded and has helped women negotiate society. In traditional society, !Kung girls began to explore sex through genital touching among themselves. Married Kgatla women masturbated one another. Lesbianism is recorded in large polygynous Azande families as a bond of love and friendship. Lesotho, like the Copperbelt, has a male migrant labor system, which periodically removes men for long periods, makes women economically insecure, destabilizes marriages, and has encouraged the development of close bonds among women. Preadolescent and adolescent girls participate in a structured friendship called "babies and mummies," which enables girls to play out their developing sexuality in romantic dramas when heterosexual involvements are forbidden. As in the mine marriages, there is asymmetry, which, along with the physical intimacy involved in the friendship, suggests a similarity to marriage. But unlike male homosexual relationships they involve fictive kinship, not marriage, do more than provide sexual release, and are structurally compatible with heterosexuality.

In Mombasa, Kenya, a Swahili Muslim society where homosexuals are open about their behavior, men may maintain a heterosexual marriage and homosexual relationships simultaneously, whereas women may substitute lesbianism for heterosexuality. It is estimated that at least 50 percent of Swahili women, primarily older ones, live apart from a husband, on their own or supported by him. Like men, women develop a circle of dependents, some of whom may be homosexual men who enjoy being around women because the latter treat them well. Women of lowly birth are drawn to lesbianism because it provides financial security or escape from an unhappy marriage. A woman need not be a lesbian to wield power, but society regards this attached lifestyle as more respectable than her living on her own.

Of related interest is the institution of woman-woman marriage. Unknown outside of Africa, it is practiced in western Africa (mainly Nigeria), South Africa, eastern Africa, and Sudan. As reported in the literature, the female husband marries but does not have sexual intercourse with her wife. In all cases, the female husband is a "social male": for the southern Bantu in terms of political status, among the Nandi of Kenya to produce male heirs for themselves, among the Igbo (Ibo) of southeastern Nigeria to accumulate wealth and prestige and produce male heirs. As in mine marriages, the female husband is the senior of the couple, but while she does not engage in sex with men, her wife does.

Arguments that homosexual relations represent an interim break in the "normal" routine of heterosexuality leading to marriage due to the scarcity of marriageable women, that they are for status and not sexual pleasure, that partnerships like female-female marriage have no sexual content, have come to be being questioned through the lens of queer theory. (This theory addresses the ways in which heterosexual-homosexual binaries operate and contests both homophobia and the notion of unified identity.) New explorations of homosexuality, in southern Africa especially, have also been motivated by Zimbabwe president Robert Mugabe's scathing attack on homosexuals at the opening of the 1995 Zimbabwe International Book Fair. Did homosexuality exist in southern Africa prior to the coming of colonial rule? Scholars like Marc Epprecht, examining court records, offer as proof the appearance of homosexual "crimes" in the first year that the colonial courts operated. Nearly 90 percent of all cases of homosexual assaults involved African men or boys. Moreover, Zimbabwe court records reveal long-term homosexual relationships with real ties of affection, where women were not scarce and many of the accused were locally married with children.

COMMERCIAL SEX
Prostitution has been prevalent and visible in African cities since the nineteenth century, rooted in the colonial past and poverty. It is a way in which women have used and manipulated their sexuality because they have been denied active participation in the economy. During the colonial period, men migrated to the mines and plantations for work;

women followed to sell sex. Labor migration carries with it the ethos of multiple sex partners, the change from polygyny to multiple girlfriends (functional polygyny), and extramarital sex as normative. While there is evidence in the literature and in ideal tales of the social regulation of (especially female) sexual behavior, all sorts of factors of cultural change have had a weakening effect. Prostitution itself was encouraged by migratory labor patterns. In Nairobi, where marriage was unstable, women became prostitutes out of economic necessity. As a result, they profited socially and economically, while avoiding male control. Prostitution can be characterized as a way of playing sexual politics; it can also be characterized as domestic labor. In colonial Nairobi, *malaya* and *waziwazi* supplied domestic services (sex, companionship, bath water, beer, cooked food) that made life tolerable to men living in cramped quarters on low wages.

With modernization, better roads, and export economies, trucking routes opened. The open road has helped further establish prostitution. Truck drivers are away from home for long periods of time, and prostitutes are located in bars and hotels along major truck routes. With independence, migration from rural areas increased and prostitution did as well. Africa has urbanization without industrialization, so that wage-sector jobs are scarce. And women often have less education than men. Thus, women turn to informal-sector jobs: trade in goods and services, legal and illegal. Prostitution is one of the main roles to have emerged for women in urban Africa. In Muslim northern Nigeria, where marriage is normative for Hausa women but rarely stable, women become *karuwai* out of economic need because they do not want to be married; in other words, prostitution provides an alternative lifestyle. Always available, prostitutes subvert the culturally prescribed seclusion of women.

See also **Childbearing; Disease: HIV/AIDS, Social and Political Aspects; Disease: Sexually Transmitted; Gender; Initiation; Labor: Industrial and Mining; Labor: Migration; Marriage Systems; Mugabe, Robert; Prostitution.**

BIBLIOGRAPHY

Ahlberg, Beth M. "Is There a Distinct African Sexuality? A Critical Response to Caldwell et al." *Africa* 64, no. 2 (1994): 220–242.

Caldwell, John C.; Pat Caldwell; and Pat Quiggin. "The Social Context of AIDS in Sub-Saharan Africa." *Population and Development Review* 15 (1989): 185–234.

Caplan, Pat, ed. *The Cultural Construction of Sexuality.* London: Tavistock Publications, 1987.

Evans-Pritchard, E. E. "Some Notes on Zande Sex Habits." *American Anthropologist* 75 (1973): 171–175.

Gaudio, Rudolf Pell. *Allah Made Us: Sexual Outlaws in an Islamic African City.* Malden, MA: Blackwell, forthcoming.

Green, Edward C. *AIDS and STDs in Africa: Bridging the Gap between Traditional Healing and Modern Medicine.* Boulder, CO: Westview Press, 1994.

Heald, Suzette. "The Power of Sex: Some Reflections on the Caldwells' 'African Sexuality' Thesis." *Africa* 65 (1995): 489–505.

Kalipeni, Ezekiel; Susan Craddock; Joseph R. Oppong; and Jayati Ghosh; eds. *HIV and AIDS in Africa: Beyond Epidemiology.* Malden, MA: Blackwell Publishing, 2004.

Lane, Sandra D., and Robert Rubinstein. "Judging the Other: Responding to Traditional Female Genital Surgeries." *Hastings Center Report* 26 (1996): 31–40.

LeVine, Robert A. "Gusii Sex Offenses: A Study in Social Control." *American Anthropologist* 61 (1959): 965–990.

Moodie, T. Dunbar, with Vivian Ndatshe. *Going for Gold: Men, Mines, and Migration.* Berkeley: University of California Press, 1994.

Runganga, Agnes; Marian Pitts; and John McMaster. "The Use of Herbal and Other Agents to Enhance Sexual Experience." *Social Science and Medicine* 35 (1992): 1037–1042.

Schapera, Isaac. *Married Life in an African Tribe.* Evanston, IL: Northwestern University Press, 1966.

Shostak, Marjorie. *Nisa: The Life and Words of a !Kung Woman.* New York: Vintage Books, 1981.

Walker, Liz; Graeme Reid; and Morna Cornell. *Waiting to Happen: HIV/AIDS in South Africa, the Bigger Picture.* Boulder CO: Lynne Rienner, 2004.

White, Luise. *The Comforts of Home: Prostitution in Colonial Nairobi.* Chicago: University of Chicago Press, 1990.

DEBORAH PELLOW

SEYCHELLES

This entry includes the following articles:
GEOGRAPHY AND ECONOMY
SOCIETY AND CULTURES
HISTORY AND POLITICS

GEOGRAPHY AND ECONOMY

The Seychelles are an archipelago of about 115 islands scattered over 622,000 square miles of the western Indian Ocean between 4 degrees and 11 degrees south latitude and 46 degrees and 56 degrees east longitude. The central Mahé group consists of some forty mountainous, granitic islands while the outlying islands of the Aldabra, Amirante, and Farquhar groups are coralline. The largest island is Mahé, situated 995 miles east of Mombasa, Kenya, with a surface area of 91 square miles. More than 80 percent of all Seychellois live on Mahé; most of the rest of the country's population lives on the neighboring islands of Praslin and La Digue, 26 miles to the northeast. Including the Aldabra lagoon, the country's surface area totals 175 square miles.

The islands' climate is tropical-oceanic. Temperatures vary little during the year, ranging from a minimum of 76 degrees Fahrenheit to a maximum of 86 degrees Fahrenheit, with humidity levels averaging from 75 to 80 percent. The amount of rainfall varies widely from island to island; on Mahé the average annual rainfall at sea level is 90 inches, but increases to 140 inches on the island's mountain slopes. Only five percent of the islands' land surface area is arable, while another 45 percent is suitable for tree crops. The remainder of the islands' surface area is forested or comprised of beach areas.

From its initial settlement in the late eighteenth century until the 1970s, the Seychellois economy depended on agriculture, with an emphasis on the production of food crops for local consumption and small quantities of export commodities. Cotton was the principal export during the late eighteenth and early nineteenth centuries. Competition from American producers led to the demise of the cotton industry during the 1820s, with the result that local plantation owners turned to coconut production, initially for oil and then, at the beginning of the twentieth century, increasingly for copra. Other cash crops included vanilla (the

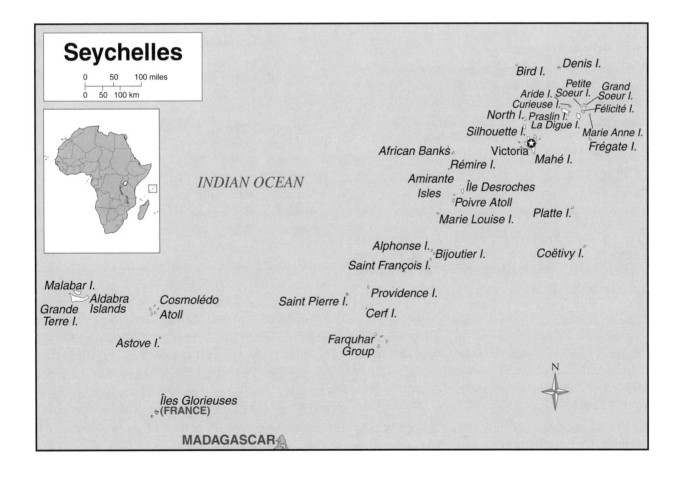

importance of which dwindled sharply after disease obliterated the crop in 1904), cinnamon, and patchouli.

The islands' economy remained dependent into the 1960s on grants-in-aid from the United Kingdom and the exportation of copra and cinnamon. The opening of an international airport on Mahé in 1971, coupled with the islands' fabled natural beauty, quickly made tourism the most important sector of the economy. By the twenty-first century, tourism provided more than 70 percent of all foreign exchange earnings. Beginning in the late 1980s commercial tuna fishing and canning also became economically important. A decline in the number of tourists coming to the islands in the wake of the Gulf War of 1990–1991 and again after the terrorist attacks on the United States in 2001 highlighted the extent to which the local tourist industry was vulnerable to factors beyond the country's control. As a result, the government has sought more recently to lessen the country's dependence on tourism by encouraging farming, fishing, and small-scale manufacturing.

See also **Mauritius: Geography and Economy; Plantation Economies and Societies; Slave Trades.**

BIBLIOGRAPHY

Benedict, Marion, and Burton Benedict. *Men, Women, and Money in Seychelles.* Berkeley: University of California Press, 1982.

Sauer, Jonathon D. *Plants and Man on the Seychelles Coast: A Study in Historical Biogeography.* Madison: University of Wisconsin Press, 1967.

RICHARD B. ALLEN

SOCIETY AND CULTURES

The Seychelles had no permanent human population until the islands were colonized in 1770. The modern Seychellois population of some 81,000 persons traces its ancestry to the peoples of Africa and Europe and, to a lesser extent, India and China. The islands' earliest settlers included small numbers of French colonists, principally from the Ile de Bourbon (Réunion), soldiers from the Ile de France and Pondichéry in southern India, and free persons of color, many of whom were of southern Indian origin.

Slaves accompanied the earliest colonists, and during the late eighteenth and early nineteenth centuries other bondmen and women were imported into the islands to supply the labor needed on local plantations. The total number of slaves imported into the Seychelles during the French era remains unknown, but by c. 1808–1810 the islands housed approximately 2,700–2,800 slaves who comprised more than 90 percent of the local population. The slave population increased substantially during the 1810s when the islands played an important role in the illegal slave trade to the Mascarenes, reaching a high of 6,740 in a total reported population of 7,022 in 1822, before beginning to decline in size. In 1834, on the eve of emancipation, the islands contained 4,673 slaves. Like those who reached the Mascarenes during the late eighteenth and early nineteenth centuries, most of these enslaved men, women, and children were exported originally from Madagascar, Mozambique, and the Swahili coast.

During the nineteenth and early twentieth centuries small numbers of Indian immigrants reached the Seychelles, usually via Mauritius. Most of these immigrants were men who appear to have come originally from South India, and many subsequently married or cohabited with local women. Small numbers of Chinese also arrived in the islands during and after the 1920s. These immigrants also tended to marry or cohabit with local women.

Anthropological fieldwork during the 1960s and 1970s characterized the modern Seychellois population as one marked by a high degree of cultural homogeneity. Seychellois culture was described as essentially a variant of European culture with strong French overtones. The absence of significant African cultural traits in the modern Seychellois population is attributed to the islands' geographical isolation and various demographic, economic and social developments that encouraged the widespread adoption of European cultural traits by the local slave population during the eighteenth and early nineteenth centuries. The cultural homogeneity of the Seychellois population is illustrated by the fact that the islands' inhabitants share a common language—Creole—which is a French-based patois, and many customs, especially those surrounding important rites of passage including birth, marriage, and death. Seychellois also share a

République des Seychelles (Republic of Seychelles)

Population:	81,895 (2007 est.)
Area:	455 sq. km (175 sq. mi.)
Official languages:	English and French
Languages:	Creole, English, French
National currency:	Seychelles rupee
Principal religions:	Roman Catholic 87%, Anglican Church 7%, other Christians 3%, other 3%
Capital:	Victoria (est. pop. 24,970 in 2002)
Main islands:	Mahé, Praslin, La Digue
Annual rainfall:	on Mahé varies from 2,300 mm (90 in.) at sea level to 3,560 mm (140 in.) on mountain slopes
Principal geographical features:	*Mountains:* Mahé Mountains (Morne Seychellois, Trois Freères)
Economy:	*GDP per capita:* US$7,800 (2006)
Principal products and exports:	*Agricultural:* coconuts, cinnamon, vanilla, sweet potatoes, cassava (tapioca), bananas, poultry, tuna *Manufacturing:* processing of coconuts and vanilla, coir (coconut fiber) rope, boat building, printing, furniture; beverages. Economy depends on upscale tourism.
Government:	Dependency of Mauritius, 1770–1903. French colony, 1756–1794. British colony, 1794–1976. Became independent republic within the British Commonwealth in 1976. Constitution approved in 1976. New constitutions adopted in 1979 and 1993. Multiparty democracy. President elected for 5-year term, with 3-term maximum, by universal suffrage. 34-member unicameral Assemblée du Peuple elected by universal suffrage, with 25 directly elected members, and 9 allocated on a proportional basis. President appoints Council of Ministers. 23 administrative districts.
Heads of state since independence:	1976–1977: President James R. Mancham 1977–2004: President France Albert René 2004–: President James Michel
Armed forces:	President is commander in chief. *Army:* 800 *Coast guard:* 250 *Paramilitary:* 1,000
Transportation:	Interisland ferry provides transportation between islands. *Roads:* 458 km (285 mi.), 96% paved *Port:* Victoria *National airline:* Air Seychelles (40% British-owned) *Airports:* Seychelles International Airport at Pointe Laru on Mahé. 14 smaller airports and airstrips among the islands.
Media:	Main periodicals include *Nation, Le Seychellois, The People, Regar, Seychelles Today, Seychelles Weekend Nation, L'Écho des Îles, The Independent, Seychelles Nation.* Radio Television Seychelles is state-controlled. Far East Broadcasting Association (a Christian mission outreach) operates Far East Broadcasting Seychelles. There are 2 radio broadcast stations and 2 television stations.
Literacy and education:	*Total literacy rate:* 87.5% (2006). Primary education is free and compulsory though Grade 10. There is no university; government scholarships for study in the Commonwealth. 3 vocational schools: Seychelles Polytechnic, Conservatory of Music and Dance, Teacher Training College.

common religious tradition; the great majority of the population is Roman Catholic.

Seychellois working-class family structure, like that in the West Indies and portions of the United States, has been described as matrifocal or matricentric. Social status is determined by a number of variables, including an individual's occupation, land ownership, ancestry, and participation in activities that are deemed to be prestigious. Fieldwork during the 1970s highlighted changes in the class structure of Seychellois society following the rapid development of the islands' tourism industry, and the emergence of heightened senses of class consciousness, especially among the islands' middle and lower classes.

See also **Creoles; Languages: Creoles and Pidgins; Mauritius: Society and Cultures; Slave Trades; Slavery and Servile Institutions.**

BIBLIOGRAPHY

Benedict, Burton. *People of the Seychelles*, 3rd edition. London: Her Majesty's Stationery Office, 1970.

Benedict, Marion, and Burton Benedict. *Men, Women, and Money in Seychelles*. Berkeley: University of California Press, 1982.

RICHARD B. ALLEN

HISTORY AND POLITICS

The Seychelles had no permanent human population until the late eighteenth century. Cartographic evidence suggests that the islands, like the Mascarene Islands of Mauritius and Réunion to the south, may have been visited by Arab seafarers before the sixteenth century. The first European visitors were probably the Portuguese, who reached the islands early in the sixteenth century. A British East India Company expedition spent ten days in the islands in 1609. Except for possible occasional visits by pirates who operated in the western Indian Ocean during the late seventeenth and early eighteenth centuries, the islands continued to be ignored until 1742 when the governor of the Ile de France (Mauritius) sent an expedition under the leadership of Lazare Picault to explore the archipelago. Picault subsequently returned to the islands in 1744. In 1756, the French formally claimed possession of the islands they named in honor of Comte Moreau de Séchelles, comptroller general of finances for Louis XV. However, the Seychelles remained uninhabited until 1770, when a small colony was established on Mahé at the instigation of Pierre Poivre, the *intendant* (comptroller) of the Ile de France, as part of a program to encourage the cultivation of spices.

During the Anglo-French wars of the revolutionary and Napoleonic eras, the Seychelles, a dependency of the Ile de France, remained undefended by French forces. The islands capitulated to the British on seven different occasions between 1794 and 1805; the local commandant, Jean-Baptiste Queau de Quinssy, kept a large blue flag bearing the words *Seychelles Capitulation* ready to be hoisted should British ships appear on the scene. The islands were ceded formally to Britain in 1814 by the Treaty of Paris, and remained a dependency of Mauritius until 1903, when they were designated as a separate British Crown colony.

During the late eighteenth century the Seychelles often served as a refreshment station for ships carrying slaves from Mozambique and East Africa's Swahili coast to Mauritius and Réunion. Following the abolition of the legal slave trade to Mauritius in 1811, outlying islands such as Providence Island in the Farquhar group served as a staging area from which significant numbers of slaves were smuggled into Mauritius until the mid-1820s. Slaves were also introduced clandestinely into the Seychelles where they underwent a certain amount of acculturation before being shipped to Mauritius under the guise of legally transferring slaves within the colony. More than 3,400 slaves reached Mauritius from the Seychelles under these circumstances between 1818 and 1827. During the second half of the nineteenth century, the islands were used as a dumping ground for two to three thousand slaves liberated by Royal Navy ships charged with suppressing the slave trade in the western Indian Ocean.

The Seychelles remained a rather neglected dependency of Mauritius throughout the nineteenth century. The islands' geographical isolation made them an ideal locale where several deposed Southeast Asian and African rulers were exiled by British authorities during the late nineteenth and early twentieth centuries. These exiles included a former king of the Ashanti in West Africa and former rulers of the kingdoms of Buganda and Bunyoro in what is now Uganda, all of whom lost their thrones during the so-called scramble for African colonies that took place during the last two decades of the nineteenth century. The islands also housed more than 1,000 prisoners of war captured by the British during the Boer War (1899–1902). In 1903 the Seychelles became a separate British Crown colony with its own governor who reported to the colonial office in London.

The Seychelles gained independence from Great Britain on June 29, 1976, as an independent republic within the Commonwealth under a constitution that provided for a democratically elected president and a multiparty national assembly. On June 5, 1977, the government led by James R. Mancham and the Seychelles Democratic Party, which had assumed office at independence, was overthrown in a coup d'état by the Seychelles People's United Party led by France Albert René. The new regime, which styled itself as a revolutionary socialist government, established a one-party system that was sanctioned by a new constitution promulgated in 1979. During the 1980s several plots to overthrow the René government were suppressed. In 1991, under increasing pressure from Great Britain and France, the government agreed to a return to multiparty politics. In June 1993 Seychelles' electorate approved a new constitution.

The following month René was reelected president and his renamed Seychelles People's Progressive Front (SSPF) won a decisive victory in the legislative election. Subsequent elections maintained René and the SSPF in power. In 2004 René resigned from office and Vice President James Michel became president.

See also **Mauritius: History and Politics; Slavery and Servile Institutions.**

BIBLIOGRAPHY

Allen, Richard B. "Licentious and Unbridled Proceedings: The Illegal Slave Trade to Mauritius and the Seychelles during the Early Nineteenth Century." *Journal of African History* 42, no. 1 (2001): 91–116.

Franda, Marcus. *The Seychelles: Unquiet Islands.* Boulder, CO: Westview Press, 1982.

Scarr, Deryck. *Seychelles since 1770: History of a Slave and Post-Slavery Society.* London: Hurst and Company, 2000.

RICHARD B. ALLEN

SHAABAN ROBERT (1909–1962).

The Tanzanian poet and writer of the Swahili language Sheikh Shaaban Robert was born at Vibambani, a village south of Machui, six miles south of Tanga in then German East Africa. He was educated in Dar es Salaam from 1922 to 1926. He was a pioneer in the development of Swahili literature and introduced the *insha* (essay) into the language. Jan Knappert wrote of him, "Sheikh Shaaban Robert opened up new ways of expression, new modes of thought (and) will for ever be known as a turning point in the evolution of the Swahili language. His work will remain a link between the classical literature of the past and the modern Swahili of the future." Sheikh Shaaban Robert is regarded as one of the greatest Swahili poets and writers of the twentieth century. His collection of literary works includes the Swahili translation of the *Rubaiyat* of Omar Khayyam. In the early twenty-first century, his collected works are read in every institution where Swahili literature is taught.

Sheikh Shaaban Robert, who considered himself an artist and a philosopher, did not claim ancestorship from Persia or from Arabia as did many upper-class Swahili of his era. He affirmed that both of his parents were of the Mganga lineage of the Yao people of northern Mozambique, an inland origin often associated with uncultured slaves. According to J. W. T. Allen, who collected his works and who interviewed his only sister, Sheikh Shaaban Robert was not his real name, but either a mispronunciation of his actual name or a name given to him when he was at school. He himself sometimes wrote his name as "Roberts."

His career was as a civil servant in the British colonial government in Tanganyika, now Tanzania, employed first as a customs clerk in Pangani from 1926 to 1944. From 1944 to 1946, he was in the service of the Veterinary Department in Longido. From 1946 to 1952, he was employed in the Provincial Commissioner's Office in Tanga. From 1952 until his retirement in 1960, he worked in the Department of Land Survey in Tanga.

Besides his employment in the civil service, Robert was a member of the East African Swahili Committee, the East African Literature Bureau, the Tanganyika Languages Board, and the Tanga Township Authority, which later became Tanga Town Council. He received the Margaret Wrong Memorial Prize for his literary works and was also awarded the medal of the Knights of the British Empire.

Sheikh Shaaban Robert's poetry often appeared in the *Mambo Leo*, a monthly newspaper that was published by the Tanganyika colonial government. Among the more important of his books are *Maisha Yangu na Baada ya Miaka Hamsini* (1949), *Kusadikika, Nchi Iliyo Angani* (1951), *Masomo Yenye Adili* (1959), *Insha na Mashairi* (1967), Utubora Mkulima (1968), *Tenzi za Marudio Mema na Omar Khayyam* (1952), *Kufikirika* (1967), *Adili na Nduguze* (1952), and *Utenzi Warita na Uhuru* (1967).

See also **Literature; Tanzania: Society and Cultures.**

BIBLIOGRAPHY

Allen, J. W. T. *Siku ya Watenzi Wote.* London: Nelson, 1968.

Robert, Shaaban. *The Poetry of Shaaban Robert,* sel. and trans. Clemet Ndulute. Tanzania: Dar es Salaam University Press, 1994.

HASSAN ADAM

SHAKA ZULU (c. 1790–1828). Shaka, a minor son of the Zulu chief Senzangkhona, succeeded to the chiefship with the support of the paramount of the neighboring Mthethwa, Dingiswayo kaJobe, on the coastal hills of northeastern modern South Africa (KwaZulu-Natal Province). When Dingiswayo was defeated and killed by his rival Ndwandwe, Shaka took the lead in establishing a firm regional basis of resistance to the Ndwandwe. Self-preservation was the initial impetus in the development of the subsequently very powerful Zulu state that came, under Shaka's leadership, to dominate the Phongolo Mzimkhulu region. Numerous small chiefdoms accepted Zulu overlordship.

The labor power brought under Zulu authority was drafted into *amabutho* (regiments), whose

Portrait thought to be of the legendary soldier, Shaka Zulu (1790–1828), awaiting battle. Shaka is credited with transforming the Zulu from a primitive tribe to a powerful nation. His methods of reform, military tactics, and innovation are widely regarded by scholars. THE GRANGER COLLECTION, LTD.

exclusive focus of allegiance was the Zulu leader. The *amabutho* were able first to repel and later to defeat the Ndwandwe, and then to raid and extract tribute from neighboring and subordinate communities. In this way the power and wealth of the Zulu rulers expanded rapidly, and the Zulu became the predominant regional power in the 1820s. Shaka remains a stereotyped, often mythologized figure, credited with setting off a half-century-long wave of violence in southeastern Africa that eventually reached as far west as the upper Zambezi and north into modern Tanzania (sometimes, but controversially, termed the *mfecane*) represented in modern popular and academic literature variously as an innovative genius and a vicious tyrant. Although he was an autocratic leader of exceptional talents, he was also a product of the broader social and political upheavals of his times.

See also **Dingiswayo.**

BIBLIOGRAPHY

Laband, J. P. C. *Rope of Sand: The Rise and Fall of the Zulu Kingdom in the Nineteenth Century.* Johannesburg: Jonathan Ball, 1995.

Taylor, Stephen. *Shaka's Children: A History of the Zulu People.* London: HarperCollins, 1995.

Wright, Carolyn, and Carolyn Hamilton. "Traditions and Transformations: The Phongolo-Mzimkhulu Region in the Late Eighteenth and Early Nineteeenth Centuries." In *Natal and Zululand from Earliest Times to 1910: A New History*, ed. Andrew Duminy and Bill Guest. Pietermaritzburg, South Africa: University of Natal Press/Shuter & Shooter, 1989.

CAROLYN HAMILTON

SHEMBE, ISAIAH (1870–1935). Very little is known, with any accuracy, about the life-history of the Zulu prophet-healer Isaiah Shembe, and what has been passed on in oral tradition among his followers in the Church of the Nazaretha, which he founded in 1911, has assumed mythical proportions. The slim historical record reveals that, as a young man, Shembe underwent a Pauline-type conversion to a life of abstinence, guided by revelations from Jehovah. As a migrant worker, he became a wandering preacher, healer, and exorcist. Joining a separatist African Baptist Church in 1906, he took instruction as a catechist and was eventually ordained a minister but broke away to found his own church in order to observe the Old Testament (Saturday) Sabbath.

While incorporating aspects of Zulu religion into his belief system, he consciously modeled his church on Old Testament precedent, and in particular on references to the Nazarites. He died in 1935 and is buried at the "High Place," the enclosed village near Durban, which he established as the center of his church. His tomb became a place of pilgrimage, and the surrounding area is called "paradise," the archetype of heaven on earth, the symbol of salvation attained. Accounts of Shembe's miraculous healing and clairvoyance circulate among the faithful and closely parallel those attributed to Christ, thus conveying the impression that he is revered as an African messiah. His church has flourished under the successive leadership of two of his sons and, despite suffering a schism, remains intact under the direction of his youngest son, Amos. Its continued success owes much to the legacy of Shembe's spiritual magnetism, his adaptation of Christianity to traditional Zulu forms, and the relevance of his vision to the needs of the poor and oppressed.

See also **Christianity; Prophetic Movements.**

BIBLIOGRAPHY

Hexham, Irving, and G. C. Oosthuizen, eds. *The Story of Isaiah Shembe*, trans. Hans-Jürgen Becken. Lewiston, NY: Edwin Mellen Press, 1996.

Oosthuizen, G. C. *The Theology of a South African Messiah: An Analysis of the Hymnal of the Church of the Nazarites.* Leiden: E. J. Brill, 1967.

Sundkler, Bengt. *Bantu Prophets in South Africa*, 2nd edition. New York: Oxford University Press, 1961.

Vilakazi, Absolom, Bongani Mthethwa, and Mthembeni Mpanza. *Shembe: The Revitalization of African Society.* Johannesburg: Skotaville, 1986.

JAMES P. KIERNAN

SHYAAM AMBUL ANGOONG (r. c. 1625–1640).

Shyaam aMbul aNgoong was the semi-legendary founder of the Kuba kingdom of central Africa. There are three different stories regarding Mbul aNgoong's origins. Some say he was foreign, from the Kwilu River area to the west,

in the Mbun or Ding territories, and illegitimately appropriated the ruling Matoon dynasty's legacy in order to stake his claim to power. The second version holds that he was a legitimate descendant of the local Matoon ruling clan, who was born during Misha miShyaang's reign. The third account maintains that aMbul aNgoong, a princess not descended from the Kuba ruling aristocracy, who is generally believed to be Shyaam's mother, was not truly his mother. In this version, aMbul aNgoong is said to have taken her female slave's son, killed the mother, and claimed Shyaam as her own in order to groom him to become the *nyim* (the Kuba paramount chief).

Mbul aNgoong impressed upon Shyaam that he was the rightful *nyim* and that the reigning *nyim*, Misha miShyaang, was both an impostor and a foreigner. While he was encouraged to believe in his kingly destiny by Mbul aNgoong, Shyaam was further persuaded by his personal opinion that Misha miShyaang was ill-mannered and boorish, unfit to rule. Upon learning of Shyaam's ambition to usurp the throne, Misha miShyaang offered a reward for Shyaam's head. Shyaam responded by disguising himself, feigning madness, and fleeing his homeland in order to search for magical charms that would enable him to claim the throne. Shyaam found refuge among the nearby Kel, thus beginning a tradition that is still in effect: even in the early twenty-first century, any enemy of the Kuba *nyim* can find shelter amid the Kel.

Shyaam then went to Mbaanc, to a man named Kaan Kabady, who hid him. Misha miShyaang asked Kaan where Shyaam was, and Kaan replied, "Underground." Misha presumed that this meant Shyaam was dead and left satisfied after he had subjected Kaan to a ritual poison ordeal in order to be sure he was telling the truth. Kaan survived the test, and Shyaam emerged from his underground hiding place with a plan. He obtained the magical Nyeeng mask, which is said to have changed shape and height according to its spectators' will, and went back to Mbaanc, where he wore the mask and danced before a crowd. The awestruck people of Mbaanc spread news of the mask to the capital, and Shyaam was invited to dance there before Misha miShyaang. In the capital, Shyaam buried magic charms in the ground to help him achieve his goal of the kingship. Unrecognized by the people, he was repeatedly invited back to dance, wearing the mask.

The *nyim* eventually became frightened of the man in the mask and fled. Soon after, Shyaam was invited to become *nyim* in his place.

Behind these stories, someone remembered in these ways as clever and powerful developed the political institutions of the Kuba people of southwestern Republic of Congo, which became well known for their elegance and wealth at the end of the nineteenth century. At this point, which was probably around 1625, Shyaam was an older man. In order to protect himself from rivals who aspired to his position as *nyim*, he repeatedly relocated the capital. With his reputation for magic, Shyaam is also given credit for the Kuba's many art forms.

See also **Dance; Social Meaning; Kingship; Masks and Masquerades.**

BIBLIOGRAPHY

Vansina, Jan. "L'influence du mode de comprehension historique d'une civilisation sur des traditions d'origine: 'example kuba." *Bulletin de l'Académie Royale des Sciences d'Outre-Mer* 2 (1972).

SARAH VALDEZ

SIERRA LEONE

This entry includes the following articles:
GEOGRAPHY AND ECONOMY
SOCIETY AND CULTURES
HISTORY AND POLITICS

GEOGRAPHY AND ECONOMY

Sierra Leone is a small country of approximately five million people, occupying a land area of 27,699 miles in the western bulge of the African continent. Its varied relief includes coastal swamps rising to a mountainous region toward the northeast, where the highest peak, the Bintumane, rises to 6,390 feet. Although half of the country is below 500 feet, less than 3 percent is above 2,000 feet. Nine rivers, flowing generally in a southeasterly direction, provide water and an increasingly exploitable source of hydroelectricity to Sierra Leone. Seasonal rainfall, generally between October and April, can amount to over 200 inches annually in higher elevations. In lower areas the annual average is 150 inches.

Much of the forest vegetation has been denuded, with an estimated 6.2 percent of forested land area remaining at the turn of the twenty-first century. Large areas of grassland mixed with farm bush now dominate the landscape, as well as coastal riverine swamps that support agriculture.

There are four administrative regions in Sierra Leone. The Western Area, which includes the capital, Freetown, is nationally the central place for administration and services. There is also the Northern Province headquartered in Makeni, the Southern Province based at Bo Town, and the Eastern Province centered on the diamond-mining town of Kenema. The provinces are split into twelve administrative districts, which in turn count for 184 further subdivisions, or chiefdoms. Paramount chiefs—heirs of traditional

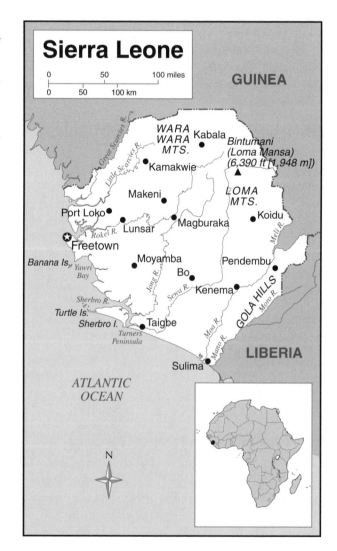

authority—work with District Officers (public officials in charge of each district) to supervise these chiefdoms. District Councils, with elected officials, provide some broad supervision and social services.

The economy was ravaged by a civil war from 1991 to 2001, and many of the services and revenue sources have picked up since the end of the war. Agriculture was traditionally the backbone of the economy, with over 60 percent of the population engaged in this sector. Production follows a typically auto-subsistence pattern primarily in rice and some root crops. It also includes tree crops, such as coffee and cocoa, that were introduced during colonial rule in the first half of the twentieth century. Soon after independence in 1961, export crops constituted over 20 percent of Sierra Leone's total exports. Over time, agricultural production saw a steady decline to the point where, by the 1970s, Sierra Leone became a net importer of rice, its staple food. This had to do partly with the diamond boom starting in the 1950s that withdrew a substantial segment of the workforce from agriculture. Subsequently, the civil war and the government's preference for imported rice further aggravated the situation, causing food imports to rise to over 30 percent of Sierra Leone's total imports. The civil war also drastically affected cocoa and coffee production, as trees were destroyed during the war. Only in the first decade of the twenty-first century did this sector begin to show about 5 percent growth.

Minerals, notably diamonds, gold, rutile, and bauxite, accounted for about 65 percent of the country's total domestic exports up to 1980. A downward slide influenced by smuggling and the civil war led to negative exports of these commodities by the end of the twentieth century. In the early twenty-first century, mining is being re-established: rutile and bauxite mining has resumed, and attention is being placed on deep-shaft diamond mining.

The Sierra Fisheries remained a prominent contributor to the economy until the civil war damaged the fishing infrastructure, reducing production to about 50 percent of prewar levels.

The value of the local currency, the leone, also declined steadily. It stood at two leones to the U.S. dollar in the early 1980s and declined to Le55 to the dollar by 1986. By 1991, just before the civil war, the rate was Le900 to one U.S. dollar and stood at Le3000 to the dollar by 2005. Whereas some of this decline is due to corruption, it is also partly due to the civil war, the impact of international finance capital, and unfruitful policies adopted under pressures imposed by international organizations.

With low salaries and marked unemployment, the postwar economy has seen the growth of a strong informal sector, particularly in Freetown which absorbs a large sector of the unemployed. This has been encouraged by the demobilization of former rebel fighters who were taught skills they now use in self-employment, or in working for unregistered contractors and other small business ventures. NGOs and the government—through the National Commission for Social Action (NaCSA)—sponsor microfinance schemes, particularly for women. Early twenty-first century reports indicate that the loans, though low-key (at 100,000 leones, the equivalent of forty U.S. dollars), show good recovery rates and have already benefited over 30,000 women.

See also **Aid and Development; Ecosystems; Energy; Freetown; Geography and the Study of Africa; Metals and Minerals; Production Strategies: Agriculture; Warfare: Civil Wars.**

BIBLIOGRAPHY

Cleeve, Emmanuel. *Multinational Enterprises in Development: The Mining Industry of Sierra Leone.* Brookfield, VT: S.I. Ashgate Publishing, 1997.

Fyle, C. Magbaily, ed. *The State and the Provision of Social Services in Sierra Leone Since Independence, 1961–1991.* Dakar, Senegal: CODESRIA, 1993.

Fyle, C. Magbaily, ed. *Historical Dictionary of Sierra Leone,* new edition. New York: Scarecrow, 2006.

Zac-Williams, Alfred. *Tributors, Supporters and Merchant Capital: Mining and Underdevelopment in Sierra Leone.* Aldershot, U.K.: 1995.

C. MAGBAILY FYLE

SOCIETY AND CULTURES

Sierra Leone is located on the Guinea coast of the Atlantic Ocean, in western Africa. A British Crown colony from 1808, it achieved political independence on April 27, 1961. The country is eight degrees north of the equator, sharing political borders with Guinea and Liberia; it runs some 200 miles east to west and north to south, for a total area of approximately 28,000 square miles. A population of 6 million live scattered in a number of geopolitical zones. The most clearly delineated region is the mountainous peninsula area in and around the capital, Freetown. But Freetown and its contiguous areas are far from the defining features of this country. Freetown, originally a home for repatriated slaves, is historically, hence politically, tied to the interior through extensive trade plied along coastal areas, inland waters, estuaries, and rivers. An extensive low coastal plain runs north to south, connecting the peoples of the rainforest in the south to the peoples of the rolling grasslands, mountains, and savanna of the north. While Sierra Leone's overall population density is some sixty people per square mile, its demographics and density are uneven. Most citizens live in Freetown and in the southern and eastern provinces. The northern region remains underpopulated and politically estranged.

In general, Sierra Leone's people are warm and welcoming. They are rich in national identity and natural resources. But the country's infrastructure remains fragile. Despite the fact that its economy is defined by extensive basic resources such as rice and fish, by export resources that include diamonds, gold, and rutile, and by a tourist industry, Sierra Leone continues to be one of the poorest countries in Africa. Per capita income is less than $150 a year, and the infant mortality rate is among the highest in the world. Beyond urban centers such as Freetown, Bo, Kenema, Koidu, Makeni, Kabala, and Kamakwie, most Sierra Leonians continue to live in rural areas. People often engage in cyclical migration to cities in search of wage labor and prestige goods.

There is no clear division of peoples and cultures in Sierra Leone. The two major language families are West Atlantic and Mande. Historically, indigenous West Atlantic speakers such as the Sape and Limba assimilated fifteenth- and sixteenth-century migrations of Mande speakers from the south (now Liberia) and from the east (Guinea). Small groups met, intermarried, and took up the local beliefs and customs. Loko, Kono, Vai, and Mende clearly resulted from this process. Later, a number of internal

groups arrived from Futa Jallon in the north. Still later, a small number of European traders took up residence. All of these groups, large or small, aggressive or passive, brought new ideas, forms of trade and technology, beliefs, and institutions. These early cultural encounters were often peaceful, but some were violent. Overall, this fusion of internal and external groups resulted in a range of ethnic populations, including Bullom, Fula, Gola, Kissi, Kono, Krio, Krim, Kuranko, Landogo, Limba, Mandingo, Sherbro, Susu, Temne, Yalunka, and Vai, as well as those of Afro-European descent.

Specifically, West Atlantic and Mande speakers share similar cultural notions of a distant God, lineage use rights in land, animal husbandry, and initiations that define role, status, and gender differences, which are informed by belief in an ongoing conflict between benevolent and malevolent forces. Each ethnic group defines itself through situational and contextual articulations of myth, ancestors, and land, a hierarchy of belief, the influence of Islam or Christianity, and access to technology, as well as through Western education and connections to national government. Ethnic difference is also found in local articulations of the relationship between the political authority of chiefs and the mystical power of religious agents. By the late 1990s ethnic differences had been elevated to the level of political identity.

Traditionally, the duty of leaders and religious agents was to ensure the fertility of people, land, and trade. This created a social covenant between land, ancestors, and people. Ideally, the powerful ruled wisely, with the rights of power sanctioned by the community. The abuse of power at local and state levels has a long history. But since the Organization of African Unity (OAU) meetings in Freetown (1980) the ideal of ruling wisely has been subverted by ever widening gaps of hunger, shortages, strikes, cycles of violence, greed, and fragmented leadership. The OAU meetings stimulated lavish government spending, which bankrupted the treasury, made more public the abuse of power, created spiraling inflation, and aggravated hunger and starvation.

While the conflicts have changed, the issue is still who has the power to be tribute-taking versus tribute-giving. From this perspective, what analysts have called the new seeds of civil war—the violence, soldier youth, mercenaries, refugee camps, social unrest, tribalism, and nepotism of the 1990s and early 2000s—have very old historical roots. There is a relationship between levels of dissatisfaction and kinds of disturbance. Now the key issue is one of scale and consequence.

Events such as the creation of Freetown as a center for repatriated Africans and recaptive slaves in 1787 set in motion a process that is still unfolding. In Freetown, and later in the interior, the search for trade and profit generated conflict between local people, the growing population of Krio (Westernized Africans), African recaptives, recent migrants to the interior, and new arrivals. In each encounter, new forms of technology, profit, and scale forced local people to adopt new forms of agency. These quickly became new institutions. New institutions generated new consequences, some intended and many unintended. This process can clearly be seen in the search to institutionalize profit and authority. The Sierra Leone Company (1791), a trading concession, for example, soon became a British Crown colony (1808).

Throughout the nineteenth century, new and more profitable forms of trade, with local people coming to outcompete the British, meant increased British intervention and mediation of the region's large states and kings, war groups, religious groups, small clans, secret societies, and even the weak subordinate groups of the interior. All negotiated their place within a new asymmetry of power. Trade became very profitable for local groups and the colonial government. Trade plus literacy extended the scale and consequences of the conflict among local groups and of local groups versus the British. When local people came to out-compete the British, the British response was to annex the interior to protect their interests and profits, and later to make it a protectorate in 1896. To support colonial administration a hut tax was imposed on indigenous peoples in the same year. Local people organized resistance to imposed British rule in what became the Hut Tax War (1898). Parallel forms of violence and resistance developed in guerrilla movements of the *poro*, Leopard, Baboon, and Alligator societies (1882–1922). These events find recent parallels.

The fusion of local and British interests created a new, more complex world, one redefined by cultural schisms, social fractures, and competing religious formations. These forces generated ever-greater forms of inequality and class (c. 1895–1935). In many cases, the push and pull of contradictory forces became a defining feature of individuals and groups maximizing profit and position. The contradictions inherent in the country's social imbalance could be seen in the waning of Krio and Freetown's influence versus the growth of an educated protectorate elite, an emerging Lebanese influence in Freetown and in the interior, and more centralized European economic and political interests. All of these groups sought to advance their interests in a situation that led to resistance and accommodation. Anti-British and anti-Lebanese sentiment coexisted in the country alongside ever-increasing social and economic ties to British and Lebanese interests. Social tensions erupted in protests, violent riots, and forms of guerrilla warfare.

Seen in this light, the anti-Lebanese riots (1919), the antislavery laws for the protectorate (1926), the total abolition of slavery in the protectorate (1927), and various constitutional changes (1924, 1947, 1951, 1967, and 1971) represent the aims of the protectorate centralization over the expanding economic opportunity of the new elites and an ever-widening world of poverty for the majority. Twentieth- and twenty-first-century events such as the Republican constitution bill (1967), the election of Siaka Stevens as president (1971), the establishment of a one-party state (1978), the OAU conference that bankrupted the treasury (1980), the so-called election of Joseph Saidu Momoh as president (1986), the civil war (1991–2002), the military coup in 1992 that replaced Momoh with the National Provisional Ruling Council (NPRC), and the democratic elections held in 2002 reveal contradictions whose genesis is in the nineteenth century. The contradictions and tensions reflected in these events may be insurmountable.

In the past as in the present, politics, control of trade, and extremes of wealth and poverty were cloaked, resisted, and justified by beliefs that those with power, authority, prestige, and resource have such benefits through the will of God, or, alternately,

Republic of Sierra Leone

Population:	6,144,562 (2007 est.)
Area:	71,740 sq. km (27,699 sq. mi.)
Official language:	English
Languages:	English, Krio, Temne, Mende, and 15 other indigenous languages
National currency:	leone
Principal religions:	Muslim 60%, Christian, animist
Capital:	Freetown (est. pop. 786,900 in 2006)
Other urban centers:	Bo, Koindu, Kenema, Makeni
Annual rainfall:	varies from 5,000 mm (200 in.) on the coast to 2,160 mm (85 in.) in the north
Principal geographical features:	*Mountains:* Loma Mountains, Wara Wara Mountains, Gola Hills, Gori Hills, Jojina Hills *Rivers:* Rokel, Jong, Gbangbar, Sewa, Waanje, Great Scarcies, Little Scarcies, Moa, Mano *Lakes:* Lake Mabesi
Economy:	*GDP per capita:* US$900 (2006)
Principal products and exports:	*Agricultural:* rice, coffee, cocoa, palm kernels, palm oil, peanuts, poultry, cattle, sheep, pigs, fish *Manufacturing:* small-scale manufacturing (beverages, textiles, cigarettes, footwear); petroleum refining, small commercial ship repair *Mining:* diamonds, rutile, bauxite, gold, some iron ore
Government:	Independence from Great Britain, 1961. Republic proclaimed in 1971. From 1997–2002, Sierra Leone was under the rule of a military junta due to civil war. The country now has a democratically elected president and a 124-seat parliament. For purposes of local government there are 3 provinces, headed by cabinet-rank ministers; 12 districts, controlled by the central government; and 147 chiefdoms, each headed by a paramount chief and a council of elders. The chiefdoms are further broken down into sections and villages. In the western area of the country, Freetown is an independent city, broken down into wards and headed by a major and eldermen. Rural areas have rural councils, and villages are headed by village committees.
Heads of state since independence:	1961–1964: Prime Minister Sir Milton Margai 1964–1967: Prime Minister Sir Albert M. Margai 1967: Brigadier David Lansana 1967–1968: Brigadier Andrew T. Juxon-Smith, chairman of the National Reform Council 1968–1971: Prime Minister Siaka Stevens 1971–1986: President Siaka Stevens 1986–1992: President Joseph Saidu Momoh 1992–1996: Captain Valentine Strasser, chairman of the National Provisional Ruling Council (renamed the Supreme Council of State in 1992) 1996: Brigadier Julius Maada Bio, chairman of the Supreme Council of State 1996–1997: President Ahmed Tejan Kabbah 1997–1998: Major Johnny Paul Koroma, chairman of the Armed Forces Revolutionary Council 1998–: President Ahmad Tejan Kabbah
Armed forces:	The Republic of Sierra Leone Armed Forces consists of an army, including an air wing and maritime wing. President is commander in chief. Voluntary enlistment.
Transportation:	*Rail:* Rail system was largely dismantled in 1973 and sold to Japan as scrap. *Waterways:* 800 km (500 mi.), 600 km (370 mi.) navigable all year on the Little Scarcies, Rokel, Jong, Sewa, and Moa Rivers. *Ports:* Freetown, Pepel, Bonthe, Sulima *Roads:* 11,674 km (7,238 mi.), 8% paved *National airline:* Sierra Leone Airways, 51% government-owned *Airports:* Major international airport at Lungi. 9 smaller airports in the interior. There are 2 heliports.
Media:	1 daily newspaper: *Daily Mail* (government-owned). 9 non-dailies, 26 periodicals. Publishing: Njala University Publishing Center, Sierra Leone University Press, the Provincial Literature Bureau, and the Government Printing Office. Sierra Leone Broadcasting Service operates both Radio Sierra Leone and television broadcasting. 10 radio broadcast stations, 2 television stations.
Literacy and education:	*Total literacy rate:* 36% (2006). Free, universal, and compulsory education has not yet been introduced. Most schools are run by religious groups. Secondary education provided through Freetown Technical Institute, and through trade centers at Kissy, Kenema, and Mazburaka. University of Sierra Leone has 2 campuses: Fourah Bay College and Njala University College, both in Freetown.

that those with power have made mystical covenants with spirits and witches that give and protect their authority, wealth, and rights to rule. Even where forms of resistance and revolt occur, they, too, are sanctioned by a cosmological system. For example, historically, when forms of resistance and revolt occurred, litigants often wore traditional forms of medicine thought to protect the body from attack while also attacking the body of one's enemy. This reality was seen most recently in the civil war, where groups used traditional specialists for medicine to destroy the enemy as well as protect the body.

A Sierra Leonian expression—"As the clock-bird flies in the air, the number of eggs it carries in its belly is known"—reflects the fact that although some of Sierra Leone's people practice forms of secrecy, most know what their business is and know that they cannot change it. Put simply, the social history transforms yet reproduces specific social oppositions and dichotomies that fracture the social fabric holding people together. In Sierra Leone there are few winners in the process of social change. Since 1787, tensions such as internal versus external, Freetown versus Upland, North versus South, indigenous versus immigrant, African versus European, local religions versus Christianity or Islam, pro-British versus anti-British, Western literate versus oral literate, labor versus technology, paramount chief versus district commissioner, have continually been reproduced, leading to short- and long-term consequences.

These consequences are felt by all, whether by a lineage-based rice farmer, a professor at Fourah Bay College, a bush trader in Kono, a gunrunner from Guinea, a police officer in Kamakwie, a cab driver, a Mandingo businessperson in Freetown, a Christian pastor in Kagbere, an imam in Bo, a minister with a large portfolio in Freetown, or a person with a Ph.D. in African history who teaches in Ohio. In essence, the politics of chaos and contradiction in Sierra Leone, even when exposed, force the powerful and weak to act on new and old forces that act on them. In efforts to move past these contradictions, leaders endlessly redesign various internal and external institutions and agencies. Some changes appear to facilitate higher levels of profit and social welfare; some extend existing schisms. Still other agencies and transactions merely render an entire nation helpless.

Inequality has become more entrenched. All people are conscious of violence, inequalities, and greed that remain unchanged since the end of the civil war (2002). The powerless majority remain rural, lineage-based, subsistence rice farmers who trade locally. The powerful minority elite remain defined by their educational, political, military, business, or religious status. Two worlds coexist. Most will remain tied to farming cycles while a few

elites secure their positions of Western prestige. In rural areas, dissatisfaction may or may not overcome a fragile peace and democratic reforms that obscure four hundred years of mystical sanction and esoteric knowledge that give rights to a few to take a lion's share. As testimonies in Sierra Leone's Truth and Reconciliation Commission (2002–2003) confirmed, power and position merely mask greed and envy. Indeed, the new seeds of civil war have very old roots.

See also **Colonial Policies and Practices; Ethnicity; Freetown; Geography and the Study of Africa; Languages; Organization of African Unity; Political Systems; Postcolonialism; Religion and Ritual; Warfare: Civil Wars.**

BIBLIOGRAPHY

Alie, Joe A. *A New History of Sierra Leone.* New York: St. Martin's Press, 1990.

Foray, Cyril P. *Historical Dictionary of Sierra Leone.* Metuchen, NJ: Scarecrow Press, 1977.

Fyle, C. Magbaily. *The History of Sierra Leone: A Concise Introduction.* London: Evans, 1981.

Mukonoweshuro, Eliphas G. *Colonialism, Class Formation, and Underdevelopment in Sierra Leone.* Lanham, MD: University Press of America, 1993.

Reno, William Sampson Klock. *Corruption and State Politics in Sierra Leone.* Cambridge, U.K.: Cambridge University Press, 1995.

Richards, Paul. *Coping with Hunger: Hazard and Experiment in an African Rice-Farming System.* London: Allen and Unwin, 1986.

Riley, Stephen P. *Liberia and Sierra Leone: Anarchy or Peace in West Africa.* London: Research Institute for the Study of Conflict and Terrorism, 1996.

Rodney, Walter. *A History of the Upper Guinea Coast, 1545–1800.* Oxford: Clarendon Press, 1970.

CLARK K. SPEED
REVISED BY ROSALIND SHAW

HISTORY AND POLITICS

Contemporary Sierra Leone has been molded by the legacies of many forces. Especially important have been: the impact of indigenous political systems; the period of settlement by returned Africans; British colonial occupation and control; the struggle for political control after independence, in particular the period from 1961 to 1968; and the efforts to create a viable democracy and economy in the 1990s.

Sierra Leone had many indigenous political structures before the period of settlement and colonial occupation, ranging from those based on the personal rule of powerful warriors and headmen to those that involved public participation in the choosing of leaders and chiefs. For many people in precolonial Sierra Leone, there had been a long tradition of regular participation in decision making. Particularly interesting were a number of societies (sometimes called secret societies) that cut across ethnic lines, such as Poro and Sande, which both educated and linked men and women in different chiefdoms in what was to become Sierra Leone.

Throughout the precolonial period there was a great deal of contact with coastal traders. The settlement in 1787 of a small number of poor Africans from England on the peninsula where Freetown is today marked the beginning of almost continuous external involvement and occupation of the coastal area. Following these settlers were ex-slaves from the United States and Jamaica, and captives from ships seized by the British on the high seas. They established what was set up to be a self-governing Land of Freedom with a complex system of representative government. Not long after, this territory came under the control of the Sierra Leone Company, a British trading company. In 1808 it became a British colony that eventually expanded to encompass what is Sierra Leone today.

In 1863 the colonial government set up an Executive and a Legislative Council, with the former representing the government and the latter having twelve appointed members, primarily representing merchants, with its first black member appointed in 1882. There were elections in Freetown starting in 1895 and in the colony villages outside Freetown in 1901, though the franchise was extremely limited. Constitutional changes in 1924 allowed for the election in the colony of three members of the Legislative Council. The rest of Sierra Leone, beyond what is today the western area, was known as the protectorate and was governed largely through the chiefs. An African majority was provided for in the 1951 constitution, and by 1957 the vote was extended to the protectorate. Party competition began in the elections of 1951,

expanding in 1957 and 1961. Thus, by independence in 1961, a tradition of representative government and elections was clearly established with a history of largely free and open contests. Much of the credit for this success goes to the nation's first prime minister, Sir Milton Margai. During his rule, there was a free and lively press, spirited debate in parliament, and effective participation in the political process by people throughout the country. Sir Milton was succeeded in 1964 by his half-brother, Albert Margai, who was elected leader of the Sierra Leone People's Party (SLPP).

Elections in 1967 resulted in the victory of the opposition All People's Congress (APC) over the SLPP incumbents. The victory was due in part to a reaction against the corruption of some SLPP politicians, and in part to opposition of people to the efforts of Margai and his close associates to set up a one-party state. Though unsuccessful, the attempt gave the APC a major campaign issue and added to its populist appeal. The APC victory was one of the first successes for an opposition party in Africa. That victory was short-lived when the military intervened soon after Siaka Stevens was sworn in as prime minister, ushering in a brief and unpopular period of military rule. Although Siaka Stevens was returned to power about one year later, the coup created a legacy of distrust, conflict, and violence that continued to plague Sierra Leone at the end of the twentieth century.

The return to civilian rule in 1968 was deeply affected by the legacy of the coup, making Stevens and those close to him in the governing APC wary of both the military and opposition parties. Thus began a period of escalating violence, political manipulation, and power politics leading to a one-party APC government in 1978 (largely based, ironically, on the one-party constitution drawn up by the SLPP in its own failed effort for one-party rule in 1965). In the early years, Stevens was a popular leader, a shrewd politician, and a successful champion of national integration. However, by 1985 Stevens' popularity had fallen, in part because of the decline of the economy, but mainly because of the growing corruption, intimidation, and greed of the APC leaders. Hoping to retain the reins of power when it became clear he could no longer remain in office, Stevens named the well-liked head of the armed forces, Major General Joseph Momoh, to succeed him.

Momoh's nomination was supported within the party, and, following constitutional guidelines, he campaigned and was elected president as the only candidate under the one-party constitution. Momoh's early years were spent asserting his control over the party and the country. As president, Momoh moved to liberalize politics, control violence and intimidation, and focus attention on the ailing economy. He reopened negotiations with the International Monetary Fund (IMF) and instituted a government austerity program of raising taxes and improving duty collection to increase revenue. Momoh also intervened to protect the press from official repression when the minister of information tried to suspend the licenses of five newspapers.

In 1989 and 1990, President Momoh turned his attention to returning the political system to an open, competitive democracy. He appointed a commission to review the changes necessary for multiparty elections and suggested steps to transform the political system. In March 1991, the commission recommended the return to a multiparty system and presented a new constitution to enable it. The constitution was put to the people in a national referendum and approved overwhelmingly. Political parties were free to form and elections were scheduled for late 1991.

President Momoh appointed former governor of the World Bank, Dr. James Funah, as minister of finance. Under his financial leadership major progress was made in controlling government expenditures and improving the economy. This progress resulted in an IMF-supported adjustment program and the renewal of World Bank assistance, suspended some years earlier during Steven's presidency. Some advances were made in restoring water and electric services in Freetown.

The invasion of southern Sierra Leone by supporters of the Liberian rebel leader Charles Taylor (and some Sierra Leonean allies) in early 1991 soon put serious strains on a military ill-prepared for an invasion. The already ailing economy deteriorated further. The move to multiparty competition was crippled by the war, which quickly expanded to affect one-third of the territory of Sierra Leone. The war diverted attention from development, drained scarce economic resources, and sowed discontent. By mid-1991 it was

increasingly clear that holding elections might be difficult in as much as one-third of the country, most of it the stronghold of the SLPP. During this period, political parties continued to campaign, while the government looked for a way to end the war. The Taylor forces moved into the diamond areas (using diamond-industry revenue to support their war efforts in Sierra Leone and Liberia) and increasingly resorted to pillaging villagers and robbing travelers. The government rapidly mobilized troops and increased its army from three thousand to seven thousand in short order. Most of these soldiers were poorly trained, badly armed and equipped, and did poorly at the front. Nigerian troops helped secure the cities so that more experienced Sierra Leone troops could go to the front. Ghanaian and Nigerian aircraft were used against the invaders but proved largely ineffective against guerrilla armies. There were few successes against the Taylor forces that were joined by Sierra Leone opposition elements formerly in exile.

In this context, junior officers took advantage of the unhappiness at the front, the disorganization of the army in Freetown, and public dissatisfaction with the government and President Momoh. They organized and carried out a coup. The military action began on April 29, 1992 as an expression of grievances, but it was soon evident that it was a well-planned, full-blown coup with broad military participation. After some fighting in Freetown, President Momoh fled to Guinea. The plotters announced the formation of the National Provisional Ruling Council (NPRC) in Freetown under the leadership of Captain Valentine E. M. Strasser.

The NPRC criticized the inefficiency and corruption of the Momoh government, promised to bring the war to a speedy end, and, in due course, to restore democracy. Efforts were made to increase the size of the army further; some progress was made against the invading Liberian forces soon after the coup, but these gains were quickly reversed. By 1994 much of the interior of the country was outside government control and increasingly run by a combination of Charles Taylor's troops, a Sierra Leone rebel force called the Revolutionary United Front (RUF), and a growing number of warlords, opportunists, and armies of unknown attachment. Although the Sierra Leonean army grew in size, it was increasingly undisciplined and unsuccessful at the front, with many reports of atrocities and human rights violations against Sierra Leonean citizens and others.

By the beginning of 1995, only the cities were controlled by government forces, and only the greater Freetown area was fully in the hands of the government. A variety of peace initiatives involving the Economic Community of West African States (ECOWAS), the European powers, Nigeria, and others were made, and some agreements were signed, but nothing led to a reduction in fighting. In January 1995 rebel forces captured the mining facilities of Sierra Rutile Ltd. and the bauxite facilities of the Sierra Leone Ore and Metal Company (SIERAMCO), depriving the government of its only important source of income.

By 1995 the strength of the RUF seemed to be growing, as did the anarchy caused by warlords, rogue government units, bandits, and adventurers. The kidnapping of foreign aid volunteers and employees of foreign companies, coupled with the continued attack on Sierra Leone citizens, fueled the sense of disorder and decay. Peace overtures continued to be made, but the inability to establish regular contacts with the RUF and other opposition elements persisted in plaguing both national and international efforts to find a peaceful solution to the political crisis. External support for the government also faded as knowledge of human-rights abuses mounted, including the revelation of the execution of more than two dozen people alleged to be involved in planning a coup; evidence of political corruption was also on the rise. Britain and the European Economic Community reviewed their support of the government. In mid-1995 the government employed a South Africa-based company, Executive Outcomes, to assist in restructuring its army—a move that sparked criticism and allegations about the use of mercenaries. The government scheduled national elections for late in 1995, but given the fighting and lack of government control of large sectors of the country, success was problematic.

The Strasser regime continued to try to end the war by military means during 1995 and early 1996. There were periodic peace initiatives but peace remained elusive. The economy continued to suffer as a result of the continued fighting, which resulted in the displacement of more than one third of the population, failure to plant crops in the most fertile parts of the country, and

closure of major mining concerns with the loss of this major source of government revenue. The ban on political parties was lifted in June 1995, but only limited headway was made to return the country to civilian rule in the months that followed.

On January 16, 1996, Captain Strasser was overthrown in a coup led by his deputy, Brigadier Julius Maada Bio. Brigadier Bio asserted that the coup was only a change of leadership of the NPRC and that the two major aims of his government were to promote peace and to continue the process toward a democratic multiparty government.

In March 1996, in spite of continued fighting in parts of the country by the remnants of Charles Taylor's invading forces, the RUF, local warlords, and bandits, coupled with the reluctance of the outgoing military ruler Brigadier Bio, elections were held to return the country to democratic multiparty rule. An estimated 60 percent of eligible voters participated in the elections, despite threats from the RUF and the existence of large 'no go' zones in the southeastern part of the country. Thirteen parties participated, with five gaining seats in the eighty-member parliament. While no party received a majority, Ahmed Tejan Kabbah of the SLPP was elected president in the runoff election and was sworn in on March 29, 1996.

While fighting continued in the interior, Foday Sankoh, leader of the RUF, indicated a willingness to discuss peace with the new regime. Talks were held in Côte d'Ivoire that produced a peace agreement in November 1996, though it rapidly fell apart. The government began to arm militias of traditional hunters from SLPP's base in the southeast, which made some key advances against the RUF. An army mutiny against Kabbah overthrew his government in May 1997. Kabbah fled to Guinea, and the most violent phase of the civil war ensued. Major Johnny Koroma became head of the Armed Forces Revolutionary Council (AFRC), a military junta. The AFRC entered into a power-sharing agreement with the RUF shortly after, in a horribly illegitimate and ineffective arrangement. In the Conakry Accord of October 1997, the AFRC agreed to a peace plan that would reinstate Kabbah within six months. The following February the international community, fearing a downward spiral in the conflict, stepped in to reinstate Kabbah through a Nigerian-led military force called the Economic Community of West African States Ceasefire Monitoring Group (Ecomog).

Their efforts were challenged, however, by groups of the AFRC-RUF alliance that moved out of the bush to retake parts of Freetown by December 1998, financed in part by resources from the Kono diamond fields. Large sections of Freetown were captured and looted. The militants were then driven out under a new ceasefire in May 1999, followed by the Lomé peace agreement in July which pardoned Sankoh and gave the RUF several government positions.

A United Nations peacekeeping mission known as the UN Mission in Sierra Leone (Unamsil) was deployed in November to reinforce the Lomé agreement, as it was quickly unraveling in 2000. Sankoh attempted another coup and was arrested as UN and U.K. diplomats stepped up efforts to build confidence among the parties. Demobilization and disarmament of armed groups began in earnest in 2001, and captives and child soldiers started to be released. President Kabbah officially declared an end to the war in January 2002. Shortly after, then-UN Secretary General Kofi Annan called for the establishment of the UN Special Court for Sierra Leone to deal with war crimes. A Truth and Reconciliation Commission was established, as well.

Presidential and legislative elections held in 2002 brought the SLPP a large majority in parliament and kept Kabbah in power as president through a landslide victory, though the APC remained most popular in the capital. The next presidential elections are scheduled for August 2007. Kabbah, in accordance with the constitution, is not eligible to run for a third term and has chosen his vice president, Solomon Berewa, as his successor in the SLPP. Ernest Koroma will run as the APC's presidential candidate. These will be the first elections since the war's end and will be carried out without the substantial resources of Unamsil, which reduced its numbers in the years after the official end of the war, finally withdrawing in 2005.

See also **Annan, Kofi; Colonial Policies and Practices; Crowther, Samuel Ajayi; Economic Community of West African States (ECOWAS); Freetown; Human Rights; International Monetary Fund; Political Systems; Postcolonialism; Secret Societies; Slavery and Servile Institutions; Stevens, Siaka; Taylor, Charles Gahnhay; United Nations; World Bank.**

BIBLIOGRAPHY

Cartwright, John R. *Politics in Sierra Leone: 1947–67.* Toronto: University of Toronto Press, 1970.

Cox, Thomas S. *Civil-Military Relations in Sierra Leone: A Case Study of African Soldiers in Politics.* Cambridge, MA: Harvard University Press, 1976.

Hayward, Fred M. "Sierra Leone: State Consolidation, Fragmentation, and Decay." In *Contemporary West African States,* ed. Donal Cruise O'Brien, John Dunn, and Richard Rathbone. Cambridge, U.K.: Cambridge University Press, 1989.

Hayward, Fred M. "Sierra Leone: First Steps in the Return to Multiparty Democracy." In *Africa Contemporary Record* vol. 22, 1989–90. eds. Marion E. Doro and Colin Legum. New York: Africana Publishing Company, 1995.

Hayward, Fred M., and Jimmy Kandeh. "Perspectives on Twenty-Five Years of Elections in Sierra Leone." In *Elections in Independent Africa.* Boulder, CO: Westview Press, 1987.

Jones, W. S. Marcus. *Legal Development and Constitutional Change in Sierra Leone (1787–1971).* Stockwell, U.K.: Elms Court, 1988.

Kilson, Martin. *Political Change in a West African State: A Study of the Modernization Process in Sierra Leone.* Cambridge, MA: Harvard University Press, 1966.

Koroma, Abdul Karim. *Sierra Leone: Agony of a Nation.* Freetown, Sierra Leone: Andromeda Publications, 1996.

Sierra Leone Country Profile 2007. London: Economist Intelligence Unit, 2007.

Spitzer, Leo. *The Creoles of Sierra Leone: Responses to Colonialism, 1870–1945.* Madison: University of Wisconsin Press, 1974.

FRED M. HAYWARD
REVISED BY NANCY RHEA STEEDLE

SIJILMASA. Located in the Tafilalt oasis of southeastern Morocco, Sijilmasa was the major point of departure from the north of the Sahara where large camel caravans gathered to make the long trek south to Timbuktu to trade for gold. As far back as 500 CE, the oasis at first served as a seasonal gathering place for Berber tribes. It became a city when Khariji Muslims settled there as religious refugees in the middle of the eighth century.

For two centuries thereafter, Sijilmasa was an independent city-state under the control of the Bani Midrar. For the next century, local rulers struggled to maintain its independence from two competing superpowers, the Umayyads of Cordoba and the Fatimids of Ifriqiya. In 1054–1055, Sijilmasa fell to another Berber tribe, the Almoravids. In his *Masalik wa-l-Mamalik*, al-Bakri provided the most complete medieval description of Sijilmasa: a circular wall with twelve gates, beautiful houses within—many with gardens—magnificent public buildings, a solidly built mosque, and poorly built baths. He also described abundant agriculture irrigated with water collected in cisterns.

Arab writers of the first half of the fourteenth century also described a city at its height. While Sijilmasa was under the control of the Marinid dynasty, al-'Umari called it one of the mightiest cities of Morocco. In a civil war in 1393, the inhabitants killed the governor, destroyed the walls of the city, and built *qsur* (fortified villages) in the surrounding area.

Following the civil war, Sijilmasa was neglected by the Moroccan Sa'adian dynasty (1549–1659). In the seventeenth century, the 'Alawi dynasty, which still rules Morocco in the early twenty-first century, emerged from the Tafilalt. They fortified the garrison of Sijilmasa in the late seventeenth century and built an impressive system of irrigation that generally improved their quality of life. Sijilmasa in the early twenty-first century is replaced by the town of Rissani that serves as the principal market for some 125–130 villages in the oasis. Monuments and shrines on the outskirts of Rissani identify it as the 'Alawi spiritual hearth. The physical remains of Sijilmasa lie buried just to the west of Rissani.

See also **Morocco; Morocco: History of (1000 to 1900); Timbuktu; Transportation: Caravan.**

BIBLIOGRAPHY

Bovill, Edward W., and Robin Hallett *The Golden Trade of the Moors: West African Kingdoms in the Fourteenth Century*, 2nd edition. Princeton, NJ: Markus Wiener, 1995.

Garrard, Timothy F. "Myth and Metrology: The Early Trans-Saharan Goldtrade." *Journal of African History* 23 (1982): 443–461.

Jaques-Meunie, D. *Le Maroc Saharien des origines a 1634*. Paris: Librairie Klinksieck, 1983.

Levtzion, Nehemia, and J. F. P. Hopkins. *Corpus of Early Arabic Sources for West African History*, 1st Markus edition. Princeton, NJ: Markus Wiener, 2000.

Lightfoot, Dale, and James Miller. "Sijilmassa: The Rise and Fall of a Walled Oasis in Medieval Morocco." *Annals of the Association of American Geographers* Vol. 86, Malden, MA: Blackwell, 1996.

Mauny, Raymond. *Tableau Geographique de l'Ouest Africain au Moyen Age*. Lisboa, Portugal: Centro de Estudos Históricos Ultramarinos, 1960.

McCall, Daniel F. "The Traditions of the Founding of Sijilmassa and Ghana," *Transactions of the Historical Society of Ghana* 1 (1961): 15–20.

Mercier, E. "Sidjilmasa selon les auteurs Arabes," *Revue Africaine* 233–274. 1867.

Messier, Ronald A. "The Almoravids, West African Gold, and the Gold Currency of the Mediterranean Basin." *Journal of the Economic and Social History of the Orient* 17 (1974): 31–47.

Messier, Ronald A. "Quantitative Analysis of Almoravid Dinars." *Journal of the Economic and Social History of the Orient* 23 (1980): 104–120.

Messier, Ronald A. "Sijilmasa: l'intermédiaire entre la Méditerranée et l'Ouest de l'Afrique." In *L'Occident Musulman et l'Occident Chrétien au Moyen Age*, ed. Mohammed Hammam. Rabat, Morocco: Publications de la Faculté des Lettres, 1995.

Messier, Ronald A. "Sijilmasa: Five Seasons of Archaeological Inquiry by a Joint Moroccan-American Mission." *Archéologie Islamique* 7 (1997): 61–92.

Mezzine, Larbi. *Le Tafilalt: Contribution à l'histoire du Maroc aux XVIIè et XVIIIè siècles*. Rabat, Morocco: Publications de la Faculté des Lettres et des Sciences Humaines, 1987.

RONALD A. MESSIER

SLAVE TRADES

This entry includes the following articles:
ATLANTIC, CENTRAL AFRICA
ATLANTIC, WESTERN AFRICA
INDIAN OCEAN
NORTHEASTERN AFRICA AND RED SEA
NORTHERN AFRICA AND SAHARA

ATLANTIC, CENTRAL AFRICA

Central Africa, in the context of the Atlantic slave trade, refers to the African coast and hinterland south of the equator (roughly Cape Lopez, in modern Gabon) as far as the mouth of the Kunene River (at the border of modern Angola and Namibia). In British studies, it is designated

"West-Central Africa," to distinguish it from colonial British Central Africa (now Zambia, Malawi, and Zimbabwe.) The low population densities of the forests to the north of this region separated it as an integrated set of demographic and economic units from "western Africa" (Cameroon to the west and north); beyond the Kunene to the south lay the virtually uninhabited Namib Desert. The western Central African region economically integrated into the commercial economy of the Atlantic, expanded from 120 miles inland from the coast or less at the dawn of slaving in the early sixteenth century to the very center of the continent, as much as 900 miles inland, by the decline of exports in the 1860s.

Central Africa contributed nearly half of the more than 12 million or so captives sent across the Atlantic from all parts of Africa. From the principal source of the sixteenth century's relatively small numbers of slaves, Central Africa's contribution declined toward one-third as western African exports surged at the end of the seventeenth century, and then rose again, becoming the principal region of origin for captives sent to the Americas after 1800—about 45 percent overall. These captives came from populations less numerous than those on which the slave-trading networks in western Africa preyed. Most of them had lived along the margins of the equatorial forest and from the grassland savannas, in a band which ran east from the mouth of the region's greatest river, the Congo (Zaire). Relatively moist highlands in central Angola drained by the Kwanza and Kunene rivers supported a second comparatively dense area of human habitation, while smaller vulnerable populations lived further to the east, around the valleys of other major rivers running through lands that were generally dry, subject to periodic drought, and covered in large part by porous, sandy soils. The fragility of agriculture under these conditions in the more southerly regions, where nearly everyone relied on farming for their food, forced people to disperse when the rains failed and thus exposed them periodically to capture and enslavement once European slavers supported raiders who created military bands, and eventually commercial communities and wide-ranging caravans, to do so.

Portuguese ships first felt their way south along the western Central African coast during the 1480s, but they turned to loading slaves only gradually, over the following century. The first Europeans were motivated by the royal sponsors' futile quest for precious metals, gold or silver; they also sought military allies, whom they found in the early sixteenth century in the ambitious heads of the largest African polity, or network of trading chiefs, near the coast, just south of the Zaire (Congo) River mouth, lords (*mani*) whom they treated as "kings" of Kongo analogous to the European monarchs they knew at home.

A second wave of Portuguese brought a more commercial orientation after the 1520s. Backed by Italian capital, they extended the sugar industry then growing on the islands off northwestern Africa (Madeira, the Canaries) to equatorial São Tomé (Saint Thomas), lying between Kongo and the main destination at that time for captives from Central Africa, the Portuguese fort at Elmina, on the Gold Coast in western Africa. Cane thrived in the island's humid equatorial climate, and sugar production required field laborers in large numbers. The planters of the island turned to the mouth of the Kwanza River, to the south of the sheltered Bay of Luanda, to buy them, particularly after the *mani* of Kongo protested the disruptions to their own political agendas done by Portuguese merchants drawing captives from their wars of expansion. In the hills above the upper valley of the Kwanza, the São Tomé planters brought captives taken by warlords known by their title, the *ngola*. By the 1560s, São Tomé had assembled perhaps thirty thousand slaves from the highlands above both sides of the Kwanza.

Large-scale slaving south of the Zaire River grew between the 1570s and the 1620s from these roots, with annual exports probably ranging between five and ten thousand individuals. This massive growth started from a severe drought that engulfed the Kwanza Valley region in violent conflict during the 1570s. A royally sponsored expedition from Portugal arrived in the same decade to challenge the São Tomé planters for control of the region. The metropolitan troops sought mythical "mountains of silver" but turned to systematic raiding for captives when they failed to materialize. They succeeded mostly by collaborating with marauding bands of young Africans, known as Imbangala (but exaggeratedly characterized by the Portuguese as cannibalistic "Jaga"), driven by hunger to a violent, predatory style of living in the midst of widespread social disintegration.

The union of the Spanish and Portuguese Crowns in Iberia in the 1580s fortuitously converted this temporary collapse in Africa to two and one-half centuries of systematic slaving. Spain took advantage of its new authority over the Portuguese fortress built at Luanda Bay to award the famous *asiento* contracts for delivering Africans as slaves to their silver-mining colonies in the Americas to merchants from Lisbon. The enormous profits obtained from selling captive Africans for Spanish pieces of eight covered the high costs in mortality among the slaves as the Europeans learned to carry larger numbers—300 and more per ship—of people alive across the Atlantic Ocean to the New World.

The sugar industry of northeastern Brazil, just then taking shape under the stimulus of Dutch investment, bought some of these captives en route to Spanish ports in the eastern Caribbean region. Along with other captives from Portuguese outposts in Upper Guinea (modern Guinea [Bissau]), these Africans enabled sugar barons in Pernambuco and then Bahia to replace São Tomé as the principal, and vastly greater producers of sugar and a much larger market for "Angolan" slaves from Central Africa. Most captives left through a port that developed at Luanda, under the guns of the fortresses commanding the bay. The Iberian government presence, under a governor and commander of the local troops, made the Luanda trade, uniquely in Africa, subject to Europe-based government regulation and taxation. The town remained the principal locus of Portuguese government authority for the duration of the trade, except for a brief loss of control to the Dutch from 1641 to 1648. Slaves regularly accounted for 90 percent of the area's exports (in European currency values), with ivory a very distant second.

Portuguese military intervention in the politics of slaving from Kongo to the central highland region, backed by sugar-planting interests in Pernambuco (in Brazil), extended the conflicts among the Africans through the late seventeenth century, in what have become known as the "Angolan wars" These wars spread slaving east to the valley of the Kwango River, where in the 1630s an Imbangala band established a military and commercial base known as Kasanje. As the slaving wars moved east beyond the Kwango at the end of the century, Kasanje became the primary supplier of slaves to Luanda for more than a century. These wars also spread slaving up to the highlands south of the Kwanza, where other Imbangala bands created several similar regimes—later known as the Ovimbundu "kingdoms"—between about 1670 and 1730. Other Brazilian planter interests, particularly from Rio de Janeiro, grew desperate for slaves from Central Africa after the discovery of gold and diamonds in Minas Gerais at the end of the seventeenth century. In order to evade the taxes, bribes, and government regulations imposed at Luanda, these Brazilian slavers developed the small southerly settlement at Benguela into the outlet for slaves from the populous highlands just to the east. Exports of captives from Benguela grew steadily to about eight thousand per year, until they approached those from Luanda—then shipping from ten thousand to fifteen thousand annually—in some decades of the late eighteenth century.

The 1670s also marked the extension of English, French, and Dutch slaving in western Africa south to the coasts of Central Africa, starting in the region north of the mouth of the Zaire River known as Loango, from the name of the largest African trading principality there. The northern Europeans bought slaves primarily for sugar plantations on the islands they held in the West Indies and, very secondarily, for South Carolina and the Chesapeake region in North America, where the captives from western Central Africa were known as "Angolas," even though they had only indirect connections with the Portuguese colony of the same name south of the mouth of the Zaire River. In the eighteenth century these northern Europeans, commercially wealthier than the Portuguese, boarded Central African captives from Kongo, Kasanje, and even further south, through ports in this northerly region at Loango, Cabinda, and Molembo. Government authorities in Luanda were responsible for maintaining a Portuguese monopoly over slaving from the coasts south of Cape Lopez but never inhibited these European competitors to their north. Central Africans—known as "Angolas" or as "Congos"—became significant components of the enslaved populations of the Caribbean, the Carolina Lowcountry (where the designation connoted the population known as "Gullahs"), and the Chesapeake.

Though Lisbon (or its contracted private agents) taxed the trade at its port at Luanda and its network of military posts to the east, it did not dominate commercially. Rather, its own colonial subjects, both Angolans and Brazilians, handled nearly all of the imports, dominated by textiles and Brazilian cane brandy, and the exports in the form of captive people. Metropolitan merchants tended to limit their involvement to supplying commercial credit, often in the form of textiles from India, wines from Madeira and Portugal, and northern European linens and woolens sent to Luanda; by leaving ownership of the slaves themselves to their colonial subjects, they passed along to them the primary risk of the trade—mortality among the slaves carried. Brazilians operated the ships that plied the south Atlantic back and forth from Rio, and secondarily from Bahia and Recife (in Pernambuco), and contributed the rotgut cane brandy prominent among the Angolan imports. They owned the slaves at most periods, together with a "Luso-African" community of families descended from women associated with the African suppliers of the slaves and from immigrant Brazilian and Portuguese traders and officials. These Angolans worked with criminals and gypsies exiled to Angola from Portugal and Brazil, as well as with their skilled African slaves, to run the caravans that linked Luanda and Benguela to the main trading fairs of the interior—at Kasanje, in southern Kongo, in the Central Highlands, and elsewhere. The ambitious Portuguese first minister of the 1750s and 1760s, the Marquis of Pombal, chartered two metropolitan companies to expand Lisbon's limited role at Luanda, but both sank beneath a sea of debt when they tried to buy their way into the Brazil-dominated trade with liberal loans of trade goods.

The numbers of Central Africans sent off to slavery in the Americas repeatedly surged because of droughts that recurred during the 1670s, again in the middle of the eighteenth century, and particularly in the 1790s and after. Kasanje drew many of the captives it sent to Luanda from "Lunda," the sandy plains reaching to the very center of the continent, through a loose but extensive network of warlords there who raided the large populations along the southern margins of the forest. The highland Ovimbundu developed large armed caravans of their own to buy the captives taken in these wars and also sent them to the southeast around the headwaters of the Zambezi River to promote the slave trade there. Kongo became a transit region for slaves who originated from far to the east and southeast and were sold to the French and English along the northern coasts. By the early nineteenth century, slaving was also advancing northeastward up the Zaire River into the heart of the equatorial forests under the stimulus of canoe traders, known as Bobangi, who dominated the trade of the lower river.

Communities in nearly every part of Central Africa were raided by slavers or lived in one way or another off slaving. Smaller, more remote communities suffered as victims of the large raiding states. By the eighteenth century, nearly all of the African polities of the region either derived their power from the control of slaving routes passing through their lands or to defensive strengths developed to protect themselves from raiding. The older kingdoms near the coast—chiefs and warlords in the Kongo region, Kasanje, the Ovimbundu states—abandoned raiding and became commercial brokers between the zones of violence farther in the interior, where many captives originated, and the commercial agents of buyers on the coast. In these more commercialized regions, political authorities exploited their power and used their wealth in trade goods to sink their subjects in debt and then condemned failed debtors, and often also the debtors' families, to exile, sale, and slavery.

In the absence of population counts, scholars disagree about the demographic impact of this pervasive slaving. After the clearly devastating drought of the early seventeenth century, total numbers of people embarked along the coasts of western Central Africa dropped to around five thousand per year in 1700 and then rose toward ten thousand each year by the end of the eighteenth century. The extent of the new regions afflicted may have increased fast enough, while African slavers may have retained enough women (since the people they sold for export were predominantly males) to have sustained overall levels of population, within the recurrently harsh limits imposed by the region's susceptibility to drought.

One very selective count made in the 1740s revealed twice as many women as men in the reproductive age cohorts, exactly complementing the 2:1 majorities of males among the people shipped off. Some scholars have hypothesized that overall population densities in the area may have been too low to support the decades of intense slaving at the end of the eighteenth century without at least a temporary decline in population. The total number of captives exported exceeded 5.5 million; the additional casualties—those displaced and enslaved within Africa and those who died in the course of the tragedy—are uncountable but would have been at least as great.

The Africans subjected to this turmoil regarded the European slavers as "red cannibals" who rendered the bones of the captives taken beyond the sea into the gunpowder with which they returned to buy more. They interpreted the butter and cooking oil among these imports as rendered from the fat of the captives' bodies, and the red wine they saw as distilled from the blood of those sent into the Atlantic, the "land of the dead." The commercially oriented warlords who dominated the trading polities they viewed as "witches."

Those enslaved in the interior reached the coast only after prolonged starvation and abuse along the way, though conditions were less severe along the northerly trails leading to the Loango coast and on the riverine canoe trade in the forests than in the drier lands to the south. Death rates at sea were correspondingly very high—averaging around 10 percent from Luanda to Rio at the end of the eighteenth century (that is, a rate that would have killed all aboard within ten months, had the voyages lasted longer than the normal four to six weeks), probably twice that earlier in the century, and perhaps lower later in the nineteenth—in spite of clumsy Portuguese medical and sanitary efforts to salvage their investments in vulnerable human capital. Smallpox epidemics in Africa, often following droughts, briefly raised mortality rates at sea to dramatically higher levels. The slaves' survival on the "middle passage" also depended on the adequacy of the food and—especially—water provided for them. Divided responsibilities for the slaves' welfare, distributed among Lisbon financiers, Africa-based traders, Brazilian shippers, and planter-buyers in Brazil left none of them in

positions to protect themselves, or the slaves, adequately. The so-called "slave risk," of mortality, became a calculation made in terms of each of the slavers' narrow economic interests, not the lives of the enslaved.

Nineteenth-century British efforts to suppress the Atlantic slaving of all other European powers north of the equator, in the wake of Britain's abolition of its own trade in 1808, only stimulated the trade from Central Africa. Portuguese and Brazilian (independent of Portugal after 1826) slavers, protected by treaty provisions and stimulated by growing production of sugar, cotton, and coffee in Brazil, drove the volume of Central African slaving to record levels—as many as thirty-five thousand captives in the final, most intense years (see Table 1). Surreptitious support from French, Spanish, and U.S. merchants, the financial backing of the British themselves for Brazil's export agriculture, and the chaotic aftermath of searing drought in Africa also contributed to the high volume. International treaties declared this trade illegal after 1830, but shipments to Brazil ended only in 1850. The booming sugar and coffee plantations of Cuba became the other principal destination of Central African captives from the 1840s until well into the 1860s.

Much of this later trade moved through ports remote from the Portuguese government posts at Luanda and Benguela. Luso-African families in Angola, deprived of profits and taxes from the slave exports that had overwhelmingly dominated the colony's economy for so long, turned to growing sugar and coffee on a minor scale and to exporting beeswax, ivory, and wild ("red") rubber that they purchased from African traders from the remote regions to the east. These African suppliers staffed their extraction and processing of the new commodities with captives whom they continued to buy and to seize; other traders put them to work in their caravans and gathering parties. The Portuguese in Angola developed their own nascent plantation agriculture—coffee, then sugar—with African laborers legally termed "servants," (serviçaes) but in fact slaves, whom they continued to buy from the same African suppliers into the early 1900s. The Angolan government sent several thousand such "servants" to cocoa plantations developed on the island of São Tomé until 1910,

Estimated volume of the transatlantic slave trade by African region and half-century

African regions	Western Africa	West Central Africa	Southeast Africa	Total	West Central Africa %
1501–1600	126,999	**149,294**	0	276,293	**54.0%**
1601–1650	146,321	**526,522**	934	673,777	**78.1%**
1651–1700	771,932	**408,618**	29,876	1,210,426	**39.7%**
1701–1750	1,833,573	**728,344**	17,674	2,579,591	**28.2%**
1751–1800	2,496,420	**1,417,562**	61,773	3,979,755	**35.6%**
1801–1850	1,491,348	**1,736,772**	394,183	3,622,303	**47.9%**
1851–1867	46,870	**84,077**	89,447	220,394	**38.1%**
1501–1867	6,974,586	**5,051,189**	593,887	12,558,491	**40.2%**

*Data in columns for West Central Africa and Southeast Africa and the Total trade are summed from the source table; the data in the column for Western Africa are calculated from these sums. Percentage column is calculated from the bolded column for West Central Africa and the totals for each period. The original data include varying estimated components, and the numbers are not in fact known as precisely as their expression in the table. Confidence levels are generally in the 95% range, or above.

SOURCE: Calculated* from "Introduction," in Eltis, David, and David Richardson, eds. "Introduction." *Extending the Frontiers: Essays on the New Transatlantic Slave Trade Database.* New Haven: Yale University Press, 2007.

Table 1.

where four hundred years of some of the most intense slaving anywhere in Africa finally ended, amidst a storm of international protest, on the same small island where it had begun.

See also **Benguela; Colonial Policies and Practices; Congo River; Ecosystems; Luanda; Production Strategies: Agriculture; Slavery and Servile Institutions; Women: Women and Slavery.**

BIBLIOGRAPHY

Alencastro, Luis Felipe de. *O trato dos viventes: Formação do Brasil no Atlântico sul.* São Paulo: Companhia das Letras, 2000.

Conrad, Robert E. *World of Sorrow: The African Slave Trade to Brazil.* Baton Rouge: Louisiana State University Press, 1986.

Curto, José C. *Enslaving Spirits: The Portuguese-Brazilian Alcohol Trade at Luanda and its Hinterland, c. 1550–1830.* Leiden: Brill, 2003.

Duffy, James. *A Question of Slavery.* Cambridge, MA: Harvard University Press, 1967.

Elbl, Ivana. "The Volume of the Early Atlantic Slave Trade, 1450–1521." *Journal of African History* 38, no. 1 (1997): 31–75.

Eltis, David. *Economic Growth and the Ending of the Transatlantic Slave Trade.* Cambridge, U.K.: Cambridge University Press, 1987.

Eltis, David; Stephen Behrandt; and David Richardson. "National Participation in the Transatlantic Slave Trade: New Evidence." In *Africa and the Americas: Interconnections during the Slave Trade,* ed. José C. Curto and Renée Soulodre-LaFrance. Trenton, NJ: Africa World Press, 2005.

Eltis, David, and David Richardson, eds. "Introduction." In *Extending the Frontiers: Essays on the New Transatlantic Slave Trade Database.* New Haven: Yale University Press, 2007.

Eltis, David, David Richardson, Stephen D. Behrendt, and Herbert S. Klein, eds. *The Atlantic Slave Trade: A Database on CD-ROM Set and Guidebook.* Cambridge, U.K.: Cambridge University Press, 1999.

Harms, Robert W. *River of Wealth, River of Sorrow: The Central Zaire Basin in the Era of the Slave and Ivory Trade, 1500–1891.* New Haven, CT: Yale University Press, 1981.

Henriques, Isabel de Castro. *O pássaro do mel: Estudos de história africana.* Lisboa: Edições Colibri, 2003.

Heywood, Linda M., ed. *Central Africans and Cultural Transformations in the American Diaspora.* Cambridge, U.K.: Cambridge University Press, 2002.

Manning, Patrick. *Slavery and African Life: Occidental, Oriental, and African Slave Trades.* Cambridge, U.K.: Cambridge University Press, 1990.

Marques, João Pedro. *The Sounds of Silence: Nineteenth-Century Portugal and the Abolition of the Slave Trade.* New York: Berghan Books, 2006.

Martin, Phyllis M. *The External Trade of the Loango Coast, 1576–1870.* Oxford: Clarendon Press, 1972.

Medina, João, and Isabel Castro Henriques, eds. *A rota dos escravos: Angola e a rede do comércio negreiro.* Lisbon: Cegia, 1996.

Miller, Joseph C. "The Significance of Drought, Disease, and Famine in the Agriculturally Marginal Zones of West-Central Africa." *Journal of African History* 23, no. 1 (1982): 17–61.

Miller, Joseph C. "The Paradoxes of Impoverishment in the Atlantic Zone." In *History of Central Africa*, Vol. 1, ed. David Birmingham and Phyllis Martin. London: Longmans, 1983.

Miller, Joseph C. *Way of Death: Merchant Capitalism and the Angolan Slave Trade: 1730–1830.* Madison, WI: University of Wisconsin Press, 1988.

Needell, Jeffrey D. "The Abolition of the Brazilian Slave Trade in 1850: Historiography, Slave Agency and Statesmanship." *Journal of Latin American Studies* 33, no. 4 (2001): 681–712.

Rodrigues, Jaime. *O infame comércio: Propostas e experiências no final do tráfico de africanos para o Brasil (1800–1850).* Campinas: Editora da UNICAMP/CECULT, 2000.

Rodrigues, Jaime. *De costa a costa: Escravos, marinheiros e intermediários do tráfico negreiro de Angola ao Rio de Janeiro, 1780–1860.* São Paulo: Companhia das Letras, 2005.

Sweet, James H. *Recreating Africa: Culture, Kinship, and Religion in the African-Portuguese World, 1441–1770.* Chapel Hill: University of North Carolina Press, 2003.

Thornton, John K. *Africa and Africans in the Making of the Atlantic World, 1400–1680.* Cambridge, U.K.: Cambridge University Press, 1992.

Thornton, John K. "Cannibals, Witches and Slave Traders in the Atlantic World." *William and Mary Quarterly* 60, no. 2 (2003): 273–294.

JOSEPH C. MILLER

ATLANTIC, WESTERN AFRICA

Thanks to the research conducted since the mid-twentieth century, historians' knowledge of the African past has grown considerably. This advance in knowledge, however, has been uneven. Economic history remains an underdeveloped field in African studies. In particular, several aspects of the political economy of the Atlantic slave trade have yet to attract serious research employing rigorously analytical tools employed in the study of other regions of the world by development economic historians. Why did European merchants trading to the Americas seek slave labor rather than free wage labor? If they had to procure slave labor, why did they not do so in Europe or in Asia instead of Africa? How did the European trade in African slaves compare with the one in European and Asian slaves that preceded it? What effect did the loss of millions of young men and women have on the processes of socioeconomic development in western Africa? For this purpose, a clear distinction is drawn between the short-term private gains of a few African individuals and groups, and the long-term developmental consequences for the economies and societies of the region as a whole.

CONCEPTUAL FRAMEWORK

The most challenging problem in comprehending and demonstrating how the Atlantic slave trade affected long-term socioeconomic development in sub-Saharan Africa is a conceptual one. While discovering the extant archival sources, and evaluating and establishing the basic facts about the trade are by no means easy tasks, even more difficult is knowing what information to look for and what meaning to give to that information once it has been procured. Only a carefully thought out conceptual framework can help solve this problem.

With the focus on long-term socioeconomic development in western Africa, an appropriate analytical framework must identify, in general terms, the central elements in the development process, given agricultural economies and societies in which subsistence production is still dominant, as was the case in western Africa in 1450. Put simply, the ultimate goal of socioeconomic development in organized societies is to raise societal capacity to regularly produce goods and services, which the members wish to consume, in a steadily expanding quantity and steadily improving quality. This requires cooperation and coordination within and between societies on a very large scale and over extensive geographical areas. At the center of this cooperation and coordination over vast and diverse geographical regions is the market. The growth of markets and market institutions makes possible the development of specialization and division of labor. Extensive development of the division of labor (interpersonal, interregional, and international) on a market basis enlarges the scale of production and offers the best opportunity for improving the skills of individual producers and the overall techniques of organization, production, and distribution.

Thus for agricultural societies still dominated by subsistence production (that is, a form of production in which the bulk of the output is not exchanged on the market but rather is consumed directly by the producer), the first prerequisite for development is generalized commercialization of socioeconomic life. The bulk of agricultural and manufacturing output must be deliberately aimed at the market and exchanged therein, and all factors of production (land, labor, and capital) must also be freely exchanged on the market as a matter of course. All of these are necessary preconditions for the full development of all the sectors of an economy (agriculture, mining, manufacturing, trade, transportation, and other services). An analysis of the impact of the Atlantic slave trade on western Africa at this level requires an understanding of how the conditions created by the trade facilitated or hindered the generalized development of these necessary preconditions.

Cooperation and coordination in a complex market economy also need rules and regulations, along with enforcement mechanisms, that must guide the production and consumption decisions of individuals and social groups. When these laws and enforcement mechanisms function properly, they provide opportunities and incentives for individuals to acquire economically useful skills and attitudes, and to evolve organizations that help to increase the social output of individuals' productive efforts. When they do not, they offer disincentives to the acquisition of productivity-increasing skills and encourage activities that disrupt productive efforts, while offering at the same time short-term rewards to a few individuals. Which of these two outcomes prevails at a given moment depends on the character of ruling elites and the conditions that inform their perception of their self-interests and determine the governmental instruments they fashion to secure them. As the fundamental conditions change, all the elements mentioned also change in the long run, including the type of ruling elites, their perception of their self-interests, and the governmental instruments they create to attain them.

It must be understood that governmental institutions are created to meet the private needs of those with the power and influence to design them. Socioeconomic development requires the establishment of socioeconomic and political structures that regularly promote the acquisition and employment of economically useful skills and attitudes, and

adequately reward productive efforts in a structurally sustained manner. Such development takes place only if the interaction of internal and external factors creates conditions that produce ruling elites whose rational choice, induced by the conditions of their existence, simultaneously secures their self-interests and fulfills the requirements for long-term socioeconomic development. If a set of conditions favoring the reproduction of such a happy coincidence does not exist, then the alternative outcome will result. Analysis of the impact of the Atlantic slave trade on the societies of western Africa at this level has to examine how the conditions that the trade both created and prevented determined the type of ruling elites that emerged, the choices made by political and economic entrepreneurs, and how those choices, in turn, affected the process of economic development in western Africa in the very long run.

THE ATLANTIC SLAVE TRADE AND ITS FORERUNNERS

From biblical evidence, historians know that a large number of Hebrew slaves were employed by African rulers in ancient Egypt. The Greeks who followed the Egyptians employed slaves procured from Europe and Asia. Then came the most elaborate slave system of the ancient world, Roman slavery. The slave population in Rome was built up initially with captives taken in the imperial wars. Subsequently, the slave markets in Rome were supplied with slaves from the British Isles and continental Europe. The rise of Islam from the seventh century CE, and the socioeconomic and political system to which it gave rise in the Middle East and northern Africa, occasioned the development of yet another major slave system that supported an important international trade in slaves. Again, the main supply sources for the Middle East and North African slave markets were, for many centuries, in Europe, especially central and eastern Europe. Italian slave traders were in charge. When the Roman Church decreed that European Christians must not be sold as slaves to Muslims in North Africa and the Middle East, they ignored the papal injunctions.

The early centuries of the present millennium witnessed the consolidation of politically and militarily strong state systems all over Europe. The weakly organized communities in Europe were incorporated into empires and other state systems sufficiently strong to defend their territorial integrity and their citizens. With this development, the taking of captives became very costly to captors. As the European supply of captives to the Middle East and North African markets dwindled and became more expensive, North African and Arab merchants trading across the Sahara to western Africa began to take more interest in procuring captives from that region. By the middle centuries of the second millennium CE, a regular trade in western African captives across the Sahara had been well established. Arab merchants trading to the eastern African coast added some numbers from that region. The main difference between Europe and sub-Saharan Africa, in terms of captive taking at this time, was the existence of a balance of power of large states in the former, and the continuing existence of political fragmentation in the latter. Sub-Saharan Africa was still characterized by a multiplicity of small-scale political systems coexisting with a smaller number of larger and stronger political organizations, such as Mali and Songhay. This political contour facilitated the taking of captives from the weakly organized sub-Saharan communities by the stronger polities at very little cost to the latter.

European colonization of the Atlantic islands and the Americas, following the fifteenth-century explorations, became the source of an unprecedented demand for slave labor. Commercial exploitation of the vast resources of the Americas needed a large amount of workers separated from their means of production and the products of their labor, and under the effective control of profit-seeking entrepreneurs. Such workers could be free wage laborers, indentured servants, or slaves. European experimentation with the enslavement of the American Indians had a disastrous outcome. Humiliated, overworked, and infected with European diseases, the American Indian populations were almost wiped out everywhere in a few decades. The experiment with European indentured servants was not any more successful; with vast unoccupied lands available in the Americas, the few European migrants to the New World at this time preferred independent employment. Large-scale commercial exploitation of the American resources, therefore, had to depend on slavery.

But where would the slaves come from? Supplies within the Americas had already dried up. The taking of captives in Europe had become so costly that even the limited demand in the Middle East and North Africa could not be met as in previous centuries. This left sub-Saharan Africa and East Asia as possible sources. Asian slaves were utilized by European entrepreneurs who operated in East Asia for centuries following the arrival of the Portuguese in 1498. But, relative to western Africa, the cost of transporting Asian slaves to the Americas would be prohibitive, given the rudimentary ocean transportation technology of the time. Thus, given the politico-military situation in sub-Saharan Africa already stated, cost considerations ensured that the supply of slaves to the Americas would come mostly from that region. The same cost considerations virtually ruled out eastern Africa until the British anti-slave trade naval patrols significantly raised the cost of procuring slaves from several subregions in western Africa in the nineteenth century.

What made the European slave trade from Africa different from preceding trades in captives was its scale and character. For the first time in human history, the demand for slave labor was based on the employment of slaves to produce commodities on a very large scale for a growing capitalist market that embraced all parts of a vast ocean. It has been estimated that in the last decades of the eighteenth century, the value of commerce conducted across that ocean was at least over £100 million (sterling) per annum, and that of the New World produce that formed the basis of this commerce, over three-quarters came from the labor of African slaves. The use of African slave labor to exploit commercially the vast natural resources of the Americas was big business, the trade that supplied the slave labor was big business, distributing the slave-produced commodities was big business, and supplying in Europe the resources that supported the entire enterprise was very big business that was highly profitable, privately and socially. This was a new phenomenon in world history.

Consequently, European slave traders were able to pay on the African coast slave prices that made captive taking privately rewarding for some political and economic entrepreneurs in the short run. In the second half of the eighteenth century, the European traders carried to western Africa alone various manufactures worth more than £2 million (sterling) annually, over 90 percent of which were exchanged for slaves. This amount of manufactures looks ridiculously small in light of the value of commerce based on the produce of the labor of those slaves, as stated above. This in itself is an indication of the low cost of captive taking in western Africa. Nevertheless, the amount of manufactures involved was sufficiently great to encourage a sustained supply of large numbers of captives, provided by a few individuals and some ruling elites, since initially the short-term costs were borne in the weaker polities and the short-term benefits were accrued in the stronger ones, until all were ravaged in the long run by the cumulative effects. It must be stressed that people on the continent of Africa during the period did not see themselves as Africans. They identified only with their more locally defined polities and communities. Ruling elites were, therefore, not constrained by ideological considerations in taking captives from other polities and selling them to European traders in exchange for imported manufactures.

EFFECTS ON WESTERN AFRICA'S POPULATION

An important aspect of the consequences of the European slave trade for western Africa was its effects on the region's population. Although the total numbers shipped from Africa are still being debated by historians, it is well established by research that whichever estimate one accepts, from 11 million to 20 million, as the number of Africans exported across the Atlantic from 1500 to 1870, the process of procuring those numbers led to a huge loss of population in sub-Saharan Africa. The socioeconomic disruptions arising from the wars caused by the trade and the attendant demographic consequences have been elaborately documented by recent research, especially for West-Central Africa, the slave coast (from the Volta River in Ghana to Lagos in Nigeria), the Gold Coast (present-day Ghana), and the Middle Niger River valley.

The debate has shifted to whether the agricultural resources and the disease environment could have sustained the population destroyed by the slave trade and its attendant consequences. On this there is ample evidence. In the decades immediately following the ending of the Atlantic slave trade—1870 to 1939—population grew in most

areas of western Africa at 0.5 to 1.0 percent per annum, long-run average. During the same period, there was a phenomenal expansion of land-intensive commodity production for export. Yet, there was more than enough arable land to sustain both developments without the need to import food from outside. Similarly, with no contribution from Western medicine worth considering, the population expansion was sustained by traditional African medicine that was available throughout the slave trade era. While many regions shared the impact, two were hardest hit: West-Central Africa and what geographers call the West African Middle Belt. The extremely low population densities of both regions in the late nineteenth century are historically explained in terms of the slave trade's effects rather than in terms of rainfall and the physical environment, which in fact are broadly similar to those of the more densely populated regions of western Africa.

While the trade lasted from the 1440s to the 1860s, the exports were concentrated in the 1650 to 1850 period, particularly 1700 to 1850. On the average, 36 percent of the exports were female and 64 percent were male. The very young and the very old were rarely included, the bulk of the exports being ages fifteen to thirty. These export characteristics were determined primarily by the preferences of the employers of slave labor in the Americas.

Some historians treat the introduction of American food plants into western Africa as a benefit associated with the slave trade, but this is a misconception. The American crops were introduced at a time when European trade with western Africa was predominantly in African products, such as gold, copper, ivory, cotton cloth, wood, and pepper. The introduction of American crops in sub-Saharan Africa, like their introduction in Europe at about the same time and the earlier introduction of Asian crops, was independent of the slave trade. Also, those crops were not adopted on a significant scale in western Africa until the late nineteenth century, or even the twentieth century in some areas. In West-Central Africa, where they seem to have been adopted much earlier, they still could not prevent the devastating effects of the trade, which attacked the region's populations at a time when the societies of Bantu migrants were still going through the process of diffusing new techniques of production and sociopolitical organization.

POLITICAL AND SOCIOECONOMIC EFFECTS ON WESTERN AFRICA

As stated earlier, European demand for captives to be shipped as slaves began at a time when the political scene in western Africa was still characterized by a multiplicity of small-scale autonomous political units. Growing population and expanding internal and external trade provided the main driving force for the incorporation of these independent units into larger political organizations by economic and political entrepreneurs. Some remarkable advances had already been made in this regard. In the western Sudan, a succession of large and complex political organizations developed from the last centuries of the first millennium CE; Mali and Songhay were the climax of that process. Other early complex political organizations included the kingdom of Kongo and a host of city-states. These polities were still going through their early stages of formation when the Europeans arrived. All over western Africa at this time the foundations were being laid for the competitive process of building large and complex state systems.

Initially European demand for African products such as gold, copper, pepper, and cotton cloth tended to encourage the emergence of state systems and ruling elites with vested interests in peaceful relations and trade with their neighbors. A good example here is the Akan trading empire ruled by merchant corporations in present-day Ghana. The combination of European and trans-Saharan demand for gold in the region stimulated general production and trade, which gave rise to the Akan sociopolitical system dominated by merchants. Early Portuguese demand for copper also tended to reinforce the central elements in the Kongo system, based originally on the production and distribution of copper and shell money.

As European demand shifted increasingly from products to captives, a fundamental change occurred in the political process. At the beginning the Europeans arranged with the rulers of the more strongly organized states, such as Bénin and Kongo, to supply captives from their weaker neighbors. But the expanding European demand for more and more

captives soon gave rise to banditry all over western Africa. In places where the foundations already laid had not yet given rise to firmly established large political organizations, the process of state building was hijacked by bandits who became successful political entrepreneurs as their self-interests demanded. All the states created in this way, such as Dahomey, the Segu Bambara state in the middle Niger Valley, and several Akan states on the Gold Coast, were dominated by military aristocracies and constantly at war with their neighbors. The activities of bandits also led to major changes in the character of the established states, some of which collapsed and gave way to more militaristic states, such as Asante and Ibadan.

The prices paid for captives by the European traders made it privately more rewarding in the short run for the predominantly military rulers of hegemonic states to take captives from the weaker communities rather than to incorporate those communities and exploit their resources through the peaceful organization of production and trade. On the other hand, the taking of prisoners for sale overseas offered the weaker communities no incentives to be part of the hegemonic polities. On the contrary, predation forced the prey to organize militarily and thus to form hostile neighboring states of their own. Thus, the existence of a large-scale export market for captives induced the development of state systems characterized by hostile relations with neighbors, which both imposed strict limits on the size of states and created the conditions for their eventual demise. The atomistic nature of the political market made it impossible for any individual state to arrest or contract out of the situation.

Overall, the conditions created by the large-scale European demand for captives for more than three hundred years severely retarded long-term socioeconomic development in western Africa. The Atlantic slave trade arrested population growth at a time when the agricultural societies of western Africa were in transition from predominantly subsistence production of food and manufactures to the generalized commercialization of socioeconomic life. By doing so, it neutralized one of the main factors behind the creation of the necessary conditions for the development of market economies and capitalism in western Africa. The growth of export demand for captives also acted against the development of commodity production in western Africa for export to other regions in the Atlantic Basin. In western Africa's competition for Atlantic markets with other tropical and semitropical regions, the export of its human resource transferred its main advantage to its competitors, while at the same time creating internally unfavorable conditions for the development of efficient production of goods and services. Hence, by the end of the eighteenth century commodity exports were less than 10 percent of the value of western Africa's seaborne commerce. The history of the Gold Coast from the sixteenth to the eighteenth centuries vividly illustrates the consequences of this phenomenon.

From the late fifteenth to the early seventeenth centuries, the external trade of the Gold Coast (with both the trans-Saharan and the European traders) was overwhelmingly dominated by gold (and to a lesser extent kola nut) exports. The growth of this commodity production for export stimulated population growth, urbanization, forest clearing for agriculture, and the expansion of internal trade. In particular, peasant production for market exchange increased. The decline of subsistence production in the countryside allowed manufacturing to concentrate in the expanding cities, further stimulating the growth of town-country trade. Evidence shows a gradual evolution of land markets in the area during the period.

But the entire process was halted and reversed when the Gold Coast was transformed from gold to slave exports, following a shift in European traders' demand from gold to captives as the Americas expanded commodity production for Atlantic commerce, employing enslaved Africans. During the seventeenth and eighteenth centuries, major areas of the Gold Coast suffered depopulation and deurbanization, peasant market production declined, subsistence production increased, manufacturing and agriculture were once again reintegrated in the countryside, and internal trade generally contracted. The evolving constituent elements of capitalism on the Gold Coast had to wait until the late-nineteenth-century demand for cocoa and resumption of population expansion gave them a new lease on life.

Some contributors to the literature on the Atlantic slave trade mistake the growth of market activities in export enclaves for a "commercial revolution" in western Africa induced by the production and sale of captives. In reality, however, the "booming" trade of the slave-trading enclaves concealed the general destruction and retardation of town-country and interregional commercial development by the multiple effects of the violent procurement of captives for export. As a simple illustration of one of the many ways captive taking retarded the development of commerce, there was no market transaction between captive takers and the communities that expended their resources to raise the people seized as captives, unlike the market exchanges that characterized the relationship between gold or cocoa producers and distributors. It was the dislocation in market circuits imposed by the violent production of captives that compelled those involved in the slave trade (merchants, warriors, and ruling elites) to accumulate servile producers employed primarily to produce their own subsistence.

The rather low-level development of the market economy in western Africa in the late nineteenth century, relative to other major regions of the Atlantic basin at the time, was largely a function of the adverse impact of the Atlantic slave trade on both population growth and the development of commodity production for export in western Africa during the critical period of 1650 to 1850. This limited development of the market economy explains the absence of proto-industrialization in all but one region—the cotton textile industry in Kano, Nigeria—of late nineteenth-century western Africa.

The delayed development of the market economy (and its associated commercialization of socioeconomic life) gave rise logically to socioeconomic characteristics wrongly labeled by some historians as uniquely African institutions—"African economic system," "African legal system," "African land law," "African social system," and so on. It is important to note that under favorable conditions—like those in pre-1650 Gold Coast (modern Ghana), nineteenth-century Kano, and late-nineteenth- and early-twentieth-century western Africa generally—the growth and development of the market economy and its cultural underpinnings followed essentially historically predictable patterns. The issue of African agency is also erroneously argued in the literature. Clearly individuals and states in Africa made self-interested choices during the period. But the conditions, under which those rational choices were made, were created by the shift of European traders' demand from products to captives. As can be seen from the Gold Coast evidence presented, that shift was beyond the control of anyone in Africa during the period.

See also **Colonial Policies and Practices; Economics and the Study of Africa; Kano; Labor; Research: Historical Resources; Slavery and Servile Institutions; Textiles; Women: Women and Slavery.**

BIBLIOGRAPHY

Iliffe, John. *The Emergence of African Capitalism*. Minneapolis: University of Minnesota Press, 1983.

Iliffe, John. *Africans: The History of a Continent*. Cambridge, U.K.: Cambridge University Press, 1995.

Inikori, Joseph E. *Forced Migration: The Impact of the Export Slave Trade on African Societies*. London: Hutchinson, 1982.

Inikori, Joseph E. *The Chaining of a Continent: Export Demand for Captives and the History of Africa South of the Sahara, 1450–1870*. Kingston, Jamaica: Institute of Social and Economic Research, University of the West Indies, 1992.

Inikori, Joseph E. "Slavery in Africa and the Transatlantic Slave Trade." In *The African Diaspora*, ed. Alusine Jalloh and Stephen Maizlish. College Station: Texas A&M University Press, 1996.

Kea, Ray A. *Settlements, Trade, and Polities in the Seventeenth-Century Gold Coast*. Baltimore: Johns Hopkins University Press, 1982.

Law, Robin. *The Slave Coast of West Africa, 1550–1750: The Impact of the Atlantic Slave Trade on an African Society*. Oxford: Clarendon Press, 1991.

Manning, Patrick. *Slavery and African Life: Occidental, Oriental, and African Slave Trades*. Cambridge, U.K.: Cambridge University Press, 1990.

Meillassoux, Claude. *The Anthropology of Slavery: The Womb of Iron and Gold*, trans. Alide Dasnois. Chicago: University of Chicago Press, 1991.

Phillips, William D., Jr. *Slavery from Roman Times to the Early Transatlantic Trade*. Minneapolis: University of Minnesota Press, 1985.

Roberts, Richard L. *Warriors, Merchants, and Slaves: The State and the Economy in the Middle Niger Valley, 1700–1914*. Stanford, CA: Stanford University Press, 1987.

Savage, Elizabeth, ed. *The Human Commodity: Perspectives on the Trans-Saharan Slave Trade*. London: Frank Cass, 1992.

Searing, James F. *West African Slavery and Atlantic Commerce: The Senegal River Valley, 1700–1860*. Cambridge, U.K.: Cambridge University Press, 1993.

JOSEPH E. INIKORI

INDIAN OCEAN

Histories of the trans-Atlantic slave trade have largely shaped the way in which scholars based in the West have viewed the slave trade in the Indian Ocean. The conventional view is that the Indian Ocean slave trade was considerably smaller than the Atlantic slave trade and largely comprised a traffic in black Africans initially to Middle Eastern markets, with the addition from the mid-eighteenth century of the plantation economies of the Francophone Mascarene islands (Réunion and Mauritius) in the Western Indian Ocean, and in the nineteenth century of Cuba and Brazil and the East African islands of Zanzibar and Pemba (and opposite continental littoral). As in West Africa, violence was the hallmark of enslavement, the victims being chiefly captured in military expeditions or kidnapped.

Moreover, while some Africans were slavers, the main culprits were foreigners, notably Muslims, who sought slaves from the entire sub-Saharan region of East Africa, comprising the Sudan and Ethiopia in the north and the entire east African littoral between Somalia and Mozambique. Moreover, at the peak of the trade in the nineteenth century, the slaving frontier moved deep into the interior, sweeping through the Great Lakes region into Central Africa. By then, most slaves were exported through Cairo, the Muslim-dominated Red Sea coastline of Ethiopia, and Zanzibar.

As in West African waters, the slave trade in the Indian Ocean was in the nineteenth century attacked by an abolitionist movement backed by the full diplomatic and naval power of Britain, then the world superpower. The British government signed a series of anti–slave trade treaties with local powers that were backed by naval searches, notably of Arab dhows. Only in the 1890s with the establishment of colonial rule in the region did the slave export trade from the east African coast finally end. However, this marked neither the end of slave exports, which continued, albeit in smaller quantity, across the Red Sea to Arabia and the Persian Gulf, nor of the internal slave trade, which has in strife-torn regions such as the Sudan witnessed a resurgence.

Historians of the Atlantic slave trade have also stimulated an extension into the Indian Ocean research into the African diaspora. Concentrating chiefly on Muslim regions, diaspora scholars have highlighted the role of African slaves who in the Middle East and South Asia rose to become great military leaders, court councilors and administrators, and even rulers. More recently, diaspora studies have enlarged to examine the African cultural heritage of communities of ex-African slaves such as the Sidis of Western India.

By contrast, revisionist scholars have eschewed the Atlantic model to study the Indian Ocean slave trade from the perspective of the regions concerned. They have highlighted the development by at least the tenth century CE of a "global economy" based on transoceanic trade that linked the entire region from the Middle East to South Asia and Southeast Asia to the Far East. Within that global economy, the main productive centers and centralized administrations of China, India, Mesopotamia, and Egypt established a strong demand not only for exotic luxuries such as cloves and ivory but also for servile labor.

In the revisionist view, the slave trade of the Indian Ocean world (IOW) global economy contrasted significantly with that of the Atlantic slave trade. First, demand was largely color blind. For long, slaves were obtained from both regional (from wars of conquest to raids against "primitive" hill or island tribes) and distant sources (e.g., for Middle Eastern markets from Eastern Europe and Central Asia). Some scholars consider that the slave trade was greatly stimulated by the rise of Islam, although more important was the demand for labor that accompanied the concomitant growth in IOW global economy (notably from the ninth to thirteenth centuries) as occurred in other periods of sustained economic development in the last centuries BCE and first centuries CE, and during the rapid expansion of the international economy in the nineteenth century.

Although small numbers of slaves were from early times shipped from Nubia and Ethiopia, East Africa did not become a significant source of slaves for IOW markets until the ninth century. Even then, traditional assumptions that African slave exports were very high have been undermined by evidence that most of the supposedly mass "Zanj" and hence "East African" slave rebels in late-ninth-century Iraq were either of local or North African origin. The export of Malagasy and East African slaves to Southeast and East Asia increased from the sixteenth century due to demand from European enclaves, notably Portuguese settlements in Macao and Japan, and Dutch forts in Indonesia; in 1694 there were about 25,000 slaves—of many different origins—in Batavia alone. However, the import of African slaves into Southeast Asian markets was limited due to the availability of slaves within the region (the hill "tribes" of Southeast Asia and the islands) and slave mortality on long-distance routes. For instance, of the 278 Malagasy slaves shipped to Batavia on one ship in 1684, only 108 survived the voyage.

From the late eighteenth century, with the rise in demand for slaves for the Mascarene plantations, East African slave exports increased sharply but only in the nineteenth century did black Africans come to dominate the slave markets of Western India (until about mid-century) and the Middle East. Moreover, the vibrant slave markets of Southeast Asia and the Far East continued to be supplied predominantly by slaves from within the region, some of whom were also exported to meet Middle Eastern demand. Moreover, for the nineteenth century, revisionists have emphasized the existence of Madagascar as a hitherto neglected market for East African slaves.

The IOW slave trade was thus multidirectional and changed over time. East African slaves were exported in cumulatively large numbers over the centuries to other regions of Africa, such as Ethiopia and Egypt, Arabia, the Persian Gulf, India, and to a lesser degree to the Far East. From the mid-eighteenth century, export markets in Africa expanded and considerable numbers of East Africans were shipped to Zanzibar, Pemba, Somalia, Madagascar, the Mascarenes, and some to Cape Town. They were also exported to Portuguese enclaves in India and the Americas. Malagasy slaves were sent in small quantities to Muslim markets, and to European settlements in the Americas, the Cape and Batavia, and from the mid-eighteenth century in considerable numbers to Réunion and Mauritius. Indian slaves were shipped to Indonesia, Mauritius, Cape Town, and the Middle East. However, most slaves to the Middle East initially originated from the Caucasus, Eastern Europe, and Africa. These were joined in the nineteenth and early twentieth centuries by slaves from the Makran coast of Iran, some from Western India, and a few from Indonesia and China. Indonesians were dispatched mainly to markets across Southeast Asia and to Cape Town, while Indochinese and Korean slaves were exported to China, and, in the nineteenth century, Chinese slaves were sent to Singapore and San Francisco.

Revisionists have also challenged the traditional concept that the IOW slave trade was of less demographic significance than the Atlantic slave trade in which for about 400 years from circa 1500 to 1850 some 10 million to 12 million slaves were transported to the Americas. The IOW slave trade, started by at least 2000 BCE, is at least 4,000 years old and is still vibrant. It is impossible to estimate with any precision the number of slaves traded in the IOW given the duration of the slave trade there, the limited nature of extant records, and the fact that, in contrast to the Atlantic system, IOW slaves rarely constituted a specialist cargo. Moreover, the IOW slave trade involved both maritime and overland routes.

As the nineteenth century progressed, the IOW slave trade came under increasing international scrutiny, which induced slavers to adopt indirect routes and pass slaves off as non-slave porters, sailors, domestics, and even as children or other kin. Unlike the trans-Atlantic slaving system, which was dominated by European finance, the ships, personnel, and finance of the IOW slave trade was dominated by indigenous agents; coastal Chinese, Bugis and "Malays" in the eastern sector, and coastal Arabs and Indians, notably Gujaratis, in the western sector. In the nineteenth century, when the IOW slave trade peaked, an estimated 1.5 million slaves were exported from East Africa alone and slaves comprised between 20 percent and 30 percent of the population of many IOW societies, rising to 50 percent and over in parts of Africa

and in Indonesian ports. Overall, however, it is possible that the greatest IOW slave traffic was overland, notably within Africa, Hindu India, and the Confucian Far East. The total number of slaves traded across the Indian Ocean world in a trade that has endured ten times as much as the Atlantic trade is thus likely to have been considerably larger than those shipped across the Atlantic.

Moreover, whereas some two-thirds of slaves landed in the Americas were male, most of them adults, it is probable that many more females and children than adult males were trafficked in the Indian Ocean. Also, whereas the typical employment of New World slaves was unskilled labor on plantations or in mines, that of Indian Ocean world slaves varied enormously according to region and the time period concerned. Some female slaves worked as water carriers, and in agriculture, textile production, and mining, although girls and young women were valued particularly for their sexual attractiveness and reproductive capacity. This profoundly affected the shaping of African-Asian communities. Rulers and the wealthy, most of whom were men, surrounded themselves with female slaves. In terms of Middle Eastern demand for Africans, Berber, Nubian, and Ethiopian females were valued as sexual partners. Ethiopians were considered excellent entertainers, and Berbers and Nubians as good child rearers and domestic servants. Sub-Saharan women were considered docile, robust, and excellent wet nurses, but were less sought after as concubines than Circassians and North Africans. Slaves as secondary wives, concubines, entertainers, and domestic servants enjoyed a lifestyle and a respect often superior to that of female peasants, while their lot was generally much easier than that of male slaves. There are instances of concubines in the Middle East sending for family members to join them—albeit as non-slaves. Female slaves were also less likely to be sold.

Young female slaves commanded generally higher prices than male and older female slaves but not eunuchs ("males made female") who were universally the most highly prized (e.g., in medieval times, black eunuchs sold for three times the price of ordinary Negro male slaves on the Egyptian market). In the Islamic Middle East, eunuchs were in high demand as bodyguards, household and harem guards, and servants and doorkeepers of the Friday mosques of Mecca and Medina. Whites castrated in Spain were initially the source of most eunuchs in the Middle East, but as time progressed were increasingly replaced by Africans, notably from Sudan (exported via Egypt), followed by Lower Senegal, the Maghreb (Berbers), and Ethiopia. As Islam forbade castration, it was generally carried out before the slaves entered the Muslim world. Moreover, it was sometimes performed at the behest of the slaves who viewed it as a means to a privileged position.

Demand for black African male slaves in the Middle East during the initial expansion of Islam was probably for arduous tasks like clearing the Mesopotamian marshes for cultivation, and the mining and smelting of gold and silver. Later occupations included date plantation labor, pearl diving, dock work, and soldiery. However, African slaves also became famous scholars, poets, military commanders, and even rulers. Many of Mecca's Qurayshī elite were the progeny of Arab males and African concubines, and the three greatest early Arab poets, 'Antara bin Shaddād al-Kalbī, Khafāf bin Nudba al-Sulakhī, and Sulayk bin al-Sulaka, were known as the Crows of the Arabs because they possessed black mothers (Hassad, Mufuta, and Mutunda).

Similarly, in the early ninth century Abū Al-Djāhiz, of probably Ethiopian slave origin, achieved fame and influence in Basra and Baghdad as author of sociological commentaries, theology, and politico-religious polemics. In India, imported African slaves were used primarily as domestic servants, soldiers, and sailors. A few Africans rose to positions of great political power in the Deccan states of the Bahmani (1347–1538), Nizam Shahi (1589–1626), and Bijapur (1580–1627). Indeed, at much the same time as Mamluks transformed themselves into the ruling elite in Egypt, some African slaves transformed themselves into rulers in India. Such was the dynasty established by the African slave Mubārak Shāh in the Dehi sultanate (c. 1399–1440) and the rule of African military commanders in Bengal from 1486–1493. The Sidis of Janjira, an island forty-five miles south of Bombay, from 1618 established a naval and military presence and a considerable political autonomy that endured well into the nineteenth century. However, the African slaves who ascended to power presented no real challenge to a political system the parameters of which they accepted and worked within.

The further away from Africa, the more expensive and valued African slaves became. In East Asia, many were acquired as symbols of conspicuous consumption, to reflect the power and wealth of slave owners. In Mongol China (1260–1368), it was *à la mode* for elite households to possess Korean maidservants and Negro manservants, while African males were also valued as divers. European powers also used African soldiers. For example, in the 1630s some three hundred Africans served in the Portuguese army in Sri Lanka. In the seventeenth century, the Dutch used African slaves to build their forts, work on pepper plantations, and mine gold in West Sumatra.

Overall, slave conditions in the IOW were rarely universally harsh. Some slaves depended for sustenance on their owners, while others were given land for subsistence cultivation. Yet others were rented out or left free to seek livelihoods: Although generally remitting from 50 to 75 percent of their earnings to their owner, they were often able to accumulate funds. Indeed, non-slave commoners were frequently described as poorer and less content than domestic slaves, despite the inferior legal status of the latter, while the particularly good treatment of skilled slaves contrasts sharply with the position in some regions of non-slave artisans subject to state imposed forced labor.

See also **Cairo; Cape Town; Colonial Policies and Practices; Diasporas; Heritage, Cultural; Labor: Conscript and Forced; Réunion; Slavery and Servile Institutions; Women: Women and Slavery.**

BIBLIOGRAPHY

Campbell, Gwyn, ed. *The Structure of Slavery in Indian Ocean Africa and Asia.* London: Frank Cass, 2004.

Campbell, Gwyn, ed. *Abolition and Its Aftermath in Indian Ocean Africa and Asia.* London: Routledge, 2005.

Campbell, Gwyn; Suzanne Miers; and Joseph C. Miller; eds. *Africa*, Vol. 1: *Women and Slavery.* Athens: Ohio University Press, 2006.

Clarence-Smith, William Gervase, ed. *The Economics of the Indian Ocean Slave Trade.* London: Frank Cass, 1989.

Harris, Joseph E. *The African Presence in Asia: Consequences of the East African Slave Trade.* Evanston: Northwestern University Press, 1971.

Hunwick, J. O. "Black Africans in the Islamic World: An Understudied Dimension of the Black Diaspora." *Tarikh* 20 (1978): 20–40.

Klein, Martin A., ed. *Breaking the Chains: Slavery, Bondage and Emancipation in Modern Africa and Asia*. Madison: University of Wisconsin Press, 1993.

Watson, James L., ed. *Asian and African Systems of Slavery*. Berkeley: University of California Press, 1980.

GWYN CAMPBELL

NORTHEASTERN AFRICA AND RED SEA

Slaves were brought across—and settled in—the frontier regions of northern and northeastern Africa for almost twelve hundred years, beginning with the Islamic conquests of the eighth century CE and ending during the twentieth century. This commerce has attracted more than its share of debate, since it touches on questions of European attitudes toward Islam, the unity of the African continent, and the ability of modern scholars to measure and evaluate developments for which they have limited and often far from "objective" records.

What scholars know for sure about the Saharan and Red Sea slave trades is that their victims were black-skinned inhabitants of the Upper Nile Valley, southern Ethiopia, and the regions south of the great African desert. Most of these captives were settled in the Arab-speaking countries of Mediterranean Africa (Morocco, Algeria, Tunisia, Libya, and Egypt), the Arabian Peninsula, and the Persian Gulf, as well as the South Asian subcontinent. Many imported slaves did, however, remain within the Sahara, the northern Nilotic Sudan, and the political centers of Ethiopia. Others, especially those entering Libya, were further sold on to ships that took them to the Islamic lands in the eastern portions of the Mediterranean and, around the fourteenth and fifteenth centuries, north into Italy and other European territories. A few also seem to have reached Southeast and East Asia.

The best-known (and also the largest) component of this trade was conducted via camel caravans organized by the Berber and Arab-speaking peoples of North Africa and the Sahara. This included both the trans-Saharan trade as normally understood and the trade from Darfur in the western Nilotic Sudan along the notorious Darb al-Arbain (Forty Day Road) to Asyut in Egypt. Along these routes most of the slaves had to transport themselves on foot, and the evidence suggests that many of them perished along the way.

The pedestrian caravan routes through various parts of Ethiopia were not as long or as arduous as those across the desert, although slaves forced along them often experienced very harsh conditions. Slaves captured in or brought to the southern Sudan were sometimes marched across a shorter desert route to such Red Sea ports as Sawakin or Aydhab. If en route for their more common destination of Egypt, however, they would travel most of the distance by Nile river craft.

Descriptions of these trades as well as the price data from various markets indicate that the majority of the human cargo consisted of women, sought for domestic service and concubinage. However, males were also recruited for employment in agriculture (especially in the Persian Gulf), mining, shipping, pearl fishing (again primarily in the Gulf), as well as urban street cleaning and porterage. A particular area of intensive but fluctuating male demand was military service: various North African and Egyptian regimes relied on servile black troops, as did a number of South Asian states (whose Ethiopian forces were known as Hubshi) prior to the seventeenth-century hegemony of the Mogul Empire. Some boys (up to a few hundred per year) were also castrated for service as eunuchs in the courts and shrines of the Middle East.

There are records of a slave trade across the Sahara and the Red Sea from very early Islamic times. The precise routes varied over time and were often quite complex, especially in the Sahara, the physical conditions of which shifted over time. Everywhere, the slave trade was closely tied to the rise and fall of various political centers as well as alliances between merchants and populations along the routes, particularly the Berber communities of the Sahara. For most of their history, these slave trades were integrated into broader systems of long-distance commerce in goods such as gold, ivory, and ostrich feathers.

THE SIZE OF THE TRADES

Both the demand for and supply of slaves could go up sharply depending upon factors at both ends of the trade routes. There appears to have been a major increase of slave exports to both the

Mediterranean and the Red Sea during the eighteenth and nineteenth centuries, when the entire international economy was undergoing major expansion. During this same period the Islamic world was cut off from alternative sources of slaves in the Caucasus by the expansion of the Russian Empire. Slaves also became available for export during this period due to jihads in the western and central Sudan, the Egyptian invasion of the Sudan, and the rise of mutually competing imperial centers in Ethiopia.

A consistent factor in creating demand for all categories of slaves in northern Africa and the Middle East was the need to replace existing servile populations. Forced immigrants from tropical Africa seemed particularly susceptible to the diseases of the Mediterranean zone. They had remarkably few children while in captivity there, and were much more frequently manumitted in Muslim societies than in the European plantation colonies of the New World. In portions of Arabia and Iraq, African slaves seem to have survived at least as well as native populations, but in the higher altitudes of Iran and (their more frequent location) the palm plantations and pearl fisheries of the Persian Gulf, life expectancies were quite low.

The Atlantic trade, when first undertaken by the Portuguese in the fifteenth century, drew on slaves who would otherwise have been transported across the Sahara. In the long run, however, the two trades seem to have complemented each other, in part because European buyers had a strong preference for male over female slaves. More important, European overseas expansion stimulated the growth (if not the "development") of non-European economies, thus increasing both the capacity to sell slaves in exporting areas and the demand for them in receiving zones.

One of the most controversial issues surrounding both the trans-Saharan and Red Sea trades is their actual size. This question has arisen in response to attempts by historian Philip Curtin and others to calculate the scale of the Atlantic slave trade. The Saharan and Red Sea counts have been restricted to slaves moving beyond the desert, the Nilotic Sudan, or Ethiopia since, in standard terminology, they were thus being removed from "sub-Saharan" Africa. In any case, it is harder to count slaves settled in the areas of transit, although

these probably exceeded (as they did on the Indian Ocean coast) the number who traveled farther.

Even if one restricts oneself to the trans-Saharan and Red Sea export slave trade, one can never produce statistics as precise as those for the Atlantic, since researchers of the former have been able to find very few commercial accounts, customs documents, or census records. Best estimates are based mainly on observations by European travelers and diplomats that are concentrated in the period after 1700. For earlier centuries one can only make projections, based on scattered numerical statements in Arabic sources and a consideration of supply and demand conditions.

The resulting uneven calculations suggest that somewhere in the region of 3.5 to 4 million slaves crossed the Sahara and another 2 million crossed the Red Sea throughout the twelve-century history of the trade. By comparison, the Atlantic slave trade took at least 10.5 million people out of Africa—three times as many as the trans-Sahara and Red Sea trades, in less than four centuries. (Another comparison might add the Indian Ocean trade to the trans-Sahara and Red Sea total, which then comes to somewhere around 8 million.) Even if one adds some 10 percent to the Saharan sum so as to take into account deaths in the desert crossing—which appears to have been more dangerous than the notorious Atlantic Middle Passage—the final figure is still below that of the Atlantic and spread out over a much longer time period. However, when compared with systems other than that of the Atlantic, the Saharan and Red Sea slave trades remain among the major examples of enslavement in world history.

DEFINING THE TRADES

The trans-Saharan and Red Sea routes have also been referred to as Islamic and Oriental, designations that indicate some of the other issues involved in studying these slave trades. In addition to the moral questions that frame modern views on all histories of slavery, this topic calls into question the very identity of the participants on both sides. The immediate recipients of the slaves in question and the overwhelming majority of those who ultimately held them were non-Europeans and at least nominally Muslim. But to speak of an "Islamic" trade suggests that Islam as a religion and cultural system is somehow to blame for the abuses of slavery. Many who documented the trade while it was in progress held such a view, and it is sometimes invoked in contemporary Western polemics about the threat of Islam to liberal values throughout the world. This is not the place to discuss the relationship between slavery and Islam, but it should be noted that a number of prominent Islamic scholars and political leaders of both northern and western Africa publicly criticized the abuses of the Saharan trade (especially where it victimized free Muslims), even if the only arguments for its abolition came after the demand for slaves had receded.

The geographical terms for this system likewise raise questions. The historian Patrick Manning and others refer to all the trades out of Africa not controlled by Europeans as "Oriental." But this term, besides being literally inaccurate about the spatial direction of Saharan commerce, raises the specter of "Orientalism" as a demeaning Western form of knowledge about the exotic and amoral non-European "Other." One critic of Manning's terminology, the African economic historian Paul Tiyambe Zeleza, is even more concerned about the use of the Saharan slave system to draw what he sees as a "racist" line between those portions of Africa on either side of the desert. For Zeleza, slaves are just one of many items of a commercial traffic that linked northern Africa and western Africa more closely to one another than to any other regions within the continent.

The major role of slaves in the commerce across the Sahara and Red Sea can most easily be explained in seemingly neutral economic terms. The transport of any goods to the northern or northeastern shores of Africa involved high costs that could only be born by a limited range of available commodities. Gold fitted such a role particularly well since it has extremely high value in proportion to its bulk. However, slaves could be supplied by a wider range of interior African regions and, even if not in as much demand in the Mediterranean as in the Atlantic, fetched a price that covered the relatively low cost of feeding them while they walked to their points of resale. Also, those slaves not exported could be used along the routes for both military and economic purposes. Thus some slaves supported the trade as they served in the armies of Sudanic and Ethiopian raiders or provisioned merchants and transporters.

Franco-Algerian singer Rachid Taha. Rachid Taha performs during the ninth annual festival Gnaoua and world music festival of Essaouira on the Moroccan Atlantic coast, June 2006. The Moroccan Gnaoua, believed to be descended from slaves, are master musicians or maalems near to the Sufi brotherhoods. Their music is a mixture of Arabo-berber and African. ABDELHAK SENNA/AFP/GETTY IMAGES

Others, however, contributed to the intensification of local agricultural, salt, and handicraft production, thus providing alternative commodities for markets within and outside their own regions.

THE DECLINE OF THE TRADES
Whether such industry would eventually have discouraged slave exports by raising the value of local labor, as argued for all of Africa by Stefano Fenoaltea, is difficult to determine. As it turned out, the Saharan and Red Sea trades were terminated by a combination of exogenous political and economic forces. During the second half of the nineteenth century European abolitionists gradually imposed restrictions on the Mediterranean and Arabian dealers in African slaves, thus cutting off much—if by no means all—of the demand.

With the advent of colonial rule, the trans-Saharan trade was more effectively ended than that of the Red Sea, which has lingered close to the present. By the early twentieth century European railroads provided transport from the western and central Sudan to the Atlantic, which was less costly than caravan carriage across the desert, thus reducing the entire Saharan commercial system to very local dimensions. Colonial governments then interfered directly with slavery in the desert regions, although never eliminating entirely the traffic in human beings, to say nothing of its social residue.

The trade to Egypt from both the Sahara and the Nile Valley diminished drastically as early as the late nineteenth century, due to both European intervention and the rapid rise of the indigenous population, reducing any serious demand for servile labor. Ethiopia, which remained independent throughout most of the twentieth century, could not be as effectively policed, particularly when conditions of famine in densely populated areas created a ready supply of human—particularly juvenile—exports. Meanwhile, on the eastern side of the Red Sea, demand for slaves was stimulated by rising oil wealth amid relatively low population densities. However, the pressure placed on local governments by their European and American patrons has reduced this trade to fairly small and clandestine forms that may well still persist.

See also **Colonial Policies and Practices; Labor: Conscript and Forced; Sahara Desert; Slavery and Servile Institutions; Transportation: Caravan; Transportation: Railways; Women: Women and Slavery.**

BIBLIOGRAPHY

Austen, Ralph A. "Marginalization, Stagnation and Growth: The Trans-Saharan Caravan Trade in the Era of European Maritime Expansion, 1500–1900." In *The Rise of Merchant Empires: Long-Distance Trade in the Early Modern World*, Vol. 1, ed. James D. Tracy. Cambridge, U.K.: Cambridge University Press, 1990.

Baer, Gabriel. *Studies in the Social History of Modern Egypt.* Chicago: University of Chicago Press, 1969.

Clarence-Smith, William Gervase, ed. *The Economics of the Indian Ocean Slave Trade in the Nineteenth Century.* London: Cass, 1989.

Derrick, Jonathan. *Africa's Slaves Today.* New York: Schocken, 1975.

Fenoaltea, Stefano. "Europe in the African Mirror: The Slave Trade and the Rise of Feudalism." *Rivista di storia economica* 25, no. 2 (August 1999): 123–165.

Hunwick, John O. "Islamic Law and Polemics over Race and Slavery in North and West Africa (16th–19th Century). In *Slavery in the Islamic Middle East*, ed. Shaun E. Marmon. Princeton, NJ: M. Wiener, 1999.

Hunwick, John O., and Eve Trout Powell. *The African Diaspora in the Mediterranean Lands of Islam.* Princeton, NJ: M. Wiener, 2002.

"Khasi [eunuchs]." *Encyclopaedia of Islam*, Vol. 4, 2nd edition. Leiden: Brill, 1960.

Manning, Patrick. *Slavery and African Life: Occidental, Oriental and African Slave Trades.* Cambridge, U.K.: Cambridge University Press, 1990.

Savage, Elizabeth, ed. *The Human Commodity: Perspectives on the Trans-Saharan Slave Trade.* London: Cass, 1992.

Zeleza, Paul Tiyambe. *A Modern Economic History of Africa*, Vol. 1: *The Nineteenth Century.* Dakar: CODESRIA, 1993.

RALPH A. AUSTEN

NORTHERN AFRICA AND SAHARA

The slave trade in Northern Africa and the Sahara began before 1000 CE. Initially, individuals captured in small raids on villages or nomadic camps were integrated into their captors' kin groups. By the ninth century, savanna kingdoms formed along the Sahara's southern edge, and gradually large empires such as ancient Ghana, Mali, and Songhay grew, increasing both the complexity of local social systems and the potential uses for slaves. Slaves who were captured in war or traded with other kingdoms grew food for the royal courts, dug wells or constructed buildings, fought in the new armies, and served in the royal households as concubines, washerwomen, cooks, pages, retainers, and stable workers, and performed other menial tasks. Because the enslaved were neither members of local ethnic groups nor royalty, they were disqualified as rulers. Paradoxically, they were ideal for trusted political and military positions because they had no obvious constituency, no clear loyalties in court intrigues, and derived their power solely from their royal masters.

Several factors had to be in place before the trans-Saharan slave trade could flourish. The camel, introduced to the Sahara in late Roman times, greatly increased the ability of nomadic groups north and south of the desert to travel in and across the Sahara. The Muslim expansion across North Africa in the eighth century, and the consequent development of towns, ports, and kingdoms there brought in new Arab overlords and provided political challenges and economic stimulus to the local populations and to Egypt. Local nomadic populations at the Sahara's margins, including Berbers in the Maghreb (present-day Morocco, Algeria, Tunisia, and Libya), Tuareg in West Africa, and Arab-speaking groups in Egypt, Sudan, and elsewhere, ventured into the desert, established

Trans-Saharan slave trade, 650–1900		
Period	Annual average	Estimated total
650–800	1,000	150,000
800–900	3,000	300,000
900–1000	8,700	1,740,000
1100–1400	5,500	1,650,000
1400–1500	4,300	430,000
1500–1600	5,500	550,000
1600–1700	7,000	700,000
1700–1800	7,000	700,000
1800–1900	12,000	1,200,000
Total		7,420,000

SOURCE: Lovejoy, Paul E. *Transformations in Slavery*, 2nd edition. Cambridge, U.K.: Cambridge University Press, 2000.

Table 1.

communities in the oases, and exploited local salt, natron, and copper deposits.

The stage was now set for the slave trade in the region. On top of the local patterns of small wars and village raids, the savanna kingdoms fought larger wars of conquest as they struggled to create the new empires. Desert nomads brought goods from the desert mines and oases to towns at the northern and southern ends of the trans-Saharan trade routes, and soon gold, ivory, and slaves were traded north across the desert, while war horses, textiles, paper and books, and assorted hardware from chain mail and fine swords to cooking pots and hoes, flowed southward. Islam spread in the region as traders ventured southward, as desert populations converted, and as Muslim groups, such as the al-Moravids in western Morocco, gained control over specific trans-Saharan routes.

The trans-Saharan traders left the actual collection of the goods they bought, including slaves, to their local partners. Thus local rulers sought control over the gold-producing areas of Bambuk and Buré, and later, farther east in Gyaman and eastern Sudan, as well as areas with large elephant herds, to harvest their tusks for ivory.

Increasingly, the trans-Saharan traders adopted Muslim law to regulate their commercial interactions, and as the savanna empires became more thoroughly Muslim over time, the Muslim strictures on slavery also began to apply in the lands south of the desert. Many laws regulate the correct behavior of Muslims toward slaves. For example,

it is unlawful for a Muslim to enslave another Muslim. This made determining the religion of captives important, and gave additional incentives for conversion to Islam. Slave women who became pregnant by their masters were to be freed. Several masters could share a slave, but if one of the masters freed his share of the slave, the others were urged to free their shares as well. There were also limits on the physical and verbal abuse of slaves. Of course, the existence of religious strictures did not guarantee lawful human behavior.

THE SLAVE CARAVANS

The desert crossing was a huge enterprise. Two main factors affected the timing of the crossing: avoidance of the hottest part of the year to reduce fatalities in the Saharan Middle Passage, and the desire of Muslim pilgrims who accompanied the trans-Saharan caravans to reach North Africa in time to continue on to Mecca for the *hajj*. There were both official caravans that had their leaders appointed by the rulers of large sub-Saharan empires such as Darfur or Sinnar, and unofficial caravans organized around regional nomadic groups—Berber, Tuareg, or Arab. The official caravans could number up to five or six thousand people and an equal number of camels. Such large caravans were often subdivided into smaller sections for easier management and communication, and to limit the peak demand for water at the smaller oases. Caravans faced attacks from hostile groups along the way, and this discouraged smaller groups from attempting the crossing. The members of a large northbound caravan would gather in a town at the desert's edge shortly before the starting date to collect equipment such as ropes, water bags, and saddles, supplies such as grain and dried foods, and trade goods including slaves, ivory, and gold. The local market place would be abuzz with activity to supply all those items.

The caravan leader was as the captain of a ship, with responsibility for those who traveled with him, for discipline, for choosing the times of departure and rest periods, for selecting the basic route, and for consulting with the expert guides who knew the route, water supplies, and local populations in great detail. In some cases, he traded on behalf of the ruler, and had an official written appointment from him.

Individual merchants traded for themselves and their partners who were related by kinship or marriage. Each had his stock of goods, some camels or donkeys to carry the goods, a few assistants—slaves or younger relatives—and slaves to trade. The richest merchants might also have a wife or several female slaves to cook for them. These merchants rode donkeys, or occasionally horses, while the less wealthy walked or rode camels. The slaves usually walked, though some select slaves—usually beautiful young women destined to be sold as concubines—might ride. In the nineteenth century, boats were used for part of the journey along the Nile to reduce the exhaustion of the slaves and their subsequent mortality. The wealthiest merchants had the best food and most water, and slaves got gruel and a minimal amount of water. Many slaves died in the desert crossing, most commonly of dehydration and exhaustion. Some travelers claimed to recognize the trans-Saharan route by the bodies along the way. Occasionally entire caravans perished, having lost their way or misjudged their water supplies.

SLAVES IN THE DESERT AND THE OASES

Within the desert societies, slaves did vital work. Drought was common in the desert, and slave raiding and slave trading served as means of restocking nomadic and oasis populations. Slaves did the hard work of desert life: digging deep wells with the attendant risk of cave-ins, drawing and hauling water, slaughtering animals, growing and irrigating crops in the oases or in the nomadic base camps at the desert's edge, mining for salt under harsh conditions, tanning leather, tending livestock, and cooking. Slave women might also spin, weave, and serve as concubines to their masters. Sometimes the free nomadic populations placed their slaves in remote villages to grow crops, returning periodically to collect the grains they needed for life in the desert. In the oases, Muslim religious communities—*zawiyas*—provided hospitality to passing caravans. Their slaves did the hard work of irrigating and growing sufficient supplies of food for these periodic visits, and then preparing meals, supplying water, and restocking the equipment and supplies for the caravans.

SLAVE MARKETS IN THE MAGHREB AND EGYPT

Although slave caravans might sell slaves at any point during the desert crossing, they generally brought the bulk of their slaves to slave merchants in northern Saharan towns. North African merchants with the caravan took their stock to their trading partners, and distributed their slaves through them. Merchants who lived south of the desert sold their slaves to northern merchants or accompanied their slaves to the larger towns and cities of the Maghreb and Egypt. There the arriving caravans were met by government officials and required to pay a standard customs duty.

Most major towns had large markets with a section for the sale of products from sub-Saharan Africa, including slaves. These were open-air markets or large buildings with a central courtyard, with an arcade for shops and storage rooms, and lockups for the slaves who were not on display. Prior to sale, slaves washed and oiled their bodies and hair, and dressed in suitable jewelry and clothing for their eventual employment.

Potential buyers approached the slave merchants there and discussed the type of slave desired. Typically the most expensive slaves were the eunuchs and best-looking young women, and males, girls, older women, and slaves with obvious defects were the least expensive. Before purchasing, buyers inspected various individuals in detail, looking at their eyes, teeth, tongues, limbs, and the shape of their heads, trying to judge the slaves' age, health, and character. At the same time, bargaining began between buyers and sellers. Buyers not satisfied with what they saw could approach a broker to locate traders with additional stocks of slaves.

Once a deal was reached, the buyer and seller might write up an agreement and have it recorded. Muslim commercial practice required that each slave in effect came with a warranty against defects such as snoring, bed-wetting, mental conditions that caused seizures, hidden handicaps, infectious diseases that had incubation periods, and, for females, unannounced pregnancies or a lack of promised virginity.

Most slaves in the market were freshly imported, but some were being resold. Potential buyers viewed them with some suspicion, wondering if they were ill, dangerous, conniving, or lazy. Consequently, sellers tried to pass them off as new arrivals, and buyers devised tests to determine their understanding of Arabic and for other signs of acculturation.

North of the Sahara, there was often a hierarchy of slaves by place of origin or ethnicity, and by race. In the Maghreb, slaves of European origin included European sailors, merchants, and passengers captured by the Barbary corsairs. The best-known were held for ransom, often for years, and served as slaves while they waited. Slaves from the Balkans and the Black Sea area (north of Turkey) were also available, as were Circassian and Greek women in the early nineteenth century and, later, Abyssinian women. Powerful rulers and wealthy men sought such women as slave concubines, or even as wives. Buyers had notions that certain African ethnic groups were better as concubines or cooks or doormen. Women were favored over men in the cities. But men may have been preferred for agricultural labor, and rulers, notably in Morocco and Egypt, built black slave armies.

Some of the most expensive slaves were eunuchs, castrated males. Muslims considered the operation itself immoral, so it was often performed south of the desert on prepubescent boys. Without proper expertise this was often fatal, and the high price of eunuchs reflected the many slaves lost during castration. Eunuchs served to guard the large harems of nobles and the rich, and often helped to manage large households.

INTERACTIONS WITH THE ATLANTIC TRADE

The slave trade in northern Africa and the Sahara interacted with the better-known Atlantic slave trade in multiple ways. So long as there were Muslim kingdoms in the Iberian Peninsula, the Maghreb supplied sub-Saharan slaves to Spain and Portugal. From the fifteenth century, the trans-Saharan trade was an alternative source of slaves for this region. The Portuguese exploration of the West African coast from 1415 led to competition between Saharan and Atlantic routes for slaves captured in the Senegal River region. Those who captured and traded slaves there had to choose whether the enslaved should be retained locally, sold into the desert, sold in exchange for European and Atlantic goods, or sold to trans-Saharan traders. The answers were affected by price, scales of demand for particular types of slaves, access, and local and regional power struggles. Except along the Atlantic coast in Senegal and Mauritania, it was often cheaper to send European goods from the Mediterranean via the Sahara to the savanna region rather than through West African forest kingdoms until late in the nineteenth century.

SUPPRESSION

As opposition to the trans-Atlantic slave trade increased in the early nineteenth century, there were consequences for the trans-Saharan slave trade and slavery in northern Africa. Historians generally agree that there was an expansion of the trade in the nineteenth century, but disagree about its causes: some suggest that the slowing down of the Atlantic slave trade in effect left more slaves to be traded within Africa, but others believe that growth in internal markets in the savanna and Sahara created a demand for labor met largely through the local use of slaves. The process of abolition of the trans-Saharan slave trade began in the 1830s with the French occupation of part of Algeria, and growing British abolitionist pressure. Tunisia was the leader, banning the export of slaves via the Mediterranean in 1841, the trans-Saharan slave trade to Tunisia in 1841, and slavery itself in 1846.

Egypt followed Tunisia's lead, but at a slower pace. It initially banned the slave trade in 1854, the import, export, and transit of slaves in 1877, and slavery itself banned within seven years of that. A more thorough and detailed measure on slavery and the slave trade in Egypt was signed in 1895. From the 1840s, the other states of the Maghreb were under considerable pressure from European abolitionists to outlaw slavery. Morocco initially demurred, stating that slavery was a recognized by Islam. A second wave of pressure led to the banning of the public sale of slaves in 1885. Events in Algeria as the French expanded their control over the country, and in sub-Saharan Africa as European nations took over the kingdoms of the savanna during the scramble for Africa, diminished the supplies of slaves and reduced the trans-Saharan trade, though slave caravans were still reported in the first two decades of the twentieth century.

See also **Colonial Policies and Practices; Ivory; Metals and Minerals: Gold and Silver; Slavery and Servile Institutions; Textiles; Transportation: Caravan; Women: Women and Slavery.**

BIBLIOGRAPHY

Austen, Ralph. "The Trans-Saharan Slave Trade: A Tentative Census." In *The Uncommon Market: Essays in the*

Economic History of the Atlantic Slave Trade, ed. Henry A. Gemery and Jan S. Hogendorn. New York: Academic Press, 1979.

Austen, Ralph A. "The Mediterranean Islamic Slave Trade Out of Africa: A Tentative Census." In *The Human Commodity: Perspectives on the Trans-Saharan Slave Trade*, ed. Elizabeth Savage. London: Frank Cass, 1992.

Austen, Ralph, and Dennis D. Cordell. "Trade, Transportation, and Expanding Economic Networks: Saharan Caravan Commerce in the Era of European Expansion, 1500–1900." In *Black Business and Economic Power*, ed. Alusine Jalloh and Toyin Falola. Rochester, N.Y.: Rochester University Press, 2002.

Hunwick, John, and Eve M. Troutt Powell, eds. *The African Diaspora in the Mediterranean Lands of Islam*. Princeton, N.J.: Markus Wiener, 2002.

La Rue, George Michael. "The Frontiers of Enslavement: Bagirmi and the Trans- Saharan Slave Routes." In *Slavery on the Frontiers of Islam*, ed. Paul Lovejoy. Princeton, N.J.: Markus Wiener, 2004.

Lovejoy, Paul E. *Transformations in Slavery*, 2nd edition. Cambridge, U.K.: Cambridge University Press, 2000.

McDougall, E. Ann. "In Search of a Desert-Edge Perspective: The Sahara-Sahel and the Atlantic Trade, c. 1815–1900." In *From Slave Trade to "Legitimate" Commerce*, ed. Robin Law. Cambridge, U.K.: Cambridge University Press, 1995.

Walz, Terence. *The Trade between Egypt and Bilad as-Sudan, 1700–1820*. Cairo: Institut Français d'Archéologie Orientale du Caire, 1978.

GEORGE LARUE

SLAVERY AND SERVILE INSTITUTIONS

This entry includes the following articles:
OVERVIEW
ANTHROPOLOGICAL PERSPECTIVES
COLONIAL
SUDAN

OVERVIEW

Institutions of servility have been associated with human society in Africa, as elsewhere, since time has been recorded. The earliest records attest to the existence, and often extensive practice, of slavery and other types of servile relationships. Institutions of servility in medieval times are sometimes referred to as serfdom, although a lack of sources makes it difficult to establish more than people imprisoned in war, sometimes settled in servile villages to produce agricultural commodities, and sometimes bought and sold on the market. Moreover, Islamic legal precedents and traditions that clearly recognized slavery often applied. Whether in areas influenced by Islam or not, servile institutions appear to have been pervasive, closely identified with issues of gender and ethnicity, as well as with political and economic developments. Slavery also appears to have been common in relatively undifferentiated societies beyond the control of centralized states, although, again, the absence of source material makes it impossible to establish the antiquity of such practices. Nonetheless, slavery and related institutions have been integral to all periods of history in Africa, up to and including the early twenty-first century, for which there are historical records.

VARIETIES OF SERVILE CONDITIONS

The types of servile institutions that developed in Africa ranged from formal slavery to debt bondage or pawnship. Slavery could and did exist alongside other types of labor, including wage-labor (in which there was monetary compensation for work), pawnship (in which labor was for interest on debts and the person was collateral for the debt), and communal work (often based on kinship or age grades, in which work was a reciprocal activity based on past and future exchanges). These other forms of labor could involve coercion but usually not to the point at which they could be called slavery. In addition, slaves could be attached to political office, living on land that was subject to patronage. In theory, these situations approximated serfdom. Concubinage, especially under Islamic law, was a special category of slavery. Children of concubine slave women were usually treated as equal to the children of free mothers. Under slavery, individuals were considered property whose ownership conferred on masters the right to buy, sell, and otherwise exploit the labor or the person of the slave without that individual's consultation or agreement. Only in instances of concubinage (in which slave women gave birth to children by their masters) was it not legally possible to sell slaves—neither the concubines nor their children could be sold. In some areas where lineage structures were particularly strong, servile relationships, including slavery, expanded the size of families and villages through the incorporation of girls and women whose children were assimilated. Under matrilineal custom, the children of servile women could only acquire rights to land and other communal holdings through their fathers, thereby structurally bypassing the usual kinship links between uncles and their nephews and nieces.

Debt bondage differed from slavery in that individuals were held as collateral for loans and, during the period of servitude, individuals were expected to work for the creditors, being released from bondage only when the full debt had been repaid. Because pawns often were not the individuals who had contracted the debt, but relatives of debtors, the conditions of servitude varied according to the social and political influence of larger kinship groups. Pawnship, like slavery, circumvented matrilineal practices of marriage and labor recruitment, which reinforced relationships between children and the senior brother of their mother, rather than their father. As in patrilineal societies, pawns usually came under the direct control of the male head of the house.

Some practices associated with slavery and pawnship suggest a series of intermediate stages of servitude. War captives, political prisoners, and victims of kidnapping could be redeemed from servitude; slavery resulted only if ransom was not paid. Former slaves and freed slaves sometimes had special status, as among the Tuareg of the Sahara. Pawns could find themselves sold as slaves when contracts for repayment of debts were not be satisfied or when creditors found themselves in debt. Although individuals could be pledged as surety for loans in formal arrangements, there were times when individuals or groups of individuals were seized in compensation for injuries or debts. This practice, sometimes referred to as *panyarring*, could result in enslavement, or in death or other forms of retaliation. Moreover, individuals held as commercial hostages could sometimes become slaves if the ransoms were unpaid. There were variations in these institutions, and their relative importance in society changed over time in ways that are not always clear.

As the range of servile relationships suggests, slavery, pawnship, and related institutions were fundamental features of social structure, at least since the fifteenth century in those places that can be documented. By the eighteenth century, slaves

and pawns were concentrated in the most centralized states and societies, and in the most economically developed areas of Africa. The political and commercial elite had acquired the most slaves. Indeed, in many places political power depended upon the accumulation of a large, servile following. By the nineteenth century, and likely earlier still, it appears that a majority of the servile population was female, usually residing in the households of the masters, where the women's acculturation and language use could be controlled. Many male slaves were inducted into the army, which served as another institution of acculturation.

Other instances of servile relations included voluntary enslavement, particularly when the threat of starvation left the person with no other recourse. This structural dimension may well have carried with it a dimension that was ultimately exploitative and violent. Nonetheless, voluntary enslavement was unusual, and it probably accounted for only a small percentage of slaves in most places. Furthermore, the possibility of voluntary enslavement depended on the existence of an institution of slavery in which violence was fundamental. If no such institution existed, a person would not become a slave but a client or some other dependent. That the status of slaves was even assigned in such instances indicates that other servile statuses were not appropriate, either because they were lacking or because they were defined to exclude such cases.

GENDER RELATIONS, ETHNIC IDENTITY, AND RELIGIOUS ISSUES

Institutions of servility strongly affected gender relationships, especially in the governing of marital and sexual arrangements. Slaves tended not to maintain their numbers naturally, and slave populations usually had to be replenished. One reason for this was the relatively short life span for many slaves. Death could result from particularly harsh work, while funeral sacrifices and unsuccessful castration operations took their toll. Travel conditions for slaves destined for distant markets were also a factor, both because individuals were moved from one disease environment to another and because rations were often inadequate. Another reason was the demographic imbalance between the sexes in slave populations. Populations with an excess number of males led to general decline in total population, not just slaves, unless more slaves were imported. When slave women were distributed unevenly, the general population did not necessarily decline, only the proportion of slaves in the population. Islamic law only sanctioned marriage with free women, but free males could have female slaves as concubines. In non-Muslim areas, men could take as many wives as they could afford and the types of marital arrangements varied with the status of the women.

Pawnship was closely tied to marriage, serving as an alternate mechanism for obtaining women as junior wives in polygynous households. Whereas slave wives were obtained through outright purchase or capture, pawn wives were obtained in return for canceling the debts of the pawns. Islamic law guaranteed children of slave concubines equal treatment to the freeborn; after the father, children could indeed inherit property, succeed to office, and marry within royalty. Children of servile women in non-Muslim areas could suffer from the absence of kinship ties with the families of their mothers, but otherwise were incorporated into the lineages of their masters. Biologically, they were the offspring of the slaves, but a slave's right to raise her children could be denied. Instead, slave children could be taken away, and even when they were not sold, could be redistributed as part of marriage arrangements, trained for the army or administration, or adopted by the master's family. Many children were brought up in aristocratic or merchant households that had many women, almost none of whom were native-born but had entered their households as slaves from different ethnic and cultural backgrounds.

Servile relationships also affected ethnic identity. Because slave women often came from cultures other than those of their masters, the diversity of ethnic and linguistic backgrounds influenced the upbringing of children in complicated ways. The presence of women of different cultural origins raises questions about the meaning of ethnic categories and how these changed over time. Moreover, as the case of the Yoruba-speaking people makes clear, the acquisition of foreign-born slaves and their incorporation into society helped to establish and maintain sub-ethnic distinctions. Ethnic categories could reflect a dichotomy between the freeborn and the enslaved. But slaves did not

necessarily come from great distances. In the Yoruba wars of the nineteenth century, many people were enslaved and many were in fact re-enslaved. Because slaves did not always come from a radically different culture, individual cases have to be examined carefully to determine the possible relationship between slave status and ethnicity.

In the early seventeenth century, the Muslim jurist Ahmad Baba (1556–1627) examined ethnicity in the context of the debate over slavery within the Islamic world of western Africa. His discourse identified categories of people who, he considered, could be legally enslaved and those who could not. Later Muslim writers, following the lead of Ahmad Baba, continued to debate issues of slavery in the context of the transatlantic slave trade. It should be noted by these examples that debates over the meaning and legitimacy of slavery were not confined to the European Enlightenment, as many Western scholars have concluded; there was an active dialogue about the subject of slavery, its legitimacy, and ethnicity in Africa itself. Because of the literate tradition of Islam, the early modern debate is known. Various legal restrictions and cultural prohibitions in other parts of Africa make it clear that most societies were concerned about the legitimacy of slavery, although usually such reservations were limited to specific categories of people, particularly kin. In both Islamic and lineage contexts, however, prohibitions were not always followed. The difficulty of verifying the status of individuals, the increasing commercialization of society, and outright illegal actions undermined internal efforts at critical reflection.

As the writings of Ahmad Baba and his successors make clear, servile relationships were sometimes closely associated with issues of religion. In a treatise written for the Bey of Tunis in the early nineteenth century, the religious practices of black slaves were described as deviant behavior that justified enslavement; this viewpoint provided an apology for slavery in the regency, although eventually slaves were emancipated. Christian slaves were freed in 1816; black slaves in 1846. Such writings indicate that the nature of Islamic orthodoxy was being debated—the position of spirit cults such as *bori* and *zar* reflected the ways in which Islamic and supposedly non-Islamic practices were interconnected with issues of servility. Only later did slavery itself come under attack, resulting in emancipation in parts of the Muslim world. Many Muslims of the jihad movement opposed the sale of slaves to Christians and protested the reduction of freeborn Muslims to slavery, yet sanctioned the enslavement of non-Muslims and Muslim enemies.

In non-Muslim areas, religion also made its imprint on the institution of slavery, although in different ways. Religious practices that were connected with kinship, including access to family shrines and funeral customs, reinforced the relationships of power between masters and their kin on the one hand, and slaves and pawns on the other. In some places, slaves were sacrificed at funerals—among the Igbo (Ibo) in the nineteenth century the execution of several slaves was a sign of great wealth on the part of the deceased. Dahomey also staged public executions of war captives, and slaves were executed in cult houses within the palaces of Dahomeyan kings. The bricks for these houses were made with the blood of slaves. Cult slavery was common elsewhere along the West African coast. Known as *osu* among the Igbo, slaves were presented to a shrine and their labor and bodies were made available to the shrine's priests. These slaves could not be sold because they technically belonged to the shrine, but they and their offspring were ostracized. Such slavery has persisted in Ghana into the early twenty-first century.

THE SLAVE TRADE

In the context of African history, the interrelationship of internal forms of slavery and servility with the export trade in slaves is an important consideration and topic of debate among scholars. The transatlantic and transsaharan slave trades removed millions of enslaved Africans from their homelands; the history of this diaspora and its relationship to Africa raises questions that are not explored in this article. The relative impact of the external trade in slaves to internal developments within Africa is also a subject of debate. Most estimates of the numbers of enslaved Africans who were shipped to the Americas range in the order of twelve million people; the numbers of people sent as slaves across the Sahara Desert, the Red Sea, and the Indian Ocean have been more difficult to establish, but the scale of this trade was historically large.

Whatever the actual figures, the political developments of the several centuries before the institution of formal European rule resulted in the massive enslavement of people in Africa. The emergence of new states along the Atlantic coast of Africa and its immediate hinterland was closely associated with the development of the transatlantic slave trade. Dahomey emerged as a state with a structure that required the enslavement of people. Slaves were either killed in public ceremonies associated with the political power of the Dahomeyan monarchy; were sold to Europeans to raise essential revenue for the state; or, after the end of the transatlantic trade in slaves, were settled on plantations in Dahomey to produce palm oil and harvest palm kernels. A series of Muslim holy wars that began in the Senegambia region in the late seventeenth century and spread across the savanna as far as the Red Sea by the end of the nineteenth century also accounted for great numbers of slaves. Thus, although there was resistance to enslavement as a political and religious weapon, the frontiers of slaving expanded greatly, particularly in the nineteenth century, resulting in a dramatic increase in the number of people who were enslaved.

The Fluctuating Status of Slaves. Not all of these newly enslaved individuals remained in slavery. Many were ransomed, regained their freedom, returned to their homes, and resumed their lives as best they could. Pawns were redeemed, as well. Ransoming and redemption, in effect, imposed forms of servile status on individuals that were temporary and could lead either to freedom or to continued enslavement and sale. The distinction between prisoners who were being held for ransom and slaves who had been bought in the market has sometimes been highlighted through the use of the term captive to describe the newly enslaved. By contrast, trade-slaves have been used to describe those individuals who were being sold. These distinctions highlight the continuum along which individuals may slide into slavery. In the African context, individuals were sometimes able to achieve emancipation or various stages of partial freedom under bondage, and thereby move out of slavery. But individuals also found themselves suddenly enslaved through kidnapping, raid, or war, and servile relationships that involved safeguards could be violated. The status of slavery and other service institutions fluctuated, either following a course toward greater oppression and even death, or leading to various methods of emancipation. Slavery was not a static institution.

ECONOMIC CONTEXTS

Economic developments strongly influenced the incidence and nature of slavery and other servile institutions. Even before the rise of the transatlantic trade, slaves were used extensively in agricultural production in the Sahel, and the import of enslaved people into such marginal areas until the late nineteenth century reveals a continuity that was virtually autonomous. Along the Atlantic shores of Africa, slaves were also used extensively in the economy, often in agricultural production and in transporting commodities to market. In Akwamu, the most important state on the Gold Coast (twenty-first century Ghana) in the late seventeenth century, slaves were a noticeable portion of the population. Asante, Dahomey, and Oyo were the dominant powers of coastal western Africa in the eighteenth and early nineteenth centuries, when slave exports were at their peak. In the Bight of Biafra, a political confederation under Aro domination controlled the interior and dominated the slave trade. The abolition of the transatlantic slave trade affected these states differently, both in timing and impact. Asante was able to adjust to declining slave exports by shifting to gold and kola production. The Igbo interior of the Bight of Biafra benefited from dense palm forests and a series of rivers and lagoons that made transport of palm oil relatively easy. As palm oil prices rose in Europe, the profits of exports also flowed to Dahomey, the southern Yoruba states, Sierra Leone, and elsewhere.

Colonial Slavery. European and Arab colonies in southern and eastern Africa made use of slaves in the nineteenth century, especially in the production of export goods. As elsewhere in Africa, local variations were profound. It is safe to generalize that slavery was a major theme in almost every area of Africa and it is also safe to say that the reasons for that importance differed substantially. South Africa, dominated by the expansion of a racialist, white slave regime at Cape Town, stands out as one discrete setting for slavery. The consolidation of Omani rule along the Swahili coast, and

commercial expansion into the interior also relied on a combination of forces that included slavery. The development of slave plantation economies in Zanzibar and Pemba (clove production), and along the Swahili coast (grain production) has been compared to the cotton plantations in America. The Portuguese, including a mulatto community, developed sesame-producing slave plantations and experimented with other crops along the Mozambique coast and the Zambezi Valley. Coffee, cotton, and other crops were grown in plantation enclaves in Angola, and also by a mixed Portuguese population. These developments in the exploitation of slave labor had several features in common, including the key entrepreneurial role of expatriates, whether European, Arab, Indian, or mulatto. Moreover, the attempt to capture export markets in agricultural commodities and mineral wealth through the use of slave labor reflects a trend that was seen elsewhere in the tropical world, both in the Americas and in Asia.

SOCIAL AND POLITICAL CONTEXTS

The history of Africa demonstrates that slavery has occurred in a variety of social and political environments. These became increasingly commercialized, so it is essential to distinguish between the extremes of market-oriented slavery, and the enslavement of individuals in relatively undifferentiated societies isolated from long-distance trade and world markets. The concentration of slaves and the scale of slavery increased with the degree of commercialization, either internationally across the Atlantic and Indian Oceans, or across ecological zones within Africa itself. The extent of the market penetration is important to consider because slavery was not just a form of property, but also a relationship between people that arose from differences in power.

Abolition. The movement to end the export of slaves from Africa, and then to end slavery as an institution, developed in the context of this more extensive use of slaves within Africa. On the one hand, international market forces encouraged the exploitation of slave labor and probably resulted in a rise of pawning. On the other hand, the abolition of slave trading and the emancipation of slaves became increasingly likely as the nineteenth century progressed. The spread of evangelical Christianity was closely associated with this reform movement. Missionary activity that involved many liberated slaves spread the discourse of the abolition movement along the coast of western Africa. Former slaves returned to slave-trade ports and sometimes traveled inland. The missionary enterprise and the abolition movement involved both Europeans and Africans.

Sometimes consciously and sometimes not, the spread of Christianity and its associated reforms ultimately had a profound impact in undermining servile institutions and helped Europeans justify their conquest of Africa that resulted in the consolidation of colonial rule in the last decade of the nineteenth century and the early years of the twentieth century. European imperialism, the Christianization of the African population, the spread of Islam under the threat of European colonialism, and reactions to colonial policies all affected the transition in servile relationships. Abolition, emancipation, and the transition to post-slavery relationships are subjects in themselves. Colonial rule imposed changes on social structures that altered the relationship of servility to political power. In some cases, antislavery ideology was used as a convenient justification for European occupation. However, slavery and pawnship were subject to gradual reforms owing to colonial regimes using conscript labor on a massive scale and otherwise exploiting labor through taxation. Moreover, local elites who allowed themselves to be co-opted into the colonial regime were usually allowed to maintain coercive power over previously servile populations. Although illegal under European colonialism, the buying and selling of slaves continued for decades in many places and even survived into the postcolonial era in some areas.

The longevity of slavery is not surprising, whether in Africa or elsewhere. Slavery is based on the absolute power of one individual over another, which may be articulated as a property relationship and ultimately has as its enforcement the threat of, or the administration of, violence. The coercion inherent in slavery is always prominent. Even when individuals were reduced to slavery during periods of famine and environmental disaster, violence or the threat of violence was usually present; political intrigue and war inhibited the movement of refugees, unless as slaves or as pawns.

The correlation of slavery with violence and hardship suggests that politically induced conditions made famines and natural disasters worse than they may otherwise have been. Slavery and the threat of enslavement limited the access of people to resources and servile status stripped people of their fundamental human rights.

See also **Baba, Ahmad; Cape Town; Christianity; Colonial Policies and Practices; Ethnicity; Gender; Household and Domestic Groups; Islam; Kinship and Descent; Labor: Conscript and Forced; Law: Islamic; Marriage Systems; Plantation Economies and Societies; Slave Trades; Women: Women and Slavery; Women: Women and the Law.**

BIBLIOGRAPHY

Cooper, Frederick. *Plantation Slavery on the East Coast of Africa*, 2nd edition. Portsmouth, New Hampshire: Heinemann, 1997.

Eltis, David. *Economic Growth and the Ending of the Transatlantic Slave Trade*. New York: Oxford University Press, 1987.

Hawthorne, Walter. *Planting Rice and Harvesting Slaves: Transformations along the Guinea-Bissau Coast, 1400-1900*. Portsmouth, New Hampshire: Heinemann, 2003.

Lovejoy, Paul E. *Transformations in Slavery: A History of Slavery in Africa*, 2nd edition. Cambridge, U.K.: Cambridge University Press, 2000.

Lovejoy, Paul E., and Jan Hogendorn. *Slow Death for Slavery: The Course of Abolition in Northern Nigeria, 1897–1936*, New ed. edition. Cambridge, U.K.: Cambridge University Press, 1993.

Lovejoy, Paul, and Toyin Falola, eds. *Pawnship, Slavery and Colonialism in Africa*. Trenton, NJ: Africa World Press, 2003.

Manning, Patrick. *Slavery and African Life: Occidental, Oriental, and African Slave Trades*. Cambridge, U.K.: Cambridge University Press, 1990.

Meillassoux, Claude, ed. *L'esclavage en Afrique precoloniale*. Paris: F. Maspero, 1975.

Miers, Suzanne, and Igor Kopytoff, eds. *Slavery in Africa: Historical and Anthropological Perspectives*. Madison: University of Wisconsin Press, 1977.

Miers, Suzanne, and Richard Roberts, eds. *The End of Slavery in Africa*. Madison: University of Wisconsin Press, 1988.

Miller, Joseph C. *Slavery and Slaving in World History: A Bibliography, 1900–1991*. Millwood, NY: Kraus International Publications, 1993.

Robertson, Claire, and Martin Klein. *Women and Slavery in Africa.* Madison: University of Wisconsin Press, 1983.

Savage, Elizabeth, ed. *The Human Commodity: Perspectives on the Trans-Saharan Slave Trade.* London: Frank Cass, 1992.

Shell Robert C.-H. *Children of Bondage: A Social History of the Slave Society at the Cape of Good Hope, 1652–1838.* Middletown, CT: Wesleyan University Press, 1994.

Willis, John Ralph, ed. *Slaves and Slavery in Muslim Africa.* 2 vols. London: Frank Cass, 1986.

PAUL E. LOVEJOY

ANTHROPOLOGICAL PERSPECTIVES

The conventional Western notion of slavery involves several diagnostic elements: slavery is understood to be the ownership of people as property, who lack freedom, whose labor is appropriated, and who constitute the lowest stratum in the population. Some Africanist scholars take these features to be the essence of slavery in Africa as elsewhere and deal with African slavery as primarily an economic institution. By contrast, other scholars stress a relativistic anthropological perspective, insisting that the Western notion loses its diagnostic and analytical value when applied to core African societies (as opposed to some peripheral areas of Saharan, Sahelian, and eastern Africa and of southern Africa, where intrusions of Islamic and Western systems of slavery occurred).

THE CULTURAL CONTEXT

The Western model of slavery is alien to African models in several respects, including the notion of property. The fundamental social units in most African societies were exclusive sets of kinsmen, real or fictive, operating as corporate kin groups (often referred to as "lineages"). Each such kin group persisted over the generations as a corporation, and it controlled an estate that included various rights over its own members and other persons (members' wives and children, for example), as well as land. The kin group "owned" its members; it could sell or kill them, and it controlled their assets. These rights over "free" or full members are, of course, precisely those that are diagnostic of slavery in the conventional Western definition, except that they were vested in the group in which the people thus "owned" had a voice rather than in an entirely

separate and autonomous individual. Moreover, rights to people were regularly transacted between kin groups in exchange for material goods or money—another feature of Western slavery in transactions between independent individuals. For example, payments procured marital rights over women and determined the kin group's rights over children, and loans between groups were secured by pawning members of the debtor community to their creditors. The acquisition of group rights over slaves partook of the same cultural logic that underlay the system of African kinship relations. This parallel made for an easy integration of the systems of kinship and of slavery, in contrast to the incompatibility of slavery and kinship in the West.

Another diagnostic feature of Western slavery—uncompensated labor—makes slavery into a primarily economic institution. But African slavery was concerned with social and political rights over persons, not merely rights to economic or material product. To focus on African slavery as a labor institution is to deny the importance of noneconomic motives in acquiring persons, evident in the great range of uses to which acquired people and their descendants were put. As to absence of freedom as a criterion of slavery, one must remember that "freedom"—in the sense of complete individual autonomy—is a modern Western ideal. Such an abstract notion could have no more currency in African societies than it could in medieval Europe or indeed in any premodern or communal society, where security lay in one's dependence on a social group or a patron. Finally, there is the question of the semantics of the term "slave." African terms that approximate "slave" are far more expansive than the Western term; they encompass many more and different kinds of people, many of whom would not qualify as slaves under the Western definition. This expansive notion calls for special caution in attributing Western characteristics to African slavery.

THE SLAVERY-TO-KINSHIP CONTINUUM

At the moment of acquisition, captured or purchased slaves were torn out of their social niches and stripped of their personhood and social identities. They were truly commodities, objects rather than persons in their lack of the all-important relationships that constituted African kin groups, and they remained isolated nonpersons if they were to be resold or sacrificed. It is at this initial stage of the process of uprooting that the conventional Western image of slavery is most applicable to Africa. But in Africa, if the slaves were to become social actors in the host society, living in daily interaction with others in it, they had to be repersonified and rehumanized. At a minimum, each had to be given a new name, which signified entry into a new personhood of relationships. This step called for careful ritual handling, and the ritual shared its cultural logic with other rites of passage, such as adoption.

The crucial question in slavery, then, is not the bare fact of acquisition but rather the acquired person's normal trajectory after it. The question points to one solution to the definitional conundrum: to abandon an all-or-nothing, static view of African slavery and to see it in terms of its defining processes. In the same sense that the defining processes in Western slavery were the loss of freedom and its possible recovery through individual manumission, in Africa they were the loss of kinsmen and a possible acquisition of new pseudo-kinsmen. African semantics usually emphasize the slaves' initial position as strangers, outsiders, aliens, or recent arrivals—people who do not "belong." It is not unusual for the same term to indicate both stranger and slave. Since in precolonial African societies one's fundamental identity derived from one's place in one's kin group, a lack of belonging to such a group provided the central meaning of slavery: a person who had broken all ties to kin or patrons—fitting precisely the Western conception of total individual freedom—can be seen as analogous to a slave.

There are two sides to the concept of belonging. "Belonging to" stresses the rights of the owner (which in Africa was the kin group); in this sense, ordinary members and slaves belonged equally to the kin group. On the other hand, "belonging in" stresses the person's rights and relationships within the kin group and his or her access to its material resources, its physical and ritual protection, exercise of authority within it as one aged, and, most importantly, the fully rooted social identity and personhood that numerous relationships within it conferred. Newly acquired outsiders did not enjoy these connections or benefits,

but they and their descendants could in time acquire some of them, sometimes all of them, as they became assimilated into the kin group. The desirable trajectory in life was the gradual movement on the slavery-to-kinship continuum from dependence with no rights to dependence with rights—or from the periphery toward the center of the group.

THE DYNAMICS OF KINSHIP IN AFRICAN SLAVERY

The centrality to African slavery of the slavery-to-kinship continuum does not mean that all African slaves and their descendants eventually became quasi-kinsmen, let alone full kinsmen. Most remained somewhere in the middle of the continuum, and this ambiguity often played a role in kin-group politics. In the perpetual competition among kin groups, success depended on size—hence, every group strove to acquire new members, be it by marriage, adoption, alliance, or purchase. Acquisition by these varied means in turn created the problem of having newcomers and strangers in one's midst. In times of dissension—over material resources, or suspicions of witchcraft, or political succession—one readily brought up accusations (often reciprocal) of slave descent. On the other hand, when group cooperation was needed, particularly against outsiders, one resorted to the kinship idiom.

The existence of the slavery-to-kinship continuum does not mean that, as quasi-relatives, slaves were necessarily treated benignly (one should beware of applying to Africa the modern Western notion of kinship relations as inherently benign). What it means is that relations with slaves were, like so many other relations in Africa, phrased in the idiom of kinship (which in Africa is strongly hierarchical) and that improvement in the condition of a slave lay in belonging, in integration into the master kin group—whereas in Western slavery it lay in manumission and personal autonomy. There were times, historically, when such autonomy was open and even attractive to African slaves, when, for example, colonial authorities were promoting abolition and offering individual wage employments. But grasping at autonomy was not the dominant response: it made little sense to move into social isolation by detaching oneself from the power of one's kin group, unless one had access to another such group. To be sure, in areas where the impact of colonial occupation was more pronounced, emancipated slaves could form their own kin groups within the protected communities emerging around mission stations; alternatively, they could become attached to European employers, seeing themselves as clients and retainers even while their new masters or patrons were more likely to see them as being merely hired hands.

VARIETIES OF AFRICAN SLAVERY

Compared with the relatively uniform slave systems of the United States South, the Caribbean, and Latin America, slaveries in Africa were strikingly varied in the uses to which acquired persons and their descendants were put. There is thus no easy generalization to be made in answer to the question often asked in the literature on slavery: was the slave system harsh or relatively benign? An important variable in the nature of any African slave system was the structure of the host society into which the slave was brought. At one extreme lay the small-scale, segmented, and socially undifferentiated societies, with local kin groups making up sovereign units with limited social and economic specialization and few sharply defined social niches. That slaves in these societies were usually made into something akin to adopted relatives is understandable: there was little else that could be done. The relatively uniform economy offered few possibilities for economic exploitation. Control over the slaves was problematic (one of the reasons for preferring young women and children over adult men). And in the competition among kin groups fostered by political fragmentation, acquired strangers could most profitably be used as adherents, retainers, and relatives—that is, as social and political rather than economic capital.

In such small-scale societies, an acquired person might attain the status of a legal minor in the master kin group: an old slave might enjoy the respected position of an elder but still be barred from central ritual and political offices. The acquisition of full status usually took several generations of repeated marriages of the children of new slaves into the local community. One difference between the "free," or person of deep local ancestry, and the newly acquired stranger lay in the fact that the free person was not totally dependent on his or her kin group: the "free" person had a complementary

kinship network outside of it, provided by maternal kinsmen in patrilineal systems and by paternal kinsmen in matrilineal ones. By contrast, a new slave's dependence on the acquisitor kin group was total, without any dilution by other ties. But as slaves and their descendants intermarried with other kin groups, they became enmeshed, like the "free," in many networks of kin, which gave them extensive local connections and embedded them more deeply in their communities. Since the boundaries between those of free descent and those distantly descended from a slave were seldom clear; in the course of community political conflicts, the accusation of slave descent could thus be plausibly flung at most established kin groups.

At the other extreme of variation were complex African societies with many social and economic niches, which exercised effective political control over large regions and were distinguished by cities, bureaucracies, armies, and wealth from producing, trading, and raiding. Here, as in the simpler societies, kin groups were also interested in expanding, and very large numbers of slaves became retainers and quasi-relatives under what one might characterize as a benign domestic regime. But complex societies, with their monetized economies and chances for profits, also offered a diversity of other uses, including some harsh ones. Slaves could be commercial agents, elite troops, bureaucrats, courtiers, and wives and mothers of rulers—but also workers who remained permanently marginal to their master kin groups as they labored in mines, plantations, and agricultural slave villages.

Complex societies could offer considerable social mobility for some slaves. Becoming a retainer in a rich and politically important kin group or particularly at a ruler's court could open the way to occupations and a lifestyle superior to those of most of the free. This closeness to power and its consequent benefits to the slave make it problematic to see slavery in Africa as an aspect of social stratification (as slavery is conventionally treated). African slaves seldom constituted a discrete social class. In complex societies, they were scattered across the strata—attached, so to speak, spread out all along the side of the social ladder rather than concentrated at its bottom. Conversely, in unstratified societies, their lifestyle differed little from everyone else's, and they identified with their respective kin groups and not with one another. The social structural ingredients for slave revolts, therefore, were almost entirely absent.

In the kinship-to-slavery continuum, the distinction between slave and "free" was imprecise and situational, and one must be cautious in interpreting statistical statements about the proportion of slaves in African populations. What is clear is that transactions in people, in both complex and small-scale societies, were frequent and their effects cumulative. Hence, the number of descendants of acquired people among kin-group members was great. Using the term "slave" in the very broad African sense results in the common estimate that between one-quarter and one-half of the populations of most West and Central African societies were of this status by the end of the nineteenth century. Some scholars take these proportions as indicative of the existence in Africa of "slave societies," defined as those in whose economy slaves played an essential role. But this reasoning begs the crucial question of who is being classified as a slave. The large numbers are themselves a consequence of using African categories. But if one used the term "slave" solely in the Western sense, considering only economic functions, the estimate of African slaves would shrink dramatically, eliminating, perhaps, any question of the existence of slave societies.

THE QUESTION OF ORIGINS

African slavery was an integral part of a pattern in which various rights in persons were constantly transacted. The pattern directed the routine workings of the social organization, operating in terms of a cultural logic that informed kinship, marriage, adoption, and various forms of dependence besides slavery. And the pattern is so nearly universal a feature of sub-Saharan African cultures that it—and the kind of slavery associated with it—must be of great cultural-historical depth. In this perspective, the origins of African slavery are to be found in the timeless functioning of kinship-based, or communal, African social systems rather than in discrete historical events such as, say, the influence of the Mediterranean and Middle Eastern slave trade or of that of the New World.

See also **Anthropology, Social, and the Study of Africa; Kinship and Descent; Labor; Marriage Systems; Slave Trades; Warfare; Witchcraft; Women: Women and Slavery.**

BIBLIOGRAPHY

Austin, Gareth. *Labor, Land, and Capital in Ghana: From Slavery to Free Labour in Asante, 1807–1956.* Rochester, NY: University of Rochester Press, 2005.

Baum, Robert Martin. *Shrines of the Slave Trade: Diola Religion and Society in Precolonial Senegambia.* New York: Oxford University Press, 1999.

Curtin, Philip D. *Economic Change in Precolonial Africa: Senegambia in the Era of the Slave Trade.* Madison: University of Wisconsin Press, 1975.

Fisher, Allan G. B., and Humphrey J. Fisher. *Slavery and Muslim Society in Africa: The Institution in Saharan and Sudanic Africa and the Trans-Saharan Trade.* Garden City, NY: Doubleday, 1971.

Fisher, Humphrey J. *Slavery in the History of Muslim Black Africa.* London: C. Hurst & Company, 2001.

Fomin, E. S. D. *A Comparative Study of Societal Influences on Indigenous Slavery in Two Types of Societies in Africa 1600–1950.* Lewiston, NY: Mellen Press, 2002.

Lovejoy, Paul E., ed. *The Ideology of Slavery in Africa.* Beverly Hills, CA: Sage, 1981.

Lovejoy, Paul E., ed. *Transformations in Slavery: A History of Slavery in Africa.* Cambridge, U.K.: Cambridge University Press, 2000.

Lovejoy, Paul E., and Toyin Falola, eds. *Pawnship, Slavery and Colonialism in Africa.* New Brunswick, NJ: Africa World Press, 2003.

Manning, Patrick. *Slavery and African Life: Occidental, Oriental, and African Slave Trades.* Cambridge, U.K.: Cambridge University Press, 1990.

Meillassoux, Claude, ed. *L'esclavage en Afrique precoloniale.* Paris: Presses Universitaires de France, 1975.

Meillassoux, Claude, ed. *The Anthropology of Slavery: The Womb of Iron and Gold,* trans. Alide Dasnois. Chicago: University of Chicago Press, 1991.

Miers, Suzanne, and Igor Kopytoff, eds. *Slavery in Africa: Historical and Anthropological Perspectives.* Madison: University of Wisconsin Press, 1977.

Miers, Suzanne, and Richard Roberts, eds. *The End of Slavery in Africa.* Madison: University of Wisconsin Press, 1988.

Perbi, Akosua Adoma. *A History of Indigenous Slavery in Ghana: From the Fifteenth to the Nineteenth Centuries.* Accra, Ghana: Sub-Saharan Publishers, 2004.

Robertson, Claire C., and Martin A. Klein, eds. *Women and Slavery in Africa.* Portsmouth, NH: Heinemann, 1997.

Shaw, Rosalind. *Ritual Memories of the Slave Trade: Ritual and the Historical Imagination in Sierra Leone.* Chicago: University of Chicago Press, 2002.

IGOR KOPYTOFF

COLONIAL

The partition of Africa took place during what was probably the bloodiest quarter century in African history. Armed increasingly with powerful repeating rifles, African armies found themselves forced to enslave to pay for their new weapons. Those slaves provided labor to produce the products Africa exported. Female slaves cooked for the soldiers and staffed the harems of the powerful. The armies that conquered Africa for various European powers were, like their African rivals, made up mostly of slaves, often freed in exchange for military service. With European parliaments reluctant to underwrite costly military operations, colonial military commanders relied on African slave soldiers and on alliances with African chiefs, most of them large slave holders, but they often justified their "civilizing mission" as a crusade against the slave trade in order to influence a European public opinion influenced by descriptions of the ravages of the slave trade in writing of missionaries and explorers.

The problem was not new. The areas under European authority during the first three- quarters of the nineteenth century were very small trading operations. Abolition of slavery by the British in 1833 and by the French in 1848 led to threats by neighboring African states to suspend trade. In coastal entrepôts, slaves were freed, but slave flight was limited and fleeing slaves were often returned to their masters. In the Gold Coast, Governor George Maclean was able to avoid applying the 1833 act because the Gold Coast was controlled by a Committee of Merchants and was not a Crown colony. The British Abolition Act of 1833 was most effective in South Africa, the only British colony in Africa that was more than an entrepôt. Freeing of the slaves was, however, a contributing factor to the Great Trek that founded two Afrikaner Republics in the interior, which preserved forms of servility. As colonial armies extended their control of the interior, the fiction of a protectorate was used to avoid being forced to apply European law. In Senegal, France disannexed a large conquered area in the 1880s and ruled it as a protectorate. Each of the British West African territories consisted of a small Crown colony and a large protectorate. In the wake of various abolition acts, it was illegal for citizens of the mother country to own slaves, but many had slave concubines, servants, and workers.

The first West African colony to confront the slavery issue was the Gold Coast. After the defeat of Asante in 1874, the colonial office wanted to act against slavery without burdening the colonial state with an act it could not enforce. As a result it used the approach adopted in India in 1843. The courts were instructed to refuse any claims to ownership of one person over another. A runaway slave could not be returned to his master. The number of slaves who took advantage of this act was small, though Getz argues that the act improved their negotiating position. During the same period, abolitionist pressures led to a more welcoming attitude toward runaway slaves making it to territories of direct administration in Senegal.

After completion of the conquest, almost all colonial regimes moved quickly to abolish slave raiding and to prohibit the trade in slaves. These were activities that threatened economic growth. The end of significant raiding and trading meant that new slaves were no longer available to those who depended on their services, but increased security made possible the emergence of a free labor market. The Portuguese abolished slavery in 1878, but enforcement was limited outside the cities.

The most dramatic attack on slavery took place in French West Africa. In 1903 field administrators received a new law code along with instructions that they were no longer to receive claims for runaway slaves from masters—once again the Indian formula. In 1905 the administration brought in a comprehensive antislavery law, which abolished all transactions in persons: sale, bequeathal, gift, and exchange. It did not actually abolish slavery, but is often interpreted as having done so. In the spring of 1906 most of the slaves working plantations around the market town of Banamba, Mali, left their masters. Over the next five or six years, the exodus spread from one area to another. All in all, close to 1 million slaves probably left their masters and returned to earlier homes.

In spite of their strong abolition movement, British were more cautious. During the conquest of Northern Nigeria (1897–1903), many slaves fled. Once in control, Governor Sir Frederick

Lugard tried to limit slave flights, fearing that they would deprive northern Nigerian society of its major source of labor. The law encouraged slaves to purchase their freedom through *murgu*, a traditional procedure based on Muslim law. Only about 55,000 did so between 1906 and 1917, but gradually, the development of a cash crop economy made it possible for large numbers of slaves to acquire their own land.

Relations of dependency persisted for several generations. Slavery was formally abolished only in 1936. In Zanzibar the economy was dominated by slave-worked clove plantations and slaves made up a majority of the population. The British abolished slavery in 1897, but coupled abolition with recognition of planter control of land, corvée labor obligations, and strong antivagrancy laws. They limited access to land, facilitated recruitment of labor from the mainland, and tried to limit departures from the plantations. By contrast, the abolition of slavery in 1907 in coastal areas of British East Africa (Kenya) became quickly effective. The British were similarly cautious in Sierra Leone, the Sudan, and southern Nigeria.

In East Africa, Germans hoped to gradually convert slavery into a form of serfdom, but there were procedures set up for slaves to acquire freedom letters. Only about 60,000 were issued, many of them to slaves who bought their freedom or to women purchased as concubines. In spite of this, the number of slaves dropped from about a half million in 1890 to about 160,000 in 1914. By contrast, German authorities in Cameroon were determined to do as little as possible. The slave trade was abolished in 1895, but the act was not strictly enforced. Free labor gradually replaced slave labor in the south but in the northern province of Adamawa, slave raiding and slave trading continued into World War I and forms of slavery were still important in the 1950s. In the Congo Free State, slavery was replaced by a more generalized and brutal servitude to which everyone was subject. In Italian Somalia, three ordinances in 1903 and 1904 provided a ban on the slave trade and a gradual end of slavery.

By World War I slave raiding and trading had disappeared in most of Africa. The major exception was Saharan colonies, where the high cost of policing meant that colonial regimes often ignored the persistence of slavery and a small slave trade. Mauritania only abolished slavery in 1980. By contrast, in the more decentralized societies, slave holding was never important and quickly disappeared. In more complex societies with large servile populations, the process was slower and many former slaves remained in positions of dependence. Gradually, social relationships were renegotiated. Slaves generally insisted on two things. They wanted control over their family life and they wanted to work for themselves. Over the years, more and more former slaves drifted away and others reduced their obligations. In this, the colonial state did little. It distanced itself from slavery, but took little interest in slaves. The only help the slaves received came from Christian missions and Muslim religious brotherhoods. Although the end of slavery created a mobile work force and facilitated the emergence of migrant labor, colonial regimes were generally cautious about undercutting elites.

The most important variables for slaves were access to land and control of their work. Where land was freely available, former slaves took advantage of that availability to clear and work it. On the coast of East Africa, slavery vanished quickly because the hinterland was lightly peopled. Neither the colonial state nor the slave owners had the power to prevent movement to new lands. Where land was in short supply, slave owners were able to control it and exact rent. Some slaves were able to acquire property, but many remained in a sharecropper relationship. At the same time, former slaves proved willing to take on new kinds of work and to do kinds of work that had low status. They thus became labor migrants, taxi drivers, mechanics, and butchers. Those who earned enough were able to buy land. Their struggle was often aided by Christian missions. Slave converts received land around mission stations. Freed slaves were often among the first to receive an education.

Similarly, Muslim religious brotherhoods helped former slaves. Among the Murids of Senegal, former slaves participated in efforts to colonize new areas and received land as a reward. Former masters often clung to status distinctions, for example, the right to sit in the front of the mosque or the expectation that former slaves would do the cooking at naming ceremonies and marriages. Former slaves can often turn conceptions of honor to their advantage by demanding gifts in exchange for their services. Freed slaves achieved complete equality only where they left the communities in which they were slaves. The struggle for complete equality continued after independence and is still important in many areas.

See also **Colonial Policies and Practices; Labor; Law: Islamic; Slave Trades; Women: Women and Slavery; World War I.**

BIBLIOGRAPHY

Cooper, Frederick. *From Slaves to Squatters: Plantation Labor and Agriculture in Zanzibar and Coastal Kenya, 1890–1925.* New Haven, CT: Yale University Press, 1980.

Getz, Trevor. *Slavery and Reform in West Africa: Towards Emancipation in Nineteenth Century Senegal and the Gold Coast.* Athens: Ohio University Press, 2004.

Klein, Martin A. *Slavery and Colonial Rule in French West Africa.* Cambridge, U.K.: Cambridge University Press, 1998.

Lovejoy, Paul, and Jan Hogendorn. *Slow Death for Slavery: The Course of Abolition in Northern Nigeria, 1897–1936.* Cambridge, U.K.: Cambridge University Press, 1993.

Miers, Suzanne, and Martin Klein, eds. *Slavery and Colonial Rule in Africa.* London: Frank Cass, 1999.

Miers, Suzanne, and Richard Roberts, eds. *The End of Slavery in Africa.* Madison: University of Wisconsin Press, 1988.

Northrup, David. *Beyond the Bend in the River: African Labor in Eastern Zaire, 1865–1940.* Athens: Ohio University Press, 1988.

Scully, Pamela. *Liberating the Family: Gender and British Slave Emancipation in the Rural Western Cape, South Africa, 1823–1853.* Portsmouth, NH: Heinemann, 1997.

MARTIN A. KLEIN

SUDAN

As both cause and effect, slavery stratified races, ethnicities, religions, and cultures, placing some into the category of slave masters and others into that of the target populations, denigrated and dehumanized to justify their enslavement. In the Sudanese context, the master race comprised the northern Sudanese who had become assimilated into the Arab-Islamic mold and made to pass as Arabs, although they were, and still are, in effect a visible African-Arab mixture, with the African element predominant. The enslaveable groups were the black Africans, especially those in the non-Arab, non-Muslim south, who practiced indigenous religious beliefs and were therefore viewed as heathens and infidels. But those who were first affected by slavery, even before the south became exposed to it, were the ethnic groups in non-Muslim parts of the north, in particular, the areas bordering the south, the Nuba Mountains and the southern Blue Nile, the Beja region to the east and Darfur in the far west.

The long-term implications of the normative framework in which the non-Muslim and non-Arab groups became the primary victims of slavery is obvious in the fact that they are still the most marginalized and discriminated against in the Sudan in the twenty-first century. Their resistance to this position has taken the form of insurgencies that have provoked genocidal counterinsurgencies by the Arab-dominated governments, inflicting atrocities on the civilian populations believed to support the insurgencies and tolerating, even encouraging, the resurgence of slavery in its crude form.

SLAVERY IN THE EVOLUTION OF IDENTITIES

Slavery was central to the classification of groups along racial, religious, and cultural lines. While the broader context of Arabization and Islamization provided the framework for the formation of identity categories, slavery contributed significantly to the consolidation of those qualitative identities. The historical evolution of identities crystallized into north and south, until the recent realignment began to challenge that racial divide and the monolithic perception of the whole north as Arab-Islamic.

Slavery was the decisive factor that classified people into the master race, comprising Arab Muslims, and the enslaveable race, the black Africans, who were deemed to have no culture but could be redeemed by their adoption of Islam, the Arabic language, Arab culture, and the fusion of blood with the master race. This process eventually resulted in the transformation of the pre-Islamic society.

The Turko-Egyptian conquest in 1820–1821 had clear objectives, one of which was to recruit blacks as slave soldiers for the Egyptian army. During most of the period of Turko-Egyptian rule, the slave trade flourished and the victims were the Blacks in the surrounding regions of the south, the neighboring Nuba and the Ingassana, and the people of Darfur farther west. Under pressure from Europe, the government later began to suppress slavery. General Charles Gordon was sent first to the south and then to the Sudan as governor-general with the objective of suppressing slavery. His efforts produced no significant results and he became a symbol of the detested Turko-Egyptian rule. With Gordon's death in the hands of the Mahdists in 1885, Turko-Egyptian rule collapsed.

The Mahdi's principal source of support against the Turko-Egyptian government was the slave-raiding militant Arab tribes of southern Kordofan and Darfur, who were vehemently antagonized by the government's antislavery campaign. The Mahdist revolution promised them the restoration of slavery. The Mahdiyya movement, both in its initial campaigns and in what happened during the Mahdist state, resulted in the breakdown of law and order; famine due to drought, and war. It is estimated that the population of Sudan fell from around 7 million before the Mahdist revolt to somewhere between 2 and 3 million after the fall of the Mahdist state. A positive consequence of the Mahdist movement was to provide the Sudan with a common vision against foreign rule, even offering the prospect of independence. On the other hand, it generated internal divisions, intertribal conflict, and a general turmoil from which the country suffered much and has never fully recovered.

The evolution of the southern identity of resistance began in the period prior to the Anglo-Egyptian condominium rule. At that time, the south was a hunting ground for slaves. In the eighteenth century, state expansion southward was effectively halted by the Shilluk kingdom and Dinka resistance. It was only in the nineteenth century that slave raids began to extend to the south and with it the emergence of north-south divide.

Northern invaders, including Arabs, persistently raided the south for slaves; they never penetrated deeply and did not attempt to settle. Swamps, flies, tropical humidity, and the fierce resistance of the southern tribes kept the contact marginal. It was not until the Turko-Egyptian government opened the Bahr al-Ghazal and Equatoria provinces in the 1820s and established more security that the slave trade became well established and assumed large proportions. European traders with Arab partners and servants established slave camps, or *zaribas*, as centers for trade and local control.

Sir Samuel Baker, whose mission in 1869 from Ismail Pasha, the viceroy of Egypt, was to establish a chain of forts and to suppress slavery, recorded his impressions of the destruction inflicted on the people: "It is impossible to describe the change that has taken place since I last visited this country. It was then a perfect garden, thickly populated and producing all that man would desire. The villages were numerous, groves of plantens fringed the steep cliff on the river bank, and the natives were neatly dressed in the bark cloth of the country. The scene has changed: All is wilderness. The population has fled. Not a village is to be seen. This is the certain result of the settlement of Khartoum traders. They kidnap the women and children for slaves and plunder and destroy wherever they set their foot" (Deng, 28).

Baker did not succeed either in conquering the south or in suppressing the slave trade. The Turkish administration brought a general devastation on the whole country, north and south, which made the Mahdist revolt initially popular as an anti-Turkish alliance against a common enemy. Although the southerners were anxious to rid themselves of Egyptian rule, they did not want new alien masters, especially slave traders.

BRITISH RULE AND THE AMBIVALENT ABOLITION OF SLAVERY

The British-dominated Anglo-Egyptian condominium administration unified the country, but created separate administrations for the north and south. This dual system reinforced Arabism and Islam in the north and encouraged southern development along indigenous African lines and also introduced Christian missionary education and rudiments of western civilization in the south. With respect to slavery, British perspectives on the stratification of races, cultures, and religions, on which slavery was founded, did not differ profoundly from that of the Arab-Islamic north.

As the dominant power in the Anglo-Egyptian administration, the British decided to abolish slavery gradually. As Gabriel Warburg noted, "The end of slavery . . . came about as a result of economic, rather than moral, reasons once wage-earning labor became more easily accessible" (1990, 155). The British distinguished between the slave trade and slavery, abolishing the former and tolerating the latter.

BRITISH PARADOXICAL PROTECTION OF THE SOUTH

If the British administration in the Sudan was tolerant toward the ongoing practice of slavery in the north, it was more decisive in stopping northern slave raids against the southerners and protecting the south against any exploitive adventures by northern traders. Toward that goal, they adopted a policy of separate development of the north and the south, which became known as the Southern Policy. It entailed the creation of separate military units in the south staffed with southern recruits under the command of British officers, with northerners and Egyptians totally excluded. The use of English as a lingua franca and the return of indigenous southern customs were encouraged to the exclusion of all persons and things northern.

As the Sudan approached independence in 1956, the British accelerated the pace of creating a unified Sudan but with unintended consequences. One incident after another intensified southern fear of the north, which peaked with the announcement that eight hundred posts previously held by the British would now be Sudanized. In fact, these posts were northernized, with only eight junior positions allocated to southerners. Southern outrage erupted in a violent revolt on August 18, 1955, in the southern town of Torit, less than four months before independence, triggering hostilities that lasted for seventeen years.

Northern political leaders accelerated the pace toward independence with near total insensitivity to southern concerns. The Sudanese Parliament passed a resolution on August 19, only a day after the revolt in the south, which provided for the holding of a direct plebiscite to ascertain the wishes of the Sudanese people. This decision was soon reversed. The reason given was that the organization of a plebiscite, in a country as vast and diversified as the Sudan with its largely illiterate population,

would create many problems and solve none. Moreover, it would be virtually impossible to conduct a plebiscite in the south, because the rebellion had caused a collapse in security and the administrative system.

LIBERATION MOVEMENT AGAINST SLAVERY-LIKE DOMINATION

The war in the south went though two phases. The first, led by the southern Sudan Liberation Movement and its military wing, the Anya-nya (1955–1972), aimed at the independence of the south, but settled seventeen years later for an autonomous south under the 1972 Addis Ababa Agreement. The second phase, championed by the Sudan People's Liberation Movement and Army (SPLMA), began in 1983 with the government's unilateral abrogation of the Addis Ababa Agreement. The declared objective was to create a new Sudan that would be free from any discrimination on the ground of race, ethnicity, religion, culture or gender.

The central government viewed the southern Sudanese struggle against Arab-Islamic domination following independence as a violation of law and order that must be crushed. Accounts of the gruesome brutality inflicted by the government forces during the first phase of the war indicate a dehumanizing treatment reminiscent of the days of slavery. Northerners generally assumed that their identity was the national model.

Since the late 1980s, slavery in the Sudan intensified under the military regime of the National Islamic Front. The Swiss-based Christian Solidarity International (CSI), the British-based Christian Solidarity International Worldwide, and the U.S.-based American Anti-Slavery Group embarked on a massive and highly controversial program of redeeming southern slaves from their Arab slavers. Instead of condemning the practice, the government argued that what was involved was not slavery but abductions, a practice that it claimed was associated with intertribal warfare. Although many found the redemption program morally objectionable because it paradoxically encouraged the practice, it provided ample evidence of slavery in modern Sudan.

As a result of mounting international pressure against slavery in the Sudan, the government created a Committee for the Elimination of Abduction of Women and Children (EAWAC) with the mandate "to facilitate the safe return of affected women and children to their families; investigate abduction of women and children and to bring to trial any person suspected of supporting or participating in such activities; and investigate into causes of abduction of women and children, forced labor or similar practices and recommend ways and means for the eradication of such practices." It is obvious from the name of the committee that the government still resists putting the label of slavery on the practice. The U.S.-sponsored International Eminent Persons Group on Slavery, Abduction, and Forced Servitude in the Sudan noted, "the use of the term abduction instead of slavery is controversial. Southerners affected by the practice are insulted that slavery is referred to as anything less" (International Eminent Persons Group, 97). While large numbers of women and children (most of them now adults) have been found and returned to their families through arrangements with tribal leaders, many more remain in captivity, and as of 2007, there have been no reports of criminal investigations, trials or punishments connected with these practices.

The revival of slavery is only one aspect of the humanitarian tragedy the proliferating regional wars of identity have inflicted on the Sudan, especially in the south. In the early twenty-first century, the Sudan appears to be at a critical juncture, poised between the threat of disintegration and the promise of genuine unity within a restructured national identity framework. With the people of the south, the Nuba Mountains, the southern Blue Nile, the Beja, and now the predominately non-Arab groups in Darfur challenging the one-sided Arab orientation of the national identity framework, the Sudan is challenged to create a new common and inclusive framework of national identity in which all Sudanese can find a sense of belonging as citizens with the equality and dignity of citizenship.

See also **Addis Ababa; Gordon, Charles George; Islam; Labor: Conscript and Forced; Slave Trades; Sudan: Wars; Women: Women and Slavery.**

BIBLIOGRAPHY

Baldo, Suleyman Ali, and Ushari Ahmad Mahmud. *Al-Dhein Massacre: Slavery in the Sudan.* Khartoum: n.p., 1987.

Burr, Millard. *Working Document II Quantifying Genocide in Southern Sudan and the Nuba Mountains 1984–1998.* Washington, DC: U.S. Committee for Refugees, December 1998.

Collins, Robert O. *Shadow in the Grass: Britain in the Southern Sudan, 1918–1956.* New Haven, CT: Yale University Press, 1983.

Daly, M. W. *Empire on the Nile: The Anglo-Egyptian Sudan, 1898–1934.* Cambridge, U.K.: Cambridge University Press, 1986.

Deng, Francis M. *Tradition and Modernization: A Challenge for Law Among the Dinka of the Sudan.* New Haven, CT: Yale University Press, 1971.

Deng, Francis M. *Dynamics of Identification: A Basis for National Integration in the Sudan.* Khartoum: Khartoum University Press, 1973.

Deng, Francis M., and Larry Minear. *The Challenges of Famine Relief: Emergency Operations in the Sudan.* Washington, DC: Brookings Institution, 1992.

International Eminent Persons Group. "Slavery, Abduction and Forced Servitude in Sudan." Report of the International Eminent Persons Group, May 2002.

Johnson, Douglas H. *The Root Causes of Sudan's Civil War.* Bloomington: Indiana University Press, 2003.

O'Ballance, Edgar. *The Secret War in the Sudan: 1955–1972.* Hamden, CT: Archon Books, 1977.

Warburg, Gabriel R. "National Identity in the Sudan: Fact, Fiction and Prejudice in Ethnic and Religious Relations." *Asian and African Studies* 24, no. 2 (July 1990).

FRANCIS M. DENG

SMUGGLING. *See* **Trade, National and International Systems.**

SMUTS, JAN CHRISTIAAN (1870–1950). Born to Boer (Afrikaner) parents in Cape Colony, Jan Smuts took a degree in literature and science, and later read law at Cambridge University. In the Anglo-Boer War (1899–1902) he was a daring guerrilla leader and later helped to unite South Africa under predominantly Afrikaner leadership in 1910. Yet Smuts never lost his attachment to Britain, and during World War I he supported South Africa's participation in the struggle against Germany. Smuts took part in the conquest of German Southwest Africa and commanded the British forces in the East African believe that Africans should share power with whites. Nevertheless, he opposed the policy of apartheid, introduced by the Nationalists after 1948.

See also **Apartheid; Namibia: History and Politics; South Africa, Republic of: History and Politics (1850–2006); World War I; World War II.**

BIBLIOGRAPHY

Hancock, William Keith. *Smuts: The Sanguine Years.* Cambridge, U.K.: Cambridge University Press, 1962.

Hancock, William Keith. *Smuts: The Fields of Force.* Cambridge, U.K.: Cambridge University Press, 1968.

Ingham, Kenneth. *Jan Christian Smuts: The Conscience of a South African.* New York: Palgrave Macmillan, 1986.

KENNETH INGHAM

Jan Smuts (1870–1950). After World War II, Smuts established the Fagan Commission, which advocated the end of segregation in South Africa. CORBIS

campaign until 1916, when he went to England. There he became a member of the Imperial War Cabinet (1917) and was one of the architects of the Balfour Declaration, which recommended a Jewish national home in Palestine. During the peace negotiations in Paris, he was a powerful advocate of the League of Nations and secured the Union of South Africa's mandate authority over Southwest Africa.

Smuts became prime minister of South Africa in 1919, but his efforts to strengthen his country's links with the British Empire (later Commonwealth) antagonized the more nationalistically inclined Afrikaners. Defeated in the 1924 elections, he did not regain office until 1939, when he overcame Nationalist opposition to South Africa's entry into World War II against the fascist Axis powers. His lifelong aim was to unite the British and Afrikaner settlers in governing South Africa in accordance with Western European principles. Smuts did not

SOBHUZA I AND II (1780–1839; 1899–1982). Sobhuza I (Sobhuza wandvungunye Dlamini; Ngwane IV; Somhlohlo, "The Wonder") fashioned the Swazi kingship out of disparate Nguni-speaking clans in southern Swaziland. His father, Ndvungunye (c. 1760–1815), by the turn of the nineteenth century had made the Dlamini the dominant clan among numerous contesting tribes in the area. To establish the kingship, Sobhuza brought the important clans together under his hegemony, which was quite tenuous at first. Sobhuza incorporated some families under the Dlamini by force; others he incorporated by various diplomatic means of persuasion and enticement, including marriage alliances, the appointing of positions of status, and granting choice lands. He then campaigned northward with the dual objectives of escaping the powerful and aggressive Ndwandwe to the south and occupying the fertile and defensible heartland of the country. Sobhuza defeated or incorporated various clans living in central Swaziland, then refashioned his strengthened kingdom along military regimental lines fashioned after Shaka's very successful Zulu. By the time of his death, Sobhuza had successfully fended off powerful Ndwandwe and Zulu attacks from the south, captured Sotho land and cattle far northward into the Transvaal high veld, and was attempting to consolidate his kingdom through diplomacy with missionaries.

Sobhuza II (Sobhuza wabhunu Dlamini), whose original name was Nkhotfotjeni, was a later direct

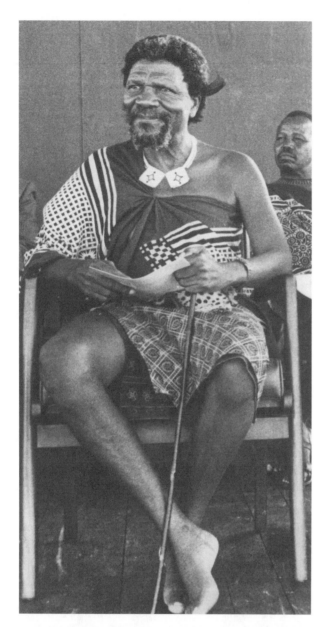

King Sobhuza II of Swaziland (1899–1982). Sobhuza II's 82-year reign is the longest monarchical reign on record. On April 12, 1973, Sobhuza repealed Swaziland's constitution and dissolved parliament to make himself absolute ruler, a role that lasted for nine years, until his death. AP IMAGES

descendant of Sobhuza I. Nkhotfotjeni was given the name Sobhuza II upon being designated heir to the Swazi throne in 1900. Crowned in 1921, and surrounded by the powerful and industrializing Union of South Africa, he inherited an enfeebled monarchy. He proceeded to restore it brilliantly over the following two generations using a number of stratagems: invoking tradition and ritual; assiduously courting an array of powerful allies, black and white;

and playing British colonials, European settlers, and domestic rivals against each other to achieve his ends. Consequently, at independence in 1968 his control over the levers of power was unmatched by any other postcolonial monarchy in all of sub-Saharan Africa. Sobhuza consolidated his rule in 1973 by scrapping Swaziland's Westminster-style constitution and ruling without official political opposition. He maintained a high degree of popularity until his death as the result of a longstanding illness, probably leukemia.

See also **Kings and Kingdoms; Kingship; Law: Southern Africa; Swaziland.**

BIBLIOGRAPHY

Bonner, Philip L. *Kings, Commoners, and Concessionaires: The Evolution and Dissolution of the Nineteenth-Century Swazi State.* New edition. Cambridge, U.K.: Cambridge University Press, 2002.

Jones, Huw M. *A Biographical Register of Swaziland to 1902.* Pietermaritzburg, South Africa: University of Natal Press, 1993.

Kuper, Hilda, *Sobhuza II: Ngwenyama and King of Swaziland.* New York: Africana Publishing Co., 1978.

ALAN R. BOOTH

SOCIALISM AND POSTSOCIALISMS.

In the struggle to liberate themselves from colonial rule, many Africans found in socialism an attractive ideology, one that promised freedom from exploitation and posed an alternative to the capitalism upon which colonialism was based. Emerging nationalist sentiment may have helped mobilize Africans in the fight for independence but was less effective in maintaining popular support following independence. Thus, some leaders and political parties adopted socialist platforms immediately upon forming their new governments; others adopted it after attempts at instituting democracy failed. Socialist ideology and policy offered several attractive elements, including a language to promote the modernization and unification of emerging nation-states; centralized control of the economy; consolidation and expansion of the state; emphasis on revolutionary change; and international bonds to the wider community of socialist/communist states. With these, governments could, in theory, facilitate rapid growth and distribute resources equitably while securing economic, political, and military assistance from abroad.

Although socialist movements in Africa took many forms, analysts speak of two primary categories: African socialism and Afro-Marxism (sometimes referred to as Afro-Communism). African socialism dominated the early period of the 1950s and 1960s and encompassed the approaches taken in Ghana, Guinea, Mali, Senegal, Tanzania, Zambia, Egypt, Libya, Algeria, and Tunisia. Positioned in opposition to both capitalism and scientific socialism, African socialists drew parallels between socialism and indigenous African (or, in the case of North Africa, Islamic) practices. Communal ownership of land, egalitarianism and relatively low degrees of stratification, and extensive networks of cooperation were forwarded (somewhat problematically) as essentially African/Islamic and socialist traits. Exclusive vanguard parties of the Leninist variety were eschewed in favor of mass parties with open membership, and orthodox Marxist belief in the necessity of class struggle as a precursor to socialist revolution was replaced with ideas of noncapitalist development and multiple paths to socialism. By and large, these states disputed the Marxist dismissal of religion as false consciousness; indeed, Algeria's second president Houari Boumediene (1932–1978) called Islam the world's first socialist movement. Finally, insistence on the African or Arab grounding of their policies allowed these regimes to sidestep Cold War divisions and claim nonaligned status.

Despite their many shared attributes, attempts were made to distinguish African socialist programs from each other: Consciencism in Kwame Nkrumah's Ghana, African socialism in Léopold Senghor's Senegal, Destourian socialism in Habib Bourguiba's Tunisia, *Ujamaa* (familyhood) in Julius Nyerere's Tanzania, Communocracy in Sékou Touré's Guinea, and Humanism in Kenneth Kaunda's Zambia. These movements hit their apogee in the mid-1960s, but for the most part met only mediocre success in terms of economic development. The sudden overthrows of Ahmed Ben Bella in Algeria (1965), Nkrumah in Ghana (1966), and Modibo Keita in Mali (1968) constituted heavy defeats for African socialism, yet strong adherence to its principles and policies continued in Tanzania and Algeria, and to lesser degrees in the other states.

Pessimism over African socialism contributed to the emergence of the second wave of socialism in the 1970s: the embrace of scientific socialism resulting in Afro-Marxist regimes. These tended to be states emerging from great instability in search of a programmatic approach to stability and development. With the example of the USSR's rapid transformation under Marxism-Leninism from feudal backwater to world superpower, scientific socialism appeared an appealing solution to underdeveloped African states. Military juntas declared Marxist-Leninist governments by fiat in Republic of the Congo (1969), Somalia (1970), Bénin (1974), Madagascar (1975), Ethiopia (1974), and Burkina Faso (1983). In Lusophone Africa, the prolonged guerrilla campaigns against Portuguese colonial rule radicalized liberation fighters and resulted in the creation of avowedly Marxist regimes in Angola (1977) and Mozambique (1977), as well as Marxist-influenced regimes in Guinea-Bissau, Cape Verde, and São Tomé e Princípe after independence in 1975. Similarly, a violent war of liberation in Zimbabwe also resulted in a self-proclaimed Marxist regime there (1979).

As an ideology of revolution, liberation, and modernization, Marxism-Leninism promised a fundamental break with capitalist exploitation and a road to the equitable distribution of wealth. Through rapid industrialization, African adherents sought to fundamentally alter their economic dependence on raw materials exports and reduce their reliance on external markets. Central planning of the economy coupled with a monopoly over the political sphere enabled the consolidation of power—a key attraction for new states facing unstable domestic, as well as global, conditions. Finally, emphasis on class consciousness justified the containment of ethnic, religious, and other subnationalist movements that could threaten the new regimes.

It should be noted that not all states that pursued these policies employed the language of Marxism-Leninism. Indeed, one-party states were the norm across the continent, and postcolonial centralized economies were the natural byproduct of colonial centralized economies. Scholars thus disagree on which states merit the designation Marxist. As with the African socialist states of previous decades, these regimes varied considerably in their commitment to socialist policy, with some strategically employing the label to attain revolutionary credentials or new international allies. And although violent revolution constituted a defining factor for Afro-Marxist states as the

Algeria's first president Ahmed Ben Bella delivers an opening speech during a party conference of the ruling National Liberation Front (FLN) in Algiers, April 16, 1964. The banner in the background proclaims the socialism-inflected state motto: "La revolution par le peuple et pour le peuple" ("Revolution by the people and for the people"). That the state motto has since been changed to "By the people and for the people" demonstrates postsocialist transition in Algeria. STF/AFP/GETTY IMAGES

necessary first step toward societal transformation, prolonged wars such as those in Mozambique, Angola, Namibia, and Ethiopia greatly impeded efforts to institute socialist policies.

Whether African socialist or Afro-Marxist in orientation, socialist states found economic centralization to be an elusive target. African governments simply lacked the means to take full command over the economy given the inherited constraints of their colonial past (poverty, shortage of skilled personnel, economies organized around the production of raw agricultural exports, and lack of capital to diversify). Despite the nationalization of major resources, state industrial investments, and agricultural price controls, mixed economies were the result across the board. Far from being stifled, private enterprise flourished in the informal economy and offered an

alternative to the shortages characteristic of government retailers. Efforts at political centralization proved somewhat more successful. Single-party states with governmental control of the media and limited tolerance for open dissent became the norm, both in socialist and nonsocialist states. Yet being a relatively new entity, the state often carried less legitimacy than kinship and patron-client ties (which also laid claim to citizens' labor and loyalty), producing a phenomenon referred to as the soft state.

In the 1980s, when a majority of African states irrespective of ideological orientation suffered severe economic crises, the World Bank and International Monetary Fund (IMF) stepped in with much-needed loans. Attached to the loans were conditions—including demands to downsize government bureaucracies, privatize state holdings, and institute multiparty

Political rally by Civic United Front (CUF), Tanga, Tanzania, November 7, 1994. A significant element of structural adjustment reform in Tanzania was the introduction of political pluralism in 1992. The Civic United Front emerged as one of the stronger opposition parties. PHOTOGRAPH BY KELLY ASKEW

elections—that greatly eroded socialist institutions. With the dissolution of the USSR and the demise of socialist governments in Eastern Europe (1989–1991), change proved inevitable for African socialist states. They had lost international allies and key sources of material support, but, more importantly, socialism itself had been discredited.

Processes of retreat from socialist ideology and policy have varied widely. With mass demonstrations in Bénin, Zambia, and Madagascar, the impetus for reform came from the citizenry, whereas structural adjustment programs imposed reform on Tanzania and Mozambique. A national conference in Republic of the Congo (followed soon thereafter with civil war), incremental institutional reform in Senegal, and military defeat in Ethiopia are other ways in which liberalization commenced. Unlike the situation in much of Eurasia, postsocialist transformation in Africa did not always entail a complete break with the past. Ruling parties formerly committed to socialist development in Mozambique (Liberation Front of Mozambique, FRELIMO), Tanzania (Chama Cha Mapinduzi, CCM), Angola (People's Movement for the Liberation of Angola - Party of Labour, MPLA), Namibia (South West Africa People's Organisation, SWAPO),

and Zimbabwe (Zimbabwe African National Union - Patriotic Front, ZANU-PF) remain in power in the early twenty-first century. And although Cape Verde's African Party of Independence of Cape Verde (PAICV) was defeated in the first multiparty elections in 1991, it returned to power—by a very slim margin of victory—in the January 2006 elections. Even some leaders affiliated with the socialist period retained or were returned to power after disavowing socialism and embracing neoliberal reform. These include Joaquim Chissano of Mozambique, Mathieu Kérékou of Bénin, and Denis Sassou-Nguesso of Republic of the Congo.

Postsocialist transformation offers notable advantages in the current political and economic context. With neoliberal reform comes access to financial resources that would otherwise be denied, membership in an international community of democratic states, acceptance as a modern nation (newly defined) with respect for the rule of law and universal human rights, and the tantalizing, but elusive, potential of trade relations with powerful Western diplomatic partners.

For many countries, the postsocialist moment has brought both relief and hardship. Farmers are more likely to receive competitive prices for their products and traders less likely to pay exorbitant taxes and import duties on commodities. Projects of villagization, collectivization, and industrialization that were so characteristic of authoritarian socialist states have largely collapsed as postsocialist states pursue foreign investors and funds from international financial institutions. Yet rather than stem corruption and violence, reform has brought about significant increases in rent-seeking behavior and a proliferation of ethnic and religious conflicts. Decollectivization in the agricultural sector, together with the sale of state-operated enterprises, has undercut the social safety net provided, however poorly and incompletely, by the interventionist state. Whereas socialist era government parastatals had provided lifelong employment, free or subsidized housing, food allowances, and even social clubs for workers during their leisure time, with liberalization and privatization unemployment rates have risen, wages have fallen, and subsidies for health care, education, housing, and transportation have been eliminated.

Socialist ideology in Africa, as elsewhere, has been relegated to the margins of political debate. But in the wake of austerity programs that shift responsibility for economic growth from the state to the market, values associated with socialism remain attractive, particularly social justice, respect for human beings, and equitable development. Neoliberalism champions similar values in the name of democracy, universal human rights, and poverty reduction. It remains to be seen whether or not it will prove more successful than socialism in delivering on its promises.

See also **Aid and Development; Capitalism and Commercialization; Cold War; Human Rights; International Monetary Fund; Kaunda, Kenneth; Nkrumah, Francis Nwia Kofi; Nyerere, Julius Kambarage; Sassou-Nguesso, Denis; Senghor, Léopold Sédar; Touré, Sékou; World Bank; Youth: Movements.**

BIBLIOGRAPHY

Askew, Kelly M., and M. Anne Pitcher, eds. *African Postsocialisms.* Edinburgh: Edinburgh University Press, 2007.

Friedland, William H., and Carl G. Rosberg, eds. *African Socialism.* Stanford, CA: Stanford University Press, 1964.

Hughes, Arnold. *Marxism's Retreat from Africa.* London: Frank Cass, 1992.

Keller, Edmond J., and Donald Rothchild, eds. *Afro-Marxist Regimes: Ideology and Public Policy.* Boulder, CO: Lynne Rienner, 1987.

Markakis, John, and Michael Waller, eds. *Military Marxist Regimes in Africa.* London: Frank Cass, 1986.

Munslow, Barry, ed. *Africa: Problems in the Transition to Socialism.* London: Zed Books, 1986.

Ottaway, Marina, and David Ottaway. *Afrocommunism,* 2nd edition. New York: Africana, 1986.

Pitcher, M. Anne. *Transforming Mozambique: The Politics of Privatization, 1975–2000.* Cambridge, U.K.: Cambridge University Press, 2002.

Young, Crawford. *Ideology and Development in Africa.* New Haven, CT: Yale University Press, 1982.

KELLY M. ASKEW

SOGA, JOHN HENDERSON (c. 1860–1941).

Born at the Mgwali mission in independent Xhosaland (later Eastern Cape, South Africa), John Henderson Soga was the second son of one of South Africa's most distinguished black families in European circles. Tiyo Soga (1829–1871), his father, was the first black South African to be ordained as a Christian minister, and his brothers included a medical doctor, a newspaper editor, and South Africa's first black veterinarian. Like his father, Soga was trained in Scotland for the church, and he likewise married a Scotswoman.

While working as a missionary in Elliotdale, Transkei, Soga became alarmed at the extent to which his Xhosa contemporaries were losing touch with their past. Therefore, he conceived the idea of writing a history that "might help them to a clearer perception of who and what they were, and to encourage in them a desire for reading and for studying their language" (Soga, xvii). His manuscript, "Abe-Nguni, Aba-Mbo Nama-Lala," was completed in 1926, but the Lovedale Press (which monopolized Xhosa-language printing) demanded £140 before publishing it. This sum Soga could not afford. The manuscript was eventually published in Soga's own English translation as *The South-Eastern Bantu,* and he followed up with an ethnography entitled *The Ama-Xosa: Life and Customs* (1932?). The Xhosa-language manuscript survives but has never been published. Indeed, it is a sad commentary on the difficulties facing South African vernacular literature that Soga's magnum opus has never been read in the language in which he wrote it or by the people whom he intended to read it.

Soga's strength as a historian lies in the comprehensive scope of the task he set himself, and the patient research he undertook to achieve his aim. Whereas most Xhosa historians wrote nothing more substantial than fragments, such as short biographies and newspaper articles, Soga deliberately set out to preserve the totality of Xhosa history and culture. He did, however, absorb and reproduce many colonial theories concerning tribal migrations and racial typology. These all-but-inevitable limits of the pioneering times in which he wrote, together with his somewhat stilted English style, make his work rather inaccessible in the early twenty-first century.

When he approached his eightieth year, Soga decided to retire from the wilds of rural Transkei to the peace and security of England. It was there, by a final irony of his culturally ambiguous life, that he perished during the German bombing of Southampton.

See also **Languages; Research: Historical Resources.**

BIBLIOGRAPHY

Peires, Jeffrey. B. *The House of Phalo (Perspectives on Southern Africa)*. Berkeley: University of California Press, 1982.

Soga, John H. *The South-Eastern Bantu*. Johannesburg, South Africa: The Witwatersrand University Press, 1930.

JEFF PEIRES

SOILS. Africa, with a total land area of about 19.1 million square miles and a population exceeding 746 million people, contains a wide range of soils and climatic environments. These soils have been described as poor, fragile, inherently infertile, lateritic, reddish, old, deeply weathered, acidic, and incapable of supporting intensive cultivation. However, not all soils fit these descriptions even though the statements are largely true.

THE SOILS

The U.S. Department of Agriculture soil taxonomy classification system, similar to the popular plant and animal taxonomies, has made it possible to group and name soils on the basis of their intrinsic properties. This classification has defined eleven soil orders of which the following seven are common in Africa (included with their estimated coverage of the land area): Aridisols (26.4%), Entisols (24.5%), Alfisols (14.3%), Oxisols (10.3%), Inceptisols (7.8%), Ultisols (6.2%), and Vertisols (3.2%).

Aridisols are light-colored soils of desert, semi-arid, and dry, tropical regions. They become fertile only when water (typically in the form of irrigation) is applied. Alfisols, Ultisols, and Oxisols, in decreasing order of abundance, are the predominant soils of humid and sub-humid Africa. Oxisols are strongly weathered, deep, permeable, and well drained soils. They are characterized by a large amount of clay-sized iron and aluminum oxides (sesquioxides) in the subsoil that become hardened under prolonged exposure to the sun.

The word "laterite" is used to describe Oxisols with a hardened layer, or plinthite. Soils that have developed laterites are no longer useful for agriculture. Many African soils have been erroneously referred to as laterites because of their reddish colors. African soils with rich red color and friable nature are better described as lateritic soils.

Extensive areas of lateritic soils occur across the humid to semiarid areas of West Africa. Alfisols, which occupy about 10 percent of the area, are soils that have a clayey subsoil horizon with a high base saturation (calcium, magnesium, potassium, and sodium). Alfisols are extensive in the Sahelian part of Africa. Ultisols, which occupy about 6.2 percent of the land area, are soils that have a lower base saturation in the subsoil horizon than Alfisols. They are heavily leached soils that have become acidic. Many Ultisols are actually buried Oxisols. A majority of the Alfisols and Ultisols have stone lines of variable thickness, composed of quartz or petroplinctic gravel. Alfisols are found mainly in the upland areas of the drier regions, whereas Ultisols occur largely in the upland areas of the wetter forest zones.

Inceptisols and Entisols are young soils that develop along the floodplains of the major rivers and bottoms of the inland valleys, or occur as wind-borne sand deposits on the edge of the Sahara. Entisols are soils mostly derived from alluvial materials. Inceptisols are primarily derived from colluvial and alluvial materials. They have relatively high fertility and, with the exceptions of those in the dry lands, have favorable moisture qualities. Some of these soils, often referred to as wetland soils, favor almost year-round cultivation but are largely underutilized because of water management problems and health hazards.

Vertisols are dark clay soils, often called black cotton soils, that shrink when dry and swell when wet. These soils are found mainly in the semi-arid regions and they develop cracks of considerable depth during the dry season. Most African Vertisols are generally not cultivated, because of their clayey nature. However, Vertisols of Sudan on the Gezira plains are used under irrigation.

SOIL CONSTRAINTS

With the exception of the Vertisols, most African soils are generally deep and permeable, and thus facilitate good drainage and root development. Excessive drainage, however, causes intense leaching of the soil nutrients (calcium, magnesium, and potassium) by percolating water, thereby leading to acid conditions. The consequence of variable but generally high subsoil acidity often limits the effective rooting depth and growth of many crops. Low organic matter (usually less than 3%) and low clay contents, a high content of coarse, infertile material (sand), and high afternoon soil temperature (up to 104 to 122 degrees Fahrenheit at shallow rooting zones) are common features of most surfaces soils, particularly Oxisols, Alfisols, and Ultisols. Organic matter is generally confined to the thin top layer, usually not more than six inches deep. These soils have clay minerals with sand-like qualities, referred to as low activity clays. For these reasons, the soils are weak, crumble easily, and are highly susceptible to compaction by raindrop impact and human, animal, and vehicular traffic. On water application, they slake easily to form a thin, dense, and impervious crust that curtails water entry into the soil and thus encourages runoff and erosion on sloping lands.

High activity clay soils are Vertisols, Aridisols, Inceptisols, and Entisols, about half of which are found in the dry climates. Thus, many African soils under cultivation have low nutrient and water retention capacities, or are infertile. The most limiting plant nutrients on all soils are nitrogen and phosphorus, normally associated with soil organic matter. The high phosphorus-fixing potential of sesquioxide-rich Oxisols and Ultisols further enhances this deficiency. About 55 percent of the land in Africa is considered unsuitable for any kind of agriculture except nomadic grazing. These are steep to very steep slopes and deserts. Low and erratic rainfall, coupled with an inability of the soil to hold and release moisture, create moisture deficits in plants and significant reduction in crop yield. Soil moisture stress is thus an overriding constraint in crop production in much of Africa.

The natural consequence of these severe soil constraints and the extensive degradation that has taken place is the inability of soils to produce sufficient food for humans and animals and to support industrial development. Indeed, since the 1970s food production in Africa has fallen far short of the rate of population growth.

SOIL DEGRADATION

African soils and climatic environments are fragile because of an inherent inability to resist drastic changes introduced by humans that often lead to permanent changes in the total environment. The traditional food production system of shifting cultivation is well adapted to the fragile soils because the land rests and recovers nutrients for some years following two to three years of cultivation. Rapid population growth (3.3% per annum) and the concomitant demand for food have, however, necessitated a continuous cultivation of more land, particularly more marginal land, some on steep slopes with attendant soil degradation. It has been estimated that 73 percent of African land has been degraded.

The real problem with African soils is that the fragile resource base is often exploited beyond its carrying capacity. Overexploitation, mismanagement, and misuses are the major causes of soil degradation. With a population exceeding 746 million people and 650 million livestock, human population densities as high as sixty-two people or more per square mile, overgrazing, and large-scale deforestation for fuel and timber or expansion of farmland have exposed soils to the harsh climatic elements.

Only 8 percent of original forests of Africa remains in the early twenty-first century. Forest consumption is estimated at about 7.4 million acres per annum. The rate of forest conversion in many African countries is variable but it exceeds the annual global average of 0.8 percent. The annual rate of deforestation is 6.5 percent in Côte d'Ivoire, 2.77 percent in Rwanda, and 2.3 percent in Zaire. About 50 percent of the deforestation in the tropical rainforest is by the slash and burn technique in the traditional farming system. Forest patches in Côte d'Ivoire and along the border between Nigeria and Cameroon are all that remains of the original rainforest.

Uncontrolled and excessive grazing depletes the vegetation cover, compacts the surface soil layer by trampling, and decreases water infiltration into the soil. Conventional soil cultivation, an imported technology, leads to soil compaction and accelerates the decomposition of organic matter and soil erosion. In Northern Nigeria, as in other parts of the arid and semi-arid areas, crop residue is removed or burned, thus exposing the soil. Both humans and animals compete for crop residue either as fuel or fodder.

High intensity rains concentrated in a few months, a rolling topography, soil exposure, and highly erodible soils set the stage for an accelerated soil erosion that occurs everywhere in Africa. Severe wind erosion is a common feature of areas with gusty winds north of 12 degrees north longitude. About 25 percent of the land is prone to water erosion and 22 percent to wind erosion. Losses by erosion can hardly be tolerated in Africa without adverse consequences on soil productivity and crop yield. This is because erosion removes the fertile portion of the thin topsoil. Experimental plots have measured as much as one-third an inch per year of soil losses. Once the topsoil is lost, no agricultural miracle can bring the land back to full production. Crop yields decline rapidly after bush clearing. The rate of decline of corn yield has been reported to be as high as one to three tons per acre per inch of eroded soil.

Soil mining is the result of poor resource farmers continually cultivating the land without replenishing the mineral nutrients. The economic consequences of severe erosion and soil mining therefore cannot be overemphasized. Grain yields are pegged at 2.5 tons per acre on most fields, owing in part to the inadequate use of mineral fertilizer. With the exception of countries such as Egypt and Kenya where fertilizer use ranges from 40 to 208 pounds per acre, the rate is less than 9 pounds per acre in most countries in Africa. Poor farmers cannot afford the exorbitant price of fertilizer that is generally two to six times more expensive overseas (North America and Europe).

Salinity and alkalinity, resulting from water application by irrigation and rainfall, are major problems of the arid and semiarid parts of Africa. It has affected about 24 percent of the continent and is a continuous problem in the environment. The construction and operation of several large irrigation dams in northern Nigeria bear testimony to this fact. About two million acres of African land have been so badly damaged that they cannot be economically repaired.

SOLVING SOIL PROBLEMS

Wholesale adoption of imported technologies has not always solved the problems of African soils. The inherently infertile nature of African soils, coupled with the severe nutrient depletion and degradation that have taken place, needs to be addressed by encouraging technologies that center on preventing soil exposure to the climatic elements. Mulching, crop rotation and mixed cropping (a traditional system), alley cropping (where suitable hedgerow trees are planted with the crops and their prunings add organic matter to the soil), and agro-forestry should also be used to promote the buildup of soil organic matter. Additionally, zero or minimum tillage should be allowed. To meet the nutrient needs of crops and to boost production, it has been estimated that fertilizer use for Africa has to increase by four times.

The use of local rock phosphate, limestone, and gypsum deposits to address phosphorus and acidity problems should be encouraged. The combined use of mineral (inorganic) and organic fertilizer, as well as indigenous and cultural practices that are soil-conserving and fertility-boosting should be endorsed for resource poor farmers, even though some of the techniques are labor intensive. The popularization and use of vetiver strips to combat the erosion menace hold great promise for soil and water conservation, and improved crop yields. Mechanical soil cultivation should not be used indiscriminately. Irrigation of agricultural land can put more land into production and alleviate moisture stress. Limited successes in irrigation agriculture in Africa may be due in part to a dearth of irrigation agronomists. Effective land use policies must be put in place to minimize degradation. Extension services must be strengthened to educate farmers. Although fertility is a major limiting factor, the management of soil and water resources is also critical. The need for African countries to integrate natural resource management with economic policies and establish an environment that makes agricultural inputs easily available to farmers cannot be overemphasized.

See also **Agriculture; Climate; Ecology; Ecosystems; Forestry.**

BIBLIOGRAPHY

Agyei, Yvonne. "Deforestation in Sub-Saharan Africa." *African Technology Forum* 8, no. 1 (1998): 1–4.

Babalola, O., and E. Zagal. "Physical Conditions and Degradation of Nigerian Soils." In *Proceedings of the 26th Annual Conference of the Soil Science Society of Nigeria*, ed. O. Babalola. Nigeria: Soil Science Society of Nigeria Publisher, 2000.

Dregne, Harold E., and Nan-Ting Chou. "Global Desertification, Dimensions and Costs." In *Degradation and Restoration of Arid Lands*, ed. H. E. Dregne. Lubbock: Texas Tech University, 1992.

Eswaran, Hari, et al. "An African Assessment of the Soil Resources of Africa in Relationship to Productivity." *World Soil Resources*. Soil Survey Division. Washington, DC: USDA Natural Resources Conservation Science, 1996.

Eswaran, Hari, et al. "Soil Quality and Soil Productivity in Africa." *World Soil Resources*. Soil Survey Division. Washington, DC: USDA Natural Resources Conservation Science, 1996.

Eswaran, Hari; Rattan Lal; and Paul Reich. "Land Degradation: An Overview." In *Response to Land Degradation*, ed. E. M. Bridges et al. Enfield, New Hampshire: Science Publishers, Inc., 2001.

FAO-UNESCO. *Soil Map of the World, Africa*. Paris: FAO, 1977.

FAO-UNESCO. *Animal Production and Health Series*. Edited by V. R. Welte. Rome: FAO, 1991.

Henao, Julio, and Carlos Baanante. "Nutrient Depletion in Agricultural Soils of Africa." *2020 Vision Brief* no. 62 (1999): 3.

Grimshaw, Richard G., and Larisa Helfer, eds. *Vetiver Grass for Soil and Water Conservation, Land Rehabilitation and Embankment Stabilization. A Collection of Papers and Newsletters Complied by the Vetiver Network.* Washington DC: The World Bank, 1995.

Lal, Rattan. "Managing the Soils of Sub-Saharan Africa." *Science* 236 (1987): 1,069–1,076.

Lal, Rattan. *Tropical Ecology and Physical Edaphology*. New York: John Wiley and Sons, 1987.

Lal, Rattan. "Soil Degradation and the Future of Agriculture in Sub-Saharan Africa." *Journal of Soil and Water Conservation* 43, no. 6 (1998) 444–451.

Oldeman, L. R.; T. A. Hakkeling; and Wim G. Sombroek. *World Map of the Status of Human–Induced Soil Degradation: An Explanatory Note.* Wageningen: Wageningen Netherlands International Soil Reference Centre, 1992.

Reich, Paul, et al. "Land Resource Stresses and Desertification in Africa." In *Agro-Science* 2, no. 2 (2001): 1–10.

Sanchez, Pedro A. "Soil Fertility and Hunger in Africa." *Science* 295 no. 5562 (2002): 2,019–2,020.

Shetto, Richard M. "Indigenous Soil Conservation Tillage Systems and Risks of Animal Traction on Land Degradation in Eastern and Southern Africa." In *Conservation Tillage with Animal Traction*, ed. Pascal Kaumbutho and Timothy Simalenga. Harare, Zimbabwe: ATNESA Publications, 1999.

Soil Conservation Service, USDA Soil Survey Staff, Soil Taxonomy. *A Basic System of the Soil Classification for Making and Interpreting Soil Surveys*. Washington, DC: Agricultural Handbook No. 436, 1975.

Steiner, Kurtz, and M. Bwalya. "Enhancing Conservation Tillage in Africa. The African Conservation Tillage Network." Madrid, Spain: Proceedings of 1st World Congress on Conservation Agriculture, 1996.

USDA/Natural Resource Conservation Service. *World Soil Resources*. International Program Division, 1996.

World Soil Resources Institute. *World Resources 1994–1995*. Oxford University Press, 1994.

O. BABALOLA

SOMALIA

This entry includes the following articles:
GEOGRAPHY AND ECONOMY
SOCIETY AND CULTURES
HISTORY AND POLITICS

GEOGRAPHY AND ECONOMY

Somalia is bounded to the east by the Indian Ocean and to the north primarily by the Gulf of Aden, a strategic point of entrance to the Red Sea and the Indian Ocean. The three states that surround Somalia to the west—Djibouti, Ethiopia, and Kenya—all encompass lands that traditionally have been home to the Somali people: the arbitrary borders set during the colonial era did not terminate the cultural/ethnic/religious and economic bonds between Somalis on either side of these borders. So to understand the economy of modern Somalia, largely shattered by civil war since the late 1980s, one must take into account cross-border movement of people, livestock and commodities.

TOPOGRAPHY, CLIMATE, AND VEGETATION

Most of Somalia consists of a vast plateau, but the country has two other distinct physiographic regions: a long, narrow coastal plain (1,118 miles long) and a mountain range (on average, 5,905–6,889 feet high) that runs more or less parallel to the northern coast. The highest peak in Somalia, Shimber Berris (7,900 feet high), sits near that coast; it is located near the town of Erigavo. The Golis mountain range falls within an area known as the Ogo, which also includes some shallow valleys but not the northern coastal plain. South of the Ogo lies the long, broad Nugaal Valley; the plateau region, known as the Haud, spreads out beyond this valley into the southern plains. In the far south, Somalia is defined by the country's two perennial rivers, both of which have their headwaters in Ethiopia: the Juba (about 1,994 miles long) and the Shabeelle (about 1,242 miles long). They are Somalia's only year-round bodies of water. Streams and other small bodies of water are created elsewhere in the country seasonally, depending on the amount of rain that falls. Somalia is drought prone and suffers from frequent severe droughts.

Somalia is subject to four different seasons: *gu* (the primary rainy season), which extends from April through June; *hagaa* (the dry season), usually from July through August; *dayr* (the rainy season), from October through November; and *jiilaal* (the driest season), from December through the end of March. Each season manifests differently from north to south, the north generally being hotter and drier, except in the higher altitudes in the northwest. The southern coasts tend to be somewhat cooler and more humid than the inland areas, but the northern coastal plain is quite hot and arid: in the course of the year average temperatures here range from 69 to 118 degrees Fahrenheit and average annual rainfall is only 3 inches. The vegetation on the northern coastal plain, known as Guban (means or burned), consists primarily of dry scrub bushes and grasses. Scrub bushes and grasses also grow along much of Somalia's eastern coast. Mangoves cluster at places along both coasts, but mainly from Kismayu to the Kenyan border.

Many types of trees, including aloes and acacias, thrive inland in the north, though much of the vegetation in this part of Somalia also consists of scrub bushes and grasses. Boswellia and commiphora trees (one the source of frankincense; the other, of myrrh) flourish in the arid northeastern highlands. Junipers grow elsewhere in the northern highlands, on slopes above 4,921 feet. As a rule, the higher the elevation, the denser the trees and other vegetation because the highlands get much more rain than the lowlands. Average annual rainfall across the north is only 2 to 6 inches, but rainfall in the highlands can be as much as almost 20 inches per year or more. Temperatures in the north vary considerably depending on the elevation and the time of year. In the northern lowlands during hagaa temperatures can rise to 113 degrees Fahrenheit and even higher (forcing many people to move out of these areas). Temperatures reach the other extreme in the northern highlands during jiilaal, when they drop down to readings near freezing at night. Such extremes and the general paucity of rainfall make the north, by and large, inhospitable to sedentary farming; the one exception is in an area west of the major northwestern city Hargeysa.

Sedentary farming in Somalia has traditionally been concentrated in the fertile interriverine region in the south. Some farms—primarily the large banana and sugar plantations, which (unlike most smallholders' farms in Somalia) employ modern irrigation systems—draw on the waters of the Juba and the Shabeelle. But most local farming is made possible by the relatively heavy rainfall in the region: the average amount of rainfall here, and also farther south, is 13 to 22 inches per year. Rainfall and the waters of the Juba and the Shabeelle offset the effects of the heat in the area, which can be considerable: temperatures throughout southern and central Somalia range nearly as high as those in the north, from 68 to 104 degrees Fahrenheit.

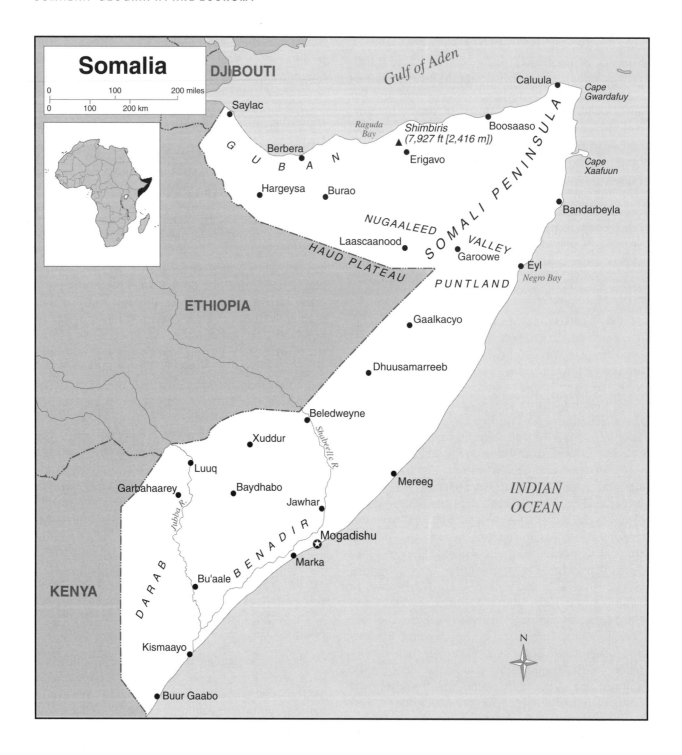

The amount of rain that falls south of the Shabeelle creates favorable conditions not only for agriculture but also for natural vegetation: acacias and other trees, as well as grasses, that grow wild in all of southern and central Somalia cluster much more thickly in the interriverine region and also in the country's southwest extreme than they do farther north on the Mudug Plain. Most of these forests have been destroyed by charcoal exporters since the mid-1990s in the absence of government regulations.

THE HAUD AND THE OGADEN
The Somali stretch of the Haud plateau is located in the northwestern part of the country and extends

west over the Ethiopian border nearly as far as the city Harar; to the south the Haud merges with the Ogaden plains, which run along Somalia's western border. Traditionally both the Haud and Ogaden have played an integral role in Somali pastoralism. Civil war in Somalia in the 1990s, as well as conflicts with Ethiopia since the late 1970s, have disrupted pastoralists' seasonal migrations. But it has been estimated that previously, in the mid-1970s, as many as three hundred thousand pastoralists cross the border (including the Ogo and the Nugaal Valley) during gu. They remained in the Haud for several months-as long as they continued to find good grazing. Subsequently some of these pastoralists would return to northern Somalia, but many others would push on to the Ogaden where they would find not only pasturage but wells. At the close of the second rainy season (day), these migrants would return to the winter grazing area in Somalia.

The rights to both the Haud and the Ogaden (officially called Somali Region in Ethiopia) have been a subject of dispute and a frequent source of regional tensions ever since borderlines were first established between Ethiopia and European colonial governments before Somalia became independent. Though the British negotiated seasonal access to the Haud for Somali pastoralists, they formally ceded the area, without Somali consent, to Ethiopia in the first Anglo-Ethiopian treaty, signed in 1897. Somali were unaware of this treaty until it was fully implemented in 1954. The discovery that the British had given away the Haud helped fuel the Pan-Somali movement, which sought to unite all Somali lands in one independent nation. The movement persisted long after the creation of the independent Somali Republic in 1960. The Ethiopian authorities denied that there was Somali territory inside Ethiopia, however, the post- 1991 regime in Addis Ababa has created a region called "Somali region" in Ethiopia. Somalia supported Somalis in Ethiopian during the 1960s and 1970s and twice-in 1964 and again during 1977-1978 became embroiled in all-out war with Ethiopia over the political status of the "Somali region."

Fighting over the border between Ethiopia and Somalia continued through the 1980s, driven in part by the fact that Somali groups dedicated to the overthrow of Mohamed Siad Barre, the Somali head of state, were using Ethiopia as a base of operations. Ethiopia supported these movements until the Somali regime collapsed and the country disintegrated in 1991. Ethiopia has continued to support different Somali factions in the civil war and this has made it difficult to advance the peace process.

ECONOMIC HISTORY

By the late 1990s Somalia's economy was in ruins, largely on account of the civil war that began in 1988. But developments of the 1970s and 1980s—among them, the accumulation of a massive national debt and a series of droughts, some particularly severe—did considerable damage to the country's economy even before the state collapsed. In 1990 the gross national product (GNP) was only $150 per capita.

Somalia's bleak economic performance in the 1970s and 1980s was not inevitable. It was a product of two mutually reinforcing factors: First, the country lacked leaders who were dedicated to developing effective public institutions. (Disunity among the elite and the lack of a system of political accountability rendered public institutions both chaotic and corrupt.) Second, during the Cold War, because of Somalia's strategic value, first Eastern and then Western donors poured large quantities of military hardware and financial assistance into the country. The combination of military and material largess fostered an unproductive and unsustainable economy but it also maintained the Somali state. Foreign support—including loans from the International Monetary Fund (IMF)—was withdrawn from Somalia in the 1980s, and government's mismanagement led to a political and economic disintegration.

TRADITIONAL AND NASCENT ECONOMIC ACTIVITIES

Livestock, sorghum, maize, rice, and other grains raised by smallholders, and bananas and citrus fruits grown on large plantations, constitute the productive anchors of the Somali economy before the onset of the civil war; sugar was another important cash crop. Cattle, which require relatively frequent watering, are raised primarily in the interriverine region and the northwestern highlands; camels, sheep, and goats are raised throughout the country.

In the late 1980s, even after the series of droughts that had ravaged Somalia during the previous two decades, pastoralists still accounted for about 50 percent of the Somali population. (About 20–25% of the population were farmers.) Herd sizes varied as Somalia was hit by drought—for example, during 1999–2000 as much as 60 percent of the livestock then in central Somalia is thought to have died—but herds have been rebuilt between droughts. Livestock were the leading Somali export: in the late 1980s livestock contributed nearly 50 percent to GNP. Bananas were the second leading export at that time, contributing about 15 percent to GNP. Another important source of foreign revenue was frankincense and myrrh, gathered from the boswellia and commiphora trees that grow in the northern highlands.

Beginning in the 1960s, efforts were made to develop economic activities in Somalia other than pastoralism and agriculture. The primary focus in the manufacturing sector was on food processing, but Somalia also established some limited facilities for produce textiles, pharmaceuticals, and other goods. In the mid-1970s a petroleum refinery was built in the capital, Mogadishu (one of the country's major ports), to process petroleum imported from Iraq and Saudi Arabia. There has been prospecting for oil and gas both on and offshore in Somalia since the 1970s, but it was abandoned due to the civil war. There has been some degree of economic recovery since the collapse of the state, fuelled by remittance from the diaspora, but Saudi Arabia's ban on livestock exports from Somalia has had debilitating economic effects. Prospecting for minerals has been more successful: reserves of a variety of minerals—including iron, uranium, gold, gypsum, and limestone—have been located in Somalia since the 1960s. However, only gypsum and limestone have been exploited commercially.

Fisheries are another undeveloped resource that potentially could be quite important economically. But Somalia had little in the way of a fishing industry before the early 1970s, when the government resettled and retrained some fifteen thousand Somali pastoralists whose traditional livelihood had been devastated by drought. (The fishing industry was designed primarily for export business, since Somalis traditionally do not eat fish.) However, once the fighting began in 1991, Somalia for the most part lost control of its waters, and its marine ecosystem has been devastated by foreign fishing fleets. Further, recent evidence has shown that toxic and radioactive waste has been dumped in Somali waters.

DEBTS, DROUGHTS, AND WARFARE

The period from 1960 to 1976 was one of relative economic prosperity in Somalia: as a whole the economy grew 2.1 percent per year, while the industrial sector grew at an annual rate of 5 percent. Several developments countered this growth and ultimately worked to undermine it. The military government that took power in 1969 nationalized many sectors of the economy; it took direct control of the manufacturing companies and monopolized the trade in agricultural goods. These actions—combined with an overly ambitious (that is, underfinanced) development program—quickly got Somalia deeply into debt. Government mismanagement of the economy also significantly diminished productivity in all areas. The once growing industrial sector stagnated and remained that way throughout the 1980s. To make matters worse, the absence of a productively growing economy meant that more pressure was exerted on pastoral and peasant resources, leading to the deterioration of range ecology as well as extensive soil erosion in crop-producing areas. Somalia depended heavily on foreign assistance and thus only continued to acquire more debt.

Severe droughts compounded the problems brought on initially by economic policy. The drought of 1974–1975 was one of the worst in the history of the region; famine affected hundreds of thousands of Somalis throughout the country (as well as Somali in Ethiopia). So much livestock died during this drought—an estimated 40 percent of all Somali livestock—that when it was over many herders were unable to resume their traditional occupation. It was then that the government resettled and retrained several thousand pastoralists as fishermen; others were resettled and retrained as farmers. Somalia was hit hard by drought again during 1983–1984, 1986–1987, and 1992. It was the drought of 1992 and the ensuing famine that provoked the United States to intervene in Somalia in the mission known as Operation Restore Hope. Some drought, and with it, famine, was also reported during 1995 and 1999. Though Somalia received substantial international aid to offset the effects of droughts in the 1970s, 1980s, and 1990s, it was also forced to increase its food imports. The expense of these imports, and also some of the cost of caring for and resettling its refugees from famine, also added to the national debt.

During the 1980s Somalia endured several other major economic setbacks. One was the continual and increasing expense of skirmishing with Ethiopian troops along the western border and also trying to suppress various rebel groups that sought to overthrow the military regime. The war with Ethiopia in 1977–1978 had also been a huge expense. In 1984 Saudi Arabia dealt Somalia a particularly heavy blow when it banned all livestock imports from the country (and other countries in eastern Africa) on account of reports of rinderpest in the region; the following year Somali export revenues plummeted by 43 percent. More recently the Saudi government claimed Somali livestock was suffering from rift valley fever and subsequently imposed a ban on exports. The civil war has devastated the economy but many legitimate and illegitimate entrepreneurs have capitalized on the absence of government regulations and the commercial and telecommunications sector has grown significantly. Much of this growth is fuelled by income transfers from Somalis who immigrated to all corners of the world since the civil war began. Despite this growth, the vast majority of the population is more impoverished than it was in the mid-1980s.

See also **Climate; Cold War; Debt and Credit; Ecosystems; Famine; Harar; International Monetary Fund; Mogadishu; Production Strategies; Warfare: Civil Wars.**

BIBLIOGRAPHY

Cassanelli, Lee V. *The Shaping of Somali Society: Reconstructing the History of a Pastoral People, 1600–1900.* Philadelphia: University of Pennsylvania Press, 1982.

Kapteins, L., with Maryan Omer Ali. *Women's Voices in a Man's World: Women and the Pastoral Tradition in Northern Somali Orature.* Portsmouth, NH: Heinemann, 1999.

Laitin, David D., and Said S. Samatar. *Somalia: Nation in Search of a State.* Boulder, CO: Westview Press, 1987.

Little, Peter. *Somalia: Economy without State.* Bloomington: University of Indiana Press, 2003.

Samatar, Abdi. *The State and Rural Transformation in Northern Somalia, 1884–1896.* Madison: University of Wisconsin Press, 1989.

Samatar, Abdi. "Destruction of State and Civil Society in Somalia: Beyond the Tribal Convention." *African Studies* 30 (1992): 625–641.

Samatar, Abdi. "Structural Adjustment as Development Strategy: Bananas, Boom and Poverty." *Economic Geography* 69 (1993): 25–44.

Samatar, Abdi, and Ahmed Samatar. "Somalis as Africa's First Democrats: Aden A. Osman and Abdirazak H. Hussen." *Bildhaan: International Journal of Somali Studies* 2 (2002): 2–66.

Samatar, Ahmed. *Socialist Somalia: Rhetoric and Reality.* London: Zed Books, 1988.

Samatar, Ahmed, ed. *The Somali Challenge: From Catastrophe to Renewal?* Boulder, CO: Lynne Rienner, 1994.

Sheik-Abdi, Abdi. *Divine Madness: Mohammed Abdulle Hassan (1856–1920).* London: Zed Books, 1992.

ABDI ISMAIL SAMATAR

SOCIETY AND CULTURES

Estimated to number between 8 and 10 million, but never systematically enumerated, the Somali people form a distinctive, single ethnic unit in the Horn of Africa, stretching from the Awash Valley (in Ethiopia) in the north to beyond the Tana River (in northern Kenya) in the south. Linguistically and culturally, the Somali belong to the Cushitic-speaking family. They are thus related ethnically to the neighboring Afar (or Danakil, or, as the Somali call them, the Oodali) of Djibouti, Eritrea, and the Awash Valley, and to the Oromo (and Borana subgroup), who form the largest ethnic group in Ethiopia. The Somali's cultural connections with these neighboring peoples are reinforced by their common profession of Sunni Islam: all the Afar and some of the Oromo tribes are Sunni Muslims (particularly the Arssi of Ethiopia's Bale Province, known to the Somali as "Somali Abo").

Like the neighboring peoples, with whom they have contended for land and water for centuries, the Somali are traditionally bellicose nomads, herding camels, sheep, and goats, and in the less arid regions, cattle. (Despite the fact that they often live side by side on the same terrain and rear the same kinds of livestock, the Somali, the Afar, and the Oromo differ in striking ways in both their herding arrangements and in their forms of social organization.) The pastoralist Somali divide their livestock into two herding units, one based on the needs of sheep and goats, which include frequent watering, and the other based on the needs of grazing camels, which can go for days without water. Cattle are treated like sheep and goats. The grazing camels, which supply milk, are put in the charge of young, typically unmarried men, while the sheep and goats and burden-bearing camels (required to carry the nomads' tents from camping ground to camping ground) travel with families. So a married man's main herds of camels may be in distant grazing areas in the care of younger kinsmen while he moves with his wife or wives and their small stock. (As Muslims, Somali may have up to four wives concurrently; divorce is common. Most men have at least two marriages in the course of their lives.)

Pastureland, as such, is not owned, traditionally, while wells and water points are subject to individual and collective rights that reflect the efforts expended in constructing and maintaining them. Livestock are owned by individuals, although camels are also subject to residual collective rights. This distinction is reflected in the fact that sheep and goats carry the brands of individual owners while camels carry the brands of the wider kinship groups to which the individual owners belong.

Although the overwhelming bias of the Somali is toward pastoralism, some cultivation is practiced in the better-watered northwestern highlands south of Harar and in the zone framed by the Shabeelle and Juba Rivers in southern Somalia. In the former, Ethiopian-style ox-drawn plows are utilized, whereas in the latter land is cultivated by hand-hoe. In the river valleys themselves, small scattered communities of non-Somali Bantu farmers and hunters have adopted irrigation cropping and commercial estates have also been developed. Bananas grown here are Somalia's main export crop.

The interriverine region is the site of the most profound cultural division in Somali society. The agropastoralists who live here are chiefly members of the Rahanwayn and Digil clan-families (clusters of clans thought to share a common ancestor) who speak a dialect, known as Maymay, that is not fully mutually intelligible to standard Somali speakers: it differs from standard Somali roughly as much as Portuguese does from Spanish. Since many Rahanwayn speakers also speak standard Somali, as do the people who make up the riverine communities, Somali provides a single medium of communication from Djibouti to the Tana River. Songs and poems in Somali compete for popularity. In the early twenty-first century as in the past, poetry, whether diffused by word of mouth, cassette, or radio, constitutes a pervasive and essential feature of Somali culture—not least in politics. The transistor radio has become as indispensible to the nomadic warrior as the Kalashnikov rifle.

Most of the Somali nation conceive of themselves as a single family, tracing descent ultimately to Arabia and the family of the Prophet Muhammad, thus validating their common Islamic identity. At the highest level of grouping, the nation consists of six major clanfamilies, of which the Digil and Rahanwayn are the most distinctive. Since, despite the Somali's centuries-long involvement in the caravan trade between the Ethiopian hinterland and the coastal ports, over 50 percent of the total Somali population is still nomadic, the pastoral tradition and its social structure dominate most aspects of Somali life—in modern towns and ports as well as in the countryside.

This applies equally to those many thousands of Somali who are migrant workers in the Gulf states and those hundreds of thousands who have become refugees in many parts of the world. It is also true of those within Somalia who are responsible for the financial organization of the vitally important livestock export trade. Only the centuries' old Somalised Arab communities in the coastal strip round and to the south of Mogadishu, with their own urban customs, live partly ouside the all-inclusive Somali clan system.

The basic principle of social and political organization is patrilineal kinship traced through the male members of the family. The Somali, in fact, have the most extensive, holistic lineage structure known to anthropologists. From the domestic family to the entire nation, all constituent groups are essentially descent groups, or lineages, led by their "elders" (all family heads) who debate all political decisions in exhaustive detail in extremely long, drawn-out council meeings. Except to some extent among the Rahanwayn, hereditary chiefs in

Somali Republic (formerly the Somali Democratic Republic)

Population:	9,118,773 (2007 est.)
Area:	637,657 sq. km (246,200 sq. mi.)
Official language:	Somali
Languages:	Somali, Arabic, Italian, English
National currency:	Somali shilling
Principal religion:	Muslim 100%
Capital:	Mogadishu (est. pop. 1,552,000 in 2005. Because of war and displacements, accurate current population figures are not available.)
Other urban centers:	Beledweyne, Kismayo, Baidoa, Jowhar, Merca, Gaalkayo, Bosasso, Hargeisa, Berbera
Annual rainfall:	less than 77 mm (3 in.) overall, but up to 550 mm (20 in.) on high ground
Principal geographical features:	*Mountains:* Shimbiris, Buuraha Cal Miskaat, Buuraha Cal Madow, Buuraha Wagar *Rivers:* Juba, Shabeelle *Other:* the Guban ("Burned Land"), the northern coastal plain
Economy:	*GDP per capita:* US$600 (2006)
Principal products and exports:	*Agricultural:* bananas, sorghum, corn, coconuts, rice, sugarcane, mangoes, sesame seeds, beans, cattle, sheep, goats, fish *Manufacturing:* light industry, including sugar refining, textiles *Mining:* limestone, gypsum; other unexploited deposits include uranium, iron ore, gold, lead barite, meerschaum, tin, titaniferous sand, quartz
Government:	The independent Somali Republic was formed in 1960 from the union of the British Protectorate of Somaliland (independence from Great Britain, 1960) and former Italian Somaliland (later a U.N. trusteeship administered by Italy, independence from Italian rule, 1960). Constitution approved in 1961, replaced in 1979. Under the 1979 constitution, Somalia was a one-party republic. Since the overthrow of Mohamed Siad Barre by the United Somali Congress (USC) in 1991, there has been no stable and effective nationwide government in the midst of the ongoing factional warfare. In May 1991, the Somali National Movement (SNM) declared the creation of an independent Somaliland Republic from what had formerly been the British protectorate. A transitional government (the Transitional Federal Government, or TFG) was formed in 2004 after a 3-year peace process led by the Inter-governmental Authority on Development. The TFG includes a 275-member parliamentary body, a transitional Prime Minister and President, and a 90-member cabinet. As of 2007, the TFI had yet to establish authority throughout the country. For administrative purposes, Somalia is divided into 18 regions.
Heads of state since independence:	1960–1967: President Aden Abdullah Osman Daar 1967–1969: President Dr. Abdirashid Ali Sharmarke 1969: Acting President Shaykh Moktar Husayn 1969–1976: Major General Mohamed Siad Barre, chairman of the Supreme Revolutionary Council 1976–1991: President Mohamed Siad Barre 1991–1997: President Ali Mahdi Mohamed, appointed by one faction of the United Somali Congress (USC) with the support of several southern factions 1991–1993: President Abdurahman Ahmed Ali "Tur," acting president of the Republic of Somaliland, chairman of the Somali National Movement (SNM) 1993–2002: President Mohamed Ibrahim Egal, president of the Republic of Somaliland 1995–1996: Interim President General Mohammed Farah Aideed, appointed by his faction of the United Somali Congress–Somali National Alliance (USC-SNA) 1996–: President Hussein Mohammed Aideed, appointed by his faction of the USC-SNA 1997–2000: 41-member National Salvation Council (NSC), created by leaders of 26 Somali factions, with 11-member National Executive Committee with 5 co-chairmen 2000–2004: Inter-governmental Authority on Development 2003–: President Dahir Rayale Kahin 2004–: Transitional Federal President Abdullahi Yusuf Ahmed
Armed forces:	The army has fallen apart into rival clan-based militias, and there is therefore no national army.
Transportation:	*Roads:* 22,500 km (13,950 mi.), 12% paved *Ports:* Mogadishu, Berbera, Kismayu, Boosaaso, Merca *National airline:* Somali Airlines *Airports:* International facilities at Mogadishu and Berbera, domestic airports at Kismayu, Hargeysa, Boosaaso, Alula, Burao. Many airstrips throughout the country.
Media:	1 official daily newspaper: *Xiddigta Oktobar,* published in Somali. Other publications include: *The Country, Dalka, Heegan, Horseed, New Era.* 11 radio stations; 4 television stations.
Literacy and education:	*Total literacy rate:* 37.8% (2006). Since the collapse of the central government in 1991, the education system has been private. Higher education provided by Somali National University at Mogadishu, School of Islamic Disciplines, Veterinary College, School of Industrial Studies, Technical College, and School of Public Health.

the African style are foreign to Somali culture. Politics are extremely uncentralized, and prior to colonization, the Somali experience of state government was peripheral and fleeting. The earliest written reference to the Somali, a sixteenth-century document, describes them as a whole as loosely organized warriors, famous for their ambushes and roadblocks.

The basic but only relatively stable political unit in the traditional Somali system is the *diya*-paying group. It is composed of those patrilineal kin who are united under the leadership of their elders by a specific treaty that details their collective responsibility to pay or to receive damages for death or injury (called *diya* in Arabic, *mag* in Somali) incurred in their fractious relations with other groups. As the remarkable efforts of the elders of the breakaway, self-declared Republic of Somaliland, in building a model democracy, in northwestern Somalia illustrate, even with conflicts as intense and casualties as widespread as those of the 1990s civil war, these traditional techniques can still be applied succesfully. For such an extensively armed, decentralized society, however, whose segments in the south are led by gangster warlords, after fourteen high profile "peace conferences" between 1991 and 2005, restoring effective statehood" still seemed remote.

In 2006 two unexpected but related developments dramatically changed the situation. Clandestine U.S. intervention led to an ad hoc counter-terrorist formation of warlords with the title Alliance for the Restoration of Peace and Counterterrorism (ARPTC). This expansion of warlord violence prompted a widespead popular reaction led by al-Itihad fundamentalist sheikhs who proceeded to extend the jurisdiction of local Islamic courts throughout southern Somalia. With the support of prosperous businessmen, the courts recruited well-armed militias that became the main agencies of law enforcement, challenging the authority of the warlords. By June 2006, the Union of Islamic Courts had defeated the U.S.-backed ARPTC and was extending its control and confronting the otiose transitional federal government, which had now moved from Kenya to Somalia, and with the hospitality of residual local Digil Mirifle warlords had established its base at Baidoa. As each side became increasingly belligerent, Ethiopia

air-lifted support for its client, the TFG, and the Union of Islamic Courts, denounced as Al Qaeda affiliates, was easily provoked into proclaiming a jihad against Somalia's old enemy. At the end of 2006, after air attacks on the Islamists a war lasting only two weeks saw the victorious Ethiopian supported TFG leader esconced in the presidential palace in Mogadishu. Two and a half years after its contested formation in Kenya, the transitional "government" (which had never governed and had no public mandate) claimed control of the capital. The Ethiopian forces that had made this possible were due to withdraw in a matter of weeks and no one knew what would happen then, with the Islamists lurking in the wings, chastened perhaps, but hardly eliminated.

See also **Ethnicity; Harar; Kinship and Descent; Production Strategies; Warfare: Civil Wars.**

BIBLIOGRAPHY

Andrzejewski, B. W., and Sheila Andrzejewski. *An Anthology of Somali Poetry.* Bloomington: Indiana University Press, 1993.

Farah, Ahmed Yusuf. *The Milk of the Boswellia Forests: Frankincense Production among the Pastoral Somali.* Uppsala, Sweden: EPOS 1994.

Farah, Ahmed Yusuf, and I. M. Lewis. *Somalia: The Roots of Reconciliation. Peace-making Endeavours of Contemporary Lineage Leaders: A Survey of Grassroots Peace Conferences in "Somaliland."* London: ActionAid, 1993.

Helander, Bernhard. *The Slaughtered Camel: Coping with Fictitious Descent among the Hubeer of Southern Somalia.* Uppsala, Sweden: University of Uppsala, 2003.

Lewis, I. M. *A Pastoral Democracy: Pastoralism and Politics among the Northern Somali of the Horn of Africa.* London and New York: Oxford University Press, 1961. Repr., New York: Africana, 1982.

Lewis, I. M. *Blood and Bone: The Call of Kinship in Somali Society.* Lawrenceville, N.J.: Red Sea Press, 1994.

Lewis, I. M. *A Modern History of the Somali.* Rev. ed, Athens: Ohio University Press, 2002.

Luling, Virginia. *Somali Sultanate: The Geledi City-State over 150 Years.* Piscataway, N.J.: Transaction, 2002.

Samatar, Said S. *Oral Poetry and Somali Nationalism: The Case of Sayyid Mahammed 'Abdille Hasan.* Cambridge: Cambridge University Press, 1982.

I. M. LEWIS

HISTORY AND POLITICS

Somalia, also known as the Somali Democratic Republic (and before 1969 as the Somali Republic) comprises the former Somaliland Protectorate as well as the United Nations Trust Territory of Somalia, which were amalgamated after their independence into a single unitary state on July 1, 1960. (The former Somaliland Protectorate proclaimed itself the Republic of Somaliland on May 18, 1991, but has not been recognized as an independent nation.) Somalia forms the figure 7 around the eastern Horn of Africa and shares borders with Djibouti, Ethiopia, and Kenya. Before the collapse of the state early in 1991, Somalia was a member of the United Nations (UN); the Non-Aligned Group of Nations; the Organization of African Unity; the Organization of Islamic States; and the Arab League. It was also an associate member of the European Economic Community.

The Somali are an ancient people indigenous to the Horn of Africa. They came to the stage of world history as businesslike people trading with most of the ancient civilizations, dealing mainly in myrrh and frankincense (native only to certain areas of southern Arabia, Eritrea, and the coast of Somalia that lies adjacent to the Gulf of Aden) but also in a variety of other valuable aromatic spices and gums. Medieval geographical and historical sources attest to the Horn of Africa's continued commercial relations with Arabia, India, and China. In the Somalian countryside pastoralism flourished, but on both the northern and the eastern coasts there were small but cosmopolitan trading communities in the busy bazaars where Somali, Arab, Indian, and other southwest Asian buyers and sellers mixed. Documents citing the names of individual Somali clans make clear that some of them were in full occupation of their present territory as early as the twelfth century CE. While developing a distinct culture and national identity based on an agropastoral economy and the Islamic faith, the Somali, however, never came under the unifying rule of a single political authority.

THE SOMALI STATE

Historical Evolution. In contrast to the people, the Somali state has a very short history. The roots of its foundation go back to the closing decades of the nineteenth century when the European "scramble"

for African possessions and the simultaneous Ethiopian expansion into Somaliland resulted in the fragmentation of the Somali territory. The French took control of the Somali-populated area Djibouti. The British and the Italians first established themselves along the edge of the Horn of Africa and the Red Sea Coast, respectively, but ultimately the Italians came to dominate the bulk of the territory that constitutes present-day Somali Democratic Republic; the British protectorate was limited to a small area (68,000 square miles) on the Gulf of Aden. Ethiopia claimed territory in the Haud and the Ogaden, traditional Somali grazing lands that fall partly within but largely to the west of present-day Somalia. The British claims for colonial Kenya included territory inhabited by many Somali. The tearing apart of their people was a momentous setback for the Somali and the inspiration for numerous resistance movements that broke out subsequently and sought to challenge the colonial regimes militarily. As elsewhere in Africa, the early resisters were defeated by the 1920s, after which time resistance took the form of peacefully organized, nationalist political agitation. The modern state of Somalia was born out of this kind of struggle against colonialism.

The nationalist campaign was spearheaded by the Somali Youth League (SYL), which was founded in Mogadishu (part of the former Italian Somaliland) in 1943. Foremost among the party's declared goals was the attainment of independence by all the Somali territories and their reunification under one national flag. This popular position enabled the party to sweep the general elections of 1959, winning 83 of the territory's 90 Legislative Council seats. In the British protectorate the Somali National League (SNL) led the drive toward independence. The central plank of this party's platform was also a call for the realization of an independent Somalia that would encompass all of the Somali territories. The SNL and the United Somali Party (USP) formed an alliance (SNL-USP) and won 32 of the 33 Legislative Council seats in the 1960 general elections in British Somaliland. With this conclusion of the largely peaceful political campaign, on June 26, 1960, the protectorate won its independence. The trust territory (administered by Italy) became free on July 1; on the same day the former protectorate and trust united to form the Somali Republic.

Independent Somalia: 1960–1991. The 33-member Legislative Council of British Somaliland and the 90-member Council of Italian Somaliland also combined on July 1 to form the parliament of independent Somalia; they elected the nation's first head of state, Aden Abdullah Osman Daar. The parliamentary form of government was ratified a year later in the constitution of 1961. The SYL and the SNL-USP formed a coalition government headed by Prime Minister Abdirashid Ali Sharmarke of the SYL. This coalition government held power until the elections of 1964, after which Abdirashid Haje Hussein formed a government composed exclusively of SYL members. But Hussein's premiership ended in 1967 when Abdirashid Ali Sharmarke became head of state and nominated Mohamed Ibrahim Egal to be prime minister. Under Egal's leadership, the SYL scored yet another, albeit short-lived, victory at the polls in 1969.

Strongly wedded to the idea of Somali reunification, the governments led by Sharmarke and Hussein sponsored secessionist rebellions in the neighboring territories inhabited by Somali. Somalia's support for these rebellions led to border clashes with Ethiopia and extremely hostile relations with Kenya. Furthermore, Somalia's irredentist policies led to its being isolated in African political circles. Worse yet, the Somali governments, distracted by their pursuit of pan-Somali goals, devoted very little time or energy to the development needs of the Somali Republic. Prime Minister Egal departed somewhat from the militant pan-Somali policies of his predecessors and normalized relations with Kenya and Ethiopia. The first decade of Somalian independence was characterized by lively political debate, the existence of a free press, and a general freedom from governmental restraints, but it also witnessed the growth of a corrupt and unwieldy bureaucracy and the flagrant misuse of public funds by the government.

On October 15, 1969, President Sharmarke was assassinated. Shortly thereafter—on October 21—as the country prepared for presidential elections, the army took over the reins of state in a bloodless coup d'état. Suspending the 1961 constitution, the soldiers quickly tightened their grip on power by appointing themselves the Supreme Revolutionary Council (SRC); their chairman,

Major General Mohamed Siad Barre, became the de facto head of state. As an indication of the region's ideological leanings, the country was renamed the Somali Democratic Republic, and on the first anniversary of the coup, the SRC adopted scientific socialism as its guiding principle. On July 1, 1976, the SRC handed over political leadership to a newly formed body, the Somali Revolutionary Socialist Party (SRSP). All the living members of the SRC automatically became members of the party's Central Committee, and Mohamed Siad Barre became its supreme boss—the general secretary. A new constitution was adopted in 1979 and elections for a new parliament—the People's Assembly—were held in December of the same year. This parliament chose Mohamed Siad Barre as president. A constitutional amendment in 1985 provided for popular election of the president, and Mohamed Siad Barre was elected under this provision for a seven-year term in 1986.

Siad Barre's regime was a crude mixture of militaristic socialism and repressive personal dictatorship. Severely curbing personal liberties, it also intervened in the economy—to detrimental effect. The combination of economic woes and political oppression made a clash between the people and the regime inevitable. In 1976 a group of disgruntled intellectuals and politicians, calling themselves the Somali Democratic Action Front (SODAF), declared war on the government. This development was followed in 1979 by the formation of the Somali Salvation Front (SSF), renamed in 1982 the Somali Salvation Democratic Front (SSDF), which waged war against the Siad Barre regime from operational bases in Ethiopia. The founding of the Somali National Movement (SNM), which operated against the regime in the north, soon followed suit. By 1989 two other major opposition groups, the Somali Patriotic Movement (SPM) and the United Somali Congress (USC), were engaged in the fight against Siad Barre. Finally, on January 27, 1991, the USC militia succeeded in driving Siad Barre out of Mogadishu.

State Demise and External Intervention. Following the ouster of Siad Barre, the USC installed Ali Mahdi Mohamed as an interim president. This appointment was condemned by all the other Somalian political fractions, and thus was ushered in the civil war that has totally destroyed the Somali state. Instead of cooperating with one another, the victorious forces—each of which were clan-based militias—fought it out in the existing power vacuum, each of them attempting to gain for its own clan the powers and privileges previously enjoyed by Siad Barre's regime. First the USC militias, which represented the Hawiye clan-family, battled a coalition of Darod militias in the southern half of the country. (Siad Barre was a member of the Darod clan.) Then in May 1991 the Isaaq-based SNM declared that the former British protectorate was seceding from the Somali union to form the independent Republic of Somaliland. Now an internal rift within the USC pitted General Mohammed Farah Aideed against Ali Mahdi Mohamed; the ensuing war caused the loss of over thirty thousand lives and the destruction of much of the once beautiful city of Mogadishu. Local militias took the cue and declared their independence from Mogadishu. By the end of 1991 Somalia was divided into a dozen or so units under the control of clan elders or local warlords. The resultant chaos combined with a continuing drought to occasion a devastating famine in which about five hundred thousand people starved to death.

Relief aid donated by the international community was repeatedly looted and denied to the starving Somalians, so in April 1992 the United Nations Security Council authorized the first of its series of peacekeeping missions to Somalia, the United Nations Operation in Somalia (UNOSOM). The first UNOSOM was a relatively small operation, designed to monitor and help maintain a ceasefire between the warring Somalian factions that had been negotiated by the United Nations in March 1992. A second, more ambitious mission, the United Nations International Task Force (UNITAF), was dispatched at the end of 1992. Part of the U.S.-led "Operation Restore Hope," UNITAF quickly secured all seaports, airports, and delivery routes in Somalia. On May 4, 1993, it handed over responsibility to another contingent of UN troops, the United Nations Operation in Somalia II (UNOSOM II). UNOSOM II was given the broadest mandate of any of the UN missions: to facilitate national reconciliation and help rebuild the country's destroyed economy. But UNOSOM II was completely unsuccessful. The UN withdrew with

its tale between its legs from Somalia at the beginning of March 1995.

Fighting in southern Somalia between the Somali militias has continued into 2006, despite repeated attempts by certain of the clan elders, as well as the international community, to foster negotiations for an enduring truce between the warring factions that might lead to the creation of a stable national government. Aideed was killed in street fighting in Mogadishu during the last week of July 1996. Clan elders chose as his replacement his son Hussein Mohammed Farah Aideed, a naturalized American raised in California, thirty-three years old at the time of his appointment.

Hopes that Hussein Mohammed Farah Aideed might be a voice for peace were soon dispelled. He boycotted peace talks convened in Ethiopia at the end of November 1996; in December he and his clan, the Habar Gidir (a member of the Hawiye clan-family), were engaged in some of the fiercest fighting of the year. Also in December 1996 there was fighting on the Somalia-Ethiopia border as Ethiopian troops pursued a Somalian faction that sought to establish an Islamic state in the repeatedly contested Ogaden region. Finally, in 2006 after two successive UN-sponsored "transitional governments" each failed spectacularly to provide a viable administration, enjoying public support, a completely new indigenous initiative entered the lists. Without the waste of European Union (EU) and UN funds on these ill-designed Eurocentric efforts, a loosely connected union of Somali Islamists, with their militias, swept through southern Somalia taking over territory previously controlled by secular warlord militias. Building from the bottom up, as in the reconstruction of Somaliland, they thus reestablished law and order and social reconstruction on a scale unseen in Somalia since the downfall of General Siad. This was truly a homemade revolution far exceeding in its effectiveness the imported and costly initiatives of the UN and EU. The residual EU-sponsored "transitional federal government," recognized by the EU but not by Somalis, began to be seen, even by its ethnocentric creators, in its true colors at last.

FORMER INSTITUTIONS OF GOVERNMENT

From 1960 to 1969 Somalia was a parliamentary democracy with a president who was elected by the legislature, the National Assembly, a unicameral institution to which 123 deputies were elected at least once every five years. The president functioned as the ceremonial head of state with powers to nominate the head of government and dissolve the assembly. The prime minister and his cabinet were drawn from the majority party in the legislature and were answerable to the legislature. The elected head of state retained life membership in the National Assembly even after giving up the office of the presidency. The constitution of 1961 also provided for a judiciary that would be independent of the executive and legislative branches of government. It consisted of a supreme court, courts of appeal, regional courts, and district courts.

Somalia was divided into eight administrative regions composed of fifty-four districts. The constitution provided for the decentralization of the administration by authorizing elected councils that constituted district and municipal authorities. The central government appointed regional governors and district commissioners to head the local governing bodies and to mediate between the local authorities and the central government. The reorganization of the country by the military regime did away with these elected district and municipal councils and instituted in their place councils appointed in Mogadishu consisting exclusively of military, police, and security personnel. The constitution of 1979 called for yet another administrative reorganization.

Since 1979 Somalia has been, constitutionally, a socialist republic with one party, the Somali Revolutionary Socialist Party (SRSP), functioning as the sole legal political organization. Before the breakdown of the state in 1991, political leadership in Somalia consisted of the general secretary of the SRSP; a five-member politburo chaired by the general secretary; the party's 76-member Central Committee; and the theoretically independent 177-person legislative People's Assembly, the members of which, though not all party loyalists, were selected by the party and then presented to the electorate for approval. Six of them became members by presidential appointment. The People's Assembly "legislated" by approving laws submitted to it by the Central Committee and/or the government. The ultimate judicial, ceremonial, executive, and legislative authority in this political hierarchy was the party's general secretary, Mohamed Siad Barre, who was also the head of state and government and chairman of the national defense, internal security, and justice councils.

After 1979, as a concession to the demands of different clans for autonomy and for their share of developmental funds, the country was divided into eighteen administrative regions plus the national capital region, all of which were further subdivided into ninety districts. The 1979 constitution restored the election of district and municipal councils. However, as in the case of the People's Assembly, the SRSP retained the prerogative not only to approve but to actually draw up the lists of candidates. The chief executives of the regional and district governments were appointed by the ministry of the interior and held the positions of party secretaries at the regional or district levels. The national capital region and its fifteen districts came directly under the authority of the presidency.

Previously (by as early as 1970) the judiciary lost its independence and came directly under the control of the executive branch. Judges lost their immunity, and the supreme judicial council was chaired by Siad Barre, who chose all its members from among his colleagues in the army or police. Structurally the judiciary remained the same: it retained its four types of courts. To them was added a novel institution, the National Security Courts, which were enacted into law in 1970. Consisting exclusively of military officers, the National Security Courts dealt with cases involving state security, treason, sedition, economic sabotage, or embezzlement of public funds. Their judgments were final and subject to review by no other courts. Only through appeals to the president could their decisions be reversed. Allegedly employed to dispatch members of the political opposition, the National Security Courts were actually abolished in October 1990, before the collapse of the Siad Barre regime.

See also **Civil Society; Mogadishu; Organization of African Unity; Postcolonialism; Socialisms and Postsocialisms; United Nations; Warfare.**

BIBLIOGRAPHY

Africa Watch. *Somalia: A Government at War with Its Own People: Testimonies about the Killings and the Conflict in the North.* New York: Africa Watch Committee, 1990.

Bongartz, Maria. *The Civil War in Somalia: Its Genesis and Dynamics.* Uppsala, Sweden: Nordiska Afrikainstitutet, 1991.

Cassanelli, Lee V. *The Shaping of Somali Society: Reconstructing the History of a Pastoral People, 1600–1900.* Philadelphia: University of Pennsylvania Press, 1982.

Drysdale, J. G. S. *The Somali Dispute.* New York: F. A. Praeger, 1964.

Farer, Tom J. *War Clouds on the Horn of Africa: A Crisis for Détente.* New York: Carnegie Endowment for International Peace, 1976.

Helander, Bernhard. *The Slaughtered Camel: Coping with Fictitious Descent among the Hubeer of Southern Somalia.* Uppsala, Sweden: Uppsala University Press, 2003.

Hess, Robert L. *Italian Colonialism in Somalia.* Chicago: University of Chicago Press, 1966.

Hoskyns, Catherine, ed. *The Ethiopia-Somali-Kenya Dispute, 1960–67.* Dar es Salaam: Published for the Institute of Public Administration, University College, Dar es Salaam, by Oxford University Press, 1969.

Laitin, David D. "Somalia's Military Government and Scientific Socialism." In *Socialism in Sub-Saharan Africa: A New Assessment,* ed. Carl G. Rosberg and Thomas M. Callaghy. Berkeley: Institute of International Studies, University of California, 1979.

Laitin, David D., and Said S. Samatar. *Somalia: Nation in Search of a State.* Boulder, CO: Westview Press, 1987.

Lewis, Herbert S. "The Origins of the Galla and Somali." *Journal of African History* 7, no. 1 (1966): 27–46.

Lewis, I. M. *A Modern History of the Somali: Nation and State in the Horn of Africa,* 4th edition. Athens: Ohio University Press, 2002.

Lewis, I. M. *Making and Breaking States in Africa: The Somali Experience.* Oxford: James Currey, 2007.

Luling, Virginia. *Somali Sultanate: The Geledi City-State over 150 Years.* Rutgers, NJ: Transaction Publishers, 2002.

Samatar, Said S. *Somalia: A Nation in Turmoil.* London: Minority Rights Group, 1991.

Sheik-Abdi, Abdi. *Divine Madness: Mohammed Abdulle Hassan (1856–1920).* London: Zed Books, 1992.

Touval, Saadia. *Somali Nationalism: International Politics and the Drive for Unity in the Horn of Africa.* Cambridge, MA: Harvard University Press, 1963.

ALI HERSI

SONG. *See* **Music.**

SONY LABOU TANSI (1947–1995). Sony Labou Tansi is widely acknowledged as one of the most talented and innovative contemporary writers from Francophone sub-Saharan Africa. From 1979 onward he published six novels with the prestigious French publisher Seuil and directed the Rocado Zulu Théatre Company, which he founded in Brazzaville, producing a number of his own plays as part of the repertoire. His novels and plays follow the tradition of resistance writing, challenging the corrupt practices of the postcolonial political elite in his native Congo and in Africa in general. However, he wrote a number of aesthetic transformations, as well, because of, he argued, the inability of ordinary discourse to describe the particularities of Africa's postcolonial circumstances. He also created these works as an attempt to distance his writings from the paradigms provided by earlier generations of Francophone authors. His technique exhibits systematic dismantling of traditional narrative linearity, and recourse to radical linguistic devices. His writings have received considerable critical acclaim, including the Prix Spécial de la Francophonie in 1979 for his first novel, *La vie et demie* (1979), the Grand Prix Littéraire de l'Afrique Noire in 1983 for his third novel, *L'anté-peuple* (1983; published in English as *The Anti-People* in 1988), and numerous prizes at theater festivals around the world.

When the People's Republic of the Congo undertook its transition toward a pluralist democracy in 1991, Sony Labou Tansi became increasingly involved in politics. In 1992 he was elected a deputy for the main opposition party. His antigovernmental rhetoric and activities resulted in house arrest and the withdrawal of his passport. He died of complications from AIDS in 1995.

See also **Literature; Theater: Southern Africa.**

BIBLIOGRAPHY

Novels by Sony Labou Tansi

Tansi, Sony Labou. *La vie et demie.* Paris: Seuil, 1979.

Tansi, Sony Labou. *L'état honteux.* Paris: Editions du Seuil, 1981.

Tansi, Sony Labou. *Les sept solitudes de Lorsa Lopez.* Paris: Seuil, 1985.

Tansi, Sony Labou. *The Antipeople,* trans. J.A. Underwood. London: Marion Boyars, 1988.

Tansi, Sony Labou. *Les yeux du volcan.* Paris: Editions du Seuil, 1988.

Tansi, Sony Labou. *Le commencement des douleurs.* Paris: Editions du Seuil, 1995.

Tansi, Sony Labou. *The Seven Solitudes of Lorsa Lopez*, new edition, trans. Clive Wake. Oxford: Heinemann, 1995.

Plays by Sony Labou Tansi

Tansi, Sony Labou. *Conscience de tracteur*, trans. Richard Miller. Dakar, Senegal: CLE, 1979.

Tansi, Sony Labou. *Je soussigné cardiaque*, Paris: Hatier, 1981.

Tansi, Sony Labou. *La parenthése de sang*, trans. Lorraine Alexander Veach. Paris: Hatier, 1981.

Tansi, Sony Labou. *The Second Ark*, 1986.

Tansi, Sony Labou. *Parentheses of Blood*. New York: Theatre Communications Group, 1986.

Tansi, Sony Labou. *Moi, veuve de l'empire*, Paris: Avant Scene, 1987.

Tansi, Sony Labou. *Le coup de vieux*, Paris: Présence africaine, 1988.

Tansi, Sony Labou. *Qui a mangé Madame d'Avoine Bergotha*, Brussels: Promotion Theatre, 1989.

Tansi, Sony Labou. *La résurrection rouge et blanche de Roméo et Juliette*, Paris, 1990.

Tansi, Sony Labou. *Une chouette vie bien osée*. Brussels: Promotion Theatre, 1992.

Tansi, Sony Labou. *Antoine m'a vendu son destin*, Paris: Acoria, 2001.

DOMINIC THOMAS

SOUSA, ANA DE. *See* Njinga Mbandi Ana de Sousa.

SOUTH AFRICA, REPUBLIC OF

This entry includes the following articles:
GEOGRAPHY AND ECONOMY
SOCIETY AND CULTURES
HISTORY AND POLITICS (1850–2006)

GEOGRAPHY AND ECONOMY

South Africa is endowed with both fine scenery and abundant natural resources but few natural ports or navigable rivers. Much of the country is a plateau, tilted up on its eastern side to form the Drakensberg mountain range. East of the Drakensberg lies a coastal strip, frequently cut through with deep valleys. Only 12 percent of the total land area is suitable for cultivation, for in the west especially the country becomes semiarid. The central portion consists of dry steppe, or grassy plains that are suitable for maize. In the southwest corner, a Mediterranean climate brings rain in winter and allows for the cultivation of vines and fruit. Offshore there are large fish stocks, though overfishing has reduced them. Gas has been piped ashore from off Mossel Bay in the south for decades, but to date no oil has been discovered. There are few natural harbors around the coast: the most significant are Table Bay, on which Cape Town was founded; Simonstown, which the Royal Navy used as a base for a century and a half; and Port Natal, which became Durban and in the early twenty-first century is the largest port. Saldanha, north of Cape Town, became an iron ore exporting port in the late twentieth century, as did Richards Bay north of Durban, and in the early twenty-first century another port designed for exports is being developed at Coega near Port Elizabeth. Even the two largest rivers, the Limpopo (which forms the northern boundary) and the Orange (or Gariep) sometimes dried up, though the waters of the Orange were harnessed in the late twentieth century to irrigate parts of the eastern Cape and then, from Lesotho, to provide water and power for the industrial heart of the country, the Witwatersrand.

ECONOMY

The past century and a half has seen spectacular but skewed economic development. Before the mineral revolution of the late nineteenth century, much of what became South Africa was given over to subsistence production. When Europeans first settled at the Cape in 1652, there were perhaps 1.5 million indigenous people living in what later became South Africa. This population increased in size over time, and always outnumbered those who came from outside Africa, whether as immigrants, slaves, or indentured laborers. Most of these indigenous people lived in the better-watered eastern half of the country. The hunter-gatherers and pastoral people of the southwest were mostly driven out or assimilated, but to the east, Bantu-speaking Africans settled early in the first millennium. West of the Drakensberg, where water was less abundant, their settlements were more dispersed. In all

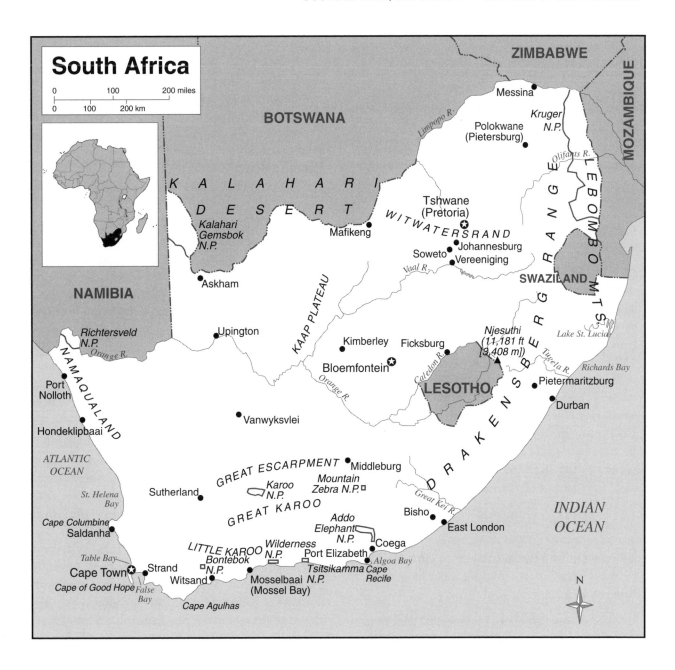

African societies, men supervised the keeping of cattle whereas women tilled the fields. In some, people skilled in one or other craft, including the working of iron, emerged. Although some of these subsistence economies engaged in modest trade, this was never sufficient to promote significant economic growth.

In the Cape, however, wine and then wool was exported on a considerable scale. The European pastoral farmers who settled in the interior, where they did not have to deal with the diseases that prevented white settlements elsewhere, severed many of their economic links with the colony but took with them guns that enabled them to conquer African states and dispossess them of land. The white-ruled states established in the interior were initially poor and divided, but in the course of time became relatively strong and involved in complex networks of trade. In the eastern Cape in particular, in the last decades of the nineteenth century, some African farmers took advantage of the new opportunities to produce successfully for the market. Most Africans, however, found themselves pushed into smaller pieces of land and unable to continue the old subsistence ways in the face of new demands for labor and taxes. Men therefore went out to work as migrant laborers, first on white farms, but from the 1870s on the diamond fields, and after 1886 in the gold mines of the Witwatersrand.

Minerals. The discovery of these minerals transformed the economy of southern Africa, and launched South Africa into the industrial age. Within a few years from the discovery of diamonds in 1867, almost at the center of the country, South Africa's first industrial community emerged not far away at the so-called dry diggings, soon given the name Kimberley. The Kimberley mines attracted labor from far away. The first modern system of laws to control labor developed there, and most black workers lived in separate locations that by 1885 evolved into closed compounds that men could not leave during the periods of their contracts. On expiry of the contract, they were searched minutely to ensure they were not hiding any diamonds. By 1880 nine companies owned the thousands of original claims in what was becoming known as the Big Hole, and the process of amalgamation continued until 1888. At that time, Cecil Rhodes's De Beers Consolidated had a monopoly of all diamond production at Kimberley that was soon, through the construction of new roads and railways and the movement of laborers, linked to many parts of the region, including southern Mozambique.

The even larger economic windfall that came in 1886 carried the process of regional integration and economic transformation that started with the discovery of diamonds much farther. Indigenous people in southern African had mined gold in southern Africa for one and a half millennia, and white prospectors had worked deposits of alluvial gold in the eastern Transvaal in the 1870s and in the early 1880s, but the Witwatersrand gold deposits were the largest ever discovered anywhere. A new town, named Johannesburg, grew dramatically on what had been open veld. Hundreds of thousands of new immigrants poured into the country from Europe, hoping to make their fortunes. Even larger numbers of men traveled from distant parts of the country and farther afield (some from as far

as present-day Malawi) to find work as laborers on the new gold fields.

By the early twentieth century, an elaborate system for the recruitment of labor had developed. Great wealth accrued to the mine owners, whereas the migrant laborers who toiled underground were paid extremely low wages. Though the Rand gold deposits were immense, the average gold content per ton of rock was low, and the gold was increasingly found deep below the surface. Deep-level mining of the gold-bearing reef, hundreds of feet underground, meant large-scale operations and huge amounts of capital, most of which came from the diamond fields or abroad. With the price of gold fixed, attempts were made to keep labor costs as low as possible. Whereas skilled jobs went to whites, many of them immigrants from Europe who were able to command high wages, wages for black migrants were pushed down to a minimum. One of the consequences of migrancy was the massive impoverishment of the rural areas from which the migrants came.

As a result of gold, the Transvaal, which had been the poorest white-ruled state in southern Africa, became the wealthiest within a decade. By 1896 gold accounted for 96 percent of its exports. Gold long remained the backbone of the South African economy, contributing massively to state revenue and earning large quantities of foreign exchange. The mineral revolution, then, wrought an immense economic transformation. Large-scale oscillating migrant labor, the job color bar, and the modern system of pass controls on labor were all entrenched for almost a century. South Africa's industrial development, based on mineral exploitation, created inequalities on a scale hardly matched elsewhere. At the same time, the mineral revolution laid the foundations for the development of manufacturing industry on a large scale, and was responsible for great advances in technology, the growth of cities (Johannesburg being only the most spectacular example), the development of infrastructure, and the expansion of trade.

Although South Africa's share of world gold production fell to only 20 percent by the end of the twentieth century, it remained the world's largest single gold producer. After World War II other minerals became increasingly important, including uranium and copper. Diamond production remained the second-most important export commodity after gold until into the 1980s, when it was overtaken by coal. South Africa possessed huge reserves of coal and iron ore, the export of which developed strongly in the late twentieth century. Two-thirds of the world's chromium and more than half of the world reserves of the platinum-group of metals were also to be found in South Africa. But though mining remained of great importance in external trade, manufacturing overtook mining to become the most important sector, responsible for 38 percent of export earnings by the end of the century. Whereas English-speaking whites controlled the economy well into the twentieth century, from the 1920s an increasing number of Afrikaner entrepreneurs were able to benefit from state policy, as their black counterparts were to do after the change of government in 1994.

From 1925 the government adopted an active policy of protecting local industry. Consumer goods were increasingly produced locally; from 1928 so was steel. Manufacturing was based in four main areas: Gauteng, the Western Cape, Durban-Pinetown, and Port Elizabeth, which was known especially for the production of automobiles. Although the economy grew rapidly in the 1960s, the growth rate began to fall from the early 1970s and fell more sharply after 1976 and from the mid-1980s. Sanctions began to affect some sectors in the late 1980s, and there was negative economic growth for some years. The economy recovered quickly in 1994, and since then it has attracted considerable foreign investment. For over a decade, the growth rate was over 3 percent per annum. At the same time, however, many jobs were lost in the formal sector as the economy restructured and opened to world markets. The textile industry was hit hard by cheap Chinese imports in the early twenty-first century. Though the government proclaimed its belief in privatization, few attempts in that direction were successful. Although a small black class prospered, benefiting from policies of affirmative action, most blacks in the rural areas continued to live in poverty, and control of much of the economy remained in white hands.

See also **Cape Town; Ecosystems; Johannesburg; Metals and Minerals; Production Strategies.**

BIBLIOGRAPHY

Bozzoli, Belinda, ed. *Labor, Townships and Protest.* Johannesburg: Ravan Press, 1979.

Callinicos, Luli. *Gold and Workers 1886–1924.* Johannesburg: Ravan Press, 1981.

Christopher, Anthony J. *The Atlas of Changing South Africa*, 2nd edition. London: Routledge, 2001.

Feinstein, Charles. *An Economic History of South Africa.* Cambridge, U.K.: Cambridge University Press, 2005.

Lester, Alan. *From Colonization to Democracy: A New Historical Geography of South Africa.* London: Taurus Academic Studies, 1996.

Lester, Alan. *South Africa, Past, Present and Future.* New York: Longman, 2000.

CHRIS SAUNDERS

SOCIETY AND CULTURES

The history of southern Africa involves complex political, economic, and social relationships among five broadly defined groups: Khoesan (hunter gatherers and herders), Bantu-speakers (agriculturalists, pastoralists, metallurgists, and traders, who began arriving in the area in the third century), and Europeans (primarily English and Dutch, but also French and Germans, who appeared in the area in the early 1600s). The final categories include the so-called Coloured (mixed-race) population, which came into being with the advent of the whites; and the Indian community, which came to South Africa in the nineteenth century.

CLASSIFYING IDENTITIES

From 1652 onward, claims to the land by the Dutch (later known as Afrikaners) and British imperial interests, culminating in the Anglo-Boer War (or South African War) of 1899–1902 led to the massive dislocation of Khoesan and Bantu-speakers in the hinterland. White expansion into the interior of southern Africa also led to a series of frontier wars, the consequences of which caused the Khoesan and the Bantu-speakers to be ultimately dispossessed of their land and resulted in their loss of subsistence capabilities.

When diamonds were discovered in Griqualand in 1867, and then gold on the Witwatersrand in 1886, white settler demands for African labor increased. Although it had been common for some African men to travel considerable distances to places of wage work in order to purchase guns and other commodities, the state's assault on African labor and movement was gradually legalized such that Africans had only approximately 13 percent of the land. These restrictions laid the foundations for the apartheid era from 1948 to 1994.

The increased demand for African migrant labor was also stimulated by the white government's imposition of various hut, poll, cattle, and marriage taxes, and the infamous and hated pass laws, which restricted the movement and employment opportunities of blacks. These laws also contributed to the breakdown of the African family and effectively criminalized sectors of the African inhabitants of South Africa. Natural disasters such as crop failures, droughts, floods, and cattle diseases led other black South Africans to flock to the urban areas. By the mid-nineteenth century African societies both in the countryside and the towns underwent rapid change.

In present-day South Africa, eleven languages are officially recognized: Afrikaans, English, isiNdebele, isiXhosa, isiZulu, Sepedi, Sesotho, Setswana, siSwati, Tshivenda, and Xitsonga. Ethnic identities carry more flexibility than can be conveyed in linguistic classification; the numerous clicks of the Xhosa language, for example, are a consequence of intimate interaction with the Khoesan. Yet these linguistic categories are highly politically salient and conceal much diversity in language and custom, and are to some extent predicated upon the policy of the apartheid era government of forcibly segregating people into ethnic-based homelands, known as Bantustans.

By the time the Afrikaner National Party came to power in 1948, the conditions for mass removals of Africans along ethnic lines were already in place. Under apartheid, and even prior to that system, black people had little attachment to the land so designated for them, when most were removed into small, densely populated rural areas, the idea being that South Africa would be a white country.

From the 1960s onward narrowly construed ethnicities emerged in conjunction with the establishment of ethnic-based Bantustans. But the growth of more inclusive organizations like the African National Congress (ANC, founded in 1913), the Pan Africanist Congress (PAC, founded in 1958), the Federation of South African Trade Unions (FOSATU, founded in 1979), the United Democratic Front (UDF, founded in 1983), and the Congress of South African Trade Unions (COSATU, founded in 1985) had mass popular support for their range and scale of activities. These organizations, among others, finally led the transition to democracy in South Africa.

The history of South Africa is characterized by movement—some voluntary and some involuntary. In southern Africa there is an anomalous relation between ethnic assertions and political claims to land. Even ethnic assertions must be seen, like nationalisms, to be conditioned by uneasy relationships with Western ideas of the nation. Ideas of nationalism and/or ethnicity are further complicated by the intersection with categories of class, gender, and race.

THE PEOPLE OF SOUTH AFRICA

The principal categories of the Bantu-speaking peoples are the Nguni, Sotho, Tsonga, Venda, and Lemba. The broad categorization of Nguni refers to Xhosa, Ndebele, Swazi, and Zulu, while smaller groupings include the Thembu, Mpondo, Mpondomise, Mfengu, and Bomvana. By contrast, Sotho speakers include the following groupings: northern Sotho (Pedi and Lobedu), western Sotho (Tswana), and southern Sotho (Basotho).

All these groups have certain similar traditions, for instance agricultural practices and cattle herding; a belief in ancestor worship, sacrifice, and witchcraft; a strong division of labor between the sexes; common facets of initiation and life cycle rituals; rank and hierarchy; strong agnatic links; the payment of *lobola* (bridewealth) upon marriage; the adoption of children into the fathers' lineage; and patrilocal residence. The major points of divergence between the Sotho and the Nguni are residential and marriage patterns.

A large-scale movement of Bantu-speakers began to take shape around 1800, following drought and famine and the incursions of the Europeans settlers. This heralded increased militarism and battles for influence and power, in which many Bantu societies were incorporated in other chieftaincies or were compelled to become refugees or seek protection with other groups. The result was the rise of the Zulu, Tswana, and Ndebele societies; but these upheavals, which altered the political structure of much of the region, also included the Sotho, Tsonga, and Pedi peoples.

In South Africa, while 75 percent of the population self-identifies itself as black, the country is also home to the largest communities in sub-Saharan Africa of whites, Indians, and Coloureds. The whites comprise about 9.5 percent (approximately 4.5 million people) of the total population. Predominant are the Afrikaners of Dutch Calvinist, French Huguenot, and German Lutheran descent. A series of nineteenth-century historical events (the Great Trek, Zulu Wars, Boer Wars) became the founding myths of the community. Out of different dialects the formal Afrikaans language emerged in the early 1900s. (A secret brotherhood, called the Broederbond, was established to ensure the political, religious, economic, social, and cultural integrity and advancement of the white Afrikaner community.) The combination of national conquest and deep religious belief convinced Afrikaners that ethnic diversity and racial superiority were both natural and stemmed from God's will. The cost of this pervasive conservatism led to the alienation of the Dutch Reformed Church from other churches in South Africa and abroad.

The discovery of gold and diamonds swelled the number of English settlers, who struggled against the Afrikaners for political domination of South Africa. As English speakers were predominantly urban and despite their divisions along class, gender, and regional lines, they tended toward a greater cosmopolitanism and more liberal political ideologies than the Afrikaners.

INDIANS AND COLOUREDS

These racial categories have a particular meaning in South Africa. Coloured and Indian communities in South Africa, with varying political rights, which were always under constant threat, were officially categorized as neither white nor black. Both communities faced discrimination at all levels, including inferior education, forced residential and business removals, and restrictions on trading, employment, and movement.

In 2006 more than 1 million South Africans (about 2.4%) identified themselves as Indians. Indentured Indian workers came to South Africa to fulfill labor demands on the sugar plantations in the province of Natal (present-day KwaZulu) in the nineteenth century. These Hindu Indians were later joined by a merchant community of predominantly Muslim Indians. The entire Indian community lived under constant threat of repatriation, but their political unity was inhibited by religious and caste systems. In the early 1900s Mohandas Gandhi, who lived in South Africa, began the passive resistance movement known as *satyagraha*, which became the cornerstone for several "disobedience" campaigns.

Over 4 million people (or 8.8% of the population) identify themselves as Coloureds. This term, in use since the 1840s, referred initially to the decimated Khoesan; to the slaves and concubines from Indonesia, Madagascar, and East Africa; and to people of mixed descent. With such great geo-biological diversity, racial identification standards of the 1950s had the effect of racially separating family members and introducing seven subcategories: Cape Coloured, Cape Malay (predominantly Muslim), Griqua, Indian, Chinese, Other Asiatic, and Other Coloured.

As the majority of Coloureds are Afrikaans-speakers, and as many belong to the Dutch Reformed Church, there are many cultural links between Coloureds and Afrikaners. Some Coloureds allied themselves with whites, some embraced a Coloured identity, and many were active in anti-apartheid resistance and members of the ANC.

ASPECTS OF BLACK CULTURE

Since 1800, in response to economic, political, and social pressures, there have been extensive transformations in systems of chiefly rule, marriage, initiation, residential patterns, ritual, and religions. It is important not to essentialize "traditional" cultures. Nevertheless it is true that a certain core pattern of beliefs and behaviors have tended to characterize the peoples of the region.

For most Bantu-speakers during the precolonial and colonial periods, the chief, who was imbued with mystical powers, set in motion the social, pastoral, agricultural, and ritual calendars, thus imposing synchronization and a central time. The chief allocated areas for pasture and land for fields. The harvest with its accompanying first-fruit ceremony and the new tilling season with rain-making festivities were ritually celebrated. The chief also settled disputes: in consultation with councilors, and in concert with the general assembly of followers, usually men. In addition there were hierarchies of courts for dispute settlement.

In most Bantu-speaking groups there was a gendered division of labor. Women were identified and associated with the more private spheres of agriculture and household domestic tasks. Men were responsible for the more public domain of jural and political decisions, and the affairs of village life and households reflect the male-female dichotomy in their spatial layout. So intense was this divide that there are many taboos regarding women and cattle. Cattle are multivalent—a form of stored wealth, a means of attracting clients, a medium of *lobola*, and a means of communicating with the ancestors—and thus, as a form of sociability, are identified with men.

The process of initiation, in which masculinity and femininity were constructed, commenced at the time of puberty. Although the time between initiation and marriage varied, Nguni speakers favored exogamy, whereas Sotho speakers generally married endogamously, choosing a spouse preferably between certain kin categories. Therefore, whereas love charms are acceptable for the Nguni, they are eschewed by the Sotho, for they may distract a girl from a preferred match. Marriage therefore helped alliances between core groups and secured inheritance rights. Marriage facilitated by *lobola* also secured certain productive, reproductive, and sexual rights over the woman concerned and over her children, who would be incorporated into her husband's patriline. Yet a woman's family remained invested in the welfare of a married daughter and her children; she would remain a jural minor, with her husband, father, or brother representing her. For the Sotho, who practiced endogamy, relations between in-laws remained less strained and formal as in the Nguni case.

The strictures placed on young men and women led inevitably to rituals expressing protest on the part of young men and women, yet in socially and culturally sanctioned forms—such as joking relations, ritual obscenities, insulting songs and competitive dancing, transvestitism, role reversals, and gender switching. There are also less subtle forms of managing social discord such as ostracism and ridicule. These social mechanisms provided an outlet to possible frustrations and tensions that inhered in difficult structural and personal relations.

Although many Bantu-speakers are practicing Christians, many engage, as they did traditionally, in ancestor worship, in which the dead of the lineage are consulted, appeased, and propitiated, usually within ritually defined spaces of the homestead. The concept of misfortune dominates African traditional belief systems; ancestors, when they are neglected, jealous, or offended, or if there is a breach of custom, may send misfortune to their descendants. Witches and sorcerers, however, often intend to send misfortune and harm thus displaying antisocial tendencies. Witches, who are members of the kin group, are the embodiment of immorality and evil as their core attacks are on the kin group itself.

Diviners and herbalists seek out the source of misfortune and provide the necessary counteractive rituals and remedies. Such remedies and rituals enforce those bonds that are ruptured, such as kinship or communal bonds, or facilitate life-cycle and fertility rituals, for example. Contingent ritual may be used to stem the power of the witch.

There is a powerful pantheon of witchcraft familiars. The influence of many of the more notorious familiars, however, has spread from other areas largely as a function of migrant labor and as a result of the interaction between peoples in the urban areas of South Africa.

Since the early 1800s the social structure of Bantu-speaking societies has been substantially altered. The National Party's policies of removal and "betterment" have led to the large-scale dislocation of cultural and social norms. The power of the chiefs has waned. Because of migrant labor, which removes men from their homes for much of the year, many marriages have disintegrated, leaving a number of matrifocal families or sibling-linked households in rural and urban districts. *Lobola* payments are for the most part no longer paid in cattle, and are adjusted to reflect the educational level and earning prospects of brides. Initiation has gone through periods of revival and neglect. Witchcraft and ancestor worship are still very common and have been integrated into the religious practices of many Zionist and Apostolic churches. Not surprisingly, then, with the approaching uncertainty of the 1994 elections heralding the

Republic of South Africa

Population:	43,997,828 (2007 est.)
Area:	1,219,912 sq. km (471,010 sq. mi.)
Official languages:	Afrikaans, English, isiNdebele, isiXhosa, isiZulu, Sepedi, Sesotho, Setswana, siSwati, Tshivenda, and Xitsonga
National currency:	rand
Principal religions:	predominantly Christian; traditional African, Hindu, Muslim, Jewish
Capital:	administrative capital: Pretoria (est. pop. 1,104,479 in 2006); legislative capital: Cape Town (est. pop. 2,415,408 in 2006); judicial capital: Bloemfontein (est. pop. 333,769 in 2006)
Other urban centers:	Johannesburg, Durban (a conurbation that includes KwaMashu, Pinetown, and Umlazi), Port Elizabeth, Springs, Benoni Germiston, Pietermaritzburg, Welkom, East London
Annual rainfall:	1,000 mm (40 in.) on east coast and the Drakensberg, decreasing to the west, with two-thirds of the country receiving less than 600 mm (23 in.) and Port Nolloth receiving only 61 mm (2.4 in.)
Principal geographical features:	*Mountains:* The Great Escarpment (Transvaal Drakens range, Natal Drakens range, Nuweveldreeks range, Roggeveld range, Bokkeveld range, Kamies range), Drakensberg, Cedarberg, Langeberg, Groot-Swartberg, Outenigrec range, Tsitsikama range, Hex River mountains. *Rivers:* Kei, Tugela, Vaal, Limpopo, Orange, Caledon, Olifants, Marico, Sand, Great Fish, Breede, Gourits *Lakes:* Fundudzi, many reservoirs throughout the country *Islands:* Prince Edward Island, Marion Island, Robben Island
Economy:	*GDP per capita:* US$13,300 (2006)
Principal products and exports:	*Agricultural:* corn, wheat, sugarcane, fruits, vegetables, beef, poultry, mutton, wool, dairy products *Manufacturing:* automobile assembly, metalworking, machinery, textiles, iron and steel, chemicals, fertilizer, foodstuffs, commercial ship repair *Mining:* diamonds, gold, platinum, chromium, iron ore, copper, manganese, lime, limestone, silver, nickel, asbestos, coal, uranium
Government:	Creation of the self-governing Union of South Africa, a British Dominion, in 1910. Became sovereign nation within the British Commonwealth in 1931. Independent republic declared in 1961. 1994 interim constitution, replacing the 1984 constitution. New constitution in 1997. Parliamentary democracy. President and executive deputy president elected by the National Assembly for 5-year term. Bicameral Parliament consisting of the National Assembly (400 seats; members elected by popular vote for 5-year terms) and the National Council of Provinces (90 seats, 10 members elected by each of the 9 provincial legislatures for 5-year terms). President appoints the cabinet.

Heads of state since independence:	*Prime ministers:* 1924–1939: James Barry Munnik Hertzog 1939–1948: Jan Smuts 1948–1954: Daniel F. Malan 1954–1958: Johannes G. Strijdom 1958–1966: Hendrik Verwoerd 1966–1978: Balthazar J. Vorster 1978–1984: Pieter W. Botha	*Presidents:* 1961–1967: Charles Robberts Swart 1967–1968: Jozua Francois Naude 1968–1975: Jacobus Johannes Fouche 1975–1978: Nicholaas Diederichs 1978–1979: Balthazar J. Vorster 1979–1984: Marais Viljoen 1984–1989: Pieter W. Botha 1989–1994: Frederick W. de Klerk 1994–1999: Nelson Mandela 1999–: President Thabo Mbeki

Armed forces:	President is commander in chief. The South African National Defense Force (SANDF) consists of an army, navy, and air force.
Transportation:	Railways previously administered by South African Railways and Harbours Administration have broken up into several parastatal companies including Portnet, Spoornet, S.A.R. Commuter Corporation, etc. *Rail:* 20,827 km (12,941 mi.). Railways previously administered by state-owned South African Transport Services, which has been broken up into 5 separate parastatals including Spoornet and the South African Rail Commuter Corporation. *Ports:* Durban, Cape Town, Port Elizabeth, East London, Saldanha, Richard's Bay, Mossel Bay *Roads:* 362,099 km (224,998 mi.), 20% paved *National airline:* South African Airways *Airports:* International facilities at Johannesburg, Cape Town, and Durban. Major domestic airports at Bloemfontein, Port Elizabeth, Kimberley, and East London. Over 700 other airports and airstrips throughout the country.
Media:	Daily newspapers: 16 in English, 5 in Afrikaans. Weeklies: 12 in English, 4 in Afrikaans, and 3 bilingual. Radio and television service provided by South African Broadcasting Corporation.
Literacy and education:	*Total literacy rate:* 86.4% (2006). Education is compulsory for all children ages 7–15. The South African Schools Act of 1996 was passed to achieve greater educational opportunities for black children. Universities include University of Cape Town, University of Durban-Westville, Medical University of Southern Africa, University of Natal, University of the North, University of the Orange Free State, University of Port Elizabeth, Potchefstroom University for Christian Higher Education, University of Pretoria, Rand Afrikaans University, Rhodes University, University of South Africa, University of Stellenbosch, University of the Western Cape, University of Witwatersrand, University of Zululand, University of Bopthuthatswana.

new democratic dispensation, witchcraft accusations, often harnessed to political agendas, increased dramatically.

URBAN ENVIRONMENT

In the 1980s and 1990s, as influx control laws were relaxed, black South Africans, who previously had been fortunate enough to gain Section 10 Rights, which enabled them to reside in urban townships, were joined by thousands of new residents. Vast squatter camps were established by the many thousands of black men and women who came to the cities usually to seek work, to engage in adventure, to escape the grinding poverty of the homelands, or to remove themselves from rural authority networks.

The townships, which are home to many black South Africans, comprise people from different areas, most of whom are polylingual. They are integrated into networks based on kinship, the church, neighborhood, community, workplaces, sports and dance, cultural interests, and civic and political organizations. The densely packed townships became a space where black people from all areas of South Africa were drawn together, and where new cultural and political forms emerged. Musical styles, for instance, were forged from diverse musical forms, which became part of daily living and were integrated into the important ritual events marking life transformations. Daily newspapers and magazines spoke to a multiethnic location. And neighborhood associations, sport clubs, and various other leisure activities were distinctly multiethnic, as were civic and political associations.

But even in the ethnically mixed townships ethnic associations still flourished. With increased migrancy to towns, ethnic-based networks or "homeboy" associations were crucial for those seeking accommodation and work. This was especially important given the residential overcrowding and high levels of unemployment. These associations also provided resources such as burial societies, rotating credit associations, and social institutions for leisure pursuits, as well as a means whereby identity could be performed through song or dance.

From the Defiance Campaign of the 1950s through the student riots of the 1970s, and up to the more integrated alliance of community and civic associations of the 1980s and 1990s, such as the UDF and COSATU, a more inclusive, nonracial, or nationalist style of politics has characterized South Africa. But these very movements have given rise to a more popular syncretic political culture. In short, even everyday rituals were politicized, and politics, while violent, was ritualized. Public displays, such as funerals and marches, epitomized symbolic power.

With the end of apartheid and the arrival of a new and radically different nationalist ideology, Bishop Desmond Tutu popularized the phrase the "Rainbow Nation" to define South Africa's diverse multicultural society.

See also **Apartheid; History of Africa; Language; Languages: Khoesan and Click; Production Strategies; Tutu, Desmond Mpilo; Witchcraft.**

BIBLIOGRAPHY

Ashford, Adam. *Witchcraft, Violence and Democracy in South Africa.* Chicago: University of Chicago Press, 2005.

Comaroff, Jean, and John Comaroff. *Of Revelation and Revolution*, Vol. 1: *Christianity, Colonialism and Consciousness in South Africa.* Chicago: University of Chicago Press, 1991.

Comaroff, Jean, and John Comaroff. *Of Revelation and Revolution*, Vol. 2: *The Dialectics of Modernity on a South African Frontier.* Chicago: University of Chicago Press, 1997.

Crapanzano, Vincent. *Waiting: The Whites of South Africa.* New York: Vintage Books, 1986.

Hammond-Tooke, W. D., ed. *The Bantu-Speaking Peoples of Southern Africa.* London: Routledge and Kegan Paul, 1974.

Kane-Berman John, ed. *South African Survey 2003/2004.* Johannesburg: South African Institute of Race Relations, 2004.

Lodge, T., and B. Nasson. *All Here and Now: Black Politics in South Africa in the 1980s.* Cape Town: David Philip, 1991.

Moodie, T. Dunbar, and Vivienne Ndatshe. *Going for Gold: Men, Mines, and Migration.* Johannesburg: Witwatersrand University Press, 1994.

Murray, Colin. *Families Divided: The Impact of Migrant Labor in Lesotho.* Cambridge, U.K.: Cambridge University Press, 1981.

Niehaus, Isak. *Witchcraft, Power, and Politics: Exploring the Occult in the South African Lowveld.* Cape Town: David Philip, 2001.

Thompson, Leonard. *The Political Mythology of Apartheid*. New Haven, CT: Yale University Press, 1985.

Thompson, Leonard. *A History of South Africa*. New Haven, CT: Yale University Press, 1995.

Wilson, Monica, and Leonard Thompson, eds. *The Oxford History of South Africa*, Vol. 2: *South Africa 1870–1966*. Oxford: Clarendon Press, 1971.

PETA KATZ

HISTORY AND POLITICS (1850–2006)

In 1850 South Africa was a geographical expression, not a country. In what became in 1910 the Union of South Africa were two British colonies, the Cape of Good Hope and Natal, two territories that had been annexed by the British High Commissioner in 1848 between the Orange and Vaal Rivers (the Orange River Sovereignty) and in the Ciskei (British Kaffraria, west of the Kei River), some Boer settlements north of the Vaal River, and a number of African states, the most powerful of which was the Zulu state north of the Tugela River.

In the decades after 1850 the area under white rule was extended until, by the end of the century, all of what became South Africa had come under white rule. The Orange River Sovereignty became the independent Orange Free State (OFS) in 1854 and the Boers north of the Vaal River consolidated themselves into the South African Republic (SAR), which claimed but did not effectively rule all the land from the Vaal to the Limpopo River in the north. In 1868 the British annexed the Basuto kingdom formed by Moshoeshoe west of the Drakensberg Mountains, and in 1871 they took over the land of the Griqua after diamonds were discovered there. Then in 1877, in order to promote the idea of a confederation of the British territories in southern Africa, the British annexed the SAR (or Transvaal) and proceeded to conquer the Zulu and the Pedi, whom the SAR had been not been able to subdue. The Cape Colony extended its control over the African peoples who lived between the Kei River and Natal between 1879 and 1894, and in the late 1890s the Venda of the far Transvaal were brought under Boer rule for the first time. The territory of Basutoland, which had come under Cape rule in the 1870s, broke away in 1884 and reverted to Direct Rule by Britain, but the Cape was enlarged in 1895

when part of what the British had annexed as Bechuanaland was added to it.

Antagonism between the Boers of the interior and the British, which had by then a long history, came to a head after the discovery of gold on the Witwatersrand in 1886. By 1899 Paul Kruger, President of the SAR, had come to believe that Alfred Milner (1854–1925), the British High Commissioner, was set on taking over his country. In October that year the SAR and the OFS declared war on Britain to preempt a British attack. By the time the Anglo-Boer (or South African) War ended on May 31, 1902, both Boer republics had been annexed by Britain, and the deaths of over 27,000 Boer women and children in the concentration camps set up by the British during a phase of guerrilla war had sown a bitterness that would help fuel the ever more exclusive Afrikaner nationalism that evolved in succeeding decades.

With the conquest of the Boer republics, all of what became a united South Africa became British, and when the ex-Boer generals who rose to political prominence in the Transvaal realized they would dominate a united country, they agreed to merge with the other states. On May 31, 1910, the Cape, Natal, the Transvaal, and the Orange River Colony became the four new provinces of a united South Africa. Its boundaries are those of present-day South Africa, except that the port enclave of Walvis Bay, then part of the Cape Colony/Province, was excised from South Africa and added to Namibia in early 1994.

POLITICAL LEADERS

A succession of Afrikaner leaders—Louis Botha (1862–1919), Jan Smuts (1870–1950), J. B. M. Hertzog (1866–1942), and then Smuts again—became successively the prime ministers of the united South Africa. Whereas Botha and Smuts tried to bring together white English speakers and Afrikaners, Hertzog, who founded the National Party (NP) in 1914, appealed to an exclusive Afrikaner nationalism, and his NP had gained sufficient support by 1924 to come to power in alliance with the Labour Party. Under Hertzog's prime ministership, South Africa became effectively independent within the British Empire, becoming the Commonwealth. After South Africa fell into economic depression from late 1929, Hertzog and Smuts came together and formed a new United Party, in opposition to which Daniel Malan (1874–1959) founded a reformed NP, which aimed to break what remained of the British connection and form a republic, a goal not achieved until 1961.

Smuts and Hertzog split in September 1939 on the issue of whether South Africa should enter World War II on the Allied side, and Smuts, who gained the majority of support in Parliament, took the country into the war. Some of those whites opposed to the war began sabotage action for which they were imprisoned, but the majority rallied behind Malan and helped his NP come to power in the general election of May 1948, though with a minority of the votes cast.

In the early twentieth century, the lawyer Mohandas Gandhi (1869–1948) led a challenge to the government on the status of Indians in South Africa and achieved some success before he left for India in 1914. Two years earlier, a South African Native National Congress (SANNC) had been formed to represent the grievances of black Africans throughout the new Union. SANNC changed its name to the African National Congress (ANC) in 1923, but in that decade was eclipsed by the Industrial and Commercial Workers' Union (ICU), formed by Clements Kadalie (1896–1951) in 1919. In the 1920s the most radical protest erupted in the rural areas, but this faded out with the advent of economic depression and the collapse of the ICU.

SEGREGATION POLICIES

The policy of racial segregation, elaborated before Union, was progressively enacted into law in stages. The 1913 Land Act, one of the key pieces in the segregation jigsaw, set aside only 7 percent of the land in which black Africans could own property (enlarged to 13% in 1936). Large numbers of Africans worked on white farms and others went as migrant laborers to the mines, leaving their families behind in the reserves that over time grew increasingly impoverished. A Natives Urban Areas Act of 1923 provided for separate locations (or townships) for black Africans in the urban areas. The ANC joined other organizations in an unsuccessful attempt to try to prevent the 1936 passage of the legislation that removed the black African vote

at the Cape, which had, since 1854, had a nonracial-qualified franchise. Though black African women were long able to resist the imposition of passes (identity documents), black Africans were increasingly controlled by a battery of legislation restricting mobility and limiting residence in townships to those with work.

The segregationist measures put in place before 1948 were extended and made more rigorous in terms of the apartheid policy of the National Party. The Population Registration Act classified the entire population into racial groups, the Group Areas Act extended residential segregation to Coloureds and Indians, and other legislation provided for the imposition of passes on African women and for a separate system of education for all black Africans. Separate amenities for racial groups in almost all areas of life became the norm, and opposition was met with harsh repression. The Communist Party of South Africa disbanded in 1950 in advance of legislation to proscribe it, and from 1952 the ANC, in alliance with other organizations, began a civil disobedience campaign. After the Congress of the People in June 1955 adopted a Freedom Charter setting out a vision of a new South Africa, those who had been involved were put on trial for treason. By the time the last of those accused were found not guilty in 1961, the leadership of the ANC and other organizations had accepted the need for armed struggle. This was in the aftermath of the Sharpeville Massacre of March 21, 1960, when the police opened fire on unarmed Africans demonstrating against the pass laws.

APARTHEID AND ITS OPPOSITION

Alongside a sabotage campaign launched by Umkhonto we Sizwe (Spear of the Nation; referred to as MK), which became the armed wing of the ANC, and the small Armed Resistance Movement of noncommunists in the early 1960s, the armed wing of the Pan-Africanist Congress (PAC), Poqo, used terrorism against civilians. The reaction of the apartheid government was to introduce yet more repressive measures, including torture. The leadership of MK was arrested at Rivonia in 1963 and put on trial, along with its commander-in-chief Nelson Mandela, who had been arrested earlier. Given life sentences, the black Rivonia defendants were sent to Robben Island, and though the chief architect of apartheid, Hendrik F. Verwoerd, was assassinated in 1966, the apartheid regime seemed stronger than ever as the 1960s ended. The economy was booming and the process of leading the former reserves toward independence as Bantustans (ethnic-based homelands), the brainchild of Verwoerd, moved forward. To consolidate such areas, millions of black Africans were forcibly removed and dumped in poor rural areas. The largest such reserve, the Transkei, was to be the first to be given nominal independence by the South African government in 1976. By then much had changed.

Perhaps the most important change was that Angola and Mozambique had become independent in 1975. The South African army was sent into Angola to try to prevent a Movimento Popular de Libertação de Angola–Partido do Trabalho (MPLA; Popular Movement for the Liberation of Angola) government coming to power, and not only failed to do this, but in response to the South African intervention, a large force of Cuban troops arrived to support the MPLA. This defeat for the apartheid regime, together with the rise of the Black Consciousness movement, founded and led by Steve Biko, together helped fuel the Soweto uprising that began on June 16, 1976, when police opened fire on unarmed schoolchildren protesting against the Bantu Education system in high schools. After hundreds had been killed in many parts of the country, the revolt was suppressed, but in September 1977, Biko was murdered in police custody. That sent shockwaves around the world, and the United Nations imposed a mandatory arms embargo on South Africa. The new prime minister from 1978, P. W. Botha, told his white electorate to adapt or die, but all he did was to relax some aspects of so-called petty apartheid and to bring Coloureds and Indians into the central government.

This was done in the constitution of 1983, which set up three houses of Parliament and provided for a strong executive president (a post to which Botha himself moved in 1984). The exclusion of black Africans from any say in central government seemed to indicate that the government had no plan ever to incorporate them as citizens. On the day the new constitution took effect, a new uprising began in the Vaal Triangle close to Johannesburg. This uprising was not suppressed until it had swept through most parts of the country and taken the country closer to civil war than

ever before. The security forces reacted by assassinations and other dirty tricks, and on the side of the resistance those said to be collaborators were killed by putting tires around their necks and setting them alight. The ANC had called for the country to be made ungovernable, and many now saw it spiraling out of control.

It was then that Mandela, from his prison cell, called for a meeting between himself and Botha to discuss a negotiated future for the country. Representatives of big business met the ANC leadership in Zambia and found them to be pragmatic. Internationally the campaign against apartheid became more vociferous than ever, persuading some governments and legislatures to impose sanctions on South Africa. MK attacks increased, and within the country black trade unions, legalized in 1979, came together and formed the Congress of South African Trade Unions (COSATU) in 1985, which allied itself to the United Democratic Front, a broad anti-apartheid front formed in Cape Town in August 1983. As the Cold War began to wind down, the ANC's links with the underground and exiled Communist Party (CP), which had long worried both government and business in South Africa, began no longer to seem so threatening. In 1988 Botha's government agreed to withdraw from Namibia after suffering a military defeat in southern Angola, where the Cubans and Angolans fought the South African Defence Force (SADF) and its allies to a stalemate outside Cuito Cuanavale and then moved south to the Namibian border.

Botha met Mandela finally in mid-1989 but could not bring himself to begin a process of negotiation with the ANC, though by then a series of talks had been taking place in secret over a period years between ANC leaders and government officials. After the communist regimes of Eastern Europe collapsed in late 1989, Botha's successor, the pragmatic F. W. de Klerk, decided on February 2, 1990, to take the risk of lifting the ban on both the ANC and the CP. He also announced the unconditional release of Mandela, who walked out of prison on February 11 and soon took over the leadership of the ANC from the ailing Oliver Tambo (1917–1993), who returned to South Africa after decades in exile. By February 1990 de Klerk knew that Namibia was on the road to independence via a liberal democratic constitution, and he hoped that he could salvage significant power for his NP in any deal he made with the ANC.

Formal talks between the ANC and the government began in May 1990, and in December 1991 a multiparty negotiating forum (known initially as the Convention for a Democratic South Africa) began work at the World Trade Centre outside Parliament. The negotiations broke down in mid-1992, amid much violence and the threat of economic collapse. After ANC supporters were shot in a massacre in Bisho, Ciskei, in September that year, the two main players agreed to return to the World Trade Centre. The assassination of the CP leader Chris Hani (b. 1942) in April 1993 by a right-wing white fanatic threatened to throw the negotiations off track again, but Mandela calmed his angry supporters; in November 1993 a new interim constitution was drawn up and took effect the following April. Constand Viljoen (b. 1933), a former head of the SADF, emerged as the most significant figure in the white far-right, which had threatened to abort the process by force. Viljoen agreed to participate in the election process, as did, at the last minute, Chief Mangosotho Buthelezi of the Inkatha Freedom Party (IFP), who had long been opposed to the ANC. With the coming into force of the interim constitution, the four Bantustans that had been given nominal independence (none of them recognized by anyone other than the South African government) were reincorporated into South Africa, and the number of provinces was enlarged from four to nine.

In the country's first democratic election, the ANC won 62 percent of the vote, the NP 20 percent, which meant that de Klerk became a deputy president and joined the cabinet, and the IFP 10 percent, so that it too joined the new Government of National Unity (GNU). The low-intensity civil war in KwaZulu Natal, which had been going on for a decade, now came to an end, and the two new houses of Parliament jointly formed a Constitutional Assembly that was given two years to draw up a final constitution. The constitution was hailed as one of the most progressive in the world and included not only liberal freedoms but also socio-economic rights to housing, education, and social services, which the government had to provide to the extent that resources were available.

The National Party left the GNU in June 1996, after which it declined; by 2005 it had disappeared. The ANC won two-thirds of the votes in the 1999 election, meaning it could in theory now change the constitution on its own, and again in the 2004 election. By then its main opponent in Parliament was the Democratic Alliance, made up of the former liberal Progressives and remnants of the NP. The IFP lost control of the province of KwaZulu Natal, and the Democratic Alliance (DA) control of the Western Cape, though a DA mayor came into office in Cape Town in 2006. Otherwise, the ANC dominated the political scene, but it was increasingly divided. Thabo Mbeki, who succeeded Mandela as president in 1999, was a remote leader, with dissident views on HIV/AIDS, and he refused to do anything significant when President Robert Mugabe of Zimbabwe increasingly used violent means to stay in power. Both Mandela and Mbeki played leading roles on the African and world stages, helping to resolve conflicts elsewhere and drawing upon the moral credit built up during South Africa's transition from apartheid to democracy.

As the end of Mbeki's second term in office approached, the ANC and its alliance partners, COSATU and the CP, were divided into those who supported Jacob Zuma, whom Mbeki fired as his deputy president in 2005 because a judge alleged he had been guilty of corruption, and those who looked for someone else to take over from Mbeki. The well-managed economy continued to do well, but South Africa remained one of the most unequal countries on earth. An increasing number of blacks entered the middle class, and some became wealthy because of the ANC's support for black business, but a substantial section of the population remained mired in chronic poverty and the rate of HIV/AIDS infection was in 2006 still one of the highest in the world.

See also **Apartheid; Biko, Steve; De Klerk, Frederik Willem; Immigrants and Immigrant Groups: Indian; Johannesburg; Kadalie, Clements; Kruger, Paul; Mandela, Nelson; Mbeki, Thabo; Moshoeshoe I; Mugabe, Robert; Political Systems; Smuts, Jan Christiaan; Verwoerd, Hendrik Frensch.**

BIBLIOGRAPHY

Barber, James. *South Africa in the Twentieth Century.* Oxford and Malden, MA: Blackwell, 1999.

Beinart, William. *Twentieth-Century South Africa*, 2nd edition. Oxford and New York: Oxford University Press, 2001.

Beinart, William, and Saul Dubow, eds. *Segregation and Apartheid in Twentieth-Century South Africa.* London and New York: Routledge, 1995.

Davenport, Thomas R., and Christopher Saunders. *South Africa: A Modern History*, 5th edition. Hampshire, U.K.: Macmillan; New York: St. Martin's, 2000.

Giliomee, Hermann. *The Afrikaners. Biography of a People.* Cape Town: Tafelberg, 2003.

Guelke, Adrian. *Rethinking the Rise and Fall of Apartheid.* New York: Palgrave Macmillan, 2005.

Maylam, Paul. *South Africa's Racial Past.* Burlington, VT: Ashgate, 2001.

Sparks, Allister. *Beyond the Miracle: Inside the New South Africa.* Johannesburg: Jonathan Ball, 2003.

Thompson, Leonard M. *A History of South Africa*, 3rd edition. New Haven, CT: Yale University Press, 2001.

CHRIS SAUNDERS

SOUTH AFRICAN REPUBLIC. *See* Cape Colony and Hinterland, History of (1600 to 1910); South Africa, Republic of.

SOUTHEASTERN AFRICA, HISTORY OF (1600 TO 1910).

Broad grasslands, rocky escarpments, and a dry, flat coastal plain shape the historical landscape of southeastern Africa. The granite of the Zimbabwe plateau, along with limestone in the central Mozambican lowlands, provided Shona-speaking inhabitants with the materials to develop a tradition of building in stone long before the arrival of the first Europeans at the end of the fifteenth century. The ruins of the elaborate enclosures at Great Zimbabwe (c. 1250–1450) serve as the grandest example of stone building among the Shona. Flourishing communities constructed other small stone settlements, known as *madzimbabwe*, throughout the area south of the Zambezi River. These centers contain evidence of a widespread material culture and integrated history in this corner of Africa.

HISTORICAL PATTERNS

This region's past is characterized by the rise and fall of spectacular states founded on an extraordinary Zimbabwe culture. For kings and commoners alike, shared political experiences, a common culture, and mutually intelligible languages led to changes and continuities in dynamic traditions over

time. Rulers presided over economies that relied primarily on intensive agricultural activities and cattle-keeping, but modest farmers also engaged in occasional mining and hunting pursuits to profit from a robust external trade. Gold and ivory were exported to the Indian Ocean trading network in return for locally valued imports of cloth and beads. The Shona also exchanged iron and salt, but there was little slave trading on the plateau. Political organization was relatively stable, save for the occasional secession crisis. The economy was based on mixed farming across a zone of uneven fertility. The exploitation of various other natural resources supplemented the seasonal agriculture cycle, especially in times of drought.

Southeastern Africa was home to both large states and small political units between the seventeenth and nineteenth centuries. In the interior, the extensive Shona political systems of the Mutapa, Torwa, and Changamire expanded rapidly on the plateau. These great states eventually disintegrated, but some political units maintained a wider authority through the formation of confederacies such as the Duma and Buhera. Amidst these changing circumstances, decentralized, segmented political structures managed to survive. Hereditary rulers controlled territories consisting of several villages, with some leaders providing tribute to larger states. Although the region is known for its impressive pattern of state-building, successful political leadership at all levels relied upon favorable environmental and economic conditions.

Nguni Migrants. During the early nineteenth century, the political and cultural terrain shifted with the invasions of several Nguni-speaking groups fleeing the disturbances in Natal after the rise of the Zulu state in South Africa. Two northern Nguni peoples, the Ndebele and Gaza Nguni, remained in different parts of the region and settled among the Shona inhabitants. In the southwest, the Ndebele under Mzilikazi formed a permanent home among the Rozvi of the Changamire state in the 1840s. The Ndebele remained highly centralized, retained their own language, and demanded tribute from the surrounding area. Military regiments of young men tended the state's cattle and formed their own territories. Many Shona subjects came to adopt Ndebele customs and speak the

Ndebele language. By 1893 about 60 percent of all Ndebele claimed Shona ancestry.

In the east, the Gaza Nguni under Soshangane first established their capital in the lower Limpopo valley of southern Mozambique among the Tsonga. They moved to the Ndau heartland for an extended occupation from 1862 to 1889 and exacted tribute over a wide region. The Gaza Nguni returned to southern Mozambique once again in 1889, forcing some Ndau to accompany them. In the Ndau region in the early twenty-first century, elders remember Gaza Nguni overrule as a turbulent time. Assimilation extended in both directions between the small core group of Gaza Nguni and their subjects. In the end, the mobility of the Gaza Nguni between central and southern Mozambique led to a loss of their own culture and the Nguni language.

POLITICS AND ETHNICITY

In the early history of southeast Africa, political divisions and alliances were formed within and across ethnic boundaries to mark cultural identities. Boundaries were fluid when both large states and small territories vied for political control and economic power to regulate trade in the wider region. Economic pursuits, particularly trade, influenced local politics and the formation of cultural identities. Political power was inextricably linked to external trade, and these precolonial contacts highlighted and reinforced cultural identities for the people who came to be called Shona.

Mutapa State. The Karanga of the northern Zimbabwe plateau were the dominant aristocracy in the Shona region in the sixteenth century when the Portuguese first arrived. The first and most prestigious Karanga state, the Mutapa state, relied on its own military power for support. A Portuguese chronicler, Damião de Goes, wrote of the Mutapa leader: "Whether in time of peace or war he always maintains a large standing army, of which the commander-in-chief is called Zono, to keep the land in a state of quietness and to prevent the lords and kings who are subject to him from rising in rebellion" (Theal 1964, vol. 3, 130). The Karanga rulers symbolized their prestige by building small *madzimbabwe* (houses of stone) in the areas where they settled, and they had better living standards than the groups they conquered.

Despite the casting of a common political identity known as Karanga over much of the northern and eastern region by the Mutapa rulers, there were some who refused to accept Mutapa overrule. Local chiefs, for instance, could decide to withhold tribute or carry out clandestine trade in perhaps grain, salt, gold, or ivory. Those within the sphere of the Mutapa's influence referred to others outside of his control, such as groups residing south of the Save River near the port of Inhambane, as *Tonga* to signify their status as outsiders.

Eastern Territories and the Portuguese. Eventually a lack of unity among the Karanga aristocracy, combined with external pressure from the Portuguese presence, led to rivalries that resulted in the formation of a series of separate secondary states in the hinterland of the port of Sofala. In the east, the Ndau and the Manica declared their independence from Mutapa overrule shortly before the beginning of the sixteenth century. From these new political subdivisions the larger states of Teve, Manica, and Barwe were formed, along with smaller territories such as Sanga and Danda. The formation of these new states over two centuries complicated the process of identity formation in the region. Some relied on the once large and powerful Mutapa state for symbolic legitimacy, and claimed—as a legitimating device—that sons of the Mutapa ruler founded these rising states.

The Portuguese persistently recognized the Mutapa ruler in the northern interior as the overlord of the entire region, for they thought that this leader controlled the gold mines in the area and thus held the key to untold wealth. This led to some hostility between the Portuguese and smaller states such as Teve and Danda who continued to trade with their Swahili partners from city-states along the East African coast. As the Portuguese challenged Swahili influence both in the hinterland and along the coast, a wider sense of being Karanga faded. In turn, states in the region came to develop their own political identities that lasted into the nineteenth century.

In the early twentieth century, Europeans and local inhabitants nonetheless revitalized these identities as ethnic markers in their quest to classify and sort the "tribes" of southeast Africa. Even though these secondary states were indeed distinct political entities over several centuries, a wider cultural

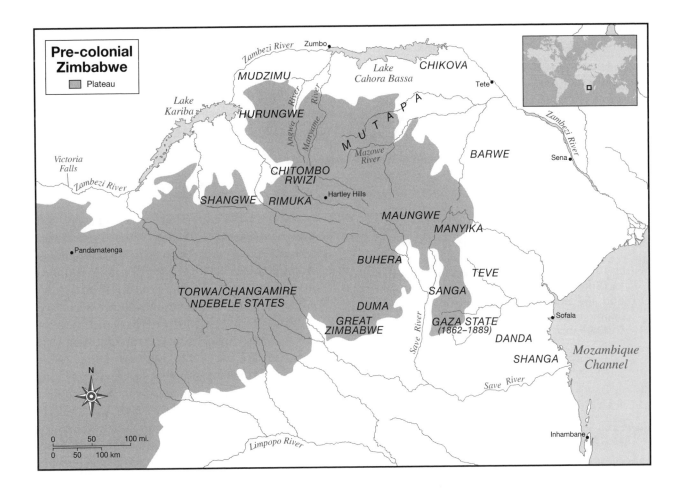

identity based on a shared history and the Shona language permeated the region.

A SHONA IDENTITY

A majority of people in Zimbabwe and a considerable number of Mozambicans living between the Zambezi and Save Rivers speak the Shona language. And on current maps and in the literature on ethnicity most of the people in Zimbabwe and central Mozambique are labeled as Shona (with Ndebele as a significant minority in Zimbabwe). Yet the use of the term Shona to encompass the various identities—historical, cultural, ethnic, or linguistic—of the people living in southeast Africa remains problematic. This is because the Nguni-speaking Ndebele first used the term Shona to refer to the Rozvi people they encountered when migrating into the southwestern area of the plateau in the 1830s. At that time Shona-speakers described themselves in terms of their region or clan, and they apparently only began to use the term Shona themselves sometime after 1890.

This relatively recent and broad characterization of people as Shona does not correspond with identities grounded in a history that signified membership within one political unit. Before the twentieth century, Shona-speakers were conscious of local chieftaincy groups rather than one overarching cultural or political identity that could be called Shona. Therefore, some historians conclude that precolonial states in this region never developed self-conscious identities with lasting legacies. While this may be the case in some situations, populations such as the Ndau drew on their specific history of a shared language and culture in the east to develop a wider sense of identity.

LOSS OF INDEPENDENCE

By 1910 southeast Africa was divided into two colonial spheres of influence. British settlers established themselves on the plateau in the 1890s and dominated over the Shona and the Ndebele in what came to be the colony of Southern Rhodesia. Meanwhile, the Portuguese conquered the Gaza Nguni in 1895 and gained control over the rest of Mozambique. Resistance to these imperial efforts was strong and widespread, most notably on the plateau during the uprisings of the *Chimurenga* struggle in 1896 and 1897. Local inhabitants throughout the region sought both military and political strategies to maintain their sovereignty, including short-lived alliances with European powers. In the end, the military threats were too great to stem the loss of African independence at the turn of the twentieth century.

See also **Cape Colony and Hinterland, History of (1600 to 1900); Colonial Policies and Practices; Immigration and Immigrant Groups; Ivory; Mozambique; Southern Africa, History of (1000 BCE to 1600 CE); Zambezi River; Zimbabwe; Zimbabwe, Great.**

BIBLIOGRAPHY

Beach, David. *The Shona and Zimbabwe, 900–1850.* New York: Holmes and Meier, 1980.

Beach, David. *The Shona and Their Neighbors.* Cambridge, MA: Blackwell, 1994.

Bhila, Hoyni H. K. *Trade and Politics in a Shona Kingdom.* Harlow, Essex: Longman, 1982.

Documents on the Portuguese in Mozambique and Central Africa, 1497–1849. Lisbon: National Archives of Rhodesia, 1962–1972.

Mudenge, Stanislaus I. G. *A Political History of Munhumutapa, c. 1400–1902.* Harare: Zimbabwe Publishing House, 1988.

Newitt, Malyn. *A History of Mozambique.* Bloomington: Indiana University Press, 1995.

Pikirayi, Innocent. *The Zimbabwe Culture: Origins and Decline of Southern Zambezian States.* Walnut Creek, CA: Alta Mira, 2001.

Randles, William G. L. *The Empire of Monomotapa: From the Fifteenth to the Nineteenth Century.* Gwelo, Zimbabwe: Mambo Press, 1979.

Schmidt, Elizabeth. *Peasants, Traders, and Wives: Shona Women in the History of Zimbabwe, 1870–1939.* Portsmouth, NH: Heinemann, 1992.

Theal, George McCall, ed. *Records of South-Eastern Africa,* 9 vols. Cape Town: C. Struik, 1964.

Vail, Leroy. *Creation of Tribalism in Southern Africa.* Berkeley: University of California Press, 1989.

ELIZABETH MACGONAGLE

SOUTHERN AFRICA, HISTORY OF (1000 BCE TO 1600 CE).

Southern Africa is the subcontinent south of the Zambezi, Cubango, Cuito, Cuando, and Kunene Rivers, and comprises southern Angola, southern Zambia, Namibia, Botswana, Zimbabwe, central and southern Mozambique, South Africa, Lesotho, and Swaziland. In physiographic terms, this region of over 3,106,856 square miles forms part of High Africa, with plateaus more than 3,281 feet above sea level, and escarpments comprising the Schwarzrand (3,281–7,218 feet), the Great Karoo (4,921–6,562 feet), the Drakensberg-Maluti mountains (8,202–11,155 feet), and the Lubombo, Chimanimani, and Vumba (4,921–8,202 feet) mountain ranges. These mountains generally face the Indian and the Atlantic Oceans, or in the case of the Chimanimani-Nyanga, the Mozambican plains. They are drained by numerous short rivers such as the Olifants, Groot Sundays, Great Fish, Great Kei, Tugela, Komati, and the Pungwe. Longer river systems such as the Gariep-Vaal-Caledon, Shashe-Limpopo, Save-Runde, Manyame-Angwa, Mazowe-Ruya, Mupfuri-Munyati, and Gwai-Shangani, drain the plateaus and highlands in the interior. The Okavango Delta and the Makgadikgadi Pans are extensive inland drainage basins. Numerous smaller inland drainage basins occur in the drier Northern Cape (Karoo), the Kalahari, and the Namib Deserts.

A moist savanna woodland biome in the eastern half of the subcontinent gives way to a dry woodland scrub to the west, which becomes the Kalahari and Namib Deserts. Overall, the climate is tropical, with subtropical inland and maritime temperate conditions experienced toward the extreme south and southeast.

Until about 1000 BCE, this subcontinent was exclusively inhabited by hunter-forager societies. Their presence is attested by a gradual transition toward advanced stone working techniques, as seen from sites with microlithic tools. Such sites would retain established time-tested technologies, along with the first inkling of new tools. The microlithic technologies that dominated the terminal Pleistocene and Holocene eras may have been instrumental in assisting humans to cope with increasingly colder climatic conditions culminating with the Last Glacial Maximum around 16,000 BCE, and facilitated the complex hunting and gathering practices that developed subsequently.

THEMES IN SOUTHERN AFRICAN HISTORY

Research coverage on the region's past remains uneven geographically, but some themes and are discernible between 1000 BCE and 1600 CE. The introduction of pastoralism encouraged societies to manufacture pottery, as it provided a durable capacity to store, transport, and heat liquids and dispersible solids better and more economically than did ostrich eggshells, gourds, or ground stone bowls. This development preceded the emergence of permanent settlement, associated with iron manufacture and crop husbandry. These farmers easily adopted ceramic manufacturing technology as pottery's ability to heat water permitted cooking of a wide range of plant foods. This encouraged not only cultivation, but also investments in long-term settlements and storage facilities near gardens. As a result, permanent hamlets of pole-and-daub house walls, agriculture, ceramic manufacture, and metallurgy became features of the southern African scene.

Though the origins of iron technology remain unresolved, by 500 CE iron was in use in much of southern Africa. Initially, there seems to be little evidence of iron effecting changes in the societies into which it was introduced. These societies still exploited wild plants and animal resources, as had their hunter-forager predecessors. Later, iron may have facilitated social transformations leading toward social complexity and urbanization in much of the region. By 1000 CE these farmers had established complex networks of trade and settlement throughout the subcontinent, so much so that social inequalities emerged from the wealth accumulated by others. Some of this wealth was expressed in monumental architecture, attesting to the ability of some of the rulers to mobilize labor resources. The export of valuable resources such as ivory, animal skins, and gold, in exchange for glass beads, cloth, and exotic ceramic wares, increasingly brought the subcontinent into the realm of the Swahili and European trading spheres.

Hunter-Forager Artistic Traditions and Interactions with Early Pastoral Societies.
Prior to the introduction of domestic stock and plants, southern Africa experienced a pattern of intensified hunting and gathering, elaboration of ritual activity, and exchange by resident hunter-foragers. The causes of this are not yet known. It is also unclear how domestic stock was introduced in southern Africa.

In discussing southern African history of the last three millennia, scholars often omit hunter-forager artistic and ritual traditions that derived from the terminal Pleistocene and continued into the Holocene era. These are paintings and engravings found in caves, rock shelters, and open spaces. This art is a product of shamanistic rituals and ceremonies connected with healing and rainmaking. Some of this art played a role in instructive teachings during certain ceremonies such as initiation, whereas other art may have expressed the local cosmological world of myths and symbolism. Some depict intergroup rivalries or conflicts.

Scholars have questioned previous interpretations that ranged from depictions of sympathetic magic to art for art's sake. An ethnographic study of the now extinct Xam (San foragers) altered scholars' understanding of a cognitive world of the artists centered on the shamanistic trance as a mechanism supporting healing, hunting, fertility, and rainmaking rituals. Many related paintings emphasize the eland, an animal important to the ritual life of these foraging peoples. However, identifying southern African rock art with the San and the purported continuities from the past to the ethnographic present is a quandary. Bantu speakers in much of this subcontinent also authored this art. The rock art from Zambia, Angola, Malawi, and Mozambique, which extends farther north into Tanzania, Kenya, and Uganda, has naturalistic representations of animals and humans painted in red. Sometimes these are covered by later geometric patterns of various shapes and patterns, which in turn are covered by paintings of geometric shapes and stylized animals in thick white paint. A later style is of schematic red and white designs. It is thought that hunter-foragers authored the naturalistic paintings, whereas the later schematic ones were the product of farming communities. It appears that this art was critical to hunter-forager and farmer economic and sacerdotal activities portraying their cosmology and their cultural and natural landscapes.

Whatever their origins—and there are indications that such processes were already taking place in the Sahara around 6000–3500 BCE—the domestication of animals and cultivation of crops in much of Africa is well attested by the presence of domestic animal bones (including cattle, sheep or goats, pigs, and sometimes donkeys), grinding stones, pottery, and permanent settlements. In southern Africa evidence of sheep or goats and cattle suggests these animals were in the region earlier than the permanent settlements associated with the first crop farmers; some has been recovered in later Holocene forager-hunter contexts.

Domestic animals in southern Africa date from the first millennium BCE, with the Cape region of South Africa and parts of Namibia showing evidence of cattle and sheep or goats. Given the absence of wild prototypes of these animals there, it is intriguing that these were established in southern Africa. The archaeological horizons have no signs of experimentation such as those in northern parts of the continent. It seemingly suggests complex interaction and shifting identities between resident hunter-foragers, pastoralists, and hunter-herders. Such identities and attempts to relate the archaeological past to an ethnographic present are difficult to discern in the archaeological record. However, San and Khoe communities, whose languages are related to those of some hunter-forager groups in eastern Africa, seem to be the first pastoral societies in southern Africa. The spread of their language and other aspects of culture are, however, still in dispute.

Early Farmers. The expansion and spread of agro-pastoral societies in the subcontinent are identified by archaeological sites containing well-fired pottery that is thick bodied with slightly concave necks and decorative motifs on the rim-neck-shoulder-body region that are either grooved or comb stamped. Some sites exhibit metalworking, the keeping of livestock, and pole-and-daub structures of permanent settlement. This pottery has been recovered near Lake Victoria in Uganda, in Rwanda, Burundi, Tanzania, much of southern and coastal Kenya, the southern part of Democratic Republic of the Congo (DRC), parts of Angola, Zambia, Malawi, Mozambique, much of the central and the eastern coastal zones of South Africa, and Swaziland. Archaeologists have described this pottery on perceived similarities between sites in terms of structure and design, and have ascribed it to certain cultural traditions. The pottery was a product of related groups of people who occupied southern Africa from the first half of the first millennium CE.

Ceramic groups such as Situmpa-Salumano, Dambwa, Kalundu, Kapwirimbwe, Chondwe, Kalambo and Kamnama (in Zambia), Bambata-Toteng (western Zimbabwe and adjacent Botswana), Mwambulambo and Nkope (Malawi), Ziwa, Kadzi, Gokomere and Chinhoyi (Zimbabwe), Matola (coastal Mozambique, Swaziland, and the coastal regions of South Africa), Lydenburg, Silver Leaves, Tzaneen, and Broederstroom (the northern and eastern highveld of South Africa) are all associated with early farming and iron-using communities formerly associated with the inception of the Iron Age on the subcontinent. This process is dated from the third centuries BCE and continues throughout the first and early second millennium CE, attesting to the expansion and spread of farming activities and iron production in southern Africa.

The people who manufactured this pottery subsisted on cattle and various domestic crops such as finger millet, pearl millet, Bambara groundnuts, cucurbits, sorghum, and cowpeas. They also exploited wild grasses and plant foods, wild animals, fish, and marine- and freshwater shells. Signs of metalworking are not as common, occurring at localities such as Divuyu and Nqoma near Tsodilo Hills in northern Botswana. The importance of cattle is attested to by the Central Cattle Pattern (CCP) that is commonly associated with a variety of social and political attitudes found in the early twenty-first century among the Sotho-Tswana and other cattle-ranging people of southern Africa. The presence of cattle at Tabazingwe in western Zimbabwe, Toutswe, Kgaswe, and other sites in Botswana suggests the importance of cattle ownership in the organization of early states on the margins of the Kalahari.

Another issue in the study of these agropastoralists is their linguistic identity. Bantu speakers populate most of sub-Saharan Africa, and a widely held, largely unquestioned assumption is that the expansion of these languages from the northern part of the equatorial forests region was part of the southward movement of the agropastoralists. The complex dynamics of languages and their associations with specific archaeologically known groups remains a thorny issue. The ceramic evidence suggests consistencies in the material correlates of southern African people from the terminal first millennium BCE until the present day. As a result, southern and eastern African Iron Age studies are dominated by discussion of the migrations of Bantu-speaking agropastoralists, with scholars identifying eastern (or Kwale tradition) and western (Kalundu) groups and attributing them to eastern and western Bantu speakers.

The populating of southern and eastern Africa by agropastoral societies may have taken on the model of slash-and-burn whereby after three to five years communities would leave a piece of land because of marginal fertility of the soils and move on to another. At the new location they would clear and burn the vegetation to get nutrient-filled ash. This practice dictated repetitive movement with the consequent result that population was always small, as were production yields. In this way, large areas of southern and eastern Africa appeared to be rapidly occupied. It is, nevertheless, difficult to verify ancient patterns of migration, though it is obvious that farmers, who displaced foragers, rapidly populated a large portion of southern Bantu-speaking Africa.

The Emergence and Development of Complex Societies. The process of political, social, and economic centralization in much of sub-Saharan Africa remains an issue of disagreement among scholars. It is generally clear that the consolidation of food production, trade in highly valued commodities, and control of certain products such as iron, copper, and gold were partly responsible for the centralization. Kings in Central Africa symbolized their power in sacred objects made of copper and iron. Manufacture of these objects implies further multifaceted relations to artisans, particularly ironworkers, who gained a role as kingmakers, as they were able to manipulate these objects into symbols of wealth and political power. The growth of social complexity depended on effective means of agricultural production embedded in a kin-based society that successfully mitigated environmental stress by the medium of transfers of resources within the kin group, orchestrated by senior members of the group. These senior members, in time, as the centers of authority—religious and secular—attained a status sufficient to become elites.

Political centralization was largely achieved through the control of the key resources—salt, cattle, ivory, hides, and gold—traded with distant communities. In southern Africa, cattle played such a significant role in the ideology and economy that by the beginning of the second millennium CE, those with the capacity to keep large herds attained social advantage, exercising control over other peoples' affairs. Some of their wealth, generated by trade, was invested in monumental architecture, defining not only special space but also status differences. Public buildings reflected communal participation in projects initiated at the level above the homestead and the village, as well as skill and innovation in extraction and construction, the existence of labor mobilization, and a system of reward for the artisans involved. Religion and ritual may not have been prime movers in state formation, but they played an important part in the development of sociopolitical systems. Authority often is achieved through manipulation of sacred places and ritual because religion and ritual express a society's expectation. The managers take on the role of mediators, embodying the hopes and aspirations of their followers. Management of religion and certain ritual obligations, as well as strategic economic resources, centralized the roles of senior managers in the sacred and the mundane. The monopolization of authority gave rise to a political technology manipulated for the purposes of political and social control.

From the tenth to the nineteenth centuries, the Zimbabwe culture was the dominant economic and political entity south of the Zambezi. Beginning at Mapungubwe (c. 1050–1240), authority passed to Great Zimbabwe (c. 1270–1650), Torwa (c. 1450–1650), Rozvi-Changamire (c. 1680–1830), and finally to Mutapa (c. 1450–1880). These polities shifted from the Shashi-Limpopo Basin toward the south-central plateau and the western and northern regions of the Zimbabwe Plateau, and their influence stretched to the Indian Ocean coastal cities as well as to polities north of the Zambezi. The center of power of this autochthonous sociopolitical tradition shifted throughout the region in response to varying environmental and security considerations, and to the economic potential of the different regions. Each state was organized around a principal lineage, associated with a major town (Zimbabwe). A sacred leadership presided over a well-defined political and settlement hierarchy.

Each town had impressive stone-built monumental architecture, an enlarged emphasis on cattle in the economy, increased specialization in domestic crafts, and long-distance connections involving gold, ivory, cloth, and glass beads with the Indian Ocean coast and the world beyond.

Although no satisfactory explanation may be posited for the demise of any individual state, observations of present-day land-use and demographic patterns suggest the difficulty of sustaining large populations without seriously upsetting the ecological balance. The territorial shifts in political power and settlement systems may be accounted, in part, to agriculture and its ranging and commercial potential. This is most evident in the transfer of economic and political power from Mapungubwe to Great Zimbabwe, from the Middle Limpopo Valley to the Plateau. Similarly, by the fifteenth century northern Zimbabwe offered better commercial opportunities through contact with Portuguese traders than did places further to the south, whereas to the southwest, the area occupied by the Torwa and Rozvi-Changamire states seems to have been more capable of supporting a pastoral economy necessary for underwriting social complexity.

Transformations South of the Limpopo. From the early second millennium CE, Bantu-language speakers south of the Limpopo developed into Nguni and Sotho-Tswana peoples. In the early twenty-first century, Zulu, Ndebele, Xhosa, and the Swazi represent Nguni speakers. The Sotho-Tswana includes the Pedi, Sotho, and Tswana. The groups extended their influence north of the Gariep River and in the southeastern Drakensburg-Maluti mountains prior to the encroachment of Europeans from the seventeenth century onward. Some of the events connected with the movements of these groups on the South African highveld are documented in European accounts, oral history, and ethnography, and historians, anthropologists, and archaeologists have tended to focus on the immediate past of these groups. Contact studies involving these groups and Europeans reveal the complex settlement processes and interactions in South Africa. Scholars' investigations continue to focus on Marothodi, the Bakgatla in the Pilanesberg, Dithakong, and other locations in the northwestern areas of South Africa. Researchers are examining these sites' spatial organization and synthesizing the oral records that outline an increasingly turbulent eighteenth century during which chiefs and

lineages competed for cattle, people, and resources to reinforce political, social, and economic power, driven in part by growing European intrusion.

Earlier pre-seventeenth-century Nguni and Sotho-Tswana settlements are known to have existed in the southeastern and central plateau regions of South Africa. Although their archaeological identities are largely based on ceramic studies, the resultant sequences are perceived in terms of transformations during the early second millennium CE that are associated with increased group interactions among agropastoral societies in regions that did not develop large-scale sociopolitical centralization, as did eastern Botswana and the Zimbabwe Plateau. The development of the Nguni and Sotho-Tswana societies should also be perceived in terms of early adjustments from the small and dispersed homesteads to large numbers of aggregated settlements. This would lead by the seventeenth century to a significant shift in the scale of production in which increasingly competitive economies and political rivalry developed between groups. In the Soutpansberg Mountains, the Venda seem to have developed from an amalgamation of Shona and Sotho-Tswana speakers, a process also linked to the developments in the area after the demise of the state based at Mapungubwe. By the late seventeenth century CE, the Venda were dominated by a Karanga/Rozvi dynasty that seems to have founded the Thovela state.

Southern Africa in World History. Over the course of the first two millennia CE, southern Africa has increasingly been in contact with the commercial worlds of the Near East and the Gulf, India and the Far East, and, latest in this period, industrialized Europe. This has generated a range of written texts reporting the contact between Africans and outsiders. Initial contact zones were coastal regions, particularly the eastern and southern African coasts, where Africans encountered new merchants and traded ivory, gold, animal skins, and other products in exchange for foreign cloth, glass beads, and ceramics. This contact transformed African societies initially into prosperous societies, but with the arrival of Europeans from the late fifteenth century onward, new patterns of trade and interaction on the continent triggered these societies' demise.

European contact with Africa is fairly well documented, and archaeology has revealed material evidence of this contact process. European attempts to control trade caused African societies to adapt to changing circumstances. Major states or empires, such as Mutapa, either became irrelevant or barriers to new commerce and were soon replaced by lesser polities that strategically placed themselves between the coast and the interior. Violent confrontations ensued. Europeans attempted to push their frontier into the interior—Dutch expansion from the Cape and the Portuguese incursions into the lower Zambezi. The underlying ethos of traditional African politics and commerce was diminished, causing the demise of many local African manufacturing capacities as the subcontinent was transformed into a source of raw materials for European home-country factories. The export of Africans as slaves, long a practice involving the Middle East, now spread to the Atlantic trade as well, further diminishing the status of Africans and their cultures in the world's view. European dominance of the region had thus begun.

See also **Art, Genres and Periods; Bantu, Eastern, Southern, and Western, History of (1000 BCE to 1500 CE); Cape Colony and Hinterland, History of (1600 to 1910); Ceramics; Desertification, Reactions to, History of (c. 5000 to 1000 BCE); Ecosystems: Savannas; Metals and Minerals: Salt; Southeastern Africa, History of (1600 to 1910).**

BIBLIOGRAPHY

Deacon, Hilary, and Jeanette Deacon. *Human Beginnings in South Africa: Uncovering the Secrets of the Stone Age.* Walnut Creek, CA: AltaMira Press, 1999.

Hall, Martin, and Andrew B. Smith, eds. *Prehistoric Pastoralism in Southern Africa.* Cape Town: South African Archaeological Society, 1986.

Huffman, Thomas N. *Iron Age Migrations: The Ceramic Sequence in Southern Zambia-Excavations at Gundu and Ndonde.* Johannesburg: Witwatersrand University Press, 1989.

Kent, Susan, ed. *Cultural Diversity among Twentieth-Century Foragers: An African Perspective.* Cambridge, U.K.: Cambridge University Press, 1996.

Lewis-Williams, James D. *Discovering Southern African Rock Art.* Cape Town: David Philip, 1990.

Mitchell, Peter. *The Archaeology of Southern Africa.* Cambridge, U.K.: Cambridge University Press, 2002.

Pikirayi, Innocent. *The Zimbabwe Culture: Origins and Decline in Southern Zambezian States.* Walnut Creek, CA: AltaMira Press, 2001.

Stahl, Ann Brower. *African Archaeology: A Critical Introduction.* Malden, MA: Blackwell, 2005.

INNOCENT PIKIRAYI

SOUTH-WEST AFRICA. *See* **Namibia.**

SOYINKA, WOLE (1934–). Soyinka was educated at the University of Ibadan (1952–1954) and the University of Leeds, where he received a B.A. degree in English. After graduation, he worked for the Royal Court Theatre, London, as a reader and director. In 1960, Soyinka returned to Nigeria and founded a theater company, which also put on his play *A Dance of the Forests* (1963), written to celebrate Nigerian independence. In 1986, Soyinka became Africa's first Nobel Laureate for literature.

His work, *Myth, Literature and the African World* (1976), while exploring literature, art, and culture, also examines the place of the artist and individual in society. Soyinka has been persistently

Nobel Prize winner Wole Soyinka (1934–) talks to the press, May 17, 2004. Soyinka was among a group of pro-democracy activists teargassed by the police while rallying in Lagos. The activists called for the resignation of President Olusegun Obasanjo two days later. PIUS UTOMI EKPEI/AFP/GETTY IMAGES

critical of Nigerian leadership. In October 1965, he was imprisoned for seizing a radio station at gunpoint and making a speech critical of the leadership. Although acquitted of those charges, he was again arrested in 1967 and imprisoned for twenty-two months for expressing sympathy towards Biafra as Nigeria plunged into a civil war (1966–1970). His prison memoir, *The Man Died* (1972), addresses that experience. In 1994, Soyinka was forced into exile by the repressive Nigerian government. Wole Soyinka remains one of Africa's most prolific writers and one of its most strident critics.

See also **Literatures in European Languages: Anglophone Western Africa; Theater.**

BIBLIOGRAPHY

George, Olakunle. "Wole Soyinka." *Encyclopedia of African Literature*, ed. Simon Gikandi. London: Routledge, 2003.

Gibbs, James, ed. *Critical Perspectives on Wole Soyinka.* Washington, DC: Three Continents Press, 1980.

Meja-Pearce, Adewale, ed. *Wole Soyinka: An Appraisal.* Portsmouth, NJ: Heinemann, 1994.

Works by Wole Soyinka

A Dance of the Forests. London: Oxford University Press, 1964.

Idanre and Other Poems. London: Methuen, 1967.

The Man Died: Prison Notes of Wole Soyinka. New York: Harper & Row, 1972.

Death and the King's Horseman. New York: Norton, 1975.

Myth, Literature and the African World. Cambridge, U.K.: Cambridge University Press, 1976.

Ake: the Years of Childhood. New York, Random House, 1981.

Isara, a Voyage Around Essay. New York: Random House, 1989.

MAUREEN EKE

SPANISH COLONIES. *See* **Colonial Policies and Practices: Spanish.**

SPANISH SAHARA. *See* **Western Sahara.**

SPIRIT POSSESSION

This entry includes the following articles:
MEDIUMSHIP
MODERNITY

MEDIUMSHIP

Spirit possession commonly refers to the control that powerful disincarnate entities exert over human beings. These entities may be imagined as ancestors or spirits, angels or demons, or as creatures of foreign origin and ontology. Depending on whether their presence among people is culturally sanctioned, they are tolerated—and occasionally invited to take over the body of their host (or medium) during episodes of possession trance—or they are expelled through exorcism. Scholars trying to transcend folk epistemologies have typified possession in Africa as mediumship, as a binary adorcism/exorcism complex, and as a form of ecstatic religion. However, it is now recognized that the diverse practices heuristically subsumed under possession do not comprise an independent type of behavior, neatly distinguishable from other practices. Some are cults such as *zar*, *bori*, or *ngoma* are widely distributed across the continent—in the case of zar, a healing cult found in North and East Africa, even spilling into the Middle East—where they have influenced other possession practices.

Like *zar* with which it is sometimes identified, *bori* is an indigenous spirit healing cult that is found principally in Niger and Nigeria. In a geographical area ranging from Cameroon to South Africa *ngoma* comprises a wide variety of practices (cults of affliction, churches, music groups, etc.) focused around the use of drums and the negotiation of spirit relationships to heal. All these religious practices have lengthy, and, in a few cases, well-documented histories. Others, such as *orpeko* among the Maasai people of Tanzania, are relatively recent phenomena that originated with foreign contacts.

In numerous cases, spirit forms—and their intervention in people's lives—have been responses to the incidence of illness. Because they are thought to both cause and cure illness, such spirits are at the centers of cults of affliction in which previously afflicted individuals go on to become healers, thanks to the knowledge that the afflicting spirits have imparted on them. Involvement with cults such as bori, ngoma, or zar generally follows a period of illness during which all other therapeutic options have failed and the sufferer is diagnosed as being afflicted by spirits. Treatment involves initiation into the cult during a propitiatory ritual where the initiates will enter into a trance, allowing the spirits to take over their bodies to manifest the spirits' identities and reveal their requirements—sacrificial offerings, gifts of alcohol, and so on.

Spirit possession cannot be reduced to therapy, however. It often intersects with other contexts and activities such as migration, marriage, social networks, memorializations of the past, political struggles, and cultural critiques. Nor can spirits be simply characterized as agents of affliction, even in cases when possession is phrased as illness. Unless spirits are exorcized, their relationships with their hosts are often complex, changing, and subject to negotiation. As purveyors of knowledge, they may teach about history, ethnicity, kinship, gender, morality, and sexuality. They may speak their own language and request special clothes. Spirits have been documented to possess their hosts not simply during ritually orchestrated ceremonies but in everyday life as well, often mediating their hosts' relationships with kin and acquaintances. In Mayotte in the Comoro Islands, spirits facilitate communication between mediums and their spouses.

In Morocco, men fall prey to a she-demon with whom they must live as husband and wife. Because this relationship precludes normal marriage for the human partner and results in a variety of ills, victims often seek treatment from the Hamadsha, an Islamic brotherhood. Members of the Hamadsha help alleviate the sufferer's symptoms by holding possession performances and sacrificial rituals. Significantly, the metaphoric equation of possession with marriage prevails elsewhere as well. In northern Sudan, zar ceremonies are patterned after weddings. In Niger, bori initiates are called brides, regardless of their gender. There, as in Nigeria among *orisa* (also spelled *orisha* or *orixá*; spiritual manifestations of Olodumare, the ultimate deity in Yoruba religious tradition) practitioners, possession is referred to as mounting and metaphorically likened to sex.

Spirit possession forms have, in numerous cases, been thoroughly impacted by Islam and Christianity, religions which they have in turn influenced. The complex ways that zar has simultaneously competed with, adapted to, and borrowed from Islam or Christianity often means that spirit devotees see no incompatibility between their commitment to zar and their identities as Christians or Muslims. To them, possession is part of a wider non-doctrinaire religious enterprise. Some disagree with this picture, however, and see zar as being antithetical to Islam and Christianity. Such divisions often follow gender lines. Thus, although zar falls squarely within the purview of Islam to northern Sudanese women, to their male counterparts, possession is sinful and contrary to the teachings of the Qur'an. That morality lies in the eye of the beholder is evidenced by the condemnatory stance taken by Nigerian and Ghanaian Pentecostal Churches—themselves cults of possession in Christian metaphors—toward the Mami Wata cult, a syncretic religion of growing popularity centered around water spirits.

Throughout the continent, Pentecostal Christians themselves engage in possession, a practice they connect to the first day of Pentecost when, the Bible says, tongues of fire descended on the heads of the apostles and they were filled with the Holy Spirit. Although they consider possession by the Holy Spirit—an experience that includes trance and speaking in tongues—a desirable event, Pentecostal Christians denounce the parallel practices centered around the worship of Mami Wata whom they identify as an instrument of the devil. These practices include dancing, spirit possession, and the maintenance of shrines where offerings of food, drinks, and incense or perfume are made to the spirits. Historically, Muslims and Christians have focused on repressing possession—which they equate with undesirable and shameful African custom—but they recognize the existence of spirits or other demonic creatures. In Madagascar, Sakalava mediums seek Protestant exorcism not because they fear opprobrium but because the requirements of the royal ancestors that possess them are too costly.

Earlier anthropological efforts to rationalize possession led previous scholars to differentiate between central cults, where possession by morally upright forces (such as ancestors) was a positive experience involving men, and marginal cults, where possession was a form of illness that typically afflicted women and socially disadvantaged individuals. In the latter case, possession functioned as the thinly disguised means of protest by the dispossessed against the powerful. More recently, a recognition that power and peripherality are relative concepts and that possession must be discussed on its own terms has prompted more culturally sensitive interpretations of what possession means for those involved. Moreover, peripherality does not necessarily imply powerlessness. In South Africa, Zionist practices (that involve possession by the Holy Spirit) empower the marginalized by allowing them to separate themselves from and actively resist neocolonial culture.

From the Hauka rebellion of Niger to Shona ancestor-led nationalist movements and subsequent guerrilla war in present-day Zimbabwe, examples abound of the subversive potential of spirit movements. Elsewhere, spirits emerge as critical commentators of cultural tradition, distilling the lessons of history, parodying the practices of outsiders, or undermining the givenness of such institutions as kinship or motherhood. Spirits also intervene in the commodities market, whether to ban goods (such as Coca-Cola among Zimbabwe's guerrillas) or to endorse them (as is the case among Kalanga women who, when possessed by lion-demons, wear store-bought cloths with lion designs).

See also **Christianity; Ethnicity; Gender; Initiation; Islam; Kinship and Affinity; Mami Wata; Myth and Cosmology; Philosophy; Prophetic Movements; Religion and Ritual; Witchcraft.**

BIBLIOGRAPHY

Boddy, Janice. *Wombs and Alien Spirits: Women, Men and the Zar Cult in Northern Sudan.* Madison: University of Wisconsin Press, 1989.

Boddy, Janice. "Spirit Possession Revisited: Beyond Instrumentality." *Annual Review of Anthropology* 23 (1994): 407–434.

Crapanzano, Vincent. *The Hamadsha: A Study in Moroccan Ethnopsychiatry.* Berkeley: University of California Press, 1971.

Janzen, John M. *Ngoma: Discourses of Healing in Central and Southern Africa.* Berkeley: University of California Press, 1992.

Lambel, Michael. *Human Spirits: A Cultural Account of Trance in Mayotte.* New York: Cambridge University Press, 1981.

Masquelier, Adeline. *Prayer Has Spoiled Everything: Possession, Power, and Identity in an Islamic Town of Niger.* Durham, N.C.: Duke University Press, 2001.

ADELINE MASQUELIER

MODERNITY

Secularization is one of the central features of modernity, according to the classical understandings of Max Weber and Jürgen Habermas. However, religion in general and possession cults in particular are still of great importance in many postcolonial societies. The insight, that modernity is not necessarily linked to processes of disenchantment with spirit, led to a reformulation of the concept of modernity itself. Alternative paths to modernity are discussed and framed in terms like multiple, alternative, or entangled modernities, thus freeing the term from its original Eurocentric rationalist connotations. Spirit possession cults are good examples to analyze the specificities of modernity in Africa, as well as their entanglements with other modernities. Their continuing success and vitality confirm that they are by no means an archaic institution but rather are deeply engaged in popular shapings their positions in the world of the twenty-first century for most people in society, in lively competition and exchange with Islam and Christianity, which are often supported by state power.

Spirit possession allows individuals to act out their (social or physical) problems as a culturally approved relationship between themselves and the spirit world being supported by an immediate community of adherents, relatives and friends. Due to the great varieties of cults a rather vague understanding exists of what possession actually is, phenomenologically, since it takes many forms and means different things to different people. For scholar Erika Bourguignon possession was synonymous with an altered state of consciousness, whereas Godfrey Lienhardt defined it as the seizure of man by divinity. Michael Lambek drew attention to the prominent aspect of communication, unfolding through dreams or voices. Others stressed the infliction of illness or misfortune by the spirits, which is especially felt in times of crises related to social change—a major experience of the last century in Africa.

Yet, spirit possession is more than healing or a form of psychotherapy. Theatrical performances are vital to its existence, as Michel Leiris pointed out already in the 1950s. Doing *ngoma*, playing drums, has become a synonym for spirit possession rituals in the Bantu-speaking societies of East, Central, and South Africa. In these rites or sessions, social issues and moral values are negotiated among cult members through songs, dance rhythms, and costumes. They are expressions of a cultural archive that allows insight into processes of social transformations being symbolised by a diversity of spirits that represent ancestors, cultural heroes or former kings as well as specific ethnic or social groups, animals, material things, abstract principles, and even emotional states.

THE SOCIOLOGY OF POSSESSION

Complexity of meaning and adaptability as an institution are outstanding features of spirit possession, and practices of it have undergone fundamental changes in membership and organization in the last decades. Whereas most cults are still organized informally, the role of healer has been transformed by undergoing professionalization through membership in national healers' associations. These professional groups enforce general standards of treatment, which in addition to control they also convey new opportunities for further qualification through attendance at courses and meetings. In addition, acting as healer has also become financially attractive since possession cults have become commercialised. Treatment is no longer free within a community of intimacy but is available to the public, who pay for it, and according to the difficulties of the case and the time involved can be very costly. Especially in areas where no paid jobs are available, healing as a profession is financially attractive.

This remunerativeness may be one of the reasons for the increase of male healers, whose prominence in spirit possession succeeds women's, with likely implications in need of more research. Although traditionally spirit possession has been judged as women's affair, male labor migrants in South Africa seem to have played important roles in disseminating ritual practices and introducing new spirits into the cults. Whereas I. M. Lewis noted only young men without any social standing as cult members during the 1970s, the number of male patients has increased as well. Urban workers who had trouble in their careers or students and schoolboys suffering from stress increasingly surrender to the spirits, either as whole groups or as individuals. They thus refute older explanations of spirit possession as a domain of the weak and the downtrodden and as being entirely dominated by women. However, possession is still a women's world in rural areas, offering cures for infertility and marital problems, or addressing gender inequalities or estrangement from home by returning wives of labor migrants. Acting out their spirits' identities as parts of their own, they symbolically transcend the limitations of their everyday worlds. This spiritual empowerment enables them to better meet the more mundane and less malleable challenges of transformed social relations. In this way, modernity is profoundly inscribed in the cults' organization as well as in their members' afflictions.

REPRESENTING AND APPROPRIATING MODERNITY

Spirit possession in the twenty-first century, however, not only is a reaction to the difficulties and conflict conveyed by modernity but also enables its adepts in its appropriation, be it materially or symbolically. By integrating luxury goods, like European food or drinks, spectacles, modern clothing or tape recorders, as well as money, the Bible and Christian songs or the Qur'an or Indian images of Mami Wata into their ritual practices, healers of spirit possession cults have shown a great openness to the appeal of "exotic" cultural artifacts. These objects of power, perhaps derived from their strangeness and still unexplored potential, are given to the spirits as confirmation of their identities and allow deep insight into the construction of African modernities. During early colonialism spirits embodied technological inventions like bicycles, trains, or airplanes, commented on and ridiculed colonial administrators, as shown in Jean Rouch's controversial Hauka film, or represented such abstract principle as Europeandom.

During the 1960s and 1970s, performances of spirits as development workers, doctors, and nurses were staged commenting and evaluating colonial and postcolonial experiences in their encounters with Western societies. Whereas these ritual performances were deeply embedded in local and regional cultures and histories, references to globalized images and ideas like Kung Fu and Adolf Hitler became more frequent during the 1990s. The violence of postcolonial relations entered into the metaphoric construction of local modernities, underlining the active roles of healers in shaping these processes. They not only actively take part in linking different modernities by integrating symbolic objects and different belief systems (Christianity, Islam, Hinduism) into their own cosmologies but also transcend the level of appropriation and representation by giving them specific forms and content. In addition, healers' success and renown enable some of them to live these changing realities themselves. As their slave ancestors before them, some distinguished healers manage to export their rituals and spiritual beliefs outside Africa, be it through emigration or, as in the case of a famous Senegalese healer, by being invited to practice her form of spirit possession in the United States.

See also **Dreams and Dream Interpretation; Gender; Religion and Ritual; Rouch, Jean; Symbols and Symbolism; Witchcraft; Women.**

BIBLIOGRAPHY

Behrend, Heike, and Ute Luig, eds. *Spirit Possession, Modernity, and Power.* London: James Currey, 1999.

Boddy, Janice. "Spirit Possession Revisited: Beyond Instrumentality." *Annual Review of Anthropology* 23 (1994): 407–434.

Janzen, John M. *Ngoma: Discourses of Healing in Central and Southern Africa.* Berkeley: University of California Press, 1992.

Lewis, I. M. *Ecstatic Religion: An Anthropological Study of Spirit Possession and Shamanism.* Harmondsworth: Penguin Books, 1971.

UTE LUIG

SPORTS

This entry includes the following articles:
OVERVIEW
FOOTBALL

OVERVIEW

Western forms of sport brought to Africa by European colonizers likely had many familiar aspects for Africans because competitive, organized games and physical activities existed in precolonial village life. Wrestling, martial arts, foot races, canoe and cattle racing, and dancing doubtless had much in common with many aspects of Western sports. In taking over modern forms of sport, then, Africans were to some extent integrating the old and the new, and appropriating European cultural forms to suit their local needs.

Soldiers, sailors, traders, and other Europeans played sports for their own entertainment, but colonial officials and missionaries also actively introduced European-style competition as a means of social control of urban Africans. In doing so, the colonizers implemented notions that derived from interactions with youth in contemporary Europe, where sports were seen as an excellent means of instilling "moral values" and a sense of structured time. Initially, missionaries and European sports enthusiasts in Africa trained Christians and the educated elite, but by the 1920s, and often in response to African demands, colonial educators and social workers were advocating investment in playing fields and equipment for the African population. It was only after World War II and especially after independence, however, that such infrastructure became widespread.

Young people encountered sports either in mission schools and youth clubs or through watching others play and then trying it for themselves informally. In South Africa, crowds of Africans watched British civilians and off-duty soldiers playing soccer in Natal and the Cape beginning in the 1860s and continuing through the South African War (1899–1902). In Léopoldville and Brazzaville, the colonial capitals of the Belgian Congo and French Equatorial Africa, the Portuguese, Flemish, British, and French communities organized teams to play soccer matches on Sunday afternoons and on special occasions such as national holidays. African crowds turned out to watch and cheer. Although predominantly a male domain, sports attracted women spectators and participants, especially in mission schools, where young girls enjoyed netball, field hockey, tennis, and athletics.

Football, or American soccer, quickly emerged as the leviathan of African sports. It was cheap, fun, easy to learn, and could be played by barefooted boys, in dusty streets, with makeshift balls of rags and paper. Men organized teams and neighborhood matches in African sections of towns. In need of specialized training, coaching, and equipment, players often enlisted the help of European sponsors interested in promoting amateur sports. After World War II, in French West Africa and Central Africa, pressure on resources caused colonial authorities to try to divert some enthusiasm into other sports, such as athletics, cycling, and volleyball. They largely failed, for soccer met the needs of players and fans far beyond physical exercise. Urban teams represented and reflected the multiple identities of townsfolk and the need to forge new identities and social networks around shared participation and observing. Teams might represent ethnic groups, urban neighborhoods, religious denominations, or workplace or class interests—for example, railroad workers, police, civil servants, or school alumni. In addition, sports expressed multiple and competing masculinities. Thus, by the 1920s and 1930s, organized sports had taken on the dominant characteristics of sports worldwide.

At the same time, African sports had a distinctive flavor. New playing styles emerged as expressions of cosmopolitanism and of cultural autonomy from colonial modes of sport. This process of "Africanization" was also exemplified by the use of magic to compete and the development of sports clubs as mutual aid associations. In the early 1920s, in Durban, South Africa, the discovery of a small bottle filled with *umuthi* (traditional medicine) in one of the goals during a championship soccer game exploded into a major controversy. In 1938, in Bulawayo, Southern Rhodesia, European administrators who were monitoring the autonomous development of boxing among urban Africans noticed fighters wearing armbands containing special medicines for success. The employment of team magicians and doctors to help win soccer matches is still common in preparations for a big game. From Abidjan to Zululand, team members might follow rituals of agrarian origins to heighten their chances of winning, and supporters may plant special charms in the middle of the playing field to impede opponents. In the Congo, where the resources of society were perceived as fixed, a game was thought to involve only the

claiming of the larger share of a preordained number of goals. The role of team magicians was to do battle with medicines and supernatural forces in order to "steal" goals from their opponents while protecting their own. Such practices indicate how far sports at the grassroots was Africanized at the same time that it was played and organized according to international rules.

Sports clubs became significant as voluntary associations that consolidated networks of relationships in cities and towns. For example, in the towns of colonial Ghana, Tanzania, Angola, Zambia, and South Africa soccer clubs became hubs of social activities, similar in this function to burial societies and dance associations. In other areas, club administrators, who were often former players and spectators with intense loyalties to a particular team, took on the role of elders to promising young players. They gave advice, collected dues, helped club members with family expenses caused by sickness, marriage, and death, and assisted young men in finding jobs.

The growth and expansion of sports in Africa assisted anticolonial mobilization after World War II. The spread of education at all levels and the teaching of sports in the schools, coupled with the growing impact of broadcast and print media familiarized students with volleyball, basketball, and athletics, as well as with soccer and boxing.

During the last four years of the Algerian War of Independence, the National Liberation Front (FLN) formed a soccer team that toured internationally to project an Algerian national identity and to raise awareness of the country's quest for freedom from France. Nnamdi Azikiwe, Nigeria's first president, made major contributions to the development of soccer in his country with his Zik Athletic Clubs (ZAC) and celebrated independence in 1960 by staging matches at the new National Stadium in Lagos. Kwame Nkrumah, the "father of African nationalism," invested resources in football to foster Ghanaian patriotism, which reached a peak after Ghana's victories in the African Cup of Nations in 1963 and 1965. In Zanzibar, the cross-class and intergenerational sociability of soccer also provided a short-term boost to the indigenous nationalist movement.

African governments have used sports not only as an instrument for promoting national unity but also to support Pan-Africanism and to heighten international recognition. The Confédération Africaine de Football (CAF), established in 1957 in Khartoum, preceded the founding of the Organization of African Unity by six years. In 1965, in Brazzaville, the first All-African Games were held, with over three thousand athletes from thirty independent countries participating. Following this event, the Supreme Council for Sport in Africa was set up with a permanent office in Yaoundé Cameroon, with the goal of promoting and coordinating sports across the continent. The potential of sports as a political instrument was shown in the successful boycott of South Africa, which was suspended from world soccer in 1961 and forbidden to compete in the Olympic Games between 1964 and 1992. At the 1976 Montreal Olympics, twenty-two African nations stayed away to protest the inclusion of New Zealand, which continued to have sporting ties with South Africa.

The most important sporting events on the international sports calendar, the Olympic Games and the Soccer World Cup, have witnessed increasingly visible and successful participation by African competitors. The first African to win an Olympic gold medal was Reginald Walker, a white South African, in the 100-meter dash at the 1908 Paris Games. In 1928, A. B. El-Ouafi, an Algerian competing for France, won a gold medal in the marathon, and Egyptians won medals in wrestling, weightlifting, and diving.

Since becoming independent, African countries have greatly increased their participation in the Olympics. In 2004, fifty-three African countries sent teams to the Athens games, and eight countries won a total of thirty-five medals (nine gold, thirteen silver, and thirteen bronze). Overall, African sportsmen and women have won 273.5 Olympic medals (2.1% of total medals awarded), with South Africa (69), Kenya (61), Ethiopia (31), Egypt (22.5), Morocco, and Nigeria (19) leading the way.

Athletes from Kenya, Ethiopia, and Morocco have dominated middle- and long-distance running since Ethiopia's Abebe Bikila won the marathon in 1960, running through the streets of Rome barefooted. In recent years Kenya has monopolized the steeplechase, winning seven of the last ten gold

medals. Morocco's Hicham El Guerrouj won gold in both the 1,500 and 5,000 meters.

African women have also had Olympic success, partially a reflection of increasing female sports participation. In 1984, the first African woman to win an Olympic medal was a Moroccan, Nawal El-Moutawakil, who captured the gold in the 400-meter hurdles. Intense pressure from Muslim fundamentalists later caused her to abandon sports. The Algerian runner Hassiba Boulmerka won the gold medal in the 1500-meter run in the 1992 Barcelona Olympics. Her compatriot Nouria Merah-Benida accomplished the same feat at the 2000 Sydney Games. In 1992 and 2000 an

Hassiba Boulmerka (1968–). In August 1995, the Algerian middle-distance athlete celebrated her gold medal victory for the women's 1500-meter dash, 5th World Track and Field Championships. In 1992, she became the first Algerian to win an Olympic title. AP IMAGES

Ethiopian runner, Derartu Tulu, won the women's 10,000-meters. West African women earned gold medals in the long jump in 1996 (Nigeria's Chioma Ajunwa) and 2004 (Cameroon's Francoise Mbango Etone).

No sport can compete in popularity with soccer, or football. It continues to be played at all levels from spontaneous street games to world-class professional matches. Within the continent, nations compete in major tournaments such as the African Nations Cup and the club competition of the Champions League run by CAF. In global competition, African teams have attracted attention and gained respect with their play in the World Cup. Until 1970, African countries had no right to representation, and an African qualifier competed with an opponent from Asia for a single slot. Egypt represented Africa for the first time in 1934. In 1966, African teams boycotted the preliminaries of the World Cup competition in protest. The visibility that can be won through sports is well illustrated in the case of Cameroon. Once a little-known nation, Cameroon first qualified as one of two countries representing Africa in 1982 and 1990. Its victory over the world champions, Argentina, in the inaugural match was one of the highlights of the 1990 competition, watched by millions all over the world. In the quarterfinals, Cameroon's near upset of England, which defeated the African team in overtime, captured the popular imagination. This success led to demands for further African representation in soccer's premier event.

In 1994 three teams—Cameroon, Morocco, and Nigeria—represented the African continent. Since 1998, Africa has fielded five teams in the 32-team final tournament. Success has also come at youth level, where Nigeria (1985) and Ghana (1991 and 1995) have claimed under seventeen world titles. In 1995 Liberian striker George Weah of Paris St. Germain earned the prestigious FIFA World Player of the Year award. In the 2002 World Cup, Senegal equaled Cameroon's earlier achievements by defeating world champions (and former colonial masters) France in the opening game and reaching the quarterfinals, where they narrowly lost to Turkey in extra-time. Nigeria and Cameroon won Olympic gold medals in soccer in

Roger Milla (1952–). The former Cameroonian football forward poses with South Africa president Thabo Mbeki after presenting the World Cup South Africa 2010 emblem, Berlin, Germany, July 2006. Milla played for the Cameroon national team in three World Cups—1982, 1990, and 1994. ALEXANDER HASSENSTEIN/BONGARTS/GETTY IMAGES

1996 and 2000. The rising prominence of the continent in world soccer will be celebrated in 2010 when South Africa will become the first African nation to host the World Cup finals: the premier sporting event on the planet. Cape Town was one of the four finalists for the 2012 Olympic games.

By 2005, more than 800 Africans played professionally for European clubs. Africans have played in Europe since the 1920s, when Larbi Ben Barek signed for a French team, Olympique Marseilles, and subsequently played for the French national team. African clubs cannot compete with the salaries offered in European leagues. The trend of top athletes in Africa going overseas, where there are greater material rewards and better opportunities for training, can be seen in other sports as well. Stars in athletics and basketball find sports scholarships to attend American colleges. In 1994 a Nigerian, Hakeem Olajuwon of the Houston Rockets, was named Most Valuable Player of the National Basketball Association.

The only other sport, apart from athletics and soccer, in which Africans have had notable international success is boxing. During the colonial period, European sponsors trained and promoted young talent. In 1922 the Senegalese Louis Faal, known as "Battling Siki," became the first African to hold a world boxing title. Nigerians such as Dick Tiger and Hogan "Kid" Bassey and Ghanaian Roy Ankrah won world titles in the 1940s and 1950s. Azumah Nelson, of Ghana, held the world super featherweight title for over a decade in the 1980s and 1990s.

Government and private gencies will continue to promote sports as well as they can, in spite of financial limitations, given the national and international prestige to be gained. When the Cameroonian soccer team qualified for the World Cup for the first time in 1982, that nation's president declared a national holiday. And in 1992, when Frankie Fredericks from Namibia won silver medals in the Olympic 100- and 200-meter, he was met on his arrival home at Windhoek Airport by the prime minister and given a state reception by the president. Talent scouts are identifying young athletes even in primary school, and the future of African sports is full of promise. The main problem for the future development of African sports is financial, largely because there are limited corporate sponsorships available and governments have reduced their funding of sports due to the multitude of more pressing national problems and spending cuts imposed by international financial institutions.

See also **Abidjan; Azikiwe, Benjamin Nnamdi; Brazzaville; Bulawayo; Colonial Policies and Practices; Games; Nkrumah, Francis Nwia Kofi; Popular Culture.**

BIBLIOGRAPHY

Akyeampong, Emmanuel K. "Bukom and the Social History of Boxing in Accra: Warfare and Citizenship in Precolonial Ga Society." *International Journal of African Historical Studies* 35, no. 1 (2002): 39–60.

Alegi, Peter. "Katanga v Johannesburg: A History of the First sub-Saharan African Football Championship, 1949–50." *Kleio* 31 (1999): 55–74.

Alegi, Peter. *Laduma! Soccer, Politics, and Society in South Africa.* Pietermaritzburg: University of KwaZulu-Natal Press, 2004.

Archer, Robert, and Antoine Bouillon. *The South African Game: Sport and Racism.* London: Zed Press, 1982.

Armstrong, Gary, and Richard Giulianotti, eds. *Football in Africa: Conflict, Conciliation and Community.* New York: Palgrave Macmillan, 2004.

Baker, William J., and James A. Mangan, eds. *Sport in Africa: Essays in Social History.* New York: Africana Publishing Co., 1987.

Bale, John, and Joe Sang. *Kenyan Running: Movement Culture, Geography, and Global Change.* London: Frank Cass, 1996.

Boer, Wiebe. "Football, Mobilization and Protest: Nnamdi Azikiwe and the Goodwill Tours of World War II." *Lagos Historical Review* 6 (2006): 39–61.

Darby, Paul. *Africa, Football and FIFA: Politics, Colonialism and Resistance.* London: Frank Cass, 2002.

Deville-Danthu, Bernadette. *Le Sport en Noir et Blanc: Du sport colonial au sport africain dans les anciens territoires français d'Afrique occidentale (1920–1965).* Paris: Harmattan, 1997.

Fair, Laura. "Kickin' It: Leisure, Politics and Football in Colonial Zanzibar, 1900s–1950s." *Africa: Journal of the International African Institute* 67, no. 2 (1997): 224–251.

Martin, Phyllis M. "Colonialism, Youth, and Football in French Equatorial Africa." *International Journal of the History of Sport* 8 (May 1991): 56–71.

Saavedra, Martha. "Football Feminine—Development of the African Game: Senegal, Nigeria and South Africa." *Soccer and Society* 4, no. 2–3 (2003): 225–253.

Schatzberg, Michael. "Soccer, Science, and Sorcery: Causation and African Football." *Afrika Spectrum* 41, no. 3 (2006): 351–369.

Vidacs, Bea. "Football in Cameroon: A Vehicle for the Expansion and Contraction of Identity." *Culture, Sport, Society* 2, no. 3 (1999): 100–117.

PHYLLIS MARTIN
REVISED BY PETER ALEGI

FOOTBALL

In terms of participation levels, attendance figures, and enthusiasm, football is without doubt the number one sport on the African continent. The significance of the game here though extends far beyond the quantitative. Football has, for decades, assumed a significant place in African society and has weaved its way through Africa's colonial and postcolonial history. Although it is difficult to generalize about the spread of football to an area that is as geographically vast and ethnically diverse as Africa, it is possible to identify a number of features that were common to the game's development throughout the continent. Football in Africa is clearly a legacy of European colonialism. The European education system that was invariably transported to African colonial societies in the late nineteenth and early twentieth centuries was central to the game's early growth. The schools that were established for the African elite were especially important because these elites, eager for the higher status that came with cultural imitation of their colonial *masters*, enthusiastically embraced the game. Thus participation in football in this period was largely dependent upon privileged contacts with European and hence the game developed as a somewhat elitist enterprise.

Opportunities for participation soon became widespread though with football's downward diffusion to the indigenous working classes. The destruction of traditional agricultural communities and massive migration into rapidly expanding industrialized, urban centers in the first four decades of the twentieth century were crucial in this regard. In this context, Africans experienced the game through contact with missionary schools, European settlers, traders, soldiers, and educators. In some of the more remote African towns and villages that came under the influence of Europeans, football developed in a relatively unplanned, haphazard fashion. However, in the larger industrial centers such as those within French North, West and Equatorial Africa, the Belgian Congo and Colonial Zimbabwe, European colonialists utilized their hegemonic position to impose football for their own ends. Alongside the belief, rooted in the cult of athleticism in the English Public School, that sport could instill positive character traits, football had been identified by European, particularly British, social reformers as having a cathartic function. Thus, in colonial Africa's crowded urban centers amidst simmering undercurrents and open expressions of resentment over the injustices of colonial rule, the game was used by the colonial authorities for the purposes or

minimizing any tendencies towards social disorder. The subsequent promotion of the game not only encouraged conformity to colonial rule but also seriously undermined indigenous sporting and cultural traditions.

What is fascinating about the role of football in African society during the colonial period is that whilst it undoubtedly served as a tool of cultural imperialism, when the game was diffused downwards to the laboring classes it came to represent a site for generating resistance to colonialism and promoting nationalist aspirations. The role of Africanized football as a conduit for anticolonial sentiment was evident throughout the continent but it was perhaps most apparent in Algeria. Here the Front de Libération Nationale (FLN) established a 'Revolutionary XI' football team in 1958 that toured the African continent agitating for Algerian and indeed, African independence. Such was the importance of football and its practical contribution to mobilizing African national consciousness that the game was used in a direct fashion by various heads of newly independent African states, such as Kenneth Kaunda in Zamia and Kwame Nkrumah in Ghana, for the purposes of nation building.

The dichotomy of football's role as a bulwark of cultural imperialism and a source of resistance during the colonial period and its immediate aftermath was also apparent within the international governance of the game and this did much to shape football's development in postcolonial Africa. Prior to the 1960s, Africa was regarded largely as an irrelevance by the world game's European dominated governing body, the Fédération Internationale de Football Association (FIFA). However, the formation of the Confédération Africaine de Football (CAF) in 1957 by four of the five independent African nations at that time (Ethiopia, Sudan, South Africa, and Egypt) was hugely significant in providing those countries that were on the verge of or had just acquired independence with a potent stage in which to respond to and root their struggle against FIFA's European bias. Thus, alongside membership of INGO's such as the United Nations, newly independent African nations immediately established national football federations, joined CAF and sought member status within FIFA.

It was perfectly reasonable for these nations to expect that their membership of FIFA, an organization that espoused philosophies of global fraternity, would allow them adequate opportunity to register their presence and passion for football on the international stage. However, this was not to be and until the election of the Brazilian, João Havelange, as FIFA president in 1974, African aspirations within international football were routinely frustrated. Since Havelange's election though, the African game has benefited from a more benevolent outlook on the part of FIFA. More places have been granted at the World Cup finals and on FIFA's committees, funding has been made available and development plans put in place. From the 1980s onwards, African nations have made great strides in the international game, both on the field of play and in the game's corridors of power. The two clearest examples of this are the fact that Africa will host its first World Cup in 2010 (South Africa) and the prediction, on the part of renowned figures in the international game such as Pele, that it will not be long before an African nation wins the World Cup.

Despite these advances African football, both domestically and internationally, continues to face major obstacles. Although the value of football in terms of nation building and creating social cohesion was recognized by African governments in the immediate aftermath of colonialism and was funded accordingly, in the context of massive foreign debts, impoverishment, and ethnic conflict, it has become increasingly difficult to divert scarce resources into the game. The domestic scene in particular has suffered and when is added into the equation the fact that the continent's best playing talent is regularly exported to Europe, the problems confronting club football become stark. Football in Africa has retained its status as the most popular sport in the continent despite such difficulties. However, unless issues such as corruption, excessive levels of government interference, poor facilities and infrastructure, violence surrounding the game, and the loss of its most talented players to the highest European bidder are tackled then this may not remain the case for too much longer.

See also **Colonial Policies and Practices; Games; Kaunda, Kenneth; Nkrumah, Francis Nwia Kofi; Production Strategies: Agriculture; United Nations.**

BIBLIOGRAPHY

Armstrong, Gary, and Richard Giulianotti. *Football in Africa: Conflict, Conciliation and Community.* London: Palgrave Macmillan, 2004.

Darby, Paul. "Football, Colonial Doctrine and Indigenous Resistance: Mapping the Political Persona of FIFA's African Constituency." *Culture, Sport, Society* 3, no. 1 (2000): 61–87.

Darby, Paul. *Africa, Football and FIFA: Politics, Colonialism and Resistance.* London and Portland, OR: Frank Cass, 2002.

Darby, Paul. "Africa, the FIFA Presidency and the Governance of World Football: 1974, 1998 and 2002." *Africa Today* 50, 1 (2003): 3–24.

Sugden, John, and Alan Tomlinson. *FIFA and the Contest for World Football: Who Rules the People's Game.* Cambridge, U.K.: Polity Press, 1998.

PAUL DARBY

STANLEY, HENRY MORTON (1841–1904).

Sir Henry Morton Stanley was born in Denbigh, North Wales, to John Rowlands and Elizabeth Parry. Abandoned by his mother, he grew up in the Saint Asaph workhouse where he remained until the age of fifteen. His account in his *Autobiography* (1909) of ill-treatment there and of a dramatic escape is almost entirely false. Not finding work locally, he embarked for America, arriving at New Orleans in 1859. There he was befriended by a merchant, Henry Stanley, whose name he adopted, later adding "Morton." John Rowlands, now Stanley, led an unsettled life as a soldier on both sides in the American Civil War, a sailor in the U.S. Navy and in merchant ships, and a traveler in Turkey, eventually coming into his own as a reporter in the Indian wars on the American frontier. In 1867 he served as a correspondent for the *New York Herald*, covering the British Expeditionary Force in Ethiopia on its campaign to free hostages held by the Ethiopian emperor at Magdala, the fall of which he was the first to report. He was later assigned to a similar position with the British in Ashanti (now part of Ghana) from 1873–1874.

Stanley's transformation from roving reporter to African explorer came when he succeeded in relieving David Livingstone, the Scottish missionary-explorer adrift in Central Africa. In November 1871, Stanley, by sheer determination, broke through to utter the famous greeting: "Dr. Livingstone, I

African explorer Sir Henry Morton Stanley (1841–1904).
Stanley became a Knight Grand Cross of the Order of the Bath in 1899 in recognition of his service to the British empire in Africa. © BETTMANN/CORBIS

Schnitzer (1840–1892, a.k.a. Emin Pasha), governor of the Equatoria province of the Anglo-Egyptian Sudan (on the upper Nile), who had been stranded by hostile forces on Lake Albert. Stanley retired in 1890. In 1895 he was elected to the British Parliament.

The ruthlessness with which Stanley drove his way through Africa earned him the dislike of many of his contemporaries, while his abrasive manners and the legacy of his deprived childhood and adolescence added to his unpopularity. He has since, however, been more fairly assessed as one of Africa's most successful explorers.

See also **Livingstone, David; Schnitzer, Eduard; Travel and Exploration: European (Since 1800).**

BIBLIOGRAPHY

Biernam, John. *Dark Safari: The Life behind the Legend of Henry Morton Stanley.* New York: Knopf, 1990.

Hall, Richard. *Stanley: An Adventurer Explored.* Boston: Houghton Mifflin, 1975.

McLynn, Frank. *The Making of an African Explorer.* New York: Cooper Square Press, 2001.

Stanley, Henry Morton. *The Autobiography of Sir Henry Morton Stanley.* London: S. Low, Marston, 1909.

DOROTHY MIDDLETON

presume?" He recounted the expedition in *How I Found Livingstone* (1872). The two men became firm friends, and on Stanley's return from Ashanti, and hearing of Livingstone's death in Africa, Stanley resolved to continue the older man's explorations. Stanley's expedition of 1874–1877 crossed the continent from east to west by way of Lake Victoria (confirmed as the source of the Nile), across to Lake Tanganyika, and thence north to the river Congo (Zaire), whose course he traced to the sea. In *Through the Dark Continent* (1878), he described the journey.

From 1879 to 1884, Stanley served King Léopold II of Belgium (1835–1909), who had virtually taken possession of the Congo Basin as his Congo Independent State. While supervising the construction of a railway up the falls from the lower to the upper river, Stanley earned the nickname Bula Mutari (Breaker of Rocks). As recorded in his *In Darkest Africa* (1890), Stanley from 1887–1889 led a west-to-east expedition across the continent from the Congo mouth to Zanzibar, to rescue Eduard

STATE FORMATION. *See* **Political Systems: States.**

STEVENS, SIAKA (1905–1988). Siaka Probyn Stevens campaigned on a platform to end corruption and promote democracy in Sierra Leone, but his tenures as prime minister (1967 and 1968–1971) and president (1971–1985) were characterized by attempted coups, violence, onerous national debt, and persistent charges of blatant governmental misconduct and fraud.

A professional trade unionist, he entered the Protectorate Assembly as the workers' representative in 1946. Five years later, he was elected to the Legislative Council and in 1952 became a minister in the first nationalist-controlled government. After various contentious political alliances, in

President of Sierra Leone Siaka Stevens (1905–1988).
Stevens served as chairman of the Organization of African
Unity from July 1980 to June 1981 and helped create the Mano
River Union, an economic committee for issues among Sierra
Leone, Liberia, and Guinea. © ALAIN NOGUES/CORBIS SYGMA

1960 he founded the All People's Congress (APC),
which he headed for the rest of his political career.
Although it won the 1967 general election,
Stevens's first tenure as prime minister ended
abruptly when a military junta overthrew his government. The following year another military government, the National Reformation Council
(NRC), intervened to reappoint him as prime minister, a post he held until April 1971 when he
introduced a republican constitution and became
executive president. In 1978, his government set
up a one-party constitution that ended overt opposition parties. Although he opened the ranks of the
APC to all sections of the community and encouraged power sharing among ethnic groups, academics,

clerics, businessmen, and traditional rulers, he did not
hesitate to employ repressive measures to ensure
political centralization and personal control. He
resigned voluntarily in 1985, but two years later he
was placed under house arrest on suspicion of participating in a coup plot.

See also **Sierra Leone: History and Politics.**

BIBLIOGRAPHY

Cartwright, John R. *Political Leadership in Sierra Leone.*
London: Croom Helm, 1978.

Conteh-Morgan, Earl, and Mac Dixon-Fyle. *Sierra Leone at
the End of the Twentieth Century: History, Politics, and
Society.* New York: Peter Lang, 1999.

Stevens, Siaka Probyn. *What Life Has Taught Me.* Bucking-
hamshire, U.K.: Kensal Press, 1984.

LaRay Denzer

STIMULANTS AND INTOXICANTS

This entry includes the following articles:
OVERVIEW
ALCOHOL

OVERVIEW

Stimulants and intoxicants are used in Africa in a
variety of ways: recreationally, functionally, cere-
monially, and medicinally. Their consumption is
often a source of tension, as people debate the
morality of being under their influence and view
them through the prism of the war on drugs. Some
substances have been consumed on the continent
for centuries, while others are recent imports.

Alcohol is the continent's most widely used
intoxicant. It is also the best documented. Its
social, cultural, and economic importance has made
it the focus of much research. Bottled beers, wines,
and spirits form a considerable proportion of alcohol consumed, although locally brewed and distilled beverages made from grain (often millet),
honey, fruit, and the sap of palm trees account for
a far larger proportion. Illicitly distilled liquor
(such as *chang'aa* in Kenya) has great notoriety
on account of dangerous adulterants added to
strengthen it.

Cannabis is cultivated and consumed throughout the continent, but has not been subject to the same degree of research as alcohol. Whereas its use in North Africa is of great antiquity, its paths of diffusion into other parts of the continent are not exactly known, although it seems that caravans venturing into Central Africa from the east may have played a significant role in spreading its use. By the late nineteenth century cannabis had taken on great significance for people such as the Luba (the Democratic Republic of Congo), amongst whom a social movement known as *bene diamba* (children of hemp) had developed. In Southern Africa—where it is known as *dagga*—reports indicate that cannabis has been consumed for over four centuries. In contrast, it is suggested that its use in West Africa began later, with former soldiers bringing back the habit after service in South Asia during World War II. In the early twenty-first century, despite its illegality, cannabis was cheap and consumed (mainly smoked alone or with tobacco and other drugs, but sometimes dissolved in spirits and then drunk) by people from all social strata. However, cannabis is not just a recreational drug, it is also used functionally in physically demanding work.

Two indigenous stimulants are khat in East Africa and kola in West Africa. Khat—the stimulant leaves and stems of *Catha edulis*—is associated with the Horn of Africa, being consumed in Somalia, Somaliland, and Djibouti, as well as throughout the Somali diaspora. The substance is usually chewed and has a long history in Ethiopia (where some believe it was first domesticated), and also in Kenya, where it has cultural resonance in the Nyambene Hills, the main production zone. Its cultivation and use stretch to the Eastern Cape and Madagascar. Although legal in some African countries, khat is illegal in Tanzania and Eritrea, and was once subject to legal restrictions in Kenya and Somalia. Like cannabis, khat is used both recreationally and functionally, being especially prized by long-distance drivers and nightwatchmen. In West Africa, the mildly stimulating kola nuts (kola comes in many varieties, *Cola nitida* being the most important) are intensively cultivated in a few regions such as Ghana, where kola once helped economically sustain the Asante kingdom. Kola is a substance with great symbolic, as well as functional, value, forming part of bride-price in some

societies. Demand for kola developed beyond West Africa in the nineteenth and early twentieth centuries, famously being used in Coca-Cola, although the demand for kola has since dwindled.

Other substances with a long history on the continent include *iboga* (*Tabernanthe iboga*) and *paan*. Iboga was used to induce visions in the *Bwiti* religion of the Fang of West-Central Africa. In the fourteenth century, Ibn Battuta mentioned the use of Paan (a mixture of areca nut, betel leaf, tobacco, and a variety of spices) in Mogadishu. Its use was still popular in early twenty-first century along the East African coast. Also, the importance of tea, coffee, and tobacco should not be underestimated, despite their familiarity: in Ethiopia and Kenya coffee is used ritually by Borana in *buna qalla*, a sacrificing of coffee beans.

The use of nonindigenous stimulants and intoxicants has grown in Africa, and there is alarm over the consumption of hard drugs like cocaine and heroin. Africa has become an important transit point for the shipment of such drugs to Europe and North America, and consumption has spilled over into African societies. A 1999 report by the United Nations found cocaine and heroin used in all ten African countries surveyed. The synthetic sedative methaqualone—mandrax—is particularly popular in South Africa (often smoked with cannabis), and Leggett (2003) provides a vivid account of its use. Other drugs familiar in Europe and North America such as ecstasy, amphetamines, and LSD are not especially common in Africa, with the exception of South Africa where they are consumed in nightclubs. Such substances are available in big cities like Nairobi, however, often to satisfy the demand of tourists, and it seems possible that their use will spread.

See also **Agriculture: Beginnings and Development; Transportation: Caravan.**

BIBLIOGRAPHY

Abaka, Edmund. *Kola Is God's Gift: Agricultural Production, Export Initiatives and the Kola Industry of Asante and the Gold Coast, c.1820–1950.* Oxford, U.K.: James Currey, 2005.

Akyeampong, Emmanuel. *Drink, Power, and Cultural Change. A Social History of Alcohol in Ghana, c. 1800 to Recent Times.* Oxford, U.K.: Heinemann, 1996.

Fabian, Johannes. *Out of Our Minds: Reason and Madness in the Exploration of Central Africa.* Berkeley: University of California Press, 2000.

Leggett, Ted. *Rainbow Vice: The Drugs and Sex Industries in the New South Africa.* London: Zed Books, 2003.

United Nations (Office of Drugs Control and Crime Prevention). *The Drug Nexus in Africa.* Vienna: United Nations, 1999.

Willis, Justin. *Potent Brews: A Social History of Alcohol in East Africa 1850–1999.* Oxford, U.K.: James Currey, 2002.

NEIL CARRIER

ALCOHOL

The production and consumption of alcoholic drinks has a deep history across the African continent, probably dating at least to the introduction of grains more than 2,000 years ago. Before the expansion of international trade into Africa, the production of alcohol was generally the province of small-scale farmers, and the presentation and consumption of alcoholic beverages were tightly interwoven into the economic, political, and ritual worlds of societies and were dependent on the structures and cycles of agricultural production. People produced and consumed a wide range of beers and wines, depending on local climates and crops, and substantial amounts of labor and agricultural produce were diverted to alcohol production.

The fermenting processes varied depending on the raw materials utilized. Millet, sorghum, and increasingly corn beers were manufactured, typically by women, through labor-intensive processes that involved the germination of some of the grain to stimulate fermentation. The result was often thick porridge-like drinks. Elsewhere, sugarcane juice, fruits, or honey were fermented to produce thinner beverages. In coastal areas, the tapping of palm trees to produce wine was a ubiquitous practice. It is impossible to estimate the levels of consumption of these drinks, but the potential for the abuse of alcohol was very much constrained by its relatively low alcoholic content (rarely more than 4% or 5%) and limited availability—and by the social controls governing its consumption.

Records dating from the eleventh century of the Sahelian kingdom of Ghana include references to alcoholic drinks, as do numerous texts that describe eighteenth- and nineteenth-century states and societies. When travelers, missionaries, and traders arrived at the capital of the Buganda kingdom in East Africa in the middle of the nineteenth century they found the royal court awash in beer. Similarly, visitors to the Zulu kingdom in South Africa in the 1820s observed long lines of young women carrying offerings of alcoholic drinks to the king's residence. Accounts drawn from a wide range of societies implicate alcoholic drinks in the central rituals of community life and state power and suggest that drinking was among the most common and important forms of socializing.

Scholars have tended to characterize drinking in precolonial African societies as an "integrated" activity in which drinking practices reinforced social and political norms and alcohol abuse was unknown. Some scholars have speculated that drinking parties provided opportunities for individuals to speak out on issues in ways that in other circumstances would be threatening or offensive. Yet there is considerable evidence to associate alcohol consumption with disorder and with the expropriation of labor and vital foodstuffs.

Only men with command over very substantial amounts of female labor could produce grain beers on a large scale, and even then production depended on the availability of grain stores and labor. Palm wine was also generally produced on a limited scale, but it was available throughout the year and tapping the trees was men's work. Controls on drinking tended to focus on restrictions on consumption by women and young men rather than on strictures against excessive individual consumption.

The perishability of grain beers and palm wine encouraged styles of drinking common in rural agricultural societies in many parts of the world. Because such drinks had to be consumed immediately or be wasted, neighbors and friends would generally be invited to share a household's wine or beer and would be encouraged to stay until all the liquor was gone. The result was ideas of moderation or temperance that differed sharply form those that developed in the West. Whereas Europeans tended to drink relatively small amounts of alcohol on a daily basis, Africans tended to drink larger amounts less frequently. And if Europeans took pride in their ability not to show the effects of alcohol, Africans generally saw mild inebriation as the point of drinking. In these circumstances drinkers often required relatively little alcohol to feel and show the effects. Observing such drinking through the lens of European drinking practice, European travelers thus tended to exaggerate the amount of drinking that went on in many African societies. In the nineteenth and twentieth centuries, as the growth of liquor markets made alcohol much more widely and continually available, these traditional drinking styles probably supported excessive drinking.

The expansion of European trade along the coasts of Africa and later into the interior transformed alcohol production and consumption. Trading ships always carried various types of distilled liquor, unknown in Africa at that time. This rum, whiskey, and later gin, were relatively minor commodities during the era of the slave trade, but these drinks were extremely important in the facilitation of commerce. In West Africa and in Angola, a rising demand for rum made this drink an increasingly important consumer item at least along the coast and its hinterland. Distilled liquors, if undiluted, had much higher alcoholic content than fermented drinks and they did not spoil. As a result, they could be stored as capital and to display wealth and they could be traded over long distances.

In the nineteenth century, the mass production of American rum and especially German and Dutch gin coupled with the development of steamship transport made cheap imported spirits increasingly affordable in West and central Africa. Many West African communities, notably in present-day Ghana, gradually integrated imported spirits into their ritual and social activities. Moreover, during the 1800s the colonies that the British had planted along the western African coast became increasingly dependent on this trade as a source of revenue. The spread and revitalization of Islam across the interior of West Africa and elsewhere on the continent in some instances challenged the spread of these new drinks and encouraged the expansion of consumption of a different narcotic, kola; similarly, missionary Christianity came to view the so-called liquor traffic as a blight and saw liquor consumption as a powerful impediment to the extension of European power and Christian

adherence. A powerful movement against the liquor trade developed in Britain and West Africa during the last decades of the nineteenth century, resulting in a series of international agreements, beginning with the 1890 Brussels Convention and culminating in the 1919 Treaty of St. Germain-en-Laye. The powers agreed in these treaties to increase duties sharply on imported spirits and ban their spread into areas where the trade was not established. The cheapest imports were banned entirely in 1919 as was any local distillation.

These measures did not apply to South Africa, where there was a long-established wine and spirits industry. Persistent overproduction led wine growers there to focus on sales of cheap liquor to black consumers, and brandy known as Cape Smoke became an important commodity in the development of trade into the interior and in the employment of agricultural workers. Industrialization gave the temperance cause much greater urgency, as prohibition advocates linked alcohol consumption by African workers to labor indiscipline and social disorder. The result was draconian restrictions which permitted Africans to drink only grain beer and gave the state control over its sale. Employers often opposed these regulations, preferring to manage alcohol sales in ways that permitted them to maintain greater control over workers. Under "Durban systems" (named for the city where the approach originated) maintained across South Africa and British East and Central Africa, municipalities relied on the revenue from their alcohol monopolies to provide minimal services to Africans and to finance residential segregation. These restrictions were widely flouted, however, and illegal brewing and distilling became major sources of income for the urban women who dominated the trade. In British West Africa and in Portuguese, French, and Belgian colonies, administrations depended heavily on alcohol revenues but imposed few restrictions on consumption of liquor other than spirits. In these dependencies illegal distillation became a highly profitable element of the informal economy.

After World War II, opposition to discriminatory legislation led gradually to reforms that legalized African consumption of all kinds of alcohol. Nationalist parties targeted the humiliating racial distinctions enshrined in alcohol regulations, while women producers—such as those in Cato Manor, South Africa, in 1959—fought state efforts to force them out of business. Independence brought an explosion in alcohol production and consumption, with states remaining heavily dependent on revenues derived from heavily regulated and often nationalized industries. Until the 1970s and 1980s, excessive consumption of alcohol had been conceived almost exclusively as a social problem linked to urbanization. The disease concept of alcoholism common in the West has attracted only limited acceptance. Across the continent, companies involved in the industrial production of beer and other kinds of alcohol (whether state controlled or private) were among the most profitable in local economies. The economic importance of brewing industries in particular has made efforts to restrict consumption politically sensitive, although it is important to note that in many areas traditional, locally produced drinks continue to dominate consumption.

In the 1990s private capital became increasingly powerful in the liquor industry, with South African Breweries emerging first as a regional giant and then establishing itself as a global corporate player. Concerns about alcohol emerge periodically in connection with drinking and driving and consumption of adulterated illegal drinks. If state efforts to control destructive drinking have been sporadic and half-hearted, temperance positions continue to draw strong support, especially among Muslims and evangelical Christians. They have made little impact, however, on the prominence of drinking in social life.

See also **Agriculture: Beginings and Development; Labor: Conscript and Forced.**

BIBLIOGRAPHY

Akyeampong, Emmanuel. *Drink, Power and Cultural Change: A Social History of Alcohol in Ghana, c. 1800 to Recent Times.* Portsmouth, NH: Heinemann, 1996.

Ambler, Charles. "Alcohol and the Slave Trade in West Africa, 15th–19th Centuries." In *Drugs, Labor, and Colonial Expansion*, ed. Daniel Bradburd and William Jankowiak. Tucson: University of Arizona Press, 2003.

Bryceson, Deborah Fahy. *Alcohol in Africa: Mixing Business, Pleasure, and Politics.* Portsmouth, NH: Heinemann, 2002.

Colson, E., and T. Scudder. *For Prayer and Profit: The Ritual, Economic and Social Importance of Beer in Gwembe District, Zambia, 1950–1982.* Stanford: Stanford University Press, 1988.

Crush, Jonathan, and Charles Ambler, eds. *Liquor and Labor in Southern Africa.* Athens: Ohio University Press, 1992.

Curto, José C. *Enslaving Spirits: The Portuguese–Brazilian Alcohol Trade at Luanda and its Hinterland, c. 1550–1830.* Boston: Brill, 2004.

Partanen, Juha. *Sociability and Intoxication: Alcohol and Drinking in Kenya, Africa, and the Modern World.* Helsinki, Finland: Finnish Foundation for Alcohol Studies, 1991.

Willis, Justin. *Potent Brews: A Social History of Alcohol in East Africa, 1850–1999.* Athens: Ohio University Press, 2002.

CHARLES AMBLER

STONE AGE. *See* **Archaeology and Prehistory: Stone Age Societies.**

STORYTELLING. *See* **Literature: Oral.**

STRATIFICATION, SOCIAL. It is commonly held that sub-Saharan Africa has no class system, that emergent modern elites constitute a single class. Yet some deny that a single class can exist in the absence of a class system. Modern class in Africa is an expression of capitalist penetration, its neocolonial form overlaying its colonial foundations. It has been said that "the emergence of class comes to dominate history" (Vincent 1982), and that "Westernization shapes class consciousness" (Kuper 1965).

Rwanda retains elements of a caste system, which has become a source of intense conflict and borders on genocide; Burundi approximates the Rwanda situation, as neighboring parts of Uganda, Democratic Republic of the Congo, and Tanzania once did. Physical differences were accentuated by selective breeding of both humans and cattle. Limited economic surplus restricted further elaboration. Modern conditions rendered the caste system untenable.

Some regard South African whites, Indians, Coloureds, and Africans as constituting a caste system, though one lacking full legitimacy. The classifications satisfy the minimum definition of caste in ascriptive membership, endogamy, clear ranking, and restricted mobility between groups, which tend also to occupy different areas of the economy. However, they lack a common system of values, and most non-whites deny the legitimacy of the caste system dominated by them. Others classify South Africa not as a caste system but as a plural society, a term that unfortunately suggests parallelism with a hint of equality in this devastatingly unequal society. The position of whites and other foreigners, such as Indians and Lebanese, approximated caste status in colonial territories but is now substantially blurred.

CLASS

Ideological and theoretical differences complicate the delineation of African classes. In North America and Europe these can be debated against a relatively agreed body of facts, but in Africa the facts are often recently emergent, subject to rapid change, and inadequately researched and known, so that consensus is more elusive. Furthermore, exogenous Western institutions, programs, and policies dominate Africa, although traditional institutions also survive and may evoke the deepest loyalties. It is difficult to give a coherent and valid presentation of modern African stratification, which is still in an inchoate stage of becoming. Current uncertainties, contradictions, and confusions may never sort themselves out and crystallize into a clear system, because new forces of change, differentiation, and contradiction are constantly being added on top of the old. For many, the likely developments seem clear, but there are radical disagreements, and fundamentally divergent directions of change are possible. Most comment has dwelt upon class consciousness and its absence, encouraged by the insistence of the elites themselves that Africa is classless.

The contemporary state of social stratification in most countries of sub-Saharan Africa may be described as an expanding elite, rather centralized and sufficiently cohesive to be termed a class, unless the existence of one class without a system of classes is excluded. Over against it is the inchoate mass of peasants, workers, migrants, shopkeepers and small businessmen, clerks, minor bureaucrats and schoolteachers, soldiers, and police; they lack a consciously unifying common interest but harbor sullen resentment for the broken promises about the advantages of independence and development,

and over the increasing gulf between them and the elite.

Building upon colonial precedents, African governments constructed or extended large housing estates, often with large grants of international aid, for particular categories of the urban population. In so doing, they committed themselves to emphasizing what inevitably became official criteria of rank and status in their fiercely contested allocation, and thus created extensive local systems of social stratification. The elite may be less cohesive than in the 1960s, when it consisted of small numbers of men, mainly from the same exclusive schools and universities. Since then it has grown much larger, more diverse and amorphous, battered this way and that by the divisions and enmities generated by civil wars, military coups, one-party governments, and ethnic favoritism.

The term system is inappropriate because there are no complete or coherent systems, nor are any likely in the foreseeable future. Emergent African systems are constantly bedeviled and confused by external shifts of policy, practice, and goals utterly beyond their control, as well as by global forces of which no agreed understanding or control is possible. African states are not puppets, and it suits Western interests to humor them, fostering the illusion that they have more autonomy and freedom of movement than is actually the case. When it comes down to it, they must bow to Western interests. The brutal Nigerian regime could thumb its nose at North America and Europe over the infamous case of the executed dissident, Ken Saro-Wiwa only because the most powerful material interests involved were those of the Shell corporation, which preferred profit to principle. Here Nigerian power was an expression of Western abdication of human and democratic values in favor of material vested interests.

THE SUPERCLASS STRUCTURE

It is through the chain of such paradoxical incidents, which constantly erupt in unexpected places and surprising forms, that the lineaments of the world power structure that dominates African and other poor nations are etched. Classes may only be defined in terms of power. The world power structure constitutes the framework of a shadowy and still amorphous global class structure, which shows more signs of growing crystallization and clarification than do the class structures of African nations. Though far from mutual self-awareness, two superclasses are clearly defined by their contrasting access to global means of production.

They consist essentially of those who own, control, and operate the dominant institutions and organizations of the global political economy on the one hand, and those who have to endure their activities on the other. However, the latter themselves occupy a similar position in the local, national arena.

The global superclass comprises the owners and high executives of the transnational corporations and conglomerates, who are all indirectly linked to one another around the world and possess deep common interests and an element of common culture, although they may also find themselves in conflict. The largest banks are obviously included. Hence by personal as well as by institutional ties the network incorporates the higher echelons of the World Bank, International Monetary Fund, United Nations and other major international agencies, and also top civil servants, ministers, and politicians of the major powers. These link at the local level with their less exalted counterparts in African countries. The latter operate as hosts to the former on their peripatetic visits and count as social equals of the former on the local, national scene. But their average wealth and power is far less, and the spatial spread of their influence far more circumscribed. They form the top layer of the local, national status and class system but the lower layer of the global system, along with all other representatives of local, national elites. They are a superclass of lower order in relation to the local status systems of the various ethnic groups and regions.

The global superclass structure impinges upon Africa through the international bureaucracies of innumerable nongovernmental organizations, from the giant World Bank and International Monetary Fund to the national aid missions and down to the smallest expatriate charitable and religious aid organizations, to which must be added the diplomatic corps and the booming commercial bureaucracies of the multinational conglomerates. Although vast in range of status and wealth, all members of the expatriate elite have to be recognized as a permanent element in the stratification of African nations, despite their high individual turnover. They are at the same time local representatives of an emergent world class and partially integrated members of the local dominant class in the country where they sojourn. They may have no formal power, but through their numbers and dispersion they exert ubiquitous influence. Their standards of living, elite housing, and ample transport represent conspicuous consumption in the African context and position them firmly in the upper stratum.

Many of them interact with local African elites on closer terms of informal socialization than did the old colonial cadres. Relations of sexual intimacy and marriage between expatriates and Africans are more frequent and acceptable. They are agents, overseers, and advisers in the disbursement of much of the foreign aid that enables African countries to survive. Their cultural influence promotes an unintentional but ineluctable Westernization of general styles of life and behavior, accelerating the erosion of African culture and institutions. The ever-spreading, ever-tightening global net of communications media instills in them a more and more clearly implied common culture, making them insidiously attractive as models to local populations, however far out of reach in reality. They contribute significantly to processes of role formation, transformation, and stratification. They are integral to society, although they usually are not citizens, they do not vote, and they have no local ancestors and probably no permanent local descendants.

In this and throughout the political economy, Africa is sucked into the globalizing dual structure of the superwealthy dominant nations and the superdeprived poor nations they exploit. African elites are enticed to play a double game, co-opted into subaltern, yet temptingly profitable, participation in the global network, though indissolubly tied by cultural roots and political destiny to the African homelands from which they come and to which they are, in this context, structural traitors. Thus, in the nascent worldwide two-class system of rich and poor, the rich lean down to participate profitably through their agents in the poor countries, whereas the leaders of the latter lean up to participate minimally and less profitably in the emergent global upper class of the rich countries.

CLASS AND AFRICAN POLITICAL ECONOMY

The whole process could be summarized as phases in the progressive penetration of capitalism. This is manifested especially in the commoditization of goods and relationships, urbanization, and the transformation of peasants into proletarians, accentuated by excessive population growth and the process of deindustrialization. It transfers the least desirable, most polluting forms of industrial labor from rich to poor countries and moves production plants to Africa to exploit cheap land and labor and lax tax and human protection laws. This transfer is accelerated in innumerable ways by the media-communications revolution.

Potential classes are defined by their relations to the means of production. African peasants and smallholders relate to the land as direct producers, often spending much of their lives as migrant workers in the capitalist labor system. Large-scale farmers, agribusinesses, and mines—usually in the hands of expatriate capitalists—demand a growing class of capitalist workers who are increasingly full-time rather than migrant. Cash crops relate the land indirectly to buyers, traders, processors, brokers, and exploiters, including the budding core of the indigenous middle class and expatriate employees of capitalist firms. Cash received by growers flows to relatives and small shopkeepers, who relay it to the government in taxes, and to wholesalers and commerce generally. The relatively low productivity of the economy as a whole, with much of its profit siphoned off to expatriate business, yields a low surplus that restricts the growth of the indigenous middle class.

The incoherence of the class system is particularly due to the fact that the upper middle class, which necessarily gives character, quality, and definition to the class system as a whole, was in Africa entirely of foreign origin and has, to a significant extent, remained so. There are numerous successful and wealthy African businessmen, but they have not been able to take over the commanding heights of their economies that still remain at critical points within the tentacles of multinationals and globalizing conglomerates, as well as the international politico-economic control system. Hence stems the importance of the political elites in the emergent class system, because they have been permitted to take over the governments of African countries completely, at least in a formal sense.

ETHNICITY

It is well known that African peoples are divided into thousands of different ethnic groups, some of them contrived, but most of them derived, through many profound transformations, from the communities that were the largest social entities known by Africans before the colonial era. Called tribes by colonialists, they have been blamed for many of Africa's difficulties in modernization and development, including the lack of a clear-cut class system. Effective classes could not develop because ethnic ties cut across them. If persons from different classes belong to the same ethnic group, to which they owe profound loyalties, class solidarities are compromised. Therefore, most commentaries explore the extent of class-consciousness rather than class action.

Large ethnic groups begin to develop class structures within themselves but cannot generate national class structures (as Ganda-led parties have constantly shown in Uganda, or Yoruba- and Hausa-led parties in Nigeria). More likely they provoke civil war. African elites are ethnically tainted and distorted by the head of state in power who displays favoritism toward his own ethnic group in appointments to every kind of office and position of power, influence, and profit. Supposedly impartial appointments boards provide little protection.

The recent history of many African countries can be read off as a succession of such debilitating favoritisms. Uganda has had Lango, Ganda, Nubi, and Ankole or Western favoritism. Kenya has passed from Gikuyu to Kalenjin favoritism. Civil wars and strife in Angola, Namibia, Mozambique, Democratic Republic of the Congo, Nigeria, Chad, Cameroon, Bénin, Liberia, Sierra Leone, and nearly everywhere else in Africa have been based on ethnic coalitions.

Compounding ethnic and racial prejudices, both black and white, South Africa was not only conquered and colonized, but received a complete white class structure: not only white rulers, entrepreneurs, and industrialists linked to international capitalism from the start, but white *petit bourgeois* shopkeepers, clerks, police, army, and civil service, as well as white mining workers. Here the landowning class, waning in Europe, flourished through Afrikaner and other white farmers as it did in Rhodesia and Kenya.

The South African ethnoracial castes could be fairly neatly ordered hierarchically in public behavior and official institutions. But although economically differentiated up to a point, there were major overlapping parallels; whites in top government, business, industrial, and professional positions, as well as landowner farmers, wine producers, and petit bourgeois and workers; Indians with their own parallel businesses and professions overlapping the whites in size and wealth, plus their own petit bourgeois and poor workers; Coloureds occupying interstitial positions in lower-middle class and working-class service jobs, but overlapping as schoolteachers and petit bourgeois in their own areas; Africans, deprived of most of their land, condemned to shift divided families between impoverished rural reserves and dilapidated urban slums, members of the agricultural, industrial, and commercial labor forces, with those who won education against heavy odds and struggled for coveted bourgeois status as teachers and businesspeople. These parallels hardly justify the plural society classification, which smacks of the separate but equal fallacy. "In some ways the entire White group is a bourgeoisie in relation to Africans" (Kuper 1965).

The formal reconciliation between Nelson Mandela and F. W. De Klerk brought this execrable system to an official termination. The economic facts of colonial and apartheid class live on, however, as do the smoldering resentments and prejudices. No less than the rest of Africa, but in a contrary sense, South Africa struggles to dismantle an imperialist, racist class system as the rest of sub-Saharan Africa moves blindly toward a more open but increasingly unequal class system of its own. The long struggle against apartheid, of which the African National Congress under heroic leadership became the dominant force, had obvious ethnic and racial aspects, but also was a clear class battle of those excluded from meaningful property and access to the means of production.

RANK

Contemporary Africa is not greatly concerned with rank as an overall instrument of social organization

and order. Rank has lost most of its importance because it is unsympathetic to most, but not all, of the exogenous values, forces, and institutions of stratification. As in most contexts, the gradient is from what is left of stable rural communities, where the rank of sibling and gender seniority pervades extended kinship groupings, up to the higher levels where, even if necessarily present, rank is not a dominant value. Traditional systems of rank were so imbued with local symbolic and ritual components as to be untranslatable into modern situations. No new African nation preserved or established hereditary rank on a national scale, except for the rare cases where the boundaries of small states coincided with ethnolinguistic borders, as in Swaziland, Lesotho, and Botswana, whose ethnic kings survive uneasily as heads of state. The king of Buganda survives informally as a regional figurehead, as do the powerful emirs of northern Nigeria and the Sahel. The emperor of Ethiopia is no more.

Rank now belongs to respect rather than respect to rank. The trappings of rank are downplayed except on the most formal occasions, and even then are modest and subdued compared with the thrones, uniforms, crowns, and headdresses of former days. The accoutrements of rank in verbal use of titles, greetings, posture, costume, and modes and tones of address are diminished, even if remaining formally on paper. A notable exception is the system of title taking in many parts of Nigeria, which is proving to be one of the most tenacious indigenous ranking systems with a capacity to adapt and even to spread. It is able to embellish and domesticate new forms of status acquisition, according honor to the few and the pleasures of feasting to the many.

Yet some rank and ceremony are still required for the smooth running of organizations. The order of precedence and seating that attends all major national festive, ceremonial, or commemorative occasions passively expresses an officially sanctioned general ranking order. Government, churches, schools and universities, sports teams, clubs, and associations all use minimal seniority systems of titles and ranks for avoidance of friction and for effective allocation and implementation of responsibility. Above all, armies and police forces maintain all-embracing ranking systems as the essential basis of their functioning. The Catholic churches retain the most rigid, elaborate, and formal hierarchy of ranks, titles, uniforms, and privileges.

The various systems and pockets of surviving rank are not coordinated, nor are they systematically related to one another or to the class system, although they make their contribution. Isolated attempts at denying rank differences, such as declaration of the one permissible title of *citoyen(ne)* in Democratic Republic of the Congo, have been hideously mocked by social realities.

The title of winner in media-promoted contests of every conceivable kind—lotteries, car races, film awards, song hits, beauty contests, fashion parades, and sports events—begins to swamp all others in popular appeal, distorting the rank and stratification spectrum. However, in Africa its influence, though remarkably penetrating, is in practice severely restricted by poverty.

CONCLUSION

Individuals and groups may attempt to perform a calculus to sum up all the various contributory components of rank and status for themselves and others, but it is too laborious, complex, and multifarious to reach any clearly accepted collective resolution as class consciousness. Rank elements are widespread but uncoordinated, caste systems are hardly reconcilable with modern contexts, and class, though a largely unwitting aspect of the social behavior of everyone, is not crystallized into generally recognized contours. Discernibly class-related action on a significant scale erupts only sporadically in crises, at critical junctures of widespread labor unrest—salary disputes and strikes— or military coups where leaders give expression to antagonisms that are class-based and have reached a boiling point. With the advent of a global superclass structure, at least conceptually, concerted class action is even harder to organize or conceive, yet isolated outbreaks of bombing and terrorism are clearly seen to threaten the establishment generally and have undeniable class implications. But Africa, with its industrial development retarded and scattered, has not yet entered significantly upon this scene.

See also **Age and Age Organization; De Klerk, Frederick Willem; Ethnicity; Gender; International Monetary Fund; Kinship and Descent; Labor; Mandela, Nelson; Nongovernmental Organizations; Saro-Wiwa, Ken; United Nations; Warfare; World Bank.**

BIBLIOGRAPHY

Kuper, Leo. *An African Bourgeoisie: Race, Class, and Politics in South Africa.* New Haven, CT: Yale University Press, 1965.

Lesorogol, Carolyn. K. "Transforming Institutions among Pastoralists: Inequality and Land Privatization." *American Anthropologist* 105, no.3 (2003): 531–542.

Lloyd, Peter C. *Africa in Social Change.* Harmondsworth, U.K.: Penguin, 1967.

Lloyd, Peter C., ed. *The New Elites of Tropical Africa.* London: Oxford University Press, 1966.

Sandbrook, Richard. *Closing the Circle: Democratization and Development in Africa.* London: Zed Books, 2000.

Tuden, Arthur, and Leonard Plotnicov, eds. *Social Stratification in Africa.* New York: The Free Press, 1970.

Vincent, Joan. *Teso in Transformation: The Political Economy of Peasant and Class in Eastern Africa.* Berkeley: University of California Press, 1982.

AIDAN SOUTHALL

SUDAN

This entry includes the following articles:
GEOGRAPHY AND ECONOMY
SOCIETY AND CULTURES
HISTORY AND POLITICS

GEOGRAPHY AND ECONOMY

GEOGRAPHY AND POPULATION

Sudan, the largest country in Africa, encompasses nearly one million square miles and a diverse ecology. The Sahara Desert dominates the northernmost third of the country, stretching about 450 miles from the capital city of Khartoum to the Egyptian border. The Sahel Belt lies between the desert and tropical biomes that are farther south. Short rains, totaling 10–20 inches, occur during the months of July, August, and September. This semiarid zone is an important domain for pastoralism in western Sudan, and irrigated agriculture in the eastern region.

Dry-savanna vegetation predominates in the central portion of the country. The climate zone here broadens near the Ethiopian uplands, which flank the eastern border of Sudan. Although the central rainlands have a lengthy dry season, stretching as long as eight months, there is sufficient

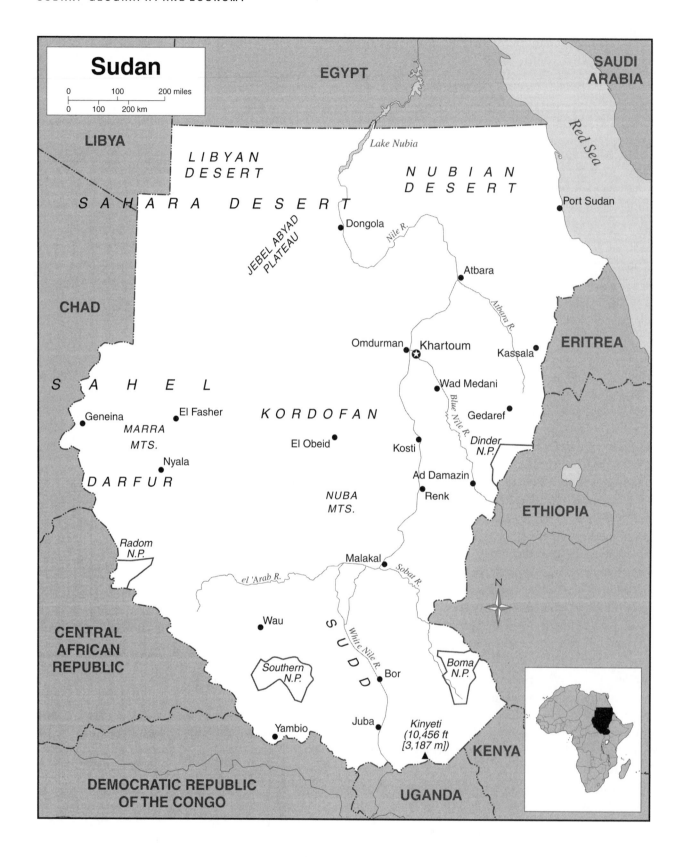

Sudan

0   100   200 miles

0   100   200 km

EGYPT

SAUDI ARABIA

LIBYA

Red Sea

L I B Y A N   D E S E R T

Lake Nubia

N U B I A N   D E S E R T

S A H A R A   D E S E R T

Port Sudan

JEBEL ABYAD PLATEAU

Dongola

Nile R.

CHAD

Atbara

Albara R.

ERITREA

Omdurman   Khartoum   Kassala

S A H E L

Wad Medani

Geneina   El Fasher

K O R D O F A N

Gedaref

MARRA MTS.

El Obeid

Blue Nile R.

Dinder N.P.

Nyala

Kosti

D A R F U R

Ad Damazin

Renk

NUBA MTS.

ETHIOPIA

Radom N.P.

Malakal   *Sobat R.*

el 'Arab R.

N

CENTRAL AFRICAN REPUBLIC

Wau

S U D D

White Nile R.

Southern N.P.

Bor

Boma N.P.

Yambio   Juba   *Kinyeti (10,456 ft [3,187 m])*

KENYA

DEMOCRATIC REPUBLIC OF THE CONGO

UGANDA

precipitation to sustain short grasses, scattered trees, and the country's principal food crops: sorghum and sesame. Most rainfed cultivation, parceled out in smallholdings or extensive farms, occurs here, in the largest climatic region of Sudan.

A more humid climate extends approximately 150 miles into southwestern Sudan from the neighboring countries of the Central African Republic and the Democratic Republic of Congo. Annual precipitation of more than 39 inches produces a mixture of diverse trees and tall grasses. Export crops (tea, tobacco, and coffee) as well as a variety of foodstuffs (most notably, corn, yams, and bananas) are grown under these moist conditions. Agriculture has been disrupted here, however, as elsewhere in the south, by Sudan's lengthy civil war.

Except for the northern border, portions of which are actively contested by Egypt, the political boundaries of Sudan are defined generally by the drainage basin of the Nile River. Flat or slightly undulating plains dominate the surface. Tebeldi trees, also known as baobabs, and rugged protrusions of volcanic rock add relief to the sweeping plains. The peak of the largest inselberg in the west, Jebel Marra, is 10,073 feet high. The highest point in Sudan is Mount Kinyeti (10,456 feet) in the far south near the border with Uganda.

Water and oil are two of the most important physical resources in Sudan. The Anglo-Egyptian administration (1899–1956) created the world's largest plantation by using the Blue and White Nile Rivers for irrigation. Devoted principally to cotton production, the Gezira (the area between the Blue and White Nile Rivers) generated the bulk of the country's export earnings until early twenty-first century.

Conflict over water resources contributed to civil war in 1983. After leaving Uganda, the White Nile flows into the Sudd, the largest permanent swamp in the world. Half of the river evaporates here each year. Serious controversy surrounded the construction of the Jonglei Canal, a 225-mile-long channel designed to divert water out of the south and into northern Sudan and Egypt. Tensions increased further with the discovery of oil nearby and northerners' subsequent attempt to redefine the north-south border. In 1983, the mutiny of a battalion of southern soldiers marked the beginning of Sudan's second civil war. The twenty-two year war suspended construction of the Jonglei Canal.

More than 50 percent of Sudan's population (39.4 million) live near the Nile or on one of its tributaries. Three towns—Omdurman, Khartoum, and Khartoum North—straddle the junction of the two Nile Rivers. Together these towns comprise the greater metropolitan area of Khartoum. Other key cities along the Nile Rivers include Juba, Bor, Malakal, Renk, Kosti, Atbara, and Wad Medani. El Fasher and El Obeid in the west, Wau in the southwest, and Gedaref in the east, are all important regional centers. In the northeast are the cities of Kassala, near the border with Eritrea, and Port Sudan, on the Red Sea.

The metropolitan area of Khartoum has experienced dramatic growth. The city has increased twelve times its size at independence (1956). Whereas the 1983 census reported 1.3 million residents in the city, estimates as of 2007 range between 2.7 and 4.0 million. Even the conservative estimate makes greater Khartoum the fifth largest city in sub-Saharan Africa. As many as two million people, displaced by the war in the south, moved to Khartoum in the 1980s. In the early 1990s, the government staged a massive demolition and relocation campaign designed to rid the capital of squatter settlements. More than 400,000 people were dispossessed and relocated to desert sites outside the city.

The combination of drought, famine, protracted civil war in the south, and a separate, new conflict in the western region of Darfur (begun in 2003) has forced between 5.3 million and 6.2 million Sudanese to leave their homes. Six hundred and sixty-five thousand Sudanese are exiled in neighboring countries. Serious ramifications are associated with such massive internal displacement. They include the marginalization of displaced people from Sudanese society, falling agricultural production, a spate of epidemics, chronic food insecurity, and accelerated environmental degradation as large-scale commercial agriculture expands into vacated rural areas. The comprehensive peace agreement signed between the Government of Sudan (GOS) and the Sudan People's Liberation Movement (SPLM) on January 9, 2005, is expected to prompt a significant return migration of displaced people to their homes in southern Sudan.

ECONOMY

Until recently, agriculture was the mainstay of the Sudanese economy. Eighty percent of the national labor force (17 million) relies on agriculture for its livelihood. Colonial administrators established cotton and gum arabic as the country's chief exports. While 90 percent of the world's supply of gum arabic still originates in Sudan, cotton from the Gezira came to dominate Sudan's economy, generating as much as 60 percent of all export earnings.

The state also encourages the expansion of commercial rainfed agriculture. Operators lease vast tracts of land for nominal fees from the government, or expropriate the land outright. Typically, they clear their tracts of all vegetative cover, deep plow the soil, and then plant sesame and sorghum. Soil depletion is rapid under these conditions. Sorghum yields in Sudan are steadily declining; the national average fell from 711 pounds per acre in the early 1960s to less than 482 pounds in the late 1980s. Land degradation and declining food security precipitated the 1984–1985 famine, the worst of the twentieth century. More than 250,000 people died in Sudan, a country once touted as the future breadbasket of the Middle East.

By the 1990s, Sudan faced a daunting economic crisis. Despite austerity measures and the reallocation of agricultural land to export crops, interest requirements on the external debt overtook Sudan's annual export earnings. Fiscal crisis remained in the interest of those few who controlled imports and the sale of basic commodities. Conditions were ideal for hoarding goods and raising prices. The inflation rate, reflected by consumer price increases, ran higher than 100 percent per year. Meanwhile, the state remained either indisposed or incapable of asserting control over illegal trading practices and the foreign currency black market. More than one million Sudanese emigrated abroad, mostly to work in the Arab Gulf countries.

Although little has changed in the agricultural sector, the national economic outlook has seen marked improvements in the early twenty-first century. In 1998, the government addressed its climbing debt by implementing the macroeconomic policies of the International Monetary Fund (IMF). In 1999, Sudan began exporting crude oil and soon was recording trade surpluses for the first time. By 2004, oil production was five times greater than domestic consumption (345,000 barrels per day). Oil revenues and new export processing zones helped revive light industrial growth. Real Gross Domestic Product (GDP) growth is has remained above 6.0 percent since 2000, and rose to an all-time high of 7.3 percent in 2004. Consumer price increases have remained below 10 percent since 2000, as well. The prospects for continued economic growth are positive, especially in view of the Naivasha Peace Treaty (January 2005), which ended the fiscal burden of a costly military campaign in the south.

See also **Climate; Ecosystems; Famine; International Monetary Fund; Nile River; Refugees; Sahara Desert; Sudan: Wars.**

BIBLIOGRAPHY

Bascom, Johnathan. *Losing Place: Refugee Populations and Rural Transformations in East Africa*. Providence, RI; Oxford: Berghahn Press, 1998.

Burr, J. Millard, and Robert Collins. *Requiem for the Sudan: War, Drought, and Disaster Relief on the Nile*, Boulder, CO; San Francisco; Oxford: Westview Press, 1995.

De Waal, Alexander. *Famine That Kills: Darfur, Sudan*, revised edition. Oxford; New York: Oxford University Press, 2005.

Kebbede, Girma, ed. *Sudan's Predicament: Civil War, Displacement and Ecological Degradation*. Aldershot, U.K.: Ashgate, 1999.

Laki, Sam L. "The Impact of the Jonglei Canal on the Economy of the Local People." *International Journal of Sustainable Development & World Ecology* 1, no. 2 (1994): 89-96.

"Sudan Country Brief." World Bank. Available from http://www.worldbank.org.

"World Fact Book—Sudan." CIA. Available from https://www.cia.gov.

B. BASCOM

SOCIETY AND CULTURES

The Republic of Sudan is home to a range of peoples, cultures, and civilizations. Cultural contrast and diversity is certainly common to both internal and external representations of the Sudanese peoples. But this picture itself has grown out of a history of contact that has woven the Sudanese together in intimate ways, sometimes through trade and patronage networks and sometimes by force, through recruitment into domestic labor or military service. The civil wars of 1956–1972 and 1983 onward have furthered contacts between all regions, though at the same time sharpening images of racial and ethnic difference.

The regime in power in 2006 was a Government of National Unity, formed after the Comprehensive Peace Agreement signed on January 9, 2005, between the Islamist-supported regime of Omar el-Bashir and the Sudan People's Liberation Army (SPLA), whose base was in the south. Unfortunately peace in the country at large has been seriously compromised by the escalation since 2003 of armed resistance in the western province of Darfur, a formerly autonomous sultanate. The government immediately mounted a heavy counter-insurgency campaign, supported by various groups of mounted militia who came to be generally known by the local term *janjawid*, roughly translated as "evil horse riders."

Despite halting moves towards peace talks supported by the international community, the war in the west has continued and has spilled over into Chad. The National Unity government continued to be led by Omar el-Bashir, and to pursue a narrowly Islamist agenda for the northern regions of the country. The south, however, has been given fresh devolved powers, including the right to a future referendum on its status, and is developing a regional secular democracy. The struggle in the west has recently taken on a heavily racist rhetoric, of "Arabs versus blacks," which contradicts older shared patterns of cooperation and family linkage. In spite of these deadly conflicts, ethnographic and historical studies reveal processes connecting rather than separating the various communities of the Sudan, through the spread of colloquial Arabic as a lingua franca, the extension of economic and political patronage, and intermarriage.

It is not possible to give accurate numerical estimates of the peoples of the country because of the inadequacy of census data and the lack of general agreement as to the categories that should be used. However, a 1995 Minority Rights Group report suggests a total figure for the country of 28 million people, who between them speak some four hundred languages. A working assumption can be made that a considerable majority of the population speak Arabic as their mother tongue and practice Islam. Most of these are resident in the north of the modern Sudan, though others (including a new generation born to parents of mixed origin) live in the towns of the modern south.

THE HEARTLAND

A wide range of present-day Sudanese link their genealogy and heritage to the Funj Sultanate of Sennar (1504–1821), which was centered on the middle Blue Nile. This kingdom was the successor to the ancient civilizations of Meroä and of medieval Christian Nubia, though these forebears are not well remembered in local tradition. The Funj rulers are remembered as Muslims, but at the same time honored as locally rooted among the indigenous people. Throughout this region, which is still arguably the heartland of the modern Sudanese state (though the Shilluk and northern Dinka districts mentioned are now part of the South as defined by the 2005 Peace Agreement), memories and myths persist of mutual interconnection and a common heritage. In this old Sudanese heartland, North and South used to be of less importance than center/periphery relations. It was the large-scale southward slave raiding of the Turco-Egyptian period (1821–1885) that tipped the balance and intensified the exploitative relationship between northern and southern Sudan.

The Riverine Central Sudanese. In the medieval period, Nubian languages were spoken along the Nile by the ancestors of the present-day northern Sudanese. Although these languages survive only in the riverine regions approaching the Egyptian border, in particular Dongola, many of the present-day social and cultural features of northern Sudanese life can be regarded as of Nubian heritage. Along the river are many communities that speak only Arabic and link themselves with a tribal genealogy deriving from Arabian sources, while practicing forms of marriage and family rituals connecting them to the pre-Islamic past. Modern studies of the riverine communities of the northern Sudan reveal these communities' internal complexity; typically they have assimilated a wide array of strangers from other parts of the country, including the South, through trade contacts and through former institutions of domestic, military, and agricultural slavery. Marriage is typically arranged by the senior male elders and is often between close kin.

Ideally, a young man's first marriage is to a paternal parallel cousin.

Women live in a relatively closed world, marrying within the village they know and remaining for much of their everyday lives within the community of their birth. In this central zone of the northern Sudan there is a long-established practice of the circumcision of girls involving the complete removal of the outer parts of the genital flesh. Married women are expected to derive health, purity, and fertility from the rite, and thus to produce a line of worthy sons for the family. Anthropological study has interpreted the widespread cult of possession by so-called foreign *zar* spirits (often representing ethnic types from the history of northeast Africa) as an imaginative and dramatic commentary by rural women upon the enclosed social world in which they live.

Hill Areas and Cultural Enclaves.

The eastern border of the Sudanese heartland, contiguous with Ethiopia, follows the foothills of the high plateau, and in the hills and valleys of the transitional zone a range of small farming communities still speak vernacular languages, though also using colloquial Arabic and in some cases observing Muslim ways. Some, like most of the Gumuz of the Blue Nile and the Berta and Koma of Bela Shangul, were formerly tributary to the old Sudan but now live within the modern Ethiopian frontier. Others, such as the Ingessana (or Gamk) and the Uduk, lived wholly within Sudanese territory until their displacement by war. Among these border populations, bride service and sister-exchange marriage tend to promote the continuity of local social groupings. Within this framework, women often have a considerable degree of control over their marriage situation. Here, as well as in the Nuba Hills, some communities organize themselves on matrilineal principles.

The Nuba Hills of the central and southern parts of Kordofan Province have sheltered, historically, a wide variety of farming communities speaking several dozen minority languages. The term "Nuba" has long been applied inclusively to them all (a term distinct from, though obviously cognate with, "Nubia" as previously mentioned). The Nuba have been stereotyped in modern Sudanese thought as strong and willing laborers, reliable recruits to the army and police, and domestic servants in the towns. While each hill community treasures its own cultural style, many of the men are engaged in long-distance labor migration and most of the people speak Arabic, sing and play Arabic music, and live for a good part of the time as Sudanese citizens would anywhere else. Both in the southern Blue Nile region adjacent to the Ethiopian border, and in the Nuba Hills, there has been very significant support for the SPLA during the civil war, and along with the area of Abyei, similarly identified as having a special character within the north, local constitutional provisions have been made in the Comprehensive Peace Agreement to protect religious and human rights.

The Shilluk Kingdom.

The Shilluk people, cattle herders and farmers on the west bank of the White Nile, speak a Nilotic language closely linked with Anuak and Luo (spoken as far south as the eastern shores of Lake Victoria). Because of the political significance of their centralized kingdom, founded at Fashoda probably in the seventeenth century, they are famous within general Sudanese historical memory. The Shilluk were never isolated but rather thrived on trading and cultural exchange with their neighbors on all sides, playing a significant role in relation to the Sultanate of Sennar itself, with whose royal institutions and rituals (including kingly execution) there were many parallels. The Shilluk have also become a key exemplar in anthropological studies of a people practicing "divine kingship," featured in historical debate about the institution of royalty in many other parts of the world.

Arab Nomads.

In addition to its importance in the central Nile Valley, Arabic is also the main language of the open arid plains to the east and west. Here, camel and cattle pastoralism thrive, supporting an often mobile population. The word "Arab," as used in many settled communities of the northern Sudan, simply means "nomad of the desert" and acquired its modern political overtones only in the late twentieth century. Some of the nomadic Arab groups preserve a memory of having migrated across the Red Sea from the Arabian Peninsula, and they retain a generally light-skinned "Arabian" appearance through a fairly strict practice of endogamy. Among these are the Rufa'a al

Hoi and Kenana of the Blue Nile, though the clearest example of such a distinctively Arabian group are the Rashaida of the coastal belt. Most Arab nomadic populations have, however, intermarried with local Sudanese communities, while many of the local settled population (of whatever origin and cultural background) have been drawn into their ranks through the expansion of the cattle- and camel-herding economies.

Best known are the Baggara, a blanket term itself building on the Arabic word for cattle that indicates "cattlemen" and including groups such as Hassaniya, Rizeiqat, Mesiriyya, and Humr, who trace their identities and interrelationship in an idiom of historical descent. Moving in the east-west belt of semiarid savanna in the south of Darfur and Kordofan, the Baggara were famous in history for their active role in supporting the Madhist movement, which led to the independent state of the nineteenth century. With regard to other nomadic Arab groups, academic research has centered on their pastoral migrations, animal management economy, and internal political organization, including the typical practice of close endogamous marriage within patrilineal descent groups. Study has also focused upon their relations with settled communities. In good years, many farmers invest in animals, and may then seek herding partners among the nomads, or even join them. In poor years, on the other hand, herders may be forced to settle with the farming villages. A historical perspective on the nomads reveals a surprising capacity for response to ecology and politics. The camel-herding peoples of the extreme northern parts of the Sudan, such as the Kababish, have also come to play active roles, on both sides, in twenty-first-century conflicts.

Twentieth-Century Immigration to the Heartland. Within the relatively accessible plains of the Sudanese heartland, a series of commercially oriented agricultural schemes was established in the course of the twentieth century. The best known is the Gezira Scheme, which dates from the completion of a dam and irrigation works on the Blue Nile at Sennar in 1925. The scheme attracted tenant settlers not only from the immediate locality but also from far afield, and in particular from the Hausa-speaking regions of Nigeria. Management of these schemes, whether governmental or (increasingly) private, seeks to attract both seasonal and permanent labor. Even those displaced by conflict from the South, or from Darfur, may find themselves absorbed as labor in this way.

EASTERN AND WESTERN EXTREMITIES

Trade often extended from the riverine market centers of the Nile Valley both to the east and to the west. In the Red Sea Hills to the east, the dominantly pastoral Beja peoples, famous in historical memory both within and outside the Sudan, continue to speak a range of vernacular languages along with Arabic. The main groups are Bisharin, Amarar, Hadendowa, and Beni Amer. They still practice camel rearing along with some cultivation and supply a series of market towns in the Red Sea Hills and along the coast. Dar Fur (meaning "the homeland of the Fur," after which are named the province of Darfur and its subdivisions), in the far west, is centered on a substantial mountain massif where dense agricultural settlement supported the old independent Fur Sultanate. Before the outbreak of civil war in this region in 2003, the political culture of the Fur people included a complex hierarchy of offices and of state rituals. Though still speaking their own language, the Fur have been successful in adopting the language and manners of national Sudanese life and in developing market production and long-distance trade. Dar Fur had its own periphery, of smaller adjacent kingdoms, for example that of Masalit to the west, nomadic camel herders such as the Zaghawa to the north, a much-exploited southern fringe of minor and rather despised groups bracketed as "Fertit," and Baggara cattle herders to the south and east. Historically, links between center and outskirts in Darfur Province were close; studies have highlighted the way in which Fur mountain farmers interacted closely with Baggara herders, joining each other's way of life for economic reasons and intermarrying. Late-twentieth-century studies on the effects of drought and famine have also emphasized the prewar regional interdependency of local communities throughout Darfur.

THE FAR SOUTH

Like the central stretches of the country around the junction of the Niles, the great basin of the upper White Nile can be represented as a heartland. Here

Jumhuriyat as-Sudan (Republic of the Sudan)

Population:	39,379,358 (2007 est.)
Area:	2,505,810 sq. km (967,498 sq. mi.)
Official language:	Arabic
Languages:	Arabic, English, tribal
National currency:	Sudanese dinar
Principal religions:	Muslim (Sunni) 70%, indigenous 25%, Christian 5%
Capital:	Khartoum (est. pop. 1,400,000 in 2006)
Other urban centers:	Port Sudan, Wad Medani, El Obeid, Atbara, Juba, Malakal, Renk, Kosti, El Fasher, Wau, Gedaref, Kassala
Annual rainfall:	from 130 mm (5 in.) in the central region to 1,270 mm (50 in.) in the south
Principal geographical features:	*Mountains:* Red Sea Hills, Jebel Marra, Nuba Mountains, Immatong Range, Dongotona Range *Rivers:* White Nile, Blue Nile, Nile, Atbara, ar-Rahad, Dindar, Bahral-Ghazal, Sobat, Jonglei Canal *Lakes:* Nuba, Khazzam, ar-Rusayris, Maleit *Other:* Libyan Desert, Nubian Desert, the Sudd (swampland)
Economy:	*GDP per capita:* US$2,400 (2006)
Principal products and exports:	*Agricultural:* cotton, groundnuts (peanuts), sorghum, millet, wheat, gum arabic, sugarcane, cassava (tapioca), mangos, papaya, bananas, sweet potatoes, sesame, sheep, livestock *Manufacturing:* cotton ginning, textiles, cement, edible oils, sugar, soap distilling, shoes, pharmaceuticals, armaments, automobile/light truck assembly *Mining:* iron ore, chromium ore, copper ore, gold, mica, manganese gypsum, oil
Government:	Ruled as an Anglo-Egyptian condominium, 1899–1956. Independence from Great Britain and Egypt, 1956. First permanent constitution approved in 1973, suspended in 1985. Interim constitution of 1985 suspended in 1989. New constitution of 1998 suspended in 1999. Interim National Constitution adopted 2005. Provisional Government established by the Comprehensive Peace Agreement of 2005 that provides for power sharing with the former southern rebels on a 70-30 basis pending national elections in 2007 or 2008. President elected for 5-year term by universal suffrage. Bicameral legislative body includes National Assembly and Council of States.
Heads of state since independence:	1956–1958: Council of State (civilian), with Prime Minister Ismail al-Azhari (1956) and Prime Minister Abdullah Khalil (1956–1958) 1958–1964: General Ibrahim 'Abboud, chairman of the Supreme Council of Armed Forces 1964–1965: Supreme Council (military) 1965–1969: Isma'il al-Azhari, president of the Supreme Council of State (civilian) 1969–1971: Colonel Ja'far Muhammad Nimeiri, chairman of the Revolutionary Command Council 1971–1985: President Ja'far Muhammad Nimeiri 1985–1986: Lieutenant General 'Abd al-Rahman Siwar al-Dahab, chairman of the Transitional Military Council 1986–1989: Supreme Council (civilian), with Prime Minister al-Sadiq al-Mahdi, who had strong executive powers 1989–1993: General Omar Ahmed el-Bashir, chairman of the Revolutionary Command Council for National Salvation 1993–: President Omar Ahmed el-Bashir
Armed forces:	The Sudan People's Armed Forces is a 100,000-member army supported by a small air force and navy. President is commander in chief. 3-year conscript service obligation.
Transportation:	*Rail:* 5,978 km (3,715 mi.), controlled by Sudan Railways Corporation *Waterways:* 5,310 km (3,292 mi.), controlled by the Sudan River Transport Company *Ports:* Port Sudan, Juba, Khartoum, Kosti, Malakal, Nimule, Sawakin *Roads:* 20,703 km (12,836 mi.), 10% paved *National airline:* Sudan Airways *Airports:* International facilities at Khartoum, Port Sudan, El Obeid, Juba. 85 other airports and airstrips throughout the country.
Media:	All press media nationalized as of 1970. 6 dailies, including *Al-Ayam, Al-Sahafa.* 9 nondailies, including the *Nile Mirror.* 25 periodicals. Book publishers (state-controlled) include El-Ayam Press, Government Printing Press, Khartoum University Press.
Literacy and education:	*Total literacy rate:* 61% (2006). Education is free, universal, and compulsory for 8 years. Postsecondary education provided by University of Khartoum, with 10 faculties; Khartoum Branch of Cairo University, with 4 faculties; Islamic University of Omdurman, with 3 faculties. University of Juba; and technical and vocational schools.

lie the great seasonal floodplains occupied by the transhumant cattle-herding peoples of the northern Nilotic language group, of whom the most numerous and widespread are the Dinka. Their close cousins, the Nuer, exemplify a long-term tendency for historical and demographic outward expansion from the floodplain area. The spatial flexibility of social relations among the Nuer and Dinka is linked to wide-reaching patterns of exogamy, or marriage between unrelated groups, and associated circulation of cattle in bridewealth. Under war conditions the great exchange cycles of the pastoral economy have been eroded, sometimes resulting in a greater degree of personal liberty for women (though their resources remain few).

The Nuer preserve in historical memory their movement eastward toward the Ethiopian hills, and indeed into territory now a part of modern Ethiopia. Other Nilotic-speaking peoples such as the Lango, Acoli, and Luo preserve legends of a southward drift as far as the territory of modern Uganda (and even Kenya and Tanzania in the case of the Luo). The Anuak to the far east of the upper Nile speak a tongue closely related to Shilluk and share some of the traditional institutions of kingship and centralized politics characteristic of the Shilluk kingdom. The northern Nilotic peoples in general have become well known throughout the Sudan from the mid-nineteenth century, the Nuer in particular having acquired a warlike reputation for fierce independence from any form of patronage and government. Studies conducted since the 1970s suggest however that the inspired religious leaders first called "prophets" by E. E. Evans-Pritchard exerted a widespread influence, drawing their authority from a capacity to mediate conflict and establish peace in the name of divinity between Nuer and non-Nuer alike from the late nineteenth century onward.

A considerable body of literature, both primary ethnography and secondary discussion, has been devoted to the spiritual beliefs, experience, and practice of the Nilotic peoples and made them prime exemplars of the imaginative power and beauty of indigenous African religion. This body of research followed upon Evans-Pritchard's pre-war masterwork on the philosophical thought of the Azande and confirmed the seriousness of his claim to demonstrate the moral and intellectual sophistication of nonliterate cultures and to bring them within the general orbit of theology, philosophy, and history.

From the mid-nineteenth century onward, interaction between different groups of the southern Sudan has been stimulated by trading networks, military recruitment, and the establishment of garrison towns. Many urban centers owe their origin to this history and in the twenty-first century include core populations who speak only Arabic and live in northern Sudanese style, though their personal family links are local. The label "Nubi" is often given to these communities associated with modern urban, merchant, and military networks, linking them in memory with the arrival of northern Sudanese "Nubians" and their mixing with local populations in the nineteenth century. The term "Nubi" extends also into Uganda and Kenya, where it is applied to Arabic- (or "Ki-Nubi"-) speaking populations associated historically with a southern Sudanese origin.

Peoples of modern-day southern Sudan have intermittently experienced civil war since the 1950s. Observers notice an extraordinary intensification of religious feeling and activity in the Sudan, not only in Islam and Christianity but also within the vernacular African traditions. A new kind of ethnographic writing about the Sudan is emerging, pursuing such themes as displacement, bereavement, and violence, along with reconstruction, renewal, and the search for meaning, justice, and peace.

See also **Bashir, Omar Ahmed el-; Initiation: Clitoridectomy and Infibulation; Kinship and Descent; Languages; Marriage Systems; Nubia; Religion and Ritual; Spirit Possession; Sudan: Wars; Warfare: Civil Wars; Women.**

BIBLIOGRAPHY

Asad, Talal. *The Kababish Arabs: Power, Authority, and Consent in a Nomadic Tribe.* London: Hurst, 1970.

Baumann, Gerd. *National Integration and Local Integrity: The Miri of the Nuba Mountains in the Sudan.* Oxford: Clarendon Press, 1987.

Boddy, Janice. *Wombs and Alien Spirits: Women, Men, and the Zar Cult in Northern Sudan.* Madison: University of Wisconsin Press, 1989.

Cunnison, Ian. *The Baggara Arabs: Power and the Lineage in a Sudanese Nomad Tribe.* Oxford: Clarendon Press, 1966.

De Waal, Alexander. *Famine That Kills: Darfur, Sudan,* rev. edition. New York: Oxford University Press, 2005.

De Waal, Alexander, and Julie Flint. *Darfur: A Short History of a Long War.* London: Zed Press, 2006.

Deng, Francis Mading. *The Man Called Deng Majok: A Biography of Power, Polygyny, and Change.* New Haven, CT: Yale University Press, 1986.

Evans-Pritchard, E. E. *Witchcraft, Oracles, and Magic among the Azande.* Oxford: Clarendon Press, 1937.

Evans-Pritchard, E. E. *The Nuer: A Description of the Modes of Livelihood and Political Institutions of a Nilotic People.* Oxford: Clarendon Press, 1940.

Evans-Pritchard, E. E. *Nuer Religion.* Oxford: Clarendon Press, 1956.

Hutchinson, Sharon E. *Nuer Dilemmas: Coping with Money, War, and the State.* Berkeley: University of California Press, 1996.

James, Wendy. *The Listening Ebony: Moral Knowledge, Religion, and Power among the Uduk of Sudan.* Oxford: Clarendon Press, 1988.

James, Wendy. *Blue Nile South: War Experiences and Transformations of Suffering in Sudan's Frontierlands.* Oxford: Clarendon Press, 2007.

Johnson, Douglas H. *Nuer Prophets: A History of Prophecy from the Upper Nile in the Nineteenth and Twentieth Centuries.* Oxford: Clarendon Press, 1994.

Johnson, Douglas H. *The Root Causes of Sudan's Civil Wars,* rev. edition. Athens: Ohio University Press, 2006.

Jok, Jok Madut. *War and Slavery in Sudan.* Philadelphia: University of Pennsylvania Press, 2001.

Kenyon, Susan M. *Five Women of Sennar: Culture and Change in Central Sudan,* 2nd edition. Long Grove, IL: Waveland, 2004.

Lienhardt, R. G. *Divinity and Experience: The Religion of the Dinka.* Oxford: Clarendon Press, 1961.

Mohamed, Abbas Ahmed. *White Nile Arabs: Political Leadership and Economic Change.* London: Athlone, 1980.

Prunier, Gérard. *Darfur: The Ambiguous Genocide.* London: Hurst, 2005.

WENDY JAMES

HISTORY AND POLITICS

Prior to the Turco-Egyptian conquest, which began in 1821, the area of what is now the early twenty-first century Republic of the Sudan did not form a unified political entity. Its inhabitants consisted of a multitude of ethnic and linguistic groups with diverse social and political organizations. The Funj Sultanate, with its capital at Sennar on the Blue Nile, ruled the eastern parts of the country, from the Gezira (the region between the Blue and the White Niles) to the riverine areas north of Khartoum. The sultanate was a loose federation of chieftaincies. Funj sultans left local chiefs in power but used their small army of mounted soldiers to collect tribute from a wide range of settled cultivators and nomadic pastoralists. The Funj Sultanate reached the height of its power in the seventeenth and eighteenth centuries, during which its armies defeated an Abyssinian invasion and came into control of the territory central to the former province, or state, of Kordofan. However, in the second half of the eighteenth century, the Funj Sultanate began to decline as a result of internal dissention and fragmentation.

The Dar Fur Sultanate ruled the western areas of Sudan. Its founders were the Fur, a local Muslim group inhabiting the area around the Jebel Marra range. The Fur emerged as a powerful group and established their sultanate in the second half of the seventeenth century. Their rulers made Islam the official religion of the sultanate and drove their former rulers, the Daju and Tunjur, into the peripheries. During the eighteenth century, the Fur expanded over the eastern part of modern Dar Fur and central Kordofan, and moved their capital to al-Fashir. The Fur Sultanate remained independent until the late nineteenth century when it was destroyed by the armies of al-Zubayr Rahma Mansur, Sudanese traders from the north.

TURCO-EGYPTIAN RULE

In 1821 the armies of Muhammad 'Ali, the Ottoman ruler of Egypt, conquered the Funj Sultanate. Muhammad 'Ali's principal objective was to recruit Sudanese slaves into his new army and to exploit Sudan's natural resources. In the early years of his rule slaves were obtained, through government-organized raids, from the Nuba Mountains and the Upper Blue Nile. Thousands of people were captured in these raids and sent to training camps in southern Egypt, but many died either as a result of the difficult journey across the desert or from the climatic conditions in Egypt. The failure of this experiment prompted Muhammad 'Ali to compel the Sudanese to grow cotton and other agricultural products in Sudan, and to impose heavy taxes on these cultivators.

Although Turco-Egyptian rule over Sudan was direct in the beginning, the government began gradually to rely on local Sudanese tribal heads. However, in the mid-1830s the government of Sudan was further centralized by the appointment of a *hakimdar* (governor-general) stationed in Khartoum, the military headquarters and the administrative center of the territory. Sudan was divided into several provinces and a governor, who had little control outside the towns and the administrative headquarters of his province, was appointed to each area. Muhammad 'Ali's successors, 'Abbas and Muhammad Sa'id, instituted several administrative and economic reforms. Arabic began to replace Turkish as the language of administration, and some Sudanese were appointed to administrative positions. Some modernizations of communications, law, and education were introduced.

The Turks' desire for Sudan's natural resources led to the opening of the Equatorial provinces for trade from the 1840s onward. Large numbers of European, Middle Eastern, and northern Sudanese traders established settlements in the area of the former provinces Bahr al-Ghazal, Upper Nile, and Equatoria, from which they exported ivory and slaves to northern Sudan and the outside world. The slave trade reached massive proportions by the mid-nineteenth century and attracted the attention of European powers that then began to pressure the Egyptian government to end it. In the 1870s the Turkish government sent several expeditions, led by European officers such as Samuel Baker (b. 1821), Charles Gordon (b. 1833), and Romolo Gessi (b. 1831), to suppress the slave trade in the South. Although these officers established several military posts and defeated the slave traders, clandestine slave trade continued.

THE MAHDIST STATE

The Turkish regime was unpopular among the Sudanese. Heavy taxation, antislavery measures, and a host of sociopolitical factors prompted a large sector of the population to support the Mahdist rebellion in 1881. The Mahdist movement was led by Muhammad Ahmad ibn el-Sayyid Abdullah (c. 1844–1885), a Muslim holy man from Dongola who declared that he was the expected *Mahdi* (divine leader) and vowed to restore the purity of Islam and liberate Sudan from Turkish rule. With armed supporters among the cattle nomads of Kordofan, the Mahdi defeated the Turks in a series of battles and captured Khartoum in 1885. Muhammad Ahmad died a few months after the fall of Khartoum. The task of establishing the Mahdist state fell to his successor, Khalifa Abdullahi (d. 1898), who established

a theocratic state. He created an administrative system of appointed provincial governors who were responsible for tax collection along with other duties. The Mahdist state ruled over at least two-thirds of the region of the Republic of the Sudan. However, the *khalifa* was constantly at war with neighboring Ethiopia and Egypt. By the end of the nineteenth century, the Nilotic Sudan became part of the European scramble for Africa. The French, Belgian, and Italian presence in the region led the British to conquer the Mahdist state in 1898.

ANGLO-EGYPTIAN RULE, 1898-1956

The Anglo-Egyptian regime in Sudan, called the Condominium, theoretically was a partnership between Great Britain and Egypt, but in reality the former had the upper hand from beginning to end. According to the terms of the Anglo-Egyptian Condominium Agreement, signed in 1899, the supreme civil and military authority was vested in the hands of a British governor-general. He would be appointed by the *khedive* of Egypt on the recommendation of the British government. The first governor-general was Horatio Herbert Lord Kitchener (1850–1916), who was succeeded in December 1899 by Sir Francis Reginald Wingate (1861–1953). The governor-general was assisted by civil, legal, and financial secretaries and by an inspector general. The country was divided into several provinces, districts, and sub-districts. A governor, assisted by British inspectors and Egyptian *mamurs* (district officers) administered each province. During the first twenty years of the Condominium, its administrators were mainly army officers. Until World War I, the Anglo-Egyptian government was preoccupied with the suppression of internal resistance movements and the extension of the government's control over the remote parts of Dar Fur and the South.

Following the mutiny of the Egyptian Army in 1924, Egyptian military and civilian personnel were evacuated from Sudan. Beginning in the mid-1920s, the colonial government began to introduce indirect rule through existing local authorities. In 1929, in line with this new administrative plan, the British announced their controversial Southern Policy, the aim of which was to check the spread of Arabic language and Islam in southern Sudan. Thereafter, the predominantly Muslim North and the non-Muslim South were ruled, in essence, as two separate entities. Education and economic developments were concentrated in the North, whereas the South remained a backwater for many decades. These factors and the policies of the post-independence Sudanese governments were responsible for the outbreak of civil war that has plagued the country from 1955 to the early twenty-first century. Another important development during the 1920s was the establishment of the Gezira irrigation scheme and the large-scale production and export of cash crops such as cotton and gum arabic.

INDEPENDENCE

In a pattern consistent with elsewhere in Africa, Sudanese nationalism was led by a small class of intelligentsia; this group formed the Graduates General Congress (GGC)—the first Sudanese political organization in 1938. However, the nationalist movement was soon fragmented and became closely associated with two rival religious sects: the Khatmiyya and the Mahdiyya. The Ashigga Party, which later became the National Unionist Party (NUP), established an alliance with the Khatmiyya sect, whereas the Umma Party, or Independence Front (IF), became the voice of the Mahdists. The former called for Sudan's unity with Egypt whereas the latter demanded complete independence. In addition to sectarian parties such as the NUP and Umma, secular organizations such as the Sudanese Communist Party (SCP) and Sudan's labor unions played a major role in the nationalist struggle in the late 1940s.

In 1953 Great Britain and Egypt signed an agreement that granted Sudan self-rule over a three-year transitional period, after which the Sudanese would decide their political status by plebiscite. In the parliamentary elections that followed, the NUP won the majority of the seats. During the next two years, the party reversed its policy of calling for unity with Egypt, and chose Sudanese independence. On December 19, 1955, the Sudanese parliament unanimously declared independence. Effective January 1, 1956, the British and the Egyptians departed, and Sudan became an independent republic. A coalition government was formed with Ismail al-Azhari (1902–1969), head of the NUP, as prime minister. However, as a result of political maneuvering and internal conflicts within the NUP, Abdullah

Khalil (1888–1970), head of the Umma Party, soon replaced Azhari.

During the negotiations for independence, the question of southern Sudan had been pushed aside: Southerners' anxieties about the prospects of northern Muslim domination, as well as demands for a federal system, were ignored. In August 1955, southern army units stationed in the South revolted and killed several hundred northern traders and officials. Although the revolt was suppressed temporarily, it signaled the beginning of the long civil war that continued into the 1990s.

POSTINDEPENDENCE PERIOD

Interparty conflicts, political maneuvering, and frequent strikes characterized the first two years of independence. The deteriorating political situation prompted Khalil to invite General Ibrahim Abboud (1900–1983), the commander in chief of the army, to assume power in November 1958. Abboud's military coup ended parliamentary rule; subsequently the Supreme Council of the Armed Forces, a military body, ruled Sudan. Political parties were dissolved, the constitution was suspended, trade unions were abolished, and strikes were outlawed. Meanwhile, the civil war in the South continued to rage and was accentuated by the government's policy of vigorous Arabization and Islamization. Abboud remained in power until October 1964 when he was forced to step down by a popular uprising.

After a transitional period of four months, general elections were held; parliamentary rule returned in May 1965. A coalition government of Umma and the NUP was formed with Muhammad Ahmad Mahjoub as prime minister and Ismail al-Azhari (1902–1969) as the president of the Supreme Council of State. However, as a result of political bickering, the continuous civil war, and the lack of economic development, the parliamentary government became unpopular. On May 25, 1969, it was overthrown by a military coup led by Colonel Jafar Muhammad Nimeiri (b. 1930). Once again, political parties were dissolved, their leaders were imprisoned, trade unions and strikes were banned, and a Revolutionary Command Council was set up to govern the country. Sudan was declared a socialist state; the Sudanese Communist Party (SCP) initially supported the new regime. However, differences between the SCP and Nimeiri's government soon emerged and culminated in the failed communist coup of July 1971.

Nimeiri's victory over the communists left him dangerously isolated. In 1972 he signed the Addis Ababa Peace Agreement with the southern rebels, which ended the civil war temporarily. The agreement gave the South regional autonomy within a unified Sudan. In 1973 a new constitution was written according to which Sudan became a one-party state and the Sudanese Socialist Union (SSU) was declared the sole political party. However, Nimeiri's isolation in the North forced him to seek a national reconciliation with the sectarian parties and the militant fundamentalist organization, the Muslim Brotherhood, in 1978. At the same time, his persistent violation of the Addis Ababa Peace Agreement and the introduction of the *shariʿa* law in 1983 led to the resumption of the civil war in the South. This time, the Sudan People's Liberation Army (SPLA) led the southern rebellion. Along with the resumption of the war was economic decline and Nimeiri's continuous repression, all of which led to a popular uprising in April 1985. Lieutenant General Abd al-Rahman Siwar al-Dahab, commander in chief of the armed forces, staged a coup and deposed Nimeiri as he returned from a state visit to the United States.

A transitional period of military rule followed; general elections were held in April 1986. Parliamentary democracy was restored and a series of coalition governments, headed by Al-Sadiq al-Mahdi (b. 1936) of the Umma Party, ruled the country for three years. However, the third democracy was characterized by continuing civil war, economic decline, and major droughts. General Umar Hasan Ahmad al-Beshir's (b. 1944) military coup on June 30, 1989 terminated Parliamentary rule. Political parties, their newspapers, and other civil associations were banned; opposition politicians were arrested. The new military dictatorship, supported (some say directed) by the National Islamic Front (NIF), the political wing of the Muslim Brotherhood, promised an eventual transition to civilian rule. It declared that Sudan would remain an Islamic state, governed strictly in accordance with the shariʿa.

SUDAN 1990–2005

The government's insistence on maintaining the Islamic legal system was one of the chief obstacles to peace in Sudan. The *shariʿa* was abolished in the South by a government decree issued on January 31, 1991, but it remained in force in northern Sudan; the SPLA leader John Garang (1945–2005) demanded that the shariʿa be lifted throughout the country. Garang's other key demand was self-determination for the southern region. Other, smaller opposition groups called for the South to secede from the republic. The fighting intensified during the 1990s despite repeated attempts at mediation that were, from 1991 to the early twenty-first century, complicated by periodic infighting among factions of the SPLA. A peace agreement between the government and several small, armed opposition groups (most of them never allied with the SPLA) announced on April 21, 1997 was rejected by Garang and failed to diminish the ongoing warfare.

The effects of the war on civilians in southern Sudan were devastating: an estimated 1.5 million non-combatants died between 1983 and 1997, thousands, apparently, from starvation. During the same period, as many as 5 million civilians might have been displaced from their homes. Though the government denied it, it was widely reported that southern women and children, primarily Dinka from the northern part of what was Bahr al-Ghazal, were seized by government-armed militias and some regular army units and sold into slavery which is illegal in Sudan. Amnesty International, the United Nations, and other organizations accused both the government and the opposition of committing atrocities against civilians.

Opposition to the government of Sudan is not confined to the country's southern region. A political organization in exile, the National Democratic Alliance (NDA), represents Sudanese opposition political parties from the North. Sudan has, in the early twenty-first century, been at odds with its neighbors Egypt and Eritrea, owing to the countries' accusations that Sudan was working in concert with Iran to export Islamic fundamentalism through the region. Tensions between Sudan and Egypt escalated considerably in mid-1995 following the discovery that Sudan was harboring three suspects in the attempted assassination of Egyptian president Husni Mubarak (b. 1928).

Relations between Sudan and Uganda began declining in 1994 when the governments of both countries alleged that the other was aiding their opposition's armed forces. Formerly an ally of Sudan, the United States has been alienated though it still maintains diplomatic relations. Beginning August 1993, Sudan was on the U.S. list of countries guilty of sponsoring terrorism. Following the bombing of U.S. embassies in East Africa in 1998, the United States launched an air strike on a pharmaceutical factory in Khartoum, claiming the factory was also involved in the production of chemical weapons.

Growing international pressure, particularly after September 11, 2001, forced the Sudanese government to make several changes in both its domestic and foreign policies. On the international level, the government sought to appease European countries and the United States by offering its willingness to collaborate on the campaign against terrorism. At the same time, it engaged in serious negotiations with the Sudanese People's Liberation Movement (SPLM) to end the civil war. These negotiations led to the signing of a comprehensive peace agreement in 2002–2003 that recognized the right of southern Sudanese people to self-determination, power sharing, and the redistribution of economic resources. Although the agreement gave hope for a lasting peace between the North and the South, it displeased people from other marginalized regions in the West and the East, who felt that they were left out of power sharing and the distribution of resources. In April 2003, a violent rebellion broke out in the western province of Darfur. The government's response was swift and severe. In addition to launching a massive military campaign involving both the regular army and the local militia, the Sudanese government used tactics that were considered by the international community to be ethnic cleansing and genocide. The Darfur conflict led to the death of hundreds of thousands of people and to the displacement of more than one million civilians. It has been described as one of the worst ongoing humanitarian catastrophes in the early twenty-first century.

See also 'Ali, Muhammad; Gordon, Charles George; Islam; Mubarak, Husni; Postcolonialism; Slave Trades; Socialism and Postsocialisms; United Nations; Warfare: Civil Wars.

BIBLIOGRAPHY

Collins, Robert O. *Shadows in the Grass: Britain in the Southern Sudan, 1918-1956.* New Haven, CT: Yale University Press, 1983.

Daly, M. W. *Imperial Sudan: The Anglo-Egyptian Condominium, 1934-1956.* Cambridge, U.K.: Cambridge University Press, 1991.

Daly, M. W. *Empire on the Nile: The Anglo-Egyptian Sudan, 1898-1934,* New ed. edition. Cambridge, U.K.: Cambridge University Press, 2004.

Flint, Julie, and Alex De Waal. *Darfur: A Short History of a Long War.* London: Zed Books, 2005.

Gray, Richard. *A History of the Southern Sudan, 1839-1889.* London: Oxford University Press, 1961.

Hill, Richard Leslie. *Egypt in the Sudan, 1820-1881.* London: Oxford University Press, 1963.

Holt, P. M. *The Mahdist State in the Sudan, 1881-1898: A Study of Its Origins, Development and Overthrow.* Oxford: Clarendon Press 1958.

Holt, P. M., and M. W. Daly, eds. *A History of the Sudan: From the Coming of Islam to the Present Day,* 5th edition. Essex, U.K.: Longman, 2000.

Johnson, Douglas H. *The Root Causes of Sudan's Civil Wars.* Bloomington: Indiana University Press, 2003.

Lesch, Ann Mosley. *Sudan: Contested National Identities.* Bloomington: Indiana University Press, 1998.

Niblock, Tim. *Class and Power in Sudan: The Dynamics of Sudanese Politics, 1898-1985.* Albany: State University of New York Press, 1987.

Woodward, Peter. *Sudan, 1898–1989: The Unstable State.* Boulder, CO: Lynne Rienner, 1990.

AHMAD ALAWAD SIKAINGA

SUDAN: WARS.

Sudan has been riddled with civil wars since the days leading to its independence. The Sudan wars are divided into the First Sudanese Civil War (1955–1972), the Second Sudanese Civil War (1983–2005), and various localized conflicts such as the wars in Darfur and eastern Sudan. The lack of comprehensive solutions to the root causes of the two Sudanese civil wars has resulted in local fighting and perpetuated the spiral of violence.

The systematic marginalization, domination, and political control imposed by an elite group, coupled with the politicization of religious and ethnic identities, have deeply divided Sudanese society. The widespread inequality in access to economic opportunities, education, and political power were not addressed when Britain granted Sudan independence in 1956. In the early twenty-first century the historical patterns of governance still exist and the country remains centrally governed by the elite in Khartoum, with large areas of the country starved of basic infrastructure. The ruling elite in the north aims to govern the country based on Islamist principles and an Islamist national identity, which has alienated non-Muslim and Muslim Sudanese alike. Sudan remains a highly factionalized country in which ethnicity—along the lines of Arab-versus-African identity, as well as among smaller ethnic groups—has become both a political tool and the motive for continued fighting. Yet, simplifying the war into a conflict of identities and of Islam-versus-Christianity glosses over the actual, strategic political and structural realities.

The local and national wars have been devastating: contemporary Sudan is marked by underdevelopment, displacement, and inequality. Every peace agreement signed during the long history of fighting has failed to pacify the country, because none have fully addressed the issues of wealth and power for the benefit of all Sudanese. The current state of official peace in the early twenty-first century, based on the Comprehensive Peace Agreement (CPA) in the south, the Eastern Sudan Peace Agreement (ESPA), and the Darfur Peace Agreement (DPA), has already proven to be unworkable.

The First Sudanese Civil War was fought over regional southern autonomy. At independence, the south was promised federalism. However, the vision of a federal Sudan remained unfulfilled, resulting in almost no political power for the south. The central political powers also have done little to tackle the dismal economic and developmental situation of most Sudanese. The ensuing war killed five hundred thousand people and displaced hundreds of thousands more. Peace negotiations began in 1971 when various southern guerrilla groups formed an alliance as the Southern Sudan Liberation Movement (SSLM) to become a unified negotiation partner to the north. The war officially ended with the signing of the Addis Ababa Agreement in 1972, granting the south regional autonomy and a distinct southern administrative

region. In spite of this effort, the agreement failed to establish a peaceful Sudan due to the lack of political will in Khartoum to implement peace. In addition, disunity amongst southern politicians and the absence of a peace dividend for most Sudanese brought the country back to war in 1983. The Second Sudanese Civil War is often seen as a continuation of the First, rather than a distinct war, as there was essentially a contestation over the same issues. In addition, the large and lucrative oilfields in southern Sudan make Khartoum even less likely to truly grant regional autonomy.

The second war was fought between the central government, which in 1989 became an Islamist government after a coup led by Omar Ahmed el-Bashir (b. 1944) and the newly established Sudan People's Liberation Army/Movement (SPLA/M) under Dr. John Garang de Mabior (1945–2005). It was one of Africa's and the world's longest conflicts. Estimates of deaths are commonly in excess of two million, the majority being civilians who died of war-related diseases or malnutrition. Twice as many people were displaced. The SPLA itself, although successful as a fighting force in control of large areas and even oilfields, was struggling with inner conflict. This eventually caused a split and an attempt by Garang's former comrades to overthrow him. That division led to some of the fiercest fighting of the war, which drew on and fuelled long-standing ethnic tensions. Various attempts at peace proved futile for over a decade until the Inter-Governmental Authority on Development (IGAD) peace process led to the signing of the Comprehensive Peace Agreement (CPA) in January 2005.

The CPA includes protocols on power- and wealth sharing, the reorganization of armed forces, an autonomous Government of Southern Sudan (GoSS) under the Government of National Unity (GoNU), and provides for a referendum in the south to decide on southern independence in 2011. The peace agreement came with big hopes for the future, but it has largely failed to fulfill its promises. The development of southern Sudan is starting from scratch and most institutions needed to implement the peace agreement have yet to be established. At the same time, ongoing conflict in other areas through Khartoum-supported militias has cast doubt on Khartoum's commitment to peace. The loss of southern Sudan, which seems likely if peace holds and the referendum goes ahead, would entail the loss of precious oil revenue by the central government in Khartoum.

Concurrent to the ongoing CPA negotiations in 2003, the central government intensified its war efforts in Sudan's west, namely Darfur. One crippling shortcoming of the CPA is its dichotomy as a peace agreement negotiated between north and south, perpetuating the neglect of other regions such as the east and Darfur. The war in Darfur has been fought over the same issues of neglect and marginalization of the mainly Muslim population of Darfur and the terror imposed upon the people of Darfur through Khartoum's proxy forces, the *Janjaweed*. A peace deal negotiated in May 2006 left little hope for improvement as not all rebel groups agreed to sign the deal and, soon after, fighting by both the Janjaweed and Sudanese military intensified. It is estimated that at least 200,000 people have been killed in four years of fighting between 2003 and 2007, with 2.5 million displaced. In August 2006, the United Nations (UN) Security Council passed a resolution calling for UN peacekeepers to support the powerless African Union Mission on the ground. In April 2007, under intense international pressure and the threat of increased sanctions, the Khartoum government agreed to allow 3,000 UN troops into Darfur. Air raids and attacks, however, continued even after the official announcement to cooperate with the UN.

Khartoum's international relations have been increasingly strained since the 1989 coup. Relations between Khartoum and the United States deteriorated after Sudan backed the Iraqi invasion of Kuwait and provided sanctuary for terrorist groups led by Osama bin Laden, among others. The U.S. Government declared Sudan a state sponsor of terrorism in 1993, imposing trade sanctions later that decade, which have been tightened during the Darfur crisis. After September 11, 2001, Sudan cooperated in giving information on international terrorism, but has also criticized U.S. interventions in Afghanistan and Iraq.

Relations between the United States and the SPLA/M were much better, with the United States being a major donor of humanitarian aid under "Operations Lifeline Sudan." The United States has played a crucial role in the negotiations leading to the CPA. Political support for Southern Sudan has been based both on alienation with the Khartoum government, but also on establishing good relations with the Government of Southern Sudan in order to maintain an open path for negotiations about oil contracts.

Sudan's oil wealth has been one of the major factors in the ongoing conflict between North and South. Oil revenues have financed much of Khartoum's war effort. Many oilfields lie in contested areas along the border between North and South, with oil contracts being signed by both the Government in Khartoum as well as the Government of Southern Sudan since the signing of the peace agreement. Exerting international pressure on Sudan over Darfur has been difficult as trade relations with China are exceptionally good. China has used its permanent seat on the Security Council to speak in favor of Sudan and avert the threat of oil sanctions. Sanctioning Sudan has thus been difficult both for the United States and the international community as Sudan relies on China for its exports and weapons supplies.

China has been delivering military equipment to Sudan since the 1960s. The 1990s saw an intensified trade and military relationship between Beijing and Khartoum. China derives most of its overseas oil supply from Sudan under contracts signed with the Khartoum government. Chinese laborers work in Khartoum-controlled areas. Little is known about conditions in the oil fields under Chinese contracts.

However, the Republic of Sudan stands accused in a lawsuit brought forth in a U.S. court that is has committed genocide in pursuit of oil. The lawsuit, brought on jointly against the Republic of Sudan and Canadian energy company Talisman Energy, highlighted issues of complicity by international corporations engaging in business with Sudan. Talisman faced intense criticism from shareholders and human rights groups when it engaged in Sudan in 1998. Facing allegations of complicity in genocide for having employed Sudanese government troops for its security operations and prolonging the war, Talisman pulled out of Sudan in 2003. In September 2006, the case against Talisman was dismissed when a judge could not see enough evidence for Talisman's complicity, although the case against the Republic of Sudan still stands. The plaintiffs appealed the judge's decision in early 2007 with a hearing scheduled for the summer that year.

While much emphasis is placed on the North/South conflict and Darfur, other parts of the country have experienced either low-level conflict, as in the east, or severe marginalization that might potentially be the powder keg for a full-blown conflict, as in the Nuba mountains that has been at the frontline between Khartoum and the SPLA. Although the Eastern Sudan Peace Agreement, signed in October 2006, gives reason for hope for this most-neglected of Sudan's regions, the difficulties surrounding its implementation will be acute. One of the main problems in ending Sudan's wars is that the CPA was not an inclusive agreement, leaving many areas and groups as isolated as before. What also remains in question is Khartoum's commitment to peace and wealth sharing.

See also **Bashir, Omar Ahmed el-; United Nations; Warfare.**

BIBLIOGRAPHY

Burr, J. Millard, and Robert O. Collins. *Darfur: The Long Road to Disaster.* Princeton, NJ: Markus Wiener, 2006.

De Waal, Alexander, and Julie Flint. *Darfur: A Short History of a Long War.* London: Zed Books, 2005.

Deng, Francis M. "Sudan: A Nation in Turbulent Search of Itself." *Annals of the American Academy of Political and Social Science* 603, no. 1 (2006): 155–162.

Dixon, Peter, and Mark Simmons. *Peace by Piece: Addressing Sudan's Conflicts.* London: Conciliation Resources, 2007.

Johnson, Douglas. *The Root Causes of Sudan's Civil Wars.* Oxford: James Currey, 2003.

Kadouf, Hunud. "Marginalization and Resistance: The Plight of the Nuba People." *New Political Science* 23, no. 1 (2001): 45–63.

Pantuliano, Sara. "Comprehensive Peace? Causes and Consequences of Underdevelopment and Instability in Eastern Sudan." Nongovernmental Organization Paper, Sudan Advocacy Coalition, 2005.

Schomerus, Mareike. *Peace and Minorities in Sudan.* London: Minority Rights Group International, 2007.

MAREIKE SCHOMERUS

SUDAN, EASTERN, HISTORY OF (1500 TO 1880 CE).

Historically North Africans referred to the land south of the Sahara Desert as *bilad al-sudan*, or "land of the blacks." In the twenty-first century the term has come to describe the Sahel and the open savanna. Eastern Sudan's most important physical features are the Nile River to the east, which flows from Uganda north to the Mediterranean, whereas to the west is Lake Chad. This comparatively fertile zone has historically been inhabited by a mosaic of ethnic groups. Around 1500 a chain of Sudanic kingdoms arose stretching along this savanna belt in what have become the modern republics of Sudan and Chad.

In the thirteenth and fourteenth centuries the genesis of Darfur emerged on what is the western boundary of present-day Sudan. Beginning with the Daju culture it sprang to life because of trade. By the fifteenth century the Nubian Tunjur had seized control only to be toppled by the Kayra, an Arabic speaking Fur dynasty.

Southeast of Lake Chad, Bagirmi emerged around 1480 in what is now Chad. From 1522 it paid tribute to Kanem-Bornu to its northwest. Although absorbed into the latter empire in the seventeenth century it later gained independence only to return to tribute paying in the mid-eighteenth century. In the nineteenth century Bagirmi was attacked by Wadai to its northeast and fell into decline.

From 1500 to 1821 the Islamic Nubian Funj kingdom of Sinnar (a successor state to the early Christian Nile kingdoms) arose and came to embrace much of the northern Nile valley in Sudan. In 1762 the matrilineal dynasty was overthrown; its patrilineal successor brought fifty years of strife. By 1821, however, the sultanate was easily conquered by the Turco-Egyptian colonizing armies.

West of Darfur in present-day Chad, northeast of Bagirmi, Wadai emerged in the sixteenth century as an offshoot of Darfur. Becoming the principal power east of Bornu, its ruling Nubian Tunjur dynasty was overthrown in the seventeenth century. During the eighteenth century Wadai resisted Darfurian hegemony while simultaneously dominating Bagirmi to its southwest.

TRADE, TRADE ROUTES, AND SLAVES

Trade was extremely important to the rise of the Sahelian states; it strengthened rulers through the accumulation of wealth and association with foreign merchants, thus affording a monopoly over strategically important items such as metals and horses. All had contact across the Sahara with North Africa. Exports to the north and in Sinnar's case also to the Red Sea included cottons, ivory, perfume, wax, hides and skins, ostrich fathers, gold and slaves. More importantly, trade encouraged a cosmopolitan presence. Sinnar, for example, had 100,000 residents in 1669 and it became an empire with traders and visitors from all over the world; after Cairo it was one of the most densely populated cities. Sinnar's trade items found markets in Western Asia and Europe, initially through Cairo. Nevertheless these Sahelian states had more frequent commercial trade east from the Nile Valley and west toward Bornu.

The sale of slaves was an institution of immense importance in Eastern Sudan, historically representing the major stimulus to the trans-Saharan trade. Slaves came into the main markets of these sultanates in three principal ways: through raids and kidnapping, as tribute, and in trade. The dwindling supply of white slaves in the latter eighteenth-century Ottoman world increased the demand for blacks. The luxury trade in eunuchs would bring immense wealth; eighteenth- and nineteenth-century Bagirmi in particular was a major exporter.

The sultanates with access to key trading routes north prospered considerably. The Wadai sultans were anxious to promote a road east of Bornu and west of Darfur. It soon profited enormously because it came to preside at the nexus of two important trade routes; one leading from the upper Nile and Darfur to Bornu and Kano and the second across the Sahara to Benghazi in Tripoli on the Mediterranean. In consequence, Darfur's long distance trade along the *darb al-arba'in* or the "forty days road" across the desert to Egypt (referred to in a 1663 source), declined around 1850 with the rise of the western Benghazi-Wadai trade route. By the beginning of the nineteenth century it was more vital than all the others. The Wadai-Benghazi route prospered until after 1900. Little is known about the volume of slave traffic across the desert. Scholars suggest that between 1800 and 1880 half a million slaves entered Egypt and a quarter of a million were taken to Morocco.

PREDATORY STATES, EXPANSION, AND DOMESTIC SLAVES

According to a theory known as the "predatory state thesis," the formation of highly militarized states was linked to the increase in demand for slaves; it sees slave production and the slave trade as crucial to the functioning and reproduction of states. The chain of sultanates that developed along the east African Sahel were predatory states and each developed a war-making machine far more destructive and organized than in previous eras. Full-time professional slave armies evolved as weapons of war became more expensive; the latter required special skills to handle firearms and cavalry horses. Most slave raids focused southward toward the small-scale stateless communities. Whereas Bagirmi sent captives to the Ottoman empire of modern-day Turkey, Sinnar organized the acquisition of slaves annually with its highly organized campaign, the "salatiya." As the Funj slave armies continued to expand south and southwest the sultanate acquired a bigger and wider influx of resources including slaves, gold, ivory, and other articles for trade. Darfur's sultans expanded east into Funj territory as well as west. Then, in 1800, Wadai discovered its new trade route north and began to mint its own coinage and import chain mail, firearms and military advisers from North Africa.

The intensification of the slave trade was paralleled by a new domestic demand. Slavery became an integral part of every economic system. This included the military, the government, in agriculture, as artisans, concubines, and eunuchs.

Another component of the predatory state was the formation of predatory satellite states, smaller entities that emerged on the periphery of their larger patrons. One of the best examples emerged southwest of Sinnar on the Nile where the Western Nilotic Shilluk kingdom evolved. Because of simultaneous wars with Sinnar as well as their bitter stateless enemies who were far more numerous (the Western Nilotic Dinka), the Shilluk centralized into a small predatory state, selling Dinka and other war captives to Sinnarian merchants on the Nile as well as to the growing Nuban kingdom of Tegali to their northwest. In return the Shilluk acquired metals and food items and correspondingly expanded their political and military power base. Similarly, south of Darfur, two petty satellites evolved, the predatory Dar Fertit kingdoms of

Feroge and Ngulgule; each fed vociferously on surrounding stateless captives which they traded north to Darfur; in the meantime they expanded southward.

ISLAM AND POLITICAL CENTRALIZATION

The period from 1480 to 1520 was a time of active Islamization in the bilad al-sudan. Islamic North Africa's relations with the Sahara and the Sudanese belt to its south centered upon the central and eastern routes across the desert. This process encouraged sultanates to develop as important centers of government and trade. Islam had begun to come in by way of Bornu, located southwest of Lake Chad and served as a transmitter of influences from North Africa to the east. The opening of the Sudanic pilgrimage route and the population movement from the west, which it facilitated had an important social, legal, and political consequence in the nineteenth century.

However, Islamization, patrilineal by nature, devastated the matrilineal Sinnarian sultanate. As the eighteenth century advanced, the opening of influences from the Islamic heartlands eroded institutions vital to the matrilineal Funj government and its state control over trade. In 1775, the kingdom lapsed into a half century of civil strife while middle class Arabic traders built dozens of villages. The sultanate collapsed with the arrival of the colonizing Egyptians. Ultimately all four states adopted the Arabic language through contact with Arabic speaking traders.

STATELESS SOCIETIES AND RESISTANCE

The predatory state thesis interprets surrounding decentralized societies as potential slaving reservoirs for captives to sell into the Atlantic and Saharan trades. It has been assumed that these stateless societies were passive victims; for many smaller cultures this model may fit the above thesis. With larger decentralized groups however, statelessness could be an advantage. This was the case with Egypt's colonization of Sudan in 1821. In its wake many states fell, Sinnar included. Egypt needed new slave recruits for its expanding armies and Sudan's most populous ethnic group, the Southern Sudanese stateless Dinka who were also the most prized of slaves, fell prey to the empires predations for decades. Khartoum traders penetrated the valley of the upper Nile and slave raiding, on a scale hitherto unknown, then took place. It is estimated that two million were killed or abducted during the nineteenth century. The violent pillaging of Dinka communities encouraged mass resistance. Armies of up to fifty thousand strong confederated; their flexible militaries acquired priest-leaders, while females became religious leaders. Unified by a new lingua franca in the region, Arabic, numerous Dinka warriors in 1884 militarily ejected the Egyptians permanently from their homelands. Officially united with the Sudanese nationalists—the Mahdi—although unofficially with little help from the latter's forces, their homelands fell into the hands of the Mahdist army, the Dervishes. Slave raids once again intensified but the Mahdists were also militarily ejected.

See also **Chad; Ethiopia and Vicinity, History of (600 to 1600 CE); Islam; Nile River; Sahara Desert; Slave Trades.**

BIBLIOGRAPHY

Beswick, Stephanie F. "Violence, Ethnicity and Political Consolidation." In *South Sudan: A History of the Dinka and Their Relations with Their Neighbors 1200–1994.* Ph.D. diss., Michigan State University, 1998.

Beswick, Stephanie F. *Sudan's Blood Memory: The Legacy of War, Ethnicity and Slavery in Early South Sudan.* Rochester, NY: University of Rochester Press, 2004.

Collins, Robert O. *The Southern Sudan in Historical Perspective.* Tel Aviv: Israel Press, 1975.

Gray, Richard. *A History of the Southern Sudan 1839–1889.* Oxford: Oxford University Press, 1961.

Holt, Peter Malcolm, and Martin W. Daly. *A History of the Sudan.* London: Weidenfeld and Nicolson, 1979.

O'Fahey, R. Sean. *State and Society in Dar Fur.* New York. St. Martin's Press, 1980.

O'Fahey, R. Sean, and Jay L. Spaulding. *Kingdoms of the Sudan.* London: Methuen, 1974.

Spaulding, Jay L. *The Heroic Age in Sinnar.* East Lansing: Michigan State University Press, 1985.

STEPHANIE BESWICK

SUDAN, WEST AND CENTRAL, HISTORY OF (1500 TO 1800 CE).

The history of West and Central Sudan from 1500 to 1800 was a period when old empires declined and new states emerged, in which major stimuli for economic change came not from the desert but from the coast, and in which the beginnings of a major religious upheaval took place. At the beginning of the period, the Sudan was dominated by Songhay in the Niger valley and Bornu in the Chad basin, but the Hausa states had already emerged as major centers of power and economic progress. The slave trade on the Senegambian coast still had no visible effect on the region.

The major polities had much in common. By 1500, they all had centralized bureaucratic states, in which offices were awarded by merit and loyalty. While members of the royal families were not unimportant, a key role was played by slave officials, some of whom had great wealth and power. Many were eunuchs. The slave trade was important, particularly in the central Sudan where slaves were the most important of Borno's exports to North Africa. Slavery was also important, providing soldiers, officials, concubines and agricultural workers. There was a high degree of social differentiation with distinct groups of merchants, soldiers, clerics, officials, and artisans. The trans-Sahara trade was probably less important than the desert-side trade between pastoralists and agriculturalists, the east-west trade and the trade between savanna and forest. Commerce was dominated by Muslim professional traders. The region was also a center of many kinds of productive activity, particularly textiles and leather.

SONGHAY AND BORNU

Sunni 'Ali (c. 1464–1492), the ruler of Gao, built a state that displaced Mali as the dominant power in the Niger valley. Using both cavalry and a fleet of canoes, he extended Songhay control along the Niger River, into the Sahara Desert and south to the Mossi kingdoms. When he died, a Muslim general, Mohammed Ture, took power as the Askia (r. 1493–1528, d. 1538). Askia Mohammed has generally been more favorably treated by scholars than Sunni 'Ali because he ended Sunni 'Ali's discrimination against the *ulema* of Timbuktu. Both rulers attempted to maintain a balanced approach to both Islam and traditional cults, but the Askias used Islam more systematically. The most important of Askia Mohammed's successors was Askia Daud (1530–1584), under whom Songhay enjoyed a long period of peace and stability. Under the patronage of the Askias, Timbuktu

was the most important center of learning in Muslim Africa.

In 1590 the Moroccan Sultan, El-Mansour, sent an army armed with muskets across the Sahara hoping to control the sources of gold and salt. Songhay forces, which had never faced firearms, were defeated at Tondibi. The Moroccans then seized Gao, Timbuktu, and Jenné, but could not hold the empire together. When the expedition did not produce economic results, El-Mansour lost interest. The descendants of the invaders, the Arma, remained important, but by 1733, Timbuktu was tributary to a Tuareg polity. The unity of the western Sudan was never restored. Islam remained important, particularly in commercial cities. In a number of areas, particularly after 1700, there developed a twin cities phenomenon in which a polity was dominated by communities of warriors and traders, who lived in separate communities, linked to each other, but inhabiting separate places.

CENTRAL SUDAN

Borno traces its origins to the relocation of the Kanem royal dynasty south of Lake Chad, away from its nomadic roots into an agricultural area. In the fifteenth century, a more bureaucratic state was developed using slave and eunuch officials, which brought much of the southern Lake Chad basin under its control. It became, as Kanem was, an important source of slaves for North Africa. It reached its greatest extent under Mai Idris Alooma (1571–1603). Where the Moroccans brought muskets to the Western Sudan, Idris Alooma brought a band of Turkish musketeers to Borno and used them to extend his power. He also opened up diplomatic relations with Tripoli, procured a steady supply of horses for his cavalry, and made Islam the official religion. During the seventeenth and eighteenth centuries, there was some decline as Borno rule was challenged in peripheral areas and the Mai's person was tied up in ritual, much of it pre-Islamic.

Bornu remained powerful, nevertheless, but increasingly the central Sudan was dominated by the Hausa. The most important of the Hausa rulers was Mohammad Rumfa, the Sarkin of Kano (1463–1499). During his reign, city walls were extended, a new market was built, and a more centralized state structure was developed with a state council as well as slave and eunuch officials. Most important, trade and politics exposed Kano to different Muslim influences, coming from Borno as well as from Mande traders called *Wangarawa*. Kano also became in this period not only a center of trade, but a center of production, particularly of dyed cotton cloth and Morocco leather, so called because Europeans bought it in Morocco.

Many writers have suggested that there was an overall decline both in the power of the central Sudanic states and in their commitment to Islam during this period. There is some suggestion, for example, that there was a reversion to pre-Islamic ritual in Borno, but certainly, when attacked by the jihads of the nineteenth century, Borno considered itself a Muslim polity. As for the Hausa, it would be better to see the conflicts of the nineteenth century as wars between two different kinds of Muslims rather than as wars between Muslims and non-Muslims.

SLAVERY AND ISLAM

The Atlantic slave trade had little impact on sudanic West Africa during the sixteenth century, though Senegambia was a major source of slaves during those years. By the late seventeenth century, demand had increased and far outpaced the trans-Sahara trade. Furthermore, as societies close to the coast became slavers, and middlemen learned to resist more effectively, the tentacles of the trade reached far into the interior. From the late seventeenth century, the largest slave exporter on the Bight of Bénin was Oyo, a cavalry state based in the savanna. Oyo fed Hausa, Nupe, Bariba and Yoruba slaves to various points along the coast. Further east, a forest state, Asante, became the dominant power in the hinterland of the Gold Coast with its victory over Denkyera in 1702. By the second half of the eighteenth century, Asante had subdued a series of northern savanna kingdoms, all of whom paid tribute to Asante in slaves. The result was a slaving vortex that fed slaves from the savanna to the coast through Oyo and Asante.

Senegambia was a major source of the early trade, but by the late seventeenth century, the slaves exported from Senegambia came mostly from the Bamana-speaking areas of western Mali. Here two states emerged in the early eighteenth century. In about 1712, Biton Kulubali created Segu on the basis of a men's association. The dominant force in Segu was a body of slave warriors called the *tonjon*. Segu was a state that lived by the slave trade and reproduced itself by the slave trade. In the 1750s, Kaarta broke away to create another *tonjon* state in desert-side areas north of Segu. Many slaving states, like Segu, started out as military formations that produced most of their slaves from warfare, but invariably, once a political center emerged, it became an important market for slaves. Most slaving states had client states and commercial allies that fed slaves through its system. The rise of the Bamana contributed to the prosperity of the Maraka, a Muslim commercial community, which provided the political-military hierarchy with trade goods in exchange for slaves. Many were taken to the coast, but others were used within the Sudan, as Maraka and *juula* traders invested in productive activity, much of it oriented to the desert-side trade.

Up to the seventeenth century, Islam spread peacefully in West Africa, its success based on the attraction of Islam to traders and political elites. By the seventeenth century, Islam was dominant in the Sudan and a presence elsewhere. Muslims were often scribes and advisers to kings. They were dominant in the cities, but many also developed rural bastions, in which ideas of reform were preached. These ideas had their greatest impact where the Muslim community felt threatened. The slave trade was not always the source of these threats, but often it was. The first jihad was led in the 1670s by Nasr al-Din, a Mauritanian marabout, who called for rulers in the Senegal valley to practice Islam, limit themselves to four wives, and stop pillaging and selling their subjects. He briefly controlled the lower Senegal river and three Wolof states, but his anti-slave trade message threatened the French who supported the traditional aristocracy. He was killed in 1673 and the traditional order was re-established by 1677. In 1776, Muslim reformers took power in the Futa Toro, where the *denianke* rulers were unable to protect people against slavers. The most important eighteenth-century jihad took place in Futa Jallon, a mountainous part of Guinea. It originated not in reaction to the slave trade, but in conflict between the Diallonke, who farmed the valleys and the Fulbe, who grazed their herds on the high slopes. During a half-century of war, the Fulbe became effective slavers in order to get the arms they needed. Once in power, the enforced *shari* law, built mosques and created schools.

Elsewhere, there were many preachers of reform. In the bend of the Niger, Sidi al-Mukhtar al-Kunti attacked pre-Islamic survivals and called for mystical studies and a revival of religious piety. Elsewhere, Muslim reformers attacked the corruption of elites and took their message to the countryside. 'Uthman dan Fodio was one of these preachers. By the end of the eighteenth century, the situation was ripe for a conflict between these Muslim reformers and the established rulers. Those conflicts erupted in the nineteenth century.

See also **Chad; Gao; Islam; Jenné and Jenné-jeno; Niger; Niger River; Slave Trades; Sunni 'Ali; Timbuktu; Western and Saharan Africa, History of (600 to 1600 CE).**

BIBLIOGRAPHY

Adamu, Mahdi. *The Hausa Factor in West Africa.* New York: Oxford University Press, 1978.

Ajayi, J. F. Ade, and Michael Crowder, eds. *History of West Africa,* Vol. 1, 2nd edition. London: Longman, 1985.

Cissoko, Sekene Mody. *Tombouctou et l'empire Songhay.* Dakar: Nouvelles Editions Africaines, 1975.

Curtin, Philip. *Economic Change in Precolonial Africa: Senegambia in the Era of the Slave Trade.* Madison: University of Wisconsin Press, 1975.

Hunwick, John. *Shari' in Songhay.* New York: Oxford University Press, 1985.

Roberts, Richard. *Warriors, Merchants, and Slaves: The State and the Economy in the Middle Niger Valley, 1700–1914.* Stanford, CA: Stanford University Press, 1987.

MARTIN KLEIN

SUNDJATA KEÏTA (c. 1205–c. 1255).

Sundjata Keïta was born in Dakajala in the vicinity of the upper Niger River, the second son of Maghan Kon Fatta (d. c. 1212), king of Manding. According to oral tradition, Sundjata had an unhappy childhood. When he was only seven years old, his father died and his elder half-brother, Dankaran-Tuma, ascended the throne. Sundjata, now persecuted, went into exile with his mother, sisters, and younger brother.

The Manding kingdom, situated on the High Niger, encompassed the Bouré, a province rich in gold. Its king was a vassal to the emperor of Ghana, an outlet to the north for the gold. Yet the Ghana Empire was torn apart by civil war and in decline. Sumanguru Kante (c. 1190–1255), the king of the intervening state of Susu and the chief of the blacksmiths (a powerful caste) in the region, subjugated Ghana and imposed his domination on Manding. Dankaran-Tuma, unable to defend his kingdom, relinquished the throne and fled. The king of Susu then brought a reign of terror to Manding and suppressed several revolts.

The Mandinka and Malinke people of Manding dispatched a secret mission to find Sundjata, who was known to have taken refuge somewhere in eastern Manding. He was found at the court of Mema, where King Mema Farin Tounkaran had entrusted him with important responsibilities. The king gave him an army, and Sundjata and his family returned to their native country. When it became known that Sundjata had come, the Malinke revolted against Sumanguru's authority. Then began a fierce battle between the Malinke and the Susu; the decisive skirmish took place in 1235 at Krina on the banks of the Niger. The Susu were routed, Sumanguru fled, and Sundjata destroyed the city of the Susu.

United, the Malinke led the way to victory after victory under the banner of their young king, assisted by two brilliant lieutenants, Tiramakhan Traoré and Fakoli Kourouma. They imposed their domination on all the kingdoms of the savanna and built up a vast kingdom extending from Timbuktu on the Niger to Banjul at the mouth of the Gambia River on the Atlantic Ocean. This kingdom, the Mali Empire, was the largest and most famous of the African empires in the Middle Ages.

Sundjata reigned from 1235 to 1255. The war of liberation of the Malinke from the yoke of Sumanguru is the subject of the Mandinka epic, that Mandinka oral tradition has transmitted through the griots (bards) from generation to generation even as of the end of the twentieth century.

In addition to being a brilliant military leader, Sundjata proved a skilled administrator and lawmaker. The vast empire under his power comprised kingdoms and many other peoples. A flexible administration gave these groups a great deal of autonomy, with each community allowed to keep its own traditions and customs. The empire was divided into two military regions and the roads and trails in the empire were secure.

Sundjata's work as lawmaker was considerable. He established the laws that have governed the lives of the Malinke people into the twenty-first century. He created a system of alliance both among Malinke clans and between Malinke clans and others. For example, among the Malinke, the patronymics Conde and Traoré correspond to the Wolof names N'Diaye and Diop, respectively. If Malinkens of the Conde or Traoré clan want to establish themselves in the Wolof country (Senegal), they take the name N'Diaye or Diop in order to be accepted as such in the clan. A similar system of correspondence was established between the Malinke and Fulani (Fulbe) patronymics.

In the Malinke oral tradition, Sundjata Keita is a man of many names and prestigious titles. He is called Nare Maghan Konate (the King of the Konate, from which the Keita dynasty arose), Marijata (Lord Lion), Maghan Sundjata (Sundjata the King), and Sogo Sogo Simbon Salaba (Master Hunter with the Venerable Bearing).

After his victory at Krina, Sundjata converted to Islam and established his capital at Niani on the Sankarani River, a tributary to the Niger. Excavations made at this site have revealed stone foundations of dwellings and public buildings dating back to the time of Sundjata.

See also **Sudan: History and Politics; Western and Saharan Africa, History of (600 to 1600 CE).**

BIBLIOGRAPHY

Histoire général de l'Afrique. Vol. 4, *L'Afrique du XIIe au XVIe siècle.* Paris, 1985.

Ly Tall, Madina. *Contributions de l'histoire de l'empire du Mali (XIIIe–XVIe sieécles).* Paris: Nouvelles Editions africaines, 1977.

Niane, Djibril Tamsir. *Recherche sur l'empire du Mali au moyenâge.* Paris, 1975.

DJIBRIL TAMSIR NIANE

SUNNI 'ALI (1464–1492). Sunni 'Ali came to power in the fifteenth-century Songhay state when Mali's suzerainty over the Middle Niger had waned so far that the nomadic Saharan Tuareg controlled the important desert-edge commercial city of Timbuktu near the northernmost part of the great bend in the Niger River. With immense energy and considerable leadership skills, Sunni 'Ali campaigned around the Middle Niger, carving out a swath of territory on either side of the river from the Dendi region (near the border of twenty-first century Nigeria and Bénin) to the area of Jenné in the southern region of the Inland Delta of the Niger River (in twenty-first century Mali). Timbuktu fell to his forces in 1468, and many of the city's scholarly elite fled to Walāta (in Mauritania), some 250 miles to the west. Some of the Muslim dignitaries were ill-treated or killed, and, among the Timbuktu scholars, Sunni 'Ali gained a reputation as a tyrant and butcher whose Islamic faith was in doubt.

Although excoriated by the Timbuktu chroniclers and in essence condemned as an apostate Muslim by the visiting North African scholar al-Maghili, Sunni 'Ali's achievement was considerable. He laid the foundations of a state that was to expand into a flourishing Sahelian empire under the subsequent dynasty of the *askiyas* (1493–1591).

See also **Islam; Jenné and Jenné-jeno; Timbuktu.**

BIBLIOGRAPHY

Adam Konare Ba. *Sonni Ali Ber.* Niamey, Niger: Institut de recherches en sciences humaines, 1977.

JOHN HUNWICK

SUSENYOS (c. 1580–c. 1632). Susenyos was emperor of Ethiopia from 1607 to 1632. A nephew of Sarsa Dengel (emperor, r. 1563–1597), Susenyos came to the Ethiopian throne after a period of civil war in which his predecessor Ya'iqob, Sarsa Dengel's son, perished. Like the Emperor Za Dengel, who had temporarily deposed Ya'iqob before being killed in a rebellion, Susenyos was convinced that the acceptance of the authority of Rome in place of that of Alexandria was desirable for reasons both political and religious. He was encouraged in this by a sympathetic Jesuit missionary, Pedro Páez, and by his own brother, Celakrestos, the governor of Gojjam, who had become a zealous Catholic. Susenyos was reconciled by Páez to the Catholic Church in 1622. Páez died shortly afterward. In 1625 a Latin patriarch, Alfonso Mendez, was solemnly received by Susenyos but at once embarked on such an insensitive program of Latinization of the Ethiopian Church that a multitude of revolts followed. Susenyos eventually abdicated in favor of his son Fasiladas, who expelled Mendez and restored the authority of Alexandria.

Susenyos appears as one of the most powerful and intelligent of Ethiopian emperors, a ruthless modernizer who misjudged his ability to change the religious commitment of his subjects and was betrayed by the uncompromising rigidity of Mendez.

See also **Ethiopia and the Horn, History of (1600 to 1910).**

BIBLIOGRAPHY

Caraman, Philip. *The Lost Empire: The Story of the Jesuits in Ethiopia, 1555–1634.* Notre Dame, IN: University of Notre Dame Press, 1985.

Pereira, F. M. E., ed. *Chronica de Susenyos, rei de Ethiopia.* Lisbon, Imprensa Nacional, 1892–1900.

ADRIAN HASTINGS

SUZMAN, HELEN (1917–).

Helen Gavronsky Suzman was a prominent anti-apartheid activist and opposition member of the South African parliament from 1953 until 1989. She was born in the Transvaal, the daughter of Jewish immigrants from Lithuania. She studied commerce at the University of Witwatersrand (Wits), left to marry Mosie Suzman (c. 1904–1994) in 1937, and returned to complete her degree after the birth of their daughter Frances in 1939. She had a second daughter, Patricia (b. 1943), and taught economic history at Wits from 1945 to 1953. Suzman first joined the United Party (UP) in 1949, just as the apartheid system was being strengthened. She was elected to Parliament in 1953. In 1959 the UP split, and she remained in the more progressive section that formed the Progressive Party (PP). For thirteen years, 1961 to 1974, she was the sole

South African politician Dame Helen Suzman (1917–). Suzman served in Parliament for 36 years. She visited Nelson Mandela in prison numerous times and was by his side when he signed the new constitution in 1996. CAMBRIDGE JONES/GETTY IMAGES

PP Member of Parliament and often the only voice opposing the increasingly stringent racial laws; in 1974 the number of PP members increased.

In 1977 the PP became the Progressive Federal Party, which continued as the official opposition party. Suzman's approach to politics is illustrated by her often-quoted comment that, "I hate bullies. I stand for simple justice, equal opportunity and human rights. The indispensable elements in a democratic society—and well worth fighting for." She retired from Parliament in 1989 and wrote her autobiography. She remained active as a commissioner on the South African Human Rights Commission from 1994 to 1998, and with the Helen Suzman Foundation, the slogan of which is "Promoting Liberal Democracy in South Africa and Southern Africa." She has received many awards and honors, including the United Nations Award of the International League for Human Rights in 1978.

See also **Apartheid; Human Rights; Judaism in Africa; Mandela, Nelson; South Africa, Republic of.**

BIBLIOGRAPHY

Helen Suzman Foundation. Available from http://www.hsf.org.za

Lewsen, Phyllis, ed. *Helen Suzman's Solo Years.* Johannesburg, South Africa: Jonathan Ball and Ad Donker, 1991.

Shain, Milton, ed. *Opposing Voices: Liberalism and Opposition in South Africa Today.* Includes a Tribute to Helen Suzman. Johannesburg, South Africa: Jonathan Ball, 2006.

Strangwayes-Booth, Joanna. *A Cricket in the Thorn Tree: Helen Suzman and the Progressive Party of South Africa.* London: Hutchinson, 1976.

Suzman, Helen. *In No Uncertain Terms: A South African Memoir.* New York: Knopf, 1993.

KATHLEEN SHELDON

SWAHILI COAST. *See* **Eastern African Coast, History of (Early to 1600).**

SWAZILAND

This entry includes the following articles:
GEOGRAPHY AND ECONOMY
SOCIETY AND CULTURES
HISTORY AND POLITICS

GEOGRAPHY AND ECONOMY

Swaziland, a former British colony that received its independence in 1968, is a small landlocked country located between the Republic of South Africa and Mozambique. To its western border lies the modern South African province of Mpumalanga (formerly eastern Transvaal). Swaziland shares its southern border with South Africa's KwaZulu Natal. It is thus almost completely surrounded by its larger and economically much more powerful neighbor, South Africa. For several hundred years, this geographical fact has shaped Swaziland's economy and politics in significant ways.

With an area of 6704 square miles, Swaziland had an estimated population of approximately 1 million in 2007. Lying between 26 and 27 degrees latitude and 31 and 32 degrees longitude, Swaziland falls into four distinct geographical regions, each with distinct physical features and climate. From the furthest point in the northwestern region of the country and covering the highest parts, the highveld ranges in altitude from 3,444 to 3,937 feet. The middleveld follows, with an average altitude between 1,476 and 1,968 feet. Further eastward lies the lowveld, rising between 492 and 300 meters. Finally, the Lubombo range at the furthest point in the east is between 450 and 984 feet in altitude. The northwestern part of the country is

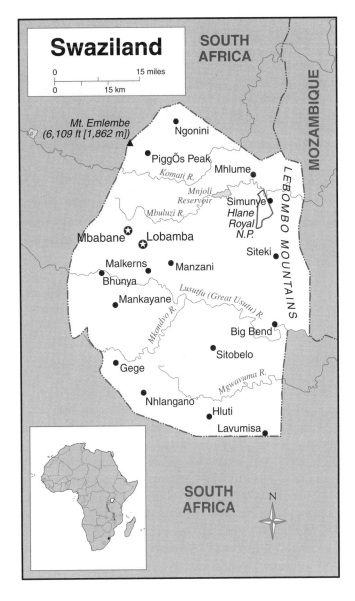

the coldest and wettest region, while the lowveld receives the least amount of rainfall and is normally the driest and hottest. In areas that do not receive nearly enough rainfall, the country's rivers provide a most significant resource for irrigation agriculture. This is particularly true of the middleveld, which produces the bulk of Swaziland's major food crops, especially in the Malkerns Valley. The middleveld not only possesses the country's richest soils, but also has the highest population and the country's main industrial city, Manzini, the "Hub of Swaziland."

Since colonial times, two principal issues have been central to Swaziland's modern economy—the contentious question of land ownership and the

Forestry near Piggs Peak, northern Swaziland. Piggs Peak is a small scenic town in the highveld region of Swaziland, located some 42 kilometers (26 miles) south of Matsamo on the South African border. To its west, at a shorter distance, lies the Bulembu border post, linking Piggs Peak with the nearby South African town of Barbatos. © NORAH NYEKO

controversy over mineral rights. Both originated in the late nineteenth century and both have continued to underline the strong connection between the economies of Swaziland and South Africa. The emergence of a dominance–dependence relationship between South Africa and Swaziland in modern times arose from the minerals and land concessions awarded to private individuals by Swazi rulers in the same period. By the start of the twentieth century, the Swazi owned only one-third of the country's land. Through a sustained buyback project led by the Swazi leadership, however, this proportion had changed by 1968, when the Swazi had just over half of the land. King Sobhuza II favored this policy rather than settle the extremely intricate issue through any extensive land reform. By 1993 only about 17 percent of the land was owned by foreigners.

Agriculture is the mainstay of Swaziland's economy. The land available for agriculture consists of two types: Swazi Nation Land (SNL), where the majority of the Swazi live and carry out subsistence farming, and Title Deed Land (TDL), on which the large foreign-dominated (mostly South African) companies, white settlers, and some wealthy Swazi undertake commercial agriculture. The subsistence farmers produce cash crops such as maize, cotton, and vegetables. The Swazi also practice livestock rearing on SNL. On TDL the

commercial farmers are engaged in the large-scale production of maize, sugar, citrus fruit, and cotton.

Swaziland's modern mining industry began only in the late nineteenth century when several small companies received concessions from the traditional rulers. These foreign companies produced gold, tin, asbestos, coal, and iron throughout the colonial period. At independence, King Sobhuza negotiated the transfer of the royalties from these minerals to a special fund, *Tibiyo Taka Ngwane* (The wealth of the nation), controlled by the monarchy. By diversifying its activities to other areas of investment such as the sugar industry, ranching, real estate, and hotels, this organization has continued to play a critical role in the country's economy. It has also helped the monarchy shore up its political hold on the country over the years.

See also **Climate; Metals and Minerals; Sobhuza I and II.**

BIBLIOGRAPHY

Forster, Peter G., and Bongani J. Nsibande, eds. *Swaziland: Contemporary Social and Economic Issues.* Aldershot, U.K.: Ashgate, 2000.

Nyeko, Balam. "Land Ownership and Swazi Agriculture: The Impact of the Concessions Revisited." In *Land, Gender and the Periphery: Themes in the History of Eastern and Southern Africa*, ed. Bahru Zewde. Addis Ababa: OSSREA, 2003.

Simelane, Hamilton Sipho. *Colonialism and Economic Change in Swaziland 1940–1960.* Kampala, Uganda and Manzini, Swaziland: JANPC, 2003.

BALAM NYEKO

SOCIETY AND CULTURES

As a society ruled by an absolute monarchy, Swaziland prides itself immensely as a country whose indigenous political system, cultures, and traditions have largely survived the encroachment of modernization. The monarchy is central to the society's existence. Allegiance to it represents the people's strongest expression of their faith in their cultures. From the moment Swazi society was confronted with foreign influences, it used tradition and cultures as weapons for resistance. This "cultural nationalism" acquired even more importance during the reign of Sobhuza II (1921–1982), who championed the need to maintain a separate Swazi cultural identity from the Europeans. Kingship was the core of "Swaziness," as reflected in the Swazi belief that the nation could not survive without it. "The Swazi nation revolved round the king. He controlled the army, was supreme judge, he distributed wealth and he possessed magic" (Kuper 1941, 347). It provided the cement that united them. The *Ngwenyama* ("king" or "lion"), usually chosen according to strict traditional custom, rules jointly with his mother *Ndlovukazi* ("Queen Mother" or "She Elephant").

The Swazi nation emerged as an amalgam of various clans, defined as groups of families related to one another by a common surname and ancestry. These coalesced around the Dlamini clan and today occupy modern Swaziland. However, a substantial minority of ethnic Swazi, whose ancestors were left out when colonial boundaries were drawn, reside within present-day South Africa. Unlike many other modern African states, Swaziland comprises one ethnic group or nationality, sharing a common historical tradition, speaking the same language and practicing one set of cultures.

The health of the king, who must always be a Dlamini, represents the general welfare of society as a whole. Kingship is strengthened through a number of rituals, the most outstanding being the annual *incwala* ceremony, which serves as a reaffirmation of the institution's place in the nation. It is a national political and religious ceremony. Since it is essentially a ritual to reinvigorate the kingship, it follows that whenever there is no reigning king, such as during the long regency of Queen Labotsibeni from 1899 to 1921, no *incwala* ceremony takes place. Hilda Kuper, the leading scholar of Swazi society, argued that the ceremony also dramatized rank and enabled the people to see which clans and people were important in the nation. Other scholars saw it as also providing an occasion for songs of "rebellion" against the king and expressions of dissent, an interpretation that Kuper rejected. She maintained, further, that her own biography of Sobhuza II was "the history not only of an outstanding man but of the culture with which he [had] deliberately identified himself" (Kuper 1978, 14). The *incwala* is also usually a celebration of the nation's First Fruits.

Other important ceremonies in the Swazi cultural calendar include the *umhlanga* ("reed dance by maidens") and the *umcwasho*, which is "a ceremony for girls who had reached or were near maturity, imposing a period of chastity and emphasizing the need for sexual restraint" (1978, 108).

The custom decreed that men should leave the maidens alone during this time. In 2003 King Mswati III imposed an *umcwasho* for a period of two years to help fight the HIV/AIDS epidemic in the country, but it is unclear how effective this was. In any case, the king himself took one such maiden as a wife soon after his declaration, leading to his being fined for breaking the tradition. Swazi traditionalists insist that the *umhlanga* ceremony is always held in honor of the Queen Mother and is not intended as an occasion for the king to choose a wife. However, King Mswati III has picked a bride from amongst the maidens at nearly every *umhlanga* since the 1990s. That some of the brides have been teenage girls who were subsequently forced to drop out of school has provoked some controversy internally and attracted international criticism of this cultural practice. In particular, opposition groups such as the People's United Democratic Movement (PUDEMO) have expressed very serious misgivings about the ceremony's relevance in the twenty-first century, its impact on the anti-HIV/AIDS campaign, and its violation of the girls' human rights by not gaining their consent to such marriage arrangements. PUDEMO also argues that the culture has been used as a way of undermining women's position in the country more generally. (PUDEMO International Office, 2002).

In a society so steeped in culture and tradition as Swaziland, and in which subordination, obedience, and respect for one's seniors are obligatory, gender relations become quite problematic. Polygamy is an integral part of kingship, as it is one means by which the monarchy can bring about unity among the various clans in the nation. However, as women must be obedient to male authority at all times, the practice has ensured that women remain largely powerless. Until the 2005 constitution came into force, women were legally treated as perpetual minors who could not own property in their own right or conclude contracts without the approval of a husband or other male relatives. Clearly, many traditional cultural practices in the areas of marriage, health, education, wife inheritance, and others have disadvantaged women and negatively affected their status in society. Many customs often violate women's human rights.

The role of cultures in Swazi society extends beyond the political arena and permeates the economy as well as religion. The control over land allocation in Swazi Nation Land, for example, resides in traditional chiefs who demand allegiance and total obedience from whomever is seeking land. Whereas the rulers use this to enhance their hold on the people, traditional religion, which cannot be separated from other aspects of Swazi life, also plays a role in sanctioning the political power of the rulers and ensuring loyalty.

In responding to Christianity, traditional Swazi authorities warned that it should not undermine their cultures, as missionaries disapproved of certain Swazi practices such as polygamy and the treatment of women as perpetual minors. Whereas Sobuza II, for example, was not overtly hostile to

Christianity, he and other members of the aristocracy remained uncoverted. Instead, Sobhuza tried to counteract the Christian influence—and thus cushion Swazi cultures against it—by establishing the Swazi National Church in 1939.

While the ordinary people have adopted Christianity more enthusiastically because it opened up more social opportunities than the traditional system did, the traditionalists preferred to adhere to Swazi religion. King Mswati III's attitude toward religion, like that of his late father Sobhuza II, was that it should be used as a vehicle for the forging of national unity and the recovery of Swazi traditional

---

The Kingdom of Swaziland

Population:	1,133,066 (2007 est.)
Area:	17,364 sq. km. (6,704 sq. mi.)
Official languages:	English, SiSwati
National currency:	lilangeni (plural: Emalangeni)
Principal religions:	Zionist (indigenous) 40%, Roman Catholic 20%, Muslim 10%, Other
Capital:	Mbabane (est. pop. 60,000 in 2006)
Other urban centers:	Manzini
Annual rainfall:	900–2,300 mm (35–90 in.) throughout most of the country; 500–900 mm (20–35 in.) in lowveld in east
Principal geographical features:	*Mountains:* Emlembe, Lebombo plateau *Rivers:* Komati, Umbuluzi, Great Usutu, Assegai, Ngwavuma
Economy:	*GDP per capita:* US$5,200 (2006)
Principal products and exports:	*Agricultural:* sugarcane, cotton, corn, tobacco, rice, citrus, pineapples, sorghum, peanuts, cattle, goats, sheep *Manufacturing:* wood pulp processing, sugar, soft drink concentrates, textile and apparel *Mining:* asbestos, iron, coal, diamonds
Government:	Independent nation within the British Commonwealth. Independence from the United Kingdom, 1968. Constitution approved in 1968, suspended in 1973. New constitution promulgated in 1978 but never formally approved. New constitution 2005. Monarchy. Advisory bicameral parliament: Senate (30 seats: 10 appointed by the House of Assembly and 20 appointed by the monarch; 5-year terms) and the House of Assembly (65 seats: 10 appointed by the monarch and 55 elected by popular vote; 5-year terms). The king may legislate by decree. The king appoints the prime minister and cabinet. For purposes of local government there are 4 regions, 9 municipalities, and 55 tinkhundla centers.
Heads of state since independence:	1968–1982: King Sobhuza II 1982–1983: Dzeliwe Shongwe (regent) 1983–1986: Ntombi Thawala (regent) 1986–: King Mswati III
Armed forces:	The military consists solely of the Umbutfo Swaziland Defense Force, loyal to and under the command of the king, and consisting of about 3,000 royal warriors organized into regiments (emabutfo). *Paramilitary:* Royal Swaziland Police Force
Transportation:	*Rail:* 297 km (184 mi.) *Roads:* 3,594 km (2,233 mi.), 30% paved *National airline:* Royal Swazi National Airways Corporation *Airports:* International facilities at Matsapa. 17 other small airports and airstrips throughout the country.
Media:	Main periodicals: *Times of Swaziland, Swaziland Observer, Swazi News, Swaziview, News from Swaziland, Swazi Life, Tikhatsi Tema Swati, Tindzaba News, Umbiki.* The Swaziland Broadcasting Service is government controlled. Television was inaugurated in 1978 and is run by the state-owned Swaziland Television Broadcasting Corporation. 5 radio stations, 12 television stations.
Literacy and education:	*Total literacy rate:* 79% (2006). Education is not compulsory. Postsecondary education provided by the University of Swaziland, Mananga Agricultural Management Centre, Swaziland College of Technology, Swaziland Institute of Management and Public Administration.

---

cultures. In modern-day Swaziland, for example, Easter services are held annually at one of the royal palaces at which the king and his mother preside. Such services have become Swazi national occasions of nearly the same status as the *umhlanga* (or reed dance) and the *incwala*. As Peter Kasenene writes, on these occasions the church leaders pray for the monarchy and the nation; "Christianity is used for political ends even when there is no commitment to it" (2000, 29). The strict adherence to tradition and culture in a changing environment in the twenty-first century poses a dilemma for the country. It might help unite a people, but it also has the potential to induce subservience and uncritical acceptance of authority. However, in modern Swaziland any attempt to question certain aspects of culture has often been met with the response that it is "unSwazi" and therefore disloyal to do so.

See also **Kingship; Queens and Queen Mothers; Religion and Ritual; Sobhuza I and II.**

BIBLIOGRAPHY

Kasenene, Peter. *Swazi Traditional Religion and Society.* Mbabane, Swaziland: Websters, 1993.

Kasenene, Peter. "Swazi Civil Religion." In *Swaziland: Contemporary Social and Economic Issues*, ed. Peter G. Forster and Bongani J. Nsibande. Aldershot, U.K.: Ashgate, 2000.

Kuper, Hilda. *Sobhuza II: Ngwenyama and King of Swaziland.* London: Duckworth, 1978.

Kuper, Hilda. "The Development of a Primitive Nation." *Bantu Studies* 15, no. 4 (1941): 339–368.

Nxumalo, Mamane. "Women and Health: The Case of Swaziland." In *Swaziland: Contemporary Social and Economic Issues*, ed. Peter G. Forster and J. Nsibande Bongani. Aldershot, U.K.: Ashgate, 2000.

Nyeko, Balam. "History, Culture and Social Change in Swaziland: A Survey of Recent Studies." *Uniswa Research Journal* 11 (June 1997): 1–16.

PUDEMO International Office. "HIV Prevention or Cultural Abuse?" H-Net List on South and Southern Africa, October 15, 2002. Available at H-SAFRICA@ H-NET.MSU.EDU.

BALAM NYEKO

HISTORY AND POLITICS

The tiny kingdom of Swaziland emerged as a state only in the late eighteenth and early nineteenth centuries. This period witnessed the Zulu-led *Mfecane* revolution ("the crushing" or "forced migration," also known as the *Difaqaane* by the Sotho) that took place among the Bantu-speaking peoples of southeast Africa during the first three decades of the nineteenth century. The core of the new state comprised the Dlamini clan, along with around ten others, who came from a northeasterly direction and settled in what is approximately present-day Swaziland. The creation of the modern Swazi state under Sobhuza I (r. c.1815–1836) resulted from the reaction of these clans to the disturbances arising from the emergence of the Zulu state during the revolutionary wars. Yet the Swazi kingdom was only one among several contemporaneous *Mfecane* states such as the Gaza, Ndwandwe, Mthetwa, Ndebele, and others. They were all preoccupied with survival as distinct entities in the face of the threat of conquest or absorption by the new powerful Zulu kingdom and the intra-African fighting that characterized this period.

Initially, the Dlamini concentrated on extending and consolidating their power over the non-Dlamini clans. However, with the passage of time, they faced new forces that subsequently affected their politics in a very significant way. The arrival of British and Afrikaner traders, farmers, travelers and concession-hunters from neighboring white settler territories posed a serious challenge. Swaziland soon became a mere pawn in the competition for power and control of the region between the British and the Transvaal Afrikaners. Although the Swazi traditional authorities often took advantage of this contest by playing one power against the other and thereby avoiding any armed conflict between themselves and the new forces, their future was finally sealed when the British and the Afrikaners agreed that Swaziland should become a British protectorate at the end of the Anglo–Boer War (1899–1902).

During the first half of the twentieth century, two major considerations dominated Swaziland's colonial history. First, the Swazi worried that their country might be formally transferred to the newly created and powerful Union of South Africa after 1910. In the face of the Union's growing anti-African policies and British ambivalence about the country's future, the Swazi put up stiff resistance to transfer and succeeded in persuading the British to abandon any such plan by the mid-1940s. However, this did not stop the country from becoming more or less an economic appendage to their strong neighbor as the British pursued a policy of neglect toward her while the South African economy expanded. The Swazi's second concern was the desire to recover control over their economic resources such as agricultural land and mineral wealth, and to win back political independence, with Sobhuza II holding executive powers as the kingdom's unchallenged leader.

In the Swazi response to these two challenges during the early twentieth century, the role of Queen Regent Labotsibeni (r. 1899–1921), Sobhuza II's grandmother, looms large. Taking over as the traditional ruler after her son Bhunu's death, Labotsibeni led the Swazi's "buyback" land campaign following the loss of massive amounts of land through the concessions granted by her husband King Mbandzeni in the late nineteenth century. The British administrators recognized her as a strong personality who sought to protect the interests of the Swazi as a people and organized resistance to the prospects of possible incorporation into the Union of South Africa during the first two decades of the twentieth century.

Internally, Labotsibeni took the initiative to start a school for Sobhuza and other children of the aristocracy. As a result of her efforts, the first Swazi national school, the Zombodze National School, enrolled its first students in 1911. Under her leadership, the Swazi played a very significant part in helping the South African Native National Congress (later the African National Congress) establish itself when the kingdom provided much-needed funds for the launching of the ANC newspaper, *Abantu-Batho*, at the party's foundation. As Kanduza argues, during her long reign Labosibeni "helped prepare Swaziland to participate in the twentieth century." When King Sobhuza II took over from her in the early 1920s, his concern was to continue her work. A related theme that ran through the history of modern Swaziland was therefore the traditional authorities' concern for the survival of the monarchy as an institution in the post-colonial period.

THE POLITICS OF DECOLONIZATION

The first nationalist political parties to champion the anticolonial struggle emerged in the early 1960s when the country's first welfare organization of educated Swazis, the Swaziland Progressive Association (SPA), transformed itself into the Swaziland Progressive Party (SPP), led by the immigrant Zulu educationist John June Nquku. Other modern political organizations formed in the period 1964 to 1967, the most notable being Dr. Ambrose Zwane's pan-Africanist Ngwane Nationalist Liberatory Congress (NNLC). A contest for power between these modern political parties and the traditionalists headed by King Sobhuza II himself ensued. Feeling threatened by the party politicians, he launched his own political organization, the Imbokodvo National Movement (INM). He preferred to describe it as a national movement of all Swazi rather than a political party. Sobhuza campaigned against multiparty politics and enlisted the support of the chiefs and other royalists, who provided the main network for the INM. In the meantime, the European settlers had formed their own organization, the United Swaziland Association (USA), with the purpose of protecting white settler interests in the country. The USA, representing a total population of less than 10,000 European businessmen and farmers, stood little chance of winning any elections on its own. However, it entered into an alliance with Sobhuza's INM in order to secure some limited representation in a new multiracial constitutional arrangement. On the eve of independence, Sobhuza and the traditionalists successfully outmaneuvered the modern political parties and swept all the seats in the parliamentary elections. Subsequently, these parties' following dwindled significantly as their leading members were steadily incorporated into the king's own movement.

SWAZILAND SINCE INDEPENDENCE

The country regained its independence in 1968 as a constitutional monarchy, but Sobhuza was clearly uncomfortable with this arrangement. Between 1968 and 1972 Swaziland experienced very serious constitutional tension as the king's INM faced a major challenge from the modern political parties, represented mainly by the NNLC, which enjoyed considerable support among the workers. The conflict came to a head at the May 1972 Parliamentary Elections when the NNLC won three seats, resulting in the defeat of a key cabinet minister who was also an important member of the royal family. The traditionalists appealed to the courts but lost, whereupon the king swiftly issued his 1973 proclamation repealing the independence constitution. He abolished parliament, banished all political parties, and declared a state of emergency empowering him to rule by decree. In his view this constitution was "foreign" in origin, unsuited to Swaziland and had allowed the courts to interfere with the nation's sovereignty.

Following the proclamation, Sobhuza ruled by decree from 1973 to 1978. In place of the old constitution, he introduced the *tinkhundla* (traditional local government structures or councils) that was later adopted by a new reconstituted parliament in 1978. The new legislature was dominated by the king's appointees and worked closely with the traditional councils and the monarchy, leading critics to describe the system as a thinly veiled mechanism for consolidating royal hegemony. All this resulted in a major polarization of political opinion within the country. A comparatively small but vocal and articulate section of the population, comprising mainly the educated, younger, and urban-based citizens protested the action and demanded constitutional reform and parliamentary democracy. A number of social and political groups emerged in the late 1980s to spearhead the agitation, among them the militant People's United Democratic Movement (PUDEMO), the Swaziland Youth Congress (SWAYOCO), and the Swaziland Federation of Trade Unions (SFTU). On the other hand, the largely rural and peasant population, mainly uneducated conservative traditionalists, supported the king's move.

Swaziland has maintained a political system based upon absolute monarchical rule. In August 1982 Sobhuza II died after over half a century on the throne. His demise prompted the outbreak of serious factional political squabbles within the inner circle of the Swazi traditional rulers that lasted for four years. Swazi politics was in a state of flux until King Mswati III, still a minor at the time of his father's death, assumed power in 1986. The country continued to face questions about the return to constitutional rule. Responding to continuing demands for parliamentary democracy and a new constitution, Mswati appointed a constitutional committee early in his rule, but its work proceeded at a snail's speed. It produced its final report only in 2004 and the new constitution was presented to the citizens in 2005, but it was not clear if it would allow for multiparty politics and greater democratization. The internal and external pressures became even stronger in the post-apartheid years following South Africa's return to democratic rule in 1994. At the same time, the African Union and other international bodies have called for an improvement in the country's governance system, but the traditionalists have resisted change, arguing that the majority of the populace prefers the "Swazi way" rather than to adopt Western parliamentary democracy.

See also **Kingship; Queens and Queen Mothers; Sobhuza I and II.**

BIBLIOGRAPHY

Bonner, Philip. *Kings, Commoners and Concessionaires: The Evolution and Dissolution of the Nineteenth-Century Swazi State.* Cambridge, U.K.: Cambridge University Press, 1982.

Booth, Alan R. *Swaziland: Tradition and Change in a Southern African Kingdom.* Aldershot, U.K.: Gower, 1984.

Booth, Alan R. *Historical Dictionary of Swaziland*, 2nd edition. Lanham, MD: Scarecrow Press, 2000.

Davies, Robert H.; Dan O'Meare; and Sipho Dlamini. *The Kingdom of Swaziland: A Profile.* London: Zed Books, 1985.

Denoon, Donald, and Balam Nyeko. *Southern Africa since 1800.* London and New York: Longman, 1984.

Kanduza, Ackson. "'You Are Tearing My Skirt': Labotsibeni Gwamile LaMdluli." In *Agency and Action in Colonial Africa: Essays for John E. Flint*, ed. Chris Youé and Tim Stapleton. New York: Palgrave, 2001: 83–99.

Kuper, Hilda. *Sobhuza II: Ngwenyama and King of Swaziland.* London: Duckworth, 1978.

Levin, Richard. "Swaziland's 'Tinkhundla' System and the Myth of Swazi Tradition." *Journal of Contemporary African Studies* 10, no. 2 (1991): 1–23.

Macmillan, Hugh. "Swaziland: Decolonization and the Triumph of 'Tradition.'" *Journal of Modern African Studies* 23, no. 4 (1985): 643–666.

Simelane, Nomtheto, ed. *Social Transformation: The Swaziland Case.* Dakar: OSSREA, 1995.

BALAM NYEKO

SYMBOLS AND SYMBOLISM

This entry includes the following articles:
OVERVIEW
ANIMAL

OVERVIEW

The word *symbol* is derived from the Greek word, *sumallein*, meaning "to throw together," and refers to the association of particular things, images, colors, odors, with particular ideas, events, and actions, which by virtue of the emotional response they evoke, often have a moral tone. In Africa, symbols play an important role in rituals, including those associated with chieftaincy and illness as well as with significant life transitions—that is, rites of passage such as death, marriage, and birth. While some symbols convey general ideas about earthly and spiritual domains or about marital relations and the social order, other symbols invoke ideas about moral values that have a specific polar cast. Symbols such as hands, for example, are associated on the right, with cleanliness and goodness, and on the left, with filth and perversion, respectively.

However, the polyvalent and sometimes discrepant qualities of symbols—that they may have different, even contradictory, meanings in different contexts—reflect the negotiability of their meanings, which is a key to understanding their importance in social life. As Victor Turner observed, "[A symbol] is alive in so far as it is 'pregnant with meaning' for men and women, who interact by observing, transgressing, and manipulating for private ends the norms and values that the symbol expresses" (1967, 44). Thus, in the Ndembu *Nkula* ritual performed in northwestern Zambia described by Turner, the redness of *mukula* tree sap is used to represent the blood of menstruation and of childbirth, as well as the blood of animals killed by the hunter. In this ritual, the physical properties of blood—its redness, heat, and fluidity—contribute to its association with ideas about relatedness and continuity, but also about hotness and danger. The symbolic representation of these somewhat contradictory qualities is reflected in the *Nkula* ritual, in which the childless female patient is prepared for fertile reproduction through references to the coagulation of menstrual blood and childbirth. Yet the association of wasted menstrual blood with the infertile blood of animals killed by hunters is also referenced in the patient's ritual performance of a hunter's dance. Indeed, the word *sumallein*, meaning "throw together," suggests a certain ambiguous arbitrariness between particular symbolic things and their meanings. Yet it is this very ambiguity and arbitrariness that allow men and women to negotiate meanings which make symbols such evocative vehicles for conveying ideas about social life and human existence.

BODY SYMBOLISM AND EMBODIED PRACTICE

Nonetheless, some things are the source of symbolic imagining more often than others, and it is the human body through which this symbolic imagining most often takes place. As T. O. Beidelman observed, "Our sight, touch, taste, and smell, and the appetites and physiological demands of our bodies . . . are all recruited both to construct and to patrol the corridors of our thoughts. Such sensations enable us not only to manufacture symbols and ideas but to evoke and contemplate them in the imaginative mind's eye of ourselves and others" (1986, 6). The importance of the body as a source of symbols in Uduk society in southeastern Sudan may be seen in beliefs about the liver (*adu*), in which the concentration of blood marks the presence of the animating life force or spirit, known as *arum*. The liver is seen as both the source of human emotions—such as anger and affection—and spiritual power, but it is also the site of spiritual vulnerability, as the liver may be invaded by external spiritual powers, which may lead to sickness. However, individuals may counter these external powers and vulnerabilities symbolized by the liver through ritual alimentary and medicinal discipline of the stomach, which when managed and strengthened through correct behavior, provides protection.

Making reference to body symbols such as the liver, heart, and blood in ritual performances may express ideas about social relations as well as human connections with spiritual domains, with the body as a resource for thinking about the natural, social, and spiritual worlds. This process may work in reverse—from the outside in—as when everyday things and habitual body practices may serve as the source of symbols and symbolic action which, upon elaboration, become part of ritual. In writing of the Kuranko people of Sierra Leone, Michael Jackson noted that "patterns of body use [in the everyday world] engender mental images and instill moral qualities . . ." (1989, 131). In other words, everyday bodily practices and the use of things provide a basis for ritual comportment and symbolic meanings. The fire-lighting techniques used by Kuranko women consists of embodied habitual practices, including the careful placement of a few pieces of wood between the firestones and the gentle pushing of these bits of wood toward the fire as they burn. Such body techniques not only conserve fuel but also represent moral qualities which, during initiation ritual, are reenacted to evoke values of moderation and constraint.

Similarly, the large wooden spoons used by Dan women in Liberia and Côte d'Ivoire in preparing quantities of rice for family events serve as models for spoons known as a *wunkirmian*. These elaborately carved spoons serve as symbols of the titled status of particular women, whose special farming, cooking, and generous hospitality skills are being honored during ritual festivals. Along with these women's special productive powers as farmers and cooks, the shape of the spoon's "belly," likened to a pregnant woman's body, makes reference to women's reproductive powers as well. *Wunkirmian* spoons, which are believed to have been given to Dan women by a spirit revealed in a dream, thus serve as symbols of women's connections with social and spiritual domains.

ANIMAL SYMBOLS IN THE NATURAL WORLD

While elements of the human bodies are primary frames of reference and sources of symbols and symbolic meanings in many African societies, Africans use a range of items in nature, such as animals, birds, reptiles, streams, termite mounds, trees, hills, the sky, and celestial bodies to express ideas about the natural world and the place of human beings and their fellow creatures in it. Representations of relationships between humans and animals in Africa have varied, both historically and culturally, reflecting ideas about nonhuman others and possible connections with them. Animals may serve as symbolic vehicles for defining human-ness by what they are not. Thus the Kaguru of Tanzania view baboons—which may try to fool humans into accepting them into society by wearing clothes and by hiding their tails—as hairy interlopers which humans then drive back into the wild, forest domain. The ways that animals are classified also contribute to their significance as symbols. The Uduk classify animals as hoofed (of whom humans are considered kin), clawed, or feathered, living in earth, water, or air.

Creatures that cross categories may be the object of elaborate rituals that play upon their ambiguous character. Thus, animals such as pythons which, as snakes, are classified as land animals confound this category by also residing in water and leaping into the air, forming rainbows. Indeed, the ambiguous attributes of pythons have contributed to their pervasive power as symbols in several African societies. Elephants, which do not neatly fit into the Uduk animal classification system, are also a source of elaborate symbolic interpretation, and the killing of an elephant is said to represent the conquest of wild animals by humans. The hunters who have managed this feat become the administrators of powerful elephant medicine, which is used to protect hunters and others who may have come into contact—through the distribution of its meat—with the spiritual essence, *arum*, of the defunct elephant.

TREES AS SYMBOLS OF ETHNIC AND POLITICAL IDENTITIES

The social relations reinforced through symbolic associations with elephant medicine and meat distribution point to another aspect of the use of symbols in Africa. Jackson noted the importance of symbols in constituting social identities, as symbols were originally thought of as a sort of half "token of identity." When matched together, these tokens "confirmed a person's identity as part of a social relationship. The meaning of a symbol thus implied a presence and absence; something always had to be brought from elsewhere to make the symbol complete, to round out its significance" (1989, 135). Trees, which are frequent sources of symbolic meaning, resemble human beings with their upright stance and blood-like sap. Knowledge of tree-symbols and of their associated meanings may be thought of as two parts of a whole, which when brought together corroborate a particular ethnic identity.

For example, in the Ndembu ritual known as *Nkang'a*, which is performed for young women at menarche, the key symbol of this ritual, the *mudyi* tree, exudes a milky white latex when its bark is scratched. The symbolism of the milk-giving tree underscores a primary theme of the ritual, namely the importance of mothers' nurturance of their infants through breast milk, not only for the continuity of the matrilineage but also for Ndembu society more generally. Knowledge of the meaning of the milk-tree, which involves an association of the physiological characteristics of white milk exuded from breasts with the white latex from the tree's bark, along with the ritual practices associated with the *mudyi* tree, confirm one's identity as a socially knowledgeable and morally responsible Ndembu person.

The symbolic meanings attributed to different trees may reflect their distinctive physical qualities. Along with trees which exude white, milky sap, other qualities such as hardness, longevity, and the seasonal shedding of leaves may be drawn upon to convey other meanings. Thus certain types of upright hardwood trees may be used in ritual practices associated with political and economic relations among living members of society—and in relations with the dead/ancestors—to represent the growth of people and ancestors, as well as to distinguish royalty, the "'one person' buried inside two fences" made with wood from specific hardwood trees, from commoners, "Every One a Thousand" (Feeley-Harnik 1991, 448).

Indeed, the expansion of the Sakalava monarchy, in the Analalava region of northwestern Madagascar, was likened to the growth of a forest, with subjects investing in the cultivation of royalty—its fields and royal tombs—in order to reap the benefits which their ancestors could bestow on the living. In the elaborate ritual process of rebuilding the exterior double fence of royal tombs known as *menaty* service, ritual workers, under the direction of knowledgeable "Ancestral People," select trees with specific characteristics—particularly hardwood trees that were perceived as either red or yellow and as dry rather than wet. After appropriate trees are chosen, they are stripped of their bark, branches, and leaves—a process referred to as washing—so that the hard inner core of wood, the *teza*, is revealed. In the ritual preparation of the hardwood *teza*, *menaty* workers symbolically handle the trees as if they were royal corpses, as the removal of the old decayed double fence and its replacement with new hardwood parallels the unwrapping/rewrapping and reburial of royal ancestral bones practiced elsewhere in Madagascar.

SENSORY SYMBOLISM: SOUND, SMELL, AND TASTE

The use of symbolic things may also convey moral meanings through reference to sensory associations with a particular category of symbols, those which have specific sounds, tastes, and smells. Particular odors may have symbolic meanings, although they may be interpreted differently in different contexts—as when sweet fragrances are interpreted as good or, when in excess, as poisonously bad. Olfactory symbols may also be associated with sacred spaces, as in African Independent Churches where censors filled with incense are swung at the beginning and conclusion of services and whose sweet scent conveys an aura of heavenly space. This practice also suggests its counterpart, that the foul smells associated with evil spirits are driven away.

In Anlo-Ewe society in southeastern Ghana, olfactory symbolism is complicated by the conflation of both smell and hearing as a sensation of air "discerned as much through the skin, eyes, and nose as through the ear" (Geurts 2002, 48). Thus the initiation of infants begins with a ritual first bath, during which any traces of *dzigbedi*, "birth dirt" (*vernix caseosa*, a waxy substance present on the skin of newborns that preserves their skins' moisture), are vigorously removed. Failure to do so may lead to the infant having a lifelong offensive body odor ("the everlasting scent"), which is perceived by others as an aural sensation that is both smelled and heard. The symbolic meaning attributed to *dzigbedi* as dirt also has moral connotations, not only for the individual but for the entire family, whose failure to address this problem properly underscores their immoral lack of social competence.

NEGOTIABILITY OF SYMBOLS AND SOCIAL LIFE

Some Anlo-Ewe women attribute the thick coating of whitish *vernix caseosa* on newborns to mothers' habit of eating a type of baked clay, known as *eye*, during their pregnancies. The aroma of baked *eye* clay balls, as well as their egg-like shape which is associated with fertility and health, contribute to women's craving for them, which some say alleviates morning sickness and promotes well-being. While some village midwives have tried to discourage this habit, by claiming that it causes a build-up of "birth dirt" on newborns, other government-trained midwives have argued that, whether *eye* clay is eaten or not, the *vernix caseosa* is a normal coating of the infant's skin in the womb. Yet the symbolic meanings and moral associations attributed to clay eating and "birth dirt," which must be removed to preclude the social stigma of "the ever-lasting scent," continue to be widely held by village women.

These different views on the meaning of *vernix caseosa*, as "birth dirt," as a natural symbol, which has negative moral implications both for the birth-mother and her family, underscore the negotiability of symbols and symbolic meaning in the presence of changing social contexts. While educated midwives have sought to redefine birth dirt, by virtue of their government training, in a value-free way, village midwives, whose authority relies on their experience and on their knowledge of traditional beliefs, continue to stress the older interpretation of this "dirt." Whether government midwives are ultimately successful in promulgating their reinterpretation of the meaning of the *vernix caseosa* as a normal consequence of fetal development will depend on the strength of state public health initiatives and the availability of primary and secondary education for young village women, who may be inclined to view "birth dirt" in a new, biomedical, way.

This negotiability of body symbols such as "birth dirt" may also be seen in the adaptation of "traditional" symbols of status, such as those used in chieftaincy rituals by the wealthy elite in southwestern Nigeria. Despite many changes in Yoruba society, including widespread Western education and conversion to Christianity or Islam, many wealthy, educated individuals—both men and women—aspire to taking chieftaincy titles, with their associated paraphernalia, which includes elaborately decorated staffs, flywhisks, and beaded caps. Together with these older symbols of office, contemporary chieftaincy title-taking rituals also incorporate new symbols of prestige, such as full-page congratulatory advertisements for chieftaincy installations published in Nigerian newspapers. However, these symbols of status associated with chieftaincy titles carry ambiguous meanings. While purporting to express traditional Yoruba values—such as royal beneficence and fairness—by their wealthy recipients, the symbolic meanings of "traditional" chieftaincy titles and things may more often be used to maintain the prevailing socioeconomic and political order. This blurring of the meanings of these old and new chieftaincy symbols, negotiated by those who are able to afford the luxury of maintaining traditional practices, enhance the moral capital of titled chiefs without raising questions about the connection between political authority and social responsibility.

CHRISTIAN, ISLAMIC, AND TRADITIONAL RELIGIOUS SYMBOLS IN AFRICA

While much of what has been written about symbols in Africa has focused on traditional religious practices and rituals, the majority of African women and men consider themselves to be Christians or Muslims. The symbols of these two monotheisms have played an important role in conversion rituals as well as in continuing disputes over the bases of belief. In Mongo Beti's novel, *Le roi miraculé* (translated as *King Lazarus*), three symbols of Christianity—rosaries, water, and white vestments—mark the conversion experience of the polygynous chief of the fictive village of Essazam, in rural Cameroon. As the chief sits, fearful that he is dying, he stares at the rosaries hanging from the local missionary's arm and considers the prospects that belief in their powers would offer him. Later he is given a rosary and is baptized with water, symbols of his Catholic faith, and upon his miraculous recovery, he is christened with the name Lazarus. The later repudiation of the symbols of his conversion—the rosary, white robe, and baptismal water—then becomes the means for him to return to prevailing local ethics and practices. Yet, during later episodes of illness, he takes them up again, temporarily, so that "On these occasions he would... insist on making his Confession so that he would be able to receive Communion and take his place in the Heavenly Feast among God's Elect, dressed in a white robe" (Beti 1970 [1958], 189). Despite the facetiousness of this example of oscillating belief, these symbols of Christian faith reflect a new basis of spiritual power and knowledge, and subsequently of social relations and identities, for women and men in many parts of Africa.

The use of symbols in recreating and constituting new religious identities, as well as delineating the qualities of immoral others, may also be seen in Islamic communities, as among the Halpulaar'en of the Fuuta Toro area in northern Senegal. For the group of artisans referred to as *nyeeybe* or men-of-skill, their use of particular tools symbolizes both their specific occupations—as fisherman, weavers, blacksmiths, carvers, and leatherworkers—and their connections with special spiritual powers. For example, the blacksmith's tongs were first revealed to a blacksmith by a spirit in a dream, while the blacksmith's furnace, in which he transforms metal into useful objects, is made with clay and material from termite mounds, which are believed throughout Africa to house powerful spirits.

This association with the spirit world puts Muslim blacksmiths and other men-of-skill in an uneasy relationship with other members of the Muslim community in Fuuta Toro, including *too-robe* Muslim clerics whose identification with the Mosque and Qur'anic schools serve as evidence of their faith. While disdaining the tools of blacksmiths as pagan objects associated with black spirits, in contrast to the holy texts and white knowledge of Muslim clerics, these men nonetheless concede the spiritual powers represented by the ownership of these things, which many believe in and fear. Yet the dominant position of Muslim clerics, whose spiritual authority is reinforced by their knowledge of the Qur'an and their practice of prayer, enables them to assert the power of the Mosque over the symbols associated with *nyeeybe* men-of-skill—such as the blacksmith's tongs and furnace as well as the termite mound. In this instance and others, the use of symbols reflects a tension between social conflict over the meanings of symbols—in which case certain groups with their own interests may have the power to make particular interpretations of a symbol prevail—and the desire for social accord, reinforced through the powerful unifying emotions which symbols can evoke, which convey a sense of moral community and enable a society to continue and prosper.

See also **Art, Genres and Periods: Rock Art, Eastern Africa; Art, Genres and Periods: Rock Art, Saharan and Northern Africa; Art, Genres and Periods: Rock Art, Southern Africa; Beti, Mongo; Childbearing; Colonial Policies and Practices; Death, Mourning, and Ancestors; Demography: Fertility and Infertility; Divination and Oracles; Dreams and Dream Interpretation; Initiation; Mami Wata; Masks and Masquerades; Myth and Cosmology; Religion and Ritual; Spirit Possession.**

BIBLIOGRAPHY

Beidelman, T. O. *Moral Imagination in Kaguru Modes of Thought*. Bloomington: Indiana University Press, 1986.

Beti, Mongo. *King Lazarus* [*Le roi miraculé*] [1958], trans. Frederick Muller. London: Heinemann, 1970.

Dilley, Roy. *Islamic and Caste Knowledge Practices among the Haalpulaar'en in Senegal: Between Mosque and Termite Mound*. Edinburgh: Edinburgh University Press for the International African Institute, 2004.

Feeley-Harnik, Gillian. *A Green Estate: Restoring Independence in Madagascar*. Washington, DC: Smithsonian Institution Press, 1991.

Fischer, Eberhard, and Hans Himmelheber. *The Arts of the Dan in West Africa*, trans. Anna Buddle. Zürich: Museum Rietberg, 1984.

Geurts, Kathryn. *Culture and the Senses: Bodily Ways of Knowing in an African Community*. Berkeley: University of California Press, 2002.

Jackson, Michael. *Paths toward a Clearing: Radical Empiricism and Ethnographic Inquiry*. Bloomington: Indiana University Press, 1989.

James, Wendy. *The Listening Ebony: Moral Knowledge, Religion, and Power among the Uduk of Sudan*. Oxford: Clarendon Press, 1988.

Lawuyi, Olatunde B. "The Social Marketing of Elites: The Advertised Self in Obituaries and Congratulations in Some Nigerian Dailies." *Africa* 61, no. 2 (1991): 247–263.

Turner, Victor. *The Forest of Symbols: Aspects of Ndembu Ritual*. Ithaca, NY: Cornell University Press, 1967.

ELISHA P. RENNE

ANIMAL

Africa boasts an exuberant variety of verbalized and artistic reflections on humankind's animal companions. The many forms of insect, reptilian, mammalian, piscine, and avian life represented on this vast continent have for countless millennia served to mirror human thought, aspiration, and foreboding in the familial, political, and cosmological spheres. Some of those zoomorphic conceptions patently resemble customs and ideas reported from other and unrelated regions of the world: thus, the regular association of descent groups with animal species among many African peoples has a correlation with Native American "totemism"; the famous "rainbow serpent" of aboriginal Australia has its counterpart in Africa; and something resembling the Central American institution of the "animal double" or *nagual* has been reported among the Banyang people of the Cameroon Highlands of western Africa. For some anthropologists, these clusters of symbolic phenomena have provided the basis for a cognitive study of natural history, based on the properties of both animal kinds and the human mind.

One cause of the extraordinary variety of zoo-morphic symbolism in Africa is the immense length of time that *Homo sapiens* have coexisted with other motile life-forms. Another is the wide range of societal structures in this continent, from hunter-gatherer bands to age-organized, acephalous communities to stratified and centralized indigenous states. All have turned to the animal world to reflect on their particular conditions, and continue to do so. As Brian Morris's work in Malawi has shown, animals remain part of contemporary life in Africa at a time when they have been pushed to the margins of social life elsewhere.

The earliest manifestation of the symbolic significance of animals in social life in Africa can be found in rock art depicting nonutilitarian animals including eland, kudu, giraffe, and elephant. The absence of a radical dichotomy between humans and other animals at this time created the possibility of transformations between various physical states, unencumbered by the notion of a uniquely human property such as a soul, language or reason. This kind of perspectivism, according to which subjects may occupy various physical envelopes, has been attributed to a number of different hunting and gathering groups. With the advent of farming, the egalitarian relationship between humans and animals was modified by the requirement of intellectual and spiritual distance between those animals that were domesticated and those that were not. However, it is not the case that spiritual unity was replaced by a complete separation. Humans and animals in Africa remained connected in complex and symbolically significant ways, as illustrated in the imminent divinity of Egyptian "natural religion" and the animal forms assumed by their deities.

When one looks more closely at the assortment of animal kinds that Africans consider of symbolic value, one soon observes, according to anthropologist Allen Roberts, that they are usually not those that appeal to the imaginations of contemporary Westerners enchanted by movies of the *Out of Africa* type. From the southern and central African savanna to the forests of western Africa, the python (*Python sebae*) represents the primal serpent out of which, according to a widely diffused myth, the world was created. Over much of the continent this

mythical beast, as in Australia, is associated with the rainbow and water. In *Le roi ivre* (1972), the Belgian anthropologist Luc de Heusch explored the many ways in which the pythonic "rainbow snake," often called Chinawezi or Chinaweji, is identified with kingship and the development of indigenous states in the central and southern African grasslands. *Serpent Worship in Africa* (1931), an early study by Wilfrid Hambly, documented the continent-wide distribution of local cults focused on python-divinities, which are often thought of as incarnations of dead kings.

Even tinier creatures can play roles of cosmic significance, as in the San origin myth featuring the praying mantis (*Mantis religiosa*), described as the creator of humankind as well as of all other creatures. In 2004 Brian Morris produced a comprehensive study of the importance of insects in the social lives of a rural matrilineal society in Malawi. In Malawi, insects create anxiety due to their role as spreaders of disease; at the same time as they bring hope because they are essential components of traditional remedies. They are both food and also parasites, destroying crops and livelihoods. Insects are not simply reviled as they are in much of the West; their relationship with people is complex and multifaceted.

No less foreign to popular Western conceptions of the hierarchy of African beasthood is the symbolic preeminence accorded over much of the Zairian rainforest to several kinds of scaly anteaters. Since the mid-twentieth century a minor anthropological industry has grown out of explaining why these seemingly humble and rarely seen creatures are the objects of such intense indigenous theorization. According to Mary Douglas, the small pangolin (*Manis tricuspis*) excited something like religious awe among the Lele, a forest-dwelling people of southern Zaire with a peculiar zest for social and natural classification. The Lele described this supremely anomalous beast as having scales like a fish but using its four legs to climb trees; instead of producing multiple offspring like other animals the pangolin gives birth singly, like human beings; most strange of all it seems to offer itself willingly to the hunter, curling into a ball to be taken and ritually sacrificed and eaten by the secret Lele society of the Pangolin Men. In *Implicit Meanings* (1975), Douglas described the small pangolin as a symbolic representation of the cosmic union of sky and earth; according to de Heusch, the same beast performs a similar symbolic function in the state ritual of the neighboring Kuba people. Its zoological cousin, the large pangolin (*Manis gigantea*), is said to symbolize the entire social structure of two other Zairian peoples, the Hamba and Lega.

Yet another scaly anteating mammal, the aardvark (*Orycteropus afer*), enjoys an extraordinary and widespread reputation as an embodied cosmic symbol. In *Animals in African Art* (1995), Allen Roberts described the multiple and contradictory meanings that the Tabwa people of southeast Zaire see in the aardvark, the oldest living ungulate. Building on Douglas's pioneering study, Roberts developed a richer and more empathetic appreciation of the symbolic significance of this widely diffused but rarely seen animal. For Tabwa, the aardvark appears to be composed of several creatures from different habitats; its elongated snout obscenely and absurdly resembles a human penis, and it has a quasi-magical ability to disappear into the ground, where it builds a seemingly unending series of subterranean tunnels. These and other remarkable qualities make the aardvark, according to Roberts, an exemplary living symbol whose very being provides a means of reflection on the infinite contradictions and puzzlements of human existence.

When it comes to zoomorphic symbols of supreme power in society it is the leopard (*Felis pardus*), rather than the lion of European fable and heraldry, that rules the African imagination. Although the spirit of a deaf chief of the Shona-speaking peoples of northern Zimbabwe is said to take the form of a lion, and the same is true of the chiefs of the Mambwe of the southern Lake Tanganyika region and the Tutsi kings of Rwanda, these are exceptions. Elsewhere in sub-Saharan Africa it is the physically smaller but more cunning and ferocious feline, the leopard, that almost universally represents the powers of kingship and elderhood.

AMBIGUITY AND COSMIC RESONANCE

As with the aardvark and pangolin, it is the leopard's appearance, as well as its nature and habits, that underlies its symbolic significance. The variegated coat of the leopard, black and white on a reddish field, makes it an apt vehicle for that combination of opposed qualities and attributes which,

as with the scaly anteaters, carries a cosmic resonance. Thus the leopard's patterned coat stands in many local African cosmologies for the alternation of day and night, and of wet and dry seasons, as well as for the contrast of human village and wild forest. The fierce and relentless character of the leopard, its unpredictable and treacherous disposition, make it a convincing animal alter ego for the human despot, as stories, sayings, and artworks all over the continent attest. In the words of a wry proverb from the Fipa of southwest Tanzania: "He who dines with the leopard is liable to be eaten."

Less physically imposing felines, notably the civet cat (*Civettictis civetta*) and the genet (*Genetta vulgaris*), are also vehicles of cosmic symbolism. According to de Heusch, both wildcats figure in central African mythology and ritual symbolism to represent the cycles of the seasons, of day and night, and life and death. In eastern Africa the skins of these animals are worn by diviners and sorcerers to indicate their paranormal powers. Another ambiguous animal, the spotted hyena (*Crocuta crocuta*), is commonly associated with sorcery or witchcraft throughout the eastern African savanna. Its category-defying ambiguity mainly resides in its hermaphroditic appearance, a consequence of the animal's peculiarly well-developed secondary sex characteristics. The hyena is both a hunter and a scavenger and, because of its stealthy habits and formidably powerful jaws, extremely dangerous. It is therefore an apt associate of such antisocial humans as witches and sorcerers, who are often said to ride on hyenas while pursuing their evil avocations.

No survey of African animal symbolism, however perfunctory, would be complete without some mention of the ubiquitous "trickster" animals of folklore. In the high grasslands of eastern and southern Africa the trickster role is assumed by the hare, and elsewhere by either the tortoise or the spider. These are all seemingly humble, even powerless, creatures. It is noteworthy, however, that like their polar opposite—the leopard—these are also all beings of solitary habit. A typical story featuring a trickster animal such as the hare shows him outwitting such seemingly powerful animals as the lion, elephant, or hyena. These tales are clearly intended to convey the message that the isolated individual is capable, despite appearances, of changing the state of worldly affairs to his advantage. A common story in eastern Africa, typical of the genre throughout the continent, tells of how the hare tricked the elephant and the hippopotamus into engaging in a gargantuan tug-of-war with each other, each believing the puny hare was at the other end of the rope. The two huge animals' unavailing exertions incidentally cleared a large area of ground which the hare was then able to use as a field for growing his crops.

BEYOND STRUCTURALISM

Academic understanding of African animal symbolism owes much to the structuralist methodology of Claude Leévi-Strauss. The major Africanist contribution in this mode has been that of de Heusch, whose magisterial studies of Bantu, and, more recently, western African and Sudanic mythology have illuminated the complex play of zoomorphic metaphor on a continental scale. Latterly, de Heusch has also turned his attention to the metonymic (part-whole) symbolism involved in African animal sacrifice, most particularly of domestic beasts. Developing earlier work by E. E. Evans-Pritchard and Godfrey Lienhardt on bovine sacrifice among the Nilotic peoples, de Heusch shows in *Sacrifice in Africa* (1985) how, among the Zulu and Tsonga peoples of South Africa, strict rules govern the cutting up and division between different social categories of the various parts of the sacrificial animal's body. Yet the most powerful symbolic complexes are those that combine metaphoric and metonymic meanings in what the classical grammar of rhetoric called synecdoche. The Lele pangolin is a metaphor conveying ideas of category-defying creativity, but the Pangolin Men's ritual sacrifice and consumption of the animal further evokes metonymic symbolism.

Synecdochal symbolism is also involved in the widespread use of animal ingredients in what some anthropologists have called African "magical medicines." These ingredients, loaded with metaphoric meanings derived from the perceived nature of particular animals, are introduced into the bodies of their clients by indigenous doctors. In the central African savanna from Malawi to southeast Zaire, magical medicines fall into two categories: herbal remedies and animal parts, generally called *vizimba*, which are thought of as vectors of cosmic power, enormously enhancing the doctor's therapeutic purpose.

Anthropology is hugely indebted to structuralist insights into the intricate architecture of human symbolic thought. But the poststructuralist, and

postmodern, "de-centering" of the anthropologist-as-observer has led to a new awareness of the irreducibly creative nature of the human imagination, particularly in its self-representation of animals. No longer, Mary Douglas asserted, can anthropologists write as if the systems of symbolic relations they describe were inherent in the natural environment: all such models are derived from humankind's experience of its own social relations. The implication is that deeper understanding of the symbolic meaning of animals, in Africa and elsewhere, entails a radical rethinking of what it is to be human.

In twenty-first century ethnography the search for meaning is complemented by a concern with extensive ethnography and with writing of considerable historical depth and political breadth. In Zimbabwe, for example, the status of animals as wild or domestic, owned or otherwise, is a political issue, determining access to resources, and providing a focus for unrest between ethnic groups. As Suzuki has shown, the saga of the wildlife parks in Zimbabwe and the classification of lions and other charismatic megafauna as game by Wildlife Industries New Development for All (WINDFALL) and Communal Area Management Program for Indigenous Resources (CAMPFIRE) in the late 1970s, rewrote the relationship between animals and particular social groups, a change that was undone in 2000 by the occupation of white-owned farms by war veterans. The case illustrates the contested nature of animal symbolism in contemporary Africa. While to some, lions and elephants are symbols of the wild, even as they are at the same time farmed and semi-domesticated, they are to others symbols of colonial oppression and alienation. This conflict is representative of a number of battles over land management and the exploitation of animals that resists a solely structuralist understanding, and requires anthropologists to combine questions of meaning with those of class, race, and gender.

See also **Anthropology, Social, and the Study of Africa; Art; Marriage Systems; Myth and Cosmology; Religion and Ritual.**

BIBLIOGRAPHY

Atran, Scott. *Cognitive Foundations of Natural History.* Cambridge, U.K.: Cambridge University Press, 1990.

Baker, Steve. *Picturing the Beast: Animals, Identity, and Representation.* New York: University of Illinois Press, 1993.

Beidelman, T. O. *Moral Imagination in Kaguru Modes of Thought*. Bloomington: Indiana University Press, 1986.

Bleek, D. F. *The Naron: A Bushman Tribe of the Central Kalahari*. Cambridge, U.K.: Cambridge University Press, 1928.

Bruno, Giordano. *The Expulsion of the Triumphant Beast*. Lincoln: University of Nebraska, 1964.

Camara Laye. *L'enfant noir*. Paris: Plon, 1953.

Douglas, Mary. *The Lele of the Kasai*. London: Oxford University Press, 1963.

Douglas, Mary. *Implicit Meanings: Essays in Anthropology*. Boston: Routledge and Kegan Paul, 1975.

Douglas, Mary. "The Pangolin Revisited." In *Signifying Animals*, ed. R. G. Willis. London: Unwin Hyman, 1990.

Evans-Pritchard, E. E., ed. *The Zande Trickster*. Oxford: Clarenden, 1967.

Glickman, Stephen. "The Spotted Hyena: From Aristotle to The Lion King." In *Humans and Other Animals*, ed. Arien Mack. Columbus: Ohio State University Press, 1999.

Hambly, Wilfrid D. *Serpent Worship in Africa*. Chicago: Field Museum of Natural History, 1931.

Heusch, Luc de. *Le roi ivre; ou, L'origine de l'état; mythes et rites bantous*. Paris: Gallimard, 1972.

Heusch, Luc de. *Sacrifice in Africa: A Structuralist Approach*. Manchester, U.K.: Manchester University Press, 1985.

Kingdon, Jonathan. *East African Mammals: An Atlas of Evolution in Africa*, Vol. 1. London: Academic Press, 1974.

Morris, Brian. *The Power of Animals*. Oxford: Berg, 1998.

Morris, Brian. *Animals and Ancestors: An Ethnography*. Oxford: Berg, 2000.

Morris, Brian. *Insects and Human Life*. Oxford: Berg, 2004.

Roberts, Allen F. *Animals in African Art*. New York: Museum for African Art, 1995.

Ruel, M. "Were Animals and the Introverted Witch." In *Witchcraft Confessions and Accusations*, ed. Mary Douglas. London: Tavistock, 1970.

Serpell, James. *In the Company of Animals*. Oxford: Blackwell, 1986.

Suzuki, Yuka. "Putting the Lion Out at Night: Domestication and the Illusion of the Wild." In *Where the Wild Things Are Now: Domestication Reconsidered*, ed. Rebecca Cassidy and Molly Mullin. Oxford: Berg, 2007.

Viveiros de Castro, Eduardo. "Cosmological Deixis and Amerindian Perspectivism." *Journal of the Royal Anthropological Institute* 4 (1998): 469–488.

Willis, Roy. *Man and Beast*. New York: Basic Books, 1974.

ROY WILLIS
REVISED BY REBECCA CASSIDY

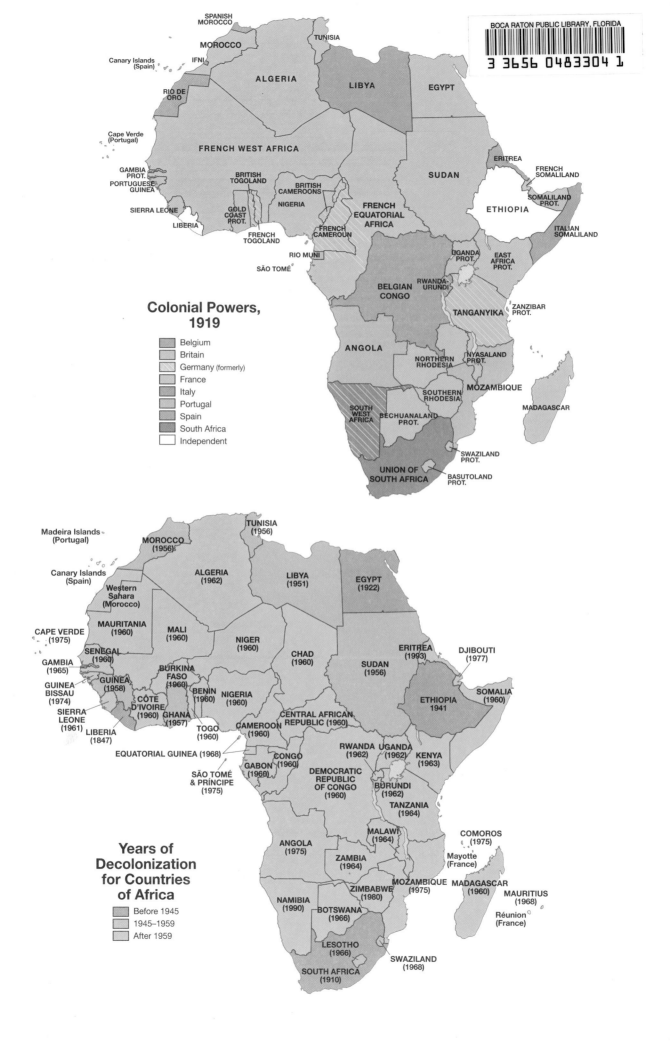

Colonial Powers, 1919

- Belgium
- Britain
- Germany (formerly)
- France
- Italy
- Portugal
- Spain
- South Africa
- Independent

SPANISH MOROCCO

MOROCCO

TUNISIA

Canary Islands (Spain)

IFNI

ALGERIA

LIBYA

EGYPT

RIO DE ORO

Cape Verde (Portugal)

FRENCH WEST AFRICA

SUDAN

ERITREA

FRENCH SOMALILAND

GAMBIA PROT.

PORTUGUESE GUINEA

BRITISH TOGOLAND

BRITISH CAMEROONS

NIGERIA

FRENCH EQUATORIAL AFRICA

SOMALILAND PROT.

SIERRA LEONE

GOLD COAST PROT.

ETHIOPIA

LIBERIA

FRENCH TOGOLAND

FRENCH CAMEROUN

ITALIAN SOMALILAND

RIO MUNI

SÃO TOMÉ

UGANDA PROT.

EAST AFRICA PROT.

BELGIAN CONGO

RWANDA-URUNDI

ANGOLA

TANGANYIKA

ZANZIBAR PROT.

NORTHERN RHODESIA

NYASALAND PROT.

MOZAMBIQUE

MADAGASCAR

SOUTH WEST AFRICA

SOUTHERN RHODESIA

BECHUANALAND PROT.

SWAZILAND PROT.

UNION OF SOUTH AFRICA

BASUTOLAND PROT.

Years of Decolonization for Countries of Africa

- Before 1945
- 1945–1959
- After 1959

Madeira Islands (Portugal)

TUNISIA (1956)

MOROCCO (1956)

Canary Islands (Spain)

Western Sahara (Morocco)

ALGERIA (1962)

LIBYA (1951)

EGYPT (1922)

CAPE VERDE (1975)

MAURITANIA (1960)

MALI (1960)

NIGER (1960)

CHAD (1960)

SUDAN (1956)

ERITREA (1993)

DJIBOUTI (1977)

GAMBIA (1965)

SENEGAL (1960)

BURKINA FASO (1960)

SOMALIA (1960)

GUINEA BISSAU (1974)

GUINEA (1958)

CÔTE D'IVOIRE (1960)

BENIN (1960)

NIGERIA (1960)

ETHIOPIA 1941

SIERRA LEONE (1961)

GHANA (1957)

TOGO (1960)

CAMEROON (1960)

CENTRAL AFRICAN REPUBLIC (1960)

LIBERIA (1847)

EQUATORIAL GUINEA (1968)

CONGO (1960)

RWANDA (1962)

UGANDA (1962)

KENYA (1963)

SÃO TOMÉ & PRÍNCIPE (1975)

GABON (1960)

DEMOCRATIC REPUBLIC OF CONGO (1960)

BURUNDI (1962)

TANZANIA (1964)

COMOROS (1975)

ANGOLA (1975)

MALAWI (1964)

ZAMBIA (1964)

Mayotte (France)

NAMIBIA (1990)

ZIMBABWE (1980)

MOZAMBIQUE (1975)

MADAGASCAR (1960)

MAURITIUS (1968)

BOTSWANA (1966)

Réunion (France)

LESOTHO (1966)

SWAZILAND (1968)

SOUTH AFRICA (1910)